THE HOUSE OF ROTHSCHILD

The House of Rothschild

MONEY'S PROPHETS

1798–1848

Niall Ferguson

~ Viking ~

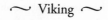

VIKING
Published by the Penguin Group
Penguin Putnam Inc., 375 Hudson Street,
New York, New York 10014, U.S.A.
Penguin Books Ltd, 27 Wrights Lane,
London W8 5TZ, England
Penguin Books Australia Ltd, Ringwood,
Victoria, Australia
Penguin Books Canada Ltd, 10 Alcorn Avenue,
Toronto, Ontario, Canada M4V 3B2
Penguin Books (N.Z.) Ltd, 182-190 Wairau Road,
Auckland 10, New Zealand
Penguin India, 210 Chiranjiv Tower, 43 Nehru Place,
New Delhi, 11009, England

Penguin Books Ltd, Registered Offices:
Harmondsworth, Middlesex, England

First American edition
Published in 1998 by Viking Penguin,
a member of Penguin Putnam Inc.

1 3 5 7 9 10 8 6 4 2

This is the first of two volumes of The House of Rothschild. In Great Britain *The House
of Rothschild* was published as one volume by Weidenfeld & Nicolson as *The World's Banker.*

ISBN 0-670-85768-8

CIP data available

This book is printed on acid-free paper.
∞
Printed in the United States of America
Set in AGaramond
Designed by Jaye Zimet

For Susan, Felix and Freya

CONTENTS

ILLUSTRATIONS IN THE TEXT

1.i: Anonymous early-eighteenth-century print of Simon of Trent and the *Judensau*. Source: Schachar, *Judensau* (Alfred Rubens Collection, Jewish Museum London.)

1.ii: The turnover of Nathan Rothschild's textile exporting business, 1801–1811 (£). Source: RAL, I/218/19–26, Invoice Books.

4.i: The average price of 3 per cent consols, 1780–1830. Source: Mitchell, *British historical statistics*, p. 455.

5.i: *Devotion in Dukes Place—or Contractors returning thanks for a Loan* (1818). Source: Jewish Theological Seminary, *Jew as Other*, p. 17. (Alfred Rubens Collection, Jewish Museum London.)

5.ii: George or Robert Cruikshank, *The JEW and the DOCTOR, or SECRET INFLUENCE BEHIND THE CURTAIN!! (Vide Times Feby. 19th 1828)*. Source: Rubens, "Rothschilds in caricature," plate VII. (Alfred Rubens Collection, Jewish Museum London.)

5.iii: Robert Cruikshank, *NEW SCENE FOR THE OLD FARCE OF THE JEW AND THE DOCTOR* (March 1828). Source: Jewish Theological Seminary, *Jew as Other*, p. 57; Rubens, "Rothschilds in caricature," plate VIII. (Alfred Rubens Collection, Jewish Museum London.)

5.iv: "Shortshanks" [Seymour], *AN UNTOWARD EVENT, OR A TORY TRIUMPH* (February 1828). Source: Rubens, "Rothschilds in caricature," plate VI. (Alfred Rubens Collection, Jewish Museum London.)

5.v: "Sharpshooter," *The HUE and CRY; or JOHN BULL between two Knaves, Stools, and the Heads of Police called to rescue him from Pickpockets. Dedicated to the holders of Foreign Bonds in General* (1829). Source: Rubens, "Rothschilds in caricature," plate XI. (Alfred Rubens Collection, Jewish Museum London.)

6.i: T. Jones, *A King bestowing favors on a Great Man's Friends—Scene near the Bank* (1824). Designed by an Amateur. Published by B. Webster. Source: Rubens, "Rothschilds in caricature," plate III. (Alfred Rubens Collection, Jewish Museum London.)

6.ii: Anon., "*To make a shambles of the parliament house—Shakespeare*," the *Looking Glass*, No. 3 (1830). Source: Jewish Theological Seminary, *Jew as Other*, no. 34. (Alfred Rubens Collection, Jewish Museum London.)

6.iii: Anon., *The Wise Men of the East and the Marquiss of West*, *McLean's Monthly Sheet of Caricatures*, No. 55 (1830). Source: Rubens, "Rothschilds in caricature," plate XII. (Alfred Rubens Collection, Jewish Museum London.)

7.i: Ernst Schalk and Philipp Herrlich, *Baron Moritz von Bethmann and Baron Amschel von Rothschild, Bilder aus Frankfurt*, Nr. 1 (1848). Source: Herding, "Rothschilds in der Karikatur," p. 51. (Historisches Museum, Frankfurt am Main.)

8.i: H. Delaporte, *James de Rothschild and Louis Philippe, La Caricature*, No. 67 (June 23, 1831). Source: Rubens, "Rothschilds in caricature," plate XVIII; Herding, "Rothschilds in der Karikatur," p. 25. (Stadt und Universitätsbibliothek, Frankfurt am Main.)

8.ii: The price of 3 per cent and 4 per cent rentes, May 1830–May 1831. Source: RAL, XI/109 series, letters from Paris to London.

8.iii: Anon., *Die Krähwinkler suchen die Papiere in die Höhe zu treiben* (1830–31). Source: Rubens, "Rothschilds in caricature," plate XVII, no. 22. (Alfred Rubens Collection, Jewish Museum London.)

8.iv: The weekly closing price of 3 per cent consols, 1828–1832. Source: *Spectator.*

9.i: S. W. Fores, *The Protocol-Society in an Uproar, or the Conferees Confounded. A Sketch in Downing Street* (1831). Source: Rubens, "Rothschilds in caricature," plate XIII. (N. M. Rothschild and Sons Limited.)

9.ii: "J.W.W.," *PLUCKING THE* GOOSE OR *BELGIUM SUPPORTED BY HER* FRIENDS AND ALLIES (1831). Source: Rubens, "Rothschilds in caricature," plate XIV. (Alfred Rubens Collection, Jewish Museum London.)

10.i: "A.C."[Crowhill], *The Great Humming Top spinning a Loan* (1820). Source: Rubens, "Rothschilds in caricature," plate XI, no. 10. (N. M. Rothschild and Sons Limited.)

10.ii: *Die Generalpumpe* (*c.* 1840). (Historisches Museum, Vienna.)

10.iii: Richard Dighton, *A View from the Royal Exchange* (1817). Source: Rubens, "Rothschilds in caricature," plate I, no. 1. (The Rothschild Archive).

10.iv: Thomas Jones, *A PILLAR of the EXCHANGE* (1829). Source: Rubens, "Rothschilds in caricature," plate IX. (N. M. Rothschild and Sons Limited)

10.v: William Makepeace Thackeray, *N. M. ROTHSCHILD ESQ.*, *National Standard,* May 18, 1833). Source: Herding, "Rothschilds in der Karikatur," p. 24.

10.vi: N. M. Rothschild & Sons, annual profits as a percentage of capital, 1830–1849. Source: appendix 2, table b.

10.vii: I. Nussgieg, after G. Geissler, *Der Musterreiter* (1825). Source: Herding, "Rothschilds in der Karikatur," p. 52. (Stadt- und Universitätsbibliothek, Frankfurt am Main.)

10.viii: "An Amateur," *A NEW COURT FIRE SCREEN* (1824), published by H. Fores. Source: Rubens, "Rothschilds in caricature," plate IV. (Alfred Rubens Collection, Jewish Museum London.)

10.ix: "A Sharpshooter," *The Man Wot Knows How to Drive a Bargain* (July 14, 1829). Source: Rubens, "Rothschilds in caricature," plate X. (Alfred Rubens Collection, Jewish Museum London.)

11.i: The weekly closing price of 3 per cent consols in 1836. Source: *Spectator.*

11.ii: Mons. Edouart, *The Shadow of a Great Man*, published by J. Knight, Standidge and Lemon (August 6, 1836). Source: Rubens, "Rothschilds in caricature," plate X, no. 20.

11.iii: R. Cullen, *SHADOW of the late N. M. ROTHSCHILD ESQ.* (1837). Sources: Rothschild, *Dear Lord Rothschild,* plate 72; Rubens, *Anglo-Jewish portraits,* p. 103.

TABLES

10a: Combined Rothschild capital, 1797–1844 (£ thousand).

10b: Average annual profits of the five Rothschild houses, 1818–1844 (£ thousand).

10c: The nominal value of loans issued by the London and Frankfurt houses, 1820–1859 (by decade, £).

10d: Loans issued by the London house, 1818–1846 (by recipient).

16a: The financial crisis of 1846–1848.

Appendix 2, table a: The sterling exchange rate of the Frankfurt gulden, 1798–1836.

Appendix 2, table b: N. M. Rothschild & Sons: profits and loss accounts, 1829–1848 (£).

ACKNOWLEDGEMENTS
───────────

Documents from the Royal Archives at Windsor Castle are quoted with the gracious permission of Her Majesty the Queen. It was Sir Evelyn de Rothschild, chairman of N. M. Rothschild & Sons, who originally suggested that the writing of a history of the firm would be a good way to mark the bicentenary of his great-great-grandfather Nathan Mayer Rothschild's arrival in England; I owe a special debt to him for opening the Rothschild Archive to me. Amschel Rothschild also took a keen interest in the project before his tragic death in 1996. Lord Rothschild, Edmund de Rothschild, Leopold de Rothschild and Baron David de Rothschild were all kind enough to agree to be interviewed. They and others also took the trouble to read and comment on substantial parts of the text. I am grateful to Miriam Rothschild for her corrections to an early version of the epilogue, and to Baron Guy de Rothschild for his looking over those passages relating to the recent history of the French bank and family. Emma Rothschild read and commented on the first draft in its entirety, a considerable distraction from her own research and writing for which I thank her. Lionel de Rothschild saved me from innumerable slips by reading and meticulously annotating the first draft, a labour for which this acknowledgement seems a very meagre wage. I should also like to thank the Earl and Countess of Rosebery for giving me access to the private papers of the 5th Earl, and for their kind hospitality at Dalmeny.

A number of directors and employees at N. M. Rothschild & Sons have also assisted me. In particular, I should like to thank Tony Chapman, Russell Edey, Grant Manheim, Bernard Myers and David Sullivan, as well as Lorna Lindsay, Hazel Matthews and Oleg Sheiko.

A project such as this depends heavily on the expertise and toil of archivists and librarians. I owe a special debt of gratitude to those at the Rothschild Archive: Victor Gray and Melanie Aspey, and their assistants Tamsin Black and Mandy Bell, who have uncomplainingly put up with my erratic work methods and unpredictable demands. I should also like to thank their predecessors, Simone Mace and Ann Andlaw. Sheila de Bellaigue, Registrar of the Royal Archives at Windsor Castle, was a model of efficiency; as were Henry Gillett and Sarah Millard at the Bank of England and Robin Harcourt-Williams at Hatfield House. I should like to record my gratitude to Dr M. M. Muchamedjanov and his assistants at the Centre for the Preservation of Historical Documentary Collections in Moscow. In addition, I and my research assistants have received invaluable help from the archivists and librarians at the Anglo-Jewish Archives, University of Southampton; the Archives Nationales, Paris; the Bayerisches Hauptstaatsarchiv, Munich; the Birmingham University Library; the Bodleian Library; the British Library; the Cambridge University Library; the Geheime Staatsarchiv Preussischer Kulturbesitz, Berlin-Dahlem; the Hessische Staatsarchiv, Marburg; the House of Lords Record Office; the Institut für Stadtgeschichte, Frankfurt; the Jewish Museum, Frankfurt; the Leo Baeck Institute, New York; the National Library of Scotland; Rhodes House, Oxford; The Times Archive; and the Thüringische Hauptstaatsarchiv, Weimar.

Lord Weidenfeld was the match-maker who suggested that I might like to write this book and for that (and many other kindnesses) I shall always be in his debt. I am indebted too to Anthony Cheetham at Orion for investing in me and offering only encouragement as deadlines passed and the manuscript overshot the agreed length. Ion Trewin has been and is a superb editor; the same goes for Peter James, my copy-editor. I should also like to thank Rachel Leyshon, Francis Gotto and Carl Stott for their contributions.

My agents, successively Gill Coleridge and Georgina Capel, provided all the shrewd advice and tenacious negotiation an author could wish for.

This book could not have been written in five years—indeed, it could not have been written—without a great deal of research assistance. I must make special mention of Mordechai Zucker, whose unique ability to decipher the archaic Hebrew script used by the first and second generations of Rothschilds was a *sine qua non.* Thanks to the translations which he had been working on for years before I came on the scene, and through his tape-recorded readings of the original *Judendeutsch,* Mordechai has been the eyes through which I have been able to read the most important of all the documents on which this book is based. Nor would I have got far with the correspondence of the French Rothschilds without the invaluable Abigail Green, who also hunted down long-lost literary allusions to the Rothschilds. Edward Lipman did great things on financial questions; while Rainer Liedtke provided vital expertise on Jewish history. Harry Seekings and Glen O'Hara slaved over nineteenth-century financial statistics. Andrew Vereker chased Natty Rothschild's dispersed political correspondence. I should also like to thank Katherine Astill, Elizabeth Emerson, Bernhard Fulda, Tobias Jones and Suzanne Nicholas.

The finished text owes much to the critical comments of other historians on earlier drafts. David Landes acted on the family's behalf as a kind of editor-cum-*Doktorvater.* It has been a rare privilege to be so attentively read by one of the acknowledged masters of modern economic history. I must also thank another master in the field, Barry Supple, for finding the time to read the first draft; as well as my old friend Jonathan Steinberg, who generously read the early chapters at a very difficult time. Fritz Backhaus and Helga Krohn of the Jewish Museum in Frankfurt gave me invaluable material which they had gathered for their outstanding exhibition; I warmly thank them and their assistant Rainer Schlott. Others who have read and commented on individual chapters include Robert Evans, Gerry Feldman, John Grigg, Lord Jenkins of Hillhead, Rainer Liedtke, Reinhard Liehr, Wolfgang Mommsen, Susannah Morris, Aubrey Newman, Sir John Plumb, Hartmut Pogge von Strandmann and Andrew Roberts. I am grateful to them all for these good works, as well as to all those who have commented on conference and seminar papers I have given on aspects of Rothschild history. I would also like to thank Amos Elon for scholarly comradeship in Moscow.

The Principal and Fellows of Jesus College, Oxford, have tolerated my absence or absent-mindedness throughout the five years this book has taken to write, as have the other members of the Oxford Modern History Faculty. I am especially grateful to my colleague Felicity Heal, who has often had to shoulder burdens we are supposed to share, as well as to Dafna Clifford, Don Fowler and Patrick McGuinness. I have also been indirectly helped by the college's staff; others will, I hope, forgive me if I single out Vivien Bowyer and Robert Haynes, who have regularly acted beyond the call of duty. I should also like to thank Doris Clifton of the Modern Languages Faculty. Nor could I omit the indispensable Amanda Hall.

Finally, I thank Susan, Felix and Freya, for whom this book was written, and to whom it is dedicated.

Note: On Being an "Authorised" Author

It may be as well to state explicitly that those members of the Rothschild family who read parts of the early manuscript were *not* acting as censors. From the outset, it was formally agreed that I would be entitled to quote freely from any material in the Rothschild Archive in London predating March 1915 (the date of the 1st Lord Rothschild's death); and, of course, from any other archives and private collections of papers as far as their curators gave me permission to do so. It was also agreed that N. M. Rothschild & Sons would have the right to comment on the manuscript. This arrangement has worked far better in practice than I could ever have hoped. For the avoidance of doubt: I have been able throughout to abide by the Rankean principle of trying to write history as far as possible "as it actually was," and the comments I have received from members of the family have only helped me in this attempt. Their commitment to historical accuracy has deeply impressed me. If the end-product falls short of Ranke's ideal, I hope it is only because relevant documents have not been read for lack of time, have not survived or never existed. Errors are, of course, my fault alone.

Niall Ferguson

Jeanette (1771–1859)
m.1795*
Benedikt Moses Worms
(1772–1824)

Amschel (1773–1855)
m.1796
Eva Hanau (1779–1848)

Salomon (1774–1855)
m.1800
Caroline Stern
(1782–1854)

Nathan (1777–1836)
m.1806
Hannah Barent Cohen
(1783–1850)

Anthony (1810–76)
m.1840
Louisa Montefiore
(1821–1910)

Anselm (1803–74)
m.1826
Charlotte (1807–59)

Betty (1805–86)
m.1824
James (1792–1868)

Charlotte (1807–59)
m.1826
Anselm (1803–74)

Lionel (1808–79)
m.1836
Charlotte (1819–84)

Mayer Anselm Léon
(1827–28)

Julie (1830–1907)
m.1850
Adolph (1823–1900)

**Hannah Mathilde
(1832–1924)**
m.1849
**Wilhelm Carl
(1828–1901)**

Sara Louise (1834–1924)
m.1858*
Baron Raimondo
Franchetti (1829–1905)

Nathaniel (1836–1905)

Ferdinand (1839–98)
m.1865
Evelina (1839–66)

**Salomon Albert
(1844–1911)**
m.1876
Bettina (1858–92)

Alice (1847–1922)

Leonora (1837–1911)
m.1857
Alphonse (1827–1905)

Evelina (1839–66)
m.1865
Ferdinand (1839–98)

**Nathaniel (Natty)
(1840–1915)**
m.1867
Emma (1834–1935)

Alfred (1842–1918)

Leopold (1845–1917)
m.1881
Marie Perugia
(1862–1937)

Constance (1843–1931)
m.1877
Cyril Flower (1st Lord
Battersea) (1843–1907)

Georg (1877–1934)

Alphonse (1878–1942)
m.1911
Clarice Sebag-Montefiore
(1894–1967)

Louis (1882–1955)
m.1946
Countess Hildegard
Auersperg (1895–1981)

Eugène (1884–1976)
m.1925
Countess Kitty
Schönborn-Bucheim (née
Wolff) (1885–1946)

Charlotte Esther
(b.&d.1885)

Victor (1910–90)
m.1933
Barbara Hutchinson
(1911–89)
m. 2nd 1946
Teresa Mayor
(1915–96)

Valentine (1886–1969)
m.1911*
Sigismund, Baron
Springer (1875–1928)

Oscar (1888–1909)

Walter (1868–1937)

Evelina (1873–1947)
m.1899*
Clive Behrens
(1871–1935)

Charles (1877–1923)
m.1907
Rozsika von Wertheimstein
(1870–1940)

Lionel (1882–1942)
m.1912
Marie-Louise Beer
(1892–1975)

Evelyn Achille
(1886–1917)

Albert (1922–38)

Bettina (b.1924)
m.1943*
Matthew Looram (b.1921)

Gwendoline (1927–72)

Sarah (b.1934)*
m.1948*
Roland Hoguet
(1920–85)

Jacob (b.1936)
m.1961
Serena Dunn (b.1935)

Miriam (b.1908)
m.1943*
George Lane (b.1915)

Miranda (b.1940)
m.1962*
Boudjemâa Boumaza
(1930–64)
m. 2nd 1967
Iain Watson (b.1942)

Elizabeth (1909–88)

Emma (b.1948)
m.1991
Amartya Sen (b.1933)

Benjamin (b. & d.1952)

Victoria (b.1953)
m.1997
Simon Gray (b.1936)

Amschel (1955–96)
m.1981
Anita Guinness (b.1957)

Kathleen (1913–88)
m.1935*
Jules de Koenigswarter
(1904–95)

Rosemary (b.1913)
m.1934*
Denis Gomer Berry
(1911–83)
m. 2nd 1942*
John Antony Seys
(1914–89)

Edmund (b.1916)
m.1948
Elizabeth Lentner
(1923–80)
m. 2nd 1982
Anne Harrison (b.1921)

Naomi (b.1920)
m.1941*
Jean Pierre Reinach
(1915–42) m. 2nd 1947*
Bertrand Goldschmidt
(b.1912)

Hannah (b.1962)
m.1994
William Brookfield

Beth (b.1964)
m.1991
Antonio Tomassini
(b.1959)

Emily (b.1967)
m.1998
Julian Freeman-Attwood

Nat (b.1971)
m.1995
Annabel Neilson (b.1969)

Kate (b.1982)

Alice (b.1983)

James (b.1985)

Katherine (b.1949)
m.1971*
Marcus Agius (b.1946)

Nicholas (b.1951)
m.1985
Caroline Darvall (b.1955)

Chloë (b.1990)

Charlotte (b.1955)
m.1990
Nigel Brown (b.1936)

Lionel (b.1955)
m.1991
Louise Williams (b.1955)

Elizabeth (b.1992)

Leopold (b.1994)

Amschel (b.1995)

Mayer Amschel (1744–1812)
m.1770 Gutle Schnapper (1753–1849)

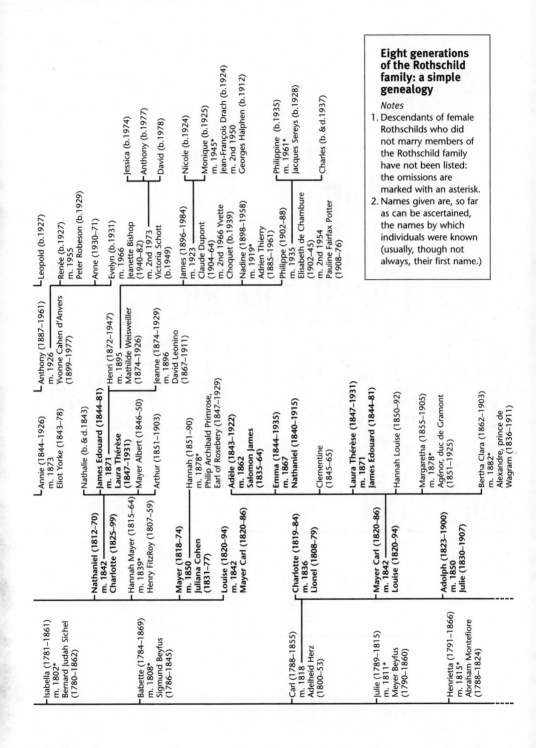

Eight generations of the Rothschild family: a simple genealogy

Notes

1. Descendants of female Rothschilds who did not marry members of the Rothschild family have not been listed: the omissions are marked with an asterisk.

2. Names given are, so far as can be ascertained, the names by which individuals were known (usually, though not always, their first name.)

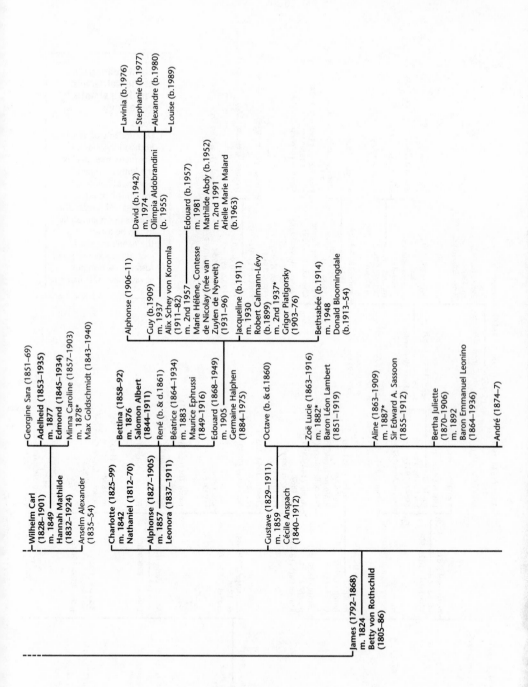

James (1792–1868)
m. 1824
Betty von Rothschild (1805–86)

Wilhelm Carl (1828–1901)
m. 1849
Hannah Mathilde (1832–1924)

Georgine Sara (1851–69)
Adelheid (1853–1935)
m. 1877
Edmond (1845–1934)
Minna Caroline (1857–1903)
m. 1878*
Max Goldschmidt (1843–1940)
Anselm Alexander (1835–54)

Charlotte (1825–99)
m. 1842
Nathaniel (1812–70)

Alphonse (1827–1905)
m. 1857
Leonora (1837–1911)

Bettina (1858–92)
m. 1876
Salomon Albert (1844–1911)
René (b. & d.1861)
Béatrice (1864–1934)
m. 1883
Maurice Ephrussi (1849–1916)
Edouard (1868–1949)
m. 1905
Germaine Halphen (1884–1975)

Alphonse (1906–11)
Guy (b.1909)
m. 1937
Alix Schey von Koromla (1911–82)
m. 2nd 1957
Marie Hélène, Contesse de Nicolay (née van Zuylen de Nyevelt) (1931–96)
Jacqueline (b.1911)
m. 1930
Robert Calmann-Lévy (b.1899)
m. 2nd 1937*
Grigor Piatigorsky (1903–76)
Bethsabée (b.1914)
m. 1948
Donald Bloomingdale (b.1913–54)

David (b.1942)
m. 1974
Olimpia Aldobrandini (b. 1955)
Edouard (b.1957)
m. 1981
Mathilde Abdy (b.1952)
m. 2nd 1991
Arielle Marie Malard (b.1963)

Lavinia (b.1976)
Stephanie (b.1977)
Alexandre (b.1980)
Louise (b.1989)

Gustave (1829–1911)
m. 1859
Cécile Anspach (1840–1912)

Octave (b. & d.1860)
Zoë Lucie (1863–1916)
m. 1882*
Baron Léon Lambert (1851–1919)
Aline (1863–1909)
m. 1887*
Sir Edward A. Sassoon (1855–1912)
Bertha Juliette (1870–1906)
m. 1892
Baron Emmanuel Leonino (1864–1936)
André (1874–7)

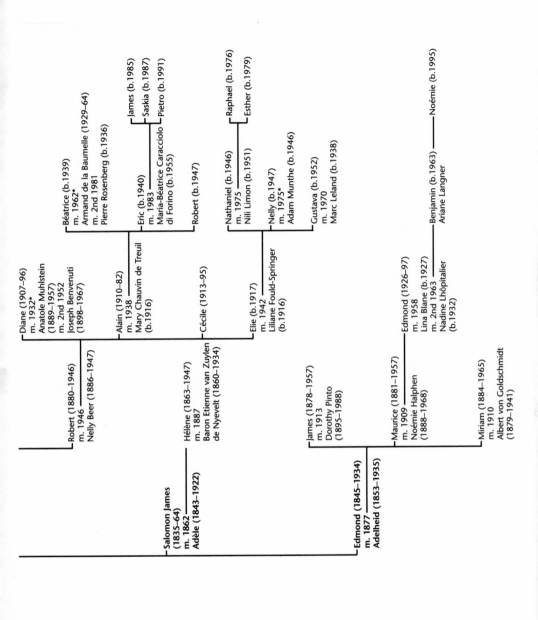

Salomon James
(1835–64)
m. 1862
Adèle (1843–1922)

Robert (1880–1946)
m. 1946
Nelly Beer (1886–1947)

Diane (1907–96)
m. 1932*
Anatole Muhlstein
(1889–1957)
m. 2nd 1952
Joseph Benvenuti
(1898–1967)

Hélène (1863–1947)
m. 1887
Baron Etienne van Zuylen
de Nyevelt (1860–1934)

Alain (1910–82)
m. 1938
Mary Chauvin de Treuil
(b.1916)

Béatrice (b.1939)
m. 1962*
Armand de la Baumelle (1929–64)
m. 2nd 1981
Pierre Rosenberg (b.1936)

Eric (b.1940)
m. 1983
Maria-Béatrice Caracciolo
di Forino (b.1955)

Robert (b.1947)

James (b.1985)
Saskia (b.1987)
Pietro (b.1991)

Cécile (1913–95)

Elie (b.1917)
m. 1942
Liliane Fould-Springer
(b.1916)

Nathaniel (b.1946)
m. 1975
Nili Limon (b.1951)

Nelly (b.1947)
m. 1975*
Adam Munthe (b.1946)

Gustava (b.1952)
m. 1970
Marc Leland (b.1938)

Raphael (b.1976)
Esther (b.1979)

Edmond (1845–1934)
m. 1877
Adelheid (1853–1935)

James (1878–1957)
m. 1913
Dorothy Pinto
(1895–1988)

Maurice (1881–1957)
m. 1909
Noémie Halphen
(1888–1968)

Edmond (1926–97)
m. 1958
Lina Blanc (b.1927)
m. 2nd 1963
Nadine Lhôpitalier
(b.1932)

Benjamin (b.1963) ——— Noémie (b.1995)
Ariane Langner

Miriam (1884–1965)
m. 1910
Albert von Goldschmidt
(1879–1941)

Reality and Myth

~ I ~

"Banking," the 3rd Lord Rothschild once remarked, "consists essentially of facilitating the movement of money from Point A, where it is, to Point B, where it is needed."[1] There is a certain elementary truth in this aperçu, even if it did reflect Victor Rothschild's personal lack of enthusiasm for finance. But if the history of the firm founded by his great-great-grandfather two centuries ago consisted of nothing more than getting money from A to B, it would make dull reading. It should not.

All banks have histories, though not all have their histories researched and written; only the Rothschilds, however, have a mythology. Ever since the second decade of the nineteenth century, there has been speculation about the origins and extent of the family's wealth; about the social implications of their meteoric upward mobility; about their political influence, not only in the five countries where there were Rothschild houses but throughout the world; about their Judaism. The resulting mythology has proved almost as long-lived as the firm of N. M. Rothschild & Sons itself.[2] The name "Rothschild" (which translates from the original German as "Redshield") may be less well known today than it was a hundred years ago, when, as Chekhov remarked, a moribund Russian coffin-maker could use it ironically as a nickname for a poor Jewish musician.[3] But most readers will recognise it, if only from its still fairly regular appearances in the press. The bank may not be the financial giant it was in the century after 1815 and the family may be a great deal more dispersed and diffuse, but the name continues to attract attention—some of it prurient. Even those who know nothing about finance and care less are likely to have come across it at least once in their lives. Thanks to an apparently hereditary aptitude for zoology and horticulture, there are no fewer than 153 species or sub-species of insect which bear the name "Rothschild," as well as fifty-eight birds, eighteen mammals (including the Baringo Giraffe, *Giraffa camelopardalis rothschildi*) and fourteen plants (including a rare slipper orchid, *Paphiopedilum rothschildianum* and a flame lily, *Gloriosa rothschildiana*)—to say nothing of three fish, three spiders and two reptiles.[4] The family's almost equally recurrent enthusiasm for the pleasures of the table has also bestowed the name on a soufflé (made with glacé fruit, brandy and vanilla) and a savoury (prawns, cognac and Gruyère on toast). There are towns and numerous streets named after members of the family in Israel,[5] Rothschild-owned vineyards at Mouton and Lafite whose wines are drunk the world over,[6] numerous Rothschild-built houses from the Vale of Aylesbury to the Riviera[7]—and there is even a Rothschild Island in the Antarctic.[8] Pieces of music have been dedicated to Rothschilds by Chopin and Rossini, as have books by Balzac and Heine. The family is as famous in the art world for its many collections (some of which can be seen in public galleries) as it is in horse-racing circles for its past Derby winners. In the course of writing this book, I have met few people who had not heard at least one Rothschild anecdote—most commonly the myth of the immense profits Nathan Mayer Rothschild made by speculating on the outcome of the battle of Waterloo; almost as often the story of the purchase of the Suez Canal shares which Disraeli did his best to make famous.[9] And, for those who know no history, books of Jewish humour still contain Rothschild jokes.[10] There have even been two Rothschild films,[11] a play[12] and a bizarre, though moderately successful, Broadway musical.[13]

It should be said right away that this book has very little to say about giraffes, orchids, soufflés, vintage wines or islands in the Antarctic. It is primarily a book about banking; and here some words of explanation and reassurance are in order for those readers who are more interested in what rich families do with their wealth than in how they get it.

In fact, the firm of N. M. Rothschild & Sons was not technically a bank at all—at least not according to that great Victorian financial journalist Walter Bagehot's definition in his *Lombard Street* (1873). "A foreigner," he wrote, "would be apt to think that they [the Rothschilds] were bankers if anyone was. But this only illustrates the essential difference between our English notions of banking and the continental":

> Messrs Rothschild are immense capitalists, having, doubtless, much borrowed money in their hands. But they do not take £100 payable on demand, and pay it back in cheques of £5 each, and that is our English banking. The borrowed money they have is in large sums, borrowed for terms more or less long. English bankers deal with an aggregate of small sums, all of which are repayable on short notice, or on demand. And the way the two employ their money is different also. A foreigner thinks "an Exchange business"—that is, the buying and selling bills on foreign countries—a main part of banking . . . But the mass of English country bankers . . . would not know how carry through a great "Exchange operation" . . . They would as soon think of turning silk merchants. The Exchange trade is carried on by a small and special body of foreign bill-brokers, of whom Messrs Rothschild are the greatest . . . [The] family are not English bankers, either by the terms on which they borrow money, or the mode in which they employ it.[14]

Having begun his business career in England as a textile exporter, Nathan Mayer Rothschild was technically a merchant who came to specialise in various financial services. He himself said in 1817: "[M]y business . . . consists entirely in Government transactions & Bank operations"—but by the latter he probably meant operations with the Bank of England. He did not mean the kind of deposit banking which Bagehot called "our English banking" and which remains the principal activity of the big high-street banks today.[15]

Nor can N. M. Rothschild & Sons really be regarded as an autonomous firm: until some time between 1905 and 1909 it was one of a group of Rothschild "houses" run by a family partnership—though the London house is the only one of these which has had an uninterrupted existence until the present day (Rothschild & Cie Banque is only an indirect descendant of the original Paris house, which was nationalised in 1981). At its zenith from the 1820s until the 1860s, this group had five distinct establishments. In addition to Nathan's in London, there was the original firm of M. A. Rothschild & Söhne in Frankfurt (after 1817, M. A. von Rothschild & Söhne), which his eldest brother Amschel took over when their father Mayer Amschel died; de Rothschild Frères in Paris, founded by his youngest brother James; and two subsidiaries of the Frankfurt house, C. M. von Rothschild in Naples, run by the fourth of the brothers, Carl, and S. M. von Rothschild in Vienna, managed by the second-born Salomon. Up until the 1860s, the five houses worked together so closely that it is impossible to discuss the history of one without discussing the history of all five: they were, to all intents and purposes, the component parts of a multinational bank. Even as late as the first decade of the twentieth century, the system of partnerships continued to function in such a way that "English" Rothschilds had a financial stake in the Paris house and "French" Rothschilds a stake in the London house. Unlike modern multinationals, however, this was always a family firm, with executive decision-making strictly monopolised by the partners who (until 1960) were exclusively drawn from the ranks of male Rothschilds.

Perhaps the most important point to grasp about this multinational partnership is that, for most of the century between 1815 and 1914, it was easily the biggest bank in the world. Strictly in terms of their combined capital, the Rothschilds were in a league of their own until, at the earliest, the 1880s. The twentieth century has no equivalent: not even the biggest of today's international banking corporations enjoys the relative supremacy enjoyed by the Rothschilds in their heyday—just as no individual today owns as large a share of the world's wealth as Nathan and James as individuals owned in the period from the mid-1820s until the 1860s (see appendix 1). The economic history of capitalism is therefore incomplete until some attempt has been made to explain how the Rothschilds became so phenomenally rich. Was there a "secret" to their unparalleled success? There are numerous apocryphal business maxims attributed to the Rothschilds—for example, to hold a third of one's wealth in securities; a third in real estate; and a third in jewels and artworks, to treat the stock exchange like a cold shower ("quick in, quick out"); or to leave the last 10 per cent to someone else—but none of them has any serious explanatory value.[16]

What exactly was the business the Rothschilds did? And what use did they make of the immense economic leverage they could exercise? To answer these questions properly it is necessary to understand something of nineteenth-century public finance; for it was by lending to governments—or by speculating in existing government bonds—that the Rothschilds made a very large part of their colossal fortune.

~ II ~

All nineteenth-century states occasionally ran budget deficits and some almost always did—that is, their tax revenues were usually insufficient to meet their expenditures. In this, of course, they were little different from eighteenth-century states. And, as before 1800, it was war and the preparation for war which generally precipitated the biggest increases in expenditure; poor harvests (or troughs in the trade cycle) also caused periodic revenue shortfalls by reducing receipts from taxes.

These deficits, though often relatively small in relation to national income, were not easily financed. National capital markets were not very developed and an internationally integrated capital market was only gradually taking shape with its first real centre in Amsterdam.[17] For most states, borrowing was expensive—that is, the interest they had to pay on loans was relatively high—because they were perceived by investors as unreliable creditors. Budget deficits were thus often financed either by the sale of royal assets (land or offices), or by inflation if the government was in a position to debase the currency. A third possibility, of course, was to raise new taxes, but, as had been the case in the seventeenth century and as was to be the case throughout the nineteenth century too, major changes in tax regimes generally necessitated some kind of political consent via representative institutions. The French Revolution was precipitated by just such a bid for new revenue from the Estates General, after all other attempts at fiscal reform had failed to keep up with the costs of the crown's military activities. One exception to the rule was the British state, which since the later seventeenth century had developed a relatively sophisticated system of public borrowing (the national debt) and monetary management (the Bank of England). Another exception was the small German state of Hesse-Kassel, which was effectively run by its ruler at a profit through the hiring out of his subjects as mercenaries to other states. Involvement in the management of his huge investment portfolio was one of the first steps Mayer Amschel Rothschild took in order to become a banker rather than a mere coin dealer (his original business).

The period 1793–1815 was characterised by recurrent warfare, the fiscal side-effects of which were profound. Firstly, unprecedented expenditures precipitated inflation in all the combatants' economies, the most extreme form of which was the collapse of the assignat currency in France. The European currencies—including the pound sterling after 1797—were thrown into turmoil. Secondly, the disruptions of war (for example, the French occupation of Amsterdam and Napoleon's Continental System) created opportunities for making large profits on highly risky transactions such as smuggling textiles and bullion and managing the investments of exiled rulers. Thirdly, the transfer of large subsidies from Britain to her continental allies necessitated innovations in the cross-border payments system which had never before had to cope with such sums. It was in this highly volatile context that the Rothschilds made the decisive leap from running two modest firms—a small merchant bank in Frankfurt and a cloth exporters in Manchester—to running a multinational financial partnership.

Nor did the final defeat of Napoleon end the need for international financial services; on the contrary, the business of settling the debts and indemnities left over from the war dragged on for most of the 1820s. Moreover, new fiscal needs quickly arose from the political crises which beset the Spanish and Ottoman Empires in this period. At the same time, fiscal retrenchment and monetary stabilisation in Britain created a need for new forms of investment for those who had grown accustomed to putting their money in high-yielding British bonds during the war years. It was this need which Nathan and his brothers successfully met. The system they developed enabled British investors (and other rich "capitalists" in Western Europe) to invest in the debts of those states by purchasing internationally tradeable, fixed-interest bearer (that is, transferable) bonds. The significance of this system for nineteenth-century history cannot be over-emphasised. For this growing international bond market brought together Europe's true "capitalists": that elite of people wealthy enough to be able to tie up money in such assets, and shrewd enough to appreciate the advantages of such assets as compared with traditional forms of holding wealth (land, venal office and so on). Bonds were liquid. They could be bought and sold five and a half days out of seven (excluding holidays) on the major bourses of Europe and traded informally at other times and in other places. And they were capable of accruing large capital gains. Their only disadvantage was, of course, that they were also capable of suffering large capital losses.

What determined the ups and downs of the nineteenth-century bond market? — The answer to this question is central to any understanding of the history of the Rothschild bank. Obviously, economic factors played an important part—in particular, the conditions for short-term borrowing and the appeal of alternative private securities. But the most important factor was political confidence: the confidence of investors (and especially of big market-making investors like the Rothschilds) in the ability of the bond-issuing states to continue to meet their obligations—that is, to pay the interest on their bonds. There were only really two things which might cause them not to do so: war, which would increase their expenditures and decrease their tax revenues; and internal instability, ranging from a change of ministry to full-blown revolution, which would not only dent their revenues but might also bring to power a new and fiscally imprudent government. It was for indications of either of these possible crises, with their intimations of default, that the markets—and the Rothschilds more than anybody—watched.

This explains the importance they always attached to having up-to-date political and economic news. Three things would give an investor an edge over his rival: closeness to the centre of political life, the source of news; the speed with which he could receive news of events in states far and near; and the ability to manipulate the transmission of that news to other investors. This explains why the Rothschilds spent so much time, energy and money maintaining the best possible relations with the leading political figures of the day. It also explains why they carefully developed a network of salaried agents in other key financial markets, whose job it was not only to trade on their behalf but also to keep them supplied with the latest financial and political news. And it explains why they constantly strove to accelerate the speed with which information could be relayed from their agents to them. From an early stage, they relied on their own system of couriers and relished their ability to obtain political news ahead of the European diplomatic services. They also occasionally used carrier-pigeons to transmit the latest stock prices and exchange rates from one market to another. Before the development of the telegraph (and later the telephone), which tended to "democratise" news by making it generally available more rapidly, the Rothschilds' communications network gave them an important advantage over their competitors. Even after they lost this edge, they continued to exercise an influence over the financial press through which news reached a wider public.

Information about the chances of international or domestic instability fed directly into the bond market, leading to the daily fluctuations in prices and yields which investors followed so closely. However, the relationship between politics and the bond market went the other way too. For the movements of prices of existing government stock—the products of past fiscal policy—had an important bearing on present and future policy. To put it simply, if a government wished to borrow more by issuing more bonds, a fall in the price (rise in the yield) of its existing bonds was a serious discouragement. For this reason, bond prices had a significance which historians have too seldom spelt out. They were, it might be said, a kind of daily opinion poll, an expression of confidence in a given regime. Of course, they were an opinion poll based on a highly unrepresentative sample by modern, democratic standards. Only the wealthy—the "capitalists"—got to vote. But then political life in the nineteenth century was itself undemocratic. Indeed, the kind of people who held government bonds were, very roughly speaking, the people who were represented politically, even if there was sometimes tension between those property owners whose assets were held primarily in the form of land or buildings and the bondholders whose portfolios were composed mainly of paper securities. These capitalists were thus to a large extent Europe's political class and their opinions were the opinions that mattered in a stratified, undemocratic society. If investors bid up the price of a government's stock, that government could feel secure. If they dumped its stock, that government was quite possibly living on borrowed time as well as money.

The singular beauty of the bond market was that virtually every state (including, as the century advanced, all the new nation states and colonies) had, sooner or later, to come to it; and most states had sizeable amounts of tradable debt in circulation. The varying fortunes of government bonds provide a vital insight into the political history of the period. They are also the key to understanding the extent and limits of the power of a bank like Rothschilds, which for much of the nineteenth century was the prime market-maker for such bonds. Indeed, it can be argued that, by modifying the existing system for government borrowing to make bonds more easily tradable, the Rothschilds actually created the international bond market in its modern form. As early as 1830 a German writer observed how, thanks to innovations in the form of bonds introduced by the Rothschilds since 1818,

> each possessor of state paper [can] . . . collect the interest at his convenience at several different places without any effort. The House of Rothschild in Frankfurt pays the interest on the Austrian metalliques, the Neapolitan rentes and the interest of the Anglo-Neapolitan obligations in either London, Naples or Paris, wherever it suits.[18]

At the core of this book, then, is the international bond market which the Rothschilds did so much to develop, though due attention is also paid to the many other forms of financial business the Rothschilds did: bullion broking and refining, accepting and discounting commercial bills, direct trading in commodities, foreign exchange dealing and arbitrage, even insurance. In addition to the inevitable web of credits and debits with other firms which arose from these activities, the Rothschilds also offered to a select group of customers—usually royal and aristocratic individuals whom they wished to cultivate—a range of "personal banking services" ranging from large personal loans (as in the case of the Austrian Chancellor Prince Metternich) to a first class private postal service (as in the case of Queen Victoria). Contrary to Bagehot's impression, they sometimes took deposits from this exclusive clientele. And the Rothschilds were also major industrial investors—an aspect of their business which has often been underestimated. When the development of railways raised the possibility of transforming Europe's transport system in the 1830s and 1840s, the Rothschilds were among the leading financial backers of lines, beginning in France, Austria and Germany. Indeed, by the 1860s James de Rothschild had built up something like a pan-European railway network extending northwards from France to Belgium, southwards to Spain and eastwards to Germany, Switzerland, Austria and Italy. From an early stage, the Rothschilds also had major mining interests, beginning in the 1830s with their acquisition of the Spanish mercury mines of Almadén and expanding dramatically in the 1880s and 1890s when they invested in mines producing gold, copper, diamonds, rubies and oil. Like their original financial business, this was an authentically global operation extending from South Africa to Burma, from Montana to Baku.

The primary concern of this book is therefore to explain the origins and development of one of the biggest and most unusual businesses in the history of modern capitalism. Nevertheless, it is not intended as a narrowly economic history. For one thing, the history of the firm is inseparable from the history of the family: the phrase "the House of Rothschild," which has often been used by previous historians (and film-makers) was used by contemporaries, including the Rothschilds themselves, to convey this unity. While the regularly revised and renewed partnership agreements regulated the management of the Rothschilds' collective business activities and the distribution of the profits which accrued, of equal importance were the nuptial agreements which, at the height of the family's success, systematically married Rothschild to Rothschild, thus keeping the family's capital united—and safe from the claims of "outsiders." When Rothschild women did marry outside the family, their husbands were prohibited from having a direct involvement in the business, as were the female Rothschilds themselves. The partners' wills were also designed to ensure the perpetuation and growth of the business by imposing the wishes of one generation on the next. Inevitably, there were conflicts between the collective ambitions of the family, so compellingly spelt out by Mayer Amschel before he died, and the wishes of the individuals who happened to be born Rothschilds, few of whom shared the founder's relentless appetite for work and profits. Fathers were disappointed by sons. Brothers resented brothers. Love was unrequited or prohibited. Marriage was imposed on unwilling cousins, and husbands and wives quarrelled. In all this, the Rothschilds had much in common with the large families which populate so much nineteenth- and early-twentieth-century fiction: Thackeray's Newcomes, Trollope's Pallisers, Galsworthy's Forsytes, Tolstoy's Rostovs and Mann's Buddenbrooks (though not, happily, Dostoevsky's Karamazovs). The nineteenth century, of course, was an era of large families—the birth rate was high and, for the rich, the death rate fell—and perhaps in this sense alone the Rothschilds were not (as Heine once called them) "the exceptional family."

Because they were so rich, the Rothschilds could plainly claim a material equivalence with the European aristocracy; their success in overcoming the various legal and cultural obstacles to full equivalence of *status* is one of the most remarkable case studies in nineteenth century social history. As men whose father had been prohibited from owning property outside the cramped and squalid Frankfurt Judengasse, the five brothers had an understandable interest in the acquisition of land and spacious residences; though it was the third generation[19] who were responsible for building most of the spectacular palaces and town houses which are the family's most impressive monuments. At the same time, the Rothschilds energetically pursued and acquired decorations, titles and other honours, securing the ultimate prize—an English peerage—in 1885. The third generation also threw themselves into hunting and horse-racing, those quintessentially aristocratic pastimes. A similar process of social assimilation is detectable in their cultural engagement. James and his nephews had a passion for collecting art, ornaments and furniture which they passed on to many of their descendants. They also extended their patronage to include writers (Benjamin Disraeli, Honoré de Balzac and Heinrich Heine), musicians (notably Fryderyk Chopin and Gioachino Rossini) as well as architects and artists. In more ways than one, they were the nineteenth century's Medicis.

Yet it would be wrong to see them as the archetype of the "feudalised" bourgeois family, "aping" the manners of the landed elite. For the Rothschilds brought to the aristocratic milieu patterns of behaviour which were distinctively commercial in origin. Initially, they bought land as an investment which they expected to pay an economic return. They regarded the large houses they built at least partly in functional terms, as private hotels for dispensing corporate hospitality. Nathan's sons and grandsons even saw the purchase of horses as a form of enjoyably speculative investment and placed bets on horse-races in much the same way that they engaged in stock market "specs." To put it cynically, mixing with members of the aristocracy was essential if it was they who governed, and almost as much political information came from informal socialising as from formal meetings with ministers.

At the same time, there is a sense in which the Rothschilds more closely resembled royalty than either the aristocracy or the middle classes. This was not just because they consciously imitated the many crowned heads they came to know. Like the extended family which provided so many of Europe's monarchs, the Rothschilds were extreme in their preference for endogamy. They relished the sense that they were *sans pareil*—at least within the European Jewish elite. In this sense, phrases like "Kings of the Jews" which contemporaries applied to them contained an important element of truth. That was exactly the way the Rothschilds saw and conducted themselves—as phrases like "our royal family" in their letters show—and the way they were treated by many other less wealthy Jews.

This relationship to Judaism and the Jewish communities of Europe and the Middle East is unquestionably one of the most fascinating themes of the family's history. For the Rothschilds, as for so many Jewish families who migrated westwards in the nineteenth century, social assimilation or integration in the countries where they settled posed a challenge to their faith, although the relaxation of discriminatory legislation allowed them to acquire not only money but many of the desirable things it could buy. Yet no matter how sumptuous their houses and how well educated their children, they constantly encountered anti-Jewish sentiment, ranging from the aggression of the Frankfurt mob to the subtle disdain of aristocrats and Gentile bankers for "the Jew." Many other wealthy Jewish families opted to convert to Christianity partly in response to such pressures. But the Rothschilds did not. They remained firmly committed to Judaism, playing an important role in the affairs of the various Jewish communities of which they were members. Moreover, they sought, from their earliest days, to use their financial leverage over individual states to improve the legal and political position of the Jews living there. They did this not only in their home town of Frankfurt, but consistently in almost every state where they did business thereafter as well as in some countries (for example, Rumania and Syria) where they had no economic interests. At least some members of the family saw such altruistic activities as in some sense linked to their own material success: by remaining true to the faith of their ancestors and remembering their "poorer co-religionists" the Rothschilds not only demonstrated their gratitude for their good fortune but ensured that it continued.

Finally, and perhaps most important, this is a political as much as it is a financial history: there are few major political figures in nineteenth-century history who do not feature in the index of this book. From the very earliest days, the Rothschilds appreciated the importance of proximity to politicians, the men who determined not only the extent of budget deficits but also the domestic and foreign policies which so influenced the financial markets; and politicians soon came to realise the importance of proximity to the Rothschilds, who at times seemed indispensable to the solvency of the states the politicians governed and who could always be relied upon to provide up-to-the-minute political news. Mayer Amschel's cultivation of the Elector of Hesse-Kassel's chief financial adviser Karl Buderus and later of Karl Theodor Anton von Dalberg, Prince-Primate of Napoleon's Rhenish Confederation, were the prototypes of countless relationships his sons cultivated with politicians throughout Europe. Beginning in 1813, Nathan became intimate with the British Commissary-General, John Charles Herries, the man responsible for financing Wellington's invasion of France. Another early Rothschild "friend" in England was Charles Stewart, brother of the Foreign Secretary Lord Castlereagh and the British delegate at the Congresses of Vienna, Troppau, Laibach and Verona. Nathan was also in direct contact with the Prime Minister Lord Liverpool and his Chancellor of the Exchequer Nicholas Vansittart in the early 1820s, and gave the Duke of Wellington important financial advice during the Reform crisis of 1830–32.

Rothschild influence extended to royalty as well. Nathan first came into contact with British royalty thanks to his father's purchase of outstanding debts owed by George, Prince Regent (later King George IV) and his brothers. These tenuous links were enhanced by careful cultivation of Leopold of Saxe-Coburg, who married George IV's daughter Charlotte and later became King Leopold I of the Belgians. Nor was his nephew Albert above turning to the Rothschilds for financial assistance after he became Queen Victoria's Prince Consort. In turn, Victoria and Albert's eldest son was on friendly terms with many members of the family before and after he succeeded his mother as Edward VII. The list of Victorian politicians who were close to the Rothschilds is a long one: Lionel's campaign for admission to the House of Commons in the 1840s and 1850s enjoyed support from Whigs like Lord John Russell and Peelites like Gladstone, but also Protectionist Tories like Disraeli and Lord George Bentinck. Later, as his sons grew disillusioned with Gladstone, they were attracted not only to Disraeli but also to Lord Randolph Churchill, Joseph Chamberlain and Arthur Balfour. In the 1880s and 1890s their advice on imperial matters was sought by both the Marquess of Salisbury and the Earl of Rosebery, Gladstone's successor as Liberal Prime Minister. Indeed, Rosebery was married to a Rothschild: Mayer's daughter Hannah.

The French Rothschilds also took a direct role in politics. They were close to the comte de Villèle in the early 1820s, shifted their allegiance skilfully to Louis Philippe in 1830, managed to survive the 1848 revolution by cultivating leading republicans, and subtly undermined the rule of Napoleon III, whose foreign adventurism they disliked. They also had a firm friend in the Third Republic in the person of Léon Say, four times French Finance Minister. In Germany and Austria, the close relationship between Salomon and Metternich was of immense importance in the years 1818–48, but it was far from unique. Other "friends" of the Restoration era included Count Apponyi, the Austrian ambassador in Paris, and members of the Esterházy family; as well as (in Prussia) Prince Hardenberg, the State Chancellor, Wilhelm von Humboldt, the educational reformer and diplomat, and Christian Rother, the finance official who rose to become president of the Prussian royal bank. Links with Bismarck proved harder to forge, though by the 1870s Mayer Carl was able to act as a channel of diplomatic communication between "old B." and the governments in London and Paris. The Emperor William II awarded Alfred de Rothschild a medal for his diplomatic services and regarded his brother Natty as "an old and much respected acquaintance."

A central aim of this book is to illuminate these relationships. As Fritz Stern said in his pioneering study of the relationship between Bismarck and Gerson Bleichröder,[20] historians used to be shy of acknowledging the role of financial factors in the policies of the great statesmen of the nineteenth century. Strangely, the many historians of a Marxist persuasion who were once so influential did hardly anything to rectify this, preferring to assert rather than to demonstrate that the interests of the ruling class were essentially the same as (or subordinate to) those of "finance capital." In recent years, historians of British imperialism have done much to refine our understanding of the relationship between the City and the Empire. But the model of "gentlemanly capitalism" advanced by Cain and Hopkins[21] does not quite fit the Rothschild case; and, given the sheer scale of the Rothschilds' role in nineteenth-century finance, this is an exception which may do more than prove the rule. The Rothschilds after the second generation may have acted like gentlemen when they were in the West End or the country. But in the "counting house" they were unalloyed capitalists, applying rules and precepts of business which had their origins in the Frankfurt Judengasse.

~ III ~

The above is a sketch of what might be called the reality of Rothschild history which this book describes in detail. In itself, it is an absorbing story. Yet it becomes doubly so when juxtaposed with the extraordinary mythology which has grown up around the family since they first began to be noticed by contemporaries as "exceptional."

The origins of the Rothschild myth—as far as surviving published records go—can be traced back to 1813, the year after the death of the founder of the firm. Despite its eulogistic title and tone, it would be wrong to describe S. J. Cohen's memoir, *The Exemplary Life of the Immortal Banker Mr Meyer Amschel Rothschild*, as an authorised biography. Nevertheless, it set the tone for what might broadly be described as the sympathetic (if not the official) explanation for the Rothschilds' financial success, essentially portraying it as a morality tale of virtue rewarded. Not only was Mayer Amschel a pious and observant Jew, Cohen argued, but his life "proved beyond doubt that a Jew, as a Jew, can be religious and at the same time an excellent man and a good citizen."[22] Like the authors of so many later works of homage, Cohen said very little about Mayer Amschel's business career. But the strong implication was that his success as a banker was a sign of divine approbation.

Some thirteen years later a more precise but comparably moralistic explanation was published. The *General German Encyclopaedia for the Educated Classes* produced by the Leipzig publisher F. A. Brockhaus was a typical example of the secular reference work of the Biedermeier era. It was popular, selling around 80,000 copies; but, though similar in form to the French encyclopaedias which had been associated with the pre-Revolutionary Enlightenment, its content was monitored by the conservative authorities. Indeed, the man who wrote the entry for "Rothschild" first published in the 1827 edition of the encyclopaedia was Friedrich von Gentz, secretary to Metternich; and the positive tone of the piece reflected the Rothschilds' growing influence over both Austrian public finance and Gentz's private affairs. This was an article which the family not only approved of but paid for: prior to publication Gentz read it aloud to Leopold von Wertheimstein, one of the Vienna house's senior clerks, and ten days later received his "actual reward" from Salomon von Rothschild himself.[23]

Though he said little about their origins in the Frankfurt ghetto in the four columns which Brockhaus published—indeed, he did not mention their religion at all—Gentz implied that they had only recently become "the greatest of all business firms." This success had its roots, he suggested, in Mayer Amschel's "hard work and parsimony . . . knowledge and proven integrity." Likewise his five sons were celebrated for "the reasonableness of their demands . . . the punctiliousness with which they carry out their duties . . . the simplicity and clarity of their schemes, and the intelligent way in which they are put into operation." Apart from their skill as businessmen, Gentz also laid considerable emphasis on "the personal moral character of each of the five brothers" as "a determining factor in the success of their undertakings":

> It is not difficult to create a party for oneself when one is powerful enough to draw many people into one's interest. But to unite the support of all parties and . . . to win the esteem of great and small, requires the possession not merely of material resources, but also of spiritual qualities which are not always found in association with wealth and power. Doing good works on all sides, never refusing help to one in need, always willing to fulfil the requests of anyone who asks for help, without regard to his class, and performing the most important services in the most gracious manner: by these means each of the five branches of the family has achieved a real popularity, and not in a calculated way but out of a natural philanthropy and kindness.[24]

Such reflections had a faintly standardised quality to them, of course: paid hacks had been writing in such glowing terms about their wealthy patrons since ancient times. Privately, Gentz was more ambivalent. His first comment on the family (in response to a suggestion by his friend Adam Müller in 1818 that he write just such an essay) had been decidedly backhanded. They were, he agreed, "a distinct *species plantarum* with its own characteristic features:" to be precise, they were "common, ignorant Jews, who exercise their craft quite naturalistically [that is, instinctively], with no idea of the more elevated relationships between things." On the other hand, they were also "gifted with a remarkable instinct which causes them always to choose the right and of two rights the better." Their enormous wealth was "entirely the result of this instinct, which the public are wont to call luck."[25] In a section of his

"Biographical Notes on the House of Rothschild" which was only published posthumously, Gentz elaborated on this last point—the relationship between ability ("virtue") and circumstances ("luck")—in a Machiavellian vein:

> There is a truth, which, although not quite new, is generally not prop-erly understood. The word *luck* as commonly used in the history of famous individuals or eminent families, becomes bereft of all meaning when we endeavour to dissociate it entirely from the personal or emi-nent factors in each case. There are circumstances and events in life in which good or ill luck may be a determining although not an exclusive factor in human destiny. Lasting success, however, and constant failure are always . . . attributable to the personal virtue or the personal failings and shortcomings of those who are blessed by the one or damned by the other. Nevertheless, the most outstanding personal qualities may some-times require exceptional circumstances and world-shattering events to come to fruition. Thus have the founders of dynasties established their thrones, and thus has the House of Rothschild become great.

The readers of Brockhaus's *Encyclopaedia* were spared these somewhat hackneyed philosophical reflections. Instead—in the form of a footnote inserted by Gentz's editor—they were given a specific and hitherto unpublicised episode which was intended to illustrate precisely the relationship between virtue and luck which Gentz was driving at:

> When the late Elector of Hesse had to flee in 1806 as the French ap-proached, his large private fortune very nearly became Napoleon's booty. R. rescued a substantial part of it by his courage and cleverness, although not without risk to himself, and conscientiously took care of it.

In the 1836 version, the story was elaborated on. Now, it was said, the Elector had:

> left the recovery of his private possessions to Rothschild, their value amounting to many million gulden. It was only by sacrificing the whole of his own property and at considerable personal risk that Rothschild contrived to save the property that had been entrusted to him. The well-known fact that all Rothschild's possessions had been confiscated by the French led the exiled Elector to believe that his own property had been lost too. Indeed he does not even appear to have thought it worth while to make enquiries about it.

But he underestimated the virtuous Mayer Amschel:

> When matters had settled down again, Rothschild immediately pro-ceeded to resume business with the property he had saved . . . When the Elector returned to his states in 1813, the House of Rothschild not merely offered immediately to return to him the capital sums with which they had been entrusted; they also undertook to pay the custom-ary rate of interest from the day when they had received them. The Elec-tor, positively astonished by such an example of honesty and fair dealing, left the whole of his capital for several more years with the firm, and refused any interest payments in respect of the earlier period, accepting a low rate of interest only as from the time of his return. By recommending the House of Rothschild [to others], especially at the

Congress of Vienna, the Elector certainly assisted greatly in extending their connections.

This, then, was "the decisive factor in the enormous . . . development of [Mayer Amschel's] business."[26] Few stories in financial history have been more frequently repeated, and the Rothschilds themselves did their share of the propagation. Nathan gave a potted version to the Liberal MP Thomas Fowell Buxton over dinner in 1834, while the version in the 1836 edition of Brockhaus was read by Carl von Rothschild and probably expanded by his sons' tutor Dr Schlemmer.[27] The story was even the subject of two small paintings by Moritz Daniel Oppenheim which the family commissioned in 1861.

Yet Gentz did not portray the morality tale of the Elector's treasure as the sole explanation for the Rothschilds' subsequent success: he also had some illuminating points to make about the Rothschilds' business methods. "Success in all great trans- actions," he argued, "does not depend purely on the choice and exploitation of the favourable moment, but much more on the application of consciously adopted and fundamental maxims." Besides their "shrewd management and the advantageous circumstances," it was these "principles" which the Rothschilds had to thank for the greatest part of their success. One of these principles obliged:

> the five brothers to conduct their combined businesses in an uninter- rupted community [of interest] . . . any proposal, no matter where it comes from, is the object of collective discussion; each operation, even if it is of minor importance, is carried out according to an agreed plan and with their combined efforts; and each of them has an equal share in its results.[28]

As in the case of the Elector's treasure, the notion of perfect fraternal harmony was very probably inspired by the brothers themselves. When they submitted a design for a coat of arms in 1817 (following their ennoblement by the Austrian Emperor), the fourth quarter depicted an arm bearing five arrows, the symbol of the unity of the five brothers which the firm of N. M. Rothschild & Sons Ltd continues to use on its notepaper to this day. The motto later adopted by the brothers—"Concordia, integritas, industria"—was intended to depict precisely the virtues listed in Brock- haus's *Encyclopaedia*.[29]

Gentz was the first of many writers to write about the Rothschilds in essentially friendly (if not sycophantic) terms. Perhaps the best of the more affectionate repre- sentations of the Rothschilds can be found in the novels of Benjamin Disraeli, who came to know the family intimately (and was also, like Gentz, not uninterested in their wealth). In Disraeli's *Coningsby* (1844), for example, the resemblance between Sidonia and Lionel de Rothschild is close (though not complete). Sidonia's father is described as having made money in the Peninsular War: he then "resolved to emi- grate to England, with which he had, in the course of years, formed considerable commercial connections. He arrived here after the peace of Paris, with his large cap- ital. He staked all on the Waterloo loan; and the event made him one of the greatest capitalists in Europe." After the war, he and his brothers lent their money to the European states and he "became lord and master of the money-market of the world." The younger Sidonia too has all the skills of a banker: he is an accomplished mathematician and "possessed a complete mastery over the principal European lan-

guages."[30] In *Tancred* (1847), the Rothschild-inspired Jewess Eva asks: "[W]ho is
the richest man in Paris?" to which Tancred replies: "The brother, I believe, of the
richest man in London." They are, of course, of her "race and faith."[31] Admittedly,
Disraeli's Rothschild-based characters often act as mouthpieces for the author's own
somewhat idiosyncratic reflections on the place of Jews in the modern world: in no
sense can they be regarded as "realistic" portraits of individual Rothschilds. Nevertheless, there are enough traces of his original models to give the novels a genuine
value to the historian.

   Other "positive" fictional representations are less substantial. An Austrian novella
of the 1850s, for example, portrayed Salomon von Rothschild as a kind of Viennese
Santa Claus, benignly siding with a carpenter's daughter who wants to marry her
rich father's gifted but poor apprentice.[32] A later example of the same genre is Oscar
Wilde's short story "The Model Millionaire, a note of admiration" (1887), which
describes how an impoverished man-about-town is helped to marry the girl he loves
by the generosity of "Baron Hausberg."[33] Such fairy stories, in which Rothschild-
inspired characters are cast as benign dispensers of largesse, have echoes in some of
the twentieth-century popular works about the family, particularly the books by
Balla, Roth, Morton, Cowles and Wilson. The consciously (and sometimes cloy-
ingly) positive tenor of such works can be inferred even from their titles: *The
Romance of the Rothschilds, The Magnificent Rothschilds, A Family Portrait, A Family
of Fortune, A Story of Wealth and Power.*[34] The 1969 musical about Mayer Amschel
and his sons represents the *reductio ad absurdum* of this sycophantic tendency. Here
the family's early history is transformed into a sentimental yarn of good Jewish boys
overcoming the deprivation and degradation of a South German version of Hell's
Kitchen: in a word, kitsch.

   Yet such positive representations account for a relatively small part of the Rothschild myth. Indeed, it is not too much to say that for every writer who has been
willing to attribute at least part of the Rothschilds' financial success to their virtues,
there have been two or three who have taken the opposite view.

   At first, in the 1820s and 1830s, it was not as easy to attack the Rothschilds in
print as it later became, especially in Germany; for one of the other favours Friedrich
Gentz did for his "friends" was to send instructions to newspapers like the *Allgemeine Zeitung* that the Rothschilds should not be criticised.[35] Even in 1843 the radical republican Friedrich Steinmann still found it impossible to find a publisher for
his detailed and highly critical history, *The House of Rothschild, Its History and Transactions*; it did not appear for another fifteen years.[36] The most that could safely be
indulged in were mild digs of the sort published in 1826 by the German economist
and journalist Friedrich List, whose brief report of a theft from the Paris house gratuitously described James de Rothschild as "the mighty lord and master of all the
coined and uncoined silver and gold in the Old World, before whose money-box
Kings and Emperors humbly bow, [the] King of Kings."[37] Even in relatively liberal
England, the earliest criticisms of the Rothschilds were made in the form of allegorical cartoons like Cruikshank's *The Jew and the Doctor*,[38] or under the protection of
parliamentary privilege, like Thomas Duncombe's contemporaneous allusion in
1828 to "a new, and formidable power, till these days unknown in Europe; master of
unbounded wealth, [who] boasts that he is the arbiter of peace and war, and that the
credit of nations depends upon his nod."[39]

It was not untypical, therefore, that the earliest critique of the Rothschilds published in France took the form of fiction. In *The House of Nucingen* (1837–8), Honoré de Balzac portrayed a roguish German-born banker who had made his fortune from a series of bogus bankruptcies, forcing his creditors to accept depreciated paper in repayment.[40] The resemblances between the overbearing, ruthless and coarse Nucingen and James de Rothschild were too numerous to be coincidental; and in his *Splendours and Sorrows of Courtesans* (1838–47), Balzac drew a famous conclusion which applied not only to Nucingen but also, by implication, to James: "All rapidly accumulated wealth is either the result of luck or discovery, or the result of a legalised theft."[41]

It may also have been Balzac who originated or at least disseminated what rapidly became one of the favourite stories in the anti-Rothschild canon; for in *The House of Nucingen* he describes Nucingen's second greatest business coup as a massive speculation on the outcome of the battle of Waterloo. This story was repeated nine years later in Georges Dairnvaell's scurrilous pamphlet, *The Edifying and Curious History of Rothschild I, King of the Jews* (1846), which claimed that, by obtaining the first news of Napoleon's defeat at Waterloo, Nathan had been able to make a huge sum of money by speculating on the stock exchange.[42] In later versions of the story, Nathan was said to have witnessed the battle himself, risking a Channel storm to reach London ahead of the official news of Wellington's victory and thereby pocketing between £20 and £135 million.[43] Other accounts have him bribing the French General Grouchy to ensure Wellington's victory; and then deliberately misreporting the outcome in London in order to precipitate panic-selling.[44]

Of course, it is possible for modern writers to retell the Waterloo legend as an illustration of Nathan's business acumen—indeed, that is what most people today seem to infer from the anecdote. According to a later American banker, Bernard Baruch, it even inspired him to make his first million.[45] However, the idea of a huge speculative profit made on the basis of advance news of a military outcome was a shocking one to many contemporaries: indeed, it epitomised the kind of "immoral" and "unhealthy" economic activity which both conservatives and radicals disliked when they contemplated the stock exchange. In refusing Gladstone's request to make Lionel de Rothschild a peer, Queen Victoria explicitly questioned whether "one who owes his great wealth to contracts with Foreign Govts. for loans, or to successful speculations on the Stock Exchange can fairly claim a British peerage" as this seemed to her "not the less a species of gambling, because it is on a gigantic scale—and far removed from that legitimate trading which she delights to honour . . ."[46]

Another contemporary interpretation of the Waterloo story was as an illustration of Rothschild political neutrality: by implication, if Napoleon had won, Nathan would have been a bear rather than a bull of British bonds. Some writers, however, chose to see his speculation as evidence of positive support for the coalition against Napoleon. To French critics especially, the Waterloo story symbolised the "unpatriotic" (sometimes German, sometimes British) sympathies of the family. As Dairnvaell put it, "The Rothschilds have only ever gained from our disasters; when France has won, the Rothschilds have lost."[47] That the Rothschilds gave their financial support to the opponents of Napoleon could equally well be taken as a sign of their political conservatism; as could the fact that they floated loans for Austria, Prussia and Bourbon France after 1815. Indeed, for radical opponents of the legitimist regimes restored at the Vienna Congress, the Rothschilds were notoriously the "chief ally of the Holy Alliance."[48] To the German writer Ludwig Börne, they were "the nation's worst enemies. They have done more than any to undermine the foundations of freedom, and it is unquestionable that most of the peoples of Europe would by this time be in full possession of liberty if such men as Rothschild . . . did not lend the autocrats the support of their capital."[49]

Nevertheless, it was not always easy to sustain the notion that the Rothschilds were politically biased towards conservative regimes. As early as 1823, in the twelfth canto of *Don Juan*, Byron had asked "Who hold the balance of the world? Who reign O'er Congress, whether royalist or liberal?" and answered: "Jew Rothschild, and his fellow Christian Baring." The crucial point is that Byron saw "Rothschild" as influential over both royalist and liberal regimes, his power stretching as far afield as the republics of Latin America.[50] Even before the 1830 revolutions, the idea was gaining currency that the Rothschilds were more than merely bankrolling the legitimist regimes; consciously or unconsciously, they were acquiring a power of their own which rivalled and perhaps might even replace that of the monarchs and emperors. The events of 1830, when Charles X was toppled from the French throne but James de Rothschild survived unscathed, seemed to confirm this notion of a new financial royalty. "Would it not be a great blessing for the world," asked Börne sarcastically in 1832, "if all the kings were dismissed and the Rothschild family put on their thrones?" William Makepeace Thackeray joked that "N. M. Rothschild, Esq. . . . play[ed] with new kings as young Misses with dolls."[51] Heinrich Heine described Nathan sitting as if on a throne and speaking "like a king, with courtiers all around him."[52] The same point underlies Heine's vision of a children's fancy-dress ball given by Salomon:

> The children wore lovely fancy dress, and they played at making loans. They were dressed up like kings, with crowns on their heads, but there was one of the bigger lads who was dressed exactly like old Nathan Rothschild. He played his part very well, kept both hands in his trouser-pockets, rattled his money and shook with bad temper when one of the little kings wanted to borrow off him . . .[53]

Elsewhere, Heine analysed the ambivalent nature of the Rothschilds' power in more detail. He acknowledged that in the short term it served to shore up the reactionary regimes because "revolutions are generally triggered off by deficiency of money" and "the Rothschild system . . . prevent[ed] such deficiencies." However, he insisted that the Rothschild "system" was also potentially revolutionary in itself:

> No one does more to further the revolution than the Rothschilds themselves . . . and, though it may sound even more strange, these Rothschilds, the bankers of kings, these princely pursestring-holders, whose existence might be placed in the gravest danger by a collapse of the European state system, nevertheless carry in their minds a consciousness of their revolutionary mission.

"I see in Rothschild," he went on, "one of the greatest revolutionaries who have founded modern democracy":

> Rothschild . . . destroyed the predominance of land, by raising the system of state bonds to supreme power, thereby mobilising property

and income and at the same time endowing money with the previous privileges of the land. He thereby created a new aristocracy, it is true, but this, resting as it does on the most unreliable of elements, on money, can never play as enduringly regressive a role as the former aristocracy, which was rooted in the land, in the earth itself.[54]

Not only had the Rothschilds replaced the old aristocracy; they also represented a new materialist religion. "[M]oney is the god of our time," declared Heine in March 1841, "and Rothschild is his prophet."[55]

Nothing seemed to illustrate better the revolutionary significance of the Roth-schilds than their role as railway developers. When the Rothschild-financed lines to Orléans and Rouen were opened in 1843, Heine wrote breathlessly of a social "tremor" with unforeseeable implications. By this time, however, a new note of scep-ticism can be detected in his allusions to the growing power of the "ruling aristoc-racy of money" and the apparent convergence of their interests with those of the old landed aristocracy.[56] In the course of the 1840s a growing number of journalists began to express a more pronounced hostility than Heine ever dared—indebted as he was (and hoped to remain) to the Rothschilds. In particular, James's securing of the rail concession to link Paris and Belgium incensed more radical critics of the July Monarchy. Thus Alphonse Toussenel's *The Jews, Kings of the Epoch: A History of Financial Feudalism* (1846) was primarily directed against the financial terms under which the concession had been granted.[57]

At one level, Toussenel was a kind of socialist who believed that the French rail network should be owned and managed by the state. However, his critique of the Rothschilds as capitalists was inseparably linked to an argument about their Jewish-ness. France had been "sold to the Jews" and the railways were directly or indirectly controlled by "Baron Rothschild, the King of Finance, a Jew ennobled by a very Christian King."[58] It was this aspect of Toussenel's book which inspired the most imitation. Like Toussenel, the anonymous author of *Judgement Passed against Roth-schild and Georges Dairnvaell* equated Judaism and capitalism: James was "the Jew Rothschild, king of the world, because today the whole world is Jewish." The name Rothschild "stands for a whole race—it is a symbol of a power which extends its arms over the entirety of Europe." At the same time, in "exploiting all that is exploitable," the Rothschilds were merely "the model of all the bourgeois and mer-cantile virtues."[59] The connections between tracts like these and what later devel-oped into Marxism are well known. In his notorious 1844 essay "On the Jewish Question," Karl Marx himself spelt out his view of "the real Jew," by which he meant the capitalist, irrespective of his religious background.[60] When, in the wake of the 1848–9 revolutions, the Rothschilds seemed to emerge intact along with the majority of the regimes temporarily overthrown, the moral was obvious to Marx: "[E]very tyrant is backed by a Jew, as is every Pope by a Jesuit."[61]

By the 1850s, then, Heine's notion that the Rothschilds were in some sense the allies of revolutionary change seemed to have been comprehensively discredited and replaced by a critique of the Rothschilds not only as defenders of the political status quo, but also as archetypal capitalists and therefore economic exploiters. It tended to be writers on the revolutionary left in the 1840s who were most keen to equate this with their Judaism—though it was never really explained *why* Jews should have such different attitudes towards economic activity from Gentiles. (For a coherent—if largely fanciful and self-referential—explanation of Rothschild business success as a function of their religion and their race, we need to turn back to Disraeli's *Coningsby* and *Tancred*.)

Further distinctions were possible. In the France of the Second Empire, some contemporaries differentiated between the Rothschilds and other Jews—between the conservative *haute banque*, personified by the Rothschilds, and the "new" bank, embodied by the Crédit Mobilier which the Saint-Simonian Pereire brothers had established. Thus the Crédit Mobilier was portrayed by many writers as a primarily political challenge to the dominance of the Rothschilds over French public finance—Napoleon III's bid to "free himself" from Rothschild tutelage.[62] Unlike most of the overtly anti-Semitic critiques of the Rothschilds, this has proved a more respectable line of argument: the Crédit Mobilier is still sometimes portrayed as a revolutionary new kind of bank, pursuing industrialisation as a developmental strategy in contradistinction to the "old" and implicitly parasitical private banks led by the Rothschilds.[63] But contemporaries—notably the financier Jules Isaac Mirès— sometimes attributed this difference in style to the different cultural backgrounds of the two families (the Pereires were Sephardic Jews, originally from Spain, the Rothschilds Ashkenazim).[64] Others conceived of the difference in more traditional political terms: Rothschild represented "the aristocracy of money" and "financial feudalism" while his rivals stood for "financial democracy" and an economic "1789."[65] In those terms, the decline and fall of the Crédit Mobilier in the 1860s seemed to be more than just a financial event: it was a harbinger of the collapse of the Second Empire itself. Even in modern historiography, James's famous epigram, "L'Empire, c'est la baisse," is often cited as the death-knell for the Bonapartist regime and a reassertion of the *haute banque's* political supremacy in France.[66]

The advent of a republic in 1870 did nothing to dam the stream of French anti-Rothschild literature, however. All that happened was that the attacks now came from the right rather than the left. To those snobbish salon conservatives, the Goncourt brothers, the Rothschilds seemed to be the "Pariah kings of the world . . . coveting everything and controlling everything."[67] Under the veil of republicanism, absolutism had been restored; but it was a corrupt and alien absolutism quite unlike the monarchical and imperial versions which had gone before. The catalyst for a fresh explosion of publications hostile to the Rothschilds was the collapse of the Union Générale bank in 1882, which its founder bitterly blamed on "Jewish finance" and its ally "governmental freemasonry."[68] In his novel *L'Argent*, Emile Zola portrayed the affair as a triumph for the Rothschildian figure of Gundermann, "the banker king, the master of the bourse and of the world . . . the man who knew [all] secrets, who made the markets rise and fall at his pleasure as God makes the thunder . . . the king of gold."[69] But Zola at least acknowledged that there had been a conscious attempt by anti-Jewish Catholics to overthrow Gundermann. It took the twisted mind of Edouard Drumont to argue—in his *Jewish France* (1886)—that the Union Générale had itself been established by the Jews to rob Catholics of their savings.[70] "The God Rothschild," Drumont concluded, was the real "master" of France.[71] Another purveyor of similar libels was Auguste Chirac, whose *Kings of the Republic* (1883)[72] and *The Speculation of 1870 to 1884* (1887) denounced the subjugation of the Republic to "a *king* named Rothschild, with a courtesan or maid called *Jewish finance*."[73]

Such polemics against the social and political power wielded by the Rothschilds were probably most numerous in France, but they had their counterparts elsewhere. In Germany, for example, the Rothschilds were attacked in books like *The Frankfurt Jews and the Mulcting of the People's Well-being* published by "Germanicus" in 1880,[74] Max Bauer's crudely racialist pamphlet *Bismarck and Rothschild* (1891),[75] or Friedrich von Scherb's 1893 *History of the House of Rothschild*.[76] Such works found an echo in the rhetoric of the anti-Semitic "People's" and "Christian Social" parties which enjoyed moderate electoral success in parts of Germany and Austria; Social Democrats also sometimes talked in this way.[77] Indeed, so all-pervasive did the idea of Rothschild power become that the academically respected (though since discredited) Werner Sombart could assert in his book *The Jews and Economic Life* (1911): "[T]he modern stock exchange is Rothschildish (and thus Jewish)."[78]

English examples can also be found. There, as on the continent, "anti-Rothschildism" was as likely to come from the left as from the right. A good illustration is John Reeves's book *The Rothschilds: The Financial Rulers of Nations* (1887), which returns a typical verdict: "The Rothschilds belong to no one nationality, they are cosmopolitan . . . they belonged to no party, they were ready to grow rich at the expense of friend and foe alike."[79]

Reeves's argument that the Rothschilds wielded international as well as internal political power was nothing new. As early as the 1830s, an American magazine could marvel: "Not a cabinet moves without their advice. They stretch their hand, with equal ease, from Petersburg to Vienna, from Vienna to Paris, from Paris to London, from London to Washington."[80] They were, according to the English diarist Thomas Raikes, "the metallic sovereigns of Europe."[81] Alexandre Weill's essay "Rothschild and the Finances of Europe" (1841) went even further (in Reeves's translation):

> There is but one power in Europe and that is Rothschild. His satellites are a dozen other banking firms; his soldiers, his squires, all respectable men of business and merchants; and his sword is speculation. Rothschild is a consequence that was bound to appear; and, if it had not been a Rothschild, it would have been someone else. He is, however, by no means an accidental consequence, but a primary consequence, called into existence by the principles which have guided the European states since 1815. Rothschild had need of the states to become a Rothschild, while the states on their side required Rothschild. Now, however, he no longer needs the State, but the State still has want of him.[82]

An anonymous German cartoonist made essentially the same point (though more vividly) in 1845 when he portrayed a grotesquely caricatured Jew—manifestly a composite Rothschild—as "Die Generalpumpe," a monstrous engine pumping money around the world, with tentacles extending to control monarchs and ministers as far away as Spain and Egypt.[83] A similar image appeared in Wilhelm Marr's *Mephistopheles* in 1850, portraying "Rothschild" surrounded by the kings of Europe, all holding out their hands for money,[84] and again in 1870, when Lionel was depicted in the same pose by the *Period*.[85] Twenty-four years later, the American populist "Coin" Harvey envisioned "Rothschilds" as a vast, black octopus stretching its tentacles around the world.[86] The French cartoonist Léandre likewise portrayed Alphonse de Rothschild as a giant vampire, grasping the world in his claws.[87]

The crucial question, however, was what *use* the Rothschilds made of this ubiquitous financial power. Was it merely an end itself, the result of a pathological appetite for interest and commissions? Perhaps the most frequent contemporary answer to this question was that it enabled the Rothschilds to prevent wars. As early as 1828 Prince Pückler-Muskau referred to "Rothschild . . . without whom no power in Europe today seems able to make war."[88] Three years later Ludwig Börne explicitly argued that Rothschild sales of Austrian government bonds had prevented Metternich from intervening to check the spread of revolution in Italy and Belgium. He also implied strongly that the Rothschilds were keen to see France adopt a more pacific policy towards Austria.[89] Similar claims were made by political insiders too, for example by the Austrian diplomat Graf Prokesch von Osten in December 1830: "It is all a question of ways and means and what Rothschild says is decisive, and he won't give any money for war."[90] After the Polish crisis of 1863, Disraeli claimed that "the peace of the world has been preserved, not by the statesmen, but by the capitalists."[91] Even a hostile writer like Toussenel took the same line: "The Jew *speculates on peace*, that is on a rise, and that explains why peace in Europe has lasted for fifteen years."[92] Later authors have echoed this time and again. Chirac purported to quote a Rothschild saying: "There will be no war because the Rothschilds do not want it."[93] According to Morton, the five sons of Mayer Amschel were "the most militant pacifists ever."[94] And few writers omit the anecdote which attributes to Gutle Rothschild the declaration: "It won't come to war; my sons won't provide money for it."[95]

To modern readers, it is axiomatic that the avoidance of war is a good thing, even if we have come to doubt the ability of bankers to achieve it. However, in the era of military conflicts which began with the Crimean War and ended with the Franco-Prussian War, there were often those who questioned the Rothschilds' motivations in seeking to preserve peace. At the time of the wars of Italian unification—which it was believed they were anxious to avert—the Earl of Shaftesbury found it "strange, fearful, humiliating" that "the destinies of this nation are the sport of an infidel Jew!"[96] The Rothschilds' New York agent August Belmont was widely attacked in the North during the American Civil War because he favoured a negotiated peace with the South and supported General George McClellan's nomination as Democrat candidate in 1864.[97] In much the same way, the Prussian government was irked by the Rothschilds' efforts to avert military confrontation during the "wars of unification," when Bismarck actively desired it.[98] Similar criticisms of Rothschild "pacifism" can be found in the diplomatic and political correspondence of the great powers before and after the turn of the century. To give a final hostile example, the foreign editor (and later editor) of *The Times*, Henry Wickham Steed, described Natty's efforts to avert a war between Germany and Britain in July 1914 as "a dirty German-Jewish international financial attempt to bully us into advocating neutrality."[99]

Yet other commentators—on both Left and Right—often took the opposite line:

that the Rothschilds positively fomented wars. In 1891 the *Labour Leader* denounced the Rothschilds as a

> blood-sucking crew [which] has been the cause of untold mischief and misery in Europe during the present century, and has piled up its prodigious wealth chiefly through fomenting wars between States which ought never to have quarrelled. Wherever there is trouble in Europe, wherever rumours of war circulate and men's minds are distraught with fear of change and calamity, you may be sure that a hook-nosed Rothschild is at his games somewhere near the region of the disturbance.[100]

The case was put in a more sophisticated form by the left-leaning Liberal J. A. Hobson, author of the classic *Imperialism: A Study* (1902). Like many radical writers of the period, Hobson regarded the Boer War as having been engineered "by a small group of international financiers, chiefly German in origin and Jewish in race."[101] The Rothschilds, in his view, were central to this group: "Does anyone seriously suppose," he asked in *Imperialism*, "that a great war could be undertaken by any European State, or any great State loan subscribed, if the house of Rothschild and its connexions set their face against it?'[102] Scherb had made much the same point from a German nationalist perspective in his *History*. "The House of Rothschild has arisen from the quarrels between states, has become great and mighty from wars [and] the misfortune of states and peoples has been its fortune."[103]

War or peace? There was, however, another possibility: that the Rothschilds saw their financial power as a means to advance the interests of their fellow Jews. To poorer Jews throughout Europe, Nathan Rothschild's extraordinary rise to riches had an almost mystical significance—hence the legend of the "Hebrew talisman," the magical source of his good luck, which became associated with him in Jewish lore. This extraordinary story—a version of which was published by an anonymous author in London just four years after Nathan Rothschild's death—imagined that the source of Nathan's financial success was his possession of a magical talisman. His wealth was in fact intended for a higher purpose: "to avenge the wrongs of Israel" by securing "the re-establishment of Judah's kingdom—the rebuilding of thy towers, Oh! Jerusalem!" and "the restoration of Judea to our ancient race."[104]

The notion that the Rothschilds had a design to reclaim the Holy Land for the Jewish people was frequently canvassed in more serious terms than these. As early as 1830 an American journal suggested that "the pecuniary distress of the sultan" might lead him to sell Jerusalem to the Rothschilds.[105] The French socialist Charles Fourier raised the same possibility in his book *The False Industry* in 1836.[106] Disraeli too spoke in 1851 of the Jews being "restor[ed] . . . to their own land" with the help of Rothschild money.[107] And the same idea can be found in popular stories from the Russian Pale of Settlement like "The Czar in Rothschild's Castle."[108]

The other possibility (also raised in this story) was that the Rothschilds might use their financial power to force the Tsar to cease his persecution of the Russian Jews.[109] This illustrated the choice which East European Jews had to contemplate throughout the nineteenth century: should one emigrate to some remote promised land, or stay and seek equality before the law? In the early part of the century, West European Jews had faced the same dilemma. Significantly, the author of the *Hebrew*

Talisman concluded his tract by accusing Nathan of preferring the comforts of social assimilation in England to the rigours of his holy mission. Indeed, he claimed that Nathan's death was the result of his decision to seek political emancipation in England—and a peerage for himself—rather than continuing to strive for the restoration of Jerusalem.

The central dilemma which confronted the Rothschilds lay here: because of their wealth, other Jews looked to them for leadership in their pursuit of equal civil and political rights. As we shall see, this leadership was forthcoming from a remarkably early stage, beginning with Mayer Amschel's efforts to achieve civil rights for the Frankfurt Jews in the era of the Napoleonic Wars, and continuing with his grandson Lionel's campaign to secure the admission of Jews to the House of Commons in the 1840s and 1850s. It was a strategy which suited the Rothschilds well, allowing them to pursue their own familial strategy of penetrating the social and political elites where they lived without converting from Judaism; and allowing them to do good works on behalf of their "co-religionists" while at the same time acquiring quasi-royal status in the eyes of other Jews. However, the more the Rothschilds sought to pursue emancipation as an international objective—intervening on behalf of Jewish communities in Syria, Rumania and Russia as well as in the countries where they themselves resided—the more they encouraged the argument of anti-Semites that the Jews were a cosmopolitan race with no real national attachment. At the same time, when other Jews, despairing of assimilation as an objective, began to press for some kind of return to the Holy Land, the Rothschilds' position was further compromised; for they themselves had no desire to forsake their palatial town and country residences for barren Palestine. But that was just what their anti-Semitic enemies desired. Hostile cartoons from the 1840s and 1890s depicted the Rothschilds in a throng of Jews leaving Germany for the Holy Land—travelling first class, but leaving nonetheless.[110] Commenting on Lionel's campaign for admission to the House of Commons, Thomas Carlyle asked: "[H]ow can a real Jew, by possibility, try to be a Senator, or even a Citizen of any country, except his own wretched Palestine, whither all his thoughts and steps and efforts tend?"[111]

This was broadly the argument (though not the language) of the early Zionists like Theodor Herzl, who came to believe that the only "solution to the Jewish question" was indeed for the Jews to leave Europe and found their own *Judenstaat*. Herzl made a succession of attempts to win the support of the Rothschilds in the belief that they were about to "liquidate" their vast capital as a response to anti-Semitic attacks.[112] But his sixty-six-page address "to the Rothschild Family Council" was never sent,[113] as he concluded from an initial rebuff that they were "vulgar, contemptuous, egoistical people." The Rothschilds, he later declared, were "a national misfortune for the Jews"; he even threatened to "liquidate" them or to "wage a barbaric campaign" against them if they opposed him.[114]

If a Zionist could use such language in the 1890s, it is perhaps not surprising that the radical anti-Semites who flourished in the defeated states of Central Europe after the First World War did so too, albeit with a very different rationale. Indeed, perhaps the most interesting thing about early National Socialist or *völkisch* propaganda directed against the Rothschilds is its very lack of originality. A good example is Dietrich Eckart's address "To All Working People" of 1919:

> The House of Rothschild owns forty billion! . . . [They] only need to
> administer their wealth, to see that it is nicely placed, they do not need
> to work, at least not what we understand by work. But who provides
> them and their like with such an enormous amount of money? . . . Who
> does this? You do it, nobody but you! That's right, it is your money,
> hard-earned through care and sorrow, which is drawn as if magnetically
> into the coffers of these insatiable people.[115]

This was little different from the kind of thing radicals had been saying in France
as well as in Germany since the 1840s. Another early National Socialist who cited
the Rothschilds as examples of the "Jewish problem" he pledged to "solve" was
Adolf Hitler. In an article in the Nazi *Völkische Beobachter* in May 1921, for example, he named them as one of a group of Jewish "capitalists" who controlled the
socialist press.[116] On at least two occasions in 1922 he gave speeches in which he
referred to "the significant difference between the achievements of a man like
Alfred Krupp, who has bequeathed an immense national achievement through his
indefatigable work as an innovator, and the rapacity of a Rothschild, who financed
wars and revolutions and brought the peoples into interest-servitude through
loans."[117] Alfred Rosenberg made a similar point in his book *The Myth of the
Twentieth Century*.[118]

Hitler's use of the past tense was not accidental, for by the 1920s there was no
longer a Rothschild bank in Frankfurt, and even the three remaining Rothschild
houses in London, Paris and Vienna had ceased to play a major role in the German
economy. Yet that did not stop the Nazis from repeatedly using the Rothschilds as a
subject for their anti-Semitic propaganda once they came to power: the old myths
were recycled and embroidered to illustrate the various racial characteristics which
Hitler so detested. For example, Eberhard Müller's play *Rothschild Wins at Waterloo*
(1936) portrayed Nathan on the field of battle, intoning lines like: "My money is
everywhere, and my money is friendly. It is the friendliest power in the world, fat,
round as a bullet and smiling"; "My Fatherland is the London Stock Exchange"; and
"The wealth of England is in my hands."[119] Similar themes were taken up in May
1938 when Julius Streicher's anti-Jewish exhibition was sent to Vienna with a room
devoted exclusively to the House of Rothschild. A later version in Frankfurt put on
display forged "facsimiles of letters" by Mayer Amschel to "an English banker"
which appeared to explain "how he planned to send his five sons all over Europe for
the purpose of dominating all Gentile commerce and finance."[120]

The culmination of the Nazis' anti-Rothschild propaganda was Erich Waschnek's
film *Die Rothschilds*, which was screened for the first time in July 1940 and then re-
released after further editing a year later with the sub-title *Aktien auf Waterloo*
("Shares in Waterloo"). This was one of a trio of films designed to prepare the
German population for harsher measures against the Jews: the others were *Jud-Süss*
and the notorious "documentary" *Der ewige Jude* ("The Eternal Jew"). It is true that
the Waterloo legend presented problems for the Propaganda Ministry at a time of
uncertainty about the correct "line" to take towards Britain. While some British
characters (Wellington and the "Finance Minister" Herries) are portrayed as corrupt
and morally degenerate, others—in particular the banker "Turner" and his Irish
wife—are cast sympathetically as victims of the Rothschilds' machinations. But the

portrayal of the Rothschilds themselves is unambiguous enough, as the plot summary drafted by the Allies after the war shows:

> In 1806 the "Landgraf" of Hesse escaping Napoleon has to entrust his fortune of £6,000,000 to somebody for safekeeping. He deposits the money with the Jewish banker, Meyer Amschel Rothschild in Frankfurt. The abusive use of this money becomes the foundation for the power of the Rothschilds. Amschel Rothschild sends the money to his son Nathan who is not respected by his business rivals. But Nathan ruthlessly outwits all of them. He gets money to Wellington in Spain with the help of his brother in Paris—Nathan is the first to receive news that Napoleon has escaped from Elba and the only one to gamble all he possesses on the reinstatement of Louis of Orleans [*sic*]. He is a joke in Society—nobody takes him seriously but his Jewish hirelings and the British Ministry of Finance. "Lord" Wellington is again sent to fight Napoleon. He has very little time to prepare for the war—the ladies keep him busy! But he has time enough (just as Fouché does in Paris) to confer with Rothschild who implies that Wellington will be well rewarded if Rothschild is the first to know the outcome of the battle. The moment Rothschild hears that Napoleon is beaten he spreads news that the English cause is lost. A panic follows—everybody sells Government Bonds—Rothschild buys them. The poor lose their money. The few honourable rich Englishmen (one of them is pictured as extremely decent due to the fact that he is married to an Irish woman!) lose all they own. The star of David lies over England—over the part of the world that Nazi Germany fights.

All the themes of Nazi anti-Semitism are here. The Jews have no allegiance to the countries where they live and merely wish to profit from the sufferings of others: "You can only make a lot of money with a lot of blood!" Mayer Amschel (Erich Ponto) tells Nathan (Karl Kuhlmann). Under their direction, "International Jewry" engages in "gigantic speculations" while "soldiers bleed to death on the battlefields." The Jews are physically different and repellent: Mayer Amschel sports a kaftan and ringlets, while his oleaginous son lusts grotesquely after the wife of his Aryan rival— a typical Goebbels touch.[121] Despite the Propaganda Minister's apparent dissatisfaction with the film, it appears to have been relatively popular: the secret police reported excitement when it was first released in Berlin and surrounding districts and it also played to large audiences in occupied France. When a British prisoner-of-war was leafing through a German newspaper in January 1945, he was so amazed to find a version of the story on the front page that he translated it and took it home when the war was over.[122]

It is instructive to compare Waschnek's film with its American precursor and model, *The House of Rothschild*, directed by Darryl Zanuck in 1934 and starring George Arliss as both Mayer Amschel and Nathan. In the earlier film, the Rothschilds are portrayed sympathetically: their rise from rags to riches is a version of the "American dream" (complete with a wholesome romance between a Rothschild daughter and the dashing young British officer who brings the news of victory at Waterloo), while the obstacles they confront—the sinister Prussian Minister Baron Ledrantz (Boris Karloff) and rioting mobs in Frankfurt—allude to contemporary developments in Germany.[123] Yet even the American version of the Rothschild story is largely myth, much of which could be construed in a less sympathetic light. Mayer Amschel may be a lovable old man with a twinkle in his eye and matinée idols for children; but he still has a plan for world domination.[124] Indeed, in places the films are like mirror images of one another. In Waschnek's version, Nathan draws a map of Europe to show the centres of Rothschild power and a family tree which, when its branches are connected, forms a Star of David; the flaming star is then superimposed over a map of England with the accompanying title: "As this film was being completed, the last members of the Rothschild family are leaving Europe as refugees and escaping to their allies in England. The fight against British plutocracy continues!" The Zanuck film uses very similar imagery: on his deathbed, Mayer Amschel tells his five sons to go to the various European cities. These are then depicted on a map, and a Star of David is again superimposed. However, the concluding sequence of the film emphasises the parallel between Nazi anti-Jewish policy and the "Hep" riots against the Frankfurt Jews in 1818. In essence, then, the two films tell the same story, albeit with the moral signs pointing in opposite directions.

This Janus-faced quality to the cinematic representations of the Rothschilds' early history is symptomatic of a more general ambiguity. For there is a sense in which all the various Rothschild legends can be thought of as a single myth—a myth of immense wealth; of meteoric social ascent; of limitless political and diplomatic power; and of some enigmatic *ultima ratio*, connected with the family's religion. Usually, the myth is told in pejorative terms: the wealth is ill-gotten, the social ascent unsuccessful, the power based on corruption and the objective sinister. But it can equally well be told in the Hollywood style, as a tale of economic over-achievement, social success, legitimate power and moral ends. Other subjects exploited by the Nazis for their propaganda have, of course, since become taboo—and in some countries even illegal. But the ambivalent quality of the Rothschild myth seems to guarantee its constant replication and modification. This is perhaps most obvious in France. Parts of the special edition of the magazine *Crapouillot* published in 1951 were undoubtedly anti-Semitic, reproducing the stories (and cartoons) from the nineteenth century radical and right-wing literature; but other "grandees" included in the magazine were not Jewish, and the tone of the text as a whole was relatively temperate.[125] As the work of writers like Coston and Peyrefitte shows, it was possible in the atmosphere of the Fourth Republic to repeat more or less verbatim the old legends about the "200 families who rule France" with only a slight modification of tone.[126] Typically, when the former de Rothschild Frères director Georges Pompidou became Prime Minister in April 1962 (and later President in 1969), *le Canard enchaîné* commented simply: "RF = République française = Rothschild frères."[127] However, similar echoes of the Rothschild myth can be found in the British press too. Hostile inferences were sometimes drawn in the 1980s from the fact that a number of Conservative politicians had worked for N. M. Rothschild & Sons Limited either before or after their political careers, at a time when the firm was handling a number of important privatisations.[128] Indeed, the Labour Shadow Chancellor Roy Hattersley went so far as to allege a "correlation between contribution to the Tory party and the receipt of business from Government" following the first Rothschild privatisation—an allegation he was later forced to withdraw.[129]

Nowhere is the continuing vitality of the Rothschild myth on the lunatic fringe more apparent than in the writings of David Icke, the erstwhile environmentalist turned "New Age" evangelist. According to Icke, the Rothschilds are members of the "Global Elite or Brotherhood"—also referred to as the "All-Seeing Eye Cult" and the "Prison Warders"—which secretly rules the world. Ever since the time of Mayer Amschel, they have "manipulated governments and worked through the Brotherhood network to create wars and revolutions." They are the hidden power which "controls" other well-known banks such as Warburgs, Schroders and Lazards, as well as being "behind" American financiers such as J. P. Morgan, the Rockefellers, Kuhn, Loeb & Co. (an "obvious Rothschild front"), the Speyers and the Lehmans—not to mention the Bank of England and the Federal Reserve system. Through this network of global power, they have been responsible for, among other things: the murder of Abraham Lincoln; the Boer War; the creation of Israel (a gambit to control the oil of the Middle East); the Russian revolution ("a coup on Russia by the United States financial arm of the Global Elite largely controlled by the Rothschilds"); the financing of Hitler; and even the floating of the dollar by President Nixon. Today, Icke alleges, they and their associates in the Conservative party and the press are plotting to monopolise the world's energy supplies—hence their interest in electricity, coal and gas privatisation.[130]

A cursory search of the Internet reveals a plethora of equally bizarre conspiracy theories. A "Study of Corporate and Banking Influence" by Don Allen purports to show the "linear connection" between the Rothschilds, the Bank of England and the Federal Reserve. The "A-albionic Research Weekly" by James Daugherty claims to have identified "The 'World Money Cartel' or 'Empire of the City (of London)' operated for the 'Crown' by the 'legendary' Merchant Bankers of the Bank of England, including the Warburgs, Rothschilds [and] Barings." "Scriptures for America" gives a more elaborate version of Icke's claims about the economic rationale behind Rothschild support for Zionism, "the single purpose" of which is supposedly "to secure permanent and secure access to [the] vast natural resources in the Far East." In a similar vein, Sherman H. Skolnick's "Conspiracy Nation" repeats the claim that the Rothschilds "arranged the murder of President Lincoln," as his "post-war policies would have wrecked [their] commodity speculations." Skolnick also repeats the allegation that "the Rothschilds . . . financed the rise of Hitler as a bulwark against the Soviet Union," adding by way of "explanation" that "the Rothschilds are interwoven with the Catholic Church and, jointly with the traditional mafia and the American CIA, interlocked with the Vatican Bank, which was pro-Nazi."

Such surreal libels are not confined to the Internet. The television preacher and Republican politician Pat Robertson's book *The New World Order* (published in 1991) states that the Rothschilds were "polluted by the occultism of . . . Illuminated Freemasonry" and that "Paul Warburg, architect of the Federal Reserve System, was a Rothschild agent." From a completely different political milieu, Khalid Muhammad—a former assistant to Louis Farrakhan, the leader of the radical African-American organisation Nation of Islam—has repeated the suggestion that "the Rothschilds . . . financed Hitler" and "aided" his anti-Semitic policies; as well—needless to say—as "gaining control of" the Bank of England and the Federal Reserve system. It might be thought that a serious banking history should scrupulously avoid reference to this kind of nonsense. Yet it is impossible to appreciate the need for a scholarly history of the subject if one blithely pretends such myths do not exist.

~ IV ~

Part of the purpose of this book, then, is to supplant Rothschild mythology with historical reality, in so far as that can be "reconstructed" from surviving documentary evidence. It might be wondered why this has not been done before; why only a tiny fraction of the books which purport to be about the Rothschilds are in fact based on serious archival scholarship. Part of the answer, of course, lies in the enduring appeal of a rich and successful family to hack writers, who are always able to turn a penny by rehashing the myths and anecdotes already in print. Another reason is that, until recently, it was far from easy to gain access to the relevant documentary material. Tragically, the vast archive of the Frankfurt house—which also included all that had been kept of the Naples house's papers—was largely destroyed in 1912, with the exception of a very few early documents which were sent to Paris.[131] Part of the archive of the Vienna house was confiscated by the Nazis in 1938 and passed into Soviet hands at the end of the war along with various papers belonging to members of the French family which were seized during the German occupation. This material lay buried in the Moscow "trophy" archive of the KGB throughout the Cold War and became available to outside researchers at the Centre for the Preservation of Historical Documents only in 1990.[132] When Count Corti wrote his two-volume study of the "Rise" and "Reign" of the Rothschilds in 1927–8, he had to rely mainly on the Austrian state archives and the published correspondence, memoirs and diaries of nineteenth-century politicians.[133] The archive of the London house was not generally open to scholars before 1978, though members of the family and "insiders" like Lucien Wolf made use of documents there to produce a number of important monographs.[134]

On the other hand, the archive of the French house—the basis of Bertrand Gille's monumental two-volume study published in the 1960s—was deposited in the Archives Nationales following the nationalisation of Banque Rothschild in 1981.[135] Considering the wealth of material which has been available in both Paris and London since the family began to relax its restrictions on access, it is remarkable how little serious research has been done. A mainly social and political history of the English family[136] and a handful of articles and monographs on quite specialised subjects[137] is a relatively low yield for such important—indeed, in many ways unique—documentary collections. Even the volume of essays produced to coincide with the successful 1994–5 exhibition at the Frankfurt Jewish Museum entitled *The Rothschilds: A European Family* contains relatively few contributions based on new archival research.[138] Pauline Prevost-Marcilhacy's volume on Rothschild architecture is the only book to date which has made use of all the major Rothschild document collections in London, Paris and Moscow.[139]

There is, however, a further explanation for this relative lack of scholarship, and that is the intractability of so much of the material. There is a vast amount of it. "We Rothschilds are inveterate scribblers," wrote Charlotte de Rothschild to her children in 1874, "and cannot live without letter writing and letter receiving."[140] It was only too true. The most important letters in the London archive[141] are the so-

called "private letters" (the XI/109 series) between the partners in the bank, which
cover the years from 1812 to 1898. Altogether, these fill 135 boxes. Of these letters,
I have referred to around 5,000 in the text. (To give an idea of the relative importance of this series, the final database of letters which I and my researchers wholly or
partially transcribed from all archives contains around 13,000 entries.) The fre-
quency of this private correspondence—which was private in the sense that, with a
few exceptions, only the partners and the scribes they occasionally used saw it—
varied enormously, depending on the volume of business, political news, the
number of partners in the various offices and the time of year. Sometimes the partners in Paris might send out only two or three letters in a quiet week; but at peaks of
activity, three partners might write one or sometimes two letters a day. To give a
single example, in March 1848, the London partners received at least sixty important private letters from their partners on the continent. These letters were often
quite lengthy, especially in the early years of the partnership, when Amschel and
Salomon routinely sent their brothers five or six sides, mingling political news,
financial information, business enquiries and answers with family gossip and personal grumblings. These were, it might be said, the telephone calls of the nineteenth-century, in that they contain the kind of information businessmen today
rarely commit to paper. They were also, it should be stressed, untypical by nineteenth century standards. Firstly, because their partners were not so geographically
dispersed, few if any of the Rothschilds' rivals corresponded in this way on a regular
basis. It is unlikely that a comparable series of letters exists in any other banking
archive. Secondly, because the Rothschilds were exceptionally well connected, the
political intelligence their letters contain was usually of a very high quality. James
did not exaggerate when he spoke in the 1840s of being able to see King Louis
Philippe "daily": at times of political crisis, he could do just that. His letters to
London—the series which I have used most fully—constitute one of the most
remarkable sources for nineteenth-century financial and diplomatic history.

   There are only two causes for regret. There is a substantial and unexplained gap
in the XI/109 series for the period 1854 to 1860, and after 1879 it trails off (though
the letters from Paris in the series XI/101 continue up until 1914). More seriously,
nearly all the copies of the outgoing letters *from* the London partners (in so far as
these were made at all) were destroyed at the orders of successive senior partners. All
that survive are eight tantalising boxes covering the period 1906–14. We therefore
have precious few letters by Nathan compared with the thousands from his brothers
which have survived; only a frustratingly small number from his eldest son Lionel;
and next to nothing from his grandsons for the period before 1906. It should also be
said that relatively few non-business letters by the partners were preserved; indeed,
the first Lord Rothschild insisted that all his private correspondence be burnt after
his death (though I have been able to find a number of letters in the archives of
politicians to whom he wrote). If at times the history of N. M. Rothschild & Sons
seems to have been written from the point of view of their continental relatives, that
is an unavoidable consequence of this imbalance in the sources. We are fortunate
that Nathan's sons (especially Nat) spent a good deal of time on the continent and
that their letters "home" to their parents and brothers have been preserved; but these
are no substitute for the letters written from London. By comparison, I have been
unable to do more than take occasional samples from the even more voluminous

general and private correspondence from the various Rothschild agents—particularly those in the major agencies in Madrid, Brussels, St Petersburg, New York, Mexico and San Francisco. There is an equally huge amount of mostly routine business letters from less important firms who merely acted as "correspondents" or did occasional business with the Rothschilds: again, I have had time only to dip into these letters, which came from as far afield as Calcutta, Shanghai, Melbourne and Valparaiso.

A further difficulty—which explains why the XI/109 files have never before been fully utilised by historians—is that, up until the late 1860s, all of the second generation and a number of key figures in the third generation of partners (as well as a few of the firm's agents) corresponded with one another primarily in *Judendeutsch*: German written in Hebrew characters. This was partly because it was the family's first language. But it was also partly to ensure that prying eyes would not be able to read the firm's private correspondence. The difficulty which even Hebrew readers find in deciphering the relatively archaic script used by the brothers has deterred previous scholars, who have been content to rely on the highly selective English extracts translated somewhat freely by a group of refugees from Germany employed as researchers in the 1950s (the so-called "T" files), or on the letters written by Nathan's children in easily legible English.[142] However, the heroic work of Mordechai Zucker in translating[143] or reading aloud the original letters on to tape has removed this obstacle for me, making available for the first time a "virgin" historical source of the very first importance.

The great benefit is that, partly because their letters were so hard for outsiders to read, the Rothschilds were able to write to one another with more or less complete candour. As a result, their correspondence has a uniquely direct and intimate quality. The partners were frank—sometimes even abusive—with one another, and made no secret of their opinions of the monarchs and ministers they had to deal with, which were rarely flattering. Their tone is colloquial, sometimes crudely so. The contrast could hardly be greater with the formal, functional business letters sent from one Rothschild house to another, or the much more carefully crafted letters they addressed to political friends and business associates outside the closed circle of the partnership and family. When used in conjunction with the other archival sources listed in the bibliography, the Rothschild letters reveal a reality which is in many ways more fascinating than even the most fantastic myth.

~ V ~

Academic historians like to contribute to historiographical debates. The Rothschilds are relevant to so many that it would be tedious to do more than merely list them, which I dutifully do now. The five Rothschild houses constitute an early version of what later became known as the "multinational:" business historians may find it illuminating to learn more about the way in which the firm worked as an international private partnership. Economic historians have for many years sought to assess the contribution of banks to industrialisation; there is ample material here on that question, especially as regards the role of the Rothschilds in the development of continental railways. The history of the Rothschilds also helps to illuminate the long-running debate about the differences between British, French and German banking, for the obvious reason that the various Rothschild houses worked in similar though not identical ways in each country. There is some new light too on the much-debated question of European capital export: those still concerned with the Hobson/Lenin paradigm may like to contrast it with the realities presented here. I would like to think that the book will also contribute, albeit indirectly, to some of the more technically sophisticated debates in the still-young specialism of financial history.[144] I fear this is not a "model" history of a bank.[145] I am conscious that I have not written anything about "asymmetrical information," "credit rationing" and "portfolio management," but I hope that those interested in such things will not be wholly disappointed by the sections of the book which concentrate on profits, losses and balance sheets. If nothing else, these data can now usefully be compared with those in other published bank histories—a task I have been able only to begin here.

Social historians will find this, I hope, a useful contribution not only to the old debates about class, but also to more voguish controversies about family structure and relations between the sexes within the wealthy elite: although the partners in the bank were exclusively male, I have taken care not to neglect their mothers, wives and daughters, who were often (as Miriam Rothschild recently pointed out) as capable as the Rothschild men, if not more so.[146]

Specialists in Jewish history may be suspicious of yet another book written about a family which has always loomed uncomfortably large in their field; I can only hope that as an atheist from a Calvinist background I have not misunderstood too much the exceedingly complicated relationship between the "exceptional family" and their "co-religionists." I do not think I am guilty of overestimating the very important role the Rothschilds have played in modern Jewish history. Though it is not my forte, I have endeavoured to satisfy cultural historians by paying due attention to the contemporary allusions to the Rothschilds in high and low literature, and by doing my best to summarise the family's contribution as art collectors and as patrons of some of the nineteenth century's most distinguished architects, writers and composers. The book should also be of use to political historians, especially those with an interest in France, Britain and Germany. I am conscious that I have probably misinterpreted some of the more obscure allusions to the high politics of nineteenth-century France in the letters of James and his nephews; but I look to French historians to correct me by doing their own research on the relevant correspondence. Perhaps, on reflection, the book will give most satisfaction to those unfashionable scholars who continue to be interested in diplomatic history. There is more here than I had originally expected to write about Belgian neutrality, Schleswig-Holstein, the Eastern Question and the origins of the various wars which were fought (or averted) in the century between Waterloo and the Marne. But after finance—or rather inseparable from it—diplomacy was what the Rothschilds themselves regarded as important.

To all these different readerships, I offer apologies for sins of omission: because the book was supposed to be written in three years (it took nearer five) there are letters which I did not read, books I merely skimmed, archives I did not visit. In deciding what not to do, I have tried to give priority to documents hitherto unknown or only partially known. Where an archive has apparently been well sifted by a previous historian, I have elected not to re-sift, at the risk of perpetuating error. This volume should thus be regarded as something of a research agenda: the London archive in particular cries out for further investigation, and I hope to see a steady stream of monographs in the coming years, correcting my broad-brush interpretations and doubtless many points of detail.

The fact that a book can at least pretend to be relevant to so many different specialisms should in itself reassure the non-academic reader, who I hope will forgive those passages of the book which betray the author's profession, just as those readers who are themselves bankers or Jews will forgive the errors and false notes which doubtless remain. If this book does something to help reintegrate economic, social, cultural, political and diplomatic history, and in the process to make both the nineteenth century world and the "exceptional family" more intelligible, it will have got the author from Point A, where he began, to Point B, where he wished to end up.

I

Father and Sons

ONE

"Our Blessed Father":
Origins

*Yes, my dear fellow, it all amounts to this: in order to do some-
thing you must be something. We think Dante great, but he
had a civilisation of centuries behind him; the House of Rothschild is rich but it has required more than one generation to
attain such wealth. Such things all lie deeper than one thinks.*

—GOETHE, OCTOBER 1828[1]

A traveller arriving in eighteenth-century Frankfurt, as he passed across the main
Sachsenhäuser Bridge leading to the Fahrtor Gate, could hardly miss the *Judensau*—the Jews' Sow (see illustration 1.i). An obscene graffito on the wall, it depicted
a group of Jews abasing themselves before—or rather beneath and behind—a fierce
sow. While one of them suckled at her teats, another (in rabbinical garb) held up her
tail for the third (also a rabbi) to drink her excrement. The "Jews' devil" watched
approvingly. If the traveller looked up, he could also see a second and still more
repellent image: that of a dead baby, its outstretched body punctured by countless
small knife wounds and beneath it nine daggers. "On Maundy Thursday in the year
1475," read a caption, "the little child Simeon, aged 2, was killed by the Jews"—an
allusion to the case of Simon of Trent, who had allegedly been a victim of "ritual
murder," the fictional practice whereby Jews murdered Gentile children in order to
put their blood in unleavened bread.[2]

Such a graphic expression of anti-Jewish sentiment was by no means unique: the
image of Jews worshipping a pig can be found in numerous woodcut and printed
versions dating as far back as the fourteenth century, while the myth of ritual
murder gained currency in Germany in the fifteenth.[3] What made the Frankfurt
pictures remarkable—at least in the eyes of the city's most celebrated son, Johann
Wolfgang Goethe—was that they were "not the product of private hostility, but
erected as a public monument."[4] The *Judensau* and the murdered child were officially sanctioned symbols of a long-standing tradition of hostility to an enemy
within the free imperial town.[5]

The first records of a Jewish community in Frankfurt date back to the middle of
the twelfth century, when it numbered between one and two hundred. Its history
was one of periodic persecution by the Gentile populace. In 1241, more than three

1.i: Anonymous early-eighteenth-century print of Simon of Trent and the *Judensau*.

quarters of the Frankfurt Jews were massacred in the so-called "Battle of the Jews" (*Judenschlacht*).[6] The community re-established itself over the subsequent decades, but just over a century later, in 1349, there was a second pogrom. In both cases, popular millenarianism played a part: in the first "battle," fears that the Jews were in league with the Mongol horde; in the second, fears instigated by members of a flagellant order that the Jews would attract the plague to the town.

There were, however, worldly reasons why both the Holy Roman Emperor—who declared the Jews "servi nostri et servi camerae nostri" in 1236—and the municipal authorities were inclined to encourage Jewish settlement. The Jews were a source of tax revenue and credit (given their exemption from the laws prohibiting usury) who could be offered "protection" and restricted privileges in return for hard cash. But protection and restriction went hand in hand. In 1458, at the order of the Emperor Frederick III, the Jews were confined to a ghetto (from the Italian *borghetto* or suburb): a single, narrow street on the north-eastern edge of the town at both ends of which gates were erected. To the 110 Jews living in the town, this capitivity in what became known as the Judengasse (Jews' Lane) suggested a "New Egypt." On the other hand, the persistent risk of popular violence could give the ghetto the character of a sanctuary. Allegations of ritual murder in 1504 and an attempt to declare the Jews heretics five years later provided a reminder of the vulnerability of the community's position, as did the conversion of the majority of the town's population to Lutheranism in 1537, given the avowed hostility of Luther towards the Jews. The Judengasse provided sanctuary of sorts in a perilous world; and between 1542 and 1610 its population grew from around 400 to 1,380 (an increase which was paralleled by Huguenot migration to Frankfurt from the Netherlands). The economic and social tensions which coincided with—or were caused by—these influxes culminated in yet another outbreak of popular violence against the Jewish community: the "Fettmilch riots," named after their shopkeeper leader Vincenz Fettmilch. However, wholesale looting of the Judengasse was this time not accompanied by mass murder (the Jews were expelled from the town) and, after a brief period of popular rule, imperial troops quashed the insurrection. Fettmilch and the other leaders of the revolt were hanged and the Jews marched back into the ghetto, their status as protégés of the Emperor reaffirmed.[7]

In practice, as before, "protection" meant extraordinarily tight regulation, the details of which were set out by the Council in the Stättigkeit, a statute which was read out each year in the main synagogue. Under its terms, which remained in force until the very end of the eighteenth century, the Jewish population was restricted to just 500 families; the number of weddings was rationed to just twelve a year and the age of marriage fixed at twenty-five. No more than two Jews from outside were allowed to settle in the ghetto each year. Jews were prohibited from farming, or from dealing in weapons, spices, wine and grain. They were forbidden to live outside the Judengasse and, until 1726, were obliged to wear distinctive insignia (two concentric yellow rings for men and a striped veil for women) at all times. They were confined to the ghetto every night, on Sundays and during Christian festivals; at other times, they were forbidden to walk in the town more than two abreast. They were barred from entering parks, inns, coffee houses and the promenades around the town's picturesque walls; they were not even allowed near the town's ancient cathedral; and had to enter the town hall by a back door. They were permitted to visit the town market, but only during set hours, and were forbidden to touch vegetables and fruit there. If he appeared in court, a Jew had to swear a special oath which reminded all present of "the penalties and maledictions which God imposed on the cursed Jews." If he heard the words "Jud, mach mores!" ("Jew, do your duty!") in the street, he was obliged—even if they were uttered by a mere boy—to doff his hat and step to one side. And if he had occasion to go outside Frankfurt—for which a special pass was required—he paid double the amount of toll paid by a Gentile when entering the town. In return for this supposed "protection," every Jew also paid a poll (or "body") tax.[8]

All this meant that the Frankfurt Jews spent most of their lives within the high walls and gates of the Judengasse. Today virtually nothing remains of this prison-cum-street. All but a couple of houses were demolished by the Frankfurt authorities in the course of the nineteenth century, and what little remained was flattened by American bombers in May 1944. However, the foundations of a part of the old street have recently been excavated, and these give at least a rough idea of the inordinately cramped conditions of life in the ghetto. Curving from the Börnheimer Gate in the north towards the Jewish cemetery in the south, it was just a quarter of a mile long and no more than twelve feet wide—in places less than ten. Having originally been designated a ghetto at a time when the Jewish population was little more than a hundred, the lane was horribly overcrowded: by 1711 there were no fewer than 3,024 people living there. Accommodating them all in such a small area required a high degree of architectural ingenuity: houses were just eight feet wide and had up to four storeys, and behind each row an additional row was constructed. Fire was an inevitable hazard—indeed, all or part of the Judengasse was destroyed by major conflagrations in 1711, 1721 and 1774. This meant that life there was both dear and cheap: dear because the demand for housing far outstripped the supply, so that a four-room house in the north of the Judengasse cost as much as Goethe's father paid for his twenty-room mansion in the Grosse Hirschgraben; cheap because lack of sanitation, light and fresh air reduced life expectancy. In the 1780s it was estimated that average mortality among Jews was 58 per cent higher than among Gentiles.[9] A traveller in 1795 observed how "most of the people among the Frankfurt Jews, even those who are in the blooming years of their life, look like the walking dead . . . Their deathly pale appearance sets them apart from all the other inhabitants in the most depressing way."[10] Later, after the walls around it had been partly demolished, the Judengasse was to some extent romanticised by artists like Anton Burger; indeed, it became something of a Victorian tourist attraction (Charles Greville and George Eliot were among the English visitors).[11] At the time, it struck the young Goethe as a hellish slum:

> The lack of space, the dirt, the throng of people, the disagreeable accents of the voice—altogether, it made the most unpleasant impression, even upon the passer-by who merely looked through the gate. It was a long time before I dared to go in there alone, and I did not return there readily when once I had escaped from that multitide of people, all of them with something to hawk, all indefatigably buying or selling.[12]

One who knew it more intimately was the poet Ludwig Börne, who (as Juda Löw Baruch) grew up there in the 1780s and 1790s. Looking back in anger rather than nostalgia, he remembered a

> long dark prison, into which the highly celebrated light of the eighteenth century has not yet been able to penetrate . . . Stretching ahead of us lay an immeasurably long street, near us just enough room to reassure us that we could turn around as soon as the wish overcame us. Over us is no longer sky, which the sun needs in order to expand in his breadth; one doesn't see sky, one sees only sunlight. An evil smell rises everywhere around us, and the cloth that is supposed to shield us from infection serves also to catch the tears of compassion or to hide the smile of malice from the gaze of the watching Jews. Tramping laboriously through the filth slows our pace down enough to permit us the leisure for observation. We set our feet down skittishly and carefully so that we don't step on any children. These swim about in the gutter, creep about in the filth innumerable as vermin hatched by the sun from the dungheap. Who would not indulge these little boys in their small desires? . . . If one were to consider play in childhood as the model for the reality of life, then the cradle of these children must be the grave of every encouragement, every exuberance, every friendship, every joy in life. Are you afraid that these towering houses will collapse over us? O fear nothing! They are thoroughly reinforced, the cages of clipped birds, resting on the cornerstone of eternal ill-will, well walled up by the

industrious hands of greed, and mortared with the sweat of tortured slaves. Do not hesitate. They stand firm and will never fall.[13]

As Börne commented, even at a time of supposed "enlightenment," when other German cities were relaxing the restrictions imposed on Jews, Frankfurt held out, refusing to implement the Emperor Joseph II's Edict of Toleration (1782) and confiscating copies of Ephraim Lessing's philo-Semitic play *Nathan the Wise*. When the Jewish community petitioned in 1769 and again in 1784 to be allowed to leave the ghetto on Sundays, the request was rejected as an attempt "to put themselves on an equal footing with the Christian residents." [14] As in the past, this policy was to some extent forced upon the Council by the majority of the Gentile townspeople. Typically, when a Jewish mathematics teacher was granted permission to live and teach outside the ghetto in 1788, there was such a popular outcry that the licence had to be revoked; and a similar request by a Jewish doctor in 1795 was turned down flat.[15] For much the same reason—as a letter of complaint signed by seven leading Jewish merchants makes clear—the rules governing travel outside the Judengasse on holidays and Sundays were made more rather than less restrictive in 1787, with the introduction of a complicated system of identity cards:

> As a human being, every Jew has the same rights as any other and a just claim for protection by his sovereign. Unfortunately, the lower classes are still so bound to the prejudices of their fathers as to doubt that a Jew is a human being like themselves. They mistreat [the Jews] in all sorts of ways and many an old man seems pleased when his son is mistreating a Jew. Even soldiers indulge in this punishable tyranny. Would they not take [the new system] as an invitation for countless acts of harassment? They would use the smallest difference in clothing, hair, beards and the like as an excuse to perform the most stringent examinations at the town gate. The slightest deviation [would] enable them to arrest the Jew and march him off to the main guard house like a common thief.[16]

There was more to this persistent and systematic discrimination than mere ancestral prejudice, however. An important factor was that the Gentile business community genuinely feared the economic challenge which they believed would be posed by an emancipated Jewish population. The fact that a slum like the Judengasse could produce mathematics teachers and doctors in itself tells us something important about its culture: it was not as closed as it seemed. As Goethe himself discovered, when he plucked up the courage to enter the ghetto, the Jews were "human beings after all, industrious and obliging, and one could not help but admire even the obstinacy with which they adhered to their traditional ways."[17] Despite—perhaps partly because of—the grim conditions in which they lived, the Frankfurt Jews were anything but an underclass in cultural terms.

Of course, the culture of the Judengasse was an unfamiliar one to a Gentile like Goethe. It was an intensely religious culture, with the rhythm of life still dictated by the religious laws of the *Halakha*. Every morning and evening, men were summoned to worship at synagogue by the *Schul-Klopper* knocking on their doors with a hammer. The Sabbath was, as an English visitor recalled, "in the picturesque phrase of their prayer-book, 'a bride,' and her welcome, week by week, was of a right bridal sort. White cloths were spread and lamps lit in her honour. The shabbiest dwellings put on something of a festive air."[18] Education at the lane's three primary schools (*heder*) and the rabbinical college (*yeshivah*) was, by the standards of the time, conservative, with children learning to read the Torah, the foundation of Mosaic teaching law, then moving on to Rashi's commentaries and finally the Talmud, the compilation of rabbinical commentaries and debates on rules of observance.[19] The community had its own fire brigade and hospitals, its own cemetery and its own voluntary associations to provide for the poor.[20]

Yet, despite the high walls which surrounded it, and despite the relatively limited impact of the Jewish Enlightenment on the community (as compared with that of Berlin), the culture of the Judengasse was far from insular. Although Gentiles sometimes sneered at their manner of speech, Heinrich Heine later insisted that the Frankfurt Jews spoke "nothing but the proper language of Frankfurt [which is] spoken with equal excellence by the circumcised as well as by the non-circumcised population." This was a slight, though pardonable, exaggeration. Those Jews who did manage to secure for themselves a secular as well as a religious education—like the doctor mentioned above—would have spoken, read and written *Hochdeutsch*. The surviving letters of Mayer[21] Amschel Rothschild, however, confirm that his was a rough and often ungrammatical German, with an admixture of Hebrew; and when he wrote to his sons he used Hebrew characters, as did they when they wrote to one another. Nevertheless, the *Judendeutsch* of the Judengasse was not the Yiddish of the Polish and Russian stetl; and in all probability many Gentile merchants in Frankfurt wrote ungrammatical letters too. When Frankfurt Jews left the Judengasse to do business—the avenue of activity most accessible to them—there was no insuperable language barrier between them and the Gentile merchants they encountered.

More than most German towns in the eighteenth century, Frankfurt was a businessman's town. At the junction of several major trade routes linking the towns of South Germany (Strasbourg, Ulm, Augsburg and Nuremberg) to the Hanseatic ports of the North (Hamburg, Bremen and Lübeck), and linking Germany as a whole to the economies of the Atlantic seaboard, the Baltic and the Near East, its prosperity was bound up with the two annual fairs in the autumn and the spring which had been held in the town since the Middle Ages.[22] And because of the enormous variety of coinage circulating in Europe up until the late nineteenth century, the town's commerce necessarily went hand in hand with banking: in particular, money-changing and bill-broking (buying and selling the IOUs generated by more complex transactions). In addition—and in some ways more importantly—Frankfurt acted as a financial centre for the princes, archdukes and electors who governed the numerous petty territories of the region. The revenues from their lands and subjects (rents, taxes and so on) and the expenditures of their courts (on grand residences, gardens and entertainments) made these rulers the biggest customers of the pre-industrial German economy, even if most of them were considerably less well off than their counterparts in the English aristocracy. In particular, the fact that the majority generally spent more than they earned created lucrative if sometimes risky opportunities for German bankers.[23]

Perhaps the most successful firm in this field prior to 1800 was that of Simon Moritz and Johann Philipp Bethmann, who imported from Amsterdam to Germany the system of "sub-bonds" (*Partialobligationen*) whereby a large loan could be subdivided into more manageable portions and sold on to a wide clientele of investors. A typical transaction was the Bethmann Brothers' loan to the Holy Roman Emperor of 20,000 gulden (around £2,000)[24] in 1778, which they sold on to investors in the form of twenty 1,000-gulden bonds, handing over the cash thus raised—minus their substantial commission—to the imperial Treasury in Vienna, and subsequently ensuring the prompt payment of interest from Vienna to the bondholders. Between 1754 and 1778 the Bethmanns floated loans totalling nearly 2 million gulden, and no fewer than fifty-four separate loans totalling nearly 30 million gulden in the following five years.[25] Other Frankfurt bankers became involved in the same kind of business, notably Jakob Friedrich Gontard.

Neither Bethmann nor Gontard was Jewish. Yet there is no question that, by the later eighteenth century, it was Jews who had come to be seen as the most enterprising operators when it came to money-changing and all kinds of lending. After more than a century of scholarly reflection on the subject, it is still hard to say quite why this was.[26] Any advantage Jews enjoyed over Gentile financiers can have been only an indirect result of their system of education: Mayer Amschel Rothschild once recalled that "in my youth I was . . . a very active merchant, but I was disorganised, because I had been a student [of the Talmud] and learnt nothing [about business]."[27] Probably membership of a tightly knit "outsider" group helped when it came to constructing credit networks. And perhaps there was a kind of business ethic derived from Judaism. But these points can be made with equal force about other religious minorities, as they were by Max Weber, who unconvincingly contrasted "the Protestant ethic" with the Jewish ethos of "politically and speculatively oriented . . . pariah capitalism."[28] The least unsatisfactory answer is that, at a time when most fields of economic activity were closed to them, Jews had little alternative but to concentrate on commerce and finance. At the same time, their Gentile rivals in these fields probably tended to exaggerate the extent of the "Jewish threat" to their business. The non-Jewish bankers of Frankfurt were complaining as early as 1685 that "the Jews had torn the bills trade from their hands"—a claim which led to a ban on Jews entering the stock exchange.[29] Twelve years later the Council was trying, not for the last time, to prevent Jews from renting warehouses in the Fahrgasse, the town's main street.

Perhaps the most notorious conflict of this sort centred around the role of Joseph Süss-Oppenheimer, who rose from being *Hoffaktor* (court agent) to Duke Karl Alexander of Württemberg to the much more political posts of privy councillor and, in 1733, envoy in Frankfurt, where his privileged position allowed him to live outside the Judengasse in the comfort of the Golden Swan Inn. Four years later Oppenheimer was executed, having been found guilty of wielding excessive political power and undermining the position of the Württemberg estates (*Stände*). Oppenheimer—the *Jud Süss* of later anti-Semitic legend—was only the most notorious of the Jewish court agents, however. By the mid-eighteenth century Frankfurt Jews were acting as agents for the Palatinate, the Electorate of Mainz, the Grand Duchy of Hesse-Darmstadt, the Kingdom of Prussia, the imperial court in Vienna, as well as Hesse-Kassel and Saxe-Weimar. Löw Beer Isaak, for example, was court agent to the Prince of Nassau-Saarbrücken in 1755,[30] while David Meyer Kupl challenged the dominance of the Kann family when he became imperial court agent at around the same time.[31] Such men formed a rich and privileged elite within the Judengasse.

Mayer Amschel

It was into this partly, but not wholly, segregated world that Mayer Amschel Roth-schild was born in either 1743 or 1744. About his parents, grandparents and more remote ancestors we know little. Benjamin Franklin once observed that in life only death and taxes are inevitable; they are also virtually the only things about which records survive for the earliest Rothschilds. It is worth noting at once that the family might never have been called "Rothschild"—literally "red shield"—at all. We know that Isak, son of Elchanan, built a house in the 1560s known as "zum roten Schild" ("the red shield"), presumably after some kind of shield of the sort often hung at the front of houses. It was common enough for residents of the Judengasse to become known by their addresses. However, Isak's grandson Naftali Herz (who died in 1685) left the house with the red shield and moved to another house, "zur Hinter-pfann" ("the warming pan"). The Rothschilds could thus conceivably have become known as the "Hinterpfanns." As it was, although Naftali Herz's son, grandson and great-grandson continued to use the name "Rothschild," they also used the name "Bauer." It was probably only in the next generation—Mayer Amschel's—that the name Rothschild stuck firmly as a surname, though even he might possibly have changed it again when he moved to another house known as "zum grünen Schild" ("the green shield").[32]

The most we can say about the early Rothschilds is that they were pious and rel-atively successful small businessmen dealing in, among other things, cloth. Five years before his death in 1585, Isak zum roten Schild had a taxable income of 2,700 gulden, and when he died he was remembered on his gravestone for his "virtue," "righteousness" and "honesty." A century later his great-grandson Kalman, a money-changer who also dealt in wool and silk, had a taxable income more than twice as large; and it seems that his son—Mayer Amschel's grandfather Moses—successfully developed his father's business, continuing the process of steady social ascent by marrying, successively, the daughters of a tax collector and of a doctor. Unfortu-nately, we know next to nothing about the economic achievements of Mayer Amschel's father, Amschel Moses—though the fact that the family continued to live in the modest house at the Hinterpfann, with its ground-floor office, its first-floor kitchen and cramped bedrooms above, suggests at best consolidation, at worst stag-nation. To judge by the lengthy and fulsome praise on his gravestone inscription, the family had done no more than attain solid respectability within the ghetto by the time he died.[33]

Amschel Moses was evidently a studious man—he was, according to his grave-stone, "a man who observed the prescribed time for the study of the Torah."[34] This may possibly explain why he sent his son Mayer Amschel away to the rabbinical school at Fürth when he had completed his primary education in Frankfurt. What-ever his reasons, it is not the case (as some historians have erroneously inferred) that Mayer Amschel was intended for the rabbinate; Cohen, who wrote a brief and laudatory biography shortly after Mayer Amschel's death and probably knew him, states that he only "studied his religion in order . . . to be a good Jew."[35] However, Mayer Amschel's studies at Fürth were cut short by the untimely death of his par-ents in 1755 and 1756, victims of one of the epidemics which still periodically swept through German towns. He was just twelve years old.

At this point, he might well have returned to rejoin his elder sister, Gutelche, and two brothers, Moses and Kalman. Instead, he was sent to Hanover to learn the rudiments of business in the firm of Wolf Jakob Oppenheim (presumably a business associate of his father's).[36] This was a formative experience, because it brought him for the first time into direct contact with the privileged world of the court agents. Of course, Mayer Amschel almost certainly knew something of this world already. Süss-Oppenheimer, after all, had been executed just six years before he was born. Moreover, we know that Süss had been involved in at least one bills transaction with Mayer Amschel's grandfather. But now the boy could see at closer quarters what it meant to be a "court Jew," since Oppenheim's grandfather Samuel had been court agent to the Austrian Emperor, and his uncle was agent to the Bishop of Cologne.[37] It was in Hanover that Mayer Amschel began to acquire an expertise which was calculated to help him acquire the status of court agent for himself. He became a dealer in rare coins and medals, a line of business in which clients were almost invariably aristocratic collectors, and in which a knowledge of Samuel Maddai's complex system of numismatic classification was indispensable.[38]

When he returned to Frankfurt—as he was obliged by residence laws to do when his apprenticeship ended—in around 1764,[39] Mayer Amschel was quick to put this expertise to good use. Within a year of his return, he had succeeded in selling rare medals to a well-born client whose future importance to the Rothschilds was to be considerable. Admittedly, Mayer Amschel's first transaction with William, Hereditary Prince of Hesse-Kassel, was small beer. Assuming that he was the "Jew Meyer" referred to in William's Privy Purse accounts for June 1765, it involved nothing more than 38 gulden and 30 kreuzers—a trifling sum, and one of many such small purchases the Prince made from various dealers in the years after 1763, as he built up his fashionable collection of medals and coins.[40] Nevertheless, this—along with "various deliveries" of which no record survives—was enough to justify a request in 1769 that Mayer Amschel be granted the title of court agent, a request which was duly granted in September of that year.[41] A year later he consolidated this new status. In August 1770 (at the age of twenty-six) he married Gutle, the sixteen-year-old daughter of Wolf Salomon Schnapper, court agent to the Prince of Saxe-Meiningen.[42] In addition to the benefits of association with her father, the match brought Mayer Amschel vital new capital, in the form of a dowry of 2,400 gulden. It was to prove the first of a succession of carefully calculated Rothschild marriages, laying a foundation of prosperous kinship every bit as important as the foundation of royal patronage represented by the title of court agent.

In the years which followed, Mayer Amschel—initially in partnership with his brother Kalman, before the latter's death in 1782—successfully established himself as Frankfurt's leading dealer not only in coins and medals, but also in all kinds of antiques. We can see how he operated from the meticulous catalogues he circulated to his widening circle of aristocratic customers. By the 1780s the items listed included ancient Greek and Roman as well as German coins, and also a variety of other antiques and "curiosities" of the sort a wealthy collector might display alongside his coin collection: carved figures, precious stones and the like. The total value of the goods for sale in each catalogue varied from around 2,500 gulden to 5,000 gulden; however, if an item interested a client, Mayer Amschel would send it for inspection and then, if the customer wished to make a purchase, negotiate a selling price, often some way below the guide price in the catalogue.[43] According to the surviving Privy Purse accounts, Prince William did not become a regular customer until 1790, after which date he made purchases almost every year. Other clients included Goethe's patron, the Duke of Weimar.

That the basis of the Rothschilds' fortune was mail-order antique sales to aristocratic numismatists may seem surprising; but there is no question that without the capital Mayer Amschel was able to accumulate by buying and selling "curiosities," he would never have had the resources to move into banking. It is not immediately obvious how successful he was as an antique dealer: his property tax assessment remained a constant 2,000 gulden between 1773 and 1794. However, the *Maaserbuch* or *Zehentbuch* in which he punctiliously recorded his charitable donations (a tenth of his annual income, according to Jewish law) suggested to his later biographer Berghoeffer that Mayer Amschel's annual *income* in the 1770s must have been in the region of 2,400 gulden—roughly the same as that of the Goethe family, and rather more than was earned at the time by a local official like a tax assessor (*Schultheiss*). On the basis of these and other available figures, Berghoeffer estimated Mayer Amschel's total wealth in the mid-1780s at around 150,000 gulden (around £15,000).[44]

We also know that Mayer Amschel was rich enough to move house in 1787. Shortly after returning to Frankfurt, he and and his two brothers had acquired complete ownership of the Hinterpfann house, buying out the distant relations with whom their parents had shared it. Now, some twenty years later, Mayer Amschel sold his three-eighths share of the Hinterpfann to his brother Moses (for 3,300 gulden) and, beginning in 1783, bought a substantially larger house, "zum grünen Schild" ("the green shield"), for more than 11,000 gulden.[45] By the standards of a Gentile family like the Goethes, this was still a wretchedly cramped place to live: just fourteen feet wide, with rooms so narrow that beds could be placed only along the side-walls at right angles to the street. It was wretched by the standards of the next generation of Rothschilds too: Mayer Amschel's sons would look back without nostalgia on the days "when we all slept in one little attic room."[46] But by the standards of the Judengasse it was a desirable residence. Located in the middle of the street— roughly opposite the middle, western gate—it had been rebuilt after the 1711 fire and, unusually, had its own waterpump. On each of the three upper storeys of the main building there was a narrow room looking over the street—each with three small windows, a stove and wall cupboard—and a similar room looking inwards over the yard. Through the back door, there was a little courtyard with a small two-storey building, part of which housed the single lavatory. Unusually (and usefully) the house had two cellars, one of which was reached through an obvious enough trapdoor in the entrance hall, and the other—a larger cellar which the house shared with its next-door neighbour—which was accessible only through a concealed opening underneath the stairs, and was unconnected to the other cellar.[47] The new space above the ground, limited though it may have been, was needed; for Mayer Amschel and his wife were proving to be a remarkably procreative couple, even by late-eighteenth-century standards. It appears that Gutle Rothschild gave birth virtually every year between 1771, the year after her marriage, and 1792. Of these nineteen or so children, ten lived: Schönche (1771), Amschel Mayer (1773), Salomon Mayer

(1774), Nathan Mayer (1777), Isabella or Betty (1781), Breunle or Babette (1784), Kalman or Carl (1788), Gotton or Julie (1790), Jettchen or Henrietta (1791) and Jakob or James (1792).[48]

It was only after the birth of his youngest child that Mayer Amschel began to engage in business which can properly be called banking. In some ways, the transition was a natural one. An antique-dealer with a growing circle of suppliers and customers naturally would extend credit to some of these from time to time. As early as 1790 we find Mayer Amschel listed as one of the creditors of Joseph Cassel in the nearby town of Deutz, albeit for a mere 365 gulden.[49] In a similar way, the coin and medal business inevitably brought him into contact with the Hessian mint, especially as his most coveted client, Prince William, often commissioned new medals to be struck. In 1794, for example, Rothschild offered to sell a quantity of silver to the Hessian war treasury "at the best possible price."[50]

However, the speed with which Mayer Amschel's wealth grew in the 1790s marked a real break with his earlier business activity. At the beginning of the 1790s Mayer Amschel Rothschild was no more than a prosperous antique-dealer. By 1797 he was one of the richest Jews in Frankfurt, and a central part of his business was unmistakably banking. The evidence for this breakthrough is unequivocal. In 1795 the official figure for Mayer Amschel's taxable wealth was doubled to 4,000 gulden; a year later he was moved into the top tax bracket, with property worth more than 15,000 gulden; and in the same year he was listed as the tenth richest man in the Judengasse with taxable wealth of over 60,000 gulden.[51] Thanks largely to Mayer Amschel, the Rothschilds had become one of the eleven richest families in the Judengasse by 1800. It was at around the same time that he began to rent a large four-roomed warehouse outside the Judengasse.[52] He also took on a talented and multilingual accountant from Bingen named Seligmann Geisenheimer.[53] Further evidence of increased wealth can be found in the generous dowries Mayer Amschel was able to give his children as they began to marry. When his eldest daughter married Benedikt Moses Worms in 1795, she received a dowry of 5,000 gulden and was promised a legacy of 10,000 after her parents' deaths. When his eldest son married Eva Hanau the following year, he was given a share of the business worth 30,000 gulden.[54]

Just what such a share meant can be seen from one of the most important documents to have been found in the recently opened Moscow "trophy" archive: the first known balance sheet of Mayer Amschel Rothschild's firm, dating back over 200 years to the summer of 1797. The total assets of the firm at this stage were given as 471,221 Reichsthaler or 843,485 gulden, the total liabilities as 734,981 gulden, leaving 108,504 gulden (around £10,000) as—in Mayer Amschel's own words—"the balance of my capital, praise God" ("Saldo meines Vermögens, Gott lob").[55] This remarkable document repays close scrutiny, for it reveals that Mayer Amschel was already far more of an international merchant banker than has previously been realised. The "assets" side of the balance-sheet evidently excluded Mayer Amschel's personal property, in that the family house does not appear there: by "my capital" he already meant his firm's capital. Most of the assets listed were either state bonds of various sorts, or personal loans and credits to a widely dispersed range of other firms. On the other side, the liabilities consisted of sums owed by Mayer Amschel to an equally broad spectrum of institutions and individuals.

The geographical range of Mayer Amschel's business credit network at this early stage was wide. The balance sheet shows that he was doing business with firms located not only in the immediate vicinity of Frankfurt (for example, in Kassel and Hanau) but also in more remote parts of Germany, ranging from Hamburg and Bremen to Regensburg, Augsburg, Leipzig, Berlin and Vienna, as well as in Amsterdam, Paris and London. Moreover, in addition to the names which might have been expected to feature in such a list of creditors and debtors (such as Mayer Amschel's son-in-law Worms and his future son-in-law Sichel), there appear the names of a number of eminent Gentile firms, including the Bethmanns, de Neufvilles and Brentanos (whom he owed a good deal of money). The celebrated art-collector Johann Friedrich Städel also had deposits with Rothschild totalling 17,600 gulden. Finally, the balance sheet provides evidence of a new kind of relationship with the government of Hesse-Kassel, which he owed some 24,093 gulden. It is not without significance that the names of two Hessian officials—Louis Harnier and Karl Buderus—appear in their own right as creditors.

This was a rapid economic ascent by any standards. Indeed, Mayer Amschel's success had been so swift and so great that it had to some extent outstripped his own capacities. In 1797 he was appalled to discover that one of his most junior employees—a youth named Hirsch Liebmann—had been able to embezzle a substantial sum virtually from under his nose. The proceedings of the subsequent criminal case have partially survived and give a good insight into the chaotic state of his rapidly expanding business at this period. According to Mayer Amschel, Liebmann, who had been with the firm some three years, had stolen between 1,500 and 2,000 gold carolins (as much as 30,000 gulden) from his office. The theft had been possible for three reasons. Firstly, Mayer Amschel allowed Liebmann to buy and sell goods on his own account to supplement his meagre wages—one and a half gulden a month after the rent of a shared room. Indeed, Rothschild even lent him a small sum on one occasion to help finance this. No one was therefore surprised when Liebmann appeared to be supplementing his wages, even if he was doing so with singular success. Secondly, the firm had no safe for valuables and scarcely any office security: the cupboard in the main office was frequently left open during business hours and employees and clients seem to have come and gone as they pleased. No one therefore noticed when coins, notes and other valuables began to disappear. And thirdly, Mayer Amschel's system of book-keeping was woefully primitive: when he came to lay charges against Liebmann, he had virtually no documents to prove how much had been stolen. No one therefore realised that money was missing until some time after Liebmann had begun stealing. It was only when a local broker appeared in the office, claiming that Liebmann wished to buy seed from him, that Mayer Amschel's suspicions were aroused. When pressed, the man admitted that this was a cover story suggested by Liebmann; in fact, he was there to buy an Austrian bill worth around 1,220 gulden which Liebmann had offered to sell him. Mayer Amschel belatedly grasped where his employee had been getting the money for his gold watches and handmade shirts. Further enquiries confirmed his suspicions: Liebmann had not only been spending money on himself, but also sending it to his parents in Bockenheim, who were notoriously "as poor as could be" but who suddenly seemed able to afford a 500 gulden dowry for Liebmann's sister. When the thief was arrested, eight thaler coins and an imperial treasury note were found among his possessions, as well as some silver spoons, a gold salt pot, a gold mug and seven medals, belying his protestations of innocence. Further proof of guilt was unwittingly provided by Liebmann's own father, who offered to return 1,000 gulden which his son had given him plus an additional 500 if Rothschild would drop his charges. Eventually, though only after prolonged interrogation, Liebmann confessed.[56]

Liebmann gave conflicting accounts of the theft, at one point saying that he took the money in small amounts over a prolonged period, later claiming that he had simply snatched two sacks of coins from the office cupboard while Mayer Amschel's second son, Salomon, was talking with some clients. Either way, the case illustrates that by 1797 at the latest the business was turning over so much cash that Rothschild himself could not keep track of it: bags of money were lying around the office, as he himself told the court, some in the cupboard, some on the floor. He always had a lot of money in his house, he said, because of his "extensive business dealings." The subsequent decade would see those dealings become more extensive still.

The Dual Revolution
In his *Biographical Notes on the House of Rothschild,* written long after Mayer Amschel's death, Friedrich von Gentz fulsomely praised his business acumen. "Nevertheless," he added wisely, "the most outstanding personal qualities may sometimes require exceptional circumstances and world-shattering events to come to fruition."[57] This was doubly true.

The epoch-making events which followed the summoning of the French Estates General by Louis XVI in 1789 took time to affect the lives of German Jews like Mayer Amschel Rothschild and his family. But when finally the Revolution reached Frankfurt, its effects were profound—indeed, literally explosive. The advance guard came as early as October 1792, when French troops temporarily occupied Frankfurt, just ten weeks after the coronation of the last Holy Roman Emperor, Francis II. We should not, of course, exaggerate the significance of this superficially symbolic change of regime. Frankfurt had been occupied by French troops before (during the Seven Years' War) and it seems that the Jewish community was no more pleased than the rest of the town's population at this renewed foreign incursion. Indeed, for all the potential benefits of French influence which could be inferred from the National Assembly's emancipation of French Jewry in 1791, the immediate, tangible effects of the French presence were distinctly negative. In June 1796, following the defeat of the Austrian army at Lodi, Frankfurt was bombarded by the victorious French forces so heavily that nearly half the houses in the Judengasse were destroyed by fire.[58]

On the other hand, the upheaval of war had its advantages. The destruction of the Judengasse obliged the Frankfurt Senate to relax its residence restrictions, granting permits (albeit for only six months) to the 2,000 or so people left homeless by the fire to live outside the Judengasse. It was presumably in the wake of this relaxation that Mayer Amschel was able to begin renting the warehouse in the Schnurgasse. Later French incursions led to a real, if temporary, improvement in the legal status of the Frankfurt Jews, an improvement foreshadowed by the emancipation of the Jews in those parts of the Rhineland which the French now annexed. (One beneficiary of this was Geisenheimer, the man Mayer Amschel hired as his bookkeeper.) Of more immediate importance, the war presented Mayer Amschel with a new and lucrative business opportunity. He and two other partners, Wolf Loeb Schott and Beer Nehm Rindskopf, were able to secure a contract to provide the Austrian army with grain and cash during their operations in the Rhine–Main region.[59]

The French Revolution was not the only revolution to transform Mayer Amschel's life and business. The British Industrial Revolution, in its first phase by the 1780s if not before, exerted an equally important influence. For although Mayer Amschel had already begun building up his banking business by the late 1790s, this did not imply a winding up of his previous coin-dealing business, which continued in a small way even after his death; and nor did it preclude expansion into other potentially profitable fields of business activity. Of these, none was more profitable in the late eighteenth century than that generated by the English revolution in textile manufacturing. In particular, the dramatic growth of (partly) mechanised cotton spinning, weaving and dyeing in Lancashire signalled an unprecedented and genuinely revolutionary change in the pace of economic life. Although this industrialisation was regionally as well as sectorally concentrated—so much so that it barely registers in the aggregate national income figures extrapolated by modern economic historians—its ramifications were felt as far as Africa, whence the slave labour of the cotton plantations came, America, where the cotton itself was grown, and India, where an established native textile industry was soon to face lethal competition from the cottages and mills of Lancashire and Lanarkshire. Those mills exerted a powerful pull in Germany too, where demand for the cheaper yet better British cloths—shawls, handkerchiefs, checks, gauzes, muslins, muslinettes, quiltings, dimities, velveteens, sallampores and jaconets—grew rapidly in the 1790s. Mayer Amschel was only one of many German businessmen to scent a unique and highly profitable opportunity. Around fifteen Jewish firms in Frankfurt alone were importing English textiles by the turn of the century, and a number of these established permanent agents in Britain at around this time. Between 1799 and 1803 no fewer than eight German merchants settled in Manchester for this purpose.[60]

It is against this background that we must see the decision to send Nathan, the third of the Rothschild brothers, to England at some point on the eve of the new century. The date of his departure from Frankfurt and the reasons for his going have long been a source of confusion to historians. Although some have Nathan arriving in England in 1797, 1799 or 1800, the majority opt for 1798.[61] There is little evidence to support this last date. We know from the balance sheet discussed above that Mayer Amschel had begun to have dealings with firms in London from at least as early as 1797, but on a fairly limited scale.[62] It was only February 1800—the date of his first letter to the London bankers Harman & Co., requesting that he be permitted to draw on them—that he began to expand his English business.[63] The first documentary evidence of Nathan's presence in England comes from 1800 too. Wolf cites a letter from Nathan dated May 29 in which he requests an acquaintance to reserve "a room with two beds in it, in some respectable lodging house" for himself and his "business manager." We also have a letter from Mayer Amschel to Harman, dated June 15, which mentions that Nathan would "soon be at your place," and a letter from Nathan dated August 15 from a London address (37 Cornhill).[64] From this Williams concluded that Nathan had actually arrived in England in 1800, spent the summer in London, then proceeded to Manchester. But this cannot be right. Not only was Nathan's first letter to Harman addressed *from* Manchester; we also have several later letters in which Nathan explicitly states that he had first come to Manchester the year before, 1799.[65] It therefore seems reasonable to conclude that Nathan did not arrive in Manchester before 1799, though he and his father were not doing English business on a large scale until the following year. This leaves the possibility—though it is nothing more—that Nathan first crossed the Channel in 1798, staying in London for some months before proceeding northwards.[66]

Why did Nathan go to England? In the absence of hard evidence, most historians have followed Nathan's own account of his emigration—which he related to the MP Thomas Fowell Buxton in 1834—in which he portrayed the decision to leave as his own:

> "There was not," he said, "room enough for all of us in that city. I dealt in English goods. One great trader came there who had the market to himself: he was quite the great man, and did us a favour if he sold us goods. Somehow I offended him, and he refused to show me his patterns. This was on a Tuesday; I said to my father, "I will go to England." I could speak nothing but German. On the Thursday I started . . ."[67]

There is no reason to think that this version of events was wholly fictitious. Nathan was a fiercely ambitious and competitive man, as quick to take offence as to give it in his business dealings, and it is not difficult to imagine him responding impetuously to such a contretemps. However, in a number of respects his retrospective account was misleading. Perhaps he could not resist romanticising his own rags-to-riches story; perhaps he was indulging in irony for the benefit of his after-dinner audience (the latter would have been more in character). In any event, it seems highly unlikely that his father would, or indeed could, have entrusted him with as large a sum of money as he suggested to Buxton—£20,000, or roughly double the net assets shown in the 1797 balance sheet—on the strength of a youthful impulse.[68] However much "start-up" capital Nathan took with him, the idea that he was doing much more than following his father's orders seems unlikely.

For political reasons, it soon became imperative to conceal the fact that Nathan was acting as the agent of a Frankfurt firm, and this has led some historians to assert that, once he arrived in England, he effectively operated independently from his father and brothers.[69] But the evidence in the firm's archives for this period is unequivocal: initially, Nathan took his orders from Frankfurt—indeed, his elder brother Salomon was sent over to assist him in 1801[70]—and it was only gradually that he began to trade on his own account. A number of Nathan's earliest letters from London and Manchester are signed "pp. Meyer Amschel Rothschild." Correspondence between father and son was evidently regular (though very little of it has survived), and Nathan wrote frequently on his father's behalf to the London firms of Salomon Salomons and Harman & Co., which handled the firm's insurance and banking business in London. It was not untypical for letters of this early period to begin with phrases like "My father wishes me to write to you" or "Agreeable to the direction I have just received from my father." On one occasion when a firm let him down, Nathan warned them that if there were more "complaints of this nature . . . [I] am certain my father will order me to turn myself to somebody that will attend more punctually."[71] On another, he informed Salomons: "I received letters from home this morn[in]g advis[in]g me of my father being very discontented w[ith] your packing, writing that I must not send any more goods to London as you have neglected the shipping."[72] And for most of this period the chests of cloth which Nathan was sending to the continent in increasing quantities all bore the insignia "MAR" for Mayer Amschel Rothschild. Nathan was not sparing his father anxiety when he concealed a brief illness from him in the summer of 1802. Rather, he did not want his father to think he had been unable—for whatever reason—to attend to business. In a letter to a recalcitrant French customer not long after this illness, Nathan left for posterity a revealing insight into his father's character, and his own view of it: "Do you think that my Father will sell . . . Goods upon his own bills . . . without Profit? You are quite mistaken, my father's Chimney will not smoke without Profit."[73] Just ten days later he received a stern letter from his father accusing him of not keeping "regular" accounts.[74]

Nathan's slapdash approach to paperwork was evidently a recurrent source of friction. Three years after this first admonition on the subject, Mayer Amschel was still harping on the same theme, in a way which makes it abundantly obvious where power lay in their relationship. This rare letter—one of the few of Mayer Amschel's private letters which survive—is worth quoting at some length to give a flavour of the early Rothschild correspondence:

> [T]o begin with, all our correspondents complain about you, dear Nathan, and say that you are so disorganised when sending consignments. Sometimes you write that you have sent, for example, the chest with this number, then later [it arrives with] another number. If you send a chest today, you only let Esriel Reiss know six months after. One of his clerks said to me that you are very disorganised. My dear friend, if you don't write down all the numbers of the chests when you send them off, if you don't write them down until you receive acknowledgement that they have arrived, if you don't pay attention, if you [don't] ask where the chest has gone when you don't receive an answer from your correspondent, if you are so disorganised and don't have someone or a friend with you, then you will be swindled. What is the good of that[?] Everyone can be a millionaire if they get the [right] opportunity. I already complained in Frankfurt about your extraordinary expenditures and disorganisation, dear Nathan; I don't like it.

This repetitive, haranguing style—which was inherited by Mayer Amschel's elder sons Amschel and Salomon—does not make for easy reading today; it cannot have given Nathan much pleasure either. However, the father's determination to bludgeon his son into mending his ways provides a fascinating insight into the business methods of the day:

> I have seen the orderly way in which Heckscher and the merchant Baresch despatch and return consignments. They have special clerks in order to keep an eye on everything. They say that without good order a millionaire can go broke the more business he does, because the whole world is not, or not very, honest. When people see that you are not orderly in your despatching, they will do business with you only in order to cheat you . . . Mostly they will pick quarrels with you in order to cheat you, the more so when they see how disorganised you are with your consignments. In sum, they will do business with you to exploit

your disorganisation. There was a man in Frankfurt called Eluzer Elfelt who made a great deal of money, but the whole world made money from him because he was so disorganised and it went as badly for him in the end as he himself had been badly organised. Dear Nathan, don't be angry with your father. When it comes to penmanship you are not much good. Take on a clerk to manage the despatching of consignments and take my advice, be more organised with your despatching, otherwise I don't give your business much chance. The more you sell the worse it will get if you aren't organised. My dear son, don't be cross that I write like this . . . You have to be careful, and Amschel says that you don't keep a proper record when he sends you remittances. That is wrong . . . It really is necessary that you keep a precise record of everything that you send us and all that we send you, you really must keep your books properly. If you can't manage to keep all our accounts in good order because of your book-keeper, write home and maybe we can suggest a plan . . . If you are organised, organised in your writing and careful in the way you give credit, I don't doubt that you will do well.

Nor did this paternal lecture end there. Mayer Amschel went on to berate Nathan for failing to calculate his profits net (as opposed to gross); for doing business with Rindskopf in precious stones ("But you are no jeweller") and for failing to discount bad debts:

My dear son, you must not be angry when a father, who has the happiness of all his children at heart, asks to know the real state of your finances, because if you have many bad debts, which God forbid, and enter them as if they are good, that is simply to pretend that you are rich . . . My dear son, you are hard-working. Do your bit like a good boy. You can't do more. I just want to encourage you to be more organised . . . You really have a good brain but you haven't learnt [the importance of] order, and here I see that all the merchants who are well organised are the ones who get very rich, and the ones who are disorganised are the ones who go broke. So dear son don't take it badly when I write you my opinion.

What is unmistakably apparent from this letter is that, in Mayer Amschel's eyes, Nathan was still just one of five subordinates within an essentially patriarchal family firm. Provided Nathan improved his business methods, he could look forward to having "as good a share in my business as your brothers" once their sisters had been married off. But until then, Mayer Amschel would give the orders.[75]

Another possibility which has been suggested is that Nathan left Frankfurt in order to escape from the religious restrictions of the ghetto. It is true that Jews—who had been readmitted to England only in 1656 after three and a half centuries of exclusion—enjoyed far greater liberty in England than in Germany in the early 1800s.[76] There were very few economic restrictions on Jews in England by this time,[77] though (in common with Catholics, Non-conformists and unbelievers) they were still excluded from Parliament, local government and the universities, and, as foreigners, new immigrants were subject to increasingly stringent supervision as the war with France intensified (Jews born in Britain were British subjects). In London, confident and prosperous Jewish communities had developed during the eighteenth century including Sephardic families like the Mocattas and Ashkenazim like the merchant Levi Barent Cohen, whose father had been a successful Amsterdam linen-dealer. In the late 1790s Benjamin and Abraham Goldsmid were already playing just the sort of dynamic financial role which Nathan would later imitate with such success, challenging the dominance of the Baring brothers and their Amsterdam correspondents Hope & Co.—and incurring in the process a version of the sort of religiously tinged but essentially economic resentment we have already encountered in Frankfurt.[78] We know Nathan had an entrée into this world through his father's business contacts with Salomons. Yet he apparently spent no more than a few months in London when he first arrived in England, before setting off northwards to the far less socially congenial environment of Manchester, where the small and still embryonic Jewish community was overwhelmingly made up of poor shopkeep-ers—dealers in old clothes, cheap jewellery, umbrellas and patent medecines.[79] Though he was subjected to much less formal discrimination in Manchester than he had been in Frankfurt, it is hard to believe that Nathan was attracted there by any-thing other than business.

How successful was Nathan in what contemporaries sometimes disparaged as the "rag trade"? Very, according to his own account, thanks mainly to his own business acumen:

> . . . the nearer I got to England, the cheaper goods were. As soon as I got to Manchester, I laid out all my money, things were so cheap; and I made good profit. I soon found that there were three profits—the raw material, the dyeing, and the manufacturing. I said to the manufacturer, "I will supply you with material and dye, and you will supply me with manufactured goods." So I got three profits instead of one, and I could sell goods cheaper than anybody. In a short time I made my 20,000£ into 60,000£. My success all turned on one maxim. I said: I can do what another man can, and so I am a match for the man with the patterns, and for all the rest of them! Another advantage I had. I was an off-hand man. I made a bargain at once.[80]

This was not a bad summary of Nathan's mode of operation, but again it greatly oversimplified matters.[81] Nathan arrived in Lancashire with orders for British tex-tiles from his father, and continued to receive these by post. Having assessed the market to establish the quality and price of cloth available, he then proceeded to place these orders with manufacturers—not only those based near Manchester, but also from firms as far afield as Nottingham, Leeds, Stockport and even Glasgow. The cloth was then manufactured (usually by sub-contracted weavers in their cottages) and "finished" by dyers and printers, usually small firms in and around Manchester. In order to drive down the price of the goods he bought, Nathan tried as far as pos-sible to pay up front "on present bill terms," which meant "drawing on" (that is, bor-rowing from) his London bankers "at three months" (for three months). As he explained in December 1802:

> On Tuesdays and Thursdays the weavers who live in the country twenty miles round Manchester bring here their goods, some twenty or thirty pieces, others more, others less, which they sell to the merchants here at two, three and six months' credit. But as there are generally some of

them in want of money and willing to sacrifice some profit to procure it, a person who goes with ready money may sometimes buy 15 or 20 per cent cheaper.[82]

Nathan did not actually have to pay the bigger manufacturers until their goods were shipped for the continent. On the other hand, it was necessary to wait—usually two months—before expecting payment from Frankfurt. Obviously, the profit to be made in such a business took the form of simple percentages. However, at a time when profit margins in the textile industry could be as high as 20 per cent, Nathan's charges were modest: 5 per cent on the cost price for purchases in cash from his warehouse, as little as 9 per cent for goods which had to be despatched to the continent.[83] This was a deliberate ploy to attract customers and increase his market share: in his letters to potential buyers, Nathan constantly stressed that his mark-up as a middle-man was lower than those charged by his competitors. As he told his father in September 1802: "No House in Manchester purchase the Goods cheaper—if so cheap—as I do and none are at so much trouble as we are to procure them to advantage."[84] "You cannot find any person in Manchester who will serve you with so small a Profit as myself," he assured one new customer. "I have the pleasure to tell you my meaning plainly, if you will do any business with me in future, you may depend that I shall send you Goods as cheap as any Person in the whole World." Moreover, as his business expanded and he began to export to firms other than his father's, Nathan began to offer not only low prices but also reasonable credit terms, telling the same buyer that he regarded his money as being "as safe in your hands as if I had it in my Pocket."[85] His continental customers were generally expected to pay with bills falling due after three months—in effect, five months after the goods had been shipped (and paid for) by Nathan. The more Nathan could pay in cash or "present bills," the less he could pay his suppliers; the more credit he could give his customers, the more customers he attracted. This seems to have been his fundamental principle.

The practical implications of this system were, as the letter copy books of the period show, nerve-racking. To begin with, Nathan himself had to do a great deal of travelling to establish a network of suppliers and customers. As early as November 1800 he left Manchester for Scotland, where he apparently found better cloth or better prices.[86] He returned there again in 1801 and 1805. Frequent trips to London (like the one he made in the summer of 1800 or 1801) were also necessary to maintain good relations with the bankers on whose overdraft facilities he depended. And although some buyers sent agents to Manchester, Nathan preferred to deal directly with continental firms, making at least two major expeditions across the Channel to drum up new business. The spring of 1802 saw him in France and the Netherlands, establishing links with firms in Paris, Nancy, Lyon, Liège, Metz, Brussels, Maastricht, Antwerp and Amsterdam. Before returning to England, he also went to Germany and Switzerland, securing orders from firms in Hamburg, Nuremberg, Heidelberg, Cologne, Munich, Memmingen, Salzburg, Leipzig, Königsberg and Basel.[87] His list of customers for 1803 even included a firm in Moscow. One of the catalogues he took with him on such trips still survives and shows—on page after page studded with small squares of cloth—the extraordinary range of patterns and textures British manufacturers were able to produce.[88] These absences in turn meant that a considerable amount of work devolved on his clerks, principally Joseph Barber, an English book-keeper he had hired shortly after arriving in Manchester.

Yet no amount of travelling could ensure that suppliers delivered their goods on time, or, for that matter, delivered the goods that had actually been ordered. Much of Nathan's correspondence was therefore concerned with cajoling manufacturers to comply with his orders.[89] At the same time, there was no guarantee that customers would always be satisfied with the goods they received, and almost as much time had to be spent in haggling retrospectively about the price and the quality of consignments.[90] As he remarked ruefully to Geisenheimer "If I send off the goods it is two months before I can draw at 3 months date and then . . . I may be kept out of my money five or six months . . . it is very easy to get commissions but not quite so easy to get paid for them."[91] Nathan also had recurrent disputes with his bankers in London over their interest charges, and the very high costs of insurance which they took care of.[92] These three pressures seem to have led to a degree of diversification on Nathan's part. It seems that in 1801 dissatisfaction with his suppliers prompted him to become directly involved in manufacturing himself—hence the purchase of a copping machine from Boulton & Watts.[93] Then, in 1805, he went into partnership with another immigrant from Frankfurt, Nehm Beer Rindskopf (the son of Mayer Amschel's business associate Beer Nehm), leaving the latter to deal with sales to customers.[94] Rindskopf soon led Nathan to diversify further, placing orders on his behalf not only for cloth but also for indigo, and later pearls, tortoiseshell and ivory (so-called colonial goods imported to Britain from her overseas empire).[95] Finally, Nathan began to concentrate increasing amounts of his own attention on the various credit transactions generated by his business. He constantly shopped around for better borrowing and bill-discounting facilities, dealing with a succession of London bankers including Lyon de Symons, Goldsmid & D'Eliason and Daniel Mocatta, as well as continental bankers, notably Parish & Co. and the Schröder brothers.[96] Like his father, he was gradually shifting from being a merchant to being a merchant banker.

The frenetic, hustling atmosphere of these formative years is vividly captured in the letter books of Nathan's which have survived. In a market crowded with numerous small businesses, subject to rapid fluctuations in prices and interest rates and almost completely unregulated, it took a combination of burning aggression and cool calculation to survive and thrive. Nathan Rothschild possessed both in abundance. He was prepared, in his earliest days, to be ingratiating, on one occasion sending Salomon Salomons a cask of wine in the hope of getting better insurance rates.[97] But soon the brash, even bullying tone which seems to have come most naturally to him began to predominate. As early as December 1800 he could write confidently to one Scottish manufacturer with whom he had placed an order: "[P]rovided you will exert your best endeavours to please me and expeditiously, [you] may rest assured that it is in my power to furnish you regularly with considerable commissions." Two weeks later he underlined the message: "I expect any day commis[sion]s from the Continent. I certainly shall give you the preference but wish to have the commis[sion]s you have . . . executed first before I can give you any more. You request to have 3 weeks more to execute it but the quicker you are in serving me, and the lower you do it, the more com[missions] you may depend on." When no response was forthcoming, Nathan was indignant: "I am astonished that I have not heard from you before this. When I was in Glasgow you promised me faithfully to execute my order instantly and now it is a long while ago that I never even heard from you. If you could execute orders in a short time you might depend upon large commission for it is of no use to give commission if they are not executed by the promised time."[98] Another Scottish firm which delayed dispatching goods he had ordered was reproached even more forcefully:

> I suppose you keep them in possession as a security untill I had sent you your very large *Bill*! which I think is very ungenteel conduct . . . I suppose you think I shall never come to Glasgow or Paisley any more but I give you my honor I will come again in 2 mo[nths] and I believe I shall be able to procure plenty of goods for my method of payment.[99]

A year later, he did not hesitate to accuse an awkward French buyer of "chicanery."[100]

At times, Nathan felt himself almost at war with his business rivals. He was on one occasion "surprized beyond measure to be informed of the most scandalous and unfounded reports that have been so industriously circulated in Frankfort by my enemies." There were, he told his father, "many people in this country that would be very glad to support their own credit and character by destroying mine—But I thank God that I am so firmly established, that they cannot effect their purpose, by their wicked and weak attempts."[101] No doubt his rivals did seek to get the better of him. However, it is hard to avoid concluding that at times he let his combative temper run away with him. "You are a great rascal," the Hamburg banker Behrens told him in the course of a minor spat:

> I . . . cannot but express my astonishment at the tune [*sic*], as well as the contents [of your letter]; to be sure you would like to make me believe you as virtuous as Cato and as rigid in being as good as your word as Regulus; however whether your wishes in this respect will ever succeed with me remains a question which I have neither the leisure nor the humour to investigate . . . You are often crazy, that's what I think. Do you fancy that you might frighten me because of your money? I have as much as you have and I am not even living in England.[102]

His partner Rindskopf once made the mistake of criticising Nathan in the early stages of their collaboration.[103] A subsequent letter from Rindskopf suggests that Nathan had not taken this well: "My speaking my mind openly to you proceeded from a real friendship I bear towards you and if any unguarded expression made its appearance it ought to be placed to the disappointment of the moment and by no means the fault of the Heart but on my part everything is buried in oblivion and I hope and wish you will on your part do the same and consider myself now writing to my old friend Mr Rothschild." When a London merchant accused him of doing business with "none but swindling houses," Nathan was incensed:

> I can assure you Sir that there is not a House with whom I have transactions but both for respectability and solidity are equal to your own; the richest and greatest Houses in London, Hamburg and other places on the Continent are not swindlers, and it is those houses with whom I do business . . . I can prove to anyone that I never made a bad debt or lost a single penny thro' any of my friends being insolvent which I presume

would not have been the case had my business been done principally
by Swindlers . . . No one abhors chicanery and complaints more than
I do.[104]

True, it was always extremely important, in the volatile world of the early-
nineteenth-century textile business, to preserve one's reputation as an honourable
businessman, for on that depended one's creditworthiness in the eyes of others. All
the same, one sympathises with another correspondent, who evidently found
Nathan's extreme belligerence hard to take:

> The great misfortune is, that as soon as you are answered on one point
> the vivacity of your imagination makes you suggest another and a
> person in business who has something better to do than eternally refute
> futile obsessions of every sort must be naturally averse to follow you
> through the labyrinth of misconceptions or erroneous statements in
> which the fertility of your mind hurries you so continually to so little
> purpose to yourself and to the dissatisfaction of others.[105]

The question remains how financially successful this aggressive young man actually was. Circumstantial evidence suggests that Nathan did indeed do well. By 1804,
when he was granted letters of denization,[106] he had a house in Downing Street,
Ardwick, a prosperous area of the town, as well as his warehouse in Brown Street.
Four years later he owned a "large and commodious" warehouse adjoining a "spacious, modern and well built" town house at 25 Mosley Street, "the most elegant
street in Manchester."[107] Such figures as it is possible to construct for the turnover of
Nathan's business between 1800 and 1811 (when he closed down his Manchester
office) confirm the impression of rapid economic ascent (see illustration 1.ii).
Indeed, if we assume that he achieved profits of, to err on the conservative side, 5
per cent on his gross sales of around £800,000 over the whole period, then his subsequent claim to Buxton that he made £40,000 as a textile merchant looks about
right. On the other hand, his progress was far from being as smooth as he later
claimed. As illustration 1.ii indicates, a good period beginning in early 1804 and
continuing until the autumn of 1805 was succeeded by nearly two years of low
turnover. This repeated itself when rapid growth in the volume of Nathan's business
in 1808 and 1809 was choked off sharply in 1810.

Such abrupt ups and downs should not surprise us. Business of the sort Nathan
was engaged in was susceptible to sharp seasonal and cyclical fluctuations at the best
of times; Nathan had to deal with the added disruption of intermittent war, with all
the restrictions on trade between England and the continent which characterised the
Napoleonic period. Even before war resumed between England and France in 1803,
he had been warned of possible embargoes on cross-Channel trade.[108] The climate
for business was already deteriorating in 1805, so that the formal imposition of a
blockade—by the Berlin decree banning British imports to the territories under
French control (November 1806)—merely set the seal on a disastrous collapse. As
one correspondent lamented as early as November 1805: "The present time is the
most critical and the most unhappy for the Continent . . . no trade whatsoever, the
market overstocked with goods [and] no debts coming in."[109] At least three firms
with which Nathan had dealings, including M. M. David in Hamburg, collapsed in
the first months of 1806, well before the imposition of the blockade in June.[110]

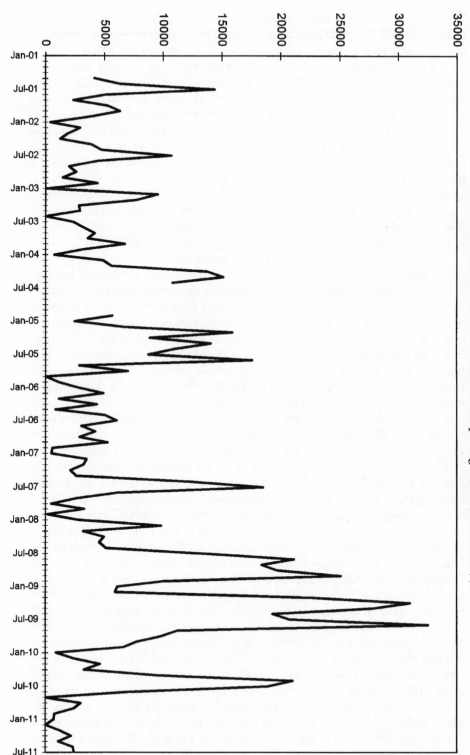

1.ii: The turnover of Nathan Rothschild's textile exporting business, 1801–1811 (£).

Thereafter, the choice for firms like Nathan's was between inactivity and sanctions-busting, with all the risks that entailed. In May 1806 the Admiralty took possession of five ships at Hull and seized contraband worth around £20,000 which had been purchased in Manchester by three Jewish merchants.[111] Another, who had merely come to settle accounts with Nathan, was arrested at Stockport.[112] The French meanwhile did the same, arresting Nathan's new Hamburg agent Parish, who was forced to sell goods of his at a heavy loss to avoid their confiscation.[113] The surviving letter copy books reveal that this was an especially difficult period for Nathan, as his bills became progressively harder and harder for Rindskopf to discount.[114] As early as April 1806 Parish complained to Mayer Amschel that his son had exceeded his credit limit by drawing on them for £2,000.[115] And by the end of August he appears to have owed Rindskopf over £28,000, on which he was paying interest at 4.2 per cent per annum.[116] Matters were improved by the Treaty of Tilsit between Napoleon and the Tsar, reports of which reached Nathan from his brother Amschel in July 1807; but the restrictions on cross-Channel trade remained in force.[117]

Under these circumstances, Nathan therefore had little option but to carry on his export business illegally—he became, in a word, a smuggler. In October 1807 he was sending a consignment of coffee to Sweden via Amsterdam, using an American-registered ship and fake Dutch documents. Other favoured routes for contraband were through Heligoland and the Baltic ports. Of course, such shipments could not legally be insured, so that the risks involved were very substantial. But so, presumably, were the potential rewards.[118] By 1808 Nathan had earned a reputation as a man who had, thanks to his superior "management, judgement, foresight and connections," regularly "succeeded in getting goods to the Continent"—though "not a word was passed about . . . *how* the goods had been sent."[119] The recovery his business enjoyed in 1808 and 1809 was short-lived, however. In September 1809 a large shipment to Riga was seized and could be released only by means of "bribery—and a heavy tax indeed it was." Another cargo suffered the same fate at Königsberg.[120]

The final blow came in October 1810, and it fell in Frankfurt. Ironically, by this date, the Edict of Trianon of August 5 had relaxed somewhat the ban on imports, legalising the import of so-called "colonial wares." However, most Frankfurt firms continued smuggling, partly in order to avoid the steep import tariff imposed under the new rules, partly so that they could continue to deal in goods defined as purely British. Mayer Amschel, for example, received no fewer than seven shipments from England in July 1810 alone, worth altogether £45,000. On October 14 the Edict of Fontainebleau was published, ordering the confiscation of all English and colonial goods found to have been smuggled into French controlled territory. Two infantry regiments occupied Frankfurt and, on the basis of reports by a spy named Thiard, some 234 firms had their premises raided. Mayer Amschel was caught with 60,000 gulden of contraband on his hands, about half of it indigo, presumably sent by Nathan. Not only was the Trianon tariff levied on the goods retrospectively (a fine which cost Mayer Amschel nearly 20,000 francs); all the goods seized—worth around 100,000 gulden in all—were also publicly burnt. As one observer reported, "The extent of general confusion which this has caused beggars description."[121] Although Mayer Amschel got off relatively lightly—the Bethmanns had to pay a fine of more than 360,000 francs—the crisis was a watershed. Henceforth, such trade in commodities would play a declining role in the Rothschilds' business.[122]

For Nathan, this transition had begun in October 1806, with his marriage to Hannah, the daughter of Levi Barent Cohen, a leading London merchant.[123] Not only did this add to Nathan's capital, to the tune of £3,248 from her dowry and a further substantial sum from his own father; it also made him the partner of one of the more eminent figures in London's Jewish community.[124] It was with Cohen that Nathan undertook much of his smuggling business in 1807; and, like his previous partner Rindskopf, Cohen encouraged his new son-in-law to widen the range of goods he exported to the continent to include Indian and Baltic products as well as British textiles.[125] This was merely a stepping stone, however; for by now Nathan had made up his mind to become a fully fledged banker. In the eyes of at least one of his Manchester associates, he had already achieved this as early as 1808, though he was not yet known as such in London, having only acquired an address in the city (12 Great St Helens) that summer.[126] Although Nathan's earliest London ledger books suggest that he was doing banking business by 1810 at the latest,[127] the move from Manchester was quite protracted, and it was not until the beginning of July 1811 that he was able formally to announce:[128]

> that the business heretofore carried on by the undersigned Nathan Meyer [sic] Rothschild at Manchester, under the firm of "Rothschild Brothers" will cease to be carried on from this day, and any persons having dealings with that firm are required to send their demands to pay their accounts to N. M. Rothschild, at his Counting-House, in No. 2 New Court, St Swithins-lane [sic], London.[129]

He had travelled a long way since leaving behind the cramped confines of the Judengasse—and the discrimination symbolised by the *Judensau*—just twelve years before. But Nathan Rothschild could not have acquired his new City address at a more propitious moment.

The Elector's Treasure

The Old Man . . . made our fortune.

—CARL ROTHSCHILD[1]

Nathan Rothschild's success in the heartland of the early Industrial Revolution was of undeniable importance to his father's business back in Frankfurt. In this sense, the Rothschilds were authentic children of the industrial age. Yet it was Mayer Amschel's parallel success in the old-fashioned role of "court Jew" which contemporaries came to believe counted for more in the family's economic rise. Indeed, even Mayer Amschel's own sons themselves tended to regard his relationship with William IX, Hereditary Prince, Landgrave and after 1803 Elector (Kurfürst) of Hesse-Kassel, as the real foundation of their fortune.[2] Since it first began to gain public currency in 1826, the myth of the Elector's treasure has been related so often and with so much embroidery that it has never seriously been questioned. Yet a close scrutiny of the surviving records suggests that the Elector's significance has been exaggerated—or at least misunderstood.

William of Hesse-Kassel was almost exactly the same age as Mayer Amschel, and shared with him an interest not only in old coins but in money of every sort. In every other respect, however, the two men were as different as could be, not least in their religious backgrounds. William's father, Landgrave of Hesse-Kassel between 1760 and 1785, had caused consternation to his Protestant relatives—not only his own father, but his father-in-law George II of England as well—by converting to Catholicism as a young man. As a result, the young William was effectively removed from his care. During the Seven Years' War, he and his brother Karl were sent to Denmark, where they came under the influence of another Protestant monarch (also linked by marriage to George II), Frederick V of Denmark, whose daughter William married in 1763. Until his father's death, William ruled independently the small Grafschaft of Hanau-Münzenberg, which lay immediately to the north and west of Frankfurt. Yet, for all the political significance of religion in his life, it cannot be said that William observed the Commandments with anything approaching the punctiliousness of his lowly Jewish contemporary. He had at least twelve illegitimate children by at least three mistresses, including four by a Hessian noblewoman, Caroline von Schlotheim, and no fewer than seven by a Swiss woman, Rosalie Dorothea Ritter. Far from seeking to conceal the fruits of his adultery, William gave them all suitably grand titles and names—von Hessenstein, von Heimrodt and von Haynau.[3]

His besetting sin, however, was avarice—a sin he was singularly well placed to commit. For, unlike the great majority of kingdoms and principalities in eighteenth-century Europe, Hesse-Kassel was rich, to the extent of between 30 and 40 million gulden at William's accession. Nor was its ruler prevented from disposing of this wealth as he pleased by any of the political restrictions which had developed in other parts of Western Europe: the assets of the state were effectively indistinguishable from the personal wealth of the Prince. This great accumulation of capital had been achieved primarily by selling the services of the Hessian army to the highest bidder—usually Britain—a system which reached its zenith during the American War of Independence. Even before succeeding his father, William was already engaged in this trade, selling a regiment of around 2,000 men from Hanau to fight for George III against the rebellious colonists. The terms were lucrative: William received 76 gulden (around £7) per man, plus an additional charge of 25 gulden for each man wounded, and 76 for each man killed.[4] This money was paid not in the form of cash, but in (non-interest-bearing) bills of exchange which were initially paid to William's account at the London bank of Van Notten & Son.[5] When he wanted to convert these into cash before they fell due, he sold them to brokers in Germany. Although he did spend considerable sums—for example, on building himself a new palace, Wilhelmshöhe—his object in realising such bills was more usually to invest his earnings so that they yielded the highest possible interest. And, as the majority of his fellow princes in Germany were frequently in want of money, he had no difficulty in doing so by lending to them.

The finances of Hesse-Kassel consequently resembled less those of a small state than those of a large bank. While the Exchequer (Kammerkasse) collected regular revenues from the royal estates and indirect taxes which were then disbursed on regular civil expenditures, the War Chest (Kriegskasse) received revenue not only from the state's property taxes but also from the hiring out of mercenaries and the interest on the Landgrave's investments, which it managed. William's total assets in 1806—adding together the assets of each financial department—stood at more than 46 million gulden (more than £4 million). More than half of this (28.8 million) was held in the form of loans to other German princes, notably the Duke of Mecklenburg-Strelitz and the Prince of Lippe-Detmold, while a further 4.6 million was invested in English annuities. The fact that his net income after all expenditures was around 900,000 gulden speaks for itself: the contemporary view that he was one of the richest of European "capitalists" was not far wrong.[6] From the point of view of an aspirant banker like Mayer Amschel, William therefore exerted a magnetic attraction. Not only was there money to be made from buying and reselling his English bills; there was also money to be made from placing his immense and constantly growing capital in secure investments. The only problem from Mayer Amschel's point of view was that other people were already making that money.

The truth was that, despite his efforts to gain a foothold at William's court while he was still residing in Hanau, Mayer Amschel was still to all intents and purposes a nobody when the new Landgrave moved north to Kassel on his father's death in 1785. We know from the fact that he requested a special Sunday pass to leave the Judengasse in 1783 and from later correspondence that Mayer Amschel had already begun to involve himself in the English bills business. But it was not until 1789 that he was able to squeeze himself into the main market for these bills at Kassel by offering to pay more than the established local firms.[7] Even then he was granted only the most meagre credit facility—£800, compared with the figure of £25,000 given to the leading Kassel broker Feidel David—and when he requested a higher credit limit the following year he got just £2,000, compared with the £10,000 he had asked for.[8] At this point, however, Mayer Amschel struck up one of those peculiarly instrumental friendships based on mutual advantage which were to become a hallmark of his sons' (and grandsons') *modus operandi*. Karl Friedrich Buderus had begun his career in William's service as the tutor of his bastards by Dorothea Ritter. In 1783 he had moved into the financial administration at Hanau and in 1792, at the age of thirty-three, he moved to Kassel to work for the all-important War Chest, rising swiftly through the civil service ranks.[9]

The first sign of tacit co-operation between Buderus and Rothschild came in 1794 when the former explicitly recommended that Mayer Amschel be allowed to join five established firms in bidding for a sale of £150,000 of English bills.[10] Evidently, his recommendation was ignored, but Buderus tried again in 1796 and this time succeeded. The two Gentile banking partnerships of Rüppell & Harnier[11] and Preye & Jordis had offered 1 million gulden of Frankfurt city bonds to the War Chest, of which the Chest had bought 900,000. Buderus then tipped off Mayer Amschel that he should offer to sell the remaining 100,000 gulden to the Chest at a more generous price (97.5 per cent of face value) than the other banks were offering (98 per cent).[12] This was hardly profitable as the bonds were quoted at par (that is, 100) on the Frankfurt bourse, but the slightly larger discount he was offering secured Mayer Amschel the foothold he had so long sought. In 1798 most of the £37,000 of English bills sold were bought either by him, by Rüppell or by Jordis for cash.[13] In the following years, Mayer Amschel steadily increased his share of William's investment business as well. Altogether, between 1801 and 1806, he was involved in at least eleven major loans, of which the most important were to Denmark, Hesse-Darmstadt, Baden and the Order of St John.[14] He also became involved in purchases of real estate on William's behalf, while continuing to supply him with his beloved medals.[15]

The negotiations leading up to the various Danish loans are of particular interest because they give us an insight into the way Mayer Amschel squeezed out his business rivals. At first, in 1800 and 1801, he was content merely to take a share of loans which were organised by the likes of Rüppell & Harnier and Bethmanns.[16] Before long, he was being treated by them as an equal partner. Finally, from around 1804, he was able to establish what amounted to a monopoly of Danish business, partly thanks to the "douceurs" and discounts he gave the obsessively penny-pinching William, partly thanks to the good relationship he established with the Hamburg banker J. D. Lawätz, who played a mediating role between Kassel and Copenhagen.[17] Altogether, Mayer Amschel sold William Danish bonds worth a total of at least 4.5 million gulden (roughly £450,000) in this period; placed three loans to the Landgrave of Hesse-Darmstadt totalling 1.3 million gulden, of which around half was taken by William; and one loan to Baden of 1.4 million gulden. These are impressive figures and, understandably, Mayer Amschel's success aroused considerable envy and resentment among his competitors. In 1806 Rüppell & Harnier complained bitterly (but vainly) about aspersions being cast on their honour by "Jewish commercial rivals" who seemed to believe that "the name Rothschild" enjoyed more credit in Hesse-Kassel than that of the Danish government itself.[18]

Nor was such ill-feeling confined to Gentile firms. In 1802 the Kassel Jewish community lodged a complaint against Mayer Amschel, on the ground that he was to all intents and purposes residing in the town (where most of the business described above was done) without having the status—and tax liabilities—of a "protected Jew." Having been obliged to pay 180 gulden to buy exemption from the relevant dues, Mayer Amschel then decided to secure protected status for his eldest son Amschel. With wonderful insincerity, he argued in his application that the presence of a Rothschild in Kassel would "not impair the activities of the local merchants in any way and those who conduct business in bills will rather profit from this, as such transactions always benefit from a large competition."[19] Opposition from the local Jewish community and hesitation on the part of Mayer Amschel as to whether the residence permit should be in his or his son's name meant that it was not actually issued until June 1806.[20]

Yet, despite the title of senior court agent (*Oberhofagent*) bestowed on him in 1803, it is important to stress that at this juncture it was not Mayer Amschel so much as William who was the real banker; Rothschild was in many ways more of a stockbroker, catering to his client's growing preference for bearer bonds as opposed to personal loans.[21] Typically, Mayer Amschel's commission when he bought bonds for William was no more than around 1.75 or 2 per cent, so that his total profits from this business probably did not exceed 300,000 gulden. Moreover, on at least two occasions, it was Mayer Amschel himself who borrowed from William. At the same time, it is important to remember that, although William was Mayer Amschel's most important client in this period, he was by no means his only client. The objective, in this era of multiple states, was to establish links with as many princely courts as possible—something which the loans business he did for Hesse-Kassel made easy. By 1803 he had been appointed court agent to the Order of St John (on the strength of a decidedly ill-starred loan), the Prince of Thurn und Taxis (hereditary postmaster of the Holy Roman Empire), the Landgrave of Hesse-Darmstadt and Karl Friedrich Ludwig Moritz zu Isenburg, Count of Büdingen.[22] The most prestigious of these appointments came in 1800, when Mayer Amschel secured the title of imperial court agent from the Austrian Emperor, in return not only for his earlier services as a supplier of war *matériel*, but also for his work in collecting the interest on the Emperor's considerable borrowings from Hesse-Kassel.[23] His only failure came in 1802, when the court of Bavaria ignored his application for the title of agent.[24]

The importance of such titles should not be exaggerated, of course. In 1803, for example, Hesse-Darmstadt customs officials simply refused to recognise Mayer Amschel's privileged status as a court agent.[25] In any case, the whole system of petty principalities and overlapping jurisdictions which had made such titles matter in the eighteenth century was on the brink of an unprecedented and revolutionary upheaval—an upheaval which was to transform the Rothschilds' relationship with their princely patrons. Up until 1806 they had depended on the Elector and his ilk for their business and the privileges they could confer. Thereafter, William found that, little by little, it was he who began to depend on Mayer Amschel and his sons.

The Origins of a Myth

As we have seen, there had already been one major collision between Hesse-Kassel and the forces of Revolutionary France in the 1790s, culminating in the bombard- ment of Frankfurt which destroyed the Judengasse in 1796. That had led to a strengthening of the traditional links between Kassel and London: not for the first time, William put troops in the field against France in return for English money.[26] True, he had subsequently accepted the terms of the Peace of Lunéville (1801), which transferred the left bank of the Rhine to France. But when war broke out again between England and France in 1803 a showdown became almost inevitable. William was too committed to England to follow the lead of those sixteen German states which seceded from the defunct Holy Roman Empire to form the Francophile Confederation of the Rhine in the summer of 1806. He was also too intent on dri- ving a hard bargain with the various powers bidding for his support to realise the vulnerability of his own position. Napoleon offered Hanoverian territory. On the other hand, the Elector (as William now was) had lent money to Austria and to Prussia, who had joined the coalition against France in 1805. When the Prussian army was defeated at Jena and Auerstadt in the autumn of 1806, he was hopelessly exposed. Neither the hasty demobilisation of his troops, nor his belated request to join the Rhine Confederation, nor even the plaintive signs he hastily ordered to be put up at his borders—"Electorat de Hesse: Pays Neutre"—could deflect the wrath of Bonaparte, in whose eyes he was now merely "a field marshal in the service of Prussia." "My object," Napoleon declared bluntly, "is to remove the House of Hesse-Kassel from rulership and to strike it out of the list of powers."[27] William had little option but to flee, heading initially for his brother's estate at Gottorp in Hol- stein (then Danish territory).[28] On November 2 General Lagrange occupied his res- idence at Kassel as Governor-General; two days later he issued a proclamation formally confiscating all his assets and threatening anyone who sought to conceal these with trial by a military tribunal.

According to legend, it was at this critical moment that William turned to his faithful court agent Rothschild, hastily leaving in his care the entirety of his movable wealth:

> The French army was actually entering Frankfurt at the moment when Rothschild succeeded in burying the prince's treasures in a corner of his little garden. His own property, which in goods and money was worth about 40,000 thalers, he did not hide, well knowing that, if he did so, a strict search would be made and that not only his own but the prince's hoard would be discovered and plundered. The Republicans who, like the Philistines of old, fell upon Rothschild, left him not one thaler's value of his own money or property. In truth, he was, like all the other Jews and citizens, reduced to utter poverty but the prince's treasure was safe . . .

According to this not untypical version of the story from an English newspaper in 1836, when Mayer Amschel finally returned the money to William, he replied: "I will neither receive the interest which your honesty offers nor yet take money out of your hands. The interest is not sufficient to replace what you lost to save mine; and further my money shall be at your service for 20 years to come and at no more than two per cent interest."[29]

As discussed in the introduction, this story first gained currency in 1827, when it appeared in F. A. Brockhaus's *General German Encyclopaedia for the Educated Classes*.[30] Though there is good reason to think that it was initially inspired by the Rothschilds themselves, it was subsequently so widely disseminated as to take on a life—and a variety of significances—of its own. Initially, it was intended to illustrate the family's exceptional probity as deposit-holders: willing to risk everything rather than fail to protect and pay interest on a client's money. That was certainly the message of Moritz Daniel Oppenheim's two paintings on the subject commissioned by the family in 1861. By the later nineteenth century, however, it was beginning to acquire an alternative reading: the Elector's treasure was "blood money" because it had been earned by the sale of mercenaries, while Mayer Amschel made the most of it rather than merely preserving it.[31] The positive and negative versions of the myth are vividly juxtaposed in the American and German films *The House of Rothschild* (1934) and *Die Rothschilds* (1940).[32]

As has long been realised, the story is fiction—though, like so much of the Rothschild myth, it contains a very tiny grain of truth. In fact, William's movable property was widely dispersed in the period after the French occupation and only a few relatively unimportant items came into Mayer Amschel's possession. Some of the most important valuables—mainly bonds (without their coupons, which were stored separately)—were successfully smuggled out of Kassel by Buderus, who made the hazardous trip through the French lines to Itzehoe in early November. The bulk, however, was stored in caches at William's country houses. According to a meticulous list drawn up by the Elector himself, twenty four chests—containing not only securities and coupons but also accounts, silverware and clothes—were hidden under the stairs of the north wing of the Wilhelmshöhe, while another twenty-four, including important War Chest papers, were concealed in another part of the palace. In the cellar of the nearby Löwenburg were hidden a further twenty-four chests, including securities belonging to the Elector's mistress, official papers, porcelain and clothes. Finally, at his hunting lodge at Sababurg, there were forty-seven chests, most of them filled with silverware. Most of this would in fact have been lost to the French—who quickly managed to obtain an inventory of the Elector's silver—had it not proved possible to strike a deal with Lagrange. In return for a bribe of 260,000 francs (modest under the circumstances) he agreed to allow forty-two of the chests to be spirited away; the rest were confiscated. Accordingly, on the night of November 8, one of the Elector's officers led a convoy of carts with the freed chests to Hof Stölzingen, where they were divided up. War Councillor Lennep took some of the most important documents (including papers relating to the Elector's London investments) back to Kassel; ten chests were deposited with the Münden firm of Thorbecke, of which two were sent on to Schleswig and the rest to Eisenach; and nineteen were smuggled into Frankfurt and left in the hands of the bankers Preye & Jordis.[33]

By this time, however, Lagrange had realised that he had undercharged the Elector's men. Having managed to recapture some of the chests he had previously released, he now demanded more money. Eventually, an agreement was reached: in return for a second, rather larger payment, Lagrange promised to understate the total value of the Elector's assets. A list was drawn up totalling 19.8 million gulden (composed mainly of the larger loans to other German princes), and this became the "official" French inventory. All documents relating to the Elector's other assets—an estimated 27 million gulden—were then handed over to Buderus. Some of these were sent to the Elector at Schleswig. Some were kept by Buderus himself. The rest, mostly routine papers from the War Chest and Privy Purse, were packed into four chests. It was these four chests which were given to Mayer Amschel. A few others containing medals and a few bonds were also temporarily left in his care in Hamburg when the Elector left Itzehoe for Austrian territory in the summer of the following year.[34] But that was all.

Yet this prosaic account understates Rothschild's importance to the exiled Elector. For one thing, William still had need of a skilled stockbroker and investment adviser. Having managed to hang on to assets worth 27 million gulden, his investment income remained substantial, even after the extra costs imposed by exile. (According to Berghoeffer's figures, the surplus was something like 740,000 gulden a year.) Part of Mayer Amschel's role in this period was to collect this income from the various borrowers concerned. In addition, he had to reinvest it in new loans. For example, he arranged a loan of 100,000 gulden to the Hanau Treasury and a large loan to Graf Karl von Hahn zu Remplin (the profligate "Theatergraf," who was shortly afterwards made a ward of court by his family). He looked after a current account for money the Elector had entrusted to Buderus. On one occasion, at Buderus's suggestion, he also borrowed money from the Elector himself. He repurchased a substantial part of the Elector's coin collection, which had been sold off and dispersed, as well as fourteen cases of wine which had been stolen from the Hanau cellars. He handled various transfers of money which the Elector had to make for military and diplomatic purposes: payments to Hessian prisoners-of-war held by the French, to the Machiavellian Prince Wittgenstein, who had offered his diplomatic services, as well as to Russia and Prussia in 1813. He lent around 160,000 gulden to the Elector's son in Berlin.[35] He looked after the finances of the Elector's mistress, Gräfin von Schlotheim.[36] He even sold the Elector a diamond ring.[37]

Much of this was trivial, admittedly, and a good deal of it was unprofitable. A lot of time was wasted in 1809 and 1810 on an abortive scheme to assist the depleted Austrian Treasury by transferring some of William's assets—with a nominal value of over 10 million gulden—to the Emperor.[38] But there was one service performed by the Rothschilds for William which made all the rest worthwhile: the management of his English investments. Nathan later claimed that "The Prince of Hesse-Cassel . . . gave my father his money; there was no time to be lost; he sent it to me. I had 600,000£ arrive unexpectedly by the post; and I put it to such good use, that the prince made me a present of all his wine and his linen."[39] This has a superficial plausibility: one of the most important financial consequences of the French wars was a large migration of capital from the continent to London.[40] As with the story of the treasure, however, the reality was rather more complex.

At the start of his time in exile, William already had a very substantial English portfolio, primarily annuities with a nominal value of £635,400 paying interest of £20,426 a year. In addition, he was owed a considerable sum—around £200,000—by the Prince of Wales and his brothers (though they were characteristically in arrears with their interest payments). As an ally of the crown, he also received subsidies totalling £100,150 between 1807 and 1810.[41] The critical question was what should be done with the interest payments and subsidies as they were paid to William's current account with Van Notten. As early as 1807—in other words, some time before his move from Manchester to London—Nathan approached William's envoy in London, Lorentz, with suggestions as to how the money might be invested, but he was rebuffed at the Elector's express instruction.[42] It was not until two years later, once again at the prompting of Buderus, that Mayer Amschel was instructed to purchase 3 per cent consols (redeemable state annuities, or what would now be called gilt-edged securities)[43] with a face value of £150,000 at 73.5 (that is, at 73.5 per cent of their face value or price at redemption). It was to be the first of no fewer than nine such purchases up until the end of 1813, totalling £664,850. This was the money to which Nathan later alluded in his conversation with Buxton. His brother Carl was also alluding to it when he observed in 1814 that "the Old Man"—meaning William—had "made our fortune. If Nathan had not had the Elector's £300,000 [sic] in hand he would have got nowhere."[44]

How could such purchases of consols on someone else's behalf have been so vital to the Rothschilds? The answer lies in the way these investments were carried out. At first sight, there was not a great deal to be made from this business, as Mayer Amschel charged only one-eighth of a per cent brokerage on each purchase. On closer inspection, however, much more stood to be made. William did not actually put up all the cash at once for each purchase; it was the Rothschilds who effectively bought the consols, albeit on his behalf, and with money they had largely borrowed. If they had wished, they could have paid only a fraction of the market price, postponing full payment until a future settlement date. But this would have involved a double speculation: on the price of the consols and on the gulden–sterling exchange rate. Mayer Amschel preferred not to do this. He was content to derive advantage from the difference between the price and the exchange rate agreed with William, and the actual price and exchange rate paid by his son in London. For the first three purchases, the difference in price was of the order of 2 per cent, reflecting the fact that, at this low ebb in Britain's campaign against Napoleon, consols were falling. It is probable (though impossible to prove) that Mayer Amschel was also deriving some benefit from differences in the exchange rate.

The Elector probably suspected what was going on: when consols reached a low of 62.5 in the summer of 1811, he called a halt to new purchases and ceased remitting money to cover previous purchases until May of the following year. But this probably suited the Rothschilds well. For the consols remained registered in Nathan's name until they were fully paid for by William. That meant, for example, that even as late as March 1813 consols with a face value of £121,000 were notionally Nathan's.[45] Of course, they had largely been bought with borrowed money, and, from the moment the Elector's remittances arrived until the stocks were formally transferred to him or his agents, the Rothschilds also had to pay interest.[46] On the other hand, a certain latitude was possible, given the difficulty of getting certificates of ownership from London to the Elector in Prague.[47] Whatever profits Nathan was able to make on the market price and the exchange rate, purchases of more than £600,000 worth of consols and the actual possession of over £100,000 signalled the advent of a new financial force in the City of London. In this sense, as Carl later noted, it gave Nathan a kind of "security"—the impression of capital resource in excess of what the family actually had.[48] Amschel spelt out the significance of this in a letter to his brothers in 1818: "The good Nathan would have been unable to draw during the war bills to the amount of £132,000 and to handle all the businesses if . . . we had not obtained for him in Prague the big deal of the Elector's stocks, which he handled . . . [U]p to then Nathan did not even know what stocks looked like."[49] In effect, the war had allowed the Rothschilds to make a part of William's financial strength their own.

On the other hand, the price of that security was a high level of insecurity on the continent. For the risks the Rothschilds ran in serving William were real. The French authorities were in earnest about tracking down the Elector's wealth and they were prepared to use all the means at their disposal to do so. Under the Berlin Convention of 1808, for example, Napoleon extended a tempting offer to the Elector's numerous debtors, inviting them to settle with the French authorities instead of the Elector in return for reductions in their debts.[50] More alarmingly, the departure of General Lagrange put paid to the deal which had been struck with him. Mayer Amschel's offices were searched by the French police, as were those of Preye & Jordis. It was probably at this time that the contents of the four chests in Mayer Amschel's possession were concealed in the secret cellar described above. In August 1808 Salomon was interrogated by a French police official, as was a representative of another bank suspected of acting for William, and the following month Buderus and Lennep were briefly arrested.[51] The same happened in the summer of the following year, in the wake of a minor anti-French revolt. The Special Commissioner of Police in Westphalia—a man named Savagner—had Buderus and Lennep arrested again and then, acting on information supplied by one of the Rothschilds' business rivals, proceeded with a senior Frankfurt police officer to Mayer Amschel's office. There followed a bizarre interrogation in which the French attempted to get Mayer Amschel to admit to having supplied money on William's behalf to the instigators of the recent revolt.

Savagner was undeniably well informed. He knew about Mayer Amschel's visits to Hamburg and Itzehoe in 1807—where he had "spent hours with [the Elector] in his office, walking in his garden and conversing with him." He also knew about his dealings with Buderus. But Mayer Amschel was apologetic: "Because of a painful illness from which he had suffered for years, he had developed a short memory." Yes, he had been in Hamburg, but only on account of some goods which had erroneously been impounded as contraband. Yes, he knew Buderus and Lennep, but he had "never trusted them, as neither of them had ever sincerely been his friends, merely appearing to be in the world's eyes." Yes, he had been the Elector's court agent and had in the past made loans on his behalf to Denmark—or was it Emden? Far from relaying money to Buderus, he had received 20,000 gulden from him, from which he had made various payments, though to whom he could not recollect. The next day, Savagner tried again with Salomon, the fifteen-year-old Jacob, Salomon's wife, Amschel's wife and even Mayer Amschel's wife Gutle. Each stonewalled in turn. Gutle in particular was the embodiment of feminine innocence: "She knew about nothing at all, she was at home throughout the year and had nothing whatever to do with business. She had never seen [Buderus], she only concerned herself with her housework." In the end, Savagner seems to have admitted defeat and, like most Napoleonic officials the Rothschilds encountered, settled for a small "loan."[52] Matters only eased in 1810 when Frankfurt was transformed into a grand duchy under the direct jurisdiction of Baron Karl Theodor Anton von Dalberg, erstwhile Archbishop of Mainz and, since 1806, Prince-Primate of the Rhenish Confederation.

Mayer Amschel had already begun to ingratiate himself with Dalberg some three years before by offering the inevitable loan.[53] He now proceeded to facilitate a payment of 440,000 gulden to secure the emancipation of the Frankfurt Jews by discounting bonds worth a total of 290,000 gulden[54] and to advance Dalberg 80,000 gulden to finance his journey to Paris for the baptism of Napoleon's son. Indeed, Mayer Amschel was soon formally acting as Dalberg's "court banker," assisting him in the speculative purchases of land he undertook with the money paid by the Frankfurt Jews.[55] It was a sign of the esteem in which Dalberg came to hold Mayer Amschel that he appointed him to the electoral college of the new département of Hanau, along with such eminent Gentiles as Simon Moritz von Bethmann.[56] Whether he was aware how far Mayer Amschel continued simultaneously to serve the man whose most fervent wish was to oust him and his French patrons from Hesse-Kassel is not known. There is a startling symmetry in the fact that, only a few years previously, Mayer Amschel had been arranging payments of some 620,000 gulden from the Elector to Austria, to pay for troops and horses in the 1809 campaign against France. Shortly after Mayer Amschel's death, his son Amschel was advancing 255,000 gulden to Dalberg, partly in order to purchase horses for the French army![57]

It is possible, of course, that Mayer Amschel—like Buderus, who also accepted an official appointment by Dalberg—no longer expected William to be restored to his estates. But if so, he never wrote him off completely. He simply backed both sides. Such a strategy has obvious attractions, and it was to become a frequent Rothschild gambit in the decades ahead. However, the double agent always runs the risk of forfeiting the trust of both sides and ending up the loser, whichever wins. For this reason, it is not surprising that during the years of the Elector's exile Mayer Amschel developed a penchant for secrecy—another of his most enduring bequests to later generations. At first, he had been blasé. He and his son Carl made numerous trips to the vicinity of Itzehoe in the first months of the Elector's exile—indeed, they established a permanent office for the purpose in Hamburg—and corresponded regularly and openly with one of William's most senior officials, Knatz.[58] As we have seen, this did not go unnoticed by the French police, and Mayer Amschel quickly came to appreciate that "these days one has to set to work carefully."[59] By the middle of 1808 correspondence between the Rothschilds and the Elector's officials, much of which was relayed via Buderus and Lawätz, was being written in a crude code. Buderus was referred to as "Baron von Waldschmidt," Knatz as "Johann Weber," Mayer Amschel as "Peter Arnoldi" or "Arnold" and William himself, variously, as "Herr von Goldstein," "Johannes Adler" or "the Principal." The Elector's English investments were known as "stock fish" (a pun on the German for cod, *Stockfisch*).[60] For additional security—"for the more care that you take, the better it is"—letters were sent not to Mayer Amschel but to Juda Sichel, whose son Bernhard had married Isabella Rothschild in 1802. When Carl and Amschel travelled to see the Elector in Prague, following his flight south from Denmark, correspondence was hidden in specially fitted secret compartments. Sometimes the Rothschilds even took the precaution of transliterating incriminating letters into Hebrew characters. And it seems highly probable that two sets of books were kept in this period, one complete, the other specially doctored for the consumption of the authorities. Such precautions were justified; in addition to the searches and interrogations described above, the French police succeeded in intercepting at least one letter in 1811.[61]

In Austrian territory too, Rothschild moves were monitored by the police. There was less reason to fear the Austrian authorities, of course, but there was no guarantee that relations between William and the Emperor would remain friendly. Indeed, after the French victory over Austria at Wagram, there was a strong likelihood that the Elector would be forced once again to move on. Nor can the failure of their financial discussions have endeared him to the authorities in Vienna. For this reason, the Rothschilds continued to operate behind a veil of secrecy even in Prague, leading the police to draw somewhat exaggerated inferences about their political role:

> [T]his Jew [Amschel] is at the head of an important propaganda scheme in favour of the Elector, whose branches extend throughout the former Hessian territories . . . These suppositions are based on facts: whenever I enter the Elector's quarters, I always find Rotschild [*sic*] there, and generally in the company of Army Councillor Schminke and War Secretary Knatz, and they go into their own rooms and Rotschild generally has papers with him. We may assume that their aims are in no sense hostile to Austria, since the Elector is exceedingly anxious to recover the possession of his Electorate, so that it is scarcely open to question that the organisations and associations, whose guiding spirit Rotschild probably is, are entirely concerned with the popular reactions and the other measures to be adopted if Austria should have the good fortune to make any progress against France and Germany. Owing to his extensive commercial connections it is probable that he can ascertain this more easily than anybody else, and can also conceal his machinations under the cloak of business.[62]

Yet for all the risks they took on his behalf, the Rothschilds were never wholly trusted by William. No part of the myth of the hidden treasure is more at variance with the truth than the idea that he was grateful to Mayer Amschel for his efforts on his behalf. On the contrary, Mayer Amschel had to endure repeated bouts of paranoia on the Elector's part. William's first concern was that Mayer Amschel might betray him to the French. Later, he began to worry that his agent had his hand in the till, suspicions which were only encouraged by envious rivals. He accused Mayer Amschel of swindling him of the interest on his English stocks. He accused him of deliberately hanging on to the valuables which had been left in his care at Hamburg.[63] Throughout this time, Mayer Amschel had to rely on Buderus to reassure the Elector. Buderus was unstinting in his praise. His reasons for entrusting so much business to Mayer Amschel were, he told William,

> the most punctual payment which one can expect of him, the certainty that he always reckons by the official exchange rate on the day of a transaction, the conviction that he never discloses Your Majesty's transactions to anyone, as he has handled the realisation [of your assets] with such care that French officials who were sent to interrogate him to find out whether he had received English money on Your Majesty's behalf, could find no trace of the money in the books which were laid before them.[64]

The irony, however, is that Buderus's assurances were themselves far from disinterested. For, unbeknown to the Elector, he had entered into an agreement with Mayer Amschel which effectively made him a sleeping partner in the Rothschild firm. In return for investing 20,000 gulden—the sum which Mayer Amschel admitted to having received when questioned by Savagner—Buderus promised "to advise that firm in all business matters to the best of his ability and to advance its interests as far as he may find practicable."[65] In the light of this—to say nothing of the deals struck by Mayer Amschel with the French authorities and with Dalberg—the Elector's mistrust begins to look rather less like paranoia. As William came to realise, the Rothschilds' skill at forging new business relationships was liberating them from their early dependence on him. When, in May 1812, he requested that one of Mayer Amschel's sons move to Prague to act as a kind of court agent in exile, he was politely but firmly rebuffed.

It is therefore something of an exaggeration to say, as Carl did, that "the old man" had made their fortune. In 1797 Mayer Amschel's capital had been 108,504 gulden (around £10,000). Ten years later the balance sheet showed a total capital of 514,500 gulden (around £50,000).[66] It seems unlikely that the business he did with William in this period accounted for as big a share of this increase as the import–export business between Frankfurt and Manchester. By 1810, to be sure, the firm's capital had risen to 800,000 gulden (around £80,000) and a substantial part of this increase probably was due to the income generated by managing William's portfolio. But the real significance of the Elector's treasure, as both Carl and Amschel implicitly acknowledged, was that it helped Nathan to make the transition from Manchester merchant to London banker. Once this was achieved, the Rothschilds needed "the Old Man" less.

Mayer Amschel's Legacy

A letter Buderus wrote to William at around this time provides a neat summary of the firm's radius of activity in the last months of its founder's life:

> Their father is old and ailing. His eldest son Amschel Mayer, and his second son Salomon, who is delicate, are indispensable to him in his extensive operations. The third [sic] son, Carl, is almost continually engaged in travelling in the service of your Electoral Highness, while the fourth [sic] son, Nathan, is very usefully established in London and the youngest, James, spends his time between London and Paris.[67]

By this stage, power in the firm had effectively passed from Mayer Amschel to his five sons. Only a few years before, however, the old man had still been playing the role of *Herr im Haus*. As we have seen, even the mercurial Nathan, far away in England, was still having to do as he was told as late as 1805. His brothers were treated even more like employees:

> Amschel writes that Kalman [Carl] would like to come to you, but what is the point of that? . . . I still need to have Kalman with me in Frankfurt for the moment and he would be much less use with you . . . He is keen to go to London. But I don't think it sensible from the point of view of our house, as Salomon has hard work to do cashing in and paying out bills. He has the obligations to deal with too . . . [If Kalman goes] then

all my commodity business will have to be done through Seligmann and
Abraham Schnapper, and Mayer Schnapper his son, because although
Jakob [James] is already in the office he has only just had his bar mitz-
vah. So it really is necessary for Kalman to stay with us. He really wants
to go to London [and] if you really need him then I will write him off.
But it is stupid not to leave Kalman here for a few more years until Jakob
has grown up. Don't write to Kalman that I said this to you ... Furthermore, my dear son Nathan, when you are writing to my son Kalman, I
advise you to praise him a lot. With God's help he is a very clever man
for his age, though he is rather too bold ... He really wants to come to
you but I really don't want this dear boy, may he live to be a hundred
years old, crossing the sea for just a three-week trip and we cannot do
without him for long[er] because as I told you Amschel has business in
Kassel. Much as I would like my son Kalman to travel to London for
three weeks it would end up being six months, and it is simply not possible to teach conceited outsiders how to run my indigo business.[68]

Mayer Amschel prevailed and Carl stayed; it may have been a sop to Nathan that
James was sent to join him for a spell three years later.[69]

As this letter also shows, Mayer Amschel's in-laws, the Schnappers, were now
involved in the business; so too were the Sichels, into which family Isabella had married, and the Beyfus brothers, Seligmann and Mayer, who married Babette and Julie
respectively in 1808 and 1811. He was also well aware of Nathan's work in partnership with Rindskopf and his own father-in-law Levi Barent Cohen. But from the
outset, Mayer Amschel kept his in-laws at one remove from the management of the
firm: the reference to the Schnappers as "outsiders" is revealing. In the same letter to
Nathan, he asked a characteristic question: "Dear Nathan, do our letters come
directly into your hands alone, so that one can write what one wants, or do you read
our letters to your whole family [meaning Nathan's in-laws, the Cohens]? Let me
know."[70] Even at this early stage, Mayer Amschel had formulated a rule which was
to be followed strictly for more than a century: his male descendants were, as far as
the running of the firm was concerned, the inner circle. In practice, this meant a distinction between family or private correspondence—almost always written in
Hebrew characters—and business correspondence, usually written in German,
French or English by clerks. Mayer Amschel more than once had to reprimand
Nathan for forgetting this distinction: "I repeat for the last time that your Hebrew
written letters may be good enough for family purposes, but for account and business matters you have to write in German, French, or English; I cannot give to my
clerks in the office your muddled Jewish letters mixed with family news, if they are
to keep good books—accordingly, a good deal of confusion arises."[71] For the historian, of course, it is precisely these letters—repetitive and unstructured though they
often were—which have by far the greater value.

The transition of the family business into "Mayer Amschel Rothschild & Sons"
happened in September 1810, when he and three of his sons—Amschel, Salomon
and Carl—issued a printed circular announcing that they would henceforth act as
partners (*wirkliche Theilhaber*) in a new firm (*Gesellschaft*).[72] When members of the
family had been interrogated by Savagner the year before, Mayer Amschel was still

calling himself the sole proprietor (*Inhaber*) of the firm, while his sons were merely his "assistants" (*Gehülfen*).[73] However, he may have been lying in order to protect them in case Savagner decided to prosecute the firm. Earlier in the year it had been Amschel, Salomon and Carl who had negotiated the purchase of a vacant lot in the Judengasse (as reconstruction work at last began) in order to build a proper office for the firm.[74] And when a formal legal partnership contract was drawn up in September 1810, its preamble explicitly stated that "a trading company already existed" in which Mayer Amschel, Amschel and Salomon were the "associates." The principal function of the 1810 agreement was to make Carl a partner, giving him a 30,000 gulden share of the total capital of 800,000 compared with Mayer Amschel's 370,000, Amschel's 185,000 and Salomon's 185,000; and to guarantee that James would become a partner (also with a share worth 30,000 gulden) when he attained his majority.

It was not only in terms of capital that Mayer Amschel remained *primus inter pares*: he alone had the right to withdraw his capital from the firm during the period of the agreement; he alone had the right to hire and fire employees of the firm; and his unmarried sons could marry only with his permission. The agreement made the grounds for this explicit. It was Mayer Amschel who had, "through the industry which he had evinced from his youth onwards, his commercial abilities and the indefatigable activity which he had maintained into his old age, laid the basis for the prosperity of the firm, and thereby established the worldly fortune of his children."

In other respects, however, the agreement would act as a model for future agreements between the brothers and their descendants for most of the nineteenth century. Profits were divided in proportion to capital shares, no partner was to engage in business independently of the others and the agreement was to run for a fixed period of years (in this case, ten). The most remarkable clause in the agreement stated what would happen were one of the partners to die. Each solemnly renounced the rights of his wife, children or their guardians to contest in any way the amount of money agreed by the surviving partners to be the deceased's share of the capital. Specifically, his widow and heirs were to be denied any access to the firm's books and correspondence.[75] This was the first formal statement of that distinctive and enduring rule which effectively excluded Rothschild women—born Rothschilds as well as those who married into the family—from the core of the business: the hallowed ledgers and letters.

The death of a partner was, of course, no longer a remote possibility. Not only was Mayer Amschel now an old man—he was sixty-six or sixty-seven when the 1810 agreement was signed—he was also a sick man. He had been seriously ill two years before, possibly with a rectal abscess arising from chronic haemorrhoids, and, although an operation was successfully performed, his health never fully recovered.[76] It was a common complaint in the Judengasse, whether because of the sedentary lives its inhabitants perforce led, or because of a genetic defect which intermarriage—also imposed by the Stättigkeit—had spread through the street's 500 families. On September 16, 1812, he was taken ill; he died just three days later.[77] But even as he lay on his deathbed, Mayer Amschel hastily revised his will, as if wishing to reinforce the message conveyed to his sons in the 1810 agreement. The new will pre-empted the agreement's provisions by withdrawing just 190,000 gulden from the firm as his notional share of the capital—obviously a substantial understatement. And it repeated emphatically the rule excluding the female line from the business:

> I hereby decree and therefore wish that my daughters and sons-in-law and their heirs have no share in the capital of the firm "Mayer Amschel Rothschild & Sons" and even less that they are able or are permitted to make a claim against it for whatever reason. Rather, the said firm shall exclusively belong to and be owned by my sons. None of my daughters and their heirs therefore has any right or claim on the said firm and I would never be able to forgive a child of mine who, against this my paternal will, allowed themselves to disturb my sons in the peaceful possession of their business.

If his daughters did do so, they would forfeit all but their minimal statutory claims as heirs under the Napoleonic code. The distinction between sons and daughters could scarcely have been more strongly expressed.[78]

That Mayer Amschel's testament was so strictly adhered to, not just by his immediate heirs but by his descendants for generations to come, confirms the impression given by those letters to his sons which have survived. Within his immediate family circle, he was a commanding and perhaps also intimidating figure. Interestingly, this is not how he was remembered by the rest of the world. To Gentiles who had dealings with him, he had tended to conform to the intelligent but deferential stereotype of the court Jew. It should be stressed that modern portrayals of Mayer Amschel— especially the screen performances by George Arliss and Erich Ponto—probably exaggerated the "Jewishness" of his appearance and manner, the former sporting a long beard and fez-like hat, the latter ringlets and a skullcap. On the other hand, the most commonly reproduced nineteenth-century lithograph—of a rather square-jawed clean-shaven man in a neat wig—was the product of an artist's imagination. One contemporary who met him in her youth remembered "a rather big man, who wore a round unpowdered wig and a small goatee beard." Another remembered him wearing the kind of hat and clothes which would have been worn by a Gentile merchant of the same generation, albeit slightly threadbare.[79]

This tallies with Mayer Amschel's somewhat ambiguous reputation within the Judengasse as relatively orthodox in matters of religion, but progressively more and more liberal in matters of education and politics. Mayer Amschel was not one of those *maskilim* who were inspired by the Jewish Enlightenment, nor did his attitudes anticipate the later Reform movement to modernise Judaism as a religion; but nor was he a staunch conservative. Cohen's unauthorised memoir (published shortly after his death) portrayed him as the personification of a kind of middle way between the new and the old—"proof that the dogmas of the Jewish religion, even according to the teachings of the Talmud, contain nothing which conflicts with the laws of morality." Rothschild had been "a zealous believer in the Talmud and chose it alone as the guiding principle of all his actions"; indeed, according to Cohen, his attitude towards religious conservatism had been "a little exaggerated." He and his brother Moses (who administered the community's poor-relief fund for some years) were active members of the Jewish community. But Mayer Amschel was also a "good citizen"—a significant phrase, as we shall see.[80]

This is evident in Mayer Amschel's attitude towards charity. As noted above, he and his brothers were conscientious in paying their tenth to the poor of the community. Ludwig Börne remembered the crowd of beggars who used to lie in wait for Mayer Amschel as he walked through the street, and the patience with which he distributed alms.[81] Yet he was less conventional in not confining his charity to the Jewish community. Cohen recalled an occasion when a street-urchin had shouted "Jew!" at him. Mayer Amschel

> calmly reached into his purse and gave the needy youth some money with the request that he might often repeat what he had said. No one could have been happier to oblige. He took what he was offered and cried at the top of his voice: "Jew! Jew!" Several other youths came up and mockingly joined in. Rothschild listened with evident pleasure, pronouncing the Hebrew blessing: "Praise be to Him, who gave the laws to His people of Israel!"[82]

In his will too he bequeathed 100 gulden to "three praiseworthy, charitable Christian foundations." Even his charitable work within the Jewish community became increasingly secular in its orientation. In 1804 he played a leading role in establishing a new school for poorer Jewish children—the Philanthropin—the curriculum of which had a thoroughly secular flavour. This seems to have reflected the influence of his book-keeper Geisenheimer and of the tutor he employed for his own children, Michael Hess, a follower of Moses Mendelssohn who later became the school's headmaster. It may also have been inspired by his younger sons, at least one of whom (Salomon) was a member of the same masonic lodge as Geisenheimer.[83] The important point is that Mayer Amschel continued to favour a communal basis for education at a time when an increasing number of Jewish families were sending their children to Gentile schools outside the ghetto.[84] Ludwig Börne was one of those who rebelled against the relatively conservative atmosphere of the Frankfurt ghetto, ultimately converting to Christianity rather than endure discrimination. But, as Heine later recalled, he could not help admiring the unaffected piety of the Rothschild household. Passing the old family home in the Judengasse in 1827, he noticed nostalgically that Mayer Amschel's widow Gutle had decorated its windows with white curtains and candles in celebration of the great feast of joy (Chanukkah):

> How gaily the candles sparkle—those candles which she has lit with her own hands in order to celebrate the day of victory on which Judas Maccabeus and his brothers liberated their fatherland as heroically as did in our own day King Frederick William, the Emperor Alexander and the Emperor Francis II! When the good lady looks at these little lights, her eyes fill with tears, and she remembers with melancholy joy her younger days when Mayer Amschel Rothschild, of blessed memory, still celebrated the Feast of Lights with her, and when her sons were still little boys who placed candles on the floor and leapt over them with childlike pleasure, as is the custom in Israel.[85]

It was Mayer Amschel's work to win full civil and political rights for the Frankfurt Jews, however, which best expressed his loyalty towards Judaism.[86] We know that his political activism predated the French Revolution because he had been one of the seven signatories of the protest to the Senate of 1787 (quoted in chapter 1) about

increased restrictions on travel outside the ghetto on Sundays and holy days. However, it was only with the advent of a French-backed regime that the possibility arose
of more substantial improvements in the lot of the Jews. Things would have moved
faster if Frankfurt had been under the direct jurisdiction of Napoleon's brother
Jérôme who, as King of Westphalia, favoured a policy of complete emancipation.
By contrast, Dalberg was cautious, partly because he could not risk alienating the
local Gentile establishment, partly because he himself feared that a liberated Jewish
community might "balance Christian injustice, as soon as they breathed some air,
with Jewish impudence." The new Stättigkeit which he issued in 1808 seemed, if
anything, a step backwards, as it reasserted the ban on Jews living outside the (still
dilapidated) Judengasse, reimposed the poll tax and confirmed the traditional
restrictions on numbers of families and marriages.[87]

It was at this point that Mayer Amschel was able to use his financial leverage over
Dalberg to force the pace of change—the first time a Rothschild acted in such a way
for what he explicitly called "our nation," and not the last. Dalberg, as we have seen,
was biddable: if a sufficiently large capital sum could be paid to compensate his
duchy for the loss of tax revenue which Jewish emancipation would entail, he was
prepared to give his consent. After preliminary discussions conducted via Dalberg's
Jewish police commissioner Itzstein,[88] the sum of 440,000 gulden was agreed on—
twenty times the sum paid each year by the Jews for their "protection"—of which
Mayer Amschel raised 290,000 on behalf of the community by discounting
bonds.[89] In December 1811, after further negotiations with the Frankfurt Senate,[90]
Mayer Amschel was able to inform his son, with understated satisfaction: "You are
now a citizen."[91] Two weeks later the decree on the "civil-legal equality of the Jewish
community" came into force.

To be a citizen of his native state, but to remain unequivocally a member of "our
nation," meaning the traditional Jewish religious community: this was Mayer
Amschel's aim. For the critical distinction between the Rothschilds and many other
successful Jewish families of this period was that, while they fervently desired social,
civil and political equality with their Gentile counterparts, they refused to abandon
Judaism as their religion in order to achieve it. Their own ambition was therefore
from the outset inseparable from the political campaign for Jewish emancipation
not only in Frankfurt, but throughout Europe.

In this, as in so much else, Mayer Amschel's influence on his descendants was
profound and enduring. Four days after their father's death, his sons sent out a circular to their most valued clients to reassure them that there would be no change in
the conduct of the family business: "His memory will never fade among us, his surviving partners . . . Our blessed father remains unforgettable to us."[92] Such pious
sentiments are not always translated into practice once the first pain of bereavement
has passed; but the sons of Mayer Amschel meant what they said. Time and again in
the years after his death, they harked back to their father's words—to his business
aphorisms, to his views on Jewish emancipation and, above all, to his paternal commandments to them, his male descendants. In many ways, these numerous allusions
to Mayer Amschel—unremarked by previous historians—reveal more about his
character than any other source.

A typical example is Amschel's request for better stock market information from
Nathan in October 1814: "Father used to say: 'A banker has to calculate, there is no

merit in making transactions in the dark.' "[93] He made a similar point in 1817: their father had told them "that Jewish fortunes as a rule don't keep longer than two generations for two reasons. One because the housekeeping and other expenses are not being considered, second because of Jewish stupidity."[94] While these echoed Mayer Amschel's criticism of Nathan's somewhat casual approach to accounting, other maxims related more to the firm's relations with governments. One point was obvious enough, given the benefits Mayer Amschel had derived from his relationship with William of Hesse-Kassel: "I [learned?] from our blessed father," Salomon told Nathan in 1818, "who always said, 'The evil eye of the court brings fewer advantages [than the title of consul or court banker].' "[95] But, as Amschel remembered, it was not enough just to acquire minor titles like "court agent": "Nowadays everybody calls himself 'Excellency.' I remember, however, what our father used to say, 'With money you become an Excellency.' "[96] The key was to establish some kind of financial leverage. As Amschel put it, "It is better to deal with a government in difficulties than with one that has luck on its side. We heard this from our father."[97]

Nor was it only the elder brothers who reminisced in this fashion. In March 1817 James remembered a tip which he would often put into practice in his relations with rival firms: "Father used to say, 'If you can't make yourself loved, make yourself feared.' "[98] As late as 1840 Carl could still be heard recalling how "his Father had often taught him, when he had occasion to apply to an inferior or a man who had little power to assist him in carrying an object he had in view, he spoke with the person as if the whole depended entirely on him, though perhaps he knew he had but the smallest possible influence in the business."[99] Of all these pieces of business advice, the one most frequently cited was probably Salomon's favourite, on the importance of cultivating politicians. He cited this in a letter to Nathan in October 1815: "You know, dear Nathan, what father used to say about sticking to a man in government."[100] It came up again a few days later: "But you remember father's principle that you have to be ready to try everything to get in with such a great government figure."[101] And Mayer Amschel had left them in no doubt as to how such politicians could best be wooed: "Our late father taught us that if a high-placed person enters into a [financial] partnership with a Jew, he belongs to the Jew" ("gehört er dem Juden").[102]

The brothers' consciousness of their Jewishness and of their responsibilities to the rest of the Jewish community also owed much to their father's influence. Intriguingly, both Salomon and Carl seem to have regarded carrying on their father's work for Jewish emancipation in an almost instrumental way. As Carl put it in May 1817, "It is the best thing on earth to be of service to the Jews. Our father did so and we see how well we are paid back."[103] Salomon made the same connection between good works and good fortune a few months later when he wrote to Nathan reminding him to put pressure on the British government on behalf of European Jewry: "If we want our children to be one day really happy, we have to do all that is in our power to bring to a good end all the work which . . . father of blessed memory . . . began in the interest of our people."[104] And he repeated the point early the next year:

> If everything depends, as it does, on God, if we want, as we do, to be fortunate, then, dear Nathan, [the interests of the entire Jewish people]

must be as important to you as the most important business deal once
was. How can we show more respect for our blessed father, than by supporting that work which he laboured at for years[?][105]

But of all their father's advice, his last commandment—to maintain fraternal
unity—had the greatest and most enduring impact. Salomon once attributed "all
our luck to the benediction which our father gave us an hour before he passed
away."[106] Amschel remembered that benediction too: "I remember what our father,
peace be with him, told me on his deathbed: 'Amschel, keep your brothers together
and you will become the richest people in Germany.' This has almost come true."[107]
That advice was often invoked when the brothers quarrelled—as they frequently did
in the turbulent years immediately after Mayer Amschel's death. "Our blessed father
ordered us to live in peace," Salomon reminded Nathan, following an especially
bitter attack by the latter on Carl.[108] He had to say it again just a week later: "My
good brother, dear Nathan, our blessed father ordered us to live in peace, otherwise
we shall lose our courage. Let us have peace."[109] More than twenty years later the
same principle was elaborately enshrined in a new partnership agreement, drawn up
following the death of Nathan himself:

> We wish to offer a proof of our reverence for the holiest memory of our
> father, whose virtuous conduct in all of life's relations is a noble example
> to us all. Through pious acceptance of the higher wishes of God,
> through faith in God's help, through conscientious honesty and inde-
> fatigable industry, this noble and philanthropic man laid the foundation
> of our good fortune, and when, almost forty years ago, he took his sons
> into partnership with him in his business, he told them that acting in
> unison would be a sure means of achieving success in their work, and
> always recommended fraternal concord to them as a source of divine
> blessing.
>   In accordance with his venerable wishes, and following the prompt-
> ings of our own hearts, we therefore wish today, through this renewed
> agreement, to reinforce our mutual dependence and hope, in this new
> league of brotherly love, to guarantee the success of the future activities
> of our House. May our children and descendants in the future be
> guided by the same aim, so that with the constant maintenance of unity
> the House of Rothschild may blossom and grow into full ripeness . . . ;
> and may they remain as mindful as we of the hallowed precept of our
> noble ancestor and present to posterity the godly image of united love
> and work.[110]

The same theme of paternally ordained brotherly unity was developed still further
in an annexe to the agreement, which solemnly hoped that "in the future [as in the
past] the blessing of our blessed father and grandfather upon our House and our
family" would be fulfilled. He had promised them "the protection of the Almighty;
the success of our undertakings; the prosperity of our family and the continuing
honour and respect of our reputation and name," but only if they "always preserved
concord, love and faith" with one another.[111]

    Of course, it is easy to detect in all this the influence of the Old Testament; and
no doubt many another Jewish (or Calvinist) patriarch before and after Mayer
Amschel tried to instil similar values into his sons. Nor was the ideal of familial

unity peculiarly biblical: Plutarch relates the parable of Scilurus, who showed his sons that a bundle of arrows could not be broken, but that the individual arrows could.[112] The impressive thing about the Rothschilds, however, is that the sons heeded their father so zealously. This was a point Gentz stressed in his article for the 1827 Brockhaus *Encyclopaedia*. The first of the Rothschilds' guiding principles, he suggested:

> obliges the five brothers to conduct their combined businesses in an uninterrupted community [of interest]. That was the rule which their dying father bequeathed them. Since his death, any proposal, no matter where it comes from, is the object of collective discussion; each operation, even if it is of minor importance, is carried out according to an agreed plan and with their combined efforts; and each of them has an equal share in its results.

In the very first paragraph of his essay, Gentz had in fact already alluded to Mayer Amschel's last commandment to his sons to maintain "unbreakable unity." "Never has a father's last testament been carried out more conscientiously and more profitably," he observed. "It is a peculiar characteristic of this family, that all its members consult the shade of their father at every important stage of their lives, and when assessing every business deal; remind themselves—often verbatim—of his wise teaching . . . and never mention his name without deep reverence."[113] In the 1836 edition it was even stated that the brothers "revere their father with such piety that that they refer back to him in the course of all important business undertakings and indeed Nathan usually decides all doubtful cases on the basis of a rule which he attributes to his father."[114]

This would not have been worth writing if it had been commonplace behaviour. It clearly was not. Even as late as 1841, nearly thirty years after Mayer Amschel's death, his eldest son could feel moved to remind all the other partners—including those who had never even met their grandfather—of the same, all-important nexus between unity and success:

> *Unity* was what our blessed father, with his last words, enjoined me to uphold as [our] first and holiest of duties—our father, who united in himself boundless integrity, the deepest of insights, the wisdom of experience and the pious habits of a sage. It is my conviction, and I am sure it is yours too, that, along with God's blessing, we owe not only our wealth but also our honourable position in society primarily to the [spirit of] unity and co-operation [that binds together] all our partners, bank houses and establishments. I therefore request most urgently that you, beloved brothers and nephews, will always take care to implant in your heirs the same consciousness of concord and togetherness, so that the same [spirit of] unity and co-operation continues to exist for as long as is at all possible. To do so will be of benefit both to you and to your descendants. It will prevent our business interests from being split up, and will stop others benefitting from our great efforts, our knowledge and the experience [we have] laboriously accumulated over many years. So I ask you, for the sake of ensuring unity, whenever there should be any differences of opinion which might lead to ill feeling, not to make an immediate decision, but to let a few days pass first to allow tempers to

cool, in order to avoid any overhasty steps being taken. May the unity, integrity, sympathy and mutual trust of the community of all Rothschild houses be always preserved and forever affirmed.[115]

In the years between 1812 and 1841, there were, as we shall see, many times when Amschel and his brothers came close to just the kind of breakdown in fraternal unity which their father had warned them against. That they always avoided it—that, even thirty years after his death, they still remembered his dying commandment—is a striking testament to the patriarchal power of Mayer Amschel Rothschild.

II

Brothers

THREE

"The Commanding General" (1813–1815)

My brother in London is the commanding general, I am his field marshal . . . —SALOMON ROTHSCHILD[1]

It is an established rule with us that no disapprobation shall be expressed by either of us at the conduct of the other, since as partners we act always for the joint interest and consequently neither of us has the right to blame the other when he has acted for the best. —SALOMON ROTHSCHILD[2]

Napoleon's celebrated aphorism—"An army marches on its stomach"—left open the question of how that stomach was to be filled. So did the Duke of Wellington's equivalent: "To gain your objects you must feed." All the armies which fought in Europe between 1793 and 1815 resorted at times to the age-old practice of requisitioning provisions from civilian populations. To varying degrees, they also relied on their own lines of supply from secure territory. But taking supplies at gunpoint has the disadvantage of making an army unpopular and food scarce, while extended supply lines are a source of vulnerability. In protracted campaigns like Wellington's in the Iberian peninsula, more sophisticated methods of procurement were necessary. Above all, it was essential to be able to purchase supplies and to pay troops. The truth of Cicero's maxim was never more apparent than in the years between 1808 and 1815: *nervos belli, pecuniam infinitam*, or, as Henry Dundas had put it to William Pitt at the outset of the wars with Revolutionary France: "All modern Wars are a Contention of Purse."[3]

As early as May 1809 Wellington was complaining to the government in London that he did not have enough of it. In March 1811 he wrote to the Prime Minister, Lord Liverpool, threatening that he would have to halt the campaign altogether because of the lack of cash. A year and a half later, on the eve of the invasion of France itself, the problem was once again acute. The outgoings of his military chest were running at around £100,000 a month, including not only payments to his own troops, but also subsidies to Portugal and Spain (now forcibly won over to the British side). But, as he explained to Earl Bathurst, he was only just able to pay for the subsidies to his allies. In the absence of cash, he was reduced to paying officers in depreciated paper money, while the lower ranks (who refused to accept payment in paper) were not being paid at all. "Unless this army should be assisted with a very large sum of money at a very early period," he warned the government,

> the distress felt by all the troops will be most severe . . . and it will be quite impossible for me to do anything . . . [The Spanish troops] are in so miserable a state, that it is really hardly fair to expect that they will refrain from plundering a beautiful country, into which they enter as conquerors; particularly, adverting to the miseries which their own country has suffered from its invaders. I cannot, therefore, venture to bring them back into France, unless I can feed and pay them . . . Without pay and food, they must plunder; and if they plunder, they will ruin us all.

The nadir was reached in February 1813, when Wellington reported that he could "scarcely stir out of my house on account of the public creditors waiting to demand payment of what is due to them."[4] As it was Wellington's financial difficulties which provided Nathan Rothschild with the decisive business opportunity of his career, it is worth saying a few words about the cause of them.

Of all the states of the *ancien régime*, Britain had the most efficient financial system. The key institutions had evolved in the century after the Glorious Revolution: a relatively cheap and centralised system of revenue collection; a fairly transparent budget-making process in parliament; a more or less stable system of public borrowing, the funded national debt; and an equally stable monetary system revolving around the Bank of England and the convertibility of paper notes into gold. It was this which enabled Britain to wage six major wars in the course of the eighteenth century without succumbing to the kind of political crisis which precipitated the overthrow of the more financially backward French state.[5] But the cost of war rose rapidly after 1789 (partly because the Revolutionary regime was able to field armies of unprecedented size): it has been estimated that the annual cost was five times higher in real terms during the Napoleonic Wars than it had been a century before. Public expenditure in Britain rose sharply between 1793 and 1815, from something like £18 million a year to around £100 million (around 16 per cent of estimated national income). The total cost of war with France in that period was around £830 million, of which some £59 million took the form of subsidies to Britain's less solvent allies. A host of new taxes had to be created, of which the income tax was the most important, but these only paid for about a quarter of the war's costs. As a result, the national debt soared from £240 million in 1793 to £900 million in 1815, close to 200 per cent of national income. Moreover, in 1797 the Bank of England felt obliged to suspend gold convertibility, ushering in a period of currency depreciation. The combination of wartime shortages and the growth of paper-money circulation led to inflation: prices roughly doubled in the twenty years before 1815.[6] Wellington's campaign was therefore being fought at a time of unparalleled fiscal "overstretch."

This does not fully explain the Duke's difficulties, however, which were partly logistical. Even if the Exchequer in London had been overflowing, it would still have been difficult to get money to Wellington in a form that Spanish merchants would accept. Up until 1813 there were two ways in which this could be done. Either bullion (in the form of gold guineas)[7] could be shipped to Portugal or Spain, and exchanged there for local coins; or the Duke could borrow from local bankers by selling them bills on London. Given the risks which attended large-scale shipments of gold, it was the latter method to which Wellington more often had recourse. The problem was that by 1812 the Iberian market for bills on London was saturated, and Wellington found that he could sell new bills only at a prohibitively steep discount: "The patriotic gentlemen at Lisbon," he complained to Bathurst, "will give us no money, or very little, for the draughts on the Treasury."[8] It was into this breach that Nathan Rothschild stepped.

War and Peace

Historians have never adequately explained how an obscure Jewish merchant banker—who only a few years before had been a smuggler, and a few years before that a minor textiles exporter—was able to become the principal conduit of money from the British government to the continental battlefields on which the fate of Europe was decided in 1814 and 1815. Of all the steps in the ascent of the house of Rothschild, this was surely the greatest; yet it is also the least understood.

Three distinct elements were required to turn Nathan into (as his brothers later said, only half in jest) the "commanding general"—the Napoleon of finance. The first was the absence of competition. This was a matter of sheer good luck, for before 1810 the City of London was not short of able bankers. Harman & Co. (whom we have already encountered among the Rothschilds' earliest correspondents in London), Reid, Irving & Co., Smith, Payne & Smith and above all Baring Brothers—all might have been expected to assist the government in its financial difficulties. Indeed, the Barings had already been involved in relaying British funds in the form of loans to Portugal. Nor was Nathan the only Jewish merchant seeking to challenge the established banks: Abraham and Benjamin Goldsmid had been doing so since the 1790s, while a succession of German bankers arrived in London in the years after 1802 (notably Schröder, Brandt and Huth) intending to emulate their achievements.[9] As the new Commissary-in-Chief who had been entrusted with the task of providing Wellington with funds observed in November 1813, "Many houses have already offered their services to me." Indeed, his first instinct was that Barings were "on every score the most proper channel for our money transactions."[10] Yet it soon became apparent that neither Barings nor any other established firm was in a position to act. In the case of Barings, this was partly because leadership of the firm had only recently passed from Francis Baring (who died in 1810) to his son Alexander. The main reason, however, was that the City as a whole was reeling from two major shocks. The first was the crisis of 1810, partly occasioned by the report of the Bullion Committee, recommending (against the advice of the Bank of England) an early resumption of gold payments. The prospect of a period of tight money—which this implied—led to a slump in the price of government stocks and left the Barings and the Goldsmids holding substantial amounts of the most recent government loan. Barings lost around £43,000. Abraham Goldsmid committed suicide, leading (as William Cobbett remarked with distaste) to "*alarm* and *dismay*" in the City and an intensification of the panic.[11] Probably of equal importance was the simultaneous collapse of the Amsterdam market occasioned by Napoleon's annexation of the Netherlands. This left Barings' continental partner Hope & Co., which had for some time played a dominant role in Russian finances, a mere "empty shell."[12]

The second factor in Nathan's favour was the appointment of John Charles Herries as Commissary-in-Chief in October 1811. Herries was to be Nathan's Buderus, his first "friend" in a high place. Himself the son of a minor merchant banker, Herries had risen through the political ranks rapidly since becoming a junior clerk at the Treasury in 1798. Three years later he was appointed private secretary to Nicholas Vansittart, the Secretary to the Treasury, and served Spencer Perceval in the same capacity when he was Chancellor of the Exchequer in 1807–9.[13] It was not only his family background in finance, however, which enabled Herries to identify Nathan Rothschild as the solution to his problem as Commissary. For Herries, unusually, was something of a Germanophile. Not only had he studied in Leipzig; he had even translated Friedrich Gentz's anti-French tract *On the State of Europe before and after the French Revolution.* It also seems possible that it was a friendship dating back to his Leipzig days which alerted him to the potential usefulness of the Rothschilds. According to one account, Herries had, as a student, been involved romantically with a woman who was now the wife of an ennobled Leipzig tobacco merchant named Baron Limburger—to the extent that he had an illegitimate child by her.[14] The Limburgers later claimed that it was on their recommendation that Herries had involved Nathan in the financing of Wellington's campaign; and it seems reasonable to infer something of the sort from the fact that they subsequently felt able to claim between £30,000 and £40,000 as a 1 per cent commission on the money made by Nathan on government business.[15] On the other hand, it was not until February 1814—after Nathan's first commission from the government—that Limburger wrote to Herries, praising the Rothschilds' "zeal and prudence," but at the same time offering his own services as "an upright and prudent individual" to superintend their operations; and Herries was initially cool in his response.[16] On reflection, he did decide to employ Limburger in the way suggested, but he was careful to emphasise that his confidence in Nathan predated Limburger's involvement.[17] Similarly, it was not until June of the same year that the Rothschilds began to regard Limburger as having influence with Herries.[18]

It is possible that Limburger was merely one of those unscrupulous and opportunistic conmen who abounded in Napoleonic Europe, and that he was subtly blackmailing Herries on account of his bastard child.[19] As Carl commented sceptically in early 1815, Limburger's wife was "a great lover of money,"[20] and Amschel suspected Limburger himself of merely "playing the great man."[21] In the end, the Limburgers had to be paid off with £15,000 in a manner which was more appropriate to blackmailers than partners.[22] Nevertheless, as Carl had to admit, Limburger "had done us a favour," if only by acting as an aristocratic go-between in the brothers' dealings with continental governments.[23]

The third and most important reason Nathan became involved in British war finance was that, unlike his rivals, he had a solution to the problem of how to get money to Wellington. As so often, Nathan subsequently made what he had done sound easy:

> When I was settled in London, the East India Company had £800,000 worth of gold to sell. I went to the sale, and bought it all. I knew the

Duke of Wellington must have it. I had bought a great many of his bills at a discount. The Government sent for me and said they must have it. When they got it, they did not know how to get it to Portugal. I undertook all that and I sent it to France; and that was the best business I ever did.[24]

And, of course, the story has been embroidered by myth-makers, attributing patriotic motives to Nathan and even imagining James crossing the French lines in woman's clothing.[25] The reality was very different. At some point before March 1811 the Rothschilds became involved in smuggling gold bullion from England to France. This was technically a breach of the Continental System, but it was tolerated by Napoleon and later actually licensed. The youngest Rothschild brother took care of the business on the other side of the Channel, at Gravelines or Dunkirk, exchanging the imported guineas for bills on London, the prices of which were naturally very low in France at that time and which could then be redeemed at a profit in London. A typical series of six shipments from Nathan to James in April 1812 amounted to some £27,300 in guineas, in return for which James sent Nathan bills from Paris bankers like Hottinguer, Davillier, Faber and Morell with a face value of £65,798.[26] The other Rothschild brothers contributed by relaying suitable bills to James from Hamburg and Frankfurt.[27]

As with the earlier covert operations on behalf of the Elector of Hesse-Kassel, an unsophisticated code was devised which more or less sufficed to allay French suspicions. Nathan became "Langbein," London became "Jerusalem," and the transfers of bullion across the Channel were codenamed "Rabbi Moses" or "Rabbi Mosche."[28] Incriminating consignments were referred to, variously, as "beer," "fish" or "children."[29] Other key figures (no longer identifiable) were known as "the fat man" and "the cursed one."[30] In addition, to ensure that cross-Channel communications were as secure and swift as possible, agents at Dover were authorised to charter boats for Rothschild business. It was one such vessel which smuggled James himself across the Channel when he visited Nathan in 1813.[31] "Playing hide and seek" with the authorities was becoming second nature to the brothers.[32] Indeed, even their sons were already being taught to attach importance to secrecy: at the age of just eleven Salomon's son Anselm refused to let his teacher correct a letter he was writing to his father. "My dear mother," the boy explained, "how can I possibly divulge the secrets which I share with my father to Mr Sachs?"[33]

It was probably the scale of Nathan's purchases of bullion in London which first brought him to Herries's attention. It may also be that some of the bills which were finding their way back to London through the Rothschilds were Wellington's, having been sold on by his Spanish, Portuguese and Maltese bankers to Paris houses. And it is just possible that James was already using the bullion sent to him by Nathan to buy bills on Spanish and Portuguese houses which were then sent across the Pyrenees to Wellington.[34] Although evidence for this assertion is scant, it is not implausible. After all, money had been sent in 1806 and 1807 from Spain's American colonies to France by an even more circuitous route starting in Vera Cruz, heading north to New York and then crossing the Atlantic, via London, to Paris. Indeed, on one occasion Mexican piasters worth over 14 million francs were shipped across the Channel to the French Treasury by a British warship![35] Generally speaking, the profits to be made from such transactions were regarded as outweighing the benefits the enemy derived from the money itself. In addition, there was a degree of theoretical confusion as to the economic significance of such transfers of bullion, which helps to explain why the French authorities tolerated James's activities in Paris and Bordeaux (about which they were quite well informed). Although some French police officials had their suspicions, Napoleon followed the advice of his Minister of the Public Treasury, François Nicholas Mollien, who argued that any outflow of bullion from Britain was a sign of economic weakness and therefore advantageous to France.[36]

This was a bad miscalculation; on the contrary, the Rothschilds' ability to relay specie across the Channel was about to become a decisive source of strength to Britain. On January 11, 1814, Nathan was officially charged with the task of financing Wellington's advance through France. In Vansittart's words, Herries was to "employ that gentleman [Nathan] in the most secret and confidential manner to collect in Germany, France and Holland the largest quantity of French gold and silver coins, not exceeding in value £600,000, which he may be able to procure within two months from the present time." These were then to be delivered to British vessels at the Dutch port of Helvoetsluys, whence they would be relayed to Wellington via St Jean de Luz, near Biarritz. It was to be "distinctly understood by Mr Rothschild . . . that he is to take upon himself all risks and losses, which may occur, prior to the delivery on board His Majesty's ship." If successful, he would be entitled to a commission of 2 per cent on the sum delivered. But, at all costs, secrecy must be maintained.[37] This was a breakthrough, in that it was the Rothschilds' first official commission from the British government and it brought Nathan into direct contact not only with Herries—by March, he was "almost continually" in Herries's office[38]—but with Vansittart and the Prime Minister himself, Lord Liverpool.[39]

Admittedly, the operation proved to be rather more difficult than Nathan had anticipated. Meyer Davidson, whom Nathan sent to Amsterdam, complained repeatedly about the short supply of suitable coins in the wake of the French occupation, and quickly concluded that new napoléons d'or (the imperial successor to the old louis d'or coin) would have to be struck if Nathan was to fulfil his contract.[40] By the end of February Davidson had been able to accumulate no more than £150,000, "Yet this is like a drop of water in the ocean. Why? Because it is . . . an English government commission and the English government could make use of all the cash that exists on the continent and even this would not satisfy them."[41] Davidson began to fear that the transaction could not be carried out, and there was talk of reducing the target figure from £600,000 to half that amount.[42]

Despite these difficulties, however, Herries was impressed. As early as February 22 Wellington was writing to thank Bathurst for "the supplies of money which are very ample."[43] By April Nathan and James were able to convert over £20,000 into guilders for immediate use by the British forces,[44] and the Rothschilds continued to furnish the advancing army with money until the end of the year, when the government resumed normal methods of payment.[45] As Herries told Sir George Burgman, the British paymaster in Amsterdam, "Rothschild of this place has executed the various services entrusted to him in this line admirably well, and though a Jew, we place a good deal of confidence in him."[46] One reason for Herries's satisfaction was that the Rothschilds delivered substantial amounts of the cash to Helvoetsluys in advance of being paid by the government, leading some historians to assume that Nathan was using Prince William's London stocks as collateral for large-scale borrowings in London and Paris.[47] This is possible, but it cannot have been the brothers' sole source of credit, given the size of the sums involved. As Neal has put it, Nathan was "financ[ing] the war against France with the resources of the continent"—merchants' bills on London which the Rothschilds were buying up and converting into bullion, which they then sent to Wellington's army on Herrries's account.[48] By the middle of May Nathan was owed as much as £1,167,000 by the government—a sum large enough to terrify his brother Salomon, and evidently more than even Nathan could sustain. As Herries told Drummond, his representative in France, he was

> not surprised at the extreme solicitude of the brother in London to obtain money from you. They are now serving us to a very considerable extent by their credit and if we fail to supply [them] with funds to meet these engagements the weight is greater than any individual however rich could be expected to support. The brother here is doing the business remarkably well and seems capable of supplying one with money to any extent.[49]

It was not only the British army which received money from the Rothschilds on Herries's account in 1814. Of rather more importance—because potentially more lucrative—were the payments which had to be made by the British government to finance the military efforts of its less solvent allies on the continent. Such payments had previously been handled by banks such as Barings and Reid, Irving, but now Nathan, having won Herries's confidence, was well placed to take them over. The only difficulty lay in persuading the recipient countries to place similar confidence in his brothers on the other side of the Channel. This was achieved most easily with Russia, rather less easily with Prussia and only to a limited extent with Austria. Smaller Allied states—including Mecklenburg and, predictably, Hesse-Kassel—also received money through the Rothschilds, as did the returning French monarch, Louis XVIII. The total amounts involved were huge. Altogether between 1811 and 1815 Britain paid around £42 million to her allies.[50] The Rothschilds became involved late in the day, but swiftly established a dominant position. In June 1814 Herries listed the payments they had so far made to Prussia, Austria, the French King and the British army. Including money that had not yet been disbursed, the total was 12.6 million francs, and more was to come.[51] Small wonder Lord Liverpool referred to "Mr Rothschild" as "a very useful friend." "I do not know," he told Castlereagh, "what we should have done without him last year [1814]."[52]

It proved relatively easy to secure a substantial share of the Russian business. The agreement reached between Britain, Russia and Prussia at Reichenbach in June 1813 had promised a total payment of £1,333,333 to Russia and £666,666 to Prussia, partly in the form of interest-bearing treasury bills. However, the cash-strapped British government repeatedly deferred payment and it was not until the end of May 1814 that an agreement was reached which provided for fifteen monthly instalments of a million Prussian thaler each (in the form of interest-bearing drafts), two-thirds to Russia, one-third to Prussia.[53] Gervais, the Russian diplomat charged with converting the subsidy into cash, initially turned to Hope & Co., seeking an advance on the first seven months' payments and offering a discount of 2 per cent. But the Hope director Labouchère hesitated and the Rothschilds—represented ably by Salomon and James—snapped up the business.[54] They offered not only to convert instalments worth 4 million thaler into louis d'or and ducats, but to deliver most of the money to Hamburg, Dresden and Warsaw, where it was urgently needed to pay Russian troops.[55]

The Rothschilds' terms were evidently attractive enough, especially in the initial absence of competition. As James said, Gervais "needed cash, and soon," and no other firm would risk delivering so much cash to remote Warsaw. It was also advantageous from a British viewpoint to let the Rothschilds handle the transaction, as they undertook to reduce the interest Britain had to pay and to secure a more favourable exchange rate from pounds to thalers than had originally been agreed.[56] Indeed, James exuberantly claimed that "a better deal had never been made for [a] government." "You can confidently tell Lord Liverpool," he told Nathan with youthful bravado, "that this transaction is a masterpiece."[57]

It was a masterpiece in more ways than one. As their father had taught them, the brothers were always careful to make their terms attractive not only to governments, but also to the individual officials with whom they were negotiating. Thus, to ensure that Gervais acquired a personal interest in doing business with Rothschilds—to make him a reliable "friend" or "helper" of the house—he and other Russian officials were discreetly plied with money in the form of commissions and interest-free loans.[58] This was, as the brothers themselves privately acknowledged, no more or less than bribery. Under the terms of a separate agreement with Russia, a 1 per cent commission went straight into Gervais's pocket.[59] "Our friend baksheesh" ("der Freund Schmiergeld") had, as James and Carl said, played a vital role not only in clinching the deal, but in paving the way for future deals.[60] For, as Davidson archly put it, "Now the Russian knows Salomon and Salomon knows the Russian." Characteristically, the brothers had widely differing views as to how much Gervais should receive. Salomon knew—or thought he knew—Gervais's price. On reflection, he felt James had given the Russian "too much of the profits" and "obviously [did] not understand how bribes are given": the gift of a watch and some English stocks would have sufficed.[61] But James dimissed this as "really stupid," assuring his brothers that he would be able to secure an even bigger commission on the next Russian transfer: "The money given to Gervais makes all the difference and I happen to know the man."[62] Carl appears to have sided with James in this argument, but could not resist pointing out that bribing Gervais had originally been his idea.[63]

Such payments to politicians and civil servants should not, of course, be judged by the standards of late-twentieth-century Britain, where holders of public office are forbidden to accept bribes, and Members of Parliament are obliged to declare their private business interests, consultancy fees and even gifts. As we shall see, bribery was common practice in most of Europe for most of the nineteenth century, and the Rothschilds frequently obliged the more venal politicians and civil servants they encountered with cash payments. To be sure, as contemporaries often remarked, "corruption" varied in its character and degree from place to place as well as over time. Even in 1814—long before the spread of Gladstonian notions of public probity—British officials were understood to be more scrupulous than Russian; or, rather, they were known to be more subject to parliamentary and press scrutiny. For this reason, the payments to Gervais were carefully concealed from Herries, and there was no question of Herries himself receiving similar sums.[64] But more subtle ways could be found of taking his private interests into consideration. In July 1814 Amschel sent Nathan a letter from Madame Limburger relating to her illegitimate child—a letter he advised his brother to show to the child's father, Herries. "It would be good [if you could]," he wrote, "because he may give you the Prussian and Russian business, as he would very much like the child to make some more money. And if the child gets a quarter of the profit, then we would have our profit, too."[65]

The Russian subsidy deal was indeed a *Meistergeschäft*—for the British government, for Gervais, and above all for the Rothschilds themselves. Taking into account their 2 per cent commission from Britain, an additional 2 per cent to cover costs and a further 4 per cent from the Russian government, their gross profit on the first tranche of 4 million thaler was of the order of 8 per cent. Later payments (of 3.7 million francs and 5.3 million thaler) yielded comparable returns.[66] Other governments were equally willing to pay substantial commissions in order to convert their subsidies into ready cash. The government of Mecklenburg "needed money like bread," James reported from Schwerin, and was willing to forgo up to 30 per cent of its 1.5 million thaler subsidy entitlement—and pay a 5 per cent commission—if the Rothschilds could arrange "immediate payment." "They would do anything we want them [to do]," wrote James gleefully, "in order to obtain money quickly."[67] The returning French King, Louis XVIII, was also furnished with money by Rothschilds in the form of bills on Paris.[68] There were equally easy pickings in Hesse-Kassel, where, following the departure of Dalberg and prior to the return of the Elector, a skeleton administration struggled to pay the costs imposed by Allied armies in transit. With the Russian Second Army Corps requisitioning already scarce grain and not a penny left in the War Chest, William's officials turned in desperation to the Rothschilds for a 250,000 gulden loan. Initially intended to be for only six months, part of this loan had to be prolonged because of the virtual impossibility of raising adequate taxation from the "plundered" and "exhausted" populace.[69]

By contrast, the Prussian subsidy business proved at once harder to secure and less lucrative. In part, this was because Prussian negotiators were less biddable than Gervais. The brothers made overtures to the Finance Minister Prince Bülow and to Prince Hardenberg's adviser Christian Rother, but elicited only a lukewarm response, despite the positive impression made by Herries's recommendation.[70] James managed to secure three instalments totalling a million thaler, but the Prussians dismissed the 2 per cent commission he asked as too high. "There's money to be made from Russia," James suspected, "but none from Prussia."[71] Six months on, he saw no reason to revise that initial judgement: "There is generally no pleasure in doing business with the Prussians," he grumbled as yet another bid was rejected.[72] In the end, the brothers had to do without a commission altogether, and although the 3 per cent profit finally realised on this deal was better than had initially been expected,[73] they had to console themselves with the thought that they had at least secured a foothold in Berlin, which might prove more profitable in the future. "At any rate," James reflected, "we have now, thank God, managed to push our way into the business, and it will be of considerable use in bringing us into contact with the Prussian court."[74]

It proved harder still to "establish contact" with the Austrian court. Under the

Treaty of Treplitz of 1813, the Austrians were to be paid a million pounds as a subsidy, and the Treaty of Chaumont of January 1814 increased the total by two-thirds,
to be paid in monthly instalments of £138,888. After the French defeat, the total
due was scaled down to £555,555.[75] Again the Rothschilds put in a bid to handle
part of the transfer, backed up as usual by Herries. The terms were deliberately generous: not only did the Rothschilds offer to waive any commission, but they offered
to convert sterling into gulden at the rate of 8.48 to the pound. But Barbier, the
Vice-President of the Austrian Treasury, and his superior, the Finance Minister
Count Ugarte, rejected the offer in the belief that Viennese banks should be
employed.[76] A second bid to transfer monies to Austria from Belgium (to defray the
costs of occupation) also fell through because the Austrians sought to attach unacceptable conditions to the Rothschild offer.[77]

All the diverse inter-governmental payments the Rothschilds succeeded in
making in 1814 had one thing in common: in each case, there were at least two ways
(and sometimes three) to make a profit. The first and most obvious took the form of
commissions, which ranged, as we have seen, from as much as 8 per cent to as little
as zero. The second—potentially more lucrative but also riskier—lay in exploiting
the often rapid and large exchange rate movements which occurred in this period.
This was how the otherwise unattractive Prussian transfer was made to yield a profit;
and it seems to have been attempted on most of the other transfers too. Essentially,
the brothers were able to take advantage of the variations in exchange rates from
place to place, which reflected the absence—especially pronounced in wartime—
of an integrated European foreign exchange market, and the effects of political
uncertainty—also at a peak in 1814–15. On a given day, a draft or bill denominated
in sterling might be worth quite different amounts in terms of gulden in London,
Amsterdam and Frankfurt. Arbitrage transactions sought to exploit those differences
by buying a currency cheap in one market and selling it dear in another. In the same
way, the exchange rate of the thaler or the ducat could vary dramatically within a
short space of time. Classic forward exchange speculation meant timing payments
so that a particular currency could be bought when its exchange rate was weakest
and sold when it was strongest.

The Rothschild brothers were singularly well placed to carry out such transactions. Not only did they have permanent bases in Frankfurt and London and semi-
permanent offices in Amsterdam and Paris; individual brothers also continued to
undertake business trips as far afield as Berlin and Prague. Moreover, thanks to their
relationship with Herries, they had a large advantage over their competitors. For one
of the main *causes* of volatility on the foreign exchanges was the very transfers of
money from Britain to the continent which the Rothschilds themselves were being
asked to undertake. Long before 1814, British observers had realised that large purchases of foreign currency with sterling bills tended to cause the pound to depreci-
ate. The bigger the deficit on the British balance of payments—in effect, the more
such unrequited subsidy payments had to be made—the more the pound's exchange
rate slid. It was precisely Nathan's commitment to Herries to undertake the transfers
with the minimum exchange rate depreciation which secured him the subsidy business in the first place; and the brothers never ceased to draw Herries's attention to
their success in this regard. (This was what James was driving at when he described
the first major Russian transfer as a "masterpiece" from the British point of view.) At

the same time, however, the Rothschilds were able to derive substantial benefits for themselves by exploiting the effects of their transactions on the various currency markets.

The key lay in controlling the sterling exchange rate, and this was in many ways the brothers' principal concern in this period. As early as June 1811, when they were first engaged in smuggling bullion across the Channel, Amschel accused James of "forcing the rate of exchange in Jerusalem [London] too high" (meaning, in fact, that the pound was falling against the franc); and James's letters to Nathan the following year frequently refer to his efforts to keep the franc from rising.[78] "It is impossible," he assured Nathan, "to do more than I do to keep [the exchange] so low as possible."[79] These early experiences explain the success with which the Rothschilds avoided substantial depreciation when transferring larger sums for Herries. To Herries's surprise and satisfaction, Nathan was able to disburse as much as "£700,000 in the purchase of bills on Holland and Frankfurt, without its having produced the smallest effect or excited any sensation on the market . . . The exchange is better now than when the operation commmenced . . . I am convinced that £100,000 negotiated by a foreign minister or an officer of the commissariat would have produced ten times the effect of Rothschild's operations."[80] The fall of Paris to the Allied armies naturally strengthened the pound,[81] but the continued payment of subsidies soon threatened to weaken it again. For this reason, the Rothschilds intervened to push it up further. By now the markets were tending to follow the Rothschild lead. As Carl noted: "When we buy, everybody buys."[82] This reflected the widespread belief that the Rothschilds were acting "on behalf of the English government and that this is being done in order to force the rate of the pound sterling up [and] . . . that we succeeded very well in doing so."[83]

In reality, of course, the Rothschilds had reasons of their own for holding up the pound. With movements of sterling more or less predictable, it was possible to engage in profitable arbitrage on the back of the big subsidy transfers. In May 1814, for example, Salomon drew Nathan's attention to the substantial gap between the Paris and London gold quotations.[84] A month later it was Nathan's turn to urge James to buy undervalued pounds in Frankfurt.[85] The subsidy payments to Gervais generated a succession of profits from exchange rate differences.[86] For example, Amschel went to Berlin in July to take advantage of the premium on ducats over louis d'or.[87] The ducats which were delivered to Gervais in August and September had been bought by James at a lower price in Amsterdam, yielding an extra profit of some 4 per cent.[88]

Such transactions probably accounted for the lion's share of the profits the Rothschilds made in this decisive period. Amschel was only half joking when, during the post-war surge in sterling, he wrote urging Salomon: "Do your stuff, make the Frankfurt house richer by a million francs, the Paris house richer by a million louis d'or and the London house richer by a million pounds, and you'll be awarded the order of the *Grande Armee!*"[89] Yet it must be stressed that this was a strategy fraught with risk. It was exceedingly difficult to accumulate the cash necessary to carry out the subsidy transfers to Russia and Prussia on time. The Frankfurt house found its sources of credit all but exhausted on more than one occasion, and Carl and Amschel frequently complained that Nathan was biting off more than they could chew.[90] Raising sums of the order of 600,000 gulden was, as Carl complained, "no

joke."[91] At the same time, the governments concerned in the subsidy transfers naturally resented the fact that the Rothschilds were making these large profits on the
side. Even Herries and Gervais on occasion complained about what was going on,[92]
while the Prussian government managed to pass at least some of the costs occasioned
by the unexpected fall of the pound in August back on to the Rothschilds.[93] The
exchange rate was also a stumbling block in the negotiations with Austria.[94]

Moreover, the success of arbitrage and forward exchange operations hinged on
rapid communication. As far as possible, the brothers sought to keep one another
abreast of news which might affect the exchange markets: the impending payment
of a new subsidy, the likelihood of further military action, the imminence of the
peace treaty being signed. And, as we have seen, they were already able to transmit
such information through their own couriers considerably faster than was possible
through official channels or the regular post. Yet the time-lags could still be substantial and Nathan was constantly being urged to speed up the system. When sterling
surged by 6 per cent in Amsterdam, James wrote impatiently for guidance:

> Now, dear Nathan, if you think the subsidies are going to stop, then you
> can be sure that the exchange rate will rise again, as there will be fewer
> bills. But if you think that there will be further transfers, then the
> exchange [rate] will fall again . . . One simply no longer knows what to
> do about the exchange rate. It is terrible that you, dear brother Nathan,
> don't bother to write me your opinion, because now it is vital to know
> what is going on over there.[95]

So anxious was Amschel to have up-to-date news from London that he asked
Nathan to send his letters by more than one route—via Paris and Amsterdam as well
as Dunkirk—and to use colour-coded envelopes so that his contact at the post office
could tell at a glance whether the exchange rate was rising (blue) or falling (red).[96]

And even with the benefit of swift communications, it was still possible to be
caught out. In July 1814 Nathan unexpectedly remitted—"like a madman"—more
than £100,000 to his brothers in Frankfurt. This caused the pound to drop at once
in Frankfurt;[97] and when the slide persisted into August and spread to Amsterdam,
a "depressed" Carl began to fear that Nathan had lost control of the market.[98]
Salomon nervously warned Nathan not to "bring the pound below a certain level":
"If you are not careful you will not remain the master of the Stock Exchange."[99]
Even as matters stood, confidence in sterling on the continent had been badly damaged.[100] These anxieties were merely compounded by Amschel's continuing confidence (which may have been due to the fact that, just as he had feared, bad news had
not reached him soon enough). It was time, Carl felt, to stop speculating in sterling:

> But if you were to write about this to Amschel [in Berlin] he would do
> exactly the contrary and would buy sterling immediately without think-
> ing things over first. No one on earth can imagine what I have to go
> through. Immediately after his arrival in Leipzig he proceeded to pur-
> chase £10,000 at 136. His opinion is that the pound will rise to 140 but
> if it were to reach 140 he still would not be able to decide whether
> he could sell or not. He would maintain the fact that it would rise to
> 150 and so forth . . . If therefore you write to him, have a fixed . . .
> amount in your mind and tell him half of it, as he will no doubt buy
> more in any case.[101]

When Amschel realised his mistake, he found it "astonishing"—the more so as he was held responsible for the fall of sterling in Berlin![102] "Could I have been more careful?" he retorted, stung by his brothers' criticisms. "You really want to be able to go out in the rain without getting wet."[103] Salomon's gloomy conclusion was that Nathan had overreached himself: "No man on earth can at any time fix the rate of the pound except a government which would be ready to risk half a million pounds during one year in order to carry out a monetary plan . . . I do not think there is any point in buying sterling for the purpose of keeping the rate of the pound from falling, because there is too much of this currency already in the world."[104] James even suggested a change of strategy: running up sterling debts on the assumption of continuing depreciation.[105] It was only gradually—and with Nathan "operating . . . as much as lies in my power" to push the rate back up—that the brothers recovered their confidence in the pound.[106] By November James found that it was once again enough for him "to put in an appearance" at the Hamburg stock exchange for the pound to rise, and the same was true when he visited Berlin early in the New Year.[107] By February he could confidently report to Nathan: "It depends solely on me whether the pound rises or falls in Paris."[108]

There was another (and not dissimilar) way of profiting indirectly from the subsidy business: by speculating on fluctuations in bond prices. Like exchange rates, bond prices were highly sensitive to large international transfers, as well as to related political developments. For example: the price of Russian bonds had plummeted from 65 per cent of their face value to just 25 between February and October 1812, for the reason that the French invasion had led to the suspension of interest payments on the government debt. News of the retreat from Moscow led to a rally: on November 30 they were quoted at 35 in Amsterdam and by March 1813 they had risen to 50, only to fall back to 41 in June on news of Napoleon's victories in Saxony.[109] As the prospect of an Allied victory neared, so Russian bonds rallied, with the payment of subsidies from Britain strongly implying an imminent resumption of interest payments. It therefore made sense for anyone who anticipated the defeat of France to buy the bonds of states allied to Britain while they were still in the doldrums. The Rothschilds attempted to do so, albeit rather late in the day. By the time Nathan sent his brother-in-law Moses Montefiore to Paris with instructions to make some speculative purchases, Russian bonds were already close to par.[110] Nevertheless, James was convinced that they would go higher, having received information (from Gervais) that interest payments would soon be resumed.[111] Amschel also made purchases of modest amounts of bonds from neighbouring German states that August.[112] And in March 1815 Rothschild purchases based on similar calculations pushed up the price of Austrian bonds.[113] However, it seems that much less money was made from these transactions than from arbitrage and foreign exchange speculation, which were on a much larger scale. Indeed, the last bond purchases very probably led to considerable losses—for reasons which will become clear.

Nathan's Waterloo

As soon as the French had been defeated, of course, and Napoleon exiled to Elba, the end of the subsidy business was in sight—or seemed to be. Nor did any major new money-making opportunity present itself. The French financial position in 1814 appeared to preclude the payment of reparations. Although the debts of the

French state accumulated in the period before around 1800 had been largely wiped out by the assignat inflation, Napoleon's wars had run up a new internal debt of 1.27 billion francs and rentes perpétuelles (the French equivalent of British consols) stood at around 58 (that is, 42 per cent below par). Napoleon had succeeded in reforming the currency, giving a monopoly on note issue to the Banque de France and effectively placing the new franc on a bimetallic (gold and silver) standard. But by 1814 the reserves of precious metal in Paris were severely depleted.[114] The most the victorious Allies therefore asked of the restored Bourbon regime was a modest contribution to the costs of the military occupation of France in the form of interest-bearing bons royaux. The Rothschilds might have expected to play a major part in these transactions, given their dominant role in the British subsidy transfers. But they were disappointed. Although they seem to have handled some franc-denominated payments to Russia, their bid to convert the Austrian share of the bons royaux into cash for a commission of 0.5 per cent was rejected, as were later proposals to the other Allied powers.[115]

For this reason, it is tempting to see Napoleon's return from Elba on March 1, 1815, as an immense stroke of luck for the Rothschilds. Just as the brothers appeared to be losing the peace, Bonaparte's "Hundred Days" plunged Europe back into war, restoring the financial conditions in which the Rothschilds had hitherto thrived. This idea that Nathan profited from the dramatic events of 1815 is central to Rothschild mythology: it has been repeatedly claimed that, by obtaining the first news of Napoleon's defeat at Waterloo—before even the government itself—Nathan was able to make a huge sum of money on the Stock Exchange.[116] The more fabulous elements of the myth—Nathan's presence at the battle itself, his riding alongside Wellington, his stormy night crossing from Ostend to Dover, his profits of between £20 and £135 million—have long ago been debunked. Nevertheless, historians—including Victor Rothschild himself—have continued to assume that the Rothschilds benefited at least to some extent from the resumption of war and the final Allied victory. Even if the money made from buying British government stock immediately after the battle can have amounted to little more than £10,000, their total profits from the Waterloo campaign have been estimated at around a million pounds.[117]

The real story is very different. It is true that the resumption of war *appeared* to promise a return to the lucrative business conditions of 1814—but not because of its effect on consols, which, as we have seen, had hitherto been of relatively minor importance to Nathan. (It was the Barings who were once again given responsibility for a new issue of gilts in 1815.) Rather, it was to a resumption of his previous business with Herries that he now looked, on the assumption that Napoleon's return would create the same urgent need for transfers of money from England to the continent as the year before. Up to a point, this was perfectly correct. But the Rothschild correspondence reveals that the resumption of payments to Wellington and to Britain's continental allies proved a source of far less easy pickings than in 1814. Indeed, it is possible that a series of miscalculations by the brothers led to losses rather than profits in the critical period before and after Waterloo. On this occasion, it seems, reality is diametrically opposite to myth.

To begin with, Napoleon's return was, as Nathan put it, nothing but "unpleasant news" for the Rothschilds. Early March had seen the brothers buying Austrian stocks in the expectation of a bull market in both Vienna and London.[118] When the news of the escape from Elba reached Nathan on March 10, this prospect evaporated. There was, he informed Salomon, "stagnation on 'Change . . . in the bill way, and I am prevented from making you a large remittance."[119] The effect on Paris was even worse: "It is practically not possible to continue business at present," reported James.[120] True, Nathan was quick to reorientate his operations. On the assumption that the British government would soon once again need cash on the continent, he began buying up bullion in London, which he then sold to Herries for shipment to Wellington. Immense sums were involved: in the first week of April alone, Nathan bought "100,000 guineas gold, £50,000 foreign and upwards of 100,000 Spanish dollars and . . . nearly £200,000 good bills."[121] To maximise the amount he could offer Herries, Nathan also sent Salomon to Amsterdam and James to Hamburg with orders "to purchase plenty of gold for the armies" and send it to London.[122] The first shipment to the continent—three ingots worth around £3,000—was despatched on April 4; around £28,000 followed on May 1, and by June 13 more than £250,000 had been sent. On April 22 Nathan sold Herries gold worth around £80,000; by October 20 he had provided gold coins worth a total of £2,136,916—enough to fill 884 boxes and 55 casks.[123] In addition, he offered his services again to relay a new tranche of subsidies to Britain's allies, which at their peak reached the unprecedented level of a million pounds a month.[124] This time, not only Russia and Prussia but the previously aloof Austrians found they had little option but to accept payment from the Rothschilds—as did a gaggle of other states, including Saxony, Baden, Württemberg, Bavaria, Saxe-Weimar, Hesse, Denmark and Sardinia.[125] Altogether, Herries's account with Nathan in 1815 amounted to £9,789,778.[126]

Assuming that the commissions charged for these transfers were, as in 1814, somewhere between 2 and 6 per cent, that figure might seem to imply profits in the region of £390,000. However, this overlooks the role of exchange rate fluctuations which, as in 1814, were the key to the profitability of the transfer payments. The immediate impact of Nathan's bullion purchases in London was to weaken sterling, pushing up the price of gold by as much as 23 per cent. This represented a major gamble, as it remained uncertain throughout March whether Britain would in fact go to war against Bonaparte once more. (Had it been postponed, Nathan might have found himself with a large stock of unwanted and depreciating bullion.) When the decision for war was finally confirmed, Nathan sought once again to strengthen sterling's exchange rate with the continental currencies—he was duly credited with pushing the pound up from 17.50 francs to the pound to 22. The Rothschilds' "commanding general" was now quite confident of his ability to control the exchanges: "You need be under no uneasiness from anywhere," he told James. "Our resources here are like lions, equal if not superior to all and every demand." He was equally sanguine in a letter to Carl: "I am not limited to a trifling difference in the exchange . . . which will give me great command over the market." Nathan was also convinced that his latest agreement with Herries was effectively risk-free, as it provided for immediate reimbursement of every amount sent to the continent (where previously he had advanced the government considerable sums).[127]

But he miscalculated in two vital respects: in assuming that it would take another lengthy war to defeat Napoleon, and in assuming that the financial paralysis which had prevailed on the continent a year before would quickly return, leaving the field empty of competition. In fact, barely three months elapsed between the return from Elba and the defeat at Waterloo, and for the first two of these there was minimal military action. As a consequence, the Rothschilds' rivals in Amsterdam, Hamburg and Frankfurt were able to compete in the money markets in a way they had not in 1814. The first signs of trouble came in Hamburg, where—to Nathan's dismay— James found himself unable to hold up the exchange rate in his purchases of bul- lion.[128] Then from Amsterdam it was reported that Wellington had more bullion than he knew what to do with, so that on May 5 Nathan "received orders from Gov- ernment this day to desist in my operations owing to your having sent off so much specie."[129] Furiously, he laid the blame on James:

> I certainly feel at a loss to understand the reason you cannot follow the instructions I have so repeatedly given you . . . I am certain you cannot be aware of the injury you are doing me . . . by your inattention I have lost at least ⅞ of the business I expected . . . What do you suppose will be the result *for they are not my orders but Government's* as I before men- tioned and I am continually blamed. I beg of you to do nothing what- ever for the present in purchasing coins or bills to draw on London a single bill, and if you do I shall not countenance your operations in any way whatever, and will not accept the bills, but let them be returned protested to you. I hope I shall not have occasion to repeat this.[130]

Yet it was hardly James's fault. It was simply—as Davidson pointed out—that he was being undercut by continental bankers like Heckscher who discerned the absurdity of the Rothschilds' shipping gold from Hamburg and Amsterdam to London only to ship it back to the continent:

> When I left London, Mr R, the Commissary in Chief in fact everyone was anxious that as much bullion might be obtained as possibly might be done. To execute this order there was no alternative but to draw on London. Things have since taken a different turn, and the long expected war remains hitherto only in preparation, and no actual war having commenced, has the effect that bullion can be collected fom all quarters. Moreover the Houses which at the time when Bony recaptured France had no desire to be connected in that line of business, appear more anx- ious to receive a share thereof.[131]

James—despatched back to Paris in disgrace—and Salomon, now joined in Am- sterdam by Carl, struggled to reverse the slide of sterling, but the damage had been done.[132]

It was at this juncture that the military situation came to its epoch-ending climax at Waterloo. No doubt it was gratifying to receive the news of Napoleon's defeat first, thanks to the speed with which Rothschild couriers were able to relay a news- paper version of the fifth and conclusive extraordinary bulletin—issued in Brussels at midnight on June 18—via Dunkirk and Deal to reach New Court on the night the 19th. This was just twenty-four hours after Wellington's victorious meeting with Blücher on the battlefield and nearly forty-eight hours before Major Henry Percy delivered Wellington's official dispatch to the Cabinet as its members dined at Lord Harrowby's house (at 11 p.m. on the 21st). Indeed, so premature did Nathan's infor- mation appear that it was not believed when he relayed it to the government on the

20th; nor was a second Rothschild courier from Ghent.[133] But no matter how early it reached him, the news of Waterloo was anything but good from Nathan's point of view. He had expected nothing as decisive so soon; indeed, just five days before the battle, he had arranged a new million pound loan for the British government in Amsterdam, and was in the middle of organising a subsidy payment to Baden even as his courier neared London.[134] Now Waterloo threatened to bring his financial operations on behalf of the anti-French coalition to a premature and highly inconvenient end. For the brothers were encumbered not only with substantial amounts of depreciating bullion, but also with over a million pounds' worth of treasury bills to be sold in Amsterdam, to say nothing of a succession of half-finished subsidy contracts which would cease the moment a peace treaty was signed.[135] As reports reached New Court confirming that the end of the war was imminent, Nathan was faced not with the immense profits of legend but with heavy and growing losses. John Roworth, his agent with the British army, described a gruelling journey on foot from Mons to Genappe, walking by day "in the midst of a cloud of dust under a burning and scorching sun" and sleeping at night "under the cannon's mouth on the ground." But when he finally caught up with Wellington's Commissary-General Dunmore, he was handed back unwanted Prussian coins worth £230,000.[136]

Although Nathan told his brothers to carry on delivering specie to Wellington's military chest, the business had ceased to be viable. Towards the end of July an "alarmed" Carl temporarily halted payments to the military chest. Two months later James found himself so strapped for cash that he had to do the same. Amschel, by contrast, was "swimming" in money in Frankfurt, but money which no one needed. As Carl admitted, "Now we don't need money for the army, as the army has enough."[137] By the end of the year James was reduced to offering Drummond deposit facilities in Paris in an attempt to get some of the specie back—a suggestion which was curtly rejected.[138] Even bigger difficulties arose in Amsterdam, where Carl found himself unable to sell the British treasury bills at the relatively modest discount agreed between Nathan and Herries. Indeed, the sudden advent of peace had made the Amsterdam market so liquid that such long-dated bills could scarcely be sold at all, precipitating another round of ill-tempered recrimination between the brothers.[139] The French collapse also had a disruptive impact on the subsidy business. In Berlin, James's negotiations with the Prussian government were thrown into confusion as the news of Waterloo caused a surge in the sterling exchange rate.[140] Other German states quickly began demanding more generous exchange rates for their subsidy payments.[141] To compound the brothers' misery came news of a family tragedy: the death of their sister Julie at the age of thirty-five. "I feel my spirits very depressed indeed," Nathan confessed to Carl just two weeks after Waterloo, "and [am] by no means able to attend to business as I could wish. The melancholy communication of the death of my sister has entirely unhinged my mind and have done but very little business today on that account."[142] Far from being hugely profitable, the aftermath of Wellington's victory was a period of acute crisis for the Rothschilds.

In London, a frantic Nathan sought to make good the damage; and it is in this context that the firm's purchases of British stocks have to be seen. On July 20, the evening edition of the London *Courier* reported that Nathan had made "great purchases of stock." A week later Roworth heard that Nathan had "done well by the early information which you had of the Victory gained at Waterloo" and asked to participate in any further purchases of government stock "if in your opinion you think any good can be done."[143] This would seem to confirm the view that Nathan did indeed buy consols on the strength of his prior knowledge of the battle's outcome. However, the gains made in this way cannot have been very great. As Victor Rothschild conclusively demonstrated, the recovery of consols from their nadir of 53 in fact predated Waterloo by over a week, and even if Nathan had made the maximum possible purchase of £20,000 on June 20, when consols stood at 56.5 and sold a week later when they stood at 60.5, his profits would barely have exceeded £7,000. Much the same can be said of Omnium (another form of government bond), which rose eight points on the news of victory.[144] In fact, the brothers' correspondence suggests that such purchases were not made on a large scale until some time later, in the period before the Paris peace treaty was finally signed.[145] An unusually anxious letter from Nathan suggests that even these were nerve-racking speculations, dependent as they were on the assumption that this time the French would not seek to resist the peace terms:

> Everything is going well, so help me God, better [even] than you would imagine. I am quite pleased. I went to see Herries, he made me feel . . . well. He swears that everything is going well. I bought stock at 61⅛ and 61½ and Herries swears . . . that everything is going well, with God's help . . . We are all in better spirits. I hope it will have the same effect on you.[146]

According to Salomon, Nathan had also purchased around £450,000 of Omnium funds at 107; if he had followed his brother's advice and sold at 120, his profit would have been around £58,000.[147] But this evidently did not strike him as a significant sum; he fretted at having bought too few in the first place, and held on for higher prices in the new year. Indeed, it may not have been until quite late in 1816 that Nathan made perhaps his most successful speculation in stocks to date: the purchase of £650,000 at an average price of 62, much of which he sold in November 1817 at 82.75, yielding a profit of £130,000. However, this was not his to keep, as the original investment had been made with government funds at Herries's suggestion.[148]

A second and more important way of recouping some of the losses caused by Waterloo lay in prolonging for as long as possible the subsidy payments to Britain's allies. In this, the Rothschilds had invaluable accomplices in the Allied powers themselves, who naturally wished to pocket as much as they could before peace was signed and the subsidies ceased.[149] In October the Prussian representative Jordan privately admitted that the continental powers were spinning out the negotiations to secure an extra month's subsidy; a gift of £1,100 in British stocks ensured that the Rothschilds handled the payment.[150] Another amenable official was, as before, the Russian Gervais, who received a generous cut (2 per cent) of the subsidy business he sent the Rothschilds' way. "The main thing," reported James from Paris, "is that Gervais, thank God, had been made Commissar in Chief for everything. Yesterday he said to me: 'Rothschild, we must make money!' "[151] The previously wary Austrian government too (thanks partly to lobbying by Limburger) now entrusted some of its subsidy business to the Rothschilds. As Carl observed, it was "not easy to do business with the Austrians . . . but once you have their confidence you can depend upon it."[152] On the other hand, the increase of competition on the continent reduced the commissions which could be charged, and it was harder to make money on the side from arbitrage. Some governments—for example, that of Saxe-Weimar—were eager to avoid "falling completely and utterly into the hands of Mr Rothschild, who is, after all, a Jew."[153] The brothers repeatedly alluded to the meagreness of the profits (often as little as 1 per cent) they were making in this period, and it seems questionable whether the various petty German states which Amschel provided with subsidy payments—including Frankfurt as well as Saxe-Coburg and Coburg-Saarfeld— were worth the "heartbreak" of which he complained.[154] Salomon and Amschel were philosophical: "You can't make millions every day," wrote the former as negotiations with Prussia dragged on. "Nothing in this world can be forced to happen. Do what you can; you can do no more." The whole world could not "belong to Rothschild." "Things here are not the way they are in England, where transactions worth millions happen every week. For a German 100,000 gulden is a big deal."[155] It is doubtful whether such fatalism impressed their brother in London.

The summer of 1815 was therefore anything but a time of unalloyed success for the Rothschilds. The agreement drawn up in March of that year would seem to suggest that the brothers' collective assets had grown substantially since the last balance sheet of 1810. But no less than two-thirds of the total capital in 1815 was credited to Nathan, and he had not been party to the 1810 agreement. Taking into account only the shares of his four brothers, there may in fact have been a contraction in the continental side's capital.[156] Moreover, this agreement predated the crisis of the Hundred Days and should therefore be regarded as evidence of earlier success (primarily, it seems reasonable to conclude, the highly lucrative business done for Herries in 1814). By the summer of 1816, it is true, the brothers estimated that their combined capital amounted to between £900,000 and £1 million, implying a doubling of their capital between March 1815 and July 1816.[157] Given that the figure agreed between them in June 1818 was £1,772,000 (a three-quarters increase over two years), this was a remarkable rate of growth.[158] But there is good reason to doubt whether the period immediately after Waterloo was when the bulk of this increase occurred.

The trouble is that it is almost impossible to say precisely how the Rothschilds performed financially in this period because they had no idea themselves. So tumultuous were the events precipitated by Napoleon's return from Elba, and so enormous the turnover of their various transfer operations during 1814 and 1815, that their already rudimentary accounting procedures collapsed altogether.

The problem first surfaced in June 1814, as Carl scrambled to raise the cash needed for an especially large subsidy instalment. The only way he had been able do this, he complained, was by "swindling" (issuing accommodation bills, or bills unrelated to "real" purchases of commodities). When James complained about this, Carl pointed out that it was not his responsibility to "keep the books."[159] At this stage, it was Salomon who was regarded as the accountant of the family—the one who could always cheer their father up by making him "on paper . . . rich in a minute."[160] But even he was soon unable to keep track of the immense commitments Nathan was making on his brothers' behalf. By August 1814 he and Amschel had to confess that they were "completely confused and do not know where the money is." "Together we are all rich and if all the five of us are taken into consideration we are worth quite a lot," wrote Salomon anxiously to Nathan. "But where is the money?"[161] Nathan's (perhaps rather acid) response was that "a book [should] be kept where [Carl] should enter business rules."[162]

The problem recurred in September 1815, when the brothers on the continent experienced a severe cash-flow crisis. "But dear Nathan," wrote Salomon, "you must have a frightful amount of money over there because here I am in debt [and] Amschel hasn't much left over. It must all be over there and [yet] you write that you are so much in debt. Where is our [cash] reserve?" Calculating that he owed as much as £120,000 in Paris alone, he repeated the question a few days later:

> You must have all our money over there with you. We here are stinking poor. We haven't a penny to spare. Amschel has less than a million left and therefore the whole lot must be with you, including what we owe . . . Work out where the family money is, my good Nathan. I don't know . . . Where is our money? Well, it's just absurd. God willing it will turn up when we do the spring cleaning![163]

When Nathan wrote back suggesting that it was Amschel who was the "big rich man," there was something close to panic.

The problem was that Amschel had a string of subsidy payments to make in Berlin and elsewhere, and virtually no cash in hand, while Carl's funds were almost entirely tied up in the British treasury bills in Amsterdam. In Paris too the position was alarmingly tight. "This eternal indebtedness is not very pleasant," complained James. "The payments we have to make are big, far too big," echoed Salomon. "Dear Nathan, you write that you have one million or two million over there. Well you really must have, because our brother Amschel is bust. We are bust. Carl is bust. So one of us must have the money." In fact, the continental Rothschilds averted "bankruptcy" at this time only by means of short-term borrowing and by making further use of accommodation bills.[164] Not surprisingly, they blamed Nathan for their predicament. Echoing their father's earlier criticisms, Salomon bitterly accused his brother of mismanagement: "We are relying on miracles and luck, and I say to you once again that you don't write clearly enough. In the name of God, such important transactions have to be carried out precisely. Unfortunately, there is absolutely no order in the way you deal with these." Too much of their accounting was being done "in the head" instead of on paper.[165] Was it any wonder the Austrian government feared that the Rothschilds might "go bankrupt?"[166]

Nathan tried to reassure his brothers that their position was secure. But Amschel continued to yearn for some tangible proof of the family's wealth. "You state that I need not enquire as to where the money actually is," he complained to Nathan. "In this respect I am like little Anselm [Salomon's son, then aged thirteen] who always inquires as to where the money is. 'People say my father possesses five millions,' he says. He would like to see it all in one single heap."[167] Were they millionaires, he demanded to know, or bankrupts? The uncertainty was making him ill: "I have to tell you that since *Sukkoth* [October 1815] I have not been well and I cannot bear it any longer. If you wish to keep your brother in good health then you must try to reduce his money worries. I have sacrificed my health. I have to take it easy . . . I have lost my spirit of speculation."[168] They were, he complained, "living like drunkards": "We don't know whether we owe money to the English Government or not."[169]

To compound the problem, this period of chaos came just as Herries was facing allegations of "maladministration" in the Commons and was therefore pressing Nathan for detailed account statements.[170] His principal parliamentary critic, Alexander Baring, had an axe to grind, needless to say. On the other hand, there was some justification for his claim. In their dealings with at least one government (the Russian) the Rothschilds had secured additional commissions and paid bribes about which Herries had not been informed. In addition, they had made the most of exchange rate differences during the early phase of subsidy payments. The need to cook books which were already in a state of some confusion no doubt explains the months of prevarication in the face of repeated requests for accounts from the "very particular" Herries.[171] Even if it meant keeping the clerks in Paris working until midnight, it was vital, as Salomon said, to avoid damaging the Rothschilds' reputation in London, "as England is our bread basket."[172] So fearful was Nathan of a scandal that in early 1816 he wrote to Amschel advising him not to purchase a new house in Frankfurt:

> I asked Herries and he gave me a rather incomplete answer saying that I should not go in for luxuries because the papers would immediately commence writing against me and officials here would start questioning . . . It would be best to take mine and Herries's advice, do not buy a house, wait until my accounts are straight.[173]

Herries was already receiving disquieting reports from Drummond in Paris about a "simulated transaction" which James assured him had been necessary to avoid disturbing the exchange rate. "This I dare say is very true," commented Drummond nervously, "but on the other hand in matters of account that are to come before the auditors nothing is more to be avoided than fiction to which a suspicion is always likely to be attached . . . Would it not be a proper general injunction to all accountants to *banish all fiction*?'[174] What Drummond did not know was the extent of the fiction. When his colleague Dunmore paid a visit on James in March 1816, the latter confessed: "My heart was beating terribly as I was scared that he might give me the order to send his money to the army." James had in fact no more than 700,000 francs, far less than the sum Dunmore could legitimately have demanded.[175]

In the end, none of the brothers was equal to the task of untangling the accounts. It was left to Benjamin Davidson to try to reconstruct the extraordinary transactions of the previous year—and then to try to conceal the numerous irregularities which had occurred.[176] The difficulties he confronted were daunting. For a start, none of the brothers had yet adopted the system of double-entry book-keeping. As Amschel put it, the Berlin banker Mendelssohn "know[s] how he stands with each of [his joint accounts] while in the House of Rothschild we have to rely on what the book keepers say. Gasser tells me: 'We have made nice profits on the Prussian transactions' and I have to believe him."[177] This in itself is remarkable: after all, the double-entry system had first been described by the Venetian Luca Pacioli in 1494 and was widely known in most European countries by the end of the sixteenth century. The fact that the Rothschilds were so slow to adopt it suggests that the capitalism of the

Frankfurt Judengasse was technically quite backward (though it also, of course, suggests that business geniuses can do without accountants—for a time). Secondly,
there were substantial gaps in the records, reflecting the habits of concealment
which had developed in Frankfurt and elsewhere during the period of French occupation.[178] Thirdly, there was the problem of the large profits which had been made
on exchange rate fluctuations without Herries's consent.[179] Finally, and most embar-
rassingly, there were the "fictional" accommodation bills which had been issued,
which totalled more than £2 million. As Davidson put it drily, "One should have
thought earlier . . . that one day Herries [would] have to look at these accounts."[180]

Fortunately, Davidson was able to arrive at figures which showed the government
rather than the Rothschilds as the principal beneficiary of the subsidy and other
payments; and in the end Salomon's verdict seems to have been accepted by Liverpool and his colleagues that "not even a hundred banking houses would have been
able to carry out a business transaction of this size within nine months and to show
a profit for the government." Herries was discharged honourably with a pension
when the office of commissary was wound up in October 1816 and a Commons
motion to prevent his appointment as auditor of the Civil List was defeated. Nevertheless, Salomon was still fretting about the accounts as late as January 1818:

> We are not yet in the clear with the government . . . As long as the gov-
> ernment leaves the accounts with Herries in suspension, we are not yet
> in the clear. [Are we] rich men or are we at ease? As far as I can see, the
> serving boy is more at ease with the little he has than we are with the
> great deal we have. Why? Because he doesn't have a bungled account
> with a government hanging round his neck . . .[181]

It is fair to conclude that the huge profits of 1814 and 1815 were made in ways
much more mysterious—and hazardous—than the traditional Waterloo myth
implies.

Fraternity

The idea of brotherhood was profoundly important in nineteenth-century Europe.
Freemasons, liberals and later socialists all idealised the fraternal relationship, creating a bewildering variety of associations which sought to forge artificial brother-
hoods beyond the narrow familial realm. This was nothing new, of course. Religious
orders had done the same for centuries. But "Alle Menschen werden Brüder" was a
line which, when penned by Schiller and set by Beethoven, had a thinly disguised
revolutionary significance. As the French Revolution's best-known slogan implied,
to imagine all men becoming brothers was as radical as to imagine them all becoming free and equal.

Contemporaries often inferred from the Rothschilds' extraordinary success that
they exemplified this ideal of fraternity. This was not because it was exceptional, as
it is in Europe today, for a family to produce five sons or, indeed, five daughters, as
Mayer Amschel and Gutle Rothschild also did. Francis Baring also had five sons.
Indeed, as late as the 1870s nearly a fifth (18 per cent) of women who married in
Britain had ten or more live births, and more than half had six or more; the statistics
for Germany are similar. What impressed contemporaries was that the Rothschild
brothers seemed to work together in uncommon harmony. This had been one of the

points strongly emphasised by Friedrich Gentz in his influential article for the Brockhaus *Encyclopaedia*:

> With the greatest conscientiousness, the brothers [have] obeyed their father's heartfelt deathbed injunction to maintain unbreakable unity and co-operation in all business transactions . . . [E]ach [business] proposition is the subject of their joint deliberations; every operation of even moderate importance is carried out according to an agreed plan and with co-ordinated efforts; and all the brothers have an equal share in the results.[182]

Simon Moritz von Bethmann, their rival in Frankfurt, echoed this view: "The harmony between the brothers contributes largely to their success. None of them ever thinks of finding fault with another. None of them adversely criticises any of the others' business dealings, even when the results do not come up to expectations."[183] "The prosperity of the Rothschilds," remarked Benjamin Disraeli later, "was as much owing to the unity of feeling which alike pervaded all branches of that numerous family as in their capital & abilities. They were like an Arabian tribe."[184] This soon hardened into the myth of "the five Frankfurters." As one German writer put it in the 1830s:

> These five brothers together formed an indomitable phalanx . . . and, true to their principle never to undertake anything individually and to agree all operations precisely among themselves, always followed the same system and pursued the same goal.[185]

Such comments would have been otiose if fraternal harmony had been the norm; the paradox is that, unlike the idealised brotherhood of the poets, real brothers seldom worked well together. Jews and Christians alike knew the story of Joseph and his brothers, one of the best biblical accounts of fraternal strife: the hatred of Gad and Asher for their half-brother, the precocious favourite Joseph; the intense affection between Joseph and his young brother Benjamin; the ambivalent feelings of Reuben, the first born; the violent confrontation and final reconciliation. Relations between the Hope brothers and the Baring brothers were less turbulent, but they failed to transcend their personal differences in the name of fraternal unity.[186] As the Rothschild brothers overtook them financially, they seemed to personify an elusive ideal.

In reality, however, brotherly love was far from easy to maintain in the chaotic circumstances of 1814 and 1815. As their resources were stretched by a succession of huge and risky undertakings, personal relations between the Rothschild brothers frequently deteriorated—on occasion, to the point of complete rupture. The main reason for this was undoubtedly Nathan's increasingly imperious treatment of his supposed partners in the business. Technically, according to the 1815 agreement, the brothers were equals: profits were divided equally, and Nathan gave each of them a promissory note worth £50,000 to compensate for his much larger share of the capital. But as Salomon and others commented at the time, the combination of Nathan's aggressive temper and the increasingly Anglocentric nature of the firm's operations effectively reduced the other brothers to the status of mere agents. Nathan was, as Salomon half joked, "the commanding general," the others were his "marshals," while the sums of "capital resources" they had to dispose of were "soldiers" who had to be "kept in readiness."[187] The implied comparison with Napoleon himself—against whom, after all, their financial operations were ultimately directed—was a revealing one, and Nathan's brothers were not alone in making it. As Swinton Holland said to his partner Alexander Baring in 1824: "I must candidly confess that I have not the nerve for his operations. They are generally well planned, with great cleverness and adroitness in execution—but he is in money and funds what Bonaparte was in war, and if any sudden shake comes, he will fall to the ground like the other."[188] To Ludwig Börne, Nathan and his brothers were all "Finanzbonaparten," and the parallel was still being drawn by writers in the 1870s.[189] But it was really Nathan who became the Bonaparte of the banking world, and he shared with the French Emperor his superhuman appetite for risks and his intolerance of inept subordinates.

As early as 1811—even before their father's death—Nathan's brothers had begun to complain about the occasionally bullying tone of his letters.[190] But it was not until the middle of 1814 that he really began to emerge as the dominant, not to say domineering, partner. The key issue was his desire to dictate his brothers' movements. In June 1814 he ordered Salomon to go to Amsterdam to assist James and took the opportunity to let fly at their brothers in Frankfurt: "I tell you, Amschel and Carl make me damned upset. You have no idea how idiotically they write and they draw on me like madmen . . . By God, they write me such idiocies that today I feel very cross. Amschel writes to James as if he could do the business by himself."[191] This evidently touched a raw nerve, and Davidson's appeal to Nathan to desist from "disparaging correspondence" came too late. A distraught Carl took to his bed, warning that "if he carried on in this way," Nathan would "soon have a partner in the other world," so ill did his letters make him feel. Salomon also complained of "severe pains in my back and legs," but his tone was angrier:

> I cannot for one moment believe that even if I were the learned Nathan Rothschild I would regard the other four brothers as stupid schoolboys, and myself as the only wise one . . . I do not wish to be upset any more and made more ill than I already am. To put it quite bluntly, we are neither drunk nor stupid. We have something you in London obviously do not have—we keep our books in order . . . If my tears were black I would write a lot more easily than with ink . . . The English mail day is a regular terror for me. Every night I dream of these letters . . . One just doesn't write that way to one's family, one's brothers, one's partners.[192]

But all their protests merely elicited from Nathan a stark threat to dissolve the business:

> I have to admit that I was thoroughly fed up with the longwinded business and its disagreeable consequences . . . And now from today on . . . I think that it would be best if Salomon would close the Paris accounts and come to London. And David[son] can bring the Amsterdam accounts with him. Then we could clear up the accounts. I expect from Frankfurt an account [too] . . . because I am fed up with the partnership . . . I know that you are all clever men and now all five of us shall have, thank God, peace.[193]

This had the desired effect; henceforth Nathan gave the orders more or less unchallenged, as Salomon acknowledged in a letter to Salomon Cohen in August 1814:

My brother in London is the commanding general, I am his field marshal and consequently I have my duty to fulfil in my capacity as such,
and therefore I have to give the commanding general reports, comments
etc. I may have made the case somewhat stronger so as to show him how
serious I am in what I say, but it is still an exaggeration to say that I lose
my head . . . Being a good general, you ought to know exactly what a
good general has to know and not think continually of advancing only,
but you ought to go on the defensive occasionally in order to safeguard
your strength.

As this letter suggests, Salomon continued to worry that Nathan was overreach-
ing himself, but he now obviously saw himself in a subordinate, advisory role:
"[W]e regard you as general-in-chief, with ourselves as lieutenants-general. God
may give us luck and blessing, and success. In this case we [remain] generals. Those,
who, God forbid, have no peace, nor luck, are not even corporals."[194] Carl too
accepted Nathan's primacy, though he employed a slightly different metaphor: "I am
only the last wheel [of the carriage] and look upon myself in the sense of a machine
only."[195] He and Salomon might not care for Amsterdam, but they stayed there if
Nathan told them to.[196] Even Salomon's requests to return to Frankfurt—where he
had spent just three weeks in the previous three years—to see his wife or to be present at his son's barmitzvah were evidently regarded by Nathan as unreasonable; the
second request was granted only on condition that Salomon return to Paris after just
a day and attend to the Frankfurt accounts while he was there.[197] Nathan had only
one concern: business. "All you ever write," complained Salomon wearily, "is pay
this, pay that, send this, send that."[198]

Since 1811 . . . I have gone where business called me. If I were needed
today in Siberia I would . . . go to Siberia . . . Please do me a favour and
desist from posting any more ill-tempered letters. One sits in his inn,
often at the light of a candle, waiting for the brothers' letters. Instead of
going to bed in a happy mood, one is depressed and remains sleepless.
What kind of pleasures are still open to us? We are all well on in years,
the pleasures of youth are out of our reach; unfortunately we have had
to say "good night" to [all] that; our stomachs are bad [so] there is no
gluttony for us. Consequently nearly all the worldly pleasures are closed
to us. Should we have to renounce the pleasure of correspondence
[too]?[199]

But Nathan gloried in his ascetic materialism:

I am writing to you giving my opinion, as it is my damned duty to write
to you . . . I am reading through your letters not just once but maybe a
hundred times. You can well imagine that yourself. After dinner I usually have nothing to do. I do not read books, I do not play cards, I do
not go to the theatre, my only pleasure is my business and in this way I
read Amschel's, Salomon's, James's and Carl's letters . . . As far as Carl's
letter [about buying a bigger house] is concerned . . . all this is a lot of
nonsense because as long as we have good business and are rich everybody will flatter us and those who have no interest in obtaining money
through us begrudge us for it all. Our Salomon is too good and agreeable to anything and anybody and if a parasite whispers something into

his ear he thinks that all human beings are noble minded[;] the truth is that all they are after is their own interest.[200]

Privately, even Gentz had to acknowledge that in reality Nathan was *primus inter pares*. It was he who had the "remarkable instinct which causes them always to choose the right, and of two rights the better":

> Baring's most profound reasoning inspires me, now that I have seen everything at close quarters, with less confidence than the sound judgement of one of the more intelligent Rothschilds—for among the five brothers there is one whose intelligence is wanting and another whose intelligence is weak—and if Baring and Hope ever fail, I can state with confidence that it will be because they have thought themselves cleverer than Rothschild and have not followed his advice.[201]

The use of the singular "Rothschild" is important. There was only one true *Finanz-bonaparte.*

It was probably Amschel and Carl whom Gentz had in mind when he spoke of "one whose intelligence is wanting and another whose intelligence is weak." This was unfair: a more accurate characterisation would be that they were more risk-averse than their brothers. Amschel was the most cautious of the five and constantly yearned to lead "a quiet life." "Me, I don't want to eat the world," he wrote in a typically homespun letter.[202] His ideal was "to work in tranquillity," without the anxieties which Nathan's Napoleonic approach necessarily generated.[203] Carl, the fourth brother, was nervous and insecure, and shared Amschel's limited ambition. "I am fed up with business," he confided to his eldest brother in a characteristic letter. "I wish God would give me but little, enough to live, garments for myself and bread to eat. I do not wish to float above the skies." This feeling doubtless intensified at the time of the Amsterdam treasury bills fiasco, which brought a torrent of recrimination down upon him. After this, as Salomon wrote, Carl was genuinely "afraid" of Nathan, though he was still capable of muttering criticisms behind "the boss's" back.[204] As we have seen, Salomon himself had the intellect and self-confidence to question Nathan's strategy; but he was too "quiet and thoughtful" and "took things too much to heart"—according to senior Rothschild employees like Davidson and Braun—to withstand his brother's belligerence.[205] He preferred, where possible, to side with Nathan against the others.[206]

Yet Nathan's dominance was never absolute: the partnership did not degenerate into a dictatorship. There were several reasons for this. Firstly, Nathan's youngest brother James—who was just twenty-three in 1815—was markedly less submissive to his will than the other three. At the height of the bitter row in June 1814, James remained cool, sardonically telling Salomon Cohen that he was allowing Nathan "to dictate to him about millions as if they were apples and pears."[207] Although there were times when James contemplated leaving Paris, it is unlikely that he stayed there just because Nathan told him to.[208] The youngest brother was intellectually and temperamentally Nathan's equal; he also had the advantage of a better schooling. Revealingly, it was James who urged his brothers to adopt double-entry book-keeping. It was only really the age difference between the two which obliged James to defer for the next twenty years to his brother.[209] Even in acknowledging Nathan's leadership, James was less than deferential. "The main point is now to work out a sensible plan for England," he wrote to Nathan in March 1818. "*You* will have to do this . . . I leave the decision to you. My duty is mainly to draw your attention to this matter and your duty, as chief commander, is to work it all out."[210] As early as December 1816 Carl had cause to complain about James's critical letters, the burden of which was that the Frankfurt house was not making enough money.[211] Already he was evincing Nathan-like traits. At the same time, Nathan (and later James) occasionally needed to be restrained by their less bullish relations. As Amschel said to James following one of the most serious setbacks of the post-war period:

> [O]ne should [n]ever lose one's head. Here lies the advantage of a part-nership. If one of the partners loses his senses, the others must remain serene. If all of them lose their heads—then good night. I hope that [this letter finds you] quietened down and that you will give thanks to God that we gained a fortune quicker than anybody else.[212]

There were indeed occasions when Nathan was only too glad to postpone a difficult decision by claiming that he needed to consult his brothers.[213] At times, this was a gambit; at times, he genuinely listened to them.

Finally, no matter how much they quarrelled, the brothers had no one else whom they could trust as much. We know that on occasion Salomon forged Nathan's signature on bills when Nathan had forgotten to endorse them; it is inconceivable that anyone else could have done so.[214] Even the best clerks were kept at one remove: when one named Feidel appeared to be gaining an undue influence over Amschel, Carl's response can only be described as jealous.[215] Similarly, their brothers-in-law—sisters' husbands and wives' brothers alike—were always viewed with a measure of suspicion, as outsiders with designs on their business.[216] James was especially worried that Nathan was confiding too much to his wife's relatives Salomon Cohen and Abraham Montefiore (Moses's brother), and was relieved to hear otherwise:

> It is rare that a man should realise that even what friends are telling him is nothing more than flattery, that there is not a true word in it; when they leave you they are laughing at your credulity. Well, dear Nathan . . . you are clever and honest, you know the world . . . Before your letter arrived, a stone fell from my heart because Salomon told me that London is now different, not only are [Abraham] Montefiore and Salomon Cohen no longer allowed to read and deliberate [about] the letters and all the business, but not even Davidson is allowed to do so. This is now confirmed by your letter.[217]

In the same way, the other brothers were kept abreast of Carl's attempts to find a wife in Hamburg because it was a matter of intense interest to all of them which family Carl married into.[218] In the end, there were authentic bonds of brotherly love, forged in the Judengasse, which no other ties could rival. "Did anyone promise us more when we all slept in one little attic room?" asked Salomon when Nathan was grumbling at having sold some consols too soon.[219] Such memories were never wholly forgotten, no matter how far apart the brothers lived and how many harsh words they exchanged by post.

The extent—and limits—of fraternal unity were most apparent as the brothers debated whether or not to modify the 1815 partnership agreement. The legacy of the great transactions of 1814 and 1815 was a tangle of financial interdependence which could not easily be undone.[220] The question now was whether James should be allowed to establish a new house in Paris under the explicitly collective name of "de Rothschild Frères." Although James was against merging the accounts of the various establishments,[221] Amschel had his anxieties, fearing that James might embroil him in risky business.[222] He and Carl were only brought round when James agreed that the capital of the partnership should not be made public—an important decision in favour of secrecy which was to set an enduring precedent.[223] The result was a compromise which it took almost two years to hammer out. The 1818 agreement accordingly defined the brothers' partnership as "three joint mercantile establishments [conducted] under their the said five partners' mutual responsibility" but at the same time "*form*[ing] *but one general joint concern*."[224] It was a nice distinction which quite accurately encapsulated the way the brothers reconciled their individual differences with a deep and enduring sense of common fraternal purpose.

FOUR

A Court Always Leads to Something (1816–1825)

*You are certainly right that there is much to be earned from a
government which has no money. But you have to take risks.*
—JAMES ROTHSCHILD TO NATHAN ROTHSCHILD.[1]

*N. M. Rothschild . . . has the money, the strength and the
power.* —NATHAN ROTHSCHILD TO CHRISTIAN ROTHER.[2]

In 1823 the twelfth, thirteenth and fourteenth cantos of Byron's Don Juan were
published in London, at a time when their author was embroiled—fatally, as it
proved—in the Greek struggle for independence. Byron's aristocratic profligacy with
money was by now as notorious as his libertinism. Nevertheless, these late verses
indicate a keen awareness of the power of money—and specifically of the new kind
of financial power personified by Nathan Rothschild. "Who hold the balance of the
world?" asked Byron in the twelfth canto, "Who reign

> O'er Congress, whether royalist or liberal?
> Who rouse the shirtless patriots of Spain?
>   (That make old Europe's journals squeak and gibber all.)
> Who keep the world, both old and new, in pain
>   Or pleasure? Who make politics run glibber all?
> The shade of Bonaparte's noble daring? –
> Jew Rothschild, and his fellow Christian Baring.[3]

Those lines have been quoted by historians before. It is worth, however, reading the
verse which follows too, for it nicely illustrates the ambivalent feelings with which
contemporaries regarded the spectacular financial boom of the early 1820s. To
Byron, Rothschild and Baring were, along with the "truly liberal Laffitte," "the true
Lords of Europe," whose every loan

> Is not a merely speculative hit,
>   But seats a nation or upsets a throne.
> Republics also get involved a bit;
>   Columbia's stock hath holders not unknown
> On 'Change; and even thy silver soil, Peru,
>   Must get itself discounted by a Jew.

Byron went on to discuss—with remarkable insight—that ascetic materialism which, as we have seen, was such a distinctive early Rothschild trait. Indeed, it seems not unreasonable to suggest that the poet's reflections on "gaunt Wealth's austerities" may have been inspired by Nathan himself:

> He is your only poet;—passion, pure
>   And sparkling on from heap to heap, displays
> *Possess'd*, the ore, of which *mere hopes* allure
>   Nations athwart the deep: the golden rays
> Flash up in ingots from the mine obscure;
>   On him the diamond pours its brilliant blaze,
> While the mild emerald's beam shades down the dyes
> Of other stones, to soothe the miser's eyes.
>
> The lands on either side are his: the ship
>   From Ceylon, Inde, or far Cathay, unloads
> For him the fragrant produce of each trip;
>   Beneath his cars of Ceres groan the roads,
> And the vine blushes like Aurora's lip;
>   His very cellars might be kings' abodes;
> While he, despising every sensual call,
> Commands—the intellectual lord of all.
>
> Perhaps he hath great projects in his mind,
>   To build a college, or to found a race,
> A hospital, a church,—and leave behind
>   Some dome surmounted by his meagre face:
> Perhaps he fain would liberate mankind
>   Even with the very ore which makes them base:
> Perhaps he would be wealthiest of his nation,
> Or revel in the joys of calculation.[4]

The allusion to "his nation" may indicate that there was more of Rothschild than of Baring in this inspired evocation of financial might.

That Byron could suggest—even satirically—that Nathan Rothschild held, along with Alexander Baring, "the balance of the world" requires some explanation. The name of Baring was, of course, well established. Like the Rothschilds the family hailed from Germany (Francis Baring had emigrated from Bremen in 1717); and, like Nathan, Francis's son John had made his fortune in the textiles business, as a wool manufacturer, before his sons established the merchant bank of Baring Brothers in 1770. However, as Lutherans the Barings had easily been absorbed into the social elite of Exeter and later London. John's younger son Francis had been an MP since 1784, a member of the board of the East India Company since 1779 and a baronet since 1793. Alexander, his son and successor at the bank, also became an MP in 1806.[5] By contrast, only a few years before *Don Juan*, the Rothschilds' role in the financing of the war against Napoleon was still largely a secret, known only to political and financial insiders. Even the Paris banker Jacques Laffitte was better known as Governor of the Banque de France between 1814 and 1820 and one of Napoleon's financial backers in the Hundred Days. What happened in the years after the upheaval of Waterloo to catapult Nathan to such celebrity—and notori-

ety—that he could be said to "reign" over royalists and liberals, "rouse" Spanish
patriots and "keep the world, both old and new, in pain / Or pleasure?"

The Economic Consequences of the Peace

The answer must be sought in what might be called (to adapt a phrase used in similar circumstances a century later) the economic consequences of the peace—the
Second Peace of Paris, imposed on France after Waterloo. The First Treaty of Paris
had imposed no reparations on the restored Bourbon regime, but the mood of the
victorious powers after Waterloo was less clement. Quite apart from any desire to
punish the French collectively for the actions of those who had rallied to Napoleon
in the Hundred Days, there was a practical need to pay for the troops occupying
northern France, who at one stage numbered more than a million. Even before the
peace was signed in November, a charge or "contribution" of some 50 million francs
was levied to pay for their upkeep. The final terms of the treaty set a total for reparations of 700 million francs to be paid over five years beginning in March 1816,
during which time an occupying force of 150,000 men would remain on French
soil. The costs of this occupation were also to be met by the French Treasury.[6]

The Rothschilds evidently hoped that the financial provisions of the peace—
which implied a new and potentially lucrative series of international transfers, this
time from Paris rather than London—would provide them with plentiful opportunities to recoup the losses of the Hundred Days.[7] At first, there were grounds for
optimism, at least as far as relations with the recipient states were concerned. Gervais
as usual promised to hand Rothschilds the better part of Russia's share, and Herries
was likewise expected to secure a large tranche of the British.[8] However, it quickly
became apparent that any business arising from the French "contributions" would
have to be shared with other bankers, who now rushed to challenge the Rothschild
monopoly on international transfer payments. Only by entering into loose partnerships—with Mendelssohn in Berlin, Bethmann and Gontard in Frankfurt, Arnstein
& Eskeles in Vienna and Parish & Co. in Hamburg—were Salomon and James able
to participate in the initial payments to Prussia and Austria.[9] Even the British and
Russian contributions could not be taken for granted.

Partly, the problem was one of declining influence. Dunmore, Herries's representative in Paris, was less "friendly" than Herries himself, while the Russian minister
Count Nesselrode had reasons for favouring Gontard. It was a serious setback when
first Gervais and then Herries left office.[10] To make matters worse, some of the other
officials they found themselves dealing with—the Russian Merian and the Prussian
Rother—declined to accept bribes.[11] But the real problem was that peace had
brought competition. As James complained, contemplating profits of 1.5 per cent
and less, there was "not much joy to be had from the contributions business, because
there are too many people here." Salomon was especially irked by the Austrian representatives, who "run from one house to the next for the sake of an extra sou." Ultimately, he and James became almost fatalistic: "There are no big, brilliant deals to be
made here. But now that we're here, we're happy to take all that we can to prevent it
going to anyone else." The only consoling thought—frequently repeated—was that
contacts with courts, no matter how unprofitable, might lead to business in the
future. The brothers never turned up their noses at small-scale transactions and

gladly advanced the contributions due to the smaller German states and the minor compensation payments which Russia had to make for damage to private property by Russian troops.[12]

Far more disappointing, however, was James's failure to win a share of the business generated on the other side of the reparations equation. That France would be able to pay reparations and the costs of occupation only by means of a large loan had become obvious by late 1816. Despite efforts to cut spending and raise taxes, there was no realistic way of achieving an annual surplus in excess of 170 million francs, not least because of the unhelpful attitude of the ultra-royalist "Incredible Chamber" which—like most nineteenth-century assemblies elected by income or property tax payers—showed little enthusiasm for raising direct taxes. Indeed, the 1816–17 budget showed a deficit of over 300 million francs, which was financed only with the greatest difficulty by short-term borrowing. Moreover, the Paris capital market by itself was far too weak to absorb unassisted the new issues of rentes which were inevitably going to be needed. With the price of 5 per cent rentes down as low as 50, the government had little option but to look abroad.

In the immediate aftermath of Napoleon's defeat, the Rothschilds' prospects of influence at the French court had been good. Not only had they been responsible for relaying a British loan to the returning French King,[13] but Dalberg, the former Prince-Primate of Napoleon's Rhenish Confederation and Grand Duke of Frankfurt, had emerged as a member of the French provisional government—one of a number of opportunists (the most famous being Talleyrand) who managed to survive yet another change of regime by a well-timed defection.[14] However, the resignation of Talleyrand and the formation of a new government under the duc de Richelieu appear to have weakened the Rothschild position. James made every effort to cultivate Richelieu's secretary, who evidently provided valuable inside information on French intentions.[15] But, when the question of a loan was raised in the autumn and winter of 1816, the Finance Minister Corvetto elected to give the business to Baring and Pierre-César Labouchère of Hope & Co.,[16] who had successfully been wooed by Gabriel-Julien Ouvrard, another survivor of the imperial era.[17] An agreement was reached in early 1817 whereby, in return for a 2.5 per cent commission, Baring provided the French government with an initial 297 million francs in return for 5 per cent rentes. Because the bonds were issued over a period of several months in three tranches at prices of 52.5, 55.5 and 61.5, this meant that the French government had increased its national debt by around 534 million francs for the sake of less than 300 million francs in cash—or to put it another way, it was paying interest at an effective rate of around 9 per cent, nearly double the nominal rate on its rentes. Contrary to later mythology, the Rothschilds found themselves more or less excluded from this immense operation, "to prevent," so Baring claimed, "a selling race at the exchanges with resulting depreciation."[18]

This was a bitter blow to James, who had expended considerable energy on his own plans for a loan, and who believed up until the eleventh hour that, at the very least, he would be able to participate in some kind of consortium.[19] "Depressed" and angry, he railed at Baring's duplicity, claiming that his rival had bribed the French government to exaggerate its inability to pay and thereby secure a six-month breathing-space.[20] His anger was redoubled when a last-ditch effort (in partnership with Laffitte and Parish) to join the Baring group for the third issue of rentes in July

1817 came to nothing.[21] Salomon, returning to Paris from London, could not help but admire the way his brother had been outmanoeuvred:

> He is quite a crook this Baring. Today he is going to dine with us, together with Laffitte . . . We must certainly watch our step as far as he is concerned. Baring's lot are and were as well versed in the way of using influence as we are. There is not a single man of importance amongst the authorities here who would not work with Baring hand in glove . . . The Russian ambassador Pozzo di Borgo is on the side of France and of Baring whose orbit he is in . . . Baring and the French Minister of Finances are sharing the profit. The Minister is reputed to be one of the most corrupt of all.[22]

Whatever the truth of these allegations, Baring was in a strong enough position to exclude James again when the negotiations began for a final loan to pay off the remainder of the indemnity. Although rentes with a face value of 290 million francs were issued directly to the public in May 1818, the government appears to have taken fright at the frantic speculation these attracted (the issue was oversubscribed almost ten times, pushing prices up to a peak of 80 compared with an issue price of 66.5), and a second issue of 480 million francs (nominal) in the same month was entrusted to Baring.[23] When James—along with the other Paris banks Baguenault, Delessert, Greffulhe, Hottinguer and Laffitte—was offered a mere 10 million francs, to be shared with David Parish, he was disgusted, fulminating at the "abominable" way he had been treated.[24] He and the others had to content themselves with shares of a 31 million franc loan to the city of Paris.[25] As the Duke of Wellington reported to Lord Liverpool, "The fact is that Baring, having the French finances in his hands, and French loans being in fashion in England, has to a certain degree the command of the money market of the world. He feels his power, and it is not a very easy task to succeed in counteracting him." If there was ever a moment when Barings deserved to be called "the sixth great power" (a probably apocryphal phrase attributed to Richelieu), then this was it.[26]

There were admittedly arguments for limiting the brothers' direct involvement in a large-scale loan to France.[27] After the trauma of the Hundred Days, Nathan had good reason to doubt the stability of the restored Bourbon regime. Salomon might reassure him that, according to best sources in Paris, there would be "no more revolution in France," but he added the important rider: "at least not in the foreseeable future, and if there is something, it is certainly not be feared in the next three months." After all, as he admitted, there was "no way of insuring against the hot heads of the French," and a future default could not be ruled out. Such comments suggest that he had no more confidence than Nathan in French funds.[28] This pessimism was reinforced by "talk of war" which James heard in Paris in May 1816.[29] A few months later he was even more alarmed by news that the British government might favour replacing Louis XVIII with the duc d'Orléans, which James warned would lead to civil war.[30] Widespread social unrest in 1817 caused by a bad harvest and high food prices reinforced such anxieties.

On the other hand, the financial position of the restored Bourbon regime was less shaky than it appeared, and this helps explain the rapid rise in the price of rentes during 1817 and the first half of 1818 which made the loan so profitable for its contractors. Because of the great assignat inflation of the 1790s, France—unlike

Britain—had more or less wiped out the accumulated debts of the eighteenth century. Its total public debt in 1815 stood at just 1.2 billion francs, roughly 10 per cent of national income—so much less than the equivalent figure for Britain that it amounted to a clean slate.[31] It was therefore easy, once Baring had started the ball rolling, for France to issue further loans without in any way depressing the price of rentes. As the price of rentes rose, Baring was getting, as James ruefully observed, "money for nothing."[32] France's resources were in reality "formidable" and the political situation stable: "If the Allies withdraw, France will remain quiet. Be assured that there is no party left here which could put up resistance to the Government, at least not soon."[33]

The Rothschilds' failure to secure the 1817 and 1818 reparations loans was therefore a costly defeat. The implication was clear: if they had stolen a march on other bankers in early 1814, now they had to face a determined effort by the Barings and Bethmanns to reclaim their earlier predominance in European public finance, as well as new competition from less established figures like Gontard and the Bavarian financier Adolph d'Eichthal.[34] As Carl had put it in 1814, "The main thing is that people are hostile towards us because we have the business."[35] "We have enemies aplenty," James lamented a year later, "though it is more a matter of envy than enmity. Every five minutes someone else is going to the [Prussian] minister and asks: 'Why does Rothschild get given everything?'" It had been easier before, commented Carl, when the risks were greater, because there had been less competition.[36] Indeed, James even acknowledged that, in seeking to exclude them from the reparations payments, the Viennese bankers were only "doing what the Rothschilds had done" over the subsidies.[37] Baring seemed to pose the biggest threat at this stage. Not only did he and his associates "want to subject all of France according to their will so that they can do what they like"; they also posed a threat to Nathan's position in London.[38] As Amschel said, Nathan seemed to be "rather upset if somebody else does any business transactions with London. He feels that he more or less owns London."[39] It cannot have pleased him to hear it said "that [because of Baring] you don't play any longer the first [role] on the Stock Exchange and that you are unable to fix the quotation" of stocks.[40] However, the growth of competition was just as marked in smaller financial markets like Kassel, where the end of the war and the return of the Elector led to frenetic efforts to end the Rothschilds' near-monopoly over his finances, built up during his years in exile, and to win a share of the Rothschilds' "mountains of gold."[41] As James put it in early 1818, "The whole world is jealous."[42]

The Rothschilds did not suffer competitors gladly. Indeed, they had a wide range of abusive terms for them, such as *Schurken* (scoundrels), *Bösewichte* (rogues) and *Spitzbuben* (rascals). Even before Waterloo, there had been much talk of "putting spokes in wheels" of rival "scoundrels" and "sharpshooters," and dealing them "blows where it hurts."[43] The question in 1818 was how best to "hurt" Baring and Labouchère. Tradition has it that the brothers did so by means of a huge intervention in the market for rentes. First, they invested heavily in the new rentes being created under the Baring scheme. Then, just as the great powers met at Aix-la-Chapelle to negotiate the final reparations payments, they allegedly turned from bulls into bears, dumping rentes on the market with devastating consequences for prices. In this way, they decisively weakened Baring's position, forcing him to call off the final loan which he had been on the point of making on behalf of France.[44] There is no doubt that we need an explanation for the remarkable speed with which the Rothschilds outstripped their more established rivals. And it is true that Baring was acutely embarrassed by the sharp drop in rentes to a nadir of 60, and was saved only by the fact that so many of the ministers present at Aix—including Nesselrode, the Austrian Chancellor Prince Metternich and his Prussian counterpart Prince Hardenberg—had themselves taken shares, and therefore had a common interest in cancelling the final loan.[45] However, no archival evidence has come to light to support the notion that the Rothschilds were directly responsible for the crisis.

The brothers undoubtedly sought to join in the bull run in the French bond market after 1816. James held rentes worth 3 million francs (nominal) at the beginning of March 1817, and by the end of the month he had acquired a further 7 million, all bought on the assumption of a sustained rise.[46] Soon he was inundated with orders to purchase rentes for Nathan and his London relatives too, though he himself still felt "in the dark" as to how long the rise could be sustained.[47] It also seems quite likely, as Ouvrard later claimed, that James took advantage of the system of part-payment to maximise his speculative purchases.[48] But there is no evidence of a concerted policy of selling at any time in 1818. When James did take profits, he took care that his sales should not be noticed, precisely to avoid weakening the market as a whole; and when rentes did weaken in the summer of 1817, the brothers actually made purchases to support the market.[49] Indeed, it is from this period that we can date that keen preoccupation with the health of the rente, and any news which might affect it, which was to be a feature of his correspondence for the next fifty years. A year later, in July 1818, he saw no reason to question Laffitte and Delessert's assumption that rentes would reach par by the end of the year.[50]

None of this should surprise us. The Rothschilds would have been taking a grave risk if they had sought to subvert the final "liquidation" of the French indemnity. In February 1818 Salomon explicitly argued against an attack on Baring: it would be counter-productive if people were able to say, "The Rothschilds organised a diversion, the loan fell through, the troops can't be withdrawn." In any case, Baring was an MP and had already asked enough awkward questions about Herries's activities as Commissary-in-Chief. There were good reasons not to antagonise him.[51] The best explanation for the downturn in the price of rentes during the Aix conference in fact lies in the policy of the Banque de France, which had fuelled the surge in rente prices after May by lending over-generously to the Paris banks. When a run on its reserves alerted the Banque to its mistake, it over-compensated by tightening its discounting terms. It was this contraction on the money market which temporarily halted the speculation in rentes and depressed prices.[52] Once the Banque had been persuaded to relax its policy again, rentes recovered rapidly, though it was not until 1821 (with prices at 87) that sufficient confidence had been recovered to float the final reparations loan. Moreover, if the Rothschilds had hoped to benefit from Baring's retreat from the French market, they were disappointed: the 1821 loan went to the Paris bankers Hottinguer, Delessert and Baguenault.[53]

In reality, it was British consols, not French rentes, which the Rothschilds sold, and they did so at the end of 1817, not in late 1818—making a profit in the process which more than compensated for any losses they may have suffered in the summer of 1815. As we have seen, at the end of that year Nathan had, at Herries's recom-

mendation, made substantial purchases of 3 per cent consols at prices of 61.1 and
61.5 as well as £450,000 of Omnium stocks at 107. Throughout 1816 he ignored
his nervous brothers' repeated advice to take profits, so that by the end of that year
he held altogether £1.2 million (nominal) worth of consols. This must have been
very nearly equivalent to the entire capital of the firm. Family opinion on this strategy was divided: cautious as ever, Amschel regarded it as "stupid . . . to invest one's
whole fortune in one single security" and continued to urge that Nathan sell, especially as he and Carl found themselves increasingly strapped for cash in Frankfurt.[54]
James was more enthusiastic—as he said, this single investment had already earned
them "as much as a loan"—but he questioned Nathan's assessment that consols
would reach 80, and by April 1817 he too was urging a halt.[55] Those closer to New
Court, however, joined in Nathan's "spec" with their own private savings. Caroline,
Salomon's wife, had evidently caught the bug while staying with her brother-in-law:
by August 1816, she was actually having dreams about consol prices reaching 86!—
a revealing insight into the indirect participation of the Rothschild women in the
family business in this period.[56] In May of 1817, when the upward trend was momentarily checked, Nathan finally gave in to his brothers' pleas by selling around
£600,000, but he evidently did so with the greatest reluctance and moved quickly to
reinvest even more before the rise resumed the following month.[57] By July, with consols leaping to above 82 and a total holding of £1.6 million (nominal), Salomon had
to acknowledge that his brother had pulled off another business "masterwork."[58]

It was at this point that Nathan began to sell, realising profits of more than
£250,000.[59] Interestingly, this was five months ahead of the market's final peak at
84.25 in December 1817 (see illustration 4.i) and this may explain why he delayed
slightly before relaying the advice to sell to others. Even his brothers-in-law and his
oldest client in the market, the Elector of Hesse-Kassel, were not tipped off until
after Nathan had sold.[60] As it became apparent that the market had indeed
peaked—by 1820 prices were back below 70—Moses Montefiore hailed his
brother-in-law's coup:

> I am very happy to learn you make as good a Bear as you formerly did a
> Bull, you must have had some difficulty with my brother Abraham,
> indeed it is quite a new character for both . . . You have beaten your
> antagonists so frequently that I am surprised there are any so hardy to
> be found in the Stock Exchange to oppose you in any considerable
> operation.[61]

There is no simple explanation for the Rothschilds' triumph over their rivals in the
1820s: but this great coup undoubtedly played an important part.

What had made Nathan decide to dispose of his consols at the end of 1817? Part
of the reason may have been a premature alarm sounded by his brothers in Paris
about the possibility of war over Spain: not for the last time, the brothers interpreted
any threat of armed conflict between the great powers as an argument for selling
government bonds.[62] But of greater importance was the invaluable inside information he was receiving about changes in British fiscal and monetary policy. This was
the fruit of Nathan's growing proximity to the Chancellor of the Exchequer,
Nicholas Vansittart, as well as his brothers' first direct contacts with the Duke of
Wellington—"old Stiff-back"—in Paris.[63] As the Rothschilds hastened to point out,

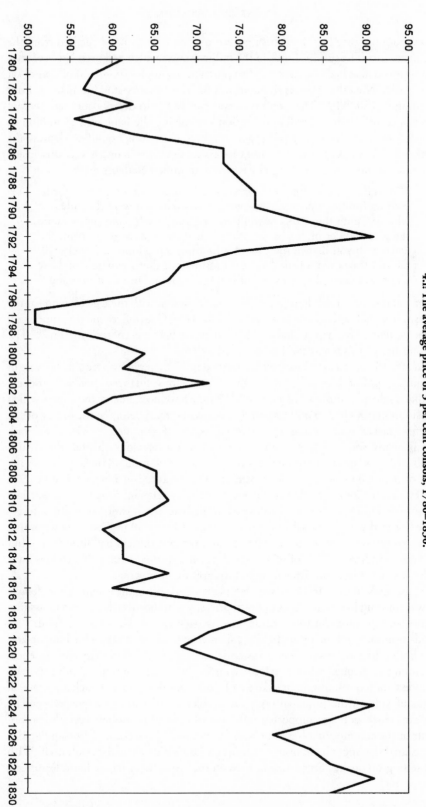

4.i: The average price of 3 per cent consols, 1780–1830.

it was not only they but the British government too which had benefited from the rise in consols. The surplus funds in the military chest which had been left over after Napoleon's defeat had also been used to purchase £650,000 (nominal) of consols at 62 in 1816. Now that consols stood at over 82, the Treasury stood to make a profit of around £130,000.[64] This good turn was clearly felt to deserve another: Nathan was tipped off about a funding operation—involving the issue of £27 million in new 3.5 or 3.25 per cent government stocks—which was bound to depress the market for 3 per cents. As Salomon's letters at this time show, it was this inside information more than anything else which determined Nathan's move:

> Vansittart is a very fine man, insofar as he gave you a hint of a forth-coming funding operation. He well knows that you were the only one who drove up the stocks, who lifted England's credit, and that you are the great holder of stocks . . . Now it is time to work out a plan. We agree with you that in the case of a funding carried out . . . stocks will fall to 80 or even a little less . . . I assure you that the whole of New Court as soon as they get wind of it are going to be "bears" of millions.[65]

As he put it to an incredulous James: "Nathan's relation with these gentlemen [of the Treasury] is such as between brothers . . . Our New Court gives me the impression of being like a Freemasons' lodge. He who enters becomes a Stock-mason."[66] The significance of this remark will be returned to below.

In fact, the operation Vansittart mentioned to Nathan ran into trouble because of mounting political opposition to the Chancellor's financial policy.[67] Indeed, Nathan's sale of consols at the end of 1817 may have been one of the abuses which Vansittart's critics had in mind when they accused him of being "at the Mercy of the Money Market" and fuelling "the inordinate spirit of gambling."[68] Vansittart's task was in many ways a hopeless one. As noted in the previous chapter, the British public debt had grown to immense proportions—£900 million, or roughly 200 per cent of national income—as a consequence of the wars against France. But in 1815 the House of Commons defied the government by refusing to renew the wartime income tax (and the malt tax), causing an immediate loss of over £14 million in revenue.[69] Faced with annual debt service charges of over £30 million, to say nothing of the continuing costs of the army and navy, the government had little option but to increase indirect taxes—of which the duty on imported corn or "Corn Law" was to become the most controversial—and to carry on borrowing.

Vansittart's strategy in 1818, which aimed at concealing the extent of the deficits he was running in order to boost consol prices, was to borrow short term by issuing exchequer bills, in order to continue making payments to Pitt's sinking fund. This hand-to-mouth system undoubtedly suited those, like Nathan, who bought and sold both bills and consols. But it was criticised, given the inflationary consequences of issuing exchequer bills to redeem consols, by those political economists who regarded the continuing depreciation of paper money and the exchange rate in terms of gold as the principal post-war problem. Led within the government by William Huskisson and supported (after initial doubts) by Robert Peel, the proponents of the resumption of gold or "cash" payments by the Bank of England gradually gained the upper hand over Vansittart and the directors of the Bank itself. With the setting up of the "Secret Committee on the Expediency of the Bank Resuming

Cash Payments" under Peel's chairmanship in 1819, the "bullionists" had effectively won.[70] Dismayed, Nathan sought to dissuade Liverpool from going back on to gold, even pursuing ministers into the country to make his case. But the Prime Minister's mind had been made up, as he indicated to Vansittart in October 1819:

> Nothing can be more foolish than Rothschild's following you, and intending to follow me, into the country. If his proceeding is known it can of course only augment the general alarm, and increase all the evils he is desirous of preventing . . . The point . . . upon which I feel most anxiety is the idea suggested by Rothschild, of a continuance of the Bank restriction. I am satisfied that no measure could be more fatal, and that the very notion of its being a matter for consideration would do harm . . . As to continuing the restriction from the dread of their diminishing their [the Bank of England's] circulation too much, this would be a ground for perpetual restriction, and is the idea of all others that it was most necessary to combat last year. Let us therefore determine to stand upon our present system, and let no one entertain a doubt that this is our determination.[71]

Given the ultimate triumph of the gold standard in the nineteenth century, it is easy to dismiss Nathan's position as special pleading. Yet Nathan's opposition to cash payments was far from unjustifiable, and it was an error on the part of the bullionists and radicals to assume that he was motivated solely by self-interest. Nathan never opposed the resumption of cash payments as a matter of theoretical principle: he and his fellow bankers made a practical argument that the short-run effects of a deflationary policy would be economically destabilising, and that this might tend to run counter to the government's goal of fiscal and monetary stabilisation.[72] The Treasury official George Harrison was right to worry in October 1818 about the consequences of tightening monetary policy at a time when the budget remained unbalanced. As he said to Vansittart,

> Its effect upon our concerns and upon the Stocks may be very considerable—for such a proceeding would drive . . . *our* Agent [meaning Nathan] in all probability to become a Seller of his stock . . . and would inevitably affect the Funds more or less . . . We could not with justice or propriety be pressing him to extend his accommodations to us, when the Bank refused to accommodate him by Discounts—as he would then be driven to become a Seller to a larger extent to enable him to meet our Wants.[73]

In fact, as we have seen, Nathan had already done most of his selling. But his brokers and their clients felt the effects of the government's deflationary policies when he issued a new loan of £12 million for the government in the summer of 1819. The decision to stick to 3 per cents more or less precluded a rapid rise in the new stock at a time when consol prices were already in the doldrums not far above the issue price of 69.[74] It was this link between monetary tightening and the continuance of government borrowing which he had sought to point out to Liverpool, who preferred to believe Baring that there would soon be "a reaction" (that is, a recovery) in consol prices. Similarly, in his evidence to the Committee of Cash Payments in 1820, Nathan did not deny for a moment that the depreciation of sterling and outflow of specie into foreign bonds was due in part to the suspension of gold payments. The key point was that the combination of tight money and a mountainous government debt was a perilous one for the economy as a whole:

> *Have the goodness to state to the Committee in detail, what you conceive would be the consequence of an obligation imposed upon the Bank to resume cash payments at the expiration of a year from the present time?*—I do not think it can be done without very great distress to this country; it would do a great deal of mischief; we may not actually know ourselves what mischief it may cause.
>   *Have the goodness to explain the nature of the mischief, and in what way it would be produced?*—Money will be so very scarce, every article in this country will fall to such an enormous extent, that many persons will be ruined.[75]

This was no exaggeration. Events would amply demonstrate that in embarking on monetary stabilisation before resolving the post-war fiscal crisis, the government was sailing into uncharted and potentially dangerous waters. As Nathan's brother-in-law Abraham Montefiore shrewdly observed in 1821, defending the record of "the poor inoffensive Old Lady, Mr. V[ansittart]": "The only really effective plan would be a good property tax properly and judiciously levied to reach only the opulent and those that can afford to spare part of their income, but unfortunately it so happens that these very persons are the law-makers themselves and their patriotism does not go so far as to reach their pockets."[76] The attempt to balance the budget with virtually no direct taxation at a time of monetary deflation would prove a recipe for instability.

"The Chief Ally of the Holy Alliance"

There was one obvious response to the difficulties experienced by the Rothschilds in London and Paris between 1815 and 1819: to seek new business elsewhere. The alternative was to assist with the financial stabilisation of the other great powers: Austria, Prussia and Russia, now grouped together, at the Tsar's suggestion, as a "Holy Alliance," as well as the various smaller states in Italy and Germany in their respective spheres of influence. Like France and Britain, the Central and East European states emerged from the war with dire financial problems which could be addressed only with the assistance of foreign capital. As Disraeli later put it in his novel *Coningsby:* "[A]fter the exhaustion of a war of twenty-five years, Europe must require capital to carry on peace . . . France wanted some; Austria more; Prussia a little; Russia a few millions."[77] Moreover, the policy of the Holy Alliance was bound to create additional financial needs from which the Rothschilds could also profit. For the principal aim of the Alliance was to avert a recurrence of the revolutionary "epidemic" which had caused such upheaval in Europe between 1789 and 1815—if necessary by military intervention. That implied further expenditure.

The first major post-war loan which the brothers succeeded in making was to Prussia, which had ended the Napoleonic period with a debt burden of around 188 million thaler (£32 million) and continued to run large deficits in 1815, 1816 and 1817.[78] Although the Frankfurt-based Rothschilds had arranged a small Prussian loan of 5 million gulden (£450,000) in early 1817 (much of which they placed with the Elector of Hesse-Kassel),[79] the size of the floating debt reached 20 million thaler by the autumn, and the government began to contemplate raising a loan in London.[80] The idea for such a loan in fact originated with the representative of the Prussian Seehandlung bank in London, a merchant named Barandon, who came close to scuppering the entire project when he rashly published details of Nathan's proposed terms in January 1818. As these were singularly tough—the issue price was to have been 60, implying an interest rate of 8.33 per cent—they provoked an outcry in Berlin, where the local bankers hastened to put together a better offer. Berating Nathan for having involved Barandon, whose reputation in Paris was that of a bankrupt small-time commodities dealer, Salomon hastened from Paris to Koblenz for fraught talks with the Prussian State Chancellor Hardenberg, and then proceeded to Berlin, where he and Carl managed to undo at least some of the damage.[81] With the connivance of the Prussian minister in London, the great educational and political reformer Wilhelm von Humboldt, Barandon was quietly sidelined—though it was not until after five days of continuous bargaining with the finance official Rother (now Director in the new Prussian Treasury) that an agreement was finally secured in London at the end of March.[82]

Historians have long claimed that the Prussian government's decision to raise a loan in London was intended to avoid the need for political concessions—such as the summoning of an assembly of the estates *(Stände)* or the creation of an independent judiciary—which the recourse to domestic sources of finance might have necessitated.[83] However, the Rothschild correspondence tells a different story. From the outset of the negotiations, Nathan argued that any loan would have to be secured by a mortgage on Prussian royal domains guaranteed by the *Stände* of the domains concerned. When Hardenberg demurred, Nathan spelt out his reasons for wishing such a guarantee in a remarkable memorandum:

> [T]o induce British Capitalists to invest their money in a loan to a foreign government upon reasonable terms, it will be of the first importance that the plan of such a loan should as much as possible be assimilated to the established system of borrowing for the public service in England, and above all things that some security, beyond the mere good faith of the government . . . should be held out to the lenders . . . Without some security of this description any attempt to raise a considerable sum in England for a foreign Power would be hopeless[;] the late investments by British subjects in the French Funds have proceeded upon the general belief that in consequence of the representative system now established in that Country, the sanction of the Chamber to the national debt incurred by the Government affords a guarantee to the Public Creditor which could not be found in a Contract with any Sovereign uncontrolled in the exercise of the executive powers.[84]

In other words, a constitutional monarchy was seen in London as a better credit-risk than a neo-absolutist regime. Was this a subtle form of political pressure—a kind of financial liberalism, lending its weight at a critical time to the efforts of the Prussian reformers who had been pressing Frederick William III to accept some kind of system of representation? Or was Nathan merely justifying the differential between his terms and those obtained by France from Baring? James's positive allusion to the (notional) ability of French deputies to go to the Treasury and "examine the books" suggests that the Rothschilds really did see some kind of constitutional control over public finances as desirable, if only as a way of reassuring British investors.[85] Admittedly, Nathan was prepared to settle for much less than parliamentary control in the Prussian case: clause 5 of the final contract merely stated that "for the security of the creditors" there would be a special mortgage on the royal domains "which are wholly disposable according to the House[hold] Law of November 6, 1809, passed by H. M. the King of Prussia and the princes of the royal house with the assent of the provincial estates."[86] The allusion to the estates could hardly have been more oblique. On the other hand, the astonishing tone of some of Nathan's letters to Rother—especially when Rother attempted to modify the terms after the contract had been signed—reveal his lack of respect for the Prussian regime:

> Dearest friend, I have now done my duty by God, your King and the Finance Minister von Rother, my money has all gone to you in Berlin . . . now it is your turn and duty to do yours, to keep your word and not to come up with new things, and everything must remain as it was agreed between men like us, and that is what I expected, as you can see from my deliveries of money. The cabal there can do nothing against N. M. Rothschild, he has the money, the strength and the power, the cabal has only impotence and the King of Prussia, my Prince Hardenberg and Minister Rother should be well pleased and thank Rothschild, who is sending you so much money [and] raising Prussia's credit.[87]

Moreover, Nathan's insistence on some kind of political guarantee had important political implications. There is an obvious link from Nathan's negotiations with Rother to the subsequent Clause 2 of the "Decree for the Future Management of the State Debt" of January 17, 1819, which imposed a ceiling on the state debt, earmarked revenues from the royal domains to service it and declared: "If the state should in future for its maintenance or for the advancement of the common good require to issue a new loan, this can only be done in consultation with, and with the guarantee of, the future imperial estates assembly."[88] Drafted by Rother himself, this meant that any future loan by the Prussian state would automatically lead to the summoning of the estates; in other words, it conceded the link between public borrowing and constitutional reform. Only by raising loans indirectly through the notionally independent Seehandlung could the Prussian state henceforth borrow money without summoning the estates. This explains why, of all the German states, Prussia borrowed the least in the 1820s and 1830s and why, when the policy of retrenchment broke down in the 1840s, the consequences were revolutionary.

Whatever its significance for Prussian politics, the 1818 Prussian loan was without question a watershed in the history of the European capital market, as contemporaries came to recognise. For Nathan's demand for some kind of political security was, in financial terms, probably the least important of the conditions he attached to the loan. Firstly, the loan was to be not in thaler, but in sterling, with the interest payable (half-yearly) not in Berlin but in London. Secondly, there was to be a British-style sinking fund to ensure the amortisation of the loan (though Rother managed to get rid of Nathan's initial stipulation that it take the form of £150,000 of British consols).[89] This deliberate Anglicisation of a foreign loan was a new departure for the international capital market. The Baring French loans had paid interest in francs in Paris, with attendant inconvenience and exchange rate risks for British investors. Now it was much easier to invest in foreign funds; and the fact that throughout the century all foreign government bonds paid higher yields than British consols meant that people did. *The Times* did not exaggerate when it later described Nathan as "the first introducer of foreign loans into Britain":

> for, though such securities did at all times circulate here, the payment of dividends abroad, which was the universal practice before his time, made them too inconvenient an investment for the great majority of persons of property to deal with. He not only formed arrangements for the payment of dividends on his foreign loan in London, but made them still more attractive by fixing the rate in sterling money, and doing away with all the effects of fluctuation in exchanges.[90]

Moreover, the loan was issued not just in London but also in Frankfurt, Berlin, Hamburg, Amsterdam and Vienna.[91] In other words, it represented a major step towards the creation of a completely international bond market. In his book *On The Traffic in State Bonds* (1825), the German legal expert Johann Heinrich Bender identified this as one of the Rothschilds' principal contributions to modern economic development: "Any owner of government bonds . . . can collect the interest at his convenience in several different places without any effort." Henceforth, an investor could receive the interest on Austrian metalliques, Neapolitan rentes or any other Rothshild-issued bonds from any of the Rothschild houses.[92] In stipulating these conditions, Nathan not only succeeded in making the Prussian loan attractive to British and continental investors; he also established a model for such international bond issues which would swiftly become standard.[93]

Although the terms of the loan were heavily criticised in Berlin (not least by the bankers there), Humboldt and Rother were impressed. Nathan, Humboldt reported to Hardenberg, was not only "the most enterprising businessman here"; he was also "dependable . . . fair, very upright and understanding" in his dealings with governments. Rother went further: "The Rothschild in this country . . . has an incredible influence upon all financial affairs here in London. It is widely stated, and is, indeed, close to the truth, that he entirely regulates the rate of exchange in the City. His power as a banker is enormous." His reputation in Berlin firmly established, Nathan was able to secure a second loan (to the Seehandlung) in 1822 for £3.5 million.[94]

In one respect, Rothschild activity in Germany was far from innovative. Hesse-Kassel was one of those states which had emerged intact from the Napoleonic period, and Amschel was careful to continue cultivating the special relationship his father had developed with the Elector. Now that he had been restored to his lands, however, William needed the Rothschilds less, and the family's old rivals in Kassel hastened to reassert their influence at court. The Rothschilds continued to manage some of the Prince's financial affairs, collecting his reparations from France, selling his English stocks (as we have seen) at a healthy profit, trying to sort out his tangled Danish investments and involving him in their post-war loans to Prussia.[95] Amschel even indulged his old coin-collecting enthusiasm.[96] But there was no doubt that the days of mutual dependence were over, especially when Buderus had ceased to be the dominant force in the Kassel bureaucracy.[97] Although the brothers lent considerable sums to William's spendthrift son, their hopes that these highly unprofitable transactions would bring more lucrative business after he succeeded his father were disappointed when this finally happened in 1821.[98] Apart from two large loans in 1821 and in 1823 for a total of 4.3 million gulden (£390,000), business in Kassel dried up.[99]

On the other hand, Hesse-Kassel was only one of thirty-nine German states which had emerged from the Napoleonic upheaval and were now grouped together as members of the loose German Confederation. And because the Confederation's Diet met in Frankfurt—in a rented hall in the Thurn und Taxis palace—it was easy for Amschel and Carl to establish contact with senior diplomatic representatives of all the member states.[100] This led to a stream of relatively small-scale loans to minor German states and princes—including the neighbouring Grand Duchy of Hesse-Darmstadt, as well as Schaumburg, Homburg, Saxe-Weimar, Anhalt-Coethen and Nassau-Usingen—throughout the 1820s. Though the individual loans only rarely exceeded 500,000 gulden (£45,000), taken together they represented a substantial amount of business. Between 1817 and 1829 total loans of this sort by the Frankfurt house amounted to more than 24.7 million gulden (£2.2 million).[101] While some were little more than personal loans to petty princes, others took more sophisticated forms, like the Hesse-Darmstadt lottery loan of 1825, one of many premium-bond-style loans issued in this period.[102] On occasion, the Rothschilds also acted as bankers to the Confederation itself. Twenty million francs—paid by France under the terms of the Peace of Paris for the construction of fortifications in Germany—were deposited with the Rothschilds in 1820, pending a decision by the Confederation to proceed with building them.[103] Given the slowness with which such decisions were reached in Frankfurt, this turned out to be a long-term deposit; but it was never certain how much notice would be needed for its withdrawal, nor indeed who had the right to request it. The difficulties this created for the Rothschilds may explain why they never did much to attract similar deposits.

Real power in Germany, however, lay not in Frankfurt, but in Vienna, the capital of the Confederation's dominant member: and it was the Austrian court more than any other which the Rothschilds sought to cultivate in the 1820s. As we have seen, the Austrians had been reluctant to leave the payment of their British subsidies to the Rothschilds in the later stages of the war against France, preferring to deal with Viennese houses like Arnstein & Eskeles,[104] Fries & Co. and Geymüller & Co.; they had driven hard bargains over the French reparations payments too. Only in partnership with the Frankfurt banker Gontard were the brothers able to handle the minor payments Austria had to receive in the wake of the peace from Russia and Naples.[105] But Vienna needed cash just as badly as the other continental states if it was to consolidate its large floating debt and stabilise its heavily depreciated currency.[106] Although its first major post-war loan of 50 million gulden was concluded—to Rothschild chagrin—with the Anglo-Hanseatic Parish brothers in partnership with Baring, Bethmann and Geymüller, it was obvious, with annual expenditure running above 100 million Austrian gulden, that more would soon be needed.[107] The breakthrough came in 1820, when Salomon jointly organised two lottery loans worth 45 million Austrian gulden (c. £4.8 million) in partnership with David Parish—a transaction so profitable that, despite the hostile comment it aroused, Salomon resolved to remain in Vienna on a more or less permanent basis.[108]

The final coup which completed the Rothschilds' emergence as "bankers to the Holy Alliance" came in 1822, with the loan to Russia. Here, as in Prussia and Austria, the war had generated acute fiscal and monetary problems: public spending had roughly quadrupled between 1803 and 1815 as had the circulation of paper roubles, leading to the inevitable inflation and currency depreciation.[109] And despite having allowed the Rothschilds to handle so much of her wartime subsidy payments and subsequent reparations contributions, Russia too turned first to others for assistance with stabilisation: it was Baring and Reid, Irving who handled the 1820 loan, for example.[110] This, however, was no great disappointment, as the Russians at this stage were still refusing to follow the Prussian example of issuing a loan denominated in sterling and with interest payable in London.[111] Two years later the Russians, like the Austrians before them, had come round. In the summer of 1822 a loan of £6.6 million was issued by Nathan in 5 per cent bonds priced at 77, which he had no difficulty in selling at prices of 80 and more to his network of London brokers, led by his brother-in-law Moses Montefiore.[112]

Thus by the end of 1822 the Rothschilds could justifiably be regarded as bankers to the Holy Alliance—"la haute Trésorerie de la Sainte Alliance."[113] Indeed, when the itinerant German Prince Pückler-Muskau first described Nathan in a letter to his wife, he introduced him as "the chief ally of the Holy Alliance."[114] There is unquestionably a sense in which it was the Rothschilds who gave the alliance substance. When the Austrian Emperor remarked to his envoy in Frankfurt that Amschel was "richer than I am," he was not being wholly facetious.[115] *The Times* correspondent reported from St Petersburg that the mere appearance of James Rothschild at the bourse was expected to boost Russian bond prices.[116] Without the financial support which Nathan in particular could provide, it would have been harder to make the Austrian strategy of "policing" Europe effective in the 1820s. Political critics of this strategy recognised this. Nathan was caricatured as the "Hollow Alliance's" insurance broker, helping to prevent political fire in Europe.[117] In 1821 he even received a death threat because of "his connexion with foreign powers, and particularly the assistance rendered to Austria, on account of the designs of that government against the liberties of Europe."[118]

Finance and Revolution

It had, of course, been assumed by the founders of the Holy Alliance that the best way of preventing a renewed revolutionary upheaval in Europe would be a policy of "containment" directed against France, the *fons et origo* of revolution since 1789. While that would prove to be the right strategy later, in 1830 and in 1848, in the 1820s it quickly had to be abandoned as it became evident that the political order established at Vienna could be challenged almost anywhere. When August von Kotzebue—a minor hack reputed to be in the pay of the Tsar—was murdered in Mannheim by a radically inclined student, Karl Sand, it suited Metternich quite well as the pretext for a crackdown on liberal tendencies throughout the German Confederation. Like the assassination of the King's nephew, the duc de Berry, in Paris in February 1820, one death did not portend a serious revolution. But the Cadiz mutiny by army units destined for South America that January was the real thing, as it led not only to the reimposition of the 1812 Cortes constitution on the Spanish King Ferdinand VIII, but also to the imposition of the same constitution on his uncle, Ferdinand I of Naples, just six months later. The "domino effect" continued in August 1820, with a military revolt in Portugal. In March 1821 there were risings by Italians in Piedmont and by Greeks throughout the Near East. The abortive Decembrist movement in Russia in 1824–5 was part of the same pattern: the unrest was often led by disenchanted soldiers (the victims of post-war cuts in defence spending), or by secret societies like the Italian Carbonari or the Spanish Freemasons. Indeed, so widespread was the political instability that France, the former outcast, had to be co-opted into the counter-revolutionary coalition. The question which came to dominate the congresses of Troppau (October to December 1820), Laibach (January 1821) and Verona (September to December 1822) was how far this coalition should intervene in the affairs of other states to prevent the success of localised revolutions. The financial question this begged, of course, was whether or not they could afford to do so. In so far as they helped to finance Austrian intervention in Italy and French intervention in Spain, the Rothschilds deserve to be thought of as financiers of "reaction."

From the Rothschild viewpoint, however, the instability of Restoration Europe was not only a source of potential new business; it was also a threat to the stability of financial markets. Existing loans to regimes which suddenly looked vulnerable slumped as alarmed investors sought to sell their bonds. Even successful armed intervention, by throwing the Austrian and French budgets into deficit, had similar negative side-effects. On the other hand, the emergence of new states in those regions where revolutions actually succeeded created a source of new business too. In particular, the creation of independent states in Brazil, in formerly Spanish America and in Greece led to numerous new bond issues as fledgling regimes rushed to the London and Paris capital markets. For that reason, the role of the Rothschilds' financial power was ambivalent.

On the Italian peninsula, matters were relatively straightforward: the Rothschilds supported Metternich's policy of divide and rule by lending to the various monarchical regimes which had his backing. As early as December 1820 Metternich wrote to Salomon from Troppau alluding suggestively to a transaction involving 25 or 30 million francs "with respect to the future fate of the Kingdom of Naples." The banker's initial response was positive.[119] "Even our financiers, led by Parish and Rothschild," so the Austrian Finance Minister Stadion assured Metternich at Laibach in January 1821, "are only anxious to see our troops across the Po at the earliest possible moment, and marching on Naples."[120] Nevertheless, Salomon was unenthusiastic when Metternich and Nesselrode invited him to Laibach to discuss possible loans, the purpose of which was evidently to pay for intervention. "My presence there," he explained to Nesselrode, "might give rise to numerous and probably highly inaccurate newspaper reports. Persons with base motives might unearth the fact that a loan to the most gracious monarchs was being discussed; rumour would be piled upon rumour, and this would not be at all agreeable in the highest quarters." Firstly, the prospect of a new Austrian loan would depress the Vienna market, already shaken by the Italian crisis. Secondly, the Rothschilds had no desire to make their role in financing the Holy Alliance so public. Instead, Salomon insisted to Stadion that any loan should be raised by Ferdinand I only after his restoration to power, the proceeds to be used to reimburse the Austrian government for the costs of intervention.[121] In the meantime, he offered Stadion short-term advances to finance General Frimont's advance south. As in the Napoleonic Wars, the Rothschilds used their extensive banking network to make cash available at reasonable rates to an army on the march. And, as before, one of the brothers—this time Carl ("un petit frère Rothschild," as he seemed to Stadion)—had to be sent to the scene of the action to ensure that all ran smoothly.[122] In March 1821 Carl set off from Vienna to join Metternich and the exiled Neapolitan king at Laibach.

To Metternich, the Neapolitan campaign was nothing less than a counter-revolutionary crusade: "We have embarked," he told Stadion,

> on a great undertaking, one that contains the possibilities of greater results than any of our time. It is great, for upon its success or failure the whole future depends; not merely the future of the Austrian monarchy, but that of the whole of Europe . . . It was impossible for us to take any other action, for it is a matter of life or death . . . everything now depends upon success. If not, the result will be the same as if we had ventured nothing; the revolution will engulf first Italy and then the world. I will spare no effort until I am killed myself.

But financial reality gave the lie to such rhetoric. There were recurrent shortages of supplies at the front, while in Vienna Stadion despairingly foresaw a return to the fiscal and monetary morass of the Napoleonic period. Indeed, Salomon had to intervene to prevent a slump in the price of "metalliques" (Austrian silver-denominated bonds).[123] The crisis deepened when reports reached Laibach of further revolutionary outbreaks in Piedmont. The impact of this news in Vienna appalled the hapless Stadion:

> If the enemy were at the gates there could not be more unreasoning panic. The whole of the population of Vienna is rushing to the Bourse to get rid of our public securities . . . Our credit (which has only just been established) is on the eve of vanishing completely. I shall be forced to suspend the conversion of paper money into cash . . . destroying in one day the labours of the preceding five years . . . This is the first step to our destruction. It is impossible that a loan should be considered, either at home or abroad, at a time when our securities are becoming worthless.[124]

By March 24, however, Naples had fallen, and Carl hurried south after Ferdinand to organise the now desperately needed loan from which the Austrians were to be reimbursed.

At this point, a conflict of interests emerged: the Austrian government wished to exact the maximum sum possible, but the Rothschilds had a low opinion of Neapolitan creditworthiness, and were willing to lend to the restored regime only at punitive rates, while the Bourbon regime itself faced the prospect of renewed unrest if it was burdened with onerous new debts. The first Neapolitan loan was a hard-won compromise, with Carl being forced to improve his initial offer to head off competition from a rival Milanese banker: instead of 10 million ducats at a discounted price of 54, he agreed to lend the government 16 million (around £2 million) at 60. To help meet the costs of the continuing Austrian occupation, a second loan was issued in November 1821, of 16.8 million ducats, underwritten at 67.3.[125] Two more loans followed for 22 million ducats in 1822 and £2.5 million in 1824, increasing the state's debt to around £13 million in all. Nevertheless, the price of Neapolitan securities rose in Paris from 65 to 103, and in London there was considerable enthusiasm for the sterling-denominated bonds.[126] This successful stabilisation partly reflected the good relationship which had developed between Carl and the new Neapolitan Finance Minister, Luigi de' Medici, whose claim that the Austrians were unnecessarily prolonging the occupation and overcharging for their presence Carl was inclined to support.[127] Even before the Congress of Verona in late 1822, it was obvious that the Austrians intended to recoup the costs of the invasion in full: of 4.65 million gulden which Metternich demanded in August 1821 as payment for the actual invasion, 4 million had been received by the following February, and to this were added occupation costs of 9 million ducats per annum. By 1825 Medici was accusing the Austrian government of deliberately profiting from the occupation and threatened to resign unless more than 1 million ducats were repaid. When the Viennese authorities stalled, Carl advanced the money to Medici—to Metternich's evident irritation.[128]

The Austrian intervention in Naples provided a classic illustration of the difficulty of maintaining good relations with both sides in a bilateral international transfer. Nevertheless, Carl had probably struck the right balance between Austrian and Italian interests. While his establishment in Naples flourished on the strength of his ties with the Bourbon regime (and also did some business with the Grand Duke of Tuscany), Metternich continued to turn to Salomon for financial assistance over other Italian matters—notably the complicated 5 million lire loan organised to provide for the children of the Archduchess Marie-Louise, the Habsburg Princess who had briefly been married to Napoleon, and who had been established after his fall in the duchies of Parma, Piacenza and Guastalla.[129] Another such case concerned the finances of Napoleon's former Governor in Illyria, Marshal de Marmont, the Duke of Ragusa.[130] At the same time, the Austrian government found itself once again having to turn to the Rothschilds to satisfy its own burgeoning financial needs. For no matter how much could be squeezed out of Naples, the costs of the military intervention there far exceeded what Stadion could raise in current revenue. There was no alternative but another loan; and although some officials were minded to reject the initial Rothschild bid, the government ended up bowing to the inevitable, although it managed to secure improved terms.[131]

Vienna's dependence on the Rothschilds was further increased in 1823, when the British government, in an attempt to exert pressure on Vienna to end its occupation of Naples, raised the question of outstanding loans—now notionally totalling £23.5 million including interest—which had been given to Austria in the early stages of the war against France. Once again Austria turned to the Rothschilds, pressing Salomon to use his brother's influence in London to get the debt scaled down—the first of many occasions when the Rothschilds would act as an unofficial channel for Metternich's diplomatic communications. When this had finally been achieved, the Rothschilds offered to organise yet another loan, in partnership with Baring and Reid, Irving, to pay the agreed sum of £2.5 million. Thirty million gulden of new metalliques were taken by the banks at an underwriting price of 82.33, and were soon trading at 93, yielding a substantial profit to the banks.[132] Another 15 million gulden loan followed in 1826.[133] Ultimately, the Austrian policy of intervention in Italy had yielded multiple profits for the Rothschilds.

By contrast, the outbreak of revolution in Spain raised more serious dilemmas. For two years after 1820, the gout-ridden despot Ferdinand VII endured the Cortes constitution, and in that period the liberal government raised a number of loans (which were needed to compensate for the shortfall in revenues caused by the revolution). Although the Rothschilds—as Salomon hastened to reassure Metternich—were not at first involved in these, they were preparing to take a hand when, in July 1822, Ferdinand and his Ultra-royalist supporters unexpectedly attempted to overthrow the Cortes, calling for foreign intervention when their coup failed.[134] At this point James became involved in an attempt by the Spanish financier Bertran de Lys to forestall an invasion by reconstituting the government on less "exalted" (that is, radical) lines.[135] It was too late, however; in April 1823, a French expedition analogous to the Austrian invasion of Naples was launched under the leadership of Louis XVIII's surviving nephew, the duc d'Angoulême, and with the enthusiastic support of revanchist diplomats like the vicomte de Chateaubriand.[136]

Ever the pragmatist—and anxious not to be out-flanked by that seasoned military paymaster Ouvrard—James now offered his services to the French Prime Minister, the comte de Villèle: just as his brother had supplied the Austrian army in Italy with cash, so he now made himself "useful" to d'Angoulême, even raising the ransom money needed to buy Ferdinand VII's release.[137] And just as military intervention had necessitated a new loan in Vienna, so too in Paris the government was obliged to fund its military adventure by borrowing: in 1823 James was at last able to overcome the suspicion of the Restoration regime and secure a major French loan. Worth 462 million francs (nominal) or £18.5 million, it was the biggest single issue of rentes by a French government between 1815 and 1848 and had been preceded by a smaller issue of 120 million in 6 per cent treasury bills, also handled by James. Given the importance of such issues throughout James's long career in Paris, it is worth noting how he pulled off this deal. Rather as his father had initially squeezed out his rivals in Kassel, James won his first rentes issue by outbidding Lafitte and three other Paris bankers, offering a price (89.55) which was actually above the current market rate. This was more than enough to beat the rival group's offer of 87.75, but it did not leave James out of pocket: the success of the operation quickly pushed rentes up above 90 and by the end of 1823 they had reached 100.[138]

The difference between Naples and Spain was that after the restoration of the Spanish Bourbon (which had been achieved by the end of 1824), the Rothschilds declined—after contemplating a joint operation with Baring and Reid, Irving—to lend to his neo-absolutist regime without guarantees which the French government was unwilling to give.[139] There were three reasons for this: the regime's refusal to recognise and redeem the bonds issued by the Cortes,[140] its refusal to repay France the costs of the invasion and, finally, the bankers' suspicion that any money lent to Ferdinand might be used in a last and probably vain attempt to recapture his former colonies in South America, which had been fighting successfully for their independence since 1808. After all, had not the 1820 revolution begun with a mutiny by soldiers about to be sent across the Atlantic? And were not Ferdinand's advisers convinced that recovering the American colonies would solve all his financial problems? It was the South American dimension which particularly concerned the British government. While London had been prepared to put up with the French expedition into Spain, despite its implicit negation of Wellington's victory in the Peninsular

War, the notion that this might be the prelude to some kind of reconquest of Latin America, with whose fledgling republics Britain was rapidly forging close economic ties, was wholly unpalatable. As the Austrian ambassador in Paris reported to Metternich: "Although the House of Rothschild may pretend that their sympathies are purely monarchist, the recognition of the engagements entered into by the Cortes Government, and the independence of the Spanish colonies, would provide a far wider field for his [Nathan's] financial enterprises and afford political security, the value of which they do not fail to appreciate."[141] In short, the Rothschild role in Spain had been ambivalent: initially showing signs of interest in the Cortes government, then financing the French invasion, but declining to bankroll the restored regime. James, Salomon and Nathan all came under conflicting pressures from the governments in Paris, Vienna and London; but the final outcome was a united and carefully calculated policy of non-commitment, which was continued throughout the decade. As James put it succinctly in 1826, "Spain's bankruptcy is uppermost in my mind."[142]

The Rothschilds kept a safe distance from the numerous bond issues by the former Spanish colonies which were generating such speculative enthusiasm in London at the time of the French intervention.[143] The years 1822–4 were the time of the great South American "bubble," as investors rushed to lend to new republics like Chile, Colombia, Buenos Aires and Guatemala. Even as unlikely a figure as Gregor MacGregor, a Scottish adventurer and former general in the Venezuelan army, was able to raise £200,000 by styling himself the "Caique of Poyais" and persuading investors that the malarial swamp in Honduras which he claimed to rule was ripe for development.[144] With a bravado it is impossible not to admire, MacGregor even wrote to Nathan outlining a project for an independent Hebrew colony in his "kingdom" on an island called Ruatan.[145] From all this the Rothschilds remained aloof, with one exception: Brazil. There were two reasons for this preference. Firstly, Brazil remained closely linked to Portugal and therefore enjoyed close commercial ties with Britain;[146] secondly, it retained a monarchical form of government even after gaining independence in 1825. (Indeed, the fact that the Brazilian Emperor was married to an Austrian princess inclined some contemporaries to regard Brazil as a kind of American representative of the Holy Alliance, though this exaggerated Austrian influence.)[147] Nathan's first step in this direction came in 1823, with a loan of £1.5 million to Portugal, secured on Brazilian revenues.[148] This once again demonstrated his willingness to lend to a constitutional regime, as the Portuguese King had accepted a Spanish-style constitution drafted by the Lisbon Cortes on his return from Brazil in 1822. The water for Brazilian bonds proper was tested in 1824 by a City group led by Thomas Wilson, which sold over a million pounds' worth of 5 per cent bonds at an issue price of 75. When these rose to 87, Nathan took over, issuing a further £2 million in 1825 at a price of 85.[149] As Heinrich Heine later joked, Nathan was now "the great Rothschild, the great Nathan Rothschild, Nathan the Wise, with whom the Emperor of Brazil has pawned his diamond crown."[150] Though it fell into disuse during the middle decades of the century, the relationship with Brazil was to prove one of the firm's most enduring.

By the summer of 1825, therefore, the Rothschilds had succeeded triumphantly in establishing themselves as the leading specialists in European public finance—and not only European. One by one, the powers of the Holy Alliance had followed the British lead, entrusting their loans to Rothschilds: first Prussia, then Austria, then Russia. Finally, France too had to abandon her preference for more established Parisian houses. In the space of three years, the brothers had provided the crucial financial assistance which enabled Austria to suppress revolution in Naples, and France to restore royal absolutism in Spain. Yet their contemporary image as "bankers to the Holy Alliance" was in some respects a caricature. It understated what might be called their political agnosticism, their tendency to assess business opportunities in financial rather than political terms. James neatly summed up the Rothschild attitude to Restoration politics in an exuberant letter to Nathan in late 1826:

> It would be a mortal sin to be dependent on a Villèle and on a Canning and on what these Gentlemen may wish to say in the Chambers, as a result of which one will be unable to sleep at night, and why so? Because they want more than they can afford to pay and we have to thank the dear Lord that we can extricate ourselves from this situation. What we now want to say is, "[You want] a loan? You can have one, as much as you want, and draw a certain profit from it. But to keep all the millions, to that we say no!"[151]

The attraction of counter-revolution, in other words, was not that it restored despots, but that it generated new financial needs. Nor were conservative regimes given preferential treatment. As the conditions attached to the 1818 Prussian loan show, Nathan in fact saw constitutional structures for controlling government finance as preferable to the extravagance and inefficiency which often characterised absolutist regimes, and which in any case tended sooner or later to generate revolutionary pressures. Ultimately, that was why he was unwilling to lend to absolutist Spain without a guarantee from constitutional France. Such views would also condition the Rothschilds' attitude to the increasingly reactionary drift of French policy under Charles X, who succeeded his brother in September 1824. And if, on the other hand, the Rothschilds preferred to lend to a constitutional monarchy like Brazil rather than a republic like Colombia, events would soon confirm the economic rationality of that preference. Where Laffitte, the follower of Saint-Simon, was "truly liberal" (in Byron's phrase), Rothschild was more politically ambivalent, a conditional supporter of the Holy Alliance at best.

Saving an Old Lady

If the French Prime Minister Villèle had hoped the large 1823 loan would ultimately "free him from the hands of these gentlemen"—meaning the Rothschilds—he quickly found himself more firmly in their grip. The sustained rise of the rentes in 1823–4 was not so much proof of "the strength and power of France"; it was proof that interest rates throughout Europe were falling.[152] This presented the Rothschilds with a new business opportunity: the conversion of government bonds bearing higher rates of interest into new bonds with lower rates. Though new to France, such operations had been undertaken in Britain before (for example, in 1717 and 1748–57). Indeed, Vansittart had converted £150 million of 5 per cents into 4 per cents in 1822; and two years later a further £75 million of 4 per cents were converted into 3.5 per cents by Frederick Robinson, his successor.[153] For the governments which undertook such conversions, the benefit was obvious: the annual burden of debt service was significantly reduced. For the Rothschilds, the benefit was obvious too: such large-scale operations justified fat fees. The only difficulty lay in persuading bondholders who had enjoyed substantial capital appreciation and wished to continue enjoying annual interest of 4 or 5 per cent to accept less. One reason for the boom in continental and Latin American bonds between 1822 and 1824 was precisely the refusal of British bondholders to do so. Confronted with the option of converting their British 5 or 4 per cents or redeeming them and reinvesting the cash in higher-yielding assets, many did the latter, fuelling the speculative fever.[154]

In France, when Villèle proposed to convert 2,800 million francs of 5 per cent rentes into 3 per cents issued at 75, the bondholders' reaction took a different form. The arguments for conversion were the same as in England: more than a third of the French budget was being consumed by the costs of servicing the state's debt and, with 5 per cents rising from 93 to a peak of 106, the time for such an operation seemed right.[155] But the proposal became mixed up with the vexed question of compensation for losses suffered by royalist émigrés during the Revolution and was narrowly rejected in the Upper House following spurious claims by Chateaubriand and others (notably financiers like Casimir Périer who had been excluded from the deal) that it was an Anglo-Austrian racket to defraud the humble French rentier.[156] A second, heavily modified scheme—which offered to convert 5 per cents on a voluntary basis in return for tax breaks—was pushed through in 1825, but only 30 million francs' worth of bonds were exchanged, leaving James with a substantial sum on his hands at a time when the market price was falling.[157] Ouvrard later claimed that the Rothschilds had doubly insured themselves against the possible failure of the first conversion scheme by not only insisting on an official safety net of 100 million in treasury bills (to be issued if the banks were left with large quantities of rentes on their hands), but also surreptitiously selling both 5 per cents and 3 per cents.[158] Suspicions that the Rothschilds were cutting their losses by selling rentes—which were justified in 1825[159]—brought to an end the brief period of harmonious relations with Villèle which had begun in 1823. In the wake of the conversion fiasco, the French premier made a concerted effort to direct government business back to James's rivals in Paris, organising Laffitte and the Receivers-General into a syndicate to undertake a loan to Haiti and to issue 1,000 million francs of 3 per cent rentes for the benefit of the dispossessed émigrés.[160]

Yet the reality was that the Rothschilds had enjoyed a lucky escape. As Nathan's well informed *Times* obituarist remembered:

> [H]ad it [the Villèle conversion] been carried, the convulsion in the money markets of Europe which shortly followed it would probably have proved fatal to him with such a burden on his shoulders, notwithstanding all his vast resources. Indeed, it was a common remark of his own at the time, that neither he nor the houses engaged in the undertaking with him could have stood the shock.[161]

It was indeed fortunate that Villèle's scheme foundered when it did. For 1825 was to be the year in which the great speculative bubble burst on the London stock exchange. And not only would it have been awkward for Nathan to have been left holding millions of 3 per cent rentes at such a time; the conversion might also have made it more difficult for his brother James to assist him in containing the English banking crisis of that year.

The 1825 crisis had in many ways been prophesied by Nathan and the other opponents of the decision to resume gold convertibility six years before. Between 1818 and 1823 the Bank of England's note circulation fell by around a third, a dramatic contraction. In 1824 a temporary influx of gold generated a big expansion in the note issue, but this was followed by an equally sharp contraction in 1825. At the same time, though fiscal policy was gradually being brought under control following Vansittart's resignation in December 1822, the enthusiasm of Huskisson at the Board of Trade for cuts in import duties made balancing the budget harder than it might have been. The medium-term aim of these first steps towards free trade was to increase the volume of commercial activity, in conformity with the principles of the political economists; but the short-term effect was to reduce revenues. Even with sharp cuts in expenditure, the government still found itself having to resort to both short- and long-term borrowing.[162] Moreover, as Nathan complained, Huskisson's policy was also giving rise to a trade deficit: as he told Herries in April 1825, "The consequence of admitting foreign goods (which had not been met by any corresponding liberality on the other side of the water) was, that all the gold was going out of the country. He had himself sent two millions within the last few weeks; the funds fell rapidly, and no advantage is gained by any human being."[163] It was this outflow of gold which lay behind the sharp monetary contraction of 1825.[164] Under these circumstances, the high prices which had been reached on the London stock exchange during the 1822–4 bubble could not be sustained. In April 1825 the market began to slide. The heaviest falls were experienced by British industrial securities and Latin American bonds: the Brazilian bonds which Nathan had issued at 85 were down to 81.25 by July and just 56 by March of the following year.[165] But the bonds of the formerly Spanish republics fared even worse: Mexican, Colombian and Peruvian all fell below 20. Even the best paper—British 3 per cent consols—was affected, falling below 75 compared with a peak of more than 97 the previous year.[166] Such a severe asset-price deflation was bound to bring a banking crisis in its wake.

There is an old anecdote which describes Nathan threatening to exhaust the Bank of England's reserve by bringing an immense number of small denomination notes to its counter and demanding gold.[167] This is another Rothschild myth which is diametrically opposed to the truth. In fact, Nathan's relations with the Bank of England were close and mutually beneficial. Beginning in the summer of 1823, when he borrowed 3 million silver dollars to finance his first loan to Portugal, he set out to establish a direct line of communication with the Governor with the intention of circumventing the Bank's established bullion brokers Mocatta & Goldsmid. It worked, though his parallel challenge to Mocatta & Goldsmid's position as the East India Company's sole bullion brokers and his later efforts to deal directly with the Mint were thwarted.[168] Thereafter, Nathan's dealings with the Bank were regular, as he later told the 1832 Committee on the Bank Charter (with characteristic oversimplification): "You bring in your bank notes, they give you the gold."[169] Much of the time, Nathan was a buyer or borrower of gold and silver.[170] In December 1825, however, it was the other way round: the Rothschilds gave the Bank their gold, supplying the "Old Lady" of Threadneedle Street with enough specie from the conti-

nent to avert a suspension of cash payments. James had in fact been sending substantial quantities of gold across the Channel since the beginning of 1825, if not
earlier. In the first week of January alone, he had sent gold worth nearly £500,000,
which he expected to "impress your Bank" (meaning the Bank of England). By the
middle of the month, he was talking about "our old established practice" of
"buy[ing] some gold whenever we can find any."[171]

It was at the end of the year, however, that his assistance mattered most. As a succession of banks stopped their payments—six failed in London alone—the Governor of the Bank informed the government that a suspension of cash payments
might be the only way to avert a general financial collapse, as he would be unable to
meet the demand for gold likely when exchequer bills fell due. Liverpool and his colleagues were determined not to sanction this, suspecting the Governor of exaggerating the shortage of bullion to undo the work of the 1819 Committee. On the other
hand, the Bank's reserve of *coined* gold which could be used immediately was running out fast, and the Cabinet was sufficiently alarmed at the prospect of an unauthorised suspension by the Bank that "orders had been given to the regiment of
Guards to remain in the City in case of disturbance."[172] Some City insiders—
notably Henry Thornton, who was battling to rescue Williams & Co.—had already
realised that "the Jew King of the City, Rothschild" had a stock of gold in reserve,
and according to one account, "by dint of a little persuasion and exhortation [by
Alexander Baring] the Jew was induced to bring out his gold, first charging 2½ per
cent commission, then saying he did it out of public spirit, and lastly begging that
they would never tell it or he would be besieged night and day."[173]

The government, however, may have hesitated to approach Nathan because of
his well-known antipathy towards Huskisson, whose policies, as we have seen, he
held responsible for the crisis. On December 17 – the turning point of the crisis—
the wife of Charles Arbuthnot, the Joint Secretary of the Treasury, recorded in her
diary "the detestation in which Mr Huskisson is held in the City" as well as their
"utmost contempt" for the Chancellor, Robinson. The feeling was evidently mutual.
According to her informant, Nathan's old friend Herries (now Financial Secretary to
the Treasury),

> Mr Huskisson has done all he can also to ruin Rothschild by spreading
> reports that their house was in danger, & he made Mr Canning write to
> Paris to enquire into the affairs of [Rothschild's] brother. Ld. Granville
> sent his private secretary to pump Rothschild. R found out what he was
> at & instantly shewed him his accounts & proved to him that he was
> worth 2½ millions.

Evidently, this led to a change of heart on both sides, which no doubt owed something to Herries's mediation and Huskisson's absence: "Rothschild has made the
most gigantic efforts to assist the Bank and he told Mr Herries that, if he had been
applied to sooner, he wd. have prevented all the difficulty. As it is, if they can hold
out till Monday or Tuesday, he will have enormous sums over in sovereigns from
Paris, & the pressure will be entirely relieved."[174]

Nathan had done two things that evening: firstly, he had advised the government
to intervene in the money market itself by purchasing exchequer bills to inject liquidity into the market; secondly, and more important, he had delivered gold to the

Bank, beginning with £300,000 of sovereigns, and continuing with larger sums in the succeeding weeks until confidence had finally been restored.[175] In fact, the reserve touched its lowest level (just over a million pounds) on December 24; however, Nathan was still delivering gold a year later, pledging a million pounds in the course of March 1826 and a total of £10 million by September.[176] His principal source was James in Paris (as he later reminded Nathan, "I emptied my coffers for your gold").[177] But, as Nathan recalled, "there was a good deal [of gold] supplied from the whole world; I imported it, and it was imported almost from every country; we got it from Russia, from Turkey, from Austria, from almost every quarter in the world." The Bank's ledgers describe the influx of myriad kinds of gold coin from France, Italy, Holland and Germany.[178]

The crisis of 1825 had come close to being another 1797 (the year when the Bank had last suspended cash payments), a monetary crisis with the potential to destabilise the British economy as a whole. As it was, 73 out of 770 country banks failed and, as Huskisson himself admitted, the country came within forty-eight hours of "putting stop to all dealings between man and man except by barter."[179] Looking back in 1839, Wellington had no doubt who had averted disaster: "Had it not been for the most extraordinary exertions—above all on the part of old Rothschild—the Bank must have stopped payment."[180] Of course, Nathan would not have made such immense deliveries of gold without asking for a generous commission in return. The operation has to be seen as part of his campaign to establish himself as the dominant force in the London bullion market. On the other hand, there is no reason why he should have bailed out the Bank and the government free of charge, when the crisis was so manifestly the product of policies he had advised against. The rescue of the Bank was a remarkable achievement which owed everything to the international nature of the Rothschilds' operations. In effect, the brothers were establishing that system of international monetary co-operation which would later be performed routinely by central banks, and on which the gold standard came to depend. Increasingly, their position in the international bullion market was becoming as dominant as their position in the international bond market.

Byron was therefore not far wide of the mark when he suggested in *Don Juan* that Baring and Rothschild reigned over both royalists and liberals, and that their loans could "seat a nation or upset a throne." He erred only in regarding the two bankers as financial equals. In 1815 they had been. By 1825 they were not. As early as August 1820 the Bremen delegate to the German Confederation's Diet in Frankfurt had a conversation with his Austrian counterpart Count Buol which acutely identified the unrivalled extent of the Rothschilds' political influence in Europe:

This house has, through its enormous financial transactions and its banking and credit connections, actually achieved the position of a real Power; it has to such an extent acquired control of the general money market that it is in a position either to hinder or to promote, as it feels inclined, the movements and operations of potentates, and even of the greatest European Powers. Austria needs the Rothschilds' help for her present demonstration against Naples, and Prussia would long ago have been finished with her constitution if the House of Rothschild had not made it possible for her to postpone the evil day.[181]

The Frankfurt banker Simon Moritz von Bethmann echoed this judgement in a letter written at around the same time:

> N. M. Rothschild, who is equipped with a vulgar talent, audacity and vanity, constitutes the centrifugal point around which the stock exchange revolves. He alone determines the exchange, buying and selling £100,000 each day . . . I can well understand why the Rothschilds are such useful instruments for the [Austrian] government.[182]

Both men had their reasons for disliking this phenomenon, as we shall see; but they did not exaggerate it.

FIVE

"Hue and Cry"
(1826–1829)

Seyd Umschlungen Millionen.

—CAPTION TO A GERMAN CARICATURE
OF NATHAN ROTHSCHILD[1]

It is not wholly surprising, in view of the decisive role they played in so many post-war financial transactions, that the Rothschilds first became famous in the 1820s. Even as early as 1816 Carl was conscious that he and his brothers were becoming "very famous" in their home town. As he told James, "these days a lot is written about us in consequence of the freedom of the Press."[2] He encountered similar publicity when he visited Berlin later the same year. Carl evidently felt uneasy about such celebrity, not least because of the inaccuracy of much that was written. "We are every day in the news," he complained to Amschel. "Last week you were mentioned in the papers in connection with the poor . . . Today you are mentioned in connection with grain, and that you are going to become [the Elector of Hesse-Kassel's] Minister at the Diet of the Confederation."[3] It was the same in Hamburg:

> Whenever any one of us arrives gossip and marvellous stories are spread by people. Lawätz told me that at some party in town the story was told that the King of Prussia wrote to us asking to arrange a bond issue of three millions. We are supposed to have replied that this was not necessary, because we were able to advance this sum from our own money.[4]

Amschel too was struck by the public propensity to exaggerate: "People think that we are ten times as rich as we really are."[5] "Wherever we go now," Carl found, "people think it is a political trip."[6] The arrival of James at the St Petersburg stock exchange, or of a ship chartered by Nathan in port, was enough to bring business to a standstill. James had only to buy a certain security in Paris for "everybody" to buy it. Unlike Carl, the youngest brother relished this new-found fame. As he told Nathan, "It is indeed nice to possess so much prestige." "They all say: 'Il n'a jamais existé à Paris une maison aussi fameuse que la nôtre.' . . . We are now regarded as *the* first . . . I sent last week [bills for] three millions to the Banque de France. There was a lot of rubbish among them—yet not a single one was returned."[7] Salomon and Nathan too could make light of publicity. "We are not going to cry about the fact that you have been caricatured," he told Nathan. "As you say, so are kings and emperors . . . May God grant that this is the worst thing that ever happens to us . . . May my Anselm and your Lionel also be caricatured, please God, as soon as they become well known in this world. I wish this for our darling children . . . [Idle] dreams!'[8] Nathan's attitude was typically robust: "*Gagesh* [nobody] is not being written about."[9] Press interest—including unsubstantiated claims that they were in financial difficulties[10]—was merely the price of success.

Public Relations

As the brothers' comments suggest, little of this publicity was good publicity. From the very earliest years of their fame, the Rothschilds were subjected to markedly more vilification than glorification in the public sphere. Of course, most monarchs, politicians and other public figures in the early nineteenth century occasionally found themselves held up to ridicule in newspapers, pamphlets and other media, especially in those parts of Europe where censorship was lax. But the Rothschilds often seemed to attract a specially intense form of criticism. One reason for this was their religion. To those who regretted the steps taken towards religious equality in the Revolutionary period, the fact that the most economically successful family of the Restoration era was Jewish was an inexhaustible source of irritation. However, other factors undoubtedly played a part, and it would be a mistake to equate anti-Semitism with anti-Rothschildism.[11] A good deal of the hostility which the brothers encountered after 1815 can be attributed to plain economic rivalry. The other Frankfurt bankers, for example, would have been envious of the meteoric rise of the Rothschilds even if they had not been Jews. Moreover, some of the Rothschilds' most determined opponents were other Jews—as in Kassel.[12] Additionally, anti-Rothschildism had a political dimension: their identification with conservative regimes and the policy of the Holy Alliance made them targets for liberal criticism. The bad publicity of the Restoration era was therefore often a synthesis of economic envy and religious antipathy, with an admixture of political radicalism.

In Frankfurt, for example, the Rothschilds' emergence as a financial great power threatened to eclipse the Bethmanns, hitherto the town's pre-eminent bankers. Simon Moritz, the dominant partner in this period, viewed his own relative decline with remarkable and indeed admirable equanimity; of all their many rivals, he yielded with the best grace. As early as September 1815 he actively sought to work in partnership with Salomon and James, observing in a letter from Paris to his own house in Frankfurt, "The more contact I have with the two Rothschilds here, the more confidence they give me."[13] Although he did not pretend to like Nathan's "audacity and vanity," he insisted that he was "far from wanting to criticise or envy" the Rothschilds, and described Salomon as "a very estimable man of character, to whom I am sincerely well disposed." He even referred to Nathan as "our fellow countryman." "The five Rothschild brothers are a remarkable phenomenon of our time," he wrote in February 1822. "What they lack in genius they make up for with relentless activity, an enviable unity and mutual consideration." However, such remarks were partly informed by Bethmann's awareness that the best place to be in the 1820s was on the Rothschilds' coat-tails.[14] His mood changed markedly when he found himself left out of the 1821 Neapolitan loan, in which he believed Carl had promised him a share. "I do not think it fair," he wrote angrily, "that I should commit myself to you for a period of months, while you find it suits you to retain the option whether you will keep your offer open or withdraw it."[15]

Such complaints about the Rothschilds' ruthless methods were nothing new: it had been the perennial complaint of the Gentile business community in Frankfurt that the Jews' business methods were "unfair." Early German caricatures of the Rothschilds emphasise this point: in I. Nussgeig's *Musterreiter*, Carl is portrayed as "Blauschild," a travelling pedlar heading south to Italy with his bedraggled pony bearing all kinds of wares, including muskets and swords.[16] A later caricature contrasts the elegant figure of Bethmann, riding his coach-and-four in fashionable apparel, with a scruffy and grotesquely ugly Amschel, standing atop a large cash box which a two-headed eagle struggles vainly to pull forward.[17]

As in the past, such business rivalry also had a political dimension. The fact that the Rothschilds were now "richer than Bethmann" was widely seen as evidence of the need to restore the traditional legal restrictions on the Jewish minority.[18] In Amschel's words, it "irked the Gentiles that a Jew should set the tone." Hostility was growing daily, he reported in September 1815: "They begrudge us Jews the eyes in our heads . . . [and want] to drink our blood."[19] Matters were not helped by the fact that other Jews were inclined to boast about the Rothschilds' wealth as a matter of communal pride, something which Amschel and Carl felt only fuelled Gentile resentment.[20] This resentment generated a spate of anti-Jewish pamphlets and plays in the post-war years—the best-known was *Unser Verkehr*, about a cowardly Jewish soldier—and finally boiled over in the so-called "Hep" riots of August 1819, when a noisy crowd rampaged through the Judengasse, chanting the traditional anti-Jewish slogan "Hep-Hep! Jude verreck!" and vandalising houses. A good deal of this hostility was specifically targeted at the Rothschild family. In 1817 noisy crowds had gathered outside Amschel's newly acquired garden, itself a symbol of Jewish social mobility, to mock his even more recent ennoblement, "chanting 'Baron Amschel' and all sorts of stupidities."[21] Caricatures were pinned to his door and the Rothschilds' office windows were among those broken during the "Hep" riots.[22] At around the same time, Amschel received death threats.[23]

Such demonstrations—which prompted Amschel to contemplate leaving Frankfurt altogether[24]—do much to explain the Rothschilds' ambivalence about popular political participation. When Metternich expressed his disapproval of the riots (a disapproval which, of course, extended to all "outbreaks of the vulgar masses") he did much to reinforce the Rothschilds' sense that conservatism might offer them more personal security than the more radical forms of liberalism. This was especially true in Germany, where traditionally the Habsburg Emperor had given the Jews "protection" from the local populace and where the proto-liberal associations of the Restoration era espoused a nationalism which was occasionally anti-Jewish in its rhetoric.[25] At the same time, the closer the Rothschilds drew to the established order, the easier it was for its critics to identify them with it. When marriage between Jews and Gentiles was legalised in Frankfurt—one of a number of minor concessions wrung from the Frankfurt Senate in the 1820s—the eighty-year-old Goethe was moved to comment:

This scandalous law will undermine all family sense of morality, intimately associated with religion as it is. When this is passed, how can a

Jewess be prevented from becoming Principal Lady of the Bed Chamber? Who knows whether or not bribery has played a role in all this; who
knows whether or not the the all-powerful Rothschilds are behind it?[26]

If so august and enlightened a figure could express such a view, it is no wonder the
Rothschilds were content to see popular participation in German political life kept
to a minimum.

Anti-Rothschildism was not confined to Frankfurt. Wherever the Rothschilds
secured a large proportion of government business, local rivals often reacted with
religiously-tinged attacks. In Vienna, for example, the 1820 lottery loan which
Salomon arranged in tandem with David Parish was widely criticised as "a shameful
Jewish ramp" because of the substantial profits the bankers stood to make.[27] Sometimes, it should be stressed, such attacks had no religious dimension. Six years later
it was Parish himself who directed one of the most vitriolic blasts against the Rothschilds of the entire period. Parish had gradually been surpassed by his erstwhile
partner: by 1823 he was the junior partner (if not the messenger boy) in Nathan's
loan to Portugal, and his eclipse was completed by the 1825–6 crisis, which claimed
Parish's Viennese bank Fries & Co. as one of its victims. On the eve of drowning
himself in the Danube, Parish wrote four letters—to his brother John, to the banker
Geymüller, to Metternich and to Salomon himself—all blaming his downfall on the
Rothschilds and pledging to discredit them publicly. Metternich, said Parish, had
"sacrificed me to the cupidity of a family who, for all their riches, are heartless men
who only care about their cash box." He had been "deceived" by Salomon "in the
most shameful way and rewarded for very considerable service with the blackest
ingratitude." The strong implication was that the Rothschilds had secured Metternich's "protection" and left Parish out in the cold by underhand means.[28] Parish's letters show that it was perfectly possible to be anti-Rothschild without being
anti-Jewish. Yet few German journalists could resist alluding to the family's religion
when reporting such stories. A good example is Friedrich List's newspaper report of
a minor case of embezzlement by a clerk at the Paris house in 1826, which referred
quite gratuitously to "Rothschild, the pride of Israel, the mighty lender and master
of all the coined and uncoined silver and gold in the Old World, before whose
money box Kings and Emperors humbly bow . . ."[29]

The brothers encountered similar kinds of hostility in Paris as well. "It's always a
case of 'The Jew has done too well, has done this, has done that,'" Salomon reported
to Nathan in October 1815.[30] These were the complaints of business rivals, who
battled to elbow the Rothschilds aside in the scramble for post-war pickings in the
French capital. Ten years later, by contrast, James found himself the target of a primarily political critique. The liberal Fournier-Verneuil's *Paris*, published in 1826,
contains the first of many French claims that the government—in this case Villèle's—was the corrupt puppet of "the aristocracy of finance, the most unfeeling and
ignoble of all aristocracies" at whose head stood none other than "M. le baron R."
Fournier quoted Chateaubriand (an unlikely ally for a liberal): "How hard it would
be if Providence had shaken the world, thrust the heir of so many kings under the
[guillotine's] blade, led our armies from Cadiz to Moscow [and] chained Bonaparte
on a rock, simply in order that MM. Villèle, Rodchild [*sic*] and company can make

money with the debris of our glory and our liberties." Even this struck Fournier as understating the problem, however:

> The Jew R. and his co-religionists . . . see in the kingdom of the heavens no more than . . . money devoted to usury . . . It is a singular race of men; I am not intolerant, but Napoleon, in calling together the grand Sanhedrin [Jewish assembly] did not create a [new] Frenchman. They . . . are still Jews, and nothing but Jews. I do not hold it against them that they retain their faith; but I reproach them for profiting from all quarrels, for charging them up; they are everywhere. They were in Poland on the corpses of our brothers; they are [currently] supplying Ibraham [Pasha], and they are dancing at this very moment on the tomb of Achilles.[31]

The references to the Ottoman oppression of the Greeks make the author's liberal sentiments obvious. Equally evident, however, is an anti-Jewish rhetoric which would only later come to be located on the political right. Fournier's was in many ways an embryonic version of that elaborate conspiracy theory which was to evolve and expand for years to come in France, and which almost invariably ascribed a central and malign political influence to the Rothschilds.

In London too—where anti-Jewish feeling is often assumed to have been less prevalent—the 1820s saw a spate of more or less hostile public allusions to Rothschild power. Indeed, the volume of such allusions was probably greater in London than anywhere else—a reflection partly of Nathan's relatively greater importance, but also of the freedom of the press. Again, hostility often had its roots in business rivalry. If the rivals were both Jews—as when Mocatta & Goldsmid denounced "the overwhelming attempt of Mr Rothschild to benefit himself at the expense of any person or establishment"—this could be acrimonious without having a religious dimension.[32] But when Alexander Baring referred to his principal rival, it was often (disdainfully) as "the Jew." According to Laffitte, it was explicitly on religious grounds that Baring sought to exclude the Rothschilds from the French reparations loan in 1817.[33] Although James tended to think this was merely a pretext, he acknowledged that a measure of prejudice was at work:

> In Frankfurt one got used to [it] so one is not astonished [there], but here the case is the contrary and if something of this kind happens here, one is more amazed . . . Yesterday Laffitte asked me to come and see him. Baring came to see him and gave clear explanations that he could not possibly make [the loan] with us. True, he himself was not of the same opinion [but] his associés and the English . . . are prejudiced against the Jews. If he were to take us in partnership, the operation would be spoiled. He is unable to do such a business with a Jew . . . It all originates in Labouchère's pride and in Sillem's envy; as these two *are* Hope [& Co.], they think that their honour would suffer if they had to get in line with a Frankfurt Jew and that we would become great by that fact . . . Baring told him: "These gentlemen are working like Jews. How could we co-operate? Their principles are different. They are working on twenty transactions at the same time . . . with the only aim to do business. It is like stock-jobbing. Take for example the Prussian business. They cut off Prussia's credit . . . then this printing [of circulars] before

anything is known." . . . He added that we are right in what we did
because we succeeded and made money. However, he does not want—
so he said—to do business in this manner. Now we try—so he said—to
bring down the English stocks after having sold ours, in order to buy
them back.[34]

It was the Rothschilds' (very successful) methods, in other words, which Baring
found objectionable; but he instinctively thought of these as "Jewish" in character.
Such attitudes were widespread. *Devotion in Dukes Place*, one of the earliest English
caricatures thought to be of Nathan, shows him at the front of a Jewish congregation in the Great Synagogue "returning thanks for a loan." (see illustration 5.i).

As elsewhere, however, there was also a political dimension to anti-Rothschildism. The Rothschilds, as we have seen, often worried in the post-war years about the
extent of Baring's political influence in London and Paris, seeing this as the key to
his dominance of the post-war reparations business. To less influential businessmen,
however, it was the Rothschilds who seemed to have the political power. As early as
1818 an anonymous member of the stock exchange wrote to Lord Liverpool, attacking Nathan for his opposition to the resumption of cash payments:

> Let me inform you, the Capitalists of Money Market . . . have set their
> faces against your Plan because it serves not their purpose or puts
> Money in their Pockets. The Jew interest alias Mr Rothschild are . . .
> straining every nerve to defeat your objects . . . If a Man asks Mr Roth-

5.i: *Devotion in Dukes Place—or Contractors returning thanks for a Loan* (1818).

schild, what is his opinion of the Funds, he answers they must be better and at the very same time he acts contrary[;] [that] in so great a country as this, Your Lordship and Colleagues should be the Sport [&] the caprice of a Jew Party . . . is truly lamentable.[35]

A cartoon of 1824 made a similar allusion to Nathan's role in the debate about resumption, portraying Nathan rising above the stock exchange in a balloon. Although the balloon is held aloft by a bull and a bear and carries the inscription "Everything must rise," it is held down by ballast labelled "Cash Bags."[36] Here too there is a religious allusion. Indeed, the most striking feature of this cartoon is the ambiguous way it portrays Nathan's relationship to a group of poorer Jews. Nathan holds two flags, bearing the mottoes "Those who give to the poor lend to the Lord" and "Charity covers a multitude of sins"; but he says: "I am going to receive my Dividends," and a figure on the left, emerging from Capel Court with a copy of *The Times*, exclaims: "We stop the press to announce that one of the greatest capitalists in the City has gone on a secret *Financial Expedition*." The six poor Jews on the right—labelled "The Old Stock reduced"—are left to direct their lamentations to King, the guard of the Royal Mail coach, who is carrying a Way-bill bearing eight Jewish names, each of which has been allotted a shilling.[37]

If these critics portrayed Nathan as an interloper within the City, it was nevertheless also plausible to portray him as the personification of the City as a whole: as the leader of the "Change-Alley People," of "Muckworm," the gang of financiers and stockjobbers whom the Tory radical William Cobbett blamed for the post-war policy of deflation. A graphic example of this sort of critique is another 1824 cartoon, *A New Court Fire Screen*, which portrays the Rothschild-founded Alliance Assurance Company as a racket for defrauding country gentlemen. At the same time, this print also attacks Nathan's connections with the Holy Alliance. The company's building has an inscription which reads "Hollow Alliance Fire and Life Preserving Office" and is surmounted by five royal busts marked "Russia," "Prussia," "Naples," "France" and "Austria." At the very top of the print is a longer inscription which alludes to the Rothschilds' counter-revolutionary role:

> Persons insured in this Office will be supplied gratis with a Box of veritable German Paste which if applied according to the directions of Prince H [or M?] & Co. will prevent fire. NB Should any Person obtain fraudulently a Box of the above miraculous Paste without being insured in this Office it will have the contrary effect and consume the House on the first appearance of the New Moon.[38]

Although the emphasis here is on the Rothschilds' foreignness—Nathan and Moses Montefiore are pictured speaking French to one another, and there is a German porter with a thick accent—there is no mistaking the Jewishness of the three brokers in the foreground, congratulating one another on their profits.

It was, however, a complex crisis at the highest level of British politics which did most to bring Nathan into the British public eye. In the wake of Lord Liverpool's illness in February 1827, a ministry had been formed by Canning which united Liberal Tories, notably Huskisson, with Whigs like Lansdowne, but excluded Ultra-Tories led by the Duke of Wellington, who shared Nathan's distaste for Huskisson's liberal economic policies. When Canning unexpectedly died in August of the same year, the King commissioned the Chancellor of the Exchequer, Robin-son (now Lord Goderich), to form a new Cabinet. But the King's insistence that Herries be appointed Chancellor (as well as his refusal to have the Whig Lord Hol-land as Foreign Secretary) meant that Goderich's term in office was exceedingly brief. At the Whig leader George Tierney's instigation, Goderich and Huskisson appointed Lord Althorp as chairman of a finance committee without consulting Herries, prompting the latter to threaten resignation unless Althorp's appointment was rescinded, and Huskisson to threaten resignation if it was. In the event, Goderich himself resigned in January 1828 and the King turned to Wellington to form a government—though the conflict between Huskisson and Herries was resolved only when Wellington agreed to replace him as Chancellor with Goulborn, demoting Herries to the office of Master of the Mint.[39]

The significance of the whole tangled affair lay in the identification of Herries with the King and his increasingly influential physician and private secretary Sir William Knighton; with the opposition within the Tory party to Catholic emanci-pation; and, perhaps decisively, with the financial interests—principally those of New Court—which were hostile to Huskisson. As early as August 1827 the Ultra-Tory *Morning Chronicle* was suggesting that Herries's close connections with Nathan disqualified him from serving as Chancellor.[40] In the debate which followed Her-ries's demotion in February 1828, this charge was repeated by the Whig MP for Hertford, Thomas Duncombe, who called for the "mystery . . . about the late change" to be "cleared up, by the rising of the curtain which concealed persons of great consequence, incorporeal as well as corporeal":

> There is . . . deny it who can, a secret influence behind the throne, whose form is never seen, whose name is never breathed, who has access to all the secrets of State, and who manages all the sudden springs of ministerial arrangement . . . Closely connected with this invisible, this incorporeal person, stands a more solid and substantial form, a new, and formidable power, till these days unknown in Europe; master of unbounded wealth, he boasts that he is the arbiter of peace and war, and that the credit of nations depends upon his nod; his correspondents are innumerable; his couriers outrun those of sovereign princes, and absolute sovereigns; ministers of state are in his pay. Paramount in the cabinets of continental Europe, he aspires to the domination of our own; even the great Don Miguel himself [see below], of whom we have lately heard and seen so much, was obliged to have recourse to this indi-vidual, before he could take possession of the throne. Sir, that such secret influences do exist is a matter of notoriety; they are known to have been but too busy in the underplot of the recent [ministerial] rev-olution. I believe their object to be as impure as the means by which their power has been acquired, and denounce them and their agents as unknown to the British consitution, and derogatory to the honour of the Crown.

Duncombe "trusted that the duke of Wellington and the right hon. Secretary for the Home Department [Peel], would not allow the finances of this great country to be controlled any longer by a Jew, or the distribution of the patronage of the Crown to be operated on by the prescriptions of a physician [a laugh]."

Responding for the government, Peel shrugged the attack off, denying knowledge of "the mysterious, incorporeal, and incomprehensible, being of which he had spoken" and denying "that the other more substantial personage had interfered, in the way stated by the hon. gentleman, with the financial affairs of the country."[41] But Duncombe's speech was widely followed up. On February 25 a letter appeared in *The Times* signed "Algernon," which declared indignantly: "We cannot suffer the destinies of a mighty Empire to be wielded by the unclean hands of a Jew and a man-midwife." Writing under the pseudonym "Malcolm Macgregor, jun.," the young Thomas Babington Macaulay contributed some satirical verses about the "mysterious two, / Lords of our fate, the Doctor and the Jew."[42] A number of satirical cartoons were also published on the subject, at least two of which were inspired by Thomas Dibdin's 1800 play *The Jew and the Doctor*. In the first to appear (see illustration 5.ii), Nathan is pictured as a pot-bellied angel, descending from the clouds with bags of gold towards the "Ex-Clerk, Ex-Commissary, Ex-Auditor, Ex-Secretary, Ex-Chancellor" Herries. "Si help me Cot!" he declares in what is supposed to be a thick German-Jewish accent, "de *Sinking Job* will go to de Bottom of de melting pot if you don't stick out Herry! You bote know dat *I* and only *I* am de Incorporial—never mind. I gave de Don Miggel and all de oder Dons de monish! plesh my hearts!'[43] A second cartoon by Robert Cruikshank (see illustration 5.iii) shows Nathan—bearded, in a broad-brimmed hat and with a sack marked "Old Rags" over his shoulder—approaching Wellington with the words: "By Cot dat Doctor is von tam Jew—he want my perquist—you know fat I do for you—you give me de monish for dat fiddle—blesh moine heats!!!—."

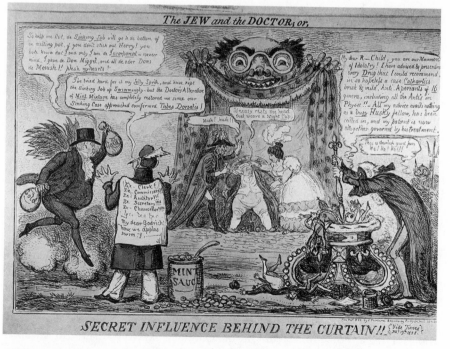

5.ii: George or Robert Cruikshank, *The JEW and the DOCTOR, or SECRET INFLUENCE BEHIND THE CURTAIN!! (Vide Times Feby. 19th 1828).*

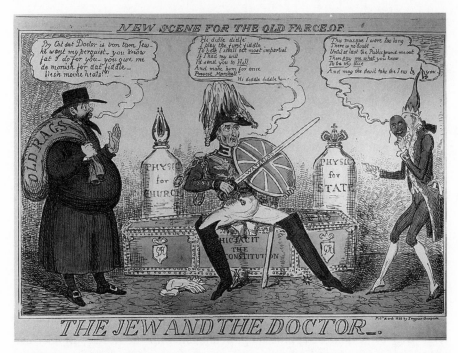

5.iii: Robert Cruikshank, _NEW SCENE_ FOR THE _OLD_ FARCE OF THE JEW AND THE DOCTOR (March 1828).

Duncombe was something of a maverick figure who moved to the left in the 1830s and 1840s, emerging as a keen supporter of Chartism, as well as of Italian and Hungarian nationalism. But it is suggestive that, though he never completed it, he also attempted to write a book entitled _The Jews of England, Their History and Wrongs_.[44] It seems reasonable to infer that he, like Fournier in France, was one of those liberals of the 1820s who saw no contradiction in attacking conservative ministers and Jewish financiers, even in terms which by modern standards seem quite anti-Semitic. The cartoonists' motives were not dissimilar. The original play _The Jew and the Doctor_ is about a generous Jew who brings up a Christian child and endows her with £5,000.[45] The cartoons invert the story by portraying Nathan in the act of trying to bribe Wellington. The recurrent theme is of a tottering government, inextricably tied not only to a corrupt court but also to a corrupting banker. In Cruikshank's cartoon, Wellington sits on a coffin marked "Hic Iacit the Constitution," with two bottles behind him marked "Physic for Church" and "Physic for State."

Another cartoon of 1828 (see illustration 5.iv) entitled _An Untoward Event, or a Tory Triumph_ shows Wellington being carried by Londonderry and two others. (Wellington carries the "Treasury Money Box," a "Treatise on the Corn Laws," the "Army Estimates," a sword marked "Waterloo" and a bone marked "Commander in Chief ship," on the end of an elaborate fork—an allusion to the post he relinquished while serving as Prime Minister.) One of the bearers says to Nathan: "Ah My good R-child, lend a hand, for he's quite a dead weight." But Nathan replies: "No, no, we'll not put our shoulders to it. He's no Daniel," and a bearded Jew whispers: "No,

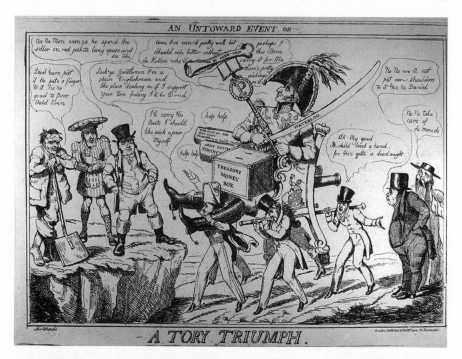

5.iv: "Shortshanks" [Seymour], *AN UNTOWARD EVENT, OR A TORY TRIUMPH* (February 1828).

No, take care of de Monish." Old Corruption and New Corruption are portrayed as two sides of the same political coin. Yet, in each cartoon, stress is laid on Nathan's Jewishness: sometimes his foreign accent is exaggerated, sometimes his appearance is altered to make him conform to the stereotype of the unassimilated immigrant, sometimes he is seen in the company of such a stereotype.

The only qualification which needs to be made is that the cartoonists of the period can scarcely be accused of singling out Jews as targets for their satire. The Irishman and the Scotsman in *A Tory Triumph* are scarcely more sympathetically portrayed than the Jews. The Irishman has simian features and leans on a spade, muttering "Devil burn peat if he [Wellington] puts a finger to it, 'tis no good to poor Erin"; while the hook-nosed Scot in his kilt exclaims: "Na na Mon wanna he spend the siller on red jackets lang spurs and sic like." Nevertheless, they conspicuously stand next to the "plain Englishman" John Bull. Nathan and the poor Jew stand on the other side of the road.

From Canning to Wellington

Was there any truth in these various allegations of hidden Rothschild influence? The answer is that there was, though the reality was more complex than the Rothschilds' critics could know. As we have already seen, Nathan Rothschild had good reason to feel loyalty towards Herries, whose patronage had given him his single most important business opportunity, and hostility towards Huskisson, whose monetary and commercial policies he had consistently opposed. However, there was an additional political dimension which explains Nathan's (at first sight puzzling) lack of sympathy with Herries. When he heard the news of his old associate's defeat, he did no more than shrug, telling Carl: "Our friend Herries is annoyed because he has been given a poor job. He is annoyed, but I cannot help him. He must be patient, and perhaps he will get another job."[46] In fact, what interested and pleased Nathan far more was the fact that the Duke of Wellington had emerged from the crisis as Prime Minister.

The cartoonists who depicted Nathan as trying to bribe Wellington or refusing to support his government were only slightly wide of the mark. Not only had the Rothschilds been cultivating the Duke assiduously since his victories over France (which they had, of course, largely financed); more importantly, his conception of British foreign policy accorded far better with Rothschild interests than that of his mercurial predecessor Canning.

George Canning no more believed in "regenerating" Europe than his predecessor Castlereagh. What distinguished the two was Canning's determination to pursue British interests, with minimal regard for the other great powers. As he put it, famously: "For *Europe* I shall be desirous *now* and *then* to read *England.*" He pointedly declined to take into account "the wishes of any other Government, or the interests of any other people, except in so far as those wishes, those feelings and those interests may, or might, concur with the just interests of England." This explains Britain's refusal to sanction the French intervention in Spain, to which Canning had responded with a strong pledge to uphold Portuguese neutrality and recognition of the Latin American republics' independence from Spain. That did not much bother the Rothschilds, who comfortably played both ends against the middle over Spain. However, in his last years—particularly in his brief period as Prime Minister (April–August 1827)—Canning took bolder steps which did much to alarm the Rothschilds.

There was already a degree of tension in their relationship even before Liverpool's death. As James said in November 1826, "It would be a mortal sin to be dependent . . . on a Canning."[47] The feeling was mutual: the following month, when Canning received details of an important speech in Paris from the Rothschilds twelve hours before the official report of the speech from the British embassy, he wrote angrily to his ambassador:

> You must make full allowance too for the day which I passed on Saturday. "Good God! what! nothing direct from Paris! Perhaps it is a mere stock-jobbing report." "Perhaps it is a trick of M. Rothschild's." . . . Such were the *propos* of the morning . . . I hope you will contrive to establish some communication with the F.O. at Paris, that will prevent Rothschild from getting official *papers*, (*news* you cannot help), before you.[48]

That this less than friendly figure was to be Prime Minister deeply alarmed the Rothschilds. James immediately anticipated "a very serious crisis on our hands in Spain and in Portugal" and "a complete standstill in business activity" in Paris.[49] For in December 1826, "to defend and preserve the independence of an Ally," Canning had sent troops to Portugal in support of the young Portuguese Queen Maria, whose claim to the throne was being challenged by her uncle Dom Miguel. Because

Miguel had the backing of the reactionary Bourbon regime in Spain, which in turn was supported by France, this raised the possibility of a confrontation between Britain and France. For the first time, the Rothschilds appreciated what a large stake they had in peace between the great powers. For nothing could do more to weaken the price of consols, rentes and every other security they and their clients held than a war. Although Villèle had reassured James in November "that I should not be silly because England and France would never go to war on account of such miserable people like the Spanish and Portuguese," James had been worried enough about Canning's attitude "to remain on the sidelines" (that is, to make no major purchases or sales) until the crisis blew over.[50] The appointment of Canning as premier revived these fears of Anglo-French conflict over Portugal. The brothers took the view that Canning was backing the wrong side in what might prove to be a bloody civil war. At an early stage they seem to have made a decision in favour of Dom Miguel, though it is not clear why.[51]

The second reason for Rothschild anxiety about Canning was his anti-Turkish (and therefore pro-Russian) policy over Greece. By 1826 the risings by Greek communities in Moldavia, the Peloponnese and Missolonghi against Ottoman rule had been largely crushed by the Egyptian Prince Ibrahim Pasha (the son of Mehemet Ali). From the point of view of Metternich, this was an entirely satisfactory outcome: another revolutionary threat to the status quo had been thwarted. However, Greek sympathisers in Britain and France, excited by reports of Byron's death at Missolonghi and of Turkish cruelty, clamoured for some kind of intervention. More seriously, traditional Russian ambitions in the region appeared to revive with the accession of Nicholas I as Tsar. In the hope of averting unilateral Russian intervention on behalf of the Greeks, Canning sent a reluctant Wellington to St Petersburg in April 1826 to agree a joint Anglo-Russian policy. The deal struck effectively gave Russia a free hand in Moldavia, while committing the two powers to impose some settlement on the Turks—forcibly, if need be—which would grant the Greeks limited self-government; a policy which Villèle endorsed in July 1827. The upshot was that in the autumn of 1827 a joint naval expedition was sent to the Eastern Mediterranean and inflicted a decisive defeat on the Ottoman forces at Navarino.[52]

As Villèle himself put it, however, "Cannon fire is bad for money';[53] and, like Canning's threat of war over Portugal, his commitment to joint military action against Turkey perturbed the Rothschilds. There were two reasons for this: firstly, they were inclined to share Metternich's pro-Turkish attitude, even if plans for a loan to Constantinople had come to nothing in 1825;[54] secondly, their relations with St Petersburg had taken a distinct turn for the worse since the appointment as Finance Minister of Count Kankrin, who made no secret of the fact that he regarded the Rothschilds' 1822 loan to Russia as "useless."[55]

All this helps to explain why Nathan was so delighted by the emergence of Wellington as Prime Minister in 1828; for it was well known that the Duke disapproved of Canning's policy abroad, sharing the King's view that he had played into the Tsar's hands by turning against Britain's "ancient ally," the Sultan. "Consols have gone up because of our [new] Ministers," Nathan reported gleefully to Carl. "Praise be to God that we have good news, as Russia will wait [before taking further military action], through Wellington everybody is for peace which does not surprise me, for our King in his speeches is nothing but *schalom aleichem* [peace be with you]."[56]

When Mrs Arbuthnot asked Nathan at around the same time "what they thought of the Duke in the City, [h]e said they had unbounded confidence in him."[57] In the two and a half years of Wellington's premiership which followed, that unbounded confidence was translated into concrete financial support for a foreign policy markedly different from Canning's. Not only did Nathan purchase substantial sums of exchequer bills in 1828 (£1 million) and 1829 (£3 million); he also provided Dom Miguel with £50,000, "under the guarantee of the British Government," to enable him to take possession of his office as Regent in Portugal.[58] At the same time, he floated a £769,000 loan to Miguel's brother Pedro, the Emperor of Brazil, in an effort to stabilise Brazilian finances, still reeling from the 1825 Latin American debt crisis.[59]

Predictably, this somewhat confused policy was grist to the satirists' mill. We have already seen the various references to "Don Miggel's monish" in the cartoons of 1828. Brazil's financial difficulties were also ridiculed in *The Hue and Cry*, a cartoon published in the wake of Pedro's default on the earlier 1823 loan (see illustration 5.v). Here Nathan is pictured advising Dom Pedro not to pay the British bondholders—represented by John Bull prostrate on the ground. "If you pay them you'll want more monies," says Nathan to Pedro, "and that is not convenient just now." The devil whispers in Nathan's ear: "Tell him to call it political expediency—*you* know how easily John Bull is *humbugg'd*."

The Rothschilds were equally in accord with Wellington when, against Nathan's expectations, Russia renewed hostilities against Turkey in 1828. A Russian request for a loan was politely turned down, much to Metternich's delight,[60] and the broth-

5.v: "Sharpshooter," *The HUE and CRY; or JOHN BULL between two Knaves, Stools, and the Heads of Police called to rescue him from Pickpockets. Dedicated to the holders of Foreign Bonds in General* (1829).

ers continued to hope for Russian military reverses throughout the campaign.[61] When, to their chagrin, the Russians won and imposed a modest indemnity on the Turks under the terms of the Treaty of Adrianople (September 1829), the Rothschilds hastened to offer their services to facilitate the payment. Their sole anxiety throughout this, the first of many Eastern crises they would have to weather, was that Wellington might feel obliged to intervene against Russia. As over Portugal, the Rothschild view was now overtly pacifist, as Nathan emphasised to Salomon:

> There are some here who want us [meaning Britain] to quarrel . . . with [the Russian ambassador] Lieven . . . and want us to send angry Notes . . . I must tell you Wellington and Peel would like to quarrel with Russia, but in the end we should have to go to war. I am not for demonstrations, and we must see to maintaining peace. What's the good of quarrelling? The Russians have gone too far, and the world will be angry with us and will say: Why didn't you do it twelve months ago? If England now says, Yes, we are angry and want to go to war, Austria and France will say, We will remain out—they will leave us in the lurch, and we shall be involved alone. I went to Wellington and congratulated him on peace. He said: "Peace is not yet. It is not yet ratified." . . . There is dissatisfaction with the Russian Peace in every respect. [But] the Cabinet has now decided for the present to remain quite calm and not to write a word to Russia, to keep quiet and to let come what may.[62]

James neatly summed up the rationality of this pacifism: "If England were earnestly to attack [over] the [Turkish] issue then I assure you that we will suffer a fall of at least 5 per cent over here. If on the other hand the reports from there turn out to be better, then we could get a small improvement."[63] The connection between international peace and bond market stability was to become a first principle of Rothschild policy in the decade to come.

Strings of Influence

It was not only a shared view of foreign policy which united the Rothschilds with politicians like Wellington or Metternich, however. Where the conspiracy theorists of the 1820s came closest to the mark was when they suggested that private financial interests also played a part.

We have already seen that it was common practice for European politicians of the period to accept favours—ranging from investment tips to outright bribes—from bankers. At the Congress of Aix-la-Chapelle, it was the fact that Baring had sold stakes in his impending French reparations loan to most of the ministers present that made them so eager to postpone the loan when the market unexpectedly crashed. The Rothschilds were adept at playing the same game. Indeed, Amschel was "convinced that we as Jews could not get by without bribing and that the Gentiles have the advantage."[64] In 1818, for example, the Frankfurt house distributed shares of the Rothschilds' new Prussian loan not only to other Frankfurt bankers like Bethmann and Gontard, but also to their old sleeping partner Buderus, the Austrian representative at the Bundestag, Count Buol, and a number of other members of the diplomatic corps.[65] In Paris, the political figures who were offered Prussian bonds included Talleyrand.[66]

Another way of securing political influence by financial means was by lending money to such individuals. The most eminent of all French recipients of Rothschild loans in this period was Louis XVIII himself, whom Nathan had advanced £200,000 on behalf of the British government to meet the costs of his return to France in 1814. This did not much endear Nathan to the Bourbon family, however, for he insisted on repayment with interest three years later.[67] By contrast, the loans made in the 1820s to the duc d'Orléans (the future Louis Philippe) were a more long-term investment which paid ample dividends in the subsequent decade.[68] Prussian recipients of loans included the son-in-law of Prince Hardenberg.[69] More routine banking facilities like current accounts were offered to other Prussian officials—notably the ambassador in London, Wilhelm von Humboldt, and the key official during the 1818 loan negotiations, Rother.[70] Because these usually led to the granting of generous overdrafts, however, such accounts often performed the same role as loans. No sooner had Caroline von Humboldt been introduced to Salomon than he asked her point blank "whether he could be of any use to me in the matter of money, and said that his purse was at my disposal."[71]

Finally, when a more subtle approach seemed appropriate, the Rothschilds gave presents to those they wished to cultivate. As Carl put it, "One must have something when going to see the great and good, either gossip or something to show them."[72] The roots of the family's later penchant for collecting art and natural curiosities can be found here; for the brothers prided themselves on their ability to find exotic gifts for jaded palates. They had an advantage in Nathan's access to the London market, by far the best in the world because of the growing superiority of British trade and manufacturing. In 1816, for example, Nathan sent Amschel two tortoises, one of which he suggested be given to the Elector of Hesse-Kassel. (When they arrived dead, Amschel had them stuffed and presented them to William anyway.)[73] Other luxury goods requested by his brothers for prospective clients included jewelled caskets for the Elector, a horse suitable for a lady and "a carving knife and fork with ivory handles" for "someone who helped us."[74]

The first British official to benefit materially from his relationship with Rothschilds was, as we have seen, Herries. Though the full extent of his personal stake in the firm's wartime operations is impossible to ascertain, he was a regular participant in post-war loans like the 1817 loan to the city of Paris. Herries—"your own Buderus over there"—was, as Salomon put it, one of the "important people whose favours are essential."[75] Another was Lord Stewart, Castlereagh's brother, the British representative in Paris in the post-war years. He first asked Salomon and James to "speculate for him in rentes" in October 1817, and thereafter became "very friendly with us. Between ourselves he likes to gamble," reported Salomon, "and I let him share in our business . . . to the amount of 50,000 francs rentes." This was the case which reminded Salomon of his father's precept that "if a high-placed person enters into a [financial] partnership with a Jew, he belongs to the Jew."[76] When Stewart came to them asking for assistance with his English affairs, Salomon urged Nathan to oblige him: "We must routinely accede to this minister's wishes, as he is everything here, and is helping us to get the loans, the liquidation [of French reparations] and everything, and is the *English* minister."[77] Twenty years later James gave the Prime Minister Lord Melbourne's brother Frederick investment tips during his time as ambassador in Vienna. "Well, Lamb is of the opinion that there will not be any war," he wrote in a typical letter. "I told him that if he sees that rentes are rising over there then I will buy 24,000 francs of rentes for him in order to resell them at a profit, for he currently has some £30,000 to his credit in London."[78] British officials who directly borrowed from the Rothschilds included George Harrison and Charles Arbuthnot at the Treasury: the former owed Rothschilds over £3,000 in 1825; the latter borrowed four times as much.[79]

It should be stressed that such relationships were not in themselves illegal—the Rothschilds had every right to extend banking services to politicians and civil servants. However, the brothers privately referred to "bribery" as a feature of their relations with Arbuthnot and with numerous foreign officials, notably the Russian Gervais.[80] And, as the case of Herries illustrates, allegations of corruption in the press could be highly damaging to the career of the politician concerned. Indeed, the brothers had been anticipating a political row of the sort which blew up in 1828 for more than a decade, ever since they first began to worry that their wartime accounts with Herries might not bear close parliamentary scrutiny.

In this context, it is not entirely surprising to find that the Duke of Wellington also banked for a time with Rothschilds. Indeed, it was Stewart who formally introduced the Duke to Salomon and James. The importance of this relationship was probably small in financial terms: the surviving 1825 balance sheet suggests that Wellington did not make much use of his overdraft facility. But in Salomon's eyes the prestige of being "Wellington's bankers" was what mattered:

> It is a great honour . . . You may say, "What does honour matter? Honour is not money." As an honest man I tell you that now I prefer honour to money. One cannot do more [with money] than to eat [from the proceeds] and we have enough to eat. [But] food does not taste good without honour. Wellington stands here higher in public esteem than the king himself.[81]

Just two months later, James was already boasting of his influence with the Duke, whom he had "already given various things."[82]

Wellington, however, was not the most senior British political figure to whom the Rothschilds "gave things." It is extraordinary to find that the family's interest in the financial affairs of King George IV predated his accession to the throne by as much as fifteen years. The earliest document referring to "bills of exchange from Prince George to the nominal amount of 150,000 Frankfurt gulden" is in Mayer Amschel's hand and is dated 1805. Two years later they figure in one of his earliest surviving balance sheets, entered with a discounted value of just over 127,784 gulden—though even this figure he regarded as questionable.[83] For, even as the heir to the throne and Prince Regent, George was regarded as a singularly unreliable debtor. How did Mayer Amschel, then the father of an obscure Manchester textile merchant, come to acquire a bill on the Prince Regent? The likeliest answer is that he bought it from the Elector of Hesse-Kassel, who had made a number of loans to the sons of George III in the 1790s. Ten years later, with Nathan firmly established as a banker in London, the sons of Mayer Amschel turned to these other royal debts with the intention of making Nathan—in Amschel's somewhat old-fashioned phrase—"court banker" in England.[84] All told, the Prince Regent owed £109,000, the Duke of York £55,000 and the Duke of Clarence £20,000, making a total of £184,000. Only the Prince Regent had ever paid interest on his loan. After pro-

tracted negotiations with the Elector's advisers—and despite the objections of
Buderus—the Rothschilds succeeded in buying these debts in return for the equivalent of their face value in consols.[85] Superficially, this was far more than they were
worth. In reality, it was an inspired investment—another of Nathan's "master-
strokes." As Salomon commented: "This makes me a very powerful man."[86] "There
is luck attached to everything English," he enthused. "Everything touching them
turns out happily. So it is with the court of our Elector. The two courts fit
together."[87]

The value of these old royal debts was that, by making Nathan one of the Prince
Regent's creditors, they brought him into direct contact with the officials charged
with managing the future King's troubled financial affairs. And not only his financial affairs: by the end of 1817 Nathan was asking Salomon and James to gather
information which might be of assistance to the so-called "Milan commission," set
up to gather evidence against "the great man's wife"—Princess Caroline of
Brunswick—whom he was determined to divorce.[88] In 1822, just after George had
finally ascended the throne, a loan of £50,000 was arranged with Nathan, secured
on the revenues of his Hanoverian possessions.[89] A year later a further £125,000
was requested. It was at around this time that he came into contact with Sir William
Knighton, though the key figure in the loan negotiations was George Harrison, who
assured the King of Nathan's "great loyalty and honesty towards your Majesty . . . in
everything relating to this transaction."[90] As we have seen, Harrison himself borrowed several thousand pounds from Nathan not long after this.

Nor was George IV the only member of the British royal family to whom Nathan
lent money in the 1820s. In 1824, for example, he lent £10,000 to the Duke of York
on the security of some jewels, as well as giving him 100 complimentary shares in
the Alliance Assurance Company.[91] The Rothschilds also looked ahead to the next
generation. In 1816 the only child of the Prince Regent, Princess Charlotte, was
betrothed to a minor German prince, Leopold of Saxe-Coburg, the youngest son of
Duke Francis Frederick. The brothers at once recognised Leopold's potential importance (his new father-in-law was, after all, in his fifties and notoriously sybaritic).
When he passed through Frankfurt on his way to England for the wedding, Carl
made his move: "We went to see him. He is a good man. We gave him a bill for £700
on you against gold as well as a letter of credit . . . He intends to buy jewellery. Please
offer him your services."[92] Nathan needed no further prompting. By April he was
being entrusted with delivery of Leopold's private correspondence to Germany, and
by August a loan of 10,000 gulden was being discussed.[93]

Only the effort Nathan put into cultivating Leopold can explain the brothers'
extraordinary reaction in May the following year to the news that Princess Charlotte
had died, apparently extinguishing Leopold's hopes of power in Britain. "We are
unable to write you fully today," wrote Salomon to Nathan,

> because of the heartbreak caused by that disaster, the death of Princess
> Charlotte. We lost our heads. I still cannot make myself believe that the
> noble woman died. We received the bad news on Saturday afternoon at
> five o'clock. We were negotiating with Baring for another million of
> rentes and we arranged with him that we are going to give him a final
> answer on Sunday . . . But when he came on Sunday for the answer, our
> consternation was so great that we told him that we could do nothing

for the time being, we are far too confused for it. Unfortunately, we are losing terribly much, my dear Nathan. It is terrible, my heart breaks when I speak about it . . . I can't write anything about business. We did not do any. We should . . . draw the moral of it: money, honours are worth nothing, we are all only dust; man should give up his pride . . . he should not make himself believe anything; we are mud and dust. It pains me very badly, this unfortunate event.[94]

"Believe me," Salomon added two days later, "I was so horrified [at the news], that since then I have had no appetite. It is as if my stomach has shrunk and I have never-ending pains in the joints." Nathan, he assumed, would also be "thrown off his feet" and "made ill" by the news. Yet the brothers were always quick to come to terms with adversity. "Nobody is immortal," reflected Salomon, "and we have to get over this . . . Unfortunately, our sorrow and sadness cannot bring her back."[95]

Another bank might have been tempted to end Leopold's privileged status now that he was a mere widower. Salomon urged Nathan to do the reverse: "According to the English papers the Prince of Coburg will stay in England and is going to remain an important person there. We should show even more friendship towards a man who fell on hard times than before. I ask you to show him more feeling than hith-erto."[96] This accounts for the subsequent efforts of Nathan to arrange life insurance not only for Leopold but for his father,[97] and for the fact that Carl happily put Leopold up at his Naples villa in 1826.[98]

It was to prove an extremely shrewd strategy. For the link forged in these years between Nathan and the man James called "your Coburg" was to prove enduring and mutually beneficial.[99] Not for nothing did one anti-Rothschild writer of the 1840s point out the similarity between the House of Rothschild and the House of Saxe-Coburg-Gotha, those two extended German families which were to rise from obscurity to glory in the course of the nineteenth century. Indeed, theirs was to be an almost symbiotic relationship.[100] The 3.5 million gulden lent to the Saxe-Coburgs by the Frankfurt house between 1837 and 1842 was only one aspect of the connection.[101] Of greater importance was the support which the Rothschilds gave to those members of the family who left Coburg in search of new thrones elsewhere.

Not that the Rothschilds lost interest in the question of the British succession fol-lowing Princess Charlotte's death. When the Prince Regent's brother, the Duke of Kent, set off for Germany to marry Victoria of Saxe-Coburg, he took with him a letter of credit on the Frankfurt Rothschilds.[102] When the marriage produced a daughter, Victoria—who at once became next-in-line to the throne—Nathan has-tened to offer the proud father financial advice and his exclusive messenger ser-vice.[103] In 1823 he also lent a substantial sum (400,000 gulden) to the Prince of Leiningen, the Duchess of Kent's son by her first marriage.[104] Nathan's sons contin-ued to act as the Duchess's banker after the Duke's death, occasionally relaying money to her brother Ferdinand of Saxe-Coburg.[105]

Yet even the English royal family were not the most influential of the Roth-schilds' clients and "friends" in this period. For, as historians generally agree, this was an era in which European politics were to a large extent dominated not by Britain but by Austria. As we have seen, the man who made Austrian policy between 1809 and 1848 was Metternich; and he too banked with Rothschilds. Indeed, the rela-tionship which developed between Metternich and Salomon Rothschild may be seen as in some respects the prototype for the relationship which later developed between Bismarck and the Rothschilds' associate in Berlin, Bleichröder—except that Metternich came to feel far closer to his banker emotionally and intellectually than Bismarck ever did.

Although he came from an aristocratic family with estates in the Mosel valley, Prince Klemens Wenzel Nepomuk Lothar von Metternich-Winneburg was "cash-poor" for much of his long political career. Within a year of their first meetings with him—in Paris during the 1815 peace negotiations[106]—he raised the possibility of a loan of 300,000 gulden with Amschel and Carl in Frankfurt.[107] Metternich had already proved a useful ally to the brothers, supplying political news in Paris, supporting their efforts to secure Austrian financial business and apparently also sympathising with their campaign for Jewish emancipation in Frankfurt.[108] The arrangement he now proposed was that the Rothschilds should advance him 100,000 gulden and sell a further 200,000 gulden of 5 per cent bonds to other investors, all secured on the new estate at Johannisberg which the Austrian Emperor had just given him. However, Carl was reluctant to lend so much to a single individual, no matter how wealthy, recalling how unsatisfactory similar loans had been for Prince Wilhelm.[109] Despite the fact that Metternich continued to prove himself "a great friend of ours"—supporting the requests for noble and consular status—the brothers preferred at this stage to limit their generosity to routine banking services and occasional gifts, like the Wedgwood china Nathan sent him in 1821.[110]

It was in October of that year that Metternich—accompanied by his mistress, Princess Dorothy de Lieven—first publicly accepted an offer of Rothschild hospitality, "taking soup" with Amschel in Frankfurt on his way back to Vienna from Hanover.[111] This was interpreted by some observers as a calculated gesture of support for the Frankfurt Jewish community at a time when conflict over the civil rights question was at its height. Less than a year later, Metternich received his thanks: a loan of 900,000 gulden, agreed just six days before the brothers received the title of "baron" from the Emperor.[112] This loan sealed the "friendship" between Metternich and the Rothschilds. At Verona in 1823, Salomon furnished Metternich with cash to meet his (considerable) personal expenses.[113] In Paris two years later, James played host to Metternich, throwing a lavish dinner for "the representatives of the Holy Alliance" which greatly impressed the *Constitutionnel* newspaper. It commented ironically:

> Thus does the the power of gold reconcile all the ranks and all the religions. One of the more curious spectacles our time—rich as it is in contrasts—is that of the representatives of the Holy Alliance established in the name of Jesus Christ attending a banquet given by a Jew on the day that the law of sacrilege is being debated in the chambers.[114]

A year later James was present at another equally grand soirée.[115] It was in this period that Metternich began to make use of the Rothschilds' courier service for important correspondence.[116] From this point onwards, he and Salomon shared political news on a regular basis, Metternich informing Salomon of Austrian intentions while Salomon provided him with news he received from his brothers in London, Paris, Frankfurt and Naples. By the end of the 1820s the Rothschilds had begun to provide Metternich—or "Uncle," as they often called him—with an unofficial diplomatic channel, through which he could relay his political views indirectly and discreetly to other governments.

All of this puts the bitter accusations of David Parish on the eve of his suicide in a new light. The Rothschilds, Parish complained to Metternich, had "understood better than I how to draw you into their [sphere of] interest" and how to secure "your special protection." It was, he insisted in his letter to Salomon, "the new alliance" between Metternich and the Rothschilds which had ruined him. "Under the protection of Prince Metternich, you succeeded in securing exclusive control over numerous transactions in which I had a moral and legal claim to a substantial share." If Salomon had given him his rightful cut of the profits from the Austrian and Neapolitan loans, he might have been able to rescue Fries & Co. "But you found it easier and more advantageous to come to an agreement with the Prince over the old rentes operation and in this way to put him wholly on your side."[117]

Although Parish's allegations cannot be taken at face value, there was real substance to his claim that an alliance had developed between Metternich and Salomon Rothschild. This can be demonstrated with reference to the contents of the silver box, recently rediscovered in Moscow, in which Salomon kept Metternich's accounts and private financial correspondence. These long-lost bank statements show that between 1825 and 1826 Metternich was in a position to repay much of the loan of 1822.[118] However, no sooner had the loan been paid off—ahead of schedule—than a new loan for 1,040,000 gulden (c. £110,000) was arranged, roughly half of which Metternich used to purchase a new estate at Plass, and the rest he took as cash.[119] The balance sheet of the Vienna house shows that Salomon retained some 35,000 gulden of the bearer bonds issued by Metternich for the purchase of Plass, on top of which the Prince owed an additional 15,000 gulden.[120] His total private debt to the Rothschilds grew in the succeeding two years to nearly 70,000 gulden.[121] In addition, the Frankfurt house advanced over 117,000 gulden to Metternich's son Viktor.[122] When Metternich married again in 1831, Salomon was on hand to help resolve the financial difficulties of his third wife, Countess Melanie Zichy-Ferraris.[123]

Nor did the Rothschilds confine themselves to loans and overdrafts. "Our friend Salomon's devotion always touches me," remarked Princess Melanie in her diary in May 1841, on receiving a present from him of American deer for their estate near Frankfurt. A few months later she described a visit by "Salomon and James, their nephew Anthony and Salomon's son and finally Amschel, who made a great point of our coming to dine with him at Frankfurt next Tuesday. James brought me a pretty mother-of-pearl and bronze box from Paris, filled with sweets, which was all to the good." At Christmas in 1843 Salomon visited the Metternichs at Ischl, bringing "lovely things to the Metternich children, such as tempted their mother to play with them herself."[124]

Metternich was not the only eminent Austrian to put his private financial affairs in Salomon's hands. In 1821—in a classic example of financial speculation based on inside information—a senior Austrian commander, General von Wolzogen, asked Salomon to purchase 100,000 gulden worth of metallic bonds on his behalf. His calculations provide a fascinating insight into the dispassionate attitude of one senior military figure to the Austrian military intervention in Italy:

My reasoning is as follows: either it will stay cold, or it will get hot. In the first case, [metalliques] will immediately go up anyway. If it turns hot, then it is probable that the [army?] will march into Naples and in that case I believe they [metalliques] will rise too . . . If peace remains, one can expect high prices. The only question is therefore whether to buy now or after the declaration of war. I am inclined to buy soon . . . But I leave it to you to do as you think best, and indeed not to buy at all if you do not think it advantageous.[125]

Other political figures who feature in the accounts of the Vienna house include Stadion and the influential diplomat Apponyi, as well as a number of the most important families of the Austro-Hungarian aristocracy.[126] Of these, the Esterházys, with their immense estates in Hungary and links to the still wealthier Thurn und Taxis family, were the most important—and problematic. Beginning with £10,000 in 1820 and 300,000 gulden in 1822, the Esterházys borrowed often from the Rothschilds.[127] Three years later Salomon went into partnership with two leading Vienna houses, Arnstein & Eskeles and Simon G. Sina, to float a large 6.5 million gulden loan (at 6 per cent). This was secured on Prince Esterházy's estates and was intended "definitively to reorder" the family finances.[128] However, balance sheets for the succeeding years show Esterházy continuing to run overdrafts with Rothschild houses in London and Vienna: £28,000 in London in 1825, 2,300 gulden in Vienna three years later.[129] By 1831 matters were bad enough for Esterházy to approach Salomon (through Metternich) for another loan. Although Salomon was hesitant, the Vienna accounts for 1832 put Esterházy's total debts at 827,000 gulden, and three years later the debt was larger still.[130] When the Prince was succeeded by his son Paul in 1836, there was another attempt at stabilisation in the form of a 7 million gulden lottery loan, issued jointly by Salomon and Sina.[131] Yet another loan (for 6.4 million gulden) followed eight years later—one of a spate of major loans to the aristocracy floated by Rothschilds and Sina in the 1840s.[132] Small wonder Esterházy "spoke very flatteringly of the family" to third parties.[133] As in the case of Metternich, financial ties were inseparable from social and political ties. In London, Prince Esterházy dined regularly with Nathan while serving as Austrian ambassador and received much of his correspondence from Metternich via Rothschild couriers.[134] In Vienna, the relationship appeared so close that in 1822 unfounded rumours appeared in the press suggesting that Esterházy had persuaded Salomon to abandon Judaism.[135]

The strategy of extending credit and other financial facilities to influential but profligate figures like Metternich and Esterházy was a highly effective way of ensuring political goodwill and "friendship." Of all the private financial relationships of this era, none illustrates this better than that between Salomon and Metternich's secretary, Friedrich von Gentz. Gentz was an intelligent, conservative and thoroughly venal man of letters—a kind of Central European Edmund Burke gone wrong—who had acquired the habit of selling the influence he had in Vienna for cash long before he came into contact with the Rothschilds.[136] Indeed, for a time it was David Parish whom he regarded as "the matador, the pearl of the merchant class of all Christendom"—a view which was not unrelated to the 100,000 gulden stake Parish had given him in the 1818 Austrian loan.[137] It did not take the Rothschilds long to purchase Gentz's fickle allegiance. After an initial encounter in Frankfurt, he, Carl and Salomon met at Aix in 1818. On October 27 Gentz recorded in his diary that Salomon had handed him 800 ducats, supposedly the proceeds of a successful speculation in British stocks. A few days later there were more "pleasant financial dealing with the brothers."[138] Gentz was soon paying regular visits to his new friends, whose apparently instinctive ability to make money deeply impressed him. He had regular business dealings with Salomon thereafter: a minor transaction in late 1820, a small loan at Laibach in 1821, a share in the Neapolitan loan of the same year which earned him 5,000 gulden within a year. His diaries in this period make repeated references to "very agreeable communications" from Salomon; "important financial arrangements" with him; "a proof of real friendship" over breakfast; "matters which, although not so elevated [as diplomacy], were far more pleasant"; and "highly welcome financial transactions with the excellent Rothschild."[139] The pattern continued throughout the decade. In 1829 Salomon lent Gentz 2,000 gulden "with the most amiable readiness," bringing his total debts to Salomon and other bankers to over 30,000 gulden. To Gentz, such loans were to be regarded as "donations pure and simple."[140] Indeed, according to one account, Salomon finally dispensed with the fiction that the money would ever be repaid by paying Gentz an annual retainer,[141] though this did not prevent Gentz from pleading for yet another loan of 4,500 gulden from Salomon, and gratefully settling for 500 gulden to tide him over.[142]

Gentz performed a number of valuable services in return for his money: supplying news and facilitating access to Metternich, for example. In addition, he was responsible for the Rothschilds' first real foray into public relations. At a time when the brothers were the objects of an increasing volume of negative comment in the press, an experienced and politically influential journalist like Gentz was a useful ally. In 1821 he wrote twice to the editor of the *Allgemeine Zeitung* to express his "grave dissatisfaction" about recent articles by the paper's Frankfurt correspondent which had been critical of the Rothschilds. "The constant attacks upon the House of Rothschild," he argued, "invariably, and sometimes in the most outrageous manner, reflect upon the Austrian government by necessary implication, since, as everybody knows, it is transacting important financial matters with that House, which is not only unimpeachable, but is honourable and thoroughly respectable."[143] Facing the threat of a ban throughout Austrian territory, the editor of the newspaper was obliged to "promise not to accept . . . anything in future relating to the value of Austrian public securities, or *anything whatever* relating to the House of Rothschild (at least affecting its relations with Austria)."[144] When Salomon heard that he had been awarded a Russian decoration in 1822, he immediately asked Gentz to arrange for a newspaper article on the subject.[145] Four years later, at Salomon's request, Gentz himself put pen to paper, writing the first "official" account of the family's history—or , as he described it, an attempt "briefly and I hope not infelicitously to explain the phenomenon of the greatness of this House." After Gentz had read it to one of Salomon's senior clerks and received his "actual pay" from Salomon, it was published in the Brockhaus *Encyclopaedia*.[146] These were the first Rothschild attempts to exert some influence on a generally hostile press, and far from the last. In 1831, with Gentz's influence waning, Salomon made overtures to the satirist Saphir in the hope of winning his services as a pro-Austrian—and implicitly also pro-Rothschild—publicist.[147]

Money Makes Money

The evidence that the Rothschilds established a network of private financial relationships with key public figures in Restoration Europe is therefore compelling. Yet
the conspiracy theorists of this and later periods misunderstood the role of such
relationships when they portrayed them as the key to Rothschild power. The image
of the Rothschilds at the centre of a web of "corruption" would become a recurrent
one in the years after 1830. But it was not, in reality, the bribes, loans and other
favours they bestowed on men like Metternich which made them the dominant
force in international finance after 1815. It was the sheer scale—and sophistication—of their operations.

In 1822 their old rival Simon Moritz von Bethmann "heard from a reliable
source that Salomon Rothschild has stated that the annual balance-sheet of the 5
brothers showed a net profit of 6 million gulden." As he observed, "This is certainly
a case where the English proverb applies: 'Money makes money.' Having regard to
their industry and judgement, we may expect their business to continue to flourish;
indeed, one hopes so, since the overthrow of this Colossus would be terrible."[148]
The evidence now available from the firm's accounts amply confirms this judgement. In 1815 the combined capital of the Rothschild houses in Frankfurt and
London was at most £500,000. In 1818 the figure was £1,772,000; in 1825
£4,082,000; and in 1828 £4,330,333.[149] The equivalent figures for the Rothschilds'
nearest rival, Baring Brothers, were £374,365 in 1815, £429,318 in 1818, £452,654
seven years later and £309,803 in 1828.[150] In other words, having been on a more or
less equal footing with Barings in 1815, the Rothschilds' resources had grown to be
more than ten times greater than their principal competitor's in as many years.
While Barings' capital had actually declined in size, the Rothschilds had increased
theirs by a factor of eight. These are astonishing figures.

The explanation for this disparity is not just that the Rothschilds made bigger
profits. Just as importantly, they ploughed the bulk of these profits back into the
business. Here, the contrast with Barings, which tended to distribute profits to the
partners (even in years when the bank made a loss) rather than allowing capital to
accumulate, is impressive. Nor did the Rothschilds lose momentum in the succeeding years. In 1836—the next time the partners met to settle accounts and renew
their contractual agreement—the capital had increased again to £6,007,707.[151]
Such figures as are available for the profits of the individual houses in this period
confirm the broad impression of rapid and sustained growth. Even in the relatively
sluggish years between 1825 and 1828, the Paris house alone made profits totalling
£414,000. Between 1823 and 1829 the profits of the Naples house totalled
7,390,742 ducats (£924,000).[152]

These figures explain the dominance of the Rothschilds on the international capital market in the 1820s; perhaps the only thing that is surprising is that they were
not more dominant. Between 1818 and 1832 it has been estimated that N. M.
Rothschild accounted for seven out of twenty-six loans contracted by foreign governments in London, and roughly 38 per cent (£37.6 million) of their total value.
This was more than twice the value of their nearest rivals, B. A. Goldschmidt.[153]
Moreover, the bank's own figures suggest that this may be an underestimate: according to Ayer, the value of loans issued by Nathan in this period was in fact £86 million.[154] The equivalent total for loans issued by the Frankfurt house in this period

was 28 million gulden (*c.* £2.5 million).[155] In Paris, James came to exercise a near monopoly over French government finance, issuing seven loans with a nominal capital of 1.5 billion francs (£60 million) between 1823 and 1847.[156]

In a sense therefore the French journalist Alexandre Weill was not exaggerating when, looking back in 1844, he declared:

> The house of Rotschild [*sic*] is merely a necessary consequence of the principle of state which has governed Europe since 1815; if it had not been a Rotschild, it would simply have been someone else . . . it is this system . . . dominant throughout Europe, which has created, produced and elevated the house of Rotschild . . . Rotschild reigns and governs on the bourse and in all the cabinets . . .[157]

This was too deterministic a view, of course. There had been moments in the 1820s when the "principles" governing the European states had come close to calling the Rothschilds back out of existence, and it is hard to imagine any other contemporary financier easily taking their place. But Weill was closer to the mark than Richelieu: if there was a sixth great power in the 1820s, it was no longer Barings, but Rothschilds. Small wonder there was such a hue and cry about them.

SIX

Amschel's Garden

Oh what joy to be in the open air
and draw breath easily!
Here alone, here alone there's life.
. . . Speak softly! Restrain yourselves!
There are ears and eyes upon us.
— *FIDELIO*, ACT 1, FINALE

The Jew, who may have no rights in the smallest German states,
decides the fate of Europe. — BRUNO BAUER[1]

Nothing symbolised the Rothschilds' escape from the gloomy confines of the Frankfurt ghetto better than their acquisition of real estate outside it. In 1815 virtually all the family's wealth was held in the form of paper—bonds and other securities—and precious metal. Such "immovable property" as they possessed was all in Frankfurt; everywhere else, the brothers still lived in rented accommodation. Inside the old Judengasse, there was of course the old *Stammhaus* "zum grünen Schild" where the brothers had grown up. It was a matter of public curiosity that their mother Gutle continued to live there until the end of her life; her sons, however, felt no such attachment. By 1817 Carl had had enough of his old room on the third floor of his mother's house: "Of course, you will say that in the ghetto we slept on the fourth floor. Yes, but one is getting old. Also [it is galling] that one should make much money and live a dog's life while others who have not a tenth of our fortune live like princes."[2] By this time the first steps out of the Judengasse had already been taken. Although the plot they had acquired in 1809–10 for their new offices was technically in the Judengasse, the sandstone neo-classical building they built there had its entrance in the Fahrgasse, the main thoroughfare off which the Judengasse ran. (In the absence of its old gates, the Judengasse itself was now increasingly referred to as the Bornheimer Strasse.)[3] Salomon had already been given permission to move his residence to a house in the Schäfergasse in 1807;[4] but the real escape came when Amschel bought a house in the suburbs on the road to Bockenheim in 1811 (10 Bockenheimer Landstrasse).[5] For the first time, he found himself living in fresh air.

Almost as soon as he had acquired the house, Amschel became consumed with the desire to buy the garden next to it. It should be stressed that the object of his desire was no country estate, merely a small suburban plot of at most a few acres, similar to those owned by Gentile banking families like the Bethmanns and the Gontards. Nor was Amschel merely bidding for social status. He seems genuinely to have fallen in love with the garden. After all, he had spent virtually all of his forty-two years cooped up in the ghetto, working, eating and sleeping in its cramped and dingy rooms, walking up and down its crowded and pungent thoroughfare. It is not easy for a modern reader to imagine how intoxicating fresh air and vegetation were to him. On a spring night in 1815—in an act as pregnant with emancipatory symbolism as the prisoners' release into the "free air" in Beethoven's *Fidelio* (1805)—he decided to sleep there. He described the experience in an excited and moving postscript to his brother Carl: "Dear Carl, I am sleeping in the garden. If God allows that the accounts work out as you and I want them to, I will buy it . . . There is so much space that you, God willing, and the whole family can comfortably live in it."[6] As that implied, Amschel regarded his purchase of the garden as dependent on the outcome of the brothers' business activities, which Napoleon's return from Elba just weeks before had thrown into turmoil.[7] He was also torn between his love of open space and his brother Carl's preference for a large and respectable town house in which visiting dignitaries could be entertained.[8] Fortunately for Amschel, Nathan categorically rejected Carl's arguments as "a lot of nonsense," but accepted the need for a garden for the sake of Amschel's health.[9] By April 1816 part of the garden had been bought and Amschel was bidding to add a further two-thirds of an acre to it.[10] Now when he slept outside—in a garden he could call his own—it was "like paradise."[11] Finally, more than a year after his first night under the stars, he bought the remainder. "From today onwards the garden belongs to me and to my dear brothers," he wrote exultantly. "There is therefore no need to remind you of what you could contribute to make it more beautiful. I would not be in the least surprised if Salomon were to buy all sorts of seeds and plants at the very first opportunity, as this garden will be inherited by the family Rothschild."[12]

As this illustrates, Amschel insisted that he had bought the garden for the family as a whole, a sense of collective experiment which his brothers were happy to encourage, sending him the seeds and plants he asked for (including African seeds from Alexander von Humboldt) and agreeing to his plans to enlarge the plot or build greenhouses.[13] Their mother Gutle also made frequent visits there.[14] But there was little doubt that it was really Amschel's garden—a place where he could potter, study and sleep, in peace and in fresh air.[15] Revealingly, he could not help regarding it as a personal indulgence—hence his need to seek his brothers' approval for what were often quite trivial expenditures, and his almost apologetic promises to earn the money back in business.[16] After much agonising about the cost, he added a greenhouse and a winter garden and, during the 1820s, had the house substantially enlarged and improved in the neo-classical style by the architect Friedrich Rumpf. Later it acquired a pond, a fountain and even a medieval folly—an early (and rare) Rothschild venture into the romantic genre.[17]

Amschel's garden was the first of many Rothschild gardens; and its story does much to illuminate the family's enduring passion for horticulture.[18] Its significance was partly religious: now the Tabernacles feast could be celebrated properly in a tent amid the greenery.[19] But the full meaning of Amschel's passion for what was, by later Rothschild standards, a tiny patch of land becomes manifest when his purchase is set in its political context. For, as we shall see, the period after 1814 saw a concerted effort by the re-established Frankfurt authorities once again to remove the civil rights which had been won by the Jewish community from Napoleon's Prince-Primate Dalberg. Under the terms of the old statute governing the position of Jews, not only had the ownership of property outside the Judengasse been forbidden; Jews had even been barred from walking in public gardens. Amschel therefore fretted that the Senate would either prevent his purchase of the garden altogether,[20] or compel him to relinquish it if the purchase went ahead—anxieties which were only exacerbated by the appearance of abusive crowds outside the garden at the time of the "Hep" riots.[21] When he was allowed to keep it, he still suspected "a kind of bribe" to keep him from leaving Frankfurt, or even a sop to avoid more general concessions to the Jewish community as a whole.[22] It became, in short, a symbol of the much bigger question of Jewish emancipation. Something of its significance in this regard can be inferred from a guidebook description from the mid-1830s, which described the garden in semi-satirical terms:

> The flowers are glittering in gold and the beds are fertilised with crown thalers, the summer houses are well papered with Rothschild bonds . . . A magnificent wealth of foreign flora spreads across the garden and each flower twinkles with ducats from Kremnitz rather than with leaves; golden figures glow from within the buds . . . To my mind, in his garden Amschel von Rothschild resembles a lord in his seraglio.[23]

"Good Jews"

It would, of course, have been a good deal easier for Amschel to have acquired his garden if he and his brothers had converted to Christianity. The fact that they did not is of the greatest significance for the history of both the family and the firm. As Ludwig Börne observed with grudging admiration, they had

> chosen the surest means of avoiding the ridicule that attaches to so many baronised millionaire families of the Old Testament: they have declined the holy water of Christianity. Baptism is now the order of the day among rich Jews, and the gospel that was preached in vain to the poor of Judaea now flourishes among the wealthy.[24]

The Rothschilds, however, remained resolutely Jewish—a fact which also impressed Disraeli, himself (like Börne) born a Jew. Disraeli's Younger Sidonia in *Coningsby*— a character partly inspired by Lionel—is "as firm in his adherence to the code of the great Legislator as if the trumpet still sounded on Sinai . . . proud of his origin, and confident in the future of his kind."[25] Eva (a character based in part on Carl's daughter Charlotte) declares in *Tancred:* "I will never become a Christian!"[26]

Such a defiant repudiation of conversion could well have come from a real Rothschild. "I am a Jew in the depths in my heart," wrote Carl in 1814, commenting on the extent to which Jewish families in Hamburg were converting to Christianity.[27] When he encountered the same thing in Berlin two years later, he was scornful: "I could marry the richest and most beautiful girl in Berlin; but I am not going to marry her for all the world because, here in Berlin, if [one is] not converted [then] one has a converted brother or sister-in-law . . . We have made our fortune as Jews and we want nothing to do with such people . . . I prefer not to mix with the *meshumed* [converted] families."[28] The brothers regarded the Bavarian banker Adolph d'Eichthal with considerable suspicion precisely because he was a convert (a mere "goy" would have been less objectionable). As James put it, "It is a bad thing when one has to deal with an apostate."[29] When the Hamburg banker Oppenheim had his children baptised in 1818, the Rothschilds were scandalised. "The only reason I find these people contemptible," Carl sneered, "is that when they convert to Christianity they adopt only what is bad but nothing that is good in it." By converting, Oppenheim had "brought about a revolution in Hamburg": "He is sorry about it. He was weeping when I left . . . after speaking to him about it . . . However, I foresee that Oppenheim's lead will be followed. Well, we are no custodians of others' souls. I will remain what I am, and my children too . . ."[30]

The brothers saw themselves as "role models" in this regard. The more they could achieve socially without converting, the weaker the arguments for conversion would seem, given that the majority of conversions were a response to continuing legal discrimination against Jews. "I am quite ready to believe that we have enough money to last us all our life," wrote James in 1816. "But we are still young and we want to work. And [as] much for the sake of our prestige as Jews as for any other reason."[31] This was the way Amschel saw Nathan's appointment as Austrian consul in London. "Though it may mean nothing to you," he wrote, "it serves the Jewish interest. You will prevent the apostasy of quite a few Vienna Jews."[32] When a newspaper reported that Salomon himself had been baptised, he hastened to publish a denial.[33] When the allegation was repeated in a French encyclopaedia fourteen years later, he insisted it be corrected in all subsequent editions.[34]

However, while their adherence to Judaism was unbending, the brothers were far from uniformly strict in their religious observance. In Frankfurt, Amschel retained his "old-Hebrew customs and habits," invariably eschewing work on the Sabbath, keeping kosher strictly and fasting and feasting on the appropriate holy days. At banquets, noted a contemporary journal, he sat "in true penance, as he never touches any viands or dishes that have not been cleansed or prepared in the Jewish fashion. This strict and unaffected observance of the religious injunctions of his faith is greatly to his honour; he is regarded as the most religious Jew in Frankfurt."[35] By the 1840s he had built a synagogue in his own house.[36] Salomon always ate his own specially prepared kosher food, even when he invited Austrian grandees like the Metternichs to dine with him; and refused to write letters on the Sabbath and holy days.[37]

Their brother Nathan too was mindful of his religious duties. We know that even when he was in Manchester, where the majority of Jews were relatively poor shopkeepers and pedlars, Nathan "conformed to all the rites and ceremonies of our faith, his dinner being cooked by a Jewess and taken to him at his warehouse every day" and the *shamas* "bringing him the palm branch and citron daily during the Tabernacle festival."[38] When Prince Pückler tried to engage him in a religious argument, he found Nathan unexpectedly well informed, reflecting afterwards that he and "his co-religionists are of older religious nobility than we Christians; they are the true aristocrats in this sphere."[39] Nathan's wife Hannah later subscribed to the Holy Society of the House of Learning of the Ashkenazim in London (Hevrah Kadisha Beit Ha-Midrash Ashkenazim Be-London), a thoroughly Orthodox institution,[40] and kept a close watch on her children's religious conduct. When he went up to Cambridge in 1837 Mayer was warned to "avoid everything possible in infringing upon our religious duties," specifically, to "abstain from these indulgencies such as riding on Horseback on Saturdays" and to refuse to attend chapel services in college;[41] while his brother Nat felt the need to apologise profusely to her for missing the Day of Atonement during a trip to Switzerland four years later.[42] James too always kept a *mahzor* (prayer book for the holidays) in his office.[43] When a new baby boy was circumcised, James "thank[ed] God . . . we have one more good Jew in the family."[44]

However, the younger brothers were regarded by Amschel as lapsing dangerously in a number of respects. When the need arose, Nathan, Carl and James all read and wrote business letters on the Sabbath—covertly if they happened to be with Amschel.[45] And one by one they abandoned the strict kosher diet (though not completely: the English family still avoided pork).[46] When Carl was trying to find himself a wife in 1814, Amschel and Salomon objected to his choice of Adelheid Herz on the ground that her family did not keep kosher. The issue was the source of constant arguments. "As to piety," wrote Carl in response to yet another complaint on the subject from Amschel, "when I am old I will be pious too. In my heart I am nothing but a Jew. I don't wish to take care of your soul, but you wrote me once that I should find means to enable you to come occasionally to my house to eat there. That [the lack of kosher food] does not mean that I am not pious."[47] In 1814 James complained bitterly from Berlin: "I am really fed up with the food here, I think it is the worst one could possibly have anywhere. [Amschel] is still concerned about eating only kosher food, as he is still pious and he knows that I am not; yet he will insist that I eat with him."[48] Some years later Heine joked that although James had "not gone over to the Christian Church," he had "gone over to Christian cooking."[49] The younger brothers also abandoned all sartorial vestiges of the ghetto.

The religious differences between—and within—branches of the family grew more acute in the next generation. In London, Nathan's elder children continued to worship more or less as their parents had done.[50] Although not deeply spiritual, they were fundamentally conservative in their habits of worship. Indeed, they found their uncle's family in Paris rather too lax. Lionel pointedly refused to work when he was in Paris for Passover in 1829, though James continued to write letters as usual.[51] Nat too, despite sharing his uncle's aversion to kosher food,[52] found it surprising that during Passover "although we go to *shul* and eat *matzot,* in Paris it is impossible to shut up shop."[53] The ascendancy of the Reform movement in Frankfurt (which essentially sought to remodel the rabbinate and Jewish forms of worship along Protestant lines)[54] perturbed them too, accustomed as they were to Amschel's old-fashioned ways. "They have a new Rabbi here who preaches uncommonly well," reported Anthony ambivalently in 1844. "He preached on Friday for the first time, I did not like anything that he said—but perhaps it was the fault of the Reformers here. They go a good deal further than they do in England. I should like to hear a man who could preach as well in England . . . I was very disquieted with the whole service."[55]

The influence of Reform on Carl's daughter Charlotte was strong, judging by the way she later critically compared Jewish practices in England with those of some Christian denominations. Yet when her brother Wilhelm Carl went to the other extreme, outdoing even Amschel in his Orthodoxy, the English Rothschilds were

even more disconcerted. His aunt Hannah reported to Lionel on his condition
rather as if "his enthusiasm in observing all the stricter duties of the Jewish religion"
were a sign of possible mental imbalance:

> I have seen him twice, he came to his Brother one Evening and
> remained an hour, and as much as propriety allowed I remarked his
> manner &c. which is very rational and not in any way different from
> others of his age and situation, tranquil and civil, plain in his dress[,]
> not conspicuous either for much attention to it . . . There is nothing in
> my opinion to fear, that this religious devotion will be followed by
> fanaticism. I saw him again at Baron A. de Rothschild['s] . . . he accom-
> panied us to look at the same things and took as much interest in all as
> any of us . . . [H]e said, I am determined to be firm and will always be
> so. Should he be fortunate to find proper and sensible Instructors, no ill
> can be anticipated from his present good principles.[56]

When Amschel withdrew a substantial donation (150,000 gulden) intended to
finance the building of a new synagogue because "they [the Jewish community's
board] have chosen a new [deputy] Rabbi for the synagogue who is not an Orthodox
one," Anthony could only shake his head: "You have no idea what a parcel of Donkeys . . . the Jews are here."[57]

To most members of the family, the conflicts between Reformers and Orthodox
Jews—which had only a muted echo in England—were an unwelcome nuisance.
Internecine theological and liturgical controversies held little interest for them; and
any weakening of Jewish unity struck them as self-defeating in a hostile world. Thus
Mayer Amschel's sons and grandsons followed his example in accepting lay offices
within their communities, but rarely intervened in religious disputes, save to appeal
for harmony. Nathan was *Parnass* (warden) of the Great Synagogue in Duke Place,
and was almost certainly behind a scheme for "an organisation of Jewish charity" to
combine the efforts of the three major Ashkenazi synagogues of the metropolis (the
Great, the Hambro' and the New)—a move foreshadowing the later emergence of
the United Synagogue.[58] For the Rothschilds, religious activism was primarily about
giving practical, material assistance to a stable Jewish community—not defining the
community, much less the nature of its faith, which they tended to regard as an
immutable given.

Of course, the relationship between the Rothschilds and the wider, poorer Jewish
community has long been the subject of myths and jokes. In the classic anecdotes on
the subject a stereotyped "Rothschild" is the target for a range of ingenious bids for
alms from *Schnorrer*—those distinctively unabashed scroungers and spongers of the
folkloric Jewish community. "Rothschild" is their long-suffering but ultimately
indulgent victim, sometimes even entering into the spirit of the game—as when a
begging letter thrown through a window onto the dinner table is thrown back with
a coin. ("Placiert"—"sold"—mutters Rothschild to himself, as if selling a bond to
an investor, when he sees the *Schnorrer* catch the coin.)[59] Such stories—which continue to be republished in anthologies of Jewish humour today—are not entirely
fanciful: they are echoes of the era when the Rothschilds, because of their great
wealth and apparent political power, had a mythic, talismanic status in the eyes of
other Jews: not only "the Jews of the Kings" but also the "Kings of the Jews"—at
once exalted by their wealth,[60] and yet mindful of their own lowly origins.[61] As

such, they were the focus of all kinds of aspiration, ranging from the mercenary to the visionary. The Rothschild archives contain numerous unsolicited letters requesting assistance from Jews and Jewish communities all over the world: the Dublin Hebrew Congregation; the friends of a Jewish doctor in reduced circumstances; the St Alban's Place Synagogue; the New Hebrew Congregation at Liverpool.[62] These were the real *Schnorrer*—rarely the cocky figures of legend, more often humble supplicants.

Because copies of outgoing correspondence were either not kept or subsequently destroyed at New Court, it is far from easy to tell which of these pleas were heeded, and therefore even harder to detect a pattern in Rothschild charitability. We know that Nathan subscribed to a number of charities for the poor and sick: the Bread, Meat and Coal Society (Meshebat Naphesh); the Jews' Hospital (Nevé Zedek) at Mile End, of which he was vice-president and later president; the Holy Society for the Assistance of the Poor for the Needs of the Sabbath in London; the charitable fund of the Great Synagogue, and the Bethnal Green Society for the Relief of the Sick Poor. He also became a Governor of the London Hospital, which had a tradition of providing for Jewish patients, in 1826.[63] But education seems to have been his main charitable interest. He subscribed to the Talmud Torah in London Society in 1820 and a year later donated 1,000 guilders to a society for the education of poor Dutch Jews.[64] In particular, he supported the Jews' Free School, donating 10 guineas to the building fund in 1817 and helping to pay for the new schoolhouse in Bell Lane, Spitalfields.[65] The school was "a charity he took so decided an interest in" that his widow made a further substantial donation to mark the third anniversary of his death.[66] It has been calculated that the firm of N. M. Rothschild & Sons gave the school an average of £9,500 a year throughout the nineteenth century, a figure which is more than doubled when individual family members' benefactions are added.[67]

In all this, Nathan may have been consciously following his father's example; but he was also falling in with the priorities of his Cohen and Montefiore relations. It was one of his sisters-in-law who made him "promise . . . to give to the poor" in 1814;[68] and it was probably his brother-in-law Joseph Cohen who involved him in the Jews' Free School, of which Hannah herself became a Life Governor in 1821.[69] When Lionel became a trustee of the Bread, Meat and Coal Society, the board was already dominated by Cohens; indeed, his mother was later described as "a zealous advocate of its prosperity & a munificent Contributor to its funds"—not surprisingly, as her father had been one of its founders.[70] Another of Hannah's pet charities was the Jewish Lying-in Charity.[71] By the later 1830s her sons were actively involved in the Jews' Hospital, of which Lionel was president and Mayer later steward,[72] and the Jews' Free School. At the same time, they continued to disburse small amounts to societies like the (Jewish) Society for Relieving the Aged Needy[73] and, through the Great Synagogue, to unfortunate individuals like a mother whose child had a club-foot.[74]

In Frankfurt, Mayer Amschel's legacy still made itself felt. Like his father, Amschel routinely gave 10 per cent of the Frankfurt house's running costs (not its income) to the poor.[75] And in 1825 Amschel and his brothers donated 100,000 gulden to the two Jewish insurance funds in Frankfurt to build a new hospital for the community in the Reichneigrabenstrasse, "in accordance with the wishes of their late father . . . [and] as a memorial to filial respect and fraternal harmony."[76] Curiously, James preferred to keep a much lower profile within the Paris Jewish community, channelling his contributions indirectly through Salomon Alkan, president of Société de Secours, and Albert Cohn, his sons' tutor (and later a leading light of French Jewry). In 1836 he even stipulated that his donations to the new synagogue in the rue Notre-Dame-de-Nazareth should be kept secret.[77]

At least one contemporary cartoonist suggested that, having made their millions, the Rothschilds were indifferent to the plight of their "poorer co-religionists" (a favourite phrase). In *A King bestowing favors on a Great Man's Friends* (1824) (illustration 6.i), a group of ragged Jews—labelled "The Old Stock Reduced"—can be seen to the right of Nathan as he prepares to ascend in a balloon "to receive my Dividends." One exclaims: "The Lord will surely hear the *Cries* of the *poor.*" Another pleads, "O! Look down from heaven and behold that we are become a mockery and derision to be buffeted and reproached." A third cries: "O Lord, have mercy on us for we are overwhelmed with contempt; overwhelmed is [*sic*] our Souls with the Scorn of those who are at ease and with the contempt of the proud." This accusation was unfounded.

Yet it is important to stress that the Rothschilds did not confine their charitable activities exclusively to the Jewish community. At times of economic hardship— 1814 in Germany, 1830 in France, 1842 in Hamburg, 1846 in Ireland—they donated money to the poor without religious distinction.[78] Nathan contributed to a

6.i: T. Jones, *A King bestowing favors on a **Great Man's Friends**—Scene near the **Bank*** (1824).

number of apparently non-denominational establishments, including the Society of Friends of Foreigners in Distress (though it is likely that some of the "foreigners" in question were poor Jewish immigrants).[79] His children also lent their support to the London Orphan Asylum, the London Philanthropic Society and the Buckinghamshire General Infirmary.[80] Especially unexpected is the fact that in 1837 either Hannah or Charlotte—more probably the latter—was "one of the most liberal contributors" to a new Church of England school at Ealing and Old Brentford.[81] It was not only Jews who applied for assistance to the Rothschilds: the *Schnorrer* even included the early socialist Robert Owen and a congregation of the secessionist Scottish Free Church![82]

"A Heavenly Good Deed": Emancipation

Although their wealth and influence allowed them to achieve what was in many respects a privileged social status, the Rothschilds never lost sight of the fact that they and their co-religionists remained subject to a wide range of discriminatory laws and regulations after 1815. They remembered Mayer Amschel's injunctions to "bring to an end all the work" which he had begun "in the interest of our people." As a result, the history of the Rothschilds is inseparable from the history of what is somewhat anachronistically called Jewish "emancipation": to be precise, the gradual process whereby Jews (with the assistance of some sympathetic Gentiles) sought to achieve full legal equality in the various European states.[83] Though self-interest undoubtedly was part of the reason for the family's sustained involvement in this, the principal motivation was a sense of moral obligation to other Jews: a point neatly made by Amschel when he ended a letter to his brothers in 1815: "I remain your brother, who wishes you, and me, and all Jews, all the best, Amschel Rothschild."[84] Those who assumed that Amschel was concerned to protect his own position misunderstood him. In 1814 he urged Nathan to maintain his "influence at the English court . . . for two reasons: firstly, in the interests of the Jewish people, secondly, in the interests of the prestige of the House of Rothschild."[85] "It is . . . good that we own so much money," he wrote to Nathan and Salomon three years later. "Thus we can lend help to the whole of Jewry."[86]

What were the handicaps under which Jews continued to labour in Restoration Europe? The situation was perhaps best in France, where the restored Bourbons, despite their devotion to Catholicism, not only preserved the legal emancipation of Jews achieved by the Revolution, but also failed to renew the so-called *décret infâme* passed by Napoleon in 1808, which had reimposed various economic restrictions. All that formally remained was a special oath which Jews had to take in court, though in practice they were also largely excluded from political life before 1830. In Britain, although native-born Jews were automatically British subjects,[87] they—along with Catholics and Non-Conformists before 1828–9—were excluded from parliament (whether as voters or members), local government and the ancient universities. On the other hand, there were few economic and social barriers.[88]

The position in Germany varied from state to state.[89] Prussia had the most liberal legislation following the emancipation edict of 1812, which granted Jews equal legal rights, though in practice they continued to be excluded from the bureaucracy and the officer corps, and after 1822 were also excluded from schoolteaching and municipal government. In Austria, by contrast, little had changed since the Tolerance

Edict of 1782 (which had reduced economic restrictions somewhat): Jews continued to be denied the right to own land in the Empire, had to pay a special poll tax, were subject to marriage restrictions and, if born outside the Empire, required a special "toleration permit" to reside there, renewable every three years. They were also excluded from the civil service, though they could and did serve in the army and some had even become officers during the Napoleonic Wars. When Lionel went on his tour through Germany in 1827, it was only in Vienna that he found the position of Jews so bad as to be noteworthy: "Jews are very much oppressed, they can hold no situation under Government nor possess any land property, not even a house in the town, they are obliged to pay a heavy tolerance tax, and must have a permission to hire lodgings."[90] All these restrictions directly affected his Uncle Salomon. He had to seek permission from Metternich in 1823, when his cousin Anton Schnapper wanted to move to Vienna to marry a relative of his senior clerk Leopold von Wertheimstein.[91] Ten years later he had to apply for renewal of "toleration" for another senior clerk, Moritz Goldschmidt (who had also been born in Frankfurt).[92] Salomon himself could only rent accommodation in Vienna, and his request in 1831 that he and his brothers be allowed "to convert part of the wealth with which a kind providence has blessed us into a form in which it will be remunerative whatever vicissitudes may befall us" was turned down—despite Salomon's ingenious argument that this would be "not wholly inconsistent with [the government's] own advantage, since it cannot regard with indifference the possibility of attracting considerable capital sums to the country which will become subject to taxation."[93] If such exceptions could not be made even for the state's most powerful and loyal banker, efforts to improve the collective position of the Austrian Jews were foredoomed to failure before the 1840s.[94]

In western Germany, matters were left in a state of flux by the end of French control in 1814. Dalberg's 1811 decree giving Jews full rights of citizenship in Frankfurt was effectively suspended shortly after his abdication as Grand Duke.[95] In March 1814 the special Jewish oath was reintroduced in the courts and Jews were dismissed from public sector posts. Later the same year, membership of the citizens' assembly was once again restricted to Christians. The situation in neighbouring Hesse-Kassel was similar. As we have seen, this reaction partly reflected popular anti-Jewish feeling, which in Frankfurt was distinctly threatening. Amschel's letters of this period are full of lurid images of impending violence: the Gentiles "could drink Jews' blood" or even "eat a grilled Jew."[96] There was, however, a chance to stem this reaction at the Congress of Vienna (1814–15), where the constitutional form of the new German Confederation was to be determined, raising the possibility of a general emancipation applicable to Germany as a whole. Although the Rothschilds were mainly preoccupied with the financial aspects of the post-war settlement, which were largely decided in Paris, they nevertheless took a close interest in this aspect of events in the Austrian capital, where a delegation had been sent by the Frankfurt Jewish community to press the Jewish case.[97] It would appear that the first member of the family to see the need for such lobbying was Salomon's wife Caroline. On July 21, 1814, she wrote to her husband, who was then in London:

It does not look rosy for us as regards our citizenship . . . As far as I can see from a distance, we still have a long struggle before us. This matter interests me so much that, if I catch a simple word about it, I listen eagerly to what is said . . . I am very curious to know what the result is going to be. Can't you, my dearest Salomon, contribute to this through your acquaintances over there? This would be a heavenly good deed, which cannot be bought even with very much money. Perhaps a minister there would give you an introduction to Austria, Russia or whomsoever has a say in this matter. You may ask what has a woman to do with public affairs? Better she should write about soap and needles. However, I see what I am doing as necessary. Nobody is doing anything about this matter. Time is passing slowly and we will reproach ourselves for not having done more . . . This matter is now most pressing; and here in Frankfurt nobody is doing anything.[98]

Amschel and Carl needed no such prompting. In August and September the former was in Berlin on business, from whence he relayed news of the likely Russian and Prussian positions on the subject to Isaac Gumprecht, one of the leaders of the Frankfurt Jews in Vienna (the other key figures were Ludwig Börne's father Jacob Baruch and the lawyer August Jassoy).[99] Carl meanwhile wrote to Nathan asking him whether an "English Lord" then on his way to Vienna—probably Castlereagh—"could possibly help in the question of the civil rights with regard to the Jews."[100]

From an early stage, the brothers pinned considerable hopes on the Prussian Chancellor Hardenberg, one of the architects of the Prussian emancipation. According to Amschel, he had "a very friendly attitude towards the Jews . . . [H]e obtained citizenship rights for the Danzig Jews. And he did this despite the anti-Jewish representations which the Danzig Gentile merchants made to the King."[101] He also urged Nathan to "send a few small presents for the Minister's [probably the Prussian Finance Minister Bülow's] wife. [He] is most certainly in a position to help the Jews."[102] The Prussian diplomat Wilhelm von Humboldt received similar blandishments: though he scrupulously refused a gift of three emerald rings from the Jewish delegation at Vienna in 1814, two years later Amschel offered to purchase some caskets from him at what he considered an excessive price "if by it something could be achieved."[103] Their other great hope was Metternich, though his apparently sympathetic attitude was known not to be shared by other senior Austrian ministers. A letter from Salomon in October 1815 asked Nathan to make a speculative purchase of British stocks worth £20,000 for "the great man who does everything for [the] Jews."[104] This could refer to either Hardenberg or Metternich, whom Salomon had seen the previous day. Buderus—who had been restored to power by the Elector in Hesse-Kassel—was also seen as a possible source of support, though the fact that the Jewish community owed him money was expected to complicate his attitude.[105]

At first, it seemed as if a compromise could be reached in Vienna. In December 1814, for example, Carl heard that citizenship could (once again) be secured for the Frankfurt Jews in return for a cash payment of 50,000 gulden; following his father's example, he offered to contribute 5,000, in addition to the 3,000 the community already owed the firm.[106] But there was a serious setback when, at the suggestion of the Bremen Bürgermeister Smidt, article 16 of the German Bundesakte—the loose confederal constitution signed by the member states in June 1815—referred only to rights previously granted to Jews "by" (as opposed to the original "in") the German states, effectively invalidating all the Napoleonic measures, and leaving future arrangements in the hands of the individual states. Nevertheless, after the interruption of Napoleon's Hundred Days, the brothers continued their efforts in the hope of bringing pressure to bear directly on the Frankfurt authorities. In September Amschel sent the latest details of the situation in Frankfurt to Paris, urging his brothers to show them to Metternich and to "Bülow who is a good friend of Hardenberg and promised me in Berlin that he would help . . . If you can help you will be blessed, for Baruch is in Vienna but will be back soon. But with such things you must strike while the iron is hot." Salomon should tell Bülow what Amschel had told Hardenberg: "That we should not be regarded as aliens. In critical times, we [Jews] served [in the army] as well as any native. I believe you will be doing good if you do this, as we have many enemies and otherwise you won't get anything; we just have far too many enemies, and I will be very sorry if we end up with nothing."[107]

Salomon was soon able to report a promise of support from Metternich as well as Hardenberg, which led to letters being sent to the Frankfurt authorities by both Austria and Prussia, urging that the agreement between Dalberg and the Jewish community of 1811 be upheld—or, as Salomon rather optimistically put it, telling them "that the devil may take all non-Jews in Frankfurt and that the Jews in Frankfurt will keep their citizenship."[108] James meanwhile urged Nathan to get a letter from a senior British figure in the same sense.[109] When Hardenberg came to Frankfurt at the end of November, Carl pressed him to receive a deputation from the community, among them Amschel, and was further encouraged to hear him speak "very graciously about our Jewish matters."[110] "You cannot do too much on acount of the Jewish matters," he exhorted his brothers.[111] Caroline even wrote to congratulate her husband on his efforts on December 7.[112]

Such congratulations were premature. Amschel sensed the coming disappointment as early as September, when he heard that Baron vom Stein might be given a decisive say in the matter, as Stein was regarded as having "turned against the Jews."[113] By November the messages he was receiving from Baruch in Vienna were gloomy,[114] while the Frankfurt authorities were unmoved by the Austrian and Prussian letters.[115] Nor was help to be had from outside Germany: according to Nathan, the British representative sent to Frankfurt, the Earl of Clancarty, was "no friend of our people."[116] Worse, the Austrian delegate to the Confederation's Diet in Frankfurt, Count Buol-Schauenstein, turned out to share the Frankfurt authorities' view that "this nation, which never integrates with any other, but always hangs together to pursue its own ends, will soon overshadow Christian firms, and with their terribly rapid increase of population they will soon spread over the whole city, so that a Jewish trading city will gradually arise beside our venerable cathedral."[117]

Although Amschel and Carl continued to lobby the representatives of the various German states and to receive encouragement from Hardenberg and Humboldt, as well as from the Russian envoy in Frankfurt, they were increasingly pessimistic.[118] Indeed, Amschel began to talk of leaving Frankfurt altogether—though this may have been intended partly as a threat to embarrass the Frankfurt authorities.[119] It was at this time that he and Carl made their first concerted efforts to overcome their social isolation in Frankfurt: the first dinners they gave were in fact primarily designed to lobby influential figures in diplomatic and financial circles "in the interests of the Jewish people."[120] They attached particular significance to winning over the banker Bethmann, whose utterances on the subject appear to have varied considerably according to the company he was in.[121] At the same time (November 1816), Amschel, Baruch and Jonas Rothschild sent a memorandum to the Federal Diet challenging the legality of the Frankfurt Senate's action.[122]

Under these circumstances, it was inevitable that the legislative settlements reached in the various states would fall far short of what had been achieved in 1811. In Kassel, although the Jews were given citizenship (in return for the inevitable payment), it was hedged around with economic restrictions preventing Jews from unrestricted ownership of real estate and prohibiting street-hawking. To Buderus's wife, Carl was fulsome in his flattery of the Elector: "I said, the Prince knows that he alone began the reform, it was his own initiative, and that the world now saw how liberally-minded he had been all along." Indeed, he pressed William to give the same rights to the Jews in his other territory of Hanau.[123] But he and his brothers knew full well that, while the conditions attached to Jewish citizenship seemed "trivial things in principle," they were "big things for those affected."[124] Moreover, as Carl privately remarked, the Elector was "an expert when it comes to going back on his word"—a verdict which seemed to be vindicated in 1820, when it was rumoured that new residence restrictions were going to be imposed on Jews in Kassel.[125] The new law was in fact typical of the kind of qualified "emancipation contract" which German states wanted to make with Jews—offering rights only in return for social "regeneration" and assimilation; it was better than nothing, but it did not satisfy the Rothschilds.

In Frankfurt, despite the example of Electoral Hesse, the debate appeared to end in an even more complete defeat in October 1816, when a revised constitution confirmed the equality of Christian citizens only, leaving Jews as second-class *Schutzgenossen* (literally "protected comrades"). It was especially galling that, even as they revoked the decree of 1811, the authorities specifically cited Amschel's garden as evidence of their enlightened attitude towards the Jewish community.[126] If this was intended to buy off the Rothschilds, however, it failed; it merely made Amschel the target for antagonism on the part of those in the town who wished even stricter measures against the Jews—namely a wholesale return to the ghetto. As we have seen, anti-Jewish feeling in Frankfurt grew more and more overt in this period, with the performance of plays like *Unser Verkehr* and the publication of numerous anti-Jewish pamphlets.[127] During the debates on the Jewish question, some members of the Senate had even been heard to propose as a "solution" that the Jews should be expelled from Frankfurt altogether "as the endeavour of these money-grabbing nomads is solely directed at the ruin of [us] Christians, so that within a few years a large part of the Christian burghers and residents will have been deprived of all happiness and prosperity."[128] In September 1816 a group of anxious representatives of the Jewish community wrote to the Rothschild brothers, noting "how tirelessly and eagerly you are working for us, how strong your solidarity with us is," but admitting: "[T]he good results which we were justified in hoping for have not been achieved . . . We fear that the fortress will not capitulate before very decisive measures are taken."[129]

What form could such measures take? In the wake of the Frankfurt defeat, Amschel angrily talked of "hurting" the Gentile bankers in Frankfurt "by doing business, even if it entails losses."[130] More plausibly, the Rothschilds might make use of their rapidly increasing wealth in a more positive way. Some German Jews looked to Nathan—the richest and most influential of the brothers at this time—to provide some kind of English *deus ex machina*. "I hope in days to come the British who conquered Napoleon," wrote one of the Frankfurt community's leaders, "are going to call the Frankfurt Senate to set free Jewish slaves here as they have freed Christian slaves elsewhere."[131] Amschel himself urged Nathan to "have the British Minister [in Bavaria, Frederick] Lamb egged on again" to support the Jewish case.[132] According to the brothers' correspondence, Nathan did what he could. A number of letters credit him with securing support on the issue from the Dutch King, as well as acting to protect the interests of other Jewish communities in British jurisdiction, notably in Corfu and Hanover.[133] "I think it might be easy to improve our lot should you approach the Prince Regent," a Hamburg Jew named Meyerstein wrote to Nathan in 1819. "Why should the Hanoverian Jews, living in an English province, not be given the same laws conceded to their brethren in England? The barbarity of the past century has got to be stopped and it is from your direction that we expect the sun to rise also for us."[134] In the case of Frankfurt, of course, British influence was minimal: the best tactic still seemed to be to apply pressure in Berlin and Vienna, in the hope that the larger German states would finally force Frankfurt to soften its attitude.[135] But here too Nathan could make a contribution. In what was to become the pattern for much of their later activities of this sort, the brothers sought to win stronger Prussian support for the Jewish case in the course of the negotiations for the 1818 sterling loan.[136] The brothers also endeavoured to raise the issue at the Congress of Aix; indeed, Amschel argued that Salomon should go there "not for business reasons but in the interest of the whole Jewry."[137] It was in fact this issue which brought them into contact with Friedrich Gentz for the first time, as he and Metternich passed through Frankfurt on their way to the Congress.[138]

Such pulling on the purse strings in Berlin and Vienna could not prevent popular antagonism in Frankfurt finally boiling over into the violence of the "Hep" riots of August 1819. On the other hand, the unrest served to strengthen the case against the town authorities, and the Rothschilds sought to press home the point by reiterating Amschel's threat to leave Frankfurt for good. A letter by James to the Vienna banker David Parish, which was evidently intended for Metternich's eyes, illustrates the way the brothers were now explicitly using their financial leverage on behalf of their "nation" (a phrase they often used):

> What can be the result of such disturbances? Surely they can only have the effect of causing all the rich people of our nation to leave Germany and transfer their property to France and England; I myself have advised my brother to shut up house and come here. If we make a start, I am convinced all well-to-do people will follow our example and I question whether the sovereigns of Germany will be pleased with a development which will make it necessary for them to apply to France or England when they are in need of funds. Who buys state bonds in Germany and who has endeavoured to raise the rate of exchange if it be not our nation? Has not our example engendered a certain confidence in the state loans so that Christian firms have also taken heart and invested

part of their money in all kinds of securities? . . . The object of the agi-
tators at Frankfurt seems to have been . . . to collect all the Israelites into
a single street; if they had been successful in doing this, might it not
have led to a general massacre? I need not point out how undesirable
such an occurrence would be, especially at a time when our house might
be holding large sums for the account of the Austrian or Prussian Court.
It seems to me to be really necessary that Austria and Prussia should
devise measures to be applied by the Senate at Frankfurt for energetically dealing with occurrences such as those of the 10th of this month,
and thus making each man secure in his possessions.[139]

In the view of their avowed adversary, the Bremen delegate to the Frankfurt Diet,
the Rothschilds were making full use of their financial leverage. Besides Austria and
Prussia, "several minor states have also had recourse to this financial Power in their
difficulties, which puts it in a strong position to ask for favours, especially for a
favour of such an apparently trivial nature as the protection of a few dozen Jews in a
small state."[140]

   The brothers kept up the pressure in 1820, pressing Metternich to lean on Buol,
who continued to support the Frankfurt authorities.[141] They also lobbied the Badenese government on behalf of the Jews there.[142] When Metternich visited Frankfurt
in October 1821, he signalled his own sympathies by lunching with Amschel;
Salomon meanwhile came to an "important financial arrangement" with Gentz,
after he had once again "bent his ear about the fatal Frankfurt 'Jews' affair."[143] In
1822 Amschel even wrote to Metternich's lover Princess Lieven "asking for the withdrawal of certain instructions towards [the Frankfurt Jews] that Count Münster
must have sent to the Minister of Hanover."

   This campaign was not a total failure. A year after his letter to Princess Lieven, for
example, Amschel was able to celebrate Buol's recall and the arrival of the more sympathetic Münch-Bellinghausen.[144] And, writing from Berlin in March 1822, Heine
detected "better prospects" that the Jews would win back their citizenship. Yet
Princess Lieven's private reaction to Amschel's letter was revealing: it was, she told
Metternich, "the funniest letter imaginable . . . Four pages of sentiment, begging my
help for the Jews of his town, and I, the patroness of the Jews! There is a kind of
naive confidence in it all, which is at once laughable and touching."[145] If this was
how Metternich felt too, the brothers' efforts in Vienna may have been less productive than they imagined. In the end, the Frankfurt authorities made only the most
minimal concessions. Although there was to be no return to the ghetto—in itself a
cause for relief rather than rejoicing—a plethora of restrictions on Jews remained,
and their citizenship was clearly of the second-class variety. The new law confirming
the "private citizen's rights" of the "Israelite citizens" (1824) excluded the Jews from
political life as before; imposed restrictions on their economic activities; subordi-
nated the community to a Senate commissioner; permitted, as before, only fifteen
Jewish marriages a year (only two of which could be with outsiders); and restored
the Jewish oath in the law courts.[146] It is important to bear in mind that these regulations applied to more than a tenth of the town's population (some 4,530 people).
Most of the rules—including the restriction on marriages to Jews from outside
Frankfurt—remained in place until 1848. Indeed, the Frankfurt Jews did not secure
full legal equality until 1864.

Heine used the Rothschilds' role in the emancipation debate to make a sarcastic joke about businessmen in general:

> Frankfurt citizenship papers . . . are said to have dropped 99 per cent below par—to adopt the language they speak in Frankfurt . . . But—to speak like a Frankfurter again—have not the Rothschilds and the Bethmanns stood at par for a long time? A businessman's religion is the same all the world over. The businessman's . . . office is his church; his desk is his pew, his copybook is his bible, his warehouse his holiest of holies, the bourse bell his church bell, his gold his God, his credit his faith.[147]

But this was to miss the point. It was not the position of the Rothschilds which was at issue, but the position of Jews in general. What Heine had to say about the religion or lack of religion of businessmen would be echoed by that other apostate Marx (who argued conversely that capitalism was the universalisation of Jewish "huckstering"); it was not, however, true in the case of the Rothschilds. In any case, the idea that Bethmann and Rothschild stood at par was not one which many Gentiles in Frankfurt accepted.

There is an obvious continuity running from the battle for Jewish rights in Frankfurt to the involvement of Nathan and his sons in the campaign to secure emancipation in Britain after 1828. For here the remaining legal discrimination to which Jews were subject did not in any way personally inconvenience the Rothschilds. Nothing prevented Nathan doing the business he did at the Royal Exchange; nothing prevented him buying the houses where he wished to live. The fact that British Jews were excluded from political life and the English universities could have been a matter of complete indifference to him, as he had no desire or need to enter any of these institutions. Yet it was not. Even Nathan, of all the brothers the most single-minded in his pursuit of profit, felt an obligation to act on behalf of the Jewish community as a whole, even for the sake of rights he himself had no intention of exercising.

In 1828 and 1829 Protestant Dissenters and then Catholics secured the repeal of the laws excluding them from political life, but Jews did not—thanks to the parliamentary Oath of Abjuration (originally intended to exclude "popish recusant convicts"), which contained the phrase "upon the true faith of a Christian."[148] This inconsistency appears to have galvanised Nathan—or, rather, to have galvanised his wife. For, like his brother Salomon, Nathan was evidently susceptible to feminine pressure on the issue. On February 22, 1829, his brother-in-law Moses Montefiore recorded in his diary how he and his wife Judith

> took a ride to see Hannah Rothschild and her husband. We had a long conversation on the subject of liberty for the Jews. He said he would shortly go to the Lord Chancellor and consult him on the matter. Hannah said if he did not, she would. The spirit manifested here by Mrs. Rothschild, and the brief but impressive language she used, reminded me most strikingly of her sister, Mrs. Montefiore.[149]

In the subsequent manoeuvrings, Nathan and Montefiore worked closely together. Broadly speaking, they tended to urge a more cautious strategy than the leading figure on the London Committee of Deputies of the British Jews (later generally known as the Board of Deputies), Isaac Lyon Goldsmid.

For Nathan, the issue revealed with sudden clarity the limits of his relationship with the Tory government, and particularly with the Prime Minister Wellington. Perhaps somewhat naively, he offered to sound out his Tory contacts about the possibility of emancipation in early April, at the height of the political crisis over Catholic emancipation which was close to toppling the government. The Lord Chancellor, Lord Lyndhurst, was evasive:

> He advised them to remain quiet until . . . the Catholic business . . . was settled, but if they thought it more to their own interest to bring the matter forward immediately, to set Lord Holland to do so, and he would support him, as he considered it right that the Jews should be relieved from their present disabilities; at the same time they must be guided by public opinion.[150]

On the basis of this ambiguous message, Nathan recommended to the Board of Deputies "that a petition praying for relief should be prepared, in readiness to be presented to the House of Lords whenever it may be thought right."[151] At Nathan's suggestion the petition dealt solely with British-born Jews, and he advised that only British-born Jews sign it (hence his son Lionel's name appeared, rather than his own). He and Montefiore then took it to their old friend, the former Chancellor Vansittart (now Lord Bexley), who agreed to present it in the Lords after some minor alterations.[152] The Deputies were impressed, and wrote thanking Nathan "for the zeal and attention he has manifested on behalf of his Hebrew Brethren, and more especially for his personal Attendance this day and evincing so ardent a desire in promoting through his powerful influence a relief to the Jews of this Kingdom from those disabilities under which they are labouring."[153] Work was begun on drafting a bill.

Yet in the course of the following month it became evident that Wellington was opposed to the introduction of any such bill that year; nor would he commit himself as to the next parliamentary session. When Nathan went to see him in February 1830 to "entreat" him "to do something for the Jews," the Duke replied that "he would not commit the Government on the question of the Jews, and advised them to defer their application to Parliament, or, if they did not . . . it must be at their own risk, and he would make no promise."[154] In the face of this, Nathan became pessimistic. The Liberal Tory Robert Grant proceeded to introduce a petition in favour of the Jews a week later, followed on April 5 by the first of many bills—an event Nathan himself may have witnessed. Two days later, however, he informed his brother James "that the Jewish matter is not going through."[155] He lobbied another old Tory friend on the subject—Herries, now President of the Board of Trade—but the government position remained unchanged and the bill was duly defeated by 228 to 165 on its second reading.[156] It was now obvious that support for Jewish emancipation was much more likely to come from the Whigs. After years of proximity to the Tories, Nathan suddenly found himself siding with the Opposition.

The emancipation issue cut across party lines: supporters included the socialist Robert Owen, the Irish Catholic Daniel O'Connell and the Liberal Tory William Huskisson, while its most vehement early opponents included William Cobbett. A flavour of the more radical opposition can be gleaned from the numerous cartoons devoted to the subject. A caricature produced shortly after the introduction of

6.ii: Anon., "*To make a shambles of the parliament house—Shakespeare*," the *Looking Glass*, No. 3 (1830).

Grant's bill (though dated March 1, 1830) depicts a bearded Jew in the House of Commons listening to Thomas Babington Macaulay's maiden speech in support of the bill and declaring: "It's *Liberty of Conscience my peoples vants*—that's all" (illustration 6.ii). The figure bears no physical resemblance to Nathan, but the fact that he has a bill in his coat pocket bearing the legend "Cent per cent interest" makes the connection between the Jews and finance clear enough.

In a contemporaneous cartoon entitled *The Wise Men of the East and the Marquiss of West*, Nathan himself is depicted in conversation with Grant (see illustration 6.iii). "I did all I could to procure you the power of legislating for a religion you mock at," Grant says, "but the narrow-minded House threw out *the Bill*." Nathan replies, "Ah well, never mind: have you any Spanish to sell, I'll give you 48 for it." A more stereotyped Jew behind Nathan whispers, "Dat's right, we can easily run it up to 50"; while another exclaims, "Mine Cot, Beards will not be de fashion yet, den!"[157] In both cases a pun is intended on the word "bill": the implication is that the Jews were more interested in the financial variety and that the proponents of a parliamentary bill for emancipation were ingenuous.

Tory opposition continued to thwart emancipation even when the Whigs returned to power after the Reform crisis. A second bill passed its third reading in the Commons in 1833, only to founder in the Lords in the face of opposition led by Wellington and the majority of bishops; a pattern repeated the following year. During Peel's brief ministry of 1834–5, Nathan was one of the signatories of a letter

6.iii: Anon., *The Wise Men of the East and the Marquiss of West*, McLean's Monthly Sheet of Caricatures, No. 55 (1830).

to the Prime Minister—known to be more pragmatic in his views—suggesting that the government at least back a bill for Jewish enfranchisement. But Peel declined; and the measure was taken up only when the Whigs came back in the following month. A year later, in 1836, when the Chancellor of the Exchequer Thomas Spring Rice introduced yet another emancipation bill, it too failed to get past the Lords.

It is hard to believe that the Tories' opposition to emancipation had no influence on Nathan's political views. As we shall see, his attitudes to the Reform Bill crisis underwent a sea-change between 1830 and 1832, and it seems likely that this was linked to disappointment with Wellington over emancipation. Certainly, when his sons took up the cudgels in the one major battle their father had failed to win, they did so as avowed Whigs, and even Liberals. Amschel's garden had been saved in Frankfurt; but the next symbol of the Rothschild role in Jewish emancipation— Lionel's seat in the House of Commons—would not be secured until twenty-two years after his father's death. And it would be another three decades more before the Rothschilds and the Tories were reunited.

"The Exceptional Family"

Yet for all their commitment to Judaism and to the interests of their "co-religionists," there was one important respect in which the Rothschilds sought to distance themselves from the wider Jewish community. By the 1820s they were unquestionably exceptional in financial terms. They were also exceptional in the privileged status they enjoyed relative to other Jews: this was what Heine was specifically alluding to when he used the phrase "exceptional family."[158] But they were also exceptional in the way they operated *as* a family.

Most eighteenth- and nineteenth-century family firms had a limited life-span. The idea that successive generations would lose the economic motivation—the "work ethic"—which had driven their fathers and grandfathers was far from being an invention of Thomas Mann, whose *Buddenbrooks* immortalised the phenomenon. It was all too obvious to Francis Baring. As he wrote ruefully in 1803, conscious already of his progeny's lack of business acumen, "Families founded on the acquirements of an individual do not last above sixty years one with another . . . [T]he posterity of a Merchant, Banker etc., particularly when they are young, abandon the pursuit of their predecessor as beneath them, or they follow it by agents without interfering themselves, which is only a more rapid road to ruin."[159] In fact, the Barings survived relatively well as a financial dynasty, relinquishing control over their own bank only in the 1990s. Innumerable other nineteenth-century family businesses had far shorter lives, lasting just one or two generations. The Rothschilds took exceptional precautions to avoid this decadence.

The necessary first step towards perpetuating the firm was, of course, to produce "posterity"; and, given the terms of Mayer Amschel's will (as well, needless to say, as the social conventions of the period), that meant sons. While Amschel failed to produce any children whatsoever, his brothers produced heirs aplenty—thirteen in all. Salomon had the first, Anselm, born in 1803; Nathan had four sons, Lionel (b. 1808), Anthony (b. 1810), Nathaniel (b. 1812) and Mayer (b. 1818); Carl also had four, Mayer Carl (b. 1820), Adolph (b. 1823), Wilhelm Carl (b. 1828) and Anselm Alexander (b. 1835); and so did James: Alphonse (b. 1827), Gustave (b. 1829), Salomon (b. 1835) and Edmond (b. 1845).

When this generation duly married, male children continued to be at a premium. Indeed, the pressure to produce sons was if anything rather greater. "What do you think of my new little girl?" Anselm asked Anthony, following the birth of his second daughter Hannah Mathilde in 1832. "A boy would have been more acceptable."[160] (His wife Charlotte's first child had been a boy, but he had died in infancy in 1828.) When Lionel too was presented with a daughter, Leonora, one of the senior clerks in Paris wrote to console him: "I actually compliment you that it is a daughter which our dear lady has given you—for you know it is necessary that the first child in our family is of that sex . . . it is a superstition, but that's the way it is." "You may have wished for a son," he added, "but he will come—in two years you will announce him."[161] But when, at the appointed date, another girl was born, Anthony could not disguise his disappointment: "Congratulations to you & your good lady. In these affairs one must take what one can get."[162] He too had to rest content with two daughters; his brother Mayer with just one. Carl's sons Mayer Carl and Wilhelm Carl had no fewer than ten girls between them, but no sons. It was not until 1840 that the third generation produced a boy (Lionel's son Nathaniel, followed by Alfred two years later); and when news broke that Nat's wife was pregnant, there was hope of a winning streak. "Nat has determined not to be outdone by the Rest of the family & intends next year to present you to his son & heir—that is the great news of the day," enthused Anthony. "It is quite [certain] & if he intends keeping par with his eldest brother a pretty lot of little ones will be in the family & the more the happier."[163] It was another girl, and she died before her first birthday.[164]

It would be wrong to infer from such remarks a crude "sexism," however. They were more indicative of an anxiety—which lasted for some years—that the third generation would fail to produce male heirs altogether. In the eyes of Nathan's wife Hannah, as she put it in 1832, it was "of no consequence to our gratification whether a boy or a girl, so [I] have no pity for any who choose to grumble."[165] Nor was this just the female point of view. Once his wife had produced a son, Anselm lost his preference for male children, as he revealed when she became pregnant again:

> If Carlo Dolee [apparently a nickname for Nat, whose wife was also pregnant] has fabricated a little girl or boy my offspring will . . . be very acceptable as for a husband or for a wife . . . The Public will not say the Rothschild family has been idle that year. I hope Billy will soon follow the good example, if he goes to [the spa at] Ems, he may be sure of success.[166]

So far, so conventional. But Anselm's light-hearted letter also touches on what was perhaps the most remarkable aspect of the Rothschilds' history as a family. For the principal reason daughters were not regarded as much less desirable than sons was that the family practised a remarkably sustained strategy of endogamy.

Before 1824 Rothschilds had tended to marry members of other, similar Jewish families, often those with whom they did business. That was true of the wives of all but one of Mayer Amschel's sons—who married, respectively, Eva Hanau, Caroline Stern, Hannah Cohen and Adelheid Herz—as well as of his daughters' husbands— Messrs Worms, Sichel, Montefiore and the two Beyfuses. This was not unusual by nineteenth-century standards. As we have seen, the Stättigkeit imposed on the Frankfurt Jews had more or less made intermarriage within the small community of the Judengasse compulsory. Even without that compulsion, however, most people— and not only Jews—tended to marry within their own religious community, seeking out an equivalent community (as Nathan did in London) if they happened to leave their home town. After 1824, however, Rothschilds tended to marry Rothschilds. Of twenty-one marriages involving descendants of Mayer Amschel between 1824 and 1877, no fewer than fifteen were between his direct descendants. Although marriage between cousins was far from uncommon in the nineteenth century—especially among German-Jewish business dynasties—this was an extraordinary amount of intermarriage. "These Rothschilds harmonise with one another in the most remarkable fashion," declared Heine. "Strangely enough, they even choose marriage partners from among themselves and the strands of relationship between them form complicated knots which future historians will find difficult to unravel."[167] It is only too true; not even the royal families of Europe were as closely inbred, though self-conscious references to "our royal family" suggest that the Rothschilds regarded them as a kind of model.[168] This was one of the other things the Rothschilds had in common with the Saxe-Coburgs.

It began in July 1824 when James married his own niece, his brother Salomon's daughter Betty. (Because he was so much younger than Salomon, the gap in age was not impossibly large: he was thirty-two, she nineteen.) Two years later Salomon's son Anselm married Nathan's eldest daughter Charlotte.[169] There was then a ten-year lull, until the marriage of Nathan's eldest son Lionel to Carl's eldest daughter

Charlotte—at a decisive turning point in the history of the family, as we shall see. Six years after that, Nat married James's daughter Charlotte (the limited range of names adds to the genealogical complexity); and Carl's son Mayer Carl married Nathan's third daughter Louise. Although their wives did not have the surname "Rothschild," Nathan's other sons Anthony and Mayer also married first cousins: Louisa Montefiore (in 1840) and Juliana Cohen (in 1850). (The former was also a descendant of Mayer Amschel as her mother was Nathan's sister Henrietta; the latter was Hannah's niece.)[170] And so it went on, into the fourth generation. In 1849 Carl's third son Wilhelm Carl married Hannah Mathilde, Anselm's second daughter; a year later his brother Adolph married her sister Caroline Julie. In 1857 James's son Alphonse married Lionel's daughter Leonora; in 1862 his brother Salomon James married Adèle, Mayer Carl's daughter; and in 1877 James's youngest son Edmond married Adelheid, Wilhelm Carl's second daughter. Anselm's sons Ferdinand and Salomon both married fellow Rothschilds: Lionel's second daughter Evelina (in 1865) and Alphonse's first daughter Bettina (in 1876). Finally, Lionel's eldest son Nathaniel—usually known as "Natty"—married Mayer Carl's daughter Emma Louise (in 1867); and Nat's son James Edouard married her sister Laura Thérèse (in 1871).

Why did they do it? Romantic love, the conventional modern rationale for marriage, was plainly a minor consideration in the eyes of the older generation, who drew a distinction between a "marriage of convenience" and a "marriage of affection"—Carl's typology when scouring Germany for a suitable wife for himself. "I am not in love," he assured his brothers, when justifying his choice of Adelheid Herz. "On the contrary. If I knew [of] another, I would marry her."[171] Nor did Amschel marry Eva Hanau for love; according to one contemporary account, he openly acknowledged that "the one creature that I ever really loved I have never been able to call mine"; and his nephew Anselm regarded their golden wedding anniversary as marking "fifty years of matrimonial struggle."[172] Caroline and Salomon were less ill suited to one another; but we have already seen how little time they spent together in the years 1812–15, when he was constantly on the move as business—or rather as Nathan—dictated. Five years later not much had changed: Caroline (in Frankfurt) was urging Salomon (in Vienna) not to go to St Petersburg merely because "your Nathan wants you to":

> That is really incomprehensible; is there anywhere you aren't expected to go? Please, dear Salomon, do not let yourself be *talked into it*, [resist it] with all your strength and your considerable intelligence. Moreover, I do not understand your letter very clearly. For there are places in it which seem to suggest that you are going to have to go to Paris or even London. I am usually willing to accept your Nathan's arguments for the above-mentioned business. But I cannot see the justification for this . . . Your Nathan cannot simply ignore the views of all of you . . . In any event, dear Salomon, you are *not* going to London without my knowing the reason why. Understood, my dear husband? You are *not* doing it.[173]

If there ever had been a romantic relationship between these two, there was not much left of it by the time Salomon finally ended his years of nomadism and settled in Vienna. She never joined him there, and the son of one of Salomon's senior clerks recalled that by the 1840s he had developed a somewhat reckless enthusiasm for young girls.[174]

To be sure, love could and did develop within such marriages. Nathan's relationship with Hannah illustrates this well: her letters to her "dear Rothschild" suggest a genuine affinity, albeit one based in large part on a shared enthusiasm for making money.[175] But such affinities were supposed to follow rather than precede marriage; they were not elective. As for James, he evidently treated his niece and wife, beautiful and intelligent though she was, primarily as a useful social asset. "To deprive oneself of one's wife is difficult," he confided in Nathan after just months of marriage. "I could not deprive myself of mine. She is an essential piece of furniture."[176] The James fictionalised as Nucingen by Balzac was respectful of his wife—indeed, treated her as an equal—but went to a succession of mistresses to satisfy his sexual needs and fell in love only once: with a courtesan.

The next generation might have been expected to be less hard-nosed in their attitudes towards marriage, following the trend we associate with the reign of Victoria (who successfully converted her own arranged marriage into a passionate romance). There is some evidence to suggest such a softening. Lionel's letters from Paris to his cousin Charlotte, before their wedding in Frankfurt in 1836, seem to indicate a genuine passion. "Now that I am separated," he effused on January 7, "I only know the meaning of the word and am only able to judge of my love, of my entirely and devoted love for you Dear Charlotte, & wish I were able to express it in words. But I cannot, even in endeavouring to do so my pen has fallen from my hand and more than an hour has passed thinking of you, without taking it up—"[177] Her reply spurred him on:

> I had passed several long days anxiously and tediously without hearing one word from you Dearest Charlotte, when I received your few lines and was then, for the first time since I have left, rendered happy for a few minutes, but I am now again in my melancholy state, your letter I have read over and over, and each time have regretted more and more the great distance that now separates us. I was also grieved to see that you still have such an indifferent opinion of me; you talk of Amusements, Occupations etc. Do you think I can have any that I do not enjoy with you Dear Charlotte? I have been invited everywhere, been entreated to join in some parties of amusement with old friends, but have declined. The only manner of passing my time without being annoyed is when I am alone at my Hotel, thinking and only thinking of you Dearest Charlotte . . .[178]

A week later, his tone was was even more desperately romantic:

> It is a little gratification in obliging you to occupy yourself with and to think of, if only for a few minutes, an absent friend, whose thoughts have never strayed for you, since his departure. Is it the case with others or am I different to the world in large? I have so much to say to you and feel so much the want of conversing with you Dearest Charlotte, that my ideas are confused. I begin with the same and end with the same, and then find myself in the same place; if I cannot have the happiness of telling you so verbally within a short time, I shall go mad.

Yet Lionel rather spoiled the effect of his love-letters when he added: "How happy [my parents] are to see me so attached to you and so fortunate as to have obtained the favours of a person of whom every person speaks in such high terms, and whose acquaintance they are so anxious to make."[179] And only months before, while still on business in Madrid, he had expressed altogether less passionate sentiments in a letter to his brother Anthony:

> I will do whatever my parents and uncles think best about staying or returning. If Uncle Charles [Carl] is gone to Naples, it will not be necessary for me to go soon to Frankfurt. Everything will therefore depend upon the family plans, as I think it makes very little difference for me to go to Frankfurt a few months earlier or later as I have no particular fancy to get married just immediately, a few weeks earlier or later makes no difference without our good parents' wish to go to Frankfurt.[180]

Moreover, it seems that Charlotte (as Lionel evidently realised) was still less excited at the prospect of marrying her cousin. His letters to her in fact suggest a combination of cribbing from fashionable novels and determined auto-suggestion—which, to give Lionel his due, seems to have achieved its object. By the time they were married, as his brothers discerned with some surprise, he really did seem to love her, even if the feeling was not yet reciprocated.

In truth, then, Rothschild-to-Rothschild marriages of the third generation were no more the products of spontaneous attraction than their parents' had been, even if one or both partners managed to summon up more than affection for their chosen spouse. "They want to make some arrangement with Aunt Henrietta about Billy [Anthony] and Louisa [Montefiore]," reported Lionel to his brothers on the eve of his own wedding, rather as if reporting the performance of stocks on the Frankfurt bourse. "Joe [Joseph Montefiore] does not find much favour in H[annah] M[ayer]'s good graces. He runs after Louise who takes no notice of him. Of young Charles [Mayer Carl] and Lou [Louise] there is nothing going on; they have only spoken but a few words with each other."[181] Immediately after the wedding, he was able to provide an update: "H[annah] M[ayer] and J[oseph Montefiore] do not take much notice of each other. The latter runs after L[ouise] who is also courted by another cousin [Mayer Carl] who has taken a fancy to her. Please God, it will be a match and he will be doubly my Brother in Law."[182] His mother was watching the marriage market equally closely. Mayer Carl, she reported, "is more agreeable & communicative than I expected and very capable if he pleases to make an impression on a young lady's heart. I fancy him now to be more manly than our other young beau; there is no alteration in Mayer, no flirtation between him and the other Charlotte Rothschild, therefore whoever is to be the happy man at a future period, will have no cause for jealousy." Six years later she married her daughter Louise off to the said Mayer Carl, while the "other Charlotte"—who had been barely eleven years old when she first discussed her prospects—married her son Nat.[183]

The typically Victorian corollary of this system of arranged marriages was that male Rothschilds were allowed to "sow wild oats": the personal letters which Nathan's sons, nephews and their friends exchanged hint at a number of premarital liaisons.[184] These were tolerated by the older generation provided nothing took place which might impede or damage the system of intermarriage. In 1829, for example, Anthony—who was evidently the playboy of the generation—overstepped the mark by forming too serious an attachment with an unidentified (but unsuitable) girl in Frankfurt. His father angrily summoned him home, accusing Amschel of having failed in his avuncular duties.[185]

The first and most important reason for the strategy of intermarriage was precisely to prevent the five houses drifting apart. Related to this was a desire to ensure that outsiders did not acquire a share in the five brothers' immense fortune. Like most arranged matches of the period, each marriage was therefore accompanied by detailed legal agreements governing the property of the two contracting parties. When James married Betty, she acquired no right to his property, but her dowry of 1.5 million francs (£60,000) remained part of her own distinct property and, had he predeceased her without issue, she would have recouped not only the dowry but a further 2,250,000 francs.[186] When Anselm married Charlotte a year later, she received not only a dowry of £12,000 (in British stocks) from her father, but a further £8,000 from her uncle and new father-in-law "for her separate use," and £1,000 from Anselm as a kind of pre-nuptial down-payment; while Anselm got £100,000 from his father and £50,000 from Nathan.[187] Such large dowries were easily given when the money was staying in the family.

But, mercenary considerations aside, there was also a genuine social difficulty in finding suitable partners outside the family. By the mid-1820s the Rothschilds were so immensely rich that they had left other families with similar origins far behind. Even as early as 1814 the brothers had found it hard to find a suitable husband for their youngest sister Henrietta, only deciding on Abraham Montefiore (to whom Nathan was already related through his sister-in-law) after much agonising. Their original choice, a man named Holländer, had seemed unsuitable to Carl not because Henrietta did not love him—that was neither here nor there—but because, as he put it, "There seems a horrible crowd connected with the Holländers . . . [T]o tell the truth young men of good class are very rare these days." On the other hand, the man she loved, Kaufmann, was "a crook."[188] A decade later, when the brothers' eldest sister Schönche (also known as Jeannette or Nettche) was persuaded by Amschel and Salomon to remarry following the death of her husband Benedikt Worms, her younger brothers disapproved. As James complained to Nathan, her new husband was merely an impecunious stockbroker from the Judengasse:

> She has nothing to live on and she told my wife that she doesn't have any bread in the house. The man is a scoundrel. He gambled her dowry away. Today he went to the Bourse again and perhaps he will earn again what he lost. However I don't believe that he will. Tell me, what is your opinion? Do we want to make something for her every year? In the meantime I personally gave her a present of several thousand francs.[189]

By this time only a Rothschild would really do for a Rothschild.

Nothing illustrates better the exclusiveness of both the partnership system and the intermarriage policy than the experience of Joseph Montefiore in August 1836. Though his mother Henrietta was born a Rothschild, his suggestion (in the wake of her brother Nathan's death) that he might be "taken as one of the partners in the Firm" elicited an icy response from Lionel. "He was averse to this," Montefiore told his uncle Moses, "alleging that there were already too many [partners] and that it would be a bad precedent, however that I might ask my Uncles at Frankfort, and that he should vote with the majority, observing that if I became a partner I must change my name to that of Rothschild." This was plainly calculated to kill the idea, and it had the desired effect: Montefiore "most decidedly did not like this condition" and indeed "approved of it so little that [he] resolved not even to speak about it to [his] Uncles." As the next best thing, this thick-skinned young man then suggested that he might join the London house without the status of a partner but with the possibility of marrying Lionel's sister Hannah Mayer.[190] But this proposal too was rejected, as we shall see.

There was a danger in the policy of intermarriage, however, which the Rothschilds can scarcely have realised. Prohibitions on cousin marriage had been widespread within Christian culture since the sixth century, when Pope Gregory ruled that "the faithful should only marry relations three or four times removed." In nineteenth-century America, eight states passed laws criminalising cousin marriage and a further thirty made it a civil offence. William Cobbett even cited the fact that "Rothschild married his own niece" as an argument against Jewish emancipation.[191] But Jewish law had no such restrictions, while the enforced exclusiveness of the ghetto in a town like Frankfurt positively encouraged cousin marriage. It was not until later in the nineteenth century that the scientific study of heredity began, and only in the second half of the twentieth century that a real understanding of the effects of cousin marriage and other forms of group endogamy has been reached by geneticists. It is now known, for example, that the high incidence among Ashkenazi Jews of Tay-Sachs disease—a condition which fatally damages the brain—is the legacy of centuries of marriage between relatively closely related individuals. Marrying a cousin—especially when the family had spent centuries in the Frankfurt ghetto—was from a strictly medical point of view risky, no matter what the financial rationale. If either Mayer Amschel or Gutle had carried a single copy of a harmful recessive gene, then every time two of their grandchildren married (and it happened four times), there would have been a one in sixteen chance of *both* partners inheriting a copy of the damaged gene; in which case their children would have had a one in four chance of receiving two copies of it and hence suffering from the disease in question.

The Rothschilds were fortunate not to fall victim to the kind of recessive gene which spread haemophilia through the ranks of nineteenth-century royalty.[192] The only indication of poor health in the next generation is the fact that, of Mayer Amschel's forty-four great-grandchildren, six died before the age of five. By modern standards that is a high level of infant mortality (13.6 per cent compared with 0.8 per cent today); on the other hand, around 25 per cent of all children died before their fifth birthday in Western Europe in the 1840s. Of course, the alternative possibility exists that there was a Rothschild "gene for financial acumen," which intermarriage somehow helped to perpetuate. Perhaps it was that which made the Rothschilds truly exceptional. But that cannot easily be demonstrated, it seems unlikely, and, even if it was the case, those concerned knew nothing of it.

SEVEN

Barons

*When [Rothschild] obtained the . . . title [of baron], it was
said, "Montmorency est le premier Baron Chrétien, et Rothschild est le premier Baron Juif."*   —THOMAS RAIKES[1]

Amschel's garden in the Bockenheimer Landstrasse was a symbol of emancipation from the ghetto. However, it would be wrong to suggest that his brothers
and their descendants were motivated solely by the same yearnings as Amschel in
their decisions to purchase property. As Carl's counter-proposal for a more imposing
town house suggests, considerations of economic utility and social prestige also
required more spacious residences—a place where members of the political elite
could be wined and dined in comfort. Two possibilities were discussed at the same
time that Amschel was buying his garden: the purchase of more elegant town
houses; and the purchase of country estates.

Carl got his way in Frankfurt with the purchase in 1818 of the relatively modest
house at 33 Neue Mainzer Strasse.[2] In Nathan's case, the need for a town house separate from New Court was, of course, even more pressing: by 1817 he and Hannah
had no fewer than five children—all under ten—and another on the way. (As yet, all
his brothers apart from Salomon were still childless, and Salomon had only Anselm
and Betty, who lived in relative comfort with their mother in the Schäfergasse house
in Frankfurt.) In June 1817 Nathan therefore offered the stockbroker James Cazenove £15,750 "payable in cash immediately" for Grosvenor House. Characteristically,
however, Nathan refused to pay more than he thought an investment was worth:
when Cazenove demanded £19,000 the deal fell through.[3] In fact, it was not until
1825—by which time there were seven children—that Nathan finally acquired the
lease on 107 Piccadilly from a member of the Coutts family. At the same time,
Moses Montefiore, his brother-in-law and neighbour in St Swithin's Lane, also
moved west to Green Street, off Park Lane.[4]

James, of all the brothers the most aesthetically and socially ambitious, was
quicker off the mark. In 1816 or 1817 he moved from his original quarters in the
rue Le Peletier to the rue de Provence in the Chaussée d'Antin (Paris's main financial
centre, in the 9th arrondissement). This did not satisfy him, however, for in December 1818 he bought the hôtel at 19 rue d'Artois (renamed rue Laffitte in 1830)
which had been built for the banker Laborde before the Revolution, and occupied
during the Empire by Hortense, the daughter of Josephine, and Napoleon's Police

Minister Fouché.[5] Twelve years later, his brother Salomon bought the house next door (17 Rue Laffitte), though it was not until the mid-1830s that the work of renovation and redecoration of both houses was complete.[6] Only in Vienna did it prove impossible to purchase a town house in this period: Salomon continued to rent the Hotel zum Römischen Kaiser in the Renngasse until in 1842 he finally secured an exemption from the rule barring Jews from owning property in the imperial capital.[7]

Nathan, Salomon and James also lost no time in acquiring places in the country—though it should be remembered that in those days, before the growth of London and Paris and the development of railways, it was neither feasible nor necessary to travel far in search of a rural retreat; "suburban retreat" might be a more accurate description. Nathan's first step in this direction was taken in 1816, when he purchased what his sister Henrietta called "a beautiful country estate"—in fact an eight-acre property on the road between Newington and Stamford Hill in the Parish of St John at Hackney.[8] It was there, rather than in New Court, that he and his family thenceforth lived—in contrast to James, who continued to live "over the shop," just a short distance away from the bourse and the Banque de France. It was not until nearly twenty years later that Nathan moved westwards (and upwards), buying the larger and more distinguished Gunnersbury Park near Acton. Built in 1802 for George III's youngest daughter Amelia, Gunnersbury was a large Italianate villa with extensive gardens including a small ornamental lake and a neo-classical "temple." Nathan commissioned the architect Sydney Smirke to enlarge the building, adding an orangerie and a dining room, and to enliven the austere façade with some fake marble decoration; he also consulted the landscape specialist John Claudius Loudon about the park.[9]

Nathan himself remained at heart an urban creature: country life—even at Stamford Hill—did not really suit him. "One of my neighbours," he told Buxton a year before the move to Gunnersbury, "is a very ill-tempered man; he tries to vex me, and has built a great place for swine, close to my walk. So, when I go out, I hear first grunt, grunt, squeak, squeak." Though he was quick to insist that "this does me no harm, I am always in good humour," it is hard to miss the confirmed city-dweller's unease with the alien world of agriculture.[10] It may just have been the smell, of course, but Nathan may also have suspected that his neighbour's choice of livestock had an anti-Jewish connotation. Nor—in marked contrast to James and his own sons—did he have the slightest desire to ride, hunt or watch horses race.[11] In this passage from *Endymion*, Disraeli evidently had Nathan (here "Neuchatel") and Gunnersbury ("Hainault House") in mind:

> [Neuchatel] was always preparing for his posterity. Governed by this passion, although he himself would have been content to live forever in Bishopsgate Street . . . he had become possessed of a vast principality, and which, strange to say, with every advantage of splendour and natural beauty, was not an hour's drive from Whitechapel.
>
> Hainault House had been raised by a British peer in the days when nobles were fond of building Palladian palaces . . . [I]n its style, its beauty, and almost in its dimensions, [it] was a rival of Stowe or Wanstead. It stood in a deer park, and was surrounded by a royal forest. The family that had raised it wore out in the earlier part of this century. It was supposed that the place must be destroyed and dismantled . . .

Neuchatel stepped in and purchased the whole affair—palace, and park, and deer, and pictures, and halls, and galleries of statue and bust, and furniture, and even wines, and all the farms that remained, and all the seigneurial rights in the royal forest. But he never lived there. Though he spared nothing in the maintenance and the improvement of the domain, except on a Sunday he never visited it, and was never known to sleep under its roof. "It will be ready for those who come after me," he would remark, with a modest smile.[12]

Although we know that Nathan did sometimes stay there during the week as well, there seems little doubt that he bought Gunnersbury primarily for the sake of his children; and it was not until two years after his death that the house was used for large-scale entertainment.[13]

In France, James and Salomon both bought houses outside Paris, beginning in 1817 when James acquired what was in effect a summer house with a three acre garden at Boulogne-sur-Seine. Nine years later Salomon bought the rather grander house across the river at Suresnes built for the duc de Chaulnes in the eighteenth century. With its ten acres situated on the banks of the Seine (near what is now the rue de Verdun), it played a similar role to Gunnersbury as a country residence within convenient distance of the city.[14] James waited until 1829 before buying the much bigger hunting estate at Ferrières, with its dilapidated château and 1,200 acres some twenty miles to the east of Paris. Unlike Nathan, James genuinely seems to have enjoyed country life. He looked forward to sleeping at Ferrières as soon as he had bought it[15] and when Hannah Mayer visited him and Betty there in 1833, she found them happily "superintending a little farm."[16]

For the Rothschilds based in Frankfurt and Vienna, however, the purchase of rural estates had to wait. Amschel himself observed that "the first question anyone asks in Germany is: 'Do you have a country estate?' "[17] But he and Carl agreed that it would be a mistake to rise to this socially alluring bait. The ownership of an estate implied a claim to aristocratic status which the ownership of a mere garden did not, and they evidently feared that evincing such delusions of grandeur would fuel the anti-Jewish backlash of the post-war period.[18] At the same time, they doubted the economic rationality of buying agricultural land. What did they know about farming? "Often these estates bring in not more than two per cent," warned Carl—indicating that the brothers were still inclined to regard land as just another form of investment.[19] Such attitudes persisted: Rothschild purchases of land in the next generation were always based on calculations of future yield; and the family managed its immovable assets as carefully as the more liquid components of its portfolio.

Society

The original and most frequently cited justification for acquiring these properties had been typically instrumental: each of the brothers needed a large and respectable house in which to entertain the ministers and diplomats who were their most important clients. The acid test of this strategy was whether the sort of figures the Rothschilds wished to entertain would accept their invitations. It was an uphill struggle.

In December 1815 Buderus—the brothers' trusted partner in their dealings with Wilhelm of Hesse-Kassel—threw a ball. "Bethmann, Gontard, and all the ministers and merchants are invited," complained Amschel bitterly. "We lent the silver. [But] the *Finanzräte* Rothschild are again left out and not invited."[20] Carl's theory was that Buderus was embarrassed by his former intimacy with them: "He thinks we do not feel the proper respect for him, and that he therefore could not appear before us in such a dignified state. For you ought to know that honours and profits do not go hand in hand."[21] There was a similar snub three months later, when Amschel was bluntly informed that, had he been invited, "rumours would have gone round that we had paid for the ball."[22] At around the same time, Amschel complained that Gontard refused to see him too frequently on business lest his friends "start to treat him as a Jew." Their exclusion as Jews from the Frankfurt Casino (gentlemen's club) also rankled. [23]

The tables could be turned, however. In May 1816 Salomon gave a dinner to which he invited the leading members of the diplomatic corps, as well as Bethmann and Gontard. All accepted. As a Rothschild cousin related with glee:

> Today Kessler [a Frankfurt broker] asked me at the Stock Exchange whether it was true that it was really so exquisite at the Rothschilds' house. Apparently there was much talk about it at the casino. He also wanted to know who was present. I mentioned the Ministers, Beth-mann, Gontard etc. I assure you that Bethmann as well as Gontard were full of praise, saying that it was a very lively affair and that Madame Rothschild knew how to arrange everything well. Bethmann especially liked the children, Anselm and Betty; he said that Betty had a fine education.

When one of the family's most ardent foes heard that "Gontard was dining with Salomon, he said: 'Mr Gontard as well?' and sighed . . . He seemed upset and that is something."[24] Three months later Amschel and Carl threw an even larger dinner, principally for the diplomatic representatives of the larger German states. Among those present was Wilhelm von Humboldt.[25] The exercise was successfully repeated a year later.[26] Only the Frankfurt Bürgermeister and one other invitee declined to attend.

The speed of this shift in attitudes astonished the Bremen Bürgermeister Smidt, one of the most determined opponents of Jewish emancipation of all the state delegates in Frankfurt. "Right up until the end of last year," he commented in August 1820,

> it was against all customs and habits of life to admit a Jew into so-called "good society." No Frankfurt banker or merchant would invite a Jew to dine with him, not even one of the Rothschilds, and the delegates to the Confederal Diet had such regard for this custom that they did the same. Since my return I find to my great astonishment that people like the Bethmanns, Gontards [and] Brentanos eat and drink with the leading Jews, invite them to their houses and are invited back, and, when I expressed my surprise, I was told that, as no financial transaction of any importance could be carried through without the co-operation of these people, they had to be treated as friends, and it was not desirable to fall out with them. In view of these developments, the Rothschilds have also been invited by some of the ambassadors.[27]

It was not long before Amschel was inviting him too. He accepted. By the 1840s Amschel was routinely giving such dinners "about once a fortnight [to] all visitors of rank."[28]

In Vienna it proved much harder to overcome the traditional social barriers. Although Metternich had no objection to "taking soup" with Amschel in Frankfurt in 1821, the Austrian capital was a different matter. Contemporary comment strongly suggests that social life in Vienna remained more segregated along religious lines than elsewhere. In the 1820s, Gentz remarked, the Jewish "aristocracy of money" tended to dine and dance together, apart from the aristocracy proper.[29] When the English writer Frances Trollope (the novelist's mother) visited Vienna in the 1830s, she encountered the same schism:

> Neither in London nor in Paris is there anything in the least degree anal-
> ogous to the station which the bankers of Vienna hold in their society.
> Their wealth as a body is enormous and, therefore, as a body they are,
> and must be, of very considerable influence and importance to the state
> . . . And yet with all this—with title, fortune, influence and a magnifi-
> cent style of living—the bankers are as uniformly unadmitted and inad-
> missible in the higher circles, as if they had continued as primitively
> unpretending in station as their goldsmith progenitors.

Trollope was no unbiased observer, of course. She herself disliked being "surrounded . . . at the the largest and most splendid parties of the monied aristocracies
. . . by a black-eyed, high-nosed group of . . . unmistakable Jews" (a prejudice which
she managed to pass on to her son). But, writing in the 1830s, it was not unreasonable for her to doubt:

> how far they are, or will ever be kindly or affectionately amalgamated
> with the other members of this Christian and Catholic Empire . . .
> Their power, as a rich body, is very great and penetrates widely and
> deeply amongst some important fibres of the body politic; but they are
> not, perhaps, the better loved for this by their Christian fellow subjects,
> and the consequence is, that their social position is more pre-eminently
> a false one than that of any set of people I have ever had an opportunity
> of observing . . . No one who visits Vienna with his eyes open and mixes
> at all in society, but will find reason to agree with me in the opinion that
> any attempt to blend Christians and Jews in social and familiar union
> may answer for an hour or a day, but will not eventually lead to affection
> or tolerance on either side.[30]

Only in the late 1830s were senior political figures willing to accept invitations to dine with Salomon in the Hotel zum Römischen Kaiser. The Metternichs did so in January 1836, along with Princess Marie Esterházy and a number of other distin-
guished guests who were duly impressed by his French chef.[31] But when Count Kolowrat accepted an invitation from Salomon (evidently for the first time) in 1838, "some people of his own position in society told him that this was giving offence. 'What would you have me do?' he said. 'Rothschild attached such enormous importance to my coming that I had to sacrifice myself to the interests of the service, as the State needs him.'"[32]

Nathan had fewer difficulties. Foreign ambassadors and other dignitaries accepted his invitations to dinner from an early stage: he dined with the Humboldts in 1818, as we have seen, Chateaubriand dined with him in 1822, and the Ester-házys were regular guests.[33] Prince Pückler's letters record a number of different social occasions at Nathan's, including a "splendid dinner" in 1828, the dessert of which was served on solid gold dishes.[34] What is not certain is whether Nathan's apparently close relations with Tory politicians like Herries, Vansittart and Welling-ton extended as far as the dinner table: quite possibly the greater part of the conver-sations he had with such figures took place in their offices. By contrast, proponents of Jewish emancipation among the Whig aristocracy like the Duke of St Albans and the Earl of Lauderdale were happy to dine with him,[35] as was the historian Thomas Babington Macaulay, a prominent supporter in the Commons, who was a Roth-schild guest in 1831.[36] It also seems reasonable to assume that most of the visiting English aristocrats whom James invited to dinner in Paris had already been enter-tained by Nathan: "your charming Lady Londonderry," for example, whom James "stuffed" with best British venison provided by Nathan in 1833; and the Duke of Richmond, whom he invited to dinner a year later.[37] The brothers' careful cultiva-tion of the British royal family and its Saxe-Coburg relations also paid social divi-dends (though it was not until after Nathan's death that the Duke and Duchess of Cambridge accepted an invitation to Gunnersbury).[38] In the winter of 1826 Carl played host to Leopold of Saxe-Coburg, entertaining him with amateur dramatics, "balls and soirees" at his villa in Naples.[39] Then, as now, members of the social elite found it difficult to resist the offer of Mediterranean hospitality in the middle of the North European winter. The Montefiores also found Carl entertaining and being entertained by the indigenous aristocracy when they visited him in 1828.[40]

Of all the Rothschild brothers, James made the most determined effort to achieve social success; perhaps his superior education gave him the confidence to do so. In 1816, equipped with a handbook of etiquette, he scored his first success, inviting the duc de Richelieu's private secretary to dinner *à deux*.[41] But he too encountered resistance. Despite the social upheavals of the Revolutionary and Napoleonic eras, the French capital was far from free of snobbery and prejudice, and he was treated to an especially flagrant snub from his rivals Baring and Labouchère in 1818.[42] It was not until March 2, 1821, that James really launched himself as a society host with his first full-scale ball in the refurbished rue d'Artois hôtel. The somewhat world-weary Berliner Henrietta Mendelssohn described how

> for the past two weeks nothing has been talked about in the world of the great and the rich here, save a ball which Herr Rothschild finally gave yesterday evening in his new and magnificently decorated house. As yet I have no details as to how it went, but I can scarcely believe it was other than as I have heard for more than ten days—I do not exaggerate—from people of every age and class: that 800 people were invited and at least as many besieged him with visits, letters and pleas in the hope of getting an invitation . . . As I am presently feeling—for whatever reason—daily more miserable and peevish, I did not make use of my invitation to this ball, though it was sent by Herr Rothschild with the most courteous billet ever written.[43]

The campaign was relentless. In April 1826 the Austrian ambassador described a sumptuous meal *chez* "M. de Rothschild" attended not only by the other ambassadors of the great powers, but also by Metternich, the Duke of Devonshire, the Russian Prince Razumovski and a small galaxy of French aristocrats: the duc and duchesse de Maillé, baron de Damas (the French Foreign Minister of the day), the duc de Duras and the comte de Montalembert.[44] A year and a half later, when the maréchal de Castellane dined with James, he encountered the English and Russian ambassadors, the duc de Mouchy and the comte Juste de Noailles.[45] On average James had around four dinners a week, each with at least ten guests and sometimes as many as sixty. The night before the birth of his first child, Charlotte, he had eighteen to dinner; the following evening twenty-six.[46]

Part of the attraction of a Rothschild event—as James well knew—was the sheer extravagance of the hospitality. As Henrietta Mendelssohn commented sardonically, invitations to James's ball in 1821 went to a premium when it was heard "that all the ladies would be given a bouquet of flowers on entering the ballroom with a diamond ring or brooch" or that there would at least be "a lottery which would give a prize to each of the ladies."[47] When Apponyi dined with him in 1826, the table was dominated by an immense silver-plated platter in the form of a candelabrum—worth, Apponyi guessed, at least 100,000 francs—and the food was prepared by the famous chef Antonin Carême, who numbered among his previous employers the Prince Regent and Tsar Alexander. So rich was the combination of turtle soup and madeira that a dyspeptic Apponyi resolved to pay the customary *visite de digestion* eight days later than usual.[48]

In many ways, Carême's elaborate cuisine was James's principal attraction in this early phase of his social ascent. The popular writer Lady Sydney Morgan was only one of many who drooled over his cooking when she dined with James at Boulogne: "[T]he delicate gravies were made with almost chemical precision . . . each vegetable still had its fresh colour . . . the mayonnaise was whipped ice cold . . . Carême deserves a laurel wreath for perfecting an art form by which modern civilisation is measured."[49] The *coup de théâtre* on this occasion was an enormous cake with her name inscribed in icing sugar, surrounded by all the supporters of the Holy Alliance. James took pains to find a worthy successor to Carême when he needed a new cook.[50] Nor was he the only member of the family to value his chef. Though they themselves never tasted a mouthful of it, both Amschel and Salomon insisted on providing their guests in Frankfurt and Vienna with the best of French cooking.[51] Disraeli was one of the most frequent recipients of Rothschild food outside the immediate family itself, and his account in *Endymion* of "delicate dishes which [guests] looked at with wonder, and tasted with timidity" gives an idea of its crucial social function.[52]

Snobbery

Yet, although their invitations were accepted, it cannot be said that the Rothschild brothers were liked. Contemporaries found Nathan Rothschild an intimidating man: unprepossessing in aspect and coarse to the point of downright rudeness in manner. Prince Pückler was given a typically rough ride when he called on "the ruler of the City" at New Court for the first time in 1826:

> I found the Russian consul there, engaged in paying his court. He was a distinguished and intelligent man, who knew perfectly how to play the

role of the humble debtor, while retaining the proper air of dignity. This was made the more difficult since the guiding genius of the City did not stand on ceremony. When I had handed him my letter of credit, he remarked ironically that we rich people were fortunate in being able to travel about and amuse ourselves, while on him, poor man, there rested the cares of the world, and he went on, bitterly bewailing his lot, no poor devil came to England without wanting something from him. "Yesterday," he said, "there was a Russian begging of me" (an episode which threw a bittersweet expression over the consul's face) "and," he added, "the Germans here don't give me a moment's peace." Now it was my turn to put a good face on the matter . . . All this in a language peculiarly his own, half English, half German, the English with an entirely German accent, yet all declaimed with an imposing self-possession which seemed to find such trifles beneath his notice.

Flattery was only partially successful. When Pückler and the visiting Russian declared "that Europe could not subsist without him" Nathan "modestly declined our compliment and said, smiling, 'Oh no, you are only jesting; I am but a servant whom people are pleased with because he manages their affairs well, and to whom they let some crumbs fall as an acknowledgement.'"[53] This was sarcasm, as the discomfited Pückler knew only too well.

In his novel *Tancred*, Disraeli—who, as we shall see, came to know Nathan's son Lionel well in the 1830s—drew on similar recollections when describing his hero's attempt to gain an audience with the elder Sidonia, a character at least partly based on Nathan:

> At this moment there entered the room, from the glass door, the same young man who had ushered Tancred into the apartment. He brought a letter to Sidonia. Lord Montacute felt confused; his shyness returned to him . . . He rose, and began to say good morning when Sidonia, without taking his eyes off the letter, saw him, and waving his hand, stopped him, saying, "I settled with Lord Eskdale that you were not to go away if anything occurred which required my momentary attention." . . .
>
> "Write," continued Sidonia to the clerk, "that my letters are twelve hours later than the despatches, and that the City continued quite tranquil. Let the extract from the Berlin letter be left at the same time at the Treasury. The last bulletin?"
>
> "Consols dropping at half-past two; all the foreign funds lower; shares very active."
>
> They were once more alone.[54]

Such bruising encounters in the office were later distilled into the famous "two chairs" joke, probably the most frequently reprinted Rothschild joke, which must surely have been inspired by Nathan. An eminent visitor is shown into Rothschild's office; without looking up from his desk, Rothschild casually invites him to "take a chair." "Do you realise whom you are addressing?" exclaims the affronted dignitary. Rothschild still does not look up: "So take *two* chairs."[55] (One of many variants has the visitor indignantly announcing himself as the Prince of Thurn *und* Taxis; Rothschild implicitly offers each a chair.)

Nor was it only on his own territory—his office—that Nathan was famed for his blithe disregard for social rank. Even to the dining rooms of polite society he brought the abrasive manners and harsh, puncturing humour of the Frankfurt Judengasse. When Prince Pückler was invited to dine with Nathan he was "diverted" to "hear him explain to us the pictures around the dining room, (all portraits of the sovereigns of Europe, presented through all their ministers) and talk of the originals as his very good friends, and, in a certain sense, his equals":

> "Yes," said he, "the _____ once pressed me for a loan, and in the same week in which I received his autograph letter, his father wrote to me also with his own hand from Rome to beg me for Heaven's sake not to have any concern in it, for that I could not have to do with a more dishonest man than his son. '*C'était sans doute très Catholique*'; probably, however, the letter was written by the old _____ who hated her own son to such a degree that she used to say of him,—everybody knows how unjustly,— 'He has the heart of a t_____ with the face of an a_____ .' "⁵⁶

After a dinner at which Nathan had brutally deflated a fellow guest, the German ambassador Wilhelm von Humboldt wrote to his wife:

> Yesterday Rothschild dined with me. He is quite crude and uneducated, but he has a great deal of intelligence and a positive genius for money. He scored off Major Martins beautifully once or twice. M. was dining with me too and kept on praising everything French. He was being fatuously sentimental about the horrors of war and the large numbers who had been killed. "Well," said R., "if they had not all died, Major, you would probably still be a drummer." You ought to have seen Martins" face.⁵⁷

Even in less exalted company Nathan could seem a boor: witness the Liberal MP Thomas Fowell Buxton's account of Nathan's table talk at a dinner they both attended at Ham House in 1834. Here, it seems, is the self-made millionaire at his self-satisfied worst, proffering pat explanations for his own success and banal advice to others:

> "I have seen . . . many clever men, very clever men, who had not shoes to their feet. I never act with them. Their advice sounds very well, but fate is against them; they cannot get on themselves; and if they cannot do good to themselves, how can they do good to me? . . .
> "To give . . . mind, and soul, and heart, and body, and everything to business; that is the way to be happy. I required a great deal of boldness and a great deal of caution to make a great fortune; and when you have got it, it requires ten times as much wit to keep it. If I were to listen to all the projects proposed to me, I should ruin myself very soon. Stick to one business, young man . . . stick to your brewery, and you may be the great brewer of London. Be a brewer, and a banker, and a merchant, and a manufacturer, and you will soon be in the Gazette."⁵⁸

When a guest at the same dinner expressed the hope "that your children are not too fond of money and business, to the exclusion of more important things. I am sure you would not wish that," Nathan retorted bluntly: "I am sure I should wish that."

Nathan struck some who encountered him as a tight-fisted philistine. The ornithologist Audubon recalled failing to persuade Nathan to subscribe to his lav-

ishly illustrated *Birds of America*, instead sending him the work in advance of payment. But when Nathan was presented with the bill he "looked at it with amaze-
ment and cried out, 'What, a hundred pounds for birds! Why sir I will give you five
pounds, and not a farthing more!'"[59] A frequently repeated anecdote has Nathan
telling the composer Louis Spohr: "I understand nothing of music. This"—patting
his pocket and making his money rattle and jingle—"is my music; we understand
that on 'Change."[60] In another he responds irritably to a request for a charitable
contribution: "Here! Write a cheque; I have made one [damned] fool of myself!"[61]
Buxton was shocked by Nathan's somewhat crass attitude towards philanthropy.
"Sometimes," he explained, "to amuse myself, I give a beggar a guinea. He thinks it
is a mistake, and for fear I shall find it out, off he runs as hard as he can. I advise you
to give a beggar a guinea sometimes; it is very amusing."[62] It was entirely in character for him to point out to his own dinner guests that a particular service had cost
£100. [63]

The notion that an ill-educated Jew could behave this way in polite society and
get away with it purely on account of his newly acquired and largely paper wealth
variously fascinated and appalled contemporaries, depending on their social position and philosophical attachment to the traditional hierarchical order. Prince Pückler, for example, did not apparently resent the way Nathan teased him when he first
presented himself at New Court with his credit note. On the contrary, he summed
him up as "a man who one cannot deny has geniality and even a kind of great character . . . really *un très bon enfant* and generous, more than others of his class—as
long, that is, as he is sure he is not risking anything himself, which one can in no way
hold against him . . . This man is really a complete original."[64] As we have seen,
Humboldt was also condescendingly amused by the combination of bad manners,
sharp wit and lack of deference which Nathan brought to polite society.

In the Paris of the Bourbon Restoration, by contrast, James's many *faux pas*—his
unprompted introduction of his own wife to the duc d'Orléans, for example, or his
use of Count Potocki's Christian name Stanislas—were viewed with distaste.[65] Like
so many of James's socially superior guests, the maréchal de Castellane did not much
care for his host even as he accepted his hospitality: "His wife . . . is pretty enough
and very well-mannered. She sang well, though rather tremulously; her German
accent is disagreeable. James . . . is small, ugly, arrogant, but he gives banquets and
dinners; the grand seigneurs make fun of him and yet are no less delighted to go to
his house, where he brings together the best company in Paris."[66]

According to Moritz Goldschmidt's son Hermann, whose memoir is one of the
few detailed first-hand descriptions we have, Salomon was even more lacking in
social graces. "Why should I eat badly at your place, why don't you come and eat
well at mine," he was once heard to reply to a dinner invitation from the Russian
ambassador. Another "highly placed personality" who asked for a loan received a
blunt negative: "Because I don't want to." Salomon therefore "seldom went into
high society, [because] he felt that because of his lack of education he would have to
play a difficult and uncomfortable role," and preferred to leave "intercourse with the
beau monde" to Goldschmidt's father.[67] On the rare occasions when he did have the
Metternichs to dine with him, he could not resist vulgar displays of wealth, showing
them the contents of his safe as a post-prandial treat.[68] Even in his own more familiar (that is, Jewish) circle, he cut a coarse figure. If his barber was late in the morn-

ing—and Salomon habitually rose at 3 a.m.—he would be reviled as "an ass." If
someone came into the office smelling slightly, Salomon would press his handker-
chief to his nose, open the window, and shout: "Throw him out, the man stinks."
He dined unsociably early at 6.30 p.m. and habitually drank two bottles of wine
before going for a stroll in the park with "blindly loyal toadies and hangers-on."
When he visited the Goldschmidts at their house in Döbling on Sundays he flirted
with the prettier girls present "in a manner which was not always proper or polite."
This included cracking crude jokes if any women present were pregnant.[69]

It is not that all these stories are wholly misleading; no doubt Nathan and his
brothers did seem to many who met them like the incarnation of "new money,"
with all its rough edges. Nothing makes the point more explicit than the 1848 cartoon (produced as the first of a series of "Pictures from Frankfurt") which cruelly
juxtaposed Moritz von Bethmann and Amschel, the former elegant on his coach and
four, the latter slouched atop a money box (see illustration 7.i). Yet such judgements
are not the best kinds of historical evidence. Firstly, they tell us only how the Rothschilds *seemed* to others. Secondly, because "new money" has been the object of
scorn for more than 2,000 years, there are tropes which tend to be repeated no
matter how little the *nouveau riche* individual in question actually conforms to the
stereotype. The brothers' own letters tell a very different story.

In fact, the brothers themselves disliked intensely the great majority of social
functions they gave. Amschel "thanked God" when his dinners were over, and Carl
thought them expensive "humbug"—"it was very nice, but the money was nicer," he
commented when the chef they had hired presented his bill. "However," he con-

7.i: **Ernst Schalk and Philipp Herrlich,** *Baron Moritz von Bethmann and Baron Amschel*
von Rothschild, Bilder aus Frankfurt, **Nr. 1 (1848).**

ceded, "it is as good as bribes": it is noteworthy that at least five of the guests at the 1817 dinner also received parcels of the new city of Paris loan.[70] In Berlin too, where he had relatively little difficulty in securing prestigious invitations from Hardenberg and the British and Austrian ambassadors, Carl retained his scepticism about the value of such socialising: "I don't really care, because I find we always do better business with those who do not invite us."[71] Nathan was as much out of his natural element in the ballroom or the salon as in the countryside. As Amschel said of him in 1817, if Nathan gave a mere tea party, he felt his morning had been "stolen."[72] Even his daughter Charlotte expressed a utilitarian view in 1829 when she hoped that "the Season will be very lively as this is always, I think, an encouragement for trade."[73]

James shed light on his brother's fundamentally anti-social temperament when, contemplating yet another ball, he said: "I now feel exactly as you do. I would gladly stay at home and don't want to drive myself crazy with all the rubbish."[74] He too was much less enamoured of such occasions than his condescending guests generally assumed. From the outset, he took much the same functional view of socialising. "I think of nothing else but business," he assured Nathan. "If I attend a society party, I go there to become acquainted with people who might be useful for the business." To prove the point, early social contacts like Richelieu's secretary were pumped for useful information.[75] Privately, James admitted to being weary of his lavish balls; he continued to give them, he confessed to Nathan in January 1825, only lest people think he could no longer afford to. "My dear Nathan," he wrote wearily,

> I am obliged to give a ball because the world claims that I am broke, for the people who have become accustomed to my giving three to four balls, as I did during the previous winter, will otherwise set their tongues wagging, and quite honestly the French are evil people. Well, the carnival takes place next week and I wish it were already over. I give you my word that my heart is not in it but one must do everything to put on a show for the world.[76]

Six years later, in the wake of the revolutionary crisis of 1830, Charlotte discerned the same link between her uncle's economic performance and his sociability: although Betty felt too "fatigued" to give "her customary balls," "the rentes still [continue] to rise so rapidly [that] James would be disposed to give them."[77] As we shall see, throwing balls was one of the vital ways in which James signalled to the Parisian beau monde that he had survived the financial and political storm of 1830.

The Honours "Racket"

It was not only by giving parties that the Rothschilds sought to transcend the traditional social barriers which confronted Jews, no matter how wealthy, in Restoration Europe. In a social world still dominated by a hierarchy of ranks and orders, they hastened to acquire formal marks of status for themselves. It is perhaps a sign of how fragile the restored Metternichian regime was that they found this exceedingly easy: that is the real point of the "Jew baron" story quoted at the beginning of this chapter.

Perhaps the most striking illustration of this point is the fact that the Rothschilds were able to acquire noble status from the Emperor Francis II as early as 1817. This was arranged in Vienna after lobbying by the Austrian Treasury official Schwinner, the Finance Minister Stadion and Metternich, and was seen by them primarily as a reward for the Rothschilds' role in paying British subsidies and French reparations payments to Austria.[78] The significance of this should not be exaggerated, of course. The Rothschilds were not the first Jews to be elevated in this way: six other families had been ennobled (though all the others had converted to Christianity by 1848).[79] Nor did ennoblement by the Habsburg Emperor connote social elevation of the sort achieved two generations later, when Nathan's grandson Natty Rothschild was given a hereditary peerage by Queen Victoria. Like the Austrian currency, the Austrian nobility had been debased compared with its more exclusive British counterpart. On the other hand, ennoblement gave the brothers three valuable assets: the right to the prefix "von" ("de" in France and England); a coat of arms (albeit not quite the grandiose design they had originally hoped for); and, in 1822, the title "Freiherr" ("Baron" in France and England).[80]

Nor were these the only trophies of social ascent which the Rothschilds picked up in the years after 1814. Just as their father before them had sought to enhance his prestige by acquiring the title of *Hoffaktor* and court banker from as many courts as possible, so too his sons and grandsons applied to be appointed "Financial Councillors" by the family's old friend the Elector of Hesse-Kassel, and later by the King of Prussia. Such titles were purely honorific, but socially useful because they entitled the bearer to wear a uniform, almost a *sine qua non* when attending court functions.[81] The titles of Austrian consul, which was secured for Nathan in 1820, and consul-general, which he and James received in 1821–2 as rewards for their financial support during the Neapolitan crisis, had essentially the same sartorial significance,[82] though notionally they also entailed some responsibility for protecting Habsburg commercial interests in Britain and France. That the Rothschilds made use of such uniforms can be seen from a variety of contemporary references. As early as 1817 Carl sought permission to wear the navy and gold uniform of the Hessian Kriegscollegium.[83] James was spotted in 1825 wearing his red consular outfit to Charles X's coronation at Rheims. Two years later the young Charles Bocher mistook him for an English general when saw him emerging from the Tuileries in his scarlet coat with gold epaulettes.[84]

A uniform was good; but a uniform with decorations—medals, ribbons or braid—was better. These too the brothers began to thirst after from as early as 1814.[85] In late 1817 Carl was publicly presented with a ribbon by the Prussian Chancellor Hardenberg, having found himself one of only two people at the Prussian court with nothing on his chest.[86] A year later the Grand Duke of Darmstadt bestowed orders on James.[87] When he and Salomon both received the Order of St Vladimir from the Tsar during the Congress of Verona in 1822, Salomon made sure—through Gentz—that it was reported in the German press.[88] A year later James added the Knight's Cross of the French Legion of Honour to his tally (though he did not become a full member of the Legion until 1841).[89] By 1827 Salomon was sufficiently blasé to request an order—the Constantine Order of St George— for his senior clerk, Leopold Wertheimstein, for services rendered to the Duchess of Parma.[90] When Nat went to Constantinople in 1834—the first Rothschild to do so—he could not conceal his excitement at the prospect of a new and exotic gong:

You do not know what it is to be received by the Sultan, no person of inferior rank than a minister plenipotentiary can be presented at court—I however consider myself Ambassador . . . & consequently have a right to the most brilliant reception.—The Sultan signified that it was his intention to bestow a mark of his satisfaction, but I do not know whether it is to be a ring, a snuffbox or a grand decoration—I hope the latter. I have already given them to understand that the diamond crescent will be the most acceptable.[91]

As his letter suggests, royal gifts like rings and engraved snuffboxes, though not unwelcome, were second best.

The Rothschilds' pursuit of titles and orders is often seen as a kind of absurd foible: a "weakness" for imitating the nobility, as Capefigue put it.[92] That is undoubtedly the way it seemed to established nobles. Metternich suspected them of "vanity" and "a craving for honours and distinctions"; while critics of the Restoration regime, notably Heine, mocked their apparent deference to aristocratic mores.[93] Yet the brothers themselves privately viewed these mores with a certain amount of contempt. Coats of arms were, as Carl put it, "part of the racket."[94] As for uniforms, James privately joked that "if you go to see a Minister here, you must always be made up as if on a visit to your bride."[95] The brothers even parodied their new titles on occasion: Carl, for example, addressed one letter to "James de Rothschild, Knight of the Society for the Liberation of Christian Slaves [*sic*], Financial Councillor of Electoral Hesse etc. etc. etc.."[96] When the King of Denmark also invited him "to ask for a title," he could only ask: "What are we going to do with all these titles?"[97] Indeed, when he was offered "a ribbon with a buckle such as soldiers wear" by the Elector of Hesse-Kassel, he turned it down as beneath his dignity.[98] Nor were the Rothschilds willing to pay over the odds for badges of status: when Nat heard that the Austrian government wished to provide his brother Lionel with a consular secretary—at an annual cost to the firm of £500—he was outraged: "For my part I wd. see the whole consulate at the deuce before I would pay £500 a year for it & have a disagreeable fellow to be master . . . I should like to know who will pay £500 a year for the honor of being Austrn. Consul."[99] Even Amschel, in many ways the most susceptible of all the family to such things, knew their place. As he put it in 1814, "If we had always worried about what other people were going to think, we would now be left with a great many decorations etc., but without money. And in the end, we would be left without praise, without decorations and without money."[100] "The highest decoration," in his view, was "a quiet life, God willing."[101]

There were two arguments for nevertheless accepting such honours. The first, as we have seen, was that they improved the partners' access to the corridors of power. The second argument was that titles and other honours were "a mark of distinction for our nation"—that is, for European Jewry.[102] The Rothschilds' ennoblement was widely interpreted in Frankfurt as a slap in the face for those in the town who wished to to reimpose the old disabilities on Jews. "[I]f one Jew is a Baron every Jew is a Baron:" that was how they saw it in the Judengasse.[103] In the same way, Nathan's appointment as Austrian consul in London was "a lucky thing for the Jews" according to Carl.[104] Even the fact that the brothers could be awarded decorations with explicitly Christian insignia—the names of saints, even the sign of the cross itself—

was regarded as a kind of victory. Though Amschel refused to accept such orders, Carl had no hesitation in accepting the ribbon and star of the newly founded Order of St George from Pope Gregory XVI in 1832,[105] while Lionel accepted the Order of Isabella from the Queen of Spain three years later. As Heine noted, the Order had originally been established "to glorify the expulsion of the Jews and Moors from Spain"; how piquant that "Herr von Shylock zu Paris" should thus be acknowledged as "the mightiest Baron of Christendom."[106] Certainly, it seemed that way to scandalised Christian commentators like the Austrian Baron Kübeck:

> His Holiness receives a member of the House of Rothschild, and with heavenly forbearance the representative of Jesus Christ on earth decorates a descendant of the people that allowed Christ to be put to death, with the ribbon and star of a newly founded order of St George, and in return allows his hand instead of his foot to be kissed. And still Rothschild refuses to become a Christian.[107]

In this light, perhaps the hardest thing to explain is Nathan's apparent doubt about the value of such honours. For example, a number of letters would seem to suggest that he was offered but turned down the offer of a knighthood (or "Nighthood," as James wrote it) in 1815 or 1816. When someone tried to tell Carl that his brother had accepted, he refused to believe it "because you love simplicity."[108] The 1816 ennoblement patents conspicuously omitted Nathan, and the approved coat of arms showed four arrows instead of five. Furthermore, unlike his brothers and eldest son, he rarely used the title "Baron" or the prefix "de."[109] Was this a matter of milieu, as Corti suggested—a desire not to be too publicly associated with reactionary Austria?[110] Mace argues that there is a more practical explanation: although Nathan secured the right to bear arms in 1818 (hence legitimising the fifth arrow), when he applied to the Royal College of Arms for registration of the Austrian title in 1825 he was turned down—probably because he had only received his own royal letters patent of denization eight years before.[111] However, it may also have been partly because, as Amschel thought, Nathan just "did not want" to be ennobled.[112] Thus, when Nathan declined a Prussian decoration in 1818, he suggested that it be given to Salomon instead because "here in London I have no use for such a thing" whereas "my brother . . . loves ribbons and is a Baron who intends to live in Paris, where one can decorate oneself with such things."[113] James too was at first reluctant to call himself "de Rothschild." "Let us remain merchants," he urged his brothers in 1816. "It is extremely nice to possess the title and not to make use of it, except in private." A positive business letter from a finance minister was "worth more than all the titles of nobility."[114]

But, while James's reservations faded quickly, in Nathan's case disdain for aristocratic trappings persisted, and perhaps ran deeper. When Prince Pückler visited the English Rothschilds in 1827, he was treated to a bizarre after-dinner performance, as an evidently tipsy Nathan donned "his new Austrian consular uniform, which, as he said, his friend M[etternich] had send him from Vienna":

> [He] showed it to us, and even suffered himself to be persuaded to try it on before the looking glass, and to walk about in it. And, as virtuosi when they have once begun never know when to stop, he now sent for

other magnificent Court dresses, and changed his toilette several times, as if he had been on the stage . . .

It was . . . rather droll to see how this otherwise serious tradesman-like man tried to assume the various bendings and bowings, and the light and gracious air, of a courtier, and, not in the least disconcerted by our laughing, assured us, with as much confidence as joviality that N.M.R., if he liked, could act any part; and, with the help of five or six glasses of wine extra, could make as good a figure at Court as the best of them.[115]

As Pückler's evidently somewhat mixed feelings suggest, this was surely a characteristic bid by Nathan to *épater l'aristocratie*. He might be willing on occasion to exchange his sober surtout for the gaudy apparel of the old order; but he regarded it as little more than fancy dress. In its way, this vivid scene—of a tipsy Jewish banker making fun of the Habsburg Empire's diplomatic finery in front of an impecunious prince—encapsulates the deep ambivalence of the Rothschilds' relationship with the Restoration social order.

"Fine Education"

Despite their reputation as philistines, the younger Rothschild brothers took at least some interest in what we would now call "high culture"—something of a misnomer given the rapid development of a "public sphere" in this period as a more or less free market for the production and consumption of music, drama, books and paintings. This interest was partly a logical consequence of entertaining in the ways described above: it was, at the very least, difficult to own a large house without acquiring pictures and other ornaments to decorate its rooms. At the same time, in order to be able to communicate with members of the social elite about matters other than money and politics, a basic knowledge of their favourite painters, composers and authors was a prerequisite. Yet busy middle-aged bankers (all the brothers save James were over forty in 1820) generally make poor students of the arts. True, they had all inherited from their father an appreciation of antique *objets d'art*, and were discerning about the gifts they sent their favourite politicians. They commissioned portraits of themselves, their wives and children from respectable artists like Sir William Beechey, Louis Amié Grosclaude and Moritz Daniel Oppenheim;[116] and in both Frankfurt and Paris they had regular boxes reserved at the theatre. But James was the only member of the second generation to show any serious interest in culture on his own account. He read Schiller and Goethe when he was in his twenties, for example,[117] and in the 1820s retained an artist named Allard on 5 francs a month, as well as subscribing to the *Courrier des Spectacles* and *Journal des Théâtres*.[118] His brothers tended to take the view that this sort of thing was better made available to their children.

The obvious is perhaps worth stating here: if the Rothschild brothers really had been philistines, they would not have educated their children as well as they did. Of course, Nathan wanted his sons "to give mind, and soul, and heart, and body, and everything to business"; at the time he made that much misunderstood remark, all but one of them had completed their educations and had been working for the firm for several years.[119] And he and his brothers recognised that there might be a conflict between *higher* education and a successful business apprenticeship. As Carl put it when Salomon was pondering the fifteen-year-old Anselm's future: "I advise you not to let him study . . . more than another two years so that he should enter the business when 17 years old. Otherwise he would not be deeply attached to business."[120] The subsequent business career of Mayer, the only one of Nathan's sons to attend an English university, proved that analysis to be only too accurate. But none of the brothers for a moment doubted that a successful business career was compatible with the best possible *secondary* education. Indeed, they viewed the latter as an essential preparation for the former. Moreover, the male Rothschilds of the third generation were in practice given even longer than Carl suggested before being expected to abandon their studies and enter the "counting house." Judging by the first appearance of his name in the business correspondence, Anselm was twenty-three before he took a serious part in the running of the firm (though he was admitted a partner a year earlier, and presumably did routine work for his father which has gone unrecorded). Lionel was twenty when he first began to write and receive business letters; Anthony and Nat were eighteen, and Mayer twenty-one. None of Carl's sons feature in the firm's deliberations before the age of twenty; indeed, the pious Wilhelm Carl was not really regarded as competent to act unsupervised until he was twenty-four. Both James's sons, Alphonse and Gustave, were nineteen before they began to write their own business letters. Given their parents' view that the best apprenticeship was learning by doing, there is little reason to think that any of the third generation had worked for long before these first recorded appearances.

In any case, the older Rothschilds had no desire to impose on their offspring the deprivations and rigours of their own childhoods. Anselm's mother took pride in her eleven-year-old son's precocious letter-writing not just because it would stand him in good stead in business; she genuinely wanted him and his sister to have "a fine education" for its own sake.[121] The influence on her of contemporary notions of *Bildung* is apparent in a letter she wrote to her husband in 1820 (which accompanied another letter from their now teenage son): "He is so uninhibited towards me, the good, sweet boy, which pleases me particularly, for you know, dear husband, that it has always been my aim that our dear children should not conceal from us their true, innermost feelings; and I—or rather we—have achieved it."[122] Nathan indulged his children in less sentimental ways. After work, he played with them, letting them (as a friend recalled) "make their equestrian exercises on your back';[123] indeed, on one occasion he horsed around so energetically that he managed to dislocate his shoulder.[124] He bought them a miniature carriage with four white goats to drive about the garden at Stamford Hill.[125] The family painted by William Armfield Hobday in 1821 was—as it looks today—a happy one: to the left, the three-year-old Mayer tries to pull a letter from his father's hand; at Charlotte's feet, Hannah Mayer has dropped her bonnet; and the older boys vainly attempt to restrain the family dog as it chews Lionel's hat. Small wonder the faintest hint of a smile plays on the lips of the relaxed *paterfamilias* as he reclines, legs crossed, in his armchair.[126] And he continued to indulge them—even to spoil them—as they grew up. At the age of seventeen, Hannah Mayer was enjoying life in Brighton, sitting for her first portrait.[127] When Thomas Fowell Buxton met Anthony the following year, he was already "a mighty hunter; and his father lets him buy any horses he likes. He lately applied to the emperor of Morocco for a first-rate Arab horse. The emperor sent him a magnificent one, but he died as he landed in England. The poor youth said very feelingly, 'that was the greatest misfortune he ever had suffered.'"[128]

In *Coningsby*, Disraeli portrayed the younger Sidonia as a model of modern education:

> Shut out from universities and schools, those universities and schools which were indebted for their first knowledge of ancient philosophy to the learning and enterprise of his ancestors, the young Sidonia was fortunate in his tutor . . . [He] penetrated the highest mysteries of mathematics with a facility almost instinctive . . . The circumstances of his position, too, had early contributed to give him an unusual command over the modern languages . . . When he was nineteen, Sidonia . . . possessed a complete mastery over the principal European languages . . . At seventeen he . . . commenced his travels. He resided . . . some time in Germany, and then, having visited Italy, settled at Naples . . .[129]

This was not far removed from the kind of education Lionel and his brothers and cousins actually received. One of the Montefiores recalled how in 1815 Lionel and Anthony had been taken away from their first teacher, "a Pole [who] used to wear a tall Polish hat and stride about the schoolroom with a cane ferociously stuck in his Wellington boots." Instead, their parents and some friends "got Garcia, who was previously a book-keeper at Barrow and Lousada's counting house, to establish a more select academy at Peckham, and there Lionel and Anthony . . . were sent."[130] The favoured curriculum was indeed modern, rather than classical, and that slant continued when the time came for a kind of modified grand tour in 1827. Aged respectively nineteen and seventeen, the two boys were despatched to see the sights of Germany—not Italy, the classicist's favoured destination—travelling with their tutor John Darby from Frankfurt through the principal towns of Saxony, then on to Prague and Vienna, returning via Baden and Strasbourg. (Prussia was conspicuously omitted, though they do seem to have gone to Hanover in order to visit the university at Göttingen.)[131] The aim was obviously to acquire a grounding in German *Kultur*: besides trailing round countless art galleries and princely piles, the brothers paid a respectful call on the aged Goethe.[132]

It was only after this tour that Lionel and Anthony were expected to turn their minds to business: in January 1829 one of the bookkeepers in the Frankfurt office was entrusted with the task of raising Anthony's numeracy to the level required of a banker. "I ceaselessly instruct him in all the arithmetical problems," the new tutor reported to Nathan, "and I am glad to perceive that he has the intellectual grasp and makes good use of what I have to teach him. In due course I shall give to the young Baron systematically the knowledge of the art of arithmetic and I shall continue to explain to him arbitration of exchange and all of the business circulation of the counting house."[133]

Visits like the one made by Nathan's sons to Frankfurt evidently encouraged a degree of Anglo-German parental rivalry. In 1831 Charlotte wrote to her mother Hannah urging her to "make [Mayer] write a letter in German if he can, if not, in his best writing in English to Mrs S[alomon] de R[othschild]. Uncle Charles's boys [Mayer Carl and Wilhelm Carl] both write very well and it is sure to be compared."[134] Four years later it was the English Mayer's turn to visit Germany; but this was a more academic trip than his elder brothers had made. With his tutor Dr

Schlemmer he spent several months studying at the University of Leipzig before going on to Heidelberg.[135] In this he was following in the footsteps of Anselm, the first Rothschild to attend university, who had acquired "a lively interest in science" while studying at Berlin.[136] He then returned to England, where he became the first of many Rothschilds to study at Cambridge, first at Magdalene and then, when the college proved punctilious about his attendance at chapel (still formally a requirement for undergraduates), to larger and laxer Trinity.[137] (Oxford was ruled out because matriculation was conditional on subscription to the thirty-nine articles; whereas in Cambridge non-conformists and Jews could become members of the university, though they could not be awarded degrees, scholarships or fellowships.)[138]

Not to be outdone, Carl sent his son Mayer Carl to Göttingen, where he studied law, and then to Berlin, where he attended lectures by the leading light of German jurisprudence, Friedrich Karl von Savigny, and Leopold von Ranke, the pre-eminent historian of the age.[139] His brother Wilhelm Carl was in turn subjected to an extraordinarily rigorous secondary education: at the age of fifteen he was studying twenty different subjects including five languages and five sciences under a team of tutors led by the French physiologist Henri Blanvalet.[140] His flight into religious Orthodoxy may have been partly a reaction against such state-of-the-art cramming. James's sons were no less thoroughly educated. Alphonse studied at the Collège Bourbon (later the Lycée Condorcet) and was tutored privately for his baccalauréat by Désiré Nisard, who later became director of the Ecole Normale and a member of the Académie Française.[141] Nor was it only the Rothschild boys who were given the benefit of a good education. Though little is known about her formal schooling, Carl's daughter Charlotte—perhaps the brightest Rothschild of the third generation—was a highly literate woman, to judge by her elegant English letters and intense German diaries.

If the aim of all this had been to produce great intellectuals, we would have to judge it a failure: with the exception of Charlotte, none of the third generation can be said to have had scholarly minds. But the aim was rather to produce men and women who would fit more easily into the elite social milieus of Europe than their fathers—without losing the desire to carry on their business as bankers. In those terms, the education of the third generation of Rothschilds was a success. Mayer Amschel's grandchildren no longer spoke the rough-hewn German of the Judengasse: Castellane disliked Betty's *German* accent not her Jewish accent, and no contemporary appears to have detected anything remotely unusual about the easy and idiomatic way Nathan's sons spoke English. Nor did the younger Rothschilds invariably write their letters in the Hebrew characters used by their fathers: although Salomon and Carl's sons continued to do so, the English and French Rothschilds of the third generation did not (though they could read *Judendeutsch* without difficulty). Indeed, from the late 1820s onwards, the business of the five houses was conducted multilingually, with each partner tending to write in his first language, occasionally lapsing into the language of his place of work or addressee in postscripts. To all intents and purposes, as their letters show, the third generation wrote English, German and French as well as—and in some cases rather better than—their aristocratic contemporaries. Moreover, the very conventionality of their cultural tastes was proof that the tutors had done their work well. They liked Scott's novels;[142] Meyerbeer's operas;[143] Murillo's paintings; Marie Antoinette's furniture.[144] The boys also picked up the hobbies and vices of the social elite—riding horses, hunting foxes and stags, betting on racehorses, as well as smoking cigars, drinking fine wines and chasing unsuitable women. They even had clubbish nicknames for one other: Lionel was "Rab," Anthony "Billy" or "Fat Bill" and Mayer "Muffy" or "Tup." All outward traces of the Frankfurt ghetto had been expunged, save, it might be said, those of physiognomy—and even in that respect few members of the family actually conformed to the hostile caricaturists' Jewish stereotypes, least of all James. He and his brothers had found it easy to become barons, wearers of royal orders, property-owners and society hosts. Now they had made it possible for the third generation of Rothschilds to become something more elusive: gentlemen.

EIGHT

Sudden Revolutions
(1830–1833)

> *In the present state of Europe something great & decisive must*
> *be done or its kingdoms and their population will be soon again*
> *in worse confusion than they were under the French Revolution*
> *and the influence of Napoleon. The march of mind is too rapid*
> *to permit the old arrangements of society to continue long as*
> *they are. The modern extraordinary advance in the arts and*
> *sciences, will 'ere long, if I am not greatly deceived, change the*
> *whole organisation of the social systems over the world greatly*
> *to the benefit of all; but it may very suddenly render all antici-*
> *pated wealth, as money is, of very little use. It may be well*
> *therefore, without losing the advantages which money gives*
> *under the existing arrangements of society, to secure also similar*
> *benefits in case of sudden revolutions in all the states of Europe*
> *which may now any day take place.*
> —ROBERT OWEN TO HANNAH ROTHSCHILD, JULY 1828.[1]

In July 1830 the French King Charles X was overthrown by a combination of parliamentary opposition and popular violence in Paris. In something like a political
chain-reaction, comparable changes of regime occurred or were attempted (with
varying degrees of violence) in Brussels, Warsaw, Modena and Bologna, as well as in
a number of German states, notably Brunswick, Hesse-Kassel and Saxony, and in
Portugal. In Belgium, Italy and Poland, the revolutionaries were as much concerned
to free themselves from foreign rule as to achieve constitutional reforms. Elsewhere,
constitutional reforms were enacted without the deposition of a monarch. This was
the case not only in England, Scotland and Ireland—sometimes neglected in
accounts of the 1830 revolution—but also in Hanover, where the change of
monarch was the result of George IV's not untimely death in June 1830. In Baden,
Württemberg and Bavaria, rulers felt constrained to make concessions to liberals.
Nor did political instability end in 1832, by which time the revolts in Poland and
Italy had been crushed and Holland had been obliged to accept the secession of Belgium. Uncertainty about the stability of new political arrangements persisted
throughout Europe until the middle of the decade and beyond.

The fact that the Rothschilds were able to survive these political upheavals led
many observers to conclude that, as Byron and others had earlier suspected, their

power was actually as great as, if not greater than, that of the kings to whom they lent money. In November 1931, in his tenth bulletin from Paris, Ludwig Börne explicitly "equated Rothschild . . . with kings":

[T]hat should certainly not annoy him, even if he should not wish to belong in their ranks, because he should know best how far below par a king stands in Paris today. But he is the great dealer in all state bonds, who gives monarchs the power to spite freedom and deprives peoples of the courage to resist violence. Rothschild is the high priest of fear, the Goddess on whose altar liberty, patriotism, honour and all civic virtues are sacrificed. Rothschild should sell off all his paper in one hour on the stock exchange, so that they crash into the deepest abyss; then he should rush into my arms and feel how strongly I press him to my heart.[2]

The new French King Louis Philippe would, suggested Börne sarcastically in his bulletin of January 1832,

have himself crowned if he is still king in a year's time; not at St Rémy at Rheims, but at Notre Dame de la Bourse at Paris, and Rothschild will officiate as archbishop. After the coronation, pigeons will be sent out, as usual, and one of them . . . will fly to St Helena, settle on Napoleon's grave, and laughingly inform his remains that they saw his successor anointed yesterday, not by the Pope but by a Jew; and that the present ruler of France has taken the title, "Emperor of the five per cents, King of the three per cents, Protector of bankers and exchange agents."

In both letters, to be sure, Börne continued to harp on the familiar theme that the Rothschilds were the supporters of reaction:

It is always the same game that these Rothschilds play, in order to enrich themselves at the cost of the land they exploit . . . The financiers are the nation's worst enemies. They have done more than any to undermine the foundations of freedom, and it is unquestionable that most of the peoples of Europe would by this time be in full possession of liberty if such men as Rothschild . . . did not lend the autocrats the support of their capital.

But it was rather harder to make this argument stick when the Rothschilds had so quickly lent their support to Louis Philippe's regime, which was plainly the product of a liberal revolution, even if it was not liberal enough for Börne. Moreover, the Rothschilds were also, as Börne said, lending money to establish Greece as an independent monarchy, which had been another liberal goal of the 1820s. Indeed, they even appeared to be in a position to influence the decision as to which prince would become the new Greek king. ("M. de Rothschild finds that all the princes of Europe are in his credit book except Prince Frederick of the Netherlands, and he concludes that the prince who has never asked him for credit is the most worthy of it.") It therefore made more sense to argue that the Rothschilds were beginning to *supplant* rather than merely shore up the European monarchies:

Would it not be a good thing for the world if the crowns were placed on their [the Rothschilds'] heads instead of lying at their feet as they do now? . . . Although the Rothschilds do not yet occupy thrones, they are at all events asked their advice as to the choice of a ruler when a throne falls vacant . . . Would it not be a great blessing for the world if all the kings were dismissed and the Rothschild family put on their thrones? Think of the advantages. The new dynasty would never contract a loan, as it would know better than anybody how dear such things are, and on this account alone the burden on their subjects would be alleviated by several millions a year.³

Born Löw Baruch in the Frankfurt Judengasse, a convert not only to Christianity but to German nationalism, Börne had his own complex personal reasons for disliking the Rothschilds.⁴ For a rather more nuanced assessment of Rothschild power in the age of revolution, we need to turn to Börne's friend, the poet and journalist Heinrich Heine. Before 1830 Heine thought of the Rothschilds in much the same way as other liberally inclined writers. In his "Travel Sketches," for example, "Rothschild I" appears alongside Wellington, Metternich and the Pope as a bulwark of reaction.⁵ Even at this stage, however, Heine had an awareness of the ambivalent nature of the relationship between the Rothschilds and the established monarchies. In "The Baths of Lucca," the Jewish Figaro-figure Hirsch-Hyacinth recalls cutting Nathan Rothschild's corns:

> This happened in his inner sanctum while he sat on his green armchair as though it were a throne. He spoke like a king, with courtiers all around him; he ordered them about and sent messages to all the kings of the world; and while I was cutting his corns, I thought to myself: what you now have in your hand is the foot of the man whose own hands hold the whole world. Now you are somebody too: if you cut too deep down below he'll lose his temper up above and he'll cut the kings more sharply. That was the greatest moment of my life.⁶

For Heine, Nathan already has the power to "cut" the kings to whom he lends. Yet his Rothschilds have not lost sight of their own lowly and Jewish origins. Nathan's bank in London is a glorified "pawnshop" and when Hirsch-Hyacinth is introduced to Salomon as a former seller of lottery tickets, he invites him to dine with him, saying: "I am something like that myself, I am the chief agent of the Rothschild lottery." "He treated me," says Hirsch-Hyacinth, "like his equal, quite famillionaire" (*ganz famillionär*). That much analysed pun hints at an idea to which Heine later returned: that, despite their enormous wealth, the Rothschilds were far from being mere props of the traditional social hierarchy.

The same point underlies the memorable allegory in which Hirsch-Hyacinth describes a children's fancy-dress ball given by Salomon:

> The children wore lovely fancy dress, and they played at making loans. They were dressed up like kings, with crowns on their heads, but there was one of the bigger lads who was dressed exactly like old Nathan Rothschild. He played his part very well, kept both hands in his trouser-pockets, rattled his money and shook with bad temper when one of the little kings wanted to borrow off him—only a little lad with the white coat and red trousers [Austria] got a kindly pat on the cheek and was praised: "You're my boy, my pet, I'm proud of you; but your cousin Michel [probably Germany] had better keep away from me, I'll give nothing to a fool like that who expends more in a day than he has coming in a year; he'll make some trouble yet in the world and spoil my business." As true as the Lord shall help me, the boy played his part wonderfully well, especially when he helped a fat child dressed in white

satin with real silver lilies [France] in its effort to walk and said to it occasionally: "Now, you, behave yourself, make an honest living, and see that they don't chase you out again, or I'll lose my money." I assure you, Herr Doktor, it was a pleasure to listen to that lad; and the other children too—dear sweet children they all were—played their parts extremely well—until the cake was brought in and they all started fighting for the best piece [and] tore the crowns off one another's heads . . ."[7]

Once again, Heine's Nathan feels contempt for the various rulers who approach him for loans: it is he who is their master. In an unpublished passage, Heine made it clear that he shared that contempt for "stupid princes," "but before Nathan Rothschild I tremble with fear. Before you can say Jack Robinson, he could send a few kings, stockbrokers, and policemen to my rooms and have me carried to the fortress prison."[8]

In an unpublished passage of "The Baths of Lucca," Heine sought to analyse the nature of the Rothschilds' power more precisely. Here he acknowledges that in the short term it served to shore up the reactionary regimes:

When I think about political economy in these our latter days it becomes ever clearer to me that without the Rothschilds' help the financial embarrassment of most states would have been exploited by subversives wanting to mislead the populace into upsetting whatever order or disorder constituted the status quo. Revolutions are generally triggered off by deficiency of money; by preventing such deficiencies, the Rothschild system may serve to preserve peace in Europe. This system, or rather, Nathan Rothschild, its inventor, is still providing firm foundations for such peace: it does not inhibit one state from making war on another exactly as before, but it does make it difficult for the people to overthrow established authority . . . Religion is no longer able to guarantee the governments that the people will remain peaceful; the Rothschild system of loans can perform the task much better.

However, the Rothschild "system" is also potentially revolutionary in itself:

[I]t possesses the moral force or power which religion has lost, it can act as a surrogate for religion—indeed, it *is* a new religion, and when the old religion finally goes under it will provide substitutes for its practical blessings. Strangely enough, it is once again the Jews who invented this new religion . . . Murdered Judaea was as cunning as the dying Nessus, and its poisoned robe—poisoned with its own blood—consumed the strength of the Roman Hercules so effectively that his mighty limbs grew weary, armour and helmet fell away from his withered body, and his voice, once so mighty in battle, dwindled to a prayerful whine. Miserably, in a death-agony that dragged on through a thousand years, Rome dies by the Judaic poison.[9]

Of course, this extraordinary passage says a good deal about Heine's own highly ambivalent attitude towards Judaism (like Börne, he had converted to Christianity); but it also anticipates his later and more coherent reflections in his "Memorandum on Ludwig Börne" (1840) on the Rothschilds as revolutionaries rather than counter-revolutionaries.

Here, in perhaps the most perceptive of any contemporary commentary, Heine confronts the reader with a striking paradox:

No one does more to further the revolution than the Rothschilds themselves . . . and, though it may sound even more strange, these Rothschilds, the bankers of kings, these princely pursestring-holders, whose
existence might be placed in the gravest danger by a collapse of the
European state system, nevertheless carry in their minds a consciousness
of their revolutionary mission.

James, he suggests, is the "Nero of finance," "reigning as absolute emperor over
the stock exchanges of the world"; but, like his predecessor, the Roman Nero, he is
"ultimately a powerful destroyer of patrician privilege, and the founder of a new
democracy."

The explanation which follows purports to be based on a genuine conversation
Heine had with James—while "sauntering arm in arm through the streets of
Paris"—and though it is possible that Heine was putting his own words in someone
else's mouth, it is sufficiently different from his earlier flights of fancy to be worth
taking seriously. According to Heine, James explained how "he himself, through his
system of government bonds, had created the first conditions for, and at the same
time paved the way towards, social progress" and the "foundation of a new order of
things." For it was the development of mobile property in the form of the rente and
other government bonds which severed the link between wealth and land, allowing
the propertied classes to converge on Paris. "The importance has long been recognised of such a [common] residence for the most diverse of forces, of such a cen-
tralisation of intelligentsia and social authorities. For, without Paris, France would
never have had its revolution . . . Through the system of rentes, Paris became Paris
much more rapidly." This prompts Heine to go further:

I see in Rothschild one of the greatest revolutionaries who have founded
modern democracy. Richelieu, Robespierre and Rothschild are for me
three terroristic names, and they signify the gradual annihilation of the
old aristocracy. Richelieu, Robespierre and Rothschild are Europe's
three most fearful levellers. Richelieu destroyed the sovereignty of the
feudal nobility, and subjected it to that royal despotism, which either
relegated it to court service, or let it rot in bumpkin-like inactivity in the
provinces. Robespierre decapitated this subjugated and idle nobility.
But the land remained, and its new master, the new landowner, quickly
became another aristocrat just like his predecessor, whose pretensions he
continued under another name. Then came Rothschild and destroyed
the predominance of land, by raising the system of state bonds to
supreme power, thereby mobilising property and income and at the
same time endowing money with the previous privileges of the land. He
thereby created a new aristocracy, it is true, but this, resting as it does on
the most unreliable of elements, on money, can never play as enduringly
regressive a role as the former aristocracy, which was rooted in the land,
in the earth itself. For money is more fluid than water, more elusive than
the air, and one can gladly forgive the impertinences of the new nobility
in consideration of its ephemerality. In the twinkling of an eye, it will
dissolve and evaporate.[10]

Heine returned again and again during the 1840s to the subject of Rothschild
power. In the journal of 1840–41 later published as *Lutezia*, for example, he caricatured the relationship between James's state of health or mood and the price of
rentes, and coined the famous pun: "[M]oney is the god of our time and Rothschild

is his prophet."[11] The Rothschilds also crop up in the poems "Romanzero," "Germany" and "Simplicissimus."[12] But he never wrote with such penetrating insight as he did in "Ludwig Börne"—partly because his personal and financial relations with the family grew somewhat closer after 1840. As we shall see, Heine was singularly perceptive in identifying the Rothschilds as agents as much of social revolution as of reaction, even if their revolutionary role was less conscious than he suggested. Nor was he alone in making this point, though no one expressed it better. A lesser writer declared that "the Rothschild brothers [had] become the hierophants of the new religion," the founders of a new "Moneycracy."[13] Brooding in Venice after the fall of the Bourbon regime, the arch-conservative Chateaubriand remarked bleakly that "the Kings [had] become the chamberlains of Salomon, Baron de Rothschild."[14]

The Revolution and the Rente

It is always easy, with the benefit of hindsight, to find fault with historical figures who fail to foresee revolutions. But revolutions are not necessarily the products of predictable forces (as the case of Eastern Europe in 1989 well illustrates), much as historians may like to discover these after the fact. The accession of Charles X in 1824 and the fall of Villèle three years later following the conversion fiasco should not be seen as harbingers of crisis in France. For the government of the vicomte de Martignac formed in January 1828 seemed to be successfully steering a course between the liberal forces represented in the Chamber of Deputies and the conservative, clerical tendencies of the court. When Nathan's daughter Charlotte was in Paris in 1829 she found James giving "a dinner party for the liberals & the Ministers, [as] it is best to keep friends with all parties."[15] Although the April parliamentary session was every bit as "stormy" as Charlotte had been warned to expect, James remained optimistic.[16] There were periods of stagnation on the bourse and occasional reports of bread riots in the wake of poor harvests, but the vital barometer of financial confidence, the rente, suggested that the regime was in good health.[17] In May 1829, the price of 3 per cent rentes stood at 76.6; a year later it was above 84, having reached a peak of 86 in December. Even the dismissal of Martignac and the appointment of the ultra-conservative Jules de Polignac in his place on August 9, 1829, did not obviously herald a crisis. Rentes actually rose when the new ministry was announced, and continued to rise with only minor dips until May 1830.[18]

Under these circumstances, it was hardly rash of James to outbid the intense competition for a relatively modest government loan in early 1830, needed to finance a popularity-boosting military adventure in Algeria.[19] As he saw it, there was a contradiction between the anti-government rhetoric of the Parisian press and the reality of financial stability: "On the one hand the whole world is screaming that the Ministry is bringing about a revolution in France and on the other hand all the various consortiums are seen to be fighting among themselves to lay their hands on a lousy 4 million rentes."[20] The government might well face "some very stormy times" when the Chamber met in March; but the bourse remained "very good."[21] As a banker, James naturally put his money on the market's view. By the time fear of a major constitutional crisis began to manifest itself at the bourse, he was committed to the new loan—and hence to the regime.

The crisis of 1830 provides a classic illustration of the difficulty bankers (and investors) always have when trying to choose between selling a falling security at a loss or holding on to it in the hope of a rise—but at the risk of a further fall. Contrary to Corti's suggestion that he was blind to the impending crisis,[22] James had been given a clear warning as early as February, when the Finance Minister outlined to him yet another conversion scheme. When James expressed doubts as to whether the government would command the necessary parliamentary majority to enact such a measure, he was left in no doubt what would happen: "If . . . the Chamber should be totally opposed to the Government then they are determined to dissolve the Chamber and to pass a law calling for fresh elections and thus engineer the formation of a new Chamber." But James hesitated:

> You know very well, my dear Nathan, what chambers and ministers are like. Whether the King will have the necessary courage to follow the above plan when the time comes to do so, and whether the Chamber will allow this to happen, I don't know. It is a diabolical situation . . . and if I can manage to extricate myself I would dearly like to do so, for I am not at all enamoured of this situation where a Minister pits himself against the public.[23]

Instead of trying to "extricate" himself, he therefore opted to sit tight—and was encouraged to do so by Nathan, who advised him only to sell "at a profit" (that is, to hang on in the hope of better prices). Partly, James made the mistake of trusting too much in the assurances of Polignac, who seemed to have "the courage of the devil" when he saw him in February. "There is only one thing that can be done over here," he told Nathan shortly before the Chamber convened at the beginning of March, "and that is to remain quiet for the time being and to observe things from the sidelines because the devil is not as black as he appears to be."[24] On this basis, Nathan blithely assured Charles Greville that "Polignac's Government will stand by the King's support and Polignac's own courage."[25] The problem was that he and his brother now held a substantial amount of 4 per cent rentes—to a nominal value of around 25 million francs (£1 million)—which they had intended gradually to sell on to brokers and investors at a profit. If they began to accelerate their sales at a time when the 4 per cents already were worth slightly less than they had paid for them, prices would very probably fall further. It is no wonder James called Polignac a devil: he had made an authentically Faustian pact with him.

This became painfully obvious when the parliamentary session began. James saw at once "that the King will have to choose between the Chambers and the Ministry." But, he reasoned, "I don't want to do anything, because as long as I remain firm, the people will not have the courage to set about depressing the rentes and I will thus ride out the storm."[26] By 221 votes to 181, the deputies passed an address to the King stating that "concord between the political views of your government and the wishes of your people . . . does not exist today," whereupon (as James had been warned to expect) the King dissolved the Chamber and called for new elections. Far from selling rentes, however, James found himself having to buy them to shore up the market—and his friend the "devil":

> Well, Polignac promised me that he will not instigate a coup d'état, that is, he will not make any move that is illegal and that he will remain faithful with his Ministers, so I went ahead and bought 100,000 francs of rentes [3.3 million nominal] because I had told him, "If you remain within the law then I promise you that there will be a rise," and I kept my word for the [3 per cent] rentes now stand at 82.40 when they had opened at 81.40 . . . Well, while we don't have any Chambers the Ministry may well get

some new Ministers and matters will then be sorted out. If we manage to gain three months then everything will be resolved.[27]

James was right to think that a financial collapse could be averted for a time, though not for three months: in fact, the price of 3 per cents rallied and remained above 84 until May 3. However, he was not in a position simultaneously to support the market and to sell worthwhile amounts of rentes (though he did try to sell some "without anyone getting wind of what I am doing").[28] This meant that, when the market began to slide even before the new Chamber convened, the brothers still held not only 25 million francs of 4 per cents but also some 1.5 million francs of 5 per cents and 4.5 million of 3 per cents. The prices paid for the 5 and 4.5 per cents had been, respectively, 106.25 and 83.70. From May onwards, the losses on these accounts began to mount. Yet neither James nor Nathan could bear to write them off by selling. James continued to clutch at straws, refusing to face the possibility that the political situation might go on deteriorating.[29] At the same time, the government put its faith in him: "If you do not succeed in preventing the fall in values," a minister told him, "everyone will believe that a *coup d'état* will occur such as you so rightly fear."[30] And indeed, prices did rally slightly between June 10 and July 12. But the truth was that the limits of Rothschild power over the market had been reached. Ouvrard and others were now beginning an unstoppable bear run.[31]

The news that the government's Algerian expedition had been successful—which reached Paris in the first week of July—was completely swamped by the results of the elections, which were a resounding victory for the Opposition. Now the only hope—expressed by Salomon, who rushed to Paris to lend his assistance—was that the King might compromise with the Chamber and abandon Polignac.[32] As James realised, however, this was unlikely:

> Vitrolles [one of Polignac's ministers] has just arrived and says that during the coming month the King will take very firm measures as a result of which the life of the Chamber will be prolonged . . . but there are one hundred Deputies more on the side of the opposition than there are supporting the Ministry. Well, what can the Chamber do in such a situation? Is it not the case that in England, if a Ministry does not have the support of a majority, they then have to resign? But here the King declares: "I will hold on to my Ministry." So what can one do? Believe me, my dear Nathan, I am . . . losing my courage.[33]

Twelve days later his courage had gone completely: "The whole world is selling rentes . . . and all the Ministers, including the Finance Minister and the Minister for Internal Affairs tell me, 'Rothschild, be careful.' . . . My dear Nathan, you are an old warrior. Tell me truthfully, do you not also fear what might happen in the end?"[34]

Before Nathan could even reply, the end arrived. On July 26 Charles X invoked his exceptional powers under article 14 of the 1814 Charter and published three ordinances which ended freedom of the press, dissolved the Chamber and introduced yet another change to the electoral system, the aim of which was to produce a more pliant set of deputies. It was in fact the first of these which triggered the revolution: few deputies had yet arrived in Paris, but liberal journalists like Adolphe Thiers of the *National* lost no time in denouncing the government's coup. When attempts were made to close down the three leading opposition newspapers, crowds took to the streets. Nathan's eldest son Lionel arrived just in time to witness the ensuing confusion, and his letter perfectly captures the uncertainty of the moment:

One moment one thinks oneself on the eve of seeing a revolution, the next, that every thing in a short time will be again in order . . . [T]oday all the newspapers appeared as usual which has created a little noise, before all the newspaper offices there are soldiers & the gens d'armes who have seized all the papers & taken the Editors before the police, this alone is enough to make a disturbance in any free country: all the shops in those streets are of course closed: in the Palais Royal there was a man selling some of these papers. He was immediately seized, some of the Boys, & of the common people took his part, but in a few minutes everything was quiet again, the gates in the Palais Royal & the shops are all closed, this cirumstance in itself is trifling, but when it comes to London they make a great story of it; Before all the Ministers' Houses there are also gens d'armes. All these things make people speak, but in the end I do not think it will come to any thing very bad . . . [T]o day there is to be a meeting of all the members of the late parliament what they will do, it is not possible to say, but the report is, that they will declare themselves the only & true representatives of the people & without their sanction nothing is legal, that is done by the ministers & that after the 1st Jan[uar]y. no taxes need to be paid . . . this is the opinion of the opposition who think that we shall see very dreadful times again, but the other party, the ministerial, who have completely the command of the army, think that with force they shall be able to carry everything, the only thing papa is that the King before long will see the Danger.[35]

By the time he did see the danger, however, it was too late. In two days of intense fighting which cost the lives of 800 protesters and 200 soldiers, the troops loyal to Charles X were driven out of Paris. Talk of mediation by moderate liberals like the bankers Jacques Laffitte and Casimir Périer was suddenly redundant, as was the King's belated offer to withdraw the ordinances. With the capital on the verge of anarchy, new institutions redolent of the 1790s were hastily improvised: a municipal committee and a national guard led by that old republican warhorse Lafayette. As Salomon uneasily reported to Metternich on July 30, "the tricolour flag is flying on all public buildings."[36] Lionel described a euphorically insurgent Paris:

The streets are crowded with persons, all laughing and as gay as if they had come from some Dance, in the squares & open places all the Garde Nationale & Royal Troops who had delivered up their arms, marching & being cheered by the people, in every corner the three coloured flags & every person with a red, blue & white cockade, in the Boulevard & streets every hundred yards the fine large trees cut down and the pavement taken up & piled up against them & broken doors &c so that nothing can pass . . . these barricades, as they call them, are not only in the principal streets, but in all the small ones, so that it was impossible for the soldiers & artillery to pass anywhere.[37]

Small wonder James was beetle-browed when the historian Jules Michelet glimpsed him in his carriage.[38] Small wonder he took the precaution of burying his bonds in the grounds of Salomon's house at Suresnes.[39]

Yet James survived. The traditional explanation for this is that he was a skilful turncoat, but the reality is more complex.[40] It is undeniable that he switched sides in July 1830 with alacrity and relief. Apart from the offer of a rural hiding place to Vitrolles, he did nothing of substance to assist the outgoing regime, rejecting all requests from the ousted monarch for money until it was clear that he was leaving the country.[41] Indeed, his nephew exulted in Charles's overthrow: "Never was there a more glorious week for France, this people have [*sic*] behaved in a way that will be admired by every person, and will make them be reckoned now amongst the first of nations . . . It will be a good lesson for other governm[en]ts."[42] When Polignac was put on trial later in the year, James shed no tears: "I assure you that, as far as I am concerned, for all the good that Polignac has done for us, he might as well be damned."[43] James was also quick to broadcast his support for the new regime, ostentatiously donating 15,000 francs for the care of those wounded in the street-fighting.[44] Not only did Anselm do his bit in the national guard (a bourgeois defence force of which the family strongly approved); James even dressed up his three-year-old son Alphonse in a miniature guard's uniform.[45] It is also true that the liberals' decision to offer first the office of lieutenant general and then the crown to the duc d'Orléans was a stroke of good luck for James; as we have seen, he had already made the new King a "good friend" in the 1820s.[46] From the Rothschild point of view, a constitutional monarchy was preferable to an absolute regime, and far better than a republic: as Salomon characteristically put it after watching Louis Philippe take the coronation oath to uphold the slightly revised charter: "Thank God that we have come so far that the matter has ended so well, for otherwise the Rentes would not have stood at 79 but would have fallen to 39 God forbid."[47] James's relations with some of the key figures in the new government—notably the two bankers Laffitte and Périer—were also relatively good, though the extent of genuine amity among such business rivals should not be exaggerated.[48] Talleyrand, who was the linchpin of Louis Philippe's diplomacy in London, was persuaded to bank with Nathan.[49] Sebastiani, the Foreign Minister from late 1830, was "on the most friendly terms" with James, who called on him "every morning';[50] relations with his successor de Broglie were also close.

Heine was ultimately right, then, when he said that James "appreciated the political capacities of Louis Philippe from the first, and . . . always stayed on an intimate footing with that grand master of politics."[51] Indeed, even the later anti-Semitic writer Drumont was not far wrong when he later spoke of an "affinity" between James and Louis Philippe based on their common "adoration of money":[52] we know that James gave Louis Philippe a personal loan of over 2 million francs in April 1840 and Heine attributed the "great attentions paid to [Rothschild] at court" to the King's "financial plight."[53] Although Stendhal's witty and well-connected "Monsieur Leuwen" can hardly have been modelled on James, as has sometimes been claimed[54]—he is not Jewish, for example, and his French is much too elegant—his political influence as portrayed by Stendhal closely corresponds to that wielded by James at the time the novel was written (1836).[55] "The newspapers write so much about the ministers speculating with us," reported Lionel in 1834, "that they don't like to receive us every day."[56] The Rothschilds' private correspondence reveals the truth of such press reports, and suggests that it was only a slight exaggeration to claim, as one Austrian source did, that "in all Ministries and in all the Departments [Rothschild] has his creatures of all ranks to bring him every kind of information."[57] At the same time, the social barriers which had still existed under the Restoration all but disappeared in the reign of the "Citizen King": members of the royal family as well as ministers and ambassadors were happy to accept James's invitations to dinners, balls and hunting parties.

Nevertheless, the cosiness of the relationship which developed between James and Louis Philippe's regime in the course of the 1830s should not blind us to the fact that, at least until 1833, the Rothschilds were far from convinced that the regime would endure. And with good reason. The example of Spain suggested the possibility of a protracted civil war between rival claimants to the throne.[58] More important, recent French history gave little encouragement to proponents of a constitutional monarchy. Every time crowds took to the streets of Paris—calling for the execution of Polignac in October 1830, for example—the fear recurred that the monarchy would be swept aside by the supporters of a republic. In December "precautions" had to be taken when James received warnings "that they [republicans] intend attacking the house tonight & taking everything."[59] Lionel's assessment was not unrealistic: "This party although not so very large makes itself appear considerably more so, by their active conduct, they make use of all the nonsense of the first revolution & wish to make this one resemble it in every respect: this frightens many persons."[60]

More pessimistic observers like the Prussian ambassador Werther warned James that Louis Philippe would "go the same way as Louis XVI." "The old revolution started in a similar manner," James's dinner guests told him, "and the situation now is beginning to look ominously alike. We can't see how anyone here can feel secure and we are surprised that you, who are so wealthy, are prepared to remain in such a country, when, at any one time, one has no idea what the next day might bring."[61] Nor was a new republic all that James had to fear. There was also the more recent memory of imperial glory, which a smaller number of Bonapartists sought to rekindle.[62] Finally, there was the newer phenomenon of working class unrest, which flared up periodically not only in Paris but in Lyon and other industrial centres about which the Rothschilds at this stage knew little.[63]

Contemporaries were impressed by the way James quickly resumed the lavish entertaining for which he was already famous, throwing a "crowded and brilliant" ball as early as January 15, 1831. But this was only the day after a violent anti-clerical riot, and, as the Austrian ambassador described it, the city was still echoing to the Marseillaise as the Rothschilds' guests danced. Louis Philippe's son the duc d'Orléans relayed his apologies through an aide-de-camp, who explained that he was at the head of his regiment and that the republic was being proclaimed in the streets:

> Mme de Rothschild was dying of fear, imagining the pillage of her house; despite that, we kept on dancing. When I engaged Mlle de Laborde for a galop, her mother told me that a glow that could be seen in the sky was none other than the bishop's house at Conflans, which the rioters had set on fire.
> "It's terrifying, yes, it's frightful," said the young lady. "But let's dance while we can today. If it is true that we are going to have the republic tomorrow, that will mean the end of feasts and balls for ages." . . . The ball lasted until four in the morning and there was no trouble. M. de Rothschild, despite his great desire to appear gay, is sad in his soul, for his money is melting in his vaults like an icicle in the heat.[64]

The combination of outward bravado and inner caution continued as long as there was such violence in the streets of Paris.[65] But the mood at these events was always tense. In January 1832 the duc d'Orléans was affronted when he heard himself referred to by his nickname ("le grand poulot") by a Legitimist guest at one of

James's parties—though it is not the case that he subsequently refused invitations to the rue Laffitte.[66]

Even in periods of relative political tranquillity, French politics seemed volatile (especially to Rothschilds raised in London), with more frequent changes of ministry than in England, and more friction between crown and parliament.[67] All these intricate political shifts had to be followed closely, for, as James put it, "a lot depends on what sort of Ministry we get."[68] In February 1831, for example, an anxious James sought reassurance from Louis Philippe that the crumbling Laffitte ministry would not be replaced by a more liberally inclined administration. He and Lionel were "consoled" to hear that the most likely successor would be another banker, Périer, and that Périer intended to reduce the King's direct influence over policy.[69] As we shall see, this was one of the most important changes of government of the period—and one which James claimed to have personally brought about. However, Périer's hold on power was always tenuous. July 1831—when elections unfortunately coincided with the anniversary of revolution—was a time of renewed political unsteadiness, with Laffitte failing by only a handful of votes to secure election as president of the Chamber.[70] When Périer nevertheless resigned, James was appalled.[71] Rothschild relief when he returned to office after a matter of days was considerable.[72] Throughout 1831, the Paris letters monitored the health of his ministry—particularly its difficulties over reform of the House of Peers—with the obsessive anxiety of relatives around a loved one's bedside.[73] The cartoonist Delaporte vividly caught the volatile mood of French politics in June 1831 when he depicted it as a funfair. To the left James and Ouvrard vie for control of a see-saw; in the centre Périer struggles to register on the "Dynamometer or Test of Strength for the use and instruction of ministers"; to the right Louis Philippe slumps unconscious (see illustration 8.i).

The metaphor of an ailing government, unfortunately, became a reality in the spring of 1832—just when Lionel began to sense a real stabilisation of the domestic political situation.[74] As Salomon fretted, it was "unpleasant to admit" that stability depended "entirely upon a single individual."[75] The full significance of this dependence suddenly became clear when Paris was struck by the cholera epidemic which swept westwards from Russia in 1831–2, claiming the lives of 18,000 people. Not only did the epidemic cause new riots in the city and "complete paralysis" on the bourse; it also afflicted Périer himself.[76] Once again James was obliged to put on a public show of confidence, staying in Paris while thousands of wealthy Parisians fled to the countryside.[77] But the combination of the premier's death (on May 16) and the landing of the Bourbon duchesse de Berry in the south of the country was yet another blow to political stability.[78] It was not until November that the threat of a "Carlist" civil war was entirely dispelled by the duchesse's arrest.[79] Meanwhile Paris continued to be subjected to republican demonstrations and riots, such as those occasioned by the funeral of General Lamarque, another cholera victim.[80]

Although James and Lionel grew increasingly confident that the regime was secure after 1832—warmly welcoming every legal restriction imposed on republican activities—there were political crises of varying degrees of intensity throughout the 1830s. Quite apart from periodic ministerial crises,[81] there were a number of attempts on the King's life,[82] working class unrest in Lyon in 1834,[83] an abortive republican coup in 1839 and an equally abortive Bonapartist invasion in 1840.[84]

8.i: H. Delaporte, *James de Rothschild and Louis Philippe*, *La Caricature*, No. 67 (June 23, 1831).

On closer inspection, relations between the Rothschilds and the July Monarchy were only superficially intimate; as James's private correspondence makes clear, he regarded Louis Philippe and most of his ministers as incompetent. The King was "duplicitous"; the Finance Minister Humann "an ass"; Thiers "a little man," and so on. "Well, my dear Amschel," wrote James dismissively as yet another government fell in early 1839, "I can assure you that within two years these old Ministers will be back again in their old posts because our French Ministers are just like serviettes: after a period of time they require the attention of a washerwoman, and once they have had a rest they are as good [as new] again."[85]

James's contempt was rooted in his own traumatic economic experience during the revolution. Between May 1830 and April 1831 the price of 3 and 4 per cent rentes slid inexorably downwards to reach a nadir of 46 and 75 respectively, a fall of 30–40 per cent (see illustration 8.ii). This was despite the closing of the bourse during the July days and the injection of 50 million francs by the Banque de France in August.[86] It was not until the end of 1831 that prices showed any sign of stabilising. Given that on the eve of the crisis James and Nathan had held a total of 6 million francs "nominal" of the two kinds of security, for which they had paid 5.36 million francs, their losses could have been as much as 2.1 million francs (£86,000) on the rente account alone. James sold at least some of these rentes before the nadir was reached, but as before he was reluctant to cut his losses. "We are sitting in a bowl of soup and we must now wait for it to be cooked," he told Nathan in late August. "Every day there are so many rentes for sale but there are no buyers to be found . . . I hope that they will go up, God willing, and then one must get out of these. I no longer have the confidence which I had previously, and it will be a long time yet before the old feeling of trust returns once more."[87]

8.iii The price of 3 per cent and 4 per cent rentes, May 1830–May 1831.

He, Lionel and even Hannah—who was in Paris for her daughter's accouchement—watched hypnotised by the hourly fluctuations of the market, waiting in vain for the crisis to "blow over."[88] Indeed, James began to buy new rentes in the hope of stabilising the market: by November 1830 his total holding may have amounted to as much as 30 million francs (nominal). But still the prices fell. "We have," he lamented, "too many rentes hanging round our neck and are unable to compete with the speculators on the same level."[89] Five months later Lionel confessed to his father: "We have been all the time so misled by the abundancy of money and scarcity of stock, & by the peaceable assurances of the King, that we never could make up our minds to sell."[90] Writing from Berlin, Anselm urged a final liquidation before rentes sank any further.[91] After much prevarication—"I cannot decide to accept a loss of 40 per cent"—James was ultimately forced to sell heavily at the bottom of the market in March 1831. "Unfortunately," he told Nathan, echoing Apponyi, "my fortune has melted away because I have been realising [that is, selling]." He had "so depleted" his capital "that I do not wish to look at the balance."[92]

Moreover, the French crash affected other bonds. A German cartoon of 1830 or 1831 shows four of the Rothschilds ("the Krähwinkler," after the imaginary German town of Krähwinkel) vainly struggling to keep some falling bonds in the air with the aid of bellows (see illustration 8.iii). It is impossible to quantify exactly the extent of the losses suffered by the Paris house at this time, as the relevant accounts have not survived; but for the London house total losses in 1830 were more than £56,000, 5 per cent of the house's capital, and it seems safe to assume that the damage was worse across the Channel. Comparable losses bankrupted Laffitte, whose firm collapsed even as he reached the zenith of his political influence.[93]

Die Krähwinkler suchen die Papiere in die Höhe zu treiben.

8.iii: Anon., *Die Krähwinkler suchen die Papiere in die Höhe zu treiben* **(1830–31).**

As it was, James had to endure a measure of embarrassment. In November 1830 he was forced to suspend payments due to the government for the pre-Revolution loan.[94] Nor could he deny that "that damned Ouvrard" had supplanted him as the dominant figure on the bourse: "For the past six months, the man has had a lot of good fortune and so the whole world follows whatever he does . . . Whatever move he makes the whole stock exchange will follow suit."[95] When James sought to participate in a new government loan in March 1831, another old rival was brutally frank. "For several months now," Hottinguer told him, "your establishment no longer makes the same positive impression [as in the past] on public opinion."[96] James felt obliged to speak to the other bankers "in a stiff tone and to 'show them my teeth' as they must appreciate that we are not to be treated off-handedly."[97] But it was some time before he was able to restore his credibility in the French financial world. Indeed, Lionel began to detect in his uncle something close to a loss of nerve.[98] "Uncle James is so much shaken by this revolution," he confided in his father, "that I assure you he is no more what he was, if he sees things looking well, he says, we must go to the old prices, and if the contrary is the case and the r[ente]s fall, then he gets immediately frightened and sells at the lowest price."[99]

James himself became increasingly fatalistic in 1831. "We can now expect many years of unrest here in France," he told Nathan gloomily in July, "and regrettably, I fear we will lose our fortune here, and have no hope of preventing this from happening, because the people never know what they want."[100] "For some time now, I have been very sick," he wrote a month later, requesting that Salomon's son Anselm return to Paris to assist him:

> Every day we have new scares, and every day new surprises hit us. Good news is followed by a fall, and bad news brings a rise in its wake. At night one goes to sleep, and is then awoken by a drum making a terrible din in the street. "Please hide all your securities without delay." . . . I promise you, so help me God, my arms are trembling, as things have gone badly wrong for me. I did some buying, so prices fell. When I sell, prices go up. It is absolutely disgusting.[101]

By October he was feeling "half frantic," "nervous" and isolated: "The world is speculating against me, and I am speculating against the world."[102] It was not until early 1832 that James began to recover his confidence. Curiously, he seems to have rather relished riding out the cholera epidemic, and was pleasantly surprised when Périer's death caused only a minor fall. Only when matters began to improve in the summer was he able to retreat to his house at Boulogne, where he took to bed in a state of complete exhaustion.[103]

Consols and the Constitution

The principal reason for James's financial survival was the role played by the other Rothschild houses in bailing him out. Here, not for the last time, the bank's multinational character proved an invaluable source of strength. Nathan's first reaction to the news of the events in Paris was to purchase and borrow large quantities of silver and gold from the Bank of England—he bought gold alone worth £779,000—and send it at once to his brother.[104] This is what James meant when he repeatedly praised Nathan's "decency," for it allowed him to continue paying the money due to the French Treasury under the terms of the loan agreement concluded earlier in the year—a vital show of financial strength. As Hannah told her husband proudly, "Your exertion in sending so much money gives great pleasure . . . You have dear Rothschild behaved uncommonly well and every one is quite satisfied with you."[105] One reason Nathan was able to bail his brother out was that, as *The Times* later said, he had managed to sell a substantial proportion of his own 4 per cent rentes before the revolution broke out.[106] The London house was again a source of support in March 1831, when James was seeking to participate in a new French loan: access to the London market remained James's trump card in Paris.[107] The Naples house also seems to have assisted by sending silver; its surviving accounts show that half-yearly profits were unaffected by the revolution.[108] Indirectly, the fact that the Frankfurt and Vienna houses remained on a sound footing also helped.

Of course, this would not have been the case if the revolutionary wave of 1830–32 had affected the other Rothschild houses as directly as it affected the French house. It is important to note that it could have. There were widespread fears in 1830 that Naples would succumb once again to revolution as well as the Papal states,[109] and the German reverberations might have been felt more strongly than they were in Vienna.[110] As it was, Salomon confided in Gentz in November 1830 that he was "10 million [gulden] poorer than he had been six months before."[111] In Frankfurt too there were grounds for anxiety, not least because of events in neighbouring Hesse-Kassel. The Elector William II (who had succeeded his father in 1821) was one of those rulers who came unstuck in 1830, when citizens' assemblies in Kassel, Hanau and Fulda demanded the summoning of a parliament (*Landtag*). Initially, the main bone of contention was William's overt cohabitation with his mistress; but the looting of customs houses on the state border suggests that economic grievances also played a part.[112] Since 1823 the Elector had not had recourse to the Rothschilds for financial assistance. But in the crisis of 1830 his officials appealed to Amschel for a small advance of 150,000 gulden. As his chief minister put it: "Your most humble servants are not in a position to propose a way of obtaining the advance which is most urgently needed other than through the house of Rothschild." They were not the only ones: requests were also received from hard-pressed governments in Hanover, Württemberg and Oldenburg.[113] Given the growing risk of German revolutions on the French model, however, Amschel was prepared to lend the Elector only 100,000 gulden.[114]

Yet when the Elector's son Frederick William was installed as co-regent and accepted a constitution which was the most liberal yet seen in Germany, Amschel's attitude changed. In 1831 he arranged two loans to the new regime totalling 1.35 million gulden.[115] In many ways, this was analogous to James's defection from Charles X to Louis Philippe in Paris. And, as in France, it did not take long for the more advanced liberals to become disillusioned with the new ruler. Amschel nevertheless stuck to the new ruler even as his popularity declined, just as James stuck to Louis Philippe. He continued to act as banker to Frederick William and his unpopular wife[116] even after the Hessian government resumed a course (under the firmly anti-liberal Ludwig Hassenpflug) which led inevitably to a messy constitutional crisis.[117] In short, Amschel blew with the wind. He and his brothers evidently had little respect for the various German princes endeavouring to retain their traditional authority. Salomon advised him "not to pay attention to the declamations and discussions" of the King of Württemberg "as I know this prince better than you: his views are always wrong and his opinions are always changing, and whether he is courageous or cowardly makes no odds, [as] I have more confidence in the opinion of a child than in that of this prince."[118] But once Metternich's influence began to make itself felt in Germany after the revolutionary high-water mark of the Hambach festival, the Frankfurt house wept no tears. Even this very modest German revolution had cost Amschel money, as Anthony found when he visited Frankfurt.[119] The failure of the *putsch* in Frankfurt attempted by a small and incompetent group of radicals in April 1833 was a welcome sign that the political tide was ebbing.[120]

Nathan in London also experienced his share of political turbulence. Of course, events in Britain were less violent than those on the continent. It would nevertheless be a mistake to overlook the close parallels between British reform on the one hand and French revolution on the other, not least because contemporaries were so conscious of these, and had no way of being sure that the former would avert the latter. The issues at stake were not so different: the freedom of the press; the reduction of religious disabilities in political life (which had already caused a serious political crisis in 1829);[121] the extension of the electoral franchise; the constitutional position of the crown relative to ministers and that of the upper house of parliament relative to the lower. The cholera came to London too.[122] More importantly, the financial consequences of political crisis were very similar, if less dramatic in London. Had the Reform crisis in Britain been even slightly more serious, then James might have found his brother much less free to lend assistance.

From the vantage point of Paris, it seemed at first unlikely that the Whig ministry of Earl Grey would survive.[123] Indeed, as late as March 5, 1831—four days after Lord John Russell introduced the Reform Bill—James wrote to Salomon assuring him that "Peel, Palmerston and Wellington are coming to power."[124] But this was wishful thinking on the part of his old Tory friends (Herries was his source for this tip). For his part, James was more inclined to think that an English revolution was in preparation, similar to the one he himself had experienced the year before, "because should the Bill be passed, then this will be seen as a fatal blow to England, and if on the other hand the Bill is not passed then one can expect a great deal of unrest."[125] When Parliament was dissolved in April, James had a sense of *déjà vu*. As he put it to Lionel: "If the Reform Bill passes, it will bring the same results as the revolution did here, the King wanted to take away from the people all their rights, which brought the revolution. In England the King gives the people more than their rights, which will have consequences as bad as the contrary has had."[126] He made the same point directly to Nathan:

> I might be mistaken, but the initial impression that the dissolution of Parliament in England has made on me is the same as . . . our dissolution made when, to start with, no one viewed the matter as giving cause for concern but then we fell some 30 per cent and I hope to God this will not be repeated this time in England. But I am very anxious . . . Let us get down to the nitty gritty. I am not at all pleased with the situation in England.[127]

As James saw it, "a lot of antagonism has been generated against the wealthier classes, and England has only been strong until now precisely because they [the government] had the support of the wealthy class." The Reform Bill might seem moderate, but "the supporters of . . . Reform will almost certainly make further demands later on."[128] He fervently wished England to "put a stop to the progress of the infamous liberal spirit." "The plebeians believe that a Parliamentary reform will provide them with [free] bread and cake," he warned Nathan, "and just like here, they are revolutionaries at heart. Once the Reform Bill has been passed, they will come up with new demands."[129] The riots in Bristol and elsewhere in October 1831 seemed to confirm this diagnosis.[130]

Lionel acknowledged that there was a parallel between France and England. "We have had a revolution and are now quiet; in England you are in the middle of your revolution, & you must wait 'til it is over."[131] However, he was far less worried by this than his uncle. This was partly a reflection of his liberal outlook. "I am very pleased to see that this Reform Bill has had a little effect upon some of the aristocracy," he commented in a revealing letter to his parents. "It is a very good thing, some of those great persons were really insupportable, the great difference that they always made between the different classes will soon be done away with, & the society in England will be more like that here, which is by far more agreeable."[132] There is more than a hint of Disraeli's fictional Adrian Neuchatel here ("Well; we City men must see what we can do against the dukes").[133]

But Lionel's attitude was rooted in pragmatic considerations: it had more to do with the connection between the prospects of the Reform Bill and the price of government bonds. Between January 1830 (when they stood at 95.6) and March 1831 (75.4), consol prices fell by 20 per cent—a less dramatic fall than in Paris, but nevertheless a substantial decline. The sharpest fall came between October 1830 and January the following year (see illustration 8.iv), but prices remained below their average level in 1829 (91) until 1834.

Although international concerns were paramount in the City (as they were on the Paris bourse), domestic factors also played a part in this crisis. Notoriously, the Duke of Wellington's intransigent speech against reform on November 11 provoked a fall of more than six points, though the slide had actually begun two months before.[134] At the same time—and this was more of a problem than in France—there was a sharp monetary tightening in 1830–31 as the Bank of England's reserve fell, providing the inspiration for the Radical Francis Place's famous slogan of the following year: "To stop the Duke, go for [meaning withdraw] gold!"[135] In short, it began to seem as if the financial markets wanted the Reform Bill to pass. In Paris, James made this connection as early as March 1831, just after the bill had passed its second reading by a single vote.[136] "That the Reformers are winning," he argued in early May, "can at the present moment only have a positive effect and cause a rise in the stocks."[137] Lionel agreed, expecting the passage of the bill to produce "a very great effect," and strongly favouring the creation of new peers to force the bill through the Lords.[138] Both were prepared for the Lords' rejection of the bill to cause a further fall in prices.[139]

By contrast, the man on the spot seems to have been less ready to see the connection between Reform and financial recovery. This was partly because Nathan's identification with Wellington—which led to his windows being broken by demonstrators—made him instinctively anti-Reform.[140] But it was also partly because the fluctuations of the London market after March 1831 were less severe than those in more volatile Paris.[141] Consol prices in fact remained relatively stable when the Lords rejected the bill in October 1831. This puzzled even some members of the British government. When the Vice-President of the Board of Trade, Charles Poulett Thomson, dined with James the following month, he declared: "Thank God, I have part of my money invested in foreign stocks, but I consider our country is very sick, and am surprised that stocks stand so high."[142] Nevertheless, by February 1832

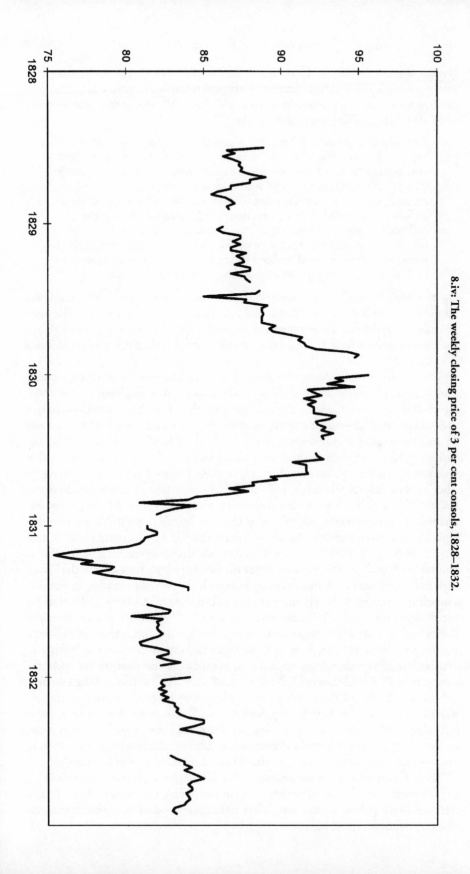

8.iv: The weekly closing price of 3 per cent consols, 1828–1832.

Nathan appears to have accepted that a Reform Bill would have to be passed.[143] There is no other way of interpreting his attitude when Wellington was called on to form an anti-Reform government following William IV's refusal to create fifty new peers. As Charles Arbuthnot told the Duke,

> Rothschild . . . came to tell me that if you let it be known, as soon as you meet Parliament that, whatever may be your own opinion of Reform, you are resolved not to disappoint expectations which are so greatly raised . . . you will surmount all your difficulties. He says that among the monied men there is an alarm lest there should be such an opposition to all Reform as would cause commotions . . . He assured me that the general feeling was that you would surmount your difficulties if men's minds were tranquillised as above stated, and if, having the reins in your hand, you were resolved to keep them. He is determined, he said, to keep up the Funds to his utmost, and he is confident he will succeed.[144]

Or, as Moses Montefiore summarised Nathan's argument more pithily, the Duke should "form a Liberal Government, and . . . consent to some reforms . . . he must go with the world, for the world would not with him."[145] This was no more than a circuitous way of telling Wellington to throw in the towel, which he duly did two days later.

What made Nathan change his mind? The obvious answer is that he genuinely feared another financial crisis of the sort which had driven Wellington from office the previous autumn. Consol prices had already fallen slightly—from 85 on May 9 to 83.25 on May 12—and it may be (as some observers suspected) that Nathan also warned Wellington of a renewed run on the Bank of England's reserve.[146] Yet the "panic" in Paris was not as great as Lionel had anticipated, and the predictions that Grey's return would boost consol prices "to their former level" proved wrong.[147] They were in fact scarcely affected by the Duke's resignation or by the passage of the Reform Bill itself; if anything, they reopened slightly lower after the royal assent was granted. Another possible explanation is that the British Rothschilds underwent a kind of political conversion. As we have seen, there is at least some evidence that from as early as 1829 Nathan, his wife and his children were shifting their political ground because of Tory opposition to Jewish emancipation. In addition, the Whigs appeared better able than the Tories to cope with the new threats of Irish political Catholicism and English radicalism.[148] The enthusiasm of Anthony and Lionel for the Whig victory in the 1832 elections was sincere;[149] and there is no evidence of Rothschild support when, largely at the King's instigation, Peel attempted to form a government in 1834. Nor is it without significance that Nathan was willing to manage the £15 million loan necessary to compensate the slave-owners after the government abolished slavery.[150] Buxton's recollections of Nathan are often quoted; but the significance of their dining together is seldom pointed out. In fact, Buxton was the leader of the Anti-Slavery Society, and his meeting with Nathan came immediately after the legislation freeing the slaves had been passed.[151] Just as James quickly aligned himself with the *doctrinaire* liberals after the revolution in France, so too, it seems, did Nathan bend with the Whiggish wind of reform in England.

Heine thus undoubtedly exaggerated when he sought to portray "Rothschild" as a revolutionary. But he was absolutely right in identifying the brothers' lack of commitment to the politics of reaction. When reform came—and even when it came by violence—they accepted it.

NINE

The Chains of Peace
(1830–1833)

Those who want war will doubtless turn to other bankers.
—FRIEDRICH GENTZ, 1830[1]

Despite the ease with which they shifted allegiances from Bourbon to Orléans, from Tory to Whig, the Rothschilds did not survive the 1830 revolution purely by adapting to domestic political change. For the internal threat—the threat which prompted James to bury bonds in the gardens at Suresnes—was in many ways the lesser threat posed by the revolutions of the period. Far more serious from a financial point of view was the possibility that the revolutions might lead indirectly to a war between the great powers. The most striking point to emerge from the private correspondence of the period is that this was the Rothschilds' real fear; and it is easy to see why. A revolution—or even a reform crisis—primarily affected bonds in one country. A war would have caused a severe slump in the price of *all* government securities in all markets. A domestic crisis in Paris could be withstood provided London, Frankfurt, Vienna and Naples stayed quiet. A European war would have hit all five houses simultaneously. The Rothschild correspondence shows that this fear was paramount in 1830–32. "You can't begin to imagine what might happen should we get war, God forbid," wrote James in October 1830, "for if that were the case, then all the securities would suffer such a fall that it would be impossible to sell anything."[2] A month later he sought to quantify the risk: "We have a holding of 900,000 rentes [30 million francs nominal]; if peace is preserved they will be worth 75 per cent, while in case of war they will drop to 45 per cent . . . I am convinced that if peace is maintained rentes will improve in three months by at least 10 per cent . . ."[3]

This helps explain why so many contemporaries believed that the Rothschilds not only favoured peace but used their financial leverage to preserve it. Ludwig Börne, for example, explicitly argued that Rothschild sales of Austrian government bonds had limited Metternich's diplomatic room for manoeuvre in 1831, when the Prince was itching to check forcibly the spread of revolution not only in Italy but in Belgium. He also implied strongly that the Rothschilds were keen to see France adopting a more pacific policy towards Austria: "If the house of Rothschild sat on the throne of France, the world would be relieved of the great dread of a war between that powerful house and the house of Habsburg."[4] Similar claims were made by political insiders too, for example by the Austrian diplomat Count Prokesch von Osten in December 1830: "It is all a question of ways and means and what Rothschild says is decisive, and he won't give any money for war."[5] Two years later the Austrian Finance Minister Baron Kübeck regarded Salomon as synonymous with "peace."[6] Nor was it only Austria which was perceived to be subject to Rothschild pressure: Metternich and his ambassador in Paris, Apponyi, alleged that the French government was even more susceptible.[7] As early as 1828, Prince Pückler was moved to compare the source of the Thames "with Napoleon who, born incognito in Ajaccio, made all the thrones of the earth quake . . . the avalanche which launches itself under the claw of a starling and five minutes later buries a village— and . . . Rothschild, whose father sold ribbons, and without whom no power in Europe today seemed able to make war."[8] The Prussian diplomat Achim von Arnim said much the same in the 1840s when he observed how few governments were unconstrained by the "golden chains of that House."[9]

Such claims very quickly became integral to the Rothschild myth. In his anti-Semitic tract *The Jews—Kings of the Epoch* (1846), Alphonse Toussenel made the point succinctly: "The Jew *speculates on peace*, that is on a rise, and that explains why peace in Europe has lasted for fifteen years."[10] Later writers put it even more crudely. Both Capefigue and Chirac purported to quote a Rothschild saying: "There will be no war because the Rothschilds do not want it."[11] In Morton's words, "the brothers became the most militant pacifists ever."[12] Gutle Rothschild is frequently credited with the declaration: "It won't come to war; my sons won't provide money for it."[13]

Publicly, the brothers liked to encourage such notions, as it made them appear both potent and benign. "Do you know who is viceroy and even king in France?" the Countess Nesselrode asked her husband in December 1840. "It is Rothschild. At his dinner, just recently, I had plenty of time for a lengthy chat with him; without saying anything to him to give away my own views, I induced him to express himself freely. He is bored with [the French premier] Thiers, and as for his ministers":

> "I know them all," he said, " I see them every day and as soon as I discern that the course they are following is contrary to the interests of the governments, I call on the king, whom I see whenever I wish, and I inform him of my observations. As he knows that I have a lot to lose, and that all I desire is peace, he has every confidence in me, listens to me and takes account of all that I say to him."[14]

But how far was this mere dinner-table bragging—like Nathan's to Prince Pückler in the 1820s? Does the brothers' private correspondence substantiate the claim that they used their position of influence to preserve peace after 1829?

Here it is necessary to distinguish the Rothschilds' use of financial leverage— principally their ability to refuse loans to governments contemplating war—from the less tangible influence which the Rothschilds were able to exercise in their capacity as a channel of diplomatic communication. This second function grew rapidly in importance in the course of the 1830s, though it had already begun to develop in the previous decade. In essence, statesmen and diplomats began to make use of the Rothschilds' network of communication for two reasons: because it was quicker than the official courier systems used for relaying diplomatic correspondence, and because messages of a non-binding nature could be sent from government to government indirectly via the brothers' own correspondence with one another. It is not hard to see why the brothers were willing to provide this service: it gave them advance knowledge of foreign policy as it was being formed, and this in turn allowed them to make better-informed investment decisions. The difficulty for the historian is that the brothers did not always explicitly distinguish their own views from those of ministers when acting as a diplomatic channel: it is from this period that they began to use the word "we" in their letters not only in the sense of "we Rothschilds," but also in the sense of "our government," the first hint of an identification with the five different states where the brothers now lived. Nor is it always apparent whether it was the Rothschilds who were actually influencing the direction of policy, or policy which was influencing the Rothschilds.

Lines of Communication

The development and nature of the brothers' communications network is therefore essential to an understanding of the financial diplomacy of the 1830s. As usual, a certain amount of mythology needs to be stripped away—above all, the notion that the Rothschilds, like Disraeli's Sidonia, were at the centre of an almost supernatural intelligence service: "No Minister of State had such communication with secret agents and political spies . . . To these sources he owed that knowledge of strange and hidden things which often startled those who listened to him . . . The secret history of the world was his pastime."[15] It is true that by the end of the 1840s they had established a formidable network of agents and regular correspondents, an important function of which was to keep New Court abreast of economic and political developments the world over. But in the twenty years after Waterloo (the news of which was the first great coup of Rothschild communications) their system was more rudimentary. Like anybody who wished to conduct international correspondence, their letters—and sometimes their lives—were at the mercy of the elements. In 1817, Salomon and his wife were "99 per cent" drowned when the carriage taking them from Paris to Rotterdam was caught in a storm while crossing a river. The whole journey lasted around seventy-two hours.[16] That was exceptional: letters sent from Paris to Frankfurt usually took just forty-eight hours in 1814; but mail from London could take up to a week to reach Frankfurt, and the service from Paris to Berlin took nine days in 1817.[17] Compulsive correspondents as they were—even scribbling letters in antechambers while waiting to see ministers—the brothers were always trying to find ways of speeding up the postal service. As we have seen, from 1815, if not before, Nathan was relying on his agents at Dover and Calais to expedite his letters by paying premiums to the captains of ships for express delivery. It seems he also sometimes sent copies of the same letter by more than one route, to reduce the risk of delays. In 1814 Amschel proposed an ingenious scheme for overcoming delays at the Frankfurt post office: if the exchange rate rose, his brothers should send their letters in blue envelopes; if it fell, in red, "then Mayer at the post office can immediately let me know if I have a red or a blue letter, which saves half a day."[18]

But this did not solve the problem that many of the offices in Germany through which the brothers' letters passed were "lodges" under the control of the Austrian secret police, so that mail was routinely opened and copied if it appeared to contain politically sensitive or useful information. The same lack of confidentiality ruled out anything more than occasional use of the diplomatic "bags" sent by courier from capital to capital.[19] There was therefore no alternative but to employ private couriers, which the Rothschilds began to do (at the latest) in 1814.[20] The problem was that couriers were expensive, and the brothers constantly bickered about when their use was justified: if couriers were sent too often, operating costs mounted, but if they were not sent, vital news could arrive late.[21] A related problem was that the very arrival of a courier alerted competitors to the probability of important news: letters to third parties were therefore sometimes backdated and couriers sent in disguise to put rivals off the scent.[22] By the mid-1820s, with costs less of a concern, couriers were being sent regularly: in December 1825 alone, the Paris house sent eighteen couriers to Calais (and hence to London), three to Saarbrücken, one to Brussels and one to Naples.[23] The practice was habit-forming: in 1827 Salomon was infuriated when he could not find a courier willing to set off from Vienna for Strasbourg at 10 p.m. on Christmas Day.[24]

Unfortunately—as with every innovation in communications—it was not long before the Rothschilds' rivals were sending just as many couriers of their own.[25] Moreover, no courier ever arrived soon enough: James's complaint in 1833 that a courier from London had arrived "one hour too late" was the classic expression of the perennial capitalist desire for faster communications.[26] From 1824, carrier pigeons were also employed, though it was apparently not until the 1840s that the brothers used these regularly enough to warrant a crude code: "A B in our pigeon dispatches means buy stock, the news is good. C D . . . means sell stock the news is bad."[27] It was not until after the mid-1830s that the development of the railway, the telegraph and the steamship opened a new era in communications—one in which it would be a good deal harder for the Rothschilds to steal a march on their competitors. In one of his first references to "telegraphic communication," James complained to Nathan: "Over here people are too well informed and there is therefore little opportunity to do anything."[28] By 1840 Carl was advising the Paris house not to send couriers to Naples, as the steamer arrived just as quickly and couriers merely alerted the "small speculators" that something was up.[29] Another important point is that as press censorship became less strict after 1830, it became unnecessary to provide so much detailed political news in private letters: by the 1840s, Nat routinely referred his brothers to the French newspapers where ten years before his uncle would have written the latest political news himself.

So it was in fact for a relatively short period—between around 1815 and 1835— that the Rothschild courier service had a real edge on alternative forms of communication. During those years, the Rothschilds were able to offer a distinctive service to those politicians and diplomats whom they wished to cultivate. Not only could they offer them private banking services; they could also deliver their letters ahead of the regular post. While in London in 1822, Chateaubriand received "an important despatch" from the duchesse de Duras through her "protégé Rothschild."[30] At Verona in the same year and at Pressburg in 1825, Metternich made use of Salomon's couriers to Vienna and London, evidently putting more trust in the Rothschilds' couriers than his own.[31] The idea soon caught on. By 1823, "receiving news from Rothschild" was an integral part of the Countess Nesselrode's routine.[32] In 1826 it was reported that:

the Rothschild clerks who travel as couriers from Naples to Paris about once or twice a month take with them all the despatches of the French, English and Spanish ministers accredited in Naples, Rome and Florence. In addition to this not inconsiderable correspondence, they also deal with the communications passing between the Courts of Naples and Rome and their legations at Turin, Paris, London, Madrid, Lisbon etc. as well as all private letters that are of any importance.[33]

When a minor crisis in Franco-Austrian relations blew up in 1826, it was a Rothschild courier who carried Villèle's placatory note to Metternich.[34] Perhaps the most distinguished—if not the most powerful—enthusiasts for the Rothschild postal service after 1840 were the young British Queen Victoria and her consort Prince Albert. It was probably the latter—whose Uncle Leopold was an old Rothschild friend—who introduced the former to the system.[35] From the moment he arrived in England, Albert (through his close adviser Christian von Stockmar and his British secretary George Anson) made regular use of Rothschild couriers for his correspondence with the continent.[36] Soon Victoria was doing the same, as well as relying on the Rothschilds to arrange minor banking services and even hotel reservations.[37] In June 1841 she assured Leopold that she "always" sent all her letters to Germany "wh. are of any *real* consequence . . . thro' Rothschild wh. is perfectly *safe* and very quick."[38]

All this meant that the Rothschilds were in a position to provide a unique news service to the European elite. Major political events as well as confidential information could be relayed from one city to another well ahead of official channels. Nathan's early news of the outcome of Waterloo was only the first of many such coups. As early as 1817 James was offering to relay details of French diplomatic despatches from Paris to London—made available by a "friend" in government circles—so that they reached Nathan before the despatches themselves reached the French ambassador.[39] The British ambassador in Paris also began to rely on Nathan for advance news from London.[40] In 1818 a British diplomat bound for the Aix Congress was "struck very much" by Nathan's "correct information as to the details of our party and his knowledge of the persons likely to compose it, some of whose names I believe had not even transpired at the Foreign Office."[41] When the duc de Berry was assassinated in February 1820, it was the Rothschilds who broke the story in Frankfurt and Vienna.[42] Likewise, when Queen Caroline died in 1821, it was again the Rothschilds who spread the news to Paris.[43] Canning, as we have seen, disliked the fact that the Rothschilds constantly scooped British ambassadorial reports; but he could hardly afford to ignore news like the Turkish capitulation at Ackerman.[44] By 1830, as Talleyrand observed, "The English Cabinet always obtain their information by [Rothschild] ten or twelve hours before the arrival of Lord Stuart's despatches, and this is not to be wondered at, seeing that the vessels which carry Rothschild's couriers belong to that firm, they take no passengers, and start at all hours . . ."[45] Villèle too had to heed Rothschild information, even though he (like Canning) strongly suspected the brothers were manipulating the news to influence the stock market.[46]

That of course was the whole idea; or rather the principal aim of Rothschild communications was, by getting political news first, to buy or sell securities before the news had influenced the markets as a whole. Yet this was not always achieved.

The fact that the Rothschilds broke the news of the French revolution of July 1830 not only to the British Foreign Secretary Lord Aberdeen in London but also (via Frankfurt) to Metternich in Bohemia is well known. But it is worth pointing out that their reports were not at first believed.[47] And, as we have seen, the outbreak of the revolution caught the Rothschilds themselves completely by surprise, plunging the French house into an economic crisis from which it was only with difficulty extricated.

Bankers' Diplomacy

The Rothschild letters reveal the extent and limitations of this communications system in the turbulent years after July 1830. In Paris, James's political connections were second to none. "I am constantly being consulted about everything," James told Nathan in 1831, and that never really changed: just as he later claimed to Countess Nesselrode, he really did see the King, his ministers and the principal ambassadors on an almost daily basis. Nathan too seems to have had access to senior government figures, notably the diplomat Frederick Lamb, in addition to key foreign diplomats in London like Talleyrand, Esterházy and Bülow; but there is no question that his influence was less than it had been under the Tories.[48] In Vienna, Salomon continued to enjoy direct access to Metternich, and relayed copies of his brothers' letters to him whenever they contained diplomatically important information. By comparison, the Frankfurt and Naples houses were somewhat out of the great power "loop." Influence in the other key capitals—St Petersburg and Berlin, as well as Brussels and the Hague—was limited to that which could be exercised through agents (for example, Gasser in Russia and Richtenberger in Belgium) or by occasional personal visits.

The first diplomatic question to be discussed via Rothschild correspondence in 1830 was whether the great powers would actually recognise Louis Philippe as king or intervene against the new regime. On July 31 James wrote to Nathan: "I hope to God that your Government is not thinking of intervening, for if they do so, then we will get a general war."[49] Lionel summed up the argument for recognition a fortnight later:

> [O]nly one thing that is completely requisite is that the king should be immediately recognised, if it is not done soon, one cannot say what may be the end . . . Until the king is recognised the neighbouring provinces may always wish to join this Governmt.[;] this will encourage also the disturbances there . . . France only wishes peace, wants nothing from other countries and knows that it only has to cultivate its own resources to be one of the greatest nations[;] at present there are in France 1,500,000 men in the National guard, all armed fit for service, besides these the whole army[;] what use [would] it be for other powers to think of making an attack on this country[?] . . . Uncle James was with the king today, being a member of a company who paid their respects to him[;] the king gave him the highest assurances of peace and of his good wishes, and of his hopes that everything will go on in the best way possible.[50]

Louis Philippe's message to James at that meeting—"My most ardent desires are centred upon the peace of Europe, and I hope that the states will resume their former friendly relations with France"—was duly passed on to Metternich through the Austrian ambassador Apponyi.[51]

However, recognition of Louis Philippe did not, as Lionel had hoped, prevent revolutionary outbreaks elsewhere. From the moment news reached Paris of the "full-blown revolution" which had broken out in Brussels on August 25, a new possibility arose: that the spread of revolution outside France would precipitate a war between France and one or more of the conservative powers, Prussia, Russia and Austria—and perhaps even England.[52] This was a far more plausible scenario than the possibility of direct foreign intervention in France for two reasons. Firstly, the other powers had not only treaty obligations (dating from 1814–15) but also strategic interests in Belgium. Secondly, foreign intervention in Belgium, or anywhere else where revolutions broke out, was likely to move the French regime to the left, because of the historic link between republicanism and revolutionary internationalism. Metternich was not the only one who remembered the 1790s, when France had combined domestic "anarchy" with dramatic military expansion.

James's first action on hearing of the Belgian revolt was thus to broker a meeting between the French Foreign Minister Molé and the Prussian ambassador, in the hope of averting a military confrontation between the two powers. He also urged Nathan to oppose any British-sponsored intervention on behalf of the Dutch King, having concluded (along with Hannah and Lionel) that Belgian claims to independence were practically (and perhaps also in principle) defensible.[53] At the same time, fearful that the revolutionary spirit might spread to Naples and Spain (as it had in the 1820s), James relayed a veiled warning from Louis Philippe to Metternich that "he was opposing revolutionaries in all countries as far as his position as a constitutional monarch allowed him to do, but . . . that he was compelled in his position to show a certain regard for Liberal aspirations"; the King of Naples should therefore make "a few concessions in the general interest of the country and in accordance with the progress of contemporary ideas."[54] A few days later Molé told James that France might be prepared to go to war if France were "surrounded by a large number of [Prussian and Austrian] troops," a fear of "general war" echoed by a number of foreign diplomats including Lamb, who raised the possibility of British intervention.[55]

There was relief when, after discussions between Talleyrand and Aberdeen, the whole Belgian question was referred to arbitration by representatives of the great powers in London.[56] However, even before an armistice had been reached between the Belgians and the Dutch, news arrived that a revolt had broken out in Warsaw against Russian rule. In fact, it may well have been this development which did most to *prevent* war over Belgium, as prior to the revolt the Tsar had been preparing to send troops from Poland to support Holland. The fact that it took the Russian army from February until October 1831 to crush the revolt may well have been the main reason there was no general war. But at the time the spread of revolution eastwards seemed only to increase the chances of international conflict.[57] The protracted arguments about the extent of the new Belgian state, its neutral status and the choice of its king served only to prolong uncertainty throughout the first half of 1831, with the Rothschilds once again relaying proposals and counter-proposals from Paris to London.[58] Then came the news of revolts in Italy: not, as had been feared, in Naples, but in the duchies of Modena and Parma (February 1831) and the Papal states (March).[59]

Between March 1831 and March 1832 there was a series of "flashpoints" when war involving more than one of the great powers seemed to come perilously close, and on each occasion the Rothschilds worked frenetically to diminish the tension. The first crisis raised the possibility not only of Austrian intervention in the Papal states but also of French moves in support of the revolutionaries. James and Salomon were much involved in the war of words which duly broke out between Paris and Vienna.[60] Ultimately, Austria did intervene, not only in Modena (which the French tacitly accepted) but also in Bologna in response to an appeal from Gregory XVI; action which, after much prevarication, elicited a more or less direct threat of war from the French government—relayed, yet again, by James.[61] This was probably the moment at which a general war came closest; it was undoubtedly the moment when both the British and French bond markets touched their lowest points. Here the evidence of Rothschild involvement in inter-government communication is especially strong, with James taking a hand in the drafting of a crucial French note to Austria calling for international arbitration (on the Belgian model).[62] By mid-April, James was sure that "the crisis in Italy [was] over" and that Anglo-French unity would avoid war over Belgium.[63]

The second flashpoint came in August 1831 over Belgium. After months of uncertainty about the election of Leopold of Saxe-Coburg as King of the Belgians (exacerbated by continued fighting in Poland and news of Austrian reprisals against Italian liberals),[64] the Dutch invasion of Belgium raised the possibility of a general war once more.[65] But again the powers drew back. Neither Prussia nor Russia supported the Dutch move and the British government—after some tense negotiations—sanctioned the French decision to send an expeditionary force to Belgium, provided it withdrew once the Dutch had been driven out.[66] It was only during October that the danger of war over Belgium gradually receded; though even the signing of the 24 Articles by Belgium on November 15 was far from the breakthrough it initially seemed, as Prussia, Austria and Russia took until May 1832 to ratify them, and the Dutch King continued to withhold his signature.[67]

The third war scare came in February 1832 as a result of fresh unrest in the Papal states. Once again Austrian troops were called in, and once again the French sought to take a hand. Indeed, this time a French force was actually sent to occupy the port of Ancona—"a serious blunder" in James's view. However, this was far less serious than the earlier crises (as the muted reaction of the markets testified) and there was never any real prospect of a serious breach between Paris and Vienna.[68] The final war scare of the post-revolutionary period came in the autumn of 1832, when France pressed once again for military intervention to force the Dutch to accept the 24 Articles. Even when Britain agreed to act jointly against Holland, this once again raised the spectre of a Prussian or Russian retaliation.[69] The Convention of London of May 1832 was a stopgap, as it left the Belgians in Luxembourg (apart from its fortress) and Limburg (apart from Maastricht) in breach of the 24 Articles. But it sufficed to preserve the peace until the definitive international settlement of 1839.

Throughout these periods of crisis, the Rothschild letters were the channel through which the views of kings, ministers and diplomats could most rapidly be exchanged. But they also allowed the Rothschilds to make their own views known not only to one another but to the political figures to whom appropriately translated copies were circulated. A central leitmotif of the brothers' own commentary was their awareness of the potentially explosive interaction between international and domestic politics. This was especially pronounced in Paris, where fear of war was inseparable from fear of a radicalisation of French domestic politics. "The Government here in France is all for peace," warned James on September 29, 1830, "but if they are threatened too much, then the king says that he would no longer be master of his house and the people don't want to be threatened like little children."[70] James constantly fretted that, if the other powers were too aggressive in countering revolution in Belgium or elsewhere, more bellicose politicians would come to power in France. The difficulty was that even those ministers to whom he and Lionel gave their qualified backing were sometimes obliged to assuage public feeling by speaking in a bellicose manner themselves; hence the repeated reassurances from James that such utterances were only for domestic consumption and should not be taken literally abroad. When Sebastiani was appointed Foreign Minister in Laffitte's new government (November 1830), James immediately rushed to see him. In fact, the message he was able to relay to London and Vienna was much the same as the King's a few weeks before: "If they are looking for an excuse to wage war against us, then we are fit and ready for them but we will make every possible effort to prevent it from happening." However, James concluded optimistically that "there is every likelihood that peace will be maintained." Provided Russia did not think of intervening on behalf of Holland, France would tell the Belgians "that they shouldn't eliminate the House of Orange from their calculations and that they will not be able to count on our support if they behave stupidly."[71] The difficulty was that, as James admitted, the government was simultaneously "asking for eighty thousand men [while] saying 'we are all for peace' . . . [T]here has been such a degree of fervour and activity at the War Department over here that it would seem that they already planned to make war in fourteen days' time. Our newspapers are now furiously screaming for war and yesterday the whole world thought that war was about to break out." Nevertheless, he still maintained that Laffitte was "for peace and he is only asking for the army so as to be able to defend peace."[72] Talk of war was merely to "keep the public mind occupied."[73] It was for this reason that James urged the Banque de France to avert Laffitte's bankruptcy in early 1831; a change of government in France, he was convinced, would increase the danger of war.[74] Throughout January he assured his brothers of the government's peaceful intent, despite the increasingly febrile mood in Paris.[75]

Yet James was soon forced to acknowledge a growing appetite for war over Belgium even within the government,[76] an appetite which was only whetted when the news reached Paris of the revolutions in Modena and Parma. James reacted promptly. According to his own account, he told Louis Philippe:

> You are being pushed into a state of war, even though you have no interest in any Belgian [territory] . . . and is it wise for the French to take on such a proud stance? And now do you want us to go ahead and declare war on the foreigners? Your Majesty, you are being deceived. Your ministers have lost the confidence of the public. You should appoint Périer and then all the people, including the wealthy section of the population, will support him, and this will demonstrate that you mean business.[77]

Laffitte, he told his brother, was bent on a course of "complete anarchy":

> This morning I was at Laffitte's and he said to me, "If France does not
> declare war on Austria, then, in a matter of three weeks, the king will no
> longer be king and will lose his head." I told him, how could he possibly
> give such bad advice to the king, to which he replied that the king no
> longer consults with him. In short, Laffitte views the situation as already
> lost . . . Tomorrow, I will ask the king and perhaps I might even go to see
> him today.[78]

It would appear that James's "talking to the king had the desired effect":[79] Laffitte
resigned just over a week later.

James's support for Périer was thus inseparable from the idea that he would
pursue a peaceful policy; by the same token, James knew that he would be able to
survive in office only if the other powers made concessions too. This was the strategy
on which he pinned his hopes of stabilisation in France. In a characteristic letter
intended for Metternich's eyes, James urged Salomon that Austria should "support"
Périer as the French politician least likely to go to war:

> Now, my dear Salomon, you must see that if my friend Périer takes
> office his ministry is supported, for thirty-two million people making a
> revolution are a danger to all countries. "And," Périer said to me, "if
> people want to do something for the king, they should try to give France
> a piece of Belgium; that would really strengthen the king's position, but
> he does not press for it." . . . Now I tell you that when Périer is in the
> saddle it depends on the [other] powers whether they have war or not
> . . . I tell the whole world that the powers only want peace . . . [W]e can't
> say yet what will happen, but I am confident because of Périer, as if we
> have war, he will suffer losses on his properties and factories; for that
> reason I believe in peace . . . When we are certain of peace abroad we
> shall have peace at home.[80]

"Périer," he assured Nathan, "is a stroke of luck from God, as he will maintain
peace, or at least I hope he will." He and Lionel were even led to believe that "if
Périer comes in, it is to be one of his conditions, that Austria should be allowed to
interfere in the Italian affairs without any notice being taken of it."[81] As soon as
Périer's appointment was confirmed, James repeated his appeal for Austrian backing:

> [W]e have a ministry which wants peace, and they want to do all that is
> in their power for peace to be maintained. [But] if the powers want
> peace to be maintained, then they will have to strengthen the "Peace
> ministry" and enable it to demonstrate [to the public] that the powers
> have no intention of attacking France. It would now be very helpful if
> both Russia and Austria were to issue a declaration that they will remain
> on the sidelines, and that they will not attack France, and such a move
> would calm the populace, for over here they firmly believe that as soon
> as Russia has resolved its problems in Poland, they will then turn their
> attention to France . . . I went to the king and pointed out to him that
> my whole fortune and family were in France and, consequently, I would
> not dream of misleading him and lulling him into believing that the for-

eign powers wanted peace when, in truth, they were planning to make war and, anyway, for whose benefit would such a ploy be? . . . If they should opt for Périer, then their credit will rise and everything will improve . . . Well, all now depends on the foreign powers and you will have to make every effort towards that end, for, should we be unsuccessful in maintaining peace, then no power will be able to preserve its credit.[82]

Five days later he "urgently begged" Salomon to continue "pestering" Metternich "as to the importance of strengthening the ministry here and . . . maintain[ing] peace, which is so necessary to Europe, the Prince alone having the power to maintain it."[83] "The whole depends upon the question of war or peace," wrote Lionel on March 31. "This govt. is for peace, but must be supported by the other powers and must not go against the public opinion, or it would give too much strength to the opposition, which would then bring us war immediately."[84]

Yet even the appointment of Périer did not wholly allay James's fears of French aggression, especially when it became known that Austria intended to intervene in the Papal states regardless of the change of ministry in Paris.[85] Events in Italy, Belgium and Poland periodically threatened to stir up liberal sentiment in Paris, leaving the government with little choice but to fight or resign. In the summer of 1831 there was even an economic argument for a more aggressive policy, as Lionel remarked: "There is [sic] in France too many young men, without employment and money and to get rid of them war is requisite, party spirit is also strong, and without a war, we should see the present king driven away."[86] Louis Philippe appeared to share this view, and James watched with apprehension as Périer's position seemed to crumble. When Périer resigned at the beginning of August, James predicted "war within four days" if an "ultra-liberal" ministry took his place.[87] Not for the last time, Périer survived politically by taking limited military action against Holland with the tacit approval of the other powers.

The same scenario was more or less replayed in January and February 1832. First James warned that Périer would resign if the final terms of the Belgian settlement were unsatisfactory to France.[88] Then Périer sent a military force to Ancona in reply to the return of Austrian troops to the Papal states. Even after Périer's death, the pattern repeated itself. With Soult eager to despatch the army against the Dutch once again in October 1832, James sought to secure British support for intervention by warning Nathan: "If the government here, God forbid, does not survive, we will then get a republican administration, and then I expect things to be very black indeed. That is why everything now depends on the Belgian problem. Should England decide not to stand by France, we will then become very sick here, for the world is opposed to the *doctrinaires*."[89]

There was a very similar link between domestic and foreign policy in Britain. The possibility, though remote, never entirely disappeared that a Tory government might revert to Pittite tradition and intervene against a revolutionary France.[90] On the other hand, when the Whigs came to power in 1830, James at once visualised an equally alarming scenario: if the new government turned out to be "radicals" then "our ministry will have to be more liberal and consequently, the Belgian problem will be that much more difficult to resolve, and England may possibly enter into a treaty with France so that we could find ourselves at war with the rest of Europe."[91] "All now depends on England," wrote James to Nathan in January 1831, during the search for a suitable Belgian king. "The foreign powers would never declare war without England as an ally . . . You see, dear Nathan, how important it is for you to be constantly vigilant, because whether or not we will have war depends on whether or not England will yield on the question of Belgium."[92] But Nathan's Tory friends were unconvinced by James's arguments, least of all when he threw his weight behind Périer. As Nathan wrote to James shortly after the start of the Reform Bill debates,

> Herries says that Peel will certainly be asked to join the ministry, that Wellington will become Foreign Minister and that, unless France gives way, he is convinced that the British Army will go to Germany . . . It would be well for you to tell the king that he must hold himself aloof, and not trifle with England, for she is not to be trifled with . . . England has no faith in your ministers who want nothing but revolutions, in which old Lafayette and I know not who else assists. Your king and his ministers have only to show that they don't want war: they must not change their tone from day to day. Go to the king and tell him that Peel, Palmerston and Wellington are coming to power.[93]

This shot across the bows does much to illuminate the Rothschilds' subsequent transition from Toryism to Whiggery. The Whig position, as relayed by Nathan on March 18, was far more congenial to James: "If France does not remain quiet, but takes action against the other three powers, we shall join the three powers, *but if the other three powers take action against France, we shall join France.*" James's fear that the Reform Bill would be defeated and the Tories returned to power was therefore more to do with the international situation than with his support for the bill itself, for "a Wellington ministry would declare war on France without hesitation."[94] As Lionel observed in June 1831, confusion about British politics tended to reduce the chances of a Belgian settlement, because "all the time the King of Holland reckons upon a change in the ministry."[95] James made the same point four months later: "The passage of your bill is being closely watched, as people believe that, should the ministry resign, we will then have war."[96] When Russia was hesitating about ratifying the 24 Articles on Holland, Lionel posed the question: "What can Russia do alone[?], everything depends upon the Reform Bill, if that passes and the present ministry remain[s] in, England & France are quite strong enough to make all the other powers tremble."[97]

This illuminates Nathan's decision not to support Wellington when he was unexpectedly returned to office in May 1832. It was not just that Nathan feared internal "commotions" if an anti-Reform government stayed in office; it was also that "the foreign ministers"—he instanced Talleyrand, Weissenburg and Bülow—were "in great anxiety lest the King of Holland should be led to expect such support from the new government as would lead to war."[98] This analysis was echoed six months later, when news of the Whig election victory was generally welcomed by James, Lionel and Anthony as "the best guarantee of peace in Europe" and the stability of the French government. In the dying moments of the Belgian crisis, when the possibility of Russian intervention surfaced for the last time, Nathan indicated the extent and nature of his conversion in a letter to James:

You must write to our brother Salomon, to tell Metternich not to let himself be bamboozled into war by Russia, for Pozzo [the Russian ambassador in Paris] is with the king and was not well received, and he and Lieven [the Russian ambassador in London] are intriguing to make Austria and Prussia declare war. I have, however, been informed in a reliable quarter [presumably Bülow] that Prussia will not go to war, and that they are making a great mistake, because England and France jointly can do a great deal. We shall keep peace, there won't be war . . . Write and tell Salomon that Neumann [the Austrian ambassador] is always spending a great deal of time with Pozzo and believes our government to be weak. The man is seven-eighths mistaken and now Pozzo has not been well received. The king invited him to Brighton and he sat six places from the king. The king asked him how long he would stay here. He replied, "Six weeks"; and now we know that Russia wants war, and Metternich is being bamboozled by those people. Pozzo and those folk are making themselves ridiculous and do not understand England, so ask our good brother Salomon to tell Prince Metternich not to let himself be bamboozled by Russia. Pozzo is here simply to spy and *I am convinced that England is stronger than she was in the time of Wellington.* Now, my dear brother, don't let yourself be bamboozled by anyone. If England and France hold together, it will be difficult to touch them. Write this to brother Salomon.[99]

In Vienna too, despite the absence of a revolutionary threat, there was a domestic political struggle with important international implications: between proponents and opponents of foreign intervention. When Salomon returned to Vienna in early October 1830, it was in order "to impress upon Prince Metternich how important it now is to maintain peace," as "the issue of peace or war depend[ed] entirely upon" him.[100] This was a slight exaggeration, as Austrian influence over the Belgian question was limited; on the other hand, Russia (and possibly also Prussia) would be more likely to go on the offensive if a lead came from Vienna—that was the implication of the Carlsbad agreement of August 1830, which had reaffirmed the counter-revolutionary intent of the Holy Alliance. Over Italy, Metternich was unequivocal. He told Salomon in November 1830 that he was prepared "to send troops . . . to keep the country quiet,"[101] and he duly did so in both Modena and Bologna, as we have seen. Until April 1831 Salomon could do little more than relay Austrian intentions to Paris (in itself an important service as his letters to James arrived as much as three days before Apponyi's official instructions). When the Tsar appealed for help in Poland, however, Salomon was able to exert real influence, forewarning Metternich's rival Count Kolowrat, who intervened "with uncharacteristic decisiveness" against such assistance.[102] By July he was able confidently to assure his brothers: "Strictly between ourselves, Austria will not make war, does not want war and is doing everything possible to avoid having a war . . . I am convinced that even if England and France declared war on . . . *Russia*, it would make no difference to Austria, we would stay . . . neutral."[103]

Even when he was away from Vienna, Salomon kept up the pressure on Metternich to avoid war. In March 1832 he wrote long and effusive letters to Metternich from Paris, urging him not to overreact to Périer's decision to send troops to Ancona.[104] In November, when French troops were descending on Antwerp,

Kübeck complained that "Prince Metternich is a veritable pendulum, swinging back and forth between Tatichev [the Russian ambassador in Vienna] and war, and Salomon Rothschild and peace."[105]

Golden Chains
Yet it is hard to assess how much the brothers' constant lobbying for peaceful policies would have achieved if it had not been linked to their financial power. As suggested above, the Rothschilds had two potential forms of leverage: not only the influence they derived from their role as a channel of informal diplomatic communication, but also actual financial pressure—if a regime bent on war asked them to lend money, they could refuse, and conversely they could give financial support to one that was peacefully inclined. Here once again it is necessary to stress the limits of Rothschild power, especially in those countries (Britain and Prussia) which did not make large increases in military expenditure during the 1830–33 crisis, but also even in those (France, Russia and Austria) where spending did create a need for new loans.

Rothschild financial leverage was most limited in the capitals where no partner was resident. In Berlin, the brothers were caught by the outbreak of revolution in 1830 halfway through a delicate conversion operation designed to reduce the interest on their earlier sterling loan to Prussia from 5 to 4 per cent. From the outset this was not a promising transaction. After much hard bargaining between Salomon, Anselm and the Rothschilds' "old friend" Christian Rother, it was agreed in February 1830 that the Rothschilds would issue a new sterling 4 per cent loan at 98, the proceeds of which would be used to redeem the old 5 per cent bonds. The total amount of the loan was £3.8 million. In addition, the possibility was raised of a similar operation for the bonds issued in 1822.[106] However, by the time the French revolution broke out in July, roughly half of the new 4 per cent bonds were still unsold. With financial markets across Europe nose-diving, there was no possibility of disposing of these other than at a steep discount: by February the new bonds were being traded at 79.5, and renewed sales would doubtless have driven the price lower. Yet the brothers were contractually bound to continue making cash payments to Prussia on the basis of the underwriting price of 98. Could the Rothschilds have stood the losses—estimated by Rother at more than £367,000—which would have ensued had the contract been honoured? Probably; but it is easy to see why, having lost so much on the earlier French 4 per cent loan, they were so determined to extricate themselves from this second costly débâcle.

Anselm was duly sent back to Berlin for a protracted and exceptionally difficult bout of wrangling, made the harder by the machinations of the various officials and ministers he had to deal with, who were united only by their opposition to an outright cancellation of the conversion agreement. Finally, after Carl had been sent to join him, it proved possible to reach a compromise. In effect, by paying an indemnity of around £140,000 (which in practice dwindled to around £50,000 after various deductions), the Rothschilds secured a postponement of the operation until European financial conditions had stabilised.[107]

From the Rothschild standpoint, this was a successful exercise in damage-limitation; but why did the Prussian authorities agree to it? Rother's argument to the Prussian King, Frederick William III, was based on self-interest. "If Nathan Mayer von Rothschild's firm were to be compelled strictly to observe the dates laid down in the contract," he pointed out, "in spite of the unfavourable conditions now obtaining, it would necessarily endeavour to sell the new 4 per cent bonds at any price in all markets, and thereby deal a severe blow to our public credit. Our experience has taught us that financial transactions in which the von Rothschild firm do not act as intermediaries, but as opponents, are apt to fall through . . ." Rothschild weakness, in other words, could have negative repercussions for Prussia too, despite the short-term benefits of insisting on the fulfilment of the contract:

> Through the recent French loan of January 1830 and the conversion . . . of the Prussian debt contracted in 1818, in which latter transaction they associated a number of other banking firms with themselves, involving them in enormous losses, the Rothschild banks have entirely lost their credit in transactions of this kind . . . Although their wealth . . . is still very considerable, they lack the cash necessary for transactions of this kind, since their property, which consists of bonds of all the European states, cannot at present be turned into money on any bourse. The Rothschild banks are therefore now refusing to take over any large loans direct, seeking as in the case of Austria, to deal with them on a commission basis, and while they will make advances on account, they proceed to sell the newly created bonds at exceedingly low prices, thus damaging the States concerned.

But this argument would not have cut any ice if Prussia too had not been in need of new funds to pay for the rising costs of her military preparations. For although Prussia was, in James's words, "of all Powers, least in a position to demand war, and most [keen] to avoid it,"[108] she could not ignore the threat of a major war (whether over Belgium or Poland) which recurred throughout 1831 and 1832. Rother's letter to the King suggests that he had been dissuaded, probably by Amschel, from attempting to float a new issue of bonds. Instead, the Rothschilds offered to make substantial short term cash-advances of up to 5 million thaler against treasury bills and to lend their support to a lottery loan. It was this offer which was decisive in securing the postponement of the conversion, discussion of which resumed only in 1833, by which time Prussian 4 per cents had recovered to 92 and "the present political situation gives no more cause for serious concern."[109] In other words, the Rothschilds still had some financial leverage in Berlin; but it was only sufficient to secure concessions over the conversion. There is no evidence of any attempt during this period to influence Prussian foreign policy: all the Rothschilds got out of Frederick William was some porcelain and (for Nat) the title of Privy Commercial Councillor, by way of grudging thanks.[110]

If their power was limited in Berlin, the Rothschilds' influence in St Petersburg was almost non-existent. True, Russia needed money more than any of the great powers to fight her war against the Poles. But relations between the Rothschilds and the the Russian Finance Minister Kankrin had never been good, so even when the Russians directly approached their agent Gasser for a loan in early 1831, James was wary. "The Minister must be terribly short of money," he reflected. "That means he will not be able to fulfil his commitments, and, should it occur to the good man not to pay his interest, we will then be left floundering." He argued for taking any loan only on commission and issuing it in small tranches, opposing Nathan's decision to

offer an immediate advance of £400,000. "In the event of war breaking out," he
warned, "neither France, nor Russia nor Prussia will meet their interest payments,
and, by God, they will all use the excuse of war to justify the non-payment of the
interest due."[111] On the other hand, as Anselm argued, if the danger of war disappeared—especially if Russia won a decisive victory in Poland—the government
would have no need of their services. Only as long as the crisis lasted would the government need money badly enough to "submit to any conditions."[112] In fact,
James's real anxiety was political: he had no objection to lending the Russian government as much as £5 million provided the fact could be kept secret in Paris, where
sympathy for the Poles was fervent. "It is a foregone conclusion," he pointed out,

> that we will be severely criticised in the newspapers, otherwise, I have no
> objections to proceeding on this basis . . . [S]hould the Poles indeed have
> achieved a victory, this will ease matters considerably, as we must make
> every effort to co-operate with the liberal[s]. Would it perhaps be possi-
> ble to claim that the minister will be arranging the loan in conjunction
> with Gasser and in his name? . . . Well, I suggest we consider . . . very
> carefully how we can possibly prevent our involvement in this matter be-
> coming public knowledge.

He repeated his misgivings a week later: "I can assure you that if we support
Russia against Poland I am not at all certain that I won't be clubbed to death,
because public opinion here is passionately behind Poland."[113] Nevertheless, he was
obviously prepared to risk public hostility if the terms of the loan were sufficiently
attractive. It is noteworthy that these discussions took place on the eve of the Poles'
decisive defeat at Ostrolenka. Indeed, Nathan managed to sell some guns to the
Russian government just a few days after the battle. James was "extremely happy" at
the profit thereby realised; once again, his only concern was to avoid bad publicity:

> I beg you, in God's name, not to provide your name unless it is
> absolutely essential, that is, to register that "Rothschild" has sold "guns"
> and please keep this information under wraps, as otherwise I am liable
> to be shot, for it will be said that I am selling guns to facilitate the shoot-
> ing of the Poles. Yesterday a friend of mine who is a newspaper corre-
> spondent came to see me and showed me a newspaper article which
> claimed that we were providing funds to Luxembourg so that they could
> suppress the Belgians. He had not written the article but believe me,
> dear Nathan, now that the general feeling amongst the public has veered
> to liberalism one must be that much more careful. That is why you
> should make every effort to prevent the information reaching the news-
> papers.[114]

The idea of a loan (now for £1 million) resurfaced again at the end of 1832.
Again, James felt nervous, this time imagining the English press "tearing us apart,
claiming that we are providing the Russian Tsar with loans which will enable him to
wage war." But once again he was prepared to run this risk. After all, "it is not as if
one can conquer the world with £1 million." And to be on the safe side Lionel argued that "in case of war the . . . clause ought to exist . . . that we are not bound to
continue our payments" (a device used for other Rothschild loans in this and later
periods, as we shall see).[115] However, as James predicted, Kankrin once again "bam-

boozled" Nathan by using the Rothschild offer merely to secure improved terms from Hope, the Russian government's traditional banker.[116] The idea that the Rothschilds had been competing to make this loan would have come as a surprise to those French émigrés—supporters of Charles X, who banked on a Russian-led counter-revolution—who were convinced that the Rothschilds had "fallen to a prodigious extent under revolutionary influence" and now served "the revolutionary movement . . . under the leadership of the London [Rothschild], and of Talleyrand."[117] After all, this was the last opportunity when a Russian intervention might have averted the imposition of the 24 Articles on Holland. It is possible that Nathan and James genuinely believed that if they handled the loan instead of Hope—especially as they envisaged lending a much smaller sum than the Dutch bank—they would be able to exert pressure on Russia not to intervene. Alternatively, Nathan's warning after the Hope coup that Russia was bent on war was disingenuous. It is tempting to conclude that he was prepared to shut his eyes to the possibility of Russian aggression if he could only win back his influence at St Petersburg.

James came to feel that his brother was trying too hard to secure Russian business. "As far as I am concerned, Russia can go to the Devil, and we can quite happily do without them," he wrote when yet another loan was bruited in 1834. "Under no circumstances should you personally write to Petersburg for you have been refused enough times. Don't give them another opportunity to embarrass you."[118] "Do you think that we will ever be on friendly terms with Russia?" he asked two years later. He evidently thought not.[119] It is hard to find a better illustration of the limits of Rothschild financial power.

Even where a partner was resident there were difficulties. In London, the disintegration of Tory power which began with Catholic emancipation and was completed by the failure of Peel's 1834–5 ministry unquestionably led to a decline of Rothschild influence over financial policy. Althorp, Grey's Chancellor, was decidedly unimpressed by Nathan when the latter sought to ingratiate himself in December 1830. "The result of a good long conversation," noted Althorp, "was that I was satisfied he must think me the greatest fool that ever existed or he never would have supposed that he could so grossly deceive me as he appeared to wish to do."[120] And whatever sympathy Nathan may have come to feel towards Grey's government, he was never given much inside political information; indeed Grey's resignation in 1834 took him wholly by surprise.[121] However, the decline of Nathan's political influence had less to do with the door being "shut in his face" by the Whigs than with the fact that British financial policy largely rendered him superfluous during the 1830s. With only one exception—the £15 million loan to compensate the slave owners in 1835—there were no major borrowings by British governments in this period. Expenditure was tending to fall and revenue, despite continuing piecemeal reductions in indirect tax, was stable.[122] For this reason, Nathan's leverage in London was much less than James's in Paris. Although Nathan was ready and willing to act as a channel for inter-governmental messages, he was not really in a position to influence their content. It was a matter of luck rather than Rothschild design that the Whig government was keen to avert war over Belgium.

By contrast, there is evidence that James succeeded in using financial leverage to discourage an aggressive policy in France, though the strength of his position should not be exaggerated. The revolution had left the Paris house in an extremely vulnerable state, saddled with large amounts of depreciating 3 and 5 per cent rentes and with payments totalling 10 million francs still outstanding to the Treasury for the 4 per cent Polignac loan.[123] On the other hand, the new French government was forced to begin borrowing almost immediately, issuing substantial quantities of treasury bills. James's immediate reaction to this was characteristic: there were, he told Nathan as early as December 1830, "big deals to be made here,"[124] and it was his intention not to be excluded from them. Despite his heavy criticism of Laffitte's foreign policy, at no point did he withdraw from the discussions about financing the government's deficit.[125] His reasons were straightforward. As he explained to his brothers in March 1831, "doing business with the current Government will, I think, bring in its wake a rise in the rentes." In any case, "the businessmen are all in agreement about the loan here, and I shall go with them, because I don't want to be out of it."[126]

The problem was that some of the money being raised was obviously wanted for military purposes (this was confirmed by "a colonel in the War Ministry who is on my payroll").[127] Indeed, James and Nathan themselves sold around 28,000 British guns and offered to sell other military supplies to the French government at around this time—a remarkable kind of "hedging," given their vocal pacifism.[128] There was no real guarantee that French armaments were for purely defensive purposes, except that the higher costs of war would be unfinanceable.[129] James pinned much hope on this idea that "an outbreak of war would be very dangerous [to the French government]," adding: "I assure you that they will have to raise loan after loan to be able to pay the interest."[130] When Sebastiani talked of France's refusing to be "bossed about" in February 1831, James was sceptical: "Basically they have no funds in reserve. With what will they wage war? Consequently, I am convinced we will have no war, no matter what others might say."[131]

This helps explain James's support for Périer, for the latter seemed to recognise the fiscal constraint on French policy:

> Périer told me, ". . . If we choose war, we will be unable to meet our debts, and I am therefore not prepared to join the ministry only to see the Treasury slide into bankruptcy the following day . . ." In short, he will not join without first being reassured that we can maintain peace . . . Should Périer not join the government, then I fear that the Treasury here faces bankruptcy for they will have to issue a loan at 5 per cent.[132]

It therefore made sense to give Périer financial as well as moral support, not least because the combination of peace and a properly funded loan would lead to a rise in the price of rentes:

> I will speak to Périer and may sell a loan on commission. The Treasury is in need of funds . . . We must assist the government by providing funds, and ensure that the bankers participate, as it is in my interest to provide these people with funds, so that . . . I can make my exit from all this . . . I think that Périer will boost the value of your stocks . . . I want to tell you that we can perhaps do business with Périer.[133]

But the fact remained that James had no way of preventing the money thus raised from being used to fight a war. He simply lacked the bargaining power to insist on the clause suggested by Nathan "that in case of war those payments that have not been made . . . are not to be enforced."[134] The most he could do was to hope that Périer would not be "too belligerent [over Austrian intervention in Bologna], as we must of course remember that the people wish to raise a loan."[135] There is some circumstantial evidence that such financial considerations inclined the French government to avoid war with Austria over the Papal states. Market expectations that the loan would stabilise the fiscal position ran counter to pessimism about the dangers of war.[136] Indeed, the fact that the French Finance Minister Louis exploited a slight rally in April to demand better terms for the loan was regarded by James as a sign of the government's peaceful intentions.[137] That the ambassadors of potentially hostile powers like Werther (Prussia) and Pozzo (Russia) were personally interested in taking a share of the loan also suggested to Lionel that peace would be preserved.[138] Nevertheless, James's overwhelming sense in the spring of 1831 was one of impotence. "I am master of nothing," he confessed to Nathan. "Times are no longer what they were. Previously, we would have taken on [such] a loan . . . by ourselves."[139]

In fact, the 1831 loan was not large enough to solve the government's financial problems, as James realised from the outset.[140] Moreover, the Treasury's parallel attempt to raise a "National Loan" by public subscription was a failure: only 25 million of a possible 80 million francs were sold, and the rest then had to be sold to the consortium of banks.[141] A more radical government than Périer's might of course have followed the example of the 1790s, pursuing an aggressive foreign policy by printing money. But, as long as Périer was in office, financial realism prevailed. In August, as the Belgian crisis abated, James was encouraged to hear talk of a new loan of 100 million francs to consolidate the floating debt.[142] Two months later he and Lionel were reassured to hear Périer say that he "would do what Villèle could not, he would make 5 per cents par and then reduce them"—an unambiguous signal of impending retrenchment.[143] The decision to maintain the sinking fund also pleased them.[144] The year 1832 saw James reasserting himself on the French financial market. In May a Rothschild-led consortium successfully bid to underwrite a 40 million franc loan by the city of Paris.[145] This paved the way for another government loan of 150 million francs, again handled by a consortium. Significantly, James insisted on delaying this until after the Dutch had relinquished their claims on Belgium.[146] By this time the idea that France might herself take unilateral military action without the express consent of England was being discounted.[147] When James was approached to consider yet another loan in early 1833, fears of French aggression had faded, as evinced when 3 per cent rentes briefly touched 80 in February.[148] In fact, the government chose to reduce the size of the army and hence the defence budget in preference to borrowing more, and there was soon talk of another conversion project to reduce the cost of servicing the existing debt.[149] The same issue was still being debated four years later.[150]

In short, the French government *was* financially constrained, but it was a constraint imposed not by the Rothschilds alone but by all the major banks in Paris. The critical point is that there was no Rothschild monopoly over French public finance in the 1830s,[151] as the loans of the period were undertaken by groups of banks, while sales of treasury bills were even more widely distributed.[152] Many of the visits paid by James to Périer and other ministers were therefore less about exerting financial leverage than about obtaining financially sensitive news. Typically, James spoke in January 1832 of "going with Salomon to see Périer to hear whether he has any news, and to formulate my future actions on the basis of any information he might provide me with, as we are currently holding a large parcel of rentes and we must therefore deal with great caution."[153]

It might therefore be suggested that, if Prussia, Russia and France *had* resolved to go to war in the 1830s over Belgium or Poland, the Rothschilds would have been powerless to avert it. Yet this is to overlook the leading role played in Central and Eastern Europe at this time by Metternich's Austria: without Austrian participation and, indeed, direction, a conservative crusade against the spread of revolution is hard to imagine. And this brings us to the role played by Salomon in Vienna, which has sometimes been portrayed as decisive in averting war after July 1830.

As early as November 1830 Salomon intimated to Gentz that, after the heavy losses suffered by himself and his brothers, financing a war was out of the question.[154] In the same way, when Metternich sent Austrian troops into Bologna, James backed up Périer's threat to intervene with an explicitly financial argument, evidently intended for official consumption. In the event of war, he asked, "how would Austria be able to pay the interest [on her debt]? . . . Better not to risk one's entire capital."[155] Yet, like James, Salomon did not occupy a monopolistic position. In the spring of 1830, when the Austrian government had issued a loan of 30 million gulden of 4 per cent metalliques, he had merely been one of a consortium of four issuing houses, along with Arnstein & Eskeles, Sina and Geymüller; and he had failed to wrest control of a planned conversion operation for the old 5 per cent bonds from the Frankfurt house of Bethmann.[156] In the wake of the revolution, he was as little able as his brother to contemplate the idea of a government loan being handled by his rivals. When Metternich requested an issue of 36 million gulden of 5 per cent metalliques to finance intervention in Italy in March 1831, Salomon took a share along with the other three Vienna houses.[157] Admittedly, a clause was inserted stating that the loan would have to be repaid within three months in the event of a war. But Salomon did nothing to oppose Metternich's covert borrowing of the 20 million francs which had been deposited with the Frankfurt house since the 1815 Treaty of Paris in the name of the German Confederation.[158] Nor did he achieve much by a thinly veiled threat to withdraw financial support if Metternich did not ratify the 24 Articles relating to Belgium in early 1832:

> Your Highness is aware that we have subscribed a quarter of the last loan of 50 million and have also purchased securities on the Bourse in order to maintain the price of metalliques, that we are carrying through other important financial operations, and that we are also negotiating new ones. As these are closely affected by the course of political events, and as I would like to see my brother happy and free from worry, I would humbly beg Your Highness to be pleased to let my manager . . . know of your opinion as to the present situation and whether the Austrian Government will recognise Belgium and allow the statement to be ratified.[159]

Metternich hastened to reassure him "that, as the fundamental attitude and will of the Russian Tsar were very well known to him, he vouched for the fact that these, without a single exception, were as peaceful as those of the Austrian Emperor."[160] But this was flannel; Austria did not ratify the articles for another three months.

Salomon's most explicit use of the financial lever came in June 1832, while he was in Paris. "I do not," he wrote with uncharacteristic bluntness in a letter he ordered to be passed on to Metternich and Kolowrat, "regard [it] with indifference . . . that Austria should issue a further metalliques loan during the year 1832, which God forbid."

> You know that, taking the sum of our holdings of metalliques at Frank-furt, Paris, London and Vienna—that is, the holdings of the four banks which really constitute one bank—the total amounts to several millions. Now, you cannot ride two horses at once; if our firm were forced to sell . . . what price could we expect to get? . . . We should be forced to realise our metalliques, whether we wished to or not. What would the capital-ists and the commercial world say to the issue of two metalliques loans in one year, when the payments in respect of the first loan are not due to be completed until December? Such action might produce a sharp fall in metalliques. The government would not be able to get further loans at a low rate of interest, a blow would be dealt to the credit of Austria's finances and the government would fail to achieve its object . . . More-over, what would the public say to a new loan? "There will be war— there must be a war, as Austria is issuing another loan." Even if we were not forced to sell, as we should be, prices would fall sharply and Austria's credit would be severely damaged . . . [This is] my conviction as to what would happen if there were to be even a whisper of a suggestion that another loan should be issued this year.[161]

At first sight, this does indeed seem like the exertion of financial pressure with a view to limiting Metternich's room for aggressive manoeuvre. But it is important to realise that it came at a time of relatively low international tension: the Austrians had by now ratified the 24 Articles and the dispute over Ancona had been resolved. On closer inspection, it looks more like a primarily financial argument to avoid a slump in the price of Austrian bonds which would have been detrimental to the Vienna house's balance sheet. Salomon was not opposing a loan altogether: for purely tech-nical reasons, he was arguing that "if it is essential to get money, it is much better to issue Treasury bills, and get in twelve millions of silver for the bank . . . a procedure which costs the government hardly anything and provides it with money for six to eight months." A year later he and the three other Vienna houses were perfectly happy to participate in another issue of metalliques worth 40 million florins, and in 1834 to a lottery loan of 25 million gulden.[162] If these were chains of peace, they did not bind tightly.

Underwriting Peace
In fact, it was not so much by denying governments money as by making it available to them that the Rothschilds were able to give weight to their diplomatic efforts. The classic illustration of this point is the way they responded to requests for credit from the areas where revolutions had broken out.

The Rothschilds had been doing business with the Belgian-based Société Gén-érale since 1827.[163] Within days of the revolution in Brussels, James had re-estab-lished contact with it and over a period of months advanced over a million francs to help it weather the storm of revolution.[164] At the same time, he and Nathan dis-

cussed a possible loan to Holland, presumably as a carrot to persuade the Dutch
King to accept the secession of Belgium; Salomon saw such a loan as a way of helping "to control our war mongers."[165] But Nathan could also wield a stick: when the
Dutch invaded Belgium in August 1831 he at once offered to sell guns to the government in Brussels.[166] Only when the Dutch had withdrawn and appeared to be
about to accept the loss of Belgium, did he and James revive the possibility of a 6 per
cent loan to the Dutch King, "for if he has the money, he will not consider any warlike actions"—and needless to say, "a lot of money could be earned from the Dutch
government."[167]

In the case of Belgium, although James was convinced there was "a fortune to be
made there," the brothers waited until the supposedly definitive 24 Articles had
been signed by Leopold before making their move.[168] At the end of 1831, in partnership with the Belgian banker Osy, they floated a loan worth some £2.75 million—five times as much as the previous year's loan to Holland. This might be
thought something of a gamble, considering that a diplomatic resolution of their
differences was anything but sure. Interestingly, a contemporary British cartoon
entitled *The Protocol–Society in an Uproar* shows the representatives of the powers
gathered in Downing Street, with Nathan stage left complaining: "Your Potecols are
no use; help mi Cot, Shentlemen, if you don't make everyting out for me, I will lend
you no more monish—vat am I to do vit your Ponds" (see illustration 9.i). An etching from the same period by "J.W.W." depicts Nathan plucking the Belgian goose,
and muttering: "cot tam you and your Pelgian Ponds! I could not find a shingle flat

**9.i: S.W. Fores, *The Protocol-Society in an Uproar, or the Conferees <u>Confounded</u>. A Sketch
in Downing Street* (1831).**

PLUCKING THE GOOSE, OR BELGIUM SUPPORTED BY HER FRIENDS AND ALLIES

9.ii: "J.W.W.," *PLUCKING THE GOOSE OR BELGIUM SUPPORTED BY HER FRIENDS AND ALLIES* **(1831).**

to puy them; upon my shoul, they are not worth as much as Spanish ponds" (see illustration 9.ii).

Anselm for one feared that it would "prove a bad concern, as I do not think that Belgium will be able to pay the Dividend for many years." On the other hand, he went on, "There is some money to be made . . . We must take things as they are and profit of the folly of the world."[169] Provided the Dutch did not resume hostilities during the period when the loan was being sold to investors, the Rothschilds as underwriters could only profit; and if they did invade again there was "a clause which provides that, in the event of war, we need not take anything further."[170] As James reported, brokers and bankers were "snapping [the loan] up like sugar pumpernickel" even before it had been issued, though by the time it was issued news of unrest in Rome and delays over the ratification of the Belgian agreement weakened demand, forcing James to support the market with repurchases.[171]

By the spring of 1832, with Holland diplomatically isolated, the brothers were ready for more. The diplomatic settlement had created a Belgian debt to Holland by allocating a portion of the pre-1830 combined Dutch debt to the new government in Brussels, and this raised an obvious possibility. "There is money to be made there," wrote James. "If you promise Talleyrand a little something, my dear Nathan, he will then arrange that you be appointed the agent for the handling of the debt, just as Baring was between France and the Powers [in 1815]." There was "money to be made if we place ourselves between Belgium and Holland"—provided of course there was no further war between the two.[172] In August 1832 proposals were drawn up for a second loan of £1.9 million, a third of which was to be issued by the Rothschilds in Paris—despite a warning from the French government that "it would be madness for us to give the Belgians money just at this moment & to give them every facility of making war."[173] The dandy and diarist Thomas Raikes took a different view. "The Belgian question is just as near settlement as it was twelve months ago," he wrote on September 12:

> The mandates of the Conference are of no avail. Holland will not abate a particle of its demands. Leopold wishes to yield, but the Belgians will not hear of it. His treasury is empty, and Rothschild will not contract for the loan without binding the Belgians not to go to war. But there will be more temporising, as the stock-jobbing interest must prevail. All the nations of Europe want money, and dread a fall in the funds more than any other calamity.[174]

However, when French troops were marching into Belgium to impose terms on the Dutch the following November, it was James's turn to think twice when the Belgian minister approached him for a short-term loan of 10 million francs. "One must help these people," he wrote somewhat wearily, "for, otherwise, they will simply not know what to do, and will only resort to stupid actions . . . In a word, these people . . . have no money and . . . don't have the intelligence to make any money."[175] Belgium, he grumbled, was "a lousy country." Only when it was apparent—and the assurances came from both Louis Philippe and Metternich—that the Dutch were diplomatically isolated and would have to acquiesce in the continuing Belgian occupation of Luxembourg and Limburg did the Rothschilds consent to the Belgian request.[176] In partnership with the Société Générale, the Paris house now took more than half of a new issue of treasury bills.[177] The decision to lend to the new state was, in many ways, a remarkable gamble, for the Rothschilds had no way of knowing that the diplomatic stand-off would end peacefully. But it was a gamble that paid off, not least because Belgium was to prove one of the dynamos of European industrialisation.

Poland was a different case, however. Although the Rothschilds had business links in Warsaw just as they had in Brussels,[178] they were never seriously interested in the success of the Polish revolt. Expressions of sympathy aside—"poor Poles, I pity them," wrote Charlotte to her mother—they did nothing to assist the revolt;[179] on the contrary, as we have seen, they sought to lend money to Russia which would have been used to crush the revolt, and actually sold guns to St Petersburg.

In Italy too there was no question of assisting the revolution. Here, even before the political situation had been brought under control, the brothers arranged a £400,000 loan to the Papacy in partnership with an Italian banker named Torlonia. Perhaps more than any other Rothschild transaction of the 1830s, this loan fascinated contemporaries, who were in varying measures amused or appalled by the notion of a Jewish bank lending to the Holy See. Carl's audience with the Pope in January 1832, for example, was widely commented upon. "Now things are getting at last into the order that God desired when He created the world," sneered Börne:

> A poor Christian kisses the Pope's feet; a wealthy Jew kisses his hand. If Rothschild had got his Roman loan at 60 per cent instead of 65 and so

been able to give the cardinal-chamberlain another 10,000 ducats, he might have been permitted to fall on the Holy Father's neck. The Rothschilds are assuredly nobler than their ancestor Judas Iscariot. He sold Christ for 30 small pieces of silver; the Rothschilds would buy Him, if He were for sale.[180]

"Like pagan Rome Christian Rome too was overcome and even obliged to pay tribute," gloated the more sympathetic Heine, conjuring up a vision of the portly Papal emissary arriving at the Rothschild office in the rue Laffitte to deliver "the tribute of Rome" to "a fair haired young man . . . who is somewhat older than he looks and whose aristocratic, grand-seigneurial nonchalance has something so solid, so positive about it that you might be inclined to think that he had in his pocket all the money of this world. And indeed—he does have all the money of this world in his pocket; his name is James de Rothschild . . . What further need, then, of the Talmud?"[181] "The Jewish banker says: '[God] has given me the royalty of wealth and the understanding of opulence, which is the sceptre of society,'" wrote Alfred de Vigny in July 1837. "A Jew now reigns over the Pope and Christianity. He pays monarchs and buys nations."[182]

In truth, the Rothschilds themselves had their doubts about the wisdom of it. At first, James was tempted to let two English banks, Wilson & Co. and Wright & Co., take the lead, for two reasons:

> First, we are Jews, and if we should have a different Pope who is an evil man, he will say to himself that he could earn a ticket to Paradise if he refuses to pay anything to Jews. Secondly, I think the Pope's financial situation is in a bad state, similar to that of Spain, and if they should decide not to pay their interest, we will then not be involved with them directly.[183]

At the same time, he and Lionel feared that while the British banks would find it easy to sell their shares, because of "the certainty of [their] being able to place amongst their Catholic friends, all their shares," the Rothschilds, "having quite a different connexion & not having the confidence of the friends of His Holiness, should have no employment for this stock & should be obliged to lock up our own money in it."[184] This partly explains the Rothschilds' uncharacteristic caution in proposing to take the loan in three separate tranches, retaining the option to withdraw after the first. On the other hand, the stabilisation of Papal finances promised at least short term and diplomatic benefits, because (as Périer, Pozzo and Apponyi all agreed) "the Pope, if he is in need of money, and he receives the same, will then ensure that peaceful conditions are maintained." Moreover, there was much more public demand for the loan than James had anticipated, leading to a hasty last-minute renegotiation of the deal to the disadvantage of Wilson and Wright, who found themselves cut out.[185] The loan, issued at 70 but soon rising above 79, turned out to be a "most excellent little business," Lionel reported with relief.[186] Although the recurrence of unrest in February 1832 caused a temporary setback, the bonds surged to a peak of 83 that summer and rose with only minor checks to reach par in 1835.[187]

At first sight, there was something contradictory about all this, an echo of Heine's point about the Rothschilds' ambivalence towards revolution: they lent at one and the same time to revolutionary states like Belgium and conservative states like the Papacy. On closer inspection, the rationale was consistent: the Rothschilds made money available to new states if they had the backing of the five great powers. Formal or informal guarantees made loans attractive whether they were to an independent Belgium or a superficially reforming Papacy. In that sense, they were merely carrying on the policy which they had begun in the 1820s and which contemporaries had misrepresented when they called them bankers to the Holy Alliance. The obvious precursor to their support for Belgium was their loan to Greece. As early as February 1830, when Leopold of Saxe-Coburg was being touted as a possible monarch for the new kingdom, James urged Nathan:

> to pay a visit to your Coburg for there is business to be made from Greece. England has already agreed that if Coburg is prepared to accept, then they will guarantee to pay the country the same every month as France and Russia and he is negotiating with them that England should join in granting the guarantee together with France and Russia.[188]

This was premature. It was not until May 1832 that a treaty was signed by the powers guaranteeing a loan to the new King, and he was a Bavarian rather than a Coburg prince (much less the Dutch prince predicted by Ludwig Börne). But the Rothschilds were still determined to handle the loan, and fought a hard battle for control against the Bavarian banker d'Eichthal and the Spaniard Aguado. Greece herself might be "worthless," but a 60 million franc loan guaranteed by France, England and Russia looked a sure thing. The feeling was mutual. Apponyi spoke for all the diplomats when he said: "Mr. Rothschild, it must not happen that such a large deal, in which all the Powers are interested, should be completed without your participation."[189] By contrast, where the powers had difficulty in agreeing—for example over Portugal, where the years 1830–34 saw the return of Dom Pedro from Brazil and his successful deposition of his brother Dom Miguel—the Rothschilds kept their distance.

In a multi-polar world, in which five powers with distinct interests sought to resolve international crises without resorting to war, the Rothschilds acted not so much to ensure peace—their power was more limited than that—as to *underwrite* it once it had been made.

TEN

The World's Bankers

*The Rothschilds are the wonders of modern banking . . . We
see the descendants of Judah, after a persecution of two thousand years, peering above kings, rising higher than emperors,
and holding a whole continent in the hollow of their hands.
The Rothschilds govern a Christian world. Not a cabinet
moves without their advice. They stretch their hand, with
equal ease, from Petersburg to Vienna, from Vienna to Paris,
from Paris to London, from London to Washington. Baron
Rothschild, the head of the house, is the true king of Judah,
the prince of the captivity, the Messiah so long looked for by
this extraordinary people. He holds the keys of peace or war,
blessing or cursing . . . They are the brokers and counsellors of
the kings of Europe and of the republican chiefs of America.
What more can they desire?* —NILES WEEKLY REGISTER, 1835–36[1]

In the years after 1832, as fears of revolution and war gradually subsided, the
Rothschilds appeared to increase the geographical extent of their financial influence. The American author of the passage quoted above was just one of many writers to comment on this expansion. At around the same time, Thomas Raikes
observed in his journal: "The Rothschilds, who began by sweeping out a shop at
Manchester, have become the metallic sovereigns of Europe. From their different
establishments in Paris, London, Vienna, Frankfurt, Petersburg [*sic*] and Naples,
they have obtained a control over the European exchanges which no party ever
before could accomplish, and they now seem to hold the strings of the public purse.
No sovereign without their assistance now could raise a loan."[2] As Prince Pückler
had put it, punning on the German word *Gläubiger* (believer or creditor), "the great
R[othschild] could be compared with the Sultan, for the latter was the ruler of all
believers, while the former was the creditor of all rulers."[3] The German economist
Friedrich List agreed: Rothschild was "the pride of Israel, the mighty lender and
master of all the coined and uncoined silver and gold in the Old World, before
whose money box Kings and Emperors humbly bow"—in short, the "King of
Kings."[4] William Makepeace Thackeray made the same point in some early and
undistinguished verses published in the short-lived *National Standard* in 1833:

Here's the pillar of 'Change! Nathan Rothschild himself,
With whose fame every bourse in the universe rings;
The first Baron Juif; by the grace of his pelf,
Not "the king of the Jews," but "the Jew of the kings."

The great incarnation of cents and consols,
The eighths, halves and quarters, scrip, options and shares;
Who plays with new kings as young Misses with dolls;
The monarch undoubted of bulls and of bears!

Cartoonists echoed and even amplified such comments. One English print
dating from 1829 shows Nathan as "the great humming top spinning a loan," with
kings bowing before him as he distributes coins to them (see illustration 10.i).

Perhaps the most potent (and pejorative) of all such images was produced by an
anonymous German cartoonist in around 1840.[5] *Die Generalpumpe* portrays a
grotesquely caricatured Jew—evidently a composite Rothschild—as a giant money
pump, a play on the double meaning of the German *pumpen*, to pump or to lend
(see illustration 10.ii). The central figure stands knee-deep in a sack full of gold; his
bulging stomach is the earth itself, with a louis d'or (labelled "earth's axis") for a
North Pole or belly-button; and on his head he wears a paper crown bearing the
names of major Rothschild loans of the 1820s and 1830s (the Prussian, Russian,

10.i: "A. C." [Crowhill], *The
Great Humming Top spinning a
Loan* (1820).

10.ii: *Die Generalpumpe* (*c.* 1840).

Neapolitan, Austrian and Portuguese). According to the badge on his waistcoat, he
is no less than "the Executor of the Court of all the World." Two diminutive figures
on either side grip the monster's fingers, as if working the pump (though it is not
clear how far they really control its motion). One on the left represents a Turk, one
on the right an Austrian. Beneath are the recipients of Rothschild money, into
whose cash-boxes and hats streams of coins flow. The Egyptian ruler Mehemet Ali
and his son Ibrahim Pasha are depicted on the left, spoon-feeding the Sultan; below
them sits a bespectacled figure with a bulldog who may represent a British Chancellor of the Exchequer (though the couple behind him "Edouard and Kunigunde" are
not easily identifiable). On the other side, there is no mistaking Louis Philippe and
the French politician Adolphe Thiers; the less instantly recognisable character to
their right is probably the Spanish general Baldomero Espartero. But although these
individuals are the recipients of Rothschild's money, they are also entangled in
thorny tendrils which sprout from his bulging money bag. So too are the smaller figures beneath them: the people standing at a closed customs post marked "Imports
Prohibited" and those passing through an open one marked "Imports Allowed or
New Income"; the soldiers massed on the right bank of the Rhine; and those
beneath Espartero begging for their "unpaid wages." Rothschild, the cartoon suggests, not only pumps money to the world, but sucks it back like a monstrous heart.

The Pillar

There was, however, something of a discrepancy between this imposing image of international power and the quite humdrum appearance of what Nathan Rothschild and his brothers actually *did*. The real Rothschilds bore little resemblance to the sinister figure portrayed in *Die Generalpumpe*. According to one of the many curious visitors drawn to the City to see him doing business at the Royal Exchange,[6] Nathan was "a very common looking person, with heavy features, flabby pendent lips, and a projected fish eye. His figure, which was stout, awkward and ungainly, was enveloped in the loose folds of an ample surtout."[7] We have numerous portraits and caricatures which bear this description out. One of the earliest is an etching by Richard Dighton entitled *A View from the Royal Exchange* and first published in October 1817 (see illustration 10.iii). It is a side view of a man in a black coat and top hat, stomach thrust forward, one hand in his pocket, the other holding a sheet of paper. The image proved a popular one with illustrators: Nathan appears in a similar pose in George Cruikshank's *The Royal Exchange* (1821) and in his *Beauties of Brighton* (1826).[8] Each time it was reproduced, however, it changed subtly. Thomas Jones added a nice detail in his 1829 version *A Pillar of the Exchange*, which depicted Nathan in front of his favourite pillar at the south-east corner of the exchange (see illustration 10.iv). There is a clever ambiguity to the juxtaposition: Nathan is like the

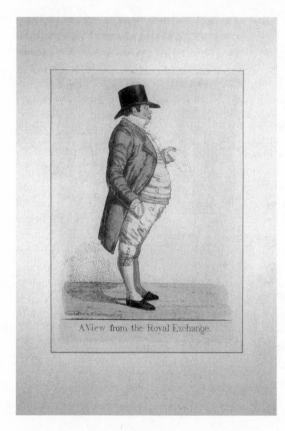

10.iii: Richard Dighton, *A View from the Royal Exchange* (1817).

A View from the Royal Exchange.

10.iv: Thomas Jones, *A PILLAR of the EXCHANGE* (1829).

pillar in his solidity and immobility, but there is also an implied contrast between the whiteness and regularity of the pillar and Nathan's black, protuberant shape.[9]

Less subtle artists went further, accentuating Nathan's protruding lower lip and stomach in ways which were unmistakably hostile. The French artist Jean-Pierre Dantan, for example, made a terracotta statuette of Nathan in 1832 which ranks as one of the most grotesque of all Rothschild caricatures. Here Nathan's lips droop obscenely from beneath the brim of his hat like those of a large cod, while his distended belly defies gravity atop his skinny legs.[10] Thackeray omitted the fat stomach in his sketch of *N. M. Rothschild, Esq.* which accompanied the lines quoted above (see illustration 10.v); but the final verses left no doubt that the author found Nathan physically repulsive:

> Oh Plutus! your graces are queerly bestowed!
> Else sure we should think you behaved *infra dig.*,
> When with favours surpassing, it joys you to load
> A greasy-faced compound of donkey and pig.
>
> Here, just as he stands with his head pointed thus,
> At full length, gentle reader, we lay him before ye;
> And we then leave the Jew (what we wish he'd leave us,
> But we fear to no purpose), *a lone* in his glory.[11]

10.v: William Makepeace Thackeray, *N. M. ROTHSCHILD ESQ., National Standard*, May 18, 1833).

While the numerous silhouettes produced after Nathan's death—most of which used the title *The Shadow of a Great Man*—were more sympathetic, they were not exactly flattering either.[12] Even the various portraits of Nathan commissioned by the family do not really attempt to glamorise him. It is true that some who saw him at work detected, or thought they detected, a faintly heroic aura. The American visitor quoted above declared that "there was something commanding in his air and manner, and the deferential respect which seemed voluntarily rendered him by those who approached him showed that he was no ordinary person. 'Who is that?' was the natural question, 'The King of the Jews,' was the reply."[13] But, whatever his temperamental resemblance to Napoleon, the Emperor's financial counterpart and nemesis was never recast by the romantic imagination in a heroic mould.[14] What contemporaries saw was a fat man buying and selling pieces of paper:

> The persons crowding around him, were presenting bills of exchange. He would glance for a moment at a paper, return it, and with an affirmatory nod, turn to the next individual pressing for an audience. Two well-looking young men, with somewhat an air of dandyism, stood beside him making a memorandum to assist in the recollections of bargains regulating the whole Continental exchanges of the day.[15]

Nor was his brother James any more ostentatious. In 1837 a Parisian journalist went in search of "M. de Rothschild in person . . . the name which is in every mouth, the Grand Orient of the rente, the key to the safes of all Europe." He was surprised to see how modestly "the sovereign" entered "his capital":

> M. de Rothschild's appearances are of short duration, between 3 and 3.25 p.m., that is to say, five or ten minutes before the close of business . . . He usually arrives accompanied by one of his nephews, but his entrance creates not the slightest sensation. People surround him eagerly, above all the brokers who are almost importunate, which does not prevent him from listening to them and replying to them with his habitual good humour. He himself greets and approaches first some of his fellow bankers; his conversation is never long and no one whispers a word of it; the bell rings [and] people start to leave; they go, and he goes just like everyone else—with no more ceremony than accompanied his arrival.[16]

Salomon was apparently even more approachable in Vienna: "Every day from the opening of the Bourse at 12 o'clock to its close at four, he [is] besieged by brokers and stockjobbers anxious to give him reports of the tendency of the market, and eager to receive and to execute his commissions."[17]

Those who were admitted into the Rothschild offices were struck by the same unpretentious—though to outsiders enigmatic—bustle. When Prince Pückler first sought out Nathan in 1826, he was surprised to find that "the ruler of the City . . . in fact . . . occupies here only an insignificant location . . . and in the little courtyard of the counting house my access to this best-connected member of the Holy Alliance was impeded by a van loaded with silver ingots."[18] No detailed descriptions of the interior of New Court in Nathan's day have survived; but we have what (allowing for authorial embroidery) may be an approximate description in Disraeli's *Tancred.* Like Pückler, Tancred finds that the Rothschild-like Sidonia is already closeted with a foreign ambassador:

> Tancred entered Sequin Court; a chariot with a foreign coronet was at the foot of the great steps which he ascended. He was received by a fat hall porter . . . who, rising in lazy insolence from his hooded chair, when he observed that Tancred did not advance, asked the newcomer what he wanted.
>
> "I want Monsieur de Sidonia."
>
> "Can't see him now; he is engaged."
>
> "I have a note for him."
>
> "Very well, give it me; it will be sent in. You can sit here." And the porter opened the door of a waiting-room which Tancred declined to enter. "I will wait here, thank you," said Tancred, and he looked round at the old oak hall, on the walls of which were hung several portraits and from which ascended one of those noble staircases never found in a modern London mansion . . .
>
> "I can't disturb master now [said the porter]; the Spanish ambassador is with him, and others are waiting. When he is gone, a clerk will take in your letter with some others that are here."
>
> At this moment, and while Tancred remained in the hall, various persons entered, and, without noticing the porter, pursued their way across the apartment.
>
> "And where are those persons going?" inquired Tancred.
>
> The porter looked at the enquirer with a blended gaze of curiosity

and contempt, and then negligently answered him . . . "Some are going to the counting-house and some are going to the Bank, I should think."

After this, the ingenuous visitor is left to cool his heels for a while until the ambassador's departure is finally heralded by "a stir":

> "Now your letter will go in with the others," [the hall porter] said to Tancred, whom for a few moments he left alone . . .
> Tancred was ushered into a spacious and rather long apartment, panelled with old oak up to the white coved ceiling, which was richly ornamented . . . A Turkey carpet, curtains of crimson damask, some large tables covered with papers, several easy chairs, against the walls some iron cabinets, these were the furniture of the room, at one corner of which was a glass door, which led to a vista of apartments fitted up as counting-houses, filled with clerks, and which, if expedient, might be covered by a baize screen which was now unclosed.[19]

The only thing which casts serious doubt on this is that the atmosphere in the other Rothschild houses was so very different. James, for instance, was always surprisingly accessible in his office. When he paid a visit in the late 1820s, Metternich's son Viktor found it was:

> like a positive magic lantern for people of the most various appearance and every kind of expression were constantly coming in and out. On that particular day the constant coming and going was specially noticeable, as securities quoted on the bourse were fluctuating violently. The great banker himself, who generally maintains an attitude of such dignified calm, betrayed a certain nervousness. Our conversation was frequently interrupted by bourse agents reporting quotations to their chief.[20]

The Frankfurt bank was also, according to a rare contemporary description, "open plan" in its design:

> He sits in his office in the midst of his clerks like a Padishah; below him are his secretaries, and around him may be seen a crowd of brokers, for ever coming and going. With a few words he dismisses each, for like a true business genius he knows at once what answer to give to every question, and what decision to arrive at on any business that may be laid before him for consideration . . . To speak to him privately on a matter of business is well nigh impossible; everything in his office is done openly as in a law court.[21]

In other words, what went on in the Rothschild offices was not so very different from what went on at the various exchanges: much toing and froing of brokers, much exchanging of pieces of paper.

Those who came expecting some visible manifestation of Rothschild power therefore were invariably disappointed by what they could glimpse of the brothers' routine activity—hence the temptation which lies behind so much Rothschild mythology to imagine some invisible mainspring: the Hebrew talisman, for example, or some sort of elaborate fraud of the sort perpetrated by Balzac's Nucingen. The only real clue contemporaries could find to illuminate the Rothschilds' prodigious success was the speed with which Nathan was able to make complex financial calculations and the ease with which he committed these to memory. "Even without [his sons'] assistance," another writer remarked, "he is said to be able to call to mind every bargain he has made." The same point was later made by his obituarist in *The Times*:

> He never hesitated for a moment in fixing the rate, either as a drawer or a taker, on any part of the world, and his memory was so retentive, that, notwithstanding the immense transactions into which he entered on every foreign post day, and that he never took a note of them, he could dictate the whole on his return home with perfect exactness to his clerks.[22]

"His ambition," wrote another writer after his death, "was to arrive at his aim more quickly and more effectually than others and to steer towards it with all his energy. When his end was reached it had lost all it charm for him, and he turned his never-wearying mind to something else."[23]

To some, this restless aptitude could seem almost diabolical. "There is," observed one who watched Nathan at work,

> a rigidity and tension in his features that would make you fancy, if you did not see that it was not so, that someone was pinching him behind and that he was either afraid or ashamed to say so. Eyes are usually denominated the windows of the soul, but here you would conclude that the windows are false ones, or that there were no soul to look out of them. There comes not one pencil of light from the interior, neither is there one scintillation of that which comes from without reflected in any direction. The whole puts you in mind of a skin to let, and you wonder why it stands upright without at least something in it. By-and-by another figure comes up to it. It then steps two paces aside, and the most inquisitive glance that you ever saw . . . is drawn out of the erewhile fixed and leaden eye, as if one were drawing a sword from a scabbard. The visiting figure, which has the appearance of coming by accident and not by design, stops but a second or two, in the course of which looks are exchanged which, though you cannot translate, you feel must be of important meaning. After these, the eyes are sheathed up again, and the figure resumes its stony posture. During the morning, numbers of visitors come, all of whom meet with a similar reception and vanish in a similar manner; and last of all, the figure itself vanishes, leaving you utterly at a loss as to what can be its nature and its functions.[24]

Overdone though it is, this account nevertheless captures another intimidating quality which contemporaries often remarked upon: Nathan's tendency to veer between sang-froid and sudden, alarming action. In 1821 he was reported to have received the threat of assassination "with a smile, and after returning his thanks for the intelligence, with the observation, that as he felt he had never done wrong to any individual, he could not entertain the idea that any persons could have formed so atrocious a design as that described, and that he really thought the affair unworthy of his attention."[25] Two years later, however, when he found a stranger occupying his usual place at the Royal Exchange, he became "so excited by being displaced that it was some time before he could compose himself and commence business."[26] The

Circular to Bankers tactfully alluded to Nathan's "strong and unfettered will" and the "pride of temper resulting from his high new position which made him bear down at any personal risk all opposition."[27] This overbearing quality, as we have seen, often spilled over into his correspondence. "The language which Mr Rothschild could use when his anger overbalances his discretion," recalled one who had evidently witnessed him in full flow, "was a licence allowed to his wealth . . . His mode of dictating letters was characteristic of a mind entirely absorbed by money-making; and his ravings when he found a bill unexpectedly protested, were translated into mercantile language ere they were fit to meet a correspondent's eye."[28]

His brothers, to whom he wrote in his own hand, were not thus spared. We have already seen how brutal Nathan could be in his private letters to his brothers; he did not much mellow with age. In 1828 Salomon's son Anselm wrote to Lionel, Nathan's eldest: "Pray tell to your good father not to write in future such violent letters against Uncle Amschel. They hurt his health I assure you, and for what reason? because he wrote to your Papa, that he is in want for [*sic*] money and that you owe him in [*sic*] Account . . . the Man gets old and weak and if you are not a little careful in your letters he will give it up . . ."[29] Six years later Nat reported that Amschel's "state of health renders him very nervous" and recommended "very strongly" that his father "coax him a little in your letters & by no means . . . scold [him] as it has more effect than you imagine."[30] There were occasional clashes with the more resilient James too. In 1832 he "protested vehemently" against making a loan to Greece, for example, and did so only when he received a letter from New Court saying: "Under no circumstances must you allow the deal to slip through your fingers." He was beside himself when Nathan then changed his mind, sending him a second letter saying: "Don't do anything concerning Greece."[31] The two had a similar contretemps over Portugal in 1835.[32]

Yet it is not enough to explain the Rothschilds' financial success purely in terms of Nathan's personality, important though it was. Increasingly in the 1830s, the main source of fraternal strife was not Nathan's dominance, which was more or less uncontested, so much as his indifference. In 1831, for example, Lionel relayed a message to his father: "Uncle James hopes Papa does not do all the business in rentes in London for your account for it will quite destroy all the business between the two Houses and in the end others will run away with the business."[33] Two years later, Nat wrote from Frankfurt that his uncle Amschel "complain[ed] my dear Papa about your doing so little business with him . . . I am sure, my dear Papa, you will see what our good uncle wants, he wishes particularly that you should do as much business with him as formerly." When this elicited no response from New Court, Nat was forced to try again:

> He begs dear papa you will be so good as to do as much business as possible with him; he complains not a little of your giving the preference to Paris & Vienna. I must say that he is a most excellent man, & if it is possible to please him one ought to do so . . . [W]ith Uncle A. however it is advisable not to pay attention to trifles.[34]

Trifles aside, there was plainly some truth in Amschel's complaint. By the early 1830s the financial ties between the London and Frankfurt houses seemed to be loosening as the brothers saw less of one another. Nor was this the only sign that centrifugal forces were at work. Just a year later Carl in Naples levelled a very similar charge against James. This time it was Nathan who had to act as arbitrator between the two. "Concerning what our brother Carl has written to you, my dear Nathan, that I have not been regularly writing to him," James wrote in response to some rebuke on the subject,

> for the sake of maintaining cordial relations and in accordance with your wishes and those of our brother Salomon, I have in fact written to him on five occasions, and I completely forgot the stupid letter which he wrote to me . . . as if it never existed. Please ask for these to be sent to you from Naples, and you will then see that I did write, for I want to maintain peaceful relations and don't want any quarrels. Well, I did all that I consider an upright man is obliged to do for his brother. [T]hey can complain about me, but I will not write any more until such time as I receive letters from them, for I am no less a Rothschild and I can stand on my honour as much as our brother Carl.[35]

Of course, the fact that the other brothers appealed to Nathan when they fell out shows how far Nathan remained "the commanding general"—the pillar on which the entire Rothschild edifice rested, as unshakeable as the pillar he stood beside at the Royal Exchange. But disputes such as these suggest that additional buttresses were needed to preserve that edifice intact.

The Rothschild System

If there was a single "secret" of Rothschild success it was the system of co-operation between the five houses which made them, when considered as a whole, the largest bank in the world, while at the same time dispersing their financial influence in five major financial centres spread across Europe. This multinational system was regulated by the partnership agreements which were drawn up and revised every few years and which were, in effect, the constitution of a financial federation. The earliest such agreement, as we have seen, had been drawn up in 1810, but this was untypical because of Mayer Amschel's continuing dominance and the wartime exclusion of Nathan. It was the three-year contract of 1815 between all five brothers which was the first authentically "federal" agreement. The crux of the matter at this stage was the superior wealth of the London house. According to the preamble of the agreement, the brothers' "partnership property in London[,] at Paris and at Frankfurt on the Main consists of the sum of £500,000 or thereabouts," but most of this was evidently Nathan's. The contract sought to redefine the brothers' collective assets by excluding some items (presumably real estate), and redistributing some £200,000 in the form of promissory notes of £50,000 each from Nathan to his four brothers. The resulting shares of a total notional capital of £336,000 were Nathan, 27 per cent; Amschel and Salomon, 20 per cent each; Carl and James, 16 per cent each. Moreover, it was agreed to defray all expenses from the London house's revenues and to share net profits at the end of each year equally.[36]

In the three years during which this contract ran, as we have seen, the brothers' capital grew at a phenomenal rate, from £336,000 to £1,772,000. So much of this increase was due to Nathan's immensely successful speculations in consols that, although the proportions of the total capital were more or less unchanged, his brothers now agreed to weight the distribution of profits in his favour. As Carl saw it,

> Nathan should have a bigger part than a fifth. He has a big family, he needs more. Whatever you arrange, I will give my agreement . . . You told me yourself that Nathan has to be given [some] prerogatives. We owe everything, really everything to him. He saved us. We wanted to take a jump earlier [that is, to sell] and he kept us back.[37]

There were now technically "three joint mercantile establishments [conducted] under . . . the . . . five partners' mutual responsibility": N. M. Rothschild in London, M. A. von Rothschild & Söhne in Frankfurt and James's new house in Paris, de Rothschild Frères. Henceforth, half of all the profits of the London house would go to Nathan, while his brothers would receive an eighth each; he would also receive four-sixteenths of the profits of the other two houses, while his brothers received three-sixteenths apiece. The 1818 agreement also introduced a new system whereby each of the partners received 4 per cent of their individual capital share per annum by way of an income to cover their expenses (both business and domestic); any lump sums spent on legacies for children, houses or landed estates were to be deducted from the individual's capital. In addition, "to preserve regularity in the books and accounts . . . it has been determined that in the running transactions of the three joint establishments *although they form but one general joint concern* each respectively is to charge exchange, brokerage, postages, stamps and interest pro and contra at the rate of 5 per cent."[38] To reinforce the sense of collective identity it was now specified that each House had to inform the others of the transactions it carried out on a weekly basis.

Although initially intended to run for just three years, this agreement in fact remained in force until 1825.[39] However, it would be wrong to infer from this a high level of fraternal harmony. Quite apart from the periodic disputes described in previous chapters, the four continental brothers on one occasion felt obliged to draw up a separate agreement between themselves, the terms of which suggest a quite serious rift between themselves and Nathan.[40] Significantly, the 1825 agreement restored the 1815 system whereby profits were shared equally, reflecting the fact that the capital of both the Frankfurt and Paris houses had grown so rapidly as to outstrip that of the London house. On the other hand, Nathan's personal share continued to be counted as more than a quarter of the joint capital, which now stood at more than £4 million. Moreover, although Salomon and Carl had more or less settled in Vienna and Naples, their houses were not given equal status with the original three, and continued to be treated as mere "branch establishments" of the Frankfurt house, without any separate capital until 1828 (and thereafter relatively little). This was probably intended to check the centrifugal tendencies discussed above. The partners now bound themselves to "mutually inform each other . . . of all the transactions, of whatever nature they may be, which have occurred" on a monthly rather than weekly basis.[41]

The 1825 agreement also saw the first steps taken to bring the next generation into the firm, with the decision to admit Salomon's son Anselm as a partner following his marriage to Nathan's daughter Charlotte. The brothers were experiencing the first intimations of mortality: the 1825 documents included a clause permitting Amschel to withdraw from the business "if the work becomes too hard for him," and sought to anticipate possible disputes over inheritance by binding each of the partners' heirs to accept whatever their share might be without resort to law. It was specifically stated that, if the heirs of a deceased partner took legal action against the surviving partners, a third of the deceased's share of capital would be forfeit and would be given to the poor of Frankfurt, London and Paris![42]

In describing their terms, it is easy to lose sight of the secrecy of these agreements, which such sanctions were intended to preserve. When the brothers met at Frankfurt in August 1828 to take stock of what had been a relatively disappointing three years, Nathan's wife and two of his sons were present but were wholly excluded from the negotiations, just as they would be eight years later. "Papa and his Brothers with Anselm are almost continually engaged in deliberating upon the arrangement of their concerns," reported Hannah, "which are held in the Tower in the Garden and are perfectly secret." The most she could say was that "every thing among the family seemed to be going on with much unanimity."[43] This was probably something of a relief to her, as the accounts drawn up in 1828 revealed that, though the partners' personal shares remained formally unchanged, the relative importance of the London house had continued to decline. Its share of the total capital was now just over 27 per cent, compared with 42 per cent in 1818.[44] This share increased only very slightly in the eight years which intervened before the next such meeting at Frankfurt—the fateful 1836 gathering during which Nathan unexpectedly died. As a result, the continental partners were able to secure new and potentially more favourable terms for the distribution of profits: henceforth, Nathan would receive 60 per cent of the profits of the London house but just 10 per cent of the profits from Frankfurt, Naples and Vienna, while his brothers would each get 10 per cent from the London house and 22.5 per cent from the continental houses.[45] This rule—which undoubtedly increased the relative autonomy of the London house—was retained despite Nathan's death: all his rights were simply transferred to his four sons.[46]

It goes without saying that the Rothschilds were financially successful; indeed, the rate of growth and size of their capital in the period before 1850 were unprecedented in banking history. Table 10a summarises the available figures for the combined capital of the various houses in the first half of the century:

Table 10a: Combined Rothschild capital, 1797–1844 (£ thousand).

	1797	1807	1810	1815	1818	1825	1828	1836	1844
Frankfurt	9.9	50.6	72.7	68.0	680.0	1,450.0	1,534.1	2,121.4	2,750.0
Paris				55.0	350.0	1,490.0	1,466.4	1,774.2	2,310.6
London				90.0	742.0	1,142.0	1,183.3	1,733.4	2,005.1
Vienna				68.0			25.0	110.4	250.0
Naples				55.0			129.6	268.3	462.5
Total	9.9	50.6	72.7	336.0	1,772.0	4,082.0	4,338.4	6,007.7	7,778.2

Notes: 1815 total may be too low: the agreement is unclear as to whether total capital was £500,000 or £336,000. Note also that in 1815 the figures are for *personal* shares, rather than for shares allocated to specific houses. 1807 figure converted from gulden @ £1 = 10.16 fl. 1828 figures converted from gulden @ £1 = 12 fl.
Sources: CPHDCM, 637/1/3/1–11; 637/1/3; 637/1/6/5; 637/1/6/7/7–14; 637/1/6/32; 637/1/6/44, 45; 637/1/7/48–52; 637/1/7/53–69; 637/1/8/1–7; 637/1/9/1–4; RAL, RFamFD, B/1; RAL, RFamFD/3; AN, 132 AQ 1.

The sheer scale of the Rothschilds' resources can hardly be over-emphasised: to take a single year—1825—their combined resources were nine times greater than the capital of Baring Brothers and eleven times larger than the capital of James's principal rival in Paris, Laffitte. They even exceeded the capital of the Banque de France (around £3 million at this time).[47] Surviving figures for the individual houses are patchy, especially before 1830. For the London house, ledgers survive from 1809 but there are no profit and loss accounts for the years before 1828. Illustration 10.vi gives the "bottom line" data for the period up until 1850: annual profits as a percentage of capital at the beginning of the year. A number of points stand out from these figures: firstly, the large fluctuations in performance, ranging from the very successful (1834), when profits were close to a quarter of capital, to the wholly disastrous (1847), when close to a third of the firm's capital was lost. Averaged out, profits were in fact rather unremarkable, though this partly reflects the fact that all expenses were deducted before net profits were calculated, rather than being paid out of profits. The figure for profits (or losses) was merely added to (or deducted from) the previous year's capital; a system quite unlike that used by the Rothschilds' great rivals Barings, who tended to calculate gross profits, and to distribute these to the partners. Perhaps the biggest difference between the Rothschilds and their rivals was that the Rothschilds ploughed back their net profits, so that their capital tended to accumulate, while the Barings kept their capital more or less constant and sought to maximise the profits on which they could then live. Between 1829 and 1846, while the capital of N. M. Rothschild increased by 90 per cent, that of Barings increased by just 50 per cent.

The other house for which detailed accounts survive is the much smaller Naples house. Considering its size, the Naples house was singularly profitable, especially in the first decade of its existence. Its average annual profits were more than £30,000 between 1825 and 1829, at a time when its capital was little more than £130,000; and throughout the 1830s and 1840s its profits averaged around £20,000.[48] Unlike the London and Paris houses, it appears never to have recorded a loss despite the financial crises of 1825, 1830 and 1836. Carl may have been regarded by contemporaries as the least gifted of the five brothers, and his letters intimate a certain dullness. Yet there can be no doubting his financial acumen.

There are, unfortunately, no complete data for the profits of the Paris, Frankfurt or Vienna houses in this period. In the French case, the only surviving figures are for the years 1824–28, and all they tell us is the extent of the damage done to James's position by the crisis of 1825 (when his losses totalled no less than £356,000) and the speed with which he recovered from the setback (his profits in the succeeding two years were £44,000 and £124,000).[49] However, it is possible to infer average annual profits for all the houses from the combined capital accounts (table 10b), though the different periods which elapsed between agreements make these a rather approximate guide to performance. These suggest—rather unexpectedly—that the London house was in fact the least economically successful of the three principal Rothschild houses: average annual profits were higher at both Frankfurt and Paris for the period 1818–44. Nathan's brothers—and Amschel in particular—have often suffered in comparison with the man they regarded as their "commanding general"; but even in the period of Nathan's dominance, the Frankfurt house was more profitable than the London house. The Vienna house too was highly profitable in view of its small capital base.

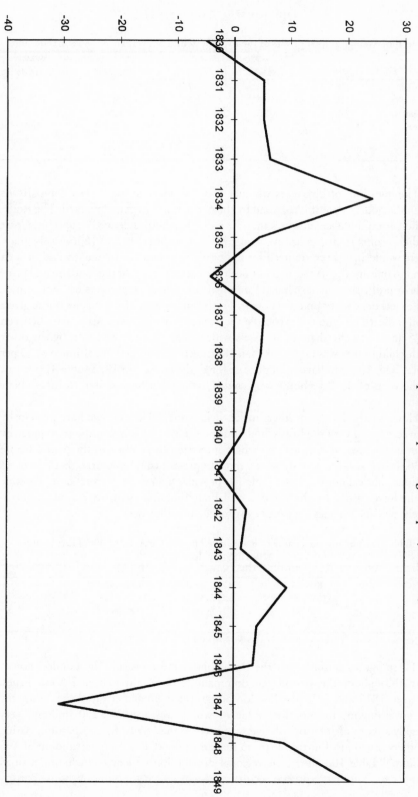

10.vi: N. M. Rothschild & Sons, annual profits as a percentage of capital, 1830–1849.

Table 10b: Average annual profits of the five Rothschild houses, 1818–1844 (£ thousand).

	1818–25	1825–28	1828–36	1836–44	AVERAGE 1818–44
Frankfurt	110	28	73	79	80
Paris	163	–8	38	67	75
London	57	14	69	34	49
Vienna		8	11	17	N/A
Naples		43	17	24	N/A
Total	330	85	208	221	204

Source: As table 10a.

The question, of course, is whether it is legitimate to make such comparisons when the houses were still regarded by the partners as inseparably linked. The Rothschild correspondence indicates that the individual houses derived a substantial part of their profits from a collective strategy whose architect before 1836 was Nathan. There would have been no need for the brothers to write so frequently and in such detail to one another if this had not been the case. Nor would the fundamental principle of profit-sharing have lasted for long if the individual partners had not continued to feel dependent on one another. The balance sheets of the Naples house give a good indication of how inextricable the activities of the five houses were: between 1825 and 1850 the share of its assets which were monies owed to it by the other Rothschild houses was rarely less than 18 per cent and sometimes as much as 30 per cent.[50] This seems to have been the case for all the houses. In 1828 some 31 per cent of the assets of the Paris house were credits to the other Rothschilds, mainly to New Court.[51]

How exactly did the brothers make their money? Thus far, we have principally been concerned with the Rothschilds' business in government bonds, as (to judge by their letters) this was the activity which interested them most in the period before 1836. It was also the activity which most impressed contemporaries, because of its obvious political implications. Table 10c provides figures for the total nominal value of the loans issued by the London and Frankfurt houses in the period (unfortunately, no lists of issues appear to exist for the other houses).

Table 10c: The nominal value of loans issued by the London and Frankfurt houses, 1820–1859 (by decade, £).

	NMR	MAR
1820–29	58,715,366	4,892,947
1830–39	43,194,150	3,599,512
1840–49	35,169,611	2,930,801
1850–59	88,485,900	7,373,825

Sources: Ayer, *Century of finance*, pp. 16–81; Berghoeffer, *Meyer Amschel*, pp. 29–42, 206–28.

These figures confirm that the Rothschilds (and especially the London house) were throughout the period the dominant force in international bond issues. Between 1815 and 1859 the London house issued altogether fifty loans, primarily for governments, the nominal value of which was around £250 million—very roughly a tenth of total British overseas assets in the 1850s. By comparison, Baring Brothers issued just fourteen loans in the same period, to a nominal amount of £66 million.[52] Table 10d shows the regional distribution of loans—including a small number of quite large private sector issues—in which the London house participated between 1818 and 1846. These figures show that the contemporary view of the Rothschilds as "bankers to the Holy Alliance" was exaggerated; the London house's biggest clients were France and Britain, with Prussia, Russia and Austria some way behind.

Table 10d: Loans issued by the London house, 1818–1846 (by recipient).

BORROWER	TOTAL (£)	PERCENTAGE OF TOTAL
Britain	44,938,547	29.2
France	27,700,000	18.0
Holy Alliance*	29,029,566	18.8
Prussia	[12,300,400]	[8.0]
Russia	[6,629,166]	[4.2]
Austria	[3,100,000]	[2.0]
Naples	[7,000,000]	[4.5]
Portugal	5,500,000	3.6
Brazil	4,486,200	2.9
Belgium	11,681,064	7.6
Other states**	5,843,750	3.8
Private sector	24,900,000	16.2
Total	154,079,127	100.0

* Prussia, Russia, Austria and Naples. ** Holland, Greece and Denmark.
Source: Ayer, *Century of finance*, pp. 14–42.

It is relatively easy to show the importance of government bonds in the balance sheets of the various houses. The earliest surviving balance sheet of the London house (that of 1828) reveals that a very large proportion of the bank's assets—more than a quarter—were invested in British government bonds. The proportion rises to 37 per cent if its holdings of Danish government stock are added.[53] In the same year, 35 per cent of the French house's assets took the form of French 3 per cent rentes.[54] The "state securities account" comprised exactly the same proportion of the Vienna house's assets, suggesting some sort of rough Rothschild policy to keep the proportion of (supposedly) "gilt-edged" securities at around a third.[55] However, it is much harder to compute the profits made from such issues. Commissions and other charges varied considerably from case to case, as we have seen; and some major issues actually lost large sums (the French loan of 1830, for example). In any case, much of the money which the brothers made on the bond market came not from issuing new bonds, but from speculating in existing bonds. Here too precise figures are hard to come by. To judge by the records which have survived, accounts were made up primarily with a view to calculating the returns on specific lines of business or transactions and ensuring that there were no discrepancies between the various inter-Rothschild accounts. Like the ledgers of most nineteenth-century firms, the London house's did not group its transactions according to type: purchases and sales of all kinds were logged as they occurred and then totted up at the end of the year. It would in theory be possible to add together the profits obtained from purchases and sales of government bonds, but it would be exceedingly laborious and it has not been attempted here. The Naples house had a "rentes account," but it also maintained separate accounts for its dealings in other government securities—Neapolitan, Roman and so on. Because it constantly changed its half-yearly accounting conventions, creating new accounts as it went along, it is well-nigh impossible to make more than an impressionistic assessment of its activities. The most that can be said is that the lion's share of its profits came from between five and ten joint accounts, some with other Rothschild houses, some with other Italian-based banks; from commissions charged on transactions for third parties; and from interest on various unspecified loans.

Of course, this would not matter if the Rothschilds had dealt only in government bonds. But their banking activities were in fact quite heterogeneous, and grew more so over time. Government finance was their first love. Of comparable importance, however, in terms of the *volume* of business, if not the profit-margins achievable, was the classic business of the London "merchant banker": the acceptance of commercial bills or bills of exchange. In the words of the 1882 Bills of Exchange Act— which gave statutory precision to a practice dating back more than three centuries—a bill of exchange was "an unconditional order in writing addressed [and signed] by one person (the drawer) to another (the drawee) . . . requiring . . . the drawee, who when he signs it becomes the acceptor, to pay at a fixed . . . future date a sum . . . to . . . a specified person or to the bearer." In other words, the seller of some goods would draw on the buyer in order to give him credit for a specific time (often three or four months), thus allowing him to put off payment until the goods had arrived and been sold on to a manufacturer or retailer. The role of the merchant banks was twofold: to act as a bill's acceptor on behalf of a buyer (charging an acceptance commission) or to buy it from a drawer at a discount (charging interest). A discount house could also rediscount a bill by selling it to a central bank, for example, and adding its own signature or endorsement. The banker who accepted a bill was effectively "selling the use of [his] name," that is, his reputation for creditworthiness.[56]

Such buying and selling of commercial bills was one of Nathan Rothschild's principal activities. Its importance can be inferred, again, from the surviving balance sheets: in 1828 "bills receivable" accounted for a quarter of the London house's assets; "bills payable" for 5 per cent of its liabilities.[57] Such business was less important to the continental houses, reflecting the greater volume of international trade conducted through London in the nineteenth century. As Nathan put it in his evidence to the Bank Committee in 1832, "this country in general is the Bank for the whole world . . . all transactions in India, in China, in Germany, in the whole world, are guided here, and settled through this country."[58] Nevertheless, the other Rothschild houses still played an important subsidiary role in his operations, as Nathan explained:

> I buy on the Exchange bills drawn from Liverpool, Manchester, Newcastle and other places, and which come to every banker and merchant in London. I purchase £6,000 or £7,000, and sometimes £10,000 of those bills in a week, and I send them to the Continent to my houses; my houses purchase against them bills upon this country which are purchases for wine, wool and other commodities . . . [I]f there be not a sufficient supply of bills abroad on this country we are obliged to get gold from Paris, Hamburg and elsewhere.[59]

This was a reasonably accurate summary of what went on. The Rothschilds did not seek to make their money from the commissions they charged for accepting bills (indeed, Nathan was well known for charging half a per cent less than other firms);[60] rather, the aim was to profit from exchange rate differentials between the various European markets. The Rothschild correspondence constantly alludes to such arbitrage transactions: was the price of "London" (short-hand for bills on London) high enough in Paris or Frankfurt to justify Nathan sending a large amount to James or Amschel? "And now, dear Nathan," wrote James in a typical letter of 1832,

> I am starting once again to busy myself with the bills of exchange business, and beg you to evaluate [precisely] what you are sending us. We are buying London here at 25.65 francs and 3 per cent [which] is equal to 25.84½ francs and you send us £21,000 Parisian at 26.07½ [and] 4 per cent, which is equal to 25.79, that is a loss of a fifth without the brokerage. Well, I am only bringing this to your attention because we don't want to operate at a loss when dealing with the bills of exchange.[61]

This gives a flavour of the complex calculations involved, and the very narrow differentials the brothers sought to exploit. As a multinational partnership, they were uniquely positioned to do such business.

Yet the Rothschilds were not as dominant in the market for bills as they were in the market for bonds. In his influential survey of the City, *Lombard Street*, Walter Bagehot called them "the greatest . . . of the foreign bill-brokers";[62] but this accolade properly belonged to the Barings.[63] In 1825 Nathan's acceptances totalled £300,000 compared with £520,000 for Baring Brothers. Twenty-five years later, acceptances at New Court had risen to £540,000, but the figure for the Barings was £1.9 million; and the gap widened still further in the second half of the century, when newcomers like the Kleinworts made the running.[64] Apart from the obvious fact that the Rothschilds put government finance first—it is almost invariably discussed before commercial business in the brothers' private correspondence—this primarily reflected the fact that the greater part of the bills business was generated by transatlantic trade, rather than by trade between Britain and continental Europe, which the Rothschilds were better placed to finance. As we shall see, there were attempts to increase the Rothschild share of the American market, but they were only fitful; throughout the first half of the nineteenth century, the Barings had the upper hand there.

Bill-broking led naturally into numerous connected avenues of activity. One of the most important of these, from an early date, was the international bullion market. As Nathan stated in his 1832 testimony, there was often a gap between the total volume of bills representing British imports and those representing exports; in the terms of contemporary classical economics, a trade deficit or surplus automatically necessitated a movement of specie out of or into London provided it was big enough to pay the cost of shipping and insuring specie, as well as melting and reminting if necessary. When the exchange rate reached the so-called "gold points" it paid to import or export gold (or silver in some countries). For the Rothschilds, transfers of gold from England to the continent had been a vital stepping stone towards direct involvement in English war finance before 1815, and the brothers never lost their interest in the bullion business, doing substantial amounts of business with the Bank of England and the Banque de France. This was what Nathan alluded to when he loftily told a Hamburg house: "My business . . . consists entirely in Government transactions & Bank operations."[65] Here too complex calculations were involved, especially when coins were being melted down into bars to be reminted in another market. "And now, dear Nathan," wrote James in another typical letter, "[when thinking of buying] silver at 11 grain gold, where you can consider the rest as profit, a lot will depend on the assay, for ½ grain is equivalent to ⅞ per cent. Well, at 59⅛, this is equivalent to 25.82 francs, and one has the chance here to make a profit when it is being assayed, and I therefore strongly urge you not to let the opportunity pass by."[66] "The van loaded with silver ingots" which blocked Prince Pückler's access to New Court was no rare sight: to judge by the brothers' letters, consignments of bullion worth tens of thousands of pounds regularly passed between Paris and London.

Another related field of activity was direct involvement in commodity trade itself.[67] Buying and selling goods rather than paper had, of course, been an integral part of Mayer Amschel's business, and Nathan himself had begun his career in Britain as a textile merchant, later branching out into "colonial goods." However, to judge by the partners' correspondence, the Rothschilds' interest in such business appears to have dwindled in the 1820s, and it was not until after 1830 that it revived. Unlike the Barings, who dealt in a wide range of traded goods, the Rothschilds preferred to specialise, aiming to establish a dominant role in a select number of markets. The key commodities which attracted their attention were cotton, tobacco, sugar (primarily from America and the Caribbean), copper (from Russia), and, most importantly, mercury (from Spain). More will be said about these below. Very occasionally they dabbled in other goods: iron, wool and wine, for example.[68] The hostile cartoonist who portrayed "Blauschild" as a travelling salesman doing business "in all branches of commerce" was therefore in error: the Rothschilds were never jacks-of-all-trades (see illustration 10.vii). To give one example: although their relatives the Worms brothers established a tea plantation in Ceylon—which they even named "Rothschild"—the bank never seriously involved itself in the tea trade.[69]

The final area of business which the Rothschilds entered as a result of their mercantile activities was insurance. The first half of the nineteenth century saw a boom in insurance, with numerous companies being founded in London and elsewhere. Nathan's involvement in the founding of the Alliance Assurance Company in 1824—the only joint-stock company in which he ever took a serious interest—has been variously explained, but never satisfactorily. According to the company's official history, it was the result of a casual meeting with his brother-in-law Moses Montefiore; others have suggested that the aim was partly to provide employment as an actuary for their relative Benjamin Gompertz, an accomplished mathematician. A third hypothesis advanced is that the existing insurance companies had been discriminating against the Jewish business community.[70] In fact, the Rothschilds had been interested in insurance for some years, understandably in view of the high premiums they themselves had been obliged to pay to insure shipments to the continent before 1815. As early as 1817 James was able to report "quite nice profits" from an unidentified French insurance company.[71] In 1823 a further impetus was provided by a request for assistance from the Duke of Saxe-Coburg, whose applications for a new life insurance policy had been rejected by two existing London companies, including the recently founded Guardian.[72] Above all, Nathan seems to have

10.vii: I. Nussgieg, after G. Geissler, *Der Musterreiter* (1825).

Der Musterreiter.

wanted to break the cartel of Lloyd's (located directly above him on the first floor of the Royal Exchange), the London Assurance and the Royal Exchange which monopolised marine insurance in London. Just days after the "Alliance British and Foreign Life and Fire Assurance Company" had been established with a capital of £5 million, the MP Thomas Fowell Buxton, one of the new company's auditors, introduced a bill into the House of Commons to end the monopoly of marine insurance. At the same time, Nathan sought to enlist the support of his old friend Herries (then Financial Secretary to the Treasury). "The object of this Society," he wrote, adopting the characteristic puffing rhetoric of the 1820s joint stock bubble,

> is to promote all kinds of national industry, by affording facilities in the advancement of Capital, and to protect Commercial men and society in general by granting insurancies [*sic*] on shipping and every species of property exposed to risks. There are other ends, equally salutary, towards which the views of the Company will be directed, all tending to give an impetus to manufactures, and to attract and retain in their ports every branch of foreign commerce.
>
> This is . . . the policy . . . of the whole European Continent at the present moment: everywhere, efforts are [afoot] to introduce a spirit of commercial enterprise, to revive trade where it has languished, and to discover new channels in which it may be directed . . . [I] request you

will bring this subject before the consideration of my Lord Liverpool, who will no doubt perceive in these facts additional grounds for persevering in that liberal principle upon which His Majesty's Government has acted, by removing every obstacle in the way of an open, free and unrestricted trade.

This was a well-judged appeal to the economic liberalism of the government; but then came the crux of the matter. According to Nathan, the existing marine insurance companies lacked:

that energy and those liberal extended views which are necessary, at the present day, to retain the advantages which they have hitherto monopolised, and I am sure I shall be borne out in the assertion that if insurancies are to be tied up by their old fashioned modes of thinking and acting, Establishments of a similar nature will arise in every part of the Continent, and will eventually wrest from their hands the business which they now conduct exclusively.[73]

The government was evidently persuaded, for the bill received the royal assent in June. However, one of the new company's shareholders (who was also an underwriter at Lloyd's) managed to obtain an injunction to restrain the Alliance from becoming involved in marine insurance on the ground that this went beyond its original objects. As a result, a second company had to be created, the "Alliance Marine Assurance Company," also with capital of £5 million.[74]

The Rothschilds' new incarnation as insurers was initially greeted with some public scepticism. A contemporary cartoon (*A New Court Fire Screen*, by "an Amateur") depicts a stagecoach loaded with a group of country investors and their bags of money drawing up in front of the "Hollow Alliance Fire and Life Preserving Office" (see illustration 10.viii). The office has three entrances: one marked "German Porter's Lodge," one marked "English Porter's Lodge" and one in the middle, in front of which three men (Rothschild, Montefiore and Gompertz) converse in French. Nathan declares, "Ma fois, c'est entre nous," Montefiore replies, "C'est bien fait pour mon beau père," and Gompertz mutters, "Experience makes men wiser." Another sign to the left reads "No Holidays except Dog Days and the Fifth of November," while on the other side the office hours are stated: "From Sun rise to Moonshine." Above the middle door there is a notice: "No Persons to be admitted but those with empty heads and full pockets." The English porter tells the newly arrived investors: "No! All full at a premium," but his German counterpart cries, "No! No! Open your door in order to get plenty of room to *take in* our Gentry Friends."[75]

Yet this cynical assessment was unfounded. Unlike so many of the joint-stock companies of the period, the Alliance was no mere vehicle for mulcting naive investors, but a securely founded enterprise with a long and prosperous future ahead of it. After two years at 4 New Court, next door to Rothschilds, it moved to Bartholomew Lane.[76] Nor was this the only Rothschild foray into insurance. In 1839 they became involved (albeit less directly) in the rapidly developing Rhineland market, lending their support to the Colonia fire insurance company set up by the Oppenheims and others. This connection survived the turbulent events of the 1840s (in particular the great Hamburg fire of 1842, which all but exhausted

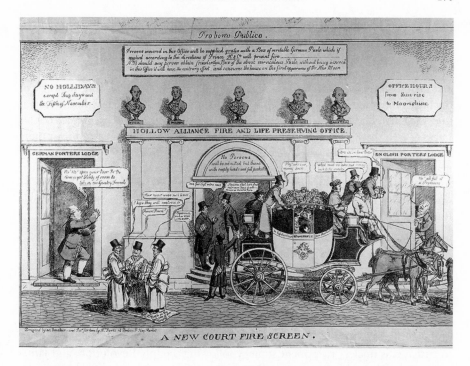

10.v.ii: "An Amateur," *A NEW COURT FIRE SCREEN* (1824), published by H. Fores.

the company's resources), and in 1852 the London, Frankfurt and Paris houses were involved again as major shareholders in the Cologne Reinsurance Society.[77]

The Rothschild Network

The ever-increasing volume of the Rothschilds' business, the diversification of their financial activities and the expanding geographical range of their interests inevitably exceeded the capacities of five brothers. It was usually possible for one of the partners to make personal visits to Brussels, the Hague, Berlin or Madrid when major government loans were being negotiated. But if they wished to conduct regular business in those capitals, other arrangements had to be made. Similarly, buying and selling commodities like cotton, tobacco, sugar, copper and mercury were impossible without effective and reliable representation in the key markets: New York, New Orleans, Havana, St Petersburg and Madrid. Throughout the 1820s and 1830s it was necessary not only to expand the number of partners by initiating the new generation into the management of the five houses, but also to increase the number of clerks in the five offices and to establish a select group of salaried agents employed to take care of the bank's interests in such new markets. Radiating out from London, Paris, Frankfurt, Vienna and Naples, the lines of communication with these agents formed a complex new network, greatly increasing the volume of correspondence, but also increasing the volume of business which could be done in the name of Rothschild. Nor was this network of formal influence all; of comparable importance was the larger but looser network of links to other banks, as well as to stockbrokers, central banks and financial newspapers. If every individual or firm which conducted regular correspondence with the Rothschilds is counted as a part of their network, then it was immense indeed.

The expansion of the partnership to include the sons of Salomon, Nathan, Carl and finally James was achieved with relatively little friction. The eldest members of the next generation—Anselm and Lionel—seem to have accepted without reservation their hereditary vocation, passing without complaint through the successive stages of a Rothschild apprenticeship: work in the paternal house, then one or more stints in an uncle's house and finally a solo foreign mission. Anselm was formally made a partner in 1826; but it was not until 1830 that the brothers had sufficient confidence to entrust him with sensitive negotiations in Berlin, and even then he was carefully coached beforehand by his anxious father, who gave him the classic Rothschild advice to "listen to everything and say little in reply":

> You are now the plenipotentiary of all the brothers . . . and in the same way all the brothers will [have to] approve everything, as fundamentally the business entails a considerable risk, so do not write too little . . . and be hard-working and busy and in all these undertakings put your reliance in the Almighty, who will give you luck and His blessing.[78]

In fact, it was not long before Anselm had the self-confidence to begin asserting his notionally equal authority as a partner. Within a year he felt sure enough of himself to criticise his uncles' investment strategy following the July Revolution, and James was soon asking for his assistance in Paris "as he really has character."[79] This was perceptive: when the next and far greater revolutionary crisis swept across Europe, Anselm would play a decisive role in limiting the damage to the five houses, even at the expense of his own father's feelings.

Nathan's eldest son Lionel also passed through his apprenticeship years with flying colours. In 1828 he was formally "initiated into the business" when he was appointed "Lieutenant General" while Nathan travelled to Frankfurt to meet his brothers. "You are now the General all on your own," wrote James, offering avuncular encouragement, "and you will no doubt attend to the business very nicely." "Make some nice business deals, like a man," he added a few days later. "Show that you are a clever and good businessman."[80] Three years later, as he struggled to remain afloat in the wake of the 1830 revolution, James's tone was altogether less patronising:

> Should you, dear Nathan, not need him [Lionel] you know how much pleasure it would give me to have him here with us. It is always better to work in pairs rather than singly. In spite of our unfortunately doing very little business here, it is nevertheless always useful to act as a pair. If it should be too inconvenient to allow him to come here, I would then be obliged if you could send one of your other sons here, whom I always treat like one of my own children. I hope that Lionel has no reason to complain about me and that he will return here.[81]

When Lionel was sent to Brussels, James expressed his unease at being left "on my own" in Paris.[82] By 1833 Lionel seemed to his sister a "complete man of business": "[He] calls to pay his respects in the morning and we do not see him again until dinner at 7."[83] His trip to Madrid in 1835 was judged a success;[84] and he stepped into his father's shoes in 1836 apparently without difficulty.

By contrast, Lionel's younger brothers were more reluctant bankers. Anthony had to cut short his first apprenticeship in Frankfurt because of a romantic entanglement of which his father disapproved, and harboured an intense dislike of "that stinking place" thereafter (a feeling shared by his brothers).[85] By comparison with Paris and London, Frankfurt had little to offer in the way of fleshpots; worse, their Uncle Amschel worked longer hours than his nephews were used to: from 8 a.m. to 7 p.m., six days a week. (Nathan plainly did not drive his sons as hard as he had once driven himself.)[86] Even in the more congenial atmosphere of Paris, Anthony was found wanting. As James put it tactfully, although he was "hard working," he failed "to bring the deals which after all will remain for future generations."[87] His uncles tried their best. James encouraged him to "observe all the wheeling and dealing" as he negotiated a major contract; Salomon sought to "instil in him a degree of steeliness which on the one hand will teach the young man not to be too quarrelsome, and on the other hand, not to be too tempestuous."[88] But Anthony never entirely lost his unreliable reputation: as late as 1840 his brother Nat felt obliged to protest at the "very coarse language" of his letters. "I do not like him to write to me exactly as if I were his servant," he complained to Lionel. "I do not think I am touchy but there is a way of saying things which is particularly offensive and our good brother Billy [Anthony's nickname] sometimes adopts that way."[89]

Nat had an altogether more placid temperament than Anthony, but he too seems to have chafed at the constraints of his apprenticeship. "You must know," he confided in his sister Charlotte, "that I have been about a month in London, I go regularly to the counting house with Papa & try as much as possible to become an accomplished man of business which however I find rather a difficult thing to do."[90] When he was sent to Naples he liked it even less, as he complained to his brother Lionel:

> I have now rather a tender subject to touch upon, namely myself. I have frequently written to you my great dislike of Naples which I assure you increases every day, I assure you however I should not mind that at all, but then I am afraid I am of no service & that I should be much better employed in London where I certainly might learn business in about a twentieth of the time & twenty times as well as here . . . [D]o my dearest Rabbi write to Papa & tell him to let us come home.[91]

In the end, it was once again James who took charge, putting Nat through a thorough year's training "just like any other apprentice, to enable him to learn how to keep the books in order." Nat was, he assured Nathan, "a very nice boy . . . and I can guarantee you that, if he is prepared to listen, he will become the most skilful of all."[92] Indeed, Nat seems to have become James's favourite nephew: soon he was talking of "teaching the good young man all that I know."[93] By 1833 he felt his protégé was ready for a foreign mission, though the choice of destination—Constantinople, during the prolonged Greek loan wrangle—was probably not a wise one.[94] Ultimately, it was Nat's fate to live and work almost all his life in his Parisian uncle's shadow, never quite ceasing to be a disgruntled English gentleman in exile, constantly dismayed by the political volatility of the French, and quietly counting the long hours he had to spend in "the stinking counting house."[95]

Why, when they had so many sons—twelve in all—did Nathan and his brothers not follow their father's example and establish at least some of them in new financial centres? This is not easy to answer. While their sons were still young, the brothers seem to have thought of establishing new houses in Madrid or St Petersburg. And later there was intermittent talk of sending one of the members of the younger generation to the United States. But the plan for a "sixth house" on the other side of the Atlantic remained no more than a pipe-dream. The best explanation for this is that they trusted five of their sons—Anselm, Lionel, Mayer Carl, Adolph and Alphonse —enough to groom them as their successors, but the others insufficiently to give them the major responsibility of setting up new houses. For if Anthony and Nat seemed to lack the spark of financial ability and dedication their uncles were looking for, they were at least competent by comparison with Nathan's youngest son Mayer, a would-be country squire, or the Orthodox zealot Wilhelm Carl. Another obstacle appears to have been Nathan's widow Hannah, who resolutely refused to allow her younger sons to be posted overseas.

Instead, the Rothschilds had to rely on a small group of paid agents. Of course, since the very early days in the Judengasse there had always been non-family members employed as clerks. We know little about these shadowy letter-writers and book-keepers, save that the partners preferred to exclude them from executive activity: they were regarded as drones, to be worked hard, treated well—and watched carefully. Some were little more than servants, like the cheerful Jakob who was injured in a coach crash in 1814 while delivering a consignment of gold to Warsaw ("better to be hurt in the legs than hurt in the gold," he joked).[96] Others were skilled linguists and accountants. In 1818 there were at least nine clerks in the Frankfurt office: Radius and Kremm, who were responsible for the book-keeping; Berend, who conducted the correspondence and ledger for all Frankfurt transactions; Geiger, who also handled Frankfurt business and matters relating to coupons; his father, who dealt with current accounts; Hamburg, who conducted all correspondence with titled customers; his brother, who dealt with foreign letters; Heisler, who looked after bills of exchange; and Kaiser, who took care of domestic matters. There was also an office boy in the accounts department and an apprentice letter-copier. To Carl, however, they were all "the young people," and when he contemplated the running costs of the office (150,000 gulden a year, or around £14,000), he suspected them of "trickery"—remembering, no doubt, his father's experience with Hirsch Liebmann.[97] The Paris house was even smaller (and cheaper): at around the same time, James estimated that he spent 34,000 francs a year (£1,700) on eight clerks, a porter, a messenger, two servants and a coachman.[98]

Often the clerks were drawn from extended families similar to the Rothschilds'. In Vienna, a key role was played by the Goldschmidt family, which included Salomon's chief clerk Moritz Goldschmidt, who had moved from Frankfurt to Vienna with Salomon in 1803, and his sons Julius, Jacob and Alexander, who worked in Vienna, Frankfurt and Paris respectively. Relations of the Goldschmidts were also regarded as trustworthy: one of Moritz's nephews worked for Rothschilds in Amsterdam, but died young. Another nephew (Moritz) worked at the London house for eighteen years, while a third (Ignaz Bauer) was sent to Spain to assist Weisweiller.

Inevitably, the numbers of staff had to be increased to keep pace with the amount of business, so that by the 1830s New Court alone employed between thirty and forty people, earning between £50 and £500 a year.[99] But the paternalistic attitudes of the partners persisted. "Pray let the Clerks have a good dinner," wrote Lionel on the occasion of his wedding in 1836, "and get all drunk or if they like . . . I think they might make a party to Greenwich; if some of them are too proud, let them make two parties and take their better halves with [them]."[100] The nearest thing to an incentive was that "on our becoming the contractors of an English and foreign loan [we] generally allowed the clerks a small interest independent of a gratuity at Christmas which of late years we have allowed them." When it became apparent that both Nat and Anthony might have to leave their posts in London and Paris to attend their father's deathbed, there was consternation: for the first time ever, it was necessary to give the senior clerks in both houses powers of attorney, a responsibility which had previously been conferred only on members of the family. In the case of London, there was some doubt about who should actually be appointed, suggesting the absence of any formal hierarchy within the office.[101] Part of the problem was that Nathan's monopoly over executive decision-making had encouraged a degree of indolence among his own employees, who were spared difficult decisions and all but guaranteed bonuses.[102]

This explains the great difficulty the Rothschilds experienced when they had to entrust their interests in remote cities like Madrid, St Petersburg or New York to men who had generally begun their careers as clerks. For inevitably these agents could not be treated as mere office-boys, subject to daily orders from the partners and denied all real responsibility. No matter how many letters were sent from New Court, the men on the ground were bound to be better informed about the places where they lived. Sometimes they had to take decisions quickly, so that consultation with London or Paris could only be retrospective. And no matter how often it was asserted that they were mere agents of the great Rothschilds, they naturally acquired considerable local status in their own right, disposing as they did over substantial resources. All this the Rothschilds found extremely hard to stomach. They constantly suspected their most valuable agents of disloyalty—above all, of trading on their own account—and complained endlessly of their insolence, independence and incompetence. "I noticed that Gasser [the St Petersburg agent] has no interest at all in our business affairs," James wrote to Nathan in 1829 on hearing of a large consignment of silver bound for Russia:

> Another man, realising that so much silver is due to arrive, would say, "I will meanwhile send you a remittance," but no, nothing of the kind occurred to him. He wrote to me and enquired whether I wanted to make with him c/meta [a joint account] for three months which would give him more courage to operate. Well, we will have to send one of our own people over there, someone who shows greater loyalty to our House. Well, thank God, you will soon have grown up sons.[103]

Gasser was repeatedly the target of such criticism. In 1838 James threatened to stop paying his salary (14,000 roubles a year), which he considered excessive, instead paying him a quarter per cent of "whatever business we do with him."[104] As so often, the charge was that Gasser was putting his own interests before those of the firm. "Under no circumstances should you write even a single word to Gasser," fumed James a year later. "That stiff dog, who is only too glad to hold on to your money at no cost to himself, is doing you more harm than any good he could possibly render."[105] Even Lazare Richtenberger—established in Brussels in 1832 as the first fully fledged Rothschild agent—was occasionally dismissed as an "ass." Despite his proximity and punctilious subservience, even he sometimes made the mistake of acting in advance of James's instructions.[106]

Perhaps the most important Rothschild agent in the 1830s was Daniel Weisweiller, their man in Madrid, whose name was first discussed for the job in 1834.[107] Weisweiller had apparently won a reputation as a "businessman" in the Frankfurt office, and his correspondence over the years was detailed to a fault. But it was not long before he too was suspected of neglecting his masters' interests.[108] By 1843 there was even talk of replacing "that young man, whose pretensions [according to Anselm] become more unagreeable [sic] every year":

> I think really the man is half cracked & fancies himself of the highest importance . . . By today's post I shall . . . write to my father about Landau that he may prepare himself for Madrid . . . [T]he best were [if] one of us could or would go to Madrid . . . but you may rely that I shall not mention Mayer in my letter to London as your good Mama wishes him to remain in England. I think Landau will do very well in Madrid when once he knows the terrain, he is very clear . . . [and,] belonging to a very respectable family[,] he will never express such ridiculous pretentions [sic] as Weisweiller does & will not fail to continue doing.[109]

Such threats were idle. Weisweiller might possess "a triple dose of vanity," but he had made himself more or less indispensable. Thus it was decided to send Mayer to Madrid only for the few months when Weisweiller was abroad getting married: as Nat put it, "Weisweiller's absence will oblige Tup [Mayer's nickname] to exert himself & will enable him at once to be master, whilst later W. will be there & it wd not be so easy for Mayer to put him immediately in his proper position."[110] When Anthony sought to bring Weisweiller to heel, he made little headway:

> He complained as usual and was as cold as ice, until I told him in plain terms that as long as he did our business in Madrid to our satisfaction, we would make no change, but if he went on giving himself airs and thought our gratitude insufficient, it would be impossible for him to stay in Madrid and one of us would be obliged to go hitherto [sic] . . . He is an uncommonly clever agent and it would be difficult to replace him, but I have seldom or never seen a more disagreeable cold hearted calculating agent. His vanity is excessive.[111]

Instead, another agent, Hanau, was sent to the United States, where he almost immediately incurred the partners' irritation by over-hasty dealings—though one suspects that, if he had taken more time to learn the ropes, he would have been criticised for idling. Only the Rothschilds could have found fault with an agent for "directing too much of his attention towards finding out all the business he could for us."[112]

To correct a long-standing misapprehension, it is important to distinguish between salaried agents like Weisweiller and associated banks with whom the Rothschilds corresponded regularly and did business on a preferential basis.[113] To list all these would be tedious: by the end of the 1840s the Rothschilds had such associates in Amsterdam, Baltimore, Berlin, Cologne, Constantinople, Florence, Hamburg, Milan, Odessa, Rome and Trieste, to name just some of the more important. Two famous German banking names are sometimes erroneously said to have been Rothschild agents in their early years: Warburg and Bleichröder. In fact, they were merely two of these many associates, and before 1848 there was nothing unusual about the modest role they played in the bank's network.[114] Nevertheless, the two cases are of interest because they illustrate how much value smaller banks (especially in Germany) attached to establishing some sort of connection—however tenuous—with the Rothschilds.

The Warburgs began lobbying for Rothschild business in Hamburg as early as 1814, though regular dealings were not established until the 1830s, and preference continued to be given to Carl Heine (the poet Heinrich's uncle) until the 1860s.[115] In much the same way, Samuel Bleichröder attempted to supplant the Mendelssohns as the Rothschilds' favoured banker in Berlin; again, despite much sycophancy, it was not until the 1860s that his son Gerson was accorded any special status, largely on account of his proximity to Bismarck and the good-quality political news this enabled him to provide.[116] Even then, he continued to be treated with a measure of disdain: "Bleichröder?" James was heard to exclaim to Herbert Bismarck. "What is Bleichröder? Bleichröder is the one per cent I let him have."[117] Many other banks performed the same role in the Rothschilds' operations, participating in major bond issues, helping to facilitate large bullion transfers and engaging in occasional arbitrage transactions: the Oppenheims in Cologne, the Schröders in London and the Banque de Bordeaux, to name just three.[118] At this stage in their histories, all were minor players.

By comparison, the Rothschilds had much more time for those larger banks whom they regarded primarily as rivals, but whose co-operation they sometimes sought for very large operations: the Barings, Thomas Wilson and Goldschmidt in London; Laffitte, Hottinguer and Mallet in Paris; Geymüller, Sina and Eskeles in Vienna; and Bethmann and Gontard in Frankfurt. Far from wishing such competitors ill—as they had in the decade of cut-throat competition after 1814—the Rothschilds increasingly came to see their existence as complementary, so long as their own position as *primus inter pares* remained unchallenged. The 1830s and 1840s saw the emergence of informal syndicates and shifting coalitions of banks in all the major financial centres. At the same time, by dint of their size, the Rothschilds came to see themselves as bearing a degree of responsibility for the stability of the banking system as a whole. This explains their reluctance to see their rivals fail. In the 1820s they had watched the collapse of Parish with almost callous indifference. In the subsequent decades, by contrast, they were occasionally willing, for the sake of financial stability, to come to their competitors' rescue, as in the case of Laffitte in 1831 and 1838.[119] Salomon's arguments for assisting Geymüller in 1841 are illuminating:

> To sit back and watch the bankruptcy of a man of 65 years—of a house which has existed for so long, a house which was in the first rank here—and not to be able to help . . . *was just impossible* . . . If Steiner and Geymüller do have to stop their payments, what a spectacle it would be,

what an impression it would make abroad, as well as in Frankfurt and other German markets, because several million—as many as 3 or 4 million—gulden of acceptances and bills would be turned away from both these houses.[120]

In this case, Salomon was overruled by his brothers and nephews. But his sense of responsibility for financial stability *in general* also informed Lionel's atttitude to the protracted debate on monetary policy in England. In 1839 he reported to his uncle on "the measures to be enacted with regard to the joint stock banks" (a new generation of which had proliferated since the mid-1820s) and their likely "effect upon our internal money concerns." "The question," as he put it, "is how to keep these gentlemen from getting too fat and getting themselves and the country into scrapes without too much cramping the circulation."[121]

In all this, the Rothschilds were increasingly beginning to think in a way fundamentally similar to that characteristic of central bankers. This is scarcely to be wondered at. In the first half of the nineteenth century, the central banks of England and France continued to be partly private institutions, albeit with evolving public responsibilities governed by statute. In terms of their financial resources, they were in fact the only banks comparable with the Rothschilds, though of course they were national where the Rothschilds were international, and the Rothschilds had no interest in resisting their monopolisation of note-issue. The relationships between the Rothschilds and the European central banks were thus almost always close and sometimes symbiotic. We have already seen how Nathan made use of the Bank of England for short-term loans during the 1820s; how, in return, he had come to its rescue in 1825; and how it had provided the advances of bullion needed to bail out James in 1830. Small wonder his evidence to the 1832 Bank Committee was so positive: "I feel the management and I know that it is good."[122] After the 1830–32 crisis, James appears to have been on a similar footing with the Banque de France; and Salomon's relations with the Austrian Nationalbank were even closer.[123]

'Change
In 1836 James gave his nephews some advice about how to sell securities on the Paris stock exchange:

> When you are buying or selling rentes, try not to look at making a profit, but rather your aim should be to get the brokers used to the idea that they need to come to you . . . [O]ne initially has to make some sacrifices so that the people then get used to the idea to come to you, my dear nephews, and as such one first has to spread the sugar about in order to catch the birds later on.[124]

It is easy for the historian to lose sight of that throng of brokers attracted by the Rothschild "sugar," for the simple reason that most of their dealings were conducted orally rather than by correspondence. Yet the brokers were the indispensable worker-ants of nineteenth-century finance. As with the banks they dealt with, the Rothschilds had their favourites: Menet & Cazenove in London, for example, who sold foreign stocks amounting to £2 million for Rothschilds in 1834 alone, and £1.4 million the following year; and the partnership founded by John Helbert Israel and his nephew John Wagg.[125] However, even these were treated rather in the manner of casually hired grouse-beaters: Alfred Wagg recalled how "on the fortnightly settlement days my grandfather or father would go over to New Court with a statement of the position across which Baron Lionel would write £500 or £1,000, being an arbitrary fee which he fixed as our renumeration, varying in amount according to the humour he was in."[126] In any case, it made tactical sense to deal with many brokers, above all because of the need to conduct some operations surreptitiously.

When contemporaries called Nathan "the master of the exchange," they were not wholly exaggerating: by the late 1820s the positions he took were watched closely by smaller traders who—not unreasonably—credited him with superior information and intuition. This meant that overt Rothschild sales or purchases could trigger a general flight from or into a particular stock, a ripple effect the brothers generally did not like to encourage. Stories abound about Nathan's techniques for averting such imitation. "If he possessed news calculated to make the funds rise, he would commission the broker who acted on his behalf [initially] to sell half a million." "It was a common practice with this mighty speculator to have one set of agents selling, and another buying the same stock so that there was no ascertaining what in reality was the object of his manoeuvres."[127] In Vienna, Salomon delegated much of his stock market business to a jobber whom he paid "a fixed salary of 12,000 gulden, irrespective of his immense commissions":

> This person used to wait upon Rothschild early every morning, when together they concerted their plans for the day's operations. The stock-jobber had his clients and customers not only in the Bourse but also in the "Panduren-Lager" [the unofficial bourse in the Grünangergasse café where out-of-hours trading went on] with whom he concluded his purchases and sales. He kept a number of runners in his employ, whose sole duty it was to run backwards and forwards from him to Rothschild's with reports of all the fluctuations in prices.[128]

Of growing importance as a non-exclusive source of financial information (and misinformation) in this period was, of course, the press. It might be thought that the proliferation of newspapers in the nineteenth century tended to erode the advantages which the Rothschilds were able to derive from their private system of communications; and to some extent this was the case. On the other hand, the existence of financial pages in newspapers presented new opportunities for influencing the markets which the Rothschilds were not slow to exploit. This was not at first easy: as we have seen, in the 1820s the Rothschilds were more often the targets of press criticism than manipulators of the media, and there were always radical and reactionary journals which remained unremittingly hostile to them. Gradually, however, a group of papers emerged over which the bank could exercise at least some influence. We have already noted how Salomon was able, through Gentz, to exert pressure on the German *Allgemeine Zeitung*, and its use of Heinrich Heine as a correspondent in the 1830s also ensured relatively positive (if satirical) coverage of James's activities. James himself appears to have steadily increased his influence over papers like the *Moniteur Universel* and the *Journal des Débats*. "Yesterday a deprecatory article concerning us was published in one of the newspapers," wrote James to Nathan in 1832. "If this article should appear in one of the larger newspapers, we will then publish a response here."[129] "Well," he told his nephews five years later, following some sensitive negotiations in Spain, "I am arranging for several articles to be printed in the newspapers for this will make an impression in Madrid and in London because your English newspapers often follow in the footsteps of our French ones and it is good if one can regulate public opinion."[130] By 1839 he could assure his nephews confidently that he would "see to it" that the French government was "attacked in all the newspapers" if it had the temerity to oppose his railway plans. "If one can't make oneself loved then one has to make oneself feared," he declared, repeating a favourite Mayer Amschel maxim. "Newspapers can make a strong impact."[131]

Nathan too responded to early press attacks by establishing what was to be an enduring relationship with the most influential of all British papers: *The Times*. In the 1820s he had been attacked on a number of occasions by the *Morning Chronicle:* for example, it alleged in 1829 that one of its rivals, the *Courier,* had used inside information from the Foreign Office about a change of ministry in France as the basis for a stock market speculation with Nathan: the editor allegedly "told Montefiore, Montefiore told Rothschild, and a very neat stock job was got up with the rapidity of lightning."[132] In fact, it was more often Nathan who was in a position to provide the papers with news—in particular, political communications relayed by his brothers from Vienna and Paris. Indeed, it was partly their common interest in speedy communication which brought the Rothschilds and *The Times* together: by the end of the 1830s they were effectively sharing a pigeon-post service between Boulogne and London.[133] Perhaps more importantly, Nathan struck up a friendship with Thomas Massa Alsager, who had joined *The Times* in 1817 as a City correspondent and was one of its leading financial writers until 1846.[134] Although the closeness of the link should not be exaggerated (Alsager at times expressed concern about the scale of British capital export, which no one had done more to encourage than Nathan), nevertheless the Radicals and Chartists who accused the paper of being "the Jew's harp" were not wholly fantasising.[135] In 1842 Anselm wrote to his cousins enclosing a new "regulation which the Prussian Govt. intends issuing about the poor Jews":

> [T]he King of Prussia being very vain & much affected when the *Journal des Débats* or the English disapprove his Govt. it would be very desirable for those papers to contain from time to time articles in favour of the Jews. As you know well the leading men of *The Times,* you will easily obtain from them the insertion of some articles, & I will then send you some German articles you may have translated.[136]

Such manipulation of the media goes on in much the same way today, of course, and it is difficult to fault the Rothschilds for seeking to influence an often hostile press. More difficult for a modern reader to judge are the financial practices of a period when there was little formal regulation and the rapid pace of financial innovation left such legislation as did exist lagging some way behind. There is no question that the Rothschilds took full advantage of the fluidity of the financial environment; but it would be quite anachronistic to level retrospective charges of "insider dealing," or any of the other modern forms of fraud which were then unknown. In the *Comédie humaine,* Balzac's Nucingen—the German-Jewish banker modelled on James—is reputed to have made his fortune by a succession of essentially bogus bankruptcies. These operations are described in considerable—and entertaining—detail, but they make little economic sense; nor do they correspond in any way to the reality of Rothschild practices.[137] In fact, there appear to have been only a few legal actions brought against Nathan alleging financial malpractice, and in only one case did the charges stick. In 1823, for example, a subscriber to the 1822 Neapolitan loan claimed that Nathan had sought to retain his deposit of £1,255 without handing over the relevant stock certificates: the case was thrown out, and it would appear that it was actually the plaintiff, a London corn-merchant named Hennings, who had acted in bad faith (refusing to pay the money due when the bonds were falling as a result of the French invasion of Spain, then attempting to pay belatedly when they began to recover).[138]

The one case which went against Nathan was filed in 1829 by a man named Brookman, who alleged that the Rothschilds had deliberately given him bad investment advice, and had then charged him for sales and purchases of stocks which had not in fact taken place. In 1818, Brookman claimed, Nathan had advised him to sell 20,000 francs of French rentes and invest in the new Prussian sterling loan then being issued by the London house. Not only had this been bad advice—rentes had promptly risen 10 per cent, while the Prussian bonds fell 7 per cent—it had also been disingenuous, for instead of selling Brookman's rentes to a third party, Nathan had kept them for himself. Contrary to Brookman's instructions, he had then sold the Prussian bonds, advising a fresh purchase of rentes worth 115,000 francs. "As in the previous cases, the moment the plaintiff bought, down went the stock into which he purchased, and the plaintiff is then advised to sell . . . The moment the plaintiff's rentes were sold, up went the market." Brookman had then asked that the money be reinvested in rentes, but shortly after that decided to sell again. According to the accounts of the Paris house, there had been "regular charges for exchange, interest, brokerage and commission" deducted from Brookman's account for each transaction; yet there had in reality been no actual purchases or sales of rentes, which had remained in the Rothschilds' hands all along. Nathan's counsel sought to argue that Brookman was merely a "veteran stock-jobber," that the accounts in question had been settled ten years before and that such book transactions were routine; but the court was unimpressed. According to the Vice-Chancellor's scathing judgement, Nathan was guilty of having made "fallacious statements," and he was ordered to pay to Brookman "the amount of all the sums which he has lost or ought to have received," plus 5 per cent interest, plus costs.[139] Predictably, the case inspired yet another cartoon of Nathan, *The Man Wot Knows How to Drive a Bargain*, which portrayed Nathan as a dealer in old clothes, carrying a sack marked "French Rentes £20,000" (see illustration 10.ix).

Yet this example of apparently Nucingen-like behaviour is worth mentioning precisely because it seems to be unique. In reality, the Rothschilds of this period were more often the victims of fraud—not to mention straightforward robbery—than its perpetrators. In 1824 a Frenchman named Doloret—who had also brought an unsuccessful action against Nathan over the Neapolitan loan—fraudulently obtained from the London house bills worth £9,670, drawn in his favour on the Paris house.[140] A year later one of James's clerks stole a quantity of banknotes (perhaps as much as 1.5 million francs) by smuggling them out of the office in a spe-

THE MAN WOT KNOWS HOW TO DRIVE
A BARGAIN,

10.ix: "A Sharpshooter," *The Man Wot Knows How to Drive a Bargain* (July 14, 1829).

cially designed belt.[141] A similar robbery occurred at New Court in 1838, when an eighteen-year-old clerk named Samuel Green absconded with a cheque for £2,900.[142] In 1839 it was the turn of the Paris house.[143] There was a much bigger robbery from the Madrid office six years later, with gold and securities worth around £40,000 being stolen.[144] And seven cases of Spanish piastres worth around £5,600 were stolen from a Rothschild coach on its way from London to Paris in 1845.[145] Nor were fraud and robbery the only threats the Rothschilds had to contend with. In 1863 a young man who had lost heavily on the bourse sought to extort 100,000 francs from James by sending him threatening letters.[146] Such crimes were perhaps the inevitable price the Rothschilds paid for their celebrity. For what more tempting target did the nineteenth century have to offer its aspirant crooks than the world's bankers?

ELEVEN

"Il est mort"
(1836)

Sidonia had foreseen . . . that, after the exhaustion of a war of twenty-five years, Europe must require capital to carry on peace. He reaped the due reward of his sagacity. Europe did require money, and Sidonia was ready to lend it to Europe. France wanted some; Austria more; Prussia a little; Russia a few millions. Sidonia could furnish them all . . . It is not difficult to conceive that, after having pursued the career we have intimated for about ten years, Sidonia had become one of the most considerable personages in Europe. He had established a brother, or a near relative, in whom he could confide, in most of the principal capitals. He was lord and master of the money-market of the world and of course virtually lord and master of everything else. He literally held the revenues of Southern Italy in pawn; and monarchs and ministers of all countries courted his advice and were guided by his suggestions. He was still in the vigour of life, and was not a mere money-making machine. He had a general intelligence equal to his position, and looked forward to the period when some relaxation from his vast enterprises might enable him to direct his energies to great objects of public benefit. But in the height of his vast prosperity he suddenly died.

—DISRAELI, CONINGSBY[1]

A Wedding and a Funeral

On June 15, 1836, a wedding took place in Frankfurt. The bride was Carl's daughter Charlotte. She had turned seventeen just two days before and was, it was generally agreed, rather beautiful. Her future mother-in-law—an exacting judge—found her as "beautiful as members have already said and her manner agreeable," "simple and amiable."[2] This was not just familial pride. When Benjamin Disraeli met Charlotte for the first time the following year, he was struck by her "tall, graceful, dark, and clear" looks: "picturesquely dressed [in] a robe of yellow silk, a hat and feathers, with a sort of "Sévigne" [bandeau] beneath of magnificent pearls," she looked "quite a Murillo" and was "universally admired."[3] The two characters in his fiction which she later inspired—Eva Besso in *Tancred* and Mrs Neuchatel in *Endymion*—are both fascinating and exotic beauties, especially the former:

> That face presented the perfection of oriental beauty; such as it existed in Eden, such as it may yet occasionally be found among the favoured races in the favoured climes . . . The countenance was oval, yet the head was small. The complexion was neither fair nor dark, yet it possessed the brilliancy of the north without its dryness, and the softness peculiar to the children of the sun without its moisture. A rich subdued and equable tint overspread this visage, though the skin was so transparent that you occasionally caught the streaky spleandour of some vein like the dappled shades in the fine peel of beautiful fruit. But it was the eye and its overspreading arch that all the Orient spake . . .[4]

Her groom—and also her cousin—was Nathan's eldest son Lionel. He was twenty-seven, and already an experienced businessman, having recently played a pivotal role in his father's intricate financial operations in Spain. To judge by his letters, he was a rather solemn, serious young man, conscious already of his daunting responsibility, as the eldest son, to preserve his father's remarkable financial achievements; but also increasingly aware of a more general obligation to advance the cause of Jewish emancipation not only in England, where he had been born and brought up, but throughout Europe. He was presentable, if not handsome, and not a little amorous.

For weeks the women of the family in Frankfurt had been preparing for the great event: Gutle, the betrothed couple's grandmother, now aged eighty-two; Eva, her eldest son Amschel's wife; the bride's mother, Adelheid; as well as Lionel's eldest sister Charlotte, who had married her cousin Anselm ten years before, and was now bringing up their three children, with another on the way. The Rothschild houses in Frankfurt were being vigorously "washed and cleaned" in preparation for the anticipated round of family dinners:[5] Amschel's house, with his beloved garden, in the northern suburbs of the town; his elegant town house on the Zeil; Anselm's newly acquired "palace" in the Neue Mainzer Strasse; and the more modest house in the same street used by Carl and his family when they were in Frankfurt rather than Naples.[6] The original family home in the former Judengasse—where Gutle stubbornly continued to live, despite her sons' great wealth—seems not to have been considered a fit venue for the festivities.

Of the London-based Rothschilds, Lionel himself was among the first to arrive; his youngest brother Mayer was already there, as he was in the process of completing his studies in Germany. Their father set off from London at the beginning of June, accompanied by his wife and two unmarried daughters, the vivacious Hannah Mayer and the musically inclined Louise. Left behind in London to mind the office at New Court was Nathan's third son, Nat. His other son Anthony was in Paris, where he would perform the same deputising role when his uncle James also left for Frankfurt. This he did on June 4, preceded by his wife Betty and their four young children: Charlotte, the eldest at eleven, Alphonse, Gustave and the baby Salomon James. They arrived in Frankfurt eight days later.[7] Just before them, James's brother Salomon had arrived from Vienna accompanied by his son Anselm. While they naturally stayed at the house in the Neue Mainzer Strasse where Anselm's wife Charlotte and the children awaited them, the less frequent visitors to Frankfurt had to be put up in hotels: the London Rothschilds were booked into the Römische Kaiser, the Paris Rothschilds stayed at the Russische Hof, and the Montefiores—doubly related to the Rothschilds by marriage—in the Englische Hof.[8] Altogether, by the time all had assembled, there were around thirty-six Rothschilds in Frankfurt. Perhaps not surprisingly, there were few other guests: the only "outsiders" referred to in the surviving correspondence are Mayer's tutor, Dr Schlemmer, and the composer Gioacchino Rossini, a friend of both James and Lionel, whose role was "to add to the gaiety of our party."[9]

Left alone in charge of the Paris office for the first time, Anthony felt ill at ease, though this was a consequence more of boredom than of the burdens of responsibility. "Am not in good spirits," he complained to his brother Nat, similarly situated in London. "Nothing is so disagreeable than to remain alone. Everything is uncommonly flat . . . How do you amuse yourself quite alone? You are better off than I am for here they have all gone and shut up the house, so I dine every day at a Cabaret [tavern]."[10] The Paris market was in the traditional summer doldrums, and his uncle James's advice from Brussels—where he and Nathan had stopped briefly on business—had scarcely been an encouragement to undertake new business:

> In my opinion you should try to leave everything alone until your good father returns, and if anyone should put a proposal to you, you should reply that you will first have to consult your father, and you will thereby gain some time and some peace and quiet. Don't take any of this to heart and take my advice, hold on to your money and don't spend any of it.[11]

Nat, by contrast, was under pressure, for his father preferred to keep his sons busy in his absence. No sooner had he arrived in Frankfurt than he despatched a characteristically restless letter, not only urging Nat to buy this security or sell that, but also exerting an indirect pressure on his brother in Paris:

> You must always put Anthony in the way of selling, as he belongs to the Bull party and does not like to sell until you have made some few purchases, therefore when the prices are low you can buy a little and encourage Billy [Anthony] to do business and write to him at the same time, that you are pleased and satisfied with his remittances and with everything he does. I have written to him, that every day he must do something whatever may be the price, the same you can write to him.[12]

A few days later—before James himself had arrived in Frankfurt—Nathan wrote directly to Anthony telling him "to keep business going" and "keep yourselves occupied."[13] Neither he nor Nat could feel comfortable on receiving such contradictory instructions from their father and uncle.

Lionel too was faintly disgruntled. He was impatient to be married. Though the match was an arranged one, intended primarily to strengthen the links between the London and Naples branches of the family—and to prevent precious family capital going to outsiders—he had fallen in love with his future wife, or at least had persuaded himself that he had. He was also eager to leave Frankfurt. As he put it to his brother Anthony, he was "heartily glad the day for me quitting beautiful Frankfurt will soon be here";[14] for, like all the younger Rothschilds who had grown up in England, he found his father's birthplace not only tediously provincial but also socially uncomfortable, in that the generality of Jews in Frankfurt were still subject to more legal discrimination than their counterparts in London or Paris, even if he and his family were to some extent exempted. His unease was only increased by his father's late arrival from Brussels,[15] and by every subsequent delay.

Besides the wedding itself, there were two ulterior motives for this large family gathering—one of the biggest Rothschild conclaves of the nineteenth century, and without question the most important. Lionel's marriage to Charlotte was not the first endogamous marriage in the family's history: as we have seen, their uncle James had married their cousin (and his own niece) Betty in 1824; and Anselm had married his cousin Charlotte two years later. More—many more—such intermarriages were to follow. The only question, as Lionel put it, was "how the younger branches of the family will agree"; or, to be precise, who would be paired off with whom. This was the real reason for the presence in Frankfurt of the numerous younger siblings and cousins: they were being assessed for their potential compatibility. Thus Carl's son Mayer Carl was tentatively identified as a suitable match for Lionel's youngest sister Louise; Louisa Montefiore was discussed as a possible wife for Anthony; Joseph Montefiore was spurned by both Hannah Mayer and Louise; and their brother Mayer ruled out as a husband for James's Charlotte. The marriage market evidently provided more entertainment for mothers than for daughters: Hannah Mayer complained of "dreadful tedious long dinners every day" punctuated by German and embroidery lessons.[16] "Only fancy," wrote a dismayed Louise to her brother in London: "to be seated as I am sometimes between *Grossmutter* and aunt Eva and to be stuffed so full as scarcely to be able to breathe."[17] The tedium was relieved only by her daily music lesson with Rossini.

The third reason for the family gathering—and the most important—was business. Accustomed though they were to reaching major business decisions on the basis of their regular correspondence, even the five Rothschild brothers sometimes found face-to-face meetings indispensable. In the years before 1836 James had often crossed the Channel to meet Nathan, and Nathan had sometimes reciprocated; Salomon, the most peripatetic of the five, had been a frequent visitor to Paris and still travelled back and forth regularly between Frankfurt and Vienna; while Carl too divided his time between Naples, where he did business, and Frankfurt, where he preferred to educate his children. Yet the regularity of such shuttling had declined over the years as the brothers had aged, and as their business and family commitments in their respective places of residence had increased. The last time all five had met together had been in 1828.

The most important item on their agenda in 1836 was nothing less than their future relations with one another. Since 1810, as we have seen, the house of Rothschild had been a partnership, based primarily on a detailed, legally binding contract as well as on the wills of the various partners, which determined how individual shares in the firm would be passed on to the next generation. It had been the custom to revise and renew the partnership agreement every few years: thus there had been new contracts in 1815, 1818, 1825—when Salomon's son Anselm had been admitted as a sleeping partner—and 1828, when he had become a "real Associé." Since then, Nathan's three elder sons, Lionel, Anthony and Nat, had all entered the firm to serve their financial apprenticeships. By 1836 Nathan felt his eldest son was ready to become a partner on the same footing as Anselm; and it was primarily to agree the terms of his elevation that the brothers now met.

Apart from the new partnership agreement, there were other matters which the brothers needed to discuss. The year 1836 was critical in the history of their operations in Spain, where a bloody civil war was raging; and there were also important transactions afoot with respect to Greece, Naples and Belgium, all countries in which the brothers had a financial interest. In addition, three of the brothers had recently begun to involve themselves in an entirely new line of business: the financing of railway construction. James in particular was deeply embroiled in battles for control of the fast-developing French rail network—business which to some extent depended on his access, through Nathan, to the larger British capital market. Yet it was far from obvious that Nathan himself approved of this new direction the firm was taking. The first British railway "mania" was reaching its peak in 1836, when no fewer than twenty-nine new railway companies were chartered; but he, in common with all but one of the established London banks, had played no part in it.[18] His preference was for stepping up the bank's involvement in the United States, continuing to concentrate on making loans to states and financing trade, rather than investing in industrial concerns. Here too, however, there was matter for discussion, not least because of the brewing financial crisis on the other side of the Atlantic, the beginnings of which had begun to manifest themselves (in the form of a monetary tightening in London) on the eve of the brothers' meeting.

The negotiations went on between the partners in strict secrecy: all other family members were excluded. "They are now all assembled," reported Lionel to his brother, "that is, the four are alone in [Papa's] room and we are shut out. Papa I believe said something about our having a share in the London profit. They all seem to let him do as he likes. I do not know . . . whether they think of getting him round by good words and coaxing."[19] "The Family arrangements go on very amicably," thought his mother. "There has been no difference."[20] By June 12 it appeared that Nathan had got his way without the "high words" his son had feared:

> Papa proposed that we should have half the profits of the London House and that he should have only half the profit the others make. Everything was agreed to immediately and not a word said. I was not in the room but this morning have heard so . . . I am sure you will be pleased in knowing that they all are pleased with each other and that there have not been any disputes . . . They all are very satisfied with the different cash accounts and did not expect to have seen the Houses so flourishing.[21]

"All parties," it seemed, were "inclined to keep the peace." Such fraternal harmony was evidently somewhat unusual. "Till now, thank heavens, there has not been one angry word between the Brothers," wrote Lionel with evident surprise. "They pass their time at [Papa's room] and the [counting] house, and dine altogether at one of the three houses quite *en famille*."[22] It was one of the rare occasions when the five brothers lived up to the first of the three ideals enshrined in their adopted motto: "Concordia." The Frankfurt artist Moritz Daniel Oppenheim captured this mood of harmony in the portraits he painted of the five brothers to mark the occasion.

Only one shadow hung over the brothers' deliberations and over the nuptial

preparations beyond their closed doors; and that was the fact that Nathan Rothschild was dying. Or rather he was ill; for no one could conceive that the man who,
since the death of his father in 1812, had been the unquestioned leader of the house
of Rothschild, might die at the very height of his powers. While at Brussels, Nathan
had suffered a recurrence of an earlier complaint, probably an ischio-rectal abscess.
As his wife put it, he had "again a visit from his most unpleasant visitor, a disagreeable boil in a most inconvenient place and [which] annoys him considerably particularly in sitting down."[23] His son was more blunt: "Papa has a most terrible boil on
his bottom and suffers very much from it. He has not yet been able to leave his bed
and has a great deal of pain. The movement of the carriage inflamed it, so that he
requires now double rest."[24]

The final illness and death of Nathan Rothschild is a case study in the inadequa-
cies of nineteenth-century medicine. The German doctors may not actually have
killed their patient by their interventions, which aimed, not unreasonably, at drain-
ing the abscess; but they inflicted excruciating pain on him, unmitigated by any
form of anaesthesia. Shortly after his arrival, an attempt was made to lance the boil,
but another swelling quickly formed which "creates the same pain and confinement
as the first." "This, dear Anthony," reported his distraught wife, "is very distressing
as these things are so painful . . . but the doctors assure us of no danger. You know
how impatient Papa is if he is ill," she concluded hurriedly, "and I therefore must go
to him."[25] "The large opening," Lionel was able to report on June 13, "has been
running famously and no other operation, it is expected, will be necessary. Professor
Chelius arrived this morning and found both wounds in a much more forward state
than he had imagined; in fact he is quite satisfied with the way they are going on and
assures us that only time is requisite to see Papa quite restored."[26] His mother was
equally reassured by this "celebrated Professor from Heidelberg, who unites great
safeness of manner and incessant attention, with renowned ability" and by his
"assurances that there is nothing more forming and the opening [is] going on
well."[27]

Needless to say, Nathan's illness blighted the wedding celebrations. Although the
bride's parents decided to proceed with the ball they had planned to give on June 13,
the bride herself was so "agitated" that she could not attend.[28] Yet Nathan—with
the phenomenal resolve which had characterised his whole life—refused to have the
wedding postponed on his account.[29] Indeed, he insisted on being present at it. On
the day of the wedding, as his wife recorded, "he took courage at 6 o'clock in the
morning to get up and walk to Charlotte's which he effected tolerably and afterwards dressed—and went to Charles's [Carl's] to be present at the celebration of the
ceremony."[30] "Everything passed off perfectly well," the relieved groom was able to
report to his absent brothers that afternoon. "Papa was well enough to come . . . and
as his complaint is only one that gives pain, it required but a little resolution, of
which you know Papa has enough. The ceremony lasted but half an hour and was
very solemn . . . [It] went off uncommonly well as Papa was there and our family
circle complete."[31] Indeed, Nathan seems to have gone out of his way to play down
his illness, trying "with jokes of every kind . . . to shorten the speech of the worthy
Rabbi and to cheer up those present."[32] It was an act. Immediately after the ceremony, "he was seized with the excessive pain which usually comes on about 2 o'clock
and lasts for 6 hours."[33] Rather than return to the hotel, he was put to bed in his

daughter's house.[34] While the newlyweds departed for a brief twenty-four-hour honeymoon at Wilhelmsbad,[35] an increasingly irritable Nathan submitted once again to the surgeon's knife. Although he bore "all his operations and dressing without a murmur," he was now worried enough to insist that his doctor and erstwhile neighbour in New Court, Benjamin Travers, be summoned.[36]

For six weeks the family waited in vain for Nathan to recover.[37] By the end of June he was well enough to resume dictating his orders to Nat via Lionel, but the final negotiation of the partnership agreement was postponed—to the evident irritation of James, who complained of eye-ache and longed for the comfort of a spa.[38] Lionel was equally impatient. "Papa is going on pretty well but slowly," he told his brothers. "Every day we have a family dinner which is long and tedious and all the day long they are running from one house to the other, doing nothing and talking of nothing."[39] But the doctors continued to open and drain the wounds of "hardness," "matter" and "fibres" with little sign of real improvement in the long-suffering patient, who sought comfort in "Soda Water, Lavender, Oranges, Arrowroot and fruit" sent by courier from England. "The second [wound] was opened this morning," reported Lionel on July 9, a month after his father had arrived in Frankfurt. "Papa underwent the operation with the greatest possible courage and all the time made jokes. The wound was larger than the first as the boil was most terribly deep and must have been very painful." And so it went on, with the gathering financial crisis eerily mirroring the patient's condition.[40]

Finally, on July 24, Nathan lapsed into a "violent" fever and was plainly "in danger"—probably the onset of septicaemia. The next day, in an agitated and near-delirious state, he summoned his son. "He has this instant called me," an anxious Lionel wrote to Nat,

> to write that he wishes you to go on selling English Securities and Exchequer Bills, as well as £20,000 India Stock more. You are also to send an account of the different Stocks on hand. I do not know if I misunderstood him, but I did not like to ask for an explanation. [He also] said you are to sell . . . the securities that the Portuguese Government has given for the money they owe us, not minding one or two per cent.[41]

To Lionel, such sales across the board—and heedless of losses as large as 2 per cent—seemed so out of character as to be almost incomprehensible. Suddenly conscious that their father was dying, Nat and Anthony prepared to leave for Frankfurt.[42] But on July 28, before they could reach him, his brothers, his wife and the two sons present gathered round what was now unmistakably Nathan's deathbed.

It was a decisive as well as fraught moment in the history of the firm: for the head of the family was dying before the new partnership agreement had been signed. As Salomon told the Austrian Chancellor Metternich in a letter written less than two weeks after his brother's death: "The agreements between us for a further period of three years [had] been drawn up, embodying every point, and they were ready for signature, for we still believed that our late brother would, with God's help, recover. However, this was not to be, fate had decided otherwise." Yet Nathan had just enough energy left for a final exercise of his domineering will. Salomon described how "three days before his death he told me all his thoughts and wishes with regard to the will which he then drew up, and which I then had written out in accordance with his intentions."[43] He was not always coherent now: his brothers remarked how he alternated between "more decisive demands" and "utterances already gradually interrupted and obscured by his sufferings." But his message to the family was intelligible enough. Above all, they were to maintain "harmony, constant love and firm unity"—a conscious echo of his own father's last words.[44] What that meant in practice he spelt out with characteristic precision.

Firstly, Nathan called on his sons to "carry on in harmony and peace the banking house founded by me under my name in London." Secondly, he stressed that they were to do so in consultation with his widow: "My dear wife Hannah . . . is to cooperate with my sons on all important occasions and to have a vote upon all consultations. It is my express desire that they shall not embark on any transaction of importance without having previously demanded her motherly advice . . ." Thirdly, he expressed his

> earnest wish that the association between my firm in London, now carried on by my four sons, and the other Houses, which my four dear brothers direct, shall be allowed to continue, that they shall continue to remain partners together . . . I thereby recommend my sons in their business always willingly to follow the advice and recommendations of my brothers . . .[45]

Finally, as his brother recalled, Nathan spelt out a series of amendments to the new partnership agreement:

> On his deathbed, Nathan asked me to have the contract renewed with his surviving sons, with the provision that it should not be terminated within a period of five years . . . The firm of N. M. Rothschild [thus] remains unaltered, the sons together acting as a unit with one vote in the partnership. The whole trading capital of the four brothers and of the late N. M. Rothschild cannot be touched for the next five years, and nobody can draw anything out of the working capital, while we have reduced the interest that we draw individually from four to three per cent, so that the partnership as a whole will, with God's help, still further improve its position in the five years, as the proportion of the funds which can be spent has been reduced, and there is no necessity for the young men to be drawn into speculative ventures.[46]

These wishes were duly incorporated in a hastily drafted annexe to the original agreement.[47]

The practical provisions for the future having been made, Nathan proffered some parting advice:

> [He] charged his eldest son, and through him all those who were not present, always to apply all their efforts to keep the business property intact and not to participate in any risky ventures. He gave them much wise counsel, bade them avoid all evil company and always to keep in the way of true virtue, religion and righteousness. My late brother told them that the world would now try to make money out of us, so that it behoved them to be all the more careful, and he remarked that, whether any son had £50,000 more or less, was a matter of indifference to him. All that mattered was that they should hold together in unity.

"He died," Salomon wrote, "in the full possession of his faculties, and ten minutes before his death he said, as he received the last consolations of religion that are customary with us: "It is not necessary that I should pray so much, for, believe me, according to my convictions I have not sinned." . . . [Then] to my daughter Betty, as she took leave of him, he said in the truly British style, 'Good night for ever.'"[48]

Five days later a carrier pigeon from Boulogne conveyed the news to London in a single, three word sentence: "Il est mort."[49]

Legacy and Legend

The deaths of only a handful of individuals in the nineteenth century can be said to have had economic effects comparable with those caused by the death of Nathan Rothschild. When the Austrian Emperor Francis had died a year before, there had been a minor panic on the Viennese stock exchange and the price of Austrian government bonds had fallen sharply; but the Rothschilds had intervened to prop up the markets.[50] When Nathan died, by contrast, it appeared that the markets' strongest prop had been removed. The financial press had been anxiously reporting on Nathan's health for nearly a week before the news of his death was first published. On July 27 *The Times* had felt able to report (wrongly) that his condition was "not at all dangerous."[51] On August 2 it categorically denied reports in other papers that he had died.[52] But, as its "Money Market and City Intelligence" column admitted, opinion in the City was less sanguine:

> The dangerous state in which Mr Rothschild remained, by the accounts from Frankfort, has again today had its effect upon Spanish and Portuguese securities, and a further depression of 1½ per cent has taken place with them . . . [I]t seems generally accepted that the firm would call in all the loans advanced upon those securities by Mr Rothschild, and hence the anxiety of the borrowers to dispose of their stock, so as to be in a position to meet the demands upon them. The sales today were extensive, but from the weak state of the market it was, in fact, possible to realize but a limited amount . . . There was very little business doing in the share market. Consols have partly recovered the depression they sustained on Saturday, in consequence of the accounts from Frankfort above referred to, but they do not, on the whole, present a very firm appearance.[53]

When the news of Nathan's death was finally confirmed the following day, there was—paradoxically—a slight rally, suggesting that the markets had been discounting the event:

> Government securities of all descriptions, but more particularly those of the foreign markets, have been falling in value during the week, in anticipation of this event, but its confirmation has had a contrary effect, probably on account of the understanding there is that his business, under the management of his sons, will go on as usual.[54]

However, this was only temporary. For Nathan's death coincided with, and perhaps also exacerbated, the onset of the international financial crisis which had been developing throughout his illness.

The period from May 1834 until July 1836 had been one of general financial sta-

bility. The price of consols had fallen below 90 only in a handful of weeks, and it
had been above 91 for the last six months of the period. But from the first week of
August—when the news of Nathan's death broke—until the end of the year, it fell
steadily, reaching a nadir of 87 in November (see illustration 11.i). Just days before,
on July 21, Bank rate (in effect, the Bank of England's base lending rate) had been
raised for the first time in nine years from 4 to 4.5 per cent; on September 1, it went
up by another half point. The Rothschilds' own profit and loss accounts show that
in 1836 the London house suffered its first loss—equivalent to more than 4 per cent
of its capital—since the revolutionary year of 1830. These losses very probably
accrued in the second half of the year.

Nathan's *Times* obituarist—probably his friend Thomas Massa Alsager—was not
exaggerating when he called Nathan's death "one of the most important events for
the city and perhaps for Europe, which has occurred for a very long time": for his
"financial transactions [had] certainly pervaded the whole of the continent, and may
be said for years past to have exercised more or less influence on money business of
every description."[55] "The variations of all stocks & their wild fluctuations,"
remarked Alexander Baring, "seem to arise much from Nathan's death. In the end
the emancipation of the money market will be a benefit, but the sudden cessation of
a despotic rule is apt to exhibit such symptoms."[56] Similar views were expressed
some months later in a pamphlet on monetary matters by David Salomons, who
described Nathan's death as "an event of some importance in the derangement of
the circulation of the country":

> It is well known with what dexterity that eminent individual managed
> the exchanges; how he prided himself in distributing his immense
> resources so that no operation of his own should abstract for a length-
> ened period the bullion of the Bank of England; and although it may be
> urged he kept the exchanges in an artificial state, and therefore produced
> no ultimate good, yet the sudden withdrawal of this artificial aid in an
> inopportune moment has tended to aggravate evils which his energy
> and promptitude might have checked. The difficulties which we have
> been experiencing since his death induce me to think that no one ever
> displayed greater ability than he did in equalising the exchanges; and I
> attribute much of the late embarrassment to the loss of that activity, zeal
> and enterprise, which he always displayed in times of financial difficulty,
> and although the operations of his important house are continued, it is
> impossible at once to replace that moral influence which the acknowl-
> edged good judgement of the head of that opulent firm had established
> for himself not only in Great Britain but throughout the whole of the
> commercial world.[57]

It is understandable, then, that the financial world paid more than ordinary
respects to the deceased. As *The Times* described it, Nathan's funeral cortège on the
morning of Monday, August 8

> was headed by a party of the city police four a-breast, followed by an
> inspector on horseback; next came several other city officers, and these
> were immediately followed by the hearse. The sons and immediate rela-
> tions of the deceased followed in mourning coaches; and the whole line
> of these vehicles consisted of 40, containing numerous branches of the

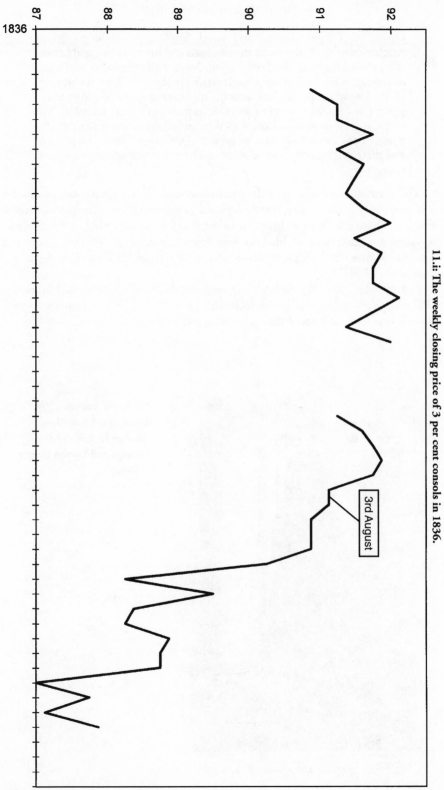

11.i: The weekly closing price of 3 per cent consols in 1836.

Goldsmid, Cohen, Samuel and Israel families. After the mourning coaches came the carriages of the deceased and his two sons, and behind these the carriages of the Lord Mayor, Mr Sheriff Salomons, and a line of foreign Ambassadors' and noblemen's carriages, in all to the number of 35. The whole procession consequently consisted of 75 carriages; and it was more than a quarter of an hour in passing through Cornhill. The crowd of people who had come to this part of the city was so great that many of the shops were shut to protect the windows from the pressure and there was scarcely a window in the line that was not crowded with spectators.[58]

The occasion was appropriately commemorated. A lithograph was produced, *The Shadow of a Great Man*, which depicted in silhouette the already well-known image of Nathan in front of his pillar in the Royal Exchange, holding four keys to represent the succession of his four sons (see illustration 11.ii). This image was reproduced by several different artists, including one of Nathan's own clerks (see illustration 11.iii).[59]

Just two days after the funeral, the poetaster William Heseltine published his "Reflections at the Grave of N. M. Rothschild Esq.," verses which tempered formulaic praise of "the Croesus of the Land" with just a hint of realism:

THE SHADOW OF A GREAT MAN.

11.ii: Mons. Edouart, *The Shadow of a Great Man*, published by J. Knight, Standidge and Lemon (August 6, 1836).

11.iii: R. Cullen, *SHADOW of the late N. M. ROTHSCHILD ESQ.* (1837).

. . . Europe's kings in adverse hour
Have sought and found thine aid.
More than their swords thy gold hath done,
In many a bloodless triumph won,
And many a panic stay'd . . .

Upon thy struggling path of life
Strong lights and shades were cast,
Which led through toil, suspense and strife
To triumph at the last!
In the continual conflict then,
With selfish, artful, flattering men
Through which thy spirit pass'd
What wonder though some stains of earth,
Were blended with thine inward worth.

Though cold unto a stranger's sight,
Thy heart was generous found,

> Nor didst thou, like the Upas, blight
> The lowly shrubs around;
> But friends, protected at thy side,
> Grew with thy growth and flourish'd wide
> In safe and prosperous ground:
> As unto Egypt's saviour came,
> All that could boast of Israel's name.[60]

Mourning rings and broaches were produced, as well as a medal featuring Nathan's face. There was even a printed silk mourning scarf, again picturing Nathan at his pillar, bearing a rather more succinct tribute (in four languages)—"Equally Distinguished for his Commercial Skill & Enterprize & for his Charitable and Benevolent Disposition"—as well as a list of his best-known loans and a statement of his total wealth. Such mementoes (as the scarf's multilingual text suggests) reached an international audience. Copies of the scarf itself were sold in Vienna;[61] Heseltine's verses inspired a similar German tribute;[62] and obituaries appeared not only in the English press but also in the *Journal des Débats* and (at Salomon's prompting) in the *Allgemeine Zeitung*.[63]

Needless to say, it was not only the financial community which mourned the great man's demise. As *The Times* mentioned, the diplomatic and political world was also well represented at the funeral: among the mourners were the Prussian, Russian, Austrian and Neapolitan ambassadors, as well Lord Stewart[64] and—according to one account—the Duke of Marlborough. And, of course, the Jewish community also turned out in force. "A great number of Jews . . . had assembled long before the hour fixed for the funeral" and a special delegation of children from the Jews' Free School preceded the coffin. At the Great Synagogue in Duke Place, the Chief Rabbi Solomon Hirschell preached a sermon; and Nathan's remains were finally buried in the north-west corner of the Jewish burial ground in Whitechapel Road.[65] Seven members of the community of the Great Synagogue attended New Court daily in the year after Nathan's death to form the required "minyan" for the Kaddish, the traditional prayers for the dead.[66]

How are we to account for this extraordinary public interest in the death of a German-born, Jewish banker? The obvious answer is that Nathan Rothschild was quite simply the richest man in Britain and therefore, given Britain's economic lead at this time, almost certainly the richest man in the world. His share of the combined capital of the five houses which he ran in partnership with his brothers was £1,478,541 when he died (a quarter of the total of just over £6 million). He had also given his children before his death around £800,000, and was able in his will to bequeath in total a further £1,192,500 to them and other members of his family. This implies that Nathan's total wealth—excluding his properties in Piccadilly and Gunnersbury Park but including money he had already given his children prior to making his will—was around £3.5 million.

This was a fortune vastly in excess of the Rothschilds' nearest banking rivals in London, Baring Brothers, whose capital in the year of Nathan's death was a mere £776,650.[67] It also easily outstripped the money accumulated by contemporary industrialists and the largely inherited fortunes of the country's wealthiest aristocratic landowners. Rubinstein's figures for British millionaires do not give precise figures for fortunes in excess of £1 million before 1858; but it seems unlikely that any of the eleven other individuals listed for the period 1810–56 left his heirs as much as Nathan: the nearest was that of the banker William J. Denison, who left £2.3 million including real estate worth £600,000 in 1849. It was not until 1857 that someone left more than Nathan to his heirs—the textile warehouseman and Anglo-American banker James Morrison, who left between £4 million and £6 million at his death. Nathan not only died richer than the ironmaster Richard Crawshay and the cotton manufacturers Robert Peel and Richard Arkwright; he also left more than the Duke of Queensberry, the Duke of Sutherland and the Duke of Cleveland.[68]

Of course, it is far from easy to compare a fortune such as Nathan's, which overwhelmingly took the form of financial assets, with the wealth of the great landowners. However, the incomes from their different forms of capital can be compared. The available figures suggest that a handful of aristocrats had incomes comparably large, if not slightly larger: the Duke of Northumberland, Earl Grosvenor, the Marquess of Stafford and the Earl of Bridgewater were all said to have £100,000 a year "clear of everything" in 1819; and not far behind them were the dukes of Bedford, Richmond, Sutherland and Buccleuch, the marquesses of Westminster and Bute, and the earls of Derby, Lonsdale, Dudley and Leicester. The 6th Duke of Devonshire, to take one example, had an income of between £80,000 and £100,000 in the decade of Nathan's death.[69] By comparison, Nathan's income in the last five full years of his life (taking the average profits of the London house as a proxy) averaged £87,623 per annum.

However, these figures overlook a vital factor which gave Nathan financial superiority over his noble contemporaries. He had debtors: they had debts. By the 1830s the Duke of Devonshire's lavish lifestyle had increased the encumbrances on his estates from £593,000 to £700,000; and interest charges on these debts consumed fully half of his income, with a further £36,000 per annum being consumed by the costs of his household at Chatsworth. Indeed, a number of the great landowners were heading rapidly for the financial rocks at the very time that Nathan died. By 1844 the Duke's debts were just short of £1 million, and he was increasingly obliged to sell off land to keep afloat. In 1848 the Duke of Buckingham actually went bankrupt, with encumbrances on his estates in excess of £1.5 million. The idea that Nathan Rothschild had died "leaving Property to the Amount of 5,000,000 Sterling" was therefore in itself a matter for public curiosity, not to say astonishment: hence its publication at the very centre of the mourning scarf described above. The figure may have been a slight exaggeration, but it was a pardonable one. In terms of *net* wealth he was in a league of his own.

What was even more remarkable was how much more Nathan Rothschild was worth when he died than when he had first arrived in Britain. According to his own account, he had arrived in England with just £20,000.[70] Moreover, he had worked his way up into the City from the much less refined textiles sector, having begun his British business career as a cloth merchant in Manchester. He, more than most wealthy Jews of the nineteenth century, really had gone from "rags" to riches. As such, he embodied perfectly the developing nineteenth-century ideal of the self-made man. And of course he was not the only rich Rothschild. Muhlstein's figures suggest that James was already probably the richest man in France.[71] In the less prosperous parts of Europe where they lived, Amschel, Salomon and Carl were even further ahead of their rivals. Together, the Rothschilds were without question the richest family in the world.

To poorer Jews in particular, Nathan's extraordinary rise to riches had an almost mystical significance—hence the legend of the "Hebrew talisman," the magical source of his good luck, which became associated with him in Jewish lore. This extraordinary story—a version of which was published by an anonymous author in London just four years after Nathan's death[72]—is one of the most bizarre early examples of what might be called the "Rothschild myth." Although apparently by a Jewish author, the possibility that (like the later and much better known *Protocols of the Elders of Zion*) it was in fact the work of an anti-Jewish *agent provocateur* cannot be ruled out, so militant is its tone. Indeed, the story anticipates many of the more fantastic allegations of the overtly anti-Rothschild French pamphleteers of the 1840s.

The story is narrated by a mysterious phantom, who describes himself as "detesting . . . the followers of the Nazarene, with a most holy and fervent detestation" and having been "doomed to long ages of agony and travail" by "the avenging one of Nazareth." He is the custodian of a talisman, which confers on its holder magical powers. "Could I not command gold? Yea . . . had I not the talisman?—Had I not the ineffable words?—Could I not buy the whole evil race, from the false prophet even to the lowest among the evil genii?—Could I not task them in the midnight incantation, and, lo! would not plenty make the hearts of my people glad at sunrise?" His aim is to give the talisman to "a zealous hater of the Nazarenes,—a man exceedingly desirous of working their degradation and destruction . . . a champion to avenge the wrongs of Israel."

Arriving in Frankfurt during the Napoleonic occupation of the town, the narrator witnesses hideous scenes of pillage by French troops. The Frankfurt Jews in particular are the objects of systematic extortion. In a looted office in the heart of the Jewish quarter, he comes across a young man, "his eyes . . . red with much weeping, and his cheeks pale and haggard, as much with sorrow and long vigils." As he looks on, a French soldier bursts into the office demanding yet more money. "'God of Abraham, Isaac, and Jacob!' [the young man] exclaimed, as, kneeling, he lifted up his trembling hands to the east, 'how long, O God! how long? . . . How long . . . shall the unbeliever triumph, and thy people be a jest and a bye word?'" Unmoved, the Frenchman seizes his last remaining object of value, the family teraphim (household shrine). After he departs, the young man "cursed the Nazarenes, and prayed in fervent tones that he might have the power to crush them, and vowed by the ineffable name of Jehovah to lose no opportunity of despoiling their wealth, and trampling down, yea, utterly bruising, their black and unsparing and unbelieving hearts." "Here," declares the narrator, "was a servant fit for the great master—here a champion fit for the great cause. His wrongs . . . would make him a faithful and very zealous foeman of the Nazarene of whatever nation. Here was, at length, the man, the long hoped, the long sought, who should build up the temple of the Lord, and make Israel and Judah feared and obeyed in all the quarters of the earth."

The phantom narrator therefore makes himself visible ("clad in the flowing robes of the far East," he is "pallid as a corpse . . . with hoary hair and beard" and "great black eyes, that shot forth lurid fires, upon which no mortal could look and not tremble"). "I spake the words of power, and the talisman was once more committed to a man of my persecuted race," on this occasion in the form of "a ring holding the keys of his rifled drawers." "I gave to that ring the influence and might of the signet of the wise Solomon. Having done this, I commanded the young man to name some wish for instant accomplishment; and ere he had thrice, according to my instructions, whirled the ring upon his forefinger, steps were heard." A man enters (later revealed to be a prince), weighed down with a huge bag of gold, which he entrusts to the young man. Needless to say, it contains "*the very sum for which he had wished aloud while making his first essay of the power of the talisman.*"

"Men of the accursed and plundering race!" the narrator exclaims, revealing at last the identity of the chosen one:

> Ye whose estates were within a brief space to have been within his grasp; ye, whose equipages and whose liveried lacquies I so lately saw following to his premature grave the man of Israel whom I thus enabled to war upon ye in your vulnerable quarter,—accursed and detested Nazarenes—the young Israelite, to whom I thus committed the Talis-man, and who thus early and thus fully experienced its mighty power— he who for years despoiled you of the gold which ye make to yourselves, even as a god—that man whom ye fawned upon, even while you hated him, and knew that he despised you—that man was NATHAN MEYER [*sic*] ROTHSCHILD. [He] waxed wealthy, more wealthy than any who had gone before him, his riches astonished the gentiles and very justly they said, such amazing wealth could not be amassed by one man, in so short a time by any human agency—they were right, it was the agency of the talisman . . .

There then follows a brief but classic mythologised account of Nathan's rise from the ruins of looted Frankfurt to fame and fortune. "He came by my direction to this paradise of loan-contracting and speculating fools, and became the leviathan of the money markets of Europe . . . the loan contractor, the jobber, and the money lender of the gentile kings." When Napoleon (encouraged by the narrator) invaded Russia, "Rothschild was right speedy to make [his] ruin utter and inevitable—not to be repaired." When the Emperor returned from Elba, "by whom was his hope blasted? . . . simply by Nathan Meyer [*sic*] Rothschild armed with the Talisman." The British government needed money not only to pay Wellington's army at Waterloo, but also to bribe "the Generals and the Senators of France" to desert Napoleon. "There was but one man on earth *who both* COULD and *would* provide the millions of golden pounds, required for the instant purposes of the English minister.— *That man was* ROTHSCHILD. By my instructions, he let the Minister have the hard gold . . ."

But all this, it transpires, was for a higher purpose: for Nathan lent the money only "on one condition . . . the re-establishment of Judah's kingdom—the rebuild-ing of thy towers, Oh! Jerusalem!":

> That most elaborate of bad jokes, history, will, no doubt, say that the Jew Rothschild lent the Nazarene elder called Lord Liverpool, the sum necessary to crush Napoleon Buonaparte, in consideration of some such Judean motive as 25 per cent interest. The writers of history, in that case, will, as usual, lie . . . Rothschild was commanded to lend the

> money . . . [in return for] the restoration of Judea to our ancient race;
> the guarantee of England for the independence of the kingdom of Judea
> . . . In twelve hours, the millions were in the possession of the minister,
> and a secret agreement, guaranteed by the sign manual of royalty, was in
> the possession of Rothschild, for the restoration of Judea in 21 years
> from the day on which Napoleon should finally be driven from France.

And here is the twist in the tale:

> This very year my task should have been completed; *would* have been
> completed, but he, Rothschild . . . at the twelfth hour proved false . . .
> His long round of success (unchecked save once when I reproved his
> presumption with the loss of a hundred thousand pounds in a single
> day's business in Spanish Stock) . . . made him more and more purse-
> proud . . . [so] that it was rather with grief than surprise that I recently
> heard from his own lips that he had basely sold the agreement for the
> restoration of Judea for the promise of a petty English Emancipation
> Bill for our people, and a petty English peerage for himself. This delec-
> table job, this high-minded bargain, was to be completed in the ensuing
> years, by which time the purse-proud, haughty renegade reckoned upon
> being worth 5,000,000 £ of money. He was already worth above four.

But of course, having betrayed his master, these vain dreams could only be
dashed. "His *talisman* disappeared, and I took care he should know it had disappeared forever. He never ventured upon the Exchange again, or the scribe who wrote
his will should have been saved much trouble and time."

> Did I give him the talisman, to enable him like Sampson to Gideon to
> intrude his family and found a peerage among the Normans? or to stifle
> his conscience with the weight of riches? or to flatter it with ostentatious
> charities? No Israelite can put his hand to the plough of this great work,
> look back and live!

In this bizarre fantasy, Nathan's death therefore becomes his punishment for his
failure to fulfil his promise to restore Palestine to the Jews; and the narrator moves
on in search of a new "heaven-appointed champion" to bear the talisman. Like a
Jewish version of the Nibelung saga, with its magic ring which corrupts as it
empowers, the story of the "Hebrew talisman" vividly illustrates the mystique that
as early as 1840 had begun to surround the career of Nathan Rothschild and his
brothers.

It is a good illustration of the wide currency of such legends that, shortly after
Nathan's death an American paper—evidently not a Jewish one—reported that

> "an extra number of watchmen, after the interment, will be placed at the
> grave for a length of time, to prevent the committal of any sacrilegious
> act towards the deceased." We suppose that this is a hint to "our peo-
> plesh" [*sic*] to keep their fingers off the fingerer of millions. A rumor is
> current that a large sum is bid for one of his ogles—in the hope that a
> "Jew's eye" would be worth a fortune.[73]

As Nathan Rothschild died, a myth was born which was to prove as enduringly
potent and dangerous as any myth of the nineteenth century.

Succession

To whom—in reality—did the "talisman" of Rothschild leadership pass on the death of "the commanding general?" The traditional assumption has been that the youngest of the five brothers, James, immediately inherited Nathan's mantle. That was his friend Heine's view. "Since the death of his distinguished brother in England, all the political significance of the House of Rothschild" was concentrated in his hands, he wrote not long afterwards. "The head, or rather the brain, of this family is Baron James, a remarkable man . . ."[74] It is not difficult to see why Heine assumed this. In an earlier piece written in March 1841, he had portrayed James only half-ironically as a kind of financial emperor, literally holding court in the rue Laffitte at the centre of "a labyrinth of halls, a barracks of wealth." Indeed, he noticed that James—in imitation of his brother Nathan—had begun to decorate his office with "busts of all the European monarchs who have contracted loans from his firm."[75] Like Nathan too, James was an intimidating figure in this, his natural habitat. "One must have respect for this man," Heine went on, "if only because of the respect he inspires in others":

> I like best to visit him in the offices of his banking house, where I can philosophically observe people—not only the Chosen People, but all the others too—bow and scrape before him. There you may watch a twisting and bending of backbones such as the most accomplished acrobat would find difficult. I have seen people who twitched convulsively when they drew near the great Baron as though they had touched a Voltaic battery. Even while approaching the door of his private office many experience a thrill of awe such as Moses once felt on Mount Horeb when he realised that he was standing on holy ground. And just as Moses then removed his shoes, so many a broker or commission agent who dared to enter Rothschild's inner sanctum would willingly remove his boots if he were not afraid that the odour of his feet might give offence.

"That inner sanctum is a remarkable place indeed," Heine continued; "it inspires sublime thoughts and feelings, like the sight of the ocean or the starry heavens. Here we may see the littleness of man and the greatness of God."

Of course, Heine was letting his comic imagination run away with him completely when he described "a stock exchange speculator" doffing his hat respectfully before James's "mighty" chamber pot; or an unidentified friend offering to "give half his nose to purchase" the honour of lunch with the Baron.[76] But the recollections of just such a minor denizen of the bourse, Ernest Feydeau, vividly confirm the quasi-regal status James enjoyed in Paris, an irascible despot in a chaotic court, besieged from nine in the morning until the bourse closed at four by a procession of sycophantic brokers, jobbers and assorted hangers-on. James, recalled Feydeau (who visited the rue Laffitte regularly in the 1850s),

> felt obliged to receive all these sullen, busy people, sometimes sickeningly banal, almost all of them obsequious in their manner, dull in their solicitations, servile in their flattery. Leaning back in his chair, he absent-mindedly took the quotation handed to him by each of these uninteresting beings, who filed from door to door in front of his desk,

barely cast a glance over it, sometimes allowing himself the malicious pleasure of dropping it in his wastepaper basket, usually giving it back to whoever had presented it to him and passing on to another.

As he ran this depressing gauntlet day after day, Feydeau never ceased to marvel at the "truly infernal din, the bewildering disorder in the middle of which the baron found the means of handling—every day, and without an instant of respite—the most colossal financial operations." The office was filled with

> the deafening and unceasing cacophony, the incessant racket produced by the banging of doors, the coming and going of employees carrying despatches or requesting signatures. The importunities of the brokers' clerks and the jobbers looking for orders added no little noise to the tumult, which gave the office of "Monsieur le baron" an air akin to the Tower of Babel. Here all the tongues of the world were spoken, including Hebrew. A crowd of friends of all three sexes—men, women and beggars—followed one after the other throughout the day, all in quest of news. There were jewellers opening their cases of precious stones before the baron's ailing eyes, porcelain dealers and art dealers coming to offer their choicest items. Pretty women wove their way everywhere, soliciting for information—or something else. And across this merciless and incessant procession, while the brain of the toiling millionaire must have been bursting under the accumulation of figures and calculations, the youngest of his sons—a large and chubby-cheeked child whom I can still picture—would periodically charge in, using his father's cane as a horse, and blowing on his trumpet like the angel of the valley of J[eh]osaphat.
>
> And the poor baron did not utter a word of complaint, did not so much as frown.

He "did not even have the right to eat and sleep in peace. From five in the morning, in winter and in summer, the bringers and takers of news besieged his door . . . When business required it, he dined with his entire family in a small room beside his office, seasoning his meal with stock exchange quotations, while the procession of brokers continued round his dinner table with merciless persistence." Indeed, at times James seemed to Feydeau less a king holding court than a prisoner of his own work ethic. What else could explain the willingess of a man who was already so rich to continue working under such gruelling conditions but "a singular tyranny of habit, as much as a commendable sentiment of professional ambition?"

Ultimately, however, James was more to be abhorred for his tyranny towards others—including Feydeau himself—than pitied:

> One of [his] malicious habits . . . consisted in not saying a word, not even lifting his eyes to look at the intermediary, leaving him there, with a look of embarrassment, his hat in his hand and standing on one leg, and passing his quotation successively to all the members of his family, who paid scarcely any more attention to it than he had. One day, when he had played this wretched trick on me, and as I was showing, despite myself, some impatience, he felt obliged to pay me a courtesy, after his fashion, in the charitable aim of calming me down. It was the month of January, and on the table there was a dish full of large, white strawber-

ries. With his fork he picked the most appetising of these strawberries, the one which lay on the top of the pile, and, presenting it to me as he might have done to a parrot, said:

"Vould you like von?"

Feydeau was naturally mortified by this humiliating treatment, especially as James's wife and daughter were evidently witnesses to it. However, he tried to put a brave face on it:

"You are a thousand times too kind," I replied, taking a step backwards, "but I would prefer an order."

The baron was not perturbed. He nailed me cruelly by saying:

"Buy five Northern shares for cash."

The price of five Northern shares then being around 50 francs, the amount I could make from such an attractive transaction was just 12 francs and 50 centimes.

Such brutal treatment of underlings was, according to Feydeau, quite routine (a view corroborated by Alexander Herzen's description of a visit to the rue Laffitte in 1849):[77]

"You are annoying me! Dat isn't true! Leaf me in peace!" were the civilities he addressed to me . . . whenever I took it upon myself to make some observation concerning an order. It is necessary to bear in mind that because of the peculiar language which he spoke and his accent, it was not always easy to understand him.

One day, prompted by a stock market price which annoyed him, he became so angry that he tore my quotation in two, obliging me to make it up again, and called me a "blested impecile!"

Others—even fellow Jews—fared just as badly: "'Ah! Dere you are, you tamned thief of a Cherman Chew!' he said one day to one of his coreligionists, a jobber, as he came into his office . . . The unfortunate man stood crushed, deflated, speechless and blank-faced. Perhaps he took it for a compliment." The occasion when a broker named Manuel dared to speak his mind to James had become part of bourse mythology. "Good day, baron," he had said, as he entered James's office. "How are you keeping?"

"Vat's dat got to do vit you?" James had retorted cantankerously.

"You are quite right," exclaimed Manuel. "You could drop down dead as I stand here, and I would no more care than if a dog died."[78]

Small wonder so many of his Parisian contemporaries assumed that James was Nathan's heir.

Yet it is far from clear that James ever wielded the same power *within* the Rothschild family that his brother had. He was undoubtedly quick to try to impose his authority on his nephews following Nathan's death. One of the first letters he wrote to Lionel and his brothers under the new dispensation of 1836 began in no uncertain terms:

I would ask you kindly, my dear nephews, to pay a little more attention to my letters, because quite frankly I was very cross today, for I would very much have wished to continue working with London in the same way that I had done in the past with your late father, and not to have to write argumentative letters, for a business can only be managed well if one pays as much attention to the smaller business transactions as one does to the larger ones.[79]

And there followed three specific sins of omission allegedly perpetrated by the London house. Such rebukes were issued on a fairly regular basis over the next decade, with James's favourite criticism being that his nephews were too busy hunting to read, much less answer, their uncle's letters.[80] Pointed allusions to the way things had been in Nathan's day were also regularly made, not only by James but by all the brothers. "You can now see how right I was," wrote Salomon patronisingly in September 1837,

> when I wrote you about the business deals and you will now have to admit it, my dear children . . . We now have to push the business with the bills, my dear children. This is what your late father had always said. Whenever he saw that others wanted to push us out of a business deal he always wrote, "My dear brother, we have to push it through." It is all the same whether we make a loss or a profit, whether we earn something or suffer a loss, we must not, nor should we let anyone grow above our heads or we will be simply pushed aside. I hope that you will now listen to my advice, my dear nephews, and irrespective of whether we make a profit or a loss we have to push.[81]

Not long after, James wrote to point out "that in the lifetime of your dear Papa he used to give us discount notes at 2½ per cent and that, as good bills can now be freely discounted in London at 3 per cent, the other houses take advantage of it . . . so that if you wish us to be able to compete with them and do business you must discount for us on the same terms."[82] Amschel harped on the same theme.[83] He and James could only agree in 1839 that "the loss of our brother Nathan was a terrible blow and one can't expect that youngsters will get the same respect, fear and trust as do the older generation."[84]

Yet—as James's complaint about preferential discounting suggests—the most serious complaint made by the continental Rothschilds was that the London house was neglecting their interests; and, as we have seen, just the same had been alleged on a number of occasions before Nathan's death. Indeed, it might be said to testify to the success of his sons in defending their relative autonomy that this charge was being heard again within just over a year of his death.[85] It was frequently repeated thereafter. In September 1839, for example, James accused the London house of collecting half the profits on their business in Spain but leaving the Paris house to run all the risks. "I think that it is only right and proper," he complained irritably, "that we share the other business operations where the Paris House runs just as much of the risk as does London, and that no House has any advantage over the other, for as soon as one House notices such behaviour in the other this will generate a feeling of mistrust and everything will then simply collapse, God forbid." A week later he repeated his grievance. "As long as I am alive," he told Nat, "I will never countenance that one of our Houses should seek to achieve an advantage over another or perpetrate an injustice [against another]." But "when you [meaning the London house] see that a deal is going well then you say, 'Let us keep it here,' whereas if it is not going well then you give a share of it to the Paris House. My dear and good Nat, this sort of attitude acts as a dampener and only gives rise to annoying correspondence."[86] Such minor disputes about the collective accounts between the houses became more frequent.[87] There was also friction in 1840 and 1841, when both James and Amschel accused their nephews of sending bills to rival banks in Paris and Frankfurt.[88]

For their part, the younger Rothschilds were often irritated by the older. "I assure you that it is a great bother to arrange with people who are so very sententious about money affairs," grumbled Anthony to Lionel, at a time when all four of his uncles seemed to be taking an inordinate interest in his marriage plans. "I assure you that although Uncle Charles is your father in law, that the less one has to do with this gentleman, the better."[89] Amschel's will, which he constantly redrafted in the hope of exerting some sort of leverage over his nephews, was another source of discontent.[90]

The reality was that, in terms of resources, the London, Paris and Frankfurt houses were now quite evenly matched, so that no one of them was really in a position to dictate to the others as Nathan once had. "My very dear nephews," James had to write apologetically, following a disagreement in March 1838, "I am very pleased with you and I fervently request of you not to take my words *à la lettre* because one has to put up with such torments over here that at times one becomes very critical and discontented. My nerves are about to snap and I am easily irritated."[91] Nor was James in a position to dominate his brothers. When Amschel made one of his periodic threats to give up business on the ground of ill health, James rushed off to Frankfurt; but it was on Salomon, his son Anselm and Carl's eldest son Mayer Carl that the onus of responsibility naturally fell, reflecting the closer community of business interest between Frankfurt, Vienna and Naples.[92] When James himself was taken seriously ill in the winter of 1838–9, any thought of his playing the role of "commanding general" had to be put aside. Indeed, there were few, if any, occasions before 1848 when he explicitly opposed his elder brothers' wishes. As Nat commented when Salomon demanded a bigger share of some railway and state loan business, "here we are in the habit of giving way to Frankfurt."[93]

As in the past, the older Rothschilds sought to counteract the firm's centrifugal tendencies by appealing to the hallowed principle of fraternal "concordia": "In what has our strength been until now?" remonstrated James in 1839, when he and his nephews were once again at odds. "Only in that people knew that one place will support the other . . . [A]s you well know, the well-being of our family is closer to my heart than anything else."[94] In 1841 Amschel felt so worried about the extent of internecine friction that he sent all his brothers and nephews a passionate appeal for family unity, invoking the memory of Mayer Amschel.[95] "Let us do business again in peace and in harmony and not quarrel with each other," pleaded James the following year. "If peace reigns between us this will only bring us good fortune and blessings and both you and we should not lack anything."[96]

Perhaps wisely, it was decided when the partners met at Paris that same year to leave the 1836 agreement unaltered, as—in Hannah's words—"the Elder Brothers appear to be content with things as they are and require no change." However, she added significantly: "The counting house of each[,] having their [*sic*] own capital[,] should be independent, and they must regulate the income of each party to make all those concerned equally so[;] the Elder Members' capital being so much greater they have more to say."[97] This was also the view of her elder sons. Two years later, Lionel was able to modify the partnership agreement in precisely that way. By formally withdrawing £340,250 from their personal share of the combined capital, he and his brothers brought their proportion—and therefore the amount of annual interest they received, calculated as 3 per cent of that proportion—into line with those of their uncles, ending the situation whereby Nathan had been the biggest "share-holder."[98]

In doing so, it might be thought, Lionel was surrendering an advantage. Indeed, he surrendered even more by leaving the 1836 system intact for the distribution of the combined profits, which had specified that 10 per cent of the continental houses' profits went to the London house. "As I was quite sure that it would have given rise to disagreeable disputes or discussions," Lionel reported to his brothers, "and I am quite certain we should have got nothing by it, I of course said not a word about our having a larger share of the profits; thank God for what we have and may we have to divide as much the next time we meet."[99] However, Lionel's objective was primarily to retain the relative autonomy of the London house. His real victory was to defeat James's proposal—first put forward nearly thirty years before—that the partnership between the five houses should be made public:

> Uncle James wanted this act of partnership, without any mention of our money matters so that he might show it at Paris, in case they wanted to know who the partners of the House are—now, *as we in London always have said that our house has nothing to do with any others* we just want to avoid having any document which anyone might show, the agreement with all the money matters is not likely to be produced but one as was proposed might very easily have been made public and will therefore not be made, they immediately agreed to my observations.[100]

Thanks to Lionel, the precise nature of the relationship between the five houses remained shrouded in mystery, a secret between the partners and their lawyers. Such secrecy was a Rothschild tradition; but it seems reasonable to conclude that Lionel already preferred not be bound too tightly to the other four houses.

"Thank God for what we have": that sentiment was typical of Nathan's sons. Both Nat and Anthony had used almost exactly the same phrase just a few months before: "We must thank God for what we have got & try to keep it."[101] Indeed, it is tempting to identify a "generation gap" in entrepreneurial attitudes as one explanation for the disagreements of the 1830s and 1840s. There is no question that New Court was a more financially staid place than it had been under Nathan: there was less bond market speculation and more bill-broking for example.[102] "We prefer dealing largely with a little less profit to keeping a very large stock on hand and holding out for very high prices," wrote Nat to his brothers from Paris, one of many essentially cautious business maxims he committed to paper.[103] Exiled as he was on the other side of the Channel, he tended to interpret differences between New Court and the rue Laffitte as national in character. "The more I see," his younger brother declared when he visited Paris in 1846, "I am convinced the more, there is no place like our old New Court. Where would the rubbishy French shares be, if we did not support them? I think we may give ourselves a few airs and be as great men as others."[104] But it is hard to imagine Nathan saying such a thing. Although only sixteen years separated Lionel and his uncle James, their attitudes to business were separated by much more. For James and his brothers retained the restless, insecure drive born of the Frankfurt ghetto. "Whenever we write to you that other people are more attentive to what is going on and do more business, you immediately assume that we are trying to pick a quarrel with you," James wrote to his nephews in a somewhat pained letter of 1845. "However, I assure you, my dear nephews, I have nothing of the sort in mind, but my heart breaks when I see how everyone is trying to push us out of [every] business deal. [Even] the stone on the wall is envious and is our enemy."[105] That tendency to regard all competition as a threat was not something the next generation could inherit.

Yet even without such differences of attitude, there would probably have been increased friction between the five houses, for it was the inevitable price of success. By the mid-1830s each of the five Rothschild houses had securely established itself as the pre-eminent force in the public finances of its respective base country. Admittedly, the great powers were inclined to draw in their horns in the wake of the revolutionary crisis of 1830–33. With the exception of the 1835 loan to indemnify the West Indian slave-owners, Britain, France and Austria did not borrow big sums until 1839–41. Nevertheless, the experience of the revolutionary alarms of the early 1830s had cemented the links between the three main Rothschild houses and the states where they were based. On the part of Lionel and his brothers, there was evidently a degree of emotional identification with England. Salomon too, influenced by his growing intimacy with Metternich, was increasingly inclined to give consideration to Austrian imperial interests. Even James, for all his disdain for the ministers of Louis Philippe, could not wholly avoid taking national priorities into account. Such national identifications did not greatly matter if peace prevailed in Europe. But when the interests of the great powers clashed, as they periodically did, it was less and less easy for the Rothschilds to remain neutral.

The Rothschilds' natural response to the reduced capital needs of the great powers was to seek business elsewhere. However, there were few regions of the world in which the European powers had no interest, and no regions in which their interests coincided perfectly. In four areas—Iberia, America, the Low Countries and the Near East—the challenge was to arrive at a policy which was in the Rothschilds' collective interest even when the national interests of their "local" governments were in conflict. This was difficult enough while Nathan was still in charge; after his death it became all but impossible.

III

Uncles and Nephews

TWELVE

Love and Debt

> *[T]he very society which you think is today rejecting you*
> *because you are not being very friendly to it over a sister who*
> *is behaving against the wishes of her family, that very same*
> *society will be just as friendly to you and will hold you in*
> *even greater esteem when they see that you stick to your princi-*
> *ples . . .*   —JAMES TO NAT, JULY 16, 1839[1]

O n April 29, 1839, a catastrophe befell the Rothschilds—or so it seemed to the
family at the time. Less than three years after the unexpected death of Nathan
at the very height of his powers, his second daughter, Hannah Mayer, renounced
Judaism to marry a Christian.

In every other respect, the Hon. Henry Fitzroy might have been thought a perfectly suitable, indeed desirable, spouse for the daughter of a German-Jewish immigrant who owed his fortune to "trade." True, he was the younger son of Lord
Southampton, and therefore unlikely to inherit much in the way of a title or land;
on the other hand, at the age of thirty-two he was already (after Magdalen, Oxford,
and Trinity, Cambridge) Deputy Lieutenant for Northamptonshire and MP for
Lewes, with realistic prospects of one day achieving political office. Not that this was
a consideration in the mind of Hannah Mayer. At some point in 1838 she had fallen
in love with the dark-haired, blue-eyed young man. It was an apostasy for which she
would never wholly be forgiven.

The Crime and Punishment of Hannah Mayer

In the classic topos of the nineteenth-century novel, it is the aristocratic family
which disapproves of the mercantile match. Fitzroy's family undoubtedly did disapprove, cutting off his allowance.[2] However, they did not disapprove nearly as violently as the Rothschilds. This was not, in fact, the first time Hannah Mayer had
formed an attachment to a Gentile: before her father's death, according to one
account, Prince Edmond de Clary had proposed to her in Paris. Then Nathan had
bluntly dismissed the idea; and when his brother James heard of her new affair with
Fitzroy, he was no more sympathetic:

Well, my dear Lionel, your letters wherein you speak about the distressing circumstances and the love affair of your sister Hannah Mayer break
our heart. You can imagine why this is so because nothing could possibly be more disastrous for our family, for our continued well-being, for
our good name and for our honour than such a decision, God forbid. I
hardly even dare mention it. To renounce our religion, the religion of
our [father] Rabbi Mayer [Amschel] Rothschild of blessed memory, the
religion which, thank God, made us so great.[3]

Yet James was from the outset pessimistic about the likelihood of stopping her a
second time. This was not so much because he felt he lacked Nathan's patriarchal
power; for Nathan had formally stated in his will that his younger daughters could
marry only with the consent of their mother and brothers, with his own brothers
having the final, binding word in the event of a disagreement. The real problem was
that the financial sanctions intended to enforce this clause were an insufficient deter-
rent. On her father's death, Hannah Mayer had received £12,500, having already
been given the same sum on attaining her majority, as well as a further £50,000
which was invested in the family bank to yield 4 per cent per annum. Had she married with her family's blessing, she would have received another £50,000 as a dowry;
but this was money she evidently felt she could do without.[4] James advised his
nephews to inform their uncle Salomon of Hannah's intentions, but was doubtful
whether he would be able "to do any more good as far as this issue is concerned than
I can." He also agreed to come to London before February 20 to try to dissuade his
niece in person. "But," he wrote gloomily,

whether our trip will turn out to be successful and what kind of impression this will make on the public, this I can't possibly predict, or whether
Hannah Mayer will take any notice of our well-meaning advice when
she well knows that the only purpose of our visit to London is to frus-
trate her love adventure. I am more inclined to believe that in view
of this girl's independent character we are more likely to exasperate her
even more than convince her to abandon this ill-starred love affair.
However, I want nothing more than the well-being of our family
and nothing will prevent me from going to London . . . I am extremely
concerned.[5]

In fact, James was prevented from visiting England by a bout of illness. Instead,
he suggested that Hannah Mayer—chaperoned by her mother—come to stay with
him in Switzerland, where he planned to continue his convalescence.[6] This suggested "diversion" came too late. The very day after James sent his invitation, the
wedding took place at St George's in Hanover Square. Only her brother Nat
attended the service, the bride's mother having escorted her no further than the
church gates. A few weeks later the scandal made it into *The Times:*

It is confirmed that the condition imposed upon Miss Rothschild on her
marrying the Hon. Mr. Fitzroy was that she should embrace the Christian religion. This is the first instance of a member of the Rothschild
family abandoning the faith of their fathers, a circumstance which
makes the deeper impression at their native place [Frankfurt], as they
had hitherto distinguished themselves by their adherence to the Jewish

creed. It is said that the bride's uncles are by no means pleased with a match which renders a change of religion necessary.[7]

This last was an understatement. "I admit quite frankly," wrote an incandescent James from Paris,

> that the story about Hannah Mayer made me so ill that I did not have the courage to pick up a pen and write about this matter. She has unfortunately robbed our whole family of its pride and caused us such harm that it can no longer be redressed. You say, my dear Nat, that she has found everything except for religion. However, I believe that [religion] means everything. Our good fortune and our blessings depend upon it. We shall therefore wipe her from our memory and never again during my lifetime will I or any other member of our family see or receive her. We now want to wish her all the best and banish her from our memory as if she had never existed.[8]

Even her own mother echoed these sentiments. "The first impressions and regrets experienced on account of the recent Marriage," she told her son Nat, "is [sic] only exceeded by a desire to avoid any similar circumstances so very much against the habits and inclinations of us all." Although she confided that she would "be most happy to receive daily bulletins of Domestic as well as all other concerns in which I so strongly participate if there should be any news from an Individual who still so much interests me," that individual had irrevocably "separated herself from me."[9] Nat—and he alone—stood by Hannah Mayer. In July he wrote to James arguing that his sister had done "no more than marry 'a Christian in a Christian country.'" The response this elicited from his uncle deserves to be quoted at length for the light it sheds on the older generation's attitudes to the subject. "From the beginning," thundered James, who had evidently been nursing his wrath, "I correctly predicted that . . . this most unfortunate matter . . . would disrupt the unity of our family . . . and I can tell you that this event has made me so ill that I honestly think that I may not survive it":

> I would like to know what more one could do than to abandon one's own religion and publicly declare that since the age of fifteen one never had any thought of doing anything else. My dear Nat, both as your friend and Uncle I want to give you my very frank and honest opinion . . . We are determined that, as long as the Almighty grants us good health, neither we nor my children will again come into contact with Hannah Mayer, for it is not only one thing [which has brought us to this decision] but so many that I could fill endless pages.

In part, James's argument was about the structure of authority within the family and the obedience the younger generation owed to their elders:

> What sort of an example will it set for our children when a girl says, "I will marry against the wish of my family?" I don't even want to take the notion of religion into account . . . I should then be expected to welcome and entertain this girl as if nothing at all had happened? Why should my children, or my children's children, ever follow the wishes of their parents if they don't get punished?

But "the main point," as he put it, was "religion":

> I and the rest of our family have . . . always brought our offspring up
> from their early childhood with the sense that their love is to be con-
> fined to members of the family, that their attachment for one another
> would prevent them from getting any ideas of marrying anyone other
> than one of the family so that the fortune would stay inside the family.
> Who will give me any assurance that my own children will do what I tell
> them if they see that there is no punishment forthcoming? What if my
> own daughter, after she has married, should say, "I am miserable because
> I didn't marry a Duke although I had enough money to do so, and I see
> that, despite the fact that this woman renounced her religion, and
> despite the fact that [she] married against the wishes of her family, she is
> nevertheless accepted [by the family]. It would have been the same with
> me?" Do you really think that all the nicely conceived projects [will
> come to fruition]—that is, that Mayer will marry Anselm's daughter,
> that Lionel's daughter will marry the child of another member of the
> family so that the great fortune and the Rothschild name will continue
> to be honoured and transmitted [to future generations]—if one doesn't
> put a stop to this?

Finally, James added some reflections on the social implications of the marriage
(evidently in response to points made by Nat):

> Of course, one could perhaps take some steps to prevent this from hap-
> pening but society may well look askance at such measures. This may
> indeed be the case but I personally don't entirely share this opinion . . .
> [T]he very society which you think is today rejecting you because you
> are not being very friendly to it over a sister who is behaving against the
> wishes of her family, that very same society will be just as friendly to you
> and will hold you in even greater esteem when they see that you stick to
> your principles and are not prepared to be upset by empty words. The
> honest and upright man will always value a man of similar character.
> Adieu.[10]

Admittedly, James added a disclaimer to this impassioned outburst. Nat "should
view this as my, and only my, thoughts and feelings and don't think that I want in
any way to influence your mother or any other member of the family. It would be
unseemly and I don't wish to do so. Everyone is entitled to do what he wants." But
these were empty words. He concluded by asking Nat to show his eldest brother
Lionel his letter "and I am sure that he shares my opinion." For the first time since
his brother's death, James was speaking in the unmistakable tone of the new head of
the family, secure in the knowledge that the majority of its members were equally
dismayed, if not more so. A letter dated the following day from Anthony—who was
in Paris during the crisis—confirms this impression:

> What they wish us to do is not to receive H[annah] M[ayer] for the pre-
> sent and that is easily understood. They say: a sister is married against
> the consent of one's family; if after two months you will receive her—
> what example will it have upon the remainder part of the family[?] They
> say: will my daughter, who sees her cousin who married against the con-

sent of all her family received by them, will she marry whom I like[?]—
no, she will also fall in love with a Christian and God knows what the
boys will also do . . . I recommend you . . . now for your own sake
and also to keep the union amongst us—not to receive H. M. for the
present.[11]

Nat made a final effort to defend his sister, but was firmly sat on by his uncle.[12]

The most striking point about James's response is, of course, the way he equated
"religion" with endogamy: "pride in religion" meant, if his words are to be taken literally, intermarriage within the Rothschild family "so that the fortune would stay
inside the family." We may well ask how much this eminently practical principle had
to do with "religion" at all. For the thrust of James's argument was not that younger
Rothschilds should marry only other Jews; it was that they should marry only *other
Rothschilds.* By encouraging other members of the family to follow their own inclinations, Hannah Mayer's rebellion had jeopardised "all the nicely conceived projects
. . . that Mayer will marry Anselm's daughter, that Lionel's daughter will marry the
child of another member of the family." In Disraeli's *Coningsby,* it is said of the
younger Sidonia that "no earthly considerations would ever induce him to impair
that purity of race on which he prides himself" by marrying a Christian.[13] Yet in
reality "earthly considerations" counted for as much in the eyes of some Rothschilds
as any racial or religious exclusivity. James came close to admitting this in his letter:
"Don't imagine, my dear Nat, that I have taken to playing the role of a religious
man, but I must admit that I take a lot of pride in my religion and very much wish
that my children will do the same." This tallies with what we know of his religiosity:
as Nat was well aware, James was far from strict in his observance. Like his brothers,
he dutifully played his part within the Jewish community, supporting the Society for
the Encouragment and Aid of [Jewish] Indigents in 1843 and asking the Education
Minister "why no Jews had been appointed to the academic council of Bordeaux" in
1847. He campaigned as energetically as any Rothschild to improve the civil rights
of Jewish communities outside France (where full religious equality had been
secured in 1830). But fundamentally his loyalty to his religion was clannish: few, if
any, Jews were on a par with the Rothschilds; nevertheless, every Rothschild had to
be a Jew.

James's appeal was heeded. When—just months after Hannah Mayer's marriage—Anthony was suspected of harbouring similar intentions, his uncle Amschel
leant on him heavily to abide by the "nicely conceived project" that he marry one of
his Montefiore cousins, Louisa (sometimes called Louise). This time the pressure
was effective, not least because Anthony was at once less romantic and more biddable than his sister. "Uncle A. was a regular bother asking me about getting married,"
he complained to his brothers, "and writing to Uncle S. that I only waited until his
death to marry a Christian . . . I told him quite short that if Aunt Henrietta [Mon-
tefiore] would cash up, I was ready, when he said of course he would not advise me
[to do so] without Louis[a] had the same fortune as Joseph and Nathaniel. So, I said
very well, and I believe he wrote to that effect—for later we left much better
friends."[14] James was apparently less worried about Anthony than Amschel. "I am
absolutely convinced," he wrote from Naples, in a letter which shows how much
attention the uncles were now paying to the marriage question,

that Anthony does not intend to marry the girl. He is a very weak person but I don't think that, even for a moment, such a silly idea could enter his head. He is weak and is easily led and I give you my word that I don't treat this matter lightly and when I am back in Paris again I will do everything in my power to bring this affair to an end. When I was in Paris I often discussed this matter with him but as you well know, my dear Amschel, people would much rather lay down in a ready-made and warm bed. Regrettably, he considers the whole matter to be rather [?humorous]. Well, you can rest assured that one can no longer tell the youngsters what to do as one could previously. As our good [brother] Salomon is coming to Paris too, God willing, so we will deal with this matter then . . . I am delighted to see that the discussions with our brother Carl's son have been successfully concluded and that everything will be well, God willing.[15]

This last allusion was to the parallel project to marry Mayer Carl to Louise, Hannah Mayer's younger sister.

In due course, James's confidence was amply vindicated. "I am pleased to note, my dear Anthony, that you are so in love," he was able to write approvingly in November 1839; a few days later came the announcement of his engagement to Louisa Montefiore; by February they were married and the recipients of pointedly warm congratulations.[16] Three years later—as planned—Mayer Carl married his cousin Louise in London.[17] In August of the same year Nat married another cousin, James's daughter Charlotte.[18] The contrast between this last, exuberant occasion and the miserable weddings of 1836 and 1839 could not have been more complete:

The ceremony was performed [at Ferrières] in a little temple erected for that purpose in the garden, the road to it strewn with rose-leaves. After the ceremony some went back to Paris, but the greater part remained, with whist, billiards, walking in the garden etc. . . . Billy & I had a bottle of champagne. At 7 we dined in the orangery, which was beautifully arranged. Lots of toasts were drunk. Your Uncle James proposed the King's health in a very good speech.[19]

A pattern had been established—or rather, re-established—which would be continued into the 1870s.

It is a moot point how far such arranged, endogamous marriages were happy. James's marriage to Betty seemed to many contemporaries to have paired beauty with the beast: "She handsome—he vulgar," was how the British diplomat Lord William Russell summed it up in 1843;[20] others were struck by Betty's more refined manners and cultural sophistication. (This was roughly the way Heinrich Heine saw the couple, though he never underrated James's intellect; and it is not too far removed from the portrayal of Nucingen and his wife by Balzac—though he never underrated Madame. Nucingen's fundamental toughness.) Yet Betty's letters suggest a genuine and deep affection for her husband and there is no evidence whatever of marital strife.

In London, Lionel and his cousin Charlotte, who were married in 1836, also seemed ill matched to some outsiders. He was an industrious, conscientious man, dedicated to his father's firm and to the cause of Jewish emancipation, but not passionate in his personal relations, nor sophisticated in his cultural tastes. When Disraeli says of Sidonia, "he was susceptible of deep emotions, but not for individuals," we are perhaps not far from the true Lionel.[21] She, by contrast, was not only very good-looking, but one of the most intellectually gifted Rothschilds of her genera- tion. It is hard to believe, judging from the frequently mordant, not to say down- right malicious tone of her voluminous letters and diaries—with their troubling subtext of frustrated boredom—that she was wholly fulfilled as "Baroness de Roth- schild," wife, mother, hostess and do-gooder. "Ever since I became your wife," she wrote to her husband in a rare outburst, "I have had to do what others want, never what I would like to do. Pray that I shall be compensated in Heaven."[22] Disraeli gives some hints of this in his fictionalised relationship between the Neuchatels in *Endymion:*

> Adrian had married, when very young, a lady selected by his father. The selection seemed a good one. She was the daughter of a most eminent banker, and had herself, though that was of slight importance, a large portion. She was a woman of abilities, highly cultivated . . . And yet Mrs. Neuchatel was not a contented spirit; and though she appreciated the great qualities of her husband and viewed him even with reverence as well as affection, she scarcely contributed to his happiness as much as became her. And for this reason . . . Mrs Neuchatel had imbibed not merely a contempt for money, but an absolute hatred of it . . . In one respect the alliance between Adrian and his wife was not an unfortunate one . . . Adrian . . . was so absorbed by his own great affairs, was a man at the same time of so serene a temper and so supreme a will, that the over-refined fantasies of his wife produced not the slightest effect on the course of his life.[23]

Yet no matter what private miseries were inflicted as a consequence of the inter- marriage strategy—and we can rarely do more than guess at them—all concerned felt or came to feel precisely the sense of clannish collective identity which it had been the intention of their elders to foster. Nothing illustrates this better than the subtly retributive way Hannah Mayer was subsequently treated by the rest of the family, and not least by Charlotte herself.

Hannah Mayer was not ostracised forever. By 1848, if not before, she and her husband were on good enough terms with her eldest brother to receive presents from him for their children, Arthur and Blanche, and to invite him to visit them at their house at Garboldisham. More surprisingly, Betty reported to her son in 1849 that she had "made my peace with HM" by "invit[ing] her to my place" when the Fitzroys visited Paris.[24] But within the family circle Hannah Mayer was always regarded with that disdain generally reserved by the Victorians for "fallen women"; and, like good Victorians, her sister Louise and her cousin and sister-in-law Char- lotte could not resist interpreting every misfortune that befell her as a kind of divine punishment. In 1852 they registered with grim satisfaction Hannah Mayer's "fury" when her husband was passed over by Lord Aberdeen for the post of Secretary at the Admiralty.[25] When the Fitzroys' son Arthur died six years later (the victim of a fall from a pony), even their niece Constance—then just fifteen—could "not help thinking that all the misfortune and distress which have overwhelmed poor Aunt Hannah Mayer have been a punishment for having deserted the faith of the fathers and for having married without her mother's consent. All the grief that she caused to that mother she now feels doubly herself."[26] The death of Henry Fitzroy himself the following year made the portrait of nemesis all but complete. All that was now lacking was a suitably wretched end for his widow and their daughter Blanche. Neither was long in coming—or so it seemed to Charlotte de Rothschild, whose letters to her youngest son Leopold chronicled with outward sympathy and inward relish each step of the Fitzroys' decline and fall.

From February 1864 onwards, Hannah Mayer was seriously ill: Charlotte reported that she had "an enormous swelling on her back, like a hump of a camel" and "looked perfectly awful—her face white and shrunk, and furrowed with deep lines expressive of intense suffering. It made one's heart break to see her in such pain. The swelling on her back is perfectly enormous, and quite hot. Yet shivering and trembling with pain, she would talk of nothing but parties . . . Her ideas are constantly running upon marriage."[27] Hannah Mayer's sole preoccupation henceforth was to find a suitable husband for her daughter. As her Rothschild relatives could hardly fail to notice, all the "candidates" considered were Christians; moreover, there was an obvious discrepancy between her ideal—"she would not hear of" Lords Loughborough, Sefton and Coventry though the Marquess of Blandford was considered acceptable—and the realistic contenders. Blanche might be pretty and artistically talented but, cut off from her Rothschild relations and low in the Fitzroy pecking-order, she was no prize catch.[28]

The successful suitor proved to be the artist and architect Sir Coutts Lindsay, a prosperous but Bohemian figure twice her age with a Scottish estate, ten thousand a year, a suspiciously close friendship with Lady Virginia Somers and a shady retinue of plebeian mistresses and bastards. When Charlotte paid one of her numerous half-patronising, half-prurient visits to her sister-in-law's house in Upper Grosvenor Square—ostensibly to offer her congratulations—she:

> found her very ill and completely overcome by her conflicting feelings; she had been crying and sobbing almost shrieking, and is indeed so much to be pitied that the congratulations died on my lips. The marriage itself, *ceci entre nous*, does not satisfy her completely, for the bridegroom elect is forty, and has grey locks, and perhaps her ambition would have soared higher, and selected a nobleman with a grand title for her daughter.[29]

With poetic justice, Blanche had followed Hannah Mayer's own example, set twenty-five years before, by choosing a husband for love and in spite of her mother's wishes. Though the latter sought to make the best of a bad job—Sir Coutts, she insisted, was "the most fascinating person I ever met"—Charlotte omitted no defect in her back-handed descriptions of the bridegroom (he was "picturesque," "one-sided," his gifts to his fiancée were miserly, and so on).

Nor was this the end of Hannah Mayer's "punishment." From the moment of her engagement, Blanche appeared to distance herself from her ailing mother, and cut herself off almost completely from the Rothschilds. According to Charlotte—who poured pity over her sister-in-law while simultaneously kindling antipathy towards the new "Lady Lindsay"—she visited her mother's bedside as infrequently as possible. She was (variously) "utterly heartless," "the heartless bride," "a heartless serpent," "quite affected and namby pamby," "an icicle," "a horrible humbug and heartless hypocrite," "that heartless, incomprehensible woman," "the unnatural daughter" and "that horrible Blanche." The object of this torrent of vituperation was "immensely happy at being Lady Lindsay, and far too much so, to feel deep anxiety for her suffering and perhaps dying mother."[30] When Charlotte paid a call on her, she found "the heartless staring creature giggling and grinning and simpering while she asked after her dying mother as if the poor sufferer had had a mere cold."

By mid-November the end was in sight. "Poor Aunt H.M.'s married life and widowed existence have become one chain of such uninterrupted sorrow and suffering," she told her son, "that, for her sake, one can hardly wish to see her days prolonged. As for Blanche—no one need waste a moment's pity upon her.—She is either a monster or an enigma. It is less disagreeable to look upon her in the light of the latter, and not to un-riddle her character." "I feel very sad," she added the next day, "when I think of such a life of torture, and of a deathbed so lonely. Blanche arrives at 5 o'clock in the evening, stays five minutes, and then departs. Do not mention this heartless behaviour as it is a perfect disgrace to our family, and must shock the domestics from whom constant fidelity is expected." And so it went on. "Upon the plea that the invalid is too weak to bear even her adored presence beyond five or six minutes in the course of the day, [she] never puts her foot into the house before 5 o'clock in the evening, viz not before the shades of evening put an end to her drawing, in Sir C. Lindsay's studio; then she arrives novel in hand, while her unfortunate mother carries on the unequal battle with disease and death."[31]

On the night of December 1, 1864, Hannah Mayer finally expired. Her life had been, Charlotte reflected, using carefully chosen words, "a long martyrdom"; indeed, in her last weeks she had sometimes looked "like one of the lovely martyrs so much admired in Italian picture-galleries and churches."[32] But Charlotte, like her uncle James, did not interpret Hannah Mayer's downfall in purely religious terms: it irked her that her sister-in-law's will had omitted to dispose of £7,000 in a savings account, money which passed by default to the Lindsays.[33] The idea of Rothschild money passing into other hands still rankled, a quarter of a century after Hannah Mayer's initial lapse from grace. Retribution even followed her to the grave and beyond, for Charlotte missed no transgression on the part of Blanche Lindsay, notably her absence from her mother's funeral (where "the Duke of Grafton, Lord Charles Fitzroy and Lord Southampton, who had known and seen the deceased so little . . . never alluded to her but talked of railroads, horses etc.") and her attempt to sell the portraits she had inherited of her Rothschild grandparents ("To sell her grandmother and her grandfather; it is not to be believed"). Everything—her louche Pre-Raphaelite dresses, her widening girth, her deteriorating eyesight—could be construed as a consequence of her mother's peculiar form of original sin. And when her marriage foundered on the rocks of Lindsay's habitual infidelity, Anselm's son Ferdinand could not resist predicting that she would "repent . . . in the long run" her decision to "leave the conjugal room."[34] Even as late as 1882, it seems, Hannah Mayer's crime, though punished, had not been forgiven.

City and Country

Nothing tells us more about the nineteenth-century Rothschilds' exceptionally acute sense of kinship than their treatment of Hannah Mayer. The paradox is that her persecution coincided with an acceleration in the pace of the family's social and cultural assimilation. By not only marrying a Christian but converting to Christianity, she had crossed one of the few barriers which remained between the Rothschilds and the European social elite, and perhaps the only one which the Rothschilds themselves wished to preserve.

In his satirical "Book of Snobs," published in *Punch* in 1846–7, Thackeray cited "the Scharlachschild family at Paris, Naples, Frankfort &c." as the archetypes of the "Banking Snob," who "receives all the world into his circle," dispensing "princely hospitalities" and "entertain[ing] all the world, even the poor, at their fêtes."[35] This was not far wide of the mark. In the decade after Nathan's death, the Rothschilds greatly increased the amount of time and energy they devoted to social and cultural pursuits, with James in the vanguard. To begin with, their residences grew grander and more numerous in both town and country. In 1836 James commissioned the architect, designer and theatre producer Charles-Edmond Duponchel to reconstruct and redecorate his rue Laffitte hôtel, with money no object. The result was the quintessential millionaire's palace, combining extravagant historicist decoration with the latest modern comforts. Among Duponchel's more spectacular touches was a wood-panelled salon in the Renaissance style which was dominated by Joseph-Nicholas Robert-Fleury's series of Renaissance scenes (including Charles V in Spain, Luther preaching and Henry VIII hunting), but which also subtly juxtaposed the Rothschild arms with those of the Medici. (There was also a billiard room with a Pompeii-style mural by François-Edouard Picot.) But this was historicism with all mod cons. Central heating was provided for the ground floor salons and dining room by four brick ovens in the cellars, and all floors had running water from tanks on the top floor. There were also four large closed tanks for waste in the cellar, to say nothing of gas lighting in the form of moustached statuettes holding mock torches. Salomon's house next door was given similar treatment, as was the new hôtel Talleyrand which James acquired in 1838 in the more fashionable rue Saint-Florentin in the 8th arrondissement.[36]

The effect was evidently imposing. In 1836, after a post-theatre ball given by James to show off the redecorated rue Laffitte house, Heine admiringly described what he called "the Versailles of the absolute reign of money":

> Here everything comes together which the spirit of the sixteenth century could invent and the money of the nineteenth century could pay for; here the genius of the visual arts competes with the genius of Rothschild. The palace and its decorations have been continuously worked on for two years and the sums expended on them are said to be enormous. M. de Rothschild smiles when someone questions him about this . . . One must, however, admire the flair with which everything has been done, as much as the costliness.[37]

A Parisian journal, the *Bon Ton*, was even more impressed: the two adjacent houses "appeared to realise the tales of the thousand and one nights. Such luxury is awesome to those who do not have at their command the bourses of Naples, Paris and London."[38] "The mantels are covered in gold-fringed velvet," observed the vicomte de Launay admiringly. "The armchairs have lace antimacassars; the walls are concealed under marvellous embroidered, brocaded, spangled fabrics of such thickness and strength they could stand alone and, if needed, actually support what they cover, should the walls give way. The curtains are fabulously beautiful; they are hung double, triple, and all over the place . . . Every piece of furniture is gilded; the walls too are gilded."[39] The Austrian diplomat Apponyi, who attended the same ball as Heine, was less easily impressed: he found the Renaissance style of the new interiors "unsuitable for a hôtel in Paris; I would prefer it in a château." But even he had to admit that it was "impossible to see a better imitation:"

> The paintings are on a gold base, executed by excellent artists, the fireplaces are admirably carved. The chairs are of ormolu bronze, with very high backs, surmounted by figures holding the arms of the house of Rothschild in enamel. The carpets, the candelabras, the chandeliers, the material of the draperies with heavy tassels of gold and silver—in short, everything is in the same style; there are clocks inlaid and enamelled on azure base, solid gold vases encrusted with precious stones and fine pearls. In a word, it is a luxury which surpasses all imagination.[40]

This was what became known as *le style Rothschild*—a style, in the words of a later critic, "which combined all the richest elements of those which had preceded it . . . The heavy golden cornices, the damask hung walls, the fringed and tasselled curtains of Genoese velvet, the marble and the parquet . . . Nothing in [it] . . . was new save the gasoliers."[41]

To a twentieth-century eye, all that gas-lit gilt is oppressive; at the time it was all the rage. "It is infinitely superior to the house of his daughter-in-law [*sic*]," reported the duchesse de Dino, after seeing Salomon's "temple," "because the proportions are more elevated and larger; the luxury of it beggars belief, but it is tasteful, pure Renaissance, without any admixture of other styles . . . In the main salon, the armchairs instead of being made of gilt wood are of gilt bronze and cost a thousand francs apiece."[42] The young Disraeli concurred. "Above all spectacles," he reported to his sister Sarah from Paris in 1843, "was the ball at B[aron] Salomon de Rothschild['s]—an hotel in decoration surpassing all the palaces of Munich—a greater retinue of servants & liveries more gorgeous than the Thuilleries [*sic*]—& pineapples plentiful as blackberries. The taste of this unrivalled palace is equal to the splendour and richness of its decorations."[43] He later paid a fictionalised tribute to the Rothschild hôtels in *Coningsby*, in a passage describing Sidonia's Paris residence, which

> had received at his hands such extensive alterations, that nothing of the original decoration . . . remained . . . A flight of marble steps, ascending from a vast court, led into a hall of great dimensions, which was at the same time an orangery and a gallery of sculpture. It was illumined by a distinct, yet soft and subdued light, which harmonised with the beautiful repose of the surrounding forms, and with the exotic perfume that was wafted about. A gallery led from this hall to an inner hall of quite different character; fantastic, glittering, variegated; full of strange shapes and dazzling objects.
>
> The roof was carved and gilt in the honeycomb style prevalent in the Saracenic buildings; the walls were hung with leather stamped in rich and vivid patterns; the floor was a flood of mosaic; about were statues of negroes of human size with faces of wild expression, and holding in

their outstretched hands silver torches that blazed with an almost painful brilliancy.

From this inner hall a double staircase of white marble led to the grand suite of apartments.

These saloons, lofty, spacious, and numerous, had been decorated principally in encaustic by the most celebrated artists of Munich. The three principal rooms were only separated from each other by columns, covered with rich hangings, on this night drawn aside. The decoration of each chamber was appropriate to its purpose. On the walls of the ball room nymphs and heroes move in measure in Sicilian landscapes, or on the azure shores of the Aegean waters. From the ceiling beautiful divinities threw garlands on the guests . . . A large saloon abounded in ottomans and easy chairs . . .[44]

James also spent substantial sums on his château house outside Paris at Ferrières, turning it into a state-of-the art gentleman's country retreat. Here the theme was English. A laundry was built by the architect Joseph-Antoine Froelicher in the mock-Tudor style and in 1840 James added a model farm, sending the estate manager to England to pick up tips. He later added an English-style dairy as well as a brick-kiln and British-made machinery to make water pipes for the estate. There were also stables, a riding school and riding track, not to mention an orangerie and a new garden laid out by Placide Massey.[45] When his sister-in-law Hannah visited Ferrières in 1842 she found it "most imposing."[46] Once again, aristocratic guests like Apponyi and Princess Lieven, who came to stay two years later, were less easy to impress. According to Apponyi—though a hint of aristocratic irony is detectable here—the Princess was much impressed by "the superb laundry" James and Betty had built in the grounds, "a veritable chef-d'oeuvre of the genre, picturesque and very convenient." However, when shown to her room—once reserved for the late duc d'Orléans—the Princess complained that the mattresses were "hard and damp," so that they had to be "changed, dried, beaten, placed and replaced." Apponyi himself ridiculed the stables James had built, "a superb and totally pompous construction in the style of Louis XIII." "Perhaps it is a little too beautiful," he mused, "as this palace somewhat overwhelms the château itself." The supercilious diplomat also found fault with the pond, which he thought "too near the house," and the absence of formal gardens and flowerbeds. "Park and garden are not separated," he observed disapprovingly, "so that the game can come right into the court of the château." Yet even this most discerning of guests had to concede that the interiors "left nothing to be desired":

> Everything is in good taste and is very magnificent. There are some beautiful pictures and an infinity of beautiful things of all descriptions, suits of armour, statuettes, ewers in silver gilt, ivory or gold, enriched by pearls and precious stones, consoles in bronze, iron, silver, in old lacquer, then vases of every kind, decorated with precious stones, then antique cabinets encrusted with ivory and silver, and Florentine mosaics. The guests' rooms are comfortably furnished, without excessive luxury, but with good carpets, good settees, armchairs, mirrors, excellent beds, wash-hand basins with plenty of towels . . .[47]

Guests could also be taken to see the gardens at the Rothschilds' other châteaux at Boulogne and Suresnes. At the former, the gardens were steadily enlarged and the

The Rothschild house "zum grünen Schild" in the Frankfurt Judengasse: photograph taken c. 1869 during demolition of much of the street. Mayer Amschel acquired the left-hand half of the central gabled building in 1785.

The Elector of Hesse-Kassel entrusts his treasure to Mayer Amschel Rothschild, Gutle and their daughter Henrietta, miniature copy of a painting by Moritz Daniel Oppenheim, 1861.

Miniature of Gutle by Moritz Daniel Oppenheim.

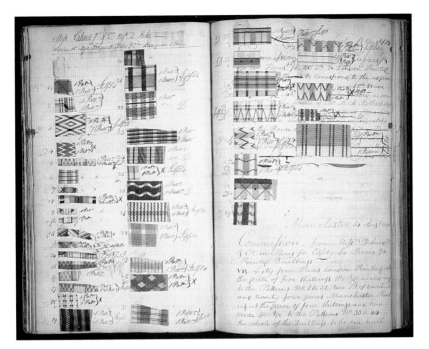

Two pages from Nathan Rothschild's sample and order book, dating from his years as a textile merchant in Manchester.

The Elector of Hesse-Kassel receives his treasure back from the five Rothschild brothers, miniature copy of a painting by Moritz Daniel Oppenheim, 1861. In commissioning these paintings, the Rothschilds were propagating their own myth: both scenes were imaginary, though the financial relationship with the Elector was real.

ABOVE Amschel von
Rothschild, by Moritz
Daniel Oppenheim,
c. 1836.

RIGHT Nathan
Rothschild, by Moritz
Daniel Oppenheim,
c. 1836. Unlike his
brothers, Nathan
hardly ever made use
of the prefix "von" or
"de."

BELOW Carl von
Rothschild, by Moritz
Daniel Oppenheim,
c. 1836.

ABOVE Salomon von
Rothschild, by Moritz
Daniel Oppenheim,
c. 1836.

BELOW James de
Rothschild, by Moritz
Daniel Oppenheim,
c. 1836.

The Rothschild family at prayer, by Moritz Daniel Oppenheim.

Hannah Rothschild née Cohen, Nathan's wife, by Sir William Beechey, 1823.

Nathan Rothschild at his desk with an imaginary classical background. It was through his letters, often harshly worded, that Nathan exerted his power.

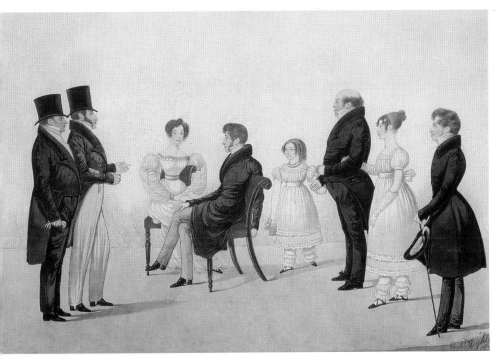

The marriage of Charlotte and Anselm von Rothschild in 1826, pencil and watercolor by Richard Dighton, 1830. LEFT TO RIGHT: Salomon, Carl, Charlotte, Anselm, Louise, Nathan, Hannah Mayer and Lionel.

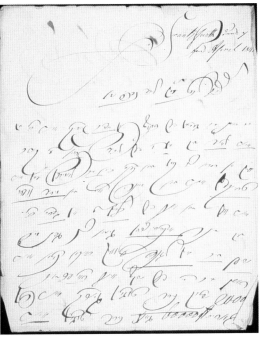

One of many thousands of letters in *Judendeutsch* exchanged between the five Rothschild brothers on an almost daily basis. This example is in Amschel's hand.

Anselm and Charlotte in her studio with their children, Nathaniel and Julie, and their nanny, painting by Charlotte, 1838.

Salomon von Rothschild's "Hôtel zum römischen Kaiser," Vienna.

The growth of New Court: the 1837 extension by John Davies seen through the arch of the rebuilt front range of the 1860s.

Betty de Rothschild, by Ingres, 1848.

The Villa Pignatelli, Carl von Rothschild's Naples house, by Carl Wilhelm Götzloff, c. 1845.

Mayer Carl von Rothschild, by Hahnisch, 1844.

ABOVE James de Rothschild's Paris hôtel, 19 rue Laffitte. In London, home and bank were separated in 1816; in Paris, one building continued to house both.

Lionel, Anthony, Nat and Mayer de Rothschild riding to hounds in the Vale of Aylesbury, by Sir Francis Grant, c. 1841.

dining room combined with an orangerie for summer dining. James also added a mock farm with cows, chickens and exotic breeds of sheep. Despite the fact that he spent little time there, Salomon lavished money on Suresnes. The château was enlarged and redecorated, acquiring elaborate glass galleries round its sides. Like his younger brother, Salomon also played at farming, building a dairy and accumulating a large stock of wildfowl; but his real love was the garden, which he extended throughout his life, later adding greenhouses and a system of irrigation.[48] As Lord William Russell reported when he visited Suresnes in 1843, "nature is made to yield to money, & produce the fruits & flowers of summer in the spring."[49] Two years later James was said to be "transplanting a great number of very large full-grown yew-trees" from Melun to Suresnes, presumably as a gift to Salomon. "Each tree," marvelled *The Times*, "is a sufficient load to require 11 horses to draw it. It was thus that Louis XIV planted the grounds at Versailles."[50] The parallel, as we have seen, had already occurred to Heine, and was one to which he and others would return.

The English Rothschilds also invested in their residences in both country and town, though on a less Bourbon scale. When Disraeli attended a fête given by Nathan's widow Hannah at Gunnersbury in 1843, it impressed him as "a most beautiful park and a villa worthy of an Italian Prince, though decorated with a taste and splendour which a French financier in the olden times could alone have rivalled . . . [with] beautiful grounds, temples and illuminated walks."[51] If the interior of Sidonia's country house in *Tancred* (1847) was partly modelled on Gunnersbury, as seems likely, there were nevertheless points of contrast with the French Rothschilds' residences:

> Passing through a marble antechamber, Tancred was ushered into an apartment half saloon and half library; the choicely-bound volumes, which were not too numerous, were ranged on shelves inlaid in the walls, so that they ornamented, without diminishing, the apartment. These walls were painted in encaustic, corresponding with the coved ceiling, which was richly adorned in the same fashion. A curtain of violet velvet covering if necessary the large window, which looked upon a balcony full of flowers, and the umbrageous Park; an Axminster carpet, manufactured both in colour and design with the rest of the chamber; a profusion of luxurious seats; a large table of ivory marquetry, bearing a carved silver bell which once belonged to a pope; a Naiad, whose golden urn served as an inkstand; some daggers that acted as paper cutters, and some French books just arrived; a group of beautiful vases recently released from an Egyptian tomb and ranged on a tripod of malachite; the portrait of a statesman, and the bust of an emperor, and a sparkling fire, were all circumstances which made the room both interesting and comfortable . . .[52]

If this was rather more cosy than the mock-Renaissance, five-star splendour of Paris, it was meant to be. To English eyes, the rue Laffitte hôtels seemed almost too grand. "When finished," Louise told her father in 1830 (after a visit to the house at number 17 which Salomon had just bought), "I think it will be most magnificent, it is immense and could hold almost three families."[53] Lionel felt the same ambivalence when he took a similar house in Paris shortly before his marriage: the ground floor would, he told his bride-to-be, "rival . . . any palace; at Paris, a rich man whether Banker or Prince can act in the same way, but in every other place, such an establishment would appear ridiculous. The first floor, the daily habitation, is nearly as splendid, so much gold that for the first few days one is quite dazzled."[54] "The houses here are splendid," Nat wrote to Lionel two years later, "you know about them. [Aunt] Betty's rooms are very nice, indeed rather too fine."[55]

There were differences too between the English and French residences in the country. For most of his life James stuck close to Paris: neither Ferrières nor Boulogne was very far from the city. His English nephews, by contrast, began looking within five years of their father's death for some more authentically rural seat than semi-suburban Gunnersbury. It still sufficed for certain social functions, and the family remained fond of it: Hannah added 33 acres to the 76 she inherited from her husband and Lionel extended the estate to no less than 620 acres between 1840 and 1873.[56] But, as Disraeli said of its fictional analogue Hainault House (in Endymion), it was not "fashionable."[57] Above all, it was too close to the city for its owners to indulge in that favourite pastime of Victorian England: hunting. No sooner had they added to the Gunnersbury property than they began looking further afield,[58] perhaps encouraged by their mother's glowing descriptions of the Devonshire and Fitzwilliam estates in Derbyshire.[59] Of course, it would have been quite impracticable for "City men" to have bought land so far from London; but Buckinghamshire seemed to offer all the advantages of genuine country life at a manageable distance. The first step in this direction came when Nathan rented Tring house in 1833 for the summer. Three years later Hannah bought some land near Mentmore, north-east of Aylesbury,[60] and in 1842, alerted by a newspaper advertisement, Mayer bought a small group of farms in the parishes of Mentmore and Wing, laying the foundation of what would rapidly become a substantial Rothschild enclave in the county.[61] Absent on duty in Paris, his elder brother Anthony was envious: "It is no harm to have your money in Land. I wish I knew of a nice place, I would do the same & I hope one of these days to have it."[62]

Contrary to what has sometimes been assumed, the purchase of rural land by the Rothschilds did not symbolise some kind of dilution of their capitalist "spirit" or compromise with the "feudal" old regime. Lionel was singularly unimpressed by the vast piles of the nobility when he visited them: Castle Howard he thought "rather a nice place but nothing wonderful. It is in fact just the same as Blenheim, only much smaller . . . altogether a place not worth putting oneself out to go to see."[63] What he and his brothers were doing in the 1840s was buying farmland, and it would have been uncharacteristic if they had not regarded their purchases at least partly as straightforward investments. There is no doubt that Lionel drove a hard bargain when the family sought to acquire another property at Creslow. "I should not mind having it," he told his brothers in 1844, "as a 33 per cent purchase would pay me 3 per cent, and there are so many little places round it which might be bought worth the money, that the whole together might be made to pay a fair rate of interest."[64] Indeed, the estates he and his brother Anthony subsequently bought to the south of Mentmore following the bankruptcy of the Duke of Buckingham in 1848 and the death of Sir John Dashwood the following year, were typical Rothschild acquisitions: bought at the bottom of the market.[65] There was also, as we shall see, a secondary and equally pragmatic rationale for buying several estates in one county: the British system of local government and parliamentary representation made such a concentration of land a useful source of political influence. (According to one account, this was why their land agents Horwood and James advised buying land in one area only.) It was not until the 1850s that the brothers began to indulge themselves by building their own "stately homes."

Outside France and England, as we have seen, there were limits on how much property the Rothschilds, as Jews, could acquire. After 1830 these restrictions began to crumble. In 1841 Carl bought himself the Villa Pignatelli near Naples, which his daughter fondly remembered as "a paradise upon earth, with a view over the bay and the islands, over the celebrated Mount Vesuvius, the most animated street and the Villa Reale, the Neapolitan Kensington Gardens."[66] It was more difficult in Vienna, however, where Salomon continued to live in the rented Hotel zum Römischen Kaiser in the Renngasse. Of course, he owned property elsewhere, in Paris as well as in Frankfurt. But there was a principle at stake—or so Salomon argued in a "special appeal" he addressed to Metternich in January 1837 concerning "the destiny of my co-religionists . . . the hopes of so many fathers of families and the highest aspirations of thousands of human beings."[67] When the government once again refused to grant any general relaxation of discrimination—lest "the public . . . suddenly draw the conclusion that full emancipation of the Jews is contemplated"—Salomon faced a dilemma; for Metternich intimated that the Emperor was willing, at his own discretion and as a special privilege, to grant *individual* Jews permission to own houses in Vienna.[68] This was the old story of the prince and the *Hofjude*, whereby the state "bought off" the Jewish banker on whom it was dependent with special exemptions. Salomon did not rush to take advantage of this offer; but in 1842—five years later—he succumbed. His request to own real estate in the city was speedily granted, allowing him finally to buy the Renngasse hotel as well as the adjoining house, which he demolished and rebuilt.[69] As he acknowledged, this—along with the grant of honorary citizenship which went with it—made him "a privileged exception in the midst of my fellow believers, who . . . [ought to] have the right to enjoy the same rights as those who belong to other religious confessions."[70]

It might be thought that this compromise ran counter to the stance taken on questions of Jewish civil rights by other members of the family; but, like Mayer Amschel before them, most Rothschilds seem to have seen general rights and individual privileges as complementary rather than dichotomous: if the former could not be had, the latter should be accepted. Salomon was not criticised for his decision to accept Metternich's offer. Indeed, even before he did, one of his English nephews was urging him "to get permission from Prince Metternich to purchase an estate in Bohemia."[71] In 1843 Salomon took his advice, though it was in fact in neighbouring Moravia that he sought the Emperor's permission not only to buy an estate but also to pass it on to his heirs. Once again he was obliged to adopt the tones of the humble but deserving court Jew, listing his various financial contributions to the Empire as "adequate proof of his unshakeable devotion to the Austrian monarchy" and expressing his "most ardent desire to own property in a country whose rulers have shown him so many signal marks of their favour."[72] Again the petition was granted, despite the reservations of the Moravian estates. As one official put it, Salomon's "position in society is so exceptional that he has been entirely removed from the ordinary circumstances of his co-religionists; his remarkable qualities and rare intelligence make it entirely inappropriate to apply strictly in his case the regu-

lations in force with regard to other Israelites." The Lord Chancellor Count Inzághy
was rather more candid: it was, he argued,

> highly desirable that Baron Rothschild should be more closely bound to
> the Imperial State of Austria by the investment of his money in real
> property in this country; and . . . it would create a very strange impres-
> sion abroad if his particular wish to settle permanently in that country,
> where he has been so actively engaged for a long period of years, and has
> been associated with the Government in more extensive and important
> transactions than has ever been the case before with a private individual,
> were to be refused after the special distinctions that have been conferred
> upon him.[73]

In addition to the estate Salomon duly purchased at Koritschau in Moravia—
which together with his property in Vienna gave him real estate in the Empire worth
2 million gulden[74]—he also acquired property in Prussia, buying the castle of
Schillersdorf in 1842.[75] It was a dispute relating to the rights attached to this estate
which prompted Heine's warning in 1846 that "Prussian aristocrats would like to
use the paw of the plebeian to stir up public opinion against the *exceptional family*
(for that term is the one constantly used to describe the house of Rothschild in proceedings regarding the right of patronage over Schillersdorf and Hültschin)."[76]

Surprisingly, in view of the protracted efforts of the town authorities to return
the Jewish community to the ghetto in the years after 1814, "the exceptional family"
encountered less of this sort of hostility when they sought to buy new properties in
Frankfurt—a reflection perhaps of the changed political climate in the town after
1830. In 1831, after much hesitation, Amschel finally commissioned the Paris-
trained Friedrich Rumpf to redesign and expand the house in his beloved garden on
the Bockenheimer Landstrasse. Rumpf transformed the original and quite modest
cube-shaped house into the central pavilion of a larger neo-classical villa, adding
two wings with Corinthian three-quarter columns and remodelling the garden itself
along strictly symmetrical lines. This mélange of Baroque and Renaissance styles
was fairly typical of the houses favoured by the town's Gentile elite in this period,
suggesting a new self-confidence on Amschel's part—in marked contrast to the
mood of insecurity when he had first acquired the property.[77] In the succeeding
years, his attachment to it showed no sign of waning: during a visit to her married
daughters Charlotte and Louise in 1844, Hannah was able to report that "a handsome and very large orangery and some magnificent trees of many sorts" had been
added to the garden.[78]

An even clearer signal of assumed equality with the Bethmanns and Gontards
came in 1834, when Amschel bought the large, four-storey town house at number
34 on the prestigious street known as the Zeil. In the same year Anselm bought a
similar "palais" (indeed, by the same architect) in the nearby Neue Mainzer Strasse
(number 45), a much grander residence than the building at number 33 acquired by
Carl in 1818 and made even more grand by Rumpf, who was commissioned to add
a new façade in the Renaissance style.[79] It was also Rumpf whom Mayer Carl commissioned to expand the house he bought on the banks of the Main in 1846; but by
this time mere imitation was no longer the Rothschild objective. Untermainkai
15—which today houses the Frankfurt Jewish Museum—had been built in 1821 at

the end of an elegant row of neo-classical houses for the banker Joseph Isaak Speyer, and was already distinguished from its neighbours by its Italian Renaissance style. Rumpf made it stand out even more. Although he preserved some original features, notably the polygonal vestibule projecting from the side wall, he doubled its length and added some distinctly Oriental features (notably two new oriels with Moorish corner pillars and arabesque balustrades).[80] The effect was to dominate, albeit subtly, the rest of the street—a symbol of the Rothschilds' now well-established dominance of the city's economic life.

The Rothschilds also acquired rural retreats in the vicinity of Frankfurt during this period. In 1835 Amschel bought a country *Schloss* at Grüneburg and two years later Carl acquired a similar property, the Günthersburg.[81] In fact, the literal translation ("castle") somewhat exaggerates the size of the original houses, and at 150 acres or so their grounds were relatively modest. In one respect, however, the Frankfurt Rothschilds were more ambitious than their relatives, for they were the first members of the family to build their own country houses rather than merely renovate the existing buildings. This gave rise to an aesthetic debate within the family, in which the English (represented at Frankfurt by Anselm's wife Charlotte and Mayer Carl's wife Louise) emphatically lost.

In 1840 Mayer Carl commissioned Rumpf to build a new "country residence" at Günthersburg. The design was not dissimilar to that of the Untermainkai house, with Doric pilasters across the ground and first floors and Corinthian ones on the upper floors of the two side projections.[82] "The house is large and when finished will be a magnificent residence," reported his mother-in-law Hannah, "but the grounds and garden do not accord with English taste."[83] Her son shared her opinion: it would be "a most magnificent house, large enough to hold us all" and the garden would be "pretty," "but it is a pity that such a large house is not in the middle of 10,000 acres about ten miles from the town."[84] The argument continued when Anselm resolved to build a new "garden house" on the Grüneburg estate.[85] Doubtless remembering her childhood at Gunnersbury, his wife Charlotte insisted that the new house be "perfectly English" in style, and asked her brothers to supply designs from London. "I am hesitating between the Elizabethan and the cottage style," she told her mother. "She wants some of the Gothic, Elizabethan and all sorts," reported Lionel somewhat dismissively. "Not a palace but a good sized House."[86] But she was evidently overruled. The design she and her husband eventually agreed on was for a long rectangular house in the style of a Loire château. With its tower-like projections at the corners, its layers of sandstone on the ground floor, its balustrades, obelisks, volutes and chimneys, it was an eclectic edifice.[87] The only concession to Charlotte was a tall neo-Gothic brick tower at the northern end of the park—a conspicuously English touch.

Elite Pursuits

Such arguments about architectural style are indicative of an important sea-change in Rothschild attitudes in the period which followed Nathan's death. Before 1836, as we have seen, he and his brothers had tended to regard the acquisition of more spacious residences in an essentially functional light: apart from simply being more comfortable, they provided settings where the great and the good could be wined and dined—and pumped for useful news or lucrative business. After 1836, the endless round of dinner parties and balls continued. The ball in March 1836 which James threw to show off his refurbished hôtel was probably not untypical: "As at all Rothschild soirées," Heine reported, the guests were "a strictly selected set of aristo-cratic illustrations, able to make an impression by reason of great name or high rank or (in the case of the ladies) beauty and finery."[88] Contemporaries generally agreed on this: whereas before 1830 there had been one or two Restoration grandees who had continued to decline James's invitations, after the advent of the "bourgeois monarchy" the faubourg Saint-Germain had less cause to remain aloof.[89] "The com-pany all the elite of Paris," was Disraeli's succinct summary of the guests invited to the ball he attended at Salomon's in 1843.[90] The guest lists of dinners given by James tell much the same story.

In London too Rothschild hospitality became more lavish, more modish. In July 1838 Lionel hosted an extravagant summer ball at Gunnersbury to which he in-vited over 500 people, among them the dukes of Cambridge, Sussex, Somerset and Wellington. After a concert by leading musicians and singers, dinner was served followed by (according to Moses Montefiore) "a grand ball . . . in a magnificent tent erected for the purpose."[91] The Cambridges dined at Gunnersbury again that Sep-tember; and five years later they were in attendance at another ball there, along with the Duchess of Gloucester and Ernst I of Saxe Coburg, Prince Albert's father—an impressive trio of royal relations.[92] Even in Frankfurt the last social constraints seemed to fall away. In 1846, for example, Lionel's sister Charlotte gave "a magnifi-cent ball" there. Among the Frankfurt Rothschilds' dinner guests in this period were the King of Württemberg, Prince Loewenstein and Prince Wittgenstein.[93] Disraeli is once again apposite (this time fictionalising in *Endymion*):

> In a very short time it was not merely the wives of ambassadors and ministers of state that were found at the garden fêtes of Hainault, or the balls, and banquets, and concerts of Portland Place, but the fitful and capricious realm of fashion surrendered like a fair country conquered as it were by surprise. To visit the Neuchatels became the mode; all solicited to be their guests, and some solicited in vain.[94]

As the frequency of such descriptions suggests, the scale and ostentation of Roth-schild hospitality never ceased to fascinate contemporaries—especially socially ambitious men of letters like Disraeli. In *Tancred*, there is an exquisite dinner at Sidonia's, "served on Sèvres porcelain of Rose du Barry, raised on airy golden stands of arabesque workmanship; a mule bore your panniers of salt, or a sea-nymph prof-fered it you on a shell just fresh from the ocean, or you found it in a bird's nest; by every guest a different pattern . . . The appearance of the table changed as if by the waving of a wand, and as silently as a dream."[95] In *Endymion*, the same author cari-catures what is unmistakably a weekend party at Gunnersbury. "Sunday was a great day at Hainault, the Royal and the Stock Exchanges were both of them always fully represented; and then they often had an opportunity, which they highly appreciated, of seeing and conferring with some public characters, MPs of note or promise, and occasionally a secretary of the Treasury, or a privy councillor."[96] At dinner a syco-phantic writer named St Barbe—a caricature of Thackeray—holds forth in praise of his hosts:

"What a family this is!" he said; "I had no idea of wealth before! Did you observe the silver plates? I could not hold mine with one hand, it was so heavy. I do not suppose there are such plates in all the world . . . But they deserve their wealth," he added; "nobody grudges it to them. I declare when I was eating that truffle, I felt a glow about my heart that, if it were not indigestion, I think must have been gratitude . . . He is a wonderful man, that Neuchatel. If I had only known him a year ago! I would have dedicated my novel to him. He is a sort of man who would have given you a cheque immediately . . . If you had dedicated it to a lord, the most he would have done would have been to ask you to dinner, and then perhaps cut up your work in one of the Quality reviews."[97]

In truth, for the Rothschilds themselves these occasions continued to be more a duty—an early form of corporate hospitality—than a pleasure. "Here we have stinking balls night after night," complained Nat to his brothers in 1843; "you have no idea how sweaty the old French ladies smell after a long waltz."[98] Nor were the nightly dinners for diplomats and politicians much more enjoyable: on April 30, 1847, when the guests included the Prince of Holstein-Glücksburg, the Duke of Devonshire and Lord and Lady Holland, Apponyi could not help noticing the "affreuses douleurs névralgiques à la tête" from which Nat's wife was all too plainly suffering.[99] As for the incessant games of whist which were such a characteristic feature of nineteenth-century elite socialising—and which seem to have been the main form of entertainment at Naples—these too palled after a time.[100] Most members of the family also had decidedly mixed feelings about the time they spent each year "taking the waters" at spas like Aix, Gastein, Wildbad and Kissingen, a practice first adopted by James in the early 1830s. Though this was the "done" thing, James rarely enthused about taking a *Kur*; indeed, he appears to have regarded it primarily as a medical necessity and often took the waters after illnesses or periods of intense and exhausting work.[101] As he grew older, he tended to spend longer and longer periods of the summer recuperating in this way, but he generally continued to bombard his nephews or sons in Paris with peremptory letters, and insisted on being kept informed of any business developments. Salomon enthused about "the air and the mountains, the waterfalls [and] the good bath water" at Gastein in 1841, and Anthony joked that the waters were good for James's libido; but Mayer's reaction to Wildbad was more typical. "You have no idea," he complained to Lionel in 1846, "how dull this place is and if I had not determined on taking the number of baths prescribed, how soon I would bolt."[102]

The image of bolting, however, was a hint at more enjoyable pastimes which, by the 1830s, James and his nephews were discovering. Of these, hunting was an early favourite. It is necessary to distinguish here between three separate, though related activities, all of which were to become staple Rothschild hobbies. Firstly, there was shooting, mainly of pheasants, which James was doing at Ferrières by the early 1830s. Secondly, there was stag-hunting, which was one of the things which attracted his English nephews to Buckinghamshire in the 1840s. Finally, there was horse-racing, an enthusiasm related to hunting, though requiring more carefully bred and trained horses—not to mention professional jockeys.

Of these pastimes, shooting was the most closely related to the pattern of social activity established in the 1820s. In September 1832, with the aftershocks of the July Revolution still reverberating, Lionel "accompanied Montalivet & Apponyi out shooting which in any other times than the present would be very amusing, but now one goes with these great personages to hear what is going on more than for the sake of the amusement."[103] That instrumental approach continued to inform his uncle James's attitude throughout the decade, most obviously in 1835, when he staged an immense slaughter of 506 partridges, 359 hares and 110 pheasants in honour of the duc d'Orleans. This was corporate hospitality at its most grotesque, with the unfortunate birds and beasts being bought in specially for the occasion, and each of the eminent guests being provided with a servant, a dog and a gun.[104] Inevitably, more discerning huntsmen looked askance at such carnage. Capefigue is quite vehement on the subject of the sport at Ferrières: "Bad kennels, bad hounds, horses dead-beat after the first gallop, greedy gamekeeper, game sold off, venison scrawny, servants scoffing and lacking in intelligence."[105] And even James's own nephews were conscious that there was room for improvement. In 1843, in an ambitious bid to re-educate their uncle, they invited him to shoot grouse with them in Scotland. "The shooting is different to what we are accustomed to see and particularly to that which our good Uncle has at Ferrières where all the game is driven to him and he has but to fire away," Lionel observed acerbically.

> Here we have to walk after the dogs and to seek for the game, which is a much greater excitement and at the same time more fatiguing. In the beginning the Baron was very eager and followed the dogs very well, and was rather lucky in killing about 15, but he soon got tired, when I was then able to shoot a little and killed about as many . . . [T]he walking is a little fatiguing, as the heath in most places is nearly up to one's knees.[106]

The younger generation evidently relished the discomfiture of "the Baron": both Nat and Anselm gleefully visualised James returning to Paris clad "as a real highlander, in a tartan dress, the claymore in his hand and exhibiting a flourishing view of stout legs and calves."[107]

The hunting preferred by James's English nephews was stag-hunting on horseback with hounds. Probably at Mayer's instigation, they began hunting with a pack of staghounds in the Vale of Aylesbury in 1839, renting stables and kennels at Tring Park. It was this new enthusiasm, more than anything else, which prompted the purchase of Mentmore three years later.[108] By 1840, "turning out the stag" was a recreation attracting not only the male Rothschilds but their wives to Buckinghamshire, though it was not until five years later that they felt ready to hold a public hunt.[109] The most passionate Rothschild testaments to the pleasures of the chase come, poignantly, from Nat, the exile in Paris, whose early letters abound with allusions to hunting. "What magic there is in a pair of leather breeches," he wrote home in 1842. "I have half a mind to put a pair on and gallop round the bois de Boulogne—old Tup [Mayer] would exclaim, "Go it, you cockney!" Write more about hunting & whether old Tup manages to tumble into the dirty black ditches, how H. Fitzroy was induced to go out with the staghounds—everything is of interest to us poor fellows who can only hunt through the columns of Bell's Life." And in the same year: "We are going to Lady Ailesbury's tonight. I'd sooner have a run for 40 minutes across the vale than look at her ugly face without a veil."[110] In 1841 Sir Francis Grant was commissioned to paint all four brothers at full tilt on their hunters, resplendent in matching scarlet coats and top hats. In fact, it was seldom that all four were able to ride to hounds together.

It is tempting to conclude from such evidence that the fad for stag-hunting was nothing more than the hedonism of wealthy youth, the stuff which would later be immortalised by Surtees and Siegfried Sassoon. Yet there is a phrase of Nat's which hints at something more. "Ride like trumps," he exhorted his brothers in 1840, "and do not let the Queen's people fancy we are all tailors."[111] As in Paris, hunting inevitably had a social significance: it meant mixing with members of the aristocracy, including courtiers, men who would tend to be accomplished riders. It mattered to the sons of the textile merchant Nathan Rothschild to prove that they were not "all tailors" by acquitting themselves well over the hedges and gates of Buckinghamshire. And of course it was good exercise: something which their grandfather, confined in the Judengasse, had been denied and their father had scorned. It is not inconceivable that the older Rothschilds' very sedentary lifestyles made them susceptible to the kind of ailment which killed Nathan. On the other hand, the fact that Nat suffered a serious injury as a result of a riding accident bore out his father's warnings many years before about the incompatibility of bankers and horses.[112]

The same was true of the brothers' first forays into horse-racing. We know from Buxton that Nathan had whetted his sons' appetites for Arab horses, and Lionel was self-confessedly "extravagant" in his expenditure on horses while serving his apprenticeship in Paris.[113] It was not until around 1840, however, that Anthony began to own and compete racehorses: in that year one of his horses won the Champs de Mars in Paris.[114] This was in some ways the height of Rothschild social pretension in the period, as the pre-eminent owner of the day in Paris was none other than the duc d'Orléans. His death in a carriage accident in July 1842 left the field to some extent open: as Disraeli wrote that October, "Anthony succeeds the Duke of Orleans in his patronage of the turf & gives costly cups to the course wh[ich] his horses always win."[115] Nat, still fondly dreaming of the Vale, was disapproving, and warned his youngest brother: "Race horses are ticklish things, very pleasant to have a lot when they win, quite the contrary when they lose . . . Dear Tupus stick to the scarlet coat, instead of the silk jacket, it is more beneficial to the health and less expensive."[116] But Mayer, evidently inspired by Anthony's success, shortly afterwards established a racing stable at Newmarket; it was he who in 1843 (after toying with the more garish combination of amber, lilac and red) registered the Rothschild colours as dark blue and yellow.[117]

Investing in Art

The pleasures of the field were not the only ones discovered by James and his nephews after 1830. An even more important new source of enjoyment—and prestige—was patronage of the arts; and here we see clearly that Rothschilds were doing much more than merely "aping" aristocratic mores.

Of course, there were those who erroneously took James de Rothschild for a philistine. "If only I had Rothschild's money!" exclaims Gumpelino in a draft of

"The Baths of Lucca" written by Heine in around 1828, three years before he left
Germany for Paris:

> But what use is it to him? He lacks culture and understands as much
> about music as an unborn calf, about painting as a cat, about poetry as
> Apollo—that's the name of my dog. When men like that lose their
> money, they cease to exist. What is money? Money is round and rolls
> away, but education endures . . . But if I—God forbid—were to lose my
> money, I would still remain a great connoisseur of art, painting, music
> and poetry.[118]

Fifteen years later, by which he time he knew James pretty well, he took a rather different view, though the compliments were—as so often with Heine—strictly back-
handed. James, he now admitted, had

> the capacity of finding (if not always of judging) the leading practition-
> ers in every other sphere of activity. Because of this gift he has been
> compared with Louis XIV; and it is true that in contrast to his colleagues
> here in Paris, who like to surround themselves with mediocrities, Herr
> James von Rothschild always appears in association with the notabilities
> of any subject; even if he knew nothing about it himself, he still always
> knew who most excelled in it. He does not, perhaps, understand a single
> note of music; but Rossini was always a friend of the family. Ary Schef-
> fer is his court painter . . . Herr von Rothschild knows not a word of
> Greek; but the Hellenist Letronne is the scholar he favours most . . .
> Poetry, whether French or German, is also very eminently represented in
> Herr von Rothschild's affections; although it seems to me as if . . . the
> Herr Baron is not as wildly enthusiastic about the poets of our own day
> as he is for the great poets of the past, for example, Homer, Sophocles,
> Dante, Cervantes, Shakespeare, Goethe—pure, dead poets, enlightened
> geniuses, who are free from all earthly dross, removed from all wordly
> needs, and do not ask him for shares in the Northern Railway.[119]

As we shall see, this last remark was a pointed allusion to Heine's own relationship with James; but leaving that aside—and making due allowance for Heine's
satirical hyperbole—it is obvious that the above passage (published in 1843 in the
Augsburger Zeitung) could hardly have been written of a man with no interest in the
arts. Even if James himself was no expert, he admired expertise—and that is a very
different thing from being a philistine. When another ambitious young man of letters (also, like Heine, a converted Jew) first met James at a dinner in Paris the year
before, he hit the nail on the head. "I found him," Benjamin Disraeli told his sister,
"a happy mixture of the French Dandy & the orange boy. He spoke to me with[ou]t
ceremony with 'I believe you know my *nephew*.'"[120] The "orange boy" in James was
most strongly evident in the strong Frankfurt accent with which he spoke French,
and in the peremptory manner which he shared with his brother in London; but the
"French Dandy" was the man within, who always enjoyed the company of artists,
musicians and writers. An English visitor to Paris in the 1850s noticed this too,
when she called on "Mme. de Roth . . . whose poetic abode has more the air of the
palace of a wealthy artist than the hôtel of a millionaire."[121] For all his rough manners, James was, in his heart, something of an aesthete—even a Bohemian—though
he indulged this trait vicariously, surrounding himself with beautiful objects and

introducing one or two of their more entertaining creators into his otherwise stuffy social round. Something similar could be said of his English nephews, whose love of hunting was only one facet of their wide-ranging activity beyond the walls of the counting house.

It was on other walls that the "acculturation" of the Rothschilds was perhaps most immediately obvious—specifically, on the walls of their houses, which gradually became covered with paintings of the very highest quality. The first picture of note bought by a Rothschild was French artist Jean-Baptiste Greuze's *The Milkmaid*—a typically rustic–romantic work of the late rococo—which James acquired as early as 1818.[122] Greuze was a favourite Rothschild artist: James bought another of his paintings—*Little Girl with Bouquet*—from the auction of Cardinal Fesch's estate in 1845, and his nephew Lionel began his collection by buying his *Virtue Faltering* at Phillips' auctioneers in 1831; he later acquired four other works by the same artist, among them *The Parting Kiss*. His brother Anthony owned another two, including *The Nursery*.[123] Such pictures complemented the numerous items of *ancien régime* furniture and ornamentation acquired by the family, like the Marie Antoinette secretaires and Sèvres porcelain owned by James. Another favourite artist was the seventeenth-century Spanish artist Bartolomé Esteban Murillo, whose work Lionel may have discovered when he went to Madrid in 1834, where, as he freely admitted, he spent "all my leisure time . . . in running about after pictures which are in very great number but few good ones."[124] By the end of the 1840s he, his uncle and his mother all owned Murillos.

But it was the art of seventeenth-century Holland which the family found most attractive. In 1840 James bought Rembrandt's *The Standard Bearer* from George IV's collection, which he hung in the grand salon at the rue Laffitte; he also owned the same artist's *Portrait of a Young Man* (which was in the sitting room) as well as Franz Hals's *Portait of a Nobleman* and works by Anthony van Dyck, Peter Paul Rubens, Jacob van Ruisdael and Philips Wouwermans. In 1836 Lionel bought Gerard ter Borch's *Young Lady with her Page* in Frankfurt, and a year later added four paintings by Wouwermans from the sale of the duchesse de Berry's collection as well as three by Jan van der Heyden, including *Rosendaal Castle* and his *View of Haarlem*.[125] He bought two more Wouwermans works and a Pieter de Hooch from George Lucy's collection in 1845. By the time the German art expert Gustav Waagen visited him in Piccadilly in around 1850, his collection included three paintings by Meindert Hobbema, three by van Ruisdael, a Paulus Potter, a Karel du Jardin, an Adam Pynacker, two Jan Wynants and an Isaac van Ostade. He later added two pictures by Nicolaes Berchem, five works by Aalbert Cuyp—including his *View on a Frozen River*—six paintings by the van Mieris, father and son, two by Gaspar Netscher, three by Gerard ter Borch and seven by David Teniers the Younger, as well as still-lifes by Jan David de Heem, Jan van Huysum, Rachel Ruysh, Jan Weenix and Peter Gysels.[126] This taste was evidently shared by his brother Anthony: in 1833 he bought a picture of a nurse and child playing with a goat which appeared to bear Rembrandt's signature (it was later reattributed to Nicolaes Maes when the signature was shown to be a forgery) and by 1850 had acquired works by Wouwermans, Teniers, Van Dyck, Rubens and van Ostade.

That something resembling a collective "Rothschild taste" developed in this period is not surprising, as to a large extent the family acted in concert, alerting one another to major sales and acting for one another in different markets. In 1840 James asked Anthony "to dispose of the Rembrandt if it could be done with advantage," but "on reflection" decided against buying a Murillo through his nephew.[127] He and his nephews sought to ensure that a major Roman collection was auctioned in Paris rather than London in 1841. "We want to do it together," wrote James. "Perhaps we will get some nice paintings."[128] Typically, when two Murillos were offered for auction in Paris in 1843, Nat considered buying them for his mother, though in the end he left them to Salomon's wife Caroline.[129] By the time of her death, Hannah owned works by Murillo, Cuyp and Teniers, all probably bought for her by her sons.[130] There was also a natural shared tendency to favour secular subjects over religious works—perhaps the best explanation for the over-representation of Dutch artists—though this was far from being a rule. Interestingly, the Rothschilds bought not only Old Testament scenes (such as Paul Delaroche's *Moses in the Bullrushes*) but also some works of explicitly Christian iconography. In 1840 Lionel acquired Murillo's *Infant Christ as the Good Shepherd* from a London dealer and he later purchased Domenichino's *Head of a Magdalene* and Andrea del Sarto's *Madonna and Child*; while James owned Jan van Eyck and Petrus Christi's *Chartreux Madonna* and a Luini *Virgin and Child*.[131] In 1846 Anthony was given Van Dyck's *The Abbot Scaglia Adoring the Virgin and Child* by his father-in-law.[132]

It would be wrong, however, to exaggerate the homogeneity of Rothschild collections even at this early period. When Nat bought Velazquez's *Lady with Fan*, he observed that "pictures are something like ladies, everyone must please himself and select according to his taste . . . It would not please everyone as the face is not a pretty one, although very well painted."[133] His brother Lionel's enthusiasm for eighteenth-century English artists was not shared by James (and was in many ways ahead of its time in Britain too). In 1846 he acquired Sir Joshua Reynolds's *Portrait of Master Braddyl* at Christie's, the first of several Reynolds works (the others were his *Portrait of Mrs Lloyd*, *Portrait of Miss Meyer as Hebe* and *Snake in the Grass: Love Unbinding the Zone of Beauty*). Later he turned to Thomas Gainsborough, buying his *Portrait of the Hon. Frances Duncombe* for £1,500 in 1871 and his *Portrait of Mrs Sheridan* the following year at Christie's. He also owned George Romney's *Portait of Emma, Lady Hamilton* and works by Sir William Beechey and John Hoppner. This enthusiasm for relatively recent portraits of individuals quite unrelated (and in all probability unknown) to the Rothschilds is especially surprising, though later in the nineteenth century such works were all the rage. Lionel's youngest brother Mayer owned a Gainsborough too—a fox-coursing scene—but he also bought works by Cranach and Titian, who are not represented in other Rothschild collections of the period.[134]

The Frankfurt Rothschilds had rather different tastes again.[135] It is hard to imagine Wilhelm Tischbein's *Goethe in the Campagna di Roma* (which Mayer Carl bought in 1846) hanging in Paris or London, for example. In any case, Mayer Carl was a good deal more interested in gold and silver ornaments than in paintings. Although his English cousins collected *objets d'art* too—among Lionel's prized possessions was the so-called "Lycurgus cup," an ancient Alexandrian or Byzantine glass goblet—they were less systematic. By the 1870s Mayer Carl had accumulated a dazzling "Goldschatz" of 5,000 items, among them such treasures as Wentzel Jamnitzer's Merkelsche Tafelaufsatz, a masterpiece of the German Renaissance, and an ivory horn on silver gilt in the same style—in fact a contemporary forgery by Rein-hold Vasters, but a brilliant one.[136]

Evidently, the Rothschilds were little interested in the art of their own day—although the myth-makers have exaggerated this indifference. The story that James antagonised two artists, Jadin and Horace Vernet, in his efforts to secure a cut-price portrait seems implausible; it cannot be right that Vernet took his revenge by depict-ing James as a cowardly Jew in *On the way to Smala*, because the figure in question bears no resemblance whatever to him or any other Rothschild.[137] What is true is that, with very few exceptions,[138] the only contemporary paintings the family owned were portraits they commissioned themselves: for example, Alfred de Dreux's portait of Lionel driving a gig (1838), Sir Francis Grant's portrait of the four broth-ers riding to hounds (1841), Ary Scheffer's portrait of James's daughter Charlotte and Jean-Auguste-Dominique Ingres' portrait of his wife Betty (1848)—not to mention the numerous family pictures painted by Moritz Daniel Oppenheim and the portraits of James by artists like Charles-Emile Champmartin, Louis-Amié Grosclaude and Hippolyte Flandrin.[139]

It would be a mistake to explain all this solely in terms of family (or individual) "taste." For the "Old Masters" were attractive to men like James and Lionel for rea-sons other than the strictly aesthetic. Quite apart from their value as "status sym-bols," celebrated paintings were as much a form of investment in the nineteenth century as they are today. The fact that James's entire collection was insured for 10 million francs (£400,000) is indicative of the scale of the investment undertaken in this period: in 1844 that sum was equivalent to a quarter of James's share in the combined capital of the five houses.[140] Moreover, the market was a lively one, still feeling the ripples generated by the French Revolution: by uprooting so much of the French aristocracy, the Revolution had made numerous private collections available to new buyers, and the practice of selling them *en bloc* at auction had continued into the nineteenth century. It was another revolution, that of 1830, which ultimately led to the sale of the duchesse de Berry's collection, one of the most important early sources of Rothschild art; 1848 saw the great Stowe auction.[141] Despite the fre-quency of such sales, the demand for Old Masters often tended to outstrip supply. It speaks for itself that a picture like Velazquez's *Lady with Fan* could sell (to Nat) for 12,700 francs in 1843, more than three times more than the banker Aguado had paid for it just six years before.[142]

Given their immense wealth, the Rothschilds could afford to outbid almost anyone, and some members of the family seemed inclined to do so. As Mayer said while shopping for Italian sculpture in 1846, "one ought always to buy the very best of everything and not to mind the price," on the ground that "the very best" could only appreciate in value.[143] But the political upheavals of 1848–9, when the art market slumped as steeply as the financial markets, called that bullish assumption into question. In later life, James was always content to let a picture go to another bidder if he felt the price was excessive. In 1860 he bid 3,000 guineas for a Rubens, only to see it go to someone else for 7,500. "Fabulous prices," commented James; "I don't have the money to pay 10,000 guineas for a Murillo" (especially when the artist's *Christ as the Good Shepherd* had cost just over £3,000 twenty years before).[144] Of course, he of all people did have the money; but, compulsive investor that he was, he hated the idea of buying at what might prove to be the peak of the market.

Piano Lessons

Art, then, was an investment as well as a form of decoration. The Rothschilds' enthusiasm for music is perhaps less easily explained. That the Rothschilds patronised some of the most famous composers and performers of the nineteenth century is well known; and the most obvious reason for this is that musicians were a prerequisite for a successful soirée or a ball. In January 1828, for example, Nathan was able to treat his dinner guests to a post-prandial performance by Ignaz Moscheles—Felix Mendelssohn's tutor.[145] Similarly, when the maréchal de Castellane had dined with James the year before, the star performer was Rossini, to whom Salomon had been introduced by Metternich at the Congress of Verona five years before.[146] It is also said—though scholars debate the authenticity of the story—that Chopin's career in Paris was launched by a performance he gave at the rue Laffitte in 1832.[147] He played there again in 1843 alongside his pupil Karl Filtsch, whose playing James was reported to "adore."[148] Other notable performers who played at Rothschild houses included Mendelssohn himself, Franz Liszt, the pianist and conductor Charles Hallé and the violinist Joseph Joachim.

Even more important than their role as performers, however, was their role as teachers. This was especially important for female Rothschilds, who were encouraged from an early age to excel at the keyboard (the piano was perhaps the nearest thing the nineteenth century had to the television, with the difference that it required skill to operate). Not surprisingly, Nathan and his brothers gave them the best tutors money could buy. Charlotte's *livre d'or*, in which she invited her teachers to jot musical mementoes, records many of their names: Moscheles appears there, as does Mendelssohn, Vincenzo Bellini (who inscribed the song "Dolente immagine di Fille mia," which he had composed in 1821), Louis Spohr (who contributed a version of his song "Nachgefühl"), Rossini (who added one of his many settings of "Mi lagnero tacendo" from Metastio's *Siroe*) and Giacomo Meyerbeer (who offered a song called "The Rare Flower"). In the 1840s Charlotte's contributors included the elderly Luigi Cherubini (who wrote in the aria "Canto d'Armida" from his opera *Armida abbandonata*) and Chopin (who added a version of the Mazurka Op. 67 no. 4).[149] Rossini also wrote a six page piano solo for her as a "Petit Souvenir."[150] Charlotte's sister Hannah Mayer was also an accomplished harpist and took lessons from Parish Alvars, who dedicated his Serenade Op. 83 to her;[151] and when the youngest sister Louise showed musical leanings, Rossini himself offered to give her singing lessons. He was, she reported to her father, "very good natured and always comes at the hour and day I like."[152] When the two were together in Frankfurt three years later, she had lessons with him every day.[153] Chopin too gave lessons to a number of Rothschild women: not only to Nathan's daughter Charlotte but also to her daughter Hannah Mathilde and to Betty's daughter, another Charlotte. Indeed, he dedicated two pieces to members of the family: the Waltz, Op. 64, No. 2 and the Ballade, Op. 52.[154] With such a source of inspiration, it is not surprising the girls themselves tried their hand at composition: the younger Charlotte published four short piano pieces while Hannah Mathilde composed piano pieces, an orchestral waltz and six sets of songs, including settings of Victor Hugo, Théophile Gautier, Goethe and Longfellow—the most successful of which ("Si vous n'avez rien à me dire") was performed at the Paris Opéra by the soprano Adelina Patti.[155]

The Rothschilds not only employed musicians to perform and teach, however;

they also mixed with them socially and enjoyed their company. Meyerbeer dined with Betty and James in 1833,[156] for example, and Rossini was invited to Lionel's wedding in 1836 primarily as a friend—"to add to the gaiety of our party"—rather than as an entertainer or teacher. As he himself put it, "the entire purpose . . . was to attend at Frankfurt the marriage of Lionel Rotschildt [sic], my very dear friend."[157] James and he remained friendly throughout their lives.[158] Similarly, Chopin was said to have "loved the house of Rothschild and that this house loved him"; after his premature death in 1848, his pupil Charlotte preserved "a touching remembrance of him"—a cushion she herself had embroidered for him.[159] Such intimacy with musicians was somewhat unconventional. When the Rossinis dined with Nathan at a fairly aristocratic gathering shortly before the wedding, Lady Grenville commented sniffily that it was "Madame Rossini['s] . . . first appearance in decent company I believe."[160] But the composer and his wife were there partly in order to liven up the proceedings. Anthony's account of the private recital he heard Liszt give in 1842 is illuminating, showing how the Rothschilds derived pleasure not only from the playing but also from the company of such stars of nineteenth-century romanticism. "The most extraordinary player in the world," he reported to his wife, was

> as curious to look at as to hear, with his long hair at times streaming over his face, at others completely thrown back by a violent toss of the head, his wild eyes which he now and then turns on every side as if to mean sometimes "Am I not wonderful?" at others that he is delighted with his own performance. Dearest, he is an agreeable and talkative man in society, and is no doubt a dear and pleasant companion.[161]

Musicians educated and entertained—and not just by their playing. In return, the family were happy to give their favourites a measure of financial assistance—usually in the form of personal banking services. Johann Strauss senior's tour of England in 1838 was partly financed by Lionel;[162] after 1842 Rossini banked at de Rothschild Frères;[163] Niccolo Paganini used the Rothschilds to relay a gift of 20,000 francs to Hector Berlioz;[164] and Adelina Patti on one occasion borrowed more than £4,000 from the Paris house while on tour in Argentina.[165] Even that most vociferous of musical anti-Semites, Richard Wagner—who demonised the influence of "Jewry in Music"—may be said to have banked with the Rothschilds as his second wife Cosima had an account with the Paris house.[166] The beneficiaries were more privileged than they may have realised: the Rothschilds generally offered such facilities only to royalty and the political elite. It was a sign of the value they attached to their relations with the musical world; and perhaps this sprang from a certain sense of affinity. Like the self-made millionaire revered for his money, the musical star idolised for his (or her) virtuosity was a nineteenth-century invention. Both were to some extent parvenus (and foreigners): Nathan as much as the Rossinis at the dinner mentioned above. Indeed, many of the nineteenth century's most gifted musicians—Meyerbeer and Joachim spring to mind—were, like the Rothschilds, beneficiaries of Jewish emancipation.

Men of Letters

Musicians gave private lessons and performances. Nineteenth-century writers, by contrast, wrote for a burgeoning public and were supposed to be freeing themselves thereby from the traditional constraints of patronage. Yet men of letters too were recipients of Rothschild favours—and two of the best-documented cases were Heinrich Heine and Honoré de Balzac, both of whom became closely associated with James in the 1830s and 1840s. (Because of its political significance, the analogous relationship between Lionel and Disraeli is discussed separately in volume II.)

On the face of it, it is amazing that the wealthiest banker in Paris, the confidant of kings and ministers, should have had anything to do with either. In political terms alone, they were extremists: Heine was exiled from Germany for his liberal views and remained a lifelong enthusiast for revolutionary and nationalist causes; Balzac, by contrast, was by temperament a romantic conservative who considered seeking election as a Bourbon legitimist in 1831–2, and devoted a lifetime to portraying the society of the July Monarchy in a less than flattering light. Financially, they were both feckless, and without question had mercenary motives for cultivating good relations with the Rothschilds. And above all they periodically depicted James in their writings in ways which would have sent a thinner-skinned man rushing to his lawyers. Yet James evidently liked both; and if the relationships he formed with them were not quite unalloyed friendships, it seems that he would have liked them to be. Nothing gives a better insight into James's complex personality than this.

We have already encountered some of Heine's most penetrating commentaries on the nature of Rothschild power before and after the 1830 revolution. It is now time to say something about his relationship to the family. The nephew of the Hamburg banker Salomon Heine, he had been intended by his mother for a career in banking and seems to have had some sort of encounter with Nathan—"a fat Jew in Lombard Street, St. Swithin's Lane"—in London in 1827. Indeed, Nathan may have been the "famous merchant, with whom I wished to be an apprentice millionaire" who told him he "had no talent for business."[167] By 1834, however, he had struck up a very different relationship with the French Rothschilds. A number of anecdotes exist which cast Heine as a kind of licensed jester at the court of Baron James. When the Austrian playwright Grillparzer dined with Heine (and Rossini) at the Rothschilds', he was shocked: "It was apparent that his hosts were afraid of Heine, and he exploited their fear by slyly poking fun at them at every opportunity. But it is not admissible to dine with people whom you don't care for. If you despise a person you should not dine with him. In point of fact, our acquaintance did not progress after this."[168]

Barbs of the sort Grillparzer alluded to invariably cast James as Heine's slow-witted straight-man. "Dr Heine," he asks, "could you tell me why this wine is called 'Lachrymae Christi'?" "All you have to do is translate," Heine answers. "Christ weeps when rich Jews can afford such good wines while so many poor folk go hungry and thirsty." "Comment trouvez-vous mon chenil?" says James, welcoming some guests to his house. "Don't you know that *chenil* means dog-kennel?" chips in Heine. "If you have so low an opinion of yourself, at least don't trumpet it abroad!" Rothschild contemplates the filthy state of the River Seine and observes that its source is perfectly clear; Heine replies: "Yes, M. le baron; and I hear that your late father was a most honest man." A third party expresses a desire to meet James. "He only wants to get to know him," quips Heine, "because he doesn't know him."[169]

Such anecdotes seem superficially plausible in the light of the more satirical passages about James in Heine's journalism. Yet the surviving correspondence suggests a rather different relationship, in which Heine increasingly came to play the more or less humble supplicant to James's indulgent patron. As we have seen, one of the first references Heine made to James was in *Ludwig Börne*, in which he suggested that James's development of financial capital made him as much of a social "revolutionary" as Richelieu and Robespierre. Though a fairly outrageous parallel, this was far from insulting; if anything, it rather exaggerated James's influence. Surprisingly, Heine felt nervous enough about the liberties he had taken—apparently quoting at length from a private conversation with James—that he took the precaution of sending a copy of the proofs to his wife Betty. "You now have in your hands the *corpus delicti* that gives me some anxiety," he wrote. "May I still appear before you? . . . Perhaps you will forgive me with a merry smile. For my part I cannot reproach myself enough for having spoken, not with ill intent, but in an unbecoming manner, of a family that conceals so much nobility of feeling and so much good will."[170]

A few months before, he had publicly denied being the author of some malicious remarks about a ball given by James which had been attributed to him in the columns of the *Quotidienne*.[171] In his *Augsburger Zeitung* articles of the early 1840s, he repeatedly went out of his way to praise James, comparing him favourably with other bankers like Benoît Fould, for example, and praising his philanthropic work.[172] The most fulsome—if faintly facetious—praise of all came in the article published in June 1843 (later incorporated in his "Lutetia") which likened James to Louis XIV for his ability to identify talent in others: "In order to make quite sure of not causing offence I will today compare M. de Rothschild to the sun. I can do this, firstly, because it costs me nothing; and secondly, because I can well justify it at a time like the present because now everyone pays homage to M. de Rothschild in the hope of being warmed by his golden rays." A few months later Heine was able to do more than merely praise James when his publisher Julius Campe sent him the manuscript of a highly critical history of the Rothschilds—the radical republican Friedrich Steinmann's *The House of Rothschild: Its History and Transactions*. Heine wrote that if the manuscript were to be suppressed it would repay the service "which Rothschild has shown me for the past 12 years, as much as this can honestly be done."[173]

Many subsequent writers have assumed that the main reason for Heine's kid-gloved treatment of James at this time was financial. But there is no record of any financial assistance from James to Heine until 1845, for the reason that before then Heine did not need such help. That, in fact, is the whole point of the passage in "Lutetia" which follows the comparison with Louis XIV, in which Heine explicitly denies wishing to join the horde of beggars who surround James:

> If I may speak in confidence, this frenzied veneration is no small affliction to the poor sun which gets no respite from its adorers . . . I really believe that money is more a curse than a blessing to him; if he had a harder heart he would endure less discomfort . . . I counsel every man who is in dire need of money to go to M. de Rothschild; not in order to borrow from him (I doubt whether he would have much success in that endeavour!) but to comfort himself with the sight of the misery money can cause.

James, argues Heine, is tortured "because he has too much money, because all the money in the world has flowed into his gigantic cosmopolitan pocket and because he has to carry such a burden around with him while all around the great rabble of starvelings and thieves stretch out their hands to him. And what terrible, what dangerous hands they are!" And Heine then tells a very different kind of joke, in which he is the straight-man and James the wit: " 'How are you?' a German poet once asked M. le baron. 'I am going mad,' the latter replied. 'I won't believe that,' said the poet, 'until you start throwing money out of the window.' The baron interrupted him with a sigh. 'That, precisely, is my madness: that I don't throw money out of the window occasionally.' "

When Heine came to rework the original newspaper articles into "Lutetia" ten years later, however, he was able to add (in his "Retrospective Explanation") a kind of postscript to this joke. Then he had been well off; but that was no longer the case.

> The indigent men whom I had liberally aided laughed at me when I said that in future I would not have enough for my own needs. Was I not related to all sorts of millionaires? Had not [Rothschild], the generalissimo of all millionaires, the millionairissimo, called me his friend? What I could never make my clients understand was that this great millionairissimo called me his friend only because I never asked him for money. Had I done so, our friendship would soon have been at an end. The days of David and Jonathan, of Orestes and Pylades are past. The poor blockheads who wanted my help thought it was easy to obtain this commodity from the rich. They never saw, as I did, the terrible locks and bars with which their great money chests are secured.[174]

To appreciate the significance of this, it is necessary to know a little of Heine's financial circumstances. Before his uncle Salomon Heine's death in December 1844, Heine had received an annual allowance from his rich relative of 4,000 marks. Salomon Heine's will left Heine a lump sum of 8,000 marks, but his allowance was promptly halved by his cousin Carl, plunging the Heine family into a protracted and bitter wrangle which was not resolved until 1847. It was at this point that Heine for the first time began to need the Rothschilds for their money as well as their friendship.[175] To begin with, he merely sought investment advice, but as his health deteriorated this gradually acquired a charitable dimension.[176] In 1846 James involved Heine in a speculation in railway shares which earned him 20,000 francs.[177] The following year he offered to give his "friend" "the most preferential treatment" in the new French government loan.[178] By 1852, however, Heine's tone was detectably that of the *Schnorrer.*

> Whenever fortune smiled on your colossal business operations with particular favour, you allowed not only the closest friends of your house, but also that great child the poet to have a bite at the cherry. At this moment, when you are again taking the leading part in a tremendous enterprise and are emerging victorious and more of a millionaire than ever from the revolutionary storms, I take the liberty of reminding you that I have not yet died, although my condition hardly deserves to be called "life."[179]

When the request was granted, Heine was pathetically grateful for "this latest proof of your goodness . . . The blessing of God is clearly upon you, and any contact with you brings good luck."[180] Three years later he made a similar request to

Anselm for shares in the new Austrian Creditanstalt; this too was granted, to the tune of 100 shares. Heine's letters of thanks—alternately sycophantic and embarrassed—indicate how hard he found it to be reduced to begging.[181] Less than two months later he was dead.

In all this, an important role was played by James's wife Betty, with whom Heine had conducted what might be described as an elegant flirtation in the 1830s. They had met at James's Boulogne château: looking back many years later, Heine recalled in a letter to Betty "the sunny day in Boulogne where you first appeared to me with all your magical charm."[182] The meeting must have taken place some time before 1834, when he sent her a copy of his new book *Der Salon*, signing himself as "Ihr ergebener Schützling"—"your faithful protégé." A year later, he described her to a friend as his "earliest patroness in Paris."[183] When he wrote promising to visit her, he could not resist adding that her "pretty, smiling face" was "constantly in his memory."[184] Nor did he confine such expressions to private communications, praising her in one of his articles of the 1830s as "not only one of the best looking women in Paris but [one] who is also distinguished in intellect and knowledge."[185] Nothing is more futile than for the historian to try to infer the intensity of such an attraction, much less the real nature of such a relationship, from a few written remnants; but these seem more than merely formal compliments to the wife of a patron. "I discovered the other day by chance," he wrote to her in 1840, enclosing the proofs of *Ludwig Börne*, "that the beautiful lady whom I took to be only intelligent and virtuous also possesses a great soul. Baron James is indeed the richest of men—but not because of his money . . . Please believe, Mme la baronne, that the interest I take in your house is of no common sort; and accept my assurance of complete devotion for the rest of my days."[186] Yet at some point in the 1840s the friendship began to fade. He continued to send her his books: in 1847 copies of *Atta Troll* and a poem called "The Angel" which may have been inspired by her;[187] in 1852 a copy of *Romancero;* two years later the *Vermischte Schriften* and in 1855 his *Poèmes et légendes.*[188] But they saw little of one another—she became, as he put it, "a doubting Thomas" towards him[189]—perhaps because of Heine's deteriorating health; perhaps because he disapproved of the Rothschilds' role in the 1848 revolutions;[190] most probably because, as Heine had foreseen, his need for money corrupted the relationship.

The contrast between Heine's relationship with the Rothschilds and that of his French contemporary Balzac is pronounced; indeed, they are like mirror images of each another. While Heine fretted that James might take umbrage at his writings, Balzac blithely caricatured him with only the most perfunctory disclaimers. While Heine decorously flirted with James's wife, Balzac sought to palm off one of his old mistresses on him. And while Heine agonised about accepting share options from the Rothschilds, Balzac happily borrowed from James and sought to avoid repaying him for as long as possible. In a famous aside, Balzac described encountering Heine and James in the street one day in 1837: "C'est-à-dire tout l'esprit et tout l'argent des Juifs."[191] It was the latter which interested him more, though with characteristic egocentricity he persistently misspelt James's name, usually as "Rostchild."

The two first met at Aix in the summer of 1832.[192] James at once took to the mercurial writer, who combined the carnal appetites of Byron with the prose output of Dickens. He immediately offered to assist him with his plan to visit Italy, offering a letter of introduction to Carl and the use of his couriers to Naples. A few months later, having heard nothing more, James wrote to remind Balzac of his offer and to invite him to dinner, chiding him affably for not calling on them since his return to Paris.[193] In Vienna two years later, Balzac took advantage of this goodwill by borrowing 500 francs from Salomon against a bill drawn on his unsuspecting publisher in Paris.[194] He also seems to have asked Betty that same November for some kind of guarantee during negotiations with another publisher.[195]

Relations were at their most cordial in the mid-1840s. In 1842 Balzac offered James tickets for his disastrous play *Les Ressources de Quinola* (appropriately enough, about the sinking of a steamship), and two years later dedicated *Un Homme d'affaires* to "Monsieur le Baron James de Rothschild / Conseil Général d'Autriche à Paris, Banquier."[196] In return, James forwarded his letters to the Polish Countess he was wooing and eased her passage through customs when she went to Naples.[197] More importantly, he provided Balzac with 150 shares in the new Northern railway line in 1846; having paid the first instalment, the writer promptly borrowed 17,000 francs from James, offering the shares as security.[198] He also borrowed a further sum—around 50,000 francs—by mortgaging his fiancée's Polish estate in order to buy a large house in the rue Fortunée. As he prepared to leave for Poland in 1846, Balzac even asked James to help him establish his former housekeeper (and mistress) in a stamp shop, for which a licence was required. Balzac's account of the negotiations is worth quoting for the light it sheds on James's capacity for Rabelaisian banter:

> Rotschild . . . asked me whether *she* was pretty, whether I had had her. "A hundred and twenty-one times," I told him, "and, if you want her, I'll give you her."
>
> "Does she have children?" he inquired.
>
> "No, but give her some."
>
> "I'm sorry, but I protect only women with children." This was his way of escaping. Had she had children he would have said he never protected immorality.
>
> "Well now, do you actually believe, Baron, that you can split hairs with me? I'm a Northern shareholder! I am going to write you out a note, and you'll take care of my business as if it were a railway with 400,000 shares."
>
> "How's that?" he said. "If you can make me do it, I'll admire you all the more."
>
> "And you shall do it," I told him, "otherwise, I'll turn your wife loose on you so she can keep an eye on you."
>
> He burst out laughing and fell back into his armchair saying: "I give in out of sheer exhaustion; business is killing me. Make out your note."
>
> I made it out and went to see Madame James.[199]

Presumably Balzac considered the complete edition of his works which he sent to Betty that same year repayment enough for all these favours.[200]

But the years after 1847 were not, as we shall see, a time when James could afford to be indulgent towards his debtors, no matter how trifling the sums involved, and no matter how amusing the debtor. In October 1848 Balzac—now ensconced in Wierzchownia—was appalled to hear from his mother that Rothschilds had refused to accept a draft for 2,500 francs drawn by one of his other bankers. Concluding that James now intended to call in the 17,000 francs he owed him, and fearing that he would accordingly deduct the money from any new remittances Balzac received, the author attempted a crude fraud: instead of having money paid to himself, he arranged for a payment of 31,000 francs to be made to his mother in her maiden name. The ruse evidently failed, and by February 1849 Balzac was frantically trying to meet the next payment due on the Northern shares by means of another banker's draft. "You have no idea," he wrote irascibly to his mother that March, "how much that debt of 17,000 francs to R[othschild] restricts me and restricts all my movements." Not that Balzac took the matter personally: veteran spendthrift that he was, he could always see the creditor's point of view. "The House of Rothschild," he acknowledged, "like beavers after a thunderstorm, has to occupy itself with repairing the disasters which 1848 has wrought in all its finances."[201] By the time he returned to Paris in the summer of 1850, normal service had been resumed: on June 11, just two months before his death from a bewildering concatenation of ailments, Balzac was arranging with Rothschilds to invest in a hundred Banque de France shares.[202] Behind his coffin, along with Victor Hugo, Alexandre Dumas and a throng of Parisian hacks and literati, as if sprung from *La Comédie humaine* itself, walked James.[203] The Rothschilds did Balzac one final favour thirty-two years later, when they bought the house in the rue Fortunée from his widow for ten times the original purchase price.[204]

Literal-minded modern scholars tend to dispute the notion that James was the model for Balzac's fictional banker Nucingen.[205] They point to obvious dissimilarities: Nucingen is said to be from Alsace, he is the son of a convert from Judaism, he has no brothers, he is too old (at sixty in 1829) to be James, has only one daughter and so on. Yet Balzac himself told his future wife in 1844 that James—"the high Baron of financial feudalism"—was "Nucingen to the last detail, and worse."[206] And a careful reading of the relevant parts of Balzac's great work shows how much of Nucingen was inspired by James. None of the other financiers of the day is more plausible as a model; fictionalised he may be, but Nucingen *is* James, to the extent that Balzac could never have created the former had he never known the latter.

Nucingen is first introduced in *Le Père Goriot* (1834–5) as the husband of one of the two self-centred daughters of the impoverished *vermicellier* Goriot. He is a "banker of German origin who had been made a baron of the Holy [Roman] Empire," speaks with a thick, phonetically-spelt German accent (for example, "quelque chose" becomes "keke chausse") and lives in the rue Saint-Lazare, "in one of those light houses, with thin columns [and] mean porches which are considered *pretty* in Paris, a true banker's house, full of expensive elegance, ornaments [and] stair landings in marble mosaic." In this early incarnation—as also in his second appearance in the *Histoire de la Grandeur et de la Décadence de César Birotteau* (1833–7)—Nucingen is portrayed as coarse and ruthless.[207] When the bankrupt *parfumier* Birotteau finally secures an audience with him—again the "superb staircase" and "sumptuous apartments" are described—he is subjected to a baffling interview and referred back to another banker, du Tillet, who is in reality the architect of his destruction. Again, Balzac makes much of Nucingen's atrocious pronunciation of French: "The shrewd baron, in order to be able to renege on promises given well but badly kept, had retained the horrible pronunciation of German Jews who flatter themselves that they can speak French."[208]

This suggestion of fraudulent practice is developed at great length in *La Maison Nucingen* (1837–8), in which Nucingen's origins and methods are discussed. The key to Nucingen's success, Balzac suggests, is a succession of bogus suspensions of payment, whereby he has forced his creditors to accept depreciated paper in payment. Having done this in 1804 and again in 1815, he is poised to unfold his third and most ambitious scheme, a swindle perpetrated at the expense of (among others) a young nobleman and the widow and daughters of the Alsatian banker from whom he had made his first fortune. Naturally, given the imputation of criminality, Balzac is careful to ensure that his character is formally distinguishable from Rothschild: thus Nucingen is described as "the son of some Jew who converted [to Christianity] out of ambition," and is said "secretly to envy the Rothschild brothers." But the resemblances are hard to miss. His second great coup involves a massive purchase of funds before the battle of Waterloo, for example. There is a description of Nucingen's appearance which also has a familiar ring: "Cubic, fat, he is as heavy as a sack, as immobile as a diplomat. Nucingen has the heavy hand and a lynx look that never lights up; his depth is not apparent but concealed; he is impenetrable, and you never see him coming." The sheer extent of Nucingen's financial influence is also suggestive: "His genius embraces everything. This elephant of finance sells deputies to the ministers and the Greeks to the Turks. For him commerce is . . . the totality of varieties, the unity of specialities." At one point Nucingen is even compared, as Nathan had been in his lifetime, with Napoleon. And, perhaps most tellingly, he is said to have been "created a peer by the July Revolution, and a grand officer of the Legion of Honour"—the latter of which honours, as we have seen, James did in fact receive from Louis Philippe.[209]

La Maison Nucingen is not, of course, intended to be a realistic portrait of James de Rothschild. The book is primarily a satire on the volatile financial markets of the 1830s, which the character of Nucingen personifies *ad absurdum*. Its underlying "moral" is that "the debtor is stronger than the creditor," and its most memorable passage summarising "the true principles of the age of gold in which we live" makes it easy to see why the political left sought to claim Balzac as one of their own after his death: "There are arbitrary acts which are criminal when committed by an individual against another individual, which are expunged when they are extended to a multitude, just as a drop of prussic acid becomes innocent in a bucket of water."

Yet this was far from Balzac's last word on Nucingen. In *Splendeurs et Misères des Courtisanes* (1838–47), he is cast in a wholly different light, as the world-weary *vieillard* who falls in love with a prostitute he has glimpsed in the bois de Vincennes. In fact, she is the lover of the amoral, ambitious Lucien Chardon, who is himself in thrall to the Mephistophelean master-criminal Vautrin, and the three aim to extort a million francs from the lovesick Nucingen. Once again Balzac takes the opportunity to develop his romantic critique of capitalism: "All rapidly accumulated wealth is either the result of luck or discovery, or the result of a legalised theft . . . The 1814 constitution proclaimed the reign of money, and success became the supreme rationale of an atheistical epoch." Once again, however, it is remarkable how many Rothschild allusions crop up. Nucingen is described here as "this Louis XIV of the counting house." Indeed, Balzac describes Nucingen's role as a patron in terms which are almost identical to those used by Heine in "Lutetia" (so much so that plagiarism seems possible):

M. de Nucingen, a pure banker, without any inventiveness beyond his calculations . . . only believed in certain values. As regards art, he had the good sense to turn, gold in hand, to the experts in such things, taking the best architect, the best surgeon, the most eminent connoisseur of paintings and statues, the most skilful lawyer, as soon as it was a matter of building a house, checking his health, acquiring some artefacts or a property.

It is also worth noting how much more sympathetically Nucingen is portrayed here, suggesting the influence of the growing friendship between Balzac and James. Nucingen knows he is making a fool of himself: "Hêdre hâmûreusse à mon hâche, cheu zai piène que rienne n'ai blis ritiquille; mai ké foullez-vû? za y êde!" ("Etre amoureux à mon âge, je sais bien que rien n'est plus ridicule; mais que voulez-vous? ça y est!") And he manages to recover some dignity when she spurns his advances, writing her an elegant and sensitive letter—in perfect French.[210]

By contrast, Nucingen's final appearances in *Un Homme d'affaires* (1845) and *La Cousine Bette* (1846) are brief: here he is merely the last resort of desperate borrowers like Maxime de Trailles, the Balzac-like wastrel Desroches and Baron Hulot, the poor Bonapartist functionary in need of a dowry for his daughter. By this time, the exigencies of his own financial position were plainly uppermost in the writer's mind: the dedication of a book about disreputable creditors to James on the eve of Balzac's own request for financial assistance is thus revealed as a characteristic joke.[211] Even the sum of money which Hulot tries to borrow from Nucingen is similar to the amount Balzac borrowed from James in the same year *La Cousine Bette* was published. Historians are usually nervous of using literature as evidence; but when art so closely imitates life, and in doing so sheds so much light on the otherwise obscure private life of a man like James de Rothschild, it would be a pity to ignore it.

THIRTEEN

Quicksilver and Hickory
(1834–1839)

I simply can't see why, when we ask you for the time being not
to do something or other, then, without any particular reason,
the very same thing happens, because everyone must know what
is best for the place where he resides.

—JAMES TO HIS ENGLISH NEPHEWS, OCTOBER 1836[1]

The Rothschild system of issuing and trading bonds for the European powers was immensely lucrative as well as giving the family real political leverage. Yet it had its limits. When the Rothschilds attempted to extend their geographical reach to new regions in the course of the 1830s, they encountered difficulties. With the benefit of hindsight, the historian can see that one of the greatest omissions of the period was the failure to establish a stable and reliable Rothschild base in the United States of America. However, to see why this did not happen it is necessary to unravel a complex story of trial and error which had its roots in the highly unstable finances of Spain and Portugal; for the route which led the Rothschilds to the Americas started here.

Iberian Dilemmas

While the rest of Europe had revolutions, it might be said, Iberia had dynastic civil wars. Superficially, there were ideological divisions, as elsewhere, between ultra-conservative clericals, moderate constitutional liberals and more radical democrats. Fundamentally, however, the politics of Spain and Portugal in the 1830s and the 1840s had more in common with the politics of the Wars of the Roses. From a banker's point of view, there is nothing *a priori* wrong with civil war in a foreign country. Like any other kind of war, civil wars require money and with domestic tax systems in disarray that money usually has to be borrowed. Though they were more cautious than other bankers, the Rothschilds proved ready and willing to lend to whichever side they thought would win in both Portugal and Spain. Their principal concern in the first phase of this involvement was that other powers might become embroiled in the conflicts, leading to the general European war which was the Rothschilds' recurrent nightmare. As it turned out, no such escalation occurred, though Britain, France and Austria all sought to interfere indirectly in the affairs of the Peninsula. The real difficulty was that, in the absence of decisive foreign intervention, the Iberian civil wars dragged on inconclusively. This meant that by the late 1830s the interest was no longer being paid on loans raised just a few years before. As a result, Spanish and Portuguese bonds performed the same role in the bond market of the 1830s as had been played by Latin American bonds in the 1820s: as James put it succinctly (and repeatedly), they were little better than "shit."

This resemblance was not coincidental. For earlier events in Latin America were not only responsible for sending inveterate troublemakers like Dom Pedro back to Europe; they also fundamentally weakened the fiscal systems of both Portugal and Spain, which had come to rely heavily on the revenues from their transatlantic empires. Portugal and Spain were thus not merely politically unstable; in many ways that was also true of France, where a similar kind of dynastic feud had seemed a possibility after 1830. The Iberian problem was one of chronic national insolvency. Trying to make money from two countries which recurrently teetered on the verge of bankruptcy proved much less easy than the more sanguine Rothschilds initially assumed.

The Portuguese story is the less complex of the two; it also proved to be the less lucrative. We have already seen that Nathan had interested himself in the affairs of Portugal and her sister-kingdom Brazil in the 1820s, arranging loans for both, secure in the knowledge that this was a traditional British sphere of interest. In doing so, he had unwittingly been lending to both the combatants in the impending civil war: Dom Miguel, whose coup he had backed in 1828, and his brother Dom Pedro, the Emperor of Brazil and father of Maria II, the Queen of Portugal whom Miguel had overthrown. In April 1831 Pedro was forced to abdicate in Brazil in favour of his son; he at once set off for France, intent on restoring his daughter to power in Portugal.[2] For no very good reason, French liberals (and some British Whigs) tended to assume that Pedro was a kindred spirit, casting Miguel as a kind of Portuguese Charles X. Pedro therefore had little difficulty in raising money in Paris and men in London, and by July 1832 was able to seize control of Oporto. However, in the absence of popular support it took him until May 1834 finally to secure Miguel's surrender—a victory which he mainly owed to the assistance he received from the English sea captain Charles Napier. Four months later Pedro himself expired, having lived just long enough to restore his daughter to power.

Yet that did not bring Portugal's political troubles to an end. Finding Maria a suitable husband proved harder than expected when her first consort, the Duke of Leuchtenberg, died after just four months of marriage, and a replacement—Ferdinand of Saxe-Coburg, nephew of the Belgian King—was not found until 1836. More seriously, Maria's supporters quickly split into two rival factions: moderate "Chartists" (loyal to the constitution of 1826) and more radical "Septembrists" (who looked further back to the more liberal 1822 version). Shortly after Maria's marriage to Ferdinand, the latter faction forcibly seized power. The Chartists attempted to do the same in 1837 and succeeded five years later. In 1846 there was yet another revolution, which precipitated joint Anglo-Spanish intervention the following year.

The Rothschilds watched the unfolding of the Portuguese civil war with mixed feelings, loath to miss out on any lucrative new business, but worried that the conflict might escalate.[3] By 1832 James had begun tentatively to participate in the operations of the Spanish financier Juan Alvarez Mendizábal, who had issued a £2 million loan for Pedro in Paris the year before. This was a gamble, for although there was indirect British and French support for Pedro, Austrian-backed support for Miguel could not be ruled out. Moreover, Miguel was able to raise a 40 million franc loan in Paris that same year. This explains why James was so pessimistic about the "Portuguese rubbish" from the outset.[4] His view was that only a guarantee from Britain and France would make a Portuguese loan into "a nice piece of business"; but this Palmerston (wisely) refused to give.[5] It is therefore not unreasonable to conclude that, when he and Nathan issued a £4 million loan for the restored government of Maria II in 1835, they were consciously dealing in what might today be called "junk bonds." For, even with Pedro dead and Miguel exiled, the likelihood of Portugal maintaining interest payments on these bonds was low. Thus James regarded those to whom he sold the bonds as, to put it mildly, naive. "We have a great many asses who have been buying this shit," he candidly reported to Nathan in early April. The 3 per cent bonds—which the Rothschilds issued at 67.5—enjoyed a temporary vogue, but within a matter of months were sliding rapidly as political instability persisted in Lisbon.[6] Within a year they had fallen to 55; and by 1839 they stood at just 25. James later explained the rationale of the Rothschild involvement: such bonds were "the only thing on which one can gamble and speculate, for what is there to gain from the French rentes? Nothing. So the world is now speculating on this shit. One can gamble with these but one can never hold on to them."[7] In other words, these high-yielding bonds were never seriously regarded as assets for long-term investors. They were mere speculative objects.

The trouble with selling "rubbish" is that some naive investors—or unlucky speculators—will inevitably be left holding it when the interest ceases to be paid; and they are unlikely to think very highly of the original vendor. For the sake of their own reputation, and therefore their ability successfully to float future bond issues, it was in the Rothschilds' interest to avoid a Portuguese default. As early as March 1835 James was nervously suggesting that the Rothschilds "should send someone over there [to Lisbon] two months before the interest falls due so as to assist the Government. We are too deeply involved in this matter not to try to render any assistance we can to these people."[8] By May it was obvious that even with a change of Finance Minister there was not going to be enough cash to pay the interest due that year. "I think that we will have to pay the interest," he concluded gloomily. The disadvantage of this, however, was that bondholders would "get accustomed to the idea that you will [always] have to extend your helping hand, and in the end you will be unable to retreat."[9]

As it turned out, however, Nathan's plan for a further £1 million advance was rejected in favour of a more generous offer by Goldschmidt, prompting a wave of retaliatory selling by the Rothschild houses in London and Paris. "There is no occasion for our supporting the market now that others have interfered in the Portuguese affairs," wrote Lionel angrily from his dying father's bedside in Frankfurt. "We can job in and out and only study our own advantage."[10] James was beside himself at the conduct of the Lisbon government: "The miserable Portuguese Minister wants to cut the throat of his own credit so that one can't tell the world with any degree of certainty that the interest will be paid, and so he makes it appear as if he wants to bring everything down."[11] "Your Portuguese are giving me a fever," he wrote to London in December 1836. "Never before in my life has anything upset me so much. These people are nothing more than the scum of the earth." The only aim now was to "persuade the public that these people have positively decided to ruin the credit and that we on our part have been doing everything in our power to prevent this." "We have to get out of this shit as quickly as we can," he reiterated a day later, "because we are dealing here with thoroughly disreputable people and with a minister who speculates on the demise of his own country."[12]

Yet when the same problem arose in 1837 Lionel had no option but to offer once again to bail the government out: after all, the bonds on which the interest was due were still the bonds which had been issued by Rothschilds two years before. James too could see no alternative but to offer another short-term advance, especially now that the Rothschilds' old friends the Saxe-Coburgs had become involved through Ferdinand's marriage to Maria.[13] The strategy in 1837 was to give Lisbon one final injection of cash "to prevent it being said that a Rothschild loan was not paid," and then to pull out.[14] Even this attempt at damage-limitation misfired, leading to a protracted and highly embarrassing legal wrangle with the Portuguese government.[15] Lionel sought to rationalise what had happened: Portuguese bonds might have fallen from 75 to 25, but "still our name is not lost."[16] His uncle was unconvinced. "I don't wish to speculate with any money whatsoever on this muck" was more or less his last word on the subject of Portugal.[17] Subsequent attempts to involve the Rothschilds in the country's finances were firmly rebuffed.[18] Nor did their rivals let them forget the débâcle. When Barings were approached for a loan in 1846, one of the partners argued strongly against any involvement on the grounds that "Portuguese credit has been so tainted by the mismanagement of the Jews and Jobbers . . . that it would not be a very desirable connexion for any House wishing to stand well with the public."[19]

Spain was politically not so very different, though economically she had much more to offer than Portugal. Here too the source of conflict was dynastic: did Salic law—giving preference to the male line—apply in Spain, in which case Ferdinand VII's brother Carlos was his rightful heir; or should the throne pass to his only child, Isabella, born in 1830? Technically, Isabella's case was the stronger: although Salic law had been introduced in 1713, it had been repealed—albeit secretly—by Carlos IV in the Pragmatic Sanction of 1789, and Ferdinand took the precaution of publicising this fact five months before his daughter's birth. On the other hand, when he fell ill in 1832, it became apparent that his brother Carlos had enough might (if not right) on his side to challenge Isabella's claim, forcing her mother Maria Christina into temporarily revoking the Pragmatic Sanction. Ferdinand's unexpected recovery forced Carlos to flee to Portugal, but civil war was now more or less inevitable. When the king finally died in September 1833, Carlos revealed that he had no intention of recognising Maria Christina's regency, returning to Spain to mobilise his supporters ten months later. As in Portugal, the dynastic dispute had an ideological significance: Carlos was the Spanish Dom Miguel, the reactionary "wicked uncle," while his sister-in-law Christina (after an initial dalliance with reforming absolutism in the person of Cea Bermudez) allied herself with "moderate" liberals like Martinez de la Rosa, and therefore enjoyed conditional support from the more "progressive" democrats who harked back to the revolution of 1820. The war also had a regional dimension: while Carlism was strongest in the countryside of Navarre and the Basque provinces, Isabella's cause appealed more to the bureaucrats of Madrid and the financiers of the country's main commercial centres.[20]

There were four reasons for offering financial support to the government of the young Queen. As in the case of Portugal, there were the short-run profits to be made from selling new, high yield bonds to investors bored with increasingly predictable consols and rentes; but of course such bonds could just as easily be issued for Don Carlos. The decision to plump for Isabella was partly diplomatic: the Quadruple Alliance of 1834 between Britain, Portugal, Spain and (later) France seemed to signal unequivocal foreign support for Isabella's regime from the two powers who traditionally wielded most influence in the Peninsula. More importantly, however, Spain (unlike Portugal) had a particular kind of asset which proved irresistibly attractive to the Rothschilds as a security for any loans: the mercury mines of Almadén to the west of Ciudad Real, one of only two major sources of the metal in the world at this time. For over three centuries, the mines had played a pivotal role in the international monetary system because of the use of mercury (or "quicksilver" as the Rothschilds preferred to call it) in the refining of silver and gold in Latin America. This in itself made them attractive to bankers. The crucial point was that the Spanish government traditionally sold the rights to work the mines and to market their output to private companies, most famously mortgaging them in the sixteenth century to the Augsburg bankers, the Fuggers.[21] Decisively, these mines were controlled by Isabella's forces for most of the civil war. Finally, despite the dramatic contraction of her American empire, Spain still had lucrative commercial ties with her remaining colonies, notably Cuba and the Philippines; the former in particular was attractive to the Rothschilds because of its importance in the tobacco trade.

There were also, on the other hand, three difficulties attendant on any financial involvement with Spain. Firstly, and most obviously, there was the confusion caused by the country's protracted and inconclusive civil war. It was not until 1839—six years after Ferdinand's death—that the Carlist forces were effectively defeated. During that period, there were repeated changes of government in Madrid, as "Moderados" and "Progresistas" (to give the factions their later names) vied for control, the latter pressing for a more parliamentary and anti-clerical regime than Maria Christina had ever intended. Matters were further complicated by the growth in political influence of the leading military commanders; indeed it was one of these, General Baldomero Espartero, who, with Progresista support, forced Maria Christina to abdicate as Regent just a year after leading her forces to victory. Espartero in turn was ousted in 1843 and replaced a year later by his rival General Narváez, who presided over what amounted to a decade of Moderado hegemony until yet another revolution in 1854.

The second argument against involvement in this unstable country was furnished by the bonds issued under the liberal regime of the early 1820s, the so-called "Cortes" (that is, parliament) bonds, which King Ferdinand had refused to honour following the suppression of the revolution. A law of 1831 formally "deferred" interest payments on these bonds for forty years, but this was scant consolation to the investors who had bought them;[22] and the English holders of the Cortes bonds were determined to oppose any further issues of Spanish paper on the London stock exchange until they had secured better terms. Events were to reveal the extreme difficulty of re-establishing Spanish credit internationally with memories of default so fresh. Finally, the support of the so-called "Northern courts"—Austria, Russia and Prussia—for the Carlist cause proved to be stronger than their support for Dom Miguel. Even if he could not contemplate direct military intervention, Metternich proved able to exert considerable diplomatic influence over events in Spain.

For all these reasons, the Rothschilds were initially reluctant to act alone in Spain. As early as December 1830 James and Nathan entered a kind of "sleeping" partnership (in return for a 2.5 per cent commission on sales) with the company which leased the Almadén mines in that year. This was intended as a first step towards greater involvement. "When the time comes that the Government wants to farm it out," James observed to his brother, "you will then be well placed to know exactly who all the customers are and how much one can sell and you will then find it that much easier to submit a proposal for the whole sum." More problematically, as it proved, James committed the Rothschilds to share all Spanish financial business with a consortium of Paris bankers led by the Spaniard Aguado.[23] This provided a degree of camouflage for speculative dealings in existing Spanish paper (for the Cortes bonds continued to be traded, though at a price of around 30);[24] but it placed awkward restrictions on Rothschild room for manoeuvre when new business had to be discussed with the Spanish government. By the summer of 1833, when a major tobacco deal came to nothing, Lionel was already finding the agreement with Aguado and his associates more a hindrance than a help.[25]

The debate over whether to increase or diminish this involvement in Spain placed a greater strain on familial harmony than any other issue the Rothschilds had to contend with before 1848; indeed, it is not too much to say that it threatened to break up the partnership between the five houses. Nathan was evidently keen to play a bigger and more independent role in Spanish finances, a position consistently supported by his nephew Anselm and rather less consistently by Lionel. James vacillated endlessly, one day seeing all the advantages, the next day seeing only the risks: "With this country there is a lot of money to be made, but on the other hand, one could lose a great deal of one's reputation"—this was James's constant refrain throughout the 1830s.[26] "You know my dear Papa how he [James] is," wrote Lionel impatiently: "One minute he is for and one minute he is against the Business."[27] Unlike his own son, Salomon was generally opposed to direct—or, to be precise, overt—involvement, primarily because of the intense pressure to which he was subjected by Metternich. But he too was inclined to waver: "Be so good as to read Uncle Salomon's letters," Lionel urged his father sarcastically in March 1834, "the first for the *Spanish*, the second *against*, the third *for*."[28]

Nathan's initial strategy seems to have been to secure some sort of agreement on the old Cortes bonds as the prelude to any new Spanish loan.[29] However, all the Spanish negotiators with whom the Rothschilds dealt carefully avoided giving a commitment on the issue.[30] After exceptionally convoluted and protracted negotiations,[31] Nathan decided to ignore the warnings of Metternich, the Austrian ambassador Apponyi, the Russian ambassador Pozzo and no fewer than three French ministers (Broglie, Rigny and Soult), all of whom strongly advised the Rothschilds to avoid Spain.[32] Despite the reservations of James and Lionel, who continued to argue for, at most, a joint and preferably anonymous operation with the Paris consortium, on April 18 Nathan unilaterally proposed to advance the Spanish government 15 million francs to pay the interest due at the end of June on its undeferred bonds.[33] He had obtained no firm guarantee from Madrid that the Cortes bonds would be revalued, merely an empty promise that the issue would be raised when the Cortes met. Nor did he receive any security for his advance when the agreement was signed with the Spanish ambassador in Paris and a representative of the Bank of San Fernando on June 7.[34] As the Carlist-inclined Duke of Wellington sardonically observed, the Rothschilds were now well and truly "in the boat";[35] and, just as Metternich and the rest had predicted, "the boat" began to sink almost at once. Given the country's notorious record of default, it is not surprising that Nathan's decision to involve himself in Spanish finances attracted satirical comment. Two cartoons portrayed him as a "Jew-dish-us cakeman," standing by his trademark pillar selling a "rice cake" marked "Loan" (see illustrations 13.i and 13.ii). "Who's for a slice? Who's for a slice?" reads the caption on the first. "All Hot! All Hot! Take care you don't burn your Fingers, Plenty of cakes but none like I make." From his pocket portrudes a bill marked "Spanish." The second cartoon shows the "cakeman" with his stall under his arm, having sold the cake. "Dat rice cake sold very well—I hope it vill agree wid my customers—I vil make anoder."

13.i: Anon., *No. 1. CITY POLITICS—JEW-DISH-US CAKEMAN: WHO'S FOR A SLICE? WHO'S FOR A SLICE?* (1834 or 1835).

13.ii: Anon., *No. 2. CITY POLITICS—JEW-DISH-US CAKEMAN. DAT RICE CAKE SOLD VERY WELL* (1834 or 1835).

It is not easy to see why Nathan acted as he did. It is possible that he (along with Anselm) was lulled by the announcement of the Quadruple Alliance into thinking that the danger of civil war would fade,[36] though there is no indication of any official nudge in this direction from Palmerston; on the contrary, Palmerston's man in Madrid, Charles Villiers, indignantly accused Nathan of "*doing*" the Spanish government with "not very advantageous conditions."[37] The most likely explanation was that he wanted to pre-empt a rival bid by Thomas Wilson or Aguado and establish himself (or James) as "court banker" to Maria Christina, in anticipation of a major new loan and conversion operation when the Cortes finally met. He plainly had a plan ready to convert the old Cortes bonds and probably also anticipated short-run speculative profits, assuming that the announcement of a Rothschild advance would boost their prices. One (admittedly hostile) Austrian diplomat recalled his saying: "I must grant it [the loan] because if I don't, somebody else will."[38] Whatever his motive, the advance was uncharacteristically reckless. As James, Lionel and Anselm had all foreseen, the other French bankers promptly sued James, on the ground that Nathan had acted without due regard to the consortium contract. Only by offering Aguado a new agreement to share any future loan was James able to avert a costly defeat in the courts.[39] Nor did the Spanish government's promise to bring the question of the deferred bonds before the new Cortes satisfy the Committee of the stock exchange in London.[40] In Paris too the markets were unconvinced by Nathan's plan: Spanish bonds fell sharply in late June.[41] Worse still, no sooner had the 15 million francs been paid over than a new Finance Minister took over in Madrid who a month later reneged on the agreement, claiming that the Rothschilds had promised to lend twice the amount; this too Nathan had been warned to expect.

It is not known for sure why the Minister in question, Toreno, was (as James put it) an "enemy." Partly, he was responding to domestic pressure to deal with Spanish bankers like Ardouin, with whom he concluded an alternative loan agreement for £4 million; more importantly, he was intent on a drastic "reduction" of the existing Spanish public debt—a conversion which would have cut the nominal value of Spanish bonds by as much as 75 per cent—something the Rothschilds regarded as a "declaration of bankruptcy."[42] To make matters worse, Toreno's appointment coincided with the return of Don Carlos to Spain and an outbreak of cholera in Madrid.[43] With Apponyi, the Austrian ambassador in Paris, issuing dire warnings as to the consequences of French intervention against Carlos, the price of Spanish bonds plummeted, occasioning suicides and murder threats on the Paris bourse. Yet the Rothschilds, while doing their fair share of selling, could not risk an all-out financial "war" against Toreno, for the top priority in the midst of this débâcle was to retrieve as much as possible of Nathan's 15 million francs, if only in the form of "those stinking [bonds] with which he is going bankrupt."[44] It was, as James said, "an awful mess"; and it revealed very starkly the limitations of financial power when confronted by a government unafraid of the international bond market. "All I want you to declare is that we will get our money back and I ask nothing further of you," James implored the Spanish representative. "My commission is now over," the latter replied, "I have been recalled." In vain, James appealed to the ambassador, to the French government and to Toreno himself. "My dear Nathan," he admitted, putting his finger on the Rothschilds' fundamental weakness, "we don't have any troops to force the Government to do that which it does not want to do."[45]

All along, the Rothschilds had suffered from a lack of first-hand knowledge of Spanish affairs: none of them had visited Madrid and there was no dedicated full-time employee there until July.[46] This explains why in August 1834 it was decided to send Lionel (accompanied by the lawyer Adolphe Crémieux) to thrash out some kind of agreement with Toreno face to face. The British ambassador was impressed by the young man's negotiating skills; however, the Rothschild correspondence reveals that Toreno was able to convince Lionel that a fully fledged loan to Spain was now the only way of averting outright bankruptcy and the advent of a republican government.[47] Anselm alone agreed. James and Nathan by now were interested solely in retrieving the money they had advanced to Toreno's predecessor.[48] In January 1835 they reluctantly agreed to accept the equivalent of 15 million francs as a share of the new loan to be issued by Ardouin.[49] Salomon later estimated their losses on the contract at 1.6 million francs.

Yet Lionel's negotiations achieved what proved to be a more important concession from Toreno; for during his stay at Madrid the contract for the Almadén mines fell due for renewal. As we have seen, the Rothschilds already had a stake in the mines and they had begun to think of increasing their control over the Spanish mercury market during 1834. Indeed, Lionel had explicitly suggested asking for the mines as a guarantee for the 15 million francs advanced.[50] He now outbid four other companies to secure the new contract—essentially by bribing Toreno and the Queen and by offering, instead of a sealed bid, to pay 5 per cent more than the highest rival bid.[51] The following year the contract was renegotiated in such a way that it became rather more advantageous for the Rothschilds.[52] This was the beginning of a long and profitable involvement. According to the Rothschilds' own estimates, the mines at the time of the 1835 agreement were producing between 16,000 and 18,000 hundredweight of mercury a year. Under the 1835 contract, they paid the government rather more (54.5 pesetas or £2.18 per hundredweight) than they had paid under the previous contract (37 pesetas); but were then able to resell the mercury in London for 76–80 pesetas or to silver refineries in Mexico for as much as 150 pesetas per hundredweight. In sterling terms, that represented a profit of at the very least £13,000 a year, with the possibility of more if the output of the mines could be increased without depressing prices. When production was stepped up in 1838, the Rothschilds' annual income from the mines rose to £32,000, though this level of output proved unsustainable. That amounted to more than 13 per cent of the total net revenue from the mines—and no less than 38 per cent of the London house's profits (though half the money was shared with the Paris house).[53] By the 1840s, 20 per cent was James's target return from Almadén.[54]

The acquisition of the mercury rights also signalled a radical change of policy. From now on, rather than issue bonds for Spain against effectively worthless paper securities, they would finance the country's chronically unreliable government by making relatively short-run advances on the royalties they had to pay for the Almadén mercury.[55] Later, similar advances would be made on the basis of copper and tobacco from Cuba.[56] Commodities thus proved to be the best kind of security for loans to unstable states. In his comic poem "Romancero" Heine joked that Mendizábal (who became Finance Minister in 1835) had pawned an ancient pearl necklace "to cover certain / deficits in state finances"; these had duly appeared "at the Tuileries . . . shimmering on the neck of Madame Solomon, baroness."[57] Contemporaries would probably have recognised the allusion to the "jewels" of Almadén.

Of course, the Spanish government may have hoped that the mercury deal would lure the Rothschilds into making a full-scale loan. But in this they were sorely disappointed. True, by the spring of 1835 James was feeling more sanguine about Spain following the success of Ardouin's loan. This, however, proved to be short-lived as the Carlists seemed to gain the upper hand.[58] The key question now became whether any foreign power would intervene to decide the outcome of the civil war.[59] This had always been a possibility: France had intervened in Spain just over a decade before and there had been abortive liberal expeditions in the wake of the 1830 revolution. The Quadruple Alliance also seemed to imply some sort of British action on behalf of Maria Christina's regime (provided the Whigs stayed in power).[60] But it was only after Toreno had wrecked his financial plans that Nathan became a convert to the idea of military intervention, as did Lionel.[61] James, summoned to London to decide the next move, once again wavered. The experience of the early 1830s had made him deeply suspicious of the more hawkish French politicians, and he was inclined to reinforce Louis Philippe's pacific inclinations against the projects for intervention hatched by Thiers. On the other hand, he found it difficult to oppose his elder brother on the Spanish issue and gradually came round to supporting intervention. By contrast, their brother Salomon—who had all along had his doubts about getting involved with Spain—now acted energetically to counter Nathan's arguments for intervention, ultimately going to extraordinary lengths to dissociate himself from his brother's actions in his correspondence with Metternich.

Metternich had been kept well informed of Nathan's actions by the Austrian chargé d'affaires in London, Hummelauer, and a junior official named Kirchner who was supposedly assisting Nathan with his consular duties. He therefore knew that Nathan was arguing for British intervention; indeed, Nathan appears to have admitted it openly to the Austrian ambassador Esterházy.[62] To clear himself of guilt by association, Salomon therefore had to write one of the most extraordinary of all Rothschild letters, addressed to his senior clerk in Vienna, Leopold von Wertheimstein, but explicitly intended for Metternich's eyes. He began by claiming that the collapse in Spanish bond prices following Toreno's appointment as Finance Minister had been engineered by the Rothschilds as an act of "vengeance" on Toreno for the losses he had caused them. According to accounts which Salomon enclosed, Nathan had sold no less than £2 million of Spanish bonds, ruining Toreno's credit and proving that the Rothschilds were now "confirmed enemies of Spain." Not only that, but Salomon and James had then gone to see Talleyrand, Guizot, Broglie and Louis Philippe himself to argue "that France's credit would go to the devil if they intervened, and that they would have to face a second and third revolution." There was therefore no question of the Rothschilds lending "a single farthing" more to Spain. As if to convince Metternich of his sincerity, Salomon's letter concluded by heaping abuse on Nathan's head. "My brother Nathan Mayer," he wrote,

> is one of the ablest men as far as the Exchequer and price movements are concerned but has no special aptitude in other matters . . . [H]e is a child in politics . . . [and] believes that the Powers will be pleased by intervention . . . In other matters that are not concerned with the Bourse, [he] is not particularly bright; he is exceedingly competent in his office, but apart from that, between ourselves, he can hardly spell his own name. This brother of mine, however, is so disgusted with Spain that he can hardly bear himself, just like all of us, only perhaps he feels it more because he realises that he made the advance of 15,000,000 francs without asking any of his partners about it.

Nor was that all. Salomon even went so far as to suggest that Nathan's error had put the entire future of the brothers' partnership in jeopardy:

> I myself do not yet know when we brothers will meet; whether the affair of the Spanish Loan will cause a split we shall see. I am sixty, my brother at Frankfurt is sixty-two; I have only two children and if I live very carefully I can live on the interest of my capital; I have fortunately only to provide for my son, as my Betty is as rich as her father. I do not mean that I intend to give up business but only to see to it that I can sleep peacefully. The Spanish affair has completely ruined my nerves; it is not the loss of money, for even if the whole 15,000,000 francs had been lost my share would have been only 3,000,000, but the unpleasantness which we have had with this business. Now Nathan Mayer Rothschild has four grown-up sons, and Carl has two younger boys, so they manage on the basis of a dozen heads. Because my father has so disposed we shall

probably have to remain together, but I must confess that it has all very much tired and exhausted
Your,
S. M. v. Rothschild.[63]

For good measure, Salomon then accused the Russian ambassador Pozzo of slandering James because he had been excluded from a profitable issue of Austrian bonds.[64] This was no mere charade: the Rothschilds' private correspondence indicates how strongly Salomon felt on this issue. As late as 1840—after Don Carlos had been defeated—James could still tell his nephews:

> [W]e can't make a loan for Spain under our own name, unless a guarantee is provided by England and by France and . . . nevertheless I tell you, my dear nephews, I don't want to have anything to do with it . . . [I]t is only if the Governments provide us with the necessary guarantees that we can give the Northern Powers a reason, otherwise I can tell you, my dear nephews, that the first thing which my good Salomon will do will be to withdraw from the business. Do you think that this deal will generate a large enough profit to justify doing something like this?[65]

It has generally been assumed that on this issue Metternich's political power prevailed over the Rothschilds' financial interests. Armed with good-quality intelligence and making the most of Salomon's desire to acquire the title of Austrian consul for his son and nephews,[66] Metternich appears to have succeeded in scuppering the project of an Anglo-French guaranteed loan to Toreno's mercurial successor, Mendizábal. Like the British ambassador in Spain, Mendizábal assumed that the Rothschilds would back this project, not least because of his business links with James, with whom he had done business in Portuguese bonds.[67] But Nathan—apparently responding to Salomon's pressure—chose to leak the Anglo-French plan to Vienna and more or less deliberately allowed the project to fall through, leaving Mendizábal high and dry. Indeed, he told Palmerston that he had no confidence in the solvency of Mendizábal's government. When the British Foreign Secretary pointed out that the planned sale of crown lands would raise money, Nathan replied with a characteristically earthy image: "Yes, in time, but not in time for the May dividend. It is like telling me at seven o'clock when I want my dinner [that] there is a calf feeding in a field a mile off."[68] Contrary to the widespread expectation in diplomatic circles that they were itching to make such a guaranteed loan, in fact Nathan and James were steadily baling out of Spanish bonds altogether.[69]

The decisive moment in the civil war coincided with the Frankfurt family "summit" and Nathan's death. Ultimately, despite pressure from the French government to come to Maria Christina's assistance, the Rothschilds kept on selling Spanish bonds; indeed, Nathan's last instructions to his sons were to liquidate all their holdings.[70] After his death, this clear-out continued, so that by 1837 the Rothschilds had more or less withdrawn completely from the market for Spanish bonds. The Spanish Prime Minister was now "that stinking Mendizábal," whom James had "never trusted"; Spanish bonds—now trading as low as 19—were simply "muck" or "shit."[71] The fact that Salomon moved so quickly after Nathan's death to secure for Lionel the Austrian consulship in London also seems to point to the importance of Metternich's leverage.[72]

However, although Metternich appeared to have won, the private Rothschild letters show that if France and Britain had intervened militarily—rather than just financially—the Rothschilds might well have resumed large-scale lending to Spain. In ditching Mendizábal, Nathan was not merely bowing to pressure from Vienna. He was acting out of self-interest, in the belief that any loan to Spain was bound to fail in the absence of military intervention: no Spanish government could now afford to pay both the interest on its external debt and an army big enough to beat the Carlists. Despite all that Salomon had said to Metternich, by March 1836 James was privately itching for France to intervene. As he put it to Nathan following an inconclusive meeting with Louis Philippe and Thiers:

> If we should be so fortunate that we, over here, decide to intervene [in Spain], this could make a difference for us of many hundreds of thousands of pounds sterling, and we could earn a great deal of money, because we could then calmly deal in bills, quicksilver and everything else, but, unfortunately, I don't have any influence, nor indeed, does anyone else have influence over the King . . . I hope to God that they will indeed decide to intervene and you can then imagine how much business this will generate. I spoke so much [in favour of intervention] that my tongue nearly fell out of my throat.[73]

When the possibility of French intervention surfaced again in July, he and Lionel were again briefly enthused, only to be disappointed at the half-heartedness of the measures taken.[74] It was the same story when Thiers failed to overcome the King's opposition to intervention in the spring of 1837.[75] Nor should it be assumed that the Rothschilds' refusal to back a full-scale loan to Mendizábal implied a complete withdrawal from Spanish finances. Before long, the practice of making advances on the mercury from the Almadén mines was resumed (despite Salomon's assurances to the contrary to Metternich), making sums of the order of £100,000 available to the government.[76] James also became increasingly interested in the revenue Spain was earning from Havana. In January 1837 some sort of deal was proposed by Mendizábal involving a buy-back of the deferred Cortes bonds in return for bills on Havana. Interestingly, the Rothschilds—Salomon included—were keen to do this, provided it could be kept secret.[77] They were also continuing to pay the salaries of Spanish diplomats in Paris at this time, an arrangement dating back to 1834.[78] Where they drew the line was at issuing bonds. Even when the idea was put forward for a loan secured on Cuban revenues, they showed little serious inclination to get involved (though this hesitation was probably reinforced by the impact of the 1837 American crisis in Cuba and by the contemporaneous gains made by Don Carlos in Spain).[79]

Of course, it would have been difficult to retain control of the lucrative mercury business without making any concessions to the Spanish government. A shot was fired across Rothschild bows when, not long after the fall of Mendizábal in August 1837, the Cortes sought to revoke the Almadén contract, arguing that it had been improperly modified two years before.[80] Defenders of the 1835 contract in Madrid warned that, if deprived of the Almadén mines, the Rothschilds might back Don Carlos "for they are the monetary dynasty of Europe, and a new lever in the balance of power, which might decide the success of the Pretender by inclining the scales in his favour." But only by agreeing to make more (and larger) advances on mercury and Havana bills were the Rothschilds able to retain the contract; and increasingly they had to allow their agent Weisweiller considerable latitude in the granting of such advances to avoid similar challenges, even turning a blind eye to the partnership he struck up with the governor of the Queen's court, Manuel Gaviria.[81] Of all the threats to their position, the biggest was probably posed by the banker Aguado, who returned to dangle the possibility of a large loan in front of the new Espartero government, with a view—so the Rothschilds suspected—to challenging their monopoly at Almadén. The new Finance Minister Alejandro Mon did his best to convince James that without a loan of £5 million the Rothschilds would lose the mines. But Salomon, with Metternich still breathing down his neck, continued to oppose involvement in any such loan unless it could be done through a "front" like the Bank of San Fernando; and James remained leery of the purely economic risks involved (not least because the Carlists managed to occupy Almadén briefly in the course of April 1838).[82] Once again it proved possible to hold on to the mines by means of large advances, which fluctuated between around £200,000 and £400,000.[83] In 1839, with the Carlist threat more or less dead, there was renewed talk of a loan, but the Rothschilds still declined to be involved, showing much more interest in establishing some kind of tobacco monopoly.[84] As James shrewdly anticipated, the defeat of Don Carlos merely unleashed the Moderado opposition to Espartero, replacing one form of political instability with another.

The price of this strategy—which gave the Spanish government as much money as a bond issue, if not more—was a good deal of Austrian irritation. Despite their best efforts, the Rothschilds could not hope to conceal what they were up to from Metternich (it was at this point that they began to realise that Kirchner was effectively spying on them). Yet the consequences were not serious: even James's fears that Lionel might lose his Austrian consulship proved unfounded.[85] Throughout the successive revolutions, coups and pronunciamentos of the early 1840s, Rothschild policy remained consistent: to hang on to Almadén (albeit on rather less lucrative terms), to expand their involvement with the Cuban and Philippines trade, but to eschew bond issues.[86] Politically, their position remained ambiguous: they apparently continued to act as Maria Christina's bankers even after Espartero had overthrown her, while at the same time leaving Weisweiller to maintain normal service first with Espartero and then with his Moderado successor Narváez. This proved to be the only way of reconciling the sharply conflicting interests of the London, Paris and Vienna houses. The agreement reached in 1843 with the Austrian government for the import of 12 million Havana cigars may be seen as a kind of Rothschild peace-offering, designed to reconcile Metternich to the continuation of such business with Spain and her colonies.[87]

A quite different diplomatic complication arose in the mid-1840s when the powers began to debate the question of Queen Isabella's marriage. The French wished to marry Isabella to her hypochondriac (and, they hoped, impotent) cousin Francisco de Asis and her sister to one of Louis Philippe's sons, the duc de Montpensier; Palmerston, appreciating that this might one day put a grandson of Louis Philippe on the Spanish throne, favoured the inevitable Coburg; while Metternich argued for a marriage between Isabella and Don Carlos's son Montemolin, to bridge symbolically the dynastic rift.[88] There was an economic subtext, as usual, with France and Britain seeking trade agreements with Spain, as well as the usual talk of internationally guaranteed loans and renewed efforts by the British bondholders to get their unpaid interest.[89] There was a good deal of excitement about this at the time, including fanciful rumours in Madrid that James was refusing to lend money to Spain until Isabella had settled the succession question by having a son.[90] However, the Rothschilds were little more than reluctant onlookers and occasional messengers in all this: it merely hardened them in their resolve to abandon Spanish bonds.[91] When Guizot and his ambassador in Madrid interpreted James's refusal to back a loan to Narváez and Mon as a vote of no confidence in their marriage schemes, they failed to see that this was merely the continuation of a Rothschild policy dating back fully ten years. Once again the great powers' conflicting interests threatened to impinge on the interests of the Rothschild houses; but this time a position of neutrality was easier to sustain as none of the Queen's possible spouses posed a threat to the Almadén monopoly. Control of the mines remained the sole object of Rothschild policy in Spain. Nor was it to be their last step away from "pure" finance and commerce, into the very different business of mineral extraction (and later also refining).

Yet even the commitment to Almadén was not unconditional. On the contrary: when the mercury contract came up for renewal in 1847, the Rothschilds were so unimpressed by the terms the Spanish government was prepared to offer that they began to contemplate withdrawal. This partly reflected their assessment of the world mercury market. Lionel Davidson's confirmation in 1845 of the existence of substantial mercury deposits in Mexico raised the possibility of discoveries elsewhere in the New World.[92] (The price which the Rothschilds had to pay for the mercury monopoly crept up steadily from 54.5 pesetas in the beginning to 70 pesetas in 1850, while the price at which it could be sold abroad began to slip following these discoveries.) With demand falling especially low in the depressed economic conditions of 1847, the Rothschilds not unreasonably expected the government to improve its terms.[93] For a government which was struggling financially, the choice was between maximising revenue from the mines and securing further cash advances from the Rothschilds. Opting for the former, the Minister elected to publish his offer, effectively ruling out further bargaining. The result was deadlock, with Spanish requests for an advance of £600,000 being firmly refused in the absence of better terms for the mercury contract.[94] As James put it, "If one could earn 20 per cent then I would be all in favour of going ahead with the deal, but as matters stand at present we stand to make only a trivial sum . . . I can't see the big fortunes we stand to make from this deal, nor why we should invest our money in such a venture in these present times."[95] By now, as we shall see, James had found more lucrative financial opportunities.

"That Blasted Country": America

The Rothschilds' interest in Spain not only led them to establish new links with Cuba, the Philippines and Mexico. More by accident than design, it also led them to establish a permanent agency in the country which was to emerge as the dominant force on the other side of the Atlantic: the United States. Yet, despite its phenomenal economic potential and the furious pace of its development after 1820, America—it might as well be said at the outset—was a challenge to which the Rothschilds never quite rose.

The reason for this has not previously been explained. Of course, it was far away, and in many ways quite different in its business culture from Europe—"very sharp and peculiar" was the phrase once used at New Court, a view echoed and immortalised by Dickens in *Martin Chuzzlewit*. But the same might easily be said *a fortiori* of Brazil, with which the Rothschilds developed an enduring relationship. It has been suggested that the American market had been "sewn up" by the Barings before Rothschilds arrived on the scene,[96] and later developed its own home-grown bankers, like J. P. Morgan, who would ultimately eclipse Rothschilds not only in the US but in the world. Yet this too will not quite do: the Rothschilds proved on numerous occasions in the nineteenth century that they had the financial muscle to oust even their most powerful rivals from business they coveted. That they did not do so in America requires a better explanation.

In fact, the answer may partly lie in the peculiarities of American democracy. The Rothschilds, as we have seen, always gave first place to public finance in their operations, and rarely conducted commercial business in a country without also lending to its government. However, this proved difficult in the US. The federal system meant that the financial needs of the central government were strictly limited, while some of the individual states proved to be among the least reliable creditors of the entire nineteenth century. A second and ultimately more serious obstacle was the American tradition of suspicion towards big banks. The Rothschilds generally liked to have a reliable local partner in their international operations, often a national or central bank in the mould of the Bank of England or the Banque de France. In Spain, that role was played by the Bank of San Fernando. In the United States, however, it proved politically impossible to establish such an institution on an enduring basis. The first Bank of the United States (BUS), set up by Alexander Hamilton in 1791, expired twenty years later when the Republican-dominated Congress refused to renew its charter on the ground that it was unconstitutional. The second BUS, established in 1816 with a capital of $25 million, became the focus of a powerful political campaign against the "money power" which was blamed for the deflationary pressures of the succeeding years. Though it survived a legal challenge by the state of Maryland, the Philadelphia-based bank fell victim to the populist President Andrew Jackson, who recognised the electoral advantages of an attack on the "monster," identified as it was with his rival Henry Clay. When the BUS's president, Nicholas Biddle, applied to have its charter renewed in 1832 (four years earlier than was necessary), Jackson vetoed it, vowing: "The Bank is trying to kill me, but I will kill it." Despite Biddle's effort to precipitate a financial panic in retaliation, "Old Hickory"—Jackson's nickname—carried the day, and in 1836 the bank lost its public status, though it continued to exist as a state bank in Pennsylvania. As we shall see, the Rothschilds' instinct was to do business with the BUS; but Jackson's attack fatally undermined its position. It should be added that American suspicion of big banks was allied to a suspicion of foreign banks, and especially Jewish ones. No sooner had the Rothschilds appeared on the American scene than Governor McNutt of Missisippi was denouncing "Baron Rothschild" for having "the blood of Judas and Shylock flow[ing] in his veins, and . . . unit[ing] the qualities of both his countrymen."[97]

Rothschild interest in the US dates from the early 1830s, when an opportunity arose to arrange the payment of a million pounds owing to the Treasury in Washington from France. This coup led to the Rothschilds replacing the Barings as the federal government's London agents.[98] At the same time, Nathan and James began to interest themselves for the first time in American state loans[99] and commercial finance. American exports of cotton and tobacco to Europe were advancing by leaps and bounds, and by the mid-1830s the London and Paris houses were doing a considerable volume of business in the bills generated by this trade, advancing substantial sums to a number of American bankers, notably J. L. and S. I. Joseph.[100] In the American financial crisis of 1836–7, they and all the other firms with which the Rothschilds had dealings got into serious difficulties;[101] and it was at this point that the Rothschilds were forced to make a decision about the future of their involvement in the US, and above all about the nature of their representation there.

The "appointment" of August Belmont (originally Schönberg) as the Rothschilds' agent in New York was an accident. Belmont had joined the Frankfurt house as an apprentice at the age of fifteen, and had risen rapidly through the ranks, getting up at 5 a.m. each morning to improve his French, English and arithmetic. By 1834 he was acting as secretary to one of the partners, visiting Paris, Naples and Rome;[102] and in 1837 it was decided to send him across the Atlantic. However, contrary to a report in the *Allgemeine Zeitung des Judenthums*, the intention was definitely not that Belmont should establish himself as the bank's New York agent.[103] His orders were to take stock of the financial crisis there—to "let us know what is going on and one can then decide accordingly what to do"—and then to proceed to Havana. This planned itinerary reveals that, in James's view, the family's interests in Cuba were what mattered: as he put it, quite apart from existing commitments there of around £100,000, "Spain receives all her income from that land and it is one of the most profitable business ventures." By contrast, he and his nephews had managed to reduce their commitments in the US to just £9,000 by the end of April, and James was prepared to write this remainder off as "a lost cause."[104] The possibility of establishing a Rothschild house in New York was not wholly ruled out, for James recognised the American market's potential and was convinced that there were bargains to be snapped up from the "shipwreck" left by the banking crisis; but he evidently regarded this as a job far in excess of Belmont's capabilities. His trip was intended to be of short duration; indeed, there was not even any question of his taking over the Havana office.[105] What James really wanted was for a Rothschild to go to America.

But who? The debate on this question illuminates the fundamental problem which was to bedevil the Rothschilds' American policy for decades to come: no one wanted to go there—witness James's vain attempts to persuade his nephews to accept the mission. Anthony, he claimed, had "long indicated that he would like to go to America [and] would gladly make use of this opportunity:"

> I am strongly urging him to do so without delay. We have so many interests in that country and in Havana that one of us should immediately go over there. However, I don't believe that you, my dear Anselm, should go there. It is Anthony's turn to do so. I know very well that it is not a pleasure trip but the business has to be attended to and you, my dear Anselm, can't go there, firstly, because my brother Amschel is not feeling

well enough to remain in Frankfurt with my brother Carl this coming summer. The latter also wants to take the waters . . . and thirdly, you are a married man whereas Anthony is a bachelor so that I can't see any reason whatsoever why it should not be Anthony rather than you who should go. Well, I don't have anyone here who knows English . . . I think that it will be possible to earn a lot of money in America. The American funds which one can sell in London will be purchasable in America for next to nothing, for no House has any credit over there and . . . one can earn some very nice profits. Well, once you are in America you can then send Belmont ahead of you to Havana . . . In short, my dear nephew, I urge you to think it over very carefully but whatever plan you decide to proceed with the main thing is that you do it without any delays.[106]

For reasons which are unclear, this proposal was abandoned or rejected, possibly because of the opposition of Anthony's mother.[107] However, a month later—and a week and a half after Belmont had reached New York—James tried again. "Don't you think," he asked his nephews somewhat disingenuously, "that Belmont should go from America to Havana, for our interests in America are no longer so substantial? I don't have anyone here and if you so want then I will go to America and Belmont can then go to Havana for the trip to America is no great deal. It is child's play."[108] If this was intended to throw down the gauntlet to his nephews, it very nearly worked, to judge by James's next letter:

Well my dear Nat, you ask me what I meant when I said that had I been younger I would have gone to Havana and whether I was trying to give you a subtle hint. I must therefore tell you quite frankly what my thoughts regarding this matter are. I would most certainly have gone to Havana in person . . . For me personally this would have been a trip which I would gladly have undertaken. However, if one of my nephews wanted to go there I would then oppose such a plan with all my strength and my love and would not permit it for [Havana] is too far away and too dangerous because of the heat and, moreover, it is not important enough for our business to justify one's exposure to such dangers.

This, of course, was mere soft soap. James now came to the point.

However, America is a different matter altogether, as the voyage there is no less safe than a voyage from Calais to Dover where one can calculate in advance how many days the trip will take. I would, however, like to put a question to you. Do we or don't we want to get involved in the American government's business schemes? If the answer is "no" then I too will say that there is no need for anyone to go there for we are unable to make good the losses suffered by Joseph and Phillips and no one there can do anything. If, however, [it is "yes"] in that case then I would say that it is necessary to take a close look at the place to see whether and how one can go about doing business there . . . [Q]uite frankly, why should Anthony not go there, and maybe he should be joined by Anselm if it is thought that such a trip would be useful and beneficial for us? If, God forbid, the good and upright Hannah does not approve, then we mustn't even think of it, but to place our trust entirely in the hands of strangers is difficult . . . I am not at all opposed to the idea of establishing a company for the American business but can such a project be realised, that is, to set up a business house with associates who are in fact not responsible? Won't the established Houses there be given preference and won't those people who agree to join us perhaps simply skim the cream off for themselves although we could do the same and get the best morsels?[109]

The Rothschilds never satisfactorily answered these questions. Despite James's reassurances that they would only be expected to stay for "three to six months," neither Nat, Anthony or Mayer went to New York;[110] and, although James's sons Alphonse and Salomon visited the US some years later, they did not stay. The fundamental problem was that while it was James who had the enthusiasm for America, his nephews conducted most of the family's business with the US, because Britain was always a bigger customer for American cotton and tobacco than France. James therefore had to defer to his nephews' greater familiarity with the American market, even when he felt that they were passing up a crucial opportunity. As he frequently admitted: "America is more suited to England than it is to France."[111] (This imbalance between the London and Paris houses also gave rise to persistent friction as to the distribution of profits—and losses.)

As a result, the decisions which determined the nature of their representation in America for the rest of the century were taken by the man on the spot. Despite James's repeated orders, Belmont did not go to Cuba.[112] Instead, and to the intense but impotent irritation of his masters, he acquired an office at 78 Wall Street and announced the establishment of August Belmont & Co., with the plan of acting as the Rothschild agent there. "We received a letter from Belmont," reported a furious James, "but I didn't have the patience to read it":

> He is a stupid young man . . . and we are not so desperate for new business and would rather sort the old business matters out so that there is no need for anyone to go to America. That is, and remains, our opinion as far as our dependence on a scoundrel such as Belmont is concerned. Instead of going to Philadelphia to collect the 300,000 francs from Cohen he says, "I shall remain in New York." Such an ass needs to be kept on a short leash.[113]

Nevertheless, James found he had little option but to reply, and a regular correspondence commenced in September.[114] When Belmont requested the right to discount bills (presumably in the Rothschild name), James was unable to refuse: "He writes every day that he wants to get the authority to discount which I well understand and the man is quite right. If one says 'A' then one must also say 'B' [a favourite James turn of phrase], though it is always dangerous to do so." The following month it was agreed to increase his salary to £500, paid jointly by the London and Paris houses.[115] By the 1840s he had a credit facility with the London house of £10,000.[116] When Belmont wished to increase that limit, he threatened to start doing business for other houses.[117]

The Rothschilds never quite forgave Belmont for taking such a profoundly important initiative, and never ceased to regard him as unreliable (feelings not alleviated by his involvement in a duel in 1841 and his conversion, evidently for the sake of social advancement, to Christianity). "We received letters today from Belmont," wrote Anthony in August 1838, "which frighten us tremendously. How can the man be so mad as to think of doing the things that he is doing . . . I should not mind going out myself . . . if you think my presence there can be of use I will go for I then can write to Anselm to come here . . . I don't think that any person is justified in doing what he has been without asking."[118] Two months later James accused Belmont of playing the London and Paris houses off against one another, giving his favour "today . . . to the English House and tomorrow to the Parisian House."[119] "I think Belmont is a great ass," declared Nat in 1840. "He treats business so lightly that I do not like him at all as an agent."[120] He was "too great a cripple to leave New York & we have been so uniformly unlucky in everything he has had the management of."[121] James agreed: "I don't have too much confidence in that man Belmont," he commented, "because . . . he deals only for himself."[122] There were fitful efforts to replace him, or at least to control him better by sending an additional agent, as Anselm suggested (following reports that Belmont was evincing suicidal tendencies).[123] In 1839 Lionel Davidson was despatched to New York, presumably for this purpose. "He seems a clever intelligent fellow," commented Nat, implying a favourable comparison with Belmont, "and will do very well if you can manage to keep him down"—a phrase which tells us much about the Rothschilds' attitude towards their agents.[124] However, it made more sense to send him on to Mexico and the American West, while Hanau, who was sent in 1843, went to New Orleans. Belmont remained ensconced in New York, and was soon embarked on a political career which would take him to the commanding heights of the Democrat Party.

The debate over the American agency thus exposed a fundamental conflict of interests between the London and Paris houses, and revealed the limits of James's power over his nephews. There is little doubt as to who was right: in refusing to establish a Rothschild house in New York, the English Rothschilds made what must have been the single greatest strategic error in the bank's history. On the other hand, it is easy to see why they hesitated. For even the limited involvement in the American market symbolised by Belmont's grudgingly conceded role as agent very soon cost the Rothschilds dear. And it is doubtful whether Anthony or Nat, in Belmont's place, would have been able to avoid the disaster which lay ahead.

Even before Belmont arrived in New York, an irresistibly tempting opportunity had arisen for the Rothschilds to step into another niche vacated by Alexander Baring. The Bank of the United States had employed Barings as its European agent; but the relationship broke down in 1836–7, and the Rothschilds hurried to offer their services.[125] Biddle had ambitious-sounding plans, including "a business with a guarantee of two million pounds sterling to provide advances for goods and stocks," and a scheme for a quasi-monopoly on cotton exports. It seemed to James like a financial marriage made in heaven: these were, he enthused, "the wealthiest people in America" and "no less solid" than the Banque de France. At once, he began to imagine "flooding the American market" with his Spanish mercury "so that in six months time we will be masters of the market."[126]

At first the partnership with the BUS went well.[127] The Rothschilds found themselves on the receiving end of large quantities of American state bonds from not only New York but also newer states like Indiana, Alabama, Missouri and even Michigan, which had only just been admitted into the Union, as well as shares in a number of new banks and a canal company.[128] However, by September 1839 James and his nephews were beginning to discern why Barings had parted company with

BUS when they had. Without its charter and its government business, the BUS was vulnerable; when the American cotton crop proved poor, it began to look seriously over-extended, its capital tied up in all kinds of long-term ventures, its managers reliant on the sale of high-yield obligations, post notes (promissory notes due in six months time) and foreign drafts.[129] In order to secure money from the Rothschilds, the BUS's agent in Europe, Samuel Jaudon, warned that he might be unable to meet his acceptances. Uncomfortably aware that their advances to him now totalled some £300,000—"upon stock which it would be most difficult to dispose of"—James and his nephews had little option but to bail Jaudon out. Reluctantly, they agreed to take over BUS drafts on Hottinguer worth 5.5 million francs (£220,000), though it was hoped to pass the buck to other investors by selling BUS debentures.[130] James raised objections to this, arguing that the Rothschilds' reputation would suffer if the BUS were to collapse "You make yourselves *uneasy* about nothing at all," Lionel assured him:

> Every person knows upon what security these Debentures are issued and if they are not paid, it is not our fault.—I think it the greatest madness in the world to give a sort of moral guarantee, that a stock which pays 10 to 20 per cent Int[erest] will be punctually paid, the purchaser must take his chance and must know that he is running some risk . . . [Even] if we take the very blackest side . . . I am still of the same opinion in thinking that we have got very well out of a nasty affair and that we ought to be delighted to get our money back so easily.[131]

This revealed a streak of ruthlessness of which, one suspects, his father would have approved. Moreover, as Nat pointed out, it had been James who had originally urged their involvement with the BUS:

> You appear to forget that it was the Paris house that accepted the 5,500,000 francs [from Jaudon] in direct opposition to our letters & wishes, you also forget that it was the Paris house and not us who encouraged Belmont to do business to such an extent and now after we try [moving] heaven & earth to get our money back by issuing a mar-ketable security . . . you write to us as if by your issuing a similar lot of debentures you run the risk of losing your good name in the event of their not being reimbursed.[132]

Nothing could better illustrate the conflict of interests and attitudes exposed by the American question—a conflict which continued throughout the next year.[133]

Yet James's pessimism was justified; for in October 1839 the BUS suspended pay-ments and in 1841 finally collapsed. Its failure coincided with a rash of defaults by states, including a number whose bonds Jaudon had handed over as securities.[134] In the wake of this fiasco, which saddled the London and Paris houses with a large quantity of thoroughly bad debts, the Rothschilds were content to hand back to Barings the position of bankers to the federal government: "You may tell your gov-ernment," James was reported as telling representatives of the US Treasury, "that you have seen the man who is at the head of the finances of Europe, and that he has told you that you cannot borrow a dollar, not a dollar."[135] The experience with the BUS had made James wish he had had "never become involved with [America]." In future, he concluded, unless the federal government were "prepared to guarantee all the States and make the payments with us" and to set up an officially backed central bank, he would keep his distance.[136] This was a view which his nephews more than endorsed. In 1842 Anthony wrote to his brothers, urging them to sell "New Yorks & all the [American] stocks which pay an interest":

> You may be certain it will be the same with all the states . . . none will pay any Interest & therefore follow my advice—let us get out of them that we can—with them that we cannot get out [of] we must make up our mind, but follow my advice & let us get rid of that blasted coun- try—as much as we profitably can. It is the most blasted & the most stinking country in the world—& we must get rid of it, & that stinking Belmont in the Bargain.[137]

Of course, such drastic disengagement did not occur: even as they were winding up the sorry remains of the BUS loan, the Rothschilds were resuming their dealings in American cotton and tobacco (hence the need to send Hanau to New Orleans). And the project of sending a Rothschild in person to the United States was revived, as we shall see, in 1848. Nevertheless, the scars left by the BUS affair are the best explana- tion we have for the lingering suspicion of the American economy which charac- terised subsequent Rothschild policy.

Trouble in Threadneedle Street

The negative repercussions of the American crisis did not end there, however. For the financial crisis of 1836–9 also strained to breaking point relations between the Rothschilds and the Bank of England. This was, to say the least, a difficult time for the Bank of England. In Britain, the deflationary tendency which had been manifest since the 1825 crash continued more or less unabated: the Bank's note circulation declined almost without interruption between 1825 and 1840, reflecting in part the restrictive effect of the bullionist system in the absence of major gold discoveries. At the same time, the American financial crisis played havoc with the international pay- ments system, drawing both gold and silver across the Atlantic. The Rothschilds found themselves torn between the need to sustain their new American commit- ments and intense pressure from both the Bank of England and the Banque de France to maintain liquidity in Europe.

The trouble began at the time of the brothers' fateful Frankfurt summit in 1836. From the outset of the American crisis, James and the ailing Nathan urged Nat "not to let the people drive you round the bend and convince you not to send any gold [just] because this might meet with the disapproval of the Governor. You should always take into consideration that whatever you don't do, others will not hesitate to do. Was Baring too timid to take some gold out for America?" "Send Gold as long as it answers," echoed Lionel, "and [do] not bother yourself with the Governor of the Bank but pay him off."[138] This was an allusion to the fact that the London house owed the Bank at least £300,000, money borrowed in December 1835 and not due for repayment until October, as well as a short-term advance of £120,000 negoti- ated on June 1 "in consequence of a pressure on the Money Market."[139] On return- ing to Paris, James promptly committed himself to supplying the Banque de France with silver, while expressing scathing criticism of the Governor in London for allow- ing his own gold reserve to sink so low. It was not until the end of November that he acted to send gold to London.[140] Not long after that he was alarmed by a rumour to the effect that

> your Government wants to try to introduce a silver standard as is the case with gold. I would consider this a great misfortune for Europe . . . If England were to do the same [gold would flow] from here over there and this will bring about a crisis everywhere. I think we have to do everything in our power to prevent such a move.[141]

What he meant, of course, was that it would be a great misfortune for *France* if England began to compete with her for silver as a reserve metal: when the Bank did start buying silver in the summer of 1837, James immediately threatened to stop sending gold to London.[142] On the other hand, he, James, accused the Bank of indecision when his offers of gold (at a price) were not immediately accepted: the Governor, he complained, "changed his mind from day to day and tomorrow he may think differently again."[143] Worse, he seemed to be ignoring James's advice "that under no circumstances should he allow any American House to collapse."[144] Timothy Curtis, the former Governor of the Bank, wrote an emollient letter, assuring James of his "sincere wish to co-operate with your nephews in everything relating to the foreign exchange" and "to act as nearly we can in union with your House," but firmly insisting that "it is your interest as well as ours that the Bank should possess a good portion of silver."[145] The damage was done: by March the following year James was convinced that "your English Bank is out to destroy our business."[146] Nor was the fence mended by a loan by the Bank to the London house of £200,000 in silver dollars the following December.[147]

The culmination of this feud came in 1839, when the Bank of England turned to the Banque de France for assistance in replenishing its reserve, now reduced by the American crisis to £3.7 million. When he heard that the Governor of the Banque, comte d'Argout, was offering assistance, James was initially wholly opposed:

> The French Bank has already been trying for a long time to reach an understanding with the English because, purely out of a sense of pride, they want to be able to claim that England is in debt to them, but where would things be if, God forbid, war were to break out? What would happen if France were to require money? Would the English Bank then open its coffers and come to the aid of the French? I read in the newspapers that the two Banks are trying to reach an understanding and that is why I am writing to you about this matter. Our own interests are very much against this scheme succeeding and we must therefore do everything we can to frustrate its success.[148]

Despite the entreaties of the Banque's Deputy Governor "that a House like ours which has rendered eminent service to the Bank of England ought to take part in the intended operation," James and Anselm were unyielding. And to reinforce the resolve of his cousins in London, Anselm added an intimidating postscript:

> Do not take any rash step in a large operation. Your mother tells me that Herries told your good father in her presence to mind and not trust the Bank without any guarantees . . . as the Bank being involved in difficulties may *stop* suddenly. Mind, you are not your good father and do not

have his influence, and he was capable of acting in other ways than prudence would direct you.[149]

The point was echoed by Hannah herself a few days later: "I would not advance any thing to the Bank without having Exchequer Bills or any other Government security for it is absolutely necessary to be well prepared and to have a sufficient supply of available property. I do not forget a former event when Herries was very apprehensive of a stoppage of the Bank."[150]

Did the Rothschilds really believe that the Bank of England might be about to suspend payments? It seems unlikely. What was really at issue was whether the Banque and Bank between them could resolve a monetary crisis without recourse to Rothschilds. However, if James thought a Rothschild boycott would suffice to undermine the agreement reached between Curtis and d'Argout, he was badly mistaken. Realising that the deal was unstoppable and that the profits would be substantial, he was forced to execute an abrupt volte-face, now resolving "to go into the business with the Bank as far as I possibly can."[151] He had left it too late, and the business was entrusted to Barings and a consortium of Paris houses.[152] This was the last straw for James:

> [In 1825] we arranged for such large quantities of gold to be brought in and thereby saved the Bank, and now it is Baring who is the recipient of everything. The Bank should at least share [the business] out . . . so that the business is properly distributed . . . You have no other defender at the Bank than that man Curtis who is a two-faced scoundrel . . . If gold should go out, and it is no different to Paris, then I will most certainly give preference to gold and [this time] I won't say, "I don't want to do it because of the Bank." No! On the one hand I will make it clear that if we have an interest in the deal we will do everything to be of service to the Bank but on the other hand they will treat us with respect . . . Only if we engage in a lot of wheeling and dealing can we stay in the public eye and make ourselves an object of fear. Baring can't say, "I won't give Rothschild anything."

This, however, was bluster. Although James talked of spoiling the market for the bills on London Baring would need to buy, he knew full well that, with the Bank of England as Baring's client, "everyone will therefore lick his backside to get the business." There was no realistic way of starting a "war with the Bank, at least not for the time being," because, as he had to admit, "they are stronger than us."[153] All he could do was ruefully assess what had gone wrong and fantasise about revenge:

> As far as the Bank of England is concerned, when the time comes and it is in our power to do so then we can show them that it is a lot better to maintain friendly relations with us. I don't know whether I should not perhaps write to Curtis that we would prefer not to renew the £5,000 next time round [possibly a reference to a private loan to Curtis]. This will need some very careful thought given to it for it will doubtless result in him bearing an enormous grudge against us. Indeed, over the recent past he has not shown himself to have been too great a friend of ours and had it not been for the English House I would not have cared the least for his friendship . . . [I]t would perhaps have been smarter if at the

time we had given him a small share of the commission from the Bank and this would have been a lot better than everything else. The man is a businessman just like us and purely out of a sense of friendship people don't always treat us preferentially.[154]

Although there were half-hearted attempts to re-establish links towards the end of the year, the damage had been done. "I am not prepared to run after the Deputy Governor and lick his backside," declared James as the negotiations over the BUS dragged on.[155] In 1843, after a period of more or less frozen relations, Lionel closed the Rothschild account at the Bank of England.[156]

In truth, the row had been allowed to grow out of all proportion: as Nat sensibly observed in its aftermath, "I think the only advantage of a [central] bank is in being able to get out money whenever you want it & that it is folly to care about what people say."[157] In his determination to get the better of Baring and to establish the Rothschilds in a pre-eminent position in the United States, James had lost sight of that. The net result of his enthusiasm for America—an enthusiasm his nephews had never wholly shared—had been a large amount of bad debts from the defunct Bank of the United States; and a comparable quantity of bad feeling at the Bank of England.

FOURTEEN

Between Retrenchment and Rearmament (1840)

> *Monsieur Rothschild knows Europe prince by prince and the bourse courtier by courtier. He carries all their bank balances in his head, those of the courtiers as well as those of the kings; he can tell them how they stand without consulting his books. He says to one such: "Your account will go into the red if you appoint that minister."* —MICHELET[1]

In the troubled years immediately after the 1830 revolution, James and his brothers had constantly urged the great powers to avoid war. To say that they were successful in this would be, as we have seen, to exaggerate their influence over great power diplomacy; nevertheless, the fact remains that the Rothschilds got what they wanted: peace. Yet there was a fundamental paradox at the heart of Rothschild pacifism. For governments which heeded their advice and avoided international confrontation were in a position to curtail their military expenditures—and therefore to dispense with the need for new loans. This meant that in the years after 1833 all the major powers effectively ceased to be Rothschild clients. Peace seemed to be making the five houses redundant.

This was especially obvious in Prussia, where the need for new loans had more or less been eliminated. With revenues rising from the new Customs Union (Zollverein) founded in 1834, and expenditure static or falling, Prussia was able to halve the proportion of total expenditure which went on debt service from 22 per cent in 1821 to 11 per cent in 1850. Having been more than three times the size of total annual revenue, public debt was just twice as much by mid century.[2] Thus, when negotiations resumed in 1844 to complete the process of converting the old 1818 sterling loan into lower-interest, thaler-denominated bonds, Rothschild hopes that this might pave the way to a new loan were unrealistic. Their old friend Rother no longer needed them.[3]

In Britain too, the period before 1848 saw public borrowing dwindle to nothing. The 1835 loan to compensate the slave-owners in the West Indies was the last major loan issued by a British government before the Crimean War. This reflected above all the liberal reformation of British public finances associated with the career of Sir Robert Peel as Conservative leader. In the years after 1835, the Whig government came under scathing attack from Peel for running what were, in view of the economic circumstances of the mid-1830s, very trifling deficits. Altogether in the five years 1836 to 1841 the government's net borrowing came to around £4 million.[4] However, there was a hand-to-mouth quality to the way this was done which strengthened Peel's case, as did the fact that much of the excess of expenditure over receipts could be blamed on a variety of overseas "adventures." The 1839 funding operation involving £5 million of exchequer bills, which the London Rothschilds happily monopolised, was a case in point.[5] Peel's remedy on coming to power after his sweeping election victory in 1841 was the product of two decades of reflection on the fiscal and monetary implications of liberal doctrine, and had four aspects. Firstly, and most conventionally, he carried out a conversion operation, reducing the interest on £250 million of stock from 3.5 to 3.25 per cent. Secondly, and unprecedentedly, he secured the reintroduction of income tax (at a flat rate of 7d in the pound on incomes above £150), hitherto regarded as a wartime expedient. Thirdly, developing a conception of monetary policy which dated back to the 1819 committee he himself had chaired, he redrafted the Bank of England's Charter in an effort to perfect the working of the bullionist system. Finally, following the practice initiated by Huskisson in the 1820s and in conformity with the classical economists' principle of laissez-faire, he stepped up the pace of trade liberalisation, reducing the number of duties on imports. Altogether 605 import duties were repealed between 1842 and 1846 and a further 1,035 were reduced. The logical culmination of this process was the repeal of the Corn Laws, a step which the majority of Peel's own backbenchers, with their pronounced agrarian interests, regarded as a betrayal of commitments made by them to their rural constituents during the 1841 election campaign.[6]

With hindsight, this programme of reforms was less coherent than it appeared to Peel at the time. Quite apart from its politically self-destructive quality (by no means unique in nineteenth-century British history), its economic consequences were far from comfortable, even by the standards of what has been called the "Age of Atonement." Theoretically, lower import duties, by increasing the volume of trade, were supposed to generate additional income. But this was unlikely to happen under the depressed conditions of the 1840s, which the Bank Charter Act tended to aggravate by restricting domestic banknote circulation as the Bank of England's gold reserve declined. As a result, the income tax—supposedly a temporary measure—soon began to look more like a permanent fact of life, even if Peel's ideological heir, Gladstone, never quite gave up hope of doing away with it. Nor was Peel able to set the nation on the course of debt redemption which he had intended: it was not until 1844–5 that the government was able to eliminate the deficit, and it proved possible to run surpluses for just three consecutive years before the 1847–8 crisis put the government back in the red. Nevertheless, there was no denying the "soundness" of Peelite finance at the time: indeed, it set the benchmark of fiscal and monetary orthodoxy for the rest of the nineteenth century. The price of 3 per cent consols rose from 87 in October 1841 to 101 just over three years later, a clear indication of City approval.

It was still possible, on the other hand, for bankers to grumble about the medicine they were being given, even when they knew it was doing the nation's finances good. It is significant in this context that, as early as 1830, Peel had conceived a revived income tax as a way of "reach[ing] such men as Baring, his [Peel's] father, Rothschild, and others, as well as absentees [from] Ireland . . . to reconcile the lower with the higher classes and to diminish the burthen of taxation on the poor man."[7] The Rothschilds were less than pleased when they were duly "reached" in 1842. Of course, they had other reasons for feeling hostile to Peel's government. Not only were the Tories opposed to Jewish emancipation, but the advent of a Tory ministry threatened to revive the possibility of an Anglo-Russian alliance against liberal France. Still, Rothschild opposition to Peel's fiscal policy was pronounced from the outset, and the main reason seems to have been the income tax.

While Nat could see the advantages of balancing the budget, and rightly foresaw the rise in consols which would follow it, he disliked the means Peel had adopted. He anticipated practical difficulties in assessment, for example. "How will it be possible," he mused shortly after Peel's Chancellor Goulborn had unveiled his first budget, "for the tax collectors to ascertain the real incomes of merchants & bankers who by and large do not know themselves what they can term their income until their balances are made?"[8] A year later he candidly asked his brothers whether, in preparing their tax return, "you value all the stock at the market price and add the increased price to your profit or whether you take unrealized stock at the valuation of last year & pay only upon realized profits & real income?"—a question which reveals some of the difficulties inherent in taxing men like the Rothschilds, whose approach to accounting had always been quite cavalier.[9] "It is a most disagreeable business with yr stinking tax gentlemen," he wrote in early 1844, "& particularly if you have to show yr books to the commissioners—let me know how yr balance is, I recommend your taking no profit in the account upon unsold stock."[10]

This is not to suggest that the Rothschilds contemplated tax evasion: on the contrary, Nat advised his brothers "most strongly to give [the Commissioners of the Income Tax] an exact amount of the profits . . . a few hundred pounds more or less [in] charges is of little consequence, whilst it would be terribly disagreeable to be fined or even blamed by the gents in offices." They were only too well aware that "the amount in question" would be one "of serious import to the Revenue."[11] Rather, their anxieties related to the possible unintended side-effects of the new tax. Their biggest concern was that, if earnings from foreign investments were taxed, bondholders would switch to domestic investments—a worrying prospect for a bank which specialised in capital export. "I think my dear Lionel," Nat urged from Paris, "you ought to make strong representations to the government about charging the income tax upon all coupons of foreign bonds paid in London . . . it is a great pity & will in a good measure stop business." At the very least, the fact that British (but not foreign) holders henceforth paid tax on their income from foreign bonds seemed likely to tempt some clients to do business through the Rothschilds under bogus foreign names.[12] The advent of income tax—a model which James feared would soon be adopted in other countries—seemed to herald an end to the golden age when governments had borrowed from capitalists like the Rothschilds and their clients, rather than taxing them.

Even in Austria and France, where such an overhaul of the fiscal system was only

a remote possibility, the years from 1834 to 1841 were relatively lean for the Rothschilds. In Austria, public spending remained more or less constant and there were
no new loans. It was even possible to repay the "fortress money" which had been
borrowed from the Rothschilds in the name of the German Confederation in
1831.[13] The same was true in France: although the July Monarchy experimented
with public works schemes, these were financed out of taxation before 1841.
Indeed, total expenditure was slightly lower in 1839 than it had been in 1831 and
the national debt was actually reduced by 169 million francs.[14] The most Molé
could offer was yet another conversion, an operation which James regarded with
little enthusiasm in the light of past experience.[15]

The financial position of Russia was altogether different, though the net effect
was essentially the same from the Rothschilds' point of view. Russian public spending continued to rise in nominal terms from 1833 until 1839, but this was to some
extent a monetary phenomenon as recurrent deficits were financed by the printing
of paper roubles. The resulting inflation was halted—albeit temporarily—by
Kankrin's reforms of the currency in 1839 and 1843, which replaced the paper
rouble with a new "hard" rouble backed by a gold and silver reserve. This reform
raised the possibility of a stabilisation loan to establish the new currency's bullion
reserve. James eagerly proposed floating such a loan simultaneously in London and
Paris. "It should not be too difficult to impress upon the Russian Government the
advantage of this," he wrote revealingly,

> not only because it will enhance their credit but also because it is in their
> own best interest to ensure that all the wealthy people [in England and
> France] have a substantial investment in Russia and would suffer a
> financial loss if ever such an unfortunate idea as to march into Russia
> and wage war or to castigate the Russian state, were to be implemented
> . . . I am extremely keen for this deal to succeed and not because of the
> profit we stand to make but rather because I want our House to resume
> the relationship we had with Russia.

Salomon wholeheartedly agreed. A loan to Russia would, he argued, be "a very desirable . . . even a very brilliant deal": "Quite apart from the pecuniary returns which it
would bring, such a loan would be of great importance for us, in that a new, close
relationship with Russia would bring us back on top with all the [great powers?] in
Europe, and a loan with Russia is always good for the morale of our house."
Amschel echoed this sentiment.[16] But not for the first time Rothschild efforts to
supplant the traditional dominance of Hope & Co. in St Petersburg came to nothing. The younger Rothschilds—and particularly those in London—evidently had
their doubts about the project, proposing terms which struck Salomon as excessively
harsh:

> For Russian 3 per cent paper you offer 70, less commission of 2 per cent
> makes 68! Is that a reasonable price, when you consider that . . . Aus-
> trian 3 per cents [stand at] 81 and Belgian 3 per cents [at] 71? When the
> bonds of a state which has scarcely emerged from revolution are valued
> at [such] prices? We must fear with good reason that such a proposal,
> coming from the House of Rothschild, would make us a laughing stock.
> In addition to this all too low price, you propose to take [only] [£] *1 mil-*

lion for yourselves and to take the rest only in commission and even this is not to be binding in the event of a war breaking out between any two of the great powers in Europe or America within six weeks [of the agreement being signed].[17]

Even when the possibility of a 40 million rouble Russian loan resurfaced in the more tranquil conditions of 1841–2, the negotiations foundered. This time it was Salomon's turn to sound the note of caution. Evidently having been briefed by Metternich, he argued that Kankrin's stated intention of investing the money in railways was merely a cover for increased expenditure on the army. He also echoed Amschel's argument that a Russian loan was unlike a loan to any of the other great powers: "In the case of a loan for England, France or Austria the money remains in circulation, and quickly returns from the government's coffers to the public. With Russia, the money that flows in is buried, poured away into the colossal European and even Asian [domains?] of this empire."[18]

Once again, the Rothschilds pitched their terms too low to break the Hope monopoly, refusing to buy more than a small proportion of the proposed loan firm ("à forfait" in contemporary parlance) as opposed to selling it in commission (with the option to return any unsold bonds). Subsequent desultory talks with St Petersburg in 1844 and 1846 were no more conclusive.[19] Once it had seemed that the Rothschilds no longer needed the great powers; now it began to seem that the powers no longer needed the Rothschilds.

Spreading the Net

As we shall see, one response to this diminution of government business—adopted most enthusiastically by James and Salomon—was to become involved in industrial finance, and especially in the formation of railway companies. The alternative was to drum up new business with smaller states. This was the strategy adopted by the Frankfurt house. To cite only the most important transactions of the period from Berghoeffer's list,[20] it issued bonds totalling 3.5 million gulden for the Duchy of Saxe-Coburg-Gotha between 1837 and 1842, and 9.9 million gulden for the Duchy of Nassau; a 6.7 million reichsthaler lottery loan for the family's oldest such client, Hesse-Kassel, in 1845, as well as loans to its neighbour Hesse-Darmstadt; and a 14 million gulden loan to Baden in the same year.[21] There was also a loan to Bavaria in 1835 which led to the appointment of Carl and Amschel as "court bankers" and various other honours (including the Bavarian consulship in Frankfurt for Anselm).[22] In the mid-1840s loans were also floated for Württemberg[23] and Frankfurt itself.[24] Hanover too was approached but this deal fell through at the eleventh hour.[25] Nor was it only in western Germany that the Rothschilds were active. There was an attempt in 1835 to revive the firm's old connection with the Danish Kingdom by issuing a £3 million loan.[26] None of this would have been possible had the other German states been as parsimonious as Prussia. But Prussia was the exception to a rule of rising indebtedness which applied to almost all other German states during the *Vormärz* period. In Hanover, Württemberg, Baden and Bavaria, the ratio of debt to revenue rose between 1825 and 1850; only in Prussia did it fall. (The difference is probably best explained by the growing involvement of the western

German states in railway construction during this period, and the restriction on Prussian borrowing established by the 1819 State Debt Decree.)

From the Rothschilds' point of view, such loans to even the medium-sized German states were relatively minor transactions; yet they often took just as much time to arrange as loans to great powers (in some cases because of the growing pressures from representative bodies on previously more or less autonomous financial bureaucracies). On the other hand, the volume of business evidently compensated for the effort involved—witness the profitability of the Frankfurt house in this period. Amschel and the nephews who assisted him in Frankfurt were apparently indifferent to the political character of the German states they did business with: while Baden (for example) was a "model" constitutional monarchy, Hanover—after the abrogation of its constitution by King Ernst August in 1837—was among the most conservative regimes in all Germany.

From the point of view of the German states, it was becoming harder and harder to raise a loan without going to the Rothschilds, so dominant were they in the German capital market. This was especially true in south-west Germany. Not only in Frankfurt, but in other commercial centres like Cologne, the Rothschilds were able to exercise all the influence of a central bank: local people talked of "Rothschild shipments" of specie and "Rothschild money."[27] This dominance inevitably aroused comment, most of it hostile. As in the 1820s, the Rothschilds were seen by liberals as shoring up reactionary regimes. "Many of the smaller German Governments," reported one Austrian diplomat, "have recourse exclusively to the House of Rothschild, and . . . refuse to be influenced by the dissatisfaction frequently expressed by their subjects."[28] This dissatisfaction was to come to a head in a matter of years. When the Hanoverian liberal Johann Stüve came to power in 1848, for example, he sought to avoid "dirty transactions with Rothschild," which he associated with the era of Metternich.[29]

Quite apart from floating bonds for medium-sized German states, the Frankfurt house also made good profits from loans to minor German princes such as Prince von Bentheim-Tecklenburg and Prince Viktor zu Isenburg (to name just two), as well as to major aristocratic landowners like Count Hugo Henckel von Donnersmarck.[30] In many ways this represented a continuation of business dating back to the time of Mayer Amschel. What was novel in the 1840s was the extension of such business to the non-German parts of the Habsburg Empire. Between 1843 and 1845 loans to the value of 12.3 million gulden were issued by Salomon and his Vienna associates to a group of Austro-Hungarian noblemen notable for the size of their estates and the extent of their political influence, all but one of whom—the Habsburg Archduke Karl Ludwig—were Hungarian. Much the largest loan, to Prince Paul Esterházy, was, of course, far from being the first Rothschild loan to that powerful family. But the sudden spate of loans to other eminent Hungarians is striking. The likes of Count Móric Sándor, Count Joseph Hunyady and Count Lajos Széchényi, eldest brother of the multi-talented Magyar reformer Istvrán Széchényi, were at the apex of Hungarian society.[31] In principle, these transactions were little different from the lending facilities provided by West End banks like Coutts & Co. to the English aristocracy. (Indeed, Esterházy had a close counterpart in the Duke of Buckingham, another land-rich but cash-poor grandee.) But this new involvement with the Magyar elite was to prove a source of political as well as financial embarrassment to the Rothschilds when, just a few years later, Hungary was plunged into a secessionist war with Austria.

In Italy, the Rothschilds pursued the same strategy of diversification. They continued to play a leading role in the finances of the Bourbon regime in the Two Sicilies, though James and his nephews worried that local bankers would sooner or later challenge Carl's dominant position there.[32] Here, as in Spain, there was a shift away from conventional bond issues in the 1830s. For example, the state-owned Sicilian sulphur mines were considered as a possible source of guaranteed revenue against which advances might be made to the government.[33] Another possibility raised was that of a lottery loan, an idea which James disliked because such loans had been prohibited on the Paris bourse.[34] It is evident from their private correspondence that the Rothschilds had a low opinion of the Neapolitan government (which was to be famously excoriated by Gladstone in 1850). On the other hand, they had no scruples about continuing to do business with "His Macaroni Majesty." "Your Finance Minister is not a man you can reliably count on," James told Carl after a visit to Naples in 1839. "He is a real blackguard. He is afraid to speak with the King and if one wants to accomplish anything at all in Naples, the only man who can do so is the King himself and [sic] the Minister of the Interior, who is a very smart fellow."[35]

Relations with the Papacy had a similar character: a fundamental contempt for the Roman government was no barrier to a profitable business relationship. As in the case of Naples, the mid-1830s saw attempts by rivals to break the monopolistic position over Papal finances which the Rothschilds had established after 1830. These were successfully seen off, and the management of the Papal debt remained firmly and profitably in the hands of their Roman partner Torlonia.[36] This gave the Rothschilds a degree of leverage over the Papal government: on at least two occasions Salomon protested through Metternich against ill-treatment of the Jewish community of Rome, reinforcing the widespread belief that (in the words of Alfred de Vigny) "A Jew now reigns over the Pope and Christianity."[37] However, this aspect of the relationship should not be exaggerated: the primary concern was profit from, not reform of, the Papal regime.

It proved rather more difficult to establish financial relations with the state which was to pose the most successful challenge to Habsburg power in Italy: the Kingdom of Piedmont–Sardinia. In 1834 the Paris house was invited by the government in Turin to bid for the management of a £1 million loan it was proposing to make. From the outset the competition for the business was fierce and Lionel was sent to Turin in an attempt to clinch the deal.[38] The correspondence between him and his uncle James during this mission sheds light not only on Rothschild negotiating techniques but also on the difficulties of dealing with an essentially absolutist regime. Finding the Piedmontese Finance Minister impossibly obtuse, Lionel sought to strike a behind-the-scenes deal with his secretary, but was unable to overcome the King's preconceptions about how the loan should be arranged. "If," James advised,

> our competitors *come to you (for in no case must you go to them yourself)*, saying that they are disposed to understand with you [sic] for the Loan, we beg you will receive their overtures and to make a contract with them, conceding to them a fourth or the half of the affair, to be disposed of as they like . . . but in this case the business must be done by

you in *our sole name*; for you were the first on the spot, and in no case can it suit us to be in the background or to join our name to another.

However, if they did not accept such a proposal, Lionel should improve his offer, for "we are disposed to take the business if not at any price, at least at a price that will make them pay dear for it if they go beyond us . . . *If the business be in the least feasible, do it, even if it should give no profit whatever, even if it were necessary to lose 2 or 3 hundred thousand francs to prove to those gent[leme]n. that we are not afraid of a sacrifice when we want to baffle them.*" James carefully outlined how Lionel should deal with the government in order to outbid the competition:

> Your principal object [he wrote] must be to do well to captivate the minister, and so clearly to prove to him that it is [in] his interest to contract with us rather than with another, never giving him your last word, and to show yourself in such dispositions that he can conclude nothing with the others without having enabled you to cover their offers—and when you must come to the *last word* you must insist that it shall in fact be the last, and that your offer shall be accepted immediately and without reserve.
>
> If however these gentlemen are clever enough to place themselves in an equal or better position than yours in this respect . . . your plan must be to make them pay as dear for it as possible, and to abandon the field to them only when you have sown so many difficulties & thorns in it that they can gather nothing but weeds. In such case we will be easily consoled . . . there are cases when victory costs more than a prudent retreat . . .[39]

This gives an indication of the way James himself would have operated had he himself been in Turin; and perhaps he might have succeeded. But the inexperienced Lionel was ultimately outmanoeuvred—or rather outbid—by what he called the "Bande Noire" of French bankers led by Hagermann.[40] It was not until 1843 that renewed attempts were made to do business with Turin and relations remained embryonic before 1848.[41]

This expansion into new areas explains why, by the early 1840s, many observers had begun to see the Rothschilds as more than merely allies of the European states: they now appeared to have acquired a unique power of their own which was independent of the great powers and nearly universal. In his essay "Rothschild and the Finances of Europe" (1844), Alexandre Weill—one of many writers of Jewish origin who were fascinated by the Rothschild phenomenon—made the point succinctly: while "Rothschild" had needed the states to become "Rothschild," he now no longer needed them.[42] In 1842, the liberal historian Jules Michelet declared in his journal that James knew "Europe prince by prince, and the bourse courtier by courtier" (see the epigraph to this chapter). This was barely an exaggeration. Leaving aside the two outstanding Rothschild failures—Portugal and the United States—and the exceptional case of Spain, where control of the country's mercury mines took precedence over the floating of loans, the list of states for which the Rothschilds raised money in the decade or so before 1848 is impressively long. Conservative states borrowed to avoid parliamentary influence over financial policy, often the necessary corollary of tax reforms. More progressive states borrowed to pay for public works, notably railways, when the private sector seemed unable or unwilling to fund investment. Few did not at least contemplate employing the Rothschilds as bankers and underwriters. The benefits of this widening of the financial net were obvious. The risks would only become apparent in 1848.

"Absolument le Maître des Finances de Ce Pays": Belgium

Perhaps the best example of Rothschild strategy in the pre-1848 period is their involvement in the finances of the newly created Kingdom of Belgium. James and his brothers had moved swiftly to establish a financial foothold in Brussels in the wake of the Belgian secession from Dutch rule in 1830, providing the new government with a lifeline of credit in the first three stormy years of its existence. In the period of relative tranquillity[43] between mid-1833 and 1838, James energetically sought to defend and develop the position of dominance he and the Société Générale had established in Brussels. A variety of transactions helped to sustain Rothschild interest—above all, state loans to finance Leopold I's policy of economic development, the centrepiece of which was the building of a railway network.[44]

In directly involving itself in railway (and canal)[45] construction, the Belgian government was to some extent breaking with the established British practice whereby the financing of railways was at first left more or less entirely to the private sector. But it was a precedent which other powers would soon follow. What the Belgians had appreciated was the strategic significance of possessing a railway network—an insight which owed much to their strained relations with Holland and, in particular, the need to avoid dependence on the established network of canals and rivers in the Low Countries which the Dutch controlled. From the Rothschild point of view, there were obvious advantages to such a policy: it always struck them as less risky to issue state bonds than private railway shares.[46] More importantly, the development of the Belgian railway system dovetailed neatly with plans for a railway link between Paris and Belgium in which James had already expressed an interest. On the other hand, the Belgian strategy of industrial development would have made little sense if it had not been accompanied by a parallel development of the country's own banking system. Having created three new institutions in partnership with the Société Générale (the Société de Commerce de Bruxelles, the Société nationale pour entreprises industrielles et commerciales and the Banque foncière), James had done his best to maintain his dominant position. But the Banque de Belgique (founded in 1835 with largely French capital) was a genuine rival and James had to decide whether to resist the challenge to his position or to join forces with it.[47] In the boom years of the mid-1830s, the Paris house worked closely with the Société Générale in floating a succession of Belgian mining companies on the Paris bourse.[48] But in the sphere of government finance, as the inconclusive negotiations over a conversion operation in 1837 revealed, even the Société Générale had to be regarded as a rival as much as an ally.[49] Intimate though their relations were with King Leopold,[50] the Rothschilds were never able to rest on their laurels as the financiers of independence, especially in view of the suspicion with which they were viewed by sections of the Belgian parliament and press. Moreover, the possibility could not be ruled out that the Belgian government might one day seek to make military use of its railway network, or indeed of the money it was borrowing to pay for it. The government spent roughly three times what it spent on railways during the 1830s on building up an army.[51]

All these conflicting factors had to be taken into consideration when the Dutch–Belgian question returned to the European diplomatic agenda in 1838–9. In essence, the question now arose whether or not the Belgian government would abide by the terms of the 1832 articles and evacuate Luxembourg and Limburg, in return for a Dutch recognition of Belgian independence. Quite apart from the territorial sacrifice, the 1832 articles entailed a financial sacrifice, because they envisaged a roughly equal division of the pre-1830 Dutch debt between the two states. It so happened that the resumption of negotiations coincided with a new Belgian proposal for a 36 million franc loan (and a parallel Dutch request),[52] giving the Rothschilds more than usual diplomatic leverage. Despite the small sum involved, James was extremely eager to secure this new loan, partly because he expected it to be relatively easy to float, but mainly because it would be the first major Rothschild bond issue since Nathan's death. It was a chance, in other words, for him to assert not only the Rothschilds' continuing dominance of the bond market, but also his own leadership within the firm. If the terms were right, he declared in May 1838, "I will immediately say yes, despite all the political problems, because there won't be any war. Belgium will have to yield and the world is so keen to do business that one really has to hurry." The Belgians might huff and puff, James reasoned, but without French support they could do little.

Momentarily, when Prussia occupied Luxembourg in order to force the Belgian government into submission, James hesitated: "the sound of cannon fire" had its usual effect on the Paris bourse. But, when it appeared that even this would not provoke a French intervention on the side of Brussels, he went ahead swiftly with the loan, aiming to issue it as quickly as possible in London, Paris and Brussels, before there could be any deterioration in the diplomatic position.[53] Although the bonds proved slightly less easy to market than James had anticipated, the issue went ahead smoothly.[54] The fact that the Belgian coal bubble also burst in 1838 may have strengthened James's position, as the sudden slump in industrial shares very nearly broke the Banque de Belgique and put even the Société Générale itself under pressure. Now it was James who stepped in to bail the two banks out.[55]

James was right to anticipate that the negotiations might sooner or later run into difficulties, though fortunately for him this did not happen until the new Belgian bonds had largely been placed. There was considerable political opposition in Belgium (and in France) to the reimposition of the 1832 settlement. Yet the fact remained that the Belgians lacked the wherewithal to resist,[56] for, although the bonds for the new loan had by now been sold, the Rothschilds had not yet finished paying over the money raised. To make the position unambiguously clear, in December 1838 James requested that a clause be inserted in the loan agreement to the effect "that if war were to break out or if any disputes were to arise then we would be at liberty to annul our contract."[57] Somewhat optimistically, the Belgians continued to negotiate with the Rothschilds in the hope of securing additional funds in the form of an advance against treasury bills.[58] "Well, the Belgians are asses," James commented on hearing reports of military preparations in Brussels. "I am not at all pleased to see all the troop concentrations, and they are quite capable of turning a joke into a serious affair, although as long as the major powers are opposed to war, they can't do anything."[59] The request for an advance was turned down flat. Playing, as usual, on Metternich's hostility to "revolutionary" regimes, Salomon (who was in Paris during the crisis) sent Apponyi a copy of his instructions to Richtenberger, the Rothschilds' agent in Brussels:

> We do not in the least resent the fact that the [Belgian] Government is somewhat angry at our refusal with regard to the Treasury Bills. It is not at all a bad thing that these gentlemen should realise that they may count on us only as long as they mean to follow a policy of wisdom and moderation. We have certainly given sufficient proof of our intention to support and help the Belgian Government but our goodwill necessarily stops short of the point of providing the rod with which we are to be beaten, that is to say, providing the money wanted to make a war which would destroy the credit that we are applying all our energies and resources to maintain. You may tell these gentlemen what I have written freely and frankly and without mincing words.

Lest there be any doubt in Austria about Rothschild policy, he followed this letter up with another to his Vienna office "for Prince Metternich's information" detailing Richtenberger's conversations with the Belgian government:

> They won't get a farthing from me until they give way, and before I go away I shall leave similar instructions with my brother James . . . I hope that Belgium will now sign the twenty-four articles especially as they lack the "nervus rerum" and as long as the articles are not accepted the Belgian Government will not get a halfpenny from us, although they have been begging for money for months. Difficult though I [have] found it to keep on refusing, I shall feel compensated, should Belgium yield and peace be restored, by the reflection that I shall have done my best to contribute to such a result.[60]

It was, of course, as much the lack of a pro-Belgian government in Paris as the lack of 4 million francs from the Rothschilds which obliged the Belgians to give way.[61] Still, the leverage which the Rothschilds were able to exert in Brussels had been considerable. Moreover, it seemed to present a perfect opportunity to consolidate Rothschild dominance in Belgian finance. Even before the treaty had been signed, James was urging his nephews that "a Belgian security is always marketable and I would suggest that one of you . . . should go to Brussels to make the acquaintance of the new Minister in order to establish a close relationship with him and to tell him that you are [now] prepared to make all the loans and to receive treasury bills"—something which had previously been refused. What James now aimed at was nothing less than a monopoly. As he put it bluntly: "[T]he arrangement of the Belgian question is going to be followed by a need for money and this will be a moment we ought to exploit in order to make ourselves the absolute masters of the finances of this country."[62] Even by Rothschild standards, this was strong stuff; but in many ways the position subsequently achieved was not far short of mastery over the government's borrowing, even if it had to be shared with the Société Générale.[63] In early 1840, when James travelled to Brussels to discuss the terms of a new loan of 60–80 million francs, he found the government "very well disposed": "I left all the people there exceedingly pleased with my visit, and I lectured them about how to put themselves on a better footing, at least for a while. They are content enough to let us guide them, now that I have pointed out to them all the mistakes they have made in attempting to act without us."[64]

After protracted discussions, a loan was duly agreed in November,[65] and another (for 28.6 million francs) followed two years later.[66] Whether to pay its indemnity to Holland or to embark on new railroad projects, the Belgian government seemed addicted to borrowing, and its reliance on the Rothschilds to find buyers for its bonds was almost complete. Typically, when James fell out with a Belgian minister in 1842, he requested Lionel "to go to Windsor on Sunday to see the King of the Belgians":

> Constantin has written a letter which you will receive in due time explaining how matters stand at Brussels & you will be able to tell the King if . . . the present minister remains there will be no market anywhere for Belgn Bonds & no possibility of undertaking a large financial operation, you must be careful not to speak against [the minister] but only let his Majesty find out yr opinion.[67]

Altogether, Belgium raised five major loans between 1830 and 1844 with a combined nominal value of close to 300 million francs; almost all had been underwritten by the Rothschilds.[68]

Nor was it only Belgian finance which the Rothschilds now sought to control. In October 1840 Anselm visited the Hague, where the Dutch government was demanding the payment of a capital sum from the Belgians (as opposed to the annuity of 5 million francs they had agreed to pay in 1839). When the Dutch blamed their deficit on the fact that the Belgians were delaying these payments, Anselm obliged with a modest advance.[69] Two years later, when an agreement was reached with Belgium to capitalise the money in the form of bonds, it was the Rothschilds who then offered to cash them (at a substantial discount) for the Dutch government.[70] It was entirely typical of the Rothschilds to act on behalf of both parties in such an international transfer.

In both Belgium and Holland, there was considerable opposition to the role played by the Rothschilds in public finances. For example, the Rothschilds were closely identified with the French government's abortive scheme for a customs union with Belgium. Protectionists in Brussels detected a sinister French plan for economic annexation, though there is in fact no evidence that the Rothschilds supported the scheme.[71] Anselm feared similar attacks by the liberal press in Holland when the possibility was raised of a conversion of the Belgian bonds given to Holland in 1841.[72] The Dutch Finance Minister, he complained, was as

> well disposed for us [sic] as can [be], but he is so much under the influence of the public opinion & the newspapers which say that he is sold to us, that really the man has not the courage to contract with us, altho he is very well aware that no other one has the means, the credit, the influence we dispose of & has the power to raise so much the public credit of the country as we might possibly do it . . . Really the Man is so terrified by every stupid Article in the news papers saying that he has sold himself to us, that he told me, "I wish most sincerely to do alone with you, if only I could save my reputation of an honest man or prove to others that they are in the impossibility [sic] of doing so well as you."[73]

The Minister was right to worry; three months later he was forced to tender his resignation in the face of opposition pressure.[74]

Although Anselm was able to retain Rothschild control over the *transfer* of the 40 million guilders still owed by Belgium to Holland, both the Dutch and Belgian governments now sought to emancipate themselves from the Rothschilds in their capacity as underwriters by selling Belgian bonds by public subscription. Needless to say, the Rothschilds viewed this development with extreme hostility, fearing a precedent which (like the British income tax) other governments might follow. Nat was characteristically fatalist: "I fear folks have become too clever everywhere & governments will not pay commission when they can manage without." "If the govt. succeeds," he told his brothers gloomily, "which is most probable, they will be able to do without us at present & in future—We can not oppose them openly." But his uncle James never gave up business without a fight. "The Baron wishes the thing not to succeed," Nat reported, "& consequently avoids helping the minister thro"—certainly it is against our interest that the Government should make open loans & if we can prevent them so doing it is our duty to act accordingly."

It would seem that James's aggressive view prevailed. "The Belgian Finance Minister will not find it a very easy job to get rid of his loan by subscription," Nat wrote some days later. "I think he will be obliged to have recourse to us after all which will very much delight us all—Try & make Belg[iu]m flat by selling a few 1840 or 1842 bonds for the J[oint] A[ccount], it will be a good thing if they write to Brussels from every where that the market is flat." This was a classic Rothschild tactic—selling off bonds to embarrass a recalcitrant government. The aim was to force the Belgian government to return to Rothschilds, cap in hand. This appears to have had its effect; for, although the public sale of the Belgian 4.5 per cents went ahead, it was not long before the government once again had to turn to Rothschilds. Meanwhile, Anselm's indefatigable negotiations in the Hague had won over the new Dutch Finance Minister to the view that Rothschilds should after all handle the sale of the £6 million Belgian 2.5 per cents he wished to realise.[75] In 1845 the Belgian government returned contritely to the Rothschild fold and James was able to exact tough conditions for relatively modest advances in 1846 and 1847. Without Rothschild, reported the French ambassador in Brussels, the Belgian government had "realised that it would be impossible for it to find a penny on any bourse, domestic or foreign."[76] This was only a slight exaggeration. To all intents and purposes, the Rothschild monopoly on Belgian public finance was complete—though the abortive attempt to sell bonds directly to the public was an intimation of how that monopoly might be challenged in the future.

Roads to Damascus

In many ways the most important aspect of the Belgian crisis of 1838–9 had been its impact in France. Along with its alleged foreign policy failures in Spain and Switzerland, the Orléanist regime's unwillingness to stand up for Belgian interests was widely criticised as appeasement of France's old enemies, conservative Austria and perfidious England. Ever since the revolution of 1830, the Rothschilds had fretted about the possibility of a French return to the old combination of internal radicalism and external aggression which had set Europe ablaze in the 1790s. When yet another international crisis—this time in the Middle East—confronted France with diplomatic isolation, that possibility threatened to become a reality. This was the first of many "Eastern Crises" the Rothschilds would have to weather. Its outcome—the fall of the bellicose Thiers government and the diplomatic humiliation of France—marked one of the high points of their political power.

In fact, James had never really stopped worrying that international developments might lead to a change of government in Paris. "Rentes will fall because Thiers is in favour of a policy of intervention [in Spain]," he warned when it was rumoured that the latter might be about to return to government in April 1837, recalling his efforts to send troops across the Pyrenees the previous year. Indeed, the very thought of another Thiers ministry was enough to convince James of the need to "get out of the [French] funds, for the end will not be good." "A good ministry," according to James's definition, was essentially one which would pursue pacific policies abroad and balance the budget at home: he liked the Molé ministry which ultimately emerged that April precisely because it was "weak."[77] When Molé survived the elections held the following November, James regarded them as having "gone well";[78] and he urged the government "to stay united and convince themselves that they are strong and powerful," promising "firm and steadfast support" when Thiers mounted a new challenge in December 1838.[79]

The Rothschilds were nervous when Molé's position finally crumbled following the elections of March 1839, fearing a ministry "composed of the Thiers party" and the *doctrinaire* liberals. "It is a very bad thing according to my opinion," wrote Anthony uneasily, "and the King is obliged to give way & to do everything as Thiers wishes—I assure you that we become a little frightened."[80] As it turned out, Thiers' insistence on a more aggressive foreign policy was still too much for Louis Philippe to accept and another moderate government was formed by Marshal Soult. But this proved short-lived, and on March 1, 1840, Thiers was at last back in office.[81] His seemingly irresistible rise made James pessimistic:

> After a new Ministry has been formed no one gives this matter any further thought, especially so during the summer, but in the long run I am very sorry to say that France will only be able to extricate herself from her current predicament by means of war. As long as Louis Philippe, may God preserve him, remains [on the throne] I think that peace will be maintained but his son, I believe, will have no option but to wage war. Well, be that as it may my dear nephews, I intend to remain faithful to my previously voiced opinion slowly but surely to sell our 3 per cent rentes . . . It is a disgrace that no Ministry can be formed and whoever may eventually head the Ministry . . . we can expect to see the various Parties in the Chamber at each other's throats, but if the securities suffer a fall then one can buy again because in France the people are just like in Spain, one day they fight each other and the next day they are good friends again.[82]

With Thiers as premier, he warned his nephews, he was "not too happy with the fundamental situation, that is, with the internal state of affairs." The regime was "losing those friends who were most dedicated to her."[83] Although James was soon talking—in his usual, adaptable way—of "build[ing] up a friendly relationship with [Thiers]," this proved to be unrealistic.[84]

The issue which led to open war between the Rothschilds and Thiers is usually referred to as the "Eastern Question": could the sprawling Ottoman Empire, which notionally encompassed most of North Africa, much of the Balkans and nearly all of the Middle East, be preserved intact? If not, what should take its place? Economically backward, religiously divided, administratively ramshackle and politically despotic—the Ottoman Empire was all of these things. So, of course, were the Romanov and Habsburg empires; but less so, and they were Christian states—hence the effective exclusion of Turkey from the "pentarchy" of European great powers in the modern period. At this time, four of the "big five" had interests in the areas where Ottoman rule appeared to be in decline. Austria and Russia, for obvious geographical reasons, had the longest history of territorial conflict with their southern neighbour; while Britain and France were becoming more and more interested in the region for a mixture of commercial, strategic and religious reasons.

In the course of the nineteenth century the future of Ottoman rule came to hinge on the interaction of these powers: the consistent theme which links all the various Eastern crises is that, while each power had her own distinct objectives, none could achieve these alone. The Rothschilds came to play a vital role in the diplomacy of the Eastern Question mainly because, whether the status quo was preserved or new structures created, money was needed; for one of the fundamental problems of governing the region was the chronic narrowness of its tax base. There was, however, a second and very different reason why the Rothschilds took an interest in Ottoman affairs: the position of their "co-religionists."

As we have seen, it was the successful Greek bid for independence which had first involved the Rothschilds in the Eastern Question. Once the diplomatic wrangles over the extent and constitution of the Greek state were over, they were only too happy to help provide the funds required to indemnify the Turks and set the new government in Athens on its feet. The loan looked at first sight a relatively straightforward business, as the Greek bonds were to be guaranteed by three of the interested powers, Britain, France and Russia. However, James had to fight hard in Paris to secure a satisfactory share from Aguado and d'Eichthal, who was in a position to dominate the transaction because of his close links—as a fellow Bavarian—with the new Greek King. Moreover, the execution of the transaction proved a good deal more difficult than had been anticipated. Essentially, 60 million francs were supposed to be issued, a third guaranteed by each of the powers. Of the money raised, 11 million francs were to be paid to Turkey through the Rothschilds, while the rest went to the Greek government via d'Eichthal.[85]

Renewed tension in the region almost immediately disrupted these arrangements, however. In November 1831 Mehemet Ali, ruling Pasha of Egypt, revolted against Sultan Mahmud II on the ground that he had been inadequately recompensed for his military efforts against the Greeks in the Balkans. Ali—himself an Albanian by birth—sent his son Ibrahim to invade Syria, the territory he most coveted. Within a matter of months he had taken possession of Gaza, Jerusalem and Damascus itself. The Sultan initially sought to enlist British support against his rebellious vassal, but Palmerston rejected the advice of his man in Constantinople, Stratford Canning, and refused assistance, seeking instead to broker some sort of compromise. The Sultan therefore turned to Russia, accepting the Tsar's offer of military assistance in February 1833.[86] Five months later, to British and French dismay, a treaty (that of Unkiar Skelessi) was concluded between Turkey and Russia which included a secret article binding the Sultan to close the Straits of the Black Sea to warships of all nations "au besoin"—in effect, if Russia requested it. The Russian diplomatic triumph was complete when Austria and Prussia endorsed the treaty at Münchengrätz.

To the Rothschilds, all this was at first just another of many threats to European peace. Salomon hastened to warn James on Metternich's behalf that France should not retaliate by backing Mehemet Ali, whose Napoleonic public image in Paris was further enhanced by his apparently progressive economic policy of state monopolies.[87] The financial implications of the crisis were, however, less clearcut because the French guarantee for the Greek loan had yet to be ratified, while the indemnity payment to Turkey was now due to be paid. Under the strained diplomatic circumstances, it was predictable that these transactions were plagued by (ostensibly) technical difficulties. The Greeks delayed sending the necessary bonds to London, for example,[88] while the Turks refused to admit a Greek delegation to Constantinople if they arrived in a warship. Nat had set off for Constantinople fantasising about the exotic decorations he would receive from the Sultan in return for facilitating the indemnity payment. By the time he left, however, he was "sick & tired of the Turks and their shameful double dealing & regret exceedingly that I ever came here to do business . . . [in] this detestable place."[89]

There were further difficulties in 1836–7, when the Greek government threatened to default on the interest payments due on its loan, a crisis which put the international guarantee to a test it only just managed to pass. In an operation similar to that which the Rothschilds had to carry out for Portugal at around the same time, new bonds were issued to raise the cash for the dividends on the existing bonds; but the financial markets quickly learned to value the various Greek bonds differently, preferring those guaranteed by Britain to those guaranteed by France and Russia.[90] The problem persisted into the 1840s, with the guarantor powers seeking to pay only the interest due, without the Rothschilds' commission.[91]

It was at this moment that French and British policy on the Eastern Question began to diverge. The period 1836–7 saw the resumption of French colonisation of another formerly Ottoman fiefdom, Algeria—a project initiated in the dying days of the Bourbon regime and now brought to a successful military conclusion.[92] Palmerston, on the other hand, was now steering British policy in a more pro-Turkish direction, in the hope of undermining the dominant Russian position in Constantinople. When war broke out again between the Sultan and Mehemet Ali in April 1839,[93] the French government gradually found itself isolated in its support for the latter.[94] In the course of tortuous diplomatic manoeuvring, an Anglo-Russian deal was struck whereby the Treaty of Unkiar Skelessi would be replaced by an international agreement on access to the Black Sea, while Mehemet Ali would be forced to quit Syria but allowed to keep the fortress of Acre. In October 1839 the Soult government rejected this proposal, but there was very little it could do. It was, as the Paris house reported to New Court, "in a rather embarrassing position. In effect . . . the French government either will be obliged to accept [Lord Palmerston's proposals] too or may well find itself completely isolated in its view of Eastern affairs."[95] Coming so soon after the government's inert response to the Belgian crisis, this diplomatic reverse seemed a compelling argument for giving Thiers' more aggressive approach to foreign policy a chance.

Up until this point, the Rothschilds had done little more than monitor diplomatic developments.[96] Then, on February 5, 1840, something happened in Egyptian-occupied Damascus which dramatically altered the complexion of the crisis. Under circumstances which remain obscure, a Sardinian Capuchin friar named Father Tommaso and his servant Ibrahim went missing without trace. As they had last been seen in the city's Jewish quarter, allegations soon began to circulate that they had been murdered there. Egged on by the French consul, the comte de Ratti-Menton, who wished to assert France's responsibility for Catholics in Damascus, the Egyptian Governor arrested a number of Jews and subjected them to torture. One Jew who alleged that he had seen Tommaso in the Muslim market was arrested and tortured to death, as was his servant. After 500 lashes, a Jewish barber alleged that he had seen Tomasso with two rabbis and seven leading members of the Jewish community, including one David Arari. They were all arrested, along with a third rabbi. When they protested their innocence, the unfortunate barber was whipped again, whereupon—in return for immunity—he claimed that the suspects had offered him money to murder the monk so that his blood could be used to make unleavened bread for Passover. Although he had refused, the barber claimed to have witnessed Tomasso's "ritual murder" at Arari's house.

After torture and a promise of immunity, Arari's servant confessed to the murder, and what were supposed to be Tommaso's remains were duly "found" in a sewer, whereupon the seven suspects were tortured until they "confessed" their guilt. One of them—who converted to Islam to save himself and his family—confirmed the ritual murder story: Tommaso's servant had, he said, been murdered in the same way. As with early modern witch-hunts, the more bizarre the story grew, the greater the number of people who were implicated. Altogether some seventy people were arrested, and almost as many children were taken hostage to force those "suspects" who had fled Damascus to give themselves up. Throughout, the French consul played the role of witchfinder–general, exploiting not only the anti-Semitism of the Catholic community but the social divisions within the Jewish community.

It was the arrest of Isaac de Picciotto, a Jewish merchant who also happened to be an Austrian subject, which transformed the witch-hunt into a major international incident. Determined to prevent his suffering the same fate as Ratti-Menton's other victims, the Austrian consul, Caspar Giovanne Merlatto, protested to the Damascus authorities and asked his superior in Egypt, the consul-general Anton Laurin, to do the same in Alexandria. On March 31 Laurin—who regarded the whole notion of ritual murder as spurious—not only complained to Mehemet Ali, but also sought to get his French counterpart in Alexandria to restrain Ratti-Menton. For good measure, Laurin simultaneously took the somewhat unusual step of sending copies of his own reports and some of those he had received from Merlatto directly to the Austrian consul-general in Paris. The latter should, Laurin suggested, press the French government to "issue a strong order . . . seriously rebuking the consul in Damascus" and "hold[ing] the government there responsible . . . [lest] the animosity of the non-Jewish population develop into a real persecution of the Jews."[97]

The Austrian consul-general in Paris and the author of the letter quoted above was, of course, James de Rothschild,[98] and Laurin's was only one of a number sent to him and to other members of the Rothschild family seeking support for the Damascus Jews, as well as those of Rhodes who were experiencing similar persecution. On March 15 letters on the subject had reached the Dutch Jewish leader Hirsch Lehren from a Beirut Jew who urged that they be passed on to the Rothschilds so that they might "speak to the kings and to their ministers." Two days later another letter from an English businessman based in the Middle East prompted Lehren to write to James, arguing that only "the renowned Rothschild family . . . has the power to save the brethren suffering persecution." On March 27 the Constantinople community had sent letters from Damascus and Rhodes to Salomon, Carl and Lionel, appealing to "the tie which so strongly binds together the whole Jewish community."[99]

James did as Laurin suggested. However, the French Foreign Ministry merely ordered that their vice-consul in Alexandria should investigate Ratti-Menton's conduct, which, as James divined, was "only a temporising measure, since the vice-consul is under the consul, so that he has no authority to call the latter to account for his actions."[100] "In such circumstances," he informed Salomon on April 7,

> the only means we have left is the all-powerful method here of calling in the newspapers to our assistance, and we have accordingly today had a detailed account, based on the reports of the Austrian consul [in Damascus], sent in to the [Journal des] Débats and other papers, and have also arranged that this account shall appear in similar detail in the Allgemeine Zeitung of Augsburg.[101]

This decision to involve the press was partly a response to the widespread support for the ritual-murder theory in French newspapers like the Quotidienne and the Univers. Determined that this should be countered as effectively as possible, James turned to Adolphe Crémieux, vice-president of the Consistory of French Jews since 1834, whose forensic skills were as celebrated as his journalistic. Crémieux's long letter on the subject appeared in the Gazette des Tribunaux and the Journal des Débats the next day.[102] In the course of the subsequent press debate, James also authorised Crémieux to publish documents Laurin had sent him—much to the irritation of Metternich who, while sympathising, abhorred the involvement of the (by Austrian standards) uninhibited press.[103]

This was only the beginning of the Rothschilds' involvement in the campaign to secure the release of the Damascus prisoners. In London, Lionel was present when the Board of Deputies met to discuss the affair on April 21 (as was Crémieux), and he was also a member of the delegation which Palmerston received nine days later.[104] Six weeks later it was Nat who suggested that Crémieux write an official letter addressed to Lionel and the British Board of Deputies, "& that will afford you an opportunity of addressing Lord Palmerston on the subject"; and it was Nat who suggested that Lionel "get up a good subscription to pay the expenses of sending Crémieux there [to the Middle East] fast."[105] This led directly to the idea of the highly publicised expedition to Alexandria by Crémieux and Sir Moses Montefiore,[106] the purpose of which was to clear the prisoners' names and secure their release. The Rothschilds contributed a substantial sum—at least £2,500—towards the costs of this venture, as well as acting as treasurers for the Damascus Jews' fund.[107] In Vienna, Salomon meanwhile persuaded Metternich to press the Vatican about rumours that Tommaso was in fact alive and hiding in a monastery (he was not).[108] In Naples, Carl loaded Montefiore's ship with provisions, gave him some negotiating tips and later helped him in his fruitless attempts to persuade the Catholic church to expunge the allegation of murder on Father Tommaso's supposed gravestone.[109] In Paris, Anselm received regular communications from Laurin, detailing the progress of Montefiore's negotiations in Alexandria.[110]

It has usually been assumed that, in taking up the cause of the Damascus Jews, the Rothschilds were motivated by sincere outrage at the way their fellow Jews were being treated. Heine—one of the journalists James tipped off—contrasted James's altruism with the indifference of other French Jews, and in particular his rival in the sphere of railway finance, Benoît Fould. James, Heine observed, had "shown a nobler spirit in his sympathies for the House of Israel than his learned antagonist."[111] There is no question that all the Rothschilds sincerely sympathised with their co-religionists. It was, said Nat, "an unpleasant business, but one must exert oneself to prevent such calumnies being spread against our religion & such horrid tortures being practised on our unfortunate brethren in the East." The aim, he added a few days later, was "to show people generally that the day is gone by when any religious sect may be neglected with impunity."[112] The French government's attempts to defend the conduct of Ratti-Menton enraged Nat: "[W]hen the Prime Minister of France declared in the Chamber that he thought the Jews committed murder for the sake of Christian blood to be used in a Hebrew religious ceremony . . . it strikes me that such a calumny upon all those who have any Jewish blood in their veins ought not only to be contradicted but proved to be false."[113] He and the rest of the family shared the widespread Jewish jubilation at the success of Montefiore's mission in securing not only a solemn *firman* from Mehemet Ali himself denying the existence of ritual murder as a Jewish practice (August 28), but also the "honourable discharge" of the prisoners a week later.[114] All this gave the lie to the charges which had been levelled at the Rothschilds in the 1830s of indifference to the fate of their fellow Jews. "Who can come forward," the editor of the *Allgemeine Zeitung des Judenthums* Ludwig Philippson had demanded to know in 1839, "to say that these people have done anything substantial for Judaism, for its external or inner emancipation, for its civil or spiritual elevation?"[115] Like the American writer who had claimed that James did not "care [about] the barren seacoast of Palestine," Philippson had to eat his words after the Damascus affair—or, alternatively, conclude that they had been heeded.[116]

On the other hand, the extent of the Rothschilds' ambitions for the Jewish communities of the Middle East should not be exaggerated. Even before 1840 it was an idea frequently canvassed in the press and elsewhere that the Rothschilds had some sort of design to reclaim the Holy Land for the Jewish people. As early as 1830, an American journal (*Niles Weekly Register*) suggested that "the pecuniary distress of the sultan" might lead him to sell Jerusalem to the Rothschilds:

> They are wealthy beyond desire, perhaps even avarice; and so situated, it is quite reasonable to suppose that they may seek something else to gratify their ambition . . . If secured in the possession, which may be brought about by money, they might instantly, as it were, gather a large nation together, soon to become capable of defending itself, and having

a wonderful influence over the commerce and condition of the east—
rendering Judah again the place of deposit of a large portion of the
wealth of the "ancient world." To the sultan the country is of no great
value; but, in the hands of the Jews, directed by such men as the Rothschilds, what might it not become, and in a short period of time?[117]

At around the same time, a correspondent asked Nathan directly: "How is it that
your people with so extensive an influence have made no efforts to re-acquire Palestine, the land of your forefathers, from the Porte, the Ruler of Egypt and the Powers
of Europe?"[118] As we have seen, this question was answered in mystical terms in the
pamphlet *The Hebrew Talisman* in 1836; and one "proto-Zionist" Jewish writer formally proposed that Amschel purchase land in Palestine that same year.[119] The early
French socialist Charles Fourier was another who thought that "The restoration of
the Hebrews would be a splendid coronation for the gentlemen of the House of
Rothschild: like Esra and Serubabel, they can lead the Hebrews back to Jerusalem
and erect once again the throne of David and Solomon, in order to call into being a
Rothschild dynasty."[120] Almost exactly the same image was conjured up at the other
end of the political spectrum by the *Univers* in October 1840.[121] British Evangeli-
cals were also attracted to this idea. As Lady Palmerston commented in the wake of
the Damascus affair, "the fanatical and religious elements . . . in this country . . . are
absolutely determined that Jerusalem and the whole of Palestine shall be reserved for
the Jews to return to; this is their only longing (to restore the Jews)."[122] Though
Stanley was surprised when Disraeli raised the subject eleven years later,[123] it was
scarcely an original thought. Indeed, it is possible to see such remarks as expressions
of Christian millenarian hopes, with the Rothschilds supposedly hastening the
Second Coming.[124] But there is no evidence that the Rothschilds harboured any
such intentions; the involvement of individual members of the family in what
became known as Zionism was a much later development.[125]

   What is more, a number of members of the family had reservations even about
the way the campaign for the release of the Damascus prisoners was conducted. It
appears from Nat's letters that Lionel was uneasy about the "rumpus" being made by
Crémieux and some of the more vociferous British Jews. They had, he felt, shown
"rather too much warmth of feeling." Indeed, one reason for suggesting that Montefiore accompany Crémieux to Alexandria was "to moderate [the latter's] zeal."[126]
Nor, it seems, did Nat or Anselm expect the expedition to achieve its objectives.[127]
When it did succeed, Anselm was "decidedly against any public demonstration" and
deplored the hero's welcome which Crémieux was accorded in Frankfurt and elsewhere.[128] The Damascus agitation galvanised Jews throughout Western Europe, and
led to a variety of schemes for improving the condition of the Jews in the Holy
Land, notably the plan for a Jewish hospital in Jerusalem devised by Philippson.[129]
At first the French Rothschilds seemed willing to follow the lead of Montefiore,
who supported the scheme; but they made their contribution conditional on the
founding of a secular school alongside the hospital. When the Jewish community in
Palestine vetoed this, the Rothschilds withdrew, and it was not until 1853–4 that the
hospital scheme was revived.[130] The Rothschilds continued to try to use their influence to improve the condition of Jewish communities elsewhere (in Russian-con-
trolled Poland for example), as they had in the past;[131] but their efforts were always

regarded with suspicion by more radical Jews who aimed at something more than economic amelioration.

For the Rothschilds, the real significance of the Damascus affair can be understood only when it is set in its diplomatic context. Sympathetic though they undoubtedly were to the Damascus prisoners, James and Salomon in particular attached more importance to the diplomatic ramifications of their plight. For the Damascus affair presented James with an ideal opportunity to undermine the position of Thiers, who had become premier a matter of weeks after the supposed "murder" of Father Tommaso. In essence, the affair tended to accentuate the problem of French diplomatic isolation which had helped bring Thiers to power. The British government had its own reasons for backing the campaign for the release of the Jews. Having decided to break the power of Mehemet Ali and isolate France, Palmerston was only too delighted to portray the Egyptian regime in Syria as barbaric. Similarly, Metternich welcomed the chance to challenge the French claim to defend the interests of Catholics in the Holy Land. Thiers, on the other hand, could hardly be seen to criticise Mehemet Ali's regime in Syria, much less disown his own consul. Instead, he went on the offensive. In early May he told James "that the case is based on truth; and we had better let the matter rest . . . [as] the Jews in the East still maintain such superstitions . . ." He said much the same to Crémieux.[132] On June 2, in response to a speech by Fould in the Chamber of Deputies, Thiers sarcastically called into question the patriotism of the French Jews:

> You protest in the name of the Jews; well, I protest in the name of the French. And if I may be permitted to say so, something extremely honourable is happening among the Jews. Once the story became public knowledge, their disquiet was apparent all over Europe, and they have handled the affair with a zeal and a fervour that profoundly honours them in my eyes. If I may be permitted to say so, they are more powerful in the world than they pretend to be, and at the very moment, they are lodging complaints at every foreign chancellery. And they do it with a zeal, an ardour that exceeds all imagination. A minister must have courage to defend his agent who is attacked in this way.[133]

This unleashed a spate of attacks on "the man who owns the splendid mansion on the rue Lafitte . . . who sought at all costs a *coup d'état* against . . . our consul at Damascus" (the *Univers*) and "the incredible arrogance" of "Mr Rothschild" (the *Quotidienne*).[134]

It is, of course, tempting to dismiss such remarks as an expression of that anti-Semitic streak which periodically surfaced in French politics throughout the nineteenth century. Yet there was a sense in which Thiers had little alternative but to defend Ratti-Menton. The Rothschilds—and James in particular—*were* determined to undermine his position, though more because of the threat he posed to international stability than because of the threat he posed to the Jews of Damascus (to say nothing of the Jews of France).

It would be an oversimplification to say that the Rothschilds toppled Thiers from power.[135] Quite apart from the events in Damascus, the summer of 1840 saw a steady worsening of the French position. Rather than accept the Anglo-Russian solution to the problem posed by Mehemet Ali, Thiers sought to engineer a bilateral agreement between Ali and the new Sultan. However, this merely provoked the other powers into signing an agreement (on July 15) to use force if necessary to compel Mehemet Ali to accept their terms, which would have confirmed him as hereditary Pasha of Egypt, given him the title of Pasha of Acre, but entrusted him with no more than the administration of southern Syria for life. It was now beyond doubt that Palmerston put the preservation of British influence in Constantinople before the preservation of the already moribund Entente Cordiale. Nor was Thiers helped by Louis Napoleon's abortive landing in August and the outbreak of unrest in Paris the following month.[136] In any case, Nat explicitly stated at the height of the crisis that it would be "almost impossible and would indeed be dangerous and altogether unwise, to overthrow him." On the other hand, when Nat inveighed against the "irresponsibility and . . . nationalistic peasant obstinacy" and the "pseudo liberalism" of "this most arrogant of all parvenus" it was obvious what kind of "happier future" he had in mind.[137] The question is how far the Rothschilds were able to hasten Thiers' downfall.

On the face of it, their sole objective in the frenetic months of August and September 1840 was to promote peace through their tried and tested channels of diplomatic communication.[138] Lionel reassured Lord Clarendon that France would not fight; James relayed to Metternich Louis Philippe's repeated pleas for an Austrian *deus ex machina*; Lionel sought to involve the King of the Belgians; James visited the bellicose duc d'Orléans; Lionel relayed Nat's warning to Palmerston not to push the French too far—and so on.[139] But the financial subtext of this diplomatic activity was calculated to undermine Thiers' position. The key was the impact of the crisis on the price of rentes. On August 3 there had been "a tremendous fall in the price of rentes" which sent Nat and James scurrying back to join Anselm in Paris. It was the beginning of a protracted slide. As the British naval expedition closed in on Ibrahim Pasha and Palmerston intransigently rejected Thiers' bids for a face-saving compromise, so, inexorably, the price of rentes declined. Three per cents fell from a high of 87 in July to 79 in early August, touching a low of 73.5 in early October. It would, no doubt, be wrong to suggest that the Rothschilds were single-handedly responsible for this fall, which was the product of a generalised panic on the Paris bourse. On the other hand, they did nothing to check it. More importantly, they had no reason to do so. For, unlike comparable crises in the early 1830s, this was costing them nothing. The clue lies in Nat's comment on August 2: "Thank God the house has scarcely any [rentes]."[140] Quite simply, they had covered themselves in advance of the crisis by clearing out of French government bonds altogether. This was what Guizot, struggling as French ambassador in London, failed to realise. "Do you think he is praying to God for the safety of his money?" he asked the Princess Lieven after a visit from Lionel on September 9.[141] Heine too was taken in by James's furrowed brow: "The rente, which had opened down two per cent, tumbled by another two per cent. M. de Rothschild, it is said, had the toothache yesterday; others say he had a colic. What does this portend? The storm draws ever nearer. The beating of the Valkyries' wings can be heard in the air."[142] In fact, James was play-acting for the benefit of Heine's readers. Nat's only regret was that he did not have more liquid funds available to speculate: "I could make a fortune," he mused.[143]

Thiers fought back. On October 12, the pro-government *Constitutionnel* fired a broadside at "M. de Rothschild and his manoeuvres":

[According to *The Times*] M. de Rothschild is a man of finance and does not want war. Nothing could be easier to understand. M. de Rothschild is an Austrian subject and the Austrian consul in Paris, and as such he has little concern for the honour and interests of France. This too is understandable. But what, pray, have you to do, M. de Rothschild, man of the Bourse, M. de Rothschild, agent of Metternich, with our Chamber of Deputies and our majority? By what right and by what authority does this King of Finance meddle in our affairs? Is he the judge of our honour, and should his pecuniary interests prevail over our national interests? We speak of pecuniary interests, but, surprisingly enough, if one can believe highly accredited reports, it is not just financial grievances that the Jewish banker would lodge against the cabinet . . . There also seems to be wounded vanity to satisfy. M. de Rothschild had promised his co-religionists to have our consul-general in Damascus dismissed for the position he took in the trial of the Jews being held in that city. Thanks to the steadfastness of the president of the council [Thiers], these insistent demands of the mighty banker have been resisted and M. Ratti-Menton upheld—hence, the irritation of the mighty banker and the fervour with which he throws himself into intrigues where he has no business.[144]

This tirade overlooked the fact that, in one fundamental respect, the "King of Finance" *was* in a position to "meddle" in government policy. If Thiers was serious about making military preparations and ultimately even fighting a war, the question inevitably arose: how was this to be paid for? The only conceivable answer in view of the already stretched budget was by borrowing. Yet the government was in no position to borrow money with the price of rentes slumping. This was the way in which not only the Rothschilds but the financial markets as a whole exerted leverage over a government they disapproved of. The financial crisis effectively destroyed the credibility of Thiers' foreign policy by depriving him of the possibility of borrowing money. In his reply to the article in the *Constitutionnel,* James made the point with subtle menace:

I have never at any time encouraged opposition to the Government, for the simple reason that I have never wished to play a political role. I am, as you state, a financier. If I desire peace, I desire it honourably, not only for France, but for the whole of Europe. *Financiers have the opportunity of rendering services to the country under any circumstances, and I think that in this respect I have never been slow to respond.*[145]

The point was that this time James's services would not be forthcoming. Less than a week later, on October 20, "the little blackguard" resigned. Ten days later a new government was formed by Soult and Guizot in which, as Nat affirmed with satisfaction, "the bourse has the greatest confidence."[146]

Of course, it took long months of negotiation to arrange a lasting peace in the Middle East—during which time the symptoms of popular "war fever" persisted not only in France but in Germany too. For the Rothschilds, however, Thiers' fall was the turning point in the crisis.[147] As Heine reported in March 1841:

Monsieur de Rothschild, who seemed somewhat indisposed for a time, is now quite restored and looks sound and well. The augurs of the Stock

Exchange, who are experts at interpreting the great Baron's physiognomy, assure us that the swallows of peace nestle in his smile, that every anxiety about the possibility of war has vanished from his countenance, that there are no electric sparks which forbode storms visible in his eyes, and that therefore the warlike stormy weather, the *Kanonendonnerwetter* which threatened the whole world, has been altogether dissipated. Even his sneezes, these augurs tell us, portend peace.[148]

Walls of Jericho

The aftermath of the Eastern Crisis demonstrated how international tension could be beneficial to the Rothschilds—provided that increased defence expenditure did not lead to outright war. To be sure, the Rothschilds had consistently used their financial power to promote peace throughout the 1830s. But when the great powers had been completely restrained in their foreign policies, as we have seen, the stream of new loan business had begun to dry up. By contrast, when they embarked on policies of rearmament, as they did from 1840 onwards, this was not necessarily detrimental to Rothschild interests.

The fall of Thiers led almost at once to new business for James. The increased expenditure on armaments which was Thiers' legacy—particularly on the costly new system of fortifications around Paris—obliged the new government of Marshal Soult to issue a major new loan in 1841.[149] The Rothschilds had every reason to dislike the fortifications project: quite apart from fuelling the bellicose mood throughout Europe, it threatened to reduce the value of Salomon's villa at Suresnes, which was close to the planned line of defences.[150] Nevertheless, they did not hesitate to meet the government's needs. Admittedly, James grumbled about the amount and issue-price proposed by the new Finance Minister, Théodore Humann—yet another former banker turned politician, and a man whom James privately regarded as a "rogue" and a "blackguard." Indeed, the negotiations were characterised by brinkmanship which was extreme even by James's standards. He bluntly refused to cut short a visit to see Salomon at Gastein and Vienna when Humann requested a meeting in Paris, and on more than one occasion intimated that he would leave the business to others if the terms were not improved. But in truth he had no intention of doing so: as he put it, "We want—indeed have—to make the loan"; and he was confident enough that Humann would not act without him to drive a hard bargain.[151] The 150 million franc loan was duly issued in October more or less exactly on James's terms.[152]

To contemporaries, this merely confirmed James's unrivalled dominance over French finances. However, the real significance of the loan may lie in the peculiar character of the "armed peace" (Guizot's phrase) which made it necessary.[153] The striking point is that now James and Nat were willing not only to justify but also to finance a policy of rearmament which they had opposed when Thiers had been in power. The new French government, they assured the London and Vienna houses, was arming merely to mollify public opinion. "No cabinet in the last ten years has pursued more peaceful policies than the one formed on Oct[ober] 9, but it has things to take into consideration, susceptibilities to overcome, ardent enemies to contend with." Once the cost of the increased armaments made itself felt, the popular mood would become more pacific.[154] On March 8 James was able to report "a triumph": "The Commission dealing with the Budget refused to ratify the establishment of the 36 new Regiments and this is a slap in the face for Thiers who wanted to increase the size of the army and this will result in a saving of 40 million and a genuine disarmament and is proof that they seek to maintain peace. I bought rentes . . ."[155]

The 1841 loan marked the resumption of "normal service" in Rothschild relations with the French Treasury. Further loans followed in 1842[156] and 1844 (for 200 million francs apiece), despite challenges to the Rothschilds' dominant position from Hottinguer, Baring and Laffitte.[157] International tension led to increased expenditure on armaments in the German states too. "As long as France continues arming," reasoned Anselm, "Germany must follow."[158] Again, this meant new business for the Rothschilds. Thus, after seven uneventful years, 1841 saw a new Austrian government loan for 38.5 million gulden, shared as usual with Sina and Arnstein & Eskeles.[159] Another loan for 40 million gulden was issued by the same banks two years later.[160] Once the Rothschilds had regarded peace as the *sine qua non* of financial stability; but an armed peace was more profitable.

Small wonder, then, that Countess Nesselrode thought James "viceroy and even King" at this time. When he told her that he knew all the French ministers, saw them daily and complained directly to the King if the policies they adopted were "contrary to the interests of the government," he was not exaggerating. "Comme il sait que *j'ai beaucoup à perdre* et que je ne désire que la tranquillité, il a toute confiance en moi, m'écoute et tient compte de tout ce que je lui dis": in that sentence, with its subtle reminder of the regime's financial reliance on the Rothschilds, lies the key to James's power over the "bourgeois monarch."[161] When Heine called James a "weathercock," he was thus underestimating the extent to which he could influence the direction of the wind. Throughout the period from 1840 to 1847, Rothschild financial support for Guizot was effectively conditional on his avoiding outright conflict with Britain—and devoting a rising share of the proceeds to constructing railways rather than fortifications.[162] At times even Nat and his brothers were surprised by the extent of their uncle's leverage in Paris. When an Anglo-French argument over the Pacific island of Tahiti blew up and then blew over in 1844, Nat remarked, "His Majesty was amazingly polite and almost kissed him so pleased was he," crediting—erroneously—the Rothschilds with having restrained Peel in London.[163]

Nevertheless, there were limits to James's power, just as there had been limits to the Rothschilds' power in the 1830s. A more serious Anglo-French dispute over Spain gave James a real scare in 1846–7, when it appeared that Louis Philippe's determination to marry his son to the Spanish Queen's sister might be seized on by Palmerston as a *casus belli*.[164] James rushed back and forth, trying to get the French to agree to an Anglo-Spanish trade treaty as a kind of compensation for the Montpensier marriage,[165] but Guizot on this occasion stood his ground. James's letter to London of September 26 gives a good insight into his unease:

> We are extremely anxious . . . for, as I was told by the English Minister [Lord Normanby], he is very concerned that they may take very firm measures. I can't imagine that they will immediately issue a declaration of war. The truth is that Montpensier is due to depart [for Spain] on Monday. Well, Guizot said to me that if England were to issue a decla-

ration of war then the wedding will [still] take place . . . Well, my dear
nephews, there is a lot of ill feeling. I did not imagine that it would be so
bad and I tell you we must be careful because in the end, something or
other will happen. The [English] Minister said to me, "We can't sit by
calmly and watch the situation unfold." Whether he made this comment so that I should then repeat it only God knows . . . I tend to see the
future as rather bleak.[166]

James went so far as to propose to Guizot that Montpensier renounce any claim
of his heirs to the Spanish throne.[167] But, as Anthony reported nervously, "Guizot
thinks that we have been intriguing against him and you have no idea how careful
we must be . . . I assure you I am very anxious—the French do not want war and
cannot go to war, but they make things quite as bad as one."[168] Indeed, Nat declined
to relay to Louis Philippe a letter from Lionel which evidently contained some
strong Palmerstonian meat:

> The arguments of our worthy uncle in favor of the alliance between
> England & France are quite conclusive but the suppositions of my Ld
> Palmerston in the event of the Queen of Spain being poisoned, of her
> not having any children & of its being the Queen dowager's interest not
> to let her daughter breed[,] that the present King of Spain & the D[uc]
> of Mont[pensier] wd fight & the Ld knows what, wd have a bad effect
> on our statesmen & make them believe Ld P . . . had talked a lot of non-
> sense with you—I should be sorry to be the bearer of such a missive.[169]

By October 1846 James was in deep gloom, expecting French and Austrian
troops to be sent to Spain at any moment and fretting at news of British naval
increases.[170] When he went to see Guizot on the 29th, he was told firmly that France
would not rule out a future claim by Montpensier's heirs to the Spanish throne.[171]
The nadir came when James sought to defend Normanby's decision not to attend a
reception for Montpensier after his return from Spain. As Nat reported, Guizot was
"very angry . . . [and] told him that situated as he was it would be just as well for him
to keep his opinion to himself."[172] James drew the obvious conclusion: "I fear that
all diplomatic communications between us here and England will be broken and the
Government here is prepared for anything that may happen. Never before have I
seen the Government so strong and stubborn. I think that even if this were to lead
to an outbreak of war, God forbid, they would still not change their stand."[173] Even
when he sought the assistance of his old friend the King of the Belgians his reception was "cold."[174]

Such open conflict between France and Britain inevitably placed a strain on
cross-Channel relations within the Rothschild family. Alphonse obviously felt
resentful of Palmerston's aggressive style of foreign policy. When he heard Lionel
argue the British case during a visit to Paris in early 1847, he sarcastically asked him
if French policy should be "to kiss humbly the British lion's claws."[175] Hannah was
somewhat embarrassed to find both Anselm and Carl taking the French side when
she visited Frankfurt at around the same time. "I now and then have rather a strong
conversation with our friends," she reported to Lionel, "particularly Anselm who is
an enthusiast in favour of Guizot."[176] Anselm also took issue with James's unhappy
efforts to play the mediator, advising his uncle tersely "not to mix personally in the
evolution of great historical events."[177]

As so often in the diplomacy of the 1830s and 1840s, the war which everyone feared failed to break out: by the end of February 1847 James was able to report that the Spanish affair was as good as settled: "Apponyi is here with me now and he says that it is now out of the question even to think of war any more. Normanby invited him and Guizot to visit him on Tuesday week. So peace will be made over a bottle of champagne and I and my dear wife will be present to witness it, God willing."[178] Yet the champagne cork was scarcely out the bottle when Palmerston seized on a new bone of contention: Greek arrears on British-held bonds. This was the cue for another Anglo-French war of words, with the Rothschilds once again acting as reluctant messengers. "Guizot told the Baron," reported Nat wearily in April 1847, "that England would be alone in her proceedings against Greece . . . & if she (England) were to kick up a row about the stupid business . . . [Guizot] wd be able to return the compliment & get his country into such a state that it wd be very hot for every body—do not repeat this at all events in these terms or as coming from us."[179]

And even if war never came between the powers, there was a second danger—one which the Rothschilds were inclined to overlook. For the tendency for so many European states to run deficits in the 1840s meant more than just good business for their bankers. It was also a symptom of a fundamental political malaise within those states. Military expenditure was not, in fact, the sole cause of the deficits of the mid-1840s. Of similar importance, as we shall see, were state subsidies for railway construction, combined with stagnant or declining tax revenues—a little-regarded side effect of slackening economic growth. As the Rothschilds insatiably added one state after another to the list of their clients, they could congratulate themselves on the diplomatic influence this gave them. The crises over Belgium and Syria really did seem to suggest that war could be averted by discreet manipulation of the European states' purse-strings. But financial power was not absolute. Above all, it depended on the internal stability of the European states. When that could no longer be maintained, the Rothschilds proved almost as vulnerable as the princes and ministers whose purse-strings they held. In the end, it was not a war which brought the defensive walls of the July Monarchy tumbling down but a revolution; and against that threat the fortifications round Paris offered no protection.

FIFTEEN

"Satan Harnessed": Playing at Railways (1830–1846)

They've got the Devil into reins!
—EICHENDORFF, *DAS INCOGNITO*

I know just how these bankers think. What they are after is a chance of immediate profit, not an affair which they have to bury in their portfolios for eighteen months, no matter how good it may be. —CASIMIR LECOMTE, DECEMBER 1841[1]

In 1836 the composer Rossini travelled by train for the first time. He was on his way from Paris to Frankfurt, and took advantage of the recently built lines in Belgium to speed up his journey. He loathed the experience, refusing ever to travel by train again; but it inspired him nonetheless. In an ironical tribute to the new mode of transport, he composed a short piece for solo piano entitled "Un petit train de plaisir (Comico Imitatif)," a humorous musical evocation of a railway journey which culminates in a derailment, the deaths of two passengers, and their journeys to Heaven and Hell. A sardonic coda evokes the celebrations of the wealthier victim's heirs.[2]

Disasters are, of course, perennially fascinating, and the nineteenth century had no shortage of both natural and man-made calamities to stir the contemporary imagination. The 1830s and 1840s, in particular, saw a succession of failed harvests, great fires and epidemics, providing encouragement to the various idealist and materialist millenarians who prophesied an impending apocalypse in the years before 1848. Railway accidents, however, were an entirely novel kind of disaster, and they provided a distinctive source of artistic inspiration. If the railways were talked up by the engineers and financiers who built them as the supreme achievements of the modern age, their susceptibility to derailments and other spectacular mishaps enthralled more sceptical observers; for the railway accident was in many ways the perfect symbol of that crisis of capitalism which malcontents on both the left and the right awaited. In his comic play *Das Incognito*, for example, the romantically inclined German playwright Joseph von Eichendorff brought the drama to a noisy climax with an on-stage railway disaster:

> *The sentry sounds the fire alarm, fleeing peasants burst suddenly on to the stage.*
> SOME. Help! Flames!
> OTHERS. They've got the Devil into reins!
> OTHERS. Nothing but murder and smoke!
> VOICES *off.* Alas! The locomotive has run amok!
> FIRST SERVANT. No, that really is impertinence,
>   It's hit the city battlements.
> *Immense crash, followed by a cloud of dust. As the dust clears, a toppled locomotive and wrecked carriages can be seen . . .*[3]

Quite apart from relishing the pyrotechnics involved in such a scene, a contemporary audience would have appreciated the potent image of a diabolical, renegade locomotive smashing down the walls of an ancient German town. For, by the time Eichendorff wrote *Das Incognito,* the railways' political potential was already widely understood. To the nationalist economist Friedrich List, the railway was "a tonic for the national spirit" and "a tight belt around the loins of the German nation" which—in conjunction with the Prussian customs union established in 1834— would bring about the long-overdue "internal unification" of Germany. For this and other reasons, railways made conservatives like Metternich uneasy: the "transformation in political and social conditions" which he saw as their inevitable consequence did not seem likely to assist him in defending the Central European status quo.[4]

That the Rothschilds came to play a leading role in the development of the European railway network might seem, at first sight, natural. It was, after all, Lionel who prevailed upon Rossini to take his first and only train ride, and Amschel who (allegedly) provided the inspiration for one of the principal characters in *Das Incognito*—the royal adviser, Paphnatius. By the late 1840s the Rothschilds had firmly established themselves as the pre-eminent private financiers of continental railway construction. Yet there was nothing inevitable about this. Indeed, the move from commercial and public finance into industrial finance was in many ways an unusual one, which relatively few established bankers even attempted, much less achieved.

The most obvious illustration of this point is Nathan's almost complete lack of involvement in industrial finance in Britain. In many ways, he of all the Rothschilds ought to have been the most keen to participate in the burgeoning new industrial sectors of the early nineteenth century; after all, it was he who had spent nearly a decade as a cotton merchant and (for a time) manufacturer. Yet apart from an apparently abortive mining venture in North Wales in 1825,[5] Nathan had virtually nothing to do with industrial finance once he had moved to London and established himself as a banker. In particular, he took no part whatever in the great railway "mania" which followed the opening of the first fully fledged passenger and freight line between Liverpool and Machester in 1830. When James visited the north of England in 1843, the traffic on this line profoundly impressed him: "What is happening here with the railways is quite amazing and had I come here earlier we would most certainly have built this railway. It must yield enormous sums. Never have I seen so many people as [are travelling] between Liverpool and Manchester."[6]

Yet his brother had sat idly by throughout the pioneering phase of British railways. A year later Nathan's wife Hannah wrote to her eldest son in a similar vein, as if he had yet to be persuaded of the utility of the new form of transport:

> The rail road travelling is so productive of good and general advantages to all classes of society [as] to make us grateful for this scientific invention—to this we are indebted for the earliest information[;] from our most distant friends we are favoured with the most constant and frequent communications, the loss of their society is lessened from the facility of obtaining this and affords great consolation and adds much to our enjoyment of life by this wonderful rapid communication.[7]

Hannah was evangelical—indeed visionary—in her enthusiasm. In 1846 she returned to the subject with equal warmth in a letter to her eldest daughter Charlotte:

> There is some luxury in going in a carriage and [being] propelled by horses: but the many delays and other inconveniences one is subject to give us a decided preference [for] railroad travelling . . . and [although] it may be objected to by many and particularly by the refined, for my part I prefer the amusement of scenes and the bustle of changes one gains . . . by this mode of travelling.[8]

The striking thing about these letters is that she felt the need to detail the advantages of railways, particularly to the younger generation who might have been expected to take these for granted. Clearly they did not. Indeed, Hannah had to conclude her effusion to Lionel with an apology: "I feel I am encroaching on your patience and you will say I am an enthusiast for rail roads." We know for certain that his brother Nat was the reverse: in 1848 he declined to meet Lionel at Calais because "railway travelling makes my head ache so terribly that I really can not make up my mind to a 30 hours shaking."[9]

Why was Hannah the sole rail "enthusiast" among the English Rothschilds, as she appears to have been? Writing more than four decades after the banker's death, Disraeli suggested that Nathan (in the guise of "Mr Neuchatel") had anticipated the inevitable bust which brought the first railway boom to an abrupt end. But Nathan was scarcely risk-averse in this sense. It seems more plausible that he preferred to concentrate on the business he knew best, namely government and commercial finance. His advice to Thomas Fowell Buxton's son on this point bears repeating:

> "If I were to listen to all the projects proposed to me, I should ruin myself very soon. Stick to one business, young man," he said to Edward, "stick to your brewery, and you may be the great brewer of London. Be a brewer, and a banker, and a merchant, and a manufacturer, and you will soon be in the Gazette."[10]

It is possible, though it cannot be proven, that Nathan had in fact burnt his fingers in 1825, when mining companies like the one he contemplated came to grief in large numbers. It is also possible that he saw too late that he had missed a golden opportunity in steering clear of home railways;[11] but it is unlikely. In fact, such specific explanations are probably unnecessary; for the English Rothschilds' lack of interest in domestic industry was wholly unexceptional in the context of the mid-nineteenth-century City of London. To put it simply, the overwhelmingly commercial and overseas orientation of the major London banks—with the single exception of Glyn's—disinclined them to involve themselves in railways. At the same time, the ease with which railway companies were able to sell their shares and scrip directly to the public—sometimes even before they had secured parliamentary incorporation—made banking intermediation more or less superfluous.[12] We know from his reports as Austrian consul that Lionel paid attention to the development of the British railway system, as well as to the almost equally revolutionary impact of steam power in sea transport. But it is also evident from such communications that he and his brothers' principal interest lay in exporting such innovations *after* they had been tried and tested in Britain.[13] Where British industry did require banking facilities, it tended to turn to the provincial joint stock banks which proliferated in the 1830s and 1840s, rather than to the City banks.

In France, by contrast, the so-called *haute banque* in Paris was not as wary of industrial investment as the City. From the 1820s onwards, there were repeated efforts to organise new kinds of financial institution large enough and ambitious enough to undertake major infrastructural investments, notably the digging of canals. But the various projects like the one instigated by Laffitte in 1825 (the Société Commanditaire de l'Industrie) foundered because of government opposition.[14] In particular, the Banque de France was extremely suspicious of attempts to create joint-stock banks—hence the need to use the word *caisse*. This suspicion was shared by James. When Laffitte revived his 1825 scheme twelve years on with a proposal for a *caisse* with a capital of up to 250 million francs to be raised by selling shares, he was sceptical, just as he would be when the Pereires attempted a similar (but better-timed) institutional challenge to the traditional Parisian banking structures in the 1850s.[15] There was no indication before 1835 that James would be any more interested than Nathan in expanding the scope of his financial operations.

Yet a subtle shift in Rothschild policy can be detected in the mid-1830s. We have already seen how the need for improved securities for Spanish government loans led Nathan and James to acquire rights over the Almadén mercury mines. This did not mean that the Rothschilds themselves directly organised the business of mining, of course. All they were buying was a monopoly over the *sale* of Spanish mercury once it had been extracted. Nevertheless, the success of this venture encouraged the brothers—and Salomon in particular—to seek similar arrangements with other governments. It was, for example, the logical complement of the Almadén deal to secure a monopoly over the mercury mines in Austrian-controlled Istria and Dalmatia.[16] It also made sense to become more directly involved in the physical process of refining silver and gold and minting coins, though it was not until the 1840s (in France) and the 1850s (in England) that the Rothschilds formalised their involvement in this industry.[17]

As bankers, the Rothschilds naturally had an interest in, and experience of, the process of manufacturing money. In the same way, it might be said, they had an interest in any technological innovation that accelerated communications within Europe, given their legendary enthusiasm for the rapid transmission of financial and political news. Railways undoubtedly represented a revolutionary breakthrough in communications; yet they were in some ways less exciting to the Rothschilds than might at first be assumed. From the vantage point of the 1830s, it would obviously be a very long time before enough railway track had been laid to reduce by much the time it took to relay a letter from Frankfurt to London. And because it was letters

and financial documents which the Rothschilds were primarily interested in trans-
porting, they stood to gain relatively less from the development of railways than
merchants and industrialists who wished to transport bulky commodities like coal
and grain, or regular travellers who latched on to the railways as an easy way to transport themselves. In any case, trains could not give the Rothschilds any advantage
even when they did begin to transport mail; for what the Rothschilds could use their
rivals could use too.

For this reason, the Rothschilds' interest in the development of railways must be
understood primarily in financial rather than developmental terms. What excited
Nathan's brothers—to be precise, what excited Salomon and James—was not really
the prospect of more rapid and more comfortable travel from Paris to Brussels,
though they doubtless looked forward to this. It was plainly not the substantial
"social savings" with which railways have retrospectively been credited by economic
historians, though the Rothschilds appreciated that railways would not only boost
the demand for coal, iron and steam engines but also integrate regional commodity
markets and facilitate labour mobility.[18] It was the short-run benefits of railway
finance which initially attracted them; in particular, the profits to be made from
issuing railway shares to the public.

In essence, the Rothschilds were inclined to see railway shares as surrogate state
bonds at a time (the mid-1830s) when European governments were issuing fewer
and fewer new bonds. And because—unlike in Britain—continental governments
became indirectly or directly involved in railway construction from a relatively early
stage, this was not an unreasonable notion. Indeed, in the case of Belgium as well as
some of the South German states, the building of national railway systems was actually financed by the sale of state bonds and carried out by the public sector.[19] The
Rothschilds were perfectly willing to underwrite such loans: after all, a state bond
was a state bond, a relatively secure asset, however the money raised was used. Of
course, the case was slightly different in those countries (such as France) where the
state did not act so directly, but contented itself with licensing and subsidising private companies. Nevertheless, the fact of state involvement meant that it was com-
paratively easy for the Rothschilds to apply their traditional underwriting
techniques to the sale of railway shares. In essence, this was how the Vienna and
Paris houses were drawn into the business of railway finance. However, the realities
of railway construction made it hard for both Salomon and James to sustain the
arm's-length role they had initially envisaged. It took time to secure a railway concession; time to acquire the land required; time to build the line and stations—usually longer than expected. Even once a line had opened, it took time to build up a
steady level of freight and passenger traffic, and it was very rare that this level
matched original projections, which were largely a matter of guesswork. Investors in
railway shares were therefore not like investors in bonds, who could count on a predictable and steady flow of interest from states, barring some unanticipated revolution or military disaster. Railway investors who bought shares were buying a stake in
a concern which would only begin to pay unspecified dividends in the future. It was
therefore practically impossible for the bankers who marketed such shares to be
indifferent to the future profitability of the companies concerned. Just as the Rothschilds could not ignore the politics of the states whose bonds they marketed, they
could not ignore the management of the railways whose shares they sold. The short-

term attractions of railway finance thus tended to lead the brothers into longer-term commitments.

Moreover, those commitments in turn exposed the Rothschilds to new and unwelcome kinds of public attention. For railways had in many ways a more direct and perceptible impact on the lives of ordinary men and women than the states which notionally governed them; and the Rothschilds were in some ways much more publicly conspicuous as railway financiers than they had ever been as the financiers of states. In theory, ordinary people might have complained that the indirect taxes they paid on articles of consumption were partly going towards paying the Rothschilds their commissions and the interest on the bonds they held for themselves; in practice, that connection was rarely made in the Vormärz period. The impact of railway companies on everyday life, by contrast, was more obvious, particularly when things went wrong—and never more glaringly than when there were railway accidents. One unintended consequence of their involvement with railway finance was that the Rothschilds were subjected to a new and militant kind of criticism, in which they were cast not as the mere paymasters of reactionary regimes, but as exploitative capitalists in their own right. Interestingly, it was in the critiques of the early railway era that, for the first time, the family's Judaism began to be thought of less as a religious identity and more as a racial explanation for their alleged exploitativeness.[20]

Salomon's Line: The Nordbahn

Given the revolutionary implications of railways, it is perhaps surprising that the first Rothschild railway should have been conceived and constructed in Habsburg territory. Salomon was not the most enterprising of the Rothschild brothers; indeed, to an extent he had allowed himself to lapse into the rather old-fashioned role of "court Jew" to Metternich, with whose political objectives he increasingly tended to identify. Nor did he himself much enjoy the experience of railway travel; as late as 1846 he still refused to take advantage of the rail link through Belgium when going from Frankfurt to Paris.[21] Taken as a whole, moreover, the Habsburg Empire was very far from being the most economically dynamic state in Europe; and the suspicious attitude of its bureaucracy towards any innovation which might have unpredictable social side-effects was notorious. Yet it was Salomon who became the first Rothschild to interest himself directly in a railway project in 1830. It was not his own idea but that of a professor at the Vienna Polytechnic Institute named Franz Xavier Riepel, a mining expert who believed that the new technology of railways could be used to link the salt mines of Wieliczka in Galicia and the iron and coal mines of Moravian Ostrau (Ostrava) to the imperial capital more than 200 miles to the south-west. Nevertheless, it is a tribute to Salomon's vision—or perhaps to his growing financial foolhardiness—that he regarded this scheme as practicable. To say the least, this was an ambitiously long line for the time. Even more remarkably, Salomon seems to have envisaged from an early stage that it would also be extended southwards from Vienna to Trieste on the Adriatic. Such things were possible in England, where Salomon despatched Riepel (along with Leopold von Wertheimstein) to acquire some practical experience of railway building and operation. But was it realistic to embark on such a long line in Habsburg territory?

Initially, the biggest obstacle to the scheme was political inertia in Vienna itself.

On the basis of a report drafted by Riepel after his visit to England, Salomon sub-mitted a petition to the Emperor to allow land to be acquired for the project. Pre-dictably, it was shelved, the Crown Prince observing with true Habsburg insight that "Even the coach to Kagran isn't always full." The postal authorities also expressed reservations, fearing a threat to their monopoly. Undaunted, Salomon pressed on. He took over the horse-drawn railway line linking the Danube and the Gmündensee from an insolvent French engineer named Zola (the novelist's father), and commis-sioned Riepel to investigate the best possible route for the line to Moravia and Gali-cia.[22] Finally, in April 1835—just six weeks after the death of the Emperor Franz —he felt ready to renew his appeal for imperial and royal backing. This time he was successful—an outcome which probably owed more to Metternich's and Kolowrat's decision to back the scheme than to the credibility of Salomon's claims that "the achievement of this great means of communication would be of benefit to the State and the public weal, no less than to those who join in the undertaking" and that the proposal was "based . . . strongly upon the interests of the common weal" and "entirely patriotic" motives.[23]

It was agreed that a joint-stock company should be set up to construct a line between Vienna and Bochnia (south-east of Cracow). As a second thought, to ensure that there would be no royal change of mind, Salomon suggested that the line be called the "Kaiser-Ferdinands-Nordbahn." This appeal to royal vanity was successful. For good measure, he also sought—as he put it to Metternich—to "take such steps as may be appropriate for inducing such statesmen as are the bearers of honoured names to place themselves as patrons at the head of this national under-taking." Specifically, he sought to enlist Metternich, Kolowrat and the head of the imperial Treasury, Count Mittrowsky, as board members. This use of noble names to lend respectability to new companies—in return for financial perks—was a device widely employed in England and elsewhere; in the Austrian case it was essential to overcome royal and bureaucratic opposition.[24]

In fact, the benefits of the Nordbahn—as the line was usually known—might well have ended up being greater for the "common weal" than for those who actually invested their money in it. The line was supposed to take ten years to build. The final stretch to Bochnia was not completed until 1858. It was supposed to cost 12 million gulden (£1 million), roughly 16,600 gulden per mile. The actual figure was closer to 27,750 gulden. Yet—as so often in the history of railways—short-term benefits to investors tended to compensate for (or at least to distract from) such long-term cost overruns. From the moment the concession was granted, demand for shares in the firm dramatically outstripped supply. Of 12,000 shares (each worth 1,000 gulden), Salomon retained 8,000, so that just 4,000 were offered to the public. There were 27,490 applications, driving the share price up well above par.[25]

These short-term capital gains help explain why other Austrian bankers hurried to compete—even when they realised better than Salomon the formidable practical problems involved. No sooner had he secured the Nordbahn concession than Sina petitioned to be granted the concession for the line from Vienna to Trieste, a peti-tion which enjoyed some official support on the familiar grounds that Sina, unlike Salomon, was Austrian born and hence a Habsburg subject.[26] It is not wholly appar-ent why, after so many years of amicable co-operation in the realm of Austrian bond issues, the major Vienna banks failed to co-operate over railways; but Salomon did not fire the first shot. Indeed, in allowing Sina and Arnstein & Eskeles substantial shareholdings in the Nordbahn and according them due influence on the company's provisional board of management, he was singularly accommodating. Unfortunately, the other bankers appear to have been intent on some sort of spoiling operation. At the second general meeting of the Nordbahn, Ludwig von Pereira (a partner at Arnstein & Eskeles) launched a well-researched technical critique of the engineering plans and financial projections, a move which succeeded in arousing the hitherto dormant anxieties of the Emperor. It was only with difficulty that Salomon and Riepel were able to rebut Pereira's criticisms, at least some of which, it must be said, were to prove quite justified.[27] The climax of this prototypical boardroom battle came in October 1836, when Salomon moved a resolution demanding that the building of the railway be commenced or the company liquidated. With 76 out of the 83 votes in favour, he was able to force Sina and Eskeles to resign.[28]

From the outset, Salomon had intended that the Nordbahn should be the basis for a succession of branch lines to the major cities on either side of it: his original petition had specifically mentioned subsidiary lines to Brünn, Olmütz and Troppau. Even while he was locking horns with Pereira—and before a single rail had been laid down—he therefore continued to secure supplementary concessions from the government to allow him to add further branches: to Pressburg, to Bielitz, to Deutsch-Wagram and so on.[29] Work finally began on the first stretch of line north from Vienna in 1837, and trains were running along the first section between Deutsch-Wagram and Florisdorf by the end of the following year.[30] It was not until 1839, however, that freight and passengers began to be carried between Vienna and Brünn, so that for more than two years the company was pouring money into materials and men (some 14,000 in all) for no return, and was kept going only by a Rothschild advance of some 8 million gulden. Small wonder Lionel felt it advisable to reassure Metternich that most English railways "will yield a profit of eight to ten per cent"; there was no sign at this stage that the Austrian line would do so, and its shares duly fell below par. As Salomon later recalled, the Nordbahn had required "the expenditure of large sums of money, and . . . patient waiting; sacrifices that I was called upon to make, to the amount of several hundred thousand."[31]

Yet from 1841 onwards Salomon's senior manager Goldschmidt began to detect an improvement on his weekly visits to monitor traffic at the main terminus.[32] As with the British railways, it was the unexpectedly large amount of passenger traffic—especially families of day-trippers on Sundays—which helped to boost receipts. As early as 1841 up to 10,000 people were regularly using the initial stretch of line from Vienna to the suburb of Vienna–Neustadt.[33] In 1843 the shares rose for the first time since their issue above par to 103; a year later they reached 129 and by 1845 they stood at no less than 228. This represented a huge if belated capital gain to the original investors—above all, to Salomon himself.[34]

Yet it would be unjust to Salomon to suggest that he operated with the short-term speculative gains solely in mind. On the contrary, he genuinely does seem to have had an entrepreneurial vision of an integrated Austrian transport system. Not only did he envisage from the outset a railway which would link Galicia and Moravia to the imperial capital and southwards to Italy; he hoped also to extend his network into Hungary.[35] A good illustration of the extraordinary—almost messianic—role Salomon saw himself playing in the Habsburg lands in this period is

provided by the police report of his trip to Pressburg in June 1844 to attend a meeting of the Central Hungarian Railway Company. It was little short of a royal visit.
The Danube steamer made an unscheduled stop at Königsplatz to allow him to dis-
embark. The occupants of rooms at the Hotel zur Sonne were unceremoniously
evicted from their rooms to make way for the Rothschild party, despite the fact that
they planned to return to Vienna by coach that night. And when it was rumoured
that the mercurial Hungarian reformer Istvàn Széchényi—who was already running
his own Danube steamship company—intended to support a challenge by Sina to
Salomon's dominance of the Central Hungarian board, the venue of the meeting
was hastily changed. To cap it all, Salomon responded to the flattering toasts proposed in his honour that evening by Carl Esterházy, Andrássy and other pro-Rothschild bigwigs with a pompous speech, concluding that he would follow the
example of his schoolmaster who told his pupils: "I am going but I am leaving my
cloak behind, and it will tell me what everybody has done, and how they have
behaved in my absence." Salomon's self-importance can hardly have been diminished by the enthusiastic welcome he had received earlier in the day from the local
Jewish community, a crowd of whom gathered on the river bank to greet him.
"Count Esterházy," the police observer reported,

> frustrated their intention of according the Baron a special welcome, as
> he would not allow the Jews to carry out their scheme of letting off forty
> rockets. They were restrained even from shouting their welcome which
> in view of the ill feeling between the citizens and the Jews here, might
> easily have led to a breach of the peace.[36]

Esterházy might be willing to ingratiate himself with the Austrian railway king, but
he had no desire to let Salomon's poor co-religionists bask in his reflected glory.

Nor was Salomon content to dominate the development of the Habsburg railway
system. He also pursued a strategy of "vertical integration" (bringing together different stages in a particular economic process under a single corporate roof). As early
as 1831 he saw the need to foster independent Austrian supplies of iron and steel,
so that the development of the imperial railways would not be reliant on imports
from the foundries of Britain. Although his first bid to purchase the Witkowitz
Ironworks company in the Ostravian coalfields was unsuccessful (because as a Jew
he was prohibited from owning land), he was able to lease the works indirectly from
the Archibishop of Olmütz, Count Chotek, in 1841 by setting up a company in
partnership with the banker Geymüller. When Geymüller went bankrupt soon
after, Salomon petitioned again to be allowed to buy the works and this time was
successful. The Witkowitz works—the first in the Habsburg Empire to use the pud-
dling process necessary for the production of rails—was to remain one of the Austrian house's principal industrial assets for almost a century.[37] At the same time,
Salomon began to interest himself in coal mining.[38]

Finally, Salomon's vision of a rail link from Vienna to Trieste led him to expand
Rothschild interests beyond land transportation into shipping, taking a leading role
in the foundation of the Austrian Steamship Company or Austrian Lloyd in 1835.
When the company got into difficulties in the 1830s, Salomon gave it the same life-
saving injection of capital he gave the Nordbahn at the same time, in the form of a
500,000 gulden loan in return for a mortgage on the company's seven steamers. As

with the Nordbahn, the investment proved a sound one, with profits rising from around 82,000 gulden to nearly 370,000 gulden between 1841 and 1847.[39] Salomon's decision to invest in a salt factory in Venice at around this time needs to be seen as part of a strategy of expansion into the Adriatic region.[40]

The question which remained to be answered was whether this bold business strategy would prove financially sustainable. As we have seen, there had been a recurrent need to inject cash into the various concerns which Salomon was seeking to knit together. Such strategies of vertical integration, though apparently rational, do not always deliver the internal gains in efficiency and economies of scale they seem to imply. Moreover, loosely connected business empires of the sort he was building are often especially vulnerable to a deterioration in economic conditions. Unfortunately for Salomon, such a deterioration was fast approaching.

Frankfurt: The Taunusbahn

By comparison with its Vienna branch, the Frankfurt house itself played a relatively modest role in railway finance before 1848. This may have been a matter of temperament; it is more likely to have reflected the different political environment of southern Germany in the Vormärz era. Although (like the British state) the Austrian state did little to facilitate the building of railways other than to grant concessions, it was at least a single entity, so that negotiations for a line stretching as far as the Nordbahn could be conducted at the imperial level. In southern Germany, by contrast, even relatively short railway lines could cross multiple state borders, and therefore required co-operation between several governments. Particularist jealousies, however, meant that such co-operation was rarely forthcoming; indeed, the larger states self-consciously pursued railway policies which were designed to maximise their own internal cohesion at the expense of inter-state communications. In Bavaria (where the first German railway was opened to link Nuremberg with Fürth less than four miles away), as well as in Baden, Württemberg and Hanover, the construction of railways was undertaken on the Belgian model by the state governments themselves. Here, therefore, the most that the Rothschilds could do was to underwrite the bonds issued to finance railway building. The state nearest to them, Hesse-Kassel, by contrast, allowed some railways to be constructed privately, as did Prussia and Saxony. The result was a degree of confusion which precluded a grand strategy of the sort adopted by Salomon in Vienna and doomed to disappointment the hope expressed in the Leipzig-based *Allgemeine Zeitung des Judenthums* in 1837 that "the House of Rothschild [would] unerringly place itself at the head of a movement which will completely reshape the European monetary system: the destruction of the trade in paper [meaning stock exchange speculation] [and] the injection of capital into industry."[41]

As early as January 1836, Amschel ran into difficulties when he sought to secure a concession for a line between Frankfurt (a free city) and Mainz (in Hesse-Darmstadt), which naturally had also to pass through Hesse-Kassel: three separate jurisdictions for a line of less than twenty miles. It took seventeen months merely to secure the legislation needed for the compulsory purchase of land in Hesse-Kassel.[42] When in 1838 a concession was secured from the Frankfurt Senate for the so-called Taunusbahn, Amschel and Bethmann had to buy out a rival company which had been authorised to build a line along a parallel route by the authorities in Kassel.[43] A similar conflict arose in the case of the plan to link Cologne to the Belgian network between the proponents (led by David Hansemann) and opponents (led by Ludolf Camphausen) of a route through Aix-la-Chapelle. A merger of their two companies to produce the Rheinische Eisenbahngesellschaft could be achieved only at the price of Camphausen's withdrawal.[44]

All this helps explain why Amschel and his nephew Anselm preferred to let other banks in the region take the lead in such negotiations. As Anselm explained in 1838, "here in Germany, railways get off the ground only with a great deal of effort." It was not untypical that the Elector of Hesse-Kassel's son expected Amschel to secure him a bribe from the company seeking the Frankfurt–Kassel concession.[45] Quite apart from the time wasted in negotiations, he grumbled, railway shares in Frankfurt were being adversely affected by such delays. The Rhineland company's, for example, fell by around 20 per cent in 1838 after cost overruns had necessitated an issue of 6,000 new shares.[46] It was therefore not the Rothschilds but the Oppenheims and Bethmanns who took the lead in private railway building in south-west Germany, though Amschel was happy to participate as a sleeping partner. It was Oppenheim who led the Rhineland consortium, taking around 25 per cent of its 3 million thaler capital, compared with a combined Paris and Frankfurt Rothschild holding of just a fortieth; similarly, it was the Bethmanns who led the £200,000 Taunusbahn consortium.[47] By comparison with these activities, there were easier profits to be made from issuing the Baden government's railway bonds, though this business also had to be shared with others; or acting as the agent for British locomotive exporters, notably George Stephenson.[48] By the mid-1840s the Frankfurt house was confining itself to floating state bonds earmarked for railways (for example, for Hesse-Kassel in 1845), turning down private schemes like the Leipzig–Frankfurt line proposed the same year.[49] When Anthony visited Frankfurt in 1844, he was impressed by the "tremendous speculation" in railway shares, but viewed the phenomenon with a marked detachment.[50]

Political fragmentation (and entrepreneurial differences) also explain the very limited involvement of the Rothschilds in Italian railway building before 1848. Although there is some evidence that the London and Paris houses bought shares in the Milanese railway line built in the mid-1830s, this interest soon waned.[51] The following year approaches to James by an Italian company planning a line between Florence and Leghorn were politely rebuffed. As James put it, "We have enough railways of our own [in France] without embarking on those of Italy as well."[52] Schemes for railways in the Two Sicilies and the Papal states were discussed in the 1840s, but—despite Metternich's (somewhat unexpected) encouragement in the latter case—did not get far beyond the drawing board.[53]

"The Chief Rabbi of the Rive Droite"

When he felt like flattering James, Heine sometimes gave the impression that he had been the *fons et origo* of the French railway network.[54] "Herr von Rothschild alone discovered Emile Pereire, the Pontifex Maximus of railways, and he immediately made him his chief engineer . . ."[55] It was really the other way round: Pereire "discovered" Rothschild, in the sense that he persuaded James to commit his enormous financial resources to railways. It was an unlikely partnership, which reflected James's susceptibility to clever men of letters as much as his financial acumen. True, Emile and his younger brother Isaac were Jews, like James; but there the resemblances ended. Where James was an immigrant from Germany, the Pereires were Sephardic Jews whose grandfather had left Spain and settled in Bordeaux. Moreover, where James had no explicit political or philosophical allegiances, the Pereires were disciples of comte Henri de Saint-Simon, the utopian prophet of a technocratic, corporatist industrial society in which the "productive" classes would displace the idle and rule benignly under the influence of a "new Christianity."[56]

For such men, partnership with the Rothschilds represented a perilous compromise, if not a Faustian pact: the Pereires' friend Prosper Enfantin hesitated to become associated with "the damned soul of a Rothschild."[57] Yet Emile Pereire was enough of a realist to grasp the indispensability of Rothschild financial support if he really was to write his projects "on the earth" rather than just on the pages of papers like the *National.* Between them, he and his brother could muster no more than 30,000 francs. Yet their pilot project—a railway from Paris to Pecq in the elegant suburb of Saint-Germain—would cost, they estimated, more than a hundred times as much to construct. As Emile put it in May 1835, "The involvement of the Rothschild bank in the railway from Paris to Saint-Germain is not only of great importance for this particular venture; it will necessarily have a determining influence on the later realisation of all the great industrial undertakings."[58]

Wisely, the Pereires did not pin all their hopes on James. Having secured political backing from Emile Legrand, the Director-General of the Ponts et Chaussées (in effect, the Department of Transport) and the more sceptical Thiers (who dismissed the railway as a "toy"), they approached Adolphe d'Eichthal and Auguste Thurneyssen for the 200,000 francs needed to secure the initial concession, and then recruited J. C. Davillier as well as James to act as shareholders. In fact, d'Eichthal had as big a stake as James—23.5 per cent of the original 5 million franc capital.[59] As an advertisement for investment in future railways, the Saint-Germain line was a qualified success. The twelve mile track cost a good deal more to build than had been anticipated (11 million francs instead of 3.9 million) and the volume of passenger traffic fluctuated much more than had been anticipated, soaring on summer Sundays and plummeting on winter weekdays.[60] On the other hand it was completed and opened ahead of schedule in August 1837, and in the first three years of its operation the Pereires succeeded in reducing running costs from 52 to 44 per cent of gross receipts, ensuring that the shareholders were not disappointed.[61] James was a convert. As he wrote to his nephew Anthony in June 1836, after himself taking the train through Belgium on his way to Frankfurt:

> I would recommend that we don't sell any St-Germain shares for the time being, because I believe that there will be a substantial rise in these. I am absolutely convinced that people in France simply have no idea how easy it is to travel by such means . . . I want to tell you, the cheaper one sets the price, the more passengers there will be, and the greater will be the profit one stands to make. Having seen what has been happening in Antwerp, I am more and more convinced that this is a lucrative and successful enterprise. I am certain that in twenty years' time there won't be a single Postmaster left in the world, and people will only travel by train . . . I am in love with the railway.[62]

The Pereires always conceived of the Saint-Germain line as the nucleus of a much larger railway system. Their hope was to concentrate as much of the traffic into and out of Paris as they could through the Saint-Germain line and into the terminus station they built at the Gare Saint-Lazare. At the same time, they always hoped to avoid financial dependence on any single banker. This was easily attained as French railways were financed from an early stage by consortiums, reinforcing a tendency towards the formation of loose business "groups" which had already manifested itself on the Paris bond market. However, the project of a Pereire-led monopoly on rail traffic in and out of Paris inevitably aroused both financial competition and political opposition. Thus, when the brothers embarked on the next phase of their programme—a line between Paris and Versailles, running along the right bank of the Seine—the move did not go unchallenged. The "Rive Droite" was a financial as well as a geographical extension of the original Saint-Germain line: de Rothschild Frères were the largest shareholder with just under a third of the 11 million franc capital; the other major shareholders were once again d'Eichthal, Davillier and Thurneyssen, with an additional 16 per cent being provided by the house of J. Lefebvre & Cie.[63]

At first James was optimistic about his investment. Shares in both the Saint-Germain and the Rive Droite soared: the former reaching a high of 950, compared with an issue price of 500 francs. "Profit smiles," wrote James gleefully as he sold a couple of hundred. "[To] go from 500 to 950 is quite nice."[64] However, he was disturbed to hear that "that miserable Fould is organising a subscription for our railway on which we have been labouring for such a long time." After "a campaign of intrigues" in the Chamber of Deputies, the Fould brothers and their partners secured a rival concession to build a parallel line to Versailles along the *left* bank of the Seine. "Well, this will ruin everything," James lamented, "and one can't do anything any more in this world."[65] The absurdity of the ensuing rivalry was not lost on contemporaries. Heine ridiculed "the Chief Rabbi of the Rive Droite, Baron Rothschild" and "the Chief Rabbi of the Rive Gauche":

> For the French Jews, as for the French as a whole, gold is the god of our times and industry the prevailing religion. In this respect, it is possible to divide the Jews of this country into two sects: the sect of the Right Bank and the sect of the Left Bank. These names refer to the two railways which lead to Versailles, the one along the right bank of the Seine, the other along the left bank, which are run by two famous rabbis of finance, who rub each other up the wrong way as much as Rabbi Shammai and Rabbi Hillel in the ancient city of Babylon.[66]

For the investors concerned, however, it was no laughing matter. There was not enough traffic between Paris and Versailles to justify the existence of two lines, and the actual returns and dividends on the shares of the new companies were correspondingly meagre (especially as there were cost overruns during construction).[67] The Saint-Germain shares also began to be affected by the rising cost of expanding the line's capacity to accommodate the increased traffic not only of the Versailles line but of other proposed branches, which necessitated a series of three loans from its bankers totalling around 10 million francs.[68] More generally, the proliferation of new industrial companies was beginning to exhaust the market's appetite for new shares: as James warned grimly in September 1837, "One of these days it will start to stink . . . because too many shares are arriving on the scene."[69] A sudden slump in the market almost exactly a year later forced the rival Versailles lines to discuss some kind of merger, the prime objective of which, as far as James was concerned, was to scrap the Rive Gauche altogether with a view to boosting the shares of the Rive Droite. In the end the Rothschild company effectively took over the Fould company and both were later absorbed into the Ouest line in 1851.[70]

These problems help explain the difficulties which beset the next phase of the Pereires' activity. From an early stage they had envisaged much longer railway lines than the initial connections to Saint-Germain and Versailles. Of the various plans they considered, the most ambitious was for a railway connection between France and Belgium, where the first state-financed lines were already operating. This project had substantial political appeal to the French government, which, as we have seen, was keen to assert its influence over its newly independent neighbour. It also appealed greatly to James, who had been impressed by the Belgian lines he had used on his way to Frankfurt, as well as attracting the interest of British railway entrepreneurs like George Stephenson and the Belgium-based John Cockerill. However, the Société Générale—which would have been the obvious financial partner for the Rothschilds—was lukewarm in its response.[71] After much prevarication, the governor of the Société Générale, Méeus, indicated that he "did not want his name to be associated with the Belgian railway," as it would be "too risky" and he put "honour before everything, money second."[72] For his part, James took the view from an early stage that "if [Méeus] is not prepared to . . . join then we will have to stay away from the project for we don't want to make enemies of them." But it was not only Méeus who had reservations about the project. James also came under pressure from the Frankfurt house to drop it: the proposed line was, as Anselm put it, just "too long."[73]

Although it was partly due to the diplomatic crisis over Belgium of 1838–9, the stalling of the plan for a Paris–Brussels connection primarily reflected the lack of confidence of continental bankers in their own ability to finance major railway lines without state assistance (or perhaps their desire to get their hands on subsidies). As early as December 1836 James was toying with the idea of some kind of state subvention to make the proposed Northern Line (or "Nord" for short) more attractive to investors. "It is a difficult business," he told his nephews in London, "because the bankers here [in Paris] are not inclined to support it. Don't you think that it [would be] possible to sell a great deal in London if the French Government [were] to guarantee an interest payment at 3 per cent?" James could see the difficulties with such an arrangement, however. "If we had chosen to go for the interest," he reported a few days later, "then every scoundrel would have appeared on the scene and would have made plans and would have placed obstacles in our path. Secondly, I believe that the [government's] credit might have suffered terribly as a result of such a move because every other département would have demanded the same terms." On the other hand, he discerned that the Nord would never be built without some sort of state support. The alternative method of subsidy he contemplated at this time was a straightforward "gift" of a third of its estimated cost: "We calculate the cost of the Railway to be 75 million and the Government will give 25 million without expecting to receive anything in return as encouragement for the boys."[74] Without a subsidy, James argued, it would be impossible to sell enough shares to the public, no matter how "crazy about railways" they were; or rather the shares would be sold, but would not rise by the 15 or 20 per cent which investors were coming to expect.[75] This, however, seems to have been unacceptable to Méeus.[76] It may also be that, as Léon Faucher suspected, the French government was wary of such involvement. James regarded "Legrand, whose assistance we much require . . . [as] no great friend of ours."[77]

Up until this point, the government had confined itself to devising bold schemes for a national network of major lines radiating outwards from Paris. For example, the Molé ministry in May 1837 had envisaged six principal railways linking Paris to Belgium in the north, Orléans in the south, Rouen in the north-west and Mulhouse in the east, with separate links to Lyon and Marseille in the far south. A year later, Legrand envisaged a total of nine major lines, adding links to Nantes and Bordeaux in the west and south-west as well as a link from Lyon to Basle.[78] However, there was opposition to the planned system of concessions, and such plans remained no more than suggestions until the 1840s. This left the private sector more or less to its own devices.

James soon formed the view that "the various railways have to be viewed as cousins of each other and when [the share price of] one rises the others will then follow."[79] However, there was a tendency for more than one "family" of railway financiers to emerge. For example, James was happy to lend financial support to Paulin Talabot, the driving force behind the Grand-Combe line, which aimed to link the coal mines of the Grande Combe (near Alès) to Beaucaire and ultimately Marseille. A visit to the Midi in 1838 seems to have convinced him that the area would be ideal for railway development, and he had no objection to advancing 6 million francs to keep the project afloat in late 1839.[80] By contrast, he was more wary of the route to Bordeaux,[81] and limited his involvement to a small shareholding in the company set up to build the line from Paris to Orléans—a wise decision, as the company folded in August 1839.[82] The concession was subsequently granted to an Anglo-French partnership of Charles Laffitte and the English financier Edward Blount, which also won the concession to link Paris and Boulogne via Amiens. Despite the fact that the Orléans line was obliged to use the Saint-Lazare terminus controlled by the Saint-Germain company, a fierce rivalry soon developed between the Laffitte–Blount group and the Rothschild group.[83]

The 1839 crisis increased James's desire to involve the state in the financing of railways, if only to bolster the performance of Saint-Germain and Rive Droite shares. Here, as with international affairs, his bullying of French politicians was unabashed. "In the event that the Government is not prepared to do anything with regard to the Rive Droite," he told his nephews in June 1839, "then I will see to it that it is attacked in all the newspapers." Two months later he went further:

> If they are indeed making things very difficult for you then you should tell them that I wrote you that I am resigning from my position as administrator [of the Rive Droite company] and at the same time I will be announcing in the newspaper that due to the implacable opposition of the present Ministry we have been forced to relinquish our position and to assure the general public that as long as the Ministry of Commerce remains in the hands of the current incumbents we will com-

pletely withdraw from doing any business in the industrials. If you put this to Marshal Soult then I can promise you that M. Dufour will change his attitude. If you can't gain someone's friendship then you have to make them fear you.[84]

As these remarks suggest, James's influence over sections of the French press was an important weapon in his railway policy.[85]

It was the question of the line to Belgium, however, which was to become the most notorious example of French governmental subservience to Rothschild financial power. Even before the various diplomatic storms of 1839 and 1840 had died away, James returned to the idea of a Northern railway more convinced than ever that it would be "a good piece of business."[86] The idea he now advanced to ministers was that the government should guarantee to pay the interest on railway *bonds* (4 per cent) for a specified period—a suggestion of Emile Pereire's designed to appeal to the more cautious investors who regarded private sector shares as too risky.[87] Now the government proved more receptive. The principle enunciated in Legrand's law of 1842 was that the state would purchase the rights of way and construct the railways and buildings, leasing the lines to the railway companies, who would provide the rolling stock and run trains for specified periods.[88] What this meant in practice, however, took years to resolve, especially in the case of the Belgian line.[89]

In James's eyes, the route north from Paris to Lille and Valenciennes promised to be the most profitable of all the main French lines because it would link the French market not only to Belgium but (via branch lines to Calais and Dunkirk) to England; the prospect of a government subsidy made it "a golden business opportunity."[90] But precisely for that reason there was bound to be political opposition to giving the Rothschilds the concession. "Well now, my dear Nat," complained James when it seemed that the government was going to deny him, "the business with our railways is not working out at all. The whole world is against us. People say we are a monopoly and that we want all the railways for they can see that it would not be possible to build the Belgian [railway] without us."[91] James was right. Although the two sides failed to reach a final agreement until 1845, the government ultimately seemed to have no alternative but to deal with the Rothschilds. A crucial factor was the government's own need to borrow precisely in order to finance the Legrand plan. James's near-monopoly on issues of rentes gave him an invaluable lever in the negotiations leading to the award of the Nord concession. As he commented with satisfaction in December 1842: "If we get the loan then we are masters over the railways. The Finance Minister said to me today, 'I won't do anything without you and the whole Ministry shares my views. The railway from Belgium will be offered to you in preference to anyone else.'"[92]

In two respects, it might be thought, James had to compromise in order to win. Firstly, the Pereires' dream that the line would terminate at the Gare Saint-Lazare had to be jettisoned, despite the negative impact this had on Saint-Germain shares.[93] Secondly, James's rivals were allowed to participate in the consortium which founded the company: with the continuing reluctance of Méeus to commit the Société Générale to a major stake in the company, James had no alternative but to allot substantial shareholdings to Laffitte–Blount, Hottinguer and other lesser rivals.[94] Yet in practice these were minor concessions. It would seem that James felt less strongly about having Saint-Lazare as the terminus than Pereire; as for his fellow investors, none of them could pretend that they were anything other than junior partners. Laffitte had hoped to revive his own long-standing ambitions by launching a single, grandiose loan to construct the entire network envisaged by Legrand; in becoming little more than a sleeping partner, he was effectively admitting defeat yet again.

When the contract was finally awarded in September 1845, the Paris and London houses were the biggest shareholders—with a 25.7 per cent stake of the 200 million franc capital, compared with Hottinguer's 20.15 per cent and Laffitte–Blount's 19.5—and held the key executive positions.[95] The only real compromises which had to be made related to the specific terms of the contract: the subsidy to be paid per mile of track constructed; the duration of the period during which the company would run it; the level of fares to be charged for the three classes of passenger; and the regularity of services.[96] But these were political rather than commercial compromises, reflecting the need to overcome opposition within the Chamber of Deputies (where an influential group of deputies favoured complete public sector construction and control of railways).[97] Similarly, James's decision to withdraw altogether from the consortium bidding three months later for the Paris–Lyon concession[98] was designed to ensure that he could make the most competitive bid for the Creil–Saint-Quentin line being auctioned simultaneously.[99]

The winning of the Nord concession needs to be seen as part of a general carving-up of the primary French railway network—a process in which the Rothschilds played a leading role. Although the Nord was the line in which James most visibly interested himself, it was by no means the only one. As we have seen, he had contemplated taking a modest share in the Paris–Lyon line. He had also thought of involving himself in the line to Bordeaux, and in 1844 formed a consortium to bid for the concession. Although the line was awarded to another company,[100] he was soon seeking some kind of partnership with it to finance the connection from Bordeaux to Cette.[101] The Rothschilds also took a substantial shareholding in the company which had won the Paris–Strasbourg concession;[102] and it had a small stake in the Lyon–Avignon concession too.[103] Smaller players vied with one another to see who could win the backing of "the all powerful name of the House of Rothschild" for their companies.[104] All this was part of an early move towards the concentration of ownership within the French railway industry which Saint-Simonians like Enfantin sought to encourage. In fact, though they lacked Enfantin's grandiose vision, the bankers did not need much persuading. As early as 1844 Hottinguer, Blanc and d'Eichthal were proposing to James that "with respect to the grand affair of the railroad from Calais to Avignon . . . we should all write & endeavour to get the whole line of railroads so as to avoid competition, that we should interest all the different companies & then all of us put together."[105] By November 1845 the craze for "fusions"—that is, mergers between railway companies—was in full swing. "You have no idea what a quantity of people are in the Counting House for the fusion of Creil & St Quentin à Lyons," reported Anselm, "which fusion creates such a confusion that our office is rather like an inn in Switzerland where all the tourists run in after a long excursion in the Mountains."[106] The time-consuming contest for concessions had begun to pall. Increasingly, collaboration seemed more rational than competition.[107]

Geographical concentration was also taking place. In securing the biggest share-holding in the Nord line and a majority of the Creil–Saint-Quentin line's capital (both in partnership with Hottinguer and Laffitte–Blount), James ensured that he controlled the two major rail links north to Belgium, to say nothing of two important routes within Paris—a total of 388 miles of line. This represented a for-midable geographical base for the pan-European railway empire he was beginning to dream of.

The English Connection

The attitude of James's English nephews towards all these projects was at first, to say the least, ambivalent. James delegated a good deal of the detailed work on railway finance to them—especially to Anthony, who consequently became more expert than his uncle. Yet he and his brothers never wholly lost the suspicion of industrial finance which they had acquired at New Court. "There is nothing new here—but Railroad Companies," complained Anthony in May 1838, "and there are so many that one gets quite sick of them—there is such a Jealousy on the part . . . of the other Companies that [one?] is a little disquieted."[108] Nat admitted that the Paris house did "not think much of our poor London house in these [railway] matters"; but he himself never tired of pointing out the disadvantages of the Nord project. "We are continually bored with Pereire & Eichtahl [*sic*] [trying] to induce us to go largely into the railroad to Chartres," he complained in the spring of 1842.[109] "The stink-ing railroads engross all our attention & for my part I wish his . . . Majesty had them all, they only give us trouble & bother & no remuneration . . . I am by no means anxious that the house shd go largely into railroad concerns." "We are up to our necks in steam," he grumbled a few weeks later, "& get nothing for all the bother & trouble." At times he denied that the railways would be profitable: "People are afraid of holding the shares and of travelling by the railroad." At other times, it was the attendant risks he objected to:

> For my part I hope & trust we shall have nothing more to do with the Be[lgia]n railroad than to take a lot of shares which we will be able to sell when good opportunity offers—I am by no means desirous of going up to one's neck in a stinking railroad & if the least thing happens one [soils?] one's breeches, whilst others know all about it & when we wish to be acquainted with the occurrence we must address ourselves to Pereire—Besides the bother & trouble with the Govt . . .

But the criticism he most frequently expressed was that becoming involved in oper-ating railways—as opposed to speculating in their shares—could tie up capital in a potentially dangerous way:

> I am against the [Belgian railway] affair because I am afraid of the anxi-ety, bother & trouble which it will surely occasion us—the moral responsibility of it will rest entirely on us, & I wd sooner leave to others the profit which the shares are likely to bring than engage in a concern of such magnitude without the possibility of attending to it properly—Such is my way of thinking & most sincerely do I trust the Baron will remain satisfied with purely financial affairs which we understand & which we can get out of when we think fit.[110]

Nat was delighted when the Nord concession appeared to fall through, and alarmed when it was finally granted. Although less hostile than his brother, Anthony could be almost as unenthusiastic. "As regards the Railroad," he told Lionel in June 1842, "I think the best thing is . . . not to have anything to do with them."[111]

These attitudes reveal a fundamental difference of attitude, though how far this was a generational difference and how far a matter of milieu is hard to say: the fact that Anselm, who had spent most of his working life in Paris or Frankfurt, also opposed too much involvement in railways suggests a generation gap of some sort.[112] In admitting that "in these times the conservative feeling has the ascendant over the acquiring sentiment—with me at least," Nat spoke for all the younger Rothschilds.[113] Like the *Journal des Débats*, they were inclined to fear that in bidding for the Nord concession James was bidding "for the privilege to ruin himself." As Nat put it, contemplating the extent of their commitments,

> by hook & by crook we shall have lots of shares in the market & proba-
> bly deeply engaged in them all—I have no doubt if things remain as
> they at present are all share concerns will turn out uncommmonly well,
> but God forbid if the least political or financial crisis were to take place
> what wd become of all the shares?[114]

"The Baron," however, was too embroiled in "wheeling and dealing" with the plethora of new scrip and shares coming on to the market seriously to contemplate such an eventuality.[115]

In this context, Nat's description of James's contrasting mood is especially illuminating:

> [T]he Baron is in a sort of fever about it, he thinks it a good business, &
> is afraid of it, he fancies the rival company will get it & then regrets it
> doubly, on the other hand he trembles head & foot at the idea of having
> to direct a railroad company of such importance without being able to
> do without such a pair of jobbers as Eichthal & Pereire.[116]

James knew the risks, in other words, but could not face losing the business to his rivals; his nephews were less furiously competitive. Nat's view "with respect to the railroad [was] not to be too greedy & not to wish to jouer le grand rôle, we may take a share & a good large one & take our profit thereon but not assume more responsibility than others."[117] James, by contrast, could not resist playing "le grand rôle." He had no illusions about the dangers and difficulties involved in "trying to do too much at once," but nevertheless exhorted his nephews to "apply themselves seriously":

> I urgently beg you to take on several new brokers so that we can do busi-
> ness on an equal footing with the others and try to put some life into the
> railway business. I feel that the world wants to find something new each
> year with which to busy itself. At the moment "industry" seems to be the
> fashionable thing. If that is the case and we decide to enter the fray then
> we have to apply ourselves seriously to the business and will have to
> engage in doing business even if there is nothing to be earned only so
> that we stay busy.[118]

Enfantin was not wrong when he suggested that "playing at railways" had supplanted even playing politics in James's affections: "Playing at gossip with Thiers,

Guizot or Molé—a game which Louis Philippe plays so well—is child's play for Rothschild, which he scarcely deigns to play; he profits from its ups and downs, but for his part he plays at railways . . . that was the great game for strong men."[119]

Yet James's project ultimately depended on the London house, in that only the resources of the London capital market could satisfy the demands of the projected line, even with government subsidies. The Nord would, as Nat saw, only be "a capital concern if we can get some good people in London to go largely into it." "[I]t is impossible for us to undertake so extensive a line unless backed by English capitalists," he advised Lionel.[120] In particular, he urged him to involve Glyn's, the one City house which had interested itself seriously in railways, and George Stephenson, whose engineering expertise would be invaluable. Given the obvious importance of the branch lines from the Nord to the Channel coast, other English businessmen were not slow to become involved, though not all were welcome: the attempts of David Salomons to elbow his way into the business were a source of considerable irritation.[121] The fact that there was so much English interest in the line may explain why Nat's opposition to involvement diminished during 1843. If nothing else, he came to believe that the shares would jump to a "famous high price" and "go like hot rolls" on issue.[122] Sure enough, French railway shares were a great success on the London market. As Mayer reported:

> The people here are quite determined upon entering every undertaking that is brought out in your good country, no matter whether it is a railroad or loan . . . [G]iven the fortune being made here by the share jobbers one has no doubt that, however immense the scheme may appear to be, a very strong party will be made.[123]

Despite their reservations about the long-term profitability of French railways, the London brothers could not help taking pride in the superior capacity of the British market. "I hope that you have sold a good lot of the Northern Shares," Anthony urged Lionel in September 1845. "Try my dear Rabbi to show that the English people can take off as many shares as the stinking French frogs."[124] His youngest brother expressed the same feeling the following year: "The more I see, I am convinced the more there is no place like our old New Court; where would all the rubbishy French shares be if we did not support them? I think we may give ourselves a few airs and be as great men as the others."[125] Such chauvinistic sentiments were another important aspect of the Rothschild generation gap.

The combination of James's entrepreneurial vision and the London market's capacity was a recipe for success. As the price of Nord shares soared from 500 francs to 760, his gamble on the line seemed amply justified.[126] Even his London nephews had to acknowledge that its prospects seemed excellent: its daily takings exceeded 20,000 francs as soon as it opened, despite the fact that the line was far from complete and the company was short of capable engine-drivers. Although that was roughly half its projected income, it still promised a respectable return to the operators—and more, with a little fine-tuning.[127] James was soon following his brother Salomon's example, exploring the possibility of "vertical integration" in the form of further investment in Belgian coal mines. "Everyone thinks that coal is like gold," he enthused, a view which even the cautious Anselm could not dispute. The 3 million franc investment which the Paris house made in coal mines (in conjunction with the

Talabot brothers) would, he was confident, "become with a little time a most capital concern as the consumption of coal becomes stronger day to day owing to so many railroads on the continent and the progress of industry . . ."[128] The Nord could get its coal at a competitive price; by the same token, the transportation of Belgian coal became a staple of the railway line's revenue.[129]

Those critics who had accused him of being interested only in a quick profit on railway issues now had to recant: like Salomon, James was building up a substantial portfolio of long-term industrial investments, at the core of which was his stake in the Nord. It was a profoundly important departure, not least because the London house chose not to do the same. This was the safer option in the short run, and undoubtedly reduced New Court's exposure when the market for railway shares slumped in 1847–8; but in the long run it meant that only the Paris house would share in the immense capital gains realised by investors in industry during the second half of the century.

The Impact of Rail

The economic significance of railways can be quantified with some degree of precision. Between 1828 and 1848 around 1,250 miles of track were built in France, with peaks of investment in 1841, 1843 and 1846–7.[130] In the first instance, the railways were financed by a multitude of small companies—between 1826 and 1838 around 500 *sociétés en commandite* were formed with nominal capital of 520 million francs. In 1845 alone, twenty-eight companies were set up with almost as much capital. The Rothschilds were without question the dominant force in this process. To be sure, their name figures in only four out of thirty-two concessions granted between 1835 and 1846. But of 225 million francs contributed by French banks to railway capital formation between 1835 and 1846, the Rothschilds accounted for 84.6 million—38 per cent of the total, and nearly a tenth of all capital subscribed.[131]

This dominance was in many ways quite natural. Apart from the superior resources of de Rothschild Frères compared with its French rivals, James had the unique advantage of a direct familial link to the London market. This was crucial, for without British capital (and technology), the progress of French railway construction would without question have been slower. It has been roughly estimated that half the capital invested in French railways by 1847 was British, and only a quarter of French locomotives were domestically produced.[132] The role of the state in the railway boom can also be quantified. From 1840, when the first state subsidies began to be paid out by the new Ministry of Public Works, until 1849, around 7.2 million francs were spent annually on railways by the state, between a fifth and a quarter of annual average gross investment.[133] In aggregate terms, this would generally be considered by modern economic historians as money well spent. Problematic though it is to calculate exactly the "social savings" generated by railways (in the form not only of more efficient internal and external communications but also of "backward linkages" to the coal, iron and steel industries), France would unquestionably have been worse off without them.

Yet contemporaries did not tend to assess the Rothschilds' role in railways in such arid, macroeconomic terms. In general, they were more concerned with the distribution of the benefits generated by the railway boom than with their developmental impact. They were also more concerned with the social costs of railways than modern economic historians. This helps to explain why the cultural and political responses to the railways were in such stark contrast to their macroeconomic impact.

To be sure, there was no shortage of writers who were ready and willing to "puff" rail travel as the wonder of the age. The 1830s and 1840s saw a spate of odes and hymns to the railway, a classic example of which was composed by an obscure poetaster named Hugelmann to mark the inauguration of the Nord line on June 14, 1846. It was entitled simply: "To Rothschild":

A dragon hurtled through space,
Throwing fire down on the lanes;
A genius covered its face;
Put its powerful hands in chains;
And turning towards our world
He threw up the dust in a whirl
With the smoking beast in his thrall
He transported it with a firm hold;
Then showing this giant in chains
To the waiting millions of men,
He says: "I will make you some reins;
Be enslaved; here is my gold . . ."
He speaks and the mountain sides yield,
They fall and their clifftops descend;
The dragon traverses the fields,
The earth it shakes under its bonds;
Germans, united with Gaul,
For this power their defences let fall
Who is come back to life to recall
The forts that the emperors quit,
And whose urn, as it inclines
Disperses his seed divine
On the running board lined with ermine
And the labourers' humble hamlet.[134]

Even the usually acerbic Heine was—on occasion—moved to write in a similar, if rather less hyperbolic, vein. "All eyes are now turned to the House of Rothschild," he reported when James's intention to bid for the Nord concession was first made public, "which represents the society formed to construct the Northern French railway system in a way that is financially as sound as it is socially praiseworthy. The House of Rothschild, which in former times directed its talents and resources exclusively to the needs of governments, now places itself at the head of great national undertakings, devoting its enormous capital and its immeasurable credit to the advancement of industry and the prosperity of the people."[135] When the lines to Orléans and Rouen were opened in May 1843, Heine was positively lyrical in his enthusiasm. He detected in Paris

a tremor, which is felt by everyone, unless he has been sent into solitary confinement. The whole population of Paris constitutes at this moment a chain, which communicates the electric shock from one person to another. While the great mass of people gapes astounded and dumbstruck at the outward manifestation of these great motive forces, the philosopher is seized by a strange horror, the way we always feel when the most monstrous, unheard of thing happens, the consequences of which are unforeseeable and incalculable. Let us just say that our entire existence is being ripped up and hurled on to new tracks; that new relationships, pleasures and torments await us, and the unknown exerts its ghastly fascination, irresistible, yet at the same time fearful. Our forefathers must have felt the same when America was discovered, when the invention of gunpowder announced itself with the first shots, when the printing press sent the first proof copies of the Word of God into the world. The railways are another such providential event . . .

Yet already Heine sounded a characteristically ambivalent note of warning when he considered the political influence which the railways were conferring on those who built them. The "ruling aristocracy of money," he suggested, exercised "more and more control every day over the rudder of state": "Soon those people will constitute not only the supervisory board of the railway company, but also the supervisory board of our entire civil society."[136] For Heine, the most intriguing aspect of the railway boom was the way that aristocratic and military elites (even admirals) flocked to associate themselves with it. They lent their names as non-executive directors and invested their savings. They were even reduced to begging for share options in new companies like the Nord:

> [E]very share which members of this house [of Rothschild] grants to individuals is really a great favour—speaking plainly I should say that it is in fact a present of money which M. de Rothschild makes his friends. The shares ultimately issued . . . are from the beginning worth several hundred francs above par, and whoever asks Baron James de Rothschild for such shares at par, begs from him in the literal sense of the word. But then—the whole world is begging from him; he is inundated by begging letters, and where the greatest aristocrats have set such a noble example, begging can no longer be considered a disgrace.[137]

Heine was not alone in portraying James's mutation into a railway baron in an essentially light-hearted light. Rothschild railway jokes were another characteristic by-product of the era. Punning on the double meaning of the French *action* (a share) the writer Prosper Mérimée told Madame de Montijo a typical one in February 1846:

> The rabbi who teaches the children of M. de Rothschild asked one of them, a young lad of seven, if he knew the difference between a good action and a bad action. "Without a doubt," replied the child. "A good action is an action of the Nord, a bad action is an action of the Rive Gauche." Believe me, that boy will not lose his father's millions.[138]

Seven years later, Count Nesselrode told his cousin a "mot de Rothschild" which may even have been true as well as archetypal. "Count Tassilo Festeticz consulted him about the investment of a considerable sum. 'M. le comte,' Rothschild told him, 'if you want your capital without interest, buy land. If you want your interest without capital, buy shares.'" "It happened in Paris," added Nesselrode, "but it is universally true."[139] Such anecdotes are too easily dismissed as apocryphal. But the

Rothschilds' private correspondence confirms that at least one of them was not far from the truth. In November 1848 Betty told her son Alphonse how his four-year-old brother Edmond had "got into the habit of taking my prayer book for his devotions. And yesterday, in one of his pious outbursts, what if he doesn't say, 'I pray to our good Lord God for Papa [and] for the *chemin de fer du Nord*!' "[140]

Yet not everyone was so amused. In the course of the 1840s, a growing number of journalists began to express hostility towards what they regarded as a dangerous and corrupting private monopoly. Above all, the Nord concession came to symbolise what more radical critics of the July Monarchy regarded as its fundamental rottenness. It began in newspapers like the *Courrier Français*, the *Réforme*, the *Univers* and the *Quotidienne*.[141] But it took its most virulent form in cheaply produced polemical books and pamphlets like Alphonse Toussenel's *The Jews, Kings of the Epoch: A History of Financial Feudalism.*

In some respects, Toussenel was in a tradition dating back to the 1820s of radical critics who laced their diatribes against political corruption with a strong dose of anti-Semitism. The thrust of his argument was directed against the financial terms under which the Nord concession had been granted (and could just as easily have been made without reference to James's Jewishness). According to Toussenel, the government had effectively ceded all the profits from the line to the Rothschild-led company for forty years, while retaining all the expenses for itself—that is "for the nation." The state would pay out an estimated 100 million francs for the land across which the railway would be built, while the company would merely advance the state the cost—around 60 million francs—of the rails and rolling stock, money which the state would reimburse when the concession expired. In effect, Toussenel argued, the company was lending the state 60 million francs in return for an income from the line of around 14 million francs a year, to say nothing of the speculative profits on the shares it issued to the public. Would it not have been more rational, he asked, for the state to have borrowed the money itself—which would have cost just 2.4 million francs a year in interest—and to have built and run the railways as a state enterprise? Why pay five times that much to acquire the line forty years in the future?[142]

At one level, this was a not implausible argument for public sector control of the railway network on the Belgian model: similar economic nationalism was being advocated in Germany at around this time. And in its critique of the distributional consequences of government policy, Toussenel's book evinced a debt to early socialist thinkers like Fourier. "The enormous profits" generated by the railways came partly from the "labour of the French worker and artisan": "Who pays for the speculator's premiums of hundred of millions? The worker, the people. Who suffers on account of the ignorance and cowardice of those in power? The people."[143]

However, Toussenel's economic argument was inextricably linked to a visceral anti-Semitism. He angrily denounced the "traitors, hacks, deputies, ministers who would sell France to the Jews . . . in these times of irritation and political senility." This identification of the railway companies with a single religious group required a considerable definitional elasticity, given the prominent role of manifestly non-Jewish investors from England and Switzerland. But Toussenel—setting an example which future generations of anti-Semites would readily follow—had no difficulty with this. Rattling off the names of the various railway companies and their principal shareholders, he portrayed them all as satellites of a single cosmopolitan, Jewish *haute banque*, personified by "Baron Rothschild, the King of Finance, a Jew ennobled by a very Christian King."[144] In the 1840s "Jew" ceased to be a purely religious category and became synonymous with the type of the exploitative capitalist.

Toussenel's book was profoundly influential, spawning a succession of imitators—who were generally only too glad to repeat verbatim his charges, and add some more for good measure. Within a year of the first edition, a still more violent pamphlet was published under the pseudonym of "Satan" by an obscure hack named Georges Dairnvaell, entitled *The Edifying and Curious History of Rothschild I, King of the Jews*. According to Dairnvaell, the Rothschilds had secured the Nord contract by corrupt means, distributing 15,000 shares to deputies; moreover, they had then defrauded these same shareholders by an unauthorised issue of shares, which reduced the value of the original stock. James was "Rothschild I . . . the speculator-monarch . . . a capitalist who enriches himself incessantly while the fathers of children lose all but their last crust of bread."[145] In the later wave of anti-Semitic journalism of the 1880s and 1890s, similar allegations were trotted out: Chirac, for example, claimed that James distributed Nord shares to friendly papers like the *Constitutionnel* or the *Journal des Débats* and even slipped a couple of shares under the serviettes of selected dinner guests![146] Drumont repeated the charges made by Toussenel; Scherb merely translated the relevant chunk of Dairnvaell.[147] The same stories were being repeated even after 1945.[148]

Was there any substance to these attacks? One modern historian has argued that "The system of [railway] finance . . . seemed to guarantee the maximum costs to the state with the maximum secure benefits to shareholders."[149] The public appetite for Nord shares was enormous. The list of names who approached James and Lionel for this purpose is an impressive one: as one contemporary joked, James must have had a "rather precious autograph collection" of the Parisian social elite by the time the deadline for applications passed.[150] Baron Stockmar was an early investor in French rails, conceivably on behalf of Prince Albert.[151] Lady Ailesbury, the widow of the 1st Marquess, was another.[152] Disraeli bought 150 shares in the Paris–Strasbourg line in 1845, though this proved a "very indifferent" speculation and he sold them just a few months later. Lionel also "gave" him some shares in the Nord.[153] Another investor in the Nord was Balzac, though he had to pay for his 150 shares—unlike a less well-known writer Jules Janin, who later wrote that "M. de Rothschild . . . saved me and my novel [*Clarisse Harlowe*] with a few Nord shares."[154] Yet evidence that shares were allocated to needy writers with the specific intention of influencing the granting of the concession is lacking. Indeed, one contemporary had the impression that most of the shares were being allocated "arbitrarily."[155] This seems plausible given the sheer number of shareholders involved. As the Minister of Public Works Dumon, pointed out, there were 12,461 subscribers for the Nord, 31,000 for the Strasbourg line and 24,000 for the line to Lyon.[156] It is also worth asking whether such large numbers would have come forward in the absence of a government subsidy. It seems unlikely. Even with the subsidy, those who held on to their Nord shares saw only a temporary (if impressive) capital gain. In the months between the granting of the concession and the opening of the line, the shares were being traded at prices above 750 francs, compared with a nominal price of 500. However, within days of its inauguration, a tragic and not wholly unpredictable event provided a reminder that, government subsidy or no, railways were a risky business. In the light of the events of 1846–8, the allegation that the Rothschilds made immense and improper profits from the Nord concession must be regarded with scepticism.

An Accident Happens

On June 14, 1846, James de Rothschild invited 1,700 guests to celebrate the open-ing of the Nord line. Transported in first class carriages of the Compagnie du Chemin de Fer du Nord, the party lunched at Lille, dined at Brussels and then returned to Paris the next day.[157] A cantata was composed specially for the occasion by Berlioz and Jules Janin and, to ensure the best possible press coverage, invitations were sent to Victor Hugo, Alexandre Dumas, Prosper Mérimée and Théophile Gau-tier, who described the inauguration in a piece for the *Presse*.[158] It was the day, in Dairnvaell's words, "when the royalty of Rothschild I was officially recognised" and James Rothschild was proclaimed "*King of Europe, Asia, Africa, America, Oceania and other places*, and above all, *King of the Jews*."[159] Just twenty-four days later, at 3 p.m. on July 8, a train running north on the same line was derailed at Fampoux when a rail gave way on an embankment running along the side of a marshy lake. Accord-ing to an eyewitness account, the first locomotive pulling the twenty-nine-carriage train kept going, but the second came to a sudden halt, snapping the connecting chains between the carriages behind it. Thirteen carriages came off the track, one was crushed by the impact and three others sank in the lake. Despite heroic efforts by passengers in the rear coaches, between fourteen and thirty-nine people died.

The conflicting estimates of the death toll were products of the subsequent, vio-lent public debate between the railway company and a chorus of hostile journalists, led by Georges Dairnvaell, for whom the accident seemed to encapsulate the wickedness not just of the company but of the political system which had granted the concession, of the Jews and above all of the Rothschilds. There had, of course, been railway accidents before. Heine had already written bitter words on the subject following a fire on the Versailles line:

> What a dreadful disaster, for instance, was the fire on the Versailles rail-way! I am not referring now to the Sunday crowd roasted or parboiled on this occasion; I refer rather to the surviving Sabbath company, whose stock tumbled by so many per cent, and which now awaits, with fear and trembling, the outcome of the lawsuits brought against it after this catastrophe. Will the promoters or founders of the company be made to disgorge some money to compensate the orphaned or maimed victims of their avid pursuit of profit? How terrible that would be! These mil-lionaires are much to be pitied . . .[160]

But Dairnvaell took his recriminations much further. The Nord company, he alleged, had ignored warnings about the poor quality of its rails and continued run-ning the normal service after the accident had happened, despite the fact that the signals were not working properly. At the same time, its directors had profited by selling their own shares before news of the accident got out.[161] This was bad enough by itself; but in truth, he argued, it was just the latest example of the way "Roth-schild" and the Jews treated the French people. Dairnvaell thus used the Nord acci-dent as the basis for a vitriolic recounting of the Rothschilds' "history" of battening off France, beginning with the battle of Waterloo and culminating at Fampoux:

> They have enriched themselves from our impoverishment and from our disasters . . . they have stayed with us the way the leech stays on a man's vein . . . [like] the vampires of commerce and the scourges of nations . . . The Rothschilds have only ever gained from our disasters; when France has won, the Rothschilds have lost. This house is our evil genius.[162]

Dairnvaell's allegations unleashed an extraordinary and protracted pamphlet war. At least seven separate publications appeared in the succeeding months, some denouncing James in similar terms, others defending him, still others claiming to judge the two sides impartially. The so-called *First Official Response of M. Baron James Rothschild* claimed that Dairnvaell was little better than a blackmailer who had demanded 5,000 francs from James in return for not publishing his *Edifying History*, and had gone into print when James had offered him only a thousand francs.[163] A similar attack on Dairnvaell appeared in the *Response of Rothschild I, King of the Jews, to Satan the Last, King of the Impostors*. In swift response came three further anti-Rothschild pamphlets: *War on the Swindlers* (by Dairnvaell himself),[164] *Roth-schild I, his Valets and his People* and *Ten Days in the Reign of Rothschild I, King of the Jews* (both anonymous). Finally, there were attempts to adjudicate. The *Letter to M. Baron de Rothschild* rebutted Dairnvaell's historical allegations, but concluded that "the Rothschild brothers have done nothing for the peoples [of the world], and con-sequently, nothing for humanity . . . M. de Rothschild . . . has a thirst for money, and that's all there is to it."[165] More overtly hostile to James was the *Grand Process between Rothschild I, King of the Jews, and Satan, last King of the Impostors*, which described James as "King of the Jews, sometime bailiff of the courts of Europe, farmer general of public works of France, Germany, England etc. etc., and sovereign of discount, usury, pawn-broking, speculation etc."[166]

Of all these works of hackery, perhaps the most sophisticated was the anonymous *Judgement Passed against Rothschild and Georges Dairnvaell*, which rejected the charge of culpability for the Fampoux disaster, but argued that "the proletarian" had been right to attack "the millionaire" with his "pockets full of banknotes and shares." Like Toussenel, the author of the *Judgement* essentially equated Judaism and capitalism: James was "the Jew Rothschild, king of the world, because today the whole world is Jewish." The name Rothschild "stands for a whole race—it is a symbol of a power which extends its arms over the entirety of Europe." Yet the Rothschilds were breaking no laws in "turning and returning" their capital and "exploiting all that is exploitable": they were merely "the model of all the bourgeois and mercantile virtues." It was the bourgeoisie as a whole which had "bent its knee before the Jewish golden calf" and embraced the "Jews" hereditary doctrine of the unlimited exploitation of property."[167] Rothschild, in short, personified "a system which is responsible for the misery and desperation of millions of men." In con-structing his railways for industrial and commercial gain, rather than to promote "the fraternisation and amalgamation of the whole human race," Rothschild was thus fulfilling "the development of the bourgeoisie."[168] This combination of anti-Semitism and socialism would prove the most dangerous of all threats to the Rothschilds' position in the years which lay ahead.

As might be expected, the Rothschilds themselves were appalled by this extensive and generally defamatory press exposure. In a letter to the Prussian government, Anselm deplored what he called "the foulest and entirely unfounded imputations upon the character and morality of our business." There was little, however, that could be done in the absence of censorship of the press in France; only when similar pamphlets appeared in Prussia could the Rothschilds lobby to have them suppressed, pointedly reminding the government in Berlin of "important services" they had rendered to Prussia in the past, and the "special claim" this implied.[169] James thundered impotently, accusing the press of mindless Luddism: "The world can no longer live without the railways and the best answer one can give to the *National* is that if France should opt to exclude herself from the railway developments and if they hope to achieve their goal of frightening the world from using the railways then the result will be that all the travellers will make use of the other railway routes":

> In an article I will ask whether the newspapers want to see France . . . pushing the bounds of civilisation back and whether they are trying to prevent the railways from being completed, for their whole thrust seems to lead in that direction, so that the remaining payments are not met [and] they can then buy them back again cheaply[;] at the same time everyone can see with what enormous strides the railways are being developed everywhere else. I am, however, convinced that the opposition will not succeed in its aim. It is best if one simply lets them scream and talk . . . I am therefore not in favour of initiating legal proceedings which will only mean that this issue will be a permanent topic of discussion when the damned Augsburg and Cologne newspapers are always opposed to us. It would be best if one would make use of these other than as reading material.[170]

Contemplating the poisonous prose of pamphleteers like Dairnvaell, the modern reader is tempted to sympathise with James's attitude. Yet it cannot be denied that the Rothschilds' private correspondence suggests at least a degree of callousness towards the victims of the Fampoux accident. Accidents were regrettable, of course, but principally because of their negative financial consequences for the railway companies concerned. The development of this attitude can be traced back to the first minor accidents on the Saint-Germain line in the 1830s. When these led to a sharp fall in the price of the company's shares, James blamed the press:

> The newspapers are astounded by the falls suffered by all the shares. They themselves are wholly responsible for this. Instead of behaving as they do in England where they don't discuss any accident and provide statistics to show how rarely accidents happen on the railways—when Huskisson lost his life in Manchester the talk was . . . not that the railway was to blame—in Paris they do exactly the opposite. Whenever an accident occurs, every newspaper asks, "Who will now want to travel [by train]? Why are the police not dealing with this?" . . . I think that

you will do well if you will arrange through Pereire for an article to be published against these newspaper articles to explain to the newspapers the true reason for the falls we have been experiencing. I see that there has been a drastic fall in the income from the St-Germain railway and this is probably the reason why.[171]

In 1842 an accident on another line persuaded James to postpone further nego-tiations for the Nord concession: it was decided, Nat reported, "to wait to see what damages will be awarded to the wounded & to the families of the Killed before entering into new affairs of this sort, you know in Paris the juries are very severe with those who are the direct or even indirect causers of accidents." When "a meet-ing of Engineers" was "silly enough to recommend all sorts of foolish plans to be adopted in order to prevent the recurrence of accidents," James immediately "called upon several of the Ministers & told them he would send in his resignation as administrateur unless they acted in concert with the direction of the railroads which they have promised to do."[172] Similarly, the collapse of a viaduct on the line from Rouen to Le Havre interested James primarily because of its likely impact on the share price.

It would be wrong to suggest that the family's response to the Fampoux accident was wholly lacking in compassion. "Poor people," wrote Anthony when the news of the "stinking slip" first reached Paris. It was he added, "a thousand pities—as it will certainly do no good for the moment—it has certainly put me out a great deal."[173] James, it was reported, was "very much affected," having used the line "only two days earlier" on his way to take the waters at Wildbad.[174] But the true nature of their distress became evident in Anthony's next bulletin to New Court:

> It is a thousand pities—as everything was going on so well. They took 27,000 fr[ancs] a day for the last four days & it is more every day. It has not stopped the working of the line & there are as many people as for-merly. It will only require very great care. I cannot give you the reason of the Accident & you must have a little patience. In the meantime it is very unpleasant & it makes our head ache most famously . . . They talk of nothing else but of this accident, & you know what an impression it makes in Paris. The price of shares have [sic] fallen to 712 & I should not at all be astonished to see them lower . . . We have just received the accounts from Pereire who says that there were only 14 [killed] in all & that the accident is not so bad as reported.—In a day or two it will be forgotten but they will try to knock the shares down.[175]

Salomon's reaction is also revealing. It was, he remarked, a "stroke of luck no person of high rank was grieved by the disaster, as the alarm about it would have been even stronger."[176]

To be fair, the Rothschilds did not—as Dairnvaell alleged—act improperly. James protested that only days before the accident he had "left [the train] at every station and inspected the carriages and then let the train continue on its way," a fact he was glad to see reported in the German press.[177] An investigation into the cause of the accident was immediately undertaken and drivers were issued with instruc-tions "to go as slow as possible over the places when there is the least danger." Yet there is no escaping the fact that Anthony and his brothers' primary concern was to limit the damage to the Nord share price by intervening on the Paris market, and resuming normal service on the line as quickly as possible.[178] Anthony's letter to Lionel of July gives an insight into his priorities in the wake of the disaster:

> There is a good deal of speculation going forward in the shares. The Baron has made so much money that they do everything that they can to make the shares fall. They spread all the lies, stories & God knows what else—The line is a most tremendously long one—it is quite new & of course as all new lines are it will require a good deal of time to get everything in to proper order—You cannot make a regiment of French frogs in a minute—They have that nationality that they think that they can do always everything better than others—I hope that they will listen to reason—& have a few people from England. They will write to you to night to engage *12 very first rate Engine Drivers* . . . They have decided upon making the line wider in a great many places & put down more [sleepers?] and to support the rails & to have the line again looked at. This accident was a great misfortune—The shares would certainly have been 800 fr[ancs] . . . the receipts have fallen a great deal within the last few days—I do not much care about it as the whole affair will be able to be better organised & when once it is en train the receipts will very soon get up again.[179]

With the share price falling towards the 650 mark and receipts down 40 per cent, the Rothschilds naturally sought a scapegoat. By July 21 Anthony was claiming "that the accident was done intentionally & that it was got up by some people for the fall of the shares," on the ground that twenty or thirty of the clamps holding the rails to the sleepers appeared to have been tampered with. One suspects this was wishful thinking. "I wish we could find it out," he told his brothers in London, "but the people who speculate for the fall are such a set of Blackguards in this part of the world that I almost think that they got [it] done . . . [I]f it was the case it would be the best thing in the world for the company."[180]

It did not prove necessary to develop this conspiracy theory any further. As the weeks passed, the traffic on the Nord line began to recover (beginning with the third class passengers), and with it the daily take.[181] By the end of August the first freight trains had begun to run and—symbolically—the Nord timetable was published for the first time in Bradshaw, the rail traveller's bible.[182] Three months later confidence was sufficiently restored for Hannah to propose to her sons "a little Spec in [100] Northern shares"—a not unreasonable proposition when James could estimate gross profits for the line at 3.2 million francs.[183] "It is a curious circumstance," noted Mayer with heroic insouciance, "that on the Austrian line a dreadful accident occurred the very first day and now the shares are at 100 per cent premium which I am positive the French Northern will be."[184]

This was hubris; and, in the light of the stark economic rationality of their reaction to the Fampoux accident, it is difficult not to see the revolutionary storm which was to break over the Rothschilds' heads less than two years later as a kind of terrible nemesis. (Perhaps a more fitting nemesis came eighteen years later, when Lionel's son Natty and his sister Evelina narrowly escaped serious injury when an express taking them from Paris to Calais collided with a goods train.)[185] To vary the dramatic image, in deciding not only to invest in but also to construct and manage railways, the Vienna and Paris Rothschilds had made a pact which contemporaries saw in Faustian terms: they had harnessed Satan, as Eichendorff put it. Yet "Satan"—in the person of Dairnvaell—now turned on Faust. The public prominence which the railways had given the Rothschilds made them obvious targets for the new social revolution which was already in preparation.

SIXTEEN

1848

Dans toute l'Europe il n'y a qu'un cris [sic]:
a [sic] bas l'infâme famille des Rothschild
NEMESIS
Le peuple se vengera!
Le peuple ne veut pas l'argent qu'il a perdu . . . mais le peuple
veut le [sic] peau de les [sic] infâmes juifs.
—ANONYMOUS LETTER TO NEW COURT, MARCH 1848[1]

The only thing we must aim at, is to maintain our name in
honour, & for that purpose, one house must support the other
with all its means & power, for the dishonour of one reflects on
the other. —ANSELM TO HIS LONDON COUSINS, APRIL 1848[2]

" [T] here is no error so vulgar," wrote Benjamin Disraeli in 1844, "as to believe that revolutions are occasioned by economical causes. They come in, doubtless, very often to precipitate a catastrophe; very rarely do they occasion one."[3] The succeeding four years were to prove him badly wrong.

Unheralded by economic crisis, the 1830 revolution had seemed to the Rothschilds like a bolt from the blue. By contrast, the 1848 revolution came after such a protracted period of economic depression that they almost grew weary of waiting for the storm to break—and perhaps even began to imagine that it never would. If they did ultimately fail to prepare themselves adequately for what was the greatest of all nineteenth-century Europe's political crises, the reason perhaps lies in the timing of the revolution. The economic nadir of the 1840s in fact came in 1847; by the spring of 1848 the worst was over. With hindsight, historians can infer that it was precisely at this point that political instability was most likely to occur, as popular expectations rose; but to contemporary bankers that was far from apparent.

Another difference between 1830 and 1848 was the Rothschilds' own position as targets of revolutionary action. In 1830 James had been sufficiently distanced from the regime of Charles X to allow a relatively easy switch to the Orléanist side. Eighteen years later he and his brothers had become much more closely identified with

16.i: Eduard Kretschmer (after Andreas Achenbach), *Apotheose und Anbetung des Götzen unserer Zeit* (1848).

the established regimes not only in France, but throughout Europe. As bankers not only to the Austrian imperial government itself but also to numerous smaller states in Germany and Italy, they appeared—especially to the nationalist elements within the revolutionary movements—as the paymasters, if not the masters, of the Metternichian system. Eduard Kretschmer's 1848 cartoon, *Apotheosis and Adoration of the Idol of our Time*, portrays "Rothschild" seated upon a throne of money, surrounded by kneeling potentates (see illustration 16.i)—a popular image of the period.[4] At the same time, the Rothschilds' financial commitments to these various states made it difficult for them to welcome the radical redrawing of Europe's boundaries implied by the first principle of political nationalism—that political and ethnic or linguistic structures should be congruent. Writing in 1846, the poet Karl Beck lamented "Rothschild's" refusal to use his financial power on the side of the "peoples"—and particularly the German people—instead of their detested princes.[5]

Nor was it as easy for the Rothschilds to contemplate defecting to the side of the revolution when that now implied a republic rather than merely a dynastic change. And not only a republic: for the 1848 revolution was, unlike its predecessor, as much concerned with social as with constitutional issues. For the first time, social*ist* (as well as ultra-conservative) arguments against economic liberalism were voiced alongside—and sometimes in contradiction to—the older arguments for political liberalism and democracy. Not only were the revolutionaries concerned with rights (to free speech, free assembly and a free press) and with representation in constitutionally secured legislatures; some among them were also concerned to combat the widening material inequality of the early industrial era. In many ways the Rothschilds had come to personify that inequality. Nothing demonstrated that better than the explosion of anti-Rothschild sentiment in the wake of the accident on the Nord railway: while third-class passengers perished, the critics suggested, "Rothschild I" callously counted his state-subsidised profits. Another cartoon of 1848 which depicted Rothschild as the object of royal (and papal) veneration also featured, kneeling in the foreground, a ragged, starving family; and in the background a group of students marching under the banner of liberty (see illustration 16.ii). When the Russian revolutionary Alexander Herzen wished to define the bourgeoisie in 1847, he called it "a solid estate, the limits of which are the electoral property qualification below and Baron Rothschild above." For Herzen liberalism was propagating a "malicious irony" when it claimed that "the destitute man enjoys the same civil rights as Rothschild," or that "the sated is . . . the comrade of the hungry."[6]

As in the 1820s and 1830s, those who inveighed against the Rothschilds as capitalists could rarely resist making a connection with their Judaism. Typically, Karl Beck too could not resist alluding to "Rothschild's . . . interest-calculating brethren," "filling the insatiable money-bag for themselves and their kin alone!" Nor is it surprising that minor figures like Beck were doing this when the man who would ulti-

16.ii: Anon., *Anbetung der Könige* (1848).

mately prove the most influential of all the period's revolutionaries had done exactly the same in February 1844 in an essay "On the Jewish Question" (though at the time, of course, there was little to distinguish Karl Marx from the numerous other radical hacks churning out anti-Rothschild abuse):

> What is the secular basis of Judaism? *Practical* need, *self-interest.* What is the worldly religion of the Jew? *Huckstering.* What is his worldly God? *Money* . . . We recognise in Judaism, therefore, a general *anti-social* element of the *present time* . . . In the final analysis, the *emancipation of the Jews* is the emancipation of mankind from *Judaism.*

Marx was not one to name names, of course, when he could couch his argument in Hegelian abstractions. But that he had the Rothschilds in mind is evident from the passage he quoted from the pamphlet by Bruno Bauer he was (ostensibly) reviewing:

> "The Jew, who in Vienna, for example, is only tolerated, determines the fate of the whole Empire by his financial power. The Jew, who may have no rights in the smallest German states, decides the fate of Europe." This is no isolated fact [continued Marx]. The Jew has emancipated himself in a Jewish manner, not only because he has acquired financial power, but also because . . . *money* has become a world power and the practical Jewish spirit has become the practical spirit of the Christian nations. The Jews have emancipated themselves insofar as the Christians have become Jews.

Only when society had "succeeded in abolishing the *empirical* essence of Judaism— huckstering and its preconditions" would "the Jew . . . become *impossible.*"[7] In fact, the socialist argument could stand unsupported by racial prejudice, as Marx came to appreciate (after all, he himself had been born a Jew, as had Karl Beck); it would be other revolutionaries of 1848 like Richard Wagner who would later develop and refine this line of argument. Either way, the Rothschilds were extremely vulnerable to radical calls for redistribution of wealth and greater regulation of the capitalists/Jews who possessed it. This made the 1848 revolution much more dangerous to them than that of 1830.

Though politically close to Marx at the time of the 1848 revolution, Heine subsequently made fun of the early socialists' motivations. In his last jottings, he wrote:

> The main army of Rothschild's enemies is made up of have-nots; they all think: "What we don't have, Rothschild has." They are joined by the main force of those who have lost their fortune; instead of ascribing their loss to their own stupidity, they blame the wiles of those who managed to hold on to what they had. As soon as a man runs out of money, he becomes Rothschild's enemy.

And he adapted a traditional Jewish story in order to provide James with a possible reply to the socialist threat: "The communist . . . wants Rothschild to share out his fortune of 300 million francs. Rothschild sends him his share, which comes to exactly 9 sous: 'Now leave me alone!'"[8] In practice, however, it did not prove quite so easy to see off the threat of expropriation. In his first surviving letter (dated 1843), a young radical named Wilhelm Marr had made exactly the argument satirised by Heine. "The time is ripe," he told his father, "to share Rothschild's property among 3,333,333.3 [*sic*] poor weavers, which will feed them during a whole year."[9] The roots of Marr's later Anti-Semitic League lie in the 1840s.

A few voices, as we have seen, were raised to defend the Rothschilds. One ingenious writer in the Paris *Globe* pointed out in 1846 that "no one today better represents the triumph of equality and work in the nineteenth century than M. le Baron de Rothschild":

> What is he, in fact? Was he born a Baron? No, he wasn't even born a citizen; he was born a pariah. At the time of his birth, civil liberty, and even less political liberty, did not exist for Jews. To be a Jew was to be less than a lackey; it was to be less than a man; it was to be a dog that children chased in the street, hurling insults and stones. Thanks to the holy principle of equality, the Jew has become a man, the Jew has become a citizen; and once his intelligence [and] his activity . . . allowed, he could rise within the social hierarchy. What better or more incontrovertible evidence could there be that the principle of equality has prevailed? Yet it is democrats who close their minds and eyes to this spectacle! Nominal democrats, no doubt. Sincere democrats would have applauded this Jew who, beginning at the bottom of the social ladder, has arrived by virtue of equality at the highest rung. Was this Jew born a millionaire? No, he was born poor, and if only you knew what genius, patience, and hard work were required to construct that European edifice called the House of Rothschild, you would admire rather than insult it . . . You tactlessly cite Figaro, without understanding that Figaro was one of the privileged by comparison with M. de Rothschild, since Figaro had only to be born in order to see before him the vast and open battlefield of labour. At his birth, M. de Rothschild found this battlefield closed to him and yet he has, aided by freedom, climbed higher than you. To abuse M. de Rothschild is to blaspheme against equality.[10]

Yet such reminders of the Rothschilds' origins in the Judengasse were rare in the 1840s. Only in England, where the issue of the parliamentary representation of the Jews was to play such an important role throughout the revolutionary period, did it really seem relevant. The continental revolutionaries did not think of the Rothschilds languishing in the Judengasse, but imagined them luxuriating in châteaus like Suresnes and Grüneburg. In Joseph Eichendorff's allegorical comedy *Liberty and her Liberators*, for example, Amschel is once again satirised in the character of Pinkus, a self-made "cosmopolitan" (misheard by a page as *Großhofpolyp*) who acquires the title of baron and with it a castle and garden. Pinkus cannot abide Nature, preferring to impose strict uniformity (complete with steam engine) on the garden; whereas Libertas wishes to set the plants, birds and animals free. When she tries to do so, Pinkus has her arrested by his "armed forces"; but the spirits of the primeval forest come to her rescue, throwing Pinkus's repressively ordered garden into chaos.[11]

The Rothschilds were far from oblivious to the animosity they were incurring. Indeed, it might be said that they took positive steps to counteract it by making generous—and ostentatious—charitable gestures. In the very dry summer of 1835, Salomon offered 25,000 gulden towards the construction of an aqueduct from the

Danube to the Vienna suburbs.[12] When Pesth and Ofen were badly flooded three years later, he hastened to offer financial assistance for the victims.[13] He donated 40,000 gulden to found an institute for scientific research in Brünn.[14] And when Hamburg was ravaged by fire in 1842 he and James made substantial donations to the fund which was set up to assist the victims.[15] Before the 1830s the Rothschild brothers' charity had been largely confined within the Jewish communities of Frankfurt, London and Paris. Now Salomon made a point of contributing to causes which were regarded as good by the Habsburg elite. Baron Kübeck recorded in his diary how the elite responded. At a dinner for Count Kolowrat in 1838, Salomon declared expansively that his guest's presence had:

> "given me as much pleasure today as if I had been given a thousand gulden, or had given them to a poor man." Thereupon Count Kolowrat replied, "Very well, give me the thousand gulden for a poor man who needs help, and has applied to me." Rothschild promised to do so and after dinner Count Kolowrat was given the thousand gulden.[16]

So frequently did Salomon act in this way that it was possible for a sentimental novella of the 1850s to portray him as a kind of Viennese Santa Claus, benignly siding with a carpenter's daughter who wants to marry her rich father's gifted but poor apprentice. The high point of this mawkish work is a description of the throng of *Schnorrer* in the antechamber of Salomon's Renngasse residence: the man who claims to be God's brother-in-law (he is sent packing); the man who wants Salomon to be the godfather to his child (he gets 50 gulden); and the woman whose five-year-old daughter can recite seventy-two poems from memory (whose reward is not recorded). That they are all drawn to the house of Rothschild is explained not just by his wealth, but by his universally acknowledged wisdom and generosity. At one point, genial old Rothschild even delivers a homily to a young Frankfurt banker on the need for those who are rich to be generous.[17]

It may well be that this was the way Salomon wished to be regarded. But not everyone who came into contact with him would have endorsed this characterisation. Moritz Goldschmidt's son Hermann—a boy in the 1840s—remembered him as an impetuous, impatient, despot: "a brutal egoist, a man without wisdom or education, who despised those around him and took the opportunity to treat them ruthlessly [just] because he was rich." He ate and drank to excess. He was habitually rude to everyone from his barber to the Russian ambassador and surrounded himself with sycophants. He had a lecherous passion for "very young girls," his "adventures" with whom had to be hushed up by the police. Above all, Salomon was extravagant. He habitually dressed in a blue suit with gold buttons and nankeen or white stockings and, when he needed a new suit or hat, bought twelve at a time for good measure. He drove around Vienna in a luxurious carriage with a liveried servant. In 1847—in the depths of the economic slump—he spent immense sums building a new residence and office in the Renngasse.[18] To be sure, Goldschmidt was looking back in anger when he wrote; but his hostility towards Salomon was probably not so different from that felt by many of his more politically radical contemporaries.

The Frankfurt Rothschilds too sought to allay popular hostility by acts of public benevolence. In May 1847 Amschel distributed bread ration cards to the poor of Frankfurt at a time of acute food shortages in the town. But, although he received "a unanimous vote of thanks" from the Frankfurt Senate, this does not seem to have done much to enhance his popularity.[19] As his nephew Anselm observed when his uncle raised the possibility of buying British grain for the German market, "We must be very careful in Germany about corn; there were a great many riots all & everywhere against corn dealers, & if the public would know that we are indirectly interested in corn transactions there might be a burst out [sic] against us."[20]

Perhaps the most successful gesture of public-spiritedness at this time was made by the English Rothschilds in response to the catastrophic potato blight and famine in Ireland—the worst of all the calamities of the 1840s, which cost the lives of around 775,000 people and drove a further two million to emigrate. Ireland was not a land with which the Rothschilds had many dealings; yet as early as 1821, hearing rumours of an impending famine there, Nathan had alerted Lord Liverpool to the possibility of buying "American and East India Rice before speculators come into the market, the price of which is at present low and the Stock large and which in case of a deficiency of the Potato Crop would supply the numerous Poor of that Country with a wholesome food during the Winter."[21] When Peel used the Irish famine twenty-five years later to justify repealing the Corn Laws (thus freeing the import of grain into the British Isles, but also bringing down his own government) the Rothschilds were ambivalent. While Alphonse viewed Peel's conversion to free trade "without admiration" as an "utter revolution,"[22] his father "very much regret-ted" Peel's fall—though probably more for the diplomatic implications of Palmer-ston's return to office.[23]

Lionel, by contrast, was a thorough-going Free Trader; but he understood that free trade alone would not alleviate the famine in Ireland, because of the general European cereal deficit. In the absence of a more than half-hearted official relief effort, he therefore took the lead in setting up at New Court the British Associ-ation for the Relief of the Extreme Distress in the Remote Parishes of Ireland and Scotland, which raised some £470,000 in the course of its existence—even soliciting a contribution from that ardent Hibernophobe and Protectionist Disraeli![24] The Rothschilds themselves contributed £1,000 to the fund, the second biggest dona-tion after the Queen's £2,000 and on a par with the Duke of Devonshire's.[25] In this instance, contemporaries were sincerely impressed by the Rothschild effort. As he declared to a friend, it did the heart of the future Liberal Irish Secretary W. E. Forster "good" to see "Rothschild, Kinnaird, and some dozen other millionaire city princes meeting every day, and working hard. A far greater sacrifice to them than mere gifts of money."[26] Lionel personally involved himself in "regulat[ing] the pur-chase and shipment of provisions to Ireland and the formation of depôts around the coast and in the interior of the country."[27] Though it is possible that this activity was partly designed to win Catholic votes at the 1847 election (in which he was a Liberal candidate), his mother's letters on the subject testify to the sincerity of the family's response to the Irish disaster.[28]

The contrast with the Paris house's role is striking. The French food crisis was, of course, far from being as disastrous as the Irish: as Nat wrote in 1847, "They talk ter-ribly of the misery of the poor devils in the provinces but I don't believe it approaches that of Ireland—it cannot be compared to it."[29] Nevertheless, the 1846 wheat harvest was an exceptionally bad one: 15 per cent lower than the average of the previous ten years, it was the worst since 1831.[30] James first began purchasing grain as early as January 1846 in anticipation of a bad harvest throughout Europe.[31] A year later he was urging the French government to make purchases of Russian grain,[32] and in the spring of 1847 he offered "to buy abroad 5 millions of francs worth of corn and flour for the consumption of Paris at our risks & peril and in the event of any loss accruing we s[houl]d bear it & the profit to be distributed in bread tickets to the poor."[33] Besides being philanthropic, James genuinely feared the social and political consequences of food shortages: as he told his nephews in November 1846, "[T]he situation with our grain, which really isn't good, does scare me a lot."[34] For this reason, there is no doubt that he wished to be seen to be alleviating distress—Salomon wrote explicitly of "making our name popular" with "the masses" by providing cheap bread and salt.[35]

Yet James had meant the grain purchases only to be non-profit-making; he had not intended to lose money outright. His assumption in early 1847, for example, was that prices would remain high; and when the improved harvest that year partly confounded that expectation he and Nat could not conceal their annoyance. "There never was anything so stupidly managed as this corn operation," grumbled Nat: "to buy up all the corn in the world & to get it just as the harvest is coming on, we shall lose a great deal of money & in future we shall be more careful."[36] This may partly explain why James received little if any credit from ordinary consumers in Paris. As Nat had predicted, "I fancy the philanthropic feelings of our good Uncle will cost a little money. If people don't attribute a wrong motive it will be all very well & charitable, but in Paris where nobody can imagine anything done disinterestedly I should not be surprised if it were said we do it for the sake of getting rid of what we have got at very high prices."[37] Violence of the sort which broke out in the faubourg Saint-Antoine in May 1847 was partly directed against grain merchants; James was widely perceived to have acted as little more.[38] Indeed, it was rumoured that Rothschild bread was laced with ground glass and arsenic.[39] Here perhaps was the origin of Heine's imagined Rothschild nightmare: "He dreams he gives 100,000 francs to the poor and becomes ill as a result."[40]

What made the agrarian crisis doubly worrying for the Rothschilds was its impact on the European banking system. All countries which found themselves obliged to import grain from relatively remote markets like Russia and America experienced a drain of gold and silver which had a direct impact on their monetary systems. The most dramatic case was that of Britain. The effect of the shift to free trade was to increase immensely the import of corn to Britain, from 251,000 tonnes in 1843 to 1,749,000 tonnes in 1847. The success of Peel's policy was thus not in reducing the price of bread, but in averting what would have been a very substantial price increase if the Corn Laws had remained in force. But the policy had an unexpected side-effect on one of Peel's other great legislative achievements, for it forced the suspension of the Bank Charter Act of 1844. It did this because the act had reinforced the link between the Bank of England's gold reserve and the British money supply. As corn imports flooded in and gold flooded out, so the reserve dwindled: from £15.8 million in 1844 to £9.8 million four years later. The Bank was obliged to increase its interest rates in steps from 2.5 per cent (March 1845) to a peak of 10 per cent (October 1847), thus causing a drastic monetary squeeze and finally forcing suspension.[41] No other European economy permitted such a large outflow of specie; but Britain's financial dominance of the continent at this period ensured that the contraction was felt everywhere. Only the grain exporters were spared, which partly accounts for the very different Russian experience in this period.

First to suffer was Frankfurt. As early as April 1846 Anselm reported: "The volume of business in Frankfurt is more and more shrinking, without a downpour of gold from heaven, I do not know how this place can recover"—a verdict echoed by James when he visited in July.[42] Soon came the inevitable casualties, this time uncomfortably close to home. In 1847 the house of Haber collapsed, threatening to take with it the Beyfus brothers' bank.[43] As two of Mayer Amschel's daughters (Babette and Julie) had been married to the Beyfuses, it was felt necessary to bail them out—to the tune of 1.5 million gulden—though this was done with extremely bad grace. The younger generation in London and Paris had little time for "old Mad Beyfus." "If we are to pay because they chose to swindle," complained Nat, "the Lord knows to what interest they may draw upon our cash box . . . the only regret I experience is that our worthy relatives have thought it fit to come to their assistance." In fact, it seems to have been James who insisted on rescuing "so near a relation," despite the grumblings of Amschel, Salomon and Carl—a good illustration of his ultimate leadership on familial matters at this time.[44] Yet the fall of the Habers—to whom the Beyfuses were also related by marriage—attracted much more attention than the survival of the Beyfuses. Once again, there were articles in the press "attributing to us the ruin of . . . German industry." "These attacks were so violent," wrote Anselm, "that we found ourselves compelled to answer these libels by a declaration signed by us and inserted in the principal papers of Germany."[45] In the Badenese parliament, a liberal deputy denounced the Rothschilds in terms which, Anselm reported, "aimed at nothing less than mobilising the masses in a religious crusade against our House, representing it as a vile monetary power . . . sitting [on] . . . all the kings, all the peoples."[46] It was even alleged that Lionel had agreed to bankrupt South German industry in return for a promise from Palmerston of a seat in the House of Commons.[47]

Banking crises have a domino effect: the problems of Haber served to exacerbate the difficulties of one of the major Vienna banks, Arnstein & Eskeles. Trouble had been brewing in the Vienna market since early 1847, prompting Metternich to request Salomon to return urgently from Paris "to contrive some plan which would ward off the crisis of the market."[48] By the end of September it seemed that he had succeeded in "averting" an "immeasurable calamity."[49] However, the failure of Haber proved to have potentially disastrous implications for Eskeles, whom he owed 1 million gulden. It may be that Salomon was already heavily committed to Eskeles, with whom he had acted in close partnership for many years in issuing Austrian government bonds. Alternatively, he felt morally bound to intercede on his behalf. At any event, he informed the Frankfurt house on December 23 that Eskeles had

> visited me a few hours ago and most frankly informed me that at present he does not need anything, however as soon as he does, he is in a position to transmit mortgages as a security to the full amount. I have in my portfolio 1,520,000 gulden drafts upon Eskeles of which 1,185,000 gulden are of Haber, the remaining with good endorsements.[50]

In effect, he and Sina had agreed to bail Eskeles out, just as Salomon had wanted to rescue Geymüller six years previously. This time, however, Salomon had acted without consulting his brothers (remembering perhaps their refusal to agree to the Geymüller rescue). Naturally, he hastened to reassure them that there was no risk involved and that Sina was "caution itself." He urged Anselm to remain "calm": "With God's help we shall remain the Rothschilds."[51] If his brothers—and son— suspected that a grave mistake had been made, Salomon had no inkling. The full gravity of his error would become apparent within the month.

In Paris, the Banque de France faced a "crisis in the supply of money" (James) from as early as October 1846.[52] On previous occasions (in 1825 and 1836–9), it had been the Banque which had come to the assistance of the Bank of England; now the Bank repaid the debt by selling its counterpart silver worth 25 million francs.[53] As in the 1830s, Rothschild attempts to play a part in this transaction were abortive: although James made a personal visit to London in December, the business was finally arranged by Hottinguer, and James's subsequent offer of an additional 5 million francs was rejected by the Banque Governor d'Argout.[54] The bad blood between New Court and Threadneedle Street since Nathan's death had yet to be purged.

Nor was Lionel successful in his attempts to mediate between St Petersburg— rich in bullion from Russian grain exports—and the Banque de France. Benjamin Davidson was packed off via Riga to the Russian capital with several carriages filled with gold, apparently with the intention of establishing a new agency. But his expe- dition was a failure. Having endured a gruelling journey on snow-covered Russian roads, Davidson found himself effectively unable to do business as a foreign Jew.[55] When the Russian government came to the Banque de France's rescue by buying 50 million francs of rentes from its securities reserve, the Rothschilds were mere onlookers.[56] In fact, the 1846–8 crisis proved a remarkably good opportunity for the Banque to enhance its power over the French monetary system: it was not sorry to see the collapse of Laffitte's ambitious Caisse Générale, nor that of the various regional banks of issue Laffitte had encouraged in his time as Banque Governor.[57] Nat summed up Rothschild feelings towards the Banque at this time succinctly: "They are a set of shits & behave to us as badly as possible, but it is not [in] our interest to quarrel with them."[58]

The position was not very different in London. As James put it in April 1847, with Bank rate climbing inexorably upwards, "Your Bank is the Master and driver of the situation. It is in a position to press its will on the world and so gold will have to be sent back."[59] Yet the Chancellor of the Exchequer, Sir Charles Wood, was less confident that the Bank would be able to master the crisis without breaching its legal gold reserve requirement. He and the Prime Minister were singularly unimpressed when they sought Lionel's views on the matter. As Wood told his confidant, Samuel Jones Lloyd, "I saw at Lord John [Russell]'s, Lionel Rothschild & [Joshua] Bates [of Barings] this morning & (low be it spoken) I am utterly confounded at the igno- rance they displayed, of facts & circumstances which I should have thought every merchant in the City must have known. They really had little or nothing to say for themselves, & admitted that things were proceeding rapidly."[60] If Nat's views give any indication of what Lionel said, the Rothschild position perhaps struck Wood as politically naive. The Bank's policy, he wrote, was "illiberal—I must say I can not understand their policy, they do all in their power to stop trade & the country will pay very dear indeed for their gold."[61] Wood knew that; what he wanted to know was how to suspend the 1844 rules without acquiring the reputation of a Vansittart. When he turned for advice (and whitewash) to the architect of the Bank Charter Act himself, Peel agreed that Lionel was not among "those who really understood the question of currency, whose prepossessions were in favour of the principles on which the Bank act was founded—and in favour of the Bank act itself." It was, Peel told him, not "Rothschild, Masterman, Glyn and the leading men of the City—but . . . those with whom he had conferred in private [who] were the very persons . . . deserving of his confidence in the matter, Jones Lloyd, W. Cotton, Norman and the Governor of the Bank."[62] This bipartisan depreciation of Lionel's expertise testifies to the Rothschilds' loss of influence over monetary policy since Nathan's death.

Deflationary monetary policies had direct effects on European industry. For the Rothschilds, it was their impact on the French railway companies which was most troublesome. It was not that railway investment and construction ceased: to the extent that these were pre-programmed by political and commercial decisions taken before the crisis, the problem was more that they were difficult to stop.[63] The strain was therefore taken by the railway companies' bankers and investors: as work proceeded, the banks found themselves being asked for loans to finance the inevitable cost overruns, while investors could only watch gloomily as the monetary squeeze drove down railway share prices. In truth, James had been over-optimistic, just as his English nephews had feared. On the very eve of the crisis, he and his son had confidently assured their relatives that, in addition to their economic benefits, the railways tended to make people politically "conservative and pro-government" too. "Every thing is calm in France," Alphonse told Mayer Carl in January 1846, "there is a strong majority for the administration. Industrialism and the railroads absorb all thoughts and divert from politics. Please God that we may enjoy for many years to come the blissful peace."[64] Within a matter of months they were singing a different tune. "Well," James confided in Anselm that August, "I must admit that when I think about the many commitments that the world has taken upon itself for the payments to be made everywhere for the railways, money which will not so quickly return into the hands of the business people, then I find myself trembling."[65] By October, he was having to reschedule payments due to the government for the Nord concession and to intervene to prop up the share price.[66]

While Nat savoured his own vindication, James's response to the crisis was to concentrate Rothschild attention on the Nord and extricate himself from the other lines in which he had a smaller interest. "If," he told his nephews, "we can't assume that when the railways draw monies from us we will then be able to get it back again, then I view the situation as being potentially very dangerous."[67] Accordingly, when "that blackguard fellow Talabot" requested additional funds for work on the Avignon–Marseille line, he was roundly rebuffed.[68] Shares in other companies were also sold off.[69] Nor did James commit more money of his own to the Nord: when the company required new funds for construction, he appealed directly to shareholders.[70] Like so many malcontents in 1847, the Rothschilds themselves blamed the government for their problems. "The gov. must change their manners of doing business," complained Anthony, "they have completely ruined their credit by the manner that they have behaved to the Railroad Companies. You can have no idea how every person cries out about losing their money & they all attribute it to the gov. & certainly they are very much to blame."⁷¹ Of such grievances, multiplied a thousand-fold, are revolutions made.

The paradox was that even as they grew more and more disgruntled with the European governments' economic policies, the Rothschilds continued—as if reflexively—to act as their lender of first resort. The transmission mechanism which linked the economic crisis of 1847 to the political crisis the following year was fiscal. All over Europe, the combination of rising expenditures (first on railways, then on social palliatives, finally on counter-revolutionary measures) and falling revenues (as earnings and consumption slumped) led inevitably to government deficits. Between 1842 and 1847, for example, the Austrian budget rose by 30 per cent.⁷² So deeply ingrained was his habit of lending to the government that, when he was approached for a new loan of 80 million gulden in February 1847, Salomon "thanked God" for "an extremely good business."⁷³ It was to prove anything but that. Along with Sina and the ailing Eskeles, he had taken on 2.5 and 5 per cent bonds worth 80 million gulden (nominal), in return for which the bankers had to pay the government 84 million in cash in instalments spread over five years.⁷⁴ This would have been a good business only if five years of peace and prosperity had been at least probable.

Ostensibly, this loan was needed to finance new railways: that was what Salomon told Gasser when he tried to sell "a considerable sum" of the new bonds to the cash-rich Tsar.⁷⁵ By November 1847, however, Austria was arming in preparation for intervention in Lombardy and Venetia, where insurrection seemed imminent. Salomon knew this because Metternich had told him, yet instead of being alarmed, he went so far as to offer more financial assistance.⁷⁶ Incredibly, he agreed to lend a further 3.7 million gulden in return for 4 per cent bonds, which he furthermore pledged not to sell on the already stretched market: they would, he promised Kübeck, remain "in his own safe," in return for interest of 4.6 per cent.⁷⁷ With short-term rates in London at this time standing at 5.85 per cent and the price of 5 per cent metalliques already ten points lower than they had been three years before, this was an extraordinary (not to say suicidal) decision. Even as Salomon's proposal was being discussed, Kübeck was warning that intervention in Italy would lead to "the complete breakdown of our finances." "We are on the verge of an abyss," he told Metternich presciently, "and the increasing demands on the Treasury arising out of the measures necessary to combat foreign revolutionary elements have led to increased disturbances within the country, as is indicated by the attitude of the provincial Estates, and by the literary outbursts in the Press of our neighbours."⁷⁸ Metternich was undaunted. When Salomon began to get cold feet in January, he angrily told him: "Politically, things are all right; the exchange is not. I do my duty but you do not do yours."⁷⁹

As with his advance to Eskeles, Salomon's undertakings to the government were made without reference to the other Rothschild houses. "We have very curious letters from Vienna," Nat wrote to New Court at around the same time. "Our good Uncle is full of Austrian Metallics 2[.5]% & 5% & how he will get out on such markets the Lord knows—Prince Metternich takes our good Uncle in so that he may continue his financial operations, I fancy the F'furt house will find a little difference in their balance the next time they make it up."⁸⁰ This was to prove a serious understatement. When the first efforts were made to compute Salomon's commitments in

February 1848, the total approached 4.35 million gulden (around £610,000).[81] That was more than double the capital of the Vienna house in 1844. Notionally, as Nat suggested, the Frankfurt house remained responsible for its Vienna branch; but it too had been accumulating the bonds of other German governments in the course of the 1840s, notably those of Württemberg and Hanover, and there was talk of a new loan to Prussia as late as March 1848![82] When Anselm finally arrived from Frankfurt to set the Vienna house in order, he was in no mood for filial generosity. His relationship with his father was to be one of the first Rothschild casualties of 1848.

French spending had also been rising steadily. By 1847 the budget was 55 per cent higher than it had been twelve years before, not least because of the various state subsidies to the railway companies. As early as the autumn of 1846 there was talk of a loan to fund the government's deficit; by the summer of the following year the difficulty of placing treasury bills on the struggling money market made such a new issue of rentes imperative. Needless to say, the Rothschilds had no intention of leaving the business to others, despite the periodic anxieties of James's nephews about French financial stability.[83] As in Vienna, so in Paris: government loans had become a matter of course, regardless of economic conditions. True, James drove what seemed to be a hard bargain.[84] The terms he secured looked generous: of the 350 million francs nominal to be raised, the Rothschilds took 250 million in the form of 3 per cent rentes priced at just 75.25, some two points below the market price.[85] Indeed, his rivals could with justice have complained of double-dealing. It seems likely that the auction of the new rentes was rigged by the Finance Minister so that James's bid was exactly equal to the Minister's supposedly secret minimum. As Nat candidly told his brothers beforehand, Dumon had "let the cat out of the bag": "[He] said he could not commmunicate his minimum as it was necessary for him to be able to state in the Chamber that his sealed letter had remained a secret for every body, but *on pourrait se mettre à peu près d'accord.*"[86]

Yet Nat was fundamentally right to regard the loan as "a most dangerous & disagreeable concern." James was less rash than Salomon, but he did not follow his bearish nephews' chorus of advice to "get out of our loan famously."[87] Some of it was sold to investors ranging from the Tsar to Heinrich Heine.[88] But not all of it. According to a number of accounts, he decided to sell only a third at once to the market, holding on to the remaining 170 million francs in the expectation that the price of 3 per cents would rise above 77. Meanwhile, of course, James had bound himself to pay the Treasury 250 million francs in instalments spread over two years.[89] It was to prove another expensive miscalculation.

In England too there was an ill-judged loan on the eve of the storm. The £8 million so-called Irish Famine Loan of March 1847 was raised ostensibly to finance the cost of aid to Ireland, though it may reasonably be assumed that there were other reasons for the government's deficit in this period. The combination of Britain's unique credit-rating and the good cause supposedly being funded boded well, and Rothschilds and Barings—who shared the underwriting equally—had no difficulty in finding buyers.[90] Indeed, James himself complained about being given only £250,000. Yet the price quickly fell from the issue price of 89.5 to 85, much to the consternation of the investing public and the embarrassment of the underwriters.[91]

Even in Italy, where the revolution may be said to have begun, the Rothschilds toyed with the possibility of state loans in 1846–7. In Naples, Carl appears to have been keen to agree a loan to the government, and was saved from doing so only by the Bourbon regime's own chronic indecisiveness.[92] In Rome too there was talk of a loan. After the advances which had been made on the basis of Rothschild loans in the 1830s, the finances of the Papacy were once again in disarray: the deficit for 1847 was double that of the previous year and Roman 5 per cents dropped below par for the first time since 1834.[93] Yet James had been intrigued by the election of Pius IX in 1846—"supposedly a liberal," as he rather acutely put it—and he ordered a halt to sales of Roman bonds in the expectation of "some really positive changes."[94] This probably referred to the position of the Jewish community in Rome, whose case for better treatment Salomon once again took up.[95] Only a stark warning from their new Italian agent Hecht "who represents the state of the Papal domains in the blackest colours & thinks that a revolution is at the eve to break out [sic]" deterred the Rothschilds from taking up Torlonia's proposal of a new loan.[96] When Adolph visited the Holy City in January 1848, he was unnerved by the combination of political debate and military preparation he encountered.[97] For the same reason, the London house's amazingly ill-timed suggestion of a loan to Piedmont— in January 1848!—was thrown out by Alphonse, who pointed out gently that this was "a country which can be considered as . . . already in full revolution."[98] The only other country whose request for a loan was turned down at this time was Belgium— ironically, one of the countries least affected by the revolutionary upheavals which were about to begin.[99]

"The Worst Revolution That Ever Happened"

To say that the 1848 revolutions began in Italy is perhaps not strictly true: civil wars in Galicia and in Switzerland were harbingers of the cataclysm, as were the abortive United Diet (Landtag) summoned—in conformity with the 1819 State Debt Decree—by Frederick William IV in Berlin in 1847, and the stirrings of liberal enthusiasm in South Germany. But, though they followed these events carefully, the Rothschilds were not worried by them. Indeed, the annexation of Cracow by Austria looked like just another Polish partition: as on previous occasions, "the poor Poles" were "very much to be pitied." "I suppose lots of them will be shot," remarked Nat dispassionately; his uncle Salomon's sole concern was that foreign governments should not challenge the Austrian move.[100] It was the outbreak of an artisans' revolt in Sicily in January 1848 and the granting of a liberal constitution by Ferdinand II which made the Rothschilds for the first time afraid. It was, commented Nat, "stinking news" (which the Rothschilds were, as usual, the first to hear).[101]

Yet he and the rest of the family continued to think primarily in diplomatic terms, wondering whether the Neapolitan crisis would harden the Austrian resolve to intervene (something Salomon anxiously denied).[102] In his letters to Lionel and Alphonse, Anselm joked about Adolph's hand shaking as he wrote his letters, suggesting that he shared his father's nervous, not to say pusillanimous temper.[103] But this was just banter. Carl's initial reaction in fact suggests sang-froid: as early as February 19 he was once again discussing the possibility of a loan to the Bourbon regime.[104] When Anselm commented on liberal attacks on Ludwig I's government in Munich, he little realised how soon his diagnosis would apply to all Europe:

"That is the way it is, alas: in the highest politics just as in the most lowly social relations, the people imposes its will and dictates the law to the higher power." He could still hope that "the unrest there" would "soon pass"—and with it the slump in the price of the Rothschilds' "low loans."[105]

As in 1830, it was the outbreak of revolution in France which turned disquiet into panic. Of course, the Rothschilds had never had unqualified confidence in the July Monarchy. The death of Louis Philippe's eldest son in 1842 had reinforced their pessimism about the future: the King himself confided "that after his death . . . the Revolution of 1830 would begin again." "I assure you it has given me the stomach ache," commented Anthony uneasily. "I do not think that there is any danger as long as the present King lives—but what will take place after his death God knows & I hope to God that the good old gentleman will live for a mighty time and that everything will go on well—nevertheless we must be prudent."[106] This explains the Rothschilds' fear of a successful assassination attempt against the King. When James himself received a death threat in 1846, he passed the letter on to the government, remarking: "The man who wants to shoot at me could just as well shoot at the King, or vice versa." When Louis Philippe survived yet another attempt on his life the following April, Nat pronounced him "one of the most admirable men that ever existed."[107]

The growing extra-parliamentary pressure for electoral reform in the course of 1847, however, raised the possibility that 1830 might repeat itself even with Louis Philippe still living. Nat's reports from Paris in January and February 1848 show that he saw the crisis coming: "[G]ood folks speak exactly as they did just before the revolution of 1830," he remarked on February 20, two days before the fateful Reform banquet was scheduled to take place, in defiance of a government ban.

> I think a change of ministry wd. remedy the evil but in the mean time it is impossible to say what will occur—no one can tell how a french mob will behave & when the [president?] of the chamber of deputies associates with the common people it is a hazardous thing to say how far they will go and when they will remain quiet—We must hope for the best, in the mean time my dear Brothers, I really recommend you most strongly to sell stocks & public securities of all sorts and descriptions.

Yet the very next day he was more optimistic:

> The nasty banquet continues exciting the public . . . It is really very much the same sort of thing as in 1830 & nevertheless I can not help thinking it will all blow over and leave us [far?] behind.—This country is so well off and in general people are so greatly interested in the maintenance of things that I believe a revolutionary movement [to be] out of the question . . . The end will be a change of ministry & Guizot will in all probability go out on the Parliamentary reform question.—I shall be very glad when that takes place, it wd. make our rentes get up and set matters right again.

"I have however no doubt that as soon as the affair of the banquet is over we shall see a great improvement," he added in another letter. "All our friends assure us there is no need of anxiety on acct. of any revolutionary demonstration on the part of the dep[utie]s of the Gauche—in my opinion their banquet will be a complete failure." "People have much too great an interest at stake in the maintenance of order to kick up rows," he concluded in his final despatch before the date set for the banquet, "& I don't think that emeutes will be again à l'ordre du jour at least p[ou]r le moment—"[108] The temperamental pessimist had picked the worst possible moment to look on the bright side.

Even in his letter of February 23, with barricades in the street and signs of mutiny in the National Guard, Nat still underestimated the gravity of the situation, hoping nervously that a change of ministry would suffice to dampen unrest:

> The ministry has changed, Guizot has just declared in the chamber of Depts. that he had sent in his resignation to the king and his majesty was at the present moment closeted with Molé—We must hope that between them they will cook up a good government but it is a danger-ous experiment to yield to the wishes of a factious minority and of a tur-bulent set of national guards—The great fault was in not sending off Guizot sooner, the people had got up the reform cry and it is impossible to resist public opinion any where nowadays.—The emeute in itself was not of a very serious nature, very little real fighting and few if any killed—but what really made the king anxious was the manifestation of the national guard in favour of reform and against Guizot . . . The emeute by all accounts is over, now they have got reform I do not see what they have got to fight for & I suppose we shall hear of illumina-tions and the Lord knows what else. I know one thing and that is your humble servant will not hold much French stock in future . . . [I]t's a dangerous job to give way to a mob incited by the National [Guard].[109]

This must have been written just hours before the fateful confrontation in the rue des Capucins, in which fifty demonstrators were shot dead by soldiers guarding the Foreign Ministry. The next day, in the face of what he called "a moral uprising," Louis Philippe abdicated in favour of his grandson and fled to England, leaving the various opposition parties to form a provisional government, including the lawyer Alexandre Ledru-Rollin, the poet Alphonse de Lamartine, the socialist Louis Blanc and a token worker named Albert. The following day a commission was set up in response to unemployed building workers' assertion of their "right to work." Nat's next despatch was short and to the point: "We are in the midst of the worst revolu-tion that ever happened—You may perhaps see us shortly after this reaches [you]."[110] Already he and James had sent their wives and children to Le Havre to take the next ship to England.[111]

Events in France were shaped as much by the memory of past revolutions as by anything else. Those who recalled how little had been achieved in 1830 were deter-mined to establish a republic on a more authentically democratic basis; those still frightened by memories of the 1790s were determined not to let power into the hands of neo-Jacobins. The issue was undecided until, at the earliest, the end of June. Although the elections to the Constitutional Assembly revealed the limited support for radical republicanism outside Paris, the possibility of a "red" coup within Paris could not be ruled out. In May this was attempted unsuccessfully by the socialists Raspail, Blanqui and Barbès. In June the closure of the national work-shops led to clashes between disillusioned workers and National Guardsmen. As late as June 1849, the so-called Montagne party took to the streets in a last vain bid to rekindle the Jacobin spirit.

The pattern was roughly similar almost everywhere the revolution broke out. Although relatively few monarchs were definitively deposed by the revolution, a number were prompted to flee their capitals and most were forced to make constitutional concessions by the outbreak of violence in the streets, which exposed the inadequacy (or unreliability) of their civilian police forces. This collective scuttle meant that a variety of constitutional innovations were possible, ranging from French republicanism (also tried in Rome and Venice) to parliamentarism (in many German states). In the Netherlands, a centre of revolution in 1830, the Dutch and Belgian monarchs hastily gave ground to liberal pressure and allowed constitutional reforms to be implemented; the same was true in Denmark. In Germany, the revolution began in Baden, where the Grand Duke was forced to concede a liberal constitution almost immediately after the Paris events,[112] an example followed in short order by Hesse-Kassel, Hesse-Darmstadt and Württemberg. In Bavaria, King Ludwig was forced to abdicate, his reputation irreparably damaged by his liaison with Lola Montez. Such changes within the monarchical system did not satisfy more radical republicans, who attempted a coup in Baden in April. The tremors were felt even in the Rothschilds' home town: contrary to Anselm's expectations, 1848 posed a threat to ancient republics like Frankfurt too if their definitions of citizenship were over-narrow and their governmental structures antiquated. The first violence in the town centre occurred in early March.[113]

Everywhere there seemed to be two (possibly successive) revolutions: one of which aimed at constitutional reform, the other of which had fundamentally economic objectives. Though they overlapped in complex ways, there was a marked social difference between the two. While educated academics, lawyers and professionals made speeches and drafted constitutions, it was artisans, apprentices and workers who manned barricades and got themselves shot.

Perhaps the biggest difference between 1848 and 1830 was that now the revolutionary epidemic spread to Austria. Metternich received the news of the Paris revolution from a Rothschild courier. "Eh bien, mon cher, tout est fini," he is said to have commented, though his subsequent remarks to Salomon were more bullish.[114] It was indeed all finished. On March 13 crowds of demonstrators clashed with troops outside the hall where the Lower Austrian Estates were meeting. The next day Metternich resigned, fleeing by a circuitous route across Europe in disguise and with barely enough money—a credit-note from his faithful banker Salomon—to pay his family's passage to England.[115] The Emperor Ferdinand replaced him with his archrival Kolowrat and promised a constitution. As elsewhere, when the new government opted for an English-style bicameral parliament with a property franchise for the lower house, radical democrats—mainly students like Hermann Goldschmidt's maverick cousin Bernhard Bauer[116]—took to the streets (May 15), prompting the Emperor himself to flee to Innsbruck. When the Constituent Assembly proved quite conservative (the peasant deputies were satisfied with the abolition of serfdom) and the revolutionary government tried to reduce the money spent on public works, there was further unrest: workers went on strike in July, and students attempted a last-ditch coup in October.

The collapse of Habsburg authority at the centre set off a chain reaction throughout Central Europe. In Prussia, unrest had already begun in the Rhineland, but it was the news from Vienna which transformed the mood in Berlin. On March 17, after days of public demonstrations, Frederick William IV appeared to capitulate by agreeing to a constitution, but simultaneously deployed troops to restore order. As in Paris, it was shots fired by nervy soldiers at demonstrators in the city centre which turned reform into revolution. For more than twenty-four hours fighting raged; then the King gave in, issuing a series of proclamations to Berliners, Prussians and—significantly—"the German nation." As in Baden, Württemberg and Hanover, liberals became ministers, though all those who accepted office soon came to realise the difficulty of reconciling their aspirations for economic and political liberty with the more radical aims of the artisans, students and workers. For a time, the best hope of unity appeared to be nationalism. Thus, from an early stage, the German revolution was more than merely a matter of constitutional reform within states: it promised a parallel transformation of the German Confederation itself.

The ramifications of the Habsburg collapse were not confined to Germany. In Prague, moderate liberals like František Palacký pressed for a modern parliament based on a property franchise in place of the antiquated Bohemian Diet. In Hungary, Croatia and Transylvania there were similar separatist tendencies with varying degrees of liberalism. It was the same in Italy, though the timing was slightly different. As we have seen, the revolution in the Two Sicilies had begun early: on March 6 Ferdinand II granted a separate parliament in Sicily and was shortly afterwards deposed there; two months later he allowed a parliament to assemble in Naples itself. In Piedmont and the Papal states, Charles Albert and Pius IX made similar concessions, both granting constitutions in March. In Venice and Milan, revolution took the form of revolt against Austrian rule. As in Germany (though on a smaller scale), some revolutionaries saw the opportunity to make Italy more than merely a geographical expression.

Why did 1848 seem "the worst revolution that ever happened" to the Rothschilds? It is important to notice that their reaction was not determined by a uniformly ideological aversion to liberal or republican forms of government. Attitudes towards the revolution varied widely from one member of the family to another. At one extreme, Salomon seemed almost incapable of comprehending the calamity which had befallen him other than in religious terms. When not trying to justify his own financial mistakes in rambling letters to his brothers and nephews, Salomon interpreted the revolution variously as an avoidable political mishap attributable to the incompetence of Louis-Philippe, the vanity of Princess Metternich and the irresponsibility of Palmerston, and a world-historical upheaval on a par not just with 1789 but with the Peasants' Wars, the Crusades and a biblical plague of locusts. Whichever it was, he regarded it as a divine test of religious faith.[117]

His nephew Nat lacked this consolation. Already more politically conservative and personally cautious than his brothers in London, he was deeply traumatised by the revolution—to the point of suffering something like a physical or nervous collapse. A worse "political cholera never yet infected the world," he lamented, before repairing to take the waters at Ems, " & I am afraid the Doctor does not exist to cure it, a great deal of blood must be shed first." Virtually every letter he wrote to his brothers during the revolutionary months concluded with a warning to sell all their stocks and shares.[118]

No one else in the family took the revolution quite as badly. Neither Amschel nor Carl seems to have reflected deeply on the subject: for them, the revolution was like a natural disaster—inexplicable, but with God's blessing survivable. The ideas of the revolution were beyond their ken—Carl dismissed talk of Italian nationality as "the stupid projects of a few deranged minds"—and as far as possible he and Amschel sought to keep their distance from political debate. Similarly, the pageantry of nationalism—the tricolours, the patriotic songs—left the older Rothschilds stone cold.[119] A contemporary cartoon depicts a puzzled Amschel asking Arnold Duck- witz, the "Reich Trade Minister" appointed by the Frankfurt parliament in the summer of 1848 (on the optimistic assumption that a new Reich was in the making): "Nothing to trade yet, Mister Minister?" (see illustration 16.iii). It was probably right to imply that he was baffled by the protracted and inconclusive debates in the parliament. James, by contrast, had a good idea what the revolution- aries were after. Increasingly of the opinion that all regimes were at once unreliable and financially biddable, he was inclined to salute whichever flag was run up the mast after the storm. His refusal to let Alphonse serve in the National Guard, for example, was more an assertion of the primacy of family interests over all politics than an explicitly anti-republican gesture.[120] James shed no tears for Louis Philippe.

This pragmatism was to some extent shared by the four eldest sons, Anselm, Lionel, Mayer Carl and Alphonse, who already tended to take a similar, sober view

16.iii: "W.V.," *Baron: "Noch niks zu handele, Härr Minister?"* **(1848).**

of political developments. Unlike James, however, they all occasionally expressed sympathy with liberal reforms, though they distinguished these from the ideas of radical democrats, socialists and communists. Anselm's commentaries on German developments suggest little sympathy with the various kings, princes and archdukes obliged to bow to "the will of the people," as well as considerable impatience with the "old wig-heads" of the Frankfurt Senate.[121] He was interested enough to attend the first debates of the German "pre-parliament" in Frankfurt before leaving for Vienna, though it was a detached kind of interest: unlike their London cousin Lionel, neither he nor Mayer Carl thought for a moment of standing for election.[122] And Anselm warmly welcomed the Austrian constitution issued in March 1849, the terms of which were in fact moderately liberal.[123] By contrast, the various younger brothers had more idiosyncratic responses. Adolph in Naples was simply terrified. Anthony, on the other hand, regarded the German princes as "a set of donkeys" and had "a very good opinion" of the Frankfurt parliament's project for a united Germany which he thought "*Right* and reasonable."[124] As for the nineteen-year-old Gustave, he itched to get back to Paris to see the action for himself—only to be disappointed by the "tristesse" he encountered there, the extent of working class unrest and the poor calibre of the republican politicians.[125]

Nowhere is the ambivalence of the Rothschilds towards the revolution more apparent than in letters and diaries of female members of the family. James's wife Betty was vehemently hostile to the revolution, applauding her four-year-old grandson James Edouar when he declared: "If I had money, I would buy a gun to shoot the republic and republicans." She expected the French republican constitution "soon to go to join its sisters whom oblivion has long since buried in the mists of time" and dismissed the deputies in the National Assembly as "the wild beasts of our great Parisian menagerie." She was equally contemptuous of the German revolution. The Frankfurt parliament was, she told her eldest son, "an agent of false doctrines and anarchy." When Robert Blum was shot in Vienna, she was delighted that "his factious voice has been extinguished" and regretted only that the same had not been done in Paris.[126] Bizarrely for one whose parents had been born in the Frankfurt ghetto, Betty even expressed nostalgia for the *ancien régime* of the eighteenth century, "that century when minds were so fertile, and when anyone knew how to bring honour to his rank with dignity without departing from it, and did not consider himself lowered by obedience to a higher authority." The nineteenth century she thought "an evil age."[127]

Her cousin, Lionel's wife Charlotte, took a very different view, however. She feared for the family's financial future, of course; yet at the same time she derived a certain moralistic satisfaction from the crisis, seeing it as an opportunity for self-denial and self-improvement. Following political events on the continent in her relatives' letters and in the newspapers gave her a sense of exhilaration, of historical acceleration. It was, she wrote in her diary, "in truth . . . the age of the railways, for the last six weeks have been almost as eventful as the six years which saw Louis XVI's death, the great Terror, the Convention and Napoleon." Above all, she was captivated by the possibilities of German unification raised at Frankfurt:

> As for Germany, there are hopes that she will soon become prosperous, powerful, united and free. In Prussia also the people have won a victory

over the army and the king is forced to grant his subjects all the reforms and concessions they demand. The ministry has changed; the prince of Prussia has fled; the press is free; the proceedings of the law courts are public . . . and all confessions and religions have equal rights. Once more as a great and united empire, strong and happy, elevated and proud, Germany will trounce the Russian storms, the Cossack invasions and the warmongering of the French.[128]

To be sure, her ideal of a united Germany was strictly monarchical: like Anselm, she repudiated republicanism. But in the French context Charlotte could find positive things to say even about republicans. Her view was that

> those at the helm of state wish to lay a foundation of prosperity and happiness for their country, even if they are mistaken in the means they adopt to achieve this . . . Ledru Rollin . . . has honest intentions for France and at this time of general turmoil, he alone, apparently, of all the members of the administration is capable of taking action as a leader.[129]

Charlotte's sister-in-law Louisa also saw positive aspects to "this wonderful Revolution." Provided "our house can only weather the storm," she felt able to bear "any losses, however severe." "I cannot say," she confessed, "that the effect it may have upon our fortunes disturbs me at all. This is not philosophy, but simple indifference, or, rather, dislike to grandeur and display . . ."[130]

In short, there was scarcely a united family front against the revolution. This can also be seen in the way individual Rothschilds treated the toppled kings and ministers who found their way into exile in England. Betty was shocked to hear that Louis Philippe and his family were living on 100 francs a day in Richmond.[131] But the most he seems to have got from the English Rothschilds was a case of good bordeaux.[132] The revolution had also left Metternich powerless and poor, as Charlotte remarked:

> His castle at Johannisberg has been appropriated because he has not paid his taxes for the past nine years . . . The Prince has never owned a large fortune. In his past youth he lived extravagantly and later had to settle the debts of his son. Now he has a large family to provide for and educate. His financial affairs have only recently been put in order by Uncle Salomon.[133]

She had little sympathy for his plight and shared the Frankfurt partners' disinclination to give him further financial assistance.[134] But Lionel felt a sense of familial obligation to "Uncle." In June Metternich was given a 323,000 gulden advance, secured against his (heavily depreciated) railway shares.[135] A further loan of 5,500 gulden to Princess Melanie appears in the Vienna house's books for November 1848, and by the following year the combined debts of the Metternichs stood at 216,500 gulden.[136] In addition, the repayments on the second half of the 1827 loan—which were supposed to be completed by 1859—were rescheduled, so that a substantial sum was still outstanding at the end of the 1870s.[137]

In two lengthy letters to Salomon—one written as he passed incognito through Arnhem, the other from the safety of England—Metternich repaid his faithful bankers with a rambling apologia which shed intriguing light on their relationship:

What disorder the world has fallen into! You always used to ask me whether war was in sight. You always heard me reassure you that this was not the case and as long as *I* had the reins in my hands I would be able to vouch for political peace. The danger of the day was not on the field of political war, but of *social* war. On this field too I have held the reins in my hands as long as was humanly possible. On the day when that possibility ceased, I stepped down from the driver's seat, for being overthrown is against my nature. If I am asked whether that could have been avoided by what naive utopians call Reform, I reply with a categorical *No*—for the logical reason that the measures which *today* are called Reforms and which might, under some conditions, have had the merit of bringing improvements, could have had no more value, given the situation of society as it was, than a dance with torches on powder kegs . . . You, dear Salomon, have understood me for years. Many others have not.

Things in France are only just beginning. Never before has there been a greater, more deep-seated confusion.[138]

Perhaps this was just a way of currying favour with those he hoped would finance his new "bourgeois life." But this avowal of mutual understanding was a fitting epitaph for a partnership which, since they had first met at Aix thirty years before, had exercised a remarkable influence over Europe. It was left to the sceptical Anselm to note that these were "theories which can't be of great help to the world now."[139]

The Threat to Property

It was not the danger the revolution posed to their own lives which most alarmed the Rothschilds. Although quick to pack their wives and younger children off to safety at moments of crisis, the male Rothschilds—most of whom ran at least some personal risk during the period—were singularly cool as the bullets and bricks began to fly. On February 24 James was seen by the young Feydeau (then serving in the National Guard) emerging arm in arm with an unidentified male companion from the rue de la Paix and walking towards the ransacked Tuileries, even as gunshots continued to emanate from its grounds.

"Monsieur le Baron," I said to him, "today does not seem to me a very fortunate choice of day for a walk. In my opinion, you would do better to return home, rather than expose yourself to the bullets which are whistling throughout this part of town."

"My young friend," he replied, "I tank you for your adfice. But tell me, vy are you here? To do your duty, isn't it? Vell then, I too, Paron de Rothschild, haf come for the same ting. Your duty is to stand armed vatch, and assure the safety of goot citizens; mine is to go to the Minister off Finance, to see vether they may not need my experience and my counsel."

And with that he left me.[140]

As early as March 4 James was ready to let his wife and sons return to Paris—though in agreeing to Betty's request he added some caveats:

All I ask is that you obtain a passport under a different name for a round trip. If you bring Alphonse, he too should have a supplementary passport with another name, because I don't want the newspapers to print a headline saying, "Madame de Rothschild has returned to London," if you decide to go back there. That would give rise to idle gossip . . . Come and bring Alphonse, although I wonder whether we shouldn't keep him out of politics. If they see him, he'll be required to enlist in the National Guard. He may come if he lies low.[141]

In May, at the time of the abortive coup by Barbès and his associates, amid talk of guillotines in the place de la Concorde, James was once again ready to send his sons abroad for safety, and indeed briefly visited London himself.[142] Yet he himself contemplated fleeing Paris only for a brief moment at the beginning of the June days.[143] The contrast with his anxiety-ridden nephew could not have been greater. Nat was even alarmed by the men sent to protect the rue Laffitte by the new prefect of police Marc Caussidière: "a most ferocious looking set of gents with red sashes and anything but agreeable to meet in a dark night alone & unarmed—They would eat you up alive."[144] Though he stayed in Paris during the revolution's most turbulent months, he retreated to England with relief at the end of November. James was contemptuous of such pusillanimity. As Betty proudly told Alphonse, her husband was one of the few who had "valiantly resisted the terrible storms which have struck down the courage and mental strength of so many."[145]

Salomon too stood his ground in Vienna though he rarely went out of doors. Despite regularly hearing the sound of "drumming in the streets" in the weeks after March 13, he did not quit the city until June, and then elected to settle with Amschel in less than tranquil Frankfurt.[146] Anselm hung on until October 6–7, when armed revolutionaries took up positions on the roof of the Rothschild offices following the lynching of Count Latour outside the War Ministry and the storming of the Arsenal, "situated only one house from our own." So dangerous had the city become by this stage that when Moritz Goldschmidt returned to rescue the bank's papers, he had to disguise himself as a milkman; and Anselm felt obliged to remain in the country for a month.[147]

Amschel never left Frankfurt, despite a number of alarming popular demonstrations. When a crowd gathered outside his house one night in March 1848, he "had gone to sleep a long time before and only learned about it the next day"; finally he hung nationalist flags out the window in the hope of being left in peace. Business continued in the Frankfurt office even when it was surrounded by barricades and hit by four bullets in September.[148] A contemporary woodcut captured Amschel's sangfroid when it depicted him remonstrating with two rifle-carrying revolutionaries. "What's going on in my house?" demands "Baron von Rotschirm," referring to the sign being nailed to his front door. The "barricade maker" replies: "Now it's begun, Herr Baron, now things will be divided up equally, but private property is sacred." At this, Amschel explodes: "What's begun? Begone yourselves! Property sacred? Divided up? What d'you say? My property has always been sacred to me, I don't need you to write that on my door. Divided up? When the Prussians come, you'll all be divided up" (see illustration 16.iv).

The "nervousness" of Nat and of Carl and Adolph in Naples was the exception, and struck other family members as such.[149] Although they often commented on the anti-Semitism which accompanied the revolution in parts of Central Europe,

16.iv: Anon., *Barrikaten-Scene am 18. September: "Was geht vor in mein Haus?"* (September 18, 1848).

the other male Rothschilds never seem to have felt themselves threatened by it. Indeed, James was more worried that he might be arrested as a German spy in the event of a war breaking out, while his wife seems to have been as concerned for James's dignity as for his life. Haughtily, she told Charlotte how the new French Minister of the Interior Louis Antoine Garnier-Pagès "always addresses our Uncle simply as 'Rothschild' without a prefix" (that is, the title "Baron" or "de")—a mark of disrespect he was spared from older revolutionaries like Lamartine.[150] Other members of the family found the revolution's self-conscious (and often backward-looking) symbolism faintly comical. Marx was not the only one to suspect that history was repeating itself, but as farce rather than tragedy. The endless illuminations of Paris, the ritualised tree-planting, and above all the elaborate neo-classical rituals involving white-clad virgins seemed absurd, especially to the English Rothschilds.[151]

It was in fact the threat to their property which worried the Rothschilds more than any threat to their persons. The marking of selected town houses and the ransacking of Salomon's villa at Suresnes—along with Louis Philippe's at Neuilly— were only the first visible expressions of this threat.[152] There were also arson attacks on some railway stations and bridges belonging to the Nord company. The Easter elections to the Constituent Assembly reassured Nat that there was no longer any danger of "a *sanguinary revolution*," but he still expected "our *purses*" to "bleed."[153] Rumours that the rue Laffitte would be plundered persisted into April;[154] and the following month, on the eve of the decisive "June days," Gustave described the appearance on walls in the city of "lists where to plunder and we are mentioned as having 600,000,000 francs."[155] In Frankfurt too—despite assurances from more moderate revolutionaries to the contrary—Rothschild properties were singled out for attacks. On three separate occasions, Amschel's windows were smashed, and he took the precaution of sending "the greater part of our disposable effects" to Brussels and Amsterdam until he was more confident that "private property will be respected."[156] In Vienna, the Goldschmidts' house was ransacked by workers building barricades outside it in May.[157] Small wonder Anselm and Nat took the precaution of sending silverware and porcelain to London for safekeeping.

A second threat to Rothschild property was that of formal confiscation by revolutionary regimes, whether in the form of expropriation or heavy direct taxation.[158] Reassurances of the sort relayed by their associate Bleichröder from Berlin on March 18—"there is absolutely no cause to fear for private property"—could hardly be taken seriously given the obvious danger that moderates like Camphausen and Hansemann might be displaced by more radical politicians.[159] As James put it in April, "They won't touch a hair on your head, but they'll pose progressively until you have nothing left to eat."[160] In Vienna, attacks on the Rothschilds in the press seemed to imply confiscation of their factories if wages and conditions were not improved.[161] In Venice, Salomon's salt factory looked vulnerable to Manin's republican regime.[162]

The most serious proposals for formal expropriation, however, came in Paris, where plans for the nationalisation of the railway network—a radical demand which predated the revolution—began to be discussed as early as March. The railway companies, it was argued, had failed to honour their commitments under the plan of 1842: having underestimated the costs of railway construction and devoted their attention to crooked share speculations, they could not even make the payments due to the government for their concessions. Without a doubt, the financial position of the railway companies in the spring of 1848 was precarious. The Nord, for example, owed the government between 72 and 87 million francs which it was quite unable to pay; and these debts could easily have justified a government takeover.[163] It must be said that nationalisation would not have been unwelcome to Nat, who had never been much enamoured of the railways. With the price of the company's shares as low as 212 and the railway workers repeatedly defying the authority of their foremen and masters—even insisting on the planting of "trees of liberty" in front of main stations—he was eager to be rid of them.[164] But James was altogether less ready to surrender the backbone of his nascent industrial empire. Unlike those companies whose lines were not yet completed, the Nord was already earning money from freight and passengers and the revolution did not much affect this.[165]

The most serious threat of all was posed to that part of the Rothschilds' wealth held in the form of government securities, the price of which fell dramatically in the first weeks of the new republic. Table 16a shows the devastating effect of the revolution on some of the principal securities held by the five Rothschild houses. Although

Table 16a: The financial crisis of 1846–1848.

SECURITY	PEAK PRICE	DATE	TROUGH PRICE	DATE	PERCENTAGE CHANGE
Austrian 5 per cent metallique	112.25	Dec. 1845	58.00	Mar. 1848	−48
French 3 per cent rente	84.25	Feb. 1846	32.00	Apr. 1848	−62
French 5 per cent rente	121.00	Jul. 1846	50.75	Apr. 1848	−58
Roman 5 per cent	105.60	1843	71.80	1848	−32
British 3 per cent consol	100.88	Jan. 1845	78.75	Oct. 1847	−22

Note: British and French prices are weekly closing prices as quoted in London; Austrian prices are monthly closing prices as quoted in Frankfurt; Roman prices are average prices as quoted in Paris.

Sources: *Spectator*, Heyn, "Private banking"; Felisini, *Finanze pontificie*.

prices had been falling generally since the onset of the economic crisis in 1846, if not before, the period February to April 1848 saw a catastrophic collapse.

As we have seen, James had held on to around 170 million francs of the new 3 per cent rentes issued the previous year. By April, the market value of these was less than half what he had paid for them. Yet he remained formally obliged to resume paying the cash instalments due to the French Treasury (which amounted to roughly 10 million francs a month over two years) in November. In addition to these heavy losses, there was also likely to be red ink on the bills account: as Nat put it, "We have 16 million francs [of] bills, but God knows how many will be paid." With bankers as substantial as d'Eichthal in difficulties, the outlook was grim.[166] At the same time, the Paris house owed around 10 million francs to railway companies, including the Nord, the Strasbourg line and the Grand-Combe.[167] Too many of its assets were depreciating stocks, shares and bills; too many of its liabilities were now due in cash. One 1848 cartoon showed a hobgoblin-like Rothschild tilting the scales of the bourse to his own advantage while above him the students demonstrate with a banner calling for the abolition of everything "except students" (see illustration 16.v). In fact the Rothschilds lost heavily in the crash.

Under these circumstances, many observers expected James to declare himself insolvent and probably also to flee Paris along with his family. The Austrian ambassador Apponyi watched him closely throughout March and April, expecting the bank to close its doors at any moment. On February 27, for example, he found James and other bankers "in a deplorable state" because their rentes had been reduced to "slips of paper, representing nothing."[168] Caussidière certainly suspected

16.v: "Alexander," *Eine Sturmpetition: Das Steigen und Fallen auf der Börse* (1848).

James of planning to leave Paris: rumours circulated that he was smuggling gold out of Paris hidden in manure carts and (as much to keep an eye on him as to protect his house from looters) James was placed under police surveillance. Throughout March and into April, rumours that de Rothschild Frères would be the next bank to fail abounded. Apponyi felt James was hanging "by a thread"; his friend Léon Faucher described him as being "bled white."[169] It was not far from the truth: at one point in April James's cash reserve was reduced to little more than a million francs. When a clerical error made it seem even less, he admitted to a moment of panic, and joked of "giving up business, going to the country and living off potatoes."[170]

If anything, the position of the Vienna house was even worse. Not only was Salomon saddled with substantial amounts of metalliques; as we have seen, he had also assumed onerous commitments as a result of his rescue of Eskeles. Altogether, he estimated his payments due in the near future to third parties at around 3 million gulden. In fact, the position was much worse than this, as Anselm soon discovered; for the money to save Eskeles had been raised by depositing three-month finance bills worth 2.75 million gulden at the National Bank, the renewal of which had never been formally agreed before the revolution. This was in addition to bills worth a further 2 million gulden, most of which Salomon had issued to finance an advance to the Nordbahn. In all, his pending obligations were therefore closer to 8 million gulden. Salomon was in no position to pay such sums when they fell due as the greater part of his assets were industrial shares which the revolution had rendered unsaleable.[171] The full extent of Salomon's insolvency can be seen in the balance sheets which were subsequently drawn up by Anselm. Fully 27 per cent of his assets were accounted for by his stakes in the Witkowitz ironworks, the Nordbahn and the Austrian Lloyd, to say nothing of various smaller industrial properties he had acquired as securities for loans. None of this could easily be realised. Small wonder he "envied his blessed brother Nathan"; he was, as he told his brothers, "in the most painful situation that ever existed."[172] This was precisely the situation his English nephews had feared when they advised James against tying up money in railways.

The plight of the Vienna house in turn jeopardised the position of the Frankfurt house: new calculations in March suggested that Salomon owed the other Rothschild houses—principally Frankfurt—some £1.7 million (half his total liabilities).[173] Salomon subsequently tried to justify this by arguing that the Frankfurt house had been milking the Vienna branch for years, but the most that can be said is that Amschel was as much to blame for allowing him to accumulate such an enormous debt.[174] For the Frankfurt house had problems enough on its own account, notably the payments still owing to the state of Württemberg for its loan, money due to Hesse-Kassel, and the substantial sum deposited with it by the German Confederation (the so-called "fortress money") which it was now feared would be withdrawn. Altogether, Anselm put its short-term liabilities at 8 million gulden, and felt sufficiently pressed to terminate support for the Beyfuses, writing off 1.3 million gulden already advanced to keep them afloat.[175] Another source of anxiety was a substantial sum (1.2 million gulden) owed to the Frankfurt house by Prussia, the payment of which could no longer be relied upon. Ironically, it was Amschel who turned to Salomon for assistance in the first weeks of March—at the very time that James was desperately seeking assistance from Frankfurt, urging Anselm to sell securities "at any price!"[176] Each house thought the other owed it money; none was in a position to pay. Salomon pledged all his houses and estates as securities for the money he owed the Frankfurt house; but, as none of these were realisable, the valuation he gave them (5 million gulden) was purely notional.[177]

With three out of the five Rothschild houses on the verge of insolvency, the future of the family as a whole evidently began to look doubtful. In London, Charlotte encountered a new, disrespectful tone from diplomats like the Austrian ambassador Count Dietrichstein, who, as she recorded in her diary,

> paid me some compliments in poor taste, saying, "Looking at you it is obvious that you no longer enjoy such a high position in the world. Now you are grateful if someone calls you beautiful whereas in the past you would have laughed your head off at such irony." I replied, "And why is it that I no longer enjoy such a high position? Is it because I no longer have a money-sack for my throne or my footstool? Or is it perhaps because I no longer am a money-sack?" "The money-sack is still there, but the revolution has half emptied it." "The world will not trouble itself about that, your Excellency, provided we do not delay our payments and make no claims upon it."

She suspected that even the Disraelis "believe in the destruction of our power," though this too she defiantly rejected: "It does not lie in our wealth alone, and God the Almighty will not withdraw his protecting hand from us. Amen!" Privately, as she admitted, "the Rothschilds, whose wealth only two months ago exceeded the reserve of the Bank of England, have lost the greatest part of that wealth."[178]

Survival

How then did they survive? The obvious answer is that the revolutions themselves did not. The degree of popular support for liberal and republican constitutional innovations outside the major cities turned out to be limited, while within the cities there were deep divisions between different occupational groups over economic issues: liberalising bankers had little in common with disgruntled artisans who yearned to revitalise the guild system. Such divisions did much to dish the republicans in France and the liberals in Germany. Secondly, there was much less danger than there had been in 1830 of a war between the great powers—which in many ways remained the Rothschilds' greatest nightmare, not least because of the remembered tendency of war to radicalise revolution.[179] James said on more than one occasion that he would leave Paris in the event of a major war; but Lamartine's France declined (once again) to play its historic role as the exporter of revolution, while Palmerston's Britain could not decide whether to back the revolution or not, when aspects of it appeared contrary to British interests (notably the German claim to the duchies of Schleswig and Holstein).[180] Prussia and Piedmont went to war, to be sure, but with strictly limited aims and even less resolve. Thirdly, the revolutionaries dissipated a good deal of their energies on national questions which implied a redrawing of state borders as well as constitutions; and here the contradictory rather than complementary nature of "the springtime of the peoples" became manifest.

As in 1830, the Poles fell victim to Russian intransigent opposition to their aspirations, despite a half-hearted Prussian flicker of support (it was all over in Posen as early as May). The minor Slav nationalities within the Habsburg Empire had everything to fear from successful Magyar secession, nothing to gain from the creation of a greater Germany and little in common among themselves, least of all language. The German project hatched in Frankfurt foundered ostensibly because the outsized and loquacious parliament could not agree on a royal figurehead for their new liberally constituted federation; in reality because there was no way of reconciling Austrian and Prussian notions of how the German Confederation should be reformed. Beyond the "Kingdom of Upper Italy" formed by Piedmont, Milan and Lombardy in May 1848, the notion of Italian unity was really an afterthought to a multiplicity of quite diverse revolts up and down the peninsula. Thus competing nationalisms tended to cancel one another out. Finally, once the Habsburg armies had regrouped under the leadership of Windischgrätz, Jelacic and Radetzky, they made short work of the revolutionaries. Prague fell in June 1848. Charles Albert's Piedmontese armies were defeated at Custozza the following month (July 25). Vienna itself capitulated in November.

Yet none of this could have been predicted with any degree of certainty. In many ways the revolution was at its most radical in the period after October 1848, and its defeat in Italy, South Germany and Hungary was not conclusive until the summer of 1849. Under the circumstances of March 1848, James and Salomon could have been forgiven for following Louis Philippe, Guizot and Metternich into exile, so closely identified were they with the ousted kings and ministers. Instead, they stayed; and their survival is one of the most remarkable aspects of 1848—from a Marxist perspective, one of the classic symptoms of the revolution's foredoomed failure.

The *sine qua non* of the Rothschilds' survival was their own "concordia." Mayer Amschel's hallowed injunction to his male progeny to maintain familial unity never counted for more, for it was the ability of the London house (and to a lesser extent the Naples and Frankfurt houses) to bail out the stricken Paris and Vienna houses which proved decisive. It helped that the revolution which had been so successful in Sicily failed so comprehensively in Naples. The accounts of the Rothschild house there reveal 1848 as a poor but not a disastrous year: profits slumped to just 2,709 ducats in the first half of 1848, but bounced back to 58,229 ducats in the second half; for the year as a whole they were down just over 40 per cent on 1847. The balance sheets show the Naples house treading water, with no major changes in the composition of its assets between 1845 and 1850.[181] It was therefore possible for Carl to send money to Frankfurt in early April.[182]

It helped even more that (as Charlotte put it) "the stirring wind of revolution which destroys the old injustices [did] not blow in England"—thanks in no small measure to the repeal of the Corn Laws and the suspension of the Bank Charter Act in 1847. The Chartist demonstration on Kennington Common on April 10 made the family nervous, but proved a damp squib; and Nat's warning to Lionel that "you will find yourselves in the same position with regard to P.A. [Prince Albert] as we are with L.P. [Louis Philippe]" proved excessively pessimistic.[183] In Ireland too the harvest proved less disastrous than had been feared. This meant that, having suffered its worst-ever year in the year of monetary crisis, 1847—with losses amounting to a staggering £660,702, or 30 per cent of capital—the London house was able to rebuild its position with some measure of success in 1848 and 1849, pushing its profits back up to £132,058 and £334,524.[184] It was true then, as Charlotte had to admit to Dietrichstein, that the Rothschilds as a family were less rich than they had been; but their "money-sack" was far from half-empty, to judge by the limited domestic economies she had to make. "We had three nursemaids and sent away two of them," she declared, "keeping one to do the dirtier and heavier chores. We shall dress the children ourselves. Our hands shall certainly lose some of their whiteness and beauty in the process, but they will still be of use to us, we hope."[185] Piano tutors for her daughter Leonora had to be content with 10 shillings an hour; when Chopin told her grandmother that he "cost" 20 guineas per performance, she "replied that of course I could play very beautifully, but that she advised me to take less, as one had to show greater 'moderayshon' this season. I gather from this that they are not so open-handed and that money is tight everywhere."[186]

Yet there was a vast difference between these expenditures and the immense sums required by the Paris, Frankfurt and Vienna houses. Lionel's hasty visit to Paris in late February seems to have convinced him that James's position could be salvaged,[187] but he was a good deal more hesitant about Salomon and Amschel. For all their sentimental appeals to their father's memory, they were made to sweat—and pay—for their salvation. Indeed, Lionel's first reaction to Salomon's pleas for support (in the form of accepting some bills of Sina's) was to refuse; and when he did respond to the appeals of the Frankfurt house to send silver (the first of which arrived on April 14), he made sure the London house turned a profit on the shipments. His uncles reproached him, but they were at his mercy and were made to feel it.[188] Lionel's tough line was reinforced by Anselm, who arrived in Vienna on April 10 to clear out his father's Augean stables, a task which he performed with a marked lack of filial compassion. Faced with a request to render yet more assistance to Arnstein & Eskeles (as well as another Vienna house, Heinrich & Wertheimer), Anselm

> immediately informed my father in the clearest possible terms, that on the basis of all my powers as representative of the [five] houses I forbade any further financial sacrifice . . . no matter what the consequences might be for the commerce and the situation of this place, and added that I would leave immediately in protest if any attempt was made here to insist on this . . . It is, believe me dear Uncle, a fatal role which I am taking on here . . . they will curse me as my father's evil angel . . . He is unfortunately in such a state of moral collapse and so bowed down by the situation, that for him to remain here any longer could only have a negative effect on his health . . . It would have been much better if he had left Vienna three months ago.[189]

The recriminations between father and son over the financial morass into which the Vienna house had sunk in many ways marked the end of the dominance of the second generation. In a sense, this was the 1848 revolution *within* the house of Rothschild.

The reality was, however, that the London house was not the lender of last resort at all. For the ability of New Court to assist Paris and Vienna depended heavily on the ability of the Rothschilds' agents in America to remit funds to New Court. The year 1848 was in many ways the decisive test of Belmont's agency: had the system failed, the Rothschilds would have been seriously at risk. Beginning in the summer of 1847, they had nervously followed Belmont as he committed substantial resources to speculating in tobacco and to financing the American war against

Mexico which had broken out in May the previous year.[190] As late as February 1848 James sanctioned his decision to advance the US government a substantial sum against treasury bills to help pay the $15 million indemnity accorded to Mexico for the territory ceded by the US under the Treaty of Guadalupe Hidalgo.[191] Typically, the Rothschilds had a man in Mexico at the same time—Lionel Davidson—who for several years had been importing Rothschild mercury from Spain to sell to Mexican silver mines; he too took a hand in the indemnity payment. Scharfenberg in Cuba and Hanau in New Orleans had also made large advances on tobacco and cotton respectively on the eve of the European crisis. These were big commitments: as James himself commented uncomfortably, "We are too much in the hands of these people."[192] Indeed, there is no better testimony to Belmont's importance at this time than the frantic letters he was sent from London and Paris, berating him for his involvement with the Mexican indemnity and accusing him of having exceeded his powers. Finally, at the end of 1848, a Rothschild—Alphonse—was sent to New York in person, as if to bring the errant agent to heel.[193]

This had its effect. Rightly fearing that Alphonse had been sent out to replace him, Belmont hastily despatched large consignments of silver to London. These were to prove one of the most important stabilising influences on the European financial situation in 1848, and without them Lionel would have been hard-pressed to assist his relatives on the continent. But Belmont wished it to be understood that he was bestowing favours, not following orders. As Alphonse reported, after a frosty reception in New York, Belmont's role was a "singular" one: "It is a position which is at once semi-dependent and semi-independent, simultaneously that of an agent and a correspondent."[194] The long-discussed plan to replace him with a family member foundered once again in the face of Belmont's doggedness and the reluctance of any of the younger Rothschilds to settle permanently in the US.[195] In the short term, Belmont packed Alphonse off to New Orleans and carried on as before, resuming the payment of the Mexican indemnity.[196]

The second factor in the Rothschilds' survival was the relaxation of monetary policy by the European central banks, which undoubtedly helped to end the collapse of security prices. The Bank of England had set the precedent by suspending its gold reserve rule in October 1847; however, it proved less than easy to persuade its counterparts on the continent to do likewise. In Frankfurt, of course, there was no central bank, and it took time to persuade the town Senate to create some emergency credit facilities.[197] In Paris, the situation was better, once the fear had receded that the republic would use the Banque de France as a milch cow for forced loans. In addition to suspending convertibility, the government set up a nationwide complex of *comptoirs d'escompte* and *magasins généraux* to supply firms with new sources of liquidity, although these proved ephemeral and the enduring effect of the revolution was to increase the power of the Banque de France by obliterating the provincial banks of issue.[198] In Vienna, the National Bank imposed a ban on exports of silver and gold and, in May, suspended convertibility.[199] In each case, of course, the danger existed that issues of paper money might be excessive, and Anselm was not alone in fearing a slide into inflation in Central Europe (no one had forgotten the assignats). Here again the Rothschilds' access to supplies of silver from America and England proved crucial, for it enabled them to replenish the reserves of the continental central banks. As early as April the Banque de France was placing orders for large silver purchases through New Court.[200] The prospect of a similar deal gave Anselm an important source of leverage in the discussions over his father's huge accumulation of due bills at the Bank, which he succeeded in prolonging for two years. Even so, it was necessary for him to issue a bald threat to clinch the deal: "Either the prolongation of the bills or the fall of the houses of Eskeles and Wertheimer, which would not only have as a consequence the fall of many other houses here and in the provinces, but would also seriously compromise the portfolio of the National Bank itself."[201]

This was one of the critical moments in the rescue of the Vienna house. For the Paris house, however, of greater importance were the deals struck over government finance. Government loans contracted in 1847 were among the Rothschilds' most burdensome obligations. The only way to reduce these was by hard bargaining. Thus, in parallel with his negotiations with the National Bank, Anselm sought to arrange a modest rescheduling of his father's obligations to the Austrian Treasury.[202] In Frankfurt too Mayer Carl sought to strike deals with Kassel and the Confederation.[203] Even in Naples an agreement had to be reached with the government regarding payment of the interest due on Neapolitan rentes.[204] The Rothschilds were most vulnerable in Paris, however, where James had been left holding around 170 million francs of 3 per cent rentes, now valued at roughly half what he had agreed to pay the government for them. Rather than swallow this heavy loss by selling (as it has sometimes been claimed he did), James sought to extricate himself from the 1847 commitments; and the way he did so is a case study in negotiation from a position of weakness.

It was far from easy. On February 24, as we have seen, James paid a visit to the Ministry of Finance, possibly to get the new regime to pay the interest falling due on the Greek bonds guaranteed by the previous regime (which normally he himself would have paid).[205] There was a quid pro quo: the next day, it was announced that he was to make an ostentatiously large donation of 50,000 francs to the fund for those injured in the street fighting and that he intended to "offer his co-operation to such a good and honest Revolution."[206] He then presented himself at the prefecture of police on February 26. When Caussidière detailed the allegations that he was smuggling money out of Paris in preparation for his own flight abroad, James categorically denied them, steering a clever course between admitting to bankruptcy and implying that he had millions at his disposal:

> People think I am made of money, but I only have paper. My fortune and my cash are converted into securities, which at the moment have no value. I am far from wishing to declare bankruptcy, and if I must die, then I am resolved to do so; but I would regard flight as cowardice. I have even written to my family, to ask them to send me funds so that I can meet my engagements; and if you like, he added, I will introduce you to my nephew tomorrow.[207]

Once again money changed hands: Caussidière requested that James open a credit for a print works to keep its 150 workers in employment, a request granted when James returned the next day with Lionel (Caussidière was handed 2,000 francs "to be distributed as [he] intended"). This was small beer to James, but the stakes were raised higher in early April when the government unexpectedly demanded

500,000 francs, the balance of a mortgage loan arranged before the revolution with Louis Philippe.[208] At the same time, he was reminded of the large sum owed by his railway company to the government.

James responded to these demands with a mixture of threats and blandishments, as Charlotte recorded in her diary:

> The failure of the House of Rothschild would be a terrible disaster for France. It would be to kill the goose that lays the golden egg with a single blow and to abandon forever the chance of [its performing] any public or private services. The government could not auction off the family's golden houses: Ferrières could not be sold; the hôtel Florentin stands empty and could not be let under the present circumstances. If, however, they spare our uncle's life—by which I mean only his financial life—then he could be of service not only to the state, but to individual members of the government . . . In England, they say, no one is grateful for favours received. We certainly do not expect that, but I think one can count on recognition for favours still to be granted. Our uncle has just granted favours to M. de Lamartine, M. Caussidière and Crémieux.[209]

At the same time, if the immediate repayment of the money owed by the Nord was demanded, "thirty or forty thousand workers would be deprived of the employment the government had guaranteed them and the expenditures of the national Treasury on unemployment would increase considerably."[210]

Not everyone was convinced by James's protestations that his "financial life" was at stake. In a good illustration of the way "socialism" made itself felt even in the financial sector, the clerks at de Rothschild Frères protested when James justified cutting their salaries on the grounds that "my business has been reduced." "Yes, you have lost nothing," declared one of them. "You are richer than anyone and we won't [accept a pay cut]." But, if nothing else, James had bought himself valuable time.[211] By the time the government's commission had decided in favour of the state's repurchasing the concessions from the companies, it was the third week of May.[212] Just over a month later, the political position in Paris was transformed by the brutal suppression of the "June days" (22–28 June)—an apparently spontaneous eruption of working class rioting—by troops under the command of General Eugène Cavaignac.

Marx's bitter diagnosis of the "June days" and their aftermath was that the "bourgeoisie" as a whole had thrown in its lot with authoritarianism and militarism in order to crush the proletarian revolution. In contrast with the revolution of 1830, however, the Rothschilds did little, if anything, to promote the restoration of "order" (just as they did little to promote resolutions of the various diplomatic conflicts of the revolution). They did no more than welcome—cautiously—the arrival of Cavaignac. Indeed, they positively avoided making a direct contribution to his efforts: James packed Alphonse off to Frankfurt to ensure that he did not take part in the fighting, which he would have done had he stayed.[213] The military restoration of "order" thus had the aspect of a *deus ex machina*. It was the same story in Naples, where Ferdinand dispensed with parliament and successfully reclaimed Sicily in August; and in Vienna, where Windischgrätz bombarded the revolutionaries into surrender in early November.[214]

Still, the Rothschilds knew how to swim with the turning political tide. For the reconstruction of the republican regime under Cavaignac provided the perfect opportunity not only to bury the railway nationalisation project but to reschedule the Nord's debts to the state[215] and to resolve the question of the 1847 loan. It was later alleged that the Paris house had been "refloated" by the government at this juncture—to the great ire of James's grandchildren, who took pains to deny that their bank had ever relied on state intervention.[216] The word "refloated" is misleading but—like the related accusations levelled at the government of excessive generosity—not without an element of truth. In essence, James had adopted the stance which Balzac had years before anticipated: that of the indispensable debtor who owes his creditors so much that they dare not let him fail. Fearing that he might otherwise be unable to resume his payments to the Treasury, the government felt obliged to renegotiate the terms of the 1847 loan. The decision was understandable: in threatening them with the death of the "golden goose," James was implicitly threatening the collapse of the French financial system. As Mérimée suggested at the time, the government's financial position was "diabolical"; the collapse of de Rothschild Frères would have made matters worse still.[217]

The easier alternative was to work in partnership with "the Baron." Thus, when Lionel visited Paris in July, he found James closeted—as of old—with the Finance Minister. He was "now a great favourite and as there is no other Banker or person with money or disposition to come forward, he is naturally very much looked up to."[218] Yet the expedient adopted by the new Finance Minister Goudchaux—to convert the 3 per cent bonds of 1847 into 5 per cents—was probably over-generous, in that it effectively turned a loss of 25 million francs into a profit of 11 million.[219] The fact that Goudchaux was a Jew (like another moderate republican linked to James, Crémieux) merely added to the radical suspicion of a conspiracy to prop up Rothschild.[220] In truth, James had probably exaggerated the danger of his own financial collapse in order to minimise his losses on the 1847 loan. Far from being in cahoots with Goudchaux, the Rothschilds regarded him as "not a practical man by any means" who knew "no more about the bourse than the man of [sic] the moon."[221]

The Rothschilds' position had in fact been stabilising for at least a month before the "June days." As early as the last week of May, it was possible for Charlotte to affirm her belief in "in a bright, European and Rothschildian future."[222] When Nat went to Frankfurt in June, he found Amschel still furious with Lionel, but financially quite secure, with a balance of at least 26 million gulden and a bullion reserve of £400,000. Indeed, the English Rothschilds were surprised to find Amschel selling on to the Vienna house silver he had received from the London house only weeks before.[223] Another sign of normalisation was the resumption in earnest of negotiations for a new mercury contract in Spain (where Baring was mounting a serious challenge). This coincided with excited reports from Davidson about new discoveries of silver in Chile and Peru which were likely to boost the mercury market.[224] By August matters were sufficiently far advanced for James, Lionel and Anselm—now the family's dominant triumvirate—to meet at Dunkirk to take stock of the combined accounts.[225] It was not until some time later, however, that it was apparent to those *outside* the family that the Rothschilds had survived. When the radical *Tocsin des Travailleurs* devoted a leader to the subject in August, its tone was ironical; yet a genuine undertone of admiration is unmistakable in its appeal to James to lend his miraculous financial powers to the cause of the republic.

> You are a wonder sir. In spite of his legal majority, Louis-Philippe has fallen, Guizot has disappeared, the constitutional monarchy and parliamentary methods have gone by the board; you, however, are unmoved! . . . Where are Arago and Lamartine? They are finished, but you have survived. The banking princes are going into liquidation and their offices are closed. The great captains of industry and the railway companies totter. Shareholders, merchants, manufacturers, and bankers are ruined *en masse*; big men and little men are alike overwhelmed; you alone among all these ruins remain unaffected. Although your House felt the first violence of the shock in Paris, although the effects of revolution pursue you from Naples to Vienna and Berlin, you remain unmoved in the face of a movement that has affected the whole of Europe. Wealth fades away, glory is humbled, and dominion is broken, but the Jew, the monarch of our time, has held his throne[.] [B]ut that is not all. You might have fled from this country where, in the language of the Bible, the mountains skip about like rams. You remain, announcing that your power is independent of the ancient dynasties, and you courageously extend your hand to the young republics. Undismayed you adhere to France . . . You are more than a statesman, you are the symbol of credit. Is it not time that the bank, that powerful instrument of the middle classes, should assist in the fulfilment of the people's destinies? Without becoming a Minister, you remain simply the great[est] man of business of our time. Your work might be more extensive, your fame—and you are not indifferent to fame—might be even more glorious. After gaining the crown of money you would achieve [your] apotheosis. Does that not appeal to you? Confess that it would be a worthy occasion if one day the French Republic should offer you a place in the Pantheon![226]

Even this struck some as premature: as late as November rumours were still circulating that James intended to go into liquidation.[227] But the Rothschilds had indeed survived. We now know how they did it. We can also see why, at the time, their escape seemed well-nigh miraculous.

Tranquillity and Order

Another important difference between 1830 and 1848 was the Rothschilds' lack of diplomatic influence. Though they fretted constantly about the danger of a European war, for most of 1848 they were far too preoccupied with their own financial problems to play their familiar part in great power politics. When the Austrian government asked Salomon to help "end the Italian difficulties" by sending "a member of his House in order to start negotiations in this sense in the name of the Austrian Government," the younger Rothschilds were reluctant to become involved. As Mayer Carl put it:

> [I]n my opinion we should not mix in politics, because, however things turn [out], it is harlequin who gets the kicks and harlequin, that is us.

Also I don't believe that Lombardy is going to pay anything to Austria. The Italian cause has aroused too much sympathy for any solution not to be inimical to Austria's interests. Also everybody [would] say that we make God knows how much out of this. People are used to assuming that Rothschild does nothing without getting something.[228]

When Radetzky "gave a good licking" to the Piedmontese armies at Custozza, Anselm and his cousins were delighted, but poorly informed about Austrian diplomatic intentions, assuming that Austria would still relinquish most of her Italian territory.[229] Although James came to realise that Bastide, the new French Foreign Minister, was unenthusiastic about Northern Italian unification, and that therefore Palmerston's efforts in that direction were unlikely to succeed, his nephews remained convinced for some time that Lombardy and Venetia would be able to buy their independence: it was, wrote Anthony, "only an affair of money."[230] Their sources of information in Germany were not much better. Mayer Carl, for example, seems to have expected Frederick William IV to accept the German crown when it was offered by the Frankfurt parliament in March, and—even more improbably—that this would help Austria and Prussia "pull together."[231] (In fact, he contemptuously spurned what he called a "diadem moulded out of the dirt and dregs of revolution, disloyalty and treason.") It was not until late February 1849 that Anselm began to receive the kind of inside information about Austrian diplomacy which his father had for so long taken for granted.[232] He was soon following in Salomon's footsteps by siding enthusiastically with Schwarzenberg in the second war with Piedmont—a tendency which his father's return in April may have reinforced.[233]

In practice, of course, the Rothschilds could not hope to exercise political influence as long as they themselves were financially weak. The traditional leverage exerted by the Rothschilds had, after all, been based primarily on the granting of loans. But throughout 1848 the British Rothschilds used their new predominance over the continental houses to veto numerous suggestions of loans to the post-revolutionary regimes in Austria, Hungary, Rome, Lombardy, Prussia, Baden and elsewhere. (Incredibly, Salomon seems to have suggested lending money to allow the Hungarians to buy guns in England—this even as he was lamenting the collapse of the Habsburg Empire!)[234] It was not until late September that anything resembling "business as usual" was contemplated, though talk of a loan to Austria proved premature.[235] The trouble was that the revolution refused to lie down and die. No sooner had "red republicanism" been defeated in Paris, Vienna and Berlin than it burst forth again in Italy. No sooner had it been defeated in Italy than it had a last lease of life in South Germany.

As long as political uncertainty remained, the Rothschilds held back. When the Austrian government approached Anselm with a 60 million gulden loan proposal in March, he was cautious, dismissing it as "a great nonsense" and "a stupid project."[236] The following month, when James was asked by the city of Paris to make a 25 million franc loan, he "refused it & said it three times, he did not wish to do any business."[237] This hesitation reflected above all the difficulty of deciding what was to be done with the Vienna house which, even after Anselm's skilful salvage operation, still owed the Frankfurt house the immense sum of £1.7 million, as well as a smaller sum to the Paris house. It was not until the summer, after a succession of meetings between the principal partners (including a full "congress" at Frankfurt in the spring), that the decision was taken to preserve the Vienna house by writing most of this money off.[238] The extent to which the London partners wished to restrain their uncles is obvious from Alphonse's comment that the "true goal" of the "congress" would be:

> to modify the bases of our house, and, with respect to the London house, to free them reciprocally from a solidarity incompatible with the political activities and the ardent business spirit of the first generation. Our good uncle [Amschel] cannot bear the reduction of our fortune, and, in his desire to re-establish it on its old basis, would not hesitate to plunge us into hazardous enterprises.[239]

It was symptomatic of the mistrust engendered by the crisis of 1848 that the London partners began to distinguish between letters they would allow their uncles to see and those they kept to themselves.[240] Considering that the circulated private letters had up until this point been the very life blood of the partnership this was a revolutionary suggestion—though it is impossible to be sure how far the London partners went in this direction since so much of their correspondence has been lost or destroyed.

Two additional factors tended to diminish Rothschild political influence. Firstly, their relations with Palmerston remained as tenuous as ever. Charlotte denounced Palmerston's policy in 1848 as "laughable," and it seems reasonable to assume that Lionel shared his wife's view; there was evidently little communication between the Rothschilds and Palmerston at this time.[241] In Nat's view, "any change in the Foreign Affairs will be an improvement on Ld. P[almerston]," a view "heartily" endorsed by his uncle James.[242] To Betty, Palmerston was "the bad genie, breathing fire everywhere and sheltering behind political puppets whom he knows how to station at the front door."[243] Indeed, the Rothschilds seem to have based their assessments of British policy more on defence estimates than on first-hand ministerial intelligence[244]—a reflection perhaps of Lionel's preoccupation at this time with the question of Jewish representation in Parliament. Secondly, they miscalculated the political future in France. James overestimated the durability of "respectable, moderate" republicanism. Assuming that Cavaignac and his fellow general Nicolas Changarnier (who combined command of the National Guard with the military governorship of Paris) would remain the key figures of the new regime, he set to work to ingratiate himself with them. Meetings with Cavaignac and other ministers to discuss French foreign policy became frequent.[245] "Our little friend" Changarnier was invited to hunt at Ferrières and was a frequent Rothschild dinner guest.[246] So close did relations become that the Austrian ambassador in Paris was able to report gossip about Changarnier's "sentiment de coeur" for Betty.[247] As it turned out, James was backing a loser, though his reason for doing so is understandable. For the alternative to the generals was Louis Napoleon Bonaparte, the nephew of the former Emperor.

Throughout the nineteenth century, no figure of political importance was viewed by the Rothschilds with more suspicion, not to say contempt, than Louis Napoleon. This was partly because of his disreputable past—the escapades at Boulogne in 1836 and Strasbourg in 1840, the idiosyncratic books, the English mistress—and the louche lifestyle which he never wholly abandoned. In April 1849, for example, Anthony reported that his aunt and uncle were "disgusted with L. N. They say he gets drunk every night & God knows what else he does." His relationship with Mrs Howard was also a subject for sardonic comment: in Anthony's words, all Louis Napoleon wanted was "plenty [of money] so that he can roger comfortably & get drunk when he likes."[248] James regarded him as "a stupid ass" but, pragmatic as ever, was prepared to put his personal aversion to one side and sup with him as early as January 16—just eighteen days after he had been sworn in as President of the Republic. "I could not refuse his invitation," he explained to his nephews apologetically. Indeed, he seems to have taken the precaution of lending Louis Napoleon 20,000 francs shortly before his election.[249] Nevertheless, this was to be no repeat of the regime change of 1830, when James and Louis Philippe had translated a private, financial relationship into a public, political one almost overnight. As soon as Louis Napoleon had access to public funds, James cut off his credit, ordering Anthony "to give Napoleon no more money, he has no credit with us . . . I promised him 20,000 francs before his budget was passed but now he is getting money from the government, so I don't want to throw away our money and so I won't give him a penny more."[250]

His wife felt an even deeper dislike, partly based on a lingering loyalty to the deposed Orléanist royal family. Disraeli recalled Betty inveighing against Napoleon "whom she hated" to Macaulay, who sought vainly to persuade her that he might be Augustus to his uncle's Julius Caesar.[251] She was unimpressed: France was "floundering between a nobody and a head garotted by a subversive, useless minority." If Cavaignac won it would be "a disaster" as he had shown "neither candour nor capacity in power." But if Louis Napoleon won it would be "a humiliation" as he was "that ridiculous flag from a wonderful past existence, a political nothing who has no other value than as a negative power, a polished socialist hiding roughness beneath the pretence of pleasant politesse." France's "love affair" with him, she predicted, "could be just like a happy love affair at the beginning of a novel; lovers in this case always end up hating each other, or by being violently separated." His victory was a "distress signal around which diverse and opposing opinions rally to protest against the country's upper crust." From the outset she assumed that "a parody of the Empire" would be restored.[252] Until April 1849 she stayed away from the President's receptions.

What concerned the Rothschilds much more, however, was the possibility that, like his uncle before him, Louis Napoleon would pursue an expansionist foreign policy which might plunge Europe once again into a general war. From the moment that Bonaparte's star began to wax in mid-1848, when he was elected to the Chamber of Deputies, it was this which coloured the Rothschilds' judgement. Identifying him as the ally of the "friends of disorder and unrest," they assumed that his popularity presaged war. As James put it, Louis Napoleon would

> spend a nice bit of money to ensure that they have him as President and in my opinion—I who have never believed in war—the situation looks blacker now, because the people now have to . . . make war. At the bourse everyone was horribly black, because they say that the working class will supposedly back him, because he is a socialist and draws his support from the most common people . . . I am trying to liquidate.[253]

Although they came to revise this assessment in the succeeding months, as the likelihood of his victory in the presidential election grew, they were far from delighted at this prospect, regarding Cavaignac as "decidedly better."[254] Both camps directly approached James to ask for support, but he told them that "not being French he was withholding all influence in this serious matter and would not support either of the two candidates, that he was waiting for the country to make its decision and would not oppose to whichever president was preferred by the majority." Privately, he expected Louis Napoleon to defeat Cavaignac.[255] But he found the new President "dull and with no charisma whatever," despite his flattering request that James should "visit him often and eat with him in the morning."[256] In the immediate aftermath of Bonaparte's victory in December, he and Betty nervously anticipated a return to the "June days," and even the outbreak of war between France and Prussia.

Such fears were only increased by the assumption—which can be detected as early as January 1849—that Louis Napoleon would "not rest till he has made himself Emperor, & that the votes of the Army and Peasantry combined will be enough to secure his success."[257] James had no doubt that this would be "a great mistake."[258] Throughout the first months of 1849 he watched with anxiety for signs of a "forward" French foreign policy which might reinforce such pretensions. In particular, the continuing instability of the situation in Italy seemed to invite some kind of French intervention. In James's words, "This question is the one which interests us the most: whether [or not] we will have peace."[259] Every flicker of unrest in Paris seemed to increase the likelihood of a gamble on war by the new government. "It will end with war," predicted James on June 9. "We are in the hands of God. We have [not only] Asiatic cholera [but also] political and financial cholera . . . I do not believe rentes will go up."[260]

The realisation that Napoleon intended to intervene in Italian affairs on the side of the Pope—who had been forced to flee Rome in November—rather than the Roman republic therefore came as a welcome relief, even if Anthony could not at first see "how they can enter & put the Pope on the throne if they have a Republic here."[261] In fact, prolonged debates on the subject meant that this ended up being the last of the foreign interventions against republicanism which finally brought the revolutionary period to an end. The first blow was dealt in March by the second, decisive Austrian victory over Piedmont, which was followed by the occupation of republican Tuscany in May. In April it was the turn once again of the Frankfurt Rothschilds to pack up their valuables as a last wave of popular unrest swept through South Germany, only to be crushed by joint action between Prussia, Saxony and Hanover.[262] As before, the Rothschilds could do little more than stand on the sidelines cheering. Anselm enthusiastically welcomed the Russian intervention in Hungary, conscious that Windischgrätz alone could not win.[263]

Only when the military defeat of the various enclaves of revolution was sure did the Rothschilds seriously think about resuming their traditional loans business. On July 4, Anselm began to talk more positively about the Austrian loan, as well as urging the Paris house to provide the Russian army in Hungary with financial assistance via the Paris house.[264] He also began to involve himself in the efforts to stabilise the Austrian exchange rate, which war and the suspension of silver convertibility had seriously weakened.[265] By mid September, a small Austrian loan had been arranged in the form of a 71 million gulden issue of treasury bills; although most of these were absorbed by the Vienna market, around 22 million were taken up and sold by Amschel in Frankfurt.[266]

Naturally, these transactions implied an explicit commitment to the forces of monarchical reaction, something which caused a degree of disquiet to members of the family in France and London, where support for Hungary was widespread. Betty can hardly have been indifferent to the bitter sentiments expressed in Heine's pro-Magyar poem, "Germany in October 1849," a copy of which he sent her.[267] But Anselm had no time whatever for his English cousins' "uneasy" expressions of pro-Hungarian feeling, advising "your good English folks [to] stick to Ireland & its Potato crop, & keep their arguments for their objects."[268] Carl's suggestion of a loan to the Pope could also be seen as lending sustenance to the counter-revolution.[269] To the disappointed revolutionaries of 1848—not least Marx—the moral was plain: "Thus we find that every tyrant is backed by a Jew, as is every Pope by a Jesuit. In truth, the cravings of the oppressors would be hopeless and the practicability of war out of the question, if there were not an army of Jesuits to smother thought and a handful of Jews to ransack pockets."[270]

It was misleading, however, to portray the Rothschilds as the financiers of reaction, as they had so often been portrayed in the past. For one thing, as Lionel reported from Wildbad in August, the revolution had made erstwhile liberals more conservative: "The Liberal party in Germany is very different from the liberals in England. All persons of property or who are in business are for the old state of things."[271] James's paramount concern was to resume normal business activity—as he reminded his nephews in London, he was "a friend of business" and wanted to "keep the wheels turning." Provided international stability could be relied upon, he was relatively uninterested in the political complexion of the regimes he lent to. Before it was confirmed that the Pope would be restored with French support, for example, James was perfectly willing to do business with the Roman Republic. Indeed, when the Republic's representative approached him with a small deposit in March 1849 to ask whether he "would do their business," he accepted it "as I am [now] a Republican"—an ironic aside from a man who at other times referred to it as the "accursed republic."[272] And when the position of the Papacy was restored at the end of June, James informed Carl that he had no desire to "run after" the Vatican for business.[273] Adolph too showed little respect for the Pope—"His old Piousness with all his nonsense." Any loan, insisted his French cousins, was to be conditional on the granting of civil rights to the Roman Jews.[274] For, as Anselm said,

> the Pope who was once so liberal and who brought Italy such misfortune through his overhasty reforms, is now not just wholly reactionary but, following the example of the Popes of the dark Middle Ages, intolerant in the highest degree, I am tempted even to say inhuman. If the Pope could do business with any other house, he would certainly break with us, and so compliments to the holy gentlemen are not in order.[275]

Nor were James and Lionel willing to allow the Vienna house to resume its traditional role as a more or less unquestioning supporter of the Habsburg regime. In

December, both expressed strong objections to Salomon's efforts to support the Austrian currency when their rivals were profiting from speculating against it.[276]

This political neutrality was most obvious in the case of Piedmont, which had been among the principal troublemakers of 1848. As Anselm pointed out, the Piedmontese indemnity to Austria promised to generate "a beautiful and safe piece of business" in the form of a loan to Piedmont as well as the transfer of part of its proceeds to Vienna.[277] Nat was initially sceptical—as Charlotte observed, the "more sensible" members of the family had not forgotten the "fearful period" of the previous year—but even he could see the appeal of such a transaction.[278] As for James, his interest in Piedmont was so great that Anselm feared he might give the Turin government the impression of "excessive keenness."[279] This underestimated James's skill as a negotiator. He had begun by sounding out the government in advance of the peace agreement with Austria, though without committing himself.[280] Then he hinted at a deal with the Italian bankers who hoped to float the bonds themselves in order to shut out rivals from Paris and Vienna.[281] In September he went in person to Vienna and Milan to offer an advance of 15 million francs on the Piedmontese indemnity due to the Austrian government.[282] Finally, in Turin, he succeeded in securing control of more than half the 76 million franc Piedmontese loan, leaving just 8 million to the Italian bankers and the rest to public subscription.[283]

This was not just because he wished to see Austria get her indemnity. As he assured a young and ambitious financier named Camillo di Cavour, he was "very anxious to have dealings with this country; he has repeatedly told me that he regards Piedmont as established on a much sounder basis than Austria."[284] For his part, Cavour was shocked by the way James had "bamboozled" the Piedmontese Finance Minister Nigra. Convinced that Piedmont should not allow herself to become dependent on "this cunning old rascal Rothschild," Cavour would prove a formidable obstacle to Rothschild ambitions in Italy in the future.[285] But, for the time being, James appeared to have established an important foothold, with the possibility—as he put it—that this would lead to a financial "marriage" with Italy as a whole.[286] In a similar way, the Frankfurt house made approaches at around the same time to German states like Württemberg and Hanover (where a liberal ministry under Johann Stüve remained in power until November 1850), though these were rebuffed.[287]

James's success in Turin brought to an end over a year of immobility induced by the revolution. Even Lionel and his brothers were now ready to contemplate new business, although they were still more interested in revolutionless Spain and America than in Central Europe. Mercury, cotton, gold, tobacco—even Nicaraguan canals and African groundnuts—seemed safer fare than loans to politically volatile states.[288]

In Paris itself there was also a slight relaxation in Rothschild attitudes. The main barometer of financial opinion—the price of rentes—points to a growing (though not unqualified) confidence in the presidential regime in the course of 1849: in the year after December 1848, 5 per cents rose from 74 to 93, and with them Nat's spirits.[289] This was in part a reflection of Napoleon's restrained foreign policy. As Nat remarked when the expedition to Rome was first bruited, "In general when troops begin to move bondholders are frightened; in this case as it is for the re-establishment of order, perhaps & I trust it will produce a good effect."[290] The return of financial confidence also reflected a growing awareness that Louis Napoleon was far from being the ally of the radical left. Although he still thought the President "a little ugly fellow," Nat was favourably impressed by the evidence of social restoration he witnessed one evening at the President's palace: "The ladies were beautifully draped in jewellery and when the carriages were called the titles were *not* omitted." "If we remain *quiet*," he added hopefully, "there will be no difference between the republic and the monarchy."[291] This was over-optimistic: in strictly financial terms, rentes never recovered to pre-war revolutionary levels under the Republic, suggesting continued doubt about the stability of the regime—witness Anthony's alternate warnings that Louis Napoleon would go the way of Louis Philippe or that the republicans would succumb to a Bonapartist coup.[292] Yet there was confidence enough for the Rothschilds to raise the inevitable subject of a new loan to France herself.[293]

There were also the first signs of a revival of the railway mania of the 1840s (Léon Faucher's appointment as Minister for Public Works was especially encouraging). In February 1849 the Pereires revealed their most ambitious scheme to date: a railway to link Paris, Lyon and Avignon, which would then fuse with the line from Avignon to Marseille (the forerunner of the Paris–Lyon–Marseille line). The aim was to revive the system on which the Nord had been based, with the state investing 147 million francs in the initial construction of line between Paris and Lyon and guaranteeing the company a 5 per cent return, while the company put up 240 million francs to operate the concession for ninety-nine years. In fact, it would seem that the Pereires were now seeking to emancipate themselves from the Rothschilds. To raise the money for the new company, they had initially approached Delessert and through him Barings—a first hint of the breach which lay ahead.[294] James was well aware of what was going on and in May fired his first shot back by forcing Isaac Pereire off the board of the Nord.[295] No one should think "that the Pereires are [the same as] Rothschild," he told Anthony. "You have no idea what scoundrels these little fellows are. They are always trying to exploit our name." But "when these people don't need you, they give you a kick in the arse."[296]

In a symbolic reassertion of his position as railway king, James had made a point of appearing alongside Napoleon and Changarnier when a new stretch of the Nord line was opened in July.[297] In November he sought to force his way into the Paris–Lyon–Avignon concession negotiations, buttonholing Louis Napoleon on the subject over dinner and haggling tenaciously with the new Finance Minister Achille Fould thereafter.[298] From the Pereires' point of view, however, this may have been an unwelcome reminder of their association with "Rothschild Ier." There was fierce opposition to their plan, which one critic warned would lead to "a vast consortium Pereire–Rothschild dominating the country from Marseille to Dunkirk and from Paris to Nantes, controlling the coasts of the Mediterranean, those of the Channel and almost all those of the Atlantic, master of the French isthmus."[299] By comparison, the more modest rival proposal put forward by Talabot and Bartholony to link Paris and Lyon seemed less monopolistic. There was similar opposition to the Pereire plan for a line linking Paris and Rennes in the west, which they hoped to link to their Rive Droite terminus. Still, the very notion that he was striving for such a "railway hegemony" testified to the extent of Rothschild recovery. As James put it in a letter to Anthony: "Above all, it is good that people realise that nothing gets off the ground without us and when we demand something, then it is a case of giving Rothschild all he wants."[300]

Nothing could better express how far things had come full circle than this renewed self-confidence—except perhaps the deeply paradoxical friendship which James formed in 1849 with Alexander Herzen. As one of the founding fathers of Russian socialism—the man who coined the phrase "Land and Freedom"—Herzen had left Russia for Paris in January 1847 and, after a brief trip to Italy, returned there at the height of the revolution in May 1848. He had already suffered internal exile as a young man for his liberal inclinations, but by the time he reached Paris his views had moved closer to those of revolutionary socialists like Michael Bakunin and Pierre-Joseph Proudhon (author of another famous aphorism of the period, *la propriété, c'est la vol*). Indeed, Herzen personally financed Proudhon's short-lived journal the *Voix du Peuple* to the tune of 24,000 francs while the latter was in prison.[301] A less likely person to become a favoured Rothschild client would be hard to imagine. The fact that he did sheds light on James's political outlook, and perhaps substantiates Heine's earlier assertion that he was at heart more a revolutionary than a reactionary.

Though born illegitimate, Herzen had inherited a substantial fortune from his aristocratic father, so it is not wholly strange that the Rothschilds obliged him with minor banking services while he was in Italy and helped him invest some 10,000 roubles when he began to sell off his Russian property.[302] Herzen later recalled how he

> made the acquaintance of Rothschild, and proposed that he should change for me two Moscow Savings Bank bonds. Business then was not flourishing, of course, and the exchange was very bad; his terms were not good, but I accepted them at once, and had the satisfaction of seeing a faint smile of compassion on Rothschild's lips—he took me for one of the innumerable princes russes who had run into debt in Paris and so fell to calling me Monsieur le Comte . . . By Rothschild's advice I bought myself some American shares, a few French ones and a small house in the rue Amsterdam which was let to the Havre Hotel.[303]

However, when the Russian government sought to prevent Herzen raising more cash by mortgaging his mother's estate at Komostra, less orthodox financial assistance was called for.[304] According to Herzen's own account, James agreed to accept a bill drawn to the value of the anticipated mortgage and, when the Russian authorities refused to authorise the mortgage, "grew angry, and walked about the room saying: 'No, I shan't allow myself to be trifled with; I shall bring an action against the bank; I shall demand a categorical reply from the Minister of Finance!'"[305] Despite receiving warnings about his new client from the Russian ambassador Count Kiselev, James now took up the cudgels on Herzen's behalf, drafting a stiff letter to Gasser in St Petersburg which threatened the Russian government with legal action and exposure in the press.

Why did he do this? He can have had no illusions about Herzen's politics because he had been given "a very unfavourable opinion" of him by Kiselev. As Herzen put it, he now "surmise[d] that I was not a prince russe." The answer seems to be that this was James's idea of a joke. Herzen was bemused by the fact that James "now took to addressing me as Baron," and even more bemused when he refused to send his letter to Gasser until Herzen increased his commission on the transaction from half a per cent to 5. This "Mephistophelean irony" was intended to test Herzen, who refused to concede more than another half per cent:

> When half an hour later I was mounting the staircase of the Winter Palace of Finance in the Rue Laffitte, the rival of [Tsar] Nicholas was coming down it.
>   . . . His Majesty, smiling graciously, and majestically holding out his own august hand [said,] "the letter has been signed and sent off. You'll see how they will come round. I'll teach them to trifle with me."
>   "Only not for half of one per cent," I thought, and I felt inclined to drop on my knees, and to offer an oath of allegiance together with my gratitude, but I confined myself to saying: "If you feel perfectly certain of it, allow me to open an account, if only for half of the whole sum."
>   "With pleasure," answered His Majesty the Emperor, and went his way into the Rue Laffitte.
>   I made my obeisance . . .[306]

Six weeks later the money was paid. "From that time forth," Herzen recalled, "I was on the best of terms with Rothschild. He liked in me the field of battle on which he had beaten Nicholas; I was for him something like Marengo or Austerlitz, and he several times recited the details of the action in my presence, smiling faintly, but magnanimously sparing his vanquished opponent."[307] After Herzen's expulsion from Paris by the Bonapartist regime, James continued to look after his investments in American and other bonds (he appears in the 1851 balance sheet owing the Paris house 50,000 francs) and secured him permits on the occasions when he wished to visit Paris. He also recommended him to the London house, which took over his account during his long English exile.[308]

Herzen's transformation from insurgent into investor, from Rothschild critic into Rothschild client, was in many ways emblematic of a Europeanwide change of mood—as was James's willingness to play this game with a notorious revolutionary. Did he know that the money he was putting in Herzen's hands was being used to finance the *Voix du Peuple*? If he did, it did not worry him. By the end of 1849 the revolution was over and the more rapid and sustained pace of economic development henceforth would make another 1848 much less likely. For his part, Herzen saw the Rothschilds as personifying this shift away from revolutionary politics:

> A Rothschild . . . must be in his office in the morning, to begin the capitalisation of his hundredth million; in Brazil there is plague, and war in Italy, America is falling to pieces—everything is going splendidly: and, if someone talks to him then of man's exemption from responsibility and of a different distribution of wealth, of course he does not listen.[309]

Of course, for a new era lay ahead: of conflicts within capitalism rather than against it, and between states rather than classes.

Prices and Purchasing Power

It goes without saying that the pound sterling was worth considerably more in the nineteenth century than it is now, mainly because of the inflation which has been a perennial feature of economic life since the 1950s. To be precise, in 1800 the pound was worth around 25 times what it is worth today. Because prices tended to fall during the nineteenth century, it was actually worth rather more in 1900: close to fifty times as much. To put it another way, the purchasing power of the pound has fallen in the past century by around 98 per cent: in 1900 terms, a pound today is worth just two (decimal) pennies.

To try to make historic prices intelligible to modern readers, historians often use price indices to calculate what a sum of money in the nineteenth century "means" in today's pounds. This is easily enough done. Let us take as an example Nathan Mayer Rothschild's total wealth at the time of his death in 1836, which I estimate at around £3.5 million (see chapter 11). Following the conventional system, in order to "convert" that figure into 1995 pounds to allow for inflation in the past 160 years, all that the reader need do is multiply by 35.5, giving £124.25 million.

The trouble with this is that it takes no account of the dramatic changes in economic structure and relative prices which have happened in the past two centuries. The cost of living is in fact a fairly meaningless concept over time because the *nature* of living—that is, what we buy with money—has changed so much in 200 years. As James de Rothschild's biographer rightly says, "A fortune . . . is essentially the power to purchase so many acres of land, to employ so many workers, to maintain so many residences."[1] Labour was much cheaper in Europe 150 years ago than it is now (hence the huge numbers of people employed as servants) and taxes were negligible; by contrast, many of the things now considered "necessaries" were expensive luxuries then, if they existed at all. The long-run price indices used for such calculations are also problematic because of definitional changes (the contents of the supposedly representative basket of goods).

A more accurate method is to relate a money value to current gross domestic product (GDP). The advantage of this is that it conveys the purchasing power of a given sum of money—that is, it gives us an approximate idea of how much of the year's total economic output expressed in current prices it could buy. As a proportion of UK GDP (£562 million in 1836), Nathan's total wealth at death was equivalent to around 0.62 per cent; 0.62 per cent of the United Kingdom's 1995 GDP (£605,100 million) is £3,752 million—a rather larger figure than the one given by the crude inflation multiplier!

Another way of conveying the significance of the original figure is to relate it to per capita GDP; this has the advantage of bringing population change into the equation. Thus Nathan's £3.5 million should be compared with a per capita GDP figure for the same period of £22—that is, Nathan had accumulated around 160,000 times per capita national income; 160,000 times the 1995 figure for per capita GDP (*c.* £10,430) is £1,669 million. It therefore seems clear that Nathan was by the standards of our own time close to being a double billionaire.

Even this measure is misleading, however, because it leaves out of account the greater inequality of the nineteenth century. In the absence of a progressively redistributive tax system and a welfare state, the distribution of income and to a lesser extent of wealth was far more unequal than in our own day. Very rich individuals and families were much rarer then than they are today, and the gulf which separated the Rothschilds from nearly everyone else in Britain was vast. As late as 1911–13, no fewer than 87 per cent of all people aged twenty-five and over in England and Wales—16 million people—had total wealth of less than £100, compared with 0.2 per cent—32,000 people—who had wealth of more than £25,000.[2] The Rothschilds remained at the very pinnacle of this wealthy elite. When they died in rapid succession in 1915, 1916 and 1917, Nathan's grandsons Natty, Leo and Alfred left between them £6,494,000—almost exactly 0.1 per cent of the total capital owned by all adults in England and Wales. To put it another way, they bequeathed between them as much as 191,000 men from the bottom 87.4 per cent of the population.

Were the Rothschilds the richest family in the nineteenth century? Rubinstein's figures for British millionaires do not give precise figures for fortunes in excess of £1 million before 1858; but it seems unlikely that any of the eleven other individuals listed for the period 1810–56 left his heirs as much as Nathan. The nearest was the banker William J. Denison, who left £2.3 million (including real estate worth £600,000) in 1849. It was not until 1857 that someone left more than Nathan to his heirs—the textile warehouseman and Anglo-American banker James Morrison, who left between £4 million and £6 million at his death. Nathan not only died richer than the ironmaster Richard Crawshay and the cotton manufacturers Robert Peel and Richard Arkwright; he also left more than the Duke of Queensberry, the Duke of Sutherland and the Duke of Cleveland.[3] Taking the period 1860–99 as a whole, only twenty-three individuals left estates worth £1,800,000 or more: four of them were Rothschilds (Nathan's sons Lionel, Anthony, Nat and Mayer). Although individually they were not the richest men of their time—Rubinstein cites two individual estates greater than £3 million—no other family could match their collective wealth. Altogether the brothers left £8.4 million: if Nathan, like all aristocratic millionaires, had left his fortune to a sole heir, Lionel would unquestionably have been the richest man in Britain. In reality, the richest man in the world was probably his uncle James who, at his death in 1868, was reported to have left his heirs around 1,100 million francs (£44 million), though a more realistic figure is probably around 193 million francs (£7.7 million) (see volume II).

From 1900 onwards, the English Rothschilds ceased to be exceptional as millionaires. Natty was the richest of his generation of English Rothschilds (leaving £2.5 million); but at least forty-six British millionaires in the period 1900–39 left as much as or more than him. It should be noted once again, however, that the partners in the French and Austrian houses were significantly richer than their English cousins. In 1905 Edouard, Gustave and Edmond each had personal shares in the combined Rothschild partnership worth £5.8 million. Albert, the head of the Vienna house, had a total share of £5.9 million. This excludes very substantial assets outside the partnership. Only seven of Rubinstein's pre-1940 millionaires could match this; nine if the South African "Randlords" are included. Taken together at its peak in December 1899, the combined capital of the Rothschild houses was £41.4 million, divided between ten partners. Again, this takes no account of private wealth, much of it held in the form of expensive art collections and prime real estate. It is almost inconceivable that any other family could match this.

Nearly a hundred years on, do the Rothschilds have a modern equivalent? The answer is no. Not even the Saudi royal family has a comparable share of the world's resources in its possession today. Nor can even the richest businessman in the world claim without qualification to be as rich in relative terms as Nathan Rothschild was when he died at the height of his fortune. At the time of writing, Bill Gates (the founder of the computer software company Microsoft) has an estimated personal fortune of $36.4 billion (£21.7 billion) and has a good claim to be the richest man in the world.[4] If we relate that to current US GDP ($7,487.6 billion), we find that Mr Gates's wealth is equivalent to 0.49 per cent of US GDP. This figure is less than Nathan's equivalent figure of 0.62 per cent of UK GDP in 1836, though Mr Gates is gaining fast. Only if we relate the Gates fortune to American GDP per head ($27,730) does he have the advantage over Nathan: Gates's wealth is 1.3 million times greater than American per capita GDP, whereas Nathan's was only 160,000 times greater than British per capita GDP. The difference, however, mainly reflects the enormous growth in population since the early nineteenth century, which has restrained the growth of American per-capita income.

Exchange Rates and
Selected Financial Statistics

The exchange rates between currencies in late-eighteenth- and early-nineteenth-century Europe varied according to the metal content of coins, and conversion of one currency into another is not always easy. In Frankfurt, the gulden was the denomination most frequently used, though sometimes figures were given in terms of the imperial thaler (Reichsthaler). One Reichsthaler was equal to around 1.79–1.89 gulden. A British pound sterling was equal to 10.2–11.2 gulden. After the return of the pound to gold convertibility, it strengthened against the gulden and for the rest of the century the exchange rate was 12 gulden to the pound (see table a).

However, simple conversion of gulden into pounds can be misleading, as it takes no account of differences in purchasing power. The cost of living was generally thought to be higher in England, and especially in London, than on the continent, but the benefits of colonisation and industrialisation meant that around this time certain commodities (for example cotton goods) were becoming much cheaper in England. For this reason, I have converted gulden figures into pounds in the text only where some sort of comparison seems helpful.

Table a: The sterling exchange rate of the Frankfurt gulden, 1798–1836.

(£)	Gulden (fl.) per pound
1798	11.25
1807	10.16
1809	11.24
1828	12.00
1836	12.00

Source: Rothschild correspondence.

A private partnership of the sort formed by the five Rothschild houses was under no obligation in the period covered by these statistics to produce balance sheets or profit and loss accounts. The profit and loss accounts for N. M. Rothschild & Sons are based on summaries (the purpose of which is not known) which begin in 1829. The accounts are simple: on one side all the year's sales of commodities, stocks and shares are listed; on the other, all the year's purchases and other costs; the difference is recorded as the annual profit or loss. Table b gives the "bottom line" data and also figures for net appropriations (withdrawals and new capital) by partners.

Nineteenth-century banks did not draw up balance sheets or profit and loss accounts in a standardised way, so comparisons with other banks for which figures are available must be made with extreme caution.

Table b: N. M. Rothschild & Sons: profit and loss accounts, 1829–1848 (£).

	Profit/loss	Net appropriations	Capital (end of calendar year)
1829			1,123,897
1830	−56,361		1,067,536
1831	56,324		1,123,860
1832	58,919		1,182,779
1833	75,294		1,258,073
1834	303,939*		1,562,011
1835	69,732*		1,733,404
1836	−72,018		1,661,386
1837	87,353		1,747,169
1838	83,124*		1,820,706
1839	52,845*		1,773,941
1840	30,937*		1,804,878
1841	−49,769*		1,755,109
1842	40,451		1,795,560
1843	23,766*		1,819,326
1844	170,977		1,990,303
1845	82,755		2,073,058
1846	73,080		2,146,138
1847	−660,702		1,485,436
1848	132,058		1,617,494

Notes: Profit and loss figures were calculated as difference between total outgoings and total income.
* Not entirely clear from books. E.g. for 1834, figure in capital account for profit (given here) is different from figure implied by actual accounts; figure for capital at end of 1839 not consistent with figure for profit.
Sources: RAL, RFamFD/13F; RFamFD/13E.

SOURCE NOTES

Abbreviations used in notes

AN   Archives Nationales, Paris
BL   British Library, London
CMR   C. M. von Rothschild (the Naples house)
CPHDCM   Centre for the Preservation of Historical Documentary
            Collections, Moscow
DeRF   de Rothschild Frères (the Paris house)
DNB   Dictionary of National Biography
HSM   Hessisches Staatsarchiv, Marburg
HoL   House of Lords Record Office
IfS   Institut für Stadtgeschichte, Frankfurt
MAR   M. A. von Rothschild & Söhne (the Frankfurt house)
NLS   National Library of Scotland
NMR   N. M. Rothschild & Sons (the London house)
RAL   Rothschild Archive, London
RA   Royal Archives, Windsor Castle
SMR   S. M. von Rothschild (the Vienna house)

Introduction:Reality and Myth
  1 Rothschild, *Meditations*, p. 17.
  2 For a suggestive if flawed discussion see Heilbrunn, "Das Haus Rothschild."
  3 Chekhov, "Rothschild's Fiddle"—a story recommended for readers who wish to be reminded how the
     great majority of nineteenth-century Europeans lived their lives: unlike the Rothschilds, in wretched
     poverty.
  4 Rothschild, *Dear Lord Rothschild*, p. 364; Rothschild, Garton and Rothschild, *Rothschild gardens*, pp.
     174–81.
  5 Heuberger, *Rothschilds*, pp. 159ff.
  6 Cf. Rothschild, *Milady Vine*; Ray, Mouton-Rothschild; *idem*, Lafite.
  7 Prevost-Marcilhacy, *Rothschild*.
  8 RAL, "Species etc." file. Cf. Rothschild, *Dear Lord Rothschild*, p. 213n.
  9 Victor Rothschild wrote useful monographs on both "legends": Rothschild, "*You have it, Madam*";
     Rothschild, *Shadow*.
 10 See e.g., Spalding, *Encyclopaedia of Jewish humour*.
 11 Browne, *House of Rothschild*; Friedman, "Rothschilds."
 12 The plot centres around a gathering of the brothers in the old house in the Judengasse in 1822 and
     Salomon's unsuccessful bid to marry his only daughter (misnamed Charlotte) to a nobleman ("the

Duke of Taunus"). She falls for James instead: Röbler, *Fünf Frankfurter*, pp. 7–91.
13 RAL, Yellen, Bock and Harnick, "The Rothschilds" MS.
14 Bagehot, *Lombard Street*, p. 104.
15 New York, Leo Baeck Institute, Nathan, London, to Behrend Brothers, Berlin, March 14, 1817.
16 Heilbrunn, "Haus Rothschild," p. 7.
17 Neal, *Rise of financial capitalism*; Riley, *International government finance*.
18 Sombart, *Juden*, pp. 115f.; Heilbrunn, "Haus Rothschild," p. 24.
19 For the sake of clarity, I refer to Mayer Amschel and his wife as the first generation, their sons (and daughters) as the second and so on. A family tree is provided at the end of the book.
20 Stern, *Gold and iron*.
21 Cain and Hopkins, *British imperialism*, 2 vols.
22 Cohen, *Denkmal*, esp. pp. 3f., 17n., 27f., 36.
23 Corti, *Rise*, pp. 372f.
24 Brockhaus, *Real-Enzyklopädie* (1827), vol. IX, pp. 431–4. Cf. Heilbrunn, "Haus Rothschild," pp. 12ff; Corti, *Rise*, pp. 368–73; Bouvier, *Rothschild*, p. 73; Sweet, *Gentz*, p. 283.
25 Corti, *Rise*, pp. 227ff.; Bouvier, *Rothschild*, p. 63f.; Sweet, *Gentz*, p. 218.
26 Brockhaus, *Real-Enzyklopädie* (1836), vol. IX, pp. 432f. See also (1847), vol. XII, p. 289. Cf. Corti, *Rise*, pp. 369ff.
27 Berghoeffer, *Meyer Amschel*, pp. 127ff.
28 Brockhaus, *Real-Enzyklopädie* (1827), vol. IX, pp. 431–4. See also (1836), vol. IX, pp. 432f.
29 Corti, *Rise*, plate opp. p. 200.
30 Disraeli, *Coningsby*, esp. pp. 114–17, 120f., 202, 213ff., 214–21, 249ff., 336f., 348.
31 Disraeli, *Tancred*, esp. pp. 115, 118–124, 133–4, 140, 145f., 186–96.
32 Bäuerle, *Baron Rothschild und die Tischlerstochter*, esp. pp. 179–87.
33 Wilde, *Works*, pp. 219–23.
34 Balla, *Romance*; Roth, *Magnificent Rothschilds*; Morton, *Rothschilds*; Cowles, *Rothschilds*; Wilson, *Rothschild*.
35 Corti, *Rise*, pp. 292f., 307f.; Sweet, *Gentz*, pp. 273f.; Gentz, *Briefe an Pilat*, vol. II, p. 105.
36 Heilbrunn, "Haus Rothschild," p. 15; Anon. [Steinmann], *Haus Rothschild*.
37 List, *Grundlinien*, p. 243.
38 See illustration 5.ii.
39 *Hansard*, New Series, vol. XVIII, Feb. 18, 1828, pp. 540–43.
40 Balzac, *La maison Nucingen*, esp. pp. 338f., 357–60, 369–72, 379f., 384–91.
41 Balzac, *Splendeurs et misères*, esp. pp. 492, 520f., 550ff., 576ff., 590ff., 598ff.
42 Dairnvaell, *Histoire édifiante*, pp. 8ff.
43 Chirac, *Rois de la République*, p. 143; Scherb, *Geschichte*, pp. 40–46; Drumont, *France juive*, p. 328. See also Reeves, *Rothschilds*, pp. 169–75; Balla, *Romance*, pp. 87–93; Morton, *Rothschilds*, p. 54.
44 For more critical accounts see Wolf, "Rothschildiana," pp. 281ff.; Rothschild, *Shadow*, pp. 24–38; Cowles, *Rothschilds*, pp. 47ff.; Chapman, "Establishment," p. 79.
45 Heilbrunn, "Haus Rothschild," p. 1f.
46 RA, R51/21, Queen Victoria to Gladstone, Nov. 1, 1869.
47 Dairnvaell, *Histoire édifiante*, pp. 9–19.
48 Pückler, *Briefe*, p. 441.
49 Börne, *Mittheilungen*, 2. Theil, pp. 136ff.
50 Byron, *Don Juan*, Canto XII, verses 4–10.
51 Prawer, *Israel at Vanity Fair*, pp. 17ff.
52 Heine, "Reisebilder: dritte Teil," in *Sämtliche Schriften*, vol. III, pp. 422–9, trans. Prawer, *Heine*, pp. 142–4.
53 *Ibid.*
54 Heine, "Ludwig Börne" in *Sämtliche Schriften*, vol. IV, p. 28.
55 Heine, "Lutetia" in *Sämtliche Schriften*, vol. V, pp. 321ff., 353.
56 *Ibid.*
57 Toussenel, *Juifs*, pp. 22ff.
58 *Ibid.*, p. 40.
59 Anon., *Jugement rendu*, pp. 6ff.
60 Marx, "On the Jewish question," esp. pp. 169ff.
61 Wilson, *Rothschild*, p. 117.

62   See e.g., Woodward, "Economic factors," p. 101.
63   Clough, *France*, p. 173; Palmade, *Capitalism*, pp. 122–4; Kindleberger, *Financial history*, pp. 88, 93, 108f. But see Landes, "The old bank and the new," which demolishes this argument.
64   Mirès, *A mes juges*, pp. 74–89. Cf. Plenge, *Crédit Mobilier*, pp. 63f.
65   Anon., *M. Mirès et M. de Rothschild*, pp. 6ff.
66   Cobban, *Modern France*, vol. II, p. 192f.
67   Goncourt, *Journal*, vol. I, pp. 586f.
68   Bouvier, *Union Générale*, pp. 147–54, 172–8.
69   Zola, *L'Argent*, pp. 21f., 91f., 202.
70   Drumont, *France juive*, vol. II, p. 98, 106f.
71   Drumont, *Testament*, p. 131.
72   Chirac, *Rois de la République*, pp. 127–54.
73   Chirac, *L'Agiotage*, esp. pp. 36, 45, 50, 52f., 56, 62, 64ff., 68f., 72, 80ff., 88, 100ff., 106.
74   Germanicus, *Frankfurter Juden*, esp. pp. 17f.
75   Bauer, *Bismarck und Rothschild*, pp. 21ff.
76   Scherb, *Geschichte*, esp. pp. 145f.
77   Wistrich, *Socialism*, pp. 217, 250, 253, 259, 273, 284, 318; Wistrich, *Jews of Vienna*, pp. 179, 233, 333.
78   Sombart, *Juden*, pp. 115ff.
79   Reeves, *Rothschilds*, p. 86.
80   *Niles Weekly Register*, quoted in Glanz, "Rothschild legend," p. 20; Muhlstein, *Baron James*, p. 105.
81   Raikes, *Journal*, vol. II, pp. 221f.
82   Weill, "Rotschild," trans. Reeves, *Rothschilds*, p. 101.
83   See illustration 10.ii.
84   Zimmermann, *Marr*, p. 68.
85   See illustration 21.i in vol. II (forthcoming).
86   See illustration 24.iii in vol. II (forthcoming).
87   See illustration 24.i in vol. II (forthcoming).
88   Pückler, *Briefe*, p. 7.
89   Börne, *Mittheilungen*, 2. Theil, pp. 136ff.
90   Corti, *Reign*, p. 10.
91   Moneypenny and Buckle, *Disraeli*, vol. IV, p. 339.
92   Toussenel, *Juifs*, vol. I, p. 2.
93   Chirac, *Rois de la République*, p. 136.
94   Morton, *Rothschilds*, p. 96.
95   Heuberger, *Rothschilds*, p. 71. See in general Poliakov, *Antisemitismus*, vol. VI, pp. 138ff.
96   Steele, *Palmerston*, pp. 91ff.
97   Katz, *Belmont*, pp. 144–8; Glanz, "Rothschild legend," pp. 15f., 20f.
98   Corti, *Reign*, p. 398; Stern, *Gold and iron*, p. 73.
99   Steed, *Thirty years*, vol. II, pp. 8f.
100 Davis, *English Rothschilds*, p. 228.
101 Rubinstein, *History of the Jews*, pp. 111ff.
102 Hobson, *Imperialism*, pp. 56ff.
103 Scherb, *Geschichte*, p. 146.
104 Anon., *Hebrew Talisman*, pp. 28ff.
105 Glanz, "Rothschild legend," p. 20.
106 Poliakov, *Antisemitismus*, vol. VI, pp. 171f.
107 Vincent, *Disraeli, Derby and the Conservative party*, p. 32.
108 Iliowzi, "*In the Pale*," p. 260.
109 *Ibid.*, pp. 255–308.
110 See illustration 24.v and 24.vi.
111 Heffer, *Carlyle*, pp. 263f.
112 Herzl, *Tagebücher*, vol. I, pp. 28, 42ff., 50, 79, 83, 90, 103, 110.
113 *Ibid.*, pp. 120–25, 144–210.
114 *Ibid.*, pp. 219, 266, 271f., 288, 307, 331, 375, 398, 423, 456f., 466ff., 472, 478, 482, 499, 504–7.
115 Lane and Rupp (eds), *Nazi ideology before 1933*, pp. 31f.
116 Jäckel and Kuhn (eds), *Hitler: Sämtliche Aufzeichnungen*, p. 405.

117 *Ibid.*, pp. 699, 755.
118 Rosenberg, *Mythus*, p. 266.
119 *Daily Telegraph*, July 11, 1936.
120 Sington and Weidenfeld, *Goebbels experiment*, p. 86.
121 Welch, *Propaganda*, pp. 162–6. See also Friedman, "One family—two films," pp. 333ff.; Heuberger, *Rothschilds*, pp. 150ff.
122 *Deutsche Allgemeine Zeitung*, Jan. 25, 1945, p. 1. I am grateful to Julian Watson for letting me see his father's translation, "The Recipe of Waterloo."
123 Heuberger, *Rothschilds*, pp. 153ff.; *Frankfurter Allgemeine Zeitung*, Jan. 30, 1995.
124 For the book of the film, see Browne, *House of Rothschild.*
125 Lefebvre, "Rothschild."
126 Coston, *Financiers; idem, Haute Banque;* Peyrefitte, *Juifs.*
127 Lottman, *Return*, p. 280.
128 *Sunday Telegraph*, Jan. 29, 1995.
129 *Daily Telegraph*, March 6, 1982.
130 Icke, *And the truth*, pp. 39–43, 59–64, 72–7, 80ff., 88, 159ff., 194, 227, 233, 242, 254, 329ff., 333.
131 Jacobson, "Auflösung." It was James's son Alphonse who opposed the idea of preserving the documents in the Baron Carl von Rothschild library in Frankfurt. He also insisted on the destruction of documents relating to the payment of French reparations in 1815, fearful that they might one day be used to impugn the patriotism of his father.
132 Trentman, "New sources." The French papers have now been returned to the family and are housed in the Rothschild Archive in London. It is hoped that the Austrian material will also be returned in due course.
133 Corti, *Rise; idem, Reign.*
134 Wolf, "Rothschildiana"; Rothschild, "*You have it, Madam*"; Rothschild, *Shadow.* See also Rothschild, *Dear Lord Rothschild;* Muhlstein, *Baron James.*
135 Gille, *Maison Rothschild,* 2 vols; Bouvier, *Rothschild.*
136 Davis, *English Rothschilds.*
137 e.g. Chapman, *Foundation; idem,* "Establishment"; McKay, "House of Rothschild." Flandreau, *Or du monde*, makes brilliant use of the French archive—the exception that proves the rule.
138 Heuberger (ed.), *Rothschilds.*
139 Prevost-Marcilhacy, *Rothschild.*
140 RAL, RFamC/21, Charlotte, London, to Leonora and Leo, Switzerland, Aug. 25, 1874.
141 See in general Knight, "Rothschildsche Banken- und Wirtschaftsarchiv"; Mace, "Archives."
142 See for example Davis, *English Rothschilds.* I have also used the T-files but, with the assistance of the archivists at the Rothschild Archive, have tried as far as possible to trace the original *Judendeutsch* letters for the purposes of quotation. This procedure is less essential but still advisable in the case of English letters which appear in the series.
143 The vast undertaking of translating the XI/109 letters has been in progress for some years. It is being financed by N. M. Rothschild & Sons in order to make the material more accessible to scholars.
144 Cassis and Cottrell, "Financial history."
145 Fase *et al.* (eds), *How to write the history of a bank, passim.*
146 Rothschild, "Silent members."

ONE *"Our Blessed Father": Origins*

  1 Quoted in Corti, *Rise*, p. 400; Heilbrunn, "Haus Rothschild," p. 28.
  2 Kracauer, *Geschichte der Juden*, vol. I, pp. 246, 369, 373; Gay, *Jews of Germany*, p. 6; Wippermann, *Leben in Frankfurt*, p. 26.
  3 Fuchs, *Juden in der Karikatur*, pp. 8f., 19, 31, 65; Schachar, "Judensau" pp. 52–64.
  4 Goethe, *Wahrheit und Dichtung*, Erster Teil, 4. Buch, p. 150.
  5 Frankfurt was one of fifty-one self-governing towns within the Holy Roman Empire (which also comprised 94 kings and princes, 103 counts and 41 church prelates).
  6 Backhaus (ed.), "*Und groß war bei der Tochter Jehudas Jammer.*"
  7 Heuberger and Krohn, *Hinaus aus dem Ghetto*, pp. 13ff.; Liberles, "Dietz's *Stammbuch*," pp. iii–v; Wippermann, *Leben in Frankfurt*, pp. 15ff. See in general Kracauer, *Geschichte der Juden*, vol. I and for the wider context Israel, *European Jewry.*
  8 Katz, *Out of the ghetto*, esp. pp. 9–27; *idem, Tradition and crisis.*

9   Elon, *Meyer Amschel,* pp. 3ff., 18, 42.

10   Gay, *Jews of Germany,* pp. 68ff.

11   Greville, *Memoirs (Second Part),* vol. II, p. 173; Eliot, *Daniel Deronda,* pp. 308–11.

12   Goethe, *Wahrheit und Dichtung,* Erster Teil, 4. Buch, pp. 149f.

13   Gay, *Jews of Germany,* p. 71.

14   Elon, *Founder,* pp. 76ff., 98. The rule was relaxed slightly in 1790, though access was granted only to a single promenade.

15   IfS, Judenschaft, Ugb D 33 Nr. 65, Conclusum in Senatu, Jan. 31, 1788.

16   Elon, *Founder,* p. 83; Heuberger, *Rothschilds,* p. 22.

17   Goethe, *Dichtung und Wahrheit,* Erster Teil, 4. Buch, p. 150. Moreover, "the girls were also pretty."

18   Magnus, *Jewish portraits,* p. 27.

19   Liberles, "Dietz's *Stammbuch,*" p. xi.

20   Backhaus, "Jewish Ghetto," pp. 23–33.

21   A word needs to be said about the spelling of Mayer Amschel's name. On his own gravestone (see Lenarz, *Friedhof,* p. 26), he is described in Hebrew characters as "Mosche Meir, Sohn Anschels, genannt Meyer Amschel Rothschild" and his three biographers have used the spelling "Meyer." However, in the course of his life, he clearly came to prefer the spelling "Mayer" (see for example the circular announcing the formation of the firm of Mayer Amschel Rothschild dated September 20, 1810 in RAL). His descendants named after him have also tended to prefer this spelling. For the sake of simplicity I have therefore used "Mayer" throughout.

22   See in general Dietz, *Frankfurter Handelsgeschichte.*

23   Forstmann, "Frankfurt am Main—Ein europäisches Finanzzentrum." Cf. Schnee, *Hoffinanz,* vol. I.

24   For a note on exchange rates, see appendix 2.

25   Jurk, "Other Rothschilds."

26   See most recently Mosse, *Jews in the German economy.*

27   RAL, RFamAD/2, Mayer Amschel, Frankfurt, to Nathan, undated, *c.* June 1805.

28   Weber, "Protestant Ethic," p. 166.

29   Jurk, "Other Rothschilds," p. 38. The ban remained in force until 1813.

30   Pohl, "From court agent," p. 52. See in general Selma, *Court Jew* and Israel, *European Jewry.*

31   Backhaus, "Last of the Court Jews," p. 80.

32   Dietz, *Stammbuch;* Berghoeffer, *Meyer Amschel,* pp. 1ff.

33   See in general Freimann, *Stammtafeln.*

34   Berghoeffer, *Meyer Amschel,* pp. 4f., 148. See also Corti, *Rise,* p. 17.

35   Cohen, *Denkmal,* pp. 5f., 13; Berghoeffer, *Meyer Amschel,* p. 6; Heuberger, *Rothschilds,* pp. 14f.

36   According to Capefigue, the firm was David & Cie. Capefigue, *Grandes opérations,* vol. II, pp. 348–61.

37   Elon, *Founder,* pp. 55f.

38   Cohen, *Denkmal,* p. 15; Backhaus, "Last of the court Jews," p. 82.

39   Bouvier, *Rothschild,* pp.17f.

40   Berghoeffer, *Meyer Amschel,* pp. 7, 149f. By 1785, the Prince's collection was sufficiently large to need a twelve-volume catalogue, compiled by his librarian Wegener. We may discount the apocryphal story that Mayer Amschel was actually introduced to William at this early stage by a general named von Estorff, as well as the fiction that Mayer Amschel impressed the Prince with his skill at chess (William is supposed to have told von Estorff: "You did not recommend a fool to me"): Hessen, " 'You did not recommend a fool'."

41   CPHDCM, 637/1/1, Wilhelm, Landgraf von Hessen, Ernennungsdekret, Philippsruhe, Sept. 21, 1769. Cf. Berghoeffer, *Meyer Amschel,* p. 7; Corti, *Rise,* pp. 19–26; Gille, *Maison Rothschild,* vol. I, pp. 35ff.

42   Berghoeffer, *Meyer Amschel,* pp. 4f.; Backhaus, "Meyer Amschel," p. 10ff.

43   Berghoeffer, *Meyer Amschel,* pp. 149f.; Gille, *Maison Rothschild,* vol. I, pp. 35–41. Thirteen of these catalogues are preserved in the Stadt- und Universitätsbibliothek, Frankfurt: Backhaus, "Last of the court Jews," p. 128n.

44   Berghoeffer, *Meyer Amschel,* p. 24.

45   Mayer Amschel did not have to pay the difference between his share of the Hinterpfann and the price of the house at the green shield all at once. He bought the house in two halves, in Dec. 1783 and Nov. 1785. In each case, as was customary, a third was paid up front, the rest in six or eight half-yearly sums.

46   RAL, T31, XI/109/4/1/53, Salomon, Frankfurt, to Nathan and James, Feb. 2, 1816.

47 Berghoeffer, *Meyer Amschel*, pp. 1–3, 17f., 147. The house was preserved more or less as Mayer Amschel had known it until 1944. After his widow's death, it had gradually fallen into disrepair and was saved from the fate of the rest of the Judengasse—compulsory purchase and demolition—only by the family's decision in the 1880s to preserve it as a historic monument. Along with its neighbour "at the golden arch" (with which it shared a roof as well as a cellar) it was completely restored and opened to the public. It also housed the offices of two Rothschild charities.

48 In the generation after Mayer Amschel, Rothschild first names underwent a confusing process of transformation according to the national milieu in which his sons found themselves. Amschel was sometimes known as Anselm, Salomon was often Salamon or even Solomon, Kalman was almost always Carl after around 1812; and Jakob became James when he moved to Paris. In much of the family's private correspondence, their sisters and wives tended to be referred to by their *Judendeutsch* names, usually in a diminutive form, though Jettchen became "Aunt Henrietta" after her English marriage. For the sake of simplicity, I employ the most frequently used forms throughout: Amschel, Salomon, Nathan, Carl and James.

49 IfS, Ugb D 52 C 137, April 28, 1790, List of creditors of Joseph Cassel in Deutz.

50 HSM, Best. 55a Nr 352, Nr 1, Mayer Amschel, Frankfurt, to Kriegs Commessarus, Feb. 21, 1794; Votum den Ankauff von einer eigesendeten Plansche Silber betr., Feb. 12; Mayer Amschel to Münzmeister Fulda, Feb. 26; Unterthäniger Bericht an Hochfürstl. Münz Direction, Feb. 27; Bericht, Feb. 28; Münzmeister Fulda to Hochfürstl. Münz Direction, April 4.

51 Berghoeffer, *Meyer Amschel*, p. 24; Elon, *Meyer Amschel*, p. 78; Heuberger, *Rothschilds*, p. 24.

52 IfS, Judenschaft, Ugb D33 Nr 106 Tom 1 Bl. 194, Befragung Lederhändler Trautwein, July 30, 1803; Nr 118 Fasz. 1, Befragung aller Juden, die sich in der Schnurgasse eingemietet haben, darunter Amschel Rothschild namens seines Vaters, Oct. 18.

53 Berghoeffer, *Meyer Amschel*, p. 26.

54 *Ibid.*, p. 25. For an example of the generous (though hard-headed) terms of a Rothschild marriage contract of the same period, see CPHDCM, 637/1/268, Ehevertrag . . . zwischen dem Herrn Salomon Rothschild und seiner Frau [Caroline Stern, daughter of Jacob Heyum Stern], Nov. 26, 1800.

55 CPHDCM, 637/1/3/1–11, Inventarium von Mayer Amschel Rothschild, Frankfurt, 11 Aug., 1797.

56 IfS, Criminalia, 1804 No. 59 (Akte Nr 11025), "den wegen eines an seinem Brodherrn Mayer Amschel Rothschild begangenen, beträchtlichen Geld-diebstahls verhafteten Judenknecht Hirsch Liebmann von Bockenheim" [hearing in presence of Senator Schweizer and Kriminalrat Siegler], Aug. 19, 1798. No records of the subsequent trial, if there was one, survive, so we do not know Liebmann's ultimate fate. Cf. Elon, *Founder*, pp. 92–7; Backhaus, "Last of the court Jews," p. 85.

57 Heilbrunn, "Haus Rothschild," pp. 12ff.

58 Fortunately, no one was killed, as the entire population (including the Rothschilds) had fled. Unfortunately, as Goethe's mother wrote to her son, this meant that "When the fire started nobody could get into the locked houses and there were no Jews there to put out the fires." Elon, *Founder*, p. 99.

59 Backhaus, "Meyer Amschel," pp. 26ff.; Heuberger, *Rothschilds*, p. 24.

60 Chapman, *Foundation*, pp. 3ff.; Williams, *Making*, p. 17.

61 1797: Wolf, "Rothschildiana," pp. 261; 1798: Berghoeffer, *Meyer Amschel*, p. 12; Corti, *Rise*, p. 40; Gille, *Maison Rothschild*, vol. I, pp. 35–41; Bouvier, *Rothschild*, p. 23; Wilson, *Rothschild*, pp. 21ff.; Chapman, *Foundation*, pp. 4f.; 1799: Pollins, *Economic History of the Jews*, p. 84; Heuberger, *Rothschilds*, pp. 36f.; 1800: Rothschild, *Shadow*, pp. 14f.; Williams, *Making*, pp. 17f. 1800 was also the date mentioned in Nathan's obituary in *The Times*, Aug. 3, 1836. Wolf's assertion that Mayer Amschel sent Nathan to England "immediately after his barmitzvah" is plainly wrong: that would have been in 1789 or 1790!

62 The firms concerned were those of Salomon Salomons and A. Goldschmidson.

63 RAL, Cole Autographs, vol. 33, U1C/1, Mayer Amschel, Frankfurt, to Harman & Co., London, Feb. 7, 1800. In this letter, Mayer Amschel claims that he is "often obliged to draw on London." But this was almost certainly a boast intended to bolster his request for credit facilities. Initially, however, the firm turned him down. It was only when he made good his promise of "substantial transactions" ("starke Geschäfte') that Harmans granted him the desired facilities: same to same, April 13, 1800. Harmans was a small but distinguished house: Jeremiah Harman was at this date a director of the Bank of England and the later firm of Harman, Hoare & Co. was one of the founders of Lloyds Bank Ltd. The Harman correspondence was discovered by Wolf and is the basis of part of his "Rothschildiana."

64   Wolf, "Rothschildiana," p. 270; RAL, Cole Autographs, vol. 33, U1C/7, MAR, Frankfurt, to Harman & Co, London, June 15, 1800.

65   RAL, I/218/35/101, Nathan to Messrs Dechapeaurouge, Hamburg, May 19, 1802 ("I have been established in this town three years"); RAL, I/218/36, Manchester Letter Copy Book, Nathan to Buderus (wrongly transliterated by a clerk as "Mr Ober Greeks Rad Boderis"!), June 30 ("I have been established in the Manufactories of Manchester Three Years"); RAL I/218/1, Manchester Letter Copy Book, Nathan to de Chapeaurouge & Co., Hamburg, Feb. 9, 1803 (Nathan states that he has been established in Manchester nearly four years); RAL, I/218/36, Nathan to S. A. Levy, London, Aug. 15, 1804 ("After having been established in business here four years").

66   Williams, "Nathan Rothschild in Manchester," pp. 35ff.

67   Buxton (ed.), *Memoirs*, pp. 288–90.

68   See Chapman, *Foundation*, pp. 1ff.; Berghoeffer, *Meyer Amschel*, p. 12.

69   Wilson, *Rothschild*, pp. 21f., 475n.

70   RAL, Cole Autographs, vol. 33, U1C/54, Mayer Amschel, Frankfurt, to Harman & Co., London, April 24, 1801; RAL, I/218/35/43, Unidentified clerk to Mr Wm McLellan, Paisley, July 21, 1801.

71   RAL, Cole Autographs, vol. 33, U1C/24, Nathan, Manchester, to Harman & Co., London, Nov. 1, 1800; RAL, I/218/35/6, Nathan to Blaydes, Loft & Co., Nov. 12; RAL, I/218/35/9, Nathan to Sal. Salomons, Dec. 7; RAL, I/218/35/67, Nathan to unidentifiable recipient, Oct. 28, 1801.

72   RAL, I/218/35/24, Nathan to Salomons, March 5, 1801.

73   RAL, I/218/36, Nathan to M. G. Gaudoit, Paris, Aug. 18, 1802. See also RAL, I/218/36, Nathan to M. G. Trenelle, Sept. 5, 1802.

74   RAL, I/218/36, Nathan to Mayer Amschel, Aug. 29, 1802.

75   RAL, RFamAD/2, Mayer Amschel to Nathan, undated, *c.* June 1805.

76   See in general Katz, *Philosemitism*; *idem, Jews in the history of England.*

77   Jews could not formally obtain the freedom of the City of London, but this restriction did not in practice prevent them from doing business there. See *The Times*, June 4, 1879.

78   Endelman, *Radical assimilation*, pp. 34f.; Kynaston, *City*, vol. I, pp. 20f.; Chapman, *Foundation*, pp. 3ff, 20f.; *idem*, "Establishment," pp. 71ff. See in general Endelman, *Jews of Georgian England.*

79   Williams, *Making*, pp. 16f.; *idem*, "Nathan Rothschild in Manchester," pp. 35ff.

80   Buxton (ed.), *Memoirs*, pp. 288ff.

81   Chapman, *Foundation*, pp. 5–17.

82   RAL, I/218/I, Nathan to J. A. Matti, Frankfurt, Dec. 29, 1802.

83   Chapman, *Foundation*, p. 17.

84   RAL, I/218/36, Nathan to Mayer Amschel, Sept. 1802.

85   RAL, I/218/36, Nathan to Sichel & Hildesheimer, Frankfurt, Oct. 17, 1802. For their original approach to Nathan, see RAL, XI/38/241A, Sichel & Hildesheimer to Nathan, July 20.

86   RAL, Cole Autographs, vol. 24, U1C/105, Nathan, Manchester, to Harman & Co., London, Nov. 12, 1800; RAL, I/218/35/7, Nathan, Paisley, to William McLellan, Dec. 6.

87   RAL, I/218/35/92, Barber to Messrs Harman & Co., May 1, 1802; RAL, I/218/35/98, Nathan to John Hatton, May 13, 1802; RAL, I/218/35, Letter Copy Book, 1800–1802.

88   RAL, Textile Order Book, so-called "Cotton Book" (copy; original at New Court). A typical order was a commission "from Messrs Sichel & Hildesheim Frankfort a/m to be forwarded immediately that the greatest part may arrive in Aug., the remaining part in Sept. to Messrs Wertheimer & Co. Hamburg, payable 3/4 of the amount as soon as the goods arrive at Hamburg, the remaining 1/4 on arrival of the goods at Frankfurt, with bills on London at 2 1/2 month, without Discount. Insurance to be effected by N. M. Rothschild: 30 1/3 pieces blk velveretts . . . 54 1/3 blk velveteens . . . 30 1/3 pieces blue velveretts . . . 221 1/3 pieces blue velveteens . . . 21 1/3 ps plain velveteens . . . 42 1/3 ps fancy velveteens . . . 42 1/3 plain thicksetts . . . 33 1/3 ps fancy cord . . . 12 1/3 ps blue fancy thicksetts newest patterns . . . 30 1/3 pieces white quilting plain and satin stripe . . . 69 1/3 printed thicksett . . . 24 1/3 ps yellow printed thicksetts newest patterns . . . 24 1/4 ps London printed quiltings, the newest patterns and good quality; 40 ps swandowns check and striped; 4 ps toilinets new fashion; 27 1/3 ps. printed thicksett same as patterns.'

89   See for example RAL, I/218/35/17, Nathan to Messrs Wormald & Gott, Leeds, Jan. 28, 1801.

90   See especially the letters to French customers in the summer of 1802 in RAL, I/218/36, NMR, Letter Copy Book, 1802–1804.

91   RAL, I/218/36, Nathan to Geisenheim, Jan. 19, 1803.

92   RAL, I/218/35/5, Nathan to Salomon Salomons, Nov. 9, 1800; RAL, I/218/35/9, Nathan to

Salomons, Dec. 7. According to Berghoeffer, when Nathan shipped a consignment of goods to his father valued at £60,500, something like £19,270 was accounted for by insurance and other charges paid to Salomons. By 1809–10, insurance could account for more than a third of the total price of a shipment: Berghoeffer, *Meyer Amschel*, p. 12.

93   RAL, I/218/35/25, Nathan to Messrs Boulton & Watts, Soho, Birmingham, March 8, 1801; RAL, I/218/35/67, Nathan to an unidentified recipient, Oct. 28; RAL, I/218/36, Nathan to G. J. Elias, Frankfurt, Oct. 31.

94   RAL, I/218/37, 38, Rindskopf Letter Copy Books. These letters from N[ehm] B[eer] Rindskopf, the Manchester representative of the firm of Rindskopf Brothers, Frankfurt, were erroneously read by Chapman as letters from Nathan himself. Cf. Dietz, *Jewish community*, pp. 282f.

95   RAL, I/218/37/173, Rindskopf to Nathan. July 9; same to same, Sept. 13. Cf. Berghoeffer, *Meyer Amschel*, pp. 11f.

96   See for example RAL, I/218/36, Nathan to Hullufson Brothers & Co., Aug. 17, 1802; RAL, I/218/36, Nathan to de Tastett & Co., London, Sept. 29, 1804; RAL, I/218/36, Nathan to M. M. David, Hamburg, Dec. 29. Cf. Chapman, *Foundation*; Roberts, *Schroders*, p. 29.

97   RAL, I/218/35/12, Nathan to Salomon Salomons & Co., Dec. 21, 1800: "You'll remember me evry [*sic*] day that you drink it as you'll find it very good and cheap. Mr Harman gives the insurance at 1pct. lower than you to do."

98   RAL, I/218/35/7, Nathan, Paisley, to Wm McLellan, Dec. 6, 1800; RAL, I/218/35/11, same to same, Dec. 21; RAL, I/218/35/14, Jan. 17, 1801.

99   RAL, I/218/35/40, Nathan to Mr Wm Bissland, Paisley, July 15, 1801.

100   RAL, I/218/36, Nathan to M. G. Trenelle, Sept. 5, 1802.

101   RAL, I/218/36, Nathan to Mayer Amschel, March 23, 1803.

102   RAL, T1/21 and 22, B. L. Behrens to Nathan, undated, 1804 or 1805.

103   RAL, I/218/37/26, Rindskopf to Nathan, Feb. 1, 1805; RAL, I/218/37/35, same to same, Feb. 7; RAL, I/218/37/40, Feb. 12; RAL, I/218/37, July 22.

104   RAL, I/218/36, Nathan to S. A. Levy, London, Aug. 15, 1804.

105   RAL, T4/35, J. Horstman, 5 Great St Helens March, to Nathan, March 8, 1809.

106   Gray (ed.), *Life and times*, p. 93. Denization was the nearest status to full naturalisation which a foreign-born Jew could be granted.

107   Williams, *Making*, pp. 17ff.; *idem*, "Nathan Rothschild in Manchester," pp. 35ff.

108   RAL, I/218/35/22, Nathan to Hewson, Guniss & Wood, Feb. 24, 1801. The outbreak of war obliged Nathan hastily to renew his passport to ensure that his right of residence in England was not called into question: RAL, I/218/1, Manchester Letter Copy Book, Nathan to Lyon de Symons, London, Aug. 18 and Aug. 20, 1803.

109   RAL, T4/12, A. Hertz of L. B. Cohen, London, to Nathan, Nov. 12, 1805.

110   RAL, I/218/38/71, Rindskopf to Nathan, Jan. 30, 1806; RAL, I/218/38/75, same to same, Feb. 3; RAL, I/218/38/99, March 11; RAL, I/218/38/100, March 12.

111   Williams, *Making*, pp. 20f.

112   RAL, T2/25, Mayer Alexander to Nathan, July 2, 1806.

113   RAL, T4/19, A. Hertz to Nathan, Nov. 29, 1806; RAL, T3/312, Parish & Co., Hamburg, to Nathan, Feb. 2, 1807.

114   RAL, I/218/38/83, Rindskopf to Nathan, Feb. 10, 1806.

115   RAL, T3/274–5, Parish & Co., Hamburg, to Mayer Amschel, Frankfurt, April 23, 1806.

116   RAL, I/218/38/137–41,149, Rindskopf to Nathan, Aug. 22, 1806.

117   RAL, T5/4, Amschel, Hamburg, to Nathan, July 8, 1807. Cf. Heuberger, *Rothschilds*, p. 39.

118   RAL, T3/31, L[evi] B[arent] Cohen to Nathan, Oct. 19, 1807; RAL, T3/32, same to same, Oct. 20; RAL, T3/33, Oct. 22; RAL, T3/34, Cohen to Mr Fox, Liverpool, Oct. 26.

119   RAL, T5/51, P. Fawcett, Manchester, to Nathan, Sept. 3, 1808.

120   RAL, T2/82, J. Aldebert & Co., Bucklesbury, to NMR, London, Sept. 26, 1809; RAL, T2/96, Anton S., Königsberg, to Nathan, Nov. 14, 1810.

121   Berghoeffer, *Meyer Amschel*, pp. 12, 15. Cf. Heuberger, *Rothschilds*, p. 40; Corti, *Rise*, pp. 106f.; Bouvier, *Rothschild*, pp. 32f.

122   In fact, Nathan burnt his fingers again with an ill-fated shipment of goods to Russia, which appears to have fallen victim to the Napoleonic invasion: RAL, T4/54, G. F. Schmidt, Copenhagen, to Nathan, Oct. 6, 1812; RAL, Cole Autographs, vol. 33, U1C/64, Nathan. London, to Messrs Latham Rice & Co., Dover, Aug. 13, 1813.

123 RAL, RFamFP/11, Marriage settlement between Nathan and Hannah Cohen, Oct. 21, 1806. Cf. Davis, *English Rothschilds*, pp. 25f.

124 The spouses of Cohen's other daughters included Moses Montefiore, Samuel Moses Samuel, John Helbert and Meyer Davidson: Loewe (ed.), *Montefiore Diaries*, vol. I, p. 2; Aspey, "Mrs Rothschild," pp. 60–7.

125 RAL, I/218/18, India Goods Book.

126 RAL, XI/112/76, Peter Fawcett, Manchester, to Nathan, Dec. 30, 1808: "I consider you a banker and am as well satisfied with your acceptance as I should be with that of any banker in London."

127 RAL, VI/10/0, Ledger book 1809/10. This includes his earliest dealings with the Bank of England.

128 Williams, *Making*, p. 20.

129 Wolf, "Rothschildiana," p. 271; Davis, *English Rothschilds*, p. 35. At the time, this now famous address was one of five three-storey houses in a prosperous professional neighbourhood. Nathan's neighbours included a surgeon and an insurance broker.

TWO   *The Elector's Treasure*

1 RAL, T27/105, XI/82/1, Carl, Frankfurt, to Amschel, Sept. 9, 1814.

2 RAL, XI/82/9/1/9, Amschel, Frankfurt, to James, undated, *c.* April 1814. William was given the title of Elector in 1803.

3 Backhaus, "Meyer Amschel," pp. 10ff.; Berghoeffer, *Meyer Amschel*, pp. 7, 51, 62.

4 Backhaus, "Meyer Amschel," pp. 17ff.; *idem*, "Last of the Court Jews," p. 82; Berghoeffer, *Meyer Amschel*, pp. 48f.; Corti, *Rise*, p. 25. Cf. Kapp, *Soldatenhandel*; Ingrao, *Hessian mercenary state*; Kipping, *Truppen von Hessen-Kassel*.

5 This system had been in operation since the Seven Years" War: Neal, *Financial Capitalism*, pp. 190–222.

6 Berghoeffer, *Meyer Amschel*, p. 56. I have converted Berghoeffer's figures from Reichsthalers to gulden.

7 *Ibid.*, pp. 20f.

8 HSM, Bestand 4 h Nr 3839, Nr 69, Unterthänigster Bericht vom Kriegs-Collegio, Kassel, to Elector William, July 31, 1789; Nr 71, Mayer Amschel to Elector William, March 10, 1790; Nr 73, Bericht des Kriegs Collegii, Kassel, March 22; CPHDCM, 637/1/2, Hessiches-Kriegscollegium, Kassel, to Mayer Amschel, April 10; HSM, Bestand 4 h Nr 3839, Nr 25, Gebot für den Verkauf englischer Wechsel, Feb. 7, 1791. Because cash was scarce in Hessen between the bi-annual fairs, it would have depressed the price of the English bills to have auctioned them for cash. For this reason, the brokers bought them on credit, paying the War Chest at a later date when the markets were more liquid. Cf. Corti, *Rise*, pp. 25f.; Backhaus, "Meyer Amschel," pp. 23ff.

9 Buderus von Carlshausen, "Carl Friedrich Buderus."

10 HSM, Bestand 4 h Nr 3839, Nr 39, Extract, Bericht von dem Ober-Kriegs-Commissario Buderus, July 6, 1794; Nr 26, Bericht des Oberkriegszahlamts, July 12. Cf. Berghoeffer, *Meyer Amschel*, pp. 21ff.; Backhaus, "Meyer Amschel," pp. 29ff.

11 Simon Rüppell was the head of the Hessen post service in Frankfurt; Louis Harnier's uncle and father were both War Councillors (like Buderus) in Kassel. They came to enjoy the support of Buderus's rival within the financial bureaucracy, Lennep.

12 Sauer, *Finanzgeschäfte*, p. 88. For subsequent sales of these bonds see HSM, Best. Rechnungen II Kassel Nr 655 C, Journal der kurfürstlichen Cabinetskasse, 1798.

13 HSM, Bestand 4 h Nr 3839, Nr 48, Schreiben des 2. Dep. des Kriegs Collegii, Kassel, Sept. 24, 1798. Interestingly, a series of sterling exchange rate figures found in the London archive dates from Aug. 1798: RAL, XI/38/59A.

14 Berghoeffer, *Meyer Amschel*, pp. 29–42; Ehrenberg, *Große Vermögen*, p. 50; Corti, *Rise*, pp. 33f., 46; Backhaus, "Meyer Amschel," pp. 41ff. Lawätz leapt to the defence of his "good" and "brave" friend: "He is a decent man who has earned respect—whatever the envious may say.'

15 HSM, Bestand 5 (Hess. Geheimer Rat), Nr 8877, Nr 2, Mayer Amschel, Munich, to Elector, Aug. 1, 1802; RAL, I/218/36, Nathan to Mayer Amschel, Frankfurt, Nov. 3; HSM, Bestand 5 (Hess. Geheimer Rat), Nr 8877, Nr 8f., Mayer Amschel, Munich, to Elector, April 26, 1804; Nr 12, Unterthänigster Bericht von der Oberrentkammer wegen der zum Ankaufen gebotenen von Castellischen Güther zu Röhrda und Netra [to Elector], Sept. 22.

16 HSM, Bestand 6b Nr 641, Kurfürstlicher Erlaß, May 1802.

17 HSM, Bestand 6b Nr 641, Elector, Kassel, to Renth-Cammer zu Hanau, May 31, 1806.

18 Berghoeffer, *Meyer Amschel*, pp. 37, 73ff.; Gille, *Maison Rothschild*, vol. I, pp. 40f.

19 HSM, 1. Best. 16 Rep. XIV Kl. 2 Nr 13, Mayer Amschel, Antrag für die Aufnahme als Schutzjude für einen seiner Söhne, Aug. 1, 1803. Cf. Berghoeffer, *Meyer Amschel*, p. 45; Backhaus, "Meyer Amschel," pp. 39f.; Heuberger, *Rothschilds*, p. 29.

20 HSM, 1. Best. 16 Rep. XIV Kl. 2 Nr 13, Mayer Amschel, Kassel, to Elector, July 8, 1805; Mayer Amschel to Elector, July 8; Ober-Renth-Cammer, Kassel, to Elector, Sept. 2, 1805; Ober-Renth-Cammer to Elector, June 14, 1806. In addition to his statutory dues and a payment of 400 thalers towards the fabric of the Neustadt church, Mayer Amschel offered to pay the Jewish community as much as the richest Kassel Jew, Oberhofagent Moses Joseph Büding, but the community was insistent that he move permanently to Kassel. In the end, no use was made of the residence permit, which was finally made out in Amschel's name, and after 1809 the Rothschilds stopped paying contributions to the Kassel community. This led to a protracted legal wrangle between 1815 and 1829 which was settled only when Amschel agreed to pay the community a fine of 2,500 thalers: see esp. HSM, Bestand 266 Nr 908, Nrn 11f., Amschel, Vollmacht, Jan. 18, 1816; Nr 903, Amschel, Erwiderung to Kurfürstliche Regierung, Jan. 18.

21 William's officials increasingly favoured the purchase of bearer bonds because they were regarded as legally more secure than personal loans; there was added safety in being one of a number of investors; they were more liquid than other forms of loan and they were a relatively anonymous form of investment, which gave little away about the total wealth of the Elector.

22 Berghoeffer, *Meyer Amschel*, pp. 41f., 138f.

23 Bayr. Hauptstaatsarchiv, Abt. II, GStA MA 8029, Nr 4, Emperor Franz II to Kurfürst von Bayern, March 6, 1800. Cf. Corti, *Rise*, pp. 46, 78.

24 Bayr. Hauptstaatsarchiv, Staatsarchiv für Oberbayern, HR Fasz. 431, Nr 115, Mayer Amschel, Frankfurt, to Kurfürst von Bayern, Nov. 3, 1802; Dekret, Nov. 10.

25 IfS, Ugb D93 Nr 90, Nichtanerkennung des Handelsfreipasses Mayer Amschel Rothschilds durch Zollverwalter in Butbach, Nov. 3, 1803.

26 HSM, Bestand 6b Nr 641, Subsidien von England, Jan. 22, 1810. Cf. Corti, *Rise*, pp. 21, 33f.

27 Corti, *Rise*, pp. 52ff.; Backhaus, "Meyer Amschel," pp. 42ff.

28 William's brother was at that time Danish Statthalter of Schleswig and Holstein, and it was to his seat, Schloss Gottorp, that William initially went. In April 1807, he moved to a modest house at Itzehoe.

29 *Morning Herald*, Aug. 5, 1836. See also *The Times*, Aug. 10; Anon., *Hebrew Talisman*, pp. 28–40; Treskow, *Nathan Meyer Rothschild*, pp. 3f.; Doering, *Ursprung, Wachstum und Schicksale*, pp. 5f.

30 See above, pp. 12ff.

31 For example, Capefigue, *Grandes opérations*, vol. II, p. 353; Chirac, *Rois de la République*, pp. 137ff.; Scherb, *Geschichte*, pp. 35–40. See also Reeves, *Rothschilds*, pp. 38ff.; Balla, *Romance*, p. 58f.

32 Friedman, "One family, two films."

33 Berghoeffer, *Meyer Amschel*, pp. 49–59; Corti, *Rise*, p. 60. The Rothschilds were evidently involved at various stages in this process: see HSM, Bestand 6b Nr 687, Nr 1, Verzeichnis der Depot Kisten (apparently in William's own hand, but undated), which lists a number of chests and chest-keys temporarily in their possession.

34 Berghoeffer, *Meyer Amschel*, pp. 68–71. This second flight was necessitated when Denmark allied herself with France, following the British seizure of the Danish fleet. For the Elector's route south: HSM, Bestand 4 a/94, 12, letzte Nr 1. Bündel. Cf. Hessen, *Wir Wilhelm*, p. 377.

35 RAL, T27/105, XI/82/1, Carl, Frankfurt, to Amschel, Sept. 9, 1814; Berghoeffer, *Meyer Amschel*, p. 143n.

36 HSM, Bestand 6b Nr 769, Carl, Hamburg, to Knatz, March 4, 1808; Nr 81, Mayer Amschel, Frankfurt, to Knatz, March 18; Nr 111, Mayer Amschel to "Reichs Frey Gnädigste Frau Insonders Gnädigste Frau Reichs Grafen," April 5.

37 Berghoeffer, *Meyer Amschel*, pp. 90f., 94ff., 100–9, 117, 143n., 149f.; Corti, *Rise*, pp. 70f., 75ff., 84ff.

38 Berghoeffer, *Meyer Amschel*, pp. 70ff., 99; Corti, *Rise*, pp. 78ff., 97ff.

39 Buxton (ed.), *Memoirs*, pp. 288ff.

40 Neal, *Financial Capitalism*, pp. 180–90. Neal also estimates that around 10 per cent of the British national debt was held by foreigners (p. 211).

41 Berghoeffer, *Meyer Amschel*, pp. 82f. In 1812 the princes' debts were rescheduled to include back interest at £225,361, of which the Prince of Wales owed £140,000, the Duke of York £66,667, the Duke of Clarence £20,000.

42 Nathan had made his first tentative foray into the gilts market in June 1803: RAL, I/218/1, Manchester Letter Book, Nathan to Harman & Co., London, June 30, 1803.

43   On the development of the 3 per cent consol as the standard British government bond after the Three
     Per Cent Consolidating Act of 1751 see Neal, *Financial Capitalism*, pp. 1ff., 117.
44   RAL, T27/105, XI/82/1, Carl, Frankfurt, to Amschel, Sept. 9, 1814. It was a point Buderus had made
     to his brother Amschel some months before: RAL, T28/20, Amschel, Frankfurt, to James, undated,
     April.
45   Berghoeffer, *Meyer Amschel*, pp. 112ff., 132; Corti, *Rise*, pp. 28–50, 75f., 105–12; Bouvier, *Rothschild*,
     pp. 34ff.
46   HSM, Bestand 340 Buderus von Carlshausen Nr 85, Buderus to Elector, Sept. 20, 1809.
47   On one occasion the sea captain to whom they had been entrusted threw them overboard when his ship
     was searched. In the spring of 1812 James was entrusted with collecting five certificates for £189,550
     in London. He and Carl, whom he met at Dunkirk, then went to Paris, from whence Carl proceeded
     to Prague. The Elector did not receive the certificates until May 20. In late 1812 Salomon picked up a
     further certificate of £250,000.
48   RAL, T28/29, Carl to unidentified recipient, July 1814.
49   RAL, T64/328/3, Amschel, Frankfurt, to his brothers, April 21, 1818.
50   Berghoeffer, *Meyer Amschel*, pp. 82, 88f.
51   CPHDCM, 637/1/4, Prozess mit Savagné: Actum in Cancellaria des Stadt und Land Gerichts, Frank-
     furt am Main, Aug. 30, 1808.
52   CPHDCM, 637/1/4, Transcript of interrogation of Mayer Amschel and his family, May 10, 11 and 14,
     1809 and Commiss. Spéciale de la haute police du Royaume de Westphalie Savagné to M. le Baron
     d'Itzstein, Directeur Général de la Police à Frankfurt, May 25, 1809. Cf. Berghoeffer, *Meyer Amschel*, p.
     120f.; Corti, *Rise*, pp. 81, 89; Bouvier, *Rothschild*, pp. 32f.
53   Corti, *Rise*, p. 69. Cf. HSM, Bestand 6b Nr 646, Auszüge aus erstatteten Berichten an Sn Kurfürstl.
     Dhln Geheimen Kriegs Rathe Lennep, May 23, 1807.
54   Bayr. Hauptstaatsarchiv, Dalberg-Nachlaß, Nr 230, Mayer Amschel to Dalberg, Feb. 20, 1810. Cf.
     Kracauer, *Geschichte der Juden*, vol. II, pp. 414–16; Huber, "Fürstprimas Dalberg"; Arnsberg, *Geschichte
     der Frankfurter Juden*, vol. I, pp. 266ff., 279; Koch, *Grundlagen*, pp. 136f.
55   Bayr. Hauptstaatsarchiv, Dalberg-Nachlaß, Nr 230, Nr 2, Abschrift Schreiben [Dalberg] An H. Rent-
     meister Ossius in Hanau d.d. Aschaffenburg, Feb. 13, 1811; Copia Schreiben an d. Hofagent und Ban-
     quier Rothschild, Feb. 15; Nr 1, unidentifiable official, Hanau, to Dalberg, Sept. 14.
56   Berghoeffer, *Meyer Amschel*, p. 139; Corti, *Rise*, pp. 108, 118f.; Cohen, *Denkmal*, pp. 26f.; Kracauer,
     Geschichte der Juden, vol. II, p. 429.
57   Forstmann, *Bethmann*, p. 215.
58   HSM, Bestand 6b Nr 769, Mayer Amschel, Hamburg, to Knatz, March 29, 1808; Nr 161, Carl, Ham-
     burg, to Knatz, April 15; Nr 171, same to same, May 13; Nr 181, May 24.
59   HSM, Bestand 6b Nr 769, Nr 201, Mayer Amschel, Hamburg, to Knatz, July 1, 1808.
60   HSM, Bestand 6b Nr 769, Nr 22l, Peter Arnoldi [Mayer Amschel] to Johann Weber [Knatz], undated,
     c. Sept., 1808; Nr 24l, "Der Sohn" [Carl], probably to Knatz, Sept. 2; Nr 33l [Carl], Frankfurt, to
     Johann Weber [Knatz], Prague, undated, *c.* Nov.; Nr 26l, Peter Arnold [Mayer Amschel], Frankfurt, to
     Johann Weber [Knatz], Prague, Nov. 4; Nr 25l, Peter Arnoldi [Mayer Amschel], Frankfurt, to Johann
     Weber [Knatz], Prague, Nov. 19; Nr 29l, Peter Arnold [Carl], Hamburg, to Johann Weber [Knatz],
     Prague, March 2, 1809; Nr 30l, Peter Arnold [Carl] to Johan Weber [Knatz], Prague, March 10; Nr 34l,
     Peter Arnoldi [Mayer Amschel], Frankfurt, to Johann Weber [Knatz], Aug. 30, 1810; Nr 35l, Carl,
     Frankfurt, to Knatz, Sept. 17. Cf. Berghoeffer, *Meyer Amschel*, pp. 64ff.; Corti, *Rise*, pp. 70f.;
     Heuberger, *Rothschilds*, pp. 32f.
61   Corti, *Rise*, p. 117.
62   *Ibid.*, pp. 83–5, 109; Bouvier, *Rothschild*, pp. 24–9; Hessen, " 'You did not recommend a fool,' " p. 32.
63   HSM, Bestand 340 Buderus von Carlshausen Nr 7, Elector, Prague, to Buderus, Nov. 18, 1808; HSM,
     Bestand 6b Nr 769, Nr 30l, Peter Arnold [Mayer Amschel] to Johan Weber [Knatz], Prague, March 10,
     1809; HSM, Bestand 6b Nr 646, Auszüge aus erstatteten Berichten an Sn Kurfürstl. Dhln Geheimen
     Kriegs Rathe Lennep, April 4. Cf. Corti, *Rise*, p. 73; Hessen, " 'You did not recommend a fool,' " pp.
     29–33; Heuberger, *Rothschilds*, pp. 30f.
64   Berghoeffer, *Meyer Amschel*, p. 79. See also HSM, Bestand 340 Buderus von Carlshausen Nr 85,
     Buderus to Elector, Sept. 30, 1809; MAR to Buderus, Jan. 7, 1814; Corti, *Rise*, pp. 107–15.
65   Corti, *Rise*, pp. 42, 85.
66   CPHDCM, 637/1/3, Inventarium nach den Handlungs Büchern v. Herrn M.A. Rothschild gezogen,
     May 12, 1807. The total assets of the firm were in excess of 970,000 gulden, 70,000 of which were

bonds of various kinds, and 110,000 of which were loans of other sorts, including a loan to William's son of 10,000 gulden and a bill on Prince George—the Prince Regent—of 127,784 gulden.

67   Corti, *Rise*, pp. 115f.

68   RAL, RFamAD/2, Mayer Amschel to Nathan, undated, *c.* June 1805.

69   RAL, XI/109J/J/43, James, Doncaster, to his nephews, Sept. 13, 1843, fondly recalling the house in Manchester when he had stayed there thirty-five years before.

70   As note 68.

71   RAL, T5/6, Mayer Amschel to Nathan, June 20, 1809.

72   Heuberger and Krohn, *Hinaus aus dem Ghetto*, p. 51.

73   CPHDCM, 637/1/4, Transcript of interrogation of Mayer Amschel and his family, May 10 and 11, 1809.

74   CPHDCM, 637/1/5, Deed sealed by Bürgermeister and Senat of Frankfurt, March 24, 1809. Cf. Berghoeffer, *Meyer Amschel*, p. 18.

75   RAL, RFamFD/3, Gesellschaftsvertrag [between] Mayer Amschel Rothschild, Amschel, Salomon and Carl, Sept. 27, 1810. Cf. Berghoeffer, *Meyer Amschel*, pp. 165ff.; Bouvier, *Rothschild*, pp. 33f.; Bergeron, *Rothschild*, pp. 38–41; Heuberger, *Rothschilds*, p. 51.

76   HSM, Bestand 6b Nr 769, Nr 24l, "Der Sohn" [Carl], probably to Knatz, undated, probably Sept. 1808; HSM, Bestand 6b Nr 659, Nr 4, Mayer Amschel, Frankfurt, to Elector, Feb. 9, 1810; HSM, Bestand 6b Nr 769, Nr 38l, Mayer Amschel to Knatz, Aug. 30. Cf. Cohen, *Denkmal*, p. 34.

77   Berghoeffer, *Meyer Amschel*, p. 146.

78   *Ibid.*, pp. 201ff. Virtually all the 190,000 gulden (apart from sums reserved for Carl's and James's marriage gifts) went to his wife and daughters however.

79   Berghoeffer, *Meyer Amschel*, pp. 145f.

80   Cohen, *Denkmal*, pp. 3f., 27f.

81   Berghoeffer, *Meyer Amschel*, p. 142; Prawer, *Heine*, pp. 361f. See also Heuberger, *Rothschilds*, pp. 14f.

82   Cohen, *Denkmal*, p. 17n.

83   Berghoeffer, *Meyer Amschel*, pp. 140ff.; Kracauer, *Geschichte der Juden*, vol. II, p. 337; Arnsberg, *Geschichte der Frankfurter Juden*, vol. I, pp. 209ff.; Elon, *Meyer Amschel*, pp. 76, 82, 87, 105. According to legend, the school originated when Mayer Amschel heard a poor Jewish boy singing in the street in Marburg: he persuaded Geisenheimer to adopt him as the first pupil in a new school.

84   Liberles, "Dietz's *Stammbuch*," p. xii. The school rapidly evolved into the main Jewish secondary school (*Realschule*) in Frankfurt.

85   Heine, "Ludwig Börne: Eine Denkschrift," in *Sämtliche Schriften*, vol. IV, p. 27, trans. Prawer, *Heine*, pp. 360ff.

86   On the background to Jewish emancipation in Germany in this period, see Katz, *Out of the ghetto* and Sorkin, *Transformation of German Jewry*. See also Rurüp, "Path to legal equality."

87   Backhaus, "Meyer Amschel," pp. 52ff.; Heuberger, *Rothschilds*, pp. 44f.; Elon, *Meyer Amschel*, pp. 103ff.; 147ff.

88   Bayr. Hauptstaatsarchiv, Dalberg-Nachlaß, Nr 230, Mayer Amschel to "Hochwohlgebohrener Herr Geheimer Hoch zu ver Ehrender Herr Geheimer Landes Registrator," Feb. 20, 1810.

89   Kracauer, *Geschichte der Juden*, vol. II, pp. 414–16; Arnsberg, *Geschichte der Frankfurter Juden*, vol. I, pp. 266ff., 279. Mayer Amschel was one of a committee of five set up by the Jewish community to negotiate with Dalberg and the Frankfurt authorities.

90   IfS, Judenschaft, Ugb D 62 No. 36, Vorstand der Judengemeinde in Frankfurt to Hohe Kommission of Senate, Nov. 22, 1811.

91   RAL, T27/5, XI/86/0, Mayer Amschel Rothschild and Salomon to James, Dec. 13, 1811. Cf. Cohen, *Denkmal*, p. 23; Corti, *Rise*, pp. 118f.

92   HSM, Bestand 6b Nr 769, 64l, MAR to Knatz, Prague, Sept. 23, 1812.

93   RAL, T29/273, XI/109/1/5/3, Amschel, Berlin, to Nathan, London, Oct. 11, 1814.

94   RAL, T61/103/2, XI/109/6, Amschel, Frankfurt, to his brothers, March 11, 1817.

95   RAL, XI/109/10/4, Salomon to Nathan, undated, 1818. See Mace, "From Frankfurt Jew," p. 192n.

96   RAL, T33, XI/109/5B/276/1, Amschel, Frankfurt, to James, Salomon and Nathan, Oct. 25, 1816.

97   RAL, T30, XI/109/2/2/170, Amschel, Frankfurt, to Salomon and James, Paris, Nov. 15, 1815.

98   RAL, T27/216, James, Paris, to Salomon and Nathan, March 8, 1817.

99   Barnett, "Diary," pp. 149ff.

100 RAL, XI/109/2/2/149, Salomon, Paris, to Nathan, Oct. 21, 1815.

101 RAL, XI/109/2/2/153, Salomon and James, Paris, to Nathan, London Oct. 25, 1815.

102   RAL, T63/138/2, Salomon and James, Paris, to Nathan, Oct. 22, 1817.
103   RAL, T62/24/1, Carl, Frankfurt, to Salomon and James, May 20, 1817.
104   RAL, T63/46/1, XI/109/8, Salomon and James, Paris, to Nathan, Dec. 17, 1817.
105   RAL, XI/109/9/1/80, Salomon to Nathan, Jan. 14, 1818.
106   RAL, T64/158/2, Salomon, Berlin, to Amschel, Nathan and James, Feb. 24, 1818.
107   RAL, T30, XI/109/2/3, Amschel, Frankfurt, to Nathan, London, Jan. 12, 1815.
108   RAL, XI/109/2/2/182, Salomon, Paris, to Nathan, London, Nov. 13, 1815.
109   RAL, XI/109/2/2/177, Salomon and James, Paris, to Nathan, London, Nov. 22, 1815.
110   CPHDCM, 637/1/7/53–69, Vollständige Abschrift des Societäts-Vertrags . . . Übereinkunft, July 30,
      1836.
111   CPHDCM, 637/1/7/70–2, Anhang, July 30, 1836.
112   Plutarch, *Apophthegmata*, p. 6. Cf. Gray (ed.), *Life and times*, p. 86. Moritz Daniel Oppenheim's 1825
      painting of Scilurus and his sons may well have been commissioned by the Rothschilds.
113   Brockhaus, *Real-Enzyklopädie* (1827), vol. IX, pp. 431–4.
114   Brockhaus, *Real-Encyklopädie* (1836), vol. IX, pp. 432f.
115   CPHDCM, 637/1/309, Amschel, Frankfurt, to his brothers and nephews, Nov. 11, 1841.

THREE   *"The Commanding General" (1813–1815)*

1   RAL, T29/159, XI/109/0/6/11, Salomon, Paris, to Nathan and Salomon Cohen, Aug. 17, 1814.
2   RAL, T5/150, Salomon to Messrs Coudere & Co. and M. P. Brantz, Aug. 8, 1817.
3   Ehrman, *Pitt: Consuming struggle*, p. 258.
4   Sherwig, *Guineas*, p. 232; Corti, *Rise*, p. 134f.
5   Dickson, *Financial revolution*; Brewer, *Sinews*.
6   O'Brien, "Power with profit."
7   In the eighteenth century, the guinea was the principal gold coin used in Britain, though the silver
     shilling (of which sixty-six were coined from the troy pound of silver) was regarded as the monetary
     standard. In 1717 the mint price was set at 21s. = 1 guinea. However, at this time the Mint switched to
     a new coin, the pound sterling (= 20s.), and the price of gold was set by Newton at £3 17s. 10 1/2d.
     This proved to be the first step towards the gold standard: in 1774 silver was effectively demoted when
     it ceased to be legal tender for sums in excess of £25.
8   Kindleberger, *Financial history*, pp. 238f.
9   Pollins, *Economic history of the Jews*, pp. 108f.
10   Chapman, "Establishment," pp. 73ff.
11   Ziegler, *Sixth great power*, pp. 43–58; Kindleberger, *Financial history*, pp. 59ff.; Kynaston, *City*, vol. I, p.
     4f.
12   Buist, *Hope & Co.*, pp. 68f., 227–61.
13   *DNB*; Herries, *Memoirs*.
14   RAL, XI/82/9/1/11, Amschel, Frankfurt, to Nathan, London, July 15, 1814. Cf. Davis, *English Roth-
     schilds*, pp. 32f. His full name was Baron Christian Theophilius de Limburger-Ehrenfels.
15   RAL, T29/6, XI/109/0/1/5, [Limburger?], Paris, to an unnamed Rothschild, probably Nathan, June
     13, 1814.
16   RAL, T37/12, [Herries Papers, Spottiswoode Collection copies], Limburger, Frankfurt, to Herries, Feb.
     16, 1814; RAL, T37/43, Herries to Limburger, March 17.
17   RAL, T37/35, Herries to Sir George Burgmann, Amsterdam, March 17, 1814.
18   RAL, XI/109/0/3/9, Amschel, Frankfurt, to Salomon, June 13, 1814; RAL, XI/109/0/1/27, Carl,
     Frankfurt, to Nathan, June 18.
19   RAL, XI/109/0/1/24, James, Amsterdam, to Nathan, London, June 17, 1814.
20   RAL, T30, XI/109/2/3/16, Carl, Frankfurt, to Nathan, London, Jan. 9, 1815; RAL, XI/109/2/2/122,
     Amschel, Frankfurt, to his brother [Carl?], Oct. 1.
21   RAL, XI/109/2/2/152, Amschel, Frankfurt, to Salomon and James, Oct. 25, 1815. Cf. RAL,
     XI/109/2/2/128, Amschel to Carl and Nathan, Oct. 2.
22   RAL, XI/82/1/1/3, Carl to Salomon and James, undated fragment; RAL, T63/55/1, Frau Limburger to
     Salomon, Dec. 7, 1817; RAL, T63/66/1, Amschel, Frankfurt, to Salomon and James, Dec. 29; RAL,
     T63/67/1, Amschel to Nathan, Dec. 31; T64/281/3, Carl to Nathan and Salomon, March 27, 1818.
     See also RAL, T3/179–86 (purchases on Limburger's account of 3 per cent consols).
23   RAL, XI/109/9/1/88, Carl, Berlin, to his brothers, Jan. 2, 1808.
24   Buxton (ed.), *Memoirs*, pp. 288–90.

25   Capefigue, *Grandes opérations*, vol. II, pp. 348–61; Longford, *Wellington: Years of the sword*, pp. 186, 341.

26   AN, F 7 4255 B, No 1, Traduction d'une lettre écrite en anglais par J. M. Rothschild à son frère à Londres [i.e. Nathan], March 28, 1812; No 2, James to Nathan, April 6; same to same, April 20. Cf. Corti, *Rise*, p. 136.

27   RAL, T27/64, Salomon to James, Dunkirk, Dec. 6, 1811; RAL, T27/66, Mayer Amschel, Frankfurt, to James, Dec. 13; T5/18, James to Nathan, Feb. 4, 1812.

28   RAL, T27/63, Amschel, Frankfurt, to James, June 17, 1811; RAL, T27/60, same to same, June 23; RAL, T27/15, XI/82/10/8, unidentified author to Nathan, Oct. 15. See also RAL, T(a)38, Davidson to Nathan, undated, *c.* Jan. 28, 1811.

29   RAL, T5/26, James, Paris, to Nathan, London, Aug. 22, 1812; RAL, T3/41, R. Cullen, Folkestone, to Nathan, April 12, 1813. See also letters from Cullen, Helvoetsluys, Jan. 26 and Feb. 6, 1814.

30   RAL, T29/25, XI/109/0/1/14, Salomon to Nathan, London, May 4, 1814.

31   RAL, T5/29, Braun, [James's clerk in] Paris, to James, London, Sept. 13, 1813. Cf. Wolf, "Rothschildiana," pp. 266f.

32   RAL, T2/98, M. A. Arnotty [Mayer Amschel?] to "Dear friend" [Nathan?], Oct. 9, 1811.

33   RAL, T29/13, Gelche [Caroline], Frankfurt, to her husband Salomon, March 23, 1814.

34   Corti, *Rise*, p. 135; Ehrenberg, *Große Vermögen*, pp. 59f.; Bouvier, *Rothschild*, pp. 36–40; Kindleberger, *Financial History*, p. 238f.; Heuberger, *Rothschilds*, p. 48f. But see also Gille, *Maison Rothschild*, vol. I, pp. 45–55. For evidence of Rothschild dealings with Maltese houses at this times see RAL, T4/44, 46, 47, 48, 49, letters from Ross, Wiggles & Co., Malta, Feb. 15, 1812, and Reimann & Meyer, Malta, May 23; RAL, T3/41, Castinet, Boulogne, to Nathan, London, May 23.

35   Kindleberger, *Financial history*, pp. 236ff. See also Neal, *Financial Capitalism*, pp. 180–90.

36   *Ibid.*, pp. 100f.; Corti, *Rise*, pp. 132–9; Gille, *Maison Rothschild*, vol. I, pp. 46f.; Bouvier, *Rothschilds*, pp. 36–40. Cf. AN, F 7 4255 B, French police report on the Rothschilds, 1814.

37   RAL, T37/8, Vansittart to Herries, Jan. 11, 1814; RAL, T37/50, Herries to Nathan, Jan. 11. Cf. Rothschild, *Shadow*, pp. 20f.; Sherwig, *Guineas*, p. 329; Chapman, "Establishment," pp. 74f.

38   RAL, T37/39, Herries to Vansittart, March 27, 1814.

39   RAL, T37/219, Herries to Nathan, Jan. 28, 1814.

40   RAL, T27/70, XI/38/81a/4, Davidson to Nathan, Jan. 20, 1814; RAL, T27/71, XI/38/81a/5, same to same, Jan. 25; RAL, T27/73, XI/38/81a/6, Jan. 28; RAL, T3/45, Feb. 1; RAL, T27/75, XI/35/81a/7, Feb. 1; RAL, T3/45, Feb. 22.

41   RAL, T27/76, XI/35/81a/9, Davidson to Nathan, Feb. 25, 1814.

42   RAL, T37/35, Herries to Sir George Burgmann, Amsterdam, March 17, 1814. The operation effectively ended in April, when Herries set off for Paris for the peace talks following the French surrender: RAL, XI/82/7/45, Nathan, London, to James, Amsterdam, April 29.

43   Rothschild, *Shadow*, pp. 16f.

44   RAL, T3/46, Drummond, Commissary-in-Chief's office, to Nathan, London, April 14, 1814; RAL, XI/82/7/38, Nathan to James, Amsterdam, April 15.

45   RAL, T3/48, Paymaster General Dunmore, Brussels, to MAR, July 15, 1814; RAL, T30, 109/2/3, James, Paris, to Nathan, London, undated, *c.* Feb. 1815.

46   RAL, T 37/52, Herries to Burgmann, Amsterdam, April 19, 1814.

47   Davis, *English Rothschilds*, pp. 30f.; Chapman, "Establishment," pp. 74f.

48   Neal, *Financial Capitalism*, pp. 180–90. This was what Walter Boyd had done in the 1790s, before going bankrupt in 1799: Cope, *Walter Boyd*, p. 3.

49   RAL, T37/56, Herries to Drummond, Paris, May 15, 1814. See also RAL, T27/11, Salomon to Nathan, London, Nov. 18, where Rothschild advances to the British government are estimated at £1,000,000.

50   Ehrenberg, *Große Vermögen*, pp. 61f.; Gille, *Maison Rothschild*, vol. I, pp. 53–5.

51   RAL, T37/73, Herries, Amsterdam, to Drummond, June 17, 1814.

52   Nicolson, *Congress of Vienna*, p. 216.

53   Buist, *Hope & Co.*, pp. 68f., 227–65. Cf. RAL, T17/133, XI/109/14 [Details of agreement between Castlereagh and Lieven], Sept. 18, 1813.

54   RAL, T29/128, XI/109/0/1/17, James, Amsterdam, to Nathan, London, May 20, 1814; RAL, T4/71, Braun, Paris, to James and Salomon, Amsterdam, May 21.

55   RAL, XI/109/0/1/22, James, Amsterdam, to Nathan, London, June 7, 1814; RAL, T34 82/7, NMR 61, Nathan to James, June 7; RAL, XI/109/0/1/26, James to Nathan, London, June 14; RAL, T37/71,

Herries, Amsterdam, to Salomon, June 17; RAL, XI/109/0/1/30, Davidson, Amsterdam, to Nathan, June 18.

56   RAL, T37/72, Herries, Amsterdam, to Drummond, June 17, 1814; RAL, XI/109/0/1/25, Carl, Frankfurt, to James, Amsterdam, June 18.
57   RAL, XI/109/0/1/24, James, Amsterdam, to Nathan, London, June 17, 1814; RAL, XI/109/0/2/6, James, Davidson and Salomon, Amsterdam, to Nathan, June 20.
58   RAL, XI/82/1/1/2, Carl, Frankfurt, to Salomon, undated, *c.* 1814.
59   RAL, XI/109/0/1/24, James, Amsterdam, to Nathan, London, June 17, 1814; RAL, XI/109/0/2/6, James, Davidson and Salomon, Amsterdam, to Nathan, June 20.
60   RAL, XI/109/0/2/12, James, Amsterdam, to Nathan, London, June 24, 1814; RAL, XI/109/0/2/14, Carl, Frankfurt, to James, June 28. Six million thalers still remained to be paid from Britain to Russia.
61   RAL, T29/129, XI/109/0/5/6, Salomon, Paris, to Nathan, London, Aug. 7, 1814.
62   RAL, T29/188, XI/109/0/8/4, James, Amsterdam, to Nathan, London, Aug. 26, 1814.
63   RAL, T29/198, XI/109/0/8/14, Carl, Frankfurt, to James, Aug. 31, 1814.
64   RAL, XI/109/0/2/7, Davidson, Amsterdam, to Nathan, London, June 21, 1814.
65   RAL, XI/82/9/1/11, Amschel, Frankfurt, to Nathan, London, July 15, 1814.
66   RAL, T29/188, XI/109/0/8/4, James, Amsterdam, to Nathan, London, Aug. 26, 1814; RAL, T29/217, XI/109/1/1/17, same to same, Sept. 9.
67   RAL, T30, XI/109/2/3/22, James, Schwerin, to Nathan, Salomon and Davidson, Feb. 18, 1815.
68   Corti, *Rise*, p. 167.
69   HSM, Bestand 5 (Hess. Geheimer Rat), Nr 13702, Nr 24, Buderus, Kassel, to Elector, May 7, 1814; Nrn 39–41, Weiterer unterthänigster Bericht der Regierung zu Hanau, den Durchmarsch Kaiserlich Russischer Armeecorps durch das Fürstenthum Hanau betr., May 19; Nr 42, Buderus, Kassel, Resolut, May 4; Nr 47, Unterthänigster Bericht der Regierung zu Hanau, die Rückzahlung des von den Hof-Banquiers Rothschild zu Frankfurt vorgeschossenen Capitals . . . betreffend, Nov. 27; Nr 51, Extract General Kriegs-Protocolli d.d. Kassel, Dec. 2; Nr 53, Unterthänigster Bericht vom geheimen Rathe und Kammerpräsidenten von Carlshausen . . . , Dec. 11; Nrn 54f., MAR to Buderus, Dec. 12.
70   RAL, XI/109/0/1/22, James, Amsterdam, to Nathan, London, June 7, 1814; RAL, T28/27, Amschel, Frankfurt, to Carl, undated, *c.* July; RAL, T29/133, XI/109/0/5/10, Amschel, Berlin, to Nathan, Aug. 8.
71   RAL, XI/109/0/1/26, James, Amsterdam, to Nathan, London, June 14, 1814.
72   RAL, T29/367(b), James, Berlin, to Salomon, Nathan and Davidson, Dec. 24, 1814.
73   RAL, XI/109/2/2/46, James to Davidson, June 27; RAL, T29/139, XI/109/0/5/15, Amschel, Berlin, to James, Aug. 9; RAL, T29/186, XI/109/0/8/2, Amschel to Nathan, London, Aug. 26; RAL, T5/7A, Bülow to Herries, Sept. 22; RAL, T3/46, Drummond to Nathan, Nov. 1; RAL, T29/308, XI/109/7/1, James, Berlin, to Salomon, Nathan and Davidson, Nov. 3; RAL, T5/43, 44, Amschel to Salomon, Dec. 9; RAL, T29/362, Amschel to Nathan and Carl, Dec. 21; RAL, T30, XI/109/2/3/7/1, James to Salomon, Nathan and Davidson, Jan. 3, 1815; RAL, T30, XI/109/2/3/13/1, same to same, Jan. 5.
74   See also RAL, XI/109/0/2/3, Carl, Frankfurt, to Nathan, London, June 20, 1814.
75   Corti, *Rise*, pp. 143f.
76   *Ibid.*, pp.152–7. In these negotiations, Limburger seems to have acted as a kind of intermediary, presumably adding a veneer of aristocratic respectability to the Rothschild bid.
77   *Ibid.*, pp.162–6. The business was given to the Bethmann Brothers, apparently on worse terms than the Rothschilds had offered—a reflection of the continuing preference in Vienna for established banks. Cf. Gille, *Maison Rothschild* vol. I, pp. 55f.; Bouvier, *Rothschilds*, pp. 56ff.
78   RAL, T27/60, Amschel, Frankfurt, to James, June 23, 1811; AN, F 7 4255 B, No. 1, Traduction d'une lettre . . . , March 28, 1812; No. 2, same to same, April 6; No. 4, April 20.
79   RAL, T3/329, James, Paris, to Nathan, London, Aug. 17, 1812.
80   RAL, T37/39, Herries to Vansittart, March 27, 1814. Cf. Ehrenberg, *Große Vermögen*, p. 67; Corti, *Rise*, pp. 156f.
81   RAL, T29/17, Amschel to Salomon, Nathan and James, April 8, 1814.
82   RAL, XI/109/0/1/23, Carl, Frankfurt, to Salomon, June 12, 1814. See also RAL, T29/37, Carl to James, Paris, June 18; RAL, XI/109/0/2/2, Carl to Nathan, June 19.
83   RAL, T29/128, XI/109/0/5/5, James, Amsterdam, to Nathan, London, Aug. 5, 1814.
84   RAL, T29/25, XI/109/0/1/14, Salomon to Nathan, London, May 4, 1814.
85   RAL, T34 82/7, NMR 59, Nathan, London, to James, Amsterdam, June 3, 1814; RAL, T34 82/7, NMR 60, same to same, June 4; RAL, XI/109/0/1/22, James to Nathan, London, June 7.

86 RAL, XI/109/0/2/6, James, Davidson and Salomon, Amsterdam, to Nathan, London, June 20, 1814.
87 RAL, T29/117, XI/109/0/4/38, Carl, Frankfurt, to James, Amsterdam, July 30, 1814. See also RAL, T29/129, XI/109/0/5/6, Salomon, Paris, to Nathan, London, Aug. 7.
88 RAL, T29/154, XI/109/0/6/6, James, Amsterdam, to Nathan, London, Aug. 14, 1814. See also RAL, T29/156, XI/109/0/6/8, unidentified Rothschild to Gervais, undated, *c.* mid-Aug.; RAL, T29/167, XI/109/0/7/7, Davidson to Nathan, Aug. 19; RAL, T29/163, XI/109/0/7/3, James to Nathan, Aug. 19; RAL, T29/188, XI/109/0/8/4, same to same, Aug. 26; RAL, T29/217, XI/109/1/1/17, Sept. 9.
89 RAL, XI/109/0/1/28, Amschel, Frankfurt, to Salomon, June 17, 1814.
90 RAL, XI/109/0/2/9, Carl, Frankfurt, to Salomon and James, June 2, 1814; RAL, T29/113, I/109/0/4/34, Amschel, Frankfurt, to Nathan and Salomon, London, July 24.
91 RAL, XI/109/0/2/2, Carl, Frankfurt, to Nathan, London, June 19, 1814.
92 RAL, T29/77, XI/109/0/3/20, James, Paris, to Nathan, London, July 8, 1814; RAL, T29/111, XI/109/0/4/32, Davidson, Amsterdam, to Nathan and Salomon, July 22; RAL, T29/110; XI/109/0/4/31, James, Amsterdam, to Nathan and Salomon, July 22; RAL, T29/148, XI/109/0/6/1, Carl, Frankfurt, to James and Davidson, Aug. 12.
93 RAL, T29/135, XI/109/0/5/12, Davidson, Amsterdam, to Nathan, London, Aug. 9, 1814; RAL, T29/139, XI/109/0/5/15, Amschel, Berlin, to James, Aug. 9; RAL, T29/145, XI/109/0/5/19, Amschel, Berlin, to Nathan, Aug. 10; RAL, T29/147, XI/109/0/5/1, same to same, London, Aug. 11; RAL, T29/172, XI/109/0/7/12, Amschel to James and Davidson, Aug. 21; RAL, T29/186, XI/109/0/8/2, Amschel to Nathan, Aug. 26.
94 RAL, T29/162, XI/109/0/7/2, Carl, Frankfurt, to Amschel, Berlin, Aug. 19, 1814.
95 RAL, XI/109/0/1/22, James, Amsterdam, to Nathan, London, June 7, 1814.
96 RAL, XI/109/0/2/1, Amschel, Frankfurt, to Nathan, London, June 19, 1814; RAL, XI/109/0/2/5, Amschel to Salomon, June 20. There appears to have been a restriction which prevented mail being collected in the morning; but letters could be seen, if not opened, in the morning: I am grateful to Lionel de Rothschild for this point.
97 RAL, T29/98, XI/109/0/4/18, Amschel, Frankfurt, to James, Amsterdam, July 18, 1814; RAL, T29/99, XI/109/0/4/19, Carl, Frankfurt, to James, July 18; RAL, T29/101, XI/109/0/4/21, Carl to Nathan, London, July 18.
98 RAL, T29/179, XI/109/0/7/19, James, Amsterdam, to Nathan, London, Aug. 2, 1814; RAL, T29/207, XI/109/1/1/7, Carl, Frankfurt, to James and Davidson, Aug. 4; RAL, T29/137, XI/109/0/5/13, Meyer Beyfus, Amsterdam, to Nathan, Aug. 9; RAL, T29/138, XI/109/0/5/14, James to Nathan, Aug. 9.
99 RAL, T29/159, XI/109/0/6/11, Salomon, Paris, to Nathan, London, Aug. 17, 1814. See also RAL, T29/161, XI/109/0/7/1, Amschel to James and Nathan, Aug. 19.
100 RAL, T29/181, XI/109/0/8/7, Salomon to Nathan, Aug. 31, 1814.
101 RAL, T29/159, XI/109/0/6/9, Carl, Frankfurt, to James, Aug. 16, 1814.
102 RAL, T29/158, XI/109/0/6/10, Amschel, Berlin, to Nathan, London, Aug. 17, 1814.
103 RAL, T29/189, XI/109/0/8/5, Amschel, Berlin, to Salomon, Aug. 26, 1814.
104 RAL, T29/335, XI/109/1/2/15, Salomon, Amsterdam, to Salomon Cohen, London, Sept. 20, 1814; RAL, T29/280, XI/109/1/5/10, Salomon to Nathan, London, Oct. 14. See also RAL, T30, XI/109/2/3/14/1, same to same, Jan. 6, 1815.
105 RAL, T27/20, James to Nathan, London, Sept. 5, 1814; RAL, T29/290, XI/109/1/5/10, Carl, Frankfurt, to James, Oct. 20.
106 RAL, T5/61, Nathan, London, to James, Nov. 18, 1814. See also RAL, T29/259, XI/109/1/4/6, Carl to Amschel, Oct. 3; RAL, T29/274, XI/109/1/5/4, James, Amsterdam, to Nathan, Oct. 11; RAL, T29/281, XI/109/1/5/11, Amschel, Berlin, to his mother and Carl, Frankfurt, Oct. 17; RAL, T24/107, Amschel to Nathan, Oct. 24.
107 RAL, T29/316, XI/109/1/7/9, James, Hamburg, to Amschel, Nov. 11, 1814; RAL, T30, XI/109/2/3/7/1, James, Berlin, to Salomon, Nathan and Davidson, London, Jan. 3, 1815; RAL, T30, XI/109/2/3/19/1, James to Nathan, Jan. 7. It was this rally which increased the profit margin on the Prussian subsidy deal from zero to a respectable 3 per cent: RAL, T29/340, XI/109/1/9/33, James, Hamburg, to Carl, Dec. 7; RAL, T27/112, Amschel to Nathan, Dec. 22.
108 RAL, T/30, XI/109/2/3/33/1, James, Paris, to Nathan, London, Feb. 14, 1815.
109 Buist, *Hope & Co.*, pp. 227–61.
110 RAL, RFamC/30/1, Moses and Judith Montefiore, Paris, to Nathan, London, March 9, 1814. Cf. Loewe (ed.), *Montefiore diaries*, vol. I, pp. 19ff.
111 RAL, T29/30, XI/109/0/1/19, Davidson, Amsterdam, to Nathan, London, May 20, 1814; RAL,

XI/109/0/1/22, James, Amsterdam, to Nathan, June 7; RAL, XI/109/0/2/8, Amschel, Frankfurt, to Nathan, June 21.

112   RAL, T29/176, XI/109/0/7/16, Amschel to Salomon, Aug. 22, 1814.

113   RAL, XI/109/2/1/40, Beyfus, Frankfurt, to Nathan, London, March 7, 1815; RAL, XI/109/2/1/42, Amschel to his brothers, March 7.

114   Braudel and Labrousse, *Histoire économique*, vol. III, pp. 356–64.

115   Corti, *Rise*, p. 161; Nicolle, *Waterloo*, pp. 29–31. See RAL, T29/188, XI/109/0/8/4, James, Amsterdam, to Nathan, London, Aug. 26, 1814; RAL, T29/186, XI/109/0/8/2, Amschel, Berlin, to Nathan, London, Aug. 26; RAL, T5/42, Amschel, Berlin, to James, Amsterdam, Oct. 29.

116   See the introduction for a full discussion of the Waterloo myth.

117   Wolf, "Rothschildiana," pp. 281ff.; Rothschild, *Shadow*, pp. 37ff.; Chapman, "Establishment," p. 79.

118   RAL, XI/109/2/1/42, Amschel to his brothers, undated but almost certainly early March 1815.

119   RAL, T5/79, Nathan, London, to Salomon, Amsterdam, March 3, 1815.

120   RAL, T5/123, James, Paris, to Nathan and Salomon, March 15, 1815.

121   RAL, T5/83, Nathan to James, Hamburg, April 7, 1815. Cf. Green, *New world of gold*, p. xiii.

122   RAL, T46/4, T5/117, James, Hamburg, to Nathan, March 17, 1815; RAL, T5/80, Nathan to Salomon, Amsterdam, March 23; RAL, T34/82/7, NMR 157, Nathan to James, March 31.

123   Longford, *Wellington: Years of the sword*, p. 395; Rothschild, *Shadow*, pp. 22f.; Gray (ed.), *Life and times*, p. 99.

124   RAL, T5/82, Nathan to James, April 7, 1815; RAL, T34/82/7, NMR 162, Nathan to Carl, April 7; RAL, T34, NMR 167, Nathan, London, to James, Hamburg, April 14; RAL, T37/89, Memorandum of a conference at Cadogan Place between Herries and Nathan, April 4; RAL, T37/111, Herries Copy Book, 1815. Cf. Chapman, "Establishment," p. 74f.; Davis, *English Rothschilds*, p. 32.

125   RAL, T5/89, Nathan, London to Carl, Amsterdam, May 2, 1815; RAL, T37/105, Herries to Nathan, May 16; RAL, T32/106, same to same, May 22; RAL, T5/94, Nathan, London, to James, Hamburg, May 23; RAL, T37/108, Herries to Rothschild, June 2.

126   Herries later stated that the total sum transferred by "a single and confidential agency" in 1814 and 1815 was £18 million: Ehrenberg, *Große Vermögen*, p. 66; Corti, *Rise*, pp. 173–7.

127   RAL, T5/84, Nathan, London to James, Hamburg, April 11, 1815; RAL, T5/86, Nathan to Carl, Amsterdam, April 14.

128   RAL, T5/87, Nathan, London, to James, Hamburg, April 18, 1815; RAL, T5/88, same to same, April 25. James was paying for his purchases by drawing on London.

129   RAL, T3/416, Van der Velde, Amsterdam, to Carl, April 28, 1815; RAL, T5/90, Nathan, London, to James, Hamburg, May 5.

130   RAL, T5/91, Nathan, London, to James, Hamburg, May 9, 1815.

131   RAL, T3/48, Davidson, Hamburg, to Benjamin Cohen, London, May 16, 1815. Cf. RAL, T5/92, Nathan, London, to James, Hamburg, May 12.

132   RAL, XI/109/2/1/45, Salomon, Amsterdam, to Nathan, May 19, 1815; RAL, T5/67, James, Paris, to Nathan and Salomon, May 30; RAL, T5/97, Nathan, London, to Carl, Amsterdam, June 13.

133   Somewhat different accounts in Wolf, "Rothschildiana," pp. 281ff.; Rothschild, *Shadow*, p. 31; Longford, *Wellington: Pillar of state*, pp. 7f. See also Corti, *Rise*, p. 137; Cowles, *Rothschilds*, pp. 47ff. and Colby, "Waterloo dispatch," p. 92. The bulletins Nathan received have not been preserved, though a letter confirming the news from a Dutch source based just six miles from the battlefield survives: RAL, T3/41, Van der Velde to Carl, June 19, 1815.

134   RAL, T5/98, Nathan, London, to Carl, Amsterdam, June 29, 1815.

135   See e.g. RAL, T3/5, Amburger & Son, St Petersburg, to NMR, June 22, 1815; RAL, T5/100, Nathan, London, to Carl, Amsterdam, June 30.

136   RAL, T3/416, Van der Velde to Carl, Amsterdam, June 25, 1815; RAL, T3/338, John Roworth, Mons, to Nathan, London, June 25; RAL, T3/339, same to same, London, July 6; RAL, T3/341, XI/112/5, Roworth to NMR, London, July 27. These letters make it unlikely that, as has sometimes been suggested, Roworth was the courier who brought the first news of Waterloo to Nathan.

137   RAL, XI/109/2/2/67, Carl, Amsterdam, to Nathan, London, Sept. 12, 1815. See also RAL, T5/103, Nathan, London to Carl, Amsterdam, July 21; RAL, T30, XI/109/2/3/28, Salomon, Paris, to Nathan, undated, *c.* Sept. For attempts to continue the business see RAL, T3/340, XI/112/51, Roworth to Nathan, London, July 25; RAL, T3/341, XI/112/5, same to same, July 27; RAL, XI/109/2/1/53, Carl, Amsterdam, to his brother, Sept. 6; RAL, XI/109/2/2/65, Carl to his brothers [Salomon and James], Sept. 11.

138 RAL, T37/174, Drummond, Paris, to Herries, Jan. 27, 1816; RAL, T37/173, James, Paris, to Drummond, Jan. 27; RAL, T37/175, Drummond to Herries, Jan. 29.

139 Characteristically, Nathan, who had intended to float as much as £3 million of these bills, blamed Carl for the Amsterdam market's lack of interest. Details in RAL, T5/107, Nathan, London, to Carl, Amsterdam, Sept. 8, 1815; RAL, XI/109/2/1/57, Carl to Nathan, Sept. 8; RAL, XI/109/2/1/59, Carl to Amschel, Salomon and James, Sept. 9; RAL, XI/109/2/1/63, Salomon, Paris, to Nathan, Sept. 10; RAL, XI/109/2/1/61, James, Paris, to Nathan, Sept. 10; RAL, XI/109/2/1/64, Salomon to Nathan, Sept. 10; RAL, XI/109/2/2/69, Carl to [Nathan?], undated, c. Sept.; RAL, XI/109/2/2/66, Carl to Salomon and James, Sept. 12; RAL, XI/109/2/2/67, Carl to Nathan, Sept. 12; RAL, XI/109/2/2/72, Salomon and James to Nathan, Sept. 13; RAL, XI/109/2/2/76, Amschel, Frankfurt, to Carl, Sept. 14; RAL, XI/109/2/2/95, Carl to Salomon and James, Sept. 20; RAL, XI/109/2/2/98, Carl to Davidson, London, Sept. 22; RAL, XI/109/2/2/108, Carl to Salomon and James, Sept. 25; RAL, XI/109/2/2/112, Carl to Nathan and Davidson, Sept. 26; RAL, XI/109/2/2/118, Carl to Nathan, Sept. 29; RAL, XI/109/2/2/123, Salomon to Nathan, Oct. 2; RAL, XI/109/2/2/124, James to Nathan, Oct. 2; RAL, XI/109/2/2/128, Amschel to Carl and Nathan, Oct. 2; RAL, XI/109/2/2/126, Carl to Nathan, Oct. 3; RAL, XI/109/2/2/130, James to Nathan, Oct. 4; RAL, XI/109/2/2/129, Salomon to Nathan, Oct. 4; RAL, XI/109/2/2/144, Carl to Nathan, Oct. 17; RAL, XI/109/2/2/150, same to same, Oct. 21; RAL, XI/109/2/2/152, Amschel to Salomon and James, Oct. 25.

140 RAL, T30, XI/109/2/3/46, James, Berlin, to Davidson, London, June 27, 1815; RAL, T5/120, James to Nathan, London, June 27; RAL, T3, XI/109/2/3, Davidson, Hamburg, to Carl, Amsterdam, July 7.

141 Thüringisches Hauptstaatsarchiv Weimar, C 2247c und d (B 113/93), Ernst August von Gersdorff, undated report, probably late June 1815. Previously, Gersdorff reported, the Rothschilds had calculated the exchange rate "à la Juifs"; now "the sinner" could be expected to "repent" and offer the London rate on the day of payment. Cf. Mecklenburgisches Landeshauptsarchiv Schwerin, Pertinanzbestand Acta Externa Nr 111, Oertzen to Grand Duke, Sept. 20, 1815; Oertzen, Paris, to Minister President, Mecklenburg-Schwerin, Dec. 8.

142 RAL, T5/101, Nathan, London, to Carl, Amsterdam, July 7, 1815; Mecklenburgisches Landeshauptsarchiv Schwerin, Pertinanzbestand Acta Externa Nr 111, Auszug aus dem Oertzenschen Berichte nr 39 aus Paris, Sept. 25.

143 RAL, T3/341,XI/112/5, Roworth to Nathan, London, July 27, 1815.

144 Rothschild, Shadow, pp. 37ff.

145 RAL, XI/109/2/2/73, Carl, Amsterdam, to Nathan, Sept. 13, 1815; RAL, XI/109/2/2/76, Amschel, Frankfurt, to Carl, Sept. 14; RAL, T30, XI/109/2/2/113, same to same, Sept. 26.

146 RAL, T34/89/7, NMR 131, Draft of a letter from Nathan, London, to Salomon, Paris, undated, c. Oct. 1815. See also RAL, XI/109/2/2/239, Davidson to Nathan, Dec. 23.

147 RAL, XI/109/2/2/149, Salomon, Paris, to Nathan, London, Oct. 21, 1815; RAL, XI/109/2/2/153, Salomon and James to Nathan, undated, c. Oct.; RAL, XI/109/2/2/156, Salomon to Nathan, Oct. 29; RAL, XI/109/2/2/230, James to Nathan, Dec. 18; RAL, T31/53/1, XI/109/4, Salomon, Frankfurt, to Nathan and James, Feb. 2, 1816.

148 Davis, English Rothschilds, pp. 34f.; Rothschild, Shadow, pp. 22f.

149 See e.g. Mecklenburgisches Landeshauptsarchiv Schwerin, Pertinanzbestand Acta Externa Nr 111, Oertzen to Grosherzog, Aug. 16, 1815; RAL, XI/109/2/1/60, Salomon, Paris, to Nathan, London, Sept. 9; RAL, XI/109/2/2/83, Amschel to Salomon and James, Sept. 17.

150 RAL, XI/109/2/2/149, Salomon, Paris, to Nathan, London, Oct. 21, 1815; RAL, XI/109/2/2/156, same to same, Oct. 29. See also RAL, T30, XI/109/2/3/50, Amschel, Frankfurt, to Salomon and James, undated, 1815; RAL, Cole Autographs, vol. 24, U1C/111, Nathan, London, to Latham Rice & Co., Sept. 13.

151 RAL, XI/109/2/2/99, James, Paris, to Nathan, London, Sept. 22, 1815; RAL, XI/109/2/2/102, Salomon, Paris, to Nathan, Sept. 23; RAL, XI/109/2/2/107, James to Nathan, Sept. 25; RAL, XI/109/2/2/109, Salomon to Nathan, Sept. 25.

152 RAL, XI/109/2/1/53, Carl, Amsterdam, to his brother, Sept. 6, 1815; RAL, T30, XI/109/2/2/160, Amschel, Frankfurt, to Salomon and James, Nov. 3. Cf. Corti, Rise, pp. 179–82, 192.

153 Thüringisches Hauptstaatsarchiv Weimar, C 2247c und d (B 113/93), Protokoll Nr 12, Gersdorff report, Sept. 16, 1815.

154 RAL, XI/109/2/1/55, Amschel to his brother, Sept. 8, 1815; RAL, XI/109/2/2/70, Amschel to his brothers, Sept. 12.

155 RAL, XI/109/2/1/63, Salomon, Paris, to Nathan, London, Sept. 10, 1815; RAL, XI/109/2/1/64,

Salomon to Nathan, Sept. 10; RAL, XI/109/2/2/76, Amschel, Frankfurt, to Carl, Amsterdam, Sept. 14; RAL, XI/109/2/2/85, Salomon to Nathan, Sept. 18.

156   CPHDCM, 637/1/6/5, Articles of Partnership between Messrs Rothschild, March 21, 1815. Cf. Gille, *Maison Rothschild*, vol. I, pp. 447f. It is not entirely clear from this document what the total value of the firm's capital was. The preamble states it to be around £500,000, but the stated shares amount to just £136,000. From comments made in correspondence in late 1815, the former figure seems more probable, though it may include valuations of real estate as well as more liquid capital. See RAL, XI/109/2/2/124, James, Paris, to Nathan, London, Oct. 2, 1815; RAL, XI/109/2/2/126, Carl, Amsterdam, to Nathan, Oct. 3.

157   RAL, T31/194/3, XI/109/4, Amschel, Frankfurt, to Salomon and James, May 5, 1816; RAL, T32/52/1, XI/109/5A, James, Paris, to Nathan, Salomon and Davidson, July 20; RAL, T32/73/1, XI/109/5A, Amschel, Berlin, to Salomon and Nathan, July 27; RAL, T32/80/1, XI/109/5A, James, Paris, to [Nathan?], July 30; RAL, T32/79/1, XI/109/5A, Amschel to Carl, Frankfurt, July 30; RAL, T32/88/2, XI/109/5A, Carl to Nathan and Salomon, Aug. 1; RAL, XI/82/9/1/70, Amschel, Frankfurt, to Nathan and Salomon, Dec. 12.

158   CPHDCM, 637/1/6/7/7–14, Articles of Partnership, June 2, 1818.

159   RAL, XI/109/0/2/13, Carl, Frankfurt, to James, Amsterdam, June 24, 1814; RAL, XI/109/0/3/7, Carl to Salomon, Amsterdam, June 30.

160   RAL, XI/109/0/3/1, Amschel, Frankfurt, to his brothers, June 27, 1814.

161   RAL, T29/173, XI/109/0/7/13, Amschel to James, Aug. 22, 1814; RAL, T29/181, XI/109/0/8/7, Salomon to Nathan, London, Aug. 31.

162   RAL, T30, XI/109/2/3/16, Carl, Frankfurt, to Nathan, London, Jan. 9, 1815.

163   RAL, XI/109/2/1/60, Salomon, Paris, to Nathan, London, Sept. 9, 1815; RAL, XI/109/2/2/86, Amschel, Frankfurt, to his brothers, Sept. 18; RAL, XI/109/2/2/94, Salomon to Nathan, Sept. 20.

164   RAL, XI/109/2/2/97, Amschel to his brothers, Sept. 21, 1815; RAL, XI/109/2/2/115, same to same, Sept. 28; RAL, XI/109/2/2/116, Amschel to Carl and Nathan, Sept. 28; RAL, XI/109/2/2/120, James and Salomon to Nathan, undated, *c.* Sept.; RAL, XI/109/2/2/119, Salomon to Nathan, Sept. 30; RAL, XI/109/2/1/58, same to same, undated fragment, *c.* Oct.

165   RAL, XI/109/2/2/129, Salomon, Paris, to Nathan, London, Oct. 4, 1815; RAL, T30, XI/109/2/2/167, Salomon and James to Nathan, Nov. 11; RAL, XI/109/2/2/175, Carl, Amsterdam, to Nathan, Nov. 20.

166   RAL, T30, XI/109/2/2/160, Amschel, Frankfurt, to Salomon and James, Nov. 3, 1815.

167   RAL, T31, XI/109/4/1/7, Amschel, Frankfurt, to Nathan, London, Jan. 5, 1816; RAL, T31/87/2, XI/109/4, Amschel to James, Paris, Feb. 1.

168   RAL, T5/139, Amschel to [James?], Jan. 21, 1816; RAL, T31/87/2, XI/109/4, same to same, Feb. 1.

169   RAL, XI/82/9/1/44, Amschel, Frankfurt, to James, Feb. 16, 1816. See also RAL, T31/85/2, XI/109/4, Amschel to Nathan, Feb. 25; RAL, XI/82/9/1/43, same to same, May 2.

170   RAL, XI/82/7, Nathan, London, to James, Amsterdam, May 10, 1814; RAL, T37/84, Herries to Nathan, Nov. 12; RAL, T37/24, Alexander Baring to Herries, Nov. 16.

171   RAL, T29/73, XI/109/0/3/16, Nathan, London, to Salomon, Carl and James, July 3, 1814; RAL, T34/82/7, NMR 73, Nathan to Davidson, Amsterdam, July 12; RAL, T30, XI/109/2/3/7, James, Berlin, to Salomon, Nathan and Davidson, Jan. 1, 1815; RAL, XI/109/2/1/52, Carl, Amsterdam, to Salomon and James, Sept. 4; RAL, XI/109/2/2/104, James to Nathan, Sept. 23; RAL, XI/109/2/2/134, Salomon and James to Nathan, Oct. 7; RAL, XI/109/2/2/168, Carl to his brothers, Nov. 11; RAL, T37/119, Herries, London, to James, Nov. 29; RAL, XI/109/2/2/227, Salomon and James to Nathan, Dec. 16.

172   RAL, XI/109/2/2/205, Salomon, Paris, to Nathan and Davidson, London, Dec. 5, 1815; RAL, XI/109/2/2/230, James, Paris, to Nathan, Dec. 18.

173   RAL, T31/1/5, Nathan to Amschel, Carl and James, Jan. 2, 1816.

174   RAL, T37/178, Drummond, Paris, to Herries, Feb. 15, 1816.

175   RAL, T31/100/2, XI/109/4, James, Paris, to Nathan, London, March 9, 1816; RAL, T31/146/3, XI/109/4, same to same, March 30.

176   RAL, XI/82/9/1/39, Amschel, Frankfurt, to James, Jan. 19, 1816.

177   RAL, T31/89/2, XI/109/4, James, Paris, to Nathan, March 2, 1816; RAL, T32/49/1, XI/109/5A, Amschel, Berlin, to Carl, July 19; RAL, T33/22, XI/109/5B, James to Nathan, Oct. 14; RAL, T33/283/1, XI/109/5B, Paris, to Nathan and Salomon, Oct. 28.

178   See e.g. RAL, T46/9, Warburg & Leidersdorf to Nathan, London, Dec. 27, 1816.

179   RAL, T31/116/2, XI/109/4, Salomon, Frankfurt, to Nathan and James, March 17, 1816.

180 RAL, T31/107/3, XI/109/4, Davidson, Frankfurt, to Nathan, London, April 15, 1816; RAL, T31/176/3, XI/109/4, same to same, April 18.

181 RAL, T63/8/1, XI/109/8, Salomon and James, Paris, to Nathan, London, Nov. 17, 1817; RAL, XI/109/9/1/83, Salomon to Nathan, Jan. 19, 1818.

182 Brockhaus, *Real-Enzyklopädie* (1836), vol. IX, pp. 425f. See also (1847), vol. XII, p. 289. Cf. Corti, *Rise*, pp. 369–72.

183 Jurk, "Other Rothschilds," p. 43. Cf. Forstmann, *Bethmann*, pp. 253f.

184 Bodleian Library, dep. Hughenden 26/2 f. 23; Swartz and Swartz (eds), *Disraeli's reminiscences*, p. 19.

185 Treskow, *Nathan Meyer Rothschild*, pp. 3f.

186 Of the five sons of Francis Baring—Thomas, Alexander, Henry, William and George—all but Alexander drifted out of the family business; see Ziegler, *Sixth great power*, pp. 43–58.

187 RAL, T27/219, Amschel, Frankfurt, to James, Paris, Feb. 28, 1817.

188 Ziegler, *Sixth great power*, pp. 94ff.

189 Heine, "Ludwig Börne: Eine Denkschrift," in *Sämtliche Schriften*, vol. IV, p. 27. Cf. Platel, *Hommes de mon temps*, p. 298: "Les écus ont besoin, comme les soldats, pour gagner une victoire, d'être jetés tout à coup, en masse, sur un point choisi." I am grateful to Lionel de Rothschild for this reference.

190 RAL, T27/61, James to Nathan, London, Aug. 17, 1811.

191 RAL, XI/109/0/1/21, Nathan, London, to Salomon, June 7, 1814. For Amschel's craven response, see RAL, XI/109/0/2/5, Amschel, Frankfurt, to Salomon, June 20.

192 RAL, XI/109/0/2/7, Davidson, Amsterdam, to Nathan, London, June 21, 1814; RAL, T28/5, same to same, June 24; RAL, XI/109/0/2/13, Carl, Frankfurt, to James, June 24; Salomon to Nathan, June 24, quoted in Rothschild, *Shadow*, pp. 6f.

193 RAL, T29/73, XI/109/0/3/16, Nathan, London, to Salomon, Carl, James and Amschel, July 3, 1814.

194 RAL, T29/159, XI/109/0/6/11, Salomon, Paris, to Nathan and Salomon Cohen, London, Aug. 17, 1814; RAL, T29/181, XI/109/0/8/7, Salomon to Nathan, undated, *c.* Aug.; RAL, XI/109/9/4/6, XI/109/10/1/6, same to same, undated, *c.* early 1818. Cf. RAL, T28/34 and 53, undated letters, *c.* April 1815. Elswhere, Salomon compared the firm to a clock, with the brothers as cogs, and, perhaps more appropriately, to a king's cabinet of ministers.

195 RAL, T29/184, XI/109/0/8/110, Carl, Frankfurt, to Salomon, James and Davidson, Aug. 30, 1814. Cf. RAL, T29/268, XI/109/1/4/15, Salomon to Nathan, London, Oct. 7; RAL, T29/364, XI/109/1/8/41, Nathan to Carl, draft of a letter, Dec. 22.

196 RAL, T30, XI/109/2/3/14/1, Salomon, Amsterdam, to Nathan, London, Jan. 6, 1815; RAL, XI/109/2/1/45, same to same, May 19; RAL, T5/104, Nathan to Carl, Amsterdam, July 28; RAL, XI/109/2/2/140, Carl to Nathan, Oct. 10.

197 RAL, XI/109/2/2/117, Amschel to his brothers, undated fragment, *c.* Sept. 1815; RAL, XI/109/2/2/123, Salomon, Paris, to Nathan, London, Oct. 2; RAL, T30, XI/109/2/2/227, same to same, Oct. 16; RAL, XI/109/2/2/209, Gelche [Caroline], Frankfurt, to Salomon, Dec. 7; RAL, XI/109/2/2/215, same to same, Dec. 10; RAL, XI/109/2/2/227, Salomon and James to Nathan, Dec. 16; RAL, XI/109/2/2/240, same to same, Dec. 23.

198 RAL, XI/109/2/2/156, Salomon, Paris, to Nathan, London, Oct. 29, 1815.

199 RAL, T64/158/2, Salomon, Berlin, to Amschel, Nathan and James, Feb. 24, 1818.

200 RAL, T31/1/5, Nathan, London, to Amschel, Carl and James, Jan. 2, 1816. See also RAL, T34/1, NMR 288, Nathan to Amschel, Frankfurt, Jan. 3, 1816. Nathan was incensed to hear that James had suffered a riding accident; in his view, to be riding at all was a sign of dilettantism.

201 Corti, *Rise*, pp. 228f.

202 RAL, XI/82/9/1/10, Amschel, Frankfurt, to Salomon and James, Paris, undated fragment, *c.* July 1814. Cf. RAL, T29/189, XI/109/0/8/5, Amschel, Berlin, to Salomon, Aug. 26; RAL, T30, XI/109/2/3/26/1, Amschel to James, Jan. 26, 1815; RAL, T31/87/2, XI/109/4, same, Frankfurt, to same, Feb. 1.

203 RAL, T33/293/2, XI/109/5B, Amschel, Frankfurt, to James, Paris, Nov. 1, 1816; RAL, T61/28/1, XI/109/6, same to same, Jan. 30, 1817.

204 RAL, T27/105, XI/82/1, Carl, Frankfurt, to Amschel, Sept. 9, 1814. Cf. RAL, T29/172, XI/109/0/7/12, Amschel, Berlin, to James and Davidson, Aug. 21; RAL, T5/107, Nathan, London, to Carl, Amsterdam, Sept. 8, 1815; RAL, XI/109/2/1/57, Carl to Nathan, Sept. 8; RAL, XI/109/2/1/63, Salomon, Paris, to Nathan, Sept. 10; RAL, XI/109/2/1/61, James, Paris, to Nathan, Sept. 10; RAL, XI/109/2/2/129, Salomon to Nathan, Oct. 4; RAL, XI/109/2/2/168, Carl to his brothers, Nov. 11;

RAL, XI/109/2/2/182, Salomon to Nathan, Nov. 13; RAL, XI/109/2/2/177, Salomon and James to Nathan, Nov. 22; RAL, XI/109/2/2/247, Carl, Kassel, to Amschel, Frankfurt, Dec. 27.

205   RAL, T4/71, H. Braun, Paris, to James and Salomon, Amsterdam, May 21, 1814; RAL, XI/109/2/2/100, Salomon, Paris, to Nathan, London, Sept. 22, 1815.

206   RAL, T31, XI/109/4/12/1, Salomon, Paris, to Nathan, Jan. 7, 1816.

207   RAL, XI/109/0/2/15, Salomon and James, Amsterdam, to Nathan and Salomon Cohen, London, June 27, 1814; RAL, XI/109/0/2/14, Carl, Frankfurt, to James, June 28; RAL, XI/109/0/3/2, Salomon and James to Nathan, June 28.

208   RAL, XI/109/2/2/125, James, Paris, to his sister [-in-law, Hannah], Oct. 2, 1815. Cf. RAL, T30, XI/109/2/2/254, James to Nathan, Dec. 30.

209   RAL, T31, XI/109/4/3/143, James, Paris, to Nathan, London, March 28, 1816.

210   RAL, T31/143/3, XI/109/4, James, Paris, to Nathan, London, March 28, 1816.

211   RAL, T33/385/2, XI/109/5B, Carl, Berlin, to Amschel, Frankfurt, Dec. 24, 1816; RAL, T5/175, Amschel to Salomon and Nathan, Jan. 26, 1817.

212   RAL, T34/2, XI/82/9/1/38, Amschel, Frankfurt, to James, Paris, Jan. 1, 1816.

213   RAL, T62/91/4, Salomon and James, Paris, to Nathan, London, June 14, 1817.

214   RAL, T63/75/2, XI/109/8, Salomon, Paris, to Nathan, Sept. 24, 1817.

215   RAL, T27/230, Carl, Hamburg, to brothers, March 8, 1817; RAL, T27/232, same to same, March 10; RAL, T27/233, same, Kassel, to same, March 16; RAL, T27/236, March 21.

216   RAL, T33/320/2, XI/109/5B, Amschel, Frankfurt, to Salomon and Nathan, Nov. 12, 1816.

217   RAL, T62/9/1, XI/109/7, James, Paris, to Nathan, London, May 19, 1817; RAL, T62/90/4, XI/109/7, Salomon, Paris, to Nathan, London, June 12. See also RAL, T64/160/2, Salomon, Berlin, to James, Feb. 26, 1818.

218   RAL, T27/206, XI/109/6, Carl, Hamburg, to Salomon, Feb. 26, 1817; RAL, T27/227, XI/109/6/2, same to same, April 4; RAL, T61/85/2, XI/109/6/2, March 7; RAL, T61/87/2, March 9; RAL, T61/100/2, XI/109/6, March 30; RAL, T61/117/2, same, Frankfurt, to Salomon and Nathan, London, April 15; RAL, T64/212/3, XI/109/9, same to James, Paris, April 20; RAL, T64/211/3, XI/109/9, Carl to Salomon, April 20.

219   RAL, T31/53/1, XI/109/4, Salomon, Frankfurt, to Nathan and James, Feb. 2, 1816.

220   RAL, T5/139, Amschel, Frankfurt, to James, Paris, Jan. 21, 1816; RAL, T32/220/1, XI/109/5B, Carl, Frankfurt, to Nathan and Salomon, Sept. 27; RAL, T61/19/1, XI/109/6, Amschel to James, Jan. 21, 1817.

221   RAL, T32/52/1, XI/109/5A, James, Paris, to Nathan, Solomon and Davidson, July 20, 1816.

222   RAL, XI/82/9/1/36, Amschel, Frankfurt, to Salomon and Nathan, Jan. 3, 1816; RAL, XI/82/9/1/43, Amschel to James, Paris, Feb. 5; RAL, T32/ 27/1, XI/109/5A, Amschel, Berlin, to Salomon and Nathan, July 11; RAL, T33/343/2, XI/109/5B, James to Nathan and Salomon, Nov. 23; RAL, T33/359/2, XI/109/5B, Amschel to James, Dec. 6; RAL, XI/82/9/1/70, Amschel, Frankfurt, to Nathan and Salomon, Dec. 12; RAL, T5/173, Amschel to James, Jan. 24, 1817.

223   RAL, T32/210/1, XI/109/5B, Carl, Frankfurt, to Nathan and Salomon, Sept. 19, 1816; RAL, T33/369/2, XI/109/5B, same, Berlin, to same, Dec. 11; RAL, T61/37/1, XI/109/6, Amschel, Frankfurt, to Salomon and Nathan, London, Feb. 6, 1817.

224   CPHDCM, 637/1/6/7/7–14, Articles of Partnership, June 2, 1818.

FOUR   *"A Court Always Leads to Something" (1816–1825)*

1   RAL, XI/109/2/2/230, James, Paris, to Nathan, London, Dec. 18, 1815.

2   GStA, I. HA Rep 92 NL v. Rother Db 5 Bd 3, Nathan, London, to Rother, Berlin, May 5, 1818.

3   Punctuation varies: this is the text in the 1986 Oxford edition. The 1930 Oxford edition has "Jew Rothschild, and his fellow-Christian, Baring" but this seems nonsensical. Byron clearly intended to suggest that the two bankers were on a par, despite their different religions.

4   Byron, *Don Juan*, canto XII, verses 5–10.

5   Emden, *Money powers*, pp. 27ff.

6   Kindleberger, *Financial history*, pp. 219ff.; Jardin and Tudesq, *Restoration*, pp. 27–44. Of the 700 million francs, some 138 million was to be spent on reconstructing strategic fortresses around France's borders. Each of the great powers was to receive between 100 and 139 million to compensate them for the costs of the Hundred Days; smaller sums went to the other states in the anti-French coalition. In addition, France had to pay substantial sums to private claimants; after prolonged wrangles, these amounted to 240 million francs. The peace also returned French borders to those of 1790, as opposed to those of

1792 which the 1814 treaty had set. It should be noted that France had previously imposed indemnities on the Netherlands, Austria, Prussia and Portugal, but the sums involved had been smaller.

7   RAL, XI/109/2/1/56, Amschel, Frankfurt, to his brothers, Sept. 8, 1815; RAL, T30, XI/109/2/2/75, Amschel to Salomon and James, Paris, Sept. 13.

8   RAL, XI/109/2/2/87, James, Paris, to Nathan, London, Sept. 18, 1815; RAL, XI/109/2/2/94, Salomon, Paris, to Nathan, Sept. 20; RAL, XI/109/2/2/161, James and Salomon to Nathan, Nov. 11; RAL, XI/109/2/2/180, James to Nathan and Davidson, Nov. 25; RAL, XI/109/2/2/183, Salomon to Nathan, Nov. 25; RAL, XI/109/2/2/200, Salomon and James to Nathan, Dec. 4. For details of contributions payments to Britain, see RAL, T32/132/2, XI/109/5A, James to Nathan and Salomon, Aug. 18, 1816; RAL, T32/170/1, XI/109/5B, same to same and Davidson, Sept. 2; RAL, T5/165, Drummond, Paris, to NMR, Oct. 11, 1817.

9   RAL, XI/109/2/1/60, Salomon, Paris, to Nathan, London, Sept. 9, 1815; RAL, XI/109/2/1/61, James, Paris, to Nathan, Sept. 10; RAL, XI/109/2/2/120, James and Salomon to Nathan, Sept. 30; RAL, XI/109/2/2/134, Salomon and James to Nathan, Oct. 7; RAL, XI/109/2/2/213, Salomon to Nathan, Dec. 9; RAL, XI/109/2/2/220, James to Nathan, Dec. 13; RAL, T31/11/1, XI/109/4, Salomon to Nathan, Jan. 6, 1816; RAL, T31/53/1, XI/109/4, Salomon, Frankfurt, to Nathan and James, Feb. 2; RAL, T31/111/2, XI/109/4, Salomon to James, March 13; RAL, T31/244/4, XI/109/4, Amschel, Berlin, to Salomon and Nathan, June 6; RAL, T32/107/2, XI/109/5, Eskeles, Carslbad, to Nathan, Aug. 6; RAL, T32/131/2, XI/109/5A, James to Eskeles, Aug. 18; RAL, T62/139/7, Carl, Berlin, to Nathan, July 15, 1817; RAL, T63/15/1, Amschel, Frankfurt, to Salomon and James, Nov. 11; RAL, T52/1, T3/290, Baron Parish de Senftenberg [John Parish], Vienna, to Nathan, July 31, 1818; RAL, T52/2, same to same, Aug. 12. Cf. Corti, *Rise*, pp. 186–90, 201, 240; Gille, *Maison Rothschild*, vol. I, pp. 81–8; Gilbert, *Bankiers*, p. xxix.

10 RAL, T31/236/4, XI/109/4, James, Paris, to Nathan and Salomon, London, June 1, 1816; RAL, T37/131, Herries to Drummond, June 21; RAL, T31/293/4, XI/109/4, James to Nathan and Salomon, June 26; RAL, T31/296/4, XI/109/4, same to same, June 29; RAL, T32/100/2, XI/109/5A, Amschel, Berlin, to James, Aug. 3. Cf. Chapman, "Establishment," pp. 74f.

11 RAL, XI/109/2/2/81, James and Salomon, Paris, to Nathan, London, Sept. 16, 1815; RAL, XI/109/2/2/84, Amschel to Carl, Sept. 17; RAL, XI/109/2/2/85, Salomon to Nathan, Sept. 18; RAL, XI/109/2/2/125, James to his sister[-in-law] Hannah, Oct. 2; RAL, XI/109/2/2/124, James to Nathan, London, Oct. 10; RAL, XI/109/2/2/142, Salomon and James to Nathan, Oct. 11; RAL, T32/41/1, XI/109/5A, James to Salomon and Nathan, July 15. The Prussian Finance Minister Bülow was less scrupulous: RAL, T5/144, G. F. Gasser to MAR, May 14, 1816; RAL, T31/238/4, XI/109/4, Carl to James, June 2. Cf. Capefigue, *Grandes opérations*, vol. III, pp. 94–7.

12 RAL, T31/39/1, XI/109/4, James, Paris, to Nathan, London, Jan. 23, 1816; RAL, T34/8, Carl, Frankfurt, to Nathan and James, Feb. 19; RAL, T31/91/2, XI/109/4, James to Nathan, March 4; RAL, T61/73/2, James to Nathan and Salomon, March 17, 1817; RAL, T64/336/3, XI/109/9, same to same, April 4, 1818. Cf. Capefigue, *Grandes opérations*, vol. III, pp. 49f.; Chirac, *Haute Banque*, p. 110.

13 On the repayment of this loan, which the Rothschilds also handled, see RAL, T63/2/1, XI/109/8, Salomon and James, Paris, to Nathan, London, Nov. 3, 1817.

14 James arranged to invest £20,000 for Dalberg in British stocks at around this time: RAL, XI/109/2/2/148, James, Paris, to Nathan, London, Oct. 21, 1815. A short time later he and Salomon joined Dalberg in a small speculation in French rentes: RAL, XI/109/2/2/158, Salomon, Paris, to Nathan, Oct. 31.

15 RAL, T32/195/1, XI/109/5B, James, Paris, to Nathan and Salomon, London, Sept. 1816.

16 The Amsterdam bank of Hope & Co. had been founded by the Boston-born Henry Hope and the Cornishman John Williams in the 1760s. Laid low by the French occupation of Holland, it had effectively been taken over by Baring Brothers. Labouchère was a Hope employee who married a Baring and later became a Hope partner: Emden, *Money powers*, pp. 33f.

17 Payard, *Ouvrard*, pp. 289–96; Kindleberger, *Financial history*, pp. 219ff.; Nicolle, *Waterloo*, p. 154; Ehrenberg, *Große Vermögen*, pp. 74ff.; Emden, *Money powers*, p. 10.

18 RAL, XI/109/2/2193, Salomon, Paris, to Nathan, London, Nov. 29, 1815; RAL, XI/109/2/2/190, 191, 192, James to Nathan, Nov. 29; RAL, XI/109/2/2/198, same to same, Dec. 2; RAL, T44/1, XI/111/110/1/3, Transcript of Baring plan. Cf. Gille, *Maison Rothschild*, vol. I, pp. 62–4. For claims that the Rothschilds profited from the reparations payments see Chirac, *Rois de la République*, pp. 144ff.; Drumont, *France juive*, pp. 333f.

19 RAL, T32/98/2, James, Paris, to Nathan and Salomon, Aug. 2, 1816; RAL, T33/232b/1, XI/109/5B,

James to unidentified recipient, probably Nathan, Oct. 5; RAL, T33/237/1, XI/109/5B, James to Nathan and Salomon, Oct. 9; RAL, T33/22, XI/109/5B, James to Nathan, Oct. 14; RAL, T33/263/1, XI/109/5B, James to Nathan and Salomon, Oct. 19; RAL, T33/301/2, XI/109/5B, same to same, Nov. 4; RAL, T33/350/2, XI/109/5B, London, Nov. 28; RAL, T33/368/2, XI/109/5B, Dec. 11; RAL, T33/379/2, XI/109/5B, Dec. 18; RAL, T34/36, Dec. 19; RAL, T33/381/2, XI/109/5B, Dec. 21; RAL, T27/114, Jan. 3, 1817; RAL, T5/138, Jan. 11; RAL, T3/281, David Parish to James, March 7; RAL, T61/69/2, XI/109/6, James to Salomon and Nathan, London, March 8.

20   RAL, T61/13/1, XI/109/6, Amschel, Frankfurt, to James, Paris, Jan. 15, 1817; RAL, T34/2, XI/82/9/1/38, same to same, Jan. 16; RAL, T61/21/1, XI/109/6, James "an den Herren Baron von Salomon nebst dem guten Herrn Knight von R[othschild] Nathan," London, Jan. 23; RAL, T61/33/1, XI/109/6, James to Amschel and Carl, Feb. 4; RAL, T61/66/2, XI/109/6, James to Nathan and Salomon, London, March 3; RAL, T62/155/8, XI/109/7, James to Nathan, July 11.

21   RAL, T62/8, XI/109/7, same to same, July 19, 1817; RAL, T62/164/8, XI/109/7, July 21; RAL, T62/166/8, XI/109/7, July 23.

22   RAL, T27/292, Salomon, Paris, to Nathan, London, Aug. 9, 1817. Cf. Kynaston, *City*, vol. I, pp. 45–6.

23   Chirac, *Haute Banque*, p. 128; Ehrenberg, *Große Vermögen*, pp. 95f.; Gille, *Banque et crédit*, pp. 162–71; Payard, *Ouvrard*, pp. 289–96. The figures cited by various authors are not easy to reconcile, partly because contemporaries tended to refer to rentes in terms of the annual interest they paid rather than their capital value, since (unlike English consols) rentes were not redeemable at a set date in the future. In order to make comparisons possible, however, I have tried to be consistent in citing the *nominal capital value* of issues of rentes.

24   RAL, T64/179/2, XI/109/9, James, Paris, to his brothers, Feb. 14, 1818; Laffitte, *Mémoires*, pp. 114f. Cf. RAL, T27/297, James and Salomon, Paris, to Nathan, London, Oct. 11, 1817; RAL, T63/144/2, same to same, Oct. 15; RAL, T63/7/1, XI/109/8, Nov. 15; RAL, T63 /46/1, XI/109/8, Dec. 17; RAL, T64/76/1, XI/109/9, Salomon to Nathan, Jan. 3, 1818; RAL, XI/109/9/1/78, Salomon and James to Nathan, Jan. 7; RAL, XI/109/9/1/108, James to Nathan, Jan. 22; RAL, T64/174/2, XI/109/9, same to same, Feb. 9; RAL, T64/286/3, XI/109/9, March 4. For James's relations with the leading French bankers of the Restoration, most of whom had made their money since the Revolution and many of whom (e.g., Perrégaux and Hottinguer) were Protestants and/or Swiss, see Muhlstein, *Baron James*, pp. 50f.; Gille, *Banque et crédit*, pp. 57–63.

25   RAL, T61/140/2, James, Paris, to Nathan and Salomon, London, April 15, 1817; RAL, T27/137, XI/109/6, James to Nathan, April 26; RAL, T27/152, XI/109/6, Carl to his brothers, April 30; RAL, T27/170, XI/109/7, Salomon and James to Nathan, May 12; RAL, T27/159, XI/109/7, same to same, May 16; RAL, XI/109/9/1/81, Jan. 15, 1818. Cf. Cadoux, *Paris*, p. 246.

26   Ziegler, *Sixth great power*, pp. 81ff.

27   RAL, XI/109/2/2/99, James, Paris, to Nathan, Sept. 22, 1815; RAL, XI/109/2/2/104, same to same, Sept. 23.

28   RAL, XI/109/2/2/156, Salomon, Paris, to Nathan, London, Oct. 29, 1815; RAL, XI/109/2/2/162, same to same, Nov. 6. See also RAL, T30, XI/109/2/2/257, Davidson to Nathan, Dec. 31; RAL, T34/2, XI/82/9/1/38, Amschel to James, Jan. 16, 1816.

29   RAL, T31/197/3, XI/109/4, James, Paris, to Nathan, London, May 4, 1816.

30   RAL, T33/339/2, XI/109/5B, James, Paris, to his brothers, Nov. 20, 1816.

31   Schremmer, "Public finance," pp. 326, 364.

32   RAL, T27/165, T62/32/2, XI/109/7, Salomon and James, Paris, to Nathan, London, May 7, 1817; RAL, T62/40/2, XI/109/7, same to same, May 19.

33   RAL, T63/5/1, XI/109/8, Salomon and James, Paris, to Nathan, London, Nov. 6, 1817.

34   Adolphe d'Eichthal was the grandson of the Bavarian court banker Aron Elias Seligmann; he changed his religion and name and moved to Paris with his son Louis.

35   RAL, XI/109/0/1/27, Carl, Frankfurt, to Nathan, London, June 18, 1814.

36   RAL, XI/109/2/2/236, Carl, Kassel, to Amschel, Frankfurt, Dec. 21, 1815. See also RAL, XI/109/9/1/106, James, Paris, to Nathan, London, Jan. 19, 1818.

37   RAL, T31/94/2, XI/109/4, James, Paris, to Nathan, London, March 6, 1816.

38   RAL, T27/162, James, Paris, to Salomon and Nathan, London, May 28, 1817.

39   RAL, T29/161, XI/109/0/7/1, Amschel to James, undated, *c.* late 1814. See also RAL, T5/61, Nathan, London, to James, Nov. 18; RAL, T5/107, Nathan to Carl, Amsterdam, Sept. 8, 1815. Nathan's "great reputation" and "influence" in London were a source of pride to other family members, however: RAL, XI/109/2/2/110, Gelche [Caroline], Frankfurt, to Salomon, Sept. 26, 1815.

40   RAL, T61/103/2, Amschel, Frankfurt, to Salomon and Nathan, London, March 21, 1817.

41   RAL, XI/109/2/2/229, Carl, Kassel, to Amschel, Frankfurt, Dec. 18, 1815; RAL, XI/109/2/2/236, same to same, Dec. 21. It was at this time that the Kassel Jewish community took Amschel to court for alleged non-payment of residence dues.

42   RAL, XI/109/9/1/82, Salomon and James, Paris, to Nathan, London, Jan. 17, 1818. Cf. RAL, T34/12, James to Nathan, March 11.

43   RAL, XI/109/0/3/4, Carl, Frankfurt, to Salomon, June 29, 1814; RAL, T29/63, XI/109/0/3/5, Amschel, Frankfurt, to Salomon, June 29; RAL, XI/109/0/3/7, Carl to Salomon, June 30; RAL, T30, XI/109/2/3/26/1, Amschel to James, Jan. 26, 1815; RAL, T30, XI/109/2/3/49, Amschel to Carl and Nathan, Aug. 31. The brothers did their utmost to challenge d'Eichthal's dominant position in Bavarian finance in 1815: RAL, XI/109/2/1/60, Salomon, Paris, to Nathan, Sept. 9; RAL, XI/109/2/1/62, Amschel to his brothers, Sept. 10; RAL, XI/109/2/1/63, Salomon to Nathan, Sept. 10; RAL, XI/109/2/1/61, James, Paris, to Nathan, Sept. 10; RAL, XI/109/2/1/64, Salomon to Nathan, Sept. 10; RAL, XI/109/2/2/70, Amschel to his brothers, Sept. 12; RAL, XI/109/2/2/145, Eichthal, London, to "verehrteste Freund" [probably Nathan], Oct. 20.

44   Emden, *Money powers*, p. 11; Ravage, *Five men*, pp. 185–97; Morton, *Rothschilds*, pp. 57f.; Cowles, *Rothschilds*, pp. 56f.; Wilson, *Rothschild*, p. 73. See also the film *The House of Rothschild*. For more cautious accounts see Corti, *Rise*, pp. 226f.; Born, *International Banking*, pp. 37f.; Gille, *Maison Rothschild*, vol. I, pp. 70–81.

45   Ehrenberg, *Große Vermögen*, pp. 95f.; Nicolle, *Waterloo*, p. 183. Baring had already agreed to advance 165 million francs to the Allies in return for 246 million of rentes at 67; the problem was the decision by the Allies at Aix to accept a final payment of 100 million in the form of 132 million of rentes which Baring rashly agreed to buy at the higher price of 74.

46   RAL, T61/71/2, James, Paris, to Nathan and Salomon, London, March 10, 1817; RAL, T27/219, also T61/72/2, same to same, London, March 11; RAL, T61/74/2, March 19; RAL, T61/75/2, March 20; RAL, T62/89b/4, XI/109/7, Salomon and James, Paris, to Nathan, June 6.

47   RAL, T27/219, T61/72/2, James, Paris, to Salomon and Nathan, London, March 11, 1817; RAL, T27/124, same to same, April 2; RAL, T61/133/2, April 4; RAL, T61/136/2, XI/109/6, April 9; RAL, T61/138/2, April 12.

48   Bouvier, *Rothschild*, pp. 60–62.

49   RAL, T62/98, XI/109/7, Salomon, Paris, to Nathan, London, June 26, 1817; RAL, T62/126/6, XI/109/7, same to same, July 5; RAL, T63/7/1, XI/109/8, Salomon and James to Nathan, Nov. 15.

50   RAL, T64, XI/109/9/4/26, James, Paris, to Nathan, London, July 8, 1818. The only allusion to a possible weakening of the market for rentes is in RAL, T42/8, XI/38/7/4/28, Abraham Montefiore, Paris, to Nathan, London, undated, c. 1818.

51   RAL, T64/158/2, Salomon, Berlin, to Amschel, Nathan and James, Feb. 24, 1818.

52   Ramon, *Banque de France*, pp. 145–8.

53   Serre, *Correspondance*, vol. IV, pp. 240, 255f., 272f.; Chirac, *Haute Banque*, pp.134–7; Gille, *Banque et crédit*, pp. 162–171; Payard, *Ouvrard*, pp. 289–96; Cameron, *France and Europe*, pp. 108–10. Cf. Clapham, *Economic development*, p. 133.

54   RAL, T3/137/2, XI/109/5A, Amschel, Frankfurt, to Nathan, Salomon and James, Aug. 21, 1816; RAL, T27/248, XI/109/6, Amschel to his brothers, March 15.

55   RAL, T61/68/2, XI/109/6, James, Paris, to Nathan and Salomon, London, March 7, 1817; RAL, T61/133/2, same to same, April 4; RAL, T61/136/2, XI/109/6, April 9; RAL, T61/140/2, April 15; RAL, T62/4/1, XI/109/7, James to Nathan, May 6.

56   RAL, T32/125/2, XI/109/5A, Salomon and his wife, Brighton, to Nathan, Hannah and Davidson, Aug. 16, 1816.

57   RAL, T62/31/2, Salomon, Paris, to Nathan, London, May 6, 1817; RAL, T27/165, same to same, May 7; RAL, T62/39/2, XI/109/2, May 17; T62/46, XI/109/7, May 31; RAL, T62/ 90/4, XI/109/7, June 12; RAL, T62/55/4, Salomon and James to Nathan, June 21.

58   RAL, T62/96/4, Salomon, Paris, to Nathan, London, July 25, 1817.

59   RAL, T62/116/5, Amschel, Frankfurt, to Carl, July 25, 1817; RAL, T27/292, Salomon, Paris, to Nathan, London, Aug. 9; RAL, T63/45/1, XI/109/8, Salomon and James to Nathan, Dec. 8.

60   HSM, Bestand 6b Nr 641, Der im Jahre 1818 beschlossene und wieder zurück gegangene Verkauf von £ 100/m St Annuitätenkapital betreffend, Abschrift, Jan. 12, 1818; Nathan, London, to Buderus, Jan. 27; Salomon to Buderus, April 6.

61   RAL, T42/4, RFamC/30/4, Moses and Judith Montefiore to Nathan, Feb. 10, 1818.

62　RAL, T63/139/2, XI/109/8, Salomon and James, Paris, to Nathan, London, Oct. 27, 1817; RAL, T63/141/2, XI/109/8, same to same, Oct. 27; RAL, T63/3/1, XI/109/8, Nov. 5; RAL, T63/58/1, XI/109/8, Carl, Berlin, to Salomon and James, Dec. 12.

63　RAL, T61/65/2, XI/109/6, James, Paris, to Nathan and Salomon, London, March 1, 1817; RAL, T27/129, same to same, April 14; RAL, T62/89b/4, XI/109/7, Salomon and James to Nathan, June 6.

64　RAL, T27/302, Salomon and James, Paris, to Nathan, London, Oct. 22, 1817; Davis, *English Rothschilds*, pp. 34f.

65　RAL, T63/44/1, XI/109/8, Salomon and James, Paris, to Nathan, London, Dec. 12, 1817.

66　RAL, T27/292a, XI/109/7, Salomon, Paris, to Nathan and James, London, Aug. 30, 1817.

67　RAL, T64, XI/109/9/1/78, Salomon and James, Paris, to Nathan, London, Jan. 7, 1818; RAL, XI/109/9/1/79, same to same, Jan. 10; RAL, XI/109/9/1/80, Salomon to Nathan, Jan. 14. Cf. *DNB*; *The Times*, Aug. 4, 1836 (which states that Nathan lost £500,000 as a consequence of this abortive operation).

68　Hilton, *Corn, cash and commerce*, p. 35.

69　Buxton, *Finance*, vol. I, pp. 12–15; Briggs, *Age of Improvement*, pp. 188–207.

70　Gash, *Mr Secretary Peel*, pp. 240f. Cf. Gille, *Maison Rothschild*, vol. I, pp. 74–7. The price of gold was £4 0s 6d in 1819 compared with the bullionists" pre-war target of £3 17s 10 ½ d.

71　Yonge, *Liverpool*, pp. 416f.

72　See e.g. RAL, XI/109/2/2/204, Heckscher, Hamburg, to Nathan, London, Dec. 5, 1815.

73　Hilton, *Corn, cash and commerce*, p. 35.

74　Ayer, *Century of finance*, pp. 16f.; Ehrenberg, *Große Vermögen*, p. 103; Chapman, "Establishment," p. 78.

75　Clapham, *Bank of England*, vol. II, pp. 67ff.; Wood, *Theories*, pp. 106f.; Hilton, *Corn, cash and commerce*, pp. 60, 87; Kindleberger, *Financial history*, pp. 62f., 79; Kynaston, *City*, vol. I, pp. 38, 46.

76　RAL, T42/12,XI/112/554/5/45, Abraham Montefiore, Clifton, to "My dear friends" [Nathan and Hannah], Feb. 27, 1821.

77　Disraeli, *Coningsby*, pp. 213f.

78　Sheehan, *German history*, pp. 291ff., 424f.; Fulda, "Loan of 1818."

79　RAL, T32/91, XI/109/5A, Amschel to Salomon and Nathan, London, Aug. 1, 1816; RAL, T33/250/1, XI/109/5B, Carl, Kassel, to his brothers, Oct. 15; RAL, T33/259/1, XI/109/5B, Carl to James, Paris, Oct. 18; RAL, T33/305/2, XI/109/5B, Carl, Berlin, to Salomon and Nathan, Nov. 5; RAL, T33/316/2, XI/109/5B, Carl to Salomon, Nov. 11; RAL, T33/342/2, XI/109/5B, Carl to Amschel and James, Nov. 13; RAL, T33/329/2, XI/109/5B, Carl to his brothers, Nov. 15; RAL, T5/178, Carl to Nathan, Jan. 21, 1817; RAL, T5/173, Amschel to James, Jan. 24; RAL, T61/26/1, XI/109/6, Carl to Amschel, Jan. 28. Cf. Berghoeffer, *Meyer Amschel*, pp. 206ff.; Corti, *Rise*, p. 203.

80　RAL, T61/36/1, XI/109/6, Carl, Berlin, to Salomon and Nathan, London, Feb. 6, 1817; RAL, T27/200, Carl, Hamburg, to Amschel, Frankfurt, Feb. 16 and 17; RAL, T61/65/2, XI/109/6, James, Paris, to Nathan and Salomon, March 1; RAL, T61/13/2, XI/109/6, Amschel to Nathan and Salomon, March 31; RAL, T62/9/1, XI/109/7, James to Nathan, May 19; RAL, T5/181, Carl to Nathan, May 22; RAL, T62/90/4, XI/109/7, Salomon, Paris, to Nathan, June 9; RAL, T62/104/5, XI/109/7, Amschel to Salomon and James, July 8; RAL, T62/135/7, XI/109/7, Carl to Nathan, July 8; RAL, T63/121/2, XI/109/8, Amschel to his brothers, Oct. 16; RAL, T63/111/2, XI/109/8, Carl to Nathan, Oct. 25; RAL, T63/28/1, XI/109/8, Carl to his brothers, Nov. 4. Cf. Ehrenberg, *Große Vermögen*, pp. 80–96, 107; Corti, *Rise*, pp. 210–15; Balla, *Romance*, pp. 94ff.; Ravage, *Five men*, pp. 169–85; Gille, *Maison Rothschild*, vol. I, pp. 70–74; Bouvier, *Rothschild*, p. 66; Heuberger, *Rothschilds*, p. 57; Chapman, "Establishment," pp. 75f.

81　RAL, T63/30/1, XI/109/8, Carl, Berlin, to Amschel and James, undated, *c.* Nov. 1817; RAL, T63/33/1, XI/109/8, Carl to Amschel, Salomon and James, Nov. 11; RAL, T63/58/1, XI/109/8, Carl to Nathan, Nov. 21; RAL, T63/37/1, XI/109/8, Carl to Amschel, Salomon and James, Nov. 22; RAL, XI/109/24/3/4, Rother, Hardenberg and Klewig [Ministry of the Treasury] to Barandon, Nov. 23; RAL, XI/109/9/1/89, Carl to Nathan, Jan. 2, 1818 [wrongly dated 1817]; RAL, XI/109/9/1/78, Salomon and James to Nathan, Jan. 7; RAL, XI/109/9/1/83, Salomon to Nathan, Jan. 19; RAL, XI/109/9/1/106, James to Nathan, Jan. 19 [wrongly dated 1817]; RAL, XI/109/9/1/105, James and Salomon to Nathan, Jan. 19; RAL, XI/109/9/1/84, Salomon to Nathan, Jan. 20; RAL, XI/109/9/1/109, James to Nathan, Jan. 22 [wrongly dated 1817]; RAL, T5/171, IX/85/1, same to same, Jan. 24; RAL, T5/186, Gasser to deRF, Jan. 27; RAL, XI/109/9/1/85, Salomon, Koblenz, to Nathan and James, Jan. 28; RAL, XI/109/9/1/110, James to Nathan, Jan. 29; RAL, XI/109/9/1/111, same to same, Jan. 31; RAL, T64/171/2, XI/109/9, Feb. 5; RAL, T64/151/2, XI/109/9, Salomon and Carl, Berlin, to their brothers and Mrs Rothschild, Feb. 12; RAL, T64/177/2, XI/109/9, James to Nathan, Feb. 12; RAL, T64 152/2, XI/109/9, Salomon to Nathan and James, Feb. 14; RAL, T64/156/2, same to same, Feb. 19; RAL, T64/158/2, Salomon to Amschel, Nathan and James, Feb. 24; RAL, T64/275/3, XI/109/9, Carl, Frankfurt, to Nathan and James, March 6; RAL, T64/272/3, XI/109/9, Salomon and Carl, Koblenz, to Amschel, Nathan and James, March 10; RAL, T64/273/3, Salomon and Carl to Nathan, March 14; RAL, T64/276/3, XI/109/9, Carl to James, March 17. See also GStA, Rep. 74 N XV Nr 47 vol. I, pp. 34f., Nathan to Hardenberg, Berlin, Jan. 15.

82   RAL, T64/301/3, XI/109/9, James, Paris, to Nathan and Salomon, March 30, 1818; RAL, T64/182/3, XI/109/9, Carl, Frankfurt, to Salomon, Nathan and James, April 2. The final terms were that 5 per cent bonds totalling £5 million would be sold in three successive tranches with the price rising from 70 (£2.5 million) to 72.5 (£1.25 million) and then to 75 (£1.25 million). £1 million of the first tranche was taken by the Prussian government itself at Rother's suggestion. Repayment was to take place over twenty-five years. Officially, as Ehrenberg says, there was no additional commission; in fact, Nathan got his 4 per cent, though this was "kept secret" to defuse criticism in Berlin. In addition, the Rothschilds kept at least £1.5 million for themselves, netting a large profit when the price rose to a peak of 83 in September. This explains why the brothers wrote in such affectionate terms to Rother after the contract was concluded: Salomon assured him that he and Nathan were his "heartfelt, eternal and faithful good friends"; it is unlikely that he would have expressed such sentiments if he had been forced to forgo a commission.

83   Kehr, "Zur Genesis," pp. 45ff. See also Obenaus, "Finanzkrise."

84   RAL, XI/109/10/3/4, undated documents relating to Prussian loan proposal, *c.* Dec. 1817, relayed to Rother via Amschel (RAL, General Copy Book 148/6, Nathan to Amschel, Frankfurt, Dec. 2) and to the Seehandlung via Carl (Nathan to Carl, Berlin, Dec. 2). Cf. See also RAL, XI/109/10/3, copy of letter probably from Nathan, London, to "Sir" [Rother or Hardenberg], Dec. 30; RAL, XI/109/9/1/89, Carl to Nathan, Jan. 2, 1818; GStA, Rep. 74 N XV, Nr. 47, vol. I, pp. 22ff., Barandon to Hardenberg, Dec. 30, 1817.

85   RAL, XI/109/9/1/108, James, Paris, to Nathan, London, Jan. 22, 1818.

86   Klein, "30-Millionen-Anleihe," p. 582.

87   GStA, I. HA Rep. 92 Db 5 Bd 3, Nathan, London, to Rother, Berlin, May 5, 1818. See also GStA, I. HA Rep. 92 Ca Nr 20 (34), same to same, May 12; GStA, I. HA Rep. 92 Ca Nr 20 (27), Carl, Berlin, to Rother, May 23; GStA, I. HA Rep. 92 Ca Nr 20 (1), Nathan to Rother, May 26.

88   Thielen, *Hardenberg*, p. 358.

89   *The Times*, Aug. 4, 1836; Dawson, *Debt crisis*, p. 20; Kynaston, *City*, vol. I, pp. 45f.; Henderson, *Zollverein*, p. 31; Gille, *Banque et crédit*, p. 225.

90   *The Times*, Aug. 4, 1836, p. 3.

91   GStA, I. HA Rep. 92 Ca Nr 20 (32), Carl, Berlin, to Rother, May 12, 1818.

92   Bender, *Verkehr*, pp. 6ff. See also p. 13n. on the Austrian loan of 1820. Cf. Heilbrunn, "Haus Rothschild," p. 24.

93   The Rothschilds had no difficulty in placing the greater part of the loan with the major Paris and Frankfurt banks, though they were less generous to their rivals in Berlin; New York, Leo Baeck Institute, NMR to Behrend Brothers & Co., Berlin, April 10, 1818; RAL, T64/199/3, Carl, Frankfurt, to Nathan and James, April 10; RAL, T64/208/3, same to same, April 17; New York, Leo Baeck Institute, Nathan, London, to Behrend Brothers, May 8. The bonds rose initially to 83 in Sept. 1818, then slipped back to 73.5 until late 1819, before rising steadily again. Rumours of a new loan in 1820 seem to have prompted the Rothschilds to sell their own holdings, but these proved unfounded; AN, 132 AQ 3, Brüderliche Übereinkunft, Aug. 12, 1820. In fact, the bonds reached par (i.e. 100) in 1824.

94   Ayer, *Century of finance*, pp. 16f.

95   RAL, XI/109/2/2/68, Amschel, Frankfurt, to Carl, Sept. 12, 1815; RAL, XI/109/2/2/90, Amschel to his brothers, undated, *c.* late 1815; RAL, T51/20, Original note of transfer of dividends to Her Serene Highness Princess Louisa of Hesse, signed by Nathan, April 21, 1816; RAL, T61/54/1, XI/109/6, Amschel, Frankfurt, to Carl, Feb. 24, 1817; RAL, T27/204, XI/109/6, Amschel to James, Paris, Feb. 25; HSM, Bestand 340 Buderus von Carlshausen, Nr 85, Buderus, Frankfurt, to kurfürstlichen Cabinetskassendirection, Feb. 28; HSM, Bestand 6b Nr 717, Nr 16, MAR to Buderus, April 15.

96   RAL, XI/109/2/2/82, Amschel, Frankfurt, to his brother [Nathan], Sept. 16, 1815; HSM, Bestand 4 a/94,1, Bd II, Amschel to Elector, Nov. 24, 1821.

97   RAL, XI/109/2/2/146, Amschel, Frankfurt, to Salomon and James, Paris, Oct. 23, 1815; RAL,

T61/60/1, XI/109/6, Amschel to Salomon, Feb. 26, 1817; RAL, T61/64/2, XI/109/6, Amschel to Carl, Feb. 28; RAL, T27/210, Amschel to James, Feb. 28; RAL, T61/62/2, XI/109/6, same to same, Feb. 28.

98 RAL, T30, XI/109/2/3/50/1, Amschel, Frankfurt, to Salomon and James, undated *c.* Sept. 1815; RAL, T30, XI/109/2/2/256, Carl, Kassel, to Amschel, Dec. 30; RAL, XI/82/1/1/4, Carl [fragment of an undated letter, probably to Amschel], *c.* late 1815; RAL, T31/4/1, XI/109/4, Carl to Amschel, Jan. 9, 1816; RAL, T31/101/2, XI/109/2, Carl to Amschel, Salomon and Davidson, March 1; RAL, T33/250/1, XI/109/5B, Carl to his brothers, Oct. 15; RAL, T61/93/2, same to same, March 19, 1817; RAL, T62/81/3, XI/109/7, Carl to Amschel, June 25; RAL, T64, XI/109/9/4, also XI/109/10/1, same to same, July 2, 1818. Cf. Berghoeffer, *Meyer Amschel,* pp. 207ff.; Corti, *Rise,* pp. 217, 200f., 227f., 274f.

99 Berghoeffer, *Meyer Amschel,* pp. 207ff.

100 See in general Sheehan, *German history,* pp. 393–425.

101 Calculated from figures in Berghoeffer, *Meyer Amschel,* pp. 206–28.

102 Doering, *Ursprung, Wachstum und Schicksale,* pp. 7ff., 21ff.

103 Corti, *Rise,* pp. 250f. Cf. AN, 132 AQ 3, Brüderliche Übereinkunft, Aug. 12, 1820.

104 Isaac Arnstein and Bernhard Eskeles were descendants of Samson Wertheimer, court banker of Charles VI. Arnstein's son Nathan married Fanny Itzig, famed for her Vienna salon.

105 Corti, *Rise,* pp. 201ff., 229, 240ff.

106 See in general Macartney, *Habsburg Empire,* pp. 205f.; Cameron, *France and Europe,* pp. 415f.

107 RAL, T33/383/2, XI/109/5B, Amschel, Frankfurt, to Carl, Dec. 22, 1816; RAL, T61/6/1, XI/109/6, James, Paris, to Nathan, London, Jan. 8, 1817; RAL, XI/109/9/1/76, Salomon, Paris, to Nathan, Jan. 3; RAL, XI/109/9/1/79, Salomon and James to Nathan, Jan. 10, 1818; RAL, T64/338/3, James to Salomon and Nathan, April 9. Cf. Ehrenberg, *Große Vermögen,* pp. 76ff. The Austrian gulden was worth slightly more than the Frankfurt gulden.

108 Corti, *Rise,* pp. 245–9. See also Ehrenberg, *Große Vermögen,* pp. 104ff., 108; Ravage, *Five men,* pp. 204–10; Bouvier, *Rothschild,* p. 67; Macartney, *Habsburg Empire,* pp. 205f.; Sweet, *Gentz,* p. 219. Rothschild and Parish paid out 35 million Austrian gulden; it was calculated that the state had to repay 76.8 million in interest and amortisation and a further 1.4 million as commission.

109 Seton-Watson, *Russian Empire,* pp. 156ff., 208f.

110 RAL, T27/227, XI/109/6/2, Carl, Hamburg, to his brothers, March 4, 1817; RAL, T5/180, Carl to Nathan, March 7; RAL, T62/90/4, XI/109/7, Salomon, Paris, to Nathan, June 9; RAL, T64, XI/109/9/4/10, also XI/109/9/1, James, Paris, to Nathan, July 15. Cf. Gille, *Maison Rothschild,* vol. I, pp. 65–70, 103–5.

111 RAL, T3/92, D. Guryev [Russian Finance Minister], St Petersburg, to Nathan, London, Nov. 21. 1819.

112 RAL, T6/23, M. Montefiore, Ramsgate, to Nathan, June 28, 1822; RAL, Cataloguing Box [letter copy book—New Russian 5 per cent Metallic Stock etc.], Nathan to Guryev, July 25; RAL, T5/210, Salomon to Nathan, Oct. 7; RAL, Cataloguing Box [letter copy book—Foreign Loans 1823–1831], Nathan to Count Lieven, March 14; same to same, March 27 (and letter of same date to Guryev). Cf. Cottrell, "Business man and financier," pp. 27ff.; Chapman, *Foundation,* p. 21. The names which figure most prominently in the list of subscribers are those of Jewish brokers and merchants, many of them related to the Rothschilds by marriage: Cohen, Mocatta, Stern, Sichel, Worms, Schnapper, Symons and Samuels. But there are also old Huguenot firms like Rougemont and Cazenove, as well as Scots like Reid, Irving. In addition, substantial parcels of the loan went to David Parish and to the Austrian Chancellor Metternich, who seems to have encouraged the Russians to turn to the Rothschilds: see Palmer, *Metternich,* pp. 215f. On the success of the loan, see the comment by the French ambassador in London, Chateaubriand: "Si cet emprunt n'était pas si modique, il pourrait faire croire à la guerre": *Correspondence générale,* vol. III, pp. 102f.

113 Capefigue, *Grandes opérations,* vol. III, p. 103.

114 Pückler, *Briefe,* p. 441.

115 RAL, XI/82/9/1/100, Amschel, Frankfurt, to James, Paris, April 30, 1817.

116 RAL, T27/262, XI/109/7, Carl, Frankfurt, to Salomon and Nathan, London, May 4, 1817; *The Times,* Sept. 10, 1822.

117 Rubens, *Anglo-Jewish portraits,* p. 299.

118 *The Times,* Jan. 15, 1821. Cf. Gille, *Banque et crédit,* p. 284.

119 CPHDCM, 637/1/18/13–14, Metternich, Troppau, to Salomon, Abschrift, Dec. 21, 1820; Salomon to Metternich, undated, *c.* end Dec.

120 Corti, *Rise*, pp. 253f.
121 CPHDCM, 637/1/18/15, Metternich, Laibach, to Salomon, Vienna, Dec. 29, 1820; CPHDCM, 637/1/18/14, Salomon to Nesselrode, Laibach, Jan. 29, 1821; CPHDCM, 637/1/18/13–14, Salomon to Metternich, Laibach, Abschrift, Feb. 4, 1821. Cf. Corti, *Rise*, pp. 254–7.
122 Corti, *Rise*, pp. 258ff.
123 *Ibid.*, pp. 260–63; Palmer, *Metternich*, p. 200.
124 Corti, *Rise*, pp. 265ff.
125 *Ibid.*, pp. 267–74, 285–8. Cf. Ehrenberg, *Große Vermögen*, p. 107; Heuberger, *Rothschilds*, pp. 80ff.; Gille, *Maison Rothschild*, vol. I, pp. 88–96; Bouvier, *Rothschild*, pp. 67–9; Schroeder, *Metternich*, pp. 109, 149.
126 Cameron, *France and Europe*, pp. 408f.; Ayer, *Century of finance*, pp. 16–35. See also Gille, *Banque et crédit*, pp. 283–92.
127 Corti, *Rise*, pp. 295ff., 375–6; Acton, *Bourbons*, pp. 688, 699. For unfounded claims that the Rothschilds had insisted on Medici's reappointment see Reeves, *Rothschilds*, pp. 65ff., 265; Balla, *Romance*, pp. 218–23.
128 Corti, *Rise*, pp. 376–80. Ultimately only around 300,000 ducats were repaid.
129 *Ibid.*, pp. 381–95, 415. The problem was that neither her son by Napoleon, the Duke of Reichstadt, nor her two children by her second husband, Count von Neipperg, stood to inherit her Italian duchies, which were to pass to the Duke of Lucca after her death.
130 *Ibid.*, pp. 354–7.
131 *Ibid.*, pp. 298–300, 324–7; Gille, *Maison Rothschild*, vol. I, pp. 96–103; Helleiner, *Imperial loans*, p. 168; Born, *International banking*, p. 39. Salomon initially offered to underwrite a loan of 42.8 million gulden at an effective price of just 67. When this was refused he proposed a smaller loan of just 12 million gulden, offering to pay "1.5 per cent more for the amount decided than is offered by any other firm." The same tactic was repeated when the loan was put out to tender; now Salomon simply offered to pay 0.5 per cent more than the highest bidder. The Austrian government wisely waited, and in April 1823 was able to secure significantly improved terms from a Rothschild-led consortium: a loan of 36 million gulden was issued at an underwriting price of 82.
132 RAL, T5/212, XI/87/OB, Salomon, Vienna, to Nathan, London, April 7, 1823; RAL, T6/34, Metternich to Salomon, Nov. 17. Cf. Helleiner, *Imperial loans*, pp. 171–5; Corti, *Rise*, pp. 322–2, 327–30; Nichols, "Britain and the Austrian war debt," pp. 342ff.; Macartney, *Habsburg Empire*, pp. 205f.; Macartney, *House*, p. 46; Katzenstein, *Disjoined partners*, pp. 60f.; Cope, *Walter Boyd*, pp. 140f.
133 Gille, *Maison Rothschild*, vol. I, pp.168f.
134 RAL, T6/18, Belin [Rothschild agent], Madrid, to deRF, Sept. 23, 1822. In fact the Cortes loans were handled by the Paris bankers Laffitte and Ardouin & Hubbard: Corti, *Rise*, pp. 306ff., 312; Gille, *Maison Rothschild*, vol. I, pp. 108f., 132; Bouvier, *Rothschild*, pp. 69–72. Cf. Carr, *Spain*, pp. 120–50; Jardin and Tudesq, *Restoration*, pp. 60ff.
135 Corti, *Rise*, pp. 314ff.; Bertier de Sauvigny, *Metternich at la France*, pp. 729–33; Gille, *Banque et crédit*, pp. 283–92. Metternich suspected that this initiative had the backing of the French government, or at least that part of it which was against intervention, but British observers believed that the Rothschilds were "pacific" for reasons of their own: RAL, T27/185, Speerman to Herries, Dec. 3, 1822.
136 RAL, T6/28, Dalberg, Paris, to Nathan, London, March 28, 1823. Dalberg predicted "a major calamity" and "a short but decisive crisis" in France.
137 Villèle, *Mémoires*, vol. III, pp. 429f.; vol. IV, p. 73; Payard, *Ouvrard*, pp. 313–39; Corti, *Rise*, pp. 316–21. As Finance Minister and then premier, Villèle had succeeded in establishing a modicum of order in the French financial system, but was disliked by the less "circumspect" Ultras, especially Chateaubriand.
138 Villèle, *Mémoires*, vol. III, p. 535; vol. IV, pp. 212f., 228; Serre, *Correspondance*, vol. IV, p. 566; Chateaubriand, *Correspondance générale*, vol. IV, pp. 315f.; vol. V, p. 16; Capefigue, *Grandes opérations*, vol. III, pp. 113–15; Marion, *Histoire financière*, vol. V, p. 36; Corti, *Rise*, pp. 313f.; Gille, *Maison Rothschild*, vol. I, pp. 81–8; *idem*, *Banque et crédit*, pp. 162–71, 180–82; Bouvier, *Rothschild*, pp. 74–81; Cameron, *France and Europe*, pp. 108–10.
139 RAL, Cataloguing Box [letter copy book Foreign Loans 1823–1831], Nathan, London, to "My Dear Brother," probably James, Paris, July 22, 1823; Chateaubriand, *Correspondance générale*, vol. V, p. 102. Cf. Corti, *Rise*, pp. 321f., 345f.; Gille, *Maison Rothschild*, vol. I, pp. 113–32; Cameron, *France and Europe*, pp. 405f.; Born, *International banking*, pp. 39f. Significantly, no Rothschild was sent to Madrid and the negotiations there were entrusted to agents, first Belin and then Renevier.

140 Villèle, *Mémoires*, vol. IV, p. 57.

141 Corti, *Rise*, pp. 357f.; Gille, *Banque et crédit*, pp. 287f.; Bouvier, *Rothschild*, pp. 69–72.

142 RAL, XI/109J/J/26, James, Paris, to Nathan, London, Nov. 27, 1826. See also RAL, XI/109J/J/27, same to same, April 23, 1827; April 24.

143 See e.g. RAL, T6/47, Vincent Gray, Havana, to Nathan, March 3, 1825, lamenting Nathan's lack of "confidence" in Peru.

144 Dawson, *Debt crisis, passim*; Clapham, *Bank of England*, vol. II, pp. 93ff.

145 RAL, T6/7, Gregor MacGregor of Poyais to Nathan, London, June 30, 1821.

146 For evidence of Nathan's commercial interests in Brazil at this time, see RAL, XI/38/215A, Samuel, Phillips & Co., Rio de Janeiro, to Nathan, London, Oct. 19, 1822.

147 In 1807 the Portuguese Crown Prince Joao had gone to Brazil at the time of the French invasion. In 1812, when the French were driven out, he refused to leave Brazil and elevated it "to the dignity, prominence and denomination of a Kingdom" equal with Portugal following his mother's death in 1816. Six years later, when Joao VI returned to Portugal, his son Pedro became Emperor and he remained as such when Brazil's independence was recognised in August 1825. When João died the following year, Pedro in turn passed the Portuguese throne to his daughter Maria, though this arrangement was subsequently challenged by Pedro's brother Miguel.

148 RAL, Cataloguing Box [letter copy book Foreign Loans 1823–1831], Nathan to Bank of England, June 16, 1823; Nathan to Baron de Teixeira, Portuguese Minister of Finance, July 1; Nathan to David Parish, July 16; James Campbell & Co., London, to Parish, July 16; Nathan to Parish, July 19; Nathan, to his brother [probably James], July 22; Nathan to the Governor and Deputy Governor, Bank of England, Sept. 10; same to same, Sept. 30; RAL, I/218/3/31, Nathan to Parish, July 16. Shares of the loan were taken by Baring and Reid, Irving; the negotiations in Lisbon were entrusted to David Parish. Disingenuously, the Rothschilds sought the French government's permission before making this loan, prompting Villèle to remark: "Voilà bien la finance cherchant à intervenir dans la politique": Villèle, *Mémoires*, vol. IV, p. 228.

149 Dawson, *Debt crisis*, esp. pp. 77f., 93, 108f., 180; Ayer, *Century of finance*, pp. 14–35.

150 Prawer, *Heine*, pp. 142–4.

151 RAL, XI/109J/J/26, James, Paris, to Nathan, London, Nov. 27, 1826.

152 Villèle, *Mémoires*, vol. III, p. 535.

153 Buxton, *Finance*, vol. I, pp. 15–27; Clapham, *Bank of England*, vol. II, pp. 93ff.; Kindleberger, *Financial history*, pp. 166ff., 221.

154 Dawson, *Debt crisis*, pp. 20f.

155 Put simply, the plan drawn up by Nathan was that the Rothschilds, Barings and Laffitte together would undertake the conversion in return for the first year's saving which resulted from it (28 million francs). To make the conversion attractive, Nathan insisted that the Banque de France must set its discount rate at 3 per cent: Villèle, *Mémoires*, vol. V, pp. 73f.; Capefigue, *Grandes opérations*, vol. III, pp. 128–132; Marion, *Histoire financière*, vol. V, pp. 36–60; Ehrenberg, *Große Vermögen*, pp. 109f.; Corti, *Rise*, pp. 337–42; Gille, *Maison Rothschild*, vol. I, pp.133–44; Gille, *Banque et crédit*, pp. 174–82; Priouret, *Caisse des Dépôts*, pp. 52f.

156 Jardin and Tudesq, *Restoration*, pp. 54ff. Brogan, *French nation*, p. 40; Bouvier, *Rothschild*, pp. 74–81. Chirac, *Haute Banque*, pp. 152–5 echoes Périer's attack on the foreign bankers involved.

157 Corti, *Rise*, pp. 350ff.; Gille, *Maison Rothschild*, vol. I, pp. 144–50. For James's over-optimistic assessment, Metternich, *Nachgelassenen Papieren*, p. 174.

158 Ouvrard, *Mémoires*, vol. III, p. 289.

159 See e.g. RAL, XI/109J/J/25, James, Paris, to Nathan, London, Jan. 28, 1825: "The Minister said to me today, 'Mr Rothschild, you have the reputation of a man who has been selling large numbers of rentes.' I must therefore be careful not to antagonise the Government. However, I think that on Monday or Tuesday when the King is due to make his speech I will be able to sell [rentes] at a better rate than today and I will profit from the situation because I don't foresee any sizeable rise."

160 Gille, *Maison Rothschild*, vol. I, pp. 151–3; Gille, *Banque et crédit*, pp. 70–76. Cf. Castellane, *Journal*, p. 210.

161 *The Times*, Aug. 4, 1836. In fact, Nathan intervened to support the rente after the rejection of the conversion bill, which unleashed a wave of selling in Paris and London.

162 Buxton, *Finance*, vol. I, pp. 15–27.

163 Healey, *Coutts*, p. 261; Kynaston, *City*, vol. I, p. 42.

164 Clapham, *Bank of England*, vol. II, pp. 93ff.

165 Powell, *Money market*, pp. 254ff. Of twenty-six foreign government loans totalling £52.4 million which had been made between 1823 and 1826, sixteen were in default within a few years.

166 Corti, *Rise*, pp. 348–50.

167 See e.g. Reeves, *Rothschild*, pp. 181ff.; Balla, *Romance*, p. 126; Morton, *Rothschilds*, p. 67.

168 Bank of England, G8 (Committee of Treasury) 21 1145/2, ff. 185–7, Nathan to Bank of England, June 16, 1823; Green, "Precious heritage," pp. 235–42, 244f.

169 Clapham, *Bank of England*, vol. II, pp. 80ff., 95.

170 See e.g. Bank of England, G8 (Committee of Treasury) 22 1145/3 f. 117, Nathan to Bank of England, Nov. 30, 1824.

171 RAL, XI/109J/J/25F1, James, Paris, to Nathan, London, undated, *c.* Jan. 1825; RAL, XI/109J/J/25, same to same, Jan. 4; Jan. 5; Jan. 7; Jan. 9; Jan. 14; Jan. 16; Jan. 17; Jan. 18; Jan. 19; Jan. 20; Jan. 25; Jan. 28; Jan. 30.

172 Stapleton, *Canning*, pp. 227ff.

173 Kynaston, *City*, vol. I, pp. 69ff.; Rothschild, *Shadow*, pp. 41ff; Morgan, *Central banking*, pp. 84f.

174 Quoted in Rothschild, *Shadow*, pp. 41ff.

175 Kynaston, *City*, vol. I, p. 70; Davis, *English Rothschilds*, pp. 22–5; Wilson, *Rothschild*, p. 87. Others, including Thomas Attwood, gave the same advice: Moss, *Attwood*, pp. 129ff.

176 RAL, T37/158, Herries to Liverpool, Sept. 27, 1826; RAL, XI/109J/J/26, James, Paris, to Nathan, London, Nov. 2; same to same, Nov. 6; Nov. 8; Nov. 11; Nov. 13; Nov. 17; Nov. 30; RAL, XI/109J/J/27, April 7, 1827; April 9. Cf. Davis, *English Rothschilds*, pp. 45f.

177 RAL, XI/109J/J/29, James, Paris, to Nathan, London, Dec. 1, 1829.

178 Green, "Precious heritage," pp. 242f.; Rothschild, *Shadow*, pp. 46f.

179 Kindleberger, *Financial history*, pp. 62f., 79.

180 Davis, *English Rothschilds*, p. 45.

181 Schwemer, *Geschichte*, vol. II, pp. 149ff.

182 Forstmann, *Bethmann*, pp. 260–64.

FIVE *"Hue and Cry" (1826–1829)*

1 Rubens, *Anglo-Jewish portraits*, p. 94.

2 RAL, T31/ 297/4, XI/109/4, Carl, Frankfurt, to James, Paris, June 30, 1816; RAL, T32/2/1, XI/109/5A, same to same, undated, *c.* July.

3 RAL, T33/390/2, XI/109/53, Carl, Berlin, to Amschel, Frankfurt, Dec. 27, 1816. See also RAL, T5/172, Carl to his brothers, Jan. 25, 1817.

4 RAL, T27/200, Carl, Hamburg, to Amschel, Frankfurt, Feb. 17, 1817.

5 RAL, T61/62/2, XI/109/6, Amschel, Frankfurt, to James, Paris, Feb. 28, 1817.

6 RAL, T62/122/1, XI/109/7, Carl, Frankfurt, to Salomon and Nathan, London, May 1, 1817.

7 RAL, T62/ 84/4, XI/109/7, James and Salomon, Paris, to Nathan, London, June 7, 1817; RAL, T63/71/2, XI/109/8, Salomon to Nathan, Sept. 6. It is surprising that the Rothschilds could still fear that bills endorsed by them might not be accepted.

8 RAL, T27/302, Salomon and James, Paris, to Nathan, London, Oct. 22, 1817.

9 RAL, T64/221/3, XI/109/9, Carl, Frankfurt, to Salomon, undated, *c.* June 1818.

10 See e.g. HSM, Bestand 6a Nr 1946, *Nouvelles de Heidelberg*, Dec. 29, 1820.

11 The first translators of the Rothschilds" *Judendeutsch* correspondence tended to do this: see e.g. RAL, T29/68, XI/109/0/3/11, Amschel, Frankfurt, to James, undated, *c.* early 1814; RAL, T28/11, Amschel, Berlin, to Carl, undated, *c.* Aug. 1814; RAL, T34/1, NMR 288, Amschel, Frankfurt, to Salomon and Nathan, Jan. 3, 1816.

12 Details of Amschel's protracted battle with the Jewish community in Kassel in HSM, Bestand 266 Nr 908, Nrn 11f., Amschel, Vollmacht, Jan. 18, 1816; HSM, Bestand 266 Nr 903, Amschel, Erwiderung to Kurfürstliche Regierung, Jan. 18; HSM, Bestand 266 Nr 908, Nr 91, Wilhelm, Landgraf von Hessen, Decret, Feb. 7, 1818.

13 Forstmann, *Bethmann*, pp. 253f.

14 For example, Bethmann and Gontard hoped to co-found a note-issuing bank in Frankfurt with Amschel, a request the Senate refused in 1824: Schwemer, *Geschichte*, vol. II, pp. 261ff.

15 Forstmann, *Bethmann*, pp. 260–64.

16 See illustration 10.vi below. The title is a pun: "Exemplary Knight" literally, but also "Knight with Samples."

17 See illustration 7.i below.

18   RAL, T30, XI/109/2/2/170, Eva, Frankfurt, to Salomon and James, Paris, Nov. 15, 1815. Cf. RAL, T27/105, XI/82/1, Carl, Frankfurt, to Amschel, Sept. 9, 1814; RAL, T29/350, XI/109/1/7/43, Carl to Salomon and Nathan, Dec. 11.

19   RAL, T5/96, Nathan, London to Carl, Amsterdam, May 23, 1815; RAL, XI/109/2/2/83, Amschel to Salomon and James, Paris, Sept. 17; RAL, XI/109/2/2/117, Amschel to his brothers, undated, c. Sept.; RAL, XI/109/2/2/115, same to same, Sept. 28. See also RAL, T31/64/2, XI/109/4/2/64, Carl, Frankfurt, to Nathan and James, Feb. 12, 1816; RAL, T31/238/4, XI/109/4, Amschel, Berlin, to his mother and Carl, June 22; RAL, T33/324/2, XI/109/5B, Amschel, Frankfurt, to Salomon, Nov. 13; RAL, T33/325/2, XI/109/5B, Amschel to James, Nov. 12.

20   RAL, T27/204, XI/109/6, Amschel, Frankfurt, to James, Paris, Feb. 25, 1817; RAL, T62/21/1, XI/109/7, Carl, Frankfurt, to Salomon, Nathan and James, May 11.

21   RAL, T5/175, Amschel, Frankfurt, to Salomon and Nathan, Jan. 26, 1817; RAL, T61/23/1, XI/109/6, Amschel to James, Paris, Jan. 27; RAL, T62/24/1, Carl, Frankfurt, to Salomon and James, May 20.

22   Arnsberg, *Geschichte der Frankfurter Juden*, vol. I, pp. 352f.; Heuberger and Krohn, *Hinaus aus dem Ghetto*, pp. 24ff.; Muhlstein, *Baron James*, p. 65. The origin of the word "Hep" is variously explained: as an acronym of "Hierosolyma est perdita," or as the sound of bleating goats, alluding to the Jews' traditional beards. There was a similar backlash against emancipation in many German towns: see e.g. RAL, T32/245/1, XI/109/5B, representative of the Hamburg Jewish community to Nathan, Oct. 1, 1816.

23   RAL, T62/63/3, XI/109/7, Amschel, Frankfurt, to Salomon, Paris, June 23, 1817; Corti, *Rise*, pp. 231ff.

24   RAL, T64/243/3, XI/109/9, Amschel, Frankfurt, to Salomon, June 1, 1818.

25   RAL, XI/109/10/3, Undated, unsigned document of around 1817–18 concerning the Tugendbund (a group of Berlin intellectuals with nationalist leanings), which explicitly links liberalism and anti-Semitism. See also RAL, T3/185, Baron de Langsdorff, Karlsruhe, to Nathan, April 16, 1819, reporting on the conspiracy of silence in Germany following the murder of Kotzebue.

26   Corti, *Rise*, pp. 398f.; Arnsberg, *Geschichte der Frankfurter Juden*, vol. I, p. 127.

27   Corti, *Rise*, pp. 246–8. Parish himself was not Jewish.

28   Ehrenberg, *Große Vermögen*, pp. 115f.; Corti, *Rise*, pp. 365–7; Gille, *Maison Rothschild* vol. I, pp. 159–61; Bouvier, *Rothschild*, pp. 72f.; Emden, *Money powers*, pp. 25f.

29   List, *Grundlinien*, p. 243.

30   RAL, XI/109/2/2/134, Salomon and James to Nathan, Oct. 7, 1815.

31   Fournier-Verneuil, *Paris*, pp. 51–2, 64f.

32   Green, "Precious heritage," p. 239.

33   Laffitte, *Mémoires*, pp. 114f.

34   RAL, T64/179/2, XI/109/9, James, Paris, to his brothers, Feb. 14, 1818.

35   Kynaston, *City*, vol. I, p. 53.

36   Roth, *Magnificent Rothschilds*, plate opposite p. 20.

37   Rubens, *Anglo-Jewish portraits*, pp. 94f. For an erroneous reading, see Herding, "Rothschilds in der Karikatur," pp. 22f.

38   See illustration 10.vii below.

39   Briggs, *Age of improvement*, pp. 218ff.; *DNB*; Bourne, *Palmerston: Early years*, p. 265; Corti, *Rise*, pp. 402ff.; Davis, *English Rothschilds*, p. 42.

40   Aspinall, *Politics and the press*, pp. 196f., 218f., 228.

41   *Hansard*, New Series, vol. XVIII, pp. 540–43, Feb. 18, 1828. Cf. *The Times*, Feb. 19, 1828.

42   His "Political Georgics," a pastiche of Dryden's Georgics, appeared in *The Times*, March 18, 1828: Pinney (ed), *Macaulay letters*, vol. II, p. 60. Macaulay later repeated the lines in a letter to his sister:

"... Oh mysterious two,
Lords of our fate, the Doctor and the Jew,
If by your care preferred th'aspiring clerk [Herries]
Quits the close alley for the breezy park,
... And you, great pair, through Windsor's shades who rove,
The Faun and Dryad of the conscious grove,
All, all, inspire me;—for of all I sing
Doctor and Jew and Marchioness and King ...
But the black stream beneath runs on the same
Still bawls in Wetherell's key, still stinks like Herries['] name."

43 Cf. Salbstein, *Emancipation*, p. 215.

44 *DNB.*

45 Jewish Theological Seminary, *Jew as Other*, p. 57.

46 Corti, *Rise*, pp. 402ff.

47 RAL, XI/109J/J/26, James, Paris, to Nathan, London, Nov. 27, 1826.

48 Stapleton (ed.), *Correspondence of Canning*, p. 173.

49 RAL, XI/109J/J/27, James, Paris, to Nathan, London, April 7, 1827; same to same, April 10; April 11; April 13; April 28.

50 RAL, XI/109J/J/26, James, Paris, to Nathan, London, Nov. 9, 1826; same to same, Nov. 11; Nov. 14; Nov. 19; Nov. 28 (two letters); Nov. 29; Nov. 30.

51 RAL, XI/109J/J/27, James, Paris, to Nathan, London, April 30, 1827.

52 Seton-Watson, *Russian Empire*, pp. 179ff.

53 Jardin and Tudesq, *Restoration*, pp. 68f.

54 Sweet, *Gentz*, p. 258.

55 Gentz, *Briefe an Pilat*, vol. II, p. 196.

56 Corti, *Rise*, pp. 402ff.

57 Kynaston, *City*, vol. I, p. 92.

58 Ayer, *Century of finance*, pp. 14–35; Davis, *English Rothschilds*, p. 44.

59 RAL, XI/109J/J/29/A, James, Paris, to Nathan, London, May 22, 1829; RAL, XI/109J/J/29, same to same, May 25; May 29. Cf. Corti, *Rise*, p. 335f. The loan was intended solely to enable Brazil to maintain interest payments on her existing debt. James "admit[ted] quite frankly that in two years" time these people will not pay anything"; but in the short run it boosted the price of Brazilian bonds.

60 RAL, T17/89, NMR, London, to Kankrin, March 31, 1828. Cf. Corti, *Rise*, pp. 404ff.; Gille, *Maison Rothschild*, vol. I, p. 169; Bouvier, *Rothschild*, p. 89.

61 RAL, XI/109J/J/28, James, Paris, to Nathan, London, Oct. 7, 1828; same to same, Oct. 10; RAL, T17/120, Anthony to Nathan, London, April 20, 1829; RAL, XI/109J/J/29, James to Nathan, May 13; same to same, May 19; June 19; June 24.

62 Corti, *Rise*, pp. 408–10. Cf. RAL, XI/109/14/1/41, Salomon, Vienna, to Stieglitz, Petersburg, copy, March 20, 1830. See also RAL, XI/109J/J/29, James, Paris, to Nathan, London, May 16, 1829; same to same, May 18; May 22; May 25; June 30; Aug. 18.

63 RAL, XI/109/J/J/29, James, Paris, to Nathan, London, Aug. 18, 1829.

64 RAL, T62/58/3, XI/109/7, Amschel, Frankfurt, to Salomon and James, Paris, June 10, 1817.

65 RAL, T64/199/3, Carl, Frankfurt, to Nathan and James, April 10, 1818.

66 RAL, T64/301/3, XI/109/9, James, Paris, to Nathan and Salomon, March 30, 1818.

67 RAL, T63/2/1, XI/109/8, Salomon, Paris, to Nathan, London, Nov. 3, 1817; RAL, T63/44/1, XI/109/8, Salomon and James to Nathan, Dec. 1.

68 By 1829 the duc was a "good friend" of James: RAL, T63/133/2, Salomon and James, Paris, to Nathan, London, Oct. 6, 1817; RAL, XI/109J/J/29/B, James to Nathan and Lionel, May 22, 1829. Cf. Corti, *Rise*, p. 282.

69 RAL, XI/109/10/2/2, Copy of letter from Hardenberg, Sept. 15, 1817; RAL, T63/83/2, XI/109/8, Carl to brothers, Sept. 18; RAL, T64/273/3, Salomon and Carl, Koblenz, to Nathan, London, March 14, 1818. Cf. GStA, I. HA, Rep 92, Amschel to Rother, Sept. 30, 1817.

70 RAL, T3/112, various letters from Wilhelm von Humboldt, 1817, relating to private financial matters; CPHDCM, 637/1/6/52–7, Balance sheet of the London house, July 31, 1825.

71 Corti, *Rise*, p. 220.

72 RAL, T32/182/1, XI/109/5B, Carl, Frankfurt, to James, Sept. 8, 1816.

73 RAL, T32/171/1, XI/109/5B, Amschel and Carl, Frankfurt, to James, Paris, Sept. 3, 1816; RAL, T32/186/1, XI/109/5/3, Carl to Nathan and Salomon, Sept. 9.

74 RAL, T62/39/2, XI/109/2, Salomon, Paris, to Nathan, London, May 17, 1817.

75 RAL, T27/170, XI/109/7, Salomon and James, Paris, to Nathan, London, May 12, 1817.

76 RAL, T63/137/2, Salomon and James, Paris, to Nathan, London, Oct. 18, 1817; RAL, T27/302, same to same, Oct. 22.

77 RAL, XI/109/9/1/81, Salomon and James, Paris, to Nathan, London, Jan. 15, 1818; RAL, T64/171/2, XI/109/9, James to Nathan, Feb. 5. Cf. NLS, Stuart MS 21293 ff. 72, 92, James, Paris, to Charles Stuart [*sic*], two business letters of 1822.

78 RAL, XI/109J/J/38, James, Paris, to his brothers and nephews, London, Nov. 10, 1838.

79 CPHDCM, 637/1/6/52–7, Balance sheet of the London house, July 31, 1825; Davis, *English Roth-schilds*, p. 33.

80 See e.g. RAL, XI/109J/J/29/A, James, Paris, to Nathan and Lionel, London, May 22, 1829.

81 RAL, T63/8/1, XI/109/8, Salomon and James, Paris, Nathan, London, Nov. 17, 1817. Cf. CPHDCM, 637/1/6/52–7, Balance sheet of the London house, July 31, 1825.

82 RAL, XI/109/9/1/108, James, Paris, to Nathan, London, Jan. 22, 1818.

83 CPHDCM, 637/1/3, Inventarium nach den Handlungs Büchern v. Herrn M.A. Rothschild gezogen, Frankfurt, May 12, 1807.

84 RAL, T29/273, XI/109/1/5/3, Amschel, Berlin, to Nathan, London, Oct. 11, 1814.

85 RAL, XI/109/2/2/121, Amschel, Frankfurt, to his brothers, Oct. 1, 1815; HSM, Bestand 6a Nr 1941, acc 1897/41 Nr 35, Nr. 1, MAR to Elector, Oct. 2; RAL, XI/109/2/2/143, Amschel to Carl and Nathan, Oct. 16; RAL, T30, XI/109/2/1/147, Schmerfeld to MAR, Oct. 19; HSM, Bestand 6a Nr 1941, acc 1897/41 Nr 35, Nr 4/5, Harrison, Treasury Chambers, to Nathan, Nov. 24; RAL, T30, XI/109/2/2/232, Carl, Kassel, to Amschel, Dec. 9; RAL, XI/109/2/2/216, same to same, Dec. 11; RAL, XI/109/2/2/224, Carl to Nathan, London, Dec. 14; RAL, XI/109/2/2/222, Carl to Amschel, Dec. 14; RAL, XI/109/2/2/234, Carl to his brothers, Dec. 20; RAL, T30, XI/109/2/2/236, Carl to Amschel, Dec. 21; RAL, XI/109/2/2/241, same to same, Dec. 23; RAL, XI/109/2/2/247, Dec. 27; RAL, XI/109/2/2/248, Dec. 28; RAL, XI/109/2/2/250, Carl to his brothers, Dec. 29; HSM, Bestand 6a Nr. 1941, acc 1897/41 Nr 35, Nr 13, Elector, decree, Jan. 8, 1816; RAL, T51/20(a), XI/148/2/342, Nathan to MAR, Jan. 23; RAL, T51/19, receipt of £148,000 signed by Nathan, Jan. 26.

86 RAL, T31, XI/109/4/12/1, Salomon, Paris, to Nathan, London, Jan. 7, 1816.

87 RAL, T27/302, Salomon and James, Paris, to Nathan, London, Oct. 22, 1817.

88 RAL, T63/6/1, XI/109/8, Salomon and James, Paris, to Nathan, London, Nov. 15, 1817.

89 RA, 31736, Note by Robert Gray, Aug. 11, 1822. See also RA, 31738, Nathan, London, to Robert Gray, Duchy of Cornwall, Somerset Place, July 23, 1822, for an earlier £6,028.

90 RAL, Cataloguing Box [letter copy book Foreign Loans 1823–1831], Nathan, London, to Amschel, Frankfurt, May 15, 1823; Aspinall (ed.), *Letters of George IV*, vol. II, pp. 1025f.; vol. III, pp. 45ff.

91 RAL, I/218/3/87, Nathan to Duke of York, Feb. 23, 1824; RA, Add. 6/44, Nathan to Charles Green-wood, July 28, 1826; RA, Add. 21/109, Statement in Chancery, Greenwood v. Taylor, Feb. 1, 1827. The loan was apparently never repaid, so Nathan kept the jewels.

92 RAL, T31/63/2, XI/109/4, Carl, Frankfurt, to Nathan, London, Jan. 11, 1816. Cf. Davis, *English Rothschilds*, p. 39.

93 RAL, T51/21, Nathan, London to MAR, April 12, 1816; RAL, T32/88/2, XI/109/5A, Carl, Frankfurt, to Nathan and Salomon, Aug. 1. See also the various letters from Leopold's aide Hardenbrook to Nathan in RAL, T3/106–11.

94 RAL, T62/34/2, Salomon, Paris, to Nathan, London, May 10, 1817.

95 RAL, T62/36/2, Salomon, Paris, to Nathan, London, May 12, 1817. See also RAL, T63/30/1, XI/109/8, Carl, Berlin, to Amschel and James, undated, c. May 1817.

96 RAL, T63/10/1, XI/109/1, Salomon and James, Paris, to Nathan, London, Nov. 24, 1817.

97 RAL, XI/4/1, Privy Counsellor Lindemann to Nathan, June 23, 1823; RAL, XI/109/21/3/1, Note regarding Prince Leopold of Saxe-Coburg's proposed life insurance, March 5, 1830.

98 Bussche, *Arnim*, pp. 10ff.

99 RAL, XI/109J/J/30, James, Paris, to Nathan, London, Feb. 20, 1830.

100 Dairnvaell, *Histoire édifiante*, pp. 8ff.

101 Berghoeffer, *Meyer Amschel*, pp. 210ff.

102 RA, Y57/10, Edward, Duke of Kent, to Thomas Coutts, Coutts & Co., May 13, 1818.

103 RAL, T51/22, Lt Col. Harvey, Kensington Palace, to Nathan, Sept. 2, 1818; RAL, T51/23, Duke of Kent's Secretary to Nathan, Aug. 4, 1819; RAL, T3/159, Correspondence relating to estate of Duke of Kent, 1820. Cf. Davis, *English Rothschilds*, p. 39.

104 Berghoeffer, *Meyer Amschel*, pp. 210ff.

105 RAL, T51/26, XI/120/3A/3/98, Duchess of Kent, Windsor Castle, to NMR, Oct. 12,

106 RAL, XI/109/2/1/63, Salomon, Paris, to Nathan, Sept. 10, 1815; RAL, XI/109/2/2/83, Amschel to Salomon and James, Sept. 17; RAL, T3/228, Metternich to MAR, Sept. 30.

107 RAL, T31/238/4, XI/109/4, Carl, Frankfurt, to James, Paris, June 2, 1816; RAL, T33/375/2, XI/109/5B, Amschel, Frankfurt, to James, Dec. 18.

108   See e.g., RAL, XI/109/2/2/153, Salomon and James, Paris, to Nathan, London, Oct. 25, 1815; RAL, XI/109/2/2/156, Salomon to Nathan, Oct. 29; RAL, T30; XI/109/2/2/155, Amschel, Frankfurt, to Salomon, Oct. 29.

109   RAL, T61/4/1, XI/109/6, Carl, Berlin, to Salomon, Nathan and James, Jan. 7, 1817; RAL, T61/9/1, XI/109/6, Carl to Amschel, Frankfurt, Jan. 10.

110   RAL, T64/125/3, XI/109/9, Carl, Frankfurt, to Nathan and Salomon, April 7, 1818; RAL, T3/229, Metternich to Nathan, London, July 2, 1820; RAL, T52/4, Captain Bauer, Chandos House, to Nathan, London, July 22, 1821. Two years later, Nathan purchased a jewel-encrusted box from Metternich: RAL, T5/212, Salomon, Vienna, to Nathan, London, April 7, 1823.

111   In fact, Amschel provided a sumptuous lunch, to which a number of leading figures in the Frankfurt diplomatic corps were also invited. The *Augsburger Zeitung* reported that "the stairs leading to the ban-quetting room were laid out with red carpet, and decorated with garlands of flowers and plants . . . Sev-eral of the most distinguished emissaries to the German Diet, as well as foreign ministers present here, enjoyed this guest luncheon prepared with no expense spared." Corti, *Rise*, pp. 290f.; Palmer, *Metter-nich*, p. 215; Harman, *Metternich*, p. 45; Heuberger, *Rothschilds*, p. 73.

112   Berghoeffer, *Meyer Amschel*, pp. 209ff.; Corti, *Rise*, pp. 301f., 357; Palmer, *Metternich*, pp. 215f.

113   Corti, *Rise*, p. 311.

114   Sauvigny, *Metternich et la France*, pp. 959f., 970. The *Courrier Français* also reported the dinner, humorously explaining the absence of the British ambassador as follows: "An Englishman was asked how it could be that the ambassador of his nation had not been present at this diplomatic feast. "Because," he replied, "England has no need of money." '

115   Apponyi, *Vingt-cinq ans*, vol. I, pp. 6ff.

116   See e.g. RAL, XI/109/10/1/11, Metternich, Pressburg, to Salomon, Vienna, Nov. 14, 1825; RAL, XI/109/10/1/12, Salomon to Metternich, Nov. 15.

117   Ehrenberg, *Große Vermögen*, pp. 115f. It is not quite clear what the "old rentes operation" was to which Parish referred.

118   CPHDCM, 637/1/18/23, Metternich's current account for the period Sept. 26, 1825, to June 30, 1826. Metternich had a gross income of 266,590 gulden for the three quarters covered by the state-ment, and outgoings totalling 78,164 gulden, leaving a credit balance of 188,426 gulden.

119   CPHDCM, 637/1/18/3–11, "Vertrag . . . zwischen seinem Durchlaucht dem hochgeborenen Herrn P. J. Fürsten Clemens, Wenzel, Lothar von Metternich Winneburg, Seinem k.k. Apostolischen Majestät Haus-, Hof-und Staatskanzler *einer-*, und dem Herrn Salomon Mayer Freiherrn von Rothschild . . . *andererseits*," March 20, 1827; CPHDCM, 637/1/18/26, Metternich to MAR, March 20; CPHDCM, 637/1/18/22, Metternich current account for the period Feb. 16, 1826 to March 31, 1827; CPHDCM, 637/1/18/24,25, Untitled statement of Metternich's mortgage on Plass, 1827–58.

120   CPHDCM, 637/1/6/22, 25, Abschluß der Wiener Filial, June 30, 1828; AN, 132 AQ 3/2 No. 5, Bal-ance, Vienna Filial of MAR, Sept. 26.

121   CPHDCM, 637/1/18/34–6, Metternich to Salomon, March 8, 1829; CPHDCM, 637/1/18/39, Met-ternich current account for the period July 16, 1827, to March 31, 1829, which shows that Metternich's income in the accounting period was 6,922 gulden, his outgoings 76,320 gulden; CPHDCM, 637/1/18/40, Salomon to Metternich, Oct. 26, 1829.

122   CPHDCM, 637/1/18/19, Ausweis, Dec. 30, 1829.

123   Corti, *Reign*, pp. 54f.

124   Metternich, *Nachgelassenen Papieren*, pp. 47, 324, 491, 493, 495; Corti, *Reign*, p. 230.

125   CPHDCM, 637/1/309, General von Wolzogen to Salomon, Jan. 11, 1821.

126   Berghoeffer, *Meyer Amschel*, pp. 224f.

127   CPHDCM, 637/1/23/99, Prince Esterházy, London, to "lieber Baron Salomon," Sept. 10, probably 1820; CPHDCM, 637/1/23/100, Salomon, Paris, to Esterházy (copy), Sept. 22; RAL, T5/200, Salomon, Vienna, to Nathan and Amschel, April 27, 1822.

128   CPHDCM, 637/1/23/10–11, Prince Esterházy to Arnstein & Eskeles and MAR, June 4, 1824; CPHDCM, 637/1/23/13–17, Prince Esterházy, contract with Arnstein & Eskeles, Simon George Sina, MAR, Nov. 10, 1824. Cf. Gille, *Maison Rothschild*, vol. I, pp. 429f.

129   CPHDCM, 637/1/6/52–57, Balance of London house, July 31, 1825; CPHDCM, 637/1/6/22, 25, Abschluß der Wiener Filial, June 30, 1828; AN, 132 AQ 3/2 No. 5, Balance, Vienna Filial of MAR, Sept. 26.

130   Corti, *Reign*, pp. 41f.; CPHDCM, 637/1/23/113, Passiv Stand [des] Fürsten Paul Esterházy, June 1,

1832; CPHDCM, 637/1/23/57, Summarischer Ausweis über dem Abschluß des [Esterházy] Passiv-Standes, June 1, 1835.

131 CPHDCM, 637/1/23/4–9, Contract with Prince Esterházy, Feb. 27, 1836; CPHDCM, 637/1/24/1–4, Schuld Verschreibung . . . Fürst Esterházy von Galantha, Feb. 29, 1836. In an effort to attract smaller investors, bonds were issued in denominations as small as 40 gulden.

132 CPHDCM, 637/1/26, Promemoria: Seine Durchlaucht der Herr Fürst Paul Esterházy von Galantha, 1844; CPHDCM, 637/1/26/9–15, Paul Esterházy, contract with MAR and S. G. Sina, Jan. 10, 1844; CPHDCM, 637/1/26/16–21, Paul Esterházy, contract with MAR and S. G. Sina, Jan. 11.

133 RFamC/1/106, Hannah, Frankfurt, to Lionel, London, undated, c. late 1846.

134 RAL, T52/5, Captain Bauer, Chandos House, to Nathan, London, Sept. 10, 1821; Loewe (ed.), *Montefiore diaries*, vol. I, pp. 34, 52.

135 CPHDCM, 637/1/310, *Allgemeine Zeitung* [article], Jan. 22, 1822, p. 87.

136 Ehrenberg, *Große Vermögen*, pp. 101ff.

137 *Ibid.*, pp. 76ff.

138 Corti, *Rise*, pp. 223–6; Sweet, *Gentz*, p. 219; Mann, *Secretary of Europe*, p. 256; Cecil, *Metternich*, pp. 154f.

139 CPHDCM, 637/1/309, Gentz to Salomon, Dec. 17, 1820; CPHDCM, 637/1/309, same to same, Jan. 8, 1821; Corti, *Rise*, pp. 267, 294, 305–10, 322f., 368, 398; Ehrenberg, *Große Vermögen*, p. 107; Sweet, *Gentz*, p. 249; Coudray, *Metternich*, p. 246.

140 Sweet, *Gentz*, pp. 283ff.

141 Corti, *Reign*, pp. 69–71.

142 Gentz, *Tagebücher*, p. 151.

143 Corti, *Rise*, pp. 292f.

144 Sweet, *Gentz*, pp. 273f.

145 Gentz, *Briefe an Pilat*, vol. II, p. 105.

146 Heilbrunn, "Haus Rothschild," pp. 12ff. See introduction.

147 Corti, *Reign*, pp. 51–3.

148 Corti, *Rise*, pp. 298f.

149 CPHDCM, 637/1/8/1–7; also RAL, RFamFD, B/1, Articles of agreement between Messrs de Rothschild [Amschel, Nathan, Salomon, Carl, Jacob and Anselm], Aug. 31, 1825; CPHDCM, 637/1/7/48–52, Abscrift [Partnership agreement], Sept. 26, 1828; CPHDCM, 637/1/6/17, General Inventarium . . . das gesamte Handlesvermögen, Sept. 26; CPHDCM, 637/1/6/44, 45, No. 4: General Capital [summary of total capital], Sept. 26.

150 Ziegler, *Sixth great power*, p. 374.

151 CPHDCM, 637/1/7/53–69, Vollständige Abschrift des Societäts-Vertrags . . . Übereinkunft, July 30, 1836.

152 AN, 132 AQ 3/2, Bilan Aug. 1825 deRF, Aug. 31, 1825; AN, 132 AQ 14/Bénéfices [Naples house] 1821–8; AN, 132 AQ 3/2, Bilan, deRF, 1er Semester, June 30, 1826, Bilan deRF, 1er Semester 1827, June 30, 1827; AN, 132 AQ 3, Paris house accounts, 1825–8.

153 Chapman, *Foundation*, p. 20. See also the figures in Cassis, *City*, p. 16.

154 Ayer, *Century of finance*. It is not entirely clear how Ayer arrived at his figures: the book seems to list the nominal value of major public and private sector securities issues.

155 Berghoeffer, *Meyer Amschel*.

156 Braudel and Labrousse, *Histoire économique*, vol. III, pp. 364–71.

157 Weill, "Rotschild et les finances de l'Europe."

SIX *Amschel's Garden*

1 Liberles, "Aristocrat and synagogue," pp. 195ff.

2 RAL, T63/58/1, XI/109/8, Carl, Berlin, to Salomon and James, Paris, Dec. 22, 1817.

3 CPHDCM, 637/1/5, Deed by Bürgermeister and Senate, March 24, 1809. Cf. Bartetzko, "Fairy tales and castles," pp. 221ff.

4 IfS, Rechtsupplikation 1808 Tom. I, ff. 138–46, 332–5, Salomon to Senate, Dec. 24, 1807. Cf. Berghoeffer, *Meyer Amschel*, p. 125.

5 Bartetzko, "Fairy tales and castles," pp. 224f.; Heuberger, *Rothschilds*, p. 175.

6 RAL, XI/109/2/1/43, Amschel, Frankfurt, to Carl, April 9, 1815.

7 RAL, XI/109/2/2/88, Amschel, Frankfurt, to his brothers, Sept. 19, 1815; RAL, XI/109/2/2/90, Amschel to unidentified recipient, Sept. 19.

SOURCE NOTES

521

8   RAL, XI/109/2/2/203, Carl, Frankfurt, to his brother, Dec. 4, 1815.
9   RAL, T31/1/5, Nathan, London, to Amschel, Carl and James, Jan. 2, 1816; RAL, T34/1, NMR 288, Nathan to Amschel, Frankfurt, Jan. 3.
10 RAL, T34/20, Amschel, Frankfurt, to James, Paris, April 6, 1816; RAL, T31/194/3, XI/109/4, Amschel to Salomon and James, May 1.
11 RAL, T31/208/3, XI/109/4, Amschel, Frankfurt, to Salomon and James, Paris, May 8, 1816.
12 RAL, T31/229/14, XI/109/4, Amschel, Frankfurt, to Salomon, Carl and James, May 25, 1816.
13 RAL, T31/63/1, XI/109/5A, Amschel, Berlin, to James, Paris, July 24, 1816; RAL, T34/35, Amschel, Frankfurt, to Salomon and Nathan, London, Sept. 15; RAL, T32/373/2, XI/109/5B, Amschel to James, Dec. 16; RAL, T61/26/1, XI/109/6, Carl, Berlin, to Amschel, Jan. 28, 1817; RAL, T27/204, XI/109/6, Amschel to James, Feb. 25; RAL, T61/62/2, XI/109/6, Feb. 28; RAL, T61/105/2, Carl, Frankfurt, to James, April 4.
14 Berghoeffer, *Meyer Amschel,* p. 173.
15 RAL, T32/246/1, XI/109/5B, Jonas Rothschild, Frankfurt, to Salomon, Oct. 13, 1816. For Amschel's homesickness for the garden when he had to leave Frankfurt in 1846, see RAL, T7/38, Anselm, Frankfurt, to his cousins, London, Nov. 6, 1846.
16 RAL, XI/82/9/1/52, Amschel, Frankfurt, to James, Paris, April 6, 1816; RAL, XI/82/9/1/71, Amschel to Salomon and Nathan, Dec. 15; RAL, XI/82/9/1/101, Amschel to his brothers, July 4, 1817. Cf. Bartetzko, "Fairy tales and castles," pp. 224f. The property was valued at £6,000 in 1818: CPHDCM, 637/1/6/7/7–14, Articles of partnership, June 2, 1818.
17 Prevost-Marcilhacy, *Rothschild,* pp. 41, 48ff., 63ff., 68f., 73ff. Cf. RAL, T22/359, XI/109/28/1/45, Henrietta Montefiore, Frankfurt, to Hannah, Sept. 22, 1832; RAL, T18/338, XI/109/47/1/70, Hannah, Frankfurt, to Lionel, undated, *c.* early 1844. The romantic dramatist Eichendorff may have had Amschel in mind when he mocked the arriviste Pinkus's aversion to untamed Nature in his *Libertas und ihr Freier.* Eichendorff, *Werke,* pp. 1443ff.
18 Rothschild, Garton and Rothschild, *Rothschild gardens,* pp. 16f.
19 RAL, T22/254, Charlotte, Frankfurt, to [her mother] Hannah, Oct. 17, 1832.
20 RAL, T31/218/4, XI/109/4, Amschel, Frankfurt, to Salomon, Carl and James, May 12, 1816; RAL, T31/224/1, XI/109/4, same to same, May 29.
21 RAL, T31/267/4, XI/109/4, Amschel, Berlin, to Salomon and Nathan, London, June 18, 1816; RAL, T61/123/2, Carl, Frankfurt, to Salomon and Nathan, April 23, 1817; RAL, T62/63/3, XI/109/7, Amschel, Frankfurt, to Salomon, Paris, June 23.
22 RAL, T31/238/4, XI/109/4, Amschel, Berlin, to his mother and Carl, Frankfurt, June 22, 1816; RAL, T32/209/1, XI/109/5B, Amschel, Frankfurt, to Salomon and Nathan, London, Sept. 19.
23 Bartetzko, "Fairy tales and castles," pp. 236f.
24 Heine, "Ludwig Börne," in *Sämtliche Schriften,* vol. IV, p. 30, trans. Prawer, *Heine,* pp. 359f.
25 Disraeli, *Coningsby,* pp. 120f.
26 Disraeli, *Tancred,* pp.191f.
27 RAL, T64/212/3, XI/109/9, Carl, Frankfurt, to James, Paris, April 20, 1814; RAL, T64/211/3, XI/109/9, Carl to Salomon, April 20. Cf. Heuberger, *Rothschilds,* pp. 80ff.
28 RAL, T33/305/2, XI/109/5B, Carl, Berlin, to Nathan and Salomon, London, Nov. 5, 1816; Carl to Amschel and James, Nov. 9; RAL, T5/174, Carl to Nathan and Salomon, Jan. 25, 1817.
29 RAL, XI/109/2/2/162, Carl, Amsterdam, to Nathan, London, Nov. 7, 1814; RAL, XI/109J/J/33, James, Paris, to Nathan, Nov. 7, 1833.
30 RAL, XI/109/9/1/90, Carl, Hamburg, to his brothers, Jan. 8, 1818; RAL, T64/99/2, XI/109/9, same to same, Jan. 23; RAL, T64/103/2, Carl, Kassel, to Amschel and Salomon, Jan. 31.
31 RAL, T31/296/4, XI/109/4, James, Paris, to Salomon and Nathan, June 29, 1816.
32 RAL, T64/326/3, Amschel, Frankfurt, to Nathan, London, April 19, 1818.
33 CPHDCM, 637/1/310, *Allgemeine Zeitung,* Jan. 22, 1822, p. 87.
34 CPHDCM, 637/1/311, *Abrégé Chronologique de l'Histoire de France* (Paris, 1836), p. 865; Salomon to M. Michaud, Académie Française, Dec. 31, 1838; CPHDCM, 637/1/310, injunction to his children to preserve these documents, Oct. 31, 1841.
35 IfS, S2/349, "Das Rheinland. Wie es ernst und heiter ist," Nr 53, ed. Fr. Wiest, May 3, 1840. Cf. Reeves, *Rothschild,* pp. 115–21.
36 RAL, XI/109/48/2/23, Lionel, Frankfurt, to his mother, London, Sept. 13, 1844.
37 Metternich (ed.), *Nachgelassenen Papieren,* p. 47; Corti, *Reign,* p. 167; RAL, XI/109J/J/37, Salomon and James, Paris, to their nephews, Sept. 28, 1837.

38 Williams, *Making*, p. 19. Of eight German-Jewish merchants in Manchester in 1806, Nathan was the only one who maintained his religious affiliation.

39 Pückler, *Briefe*, p. 660.

40 RAL, XII/158/9, receipt for £5 donation, June 22, 1840. This was the Burial Society.

41 Barnbougle Castle, Rosebery Papers, Hannah, Gunnersbury, to Mayer, Cambridge, two undated letters, *c.* Oct. 1837.

42 RAL, XI/109/18/1/39, Nat, Switzerland, to his mother, London, Oct. 2, 1831; Davis, *English Rothschilds*, pp. 55f.

43 Heuberger, *Rothschilds*, p. 98.

44 RAL, XI/109J/J42, James, Paris, to his nephews, London, Nov. 4, 1842.

45 RAL, T29/7, T29/37, Carl, Frankfurt, to James, Paris, June 18, 1814; RAL, XI/109J/J/34, James to Nathan, London, July 10, 1834.

46 See e.g., RAL, T42/13, RFamC/30/11, Judith Montefiore, Verona, to Hannah, Nov. 21, 1823; RAL, T23/234, RFamC/1/162, Hannah to Nat and Anthony, Dec. 26, 1841. Cf. Davis, *English Rothschilds*, p. 46.

47 RAL, T27/236, XI/109/6, Carl to Amschel, Frankfurt, March 21, 1817.

48 RAL, T29/309, XI/109/1/7/2, James, Berlin, to Salomon, Nov. 3, 1814. Cf. RAL, T32/19/1, XI/109/5A, Amschel, Frankfurt, to James, Paris, July 8, 1816.

49 Heine, "Lutetia," in *Sämtliche Schriften*, vol. V, pp. 273f.

50 RAL, T22/254, Charlotte, Frankfurt, to Hannah, London, Oct. 17, 1832; RAL, XI/101/3,4,5/3, Amschel, Frankfurt, to Lionel, London, Oct. 25, 1840; RAL, T23/444, RFamC/1/166, Hannah to Lionel, Sept. 8, 1842; RAL, T18/176, XI/109/45/1/45, Adolph, Paris, to Lionel, London, Sept. 23, 1843.

51 RAL, XI/109J/J/29, James and Anselm, Paris, to Nathan, London, April 25, 1829.

52 In 1844 Nat was obliged to eat "a kosher lunch and [felt] very sick in consequence. I shall smoke a 14 sou Havana to relieve my stomach": RAL, T18/287, XI/109/47/1/89, Nat, Paris, to his brothers, London, April 3, 1844.

53 RAL, XI/109/42a/2/27, Nat, Paris, to his brothers, London, March 26, 1842. See also RAL, T20/37, XI/10948/2/45, same to same, Sept. 12, 1844.

54 Heuberger and Krohn, *Hinaus aus dem Ghetto*, pp. 41ff.; Liberles, "Introduction," pp. xxi—xxvi; Heuberger, *Rothschilds*, p. 185. See in general Meyer, *Response to modernity*.

55 RAL, XI/109/47/1/74, Anthony, Frankfurt, to his brothers, undated, *c.* May 1844.

56 RAL, XI/109/47/1/102, Hannah, Frankfurt, to Lionel, London, May 14, 1844. Wilhelm attended the synagogue twice daily and studied the Talmud in the evening. On the Orthodox revival in Frankfurt, see Liberles, *Religious conflict*.

57 RAL, XI/109/47/1/31, Anthony to his brothers, London, undated, *c.* May 1844; *The Times*, May 31, 1844. The project had been discussed for some time: CPHDCM, 637/1/7/48–52, Partnership agreement, Sept. 26, 1828. In an effort to rebut newspaper accusations of "intolerant fanaticism," Amschel instead invested the money in a fund for the poor. Amschel's spat with the Reform-inclined leaders of the Frankfurt community seems to have thwarted Lionel's plan to found a new school in his father's birthplace: RAL, XI/109/48/2/11, Lionel, Frankfurt, to his brothers, Sept. 2, 1844. Details of the divisions within the Frankfurt community in Liberles, "Aristocrat and synagogue," pp. 198f.; Arnsberg, *Geschichte der Frankfurter Juden*, vol. I, pp. 516f.

58 Roth, *Great Synagogue*, pp. 235ff.; Wolf, "Rothschildiana," p. 275; Lipman, *Social service*, p. 15. I am grateful to Dr Aubrey Newman for his assistance on this point.

59 Reeves, *Rothschilds*, pp. 120f. The most common *Schnorrer* joke has Rothschild complaining about the *Schnorrer's* tactics only to be asked, "Are you trying to teach me schnorring?" Another favourite has the *Schnorrer* regarding his relative's regular hand-out as inheritable property. Sometimes the *Schnorrer* is caught out: he claims to play the bassoon, but Rothschild has one in a cupboard and asks him to play; or he sees Rothschild's daughters playing a duet and decides not to bother schnorring: the Baron has clearly fallen on hard times if they have to share a piano. See Anon., *Gewaltsachen*, p. 61; Richman, *Laughs*, pp. 118ff.; Schnur, *Jewish humour*, pp. 23ff.; Landmann, *Der jüdische Witz*, pp. 276ff.; Lears, *Filled with laughter*, pp. 214f.; Spalding, *Encyclopaedia*, pp. 30ff.

60 "So young—and already a Rothschild," says one *Schnorrer* to another as a child is wheeled past in a sumptuous perambulator or carriage. Contemplating a lavish Rothschild gravestone, the *Schnorrer* can only marvel: "They sure know how to live." There are numerous jokes in this vein.

61 The notion that there remained a fundamental affinity between the Rothschilds and poor Jews can be

traced back as far as the 1820s: see e.g. Heine, "Die Bäder von Lucca," in *Sämtliche Schriften*, vol. III, pp. 430f. Even the poorest Jew can imagine "If I were Rothschild"; equally, Rothschild can remember being a poor Jew. See more recently, Howe and Wisse (eds), *Best of Shalom Aleichem*, pp. 129–32.

62 RAL, XI/109/37, President and Treasurer of the Dublin Hebrew Congregation to Messrs N. M. Rothschild & Sons, Sept. 17, 1839; RAL, XI/109/42/4/51, two illegibile signatories to Nat, May 6, 1842; RAL, XI/109/46/2/47, Henry Levy Keeling of the St Alban's Place Synagogue, Jan. 12, 1844; RAL, XI/109/46/2/49, Deputation from the New Hebrew Congregation, Liverpool, to Lionel, Feb. 5.

63 Wolf, "Rothschildiana," p. 275; Gray (ed.), *Life and times*, pp. 95f.

64 RAL, T6/1, L. Bouquet, Amsterdam, to Nathan, London, July 6, 1821.

65 Katz, *Jews in the history of England*, p. 368; Davis, *English Rothschilds*, p. 46.

66 RAL, RFamC/1/88, Hannah, Suresnes, to Lionel and Nat, July 23, 1839. She donated a further £500 to the school on the third anniversary of his death. Cf. RAL, T23/418, XI/109/42/3/138, Nat, Paris, to his brothers, London, undated, *c.* 1842.

67 Black, *JFS*, pp. 55f.

68 RAL, T17/3, Frances Cohen to Hannah, Aug. 31, 1814.

69 Black, *JFS*, pp. 55, 59: every year she provided complete school uniforms for all the pupils.

70 RAL, XI/109/36/3, Secretary of the London Hebrew Bread, Meat and Coal Society to Lionel, Oct. 23, 1838; RAL, XI/109/77, Daniel Salomons, President of the Bread, Meat and Coal Society, to Lionel, undated, *c.* Nov. 1850.

71 RAL, XI/109/77, J. L. Cowan, President of the Jewish Lying-in Charity to Charlotte, Dec. 4, 1850.

72 RAL, XI/109/37, Resolution of the Committee of Jews' Hospital, March 21, 1839; RAL, XI/109/38, S. Solomon, Secretary of Jews" Hospital, to Lionel, Jan. 27, 1840; RAL, XI/109/38, Resolution of the General Court of the Governors, March 22; RAL, XI/109/40/1/47, S. Hart to Anthony, May 25, 1841; RAL, XI/109/44, A. Solomon to Mayer, June 20, 1843.

73 RAL, XI/109/46/2/48, "Society for Relieving the Aged Needy," 3 Bury St, to Lionel, Jan. 25, 1844.

74 RAL, XI/109/41, Simeon Oppenheim, Great Synagogue Chambers, Lionel, Nov. 16, 1841; RAL, T24/108, XI/109/43/4/14, Synagogue Board to Isaac Cohen Esq., Oct. 27, 1842.

75 RAL, X1/82/9/1/70, Amschel, Frankfurt, to Nathan and Salomon, Dec. 12, 1816.

76 *The Times*, Oct. 29, 1825. Cf. Heuberger, *Rothschilds*, pp. 121f.; Schembs, "For the care of the sick," p. 208.

77 Prevost-Marcilhacy, *Rothschild*, p. 142.

78 See e.g. RAL, T29/271, XI/109/1/5/1, Amschel, Berlin, to Salomon and James, Oct. 11, 1814; RAL, XI/109/42, Committee for the Relief of the Sufferers of Hamburg, May 19, 1842; RAL, XI/109/42, H. P. Rouquette to Lionel, June 27.

79 RAL, T3/284, John Parish to Nathan, July 23, 1818; RAL, XI/109/13/1/21, Charles Murray, Secretary of the Society of Friends of Foreigners in Distress, to Nathan, April 22, 1829; RAL, XI/109/44, Secretary of the Society of Friends of Foreigners in Distress to Lionel, May 9, 1843.

80 RAL, XI/109/37, Charlotte Somerset to Miss Rothschild, undated, *c.* Jan. 1839; RAL, XI/109/37, C. Heyward, Secretary to the Board of Governors of the Buckinghamshire General Infirmary, Aylesbury, to "Rotschild [*sic*] Esq.," Nov. 7; RAL, XI/109/41/2/3, unidentified signatory to a Rothschild, Oct. 14, 1841; RAL, XI/109/44, J. Alexander, Infant Orphans' Asylum, to Lionel, Nat and Anthony, March 1, 1843; RAL, XI/109/44/4/7, Sydney Turner, Resident Chaplain of the Philanthropic Society, London, to NMR, May 22.

81 *The Times*, Dec. 20, 1847.

82 RAL, XI/109/11/3/64, Robert Owen, New Harmony, Indiana, USA., to Hannah, Stamford Hill, near London, Great Britain, undated, *c.* July 1828; RAL, T18/293, XI/109/47/2/48, Robert Smellie, Secretary of the Free Church, Langholm by Carlisle, to Baron Rothschild, April 9, 1844.

83 See in general Katz, *Out of the ghetto*.

84 RAL, XI/109/2/2/111, Amschel, Frankfurt, to Salomon and James, Paris, Sept. 26, 1815.

85 RAL, XI/82/9/1/25, Amschel, Berlin, to Nathan, London, Oct. 27, 1814.

86 RAL, T61/20/1, XI/109/6, Amschel, Frankfurt, to Salomon and Nathan, Jan. 23, 1817.

87 A fact which pleased Amschel: RAL, T31/286/4, XI/109/4, Amschel, Berlin, to his brother-in-law [Abraham Montefiore] and sister Jettchen [Henrietta], London, June 24, 1816.

88 Henriques, "Jewish emancipation controversy"; Salbstein, *Emancipation*. Even the political rules were not strictly enforced: some individual Jews did cast votes in elections and a number held parish offices.

89 Sorkin, *Transformation*; Rurüp, "Emanzipation"; *idem*, "Path to legal equality."

90 RAL, RFam AD/1/2, Lionel, Journal [copy], April 1827, p. 59.

91 Corti, *Rise*, pp. 333f.

92 Corti, *Reign*, pp. 68f.

93 *Ibid.*, pp. 42–6.

94 For Salomon's limited efforts in this direction and his links to the Vertretung der Wiener Judenschaft, *ibid.*, pp. 174f.

95 Heuberger and Krohn, *Hinaus aus dem Ghetto*, pp. 24ff.

96 RAL, XI/109/2/2/115, Amschel, Frankfurt, to Salomon and James, Paris, Sept. 28, 1815; RAL, T33/330/2, XI/109/5B, Amschel to James, Nov. 15, 1816.

97 Kracauer, *Geschichte der Juden*, vol. II, p. 451; Arnsberg, *Geschichte der Frankfurter Juden*, vol. I, pp. 314f.

98 RAL, T29/108, XI/109/0/4/28, Caroline, Frankfurt, to Salomon, London, July 21, 1814.

99 RAL, T28/76, Amschel, Berlin, to Carl, Frankfurt, undated, *c.* Aug. 1814; RAL, T28/16, XI/82/9/1/22, Amschel to Carl, Sept. 1.

100 RAL, T28/35, Carl, Frankfurt, to Nathan, London, undated, *c.* Sept. 1814.

101 RAL, T28/76, Amschel, Berlin, to Carl, Frankfurt, undated, *c.* Aug. 1814; RAL, T28/16, XI/82/9/1/22, Amschel to Carl, Sept. 1.

102 RAL, T29/319, Amschel, Berlin, to Nathan, London, Nov. 8, 1814.

103 RAL, T61/1/1, XI/109/6, Amschel, Frankfurt, to Salomon and Nathan, Jan. 1, 1817; Corti, *Rise*, p. 171.

104 RAL, XI/109/2/2/153, Salomon and Amschel, Paris, to Nathan, London, Oct. 25, 1815.

105 RAL, XI/109/2/2/187, Carl, Frankfurt, to his brother, Nov. 28, 1815.

106 RAL, T29/370, Carl, Frankfurt, to Nathan, Salomon and Davidson, London, Dec. 28, 1814.

107 RAL, XI/109/2/2/96, Amschel, Frankfurt, to Salomon and James, Paris, Sept. 21, 1815.

108 RAL, T30, XI/109/2/2/155, Amschel, Frankfurt, to Salomon, Paris, Oct. 29, 1815; RAL, XI/109/2/2/183, Salomon to Nathan, London, Nov. 25. Cf. Corti, *Rise*, pp. 183f. An important element in the Jewish case, stressed by the Rothschilds, was that a payment had been made by the Jewish community for their rights, to finance which bonds had been issued. To revoke the 1811 agreement would therefore require this money to be refunded.

109 RAL, XI/109/2/2/190,191,192, James, Paris, to Nathan, London, Nov. 29, 1815. Cf. Heilbrunn, "Haus Rothschild," p. 1.

110 RAL, XI/109/2/2/194, Carl, Frankfurt, to Nathan, London, Nov. 30, 1815; RAL, XI/109/2/2/195, Carl to his brothers, Nov. 30; RAL, XI/109/2/2/203, Carl to Nathan, Dec. 4.

111 RAL, XI/109/2/2/206, Carl, Frankfurt, to Salomon and James, Paris, Dec. 5, 1815.

112 RAL, XI/109/2/2/209, Caroline, Frankfurt, to Salomon, Paris, Dec. 7, 1815.

113 RAL, XI/109/2/2/111, Amschel, Frankfurt, to Salomon and James, Paris, Sept. 26, 1815; RAL, T30, XI/109/2/2/170, same to same, Nov. 15.

114 RAL, T30, XI/109/2/2/164, Amschel, Frankfurt, to his brothers, Nov. 8, 1815.

115 RAL, T30, XI/109/2/2/172, Amschel, Frankfurt, to Salomon, Nov. 18, 1815.

116 RAL, XI/109/2/2/203, Carl, Frankfurt, to Nathan, London, Dec. 4, 1815.

117 Corti, *Rise*, p. 185.

118 RAL, XI/109/2/2/226, Carl, Kassel, to Amschel, Frankfurt, Dec. 15, 1815; RAL, T31/198/3, XI/109/4, Amschel to Salomon and James, Paris, May 3, 1816; RAL, T31/262/4, XI/109/4, Gasser, Berlin, to Amschel, June 15; RAL, T31/267/4, XI/109/4, Amschel, Berlin, to Salomon and Nathan, June 18; RAL, T31/272/4, XI/109/4, Amschel to Carl, June 19; RAL, T31/ 274/4, XI/109/4, June 20; RAL, T32/169/1, XI/109/53, Amschel, Frankfurt, to James, Sept. 1.

119 RAL, T34/1, NMR 288, Amschel, Frankfurt, to Salomon and Nathan, London, Jan. 3, 1816; RAL, T31/64/2, XI/109/4, Carl, Frankfurt, to Nathan and James, Feb. 12; RAL, T31/238/4, XI/109/4, Amschel, Berlin, to his mother and Carl, June 22; RAL, T32/38/1, XI/109/5A, Carl to Nathan and Salomon, July 13; RAL, T32/2/1, XI/109/5A, Carl to James, undated, *c.* July; RAL, T32/156/2, XI/109/5A, same to same, Aug. 26; RAL, T33/325/2, XI/109/5B, Amschel, Frankfurt, to James, Nov. 13; RAL, T64/243/3, XI/109/9, Amschel to Salomon, undated, *c.* June 1818.

120 RAL, T32/103/2, XI/109/5A, Carl, Frankfurt, to James, Paris, Aug. 5, 1816; RAL, T32/119/2, XI/109/5A, Carl to Salomon and Nathan, London, Aug. 15.

121 See e.g. RAL, T62/ 20/1, XI/109/7, Carl, Frankfurt, to Salomon and James, Paris, May 9, 1817; RAL, T63/24/1, XI/109/8, Amschel to Salomon and James, Nov. 28. Cf. Corti, *Rise*, p. 212.

122 Koch, *Grundlagen*, p. 152. Cf. RAL, XI/82/9/1/60, Amschel to James, Nov. 19, 1816.

123 RAL, XI/109/2/2/226, Carl, Kassel, to Amschel, Frankfurt, Dec. 28, 1815; RAL, XI/109/2/2/250,

same to same, Dec. 29; RAL, T33/266/1, XI/109/5B, Carl, Kassel, to his brothers, Oct. 21, 1816; RAL, T33/273/1, XI/109/5B, same to same, Oct. 24; RAL, T27/183, XI/109/6, Amschel to Carl, Feb. 7, 1817; RAL, T61/90/2, Carl to Amschel, March 17; RAL, T27/234, Carl to Nathan and Salomon, March 17.

124 RAL, XI/109/2/2/217, Carl, Kassel, to Amschel, Frankfurt, Dec. 12, 1815; RAL, XI/109/2/2/224, Carl to Nathan, London, Dec. 14; RAL, XI/109/2/2/222, Carl to Amschel, Dec. 14. Cf. Backhaus, "Meyer Amschel," pp. 54ff.

125 RAL, T33/278/1, XI/109/5B, Carl, Leipzig, to his brothers, Oct. 26, 1816; HSM, Bestand 6b Nr 721, MAR to Elector, Kassel, Dec. 15, 1820.

126 RAL, T32/209/1, XI/109/5B, Amschel, Frankfurt, to Salomon and Nathan, London, Sept. 19, 1816.

127 RAL, T5/175, Amschel, Frankfurt, to Nathan and Salomon, London, Jan. 26, 1817; RAL, T61/23/1, XI/109/6, Amschel to James, Paris, Jan. 27. See also RAL, T61/17/1, XI/109/6, Amschel to James, Jan. 21.; RAL, T62/24/1, Carl, Frankfurt, to Salomon and James, Paris, May 20; RAL, T62/63/3, XI/109/7, Amschel to Salomon, June 23, 1817; RAL, XI/109/10/3, undated, unsigned document discussing the role of the Tugendbund in Germany; RAL, T64/103/2, Carl, Kassel, to Amschel and Salomon, Jan. 31, 1818. Cf. Corti, *Rise*, p. 231.

128 Arnsberg, *Geschichte der Frankfurter Juden*, vol. I, pp. 314f.

129 RAL, T32/202/1, XI/109/58, Joseph Pfungst, Joseph Oppenheimer, Jonas Rothschild, Gumpertz Ellissen, Meyer Fuld, Carl Feist, Frankfurt, to Salomon and Nathan, London, Sept. 8, 1816.

130 RAL, T33/325/2, XI/109/5B, Amschel, Frankfurt, to James, Paris, Nov. 13, 1816; RAL, T33/324/2, XI/109/5B, Amschel to Salomon, Nov. 13.

131 RAL, T32/246/1, XI/109/5B, Jonas Rothschild, to Salomon, London, Oct. 13. See e.g. RAL, T32/245/1, XI/109/5B, unidentified representative of the Hamburg Jews to Nathan, late 1816.

132 RAL, XI/82/9/1/109, Amschel, Frankfurt, to Nathan, London, Dec. 12, 1817.

133 RAL, T61/25, XI/109/6, Carl, Frankfurt, to Nathan and Salomon, London, Jan. 28, 1817; RAL, T63/6/1, XI/109/8, Salomon and James, Paris, to Nathan, Nov. 15; RAL, T63 /46/1, XI/109/8, Dec. 17.

134 RAL, T3/245, J. C. Meyerstein, Hamburg, to Nathan, London, July 14, 1819.

135 RAL, T33/284/1, XI/109/5B, Carl, Berlin, to his brothers, Oct. 28, 1816; RAL, T33/316/2, XI/109/5B, Carl to Salomon, Nov. 11; RAL, T61/39/1, XI/109/6, Amschel, Frankfurt, to James, Feb. 7, 1817; RAL, T61/32/1, XI/109/6, Carl, Hamburg, to Salomon and Nathan, London, Feb. 10; RAL, T27/151, Carl, Frankfurt, to his brothers, April 29; RAL, T63/72/2, XI/109/8, same, Hamburg, to same, Sept. 2; RAL, XI/109/9/1/80, Salomon, Paris, to Nathan, Jan. 14, 1818. Cf. Corti, *Rise*, p. 203.

136 RAL, T63/58/1, XI/109/8, Carl, Berlin, to Nathan, London, Nov. 21, 1817; RAL, XI/109/9/1/85, Salomon, Koblenz, to Nathan and James, Jan. 28, 1818; RAL, T64/246/3, XI/109/9, Amschel, Frankfurt, to Nathan and James, March 3; RAL, T64/199/3, Carl, Frankfurt, to Nathan and James, April 10. Cf. Corti, *Rise*, pp. 210f., 224.

137 RAL, T64/237/3, XI/109/9, Amschel, Frankfurt, to his brothers, undated, *c.* Sept. 1818.

138 Kracauer, *Geschichte der Juden*, vol. II, pp. 488, 499; Corti, *Rise*, p. 203; Ehrenberg, *Große Vermögen*, pp. 76ff.

139 Corti, *Rise*, pp. 233f. The letter had an impact: see *ibid.* pp. 237ff.

140 Schwemer, *Geschichte*, vol. II, pp. 149ff.

141 Corti, *Rise*, p. 290.

142 Rurüp, *Emanzipation*, p. 148.

143 Kracauer, *Geschichte der Juden*, vol. II, pp. 500ff.

144 Corti, *Rise*, p. 323.

145 Lieven, *Letters to Metternich*, p. 126.

146 Heuberger and Krohn, *Hinaus aus dem Ghetto*, p. 38; Corti, *Rise*, pp. 323f.; Kracauer, *Geschichte der Juden*, vol. I, p. 509; Arnsberg, *Geschichte der Frankfurter Juden*, vol. I, pp. 314f. The economic restrictions extended the duration of Jewish apprenticeships and prohibited Jews from the trading in food and firewood.

147 Heine, "Briefe aus Berlin: Zweiter Brief," in *Sämtliche Schriften*, vol. II, p. 36.

148 The following is largely based on the definitive study by Salbstein, *Emancipation*, esp. pp. 59–72, 87f. and Loewe (ed.), *Montefiore diaries*, vol. I, pp. 60–92. See also Endelman, *Jews of Georgian England*, p. 31.

149 Loewe (ed.), *Montefiore diaries*, vol. I, p. 61; Wolf, "Rothschildiana," p. 276. Montefiore had retired from business to concentrate on philanthropy and Jewish communal matters.

150   Loewe (ed.), *Montefiore diaries*, vol. I, p. 66.
151   Davis, *English Rothschilds*, pp. 46f.
152   Loewe (ed.), *Montefiore diaries*, vol. I, pp. 71–3.
153   RAL, XI/109/13/1/18, Moses Mocatta, Joseph Cohen and other members of Board of Deputies, to Nathan, April 17, 1829.
154   Loewe (ed.), *Montefiore diaries*, vol. I, pp. 74–9.
155   RAL, XI/109J/J/30, James, Paris, to Nathan, London, April 7, 1830.
156   Loewe (ed.), *Montefiore diaries*, vol. I, pp. 79ff.; Salbstein, *Emancipation*, p. 63f.
157   See also Fuchs, *Juden in der Karikatur*, p. 55.
158   RAL [formerly CPHDCM], 58–1–403/6, Heinrich Heine, Paris, to Betty Rothschild, Paris, April 7, 1846.
159   Ziegler, *Sixth great power*, pp. 43ff.
160   RAL, T22/129, XI/109/25/2/12, Anselm, Frankfurt, to Anthony, London, March 6, 1832.
161   RAL, XI/101/0–1/8, Haas, Paris, to Lionel, London, Aug. 28, 1837. Note Haas's reference to "our family," an early example of the Rothschild employees" tendency to identify with the family as well as the firm.
162   RAL, T25, XI/103/0/1/54, Anthony, Paris, to Lionel, London, Aug. 28, 1839.
163   RAL, XI/109/43a/2/49, Anthony, Paris, to his brothers, London, undated, second half of 1842.
164   RAL, T18/211, XI/109/46/1/5, Anselm Frankfurt, to James, Paris, Jan. 3, 1844.
165   RAL, T22/169, RFamC/1/138, Hannah to Anthony, undated, *c.* 1832.
166   RAL, T23/400, XI/109/43/1/31, Anselm, Paris, to Lionel, Anthony and "Carlo Dolee," July 10, 1842.
167   Prawer, *Heine*, pp. 331–5; Heuberger, *Rothschilds*, pp. 94f.
168   RAL, T20/34, XI/109/48/2/42, Nat, Paris, to his brothers, Sept. 4, probably 1844.
169   Heuberger, *Rothschilds*, p. 95.
170   Loewe (ed.), *Montefiore Diaries*, vol. I, pp. 3ff.
171   RAL, T27/206, XI/109/6, Carl, Hamburg, to Salomon, Feb. 26, 1817; RAL, T27/227, XI/109/6/2, Carl to his brothers, March 4; RAL, T61/85/2, XI/109/6/2, Carl to Nathan and Salomon, London, March 7; RAL, T61/87/2, Carl to James, Paris, March 9; RAL, T61/100/2, XI/109/6, Carl, Frankfurt, to Salomon and Nathan, March 30; RAL, T61/117/2, same to same, April 15; RAL, T64/212/3, XI/109/9, Carl to James, April 20.
172   RAL, T7/38, Anselm, Frankfurt, to his cousins, Nov. 6, 1846. Cf. Balla, *Romance*, p. 244f.
173   CPHDCM, 637/1/122/3–5, Caroline, Frankfurt, to Salomon, Vienna, Sept. 26, 1820; CPHDCM, 637/1/122/6,7, same to same, Sept. 29. Caroline's few surviving letters to Salomon suggest above all an impatience with his over-eagerness to please Nathan and others. Their son Anselm became the main focus for her affections; that may explain the relatively cool relationship he had with his father.
174   Goldschmidt, *Erinnerungen*, p. 35: "Seine Liebhabereien für sehr junge Mädchen brachten ungezählte Skandale zutage . . ."
175   See her letters from Paris in 1830, discussed below. Hannah was supposed to be there in attendance at the birth of her first grandchild; but she was irresistibly attracted by the wild fluctuations of the bourse caused by the revolution. Despite a number of "specs," however, she had to confess to her husband: "You will see me back without having made a great deal of money": RAL, RFamC/1/136, Hannah, Paris, to Nathan, London, Sept. 5, 1830. Three years later her son wrote expressing the hope that she had been "a great Bull" during the "enormous rise in all the funds": RAL, XI/109/30/1/2, Lionel, Paris, to his mother, London, May 26, 1833.
176   RAL, XI/109J/J/25, James, Paris, to Nathan, London, Jan. 16, 1825.
177   RAL, RFam C/4/5, Lionel, Paris, to Charlotte, Frankfurt, Jan. 7, 1835.
178   RAL, RFamC/4/6, same to same, Jan. 13, 1836.
179   RAL, RFamC/4/9, Jan. 22, 1836.
180   RAL, T22/688, XI/109/33/1/6, Lionel, Madrid, to Anthony, London, March 21, 1835.
181   RAL, RFamC/4/109, Lionel, Frankfurt, to his brothers, London, June 12, 1846.
182   RAL, RFamC/4/124, Lionel, Frankfurt, to his brothers, London, undated, *c.* June 17, 1836.
183   RAL, RFamC/1/61, Hannah, Frankfurt, to Anthony, undated, *c.* June 1836.
184   See e.g. RAL, T22/688, XI/109/33/1/6, Lionel, Madrid, to Anthony, March 21, 1835 ("You had better come by way of Bordeaux, bring as many little nice things for ladies as you can you will find lots to accept them'); RAL, T22/698, XI/109/32/2/13, unidentified friend to Nat, April 4, 183; RAL, T23/21, RFamC/4/106, Lionel, Frankfurt, to Anthony, London, June 1, 1836; RAL, T25/104/0/49, Nat, Paris,

to Anthony, London, May 21, 1840 ("Have heard not a word more from any of your old female friends, the lady who annoyed you in London is very quiet here"); RAL, T23/149, XI/109/38/3/36, Lionel Davidson, New York, to Anthony, London, May 31 ("Congratulate you on the event [marriage] which depriving you of the liberty you so well knew how to use, will open to you pleasures of a different nature"); RAL, T18/413, XI/109/48/1/51, Anselm, Vienna, to Anthony and Nat, Paris, July 17, 1844 ("Pleased to know Billy is in such spirits. He is in his element, the Boulevards, the Café de Paris, the club and something else which I dare not mention. All these things he cannot enjoy in London or Frankfurt").

185 RAL, XI/109J/J/29, James, Paris, to Nathan, London, Dec. 15, 1829.

186 CPHDCM, 637/1/269/2, Marriage contract for James and Betty, July 10, 1824. See also, CPHDCM, 637/1/269, Amschel's deed guaranteeing Betty an income in the event of James's premature death, June 29.

187 CPHDCM, 637/1/8/38–42, Marriage contract for Anselm and Charlotte also signed by Salomon and Nathan, Aug. 31, 1825.

188 RAL, T28/37, Carl, Frankfurt, to his brother [probably Amschel], undated, summer 1814; RAL, T29/113, XI/109/0/4/34, Amschel, Frankfurt, to Nathan and Salomon, London, July 24; RAL, T29/233, XI/109/1/2/13, Carl to Salomon and James, Paris, Sept. 18; RAL, T29/234, XI/109/1/2/14, Carl to Salomon and Davidson, Paris, Sept. 19; RAL, T29/239, XI/109/1/2/19, Carl to Salomon and James, undated, c. Sept.; RAL, T29/247, XI/109/1/3/6, Carl to Salomon, Sept. 26; RAL, T29/250, XI/109/1/3/2, Henrietta, Frankfurt, to Salomon, Sept. 28; RAL, T29/281, Amschel, Frankfurt, to his mother and Carl, Oct. 17; Carl to Salomon, Dec. 22; RAL, T30, XI/109/2/3/16/1, Carl to Nathan, London, Jan. 9, 1815; RAL, T30, XI/109/2/3/21/1, Salomon, Amsterdam, to Nathan, Jan. 13; RAL, XI/109/2/2/136, Benedikt Worms to Carl, Oct. 8.

189 RAL, XI/109J/J/25, James, Paris, to Nathan, London, Jan. 5, 1825; same to same, Jan. 9.

190 Cohen, *Lady de Rothschild*, p. 11.

191 Melville, *Cobbett*, vol. I, p. 21.

192 Jones, *In the blood*, pp. 68ff., 151. As late as the 1920s one Jewish marriage in five in Germany was between partners with the same grandparents.

SEVEN *Barons*

1 Raikes, *Journal*, vol. II, pp. 221ff. Reeves, *Rothschilds*, p. 195, attributes this line to Nathan. In an earlier version, the phrase is attributed to Talleyrand: Herding, "Rothschilds in der Karikatur," p. 24.

2 Bartetzko, "Fairy tales and castles," pp. 224f.

3 Kynaston, *Cazenove*, p. 22.

4 Wolf, "Rothschildiana," p. 271; Davis, *English Rothschilds*, pp. 47f.

5 Muhlstein, *Baron James*, pp. 59, 81; Corti, *Rise*, p. 313; Bergeron, *Rothschild*, pp. 152f. See also on Parisian social geography in this period, Brogan, *French nation*, p. 23; Chastenet, *Contestation*, p. 77; Artz, *Restoration*, p. 264. The offices of the other leading bankers were nearby: Hottinguer and the Foulds in the rue Bergère, d'Eichthal in the rue Le Peletier and the Mallets in the rue de la Chaussée-d'Antin: Prevost-Marcilhacy, *Rothschild*, pp. 38f.

6 In 1836, Betty told a guest who admired her house: "If you had seen the hotel of M. Solomon Rothschild (which is next door), you would think our house was only the stables attached to it": Raikes, *Journal*, vol. II, p. 335.

7 Corti, *Rise*, pp. 249f.

8 Davis, *English Rothschilds*, p. 36.

9 Prevost-Marcilhacy, *Rothschild*, pp. 39, 52, 67, 75; Davis, *English Rothschilds*, pp. 47f.; Heuberger, *Rothschilds*, pp. 60f.; Surtees, *Coutts Lindsay*, p. 128. Cf. Collett-White, *Gunnersbury Park*.

10 Buxton (ed.), *Memoirs*, pp. 288–90.

11 Interestingly, the Rothschild passion for horses appears to have begun with the brothers' wives: see RAL, T5/63, Hannah, London, to James, Paris, undated, c. June 1814; RAL, T32/175/1, XI/109/5B, Carl, Frankfurt, to Salomon and Nathan, London, Sept. 5, 1816. With the exception of James, the brothers regarded horses exclusively as a means of getting from A to B, and were baffled when James began riding for pleasure: see e.g. RAL, XI/109/2/2/75, Amschel, Frankfurt, to his brothers, Sept. 15, 1815; RAL, T31/1, XI/109/4/1/1, Salomon, Paris, to Nathan, Jan. 1, 1816.

12 Disraeli, *Endymion*, pp. 130f.

13 Corti, *Reign*, p. 179.

14   Prevost-Marcilhacy, *Rothschild*, pp. 48, 74.
15   RAL, XI/109/J/J/29, James Paris, to Nathan, Anselm and his nephews, London, June 26, 1829. Cf. Corti, *Reign*, pp. 391f.; Bergeron, *Rothschild*, p. 104.
16   RAL, XI/109/30/2/12, Hannah Mayer, Paris, to her father, London, Sept. 29, 1833. See also RAL, XI/109J/J/33, James, Paris, to Nathan, March 10.
17   RAL, T29/189, XI/109/0/8/5, Amschel, Berlin, to Salomon, August 26, 1814.
18   RAL, T32/110/2, XI/109/5A, Carl, Frankfurt, to James, Nathan and Salomon, Aug. 8, 1816; RAL, T33/311/2, XI/109/5B, Carl, Berlin, to Amschel and James, Nov. 9; RAL, T63/122/2, XI/109/8, Amschel, Frankfurt, to brothers, Oct. 17, 1817.
19   RAL, T32/140/2, XI/109/5A, Carl to James, Paris, Aug. 22, 1816. It is striking that in the 1818 agreement two pieces of real estate were counted as parts of the firm's combined property, though this practice was later abandoned: CPHDCM, 637/1/6/7/7–14, Articles of partnership, June 2, 1818.
20   RAL, T30, XI/109/2/2/251, Amschel, Frankfurt, to James, Paris, Dec. 29, 1815.
21   RAL, T30, XI/109/2/2, Carl, Kassel, to Amschel, Frankfurt, Dec. 30, 1815.
22   RAL, T31/107/2, XI/109/4, Amschel, Frankfurt, to James, Paris, March 12, 1816.
23   RAL, XI/82/9/1/48, Amschel, Frankfurt, to James, Paris, Feb. 27, 1816.
24   RAL, T31/217/14, XI/109/4, S. Schnapper, Frankfurt, to Carl, May 12, 1816.
25   RAL, T32/119/2, XI/109/5A, Carl, Frankfurt, to Salomon and Nathan, Aug. 15, 1816; RAL, T32/129/2, XI/109/5A, Amschel and Carl to James, Paris, Aug. 18; RAL, T32/134/2, XI/109/5A, Amschel and Carl to Nathan and Salomon, Aug. 19; RAL, T32/157/2, XI/109/5, Carl to his brothers, Aug. 27.
26   RAL, T62/69/3, XI/109/7, Carl, Frankfurt, to Salomon and James, Paris, June 2, 1817; same to same, June 11.
27   Heilbrunn, "Haus Rothschild," p. 21; Corti, *Rise*, pp. 288f.; Heuberger, *Rothschilds*, p. 177.
28   RAL, RFamC/1/107, Hannah, Frankfurt, to her son Lionel, London, Jan. 16, 1847.
29   Spiel, *Fanny von Arnstein*, pp. 333f.
30   Trollope, *Vienna and the Austrians*, pp. 5–7, 103f., 220.
31   Metternich (ed.), *Nachgelassenen Papieren*, pp. 47, 324, 491, 493, 495.
32   Kübeck, *Tagebücher*, vol. I/2, pp. 779f., trans. Corti, *Reign*, p. 166; Woodward, "Economic Factors," p. 89.
33   Corti, *Rise*, p. 220; Chateaubriand, *Mémoires d'outre-tombe*, vol. II, p. 76; Loewe (ed.), *Montefiore Diaries*, vol. I, pp. 34f.
34   Pückler, *Briefe*, p. 656.
35   Loewe (ed.), *Montefiore Diaries*, vol. I, pp. 34f., 61, 74.
36   Kynaston, *City*, vol. I, p. 92.
37   RAL, XI/109J/J/33, James, Paris, to Nathan, London, May 18, 1833; RAL, XI/109J/J/34, same to same, May 21, 1834.
38   Loewe (ed.), *Montefiore diaries*, vol. I, pp. 142, 145f.
39   Corti, *Rise*, pp. 376f.; Bussche, *Arnim*, pp. 10ff.
40   Loewe (ed.), *Montefiore diaries*, vol. I, p. 52.
41   RAL, T31/265/4, XI/109/4, Carl, Frankfurt, to James, Paris, June 16, 1816; RAL, T32/170/1, XI/109/5B, James to Salomon, Nathan and Davidson, Sept. 2.
42   RAL, T64/338/3, James, Paris, to Salomon and Nathan, London, April 9, 1818. On James's early social career see Bertaut, *Bourse*, pp. 101–5.
43   Gilbert, *Bankiers*, pp. 45f.
44   Apponyi, *Vingt-cinq ans*, vol. I, pp. 6ff.
45   Castellane, *Journal*, pp. 200f.
46   Muhlstein, *Baron James*, pp. 79ff. Cf. Capefigue, *Grandes opérations*, vol. III, pp. 202–5.
47   Gilbert, *Bankiers*, pp. 45f.
48   Apponyi, *Vingt-cinq ans*, vol. I, pp. 6ff.
49   Bertaut, Bourse, pp. 126–30; Heuberger, *Rothschilds*, pp. 108f.
50   RAL, XI/109J/J/39, James, Rome, to his nephews, London, Jan. 29, 1839; RAL, XI/109J/J/40B, James to Nat, March 9, 1840.
51   RAL, RFamC/1/107, Hannah, Frankfurt, to Lionel, London, Jan. 16, 1847.
52   Disraeli, *Endymion*, pp. 132f.
53   Pückler, *Briefe*, pp. 441f.
54   Disraeli, *Tancred*, pp.118–24.

55 Various different versions in Anon., *Gewaltsachen*, p. 36; Landmann, *Der jüdische Witz*, p. 277; Spalding, *Encyclopaedia*, p. 200 and in all popular histories of the family, often as if true. I have come across only one instance in which the tables are turned, and it is a haughty Rothschild who is offered two chairs by a Prussian bureaucrat.
56 Pückler, *A Tour in England*, vol. III, pp. 165ff.
57 Corti, *Rise*, p. 220.
58 Buxton (ed.), *Memoirs*, pp. 288–90.
59 Rothschild, *Shadow*, pp. 7f. Audubon alleged that the volumes were reclaimed, but, according to Victor Rothschild, *Audubon's Birds of America* appears in the "Catalogue of the books belonging to the principal library of Baron N. M. de Rothschild, London, 1835" at New Court.
60 Reeves, *Rothschilds*, p. 200.
61 *Ibid.*, p. 195.
62 Buxton (ed.), *Memoirs*, pp. 288–90.
63 Pückler, *Briefe*, p. 656.
64 *Ibid.*, pp. 441f., 660, 819. See also pp. 632, 841, for Pückler's positive assessment of Hannah.
65 Castellane, *Journal*, pp. 56f., 200.
66 *Ibid.*, pp. 200f.
67 Goldschmidt, *Erinnerungen*, pp. 12–33, 35f.
68 Metternich (ed.), *Nachgelassenen Papieren*, pp. 47, 324, 491, 493, 495.
69 Goldschmidt, *Erinnerungen*, pp. 12–33, 35f.
70 RAL, T62/69/3, XI/109/7, Carl, Frankfurt, to Salomon and James, Paris, June 11, 1817.
71 RAL, T61/40/1, XI/109/6, Carl, Berlin, to Salomon and Nathan, London, Feb. 8, 1817; RAL, T63/25/1, XI/109/8, Carl to James, Paris, Nov. 1; RAL, T63/32/1, XI/109/8, Carl to Salomon and James, Nov. 11.
72 RAL, XI/82/9/1/101, Amschel, Frankfurt, to his brothers, July 4, 1817.
73 RAL, XI/109/13/1/2, Charlotte, Paris, to her mother, London, undated, *c.* early 1829.
74 RAL, XI/109J/J/25, James, Paris, to Nathan, London, Jan. 16, 1825.
75 RAL, T63/5/1, XI/109/8, Salomon and James, Paris, to Nathan, London, Nov. 6, 1817; RAL, T5/171, IX/85/1, James to Nathan, Jan. 24, 1818.
76 RAL, XI/109J/J/25, James, Paris, to Nathan, London, Jan. 16, 1825.
77 RAL, XI/109/18/1/46, Charlotte, Paris, to her mother, undated, *c.* Nov. 6, 1831. See also RAL, XI/109J/J/31B, James, Paris, to Nathan, London, Nov. 24.
78 RAL, T30, XI/109/2/2/256, Carl, Kassel, to Amschel, Frankfurt, Dec. 30, 1815; RAL, XI/82/9/1/59, Amschel to James, Paris, March 14, 1816. Details in Corti, *Rise*, pp. 192–8; Rössler, *Stadion*, vol. II, pp. 169, 185.
79 McCagg, *Jewish nobles*, p. 58n.
80 Corti, *Rise*, pp. 198–201, 302f. Cf. RAL, T61/100/2, XI/109/6, Carl, Frankfurt, to Salomon and Nathan, London, March 30, 1817; RAL, T61/13/2, XI/109/6, Amschel, Frankfurt, to Nathan and Salomon, March 31; RAL, T27/142, Carl to his brothers, April 13; RAL, XI/82/9/1/100, Amschel to James, Paris, April 30; RAL, T62/169/9, XI/109/7, Carl, Berlin, to Amschel, Aug. 15. On the coat of arms see Corti, *Rise*, plate facing p. 200. Salomon initially requested the following arms: "First quarter, or, an eagle sable surcharged in dexter by a field gules; second quarter, gules, a leopard passant proper; third quarter, a lion rampant; fourth quarter, azure, an arm bearing five arrows. In the centre of the coat a shield gules. Right hand supporter, a greyhound, a symbol of loyalty; left supporter, a stork, a symbol of piety and content." This was to be surmounted by a seven-point crown and a lion rampant. This design was substantially modified by the Vienna heralds: the final version featured only the eagle and the hand grasping *four* arrows; there were no supporters, and the shield was surmounted by a helmet, a three-pointed crown and another eagle. The version registered by Nathan in 1818 was slightly different: the arms consisted of "Azure a lion passant guardant erminois grasping with the dexter forepaw five arrows the pheons downwards or; And for the crest on a wreath of the colours out of a crown vallery gules a demi lion erminois holding between the paws five arrows as in the arms": Mace, "From Frankfurt Jew," pp. 181f. The motto, "Concordia, integritas, industria," was incorporated later.
81 RAL, XI/109/2/2/221, Amschel, Frankfurt, to his brothers, Dec. 13, 1815; RAL, XI/109/2/2/224, Carl, Kassel, to Nathan, Dec. 14; RAL, T62/167/9, XI/109/7, Carl, Hamburg, to Amschel, Aug. 8, 1817; RAL, T7/92, von der Goltz, Frankfurt, to Nathan, London, June 20, 1818; HSM, Bestand 300 Nr C 32/9, Elector, Reskript, April 11, 1829; Salomon, Vienna, to Elector, March 29, 1834; Elector, Höchtes Reskript, April 23, 1835; RAL, T25/104/0/36, Nat, Paris, to his brothers, London, May 2,

1840; HSM, Bestand 300 Nr C 32/9, Elector, Höchtes Reskript, Jan. 15, 1845. Nat became a Prussian Privy Commercial Councillor in 1834: Corti, *Reign*, p. 78. The brothers also continued to seek appointments as court bankers: see e.g. RAL, T5/168, XI/109/8A, William, Duke of Nassau, Decree, Oct. 6, 1817.

82   RAL, T63/108/2, Carl, Berlin, to Salomon and James, Paris, Oct. 21, 1817; RAL, XI/109/10/1/6, Salomon to Nathan, undated, *c.* Jan. 1818; RAL, XI/82/9/1/111, Amschel, Frankfurt, to James, March 27. Cf. Corti, *Rise*, pp. 204–6, 245, 279–84, 311f. Amschel became Bavarian consul in Frankfurt at around the same time: Heuberger, *Rothschilds*, p. 177.

83   RAL, T62/72/3, XI/109/7, Carl, Frankfurt, to Salomon and James, Paris, June 10, 1817. He later became Neapolitan consul general in Frankfurt too: Leo Baeck Institute, New York, AR 512, B30/5, Copia tratta dalla roccolta dei Decreti originali dell'anno 1830 vol. 279, Num. 1632, Aug. 17, 1830.

84   Cabanis, *Charles X*, p. 312; Bocher, *Mémoires*, p. 134.

85   RAL, T28/27, Amschel, Frankfurt, to Carl, undated *c.* July 1814; RAL, T29/198, XI/109/0/8/14, Carl, Frankfurt, to James, Paris, Aug. 31; RAL, T30, XI/109/2/3/13/1, James, Berlin, to Nathan, Salomon and Davidson, Jan. 5, 1815; RAL, XI/109/2/2/226, Carl, Kassel, to Amschel, Dec. 15; RAL, T61/92/2, XI/109/6, same to same, March 17, 1817; RAL, T63/72/2, XI/109/8, Carl, Hamburg, to his brothers, Sept. 2.

86   RAL, T63/33/1, XI/109/8, Carl, Berlin, to Amschel, Salomon and James, Nov. 11, 1817; RAL, T63/30/1, XI/109/8, Carl to Amschel and James, undated, *c.* Dec.

87   RAL, T64, XI/109/9/4/10–19, Amschel, Frankfurt, to Carl, July 1, 1818.

88   Gentz, *Briefe an Pilat*, vol. II, p. 105; Corti, *Rise*, pp. 307ff.

89   RAL, XI/109J/J/38, James, Paris, to his nephews, London, Nov. 10, 1838; RAL, XI/101/3,4,5–12, Guizot to James, Dec. 24, 1841; RAL, XI/109J/J/41, James to his nephews, Dec. 25. Cf. Corti, *Reign*, p. 55.

90   Corti, *Rise*, pp. 393ff.

91   RAL, XI/109/32/2/23, Nat, Constantinople, to his parents, London, March 4, 1834.

92   Capefigue, *Grandes opérations*, vol. III, p. 204.

93   Corti, *Rise*, pp. 393f.; Prawer, *Heine*, pp. 144f. In "The Baths of Lucca," a ball at Salomon's house is described: "Such stars and orders! The Order of the Falcon, the Order of the Golden Fleece, the Order of the Lion, the Order of the Eagle—and there was even a child, I assure you, a tiny tot, that wore the Order of the Elephant." When Macaulay dined with "the Jew" (i.e. Nathan) he "did not see one Peer, or one star, except a foreign order or two, which I generally consider as an intimation to look to my pockets": Kynaston, *City*, vol. I, p. 92.

94   RAL, T62/69/3, XI/109/7, Carl, Frankfurt, to Salomon and James, Paris, June 11, 1816.

95   RAL, T63/5/1, XI/109/8, James, Paris, to Nathan, London, Nov. 6, 1817.

96   RAL, T61/87/2, Carl to James, Paris, March 9, 1817.

97   RAL, T64, XI/104/2, Carl to his brothers, undated, *c.* early 1818.

98   RAL, T27/234, Carl, Kassel, to Salomon and Nathan, London, March 17, 1817.

99   RAL, XI/109/58b/2/37, Nat, Paris, to his brothers, London, Oct. 1, 1846.

100   RAL, T29/189, XI/109/0/8/5, Amschel, Berlin, to Salomon, Aug. 26, 1814.

101   RAL, XI/109/2/2/97, Amschel to his brothers, Sept. 21, 1815.

102   RAL, T30/49/2, James to Hannah, Aug. 26, 1815.

103   RAL, T33/262/1, XI/109/5B, Amschel, Frankfurt, to James, Paris, Oct. 19, 1816; RAL, T27/244, XI/109/6, Amschel to his brothers, March 11, 1817; RAL, T27/149, XI/109/6, Carl to his brothers, April 25. Technically, of course, use of the title "Baron" was premature.

104   RAL, T64/125/3, XI/109/9, Carl, Frankfurt, to Nathan and Salomon, London, April 7, 1818.

105   Corti, *Reign*, pp. 137–40.

106   Heine, "Shakespeares Mädchen und Frauen: Tragödien—Portia," in *Sämtliche Schriften*, vol. IV, p. 264.

107   Kübeck, *Tagebücher*, vol. I/2, p. 544.

108   RAL, XI/109/2/49, James, Paris, to Hannah, London, Aug. 24, 1815; RAL, T32/4/1, XI/109/5A, Carl, Frankfurt, to James, July 2, 1816; RAL, T32/22/1, XI/109/5A, Carl to Nathan, London, July 10.

109   See e.g. RA, Add. 21/109, Statement in Chancery, Greenwood v. Taylor, Feb. 1, 1827, in which Nathan is referred to as "Baron de Rothschild" and replies as "Baron N. M. de Rothschild"; his solicitors, however, call him "Mr Rothschild": Dawes & Chatfield to Farrers & Co., April 11, 1827. Cf. Corti, *Rise*, pp. 198, 404; *The Times*, Aug. 4, 1836.

110   The other brothers clearly relished being von (or de) Rothschilds: RAL, T32/173/1, XI/109/5B,

Amschel, Frankfurt, to Salomon and Nathan, London, Sept. 4, 1816; RAL, T32/149/1, XI/109/5B, Amschel and Carl to James, Paris, Sept. 6; RAL, T33/248/1, XI/109/5B, Carl, Kassel, to Amschel, undated, *c.* Oct.; RAL, T33/231/1, XI/109/5B, Carl to Nathan and Salomon, Oct. 3; RAL, T33/237/1, XI/109/5B, James to Salomon and Nathan, Oct. 9; RAL, T33/297/2, XI/109/5B, Amschel to James, Nov. 3. It is worth noting that Nathan's grandson dropped the "de" on receiving a British peerage, a usage followed by his descendants—hence the fact that there are "Rothschilds" as well as "de Rothschilds" today.

111 Mace, "From Frankfurt Jew," pp. 181f.; Hall, "Nathan Rothschild as an owner of paintings," p. 76.
112 RAL, T33/299/2, XI/109/5B, Amschel, Frankfurt, to Salomon, Nov. 3, 1816.
113 Heuberger, *Rothschilds*, p. 75.
114 RAL, T33/351/2, XI/109/5B, James, Paris, to Amschel and Carl, Frankfurt, Nov. 29, 1816; RAL, T27/217, James to Salomon and Nathan, London, March 8, 1817.
115 Pückler, *Briefe*, p. 819.
116 Hall, "Nathan Rothschild as an owner of paintings," pp. 70ff. Other paintings in Nathan's possession were gifts from government clients, like the portraits of Francis I of Austria, Frederick William III of Prussia, William I of Holland, John VI of Portugal and the Empress Alexandra of Russia seen by Prince Pückler.
117 RAL, T32/182/1, XI/109/5B, Carl, Frankfurt, to James, Paris, Sept. 8, 1816.
118 Muhlstein, *Baron James*, p. 64.
119 Buxton (ed.), *Memoirs*, pp. 288–90.
120 RAL, T63/32/1, XI/109/8, Carl, Berlin, to Salomon and James, Paris, Nov. 11, 1817.
121 RAL, T29/13, Gelche [Caroline], Frankfurt, to Salomon, March 23, 1814; RAL, T31/217/14, XI/109/4, S. Schnapper, Frankfurt, to Carl, May 12, 1816.
122 CPHDCM, 637/1/122/6,7, Caroline, Frankfurt, to Salomon, Vienna, Sept. 29, 1820.
123 Davis, *English Rothschilds*, p. 37.
124 *The Times*, June 17, 1825, p. 3. "Mr Holt of Tottenham was sent for, the shoulder was replaced, and Mr Rothschild was able to attend business yesterday as usual.'
125 Davis, *English Rothschilds*, pp. 36f. The cart still survives.
126 Hall, "English Rothschilds as collectors," p. 267; *idem*, "Nathan Rothschild as an owner of paintings," pp. 69f. *The Family of W. N. [sic] Rothschild, Consul General of his Austrian Majesty at the British Court* was commissioned to mark Nathan's appointment as Austrian consul general. Hobday was paid £1,000 for the work, which was shown at the Royal Academy in 1821 and then hung for a time at Austrian Consulate, before being moved to Gunnersbury. It can now be seen in the main hall of N. M. Rothschild & Sons at New Court.
127 RAL, T22/389, XI/109/29/1/86, Hannah Mayer, Brighton, to her father, London, Feb. 7, 1833.
128 Buxton (ed.), *Memoirs*, pp. 288–90.
129 Disraeli, *Coningsby*, pp. 214–21.
130 Davis, *English Rothschilds*, pp. 36f. Cf. RAL, XI/109/2/2/125, James, Paris, to his sister[-in-law], Hannah, London, Oct. 2, 1815.
131 RAL, RFamAD/1/2, Lionel, Journal through Germany [copy], 65pp., April 1827.
132 Davis, *English Rothschilds*, p. 52; Corti, *Rise*, p. 400.
133 RAL, T6/94, Abr. Crailsheim, Frankfurt, to Nathan, London, Jan. 8, 1829.
134 RAL, T22/6, XI/109/22/1/46, Charlotte, Frankfurt, to her mother, July 17, 1831.
135 RAL, T23/77, XI/109/34/1/3, Dr Schlemmer, Leipzig, to Nat, Paris, May 15, 1836. Cf. Davis, *English Rothschilds*, p. 54.
136 *The Times*, Aug. 13, 1874.
137 Barnbougle Castle, Rosebery Papers, Hannah, Gunnersbury, to Mayer, Cambridge, two undated letters, *c.* Oct. 1837.
138 Hannah also found the atmosphere less tolerant when she went there in 1841: "[T]he Place is too orthodox to be an agreeable residence for any other sect beside Protestant. Bibles and other religious Books are placed in the different apartments of the Hotel we are in but the Inhabitants are civil and attentive": RAL, RFamC/1/14, Hannah, Oxford, to her daughter-in-law Charlotte, London, Nov. 22, 1841; Davis, *English Rothschilds*, pp. 55ff.; Endelman, *Radical Assimilation*, p. 78.
139 Heuberger, *Rothschilds*, p. 179.
140 *Ibid.*, p. 99.
141 Muhlstein, *Baron James*, pp. 160f.

142   RAL, T17/233, Charlotte, Paris, to her mother, London, Nov. 6, 1831.

143   RAL, T7/3, Charlotte, Boulogne, to her mother, London, Nov. 13, 1833.

144   Davis, *English Rothschilds*, pp. 65f.

EIGHT   *Sudden Revolutions (1830–1833)*

1   RAL, XI/109/11/3/64, Robert Owen, New Harmony, Indiana, USA., to Hannah, Stamford Hill, near London, Great Britain, undated, *c.* July 1828. The utopian socialist Owen had known the Rothschilds since at least 1818: Owen, *Life*, pp. 182f., 211.

2   Börne, *Mittheilungen*, 1. Theil, pp. 170ff.

3   *Ibid*, 2. Theil, pp. 136–55. Börne of course erred in his choice of candidate for the Greek crown.

4   Rose, *Revolutionary anti-Semitism*, pp. 152f.

5   Prawer, *Heine*, pp. 128f.

6   Heine, "Reisebilder: dritte Teil," in Sämtliche Schriften, vol. III, pp. 422–9, trans. Prawer, *Heine*, pp. 142–4.

7   *Ibid.*

8   Prawer, *Heine*, pp. 145f.

9   Heine, "Skizzen zu die Bäder von Lucca," in *Sämtliche Schriften*, vol. III, pp. 628f., trans. Prawer, *Heine*, pp. 146f.

10   Heine, "Ludwig Börne," in *Sämtliche Schriften*, vol. IV, p. 28. Cf. Prawer, *Heine*, pp. 358ff.; Corti, *Reign*, pp. 215ff.

11   Heine, "Lutetia," in *Sämtliche Schriften*, vol. V, pp. 321ff., 353. Cf. Prawer, *Heine*, pp. 643f.

12   "Above all fill his purse, O king,
  With ample funds for travelling,
  And give him a letter of credit to greet
  The Rothschild brothers in Rue Lafitte.
  "Yes a letter of credit for a million or two
  Of golden ducats should seen him through;
  And Baron de Rothschild will say of him, then,
  "This elephant's surely the best of men!" '
  Sämtliche Schriften, vol. VI/1, p. 18, trans. Draper, *Heine*, p. 569. See also *ibid.*, pp. 531, 795.

13   Gutzkow, *Öffentliche Charaktere*, pp. 275–302.

14   Chateaubriand, *Mémoires d'outre-tombe*, p. 103.

15   RAL, XI/109/13/1/2, Charlotte, Paris, to "dear Mama," [undated, probably Feb. 1829].

16   RAL, XI/109J/J/29, James and Anselm, Paris, to Nathan, April 25, 1829.

17   RAL, XI/109J/J/29, James and Anselm, Paris, to Nathan and Lionel, London, May 2, 1829; same to same, May 5; May 15; James to Nathan, May 16; James and Anselm to Nathan and Lionel, May 18; James to Nathan and Lionel, May 22; James to Nathan, May 25; James to Nathan and Lionel, May 26; same to same, May 27; James to Nathan, May 29; same to same, June 5; James and Anselm to Nathan, June 10; James to Nathan, Anselm and Lionel, June 12; James to Nathan and his nephews, June 13; James to Nathan, June 15; James to Nathan, Anselm and Lionel, June 17; same to same, June 19; June 26; James to Nathan, June 27.

18   RAL, XI/109/J/J/29, James, Paris, to Nathan, Anselm and his nephews, London, July 4, 1829; James and Salomon, Paris, to Nathan, Aug. 11; James and Salomon to Nathan, Lionel and Hannah, Aug. 26; James to Nathan and Lionel, Sept. 9; James to Nathan, Lionel, Nat and Hannah, Sept. 16; James to Nathan and Lionel, Nov. 30; James to Nathan, Sept. 2. Cf. Corti, *Rise*, pp. 407f.

19   RAL, XI/109J/J/29, James, Paris, to Nathan and Lionel, London, Dec. 4, 1829; same to same, Dec. 5; Dec. 9; Dec. 11; James to Nathan and his nephews, Dec. 14; same to same, Dec. 15; Dec. 18; Dec. 19; Dec. 20; James to Nathan, Dec. 26; same to same, Dec. 28; RAL, XI/109J/J/30/F2, unidentified and undated fragment, almost certainly from James to Nathan, *c.* Dec.; RAL, XI/109J/J/30, James to Nathan and his nephews, Jan. 26, 1830. Cf. Capefigue, *Grandes opérations*, vol. III, pp. 156–8; Marion, *Histoire financière*, vol. V, pp. 105f.; Reeves, *Rothschilds*, pp. 308ff.; Corti, *Rise*, pp. 415f.; Gille, *Maison Rothschild*, vol. I, pp. 171–9; *idem, Banque et crédit*, pp. 162–71. The loan was for 80 million francs in 4 per cent rentes. To ensure that he outbid his rivals, James bid 102.725, 2.725 more than the nearest bid by the syndicate of receivers-general.

20   RAL, XI/109J/J/29/A, James, Paris, to Amschel, Frankfurt, Salomon, Vienna, and Carl, Naples, Dec. 20, 1829.

21 RAL, XI/109J/J/30, James, Paris, to Nathan and his nephew, London, Jan. 27, 1830; James to Nathan, Jan. 31; James to Nathan and Lionel, Feb. 1; same to same, Feb. 6.

22 Corti, *Rise*, p. 420.

23 RAL, XI/109J/J/30, James, Paris, to Nathan and his nephews, London, Feb. 12, 1830. As James later noted, "regarding Polignac, I had been forewarned on several occasions as far back as six months before. However, I did not want to believe it. I had a gut feeling"; RAL, XI/109J/J/31, James, Paris, to Nathan, London, Nov. 21, 1831.

24 RAL, XI/109J/J/30, James, Paris, to Nathan and his nephews, London, Feb. 16, 1830; same to same, Feb. 20.

25 Greville, *Memoirs*, vol. I, p. 279: "Went to Esterhazy's ball; talked to old Rothschild who was there with his wife and a dandy little Jew son. He . . . offered to give me a letter by his brother, who would give me any information I wanted, squeezed my hand, and looked like what he is."

26 RAL, XI/109J/J/30, James, Paris, to Nathan and his nephews, London, March 12, 1830; same to same, March 13; March 15.

27 RAL, XI/109J/J/30, James, Paris, to Nathan and his nephews, London, March 18, 1830.

28 RAL, XI/109J/J/30, James to Nathan and his nephews, March 23, 1830; same to same, March 25; March 29; March 30; April 6; April 7; April 10; April 13; April 14.

29 RAL, XI/109J/J/30, James to Nathan and his nephews, May 3, 1830; same to same, May 19; RAL, XI/109J/J/30/F3, James, Paris, to Nathan, London, undated, probably June 1; RAL, XI/109J/J/30, James and Carl, Paris, to Nathan, London, June 9; same to same, June 10.

30 Corti, *Rise*, p. 420.

31 Scherb, *Geschichte*, p. 74; Ehrenberg, *Große Vermögen*, p. 113.

32 Cf. Corti, *Rise*, pp. 421f.

33 RAL, XI/109J/J/30, James to Nathan, Carl and his nephews, July 12, 1830.

34 RAL, XI/109J/J/30, James and Salomon, Paris, to Nathan, London, July 24, 1830.

35 RAL, XI/109/16/1/3, Lionel, Paris, to his parents, London, July 27, 1830. See also RAL, T17/36, Charlotte, Paris, to her mother Hannah, London, July 27.

36 Corti, *Rise*, pp. 424f.

37 RAL, XI/109/27/1/1, Lionel, Paris, to Nathan, London, July 31, 1830.

38 Bouvier, *Rothschild*, p. 102. "Dans la journée, ma voiture croisa rapidement celle de M. Rothschild, si vite que je ne pus le saluer; son profil de singe intelligent me frappa comme une ébauche de Rembrandt, un coup de crayon qui dit tout."

39 RAL, XI/109/27/1/1, Lionel, Paris, to Nathan, London, July 31, 1830.

40 See e.g. Bertaut, *Bourse*, pp. 105f.; Chirac, *Haute Banque*, p.164.

41 RAL, XI/109/J/J/30, James, Paris, to Nathan, Hannah and his nephew, Aug. 4, 1830. Cf. Arnaud, *Mémoires*, p. 383.

42 RAL, XI/109/27/1/1, Lionel, Paris, to Nathan, London, July 31, 1830; T17/172, XI/109/16/2, Lionel, Paris, to Nathan, London, Aug. 2.

43 RAL, XI/109J/J/30B, James, Paris, to Nathan, London, Dec. 21, 1830. James was more magnanimous about Charles X when he heard of the death of that "really decent and upright man" six years later: RAL, XI/109J/J/36, James, Paris, to his nephews, London, Nov. 14, 1836.

44 Gille, *Maison Rothschild*, vol. I, pp. 203–5.

45 RAL, RFamC/1/119, Hannah, Paris, to Nathan, London, Aug. 25, 1830; RAL, RFamC/1/115, same to same, Sept. 1; RAL, XI/109/17/1/22, Charlotte, Paris, to Hannah Mayer, London, Sept. 25; RAL, RFamC/1/115, Hannah, Paris, to Nathan, London, Oct. 15.

46 RAL, XI/109J/J/30, James, Paris, to Nathan, London, July 31, 1830; RAL, XI/109J/J/30, James and Salomon, Paris, to Nathan, London, Aug. 8.

47 RAL, XI/109J/J/30, James and Salomon, Paris, to Nathan, London, Aug. 9, 1830.

48 RAL, XI/109J/J/30, James and Salomon, Paris, to Nathan, London, Aug. 12, 1830. Cf. Remusat, *Mémoires*, vol. II, p. 474.

49 RAL, T17/186, XI/109/15/2, Lionel, Paris, to his father, London, Sept. 9, 1830.

50 Corti, *Rise*, pp. 433–6.

51 Prawer, *Heine*, pp. 331–5.

52 Drumont, *France juive*, pp. 341, 358.

53 Gille, *Maison Rothschild*, vol. I, pp. 429f.; Prawer, *Heine*, pp. 328f.

54 Bouvier, *Rothschild*, pp. 50ff.

55 Stendhal, *Lucien Leuwen*. Leuwen also has no objection to his son leaving the family firm to pursue a military or political career, something James would never have countenanced. Cf. the comments in Bouvier, *Rothschild*, pp. 49–52.

56 RAL, T22/624, XI/109/32/3/38B, Lionel, Paris, to his parents, London, Aug. 19, 1834.

57 Corti, *Reign*, p. 178.

58 See e.g. RAL, XI/109J/J/30, James, Paris, to Nathan, London, Aug. 3, 1830.

59 RAL, XI/109J/J/30, Salomon and James, Paris, to Nathan, London, Aug. 24, 1830; RAL, XI/109J/J/30A, James, Paris, to Nathan, London, Sept. 20; RAL, T17/180, Lionel, Paris, to Nathan, London, Sept. 20; RAL, XI/109/16/1/18, Lionel, Paris to his parents, London, Sept. 21; RAL, XI/109J/J/30, James, Paris, to Nathan, London, Oct. 16; RAL, XI/109/17/1/14, Lionel, Paris, to his parents, London, Dec. 14; RAL, XI/109/1/16/25, same to same, Dec. 20.

60 RAL, XI/109/17/1/15, Lionel, Paris, to his parents, London, Dec. 22, 1830. Cf. RAL, XI/109/22/1/43, same to same, Dec. 27; RAL, XI/109J/J/31A, James, Paris, to Nathan, Hannah and Anthony, London, Jan. 1, 1831.

61 RAL, XI/109J/J/31B, James, Paris, to Nathan, London, Feb. 26, 1831. Cf. RAL, XI/109J/J/31, May 10; RAL, T17/339, Lionel, Paris, to his parents, London, May 10; XI/109J/J/31, James to Nathan, June 18.

62 RAL, XI/109J/J/30, James, Paris, to Amschel, Frankfurt, and Salomon, Vienna, May 6, 1831; RAL, XI/109J/J/31, James, Paris, to Nathan, London, May 11.

63 RAL, XI/109J/J/30, James and Salomon, Paris, to Nathan. London, Aug. 16, 1830; James to Nathan, Sept. 2; same to same, Sept. 4; RAL, XI/109J/J/31B, Nov. 24, 1831; RAL, XI/109J/J/31, Nov. 27; Dec. 12; RAL, XI/109/24/1/12, Lionel, Paris, to his parents and uncle, Dec. 22.

64 Apponyi, *Vingt-cinq ans*, vol. I, p. 424; Castellane, *Journal*, vol. II, p. 414. As Castellane noted: "Ce mélange des masques, de joie et d'émeutes est un spectacle curieux: notre nation est singulière." Cf. RAL, T17/227, Lionel, Paris, to his parents, London, Feb. 16, 1831. See also Apponyi, *Vingt-cinq ans*, vol. II, p. 297.

65 RAL, XI/109J/J/31, Anselm, Paris, to Nathan, London, May 12, 1831; RAL, XI/109/24/1/3, Lionel, to his mother, London, Dec. 12.

66 Corti, *Reign*, pp. 55f. See also RAL, T22/410, XI/109/29/1/8, Nat, Paris, to his parents, London, May 11, 1833; RAL, T22/414, XI/109/29/1/59, same to same, May 18.

67 RAL, XI/109J/J/30, James, Paris, to Nathan, London, Sept. 26, 1830; RAL, XI/109/16/1/21, Lionel, Paris, to his parents, London, Oct. 2.

68 RAL, XI/109J/J/30, James, Paris, to Nathan, London, Oct. 23, 1830. Cf. RAL, XI/109J/J/30, same to same, Oct. 31; Nov. 2; Dec. 27.

69 RAL, XI/109/18/1/22, Lionel, Paris, to his parents, London, Feb. 21, 1831; RAL, XI/109/18/1/25, same to same, Feb. 25; RAL XI/109/20/1/7, March 10. On relations with Périer, see Bergeron, *Rothschild*, pp. 43–6.

70 RAL, XI/109J/J/31, James, Paris, to Nathan, London, July, 1831; RAL, XI/109/22/1/6, Lionel, Paris, to his parents, London, July 4; RAL, XI/109J/J/31, James to Nathan, July 6; same to same, July 9; July 11; RAL, XI/109/22/1/9, Lionel to his parents, July 12; RAL, XI/109J/J/31, James to Nathan, July 12; RAL, XI/109/22/1/10, Lionel to his parents, July 13; RAL, XI/109J/J/31, James to Nathan, July 14; RAL, XI/109/22/1/11, Lionel to his parents, July 14; RAL, XI/109J/J/31, James to Nathan, July 18; RAL, XI/109/22/1/14, Lionel to his parents, July 18; RAL, XI/109J/J/31, James to Nathan, July 19; RAL, XI/109/22/1/15, Lionel to his parents, July 19; RAL, XI/109/22/1/16, same to same, July 20; RAL, XI/109J/J/31, James to Nathan, July 21; same to same, July 25; July 27; July 31; RAL, XI/109/22/1/21, Lionel to his parents, Aug. 1. Cf. Corti, *Reign*, p. 32, for James's offer to "use his influence" with his tenants in the Seine-et-Oise Department against the Republicans.

71 RAL, XI/109J/J/31, James, Paris, to Nathan, London, Aug. 1, 1831; same to same, Aug. 2; RAL, T22/49, XI/109/22/1/22, Lionel, Paris, to his parents, London, Aug. 2.

72 RAL, XI/109/22/1/29, Lionel, Paris, to his parents, London, Aug. 10, 1831.

73 RAL, XI/109J/J/31, James, Paris, to Nathan, London, Aug. 24, 1831; same to same, Aug. 27; Aug. 28; RAL, XI/109/22/1/39, Lionel, Paris, to his father, London, Sept. 4; RAL, XI/109/18/1/2, Lionel, Paris, to his parents, London, Sept. 17; RAL, XI/109J/J/31, James to Nathan, Sept. 18; same to same, Sept. 19; Sept. 24; Sept. 29; RAL, XI/109/23/1/10, Lionel to his parents, Sept. 29; RAL, XI/109J/J/31, James to Nathan and Lionel, Oct. 11; James to Nathan, Lionel, Anthony and Nat, Oct. 13; James to Nathan, Oct. 15; same to same, Dec. 24; Dec. 26; Dec. 28.

74 RAL, XI/109/25/1/24, Lionel, Paris, to his parents, London, Feb. 8, 1832.

75 Corti, *Reign*, pp. 57–9.
76 RAL, XI/109J/J/32, James, Paris, to Nathan, London, March 28, 1832; same to same, March 31; April 2; RAL, XI/109/26/1/1, Lionel, Paris, to his parents, April 4; RAL, XI/109/26/1/2, same to same, April 5; RAL, XI/109/26/1/4, April 7; RAL, XI/109J/J/32, James to Nathan, April 9; same to same, April 10; April 11; April 17; April 18; April 21; April 22; April 23; April 24; April 26; RAL, XI/109J/J/32A, James and Salomon to Nathan and their nephews, April 26; RAL, XI/109J/J/32, James to Nathan, April 29; RAL, XI/109/26/1/8, Lionel to his parents, April 30. Cf. Corti, *Reign*, pp. 47, 63, 218.
77 Heine, "Französische Zustände," Artikel VI, in *Sämtliche Schriften*, vol. III, p. 176. Cf. Prawer, *Heine*, p. 233. See also Castellane, *Journal*, vol. II, p. 502, noting that James had his house painted with chlorine.
78 RAL, XI/109J/J/32, James, Paris, to Nathan, London, April 30, 1832; same to same, May 1; RAL, XI/109/27/1/28, Lionel, Paris, to his parents, London, Nov. 10.
79 RAL, XI/109J/J/32, James, Paris, to Nathan and his nephews, London, May 30, 1832; RAL, T22/189, XI/109/26/1/22, Lionel, Paris, to his parents, London, June 2; RAL, XI/109/26/1/23, same to same, June 3; RAL, XI/109J/J/32, Salomon and James, Paris, to Nathan, Anthony and Nat, June 4; RAL, XI/109/28/1/6, Lionel to his parents, June 20.
80 RAL, T22/202, XI/109/26/1/26, Lionel, Paris, to his parents, London, June 5, 1832; RAL, XI/109J/J/32, James to Nathan, June 5, 1832; RAL, T22/303, XI/109/26/1/27, Lionel to his parents, June 6; RAL, XI/109J/J/32, James and Salomon to Nathan and their nephews, June 6; RAL, XI/109/25/1/38, Lionel to his parents, June 6; RAL, XI/109/28/1/1, same to same, June 9; RAL, XI/109/28/1/3, June 13. For later disturbances, see RAL, XI/109J/J/33, James to Nathan, April 4, 1833; RAL, XI/109J/J/34, same to same, Feb. 23, 1834; Feb. 24.
81 E.g. the ministerial "interregnum" of 1832 which preceded Marshal Soult's appointment as President of the King's council and Broglie's as Foreign Minister: RAL, XI/109/26/1/35, Lionel, Paris, to his parents, London, July 1, 1832; RAL, XI/109/28/1/10, same to same, July 3; RAL, XI/109/27/1/14, Sept. 10; RAL, XI/109/27/1/18, Sept. 29; RAL, XI/109/27/1/20, Oct. 3; RAL, XI/109/22/1/22, Oct. 6; RAL, XI/109J/J/32, James to Nathan, Oct. 17. For the fall of Broglie, see RAL, XI/109J/J/34, same to same, Feb. 22, 1834; March 18; RAL, XI/109J/J/34, March 26; April 2; April 4; April 5. For his brief return, see RAL, XI/109J/J/35, James to Nathan and Nat, March 1, 1835; RAL, XI/109/33/1/57, Anthony, Paris to my dear Parents, London, Oct. 12. For Thiers' short-lived first ministry, RAL, XI/109J/J/36, James to Nathan and his nephews, Feb. 16, 1836; same to same, Feb. 17; Feb. 18; Feb. 22; April 16; Sept. 24. For the fall of Molé (whom the Rothschilds liked) and the formation of a second Thiers ministry (which they regarded as a "bad thing"), RAL, XI/101/1/20/32, Anthony, Paris, to his brothers, London, Dec. 4, 1838; RAL, XI/101/1/20/38, Anthony to Nat, Dec. 29; RAL, XI/101/2/8/13, Anthony to his brothers, Jan. 1839; RAL, XI/101/2/8/15, same to same, Jan.; RAL, XI/101/2/8/19, Jan.; RAL, XI/101/2/8/22, Jan.; RAL, XI/101/2/8/23, Jan. For the fall of Thiers, RAL, XI/101/2/9/22, Anselm to his cousins, March 19. See also the detailed reports of an unidentified political source: RAL, XI/101/2/9/22a, March 22, 1839; RAL, XI, 101/2/9/22b, March 23, 1839.
82 RAL, T22/282, XI/109/27/1/33, Lionel, Paris, to his parents, London, Nov. 19, 1832; RAL, XI/109J/J/32, James, Paris, to Nathan, London, Nov. 19; RAL, XI/109J/J/33, James to Nathan and his nephews, March 19, 1833; RAL, T25/104/0/96, Nat, Paris, to his brothers, London, undated, early 1840.
83 RAL, XI/109J/J/34, James, Paris, to Nathan and Anthony, London, Feb. 18, 1834; RAL, XI/109J/J/34B, James to Nathan, April 12; same to same, April 13; RAL, XI/109J/J/34A, James to Anthony, April 13; RAL, XI/109J/J/34, James to Nathan, April 22.
84 RAL, T25/104/0/76, Nat, Paris, to his brothers, undated, early 1840; RAL, T25/104/0/75, Anselm, Paris, to his cousins, London, Aug. 7.
85 RAL, XI/109J/J/39, James, Rome, to his brothers and nephews, Feb. 2, 1839. Cf. Muhlstein, *Baron James*, p. 112.
86 RAL, XI/109J/J/30, Salomon and James, Paris, to Nathan, London, Aug. 24, 1830; RAL, XI/109/16/1/12, Lionel, Paris, to his father, London, Aug. 25; RAL, XI/109J/J/30, James, Paris, to Nathan, London, Aug. 25.
87 RAL, XI/109J/J/30, James, Paris, to Nathan, London, Aug. 18, 1830; RAL, 109/14/1/29, Lionel, Paris, to his father, London, Aug. 20; RAL, XI/109J/J/30, James, Paris, to Nathan, Aug. 21; RAL, XI/109/14/1/30, Lionel, Paris, to his father, London, Aug. 23. 236–241
88 RAL, RFamC/1/118, Hannah, Paris, to Nathan, London, Aug. 24, 1830: "You must look at it coolly, dear Rothschild. It will blow over. Salomon and James do not like the fall, you may easily suppose, but

they are very cool and not frightened. Our attention is so engrossed with the funds that I can dwell upon nothing else." See also RAL, RFamC/1/79, undated but probably Sept. 1830.

89   RAL, XI/109J/J/30B, James, Paris, to Nathan, London, Sept. 20, 1830. His only consolation was that, by holding so many rentes, he retained a certain leverage over the government; RAL, XI/109/17/1/3, Lionel, Paris, to his parents, London, Oct. 7.

90   RAL, XI/109/18/1/26, Lionel, Paris, to his parents, London, Feb. 26, 1831.

91   RAL, XI/10919/1/40, Anselm, Berlin, to his father, Vienna, Feb. 25, 1831.

92   RAL, XI/109J/J/31, James, Paris, to Nathan, London, March 3, 1831; RAL, XI/109J/J/31C, same to same, April 2; RAL, XI/109J/J/31, April 5; April 9. See also RAL, XI/109J/J/31, James, Paris, to Nathan, London, March 17; James to Nathan and Anthony, March 19; James to Nathan, March 26. By the time the market began to rise in April, all but around 17 million (nominal) had been sold.

93   RAL, XI/109J/J/31A, James, Paris, to Nathan, London, Jan. 3, 1831; RAL, XI/109J/J/31, same to same, Jan. 6; Jan. 8. Cf. Gille, *Banque et crédit*, pp. 149–56 for the comparable impact of the crisis on the syndicate of receivers-general. On the economic background, see Johnson, "Revolution of 1830," pp. 147–57.

94   RAL, XI/109/16/1/24, Lionel, Paris, to his parents, London, Nov. 16, 1830.

95   RAL, XI/109J/J/30, James, Paris, to Nathan, London, Dec. 30, 1830.

96   RAL, XI/109J/J/31, James, Paris, to Nathan, London, March 13, 1831. According to Lionel, Hottinguer said: "Our credit is no more so good, and this last six months we have lost much in the public opinion; we shall not find so many more followers when we wish to make any loans."

97   RAL, XI/109J/J/31, James, Paris, to Nathan, March 21, 1831.

98   RAL, XI/109/15/1/11, Lionel, Paris, to his parents, London, Nov. 18, 1830.

99   RAL, XI/109/21/1/22, Lionel, Paris, to his parents, London, June 18, 1831. Cf. RAL, XI/109/18/1/5, July 21: "We have been lately always on the wrong side—if we buy the next day the rentes fall & if we sell they rise."

100 RAL, XI/109J/J/31, James to Nathan, July 22, 1831.

101 RAL, XI/109J/J/31, James to Nathan, Aug. 13, 1831.

102 RAL, XI/109J/J/31, James to Nathan, Oct. 1, 1831.

103 RAL, XI/109J/J/32, James, Boulogne, to Nathan, London, July 5, 1832.

104 Interestingly, his first request for £300,000 in silver was turned down without explanation by the Bank: Bank of England, G8 (Committee of Treasury) 24 1146/2, Minutes of the Committee, July 7, 1830; he had to wait another two weeks before the Bank agreed to a loan: Bank of England, G8 (Committee of Treasury) 24 1146/2, Minutes, July 21. See also RAL, XI/109/16/1/5, Lionel, Paris to his parents, London, Aug. 2, 1830. Cf. Clapham, *Bank of England*, vol. II, p. 117. This was very much a short-term loan, and by the end of October the flow of gold was in the other direction, so that Nathan could repay the Bank: RAL, XI/109J/J/30, James, Paris, to Nathan and his nephews, London, Oct. 27, 1830. To outside observers, Nathan himself appeared to be in difficulties at this point; see Ziegler, *Sixth great power*, p. 136; Brock, *Great Reform Act*, p. 106. Cf. Capefigue, *Grandes opérations*, vol. III, pp.181f.; Chirac, *Haute Banque*, pp. 173–77.

105 RAL, RFamC/1/120, Hannah, Paris, to Nathan, London, Aug. 27, 1830.

106 *The Times*, Aug. 4, 1836: "This contract was more detrimental in proportion to his subscribers than to himself, as the greater part was distributed among them, and it was at the time a matter of severe reproach against him that he did on this occasion leave his friends completely in the lurch. But this was answered by the remark that he had always been in the practice of dealing liberally with his subscribers in sharing his contracts among them, and that the revolution which followed and made this so ruinous an operation was one that could not possibly have been foreseen by him."

107 RAL, XI/109J/J/31B, James, Paris, to Nathan, London, April 2, 1831.

108 AN, 132 AQ 13/Bilan, 1821–42.

109 RAL, XI/109/16/1/13, Lionel, Paris, to his father, London, Aug. 30, 1830; RAL, XI/109/16/1/16, Sept. 4. Cf. Corti, *Rise*, p. 431.

110 Corti, *Rise*, pp. 428–30.

111 Gentz, *Briefe an Pilat*, vol. II, p. 334.

112 Cf. Nipperdey, *Germany*, pp. 324ff.; Sheehan, *German history*, pp. 606f.

113 RAL, XI/109/23/2/13, Oldenburg loan contract between MAR, Leopold Goldschmidt and Grand Duke, September 24, 1831.

114 HSM, Bestand 6a Nr 583, Nrn 1–3, Schmincke, Cassel, to Elector, Oct. 31, 1830; Staatsministerium to Elector, Dec. 21.

115 RAL, XI/109/22/2/3c, Anselm, Berlin, to Amschel, Frankfurt, July 8, 1831. Cf. Berghoeffer, *Meyer Amschel*, pp. 207ff.

116 Frederick William had made a morganatic marriage to Gertrud Falkenstein, the divorced wife of a Prussian lieutenant. In 1831 he elevated her to the rank of Countess von Schaumburg, and later Princess of Hanau. When he was in Frankfurt, the couple and their five children regularly "took their midday meal quite *en famille* with their good business friend": Schwemer, *Geschichte*, vol. III/1, p. 387.

117 RAL, XI/109J/J/33, James, Paris, to Nathan, London, March 26, 1833. Corti, *Reign*, p. 227.

118 RAL, XI/109/23/2/12, Salomon, Munich, to his brothers, Sept. 20, 1831.

119 RAL, XI/109/27/2/5, Anthony, Frankfurt, to his father, London, Oct. 23, 1832: "The F[rank]furt house has not so much money at his command as it formerly used . . . so they cannot spare their money as well as they formerly could." See also RAL, T22/489, XI/109/30/2/10, same to same, Oct. 11, 1833.

120 RAL, XI/109/32/3/8, Anselm, Frankfurt, unaddressed, probably to James, Paris, May 3, 1833 [wrongly dated 1834].

121 "The whole land [is] in ferment and people do not even seem to trust the King": RAL, T17/118, Salomon, Vienna, to his brother [James?], Feb. 24, 1829.

122 On July 17, 1832, Thomas Raikes recorded in his journal that a Dutch broker had asked "Rothschild yesterday . . . if he would advance money on stock; the old Jew refused him, saying, 'In these times I shall not advance money to any one *by Got*; who knows what may happen? you may be dead tomorrow.' It so happened that the poor man was seized with the cholera that very evening, and the next morning he was dead": Raikes, *Journal*, vol. I, p. 62.

123 RAL, XI/109/15/1/11, Lionel, Paris, to his parents, London, Nov. 18, 1830; RAL, XI/109J/J/30, James, Paris, to Amschel, Frankfurt, Salomon, Vienna and Carl, Naples, Nov. 18; RAL, T17/186, Lionel to his parents, Nov. 20; RAL, XI/109/24/1/27, Nat, Paris, to his mother, Dec. 12; RAL, XI/109J/J/31A, James to Nathan, Anthony and Hannah, Jan. 1, 1831; RAL, XI/109/18/1/2, Lionel to his parents, Jan. 1.

124 Corti, *Reign*, pp. 12f.

125 RAL, XI/109J/J/31, James, Paris, to Nathan, London, March 5, 1831; same to same, March 7. Cf. Corti, *Reign*, pp. 13f.

126 RAL, XI/109/20/1/31, Lionel, Paris, to his parents, April 25, 1831.

127 RAL, XI/109J/J/31, James, Paris, to Nathan, London, April 25, 1831. Cf. April 26.

128 RAL, XI/109J/J/31A, James, Paris, to Nathan, London, May 7, 1831; same to same, May 12; June 2.

129 RAL, XI/109J/J/31, James, Paris, to Nathan, Hannah and his nephews, Oct. 10, 1831; James to Nathan, Oct. 15.

130 RAL, XI/109J/J/31, James, Paris, to Nathan, London, Nov. 2, 1831.

131 RAL, XI/109/20/1/34, Lionel, Paris, to his parents, London, April 29, 1831. See also RAL, XI/109/24/1/1, same to same, Dec. 11.

132 RAL, XI/109/20/1/42, Lionel, Paris, to his parents, London, April 27, 1831.

133 Disraeli, *Endymion*, pp. 131f.

134 RAL, RFamC/1/122, Hannah, Paris, to Nathan, London, Sept. 6, 1830. Cf. Buxton, *Finance*, vol. I, p. 30n.

135 RAL, XI/109/1/1/15, Lionel, Paris, to his parents, London, May 26, 1831.

136 RAL, XI/109J/J/31, James, Paris, to Nathan, London, March 23, 1831; same to same, April 21; April 23; April 25.

137 RAL, XI/109J/J/31, James, Paris, to Nathan, London, May 2, 1831.

138 RAL, XI/109/22/1/3, Lionel, Paris, to his parents, London, June 19, 1831; RAL, XI/109/22/1/6, same to same, July 4; RAL, XI/109/22/1/11, July 14; RAL, XI/109/22/1/15, July 19. Both he and James were struck by the parallel between the French debate on the hereditary peerage and the British debate on the Lords' veto: RAL, XI/109J/J/31, James to Nathan, Sept. 29; RAL, XI/109/23/1/10, Lionel to his parents, Sept. 29.

139 RAL, XI/109J/J/31, James, Paris, to Nathan, London, Oct. 3, 1831.

140 RAL, T17/316, XI/109/20/1, Lionel, Paris, to his parents, April 30, 1831. Cf. RAL, T17/242, Anthony, Paris, to his parents, Nov. 27.

141 RAL, XI/109J/J/32, James, Paris, to Nathan, London, Jan. 28, 1832: same to same, Jan. 30; RAL, XI/109/25/1/18, Lionel to his parents, Jan. 30; RAL, XI/109/25/1/23, same to same, Feb. 7.

142 RAL, XI/109J/J/31, James, Paris, to Nathan, London, Nov. 21, 1831.

143   Corti, *Reign*, p. 57.
144   *Ibid.*, pp. 63f. Cf. Butler, *Passing of the Great Reform Bill*, p. 396; Brock, *Great Reform Act*, p. 302; Thompson, *Wellington after Waterloo*, p. 125; Kynaston, *City*, vol. I, p. 98.
145   Loewe (ed.), *Montefiore diaries*, vol. I, pp. 93f.
146   Kriegel (ed.), *Holland House diaries*, p. 180.
147   RAL, XI/109/26/1/11, Lionel, Paris, to his parents, London, May 12, 1832; RAL, XI/109/26/1/10, same to same, May 12; RAL, T6/111, L. C. Beigle, Paris, to Nathan, May 16; RAL, T22/189, XI/109/26/2/7, Anselm, Frankfurt, to Lionel, Paris, May 17; RAL, XI/109/26/1/14, Lionel to his parents, May 20; RAL, XI/109/26/1/20, same to same, May 30.
148   See e.g. RAL, T22/389, XI/109/29/1/86, Hannah Mayer, Brighton, to her father, Feb. 7, 1833 (attacking O'Connell); RAL, XI/109/29/1/7, Lionel, Paris, to my dear parents, London, April 27 (attacking Attwood).
149   RAL, XI/109/27/2/22, Anthony, Frankfurt, to his parents, Dec. 3, 1832; RAL, XI/109/27/1/45, Lionel, Paris, to his parents, Dec. 8; RAL, XI/109/27/1/50, same to same, Dec. 15.
150   Ayer, *Century of finance*, p. 38f.; Gille, *Maison Rothschild*, vol. I, pp. 235–8; Davis, *English Rothschilds*, p. 70; Jenks, *Migration*, p. 44. Details in Loewe (ed.), *Montefiore diaries*, vol. I, pp. 97f.
151   Buxton (ed.), *Memoirs*, pp. 288–90; cf. *DNB*. He was also one of the auditors and parliamentary proponents of the Alliance Assurance Company.

NINE   *The Chains of Peace*

   1   Gentz, *Briefe*, vol. II, p. 334.
   2   RAL, XI/109J/J/30, James and Salomon, Paris, to Nathan, London, Oct. 10, 1830.
   3   James, Paris, to Salomon, Vienna, Nov. 24, 1830, quoted in Corti, *Rise*, pp. 433–6. By Jan. 19, he had revised his projections downwards: war would mean a fall of 10 per cent in Paris and 5 per cent in London: RAL, XI/109J/J/31, James, Paris, to Nathan, London, Jan. 19, 1831.
   4   Balla, *Romance*, pp. 191ff.
   5   Corti, *Reign*, p. 10.
   6   Kübeck, *Tagebücher*, vol. I/2, p. 593.
   7   Bouvier, *Rothschild*, p. 52: "The House of Rothschild . . . for reasons that are natural although I cannot regard them as good, and certainly not as morally satisfactory, plays a much bigger part in France than do the foreign cabinets, except possibly that of England. The great vehicle in France is money . . ."
   8   Pückler, *Briefe*, p. 7.
   9   Corti, *Reign*, p. 246.
  10   Toussenel, *Juifs*, vol. I, p. 2.
  11   Capefigue, *Grandes opérations*, vol. III, p. 198; Chirac, *Rois de la République*, p. 136. Cf. Ponteil, *Institutions*, pp.194f.
  12   Morton, *Rothschilds*, p. 96.
  13   Heuberger, *Rothschilds*, p. 71.
  14   Nesselrode, *Lettres et papiers*, vol. VIII, p. 95.
  15   Disraeli, *Coningsby*, pp. 214–21.
  16   RAL, T62/127/6, XI/109/7, Caroline, Rotterdam, to Nathan and Hannah, London, July 11, 1817.
  17   RAL, T29/181, XI/109/0/7/21, Carl, Frankfurt, to Salomon, Aug. 23, 1814; RAL, T63/28/1, XI/109/8, Carl, Berlin, to his brothers, Nov. 4, 1817.
  18   RAL, XI/109/0/2/1, Amschel, Frankfurt, to Nathan, June 19, 1814; RAL, XI/109/0/2/5, Amschel, Frankfurt, to Salomon, June 20.
  19   Corti, *Rise*, pp. 241ff.
  20   RAL, T29/138, XI/109/0/5/14, James, Amsterdam, to Nathan, London, Aug. 9, 1814.
  21   See e.g. RAL, XI/109/2/2/148, James, Paris, to Nathan, London, Oct. 21, 1815; RAL, T30, XI/109/2/2/167, Salomon and James, Paris, to Nathan, Nov. 11; RAL, Cole Autographs, vol. 33, U1C/73, Nathan, London, to Messrs Latham Rice & Co., Dover, May 26.
  22   RAL, T63/20/1, Amschel, Frankfurt, to James, Paris, Nov. 25, 1817.
  23   Gille, *Maison Rothschild*, vol. I, pp. 187f.
  24   RAL, T5/239, Salomon, Vienna, to MAR, Frankfurt, Dec. 25, 1827.
  25   See e.g. RAL, XI/109/21/2/5, Anselm, Berlin, to James, Paris, May 20, 1831; RAL, T70/1, Anselm, Frankfurt, to James and Lionel, Paris, May 22.
  26   RAL, XI/109J/J/33, James, Paris, to Nathan and his sons, London, Feb. 16, 1833.

27   RAL, T7/184, Nat, Paris, to his brothers, London, undated, *c.* 1846. See also RAL, XI/109J/J/36, James, Paris, to Nathan and his sons, London, April 20, 1836; RAL, T25/104/0/86, Isaac Cohen, Boulogne, to Lionel, Sept. 8, 1840.

28   RAL, XI/109J/J/36, James, Paris, to Nathan and Nat, London, May 19, 1836. See also RAL, XI/109J/J/46, James, Paris, to his nephews, London, May 28, 1846.

29   RAL, XI/109/39/1/5, Carl, Naples, to deRF, Paris, Aug. 18, 1840.

30   Chateaubriand, *Correspondence générale*, vol. III, pp. 663f.

31   Corti, *Rise*, pp. 308ff. See e.g. RAL, XI/109/10/1/11, Metternich, Pressburg, to Salomon, Vienna, Nov. 14, 1825; RAL, XI/109/10/1/12, Salomon, Vienna, to Metternich, Pressburg, Nov. 15.

32   Lieven, *Letters to Metternich*, p. 237. See also Nesselrode, *Lettres et papiers*, p. 234.

33   Corti, *Rise*, pp. 346f.

34   Bertier de Sauvigny, *Metternich et la France*, pp. 1157f.

35   The existing links between the House of Saxe-Coburg and the Rothschilds explain why the marriage of "your little Queen" to Albert prompted a message of congratulation from Salomon's son Anselm to his London cousins: RAL, T25, XI/104/0/13, Anselm, Paris, to his cousins, London, Feb. 11, 1840.

36   RAL, T23/143, XI/109/38/3/30, F. Schenck, Buckingham Palace, to NMR, March 13, 1840; RAL, T23/145, XI/109/38/3/31, same to same, March 19; RAL, T23/146, XI/109/38/3/33, April 10; RAL, T23/155, XI/109/39/4/5, July 7; RAL, T23/175, XI/109/39/4/13–15, Dr Praetorius, Windsor Castle, to Lionel, Nov. 10, 13 and 19; RAL, T23/204, XI/109/40/3/8, Schenck, Buckingham Palace, to Lionel, May 4, 1841; RAL, T23/209, XI/109/40/3/6, Praetorius, Buckingham Palace, to Lionel, May 21; RAL, T23/205, XI/109/40/3/7, same to same, May 25; RAL, T23/214, XI/109/41/4/1, Schenck, Buckingham Palace, to NMR, July 6; RAL, T23/262, XI/109/42/5/5, Praetorius, Windsor Castle, to Lionel, Feb. 8, 1842; RAL, T24/152, X/109/52/85, XI/109/43/4/13, same to same, Dec. 23; RAL, T24/189, X/109/53/30, XI/109/44/6/2, Mr Anson, Buckingham Palace, to Lionel, March 30, 1843; RAL, T18/245, XI/109/46/2/67, Praetorius, Windsor Castle, to Lionel, Feb. 8, 1844; RAL, T18/269, XI/109/46/2/69, Praetorius, Windsor Castle, to NMR, Feb. 29.

37   RAL, T23/157, Stockmar to Lionel, July 20, 1840; RAL, T18/270, XI/109/46/1/31, Anselm, Frankfurt, to Lionel and Billy [Anthony], London, March 2, 1844.

38   RA, Y90/22, Queen Victoria to King Leopold of the Belgians, June 7, 1841; Benson and Esher (eds), *Letters of Queen Victoria*, vol. I, p. 290. See also RAL, T51/28, XI/113/2B/2, Anson, Osborne House, to NMR, July 23, 1845. Leopold visited Amschel's garden in 1843: RA, Y70/8, King Leopold, Frankfurt, to Queen Victoria, Aug. 22, 1843.

39   RAL, T27/280, XI/109/7 (also T62/85/4), James, Paris, to Salomon and Nathan, June 18, 1817.

40   NLS, Stuart MS 21274 f. 6, deRF to Charles Stuart [*sic*], Nov. 11, 1817 (reporting on the health of Princess Charlotte).

41   Kynaston, *City*, vol. I, pp. 54f.

42   Corti, *Rise*, p. 242; Gille, *Banque et crédit*, p. 262.

43   Serre, *Correspondance*, vol. IV, p. 249. For another example, see *ibid.*, p. 418.

44   Aspinall (ed.), *Letters of George IV*, vol. III, p. 175. Cf. Stapleton (ed.), *Correspondence of Canning*, p. 173.

45   Talleyrand, *Memoirs*, vol. III, p. 315.

46   Villèle, *Mémoires*, vol. III, p. 219. Cf. Gille, *Banque et crédit*, p. 262; Bertier de Sauvigny, *Metternich et la France*, p. 899. For a similar allegation of "rig[ging] the market" from an Austrian source, see Corti, *Rise*, p. 348.

47   BL, Add. MS 43234 f. 303, Nathan to Aberdeen, undated, *c.* 1830; Corti, *Rise*, pp. 424f., 427f.; Balfour, *Life of Aberdeen*, pp. 254f.; Gash, *Mr Secretary Peel*, p. 638; Chamberlain, *Aberdeen*, pp. 237f.; Gentz, *Briefe and Pilat*, vol. II, pp. 288f.; Mann, *Secretary of Europe*, p. 298; Bertier de Sauvigny, *Metternich et la France*, p. 1361. It took three days for details of Salomon's "mysterious letter" to Frankfurt to reach Metternich.

48   See e.g. RAL, XI/109J/J/31, James, Paris, to Nathan, London, March 30, 1831.

49   RAL, XI/109J/J/30, James, Paris, to Nathan, London, July 31, 1830. See also RAL, XI/109/16/1/4, Lionel, Paris, to my dear parents, London, Aug. 1; RAL, XI/109J/J/30, James and Salomon to Nathan, Aug. 12.

50   RAL, XI/109/16/1/7, Lionel, Paris, to his parents, London, Aug. 14, 1830. Cf. XI/109/16/1/8, same to same, Aug. 16.

51   RAL, XI/16/1/8, Lionel, Paris, to his parents, London, Aug. 16. Cf. Corti, *Rise*, p. 430.

52   RAL, XI/109J/J/30, James, Paris, to Nathan, London, Aug. 28, 1830; RAL, XI/109J/J/30A, James and
     Salomon to Nathan, Aug. 30; RAL, XI/109/16/1/13, Lionel, Paris, to his father, London, Aug. 30.
53   RAL, XI/109/16/1/14, Lionel, Paris, to his father, London, Sept. 1, 1830; RAL, XI/109J/J/30, James to
     Nathan, Sept. 1; same to same, Sept. 2; Sept. 6; Sept. 11.
54   RAL, XI/109/16/1/17, Lionel, Paris, to his father, London, Sept. 7, 1830; Corti, *Rise*, pp. 432f.
55   RAL, XI/109J/J/30A, James, Salomon and Anselm, Paris, to Nathan, London, Sept. 15, 1830; James to
     Nathan, Sept. 18; same to same, Sept. 19; Sept. 20; RAL, XI/109/16/1/18, Lionel to his parents, Sept.
     21; RAL, XI/109/16/1/21, same to same, Oct. 2; Oct. 4.
56   RAL, XI/109/17/1/7, Lionel, Paris, to his parents, London, Oct. 13, 1830; RAL, XI/109J/J/30, James
     to Nathan, Oct. 27; same to same, Oct. 21.
57   RAL, XI/109J/J/30A, James, Paris, to Nathan, London, Dec. 21, 1830. For Salomon's prediction that
     the Polish revolt was doomed to end in a "bloodbath," see RAL, XI/109/23/2/11, Salomon, Vienna, to
     his brother, Dec. 19. For Anselm's fear—or hope?—that a revolt had also broken out in St Petersburg,
     RAL, XI/109/17/3/15, Anselm, Berlin, to his uncle, Dec. 23. For Salomon's warnings against Austrian
     involvement, Kübeck, *Tagebücher*, vol. I/2, p. 302. For James's hopes of a swift Russian victory, RAL,
     XI/109J/J/31, James to Nathan, March 8, 1831.
58   RAL, XI/109J/J/31, James, Paris, to Nathan, Jan. 17, 1831; RAL, XI/109J/J/31B, same to same, Jan.
     25; RAL, XI/109J/J/31, Jan. 31; Feb. 2; Feb. 4; Feb. 5; Feb. 7; Feb. 21; March 23; March 31; RAL,
     XI/109J/J/31B, April 2; RAL, XI/109J/J/31C, April 2; RAL, XI/109J/J/31, April 6; April 7; April 11;
     April 12; April 23; April 26; April 27; May 4. See also RAL, XI/109/18/1/7, Lionel to his parents, Jan.
     25; RAL, XI/109/18/1/12, same to same, Jan. 31; RAL, XI/109/18/1/15, Feb. 4; RAL,
     XI/109/18/1/17, Feb. 5; RAL, XI/109/18/1/18, Feb. 7; RAL, XI/109/18/1/18, same to same Feb. 12;
     RAL, XI/109/18/1/22, Feb. 21; RAL, XI/109/20/1/18, April 6; RAL, XI/109/20/1/22, April 12; RAL,
     XI/109/20/1/29, April 27; RAL, XI/109/21/1/5, May 9. Of crucial importance was the French gov-
     ernment's unequivocal commitment to the two protocols of January 1831, and its refusal to accept the
     Belgian offer of the crown to Louis Philippe's son the duc de Nemours, or to support Belgian resistance
     against the territorial provisions of the protocols. Needless to say, it was good news from a Rothschild
     standpoint that Leopold of Saxe-Coburg emerged as the successful candidate for the Belgian throne.
59   RAL, XI/109/18/1/16, Lionel, Paris, to his parents, London, Feb. 10, 1831; RAL, XI/109J/J/31, James,
     Paris, to Nathan, Feb. 10; RAL, T17/267, Nat, Naples, to his father, London, Feb. 13.
60   RAL, XI/109/18/1/16, Lionel, Paris, to his parents, Feb. 10, 1831; RAL, XI/109/18/1/23, same to
     same, Feb. 22; RAL, XI/109J/J/31, James to Nathan, March 5; RAL, XI/109/20/1/5, Lionel to his par-
     ents, March 7. Cf. Corti, *Reign*, pp. 10f., 13f.
61   RAL, XI/109/20/1/28, James, Paris, to Salomon, Vienna, undated, March 1831; RAL, XI/109J/J/31,
     James to Nathan, March 23; same to same, March 24; March 26; March 27; March 29; March 30. Cf.
     RAL, XI/109/20/1/14, Lionel to his parents, March 23; RAL, XI/109/20/1/15, same to same, March
     24; April 14. Cf. Corti, *Reign*, pp. 17–22; Johnson, "Revolution of 1830," p. 156.
62   RAL, XI/109J/J/31, James, Paris, to Amschel [and Salomon?], Frankfurt, March 31, 1831. Cf. Corti,
     Reign, pp. 22ff. James opposed the use of the brusque phrases "evacuez immédiatement Bologne" and
     "evacuez promptement Bologne." "I shall ensure," he told his brothers, "that the offending phrase is
     omitted." James's hope that the Austrians would refer the matter to an international conference in
     Rome was fulfilled, but it was not until July that their troops were withdrawn. The fact that Périer did
     not make withdrawal a *casus belli* was therefore significant. See also RAL, XI/109J/J/31B, James to
     Nathan, April 5, 1831; RAL, XI/109J/J/31, same to same, April 9; June 16. Cf. Corti, *Reign*, pp. 24–8.
63   RAL, XI/109J/J/31, James, Paris, to Nathan, London, April 14, 1831; same to same, May 10; May 14;
     May 15.
64   RAL, XI/109J/J/31, James, Paris, to Nathan, London, May 16; same to same, May 17; May 18; May
     19; May 21; May 23; May 24; May 28; May 30; May 31; June 1; June 2; June 6; June 7; June 8; June 9;
     June 11; June 12; June 16; June 20; June 21; June 22; June 25; June 27; June 28; July 2; July 3; July 4;
     July 5; July 6; July 7; July 9; July 11; July 16; July 21; July 22; July 25; July 27; July 30; July 31. Cf. RAL,
     XI/109/21/1/14, Lionel, Paris, to his parents, London, May 24; RAL, XI/109/21/1/18, same to same,
     June 8; RAL, XI/109/21/1/20, June 9; RAL, XI/109/22/1/1, June 10; RAL, XI/109/21/1/21, June 11;
     RAL, XI/109/22/1/4, June 24; RAL, XI/109/21/1/28, June 25; RAL, XI/109/22/1/9, July 12; RAL,
     XI/109/22/1/10, July 13; RAL, XI/109/22/1/15, July 19; RAL, XI/109/22/1/19, July 30. Cf. Corti,
     Reign, pp. 30ff.
65   RAL, XI/109/22/1/21, Lionel, Paris, to his parents, London, Aug. 1, 1831; RAL, XI/109J/J/31, James,
     Paris, to Nathan, London, Aug. 1; same to same, Aug 2; Aug. 3; Aug. 4.

66 RAL, XI/109J/J/31, James, Paris, to Nathan, London, Aug. 4, 1831; RAL, XI/109/22/1/23, Lionel, Paris, to his parents, London, Aug. 4; RAL, XI/109J/J/31A, James to Nathan, Aug. 6; RAL, XI/109J/J/31B, James and Lionel to Nathan, Aug. 6; RAL, XI/109J/J/31, James to Nathan, Aug. 9; RAL, XI/109J/J/31A&B, James and Lionel to Nathan, Aug. 10; same to same, Aug. 13; James, Fer- rières, to Nathan, Aug. 14; RAL, XI/109J/J/31, same to same, Aug. 16; RAL, XI/109/22/1/33, Lionel to his parents, Aug. 16; RAL, XI/109/18/1/20, same to same, Aug. 17; RAL, XI/109J/J/31, James to Nathan, Aug. 17; same to same, Aug. 20; Aug. 24; Aug. 27; Aug. 28; Aug. 30; Sept. 1; Sept. 3; Sept. 5; Sept. 10; Sept. 14; Sept. 27; Sept. 28; Oct. 3; Oct. 4. Cf. RAL, XI/109/22/1/38, Lionel to his father, Sept. 1; RAL, XI/109/23/1/1, same to same, Sept. 2; RAL, XI/109/23/1/2, Sept. 3; RAL, XI/109/22/1/39, Sept. 4; RFamC/1/136, Hannah, Paris, to Nathan, Sept. 5; RAL, XI/109/23/1/4, Lionel to Nathan, Sept. 7; RAL, XI/109/23/1/5, same to same, Sept. 10; RAL, XI/109/22/1/41, Sept. 11; RAL, XI/109/23/1/8, Sept. 27; RAL, XI/109/23/1/9, Sept. 28; RAL, XI/109/23/1/10, Sept. 29.

67 RAL, XI/109J/J/31, James, Paris, to Nathan, Hannah and their sons, Oct. 5, 1831; same to same, Oct. 10; James to Nathan and Lionel, Oct. 11; James to Nathan and his nephews, Oct. 13; same to same, Oct 15; Oct. 17; Oct. 18; Oct. 19; Oct. 25; Oct. 26; Oct. 31; Nov. 2; Nov. 7; Nov. 14; Nov 16; Nov. 27; Dec. 12; Dec. 18; Dec. 29; RAL, XI/109/23/1/14, Lionel to his parents, Nov. 7; RAL, XI/109/23/1/17, same to same, Nov 14; RAL, XI/109/24/1/28, Nat, Paris, to his parents, Dec. 12; RAL, XI/109/24/1/35, same to same, Dec. 30; RAL, XI/109/24/1/2, Lionel to his parents, Dec. 12; RAL, XI/109/24/1/7, same to same, Dec 17; RAL, XI/109/24/1/9, Dec. 20; RAL, XI/109/4/1/16,17, Dec. 31; RAL, XI/109J/J/31A, James to Nathan and Anthony, Dec. 31; RAL, XI/109J/J/31B, James to Nathan, Dec. 31; RAL, XI/109/25/1/1, Lionel to his parents, Jan. 1, 1832; RAL, XI/109/25/1/3, same to same, Jan 5; RAL, XI/109/25/1/8; Jan. 10; RAL, XI/109J/J/32, James to Nathan, Jan.1; same to same, Jan. 2; Jan. 3; Jan. 4; Jan. 5; Jan. 7; Jan. 8; Jan. 9; Jan. 10; Jan. 11; Jan. 14; James and Salomon to Nathan, Jan. 16; RAL, XI/109J/J/32A&B, James to Nathan and Nat, Jan. 18; James to Nathan, Jan. 17; RAL, XI/109/25/1/40, Nat to his parents, Jan. 5; RAL, XI/109/25/1/42, same to same, Jan. 7; RAL, XI/109/25/2/10, Anselm, Frankfurt, to James, Jan. 16; RAL, XI/109J/J/32, James and Salomon to Nathan and Nat, Jan. 23; same to same, Jan. 24; James to Nathan, Jan. 25; James and Salomon to Nathan and Nat, Jan. 26; James to Nathan, Jan. 28; RAL, XI/109/25/1/16, Lionel to his parents, Jan. 28; RAL, XI/109/25/1/23, same to same, Feb. 7; RAL, XI/109/25/1/33, March 24; RAL, XI/109/25/1/34, March 26; RAL, XI/109J/J/32, James to Nathan, March 26; same to same, April 3.

68 RAL, XI/109J/J/31, James, Paris, to Nathan, London, Dec. 26, 1831; RAL, XI/109/24/1/34, Nat, Paris, to his parents, London, Dec. 29; RAL, XI/109/25/1/18, Lionel, Paris, to his parents, Jan. 30, 1832; RAL, XI/109/18/1/15; same to same, Feb 1; RAL, XI/109/25/1/20, Feb. 2; RAL, XI/109J/J/32, James to Nathan, Jan 30; same to same, Jan. 31; Feb. 1; Feb. 5; Feb. 7; Feb. 29; March 4; March 5; March 6; March 31; April 2; RAL, XI/109/25/1/25, Lionel to his parents, Feb. 29.

69 RAL, XI/109J/J/32, James to Nathan, July 23, 1832; RAL, XI/109/18/1/31, Lionel, Paris, to his par- ents, London, Sept. 17; RAL, XI/109/28/1/25, same to same, Sept. 18; RAL, XI/109/18/1/32, Sept. 19; RAL, XI/109/28/1/26, Sept. 22; RAL, XI/109/27/1/17, Sept. 27; RAL, XI/109/27/1/18, Sept. 29; RAL, XI/109/27/1/20, Oct. 3; RAL, XI/109/22/1/22, Oct. 6; RAL, XI/109J/J/32, James to Nathan, Oct. 23; same to same, Oct. 24; Oct. 25; Oct. 29; Oct. 31; RAL, XI/109J/J/32A&B, Nov. 3; RAL, XI/109J/J/32, James and Anselm to Nathan and Nat, Nov. 5; James to Nathan and Nat, Nov. 7; James to Nathan, Nov. 10; same to same, Nov. 13; Nov. 14; Nov. 17; Nov. 19; RAL, XI/109/27/1/32, Lionel to his parents, Nov. 17.

70 RAL, XI/109J/J/30A, James, Paris, to Nathan, London, Sept. 29, 1830.

71 RAL, XI/109J/J/30, James, Paris, to Nathan, London, Nov. 23, 1830. Cf. Corti, *Rise*, pp. 433–8; Gille, *Maison Rothschild*, vol. I, pp. 206–9.

72 RAL, XI/109J/J/30, James, Paris, to Nathan, Nov. 29, 1830; same to same, Nov. 30.

73 RAL, XI/109/17/1/14, Lionel, Paris, to his parents, London, Dec. 14, 1830; RAL, XI/109J/J/31A, James, Paris, to Amschel, Frankfurt, and Salomon, Vienna, Jan. 2,

74 RAL, XI/109J/J/30, James, Paris, to Nathan, London, Dec. 29, 1830; same to same, Dec. 30; RAL, XI/109/18/1/3, Nat, Paris, to his parents, London, Jan. 1, 1831; RAL, XI/109/20/1/2, Lionel, Paris, to his parents, London, Jan. 6; RAL, XI/109J/J/31A, James to Nathan, Jan. 3; RAL, XI/109J/J/31, same to same, Jan. 6; Jan. 8; Jan. 19.

75 RAL, XI/109J/J/31, James, Paris, to Nathan, Jan. 17, 1831; same to same, Jan. 18; Jan. 28; Jan. 31. Lionel rightly suspected James of "thinking as he wished": RAL, XI/109/18/1/10, Lionel to his parents, Jan. 18; RAL, XI/109/18/1/4, Jan. 19; RAL, XI/109/18/1/8, Jan. 24; Jan. 27.

76 RAL, XI/109J/J/31A, James, Paris, to Nathan, London, Jan. 25, 1831; RAL, XI/109J/J/31, same to same, Feb. 9.

77 RAL, XI/109J/J/31, James, Paris, to Nathan, London, Feb. 21, 1831. Cf. Feb. 22; Feb. 24; Feb. 25.

78 RAL, XI/109J/J/31, James, Paris, to Nathan, London, Feb. 27, 1831. Cf. RAL, XI/10919/1/40, Lionel to his parents, Feb. 25; RAL, XI/109/20/1/3, same to same, March 1.

79 RAL, XI/109J/J/31, James, Paris, to Nathan, London, March 9, 1831.

80 Corti, *Reign*, pp. 15f. Cf. RAL, XI/109/20/1/6, Lionel, Paris, to his parents, London, March 9, 1831.

81 RAL, XI/109/20/1/7, Lionel, Paris, to his parents, London, March 10, 1831. Cf. Corti, *Reign*, pp. 17f.

82 RAL, XI/109J/J/31, James, Paris, to Salomon, Vienna, March 14, 1831. Cf. Corti, *Reign*, pp. 18ff.

83 Corti, *Reign*, pp. 21f.

84 RAL, XI/109/21/1/1, Lionel, Paris, to his parents, London, March 31, 1831. Cf. Corti, *Reign*, pp. 22ff.

85 RAL, XI/109J/J/31, James, Paris, to Nathan, London, March 15, 1831. The fact that Sebastiani remained Foreign Minister meant that there was less discontinuity in French policy than James claimed.

86 RAL, XI/109/21/1/22, Lionel, Paris, to his parents, London, June 18, 1831. Cf. RAL, XI/109J/J/31, James, Paris, to Nathan, London, June 20; same to same, June 21; June 22; June 25; RAL, XI/109/21/1/26, Lionel to his parents, June 28.

87 RAL, XI/109J/J/31, James, Paris, to Nathan, London, Aug. 2, 1831.

88 RAL, XI/109J/J/32, James to Nathan, Jan. 5, 1832; same to same, Jan. 7; Jan. 8; Jan. 9; Jan. 10, Jan. 11; Jan. 14; James and Salomon to Nathan, Jan. 16; James to Nathan, Jan. 17; RAL, XI/109J/J/32A&B, James to Nathan and Nat, Jan. 18.

89 RAL, XI/109J/J/32, James, Paris, to Nathan, London, Oct. 17, 1832; same to same, Oct. 20; Oct. 22; Oct. 23.

90 RAL, XI/109J/J/30, James, Paris, to Nathan, London, Nov. 3, 1830.

91 RAL, XI/109J/J/30, James, Paris, to Amschel, Frankfurt, Salomon, Vienna and Carl, Naples, Nov. 18, 1830; RAL, XI/109/15/1/11, Lionel to his parents, Nov. 18.

92 RAL, XI/109J/J/31B, James, Paris, to Nathan, London, Jan. 23, 1831; same to same, Jan. 24.

93 Corti, *Reign*, pp. 12f.

94 *Ibid.*, p. 20; RAL, XI/109J/J/31, James, Paris, to Nathan, London, March 21, 1831.

95 RAL, XI/109/22/1/3, Lionel, Paris, to his parents, London, June 19, 1831.

96 RAL, XI/109J/J/31, James, Paris, to Nathan, London, Oct. 1, 1831.

97 RAL, XI/109/4/1/6, Lionel, Paris, to his parents, London, Dec. 15, 1831.

98 Corti, *Rise*, pp. 63f. Cf. RAL, XI/109/26/1/10, Lionel, Paris, to his father, London, May 12, 1832.

99 Corti, *Reign*, pp. 74f. Emphasis added.

100 RAL, XI/109J/J/30A, Salomon, Paris, to Nathan, London, Oct. 10, 1830.

101 RAL, XI/109/17/1/12, Lionel, Paris, to his parents, London, Nov. 28, 1830. Cf. Corti, *Rise*, pp. 437f.

102 Kübeck, *Tagebücher*, vol. I/2, p. 382; Corti, *Reign*, pp. 26f.

103 RAL, XI/109/22/2/22, Salomon, Vienna, to his brothers, July 9, 1831. Cf. RAL, XI/109/22/2/25, James, Paris, to Salomon, Vienna, July 18.

104 Corti, *Reign*, pp. 58–62.

105 Kübeck, *Tagebücher*, vol. I/2, p. 593.

106 RAL, XI/109/13/1/63, Rother, Cologne, to Salomon, Vienna, Aug. 18, 1829; RAL, XI/109/12/1/12, same to same, Dec. 5; RAL, XI/109J/J/29, James, Paris, to Nathan and his nephews, London, Dec. 18; RAL, XI/109J/J/29A&B, same to same, Dec. 20; RAL, XI/109/13/1/54, Rother, Berlin, to Anselm, Frankfurt, Jan. 28, 1830; RAL, XI/109J/J/30, James to Nathan and Lionel, Jan. 30; RAL, XI/109/14/1/1, Anselm to James, Feb. 1; RAL, XI/109J/J/30B, James to Nathan, Feb. 6; RAL, XI/109/14/1/40, Salomon, Vienna, to Anselm, Berlin, Feb. 11; RAL, XI/109/14/1/2, Anselm to his uncles, Feb. 11; RAL, XI/109J/J/30, James to Nathan and his nephews, Feb. 12; RAL, XI/109/14/1/3, Anselm to his uncles, Feb. 13; RAL, XI/109/14/1/4, same to same, Feb. 14; RAL, XI/109/14/1/5, Feb. 28; RAL, T17/139, Rother, Berlin, to Salomon, Vienna, March 8; RAL, XI/109/14/1/17, Anselm to his uncles, March 21; RAL, XI/109/14/1/18, same to same, April 11; RAL, XI/109/14/1/18, April 12; RAL, XI/109/20/3/43, undated copy of contract. Cf. Corti, *Rise*, pp. 410–14; Berghoeffer, *Meyer Amschel*, pp. 206ff.; Ayer, *Century of finance*, pp. 36f. Salomon assured the Prussian government that "he had the honour of his House particularly in view, as he attached the greatest value to demonstrating to the Royal Government of Prussia that the consolidation of its public credit, and the fulfilment of the assurances which his House had given in this matter, were of more importance in his eyes than any considerations of private profit." This proved all too true, despite Nathan's decision to send Anselm to Berlin to secure modifications to the deal. In essence, the £3,809,400 of 5 per cent bonds still out-

standing from the 1818 loan were to be exchanged for 4 per cents issued to the same amount at 98 in the course of two and a half years from March 1830 until September 1832. As James realised even before the agreement was concluded, the issue price was certainly too high given the growing political uncertainty in France and the commission of 1.5 per cent too low. Interestingly, however, he seems to have regarded it as preferable that the Rothschilds undertake the risk, the extent of which he quite accurately gauged: "The worst, the very worst is that we stand to lose 15 per cent, God forbid, which amounts to £200,000 which is quite liable to ruin someone [else]."

107   RAL, XI/109/17/3/5, Anselm, Berlin, to his uncles, Dec. 11, 1830; RAL, XI/109/17/3/10, same to same, Dec. 16; RAL, XI/109/17/3/13, Dec. 20; RAL, XI/109/17/3/18, Anselm to James and Lionel, Paris, Dec. 25; RAL, XI/109J/J/31A, James to Amschel and Salomon, Jan. 2, 1831; RAL, XI/109/18/1/47, Anselm to James and Lionel, Jan. 27; RAL, XI/109J/J/31, James to Nathan, Feb. 5; RAL, XI/109/18/1/39, Anselm to Carl, Feb. 22; RAL, XI/109/20/1/25, MAR to deRF, Feb. 28; RAL, XI/109/18/1/41, Anselm to his uncles, Feb. 28; RAL, XI/109/0/2/2, same to same, March 1; RAL, XI/109/20/2/8, Anselm to Amschel, Frankfurt, March 7; RAL, XI/109/18/1/46, same to same, March 27; RAL, XI/109/20/2/14, April 7; RAL, XI/109/20/2/17, April 9; RAL, XI/109/21/2/11, undated, Anselm to his uncles; RAL, XI/109/22/2/19, SMR, CMR and NMR [to deRF?], April 13; RAL, XI/109/22/2/1, Anselm to Amschel, July 1; RAL, XI/109/22/2/2, same to same, July 5; RAL, XI/109/22/2/4, July 7; RAL, XI/109/22/2/3c, July 8; RAL, XI/109/22/2/15, Aug. 6; RAL, XI/109J/J/31A, James to Nathan, Nov. 24. Cf. Corti, *Rise*, pp. 428ff.; *idem, Reign*, pp. 1–9, 39, 76; Gille, *Maison Rothschild*, vol. I, pp. 218–21.

108   Corti, *Reign*, pp. 34f.

109   The outstanding £850,000 of 5 per cents were finally redeemed in 1834: RAL, XI/109J/J/32, James to Nathan, April 14, 1832; RAL, XI/109/26/1/8, Lionel, Paris, to his parents, London, April 30; RAL, XI/109/26/2/8, Anselm, Frankfurt, to NMR, May 21; RAL, XI/109/30/2/5, MAR to NMR, Jan. 2, 1833; RAL, XI/109/31a/1/56, Anselm, Frankfurt, to James, Paris, March 24, 1834; RAL, XI/109J/J/34, James to Nathan, March 26; RAL, XI/109J/J/34A, James to Nathan and Anthony, March 29; RAL, XI/109/32/3/6, Anselm, Frankfurt, to [James?], April 21; RAL, XI/109/31a/1/58, same to same, April 26; RAL, XI/109/31a/1/60, April 28; RAL, XI/109J/J/34A, James to Nathan and Anthony, April 28.

110   See Corti, *Reign*, p. 76.

111   RAL, XI/109J/J/31, James, Paris, to Nathan, London, Jan. 29, 1831; RAL, XI/109J/J/31B, James to Gasser, St Petersburg, Feb. 9; RAL, XI/109J/J/31, James to Nathan, Feb. 10.

112   RAL, XI/109/20/2/4, Anselm, Berlin, to his uncles, March 3, 1831; RAL, XI/109/20/2/20, Anselm to James, April 11.

113   RAL, XI/109J/J/31, James, Paris, to Nathan, London, April 28, 1831; same to same, May 7; James and Anselm to Nathan, May 12.

114   RAL, XI/109J/J/31, James, Paris, to Nathan, London, May 30, 1831.

115   RAL, XI/109J/J/32, James, Paris, to Nathan, London, Dec. 19, 1832; same to same, Dec. 20; RAL, XI/109/27/1/52&53, Lionel, Paris, to his parents, Dec. 19.

116   RAL, RFamC/1/143, Hannah, Brighton, to Nathan, London, Jan. 8, 1833.

117   Corti, *Reign*, pp. 73–5.

118   RAL, XI/109J/J/34, James, Paris, to Nathan, London, Jan. 10, 1834; same to same, May 27.

119   RAL, XI/109J/J/36, James, Paris, to Nathan and his nephews, Feb. 2, 1836.

120   Wasson, *Whig renaissance*, pp. 193f. Cf. Kynaston, *City*, vol. I, p. 92.

121   RAL, XI/109J/J/34, James, Paris, to Nathan, London, July 11, 1834.

122   Buxton, *Finance*, vol. I, pp. 28–37.

123   RAL, XI/109/16/1/24, Lionel, Paris, to his parents, London, Nov. 16, 1830.

124   RAL, XI/109J/J/30A, James, Paris, to Nathan, London, Dec. 21, 1830; RAL, XI/109J/J/31, same to same, Feb. 3, 1831.

125   RAL, XI/109/20/1/5, Lionel, Paris, to his parents, London, March 7, 1831; RAL, XI/109J/J/31, James to Nathan, March 7. The first loan proposal was for a 200 million franc bond issue secured on state-owned timber.

126   RAL, XI/109J/J/31, James, Paris, to Nathan, London, March 8, 1831; Corti, *Reign*, pp. 15f. Cf. RAL, XI/109/20/1/6, Lionel, Paris, to his parents, London, March 9, 1831.

127   RAL, XI/109J/J/31A, James, Paris, to Amschel, Frankfurt, and Salomon, Vienna, Jan. 2, 1831; RAL, XI/109J/J/31B, James, Paris, to Nathan, London, Jan. 2.

128   RAL, XI/109J/J/31, James, Paris, to Nathan, London, Jan. 26, 1831; same to same, Jan. 29; RAL,

XI/109/18/1/10, Lionel to his parents, Jan. 29; RAL, XI/109/18/1/14, same to same, Feb. 3; RAL, XI/109J/J/31, James to Nathan, Feb. 7; same to same, March 12; RAL, T22/16, XI/109/22/3/37, R. M. Marshall for the Secretary, Ordnance Office, to Nathan, July 25.

129 RAL, XI/109J/J/31A, James, Paris, to Nathan, London, Jan. 3, 1831.

130 RAL, XI/109/J/J/30, James, Paris, to Nathan, London, Nov. 23, 1830.

131 RAL, XI/109J/J/31, James, Paris, to Nathan, London, Feb. 19, 1831.

132 RAL, XI/109J/J/31, James, Paris, to Nathan, London, March 10, 1831.

133 RAL, XI/109J/J/31, James, Paris, to Nathan, London, March 12, 1831; same to same, March 13.

134 RAL, XI/109/20/1/12, Lionel, Paris, to his parents, London, March 17, 1831; RAL, XI/109J/J/31, James, Paris, to Nathan, London, March 17; March 19; March 22; April 7.

135 RAL, XI/109J/J/31, James, Paris, to Nathan, London, March 27, 1831.

136 RAL, XI/109/20/1/22, Lionel, Paris, to his parents, London, April 12, 1831; RAL, XI/109J/J/31, James, Paris, to Nathan, London, April 13; RAL, XI/109/20/1/23, Lionel to his parents, April 14; RAL, XI/109J/J/31, James to Nathan, April 14, 1831; RAL, XI/109/20/1/24, Lionel to his parents, April 15; RAL, XI/109J/J/31, James to Nathan, April 16.

137 RAL, XI/109/20/1/27, Lionel, Paris, to his parents, London, April 19, 1831; RAL, XI/109/18/1/28, same to same, April 19; RAL, XI/109J/J/31A, James to Nathan, April 19; RAL, XI/109/20/1/28, Lionel to his parents, April 20; RAL, XI/109J/J/31, James to Nathan, April 20; RAL, XI/109/20/1/36, Lionel to his parents, April 21; RAL, XI/109J/J/31, James to Nathan, April 21; same to same, April 23. All told, 120 (or 140) million francs (nominal) of 5 per cent rentes were taken at a price of 84 (81.5 to the public) by a consortium of around ten banks, with the Rothschilds taking around a fifth of the total. Lionel opposed taking the loan, but was overruled by James, who thought there was "a lot of money to be made." Cf. Corti, *Reign*, pp. 28f.; Gille, *Maison Rothschild*, vol. I, pp. 214–16; *idem*, *Banque et crédit*, pp. 174–9.

138 "Our friend Pozzo takes 50,000 in the new loan and gives the money for it. Werther also takes 15,000, if Politics were not good they would not do it": RAL, XI/109/20/1/25, Lionel, Paris, to his parents, London, April 16, 1831. However, both were quick to take their profits, which dampened Lionel's optimism: RAL, XI/109/21/1/5, same to same, May 9.

139 RAL, XI/109J/J/31, James, Paris, to Nathan, London, April 18, 1831. Cf. RAL, XI/109J/J/31B, same to same, April 19.

140 RAL, XI/109J/J/31, James, Paris, to Nathan, London, May 8, 1831.

141 RAL, XI/109/21/2/7, Anselm, Berlin, to Amschel, Frankfurt, May 23, 1831; RAL, XI/109/21/1/18, Lionel, Paris, to his parents, London, June 8, 1831; RAL, XI/109J/J/31, James, Paris, to Nathan, London, June 8.

142 RAL, XI/109J/J/31, James to Nathan, Aug. 13, 1831; RAL, XI/109/30/1/28, Lionel, Paris, to his brothers, London, Aug. 25. See also RAL, XI/109J/J/31, James to Nathan, Oct. 18; same to same, Nov. 16.

143 RAL, XI/109/1/18/33, Lionel, Paris, to his parents, London, Nov. 3, 1831.

144 RAL, XI/109J/J/32, James, Paris, to Nathan, London, Jan. 25, 1832; RAL, XI/109J/J/32, James and Salomon to Nathan and Nat, Jan. 26; RAL, XI/109/25/1/15, Lionel, Paris, to his parents, London, Jan. 26.

145 RAL, XI/109/26/1/15, Lionel, Paris, to his parents, London, May 23, 1832; RAL, XI/109J/J/32, James, Paris, to Nathan, London, May 26; RAL, XI/109/206/1/18, Lionel to his parents, May 28; RAL, XI/109J/J/32, James to Nathan, May 29; RAL, XI/109/26/1/19, Lionel to his parents, May 29.

146 RAL, XI/109J/J/32B, James, Paris, to Nathan, London, Jan. 18, 1832; RAL, XI/109J/J/32, same to same, Jan. 28; RAL, T22/258, XI/109/28/1/4, Lionel, Paris, to his parents, London, June 15; RAL, XI/109/28/1/5, same to same, June 16; RAL, XI/109J/J/32, James and Salomon to Nathan and their nephews, June 16; RAL, XI/109/26/1/29, Lionel to his parents, June 18; RAL, XI/109J/J/32, James, Boulogne, to Nathan and his nephews, London, June 19; same to same, June 23; June 24; RAL, XI/109/26/1/32, Lionel to his parents, June 25; RAL, XI/109/28/1/11, same to same, July 4; RAL, XI/109/28/1/12, July 5; RAL, XI/109J/J/32, James to Nathan and his nephews, July 23; same to same, July 29; RAL, XI/109/28/1/17, Lionel to his parents, Aug. 4; RAL, XI/109J/J/32, James to Nathan, Aug. 4; same to same, Aug. 8; RAL, XI/109/28/1/18, Lionel to his parents, Aug. 8. The other partners included Odier, Hagerman, Blanc, Fould and Cottier. Hottinguer seems to have sought a share late in the day. The 5 per cent rentes were issued at 98.5.

147 RAL, XI/109/18/1/31, Lionel, Paris, to his parents, London, Sept. 17, 1832.

148 RAL, XI/109J/J/33, James, Paris, to Nathan, London, Jan. 6, 1833; same to same, Feb. 6.
149 RAL, XI/109J/J/33, James, Paris, to Nathan and his nephews, London, Feb. 13, 1833; same to same, Feb. 20; Feb. 27; March 15. See also RAL, XI/109/29/1/7, Lionel, Paris, to his parents, London, April 27; RAL, XI/109J/J/33, James to Nathan and his nephews, July 3, for James's opposition to plans to tamper with the sinking fund; and RAL, XI/109J/J/34, James to Nathan, Jan. 30, 1834; same to same, March 2, 1834 for James's opposition to an issue of 4 per cent rentes proposed in 1834.
150 RAL, XI/101/1/14/3, Anthony, Paris, to his brothers, London, Jan. 1, 1838; RAL, XI/101/1/21/6, Anselm, Paris, to his cousins, London, Feb. 6; RAL, XI/101/1/1/7, same to same, Feb. 7; RAL, XI/101/1/15/1a, Anthony, Paris, to his brothers, London, March 2; RAL, XI/101/1/15/16, same to same, March 24; RAL, XI/101/1/15/21, April 3; RAL, XI/101/1/22/4, Anselm to his cousins, April 20; RAL, XI/101/22/4, same to same, April 24; RAL, XI/101/1/20/5, Anthony to his brothers, Nov. 1; RAL, XI/101/1/20/9, same to same, Nov. 10; RAL, XI/101/1/24/02, Anselm to his cousins, Nov. 14; RAL, XI/101/1/20/15, Anthony and Anselm to NMR, Nov. 21. Generally speaking, the Rothschilds were wary of French conversions: the memory of the Villèle fiasco and the Prussian crisis of 1830 still lingered.
151 Dupeux, *Society*, pp. 121f. Cf. Deschamps, *Belgique*, p. 544.
152 Gille, *Maison Rothschild*, vol. I, pp. 214ff., 235–8; *idem, Banque et crédit*, pp. 162–71, 180–82.
153 RAL, XI/109J/J/32, James and Salomon, Paris, to Nathan, London, Jan. 29, 1832.
154 Gentz, *Briefe and Pilat*, vol. II, p. 334.
155 RAL, XI/109/20/1/28, James, Paris, to Salomon, Vienna, undated, March 1831.
156 Corti, *Rise*, pp. 414–20.
157 Kübeck, *Tagebücher*, vol. II/2, pp. 412ff.; Corti, *Reign*, p. 17; Born, *International banking*, p. 41; Gille, *Maison Rothschild*, vol. I, pp. 216ff. The loan was for 57.1 million gulden (nominal) and was issued at 84. Cf. RAL, XI/109J/J/30, James, Paris, to Salomon and Amschel, May 6, 1831 [wrongly dated as 1830]; James to Nathan, May 28.
158 Corti, *Reign*, pp. 39f. The money was earmarked for the construction of fortresses on the Franco-German border; that was evidently not Metternich's purpose in borrowing it.
159 *Ibid.*, pp. 56f.
160 RAL, XI/109/5/2/4, Salomon, Vienna, to his brothers, Jan. 7, 1832.
161 Corti, *Reign*, pp. 66ff.
162 RAL, XI/109/29/1/34, Anselm, Frankfurt, to James and Lionel, Paris, Jan. 29, 1833; RAL, XI/109/29/2/43, submission by MAR, Eskeles, Geymüller and Sina, Feb. 7; RAL, XI/109/31a/1/72, Nat, Vienna, to his parents, London, April 22, 1834; RAL, XI/109/31a/2/62, submission for loan, April 26; RAL, XI/109J/J/34, James, Paris, to Nathan and Anthony, April 26. Cf. Gille, *Maison Rothschild*, vol. I, pp. 239f.
163 Cameron, *France and Europe*, pp. 119–24.
164 RAL, XI/109J/J/30, James, Paris, to Nathan, London, Sept. 4, 1830; same to same, Sept. 19.
165 RAL, XI/109J/J/30B, Salomon and James, Paris, to Nathan, London, Sept. 25, 1830; RAL, XI/109/17/1/1, Lionel, Paris, to his parents, London, Oct. 4; RAL, XI/109J/J/30, Salomon, Paris, to Nathan, London, Oct. 10.
166 RAL, T22/345, XI/109/28/2/2, Chr. de Stockmar, Brussels, to NMR, London, Aug. 5, 1831.
167 RAL, XI/109/23/1/15, Lionel to his parents, Nov. 12, 1831; RAL, XI/109J/J/31, James to Nathan, Nov. 14; same to same, Nov. 22.
168 For early discussions, see RAL, XI/109/16/1/31, Anselm, Berlin, to his uncle, Dec. 28, 1830; RAL, XI/109J/J/31B, James, Paris, to Nathan, London, Jan. 1, 1831. For the 1831 loan, RAL, XI/109J/J/31, James to Nathan, Nov. 14, 1831; same to same, Nov. 24; Dec. 3; Dec. 4; Dec. 6; Dec. 7; Dec. 11; Dec. 13; Dec. 14; Dec. 18; RAL, XI/109/24/1/1, Lionel to his parents, Dec. 11; RAL, XI/109/24/2/9, Anselm, Frankfurt, to his uncle, Paris, Dec. 13; RAL, XI/109/24/1/29, Nat, Paris, to his parents, London, Dec. 13; RAL, XI/109/24/1/4, Lionel to his parents, Dec. 13; RAL, XI/109/24/1/5, same to same, Dec. 14.
169 RAL, XI/109/24/1/26, Anselm, Frankfurt, to Lionel, Paris, Dec. 21, 1831; RAL, XI/109/24/1/11, Lionel, Paris, to his parents, London, Dec. 21.
170 RAL, XI/109J/J/32, James, Paris, to Nathan, March 25, 1832; same to same, April 4; April 9; April 14. This clause subsequently gave rise to unexpected, though obscure, difficulties.
171 RAL, XI/109J/J/31, James, Paris, to Nathan, Dec. 12; same to same, Dec. 24; Dec. 26; Dec. 27; Dec. 28; Dec. 31; RAL, XI/109/24/1/13, Lionel, Paris, to his parents, London, Dec. 26; RAL,

XI/109/24/1/24, same to same, Dec. 26; RAL, XI/109/24/1/33, Nat, Paris, to his parents, Dec. 27; RAL, XI/109/24/1/34, same to same, Dec. 28; RAL, XI/109J/J/32, James to Nathan, Jan. 2; same to same, Jan. 3; RAL, XI/109/26/1/26, Lionel to his parents, Jan. 4. The 5 per cent bonds were issued at 75 in London and 77 in Paris. Cf. Ayer, *Century of finance*, pp. 36f.; Gille, *Maison Rothschild*, vol. I, pp. 221–6; Cameron, *France and Europe*, pp. 119–24, 336–8.

172 RAL, XI/109J/J/32, James and Lionel to Nathan, London, March 11, 1832. Cf. James to Nathan, March 13; same to same, March 25; April 14; June 11; July 5; July 14; July 23.

173 RAL, XI/109J/J/32, James, Paris, to Nathan, London, Aug. 11, 1832; RAL, XI/109/27/1/7, Lionel, Paris, to his parents, London, Aug. 30; RAL, XI/109/28/1/23, same to same, Sept. 3; RAL, XI/109/27/1/13, Sept. 8; RAL, XI/109/27/1/14, Sept. 10. Cf. RAL, T17/222, King Leopold to NMR, deRF and Societé Générale, Sept. 22.

174 Raikes, *Journal*, vol. I, pp. 83f.

175 RAL, XI/109J/J/32, James, Paris, to Nathan and Nat, London, Nov. 19, 1832; same to same, Nov. 20; Nov. 27; Dec. 1; Dec. 27; RAL, XI/109/27/1/59, Lionel to his parents, Dec. 27.

176 RAL, XI/109J/J/33, James, Paris, to Nathan, London, Jan. 12, 1833; same to same, Jan. 15; Jan. 23; Feb 2; Feb. 4; Feb. 5; Feb. 6; Feb. 7; RAL, XI/109/29/1/67, Salomon, Vienna, to his brothers, Jan. 23; RAL, XI/109J/J/33B, James to Nathan, Feb. 9; RAL, XI/109J/J/33C, James to Lionel, Feb. 9; RAL, XI/109J/J/33, James to Nathan and his nephews, Feb. 12; same to same, Feb. 19; Feb. 23; Feb. 24; March 25; March 26; April 1; RAL, XI/109/29/1/77, Salomon to his brothers, April 28; RAL, XI/109J/J/33, James to Nathan and Anthony, April 30; James to Nathan, May 7; RAL, XI/109J/J/33A, same to same, May 21; RAL, XI/109/30/1/16, Lionel, London, to his parents, London, July 24; RAL, XI/109J/J/34, James to Nathan and Anthony, July 31.

177 Ayer, *Century of finance*, pp. 36f.; Cameron, *France and Europe*, pp. 119–24, 336–8. Cf. RAL, XI/109/30/1/24, Lionel, Paris, to his parents, London, Aug. 14, 1833; RAL, XI/109J/J/33, James, Paris, to Nathan, London, Sept. 7; James to Nathan and Anthony, Sept. 18; James to Nathan, Nov. 5.

178 RAL, T17/185, Anselm, Berlin, to James and Lionel, Paris, Dec. 13, 1830; RAL, XI/109/22/2/8&9, Anselm, Berlin, to deRF, July 19, 1831. A Polish bank had been a major partner in the abortive Prussian conversion of 1830.

179 RAL, T22/6, XI/109/22/1/46, Charlotte, Frankfurt, to her mother, London, July 17, 1831.

180 Börne, *Mittheilungen*, 2. Theil, pp. 136–55; Kübeck, *Tagebücher*, vol. I/2, p. 544.

181 Heine, *Sämtliche Schriften*, vol. III, pp. 542, 583f. Cf. Prawer, *Heine*, pp. 253f.; Sammons, *Heine*, p. 248.

182 Muhlstein, *Baron James*, p. 105.

183 RAL, XI/109J/J/31, James, Paris, to Nathan, London, Nov. 11, 1831.

184 RAL, XI/109/22/1/24, Lionel, Paris, to his parents, London, July 5, 1831.

185 RAL, XI/109J/J/31, James, Paris, to Nathan, London, Oct. 23, 1831; same to same, Oct. 31; Nov. 5; Nov. 6; Nov. 11; Nov. 15; Nov. 21; Nov. 22; RAL, XI/109/1/18/33, Lionel, Paris, to his parents, London, Nov. 3; RAL, XI/109/23/1/13, same to same, Nov. 6; RAL, XI/109/23/1/24&26, James to Nathan, Nov. 7; RAL, XI/109/24/2/1, Anselm, Berlin, to James, Nov. 9; RAL, XI/109/23/1/25, James, Paris, to Nathan and Lionel, London, Nov. 23; RAL, XI/109/23/2/19, Salomon, Munich, to his brothers, Nov. 26; RAL, XI/109J/J/31, same to same, Nov. 23; Dec. 3; Dec. 4; Dec. 6; Dec. 7; Dec. 9; Dec. 10; Dec. 11. Cf. Corti, *Reign*, pp. 132–7; Cameron, "Papal Finance," pp. 132–5; Reinerman, *Austria and the Papacy*, p. 179; Cameron, *France and Europe*, pp. 432f.; Felisini, *Finanze pontificie*.

186 RAL, XI/109/24/1/3, Lionel, Paris, to his mother, London, Dec. 12, 1831.

187 Felisini, *Finanze pontificie*, pp. 57, 78. There was a further issue of £250,000 in August 1832: RAL, T22/351, XI/109/28/1/39, Lionel, Paris, to his parents, London, Aug. 25, 1832.

188 RAL, XI/109J/J/30, James, Paris, to Nathan, Feb. 20, 1830; same to same, March 30.

189 RAL, XI/109/25/1/10, Lionel, Paris, to his parents, London, Jan. 12, 1832; RAL, XI/109/27/3/24, Anselm, Frankfurt, to James, Paris, Oct. 25; RAL, XI/109J/J/32, James, Paris, to Nathan, London, Sept. 11; same to same, Dec. 20; RAL, XI/109/27/1/54, Lionel to his parents, Dec. 22; RAL, XI/109/27/1/60, same to same, Dec. 29; RAL, XI/109/27/1/62, Dec. 31; RAL, XI/109J/J/32B&C, James to Nathan, Dec. 22; same to same, Dec. 25; Dec. 27; Dec. 29; RAL, XI/109/29/2/38, Greek loan contract, Jan. 2, 1833; RAL, XI/109J/J/33, James to Nathan, Jan. 12; same to same, Jan. 14; RAL, XI/109/30/2/3, Anselm, Paris, to Anthony, 19 Feb. The 5 per cent loan was initially issued at 94. Altogether 11 million francs were earmarked for the payment of compensation to Turkey; the parallel with the Belgian–Dutch separation is striking.

TEN *The World's Bankers*

1 Quoted in Glanz, "Rothschild legend," p. 20; Muhlstein, *Baron James*, p. 105.
2 Raikes, *Journal*, vol. II, pp. 221ff. Cf. Kynaston, *City*, vol. I, pp. 90f.
3 Pückler, *Briefe*, p. 819.
4 List, *Grundlinien*, p. 243.
5 The cartoon is usually dated 1848 or 1849 (Rubens's suggestion of 1869 is clearly wrong), but the political allusions are to the political events of 1840: cf. Fuchs, *Juden in der Karikatur*, p. 228; Rubens, "Rothschilds in caricature," pp. 84f.; Herding, "Rothschilds in der Karikatur," pp. 19ff.
6 The Royal Exchange (not to be confused with the Stock Exchange at Capel Court) was essentially a market for commercial bills and foreign exchange, though in Nathan's time bonds began to be traded there too. On the ground floor, the south-east corner was formally allocated to Jewish traders, behind the Spanish and Portuguese: Kynaston, "City of London in Nathan Rothschild's time," pp. 43–9.
7 Rumney, "Anglo-Jewry," p. 339; Cowles, *Rothschilds*, p. 84.
8 Rubens, "Rothschilds in caricature," plates II and V.
9 Rubens, *Anglo-Jewish portraits*, p. 94.
10 Herding, "Rothschilds in der Karikatur," p. 42. See also Rubens, "Rothschilds in caricature," plate XVII, no. 19.
11 Prawer, *Israel at Vanity Fair*, pp. 17ff.
12 For an exhaustive list, Rubens, *Anglo-Jewish portraits*, pp. 101–4. See for examples Herding, "Rothschilds in der Karikatur," p. 40; Rothschild, *Dear Lord Rothschild*, plate 72.
13 For a similar comment by a German visitor see Pückler, *Briefe*, p. 47: looking at a portrait of a handsome "Oriental" Jew, Prince Pückler observed: "When one of the Rothschilds looked like that, he would certainly become King of Jerusalem and Solomon's throne would no longer stand empty." Pückler was also one of the earliest writers to refer to Nathan as *Rex Judaeorum*: *ibid.*, p. 656.
14 Cowles, *Rothschilds*, p. 84.
15 Rumney, "Anglo-Jewry," p. 339.
16 Bertaut, *Bourse*, p. 41.
17 Reeves, *Rothschilds*, pp. 281f.
18 Pückler-Muskau, *Pückler's Progress*, pp. 28f.
19 Disraeli, *Tancred*, pp. 118–24.
20 Corti, *Rise*, pp. 402f.
21 Reeves, *Rothschilds*, pp. 115–22.
22 *The Times*, Aug. 4, 1836.
23 Reeves, *Rothschilds*, pp. 194ff.; Ehrenberg, *Große Vermögen*, pp. 158f.
24 Reeves, *Rothschilds*, pp. 186–93.
25 *The Times*, Jan. 15, 1821.
26 *Observer*, Dec. 1, 1822.
27 Kynaston, *City*, vol. I, pp. 105f.
28 Reeves, *Rothschilds*, pp. 194ff. Though not always: GStA, I. HA Rep 92 Ca Nr 20 (24), Carl, Berlin, to Rother, March 30, 1818, apologising for a rude letter from Nathan "because he writes as he speaks."
29 RAL, XI/109/11/3/54, Anselm, Frankfurt, to Anthony, London, Dec. 4, 1828.
30 RAL, XI/109/32/2/24, Nat, Frankfurt, to his parents, London, May 5, 1834.
31 RAL, XI/109J/J/32, James, Paris, to Nathan, London, Dec. 29, 1832.
32 RAL, XI/109J/J/35, James and Salomon, Paris, to Nathan, London, May 5, 1835.
33 RAL, T17/241, Lionel, Paris, to his parents, London, Nov. 5, 1831.
34 RAL, XI/109/30/1/8, Nat, Frankfurt, to his parents, London, undated, *c.* June 1833; RAL, XI/109/30/2/29, same to same, undated, *c.* June 1833.
35 RAL, XI/109J/J/33, James, Paris, to Nathan and Anthony, London, June 22, 1833.
36 CPHDCM, 637/1/6/5, Articles of partnership between Messrs Rothschild, March 21, 1815.
37 RAL, T64/211/3, XI/109/9, Carl, Frankfurt, to Salomon, April 20, 1818.
38 CPHDCM, 637/1/6/7/7–14, Articles of partnership, June 2, 1818. Emphasis added.
39 CPHDCM, 637/1/6/27–8, Indenture, Aug. 25, 1824.
40 AN, 132 AQ 3, Brüderliche Übereinkunft [signed by Amschel, Salomon, Carl and James], Aug. 12, 1820. Among other things, the brothers resolved to withdraw their deposits at New Court and to sell their holdings of the 1818 Prussian loan. They also agreed to ensure that they had between them sufficient liquid funds to make available the 9 million gulden of French reparations deposited with them by

the German Confederation, and to circulate monthly balance sheets for this purpose. It is not clear whether the agreement was acted upon or whether it was simply intended as a shot across Nathan's bows.

41 CPHDCM, 637/1/8/1–7; also RAL, RFamFD, B/1, Articles of agreement between Messrs de Rothschild [Amschel, Nathan, Salomon, Carl, Jacob and Anselm], Aug. 31, 1825. See also AN 132 AQ 1, unsigned, unheaded document, apparently the draft "Testament," Aug. 31, 1825.

42 CPHDCM, 637/1/7/38–42, Zusatzartikel zu dem . . . am 31 August 1825 in London unterzeichneten Societätsvertrag, Sept. 26, 1825. Anselm immediately became entitled to a fifteenth of the profits, though he did not formally acquire a share of the capital until 1828, when a million gulden was invested in his name in the Paris house. His grandmother Gutle's inheritance from Mayer Amschel was invested in the Frankfurt house, but she had no status as a partner and her share was not included in the total capital for accounting purposes.

43 RAL, RFamC/1/73, Hannah, Frankfurt, to Lionel, London, Aug. 18, 1828.

44 CPHDCM, 637/1/6/44,45, No. 4 General Capital, Sept. 26, 1828; CPHDCM, 637/1/6/17, General Inventarium, Sept. 26; CPHDCM, 637/1/6/31, [untitled deed signed by Anselm and the five brothers], Sept. 26; CPHDCM, 637/1/7/48–52, Abschrift [Partnership agreement], Sept. 26; AN, 132 AQ 3/2/No 5, General Inventarium, Sept. 26.

45 CPHDCM, 637/1/6/32, General Aufstellung, July 30, 1836; CPHDCM, 637/1/7/68, General Aufstellung, July 30; CPHDCM, 637/1/7/53–69, Vollständige Abschrift des Societäts-Vertrags . . . Übereinkunft, July 30. A clause was added, however, which stated that if the profits of the Paris, Frankfurt, Naples and Vienna houses exceeded those of the London house to the point that 22.5 per cent of their total profits exceeded 60 per cent of the London house's, then the division of the profits would revert to the old system of equal shares of the whole.

46 CPHDCM, 637/1/7/70–2, Übereinkunft, Anhang, July 30, 1836.

47 Ziegler, Sixth great power, p. 374; Gille, Maison Rothschild, vol. I, pp. 163–6, 450f.

48 AN, 132 AQ 13/Bilans, June 1821–June 1842.

49 Calculated from the fragmentary evidence (primarily half-yearly figures) in AN, 132 AQ 3/2; CPHDCM, 637/1/6/34–42.

50 Gille, Maison Rothschild, vol. I, p. 248. However, see CPHDCM, 637/1/6/20–1, Balance sheet of Naples house, Dec. 31, 1827.

51 CPHDCM, 637/1/6/34–42, Bilan de MM de Rothschild Frères, June 30, 1828.

52 Chapman, Merchant banking, p. 16. British foreign investments in 1855 totalled around £2,300 million: Kindleberger, Financial history, p. 225.

53 CPHDCM, 637/1/6/52–7, N. M. Rothschild, balance sheet, July 31, 1828.

54 CPHDCM, 637/1/6/34–42, Bilan de MM de Rothschild Frères, June 30, 1828.

55 CPHDCM, 637/1/6/22,25, Abschluss des Wiener-Filial-Etablissements, June 30, 1828; see also AN, 132 AQ 3/2 No. 5.

56 Sayers, Modern banking, p. 51. Cf. Gillett Brothers, Bill on London.

57 CPHDCM, 637/1/6/52–7, N. M. Rothschild, balance sheet, July 31, 1828.

58 Feaveryear, Pound sterling, p. 315.

59 Bright (ed.), Speeches by Richard Cobden, p. 44. Cf. Gille, Maison Rothschild, vol. I, pp. 440–45.

60 Chapman, Foundation, p. 22.

61 RAL, XI/109J/J/32, James and Anselm, Paris, to Nathan and Nat, London, Nov. 5, 1832. Countless similar examples could be cited, e.g. RAL, XI/109J/J/33, James to Nathan, April 21, 1833; RAL, XI/109J/J/33, James to Nathan, May 5; RAL, XI/109J/J/36A, James to Nathan and his nephews, April 26, 1836.

62 Bagehot, Lombard Street, p. 213.

63 Ziegler, Sixth great power, pp. 127ff.

64 Chapman, Merchant banking, p. 17; Kynaston, City, vol. I, pp. 308f.

65 New York, Leo Baeck Institute, Nathan to Behrend Brothers, March 14, 1817.

66 RAL, XI/109J/J/33, James, Paris, to Nathan, London, March 10, 1833.

67 Gille, Maison Rothschild, vol. I, pp. 401ff., 415–18, 420; vol. II, pp. 546–55; Landes, Bankers and pashas, p. 14.

68 Corti, Reign, pp. 75f.

69 Forrest, Ceylon tea, p. 52.

70 Schooling, Alliance Assurance, pp. 1f.; Morgan and Thomas, Stock Exchange, p. 129; Cottrell, "Business man and financier," pp. 29ff.; Kynaston, City, vol. I, p. 62.

71 RAL, T62/4/1, XI/109/7, James, Paris, to Nathan, London, May 6, 1817; RAL, T27/159, XI/109/7, James to Salomon and Nathan, May 16.

72 RAL, XI/4/1, Privy Councillor Lindemann to Nathan, June 23, 1823. A similar policy was apparently arranged through the Alliance for the King of Holland in 1842: see esp. RAL, XI/109/42a/3/16, Anselm, the Hague, to his cousins, May 6, 1842; RAL, XI/109/42a/3/19, same to same, May 13; RAL, XI/109/42a/3/20, May 16.

73 Rothschild, *Shadow*, pp. 39ff.

74 Ayer, *Century of finance*, p. 21. The company was not a limited-liability company, but was given a statutory existence (allowing it to be sued in its own name) by an act of Parliament passed the following year.

75 Cowles, *Rothschilds*, p. 61.

76 Schooling, *Alliance Assurance*, p. 85.

77 Stürmer *et al.*, *Striking the balance*, pp. 85ff.; Heuberger, *Rothschilds*, pp. 138ff.; Tilly, *Financial institutions*, pp. 104–5, 108, 173n.

78 RAL, XI/109/13/1/54, Rother, Berlin, to Anselm, Jan. 28, 1830; RAL, XI/109/14/1/40, Salomon, Vienna, to Anselm, Berlin, Feb. 11.

79 RAL, XI/10919/1/40, Anselm, Berlin, to his father, Feb. 25, 1831; RAL, XI/109J/J/31, James and Lionel, Paris, to Nathan, London, Aug. 13.

80 RAL, XI/109J/J/28, James and Anselm, Paris, to Lionel, London, July 28, 1828; James to Lionel, Aug. 2; same to same, Aug. 5; Aug. 8.

81 RAL, XI/109J/J/31, James, Paris, to Nathan, London, Oct. 17, 1831.

82 RAL, XI/109J/J/32, James, Paris, to Nathan, London, Dec. 9, 1832.

83 RAL, XI/109/30/2/12, Hannah Mayer, Paris, to her father, London, Sept. 29, 1833.

84 See his characteristic request for more accurate accounts from Paris and London: RAL XI/109/33/1/15, Lionel, Madrid, to Anthony, April 1, 1835.

85 RAL, XI/109J/J/29, James, Paris, to Nathan, London, Dec. 15, 1829; RAL, T22/255, XI/109/27/2/23, Anthony, Frankfurt, to Lionel, Paris, Oct. 18, 1832; RAL, T22/258, XI/109/27/2/6, Anthony to his parents, Oct. 26; RAL, T22/259, XI/109/27/2/7, Anthony to Lionel, Oct. 28; RAL, T22/260, XI/109/27/2/8, Anthony to his parents, Oct. 28; RAL, T22/263, XI/109/27/2/11, Anthony to his mother, Oct. 31; RAL, T22/262, XI/109/27/2/10, Anthony to Nat, Oct. 31; RAL, XI/109/33/1/47, Anthony, Frankfurt, to Nat, Oct. 24, 1835; RAL, T26, XI/101/1/16/16/36, Anthony to his brothers, undated, early 1838.

86 RAL, T25/104/1/4/77, Anselm, Frankfurt, to Nat, Paris, July 9, 1841; RAL, T23/243, XI/109/42/3/22, same to same, undated, 1842; RAL, T18/338, XI/109/47/1/70, Hannah, Frankfurt, to Lionel, London, undated, 1844.

87 RAL, XI/109J/J/31A, James, Paris, to Nathan, London, Feb. 9, 1831.

88 RAL, XI/109J/J/31, James, Paris, to Nathan, London, July 31, 1831; RAL, XI/109J/J/32B, same to same, Jan. 9, 1832; RAL, XI/109J/J/35, Salomon and James, Paris, to Nathan, May 9, 1835.

89 RAL, T25/104/0/59, Nat, Paris, to Lionel, London, June 13, 1840.

90 RAL, XI/109/21/1/39, Nat to Charlotte, undated, *c.* 1831.

91 RAL, XI/109/21/1/34, Nat, Naples, to Lionel, Paris, April 11, 1831.

92 RAL, XI/109J/J/31, James, Paris, to Nathan, London, July 4, 1831.

93 RAL, XI/109J/J/32, James, Paris, to Nathan, March 4, 1832.

94 RAL, XI/109J/J/33, James, Paris, to Nathan, London, May 18, 1833; same to same, June 18.

95 RAL, T18/43, XI/109/45/6/100, Nat, Paris, to his brothers, London, Jan. 14, 1843.

96 RAL, T29/122, XI/109/0/4/43, letter to Carl, Frankfurt, Aug. 1814.

97 RAL, T64/212/3, Carl, Frankfurt, to Salomon, April 1818; RAL, T61/46/1, XI/109/6, Carl, Hamburg, to Amschel, Frankfurt, Feb. 15, 1817.

98 RAL, T61/65/2, XI/109/6, James, Paris, to Nathan and Salomon, London, March 1, 1817.

99 RAL, T6/216, NMR to James Campbell Esq., Secretary of the General Post Office, March 3, 1847.

100 RAL, RFamC/4/108, Lionel, Frankfurt, to Nat, London, June 9, 1836. In the same spirit, Lionel was also chairman of the Provident Clerks' Mutual Benefit Association & Benevolent Fund: RAL, XI/109/44, Secretary to Lionel, Feb. 3, 1843.

101 RAL, XI/109J/J/36, James, Frankfurt, to Anthony, Paris, July 26, 1836; RAL, RFamC/4/149, Lionel, Frankfurt, to Nat, July 26; RAL, T23/75, RFamC/24/10, Anselm, Frankfurt, to Nat, July 26.

102 RAL, T6/233, Benjamin Davidson, Paris, to Mayer, London, Feb. 16, 1847.

103 RAL, XI/109/J/J/29, James, Paris, to Nathan and his nephews, London, June 24, 1829.

104 RAL, XI/109J/J/38, James, Paris, to his nephews, London, Feb. 10, 1838.

105 RAL, XI/109J/J/39, James, Paris, to his brothers and nephews, March 16, 1839.

106 RAL, XI/109J/J/40, James, Paris, to Amschel, Frankfurt, April 3, 1840; RAL, XI/109J/J/42A, James to his nephews, London, March 9, 1842. Cf. Gille, *Maison Rothschild*, vol. II, pp. 575–80.

107 RAL, XI/109J/J/34, James, Paris, to Nathan, London, May 25, 1834.

108 RAL, XI/101/1–20/8, Anthony, Paris, to his brothers, London, Nov. 12, 1838.

109 RAL, XI/109/45b/5/42, Anselm, Frankfurt, to Nat, Paris, Aug. 26, 1843.

110 RAL, T18/90, XI/109/45/6/122, Nat, Paris, to his brothers, London, undated, 1843; RAL, XI/109/45b/6/25, same to same, March 25.

111 RAL, T18/114, XI/109/45/6/38, Anthony, Frankfurt, to his brothers, London, May 14, 1843.

112 AN, 132 AQ 5404/1M6, NMR to deRF, March 17, 1843; AN, 13 AQ 5403/1M5, Letters to Hanau and Belmont, April 24.

113 Gille, *Maison Rothschild*, vol. I, pp.182–7.

114 See e.g. Stern, *Gold and iron*, p. 6; Born, *International banking*, pp. 53–5.

115 See e.g. RAL, XI/109J/J/36B, James, Paris, to Nathan and Nat, London, April 26, 1836. There was a threat to give Warburgs priority in 1848, but this seems not to have been carried out. See Rosenbaum and Sherman, *M. M. Warburg & Co.*, p. 27; Chernow, *Warburgs*, p. 10.

116 See e.g. RAL, XI/109J/J/36A, James, Frankfurt, to Anthony, Paris, July 8, 1836; RAL, T42/18, Moses Montefiore, Berlin, to the Barons de Rothschild, London, March 9, 1846. Cf. Stern, *Gold and iron*, p. 8. On the Mendelssohns, see Gilbert, *Bankiers*, p. xxix.

117 Stern, *Gold and iron*, p. 255n.

118 Stürmer *et al.*, *Striking the balance*, pp. 37, 64f.; Roberts, *Schroders*, pp. 31–5; Gille, *Maison Rothschild*, vol. I, pp. 424f., 435–7.

119 RAL, XI/101/1–20/32, Anthony, Paris, to his brothers, London, Dec. 4, 1838; RAL, XI/101/1–20/34, same to same, Dec. 5; RAL, XI/101/1–24/5, Anselm, Paris, to his cousins, London, Dec. 29; RAL, XI/101/2–8/4, Anthony to his brothers, Jan. 2, 1839.

120 RAL, XI/109/40/2/9, Salomon, Vienna, to his brothers, June 10, 1841; RAL, XI/109/40/2/8, Salomon to his brothers, son and nephews, July 7; RAL, XI/109/40/2/10, same to same, July 8. Cf. RAL, XI/109/41/4/12a, SMR to MAR, Oct. 28.

121 RAL, T7/5, XI/06/0, Lionel, London, to deRF, Feb. 16, 1839. Cf. Corti, *Reign*, pp. 226, 229.

122 Kynaston, *City*, vol. I, pp. 85, 90f.

123 Rudolph, "Austria," p. 34.

124 RAL, XI/109J/J/36, James, Paris, to his nephews, London, Nov. 15, 1836.

125 Kynaston, *Cazenove*, pp. 22f., 25, 29; *idem*, *City*, vol. I, p. 59.

126 Kynaston, *City*, vol. I, p. 316.

127 Reeves, *Rothschilds*, pp. 186–93; Kynaston, *City*, vol. I, p. 53. Another apocryphal anecdote has the roles reversed, with a wily stockbroker bursting into Nathan's house, feigning drunkenness, overhearing sensitive information and rushing back to the exchange to make a killing.

128 Reeves, *Rothschilds*, pp. 281f.

129 See e.g. RAL, XI/109J/J/32, James, Paris, to Nathan, Jan. 1, 1832; same to same, March 25. Cf. Deschamps, *Belgique*, p. lxxvi. The connection with the Journal seems to have lapsed in 1839, to judge by the fact that the London house cancelled its subscription in that year: AN, 132 AQ 5401, NMR to deRF, Jan. 4, 1839. See also Cameron, *France and Europe*, p. 132, on the Rothschilds" links to the *Semaine Financière*.

130 RAL, XI/109J/J/37, James, Paris, to his nephews, London, Nov. 3, 1837.

131 RAL, XI/109J/J/39, James, Venice, to his nephews, London, June 17, 1839.

132 Aspinall, *Politics and the press*, pp. 196f., 218f., 228.

133 Webster, *Foreign policy of Palmerston*, vol. I, p. 52. See e.g. RAL, T25/104/1/6/147, Anthony, Paris, to his brothers, undated, 1841.

134 In the 1840s the *Railway Times* referred to the "notorious fact that in all loan transactions of the late Mr Rothschild, *The Times* invariably, aye systematically, came in for a share of the pickings." Alsager's career ended disastrously: he left the paper after a large "inconsistency" was discovered in the accounts, and committed suicide shortly afterwards: *The Times, History of the Times*, vol. II, p. 15–22.

135 Kynaston, *City*, vol. I, p. 268.

136 RAL, T23/378, XI/109/42/3/21, Anselm, Frankfurt, to Lionel, London, June 28, 1842.

137 See esp. Balzac, *Maison Nucingen*, pp. 338ff, 371f., 379ff.

138 *The Times*, Dec. 20, 1823, pp. 2f.

139 *The Times*, June 30, 1829, p. 6; July 1, p. 3; July 17, p. 3; July 18, p. 4.

140 *The Times*, June 24, 1824, p. 3.
141 *The Times*, Dec. 15, 1825, p. 2. Cf. List, *Grundlinien*, p. 243.
142 RAL, XI/101/1–19/6, Anthony, Paris, to his brothers and Anselm, London, Oct. 15, 1838.
143 RAL, XI/101/2–10/27, Scharfenburg, Paris to NMR, Nov. 15, 1939.
144 *The Times*, May 10, 1844, p. 6.
145 *The Times*, Jan. 7, 1845, p. 5.
146 *The Times*, April 13, 1863, p. 10.

ELEVEN *"Il est Mort" (1836)*
1 Disraeli, *Coningsby*, pp. 213f.
2 RAL, RFamC/1/57, Hannah and Louise, Frankfurt, to Nat, London, undated, June 1836; RFamC/1/61, Hannah to Anthony, Paris, undated, June.
3 Monypenny and Buckle, *Disraeli*, vol. II, p. 20; Wiebe *et al.* (eds), *Disraeli letters*, vol. III, p. 22.
4 Disraeli, *Tancred*, pp. 186f. See also Disraeli, *Endymion*, pp. 133–5.
5 RAL, T22/20, RFamC/4/105, Lionel, Frankfurt, to Nat, London, May 18, 1836.
6 Bartetzko, "Fairy tales and castles," p. 228.
7 RAL, XI/109J/J/36, James, Paris, to Nat, London, June 2, 1836; James to Nathan, London, June 3; RAL, XI/109J/J/36, James, Frankfurt, to Anthony, Paris, June 13.
8 RAL, T23/78, XI/109/34/1/4, Dr Schlemmer, Frankfurt, to Nat, London, June 8, 1836.
9 RAL, RFamC/1/57, Louise, Frankfurt, to Nat, London, undated, June 1836.
10 RAL, T23/7b, XI/109/34/3/40C, Anthony, Paris, to Lionel, Frankfurt, June 4, 1836.
11 RAL, XI/109J/J/36, James and Nathan, Brussels, to Nat and Anthony, June 6, 1836.
12 RAL, RFamC/9/1, Nathan, Frankfurt, to Nat, London, June 12, 1836.
13 RAL, RFamC/9/2, Nathan, Frankfurt, to Anthony, Paris, June 12, 1836. See also RAL, XI/109J/J/36, James, Frankfurt, to Anthony, June 14; RAL, XI/109J/J/36, James and Salomon to Anthony, June 16.
14 RAL, T23/21, RFamC/4/106, Lionel, Frankfurt, to Anthony, Paris, June 1, 1836.
15 RAL, RFamC/4/108, Lionel, Frankfurt, to Nat, London, June 9, 1836.
16 RAL, T23/59, XI/109/34/1/1, Hannah Mayer, Frankfurt, to Nat, London, June 12, 1836; RAL, T23/61, RFamC/20/6, Louise, Frankfurt, to Anthony, Paris, July 7.
17 RAL, T23/60, RFamC/20/5, Louise, Frankfurt, to Nat, London, undated, June 1836.
18 Kindleberger, *Financial history*, pp. 199f.
19 RAL, RFamC/4/110, Lionel, Frankfurt, to Nat, London, June 11, 1836.
20 RAL, RFamC/9/1, Nathan and Hannah, Frankfurt, to Nat, London, June 12, 1836.
21 RAL, RFamC/4/109, Lionel, Frankfurt, to Nat, London, June 12, 1836; cf. RAL, RFamC/9/2, Lionel to Anthony, Paris, June 12; RAL, RFamC/4/112, Lionel to Anthony, June 13.
22 RAL, RFamC/4/124, Lionel, Frankfurt, to Anthony and Nat, undated, *c.* June 17, 1836.
23 RAL, RFamC/1/57, Hannah, Frankfurt, to Nat, London, undated, June, 1836; RAL, RFamC/1/58, Hannah to Anthony, Paris, undated, June. Cf. Rothschild, *Shadow*, for the argument that Nathan may have been suffering from a more serious illness which prevented the abscess from healing after it had been drained. A similar complaint seems also to have killed Nathan's father.
24 RAL, RFamC/4/110, Lionel, Frankfurt, to Nat, London, June 11, 1836.
25 RAL, RFamC/1/59, Hannah, Frankfurt, to Anthony, London, undated, June 1836.
26 RAL, RFamC/4/111, Lionel, Frankfurt, to Nat and Anthony, June 13, 1836; RAL, RFamC/4/113, Lionel to Nat, June 13.
27 RAL, RFamC/1/61, Hannah, Frankfurt, to Nat, London, undated, June, 1836.
28 RAL, RFamC/1/60, Hannah, Frankfurt, to Anthony, June 14, 1836; RAL, T23/79, XI/109/34/1/5, Dr Schlemmer, Frankfurt, to Nat, London, June 14.
29 RAL, RFamC/4/109, Lionel, Frankfurt, to Nat, London, June 12, 1836.
30 RAL, RFamC/1/62, Hannah, Frankfurt, to Nat, London, June 16, 1836.
31 RAL, RFamC/4/114, Lionel, Frankfurt, to Anthony and Nat, June 15, 1836.
32 RAL, T23/80, XI/109/34/1/6, Dr Schlemmer, Frankfurt, to Nat, London, June 16, 1836.
33 RAL, RFamC/1/62, Hannah, Frankfurt, to Nat, London, June 16, 1836.
34 RAL, RFamC/1/60, Hannah, Frankfurt, to Anthony, Paris, June 14, 1836; RFamC/1/61, same to same, undated, June; RAL, RFamC/1/62, Hannah to Nat, June 16; RAL, T23/54, RFamC/1/66, Hannah to Anthony, undated, June.
35 The marriage was apparently unconsummated, for reasons which can easily be inferred. "It appears," commented James crudely, "that the red King would not permit him to spit roast the bird despite the

fact that he had caught it in his net": RAL, XI/109J/J/36, James, Frankfurt, to Anthony, Paris, June 18, 1836. Lionel was more delicate: "Till now there is not much to relate as you well know that the fright has generally such an effect upon the young ladies that they are immediately troubled with some thing that pays them very often a visit. I can only say that she is a most beautiful person in every respect": RAL, RFamC/4/116, Lionel, Frankfurt, to Anthony and Nat, June 17. The different language illustrates nicely the difference between the generations; at the same time, the fact that both men saw fit to allude to the subject shows how few secrets there were between members of the family.

36 RAL, RFamC/1/63, Hannah, Frankfurt, to Nat, London, June 17, 1836.
37 RAL, RFamC/1/66, Hannah, Frankfurt, to Anthony, Paris, undated, *c.* June 20, 1836.
38 RAL, XI/109J/J/36, James, Frankfurt, to Anthony and Nat, June 21, 1836; RAL, RFamC/4/117, Lionel, Frankfurt, to Anthony and Nat, June 22; RAL, RFamC/4/119, same to same, June 26; RAL, RFamC/1/65, Hannah to Nat, June 27; RAL, RFamC/4/122, Lionel to Anthony and Nat, June 29; RAL, XI/109J/J/36A, James, Salomon and Carl to Anthony, June 29; RAL, XI/109J/J/36B, James to Anthony, June 29; RAL, XI/109J/J/36, James and Salomon to Anthony, July 1; RAL, RFamC/4/126, Lionel to Anthony and Nat, July 3; RAL, XI/109J/J/36A, James to Anthony, July 8; RAL, XI/109J/J/36A, James to Nat, July 9; RAL, XI/109J/J/36B, James to Anthony, July 9.
39 RAL, RFamC/4/121, Lionel, Frankfurt, to Anthony and Nat, June 28, 1836; RAL, RFamC/4/127, same to same, July 6.
40 RAL, RFamC/4/125, Lionel, Frankfurt, to Anthony and Nat, July, 1836; RAL, RFamC/1/67, Hannah to Anthony and Nat, July 1; RAL, RFamC/4/128, same to same, July 7; RAL, RFamC/4/130, Lionel to Anthony and Nat, July 9; RAL, RFamC/4/131, same to same, July 11; RAL, RFamC/4/132, July 12; RAL, RFamC/4/133, Lionel to James, Kreuznach, July 12; RAL, RFamC/4/134, Lionel to Nat, July 13; RAL, RFamC/4/138, same to same, July 14; RAL, RFamC/4/137, Lionel to Anthony and Nat, July 14; RAL, RFamC/4/136, same to same, July 15; RAL, RFamC/1/68, Hannah to Nat, July 17; RAL, RFamC/4/140, Lionel to Anthony and Nat, July 17; RAL, RFamC/4/141, same to same, July 18; RAL, RFamC/4/142, July 18; RAL, RFamC/4/144, July 20; RAL, RFamC/4/145, July 21; RAL, RFamC/4/146, July 22; RAL, RFamC/4/147, July 22.
41 RAL, RFamC/4/148, Lionel, Frankfurt, to Nat, London, July 25, 1836.
42 RAL, T23/75, RFamC/24/10, Anselm, Frankfurt, to Nat, London, July 26, 1836; RAL, XI/109J/J/36, James, Kreuznach, to Anthony, Paris, July 26; RAL, RFamC/4/149, Lionel to Nat, July 26. Powers of attorney had to be sent to allow senior clerks to act in the absence of family members—a rare if not unprecedented circumstance at this time.
43 Corti, *Reign*, pp. 150ff.
44 CPHDCM, 637/1/7/70–2, Anhang, July 30.
45 CPHDCM, 637/1/276/1–5, Nathan's will, undated. Cf. Corti, *Reign*, pp. 152f.
46 Corti, *Reign*, pp. 150ff.
47 CPHDCM, 637/1/7/68, Generalaufstellung, July 30, 1836; CPHDCM, 637/1/6/32, Generaufstellung, 10 p.m., July 30; CPHDCM, 637/1/7/53–69, Vollständige Abschrift des Societäts-Vertrags . . . Übereinkunft, July 30; CPHDCM, 637/1/7/70–2, Anhang, July 30; RAL, RFamFD/3,6, undated, statement signed by Amschel, Salomon, Carl, James and Anselm, giving Nat and Anthony three months to ratify the new agreement.
48 Corti, *Reign*, pp. 150ff. See also Loewe (ed.), *Montefiore diaries*, vol. I, p. 103.
49 *The Times*, Aug. 3, 1836.
50 Corti, *Reign*, pp. 79f.
51 *The Times*, July 27, 1836.
52 *The Times*, Aug. 2, 1836.
53 *Ibid.*
54 *The Times*, Aug. 3, 1836.
55 *The Times*, Aug. 4, 1836. I am grateful to Melanie Aspey for identifying Alsager as the likely author.
56 Kynaston, *City*, vol. I, p. 107.
57 *The Times*, Feb. 24, 1837.
58 *The Times*, Aug. 9, 1836. The family had returned to England with the body, travelling by steamboat: *The Times*, Aug. 6.
59 Rubens, *Anglo-Jewish portraits*, pp. 101, 103.
60 Heseltine, *Family scene*, pp. 53ff.
61 Corti, *Reign*, p. 180; Heuberger, *Rothschilds*, p. 59.

62 Doering, *Handelshauses Rothschild*, pp. 16–19.

63 Corti, *Reign*, p. 155.

64 Almost certainly Charles Stewart, the 2nd Marquess of Castlereagh, with whom the brothers had close dealings at the time of the Congress of Vienna.

65 *The Times*, Aug. 9, 1836; Doering, *Handelshauses Rothschild*, pp. 30ff. Cf. Katz, *Jews in the history of England*, p. 368; Corti, *Reign*, p. 155.

66 Gray (ed.), *Life and times*, pp. 114f.

67 Ziegler, *Sixth great power*, p. 375.

68 Rubinstein, "British millionaires." See Appendix 1.

69 Cannadine, *Aspects of aristocracy*, pp. 39, 165ff.

70 Buxton (ed.), *Memoirs*, pp. 228f.

71 Muhlstein, *Baron James*, pp. 162ff.

72 Anon., *Hebrew Talisman*, pp. 28ff.

73 Glanz, "Rothschild legend," pp. 22f.

74 Corti, *Reign*, p. 217; Prawer, *Heine*, pp. 331–5.

75 Heine's friend Prince Pückler had noticed Nathan's collection of royal portraits in London over a decade earlier.

76 Heine, "Lutetia," in *Sämtliche Schriften*, vol. V, pp. 355f., trans. Prawer, *Heine*, pp. 646ff.

77 "I looked about me. Every minute a small door opened and one Bourse agent after another came in, uttering a number in a loud voice; Rothschild going on reading, muttered without raising his eyes: "Yes—no—good—perhaps—enough—" and the number walked out. There were various gentlemen in the room, rank-and-file capitalists, members of the National Assembly, two or three exhausted tourists with youthful moustaches and elderly cheeks, those everlasting figures who drink—wine—at watering-places and are presented at courts, the feeble, lymphatic suckers that drain the sap from the aristocratic families, and shove their way from the gaming table to the Bourse. They were all talking together in undertones. The Jewish autocrat sat calmly at his table, looking through papers and writing something on them, probably millions, or at least hundreds of thousands": Herzen, *My past and thoughts*, vol. II, p. 762.

78 Feydeau, *Mémoires*, pp. 127–54. Cf. Capefigue, *Grandes opérations*, vol. III, pp. 202–5.

79 RAL, XI/109J/J/36, James, Paris, to his nephews, London, Oct. 25, 1836.

80 See e.g. RAL, XI/109J/J/37, James, Paris, to his nephews, Jan. 11, 1837; RAL, XI/109J/J/38A, James, Nice, to Salomon and Anthony, Paris, Oct. 2, 1838; RAL, XI/109J/J/39, James, Paris, to his nephews, London, Nov. 6, 1839; RAL, XI/109J/J/41, same to same, April 21, 1841; RAL, XI/101/3,4,5–3/60, James to Nat, May 19. In the case of Mayer, the charge may well have been justified: cf. RAL, T23/225, XI/109/41/4/7, Anthony, Paris, to his brothers, Aug. 30.

81 RAL, XI/109J/J/37, Salomon, Paris, to his nephews, London, Sept. 15, 1837.

82 RAL, XI/101/0–1/36, James, Paris, to Lionel, London, Nov. 18, 1837.

83 RAL, XI/109/46/1/88, Nat, Paris, to his brothers, undated, early 1844.

84 RAL, XI/109J/J/39, James, Kissingen, to Amschel and Carl, Aug. 1, 1839.

85 RAL, XI/101/1–13/7, Nat, Paris, to Lionel, undated, Jan. 1838.

86 RAL, XI/109J/J/39, James, Frankfurt, to Anthony, London, Sept. 1, 1839; James to Nat, Paris, Sept. 7.

87 RAL, XI/109J/J/41A, James, Paris, to Lionel, London, June 23, 1841.

88 RAL, XI/109J/J/40, James, Paris, to his nephews, London, Jan. 9, 1840; same to same, Jan. 15; RAL, XI/109/40/2/17, MAR to NMR, May 16, 1841; RAL, T25/104/0/23, Anthony, Paris, to his brothers, London, undated, probably 1841; RAL, T25/104/1/3/53, same to same, May 28, 1841.

89 RAL, T7/8, XI/103/0, Anthony to his brothers, July 11, 1839.

90 RAL, T26/101/1/4/4/18, Anthony, Frankfurt, to his brothers, London, Feb. 18, 1837. Cf. CPHDCM, 637/1/275/27–48, Draft will by Amschel, Dec. 8, 1840.

91 RAL, XI/109J/J/38, James, Paris, to his nephews, March 10, 1838.

92 RAL, XI/109J/J/37, James, Paris, to his nephews, March 4, 1837; James and Salomon to their nephews, March 5; James to his nephews, March 6; same to same, March 9; same, Frankfurt, to same, March 15.

93 RAL, XI/109/58b/2/29, Nat, Paris, to his brothers, undated, late 1846.

94 RAL, XI/109J/J/39, James, Nice, to his brothers and nephews, March 16, 1839.

95 CPHDCM, 637/1/309, Amschel, Frankfurt, to his brothers and nephews, Nov. 11, 1841.

96 RAL, XI/109J/J42, James, Paris, to his nephews, Nov. 14, 1842.

97 RAL, RFamC/1/20, Hannah, Paris, to Mayer, London, Aug. 22, 1842. Hannah also sided with her

sons-in-law, pressing Lionel to secure promotion for Mayer Carl, who she felt was being treated by Amschel as a mere clerk in Frankfurt: RAL, RFamC/1/170, Hannah, Mainz, to Lionel, London, Oct. 7.

98 CPHDCM, 637/1/7/88–92, Übereinkunft, Aug. 30, 1844; also CPHDCM, 637/1/9/1–4. Cf. the somewhat over-simplified accounts in Gille, *Maison Rothschild*, vol. I, pp. 454–61; Born, *International banking*, pp. 53–5.

99 RAL, XI/109/48/2/9, Lionel, Frankfurt, to Nat, Paris, Aug. 31, 1844.

100 RAL, XI/109/48/2/6, Lionel, Frankfurt, to Nat, Paris, Aug. 28, 1844. Emphasis added. See also RAL, XI/109/48/2/8, same to same, Aug. 29.

101 RAL, XI/109/46/1/89, Nat, Paris, to his brothers, London, undated, 1844.

102 Chapman, *Foundation*, p. 21.

103 RAL, T18/294, XI/109/47/1/92, Nat, Paris, to his brothers, London, April 10, 1844.

104 Davis, *English Rothschilds*, pp. 134f.

105 RAL, XI/109J/J/45, James, Paris, to his nephews, London, March 18, 1844.

TWELVE *Love and Debt*

1 RAL, XI/109J/J/39, James, Heinrichsbad, to Nat, Paris, July 16, 1839. See also Davis, *English Rothschilds*, p. 60; Heuberger, *Rothschilds*, pp. 94f.

2 Surtees, *Coutts Lindsay*, pp. 42ff.

3 RAL, XI/109J/J/38, James, Paris, to Lionel and Nat, London, Nov. 11, 1838.

4 CPHDCM, 637/1/276/1–5, Nathan's will, undated, 1836.

5 RAL, XI/109J/J/38, James, Paris, to Lionel and Nat, London, Nov. 11, 1838.

6 RAL, XI/109J/J/39, James, Naples, to Nat, London, April 28, 1839.

7 *The Times*, May 18, 1839.

8 RAL, XI/109J/J/39, James, Heinrichsbad, to Nat, Paris, June 29, 1839.

9 RAL, RFamC/1/83, Hannah to Nat, May 19, 1839.

10 RAL, XI/109J/J/39, James, Heinrichsbad, to Nat, Paris, July 16, 1839. See also Davis, *English Rothschilds*, p. 60; Heuberger, *Rothschilds*, pp. 94f.

11 RAL, T7/9, XI/03/0 1–40, Anthony, Paris, to his brothers, London, July 17, 1839.

12 RAL, XI/109J/J/39, James, Frankfurt, to Nat, Paris, Sept. 7, 1839.

13 Disraeli, *Coningsby*, p. 348.

14 RAL, T7/8, XI/103/0, Anthony, Frankfurt, to his brothers, London, July 11, 1839. Cf. Davis, *English Rothschilds*, p. 61.

15 RAL, XI/109J/J/39, James, Naples, to Amschel, Frankfurt, July 11, 1839.

16 RAL, XI/109J/J/39, James, Paris, to his nephews, Nov. 19, 1839; same to same, Nov. 28; Dec. 2; RAL, T25/103/0/1/66, Anselm, Paris, to his cousins, London, Nov. 27; RAL, XI/109J/J/40B, James, Paris, to Anthony, London, Feb. 27, 1840.

17 RAL, XI/109J/J/42, James, Paris, to Mayer Carl, March 3, 1842; RAL, T23/311, XI/109/42/3/15, Anselm, Frankfurt, to Lionel and Anthony, London, April 8. Cf. Heuberger, *Rothschilds*, pp. 179f.

18 RAL, T23/382, XI/109/43/1/22, Charlotte, Frankfurt, to her brothers, London, May 12, 1842.

19 RAL, T23/365, XI/109/42/4/45, Lionel, Paris, to Mayer, London, Aug. 20. Uncle Salomon gave the bride £20,000 and other gifts were doubtless equally lavish: CPHDCM, 637/1/309, Salomon to Charlotte, Aug. 9, 1842.

20 Blakiston, *Lord William Russell*, pp. 475, 479.

21 Disraeli, *Coningsby*, p. 130.

22 Davis, *English Rothschilds*, p. 63.

23 Disraeli, *Endymion*, pp. 133–5.

24 RAL, XI/109/68B/2, Hannah Mayer and Henry Fitzroy, Garboldisham, to Lionel, London, undated, 1848; RAL, Moscow 224, Betty, Paris, to Alphonse, New York, April 4, 1849.

25 Davis, *English Rothschilds*, pp. 91f. The post went to Ralph Bernal Osborne; Fitzroy had to be content with being under-secretary at the Home Office (1852–5) and later became Chief Commissioner of Works (1859): *DNB*.

26 Davis, *English Rothschilds*, p. 161.

27 RAL, RFamC/21, Charlotte to Leopold, Feb. 6, 1864; same to same, Feb. 11; Feb. 24; March 1.

28 RAL, RFamC/21, Charlotte to Leopold, May 3; same to same, May 6; June 9. Cf. Surtees, *Coutts Lindsay*, pp. 92ff., 102–31.

29 RAL, RFamC/21, Charlotte to Leopold, May 9, 1864; same to same, May 10.

30 RAL, RFamC/21, Charlotte to Leopold, Nov. 5, 1864.

31 RAL, RFamC/21, Charlotte to Leopold, Nov. 15, 1864; same to same, Nov. 16; Nov. 17.

32 RAL, RFamC/21, Charlotte to Leopold, Nov. 29, 1864; same to same, Dec. 2; Dec. 3.

33 RAL, RFamC/21, Charlotte to Leopold, Dec. 3; same to same, Dec. 10.

34 Barnbougle Castle, Rosebery Papers, Ferdinand to Rosebery, Oct. 20, 1882.

35 Thackeray, "Book of snobs," pp. 296f.

36 Prevost-Marcilhacy, *Rothschild*, pp. 38, 42–7, 54f., 66ff.

37 Heine, "Korrespondenzartikel, 1832–52," in *Sämtliche Schriften*, vol. V, pp. 140ff., trans. Prawer, *Heine*, pp. 265–8.

38 Bertaut, *Bourse*, p. 119.

39 Muhlstein, *Baron James*, p. 81.

40 Apponyi, *Vingt-cinq ans*, vol. III, pp. 471f.

41 Lancaster, *From here of all places*, p. 92. See also Jullian, *Les styles*, p. 104. I am grateful to Ian Irvine for these references.

42 Gille, *Maison Rothschild*, vol. I, p. 476.

43 Wiebe *et al.* (eds), *Disraeli letters*, vol. IV, p. 59.

44 Disraeli, *Coningsby*, pp. 336f.

45 Prevost-Marcilhacy, *Rothschild*, pp. 70–77.

46 RAL, T23/439, RFamC/1/167, Hannah, Paris, to Mayer, London, Sept. 2, 1842.

47 Apponyi, *Vingt-cinq ans*, vol. IV, p. 44.

48 Prevost-Marcilhacy, *Rothschild*, pp. 48, 51, 71, 73, 78.

49 Blakiston, *Lord William Russell*, p. 479.

50 *The Times*, Feb. 21, 1845, p. 6.

51 Monypenny and Buckle, *Disraeli*, vol. II, p. 183.

52 Disraeli, *Tancred*, pp. 133f.

53 RAL, XI/109/17/1/18, Louise, Paris, to her father, London, undated, 1830.

54 RAL, RFamC/4/6, Lionel, Paris, to Charlotte, Jan. 13, 1836.

55 RAL, XI/101/1–13/6, Nat, Paris, to Lionel, London, undated, Jan. 1838.

56 RAL, T23/163, Richard Davies, Angel Court, Throgmorton Street, to Lionel, Aug. 6, 1840; RAL, T23/16, XI/109/39/3/12, same to same, Aug. 14. I am grateful to Lionel de Rothschild for this information.

57 Disraeli, *Endymion*, pp. 132f.

58 RAL, T25/104/0/62, Nat to his brothers, undated, 1840; RAL, T25/104/1/5/136, Anthony to his brothers, undated, 1840.

59 RAL, RFamC/1/5, Hannah, York, to Charlotte, Brighton, Oct. 5, 1841.

60 Prevost-Marcilhacy, *Rothschild*, p. 73.

61 RAL, T25/104/1/3/59, Anthony to his brothers, undated, 1841.

62 RAL, T23/455, XI/109/43/2/141, Anthony to his brothers, London, undated, 1842; RAL, XI/109/43a/2/42, same to same, undated, 1842. Cf. Davis, *English Rothschilds*, pp. 92f.

63 RAL, RFamC/4/40, Lionel, Thirsk, to Charlotte, Aug. 14, 1843.

64 RAL, T20/47, XI/109/48/2/18, Lionel, Frankfurt, to his brothers, London, Sept. 7, 1844.

65 Davis, *English Rothschilds*, p. 94f. By 1873 the Rothschilds owned all the land between Cheddington, Wingrave and Wing.

66 RAL, RFamC/21, Charlotte to Leo, Cambridge, Jan. 25, 1867. Cf. Prevost-Marcilhacy, "Rothschild architecture," pp. 245ff.; *idem, Rothschild*, p. 53.

67 Corti, *Reign*, pp. 174f.

68 *Ibid.*, pp. 175f.

69 *Ibid.*, pp. 230f.

70 Heuberger, *Rothschilds*, pp. 76ff.; Heilbrunn, "Haus Rothschild," p. 33. His son Anselm received honorary citizenship in 1847: Corti, *Reign*, p. 251.

71 RAL, T23/227, XI/109/41/4/8, Anthony, Frankfurt, to Nat, Paris, Sept. 1, 1841.

72 Corti, *Reign*, pp. 232ff.

73 *Ibid.*, pp. 234–7.

74 *Ibid.*, pp. 251f. In 1847, Salomon sought to merge all the properties into a single entailed estate.

75 Prevost-Marcilhacy, *Rothschild*, pp. 50f., 67; Corti, *Reign*, pp. 238f.; Reeves, *Rothschilds*, pp. 89f.

76 RAL [formerly CPHDCM], 58–1–403/6, Heinrich Heine, Paris, to Betty, Paris, April 7, 1846. Cf. Prawer, *Heine*, pp. 516f.

77 Bartetzko, "Fairy tales and castles," pp. 226f. Later additions in 1870–71 and 1891–8 significantly increased the size of the house: see the photograph in *ibid.*, p. 227.

78 RAL, T18/338, XI/109/47/1/70, Hannah, Frankfurt, to Lionel, London, undated, 1844; Heuberger, *Rothschilds*, p. 179.

79 Bartetzko, "Fairy tales and castles," pp. 228f.; Prevost-Marcilhacy, *Rothschild*, pp. 41, 48ff., 63ff., 73ff.

80 Bartetzko, "Fairy tales and castles," pp. 231f.

81 *Ibid.*, pp. 232f. Cf. Heuberger, *Rothschilds*, pp. 177.

82 See the picture in Bartezko, "Fairy tales and castles," p. 233; Prevost-Marcilhacy, *Rothschild*, p. 62 (the two sources give differing dates for the commission). The original house was demolished in 1855 to make way for an orangerie.

83 RAL, T18/338, XI/109/47/1/70, Hannah, Frankfurt, to Lionel, London, undated, 1844.

84 RAL, T18/541, XI/109/48/1/61, Lionel, Frankfurt, to Nat, Paris, Aug. 13, 1844. The house was demolished on Mayer Carl's death in 1886 and the grounds given to the City of Frankfurt: Heuberger, *Rothschilds*, pp. 179f.

85 There appears to have been some sort of financial constraint imposed on Anselm by his father, who perhaps wished his son to reserve his energies for the Austrian estates he would one day inherit. When Anselm spotted an attractive property at Emmerich near Frankfurt in 1843, he had to ask James to put up the money and sought to justify it as a speculative investment: RAL, T18/151(a), XI/109/45/5/111, Anselm, Frankfurt, to James and Nat, Paris, July 3, 1843; RAL, T18/151(d), XI/109/45/5/35, Anselm to Nat, July 6. Revealingly, Amschel was to act as "paymaster" for the new house at Grüneburg.

86 RAL, T20/49, XI/109/48/2/19, Lionel, Frankfurt, to his brothers, Sept. 9, 1844; RAL, T20/58, XI/109/48/2/22, same to same, Sept. 13; RAL, T20/66, XI/109/48/2/96, Charlotte, Frankfurt, to her mother, London, Sept. 13, 1844.

87 Bartetzko, "Fairy tales and castles," p. 234, attributes the house to Johann Jakob von Essen; but according to Prevost-Marcilhacy, *Rothschild*, pp. 64f., the house was actually designed by the French architect Bellanger.

88 Corti, *Reign*, pp. 219f.; Prawer, *Heine*, pp. 265–8.

89 Bocher, *Mémoires*, p. 368.

90 Wiebe *et al.* (eds), *Disraeli letters*, vol. IV, p. 59.

91 Loewe (ed.), *Montefiore diaries*, vol. I, p. 142.

92 *Ibid.*, pp. 144f.; Monypenny and Buckle, *Disraeli*, vol. II, p. 183.

93 RAL, T23/411, XI/109/43/1/42, Anselm, Frankfurt, to Nat and Anthony, Paris, undated, 1842; RAL, T7/32, XI/109/58–1, Hannah, Frankfurt, to Lionel, London, Nov. 14, 1846.

94 Disraeli, *Endymion*, pp. 162–4.

95 Disraeli, *Tancred*, pp. 140f., 145f.

96 Disraeli, *Endymion*, pp. 133–5.

97 *Ibid.*, pp. 146f. Despite his confessed "bad opinion" of Jews in general, Thackeray became friendly with Anthony's wife Louisa and Lionel's wife Charlotte after a chance meeting in 1848: Cohen, *Lady de Rothschild*, pp. 33ff.

98 RAL, T18/48, XI/109/45/1/18, Nat, Paris, to his brothers, London, undated, 1843.

99 Apponyi, *Vingt-cinq ans*, vol. IV, p. 115.

100 RAL, XI/109J/J/38, James, Naples, to Anthony, Paris, Dec. 11, 1838; RAL, T24/136, X/109/52/69, XI/109/43/2/159, Nat, Paris, to his brothers, London, undated, 1842.

101 See RAL, XI/109J/J/32, James and Anselm, Milan, to Salomon and Lionel, Paris, Sept. 23, 1832; RAL, XI/109J/J/33, James, Aix, to Salomon, Lionel and Carl, Aug. 13, 1833; RAL, XI/109J/J/41, James, Salomon and Anselm, Gastein, to Nat, Paris, Aug. 11, 1841.

102 Muhlstein, *Baron James*, p. 156; RAL, T7/67, Mayer, Wildbad, to Lionel, London, undated, 1846.

103 RAL, XI/109/18/1/31, Lionel, Paris, to his parents, London, Sept. 17, 1832.

104 Doering, *Handelshauses Rothschild*, p. 13.

105 Capefigue, *Grandes opérations*, vol. III, p. 204. See also Raikes, *Journal*, vol. II, pp. 221ff.: "[G]reat efforts had been made to insure a splendid battue; but a common morning's diversion at Sudbourne, or at some other houses in England would have beat it hollow. Fifteen or sixteen guns could scarcely bring down 300 animals of every description."

106 RAL, RFamC/4/42, Lionel, Crieff, to Charlotte, Gunnersbury, Aug. 19, 1843.

107 RAL, T18/165 , XI/109/45/5/43, Nat, to Anthony, Aug. 21, 1843; RAL, T18/174, XI/109/45/5/47, Anselm to his cousins, London, Sept. 11.

108 Davis, *English Rothschilds*, pp. 92ff.; Endelman, *Radical assimilation*, p. 75.

109 RAL, T25/104/0/29, Anthony to Lionel, undated, 1840; Kessler, "Rothschilds and Disraeli," pp. 238ff.

110 RAL, T24/135, XI/109/43/2/158, Nat, Paris, to his brothers, London undated, 1842; RAL, T24/123, XI/109/43/2/160, same to same, undated, 1842; RAL, T24/98, XI/109/43/2/65, undated, 1842. The allusion to Fitzroy confirms that Nat did not sever relations with Hannah Mayer and her husband, despite James's call for ostracism.

111 RAL, T25/104/0/129, Nat, Paris, to his brothers, London, Nov. 21, 1840.

112 RAL, T34/1, NMR 288, Nathan, London, to Amschel, Frankfurt, Jan. 3, 1816.

113 RAL, XI/109/30/1/2, Lionel, Paris, to his mother, London, May 26, 1833.

114 RAL, T25/104/0/40, Nat, Paris, to his brothers, London, undated, 1840; RAL, T25/104/0/41, Nat, Paris, to his brothers, London, May 12, 1840.

115 Monypenny and Buckle, *Disraeli*, vol. II, pp. 147; Wiebe *et al.* (eds), *Disraeli letters*, vol. IV, pp. 59, 68.

116 RAL, T18/352, XI/109/47/1/105, Nat, Paris, to his brothers, London, May 26, 1844.

117 Dasent, *Piccadilly*, pp. 141ff., 292.

118 Heine, "Skizzen zu den Bäder von Lucca," p. 623, trans. Prawer, *Heine*, pp. 138–40. It is possible that the passage alludes to Nathan, whom Heine had met in London the year before. If so, it is less wide of the mark.

119 Heine, "Lutetia," in *Sämtliche Schriften*, vol. V, pp. 451f. Cf. Corti, *Reign*, p. 217; Prawer, *Heine*, pp. 331–5.

120 Monypenny and Buckle, Disraeli, vol. II, p. 151; Wiebe *et al.* (eds), *Disraeli letters*, vol. IV, pp. 59, 68.

121 Launay, *Lettres parisiennes*, p. 281.

122 Heuberger (ed.), *Rothschilds*, pp. 4ff.

123 Hall, "English Rothschilds as collectors," pp. 265ff.

124 Davis, *English Rothschilds*, pp. 65f.

125 Hall, "English Rothschilds as collectors," pp. 265ff.

126 A number of these later acquisitions came from large *en bloc* purchases of other collections such as Charles Heusch's (in 1862) and Willem van Loon's (in 1879).

127 RAL, T25/104/0/42, James, Paris, to Anthony, May 12, 1840.

128 RAL, XI/109J/J/41, James, Paris, to his nephews, London, May 1, 1841.

129 RAL, T18/85, Nat, Paris, to his brothers, London, undated, 1843.

130 See e.g. RAL, T24/124, X/109/52/57, XI/109/43/2/83, Anthony, to his brothers, London, undated, 1842.

131 RAL, T23/148, XI/109/38/3/20, T. R. de Lusuriaga, 107 High Street, Portsmouth, to Baron Rothschild, May 26, 1840.

132 Hall, "English Rothschilds as collectors," p. 273.

133 RAL, T18/76, XI/109/45/6/22, Nat, Paris, to his brothers, London, March 16, 1843; RAL, T18/80, XI/109/45/6/117A, same to same, undated, 1843.

134 Hall, "English Rothschilds as collectors," pp. 270–74. Cf. Davis, *English Rothschilds*, pp. 97f.

135 Höffner, "Frankfurter Privatsammlungen," pp. 136ff.

136 *Ibid.*, pp. 136ff.; Heuberger, *Rothschilds*, pp. 7ff.

137 Balla, *Romance*, pp. 181ff.; repeated in Cowles, *Rothschilds*, p. 97.

138 Prevost-Marcilhacy, *Rothschild*, pp. 38, 60, notes some exceptions in James's early collection: a tableau by Bonington, *Henri III*, and one by Delacroix, *Jeanne la Folle*.

139 Hall, "English Rothschilds as collectors," pp. 272f.; Prevost-Marcilhacy, *Rothschild*, p. 81; Cowles, *Rothschilds*, pp. 114f; Heuberger, *Rothschilds*, pp. 102f.

140 Muhlstein, *Baron James*, pp. 166f.

141 Reitlinger, *Economics of taste*, vol. II, p. 94f.

142 RAL, T18/76, XI/109/45/6/22, Nat, Paris, to his brothers, London, March 16, 1843; RAL, T18/80, XI/109/45/6/117A, same to same, undated, 1843.

143 RAL, XI/109J/J/46D, Mayer, Milan, to Nat and Anthony, Paris, Aug. 12, 1846.

144 AN, 132 AQ 5902, James to his son, June 30, 1860. Cf. Reitlinger, *Economics of taste*, vol. I, p. 132.

145 Pückler, *Briefe*, p. 656. See also Loewe (ed.), *Montefiore diaries*, vol. I, pp. 61, 142.

146 Castellane, *Journal*, pp. 200f.; Corti, *Rise*, p. 311.

147 Niecks, *Chopin*, vol. I, p. 247; Samson, *Chopin*, p. 85; Muhlstein, *Baron James*, p. 155. Cf. Hedley, *Selected correspondence of Fryderyk Chopin.*

148 Samson, *Chopin*, p. 196.

149   Rothschild, "Brief history," p. 3; *idem*, "Musical associations," pp. 287ff. In 1859, the book passed on
      to her equally musical daughter Hannah Mathilde, who collected autographs from, among others,
      Anton Rubinstein. He contributed his song "Hüte dich."
150   Weinstock, *Rossini*, p. 460n.
151   Rothschild, "Musical associations," p. 287.
152   RAL, T22/478, XI/109/30/2/13, Louisa and Hannah Mayer, Paris, to their father, London, undated, *c.*
      1833; RAL, RFamC/1/156, Hannah to Nathan, Oct. 17.
153   RAL, T23/61, RFamC/20/6, Louise, Frankfurt, to Anthony, Paris, July 7, 1836.
154   RAL, T7/134, Caroline [Julie] and [Hannah] Mathilde, Paris, to their grandmother, Hannah, Sept. 27,
      1847. Cf. Rothschild, "Musical associations," pp. 289f.
155   RAL, RFamC/21, Charlotte Lionel de Rothschild to Leo, Dec. 12, 1865; same to same, May 16, 1866.
      Cf. Rothschild, "Musical associations," p. 293. Charlotte de Rothschild has recorded a number of the
      songs mentioned here.
156   Corti, *Reign*, p. 213.
157   RAL, XI/109/33/1/15, Lionel, Madrid to Anthony (Billy), April 1, 1835; RAL, RFamC/1/57,
      Hannah, Frankfurt, to Nat, London, June 10, 1836. Cf. Osborne, *Rossini*, p. 89; Weinstock, *Rossini*,
      pp. 191f.
158   Weinstock, *Rossini*, pp. 328, 352.
159   Niecks, *Chopin*, vol. II, pp. 135n., 165n.
160   The other guests included "Leopold, Kent's son Leiningen, old Talleyrand . . . Prince Hohenlohe, Juste
      de Noailles [and the] Dalbergs."
161   Rothschild, "Musical associations," p. 290.
162   RAL, XI/109/36/3/1–2, Johann Strauss senior, Sheffield, to Baron Rothschild, London, Oct. 13, 1838;
      same, Leeds, to same, Oct. 17.
163   Weinstock, *Rossini*, p. 227.
164   Rothschild, "Musical associations," p. 290.
165   RAL, T15/19, E. Nicolini [Adelina Patti's second husband], Buenos Aires, to [Alphonse?], June 28,
      1889.
166   Stern, *Gold and iron*, p. 17.
167   Heine, "Memoiren," in *Sämtliche Schriften*, vol. VI/1, pp. 560f.; Prawer, *Heine*, p. 167; Sammons,
      Heine, p. 129.
168   Corti, *Reign*, p. 223; Prawer, *Heine*, pp. 425f.
169   *Ibid.*, pp. 425f.
170   *Ibid.*, p. 426.
171   *Ibid.*, pp. 329f.
172   *Ibid.*, p. 329.
173   *Ibid.*, pp. 516f.; Corti, *Reign*, p. 222; Heilbrunn, "Haus Rothschild," p. 15. The book in question was
      published anonymously in Prague fifteen years later: see Anon., *Haus Rothschild.*
174   Heine, "Lutetia," in *Sämtliche Schriften*, vol. V, pp. 452–65, trans. Prawer, *Heine*, pp. 648ff., 655f.
175   Mende, *Heine-Chronik*, pp. 181f.
176   Sammons, *Heine*, p. 286.
177   Mende, *Heine-Chronik*, p. 193, 195.
178   RAL [formerly CPHDCM], 58-1–404, James, Paris, to Heinrich Heine, Oct. 19, 1847.
179   RAL [formerly CPHDCM], 58-1–403, Heinrich Heine, Paris, to James ["Herr Baron'], Jan. 15, 1852;
      Prawer, *Heine*, pp. 740f.
180   RAL [formerly CPHDCM], 58-1–403, Heinrich Heine, Paris, to James, Jan. 19, 1852.
181   Corti, *Reign*, pp. 215–17; Prawer, *Heine*, pp. 741ff.
182   RAL [formerly CPHDCM], 58-1–403/7, Heinrich Heine, Paris, to Betty, May 16, 1849.
183   RAL [formerly CPHDCM], 58-1–403/4, Heinrich Heine, Paris, to Betty, Feb. 7, 1834; Prawer, *Heine*,
      p. 426.
184   RAL [formerly CPHDCM], 58-1–403/5, Heinrich Heine to Betty, Paris, undated, *c.* 1834.
185   Heine, "Korrespondenzartikel, 1832–52," in *Sämtliche Schriften*, vol V, pp. 140ff., trans. Prawer, *Heine*,
      pp. 265–8.
186   Prawer, *Heine*, p. 426.
187   Corti, *Reign*, pp. 220f.
188   RAL [formerly CPHDCM], 58-1–403, Heinrich Heine, Paris, to Betty, Nov. 9, 1854; Mende,
      Heine—Chronik, pp. 226, 257.

189 Draper, *Heine*, p. 898.
190 In late 1849 Heine sent her a copy of his post-revolutionary poem which contains a passionate denunciation of the powers which had crushed the Hungarian rising. The Rothschilds' support for the Russian-sponsored reaction was well known: RAL [formerly CPHDCM], 58–1–403/2, Heinrich Heine, poem: "Deutschland im Oktober 1849" [copy].
191 Sparr, "Rothschilds in literature," p. 315.
192 Balzac, *Correspondance*, vol. II, pp. 125f.
193 *Ibid.*, vol. II, pp. 227f.
194 *Ibid.*, vol. II, pp. 674ff.
195 *Ibid.*, vol. II, p. 757.
196 *Ibid.*, vol. IV, pp. 422f., 433f. James may have attended the second, disastrous performance.
197 *Ibid.*, vol. V, p. 56.
198 *Ibid.*, vol. V, pp. 167f.; Gille, *Maison Rothschild*, vol. I, pp. 429f.
199 Balzac, *Lettres à l'étrangère*, vol. III, pp. 217ff. Cf. Muhlstein, *Baron James*, p. 155; Robb, *Balzac*, pp. 237, 276.
200 Balzac, *Correspondance*, vol. V, p. 218.
201 *Ibid.*, vol. V, pp. 386, 400, 404, 454, 457f., 475, 514f., 518, 537, 634ff., 649, 709ff., 726, 779f.
202 Gille, *Maison Rothschild*, vol. I, pp. 429f.
203 Corti, *Reign*, pp. 282f.
204 Robb, *Balzac*, p. 416. They demolished it.
205 See e.g. Hunt, *Balzac's Comedie Humaine*, p. 193; Castex, "L'Univers," pp. xxxi—xxxii.
206 Sparr, "Rothschilds in literature," p. 315.
207 Balzac, *Le père Goriot*, esp. pp. 125, 157.
208 Balzac, *César Birotteau*, esp. pp. 250ff.
209 Balzac, *La maison Nucingen*, pp. 338f., 357–60, 369–72, 379f., 384–91.
210 Balzac, *Splendeurs et misères*, pp. 492, 520f., 550ff., 576ff., 590f., 598ff.
211 Balzac, *Un homme d'affaires*, p. 418; Balzac, *La cousine Bette*, pp. 178, 313.

THIRTEEN *Quicksilver and Hickory (1834–1839)*

1 RAL, XI/109J/J/36, James, Paris, to his nephews, London, Oct. 25, 1836.
2 Corti, *Reign*, p. 30.
3 RAL, XI/109J/J/31, James, Paris, to Nathan, London, Sept. 27, 1831; same to same, Sept. 28; Sept. 29; RAL, XI/109J/J/32, Feb. 5, 1832; RAL, XI/109/25/1/24, Lionel, Paris, to his parents, London, Feb. 8; RAL, XI/109/26/1/30, same to same, June 19.
4 RAL, XI/109J/J/32A, James, Paris, to Nathan, London, March 14, 1832; same to same, Dec. 19; RAL, XI/109J/J/33, March 15; April 3; RAL, XI/109/30/1/20, Lionel, Paris, to his parents, London, Aug. 6. Cf. Gille, *Maison Rothschild*, vol. I, p. 242.
5 RAL, XI/109J/J/33, James, Paris, to Nathan, London, Aug. 13; same to same, Sept. 9; RAL, XI/109J/J/34, July 19; RAL, XI/109J/J/34B, July 21.
6 RAL, XI/109J/J/35, James, Paris, to Nathan, London, April 2, 1835; same to same, April 12; April 15; April 16; April 18; April 20; May 2. Cf. Gille, *Maison Rothschild*, vol. I, pp. 241–4; Ayer, *Century of finance*, pp. 38f.
7 RAL, XI/109J/J/36, James, Paris, to his nephews, London, Jan. 4, 1837.
8 RAL, XI/109J/J/36, James, Paris, to Nathan, London, March 5, 1836. Cf. same to same, April 28; May 3; May 5.
9 RAL, XI/109J/J/36, James, Paris, to Nathan, London, May 9, 1836; same to same, May 12; May 13.
10 RAL, XI/109J/J/36, James, Paris, to Nathan, London, May 16, 1836; James, Frankfurt, to Anthony, Paris, July 1; RAL, RFamC/4/105, Lionel, Frankfurt, to Nat, London, May 18; RAL, RFamC/4/125 [and /143], same to same, London, July 1.
11 RAL, XI/109J/J/36, James, Paris, to his nephews, London, Oct. 12, 1836.
12 RAL, XI/109J/J/36, James, Paris, to his nephews, London, Dec. 16, 1836; same to same, Dec. 17. See also Dec. 21; RAL, XI/109J/J/36/F2, James to unidentified recipient, Lisbon, Jan. 1, 1837; RAL, XI/109J/J/36, James to nephews, Jan. 31; same to same, May 29.
13 RAL, XI/109J/J/36, James, Paris, to his nephews, London, Oct. 19, 1836; same to same, Oct. 24; Nov. 16; Nov. 20; Dec. 5; Dec. 7; Dec. 8.
14 RAL, XI/109J/J/37, James, Paris, to his nephews, London, May 29, 1837; same to same, June 6; June 12; June 14; June 21; July 3; July 20.

15   *The Times*, Dec. 17, 1838; Jan 12, 1839; June 25; Nov. 18; Dec. 20; Dec. 21; Dec. 23; Dec. 24; June 8,
     1841. The Rothschilds had lent the Portuguese government £88,688 for four months to pay the inter-
     est due on its 3 per cent bonds. As a security, the government handed over "Regency bonds" to the nom-
     inal value of £600,000. When the government failed to repay the £88,688, the London house sold
     these bonds, but the Portuguese government claimed that it had unnecessarily delayed this sale in order
     to collect more interest. The final judgement went in favour of the Portuguese government on a techni-
     cality. Cf. RAL, XI/101/0–1/14, Schafenburg, Paris, to NMR, London, Sept. 10, 1837.
16   AN, 132 AQ 5434/1M39, Lionel, London, to James, Anselm and Anthony, Paris, Dec. 29, 1839.
17   RAL, XI/109J/J/37, James, Paris, to his nephews, London, Nov. 6, 1837.
18   RAL, XI/109/41/4/14, SMR to NMR, Sept. 10, 1841; AN, 132 AQ 5403/1M5, deRF to NMR, April
     13, 1841.
19   Ziegler, *Sixth great power*, pp. 139ff.
20   For the political background, Carr, *Spain*, pp. 146ff.
21   Kindleberger, *Financial history*, p. 26; Corti, *Reign*, pp. 120f.
22   Gille, *Maison Rothschild*, vol. I, pp. 325–7. Very nearly half the nominal amount of Spanish debt at this
     time was in foreign hands: Martin, *Minas de Almadén*, pp. 285f.
23   RAL, XI/109J/J/30, James, Paris, to Nathan and Anthony, London, Dec. 31, 1830.
24   RAL, XI/109J/J/32A, James, Paris, to Nathan, London, Nov. 3, 1832; RAL, XI/109J/J/32B, James and
     Salomon, Paris, to Nathan, Nov. 3; RAL, XI/109J/J/32C, James, Paris, to Nathan, Lionel and Nat,
     Nov. 3; RAL, XI/109J/J/32, James and Lionel, Paris, to Nathan and Nat, Dec. 16.
25   RAL, XI/109J/J/33, James, Paris, to Nathan, London, Jan. 4, 1833; same to same, Jan. 16; Feb. 9;
     March 9; March 13; March 15; March 16; May 7; RAL, XI/109/29/1/55, Nat, Paris, to his parents,
     London, May 7; RAL, XI/109/29/1/15, Lionel, Paris, to his parents, London, May 2; same to same,
     May 7; May 15; May 28; June 12; June 19.
26   RAL, XI/109J/J/32, James, Paris, to Nathan, London, April 26, 1832.
27   RAL, XI/109/32/1/39, Lionel, Paris, to his parents, London, June 7, 1834.
28   RAL, XI/109/31a/1/29, Lionel, Paris, to his parents, London, March 8.
29   RAL, XI/109J/J/31, James, Paris, to Nathan, London, Feb. 4, 1831; same to same, Feb. 5; June 6; July
     2; Nov. 16; RAL, XI/109/20/1/14, Lionel, Paris, to his parents, London, March 23; RAL,
     XI/109/27/1/34, same to same, March 20, 1832.
30   RAL, XI/109J/J/32A, James and Salomon, Paris, to Nathan, London, April 22, 1832; James and
     Salomon to Nathan and their nephews, Oct. 25; same to same, Oct. 27; RAL, XI/109/30/1/57, Lionel,
     Paris, to his parents, London, Dec. 23.
31   RAL, XI/109J/J/33, James, Paris, to Nathan, London, Dec. 23, 1833; same to same, Dec. 30; RAL,
     XI/109/30/1/59, Lionel, Paris, to his parents, London, Dec. 30; RAL, XI/109/32/1/1, same to same,
     Jan. 1, 1834; RAL XI/109/31a/1/1, Jan. 4; RAL, XI/109J/J/34, James, Paris, to Nathan and Nat,
     London, Jan. 7; same to same, Jan. 10; RAL, XI/109/31a/1/5, Lionel to his father, Jan. 13; RAL,
     XI/109J/J/34, James to Nathan, Jan. 17; RAL, XI/109J/J/34A, same to same, Jan. 18; RAL,
     XI/109J/J/34B, Jan. 18; RAL, XI/109J/J/34, Jan. 20; Jan. 21; Jan. 26; RAL, XI/109/31a/1/1, Anselm,
     Frankfurt, to NMR, undated, Feb.; RAL, XI/109J/J/34B, James to Nathan, Feb. 1; RAL, XI/109J/J/34,
     same to same, Feb. 12; RAL, XI/109/31a/1/15, Lionel to his parents, Feb. 13; RAL, XI/109/31a/1/16,
     same to same, Feb. 16; RAL, XI/109J/J/34, James to Nathan, Feb. 19; RAL, XI/109/31a/1/19, Lionel
     to his parents, Feb. 20; RAL, XI/109/31a/1/25, same to same, Feb. 27; RAL, XI/109J/J/34, James to
     Nathan, March 1; same to same, March 3; March 4; March 5; March 6; RAL, XI/109/31a/1/26, Lionel
     to his parents, March 3; RAL, XI/109/31a/1/27, same to same, March 4; RAL, XI/109/31a/1/29,
     March 8; RAL, XI/109J/J/34, James to Nathan, March 8; RAL, XI/109/31a/1/30, Lionel to his par-
     ents, March 9; RAL, XI/109J/J/34, James to Nathan, March 16; RAL, XI/109/31a/1/35, Lionel to his
     parents, March 22; RAL, XI/109/31a/1/56, Anselm, Frankfurt, to James, Paris, March 24; RAL,
     XI/109/31a/1/37, Lionel to his parents, March 25; RAL, XI/109J/J/34, James to Nathan and Anthony,
     March 25; RAL, XI/109J/J/34A, James to Nathan, March 29; RAL, XI/109J/J/34, same to same,
     March 30; March 31; RAL, XI/109J/J/34, James to Nathan and Anthony, April 7; James to Nathan,
     April 8; RAL, XI/109/32/1/10, Lionel to his parents, April 8; RAL, XI/109/31a/1/41, same to same,
     April 9; RAL, XI/109J/J/34B, James to Nathan, April 9; RAL, XI/109J/J/34C, James to Nathan and
     Anthony, April 9; RAL, XI/109/32/1/11, Lionel to his parents, April 9; RAL, XI/109/31a/1/43, same
     to same, April 12; RAL, XI/109J/J/34A, James to Nathan, April 12.
32   RAL, XI/109J/J/34, James, Paris, to Nathan, London, Jan. 21, 1834; same to same, Feb. 11; RAL,

XI/109/31a/1/8, Lionel, Paris, to his parents, London, Jan. 25; RAL, XI/109J/J/34, James to Nathan, Feb. 20; same to same, Feb. 25; Feb. 26; Feb. 27; RAL, XI/109/31a/1/24, Lionel to his parents, Feb. 26; RAL, XI/109J/J/34, James to Nathan, March 9; same to same, March 12; March 13; March 15; March 18; March 19; RAL, XI/109/31/1/32, Lionel to his parents, March 12; RAL, XI/109/31a/1/75, Salomon, Vienna, to his brothers, April 1; RAL, XI/109J/J/34A, James to Nathan, April 9. Interestingly, Metternich made it clear that he had no objection to the Rothschilds covertly participating in Spanish business in partnership with other firms. His concern was that the name "Rothschild," if publicly associated with the Regency of Maria Christina, would strengthen its position. The warnings of Broglie to James are not easy to reconcile with his talk on March 8 of a French-backed loan to integrate Spain "dans l'ensemble des finances de l'Europe, lesquelles forment en ce moment une sorte de République, une sorte de fédération, qui sont jusqu'à un certain point solidaires les unes des autres et se soutiennent mutuellement dans une certaine mesure." When asked to define the nature of the French backing, he changed his tune: Gille, *Maison Rothschild*, vol. I, pp. 244–7.

33 RAL, XI/109/31/1/45, Lionel, Paris, to his parents, London, April 14, 1834; RAL, XI/109J/J/34, James to Nathan and Anthony, April 14; RAL, XI/109/31a/1/46, Lionel to his parents, April 15; RAL, XI/109/3/1/14, same to same, April 15; RAL, XI/109J/J/34, James to Nathan and Anthony, April 16; RAL, XI/109/32/1/16, Lionel to his father, April 17; RAL, XI/109/31a/1/57, Anselm, Frankfurt, to deRF, April 17; RAL, XI/109J/J/34, James to Nathan, April 17; same to same, April 18; RAL, XI/109J/J/34A, April 19; April 20; April 22; April 23; April 26; RAL, XI/109/32/1/17, Lionel to his parents, April 28; RAL, XI/109/32/3/8, Anselm to James, May 3; RAL, XI/109J/J/34A, James to Nathan and Anthony, London, May 13; RAL, XI/109J/J/34, same to same, May 14.

34 RAL, XI/109/33/4/8, Agreement signed by Queen Regent, May 15, 1834. The government merely promised "to submit to the approaching Cortes session the question of recognising the loans of the former sessions." See also RAL, XI/109/32/4/12, Martinez de la Rosa, Madrid, to deRF, May 17; RAL, XI/109/32/4/11, deRF to Martinez de la Rosa, May 17; RAL, XI/109J/J/34A, James, Paris, to Nathan and his nephews, London, May 20; RAL, XI/109J/J/34, same to same, May 22; May 24; May 27; May 29; RAL, XI/109/32/1/27, Lionel to his parents, May 24; RAL, XI/109/32/1/32, same to same, May 27; RAL, XI/109/32/1/35, May 31; RAL, XI/109J/J/34A, James to Nathan, May 31; RAL, XI/109J/J/34A, same to same, May 31; RAL, XI/109/32/1/39, Lionel to his parents, June 7; RAL, XI/109J/J/34, James to Nathan, June 7. Cf. Gille, *Maison Rothschild*, vol. I, pp. 248–51; Fontana, *Revolucion*, pp. 59f.; Martin, *Minas de Almadén*, ch. 4; Otazu, *Rothschild*.

35 RAL, XI/109J/J/34, James, Paris, to Nathan, London, July 3, 1834.

36 RAL, T22/567, XI/109/32/1/37B, Lionel, Turin, to James, Paris, May 7, 1834; RAL, XI/109J/J/34, James to Nathan and Anthony, London, May 12.

37 Bullen and Strong (eds), *Palmerston: Correspondence with Villiers*, pp. 140–43. The terms were in fact quite generous under the circumstances: just 5 per cent interest and a 2 per cent commission, with repayment due after a year and a quarter.

38 Corti, *Reign*, pp. 129f.

39 RAL, XI/109/31a/1/58, Anselm, Frankfurt, to James, Paris, April 26, 1834; RAL, XI/109J/J/34, James to Nathan and Anthony, London, May 1; same to same, May 5; May 11; May 15; RAL, XI/109/32/1/26, Lionel to his parents, May 22; RAL, XI/109/32/1/33, same to same, May 28; RAL, XI/109/32/1/38, June 4; RAL, XI/109J/J/34, James to Nathan and his nephews, June 2; same to same, July 3; July 5; July 8; July 9; RAL, XI/109/32/1/54, Lionel to his parents, July 5; RAL, XI/109/32/4/60, Draft agreement between deRF and Ferrère Laffitte, undated.

40 RAL, XI/109/32/1/45, Lionel, Paris, to his parents, London, June 22, 1834.

41 RAL, T22/598, XI/109/32/2/38B, Lionel, Paris, to his parents, London, June 26, 1834; RAL, XI/109J/J/34, James, Paris, to Nathan, June 26; same to same, June 28; June 30.

42 RAL, T22/601, XI/109/32/2/38B, Lionel, Paris, to his parents, London, July 5, 1834; RAL, XI/109/32/4/20, Agreement between Toreno and Ardouin, July 8; RAL, XI/109J/J/34, James to Nathan and his nephews, July 11; same to same, July 13; July 14; July 15; July 16; July 17; RAL, XI/109/32/1/60, Lionel to his parents, July 12; RAL, XI/109/32/1/65, same to same, July 17. Three months earlier James had referred to Toreno as "a gambler who has been imprisoned over here for [nonpayment] of his debts, and who had earlier been a partner with Ardouin . . . in all business deals involving the Cortes": RAL, XI/109J/J/34, James to Nathan and Anthony, April 14, 1834. Cf. Corti, *Reign*, pp. 121f.; Scherb, *Geschichte*, pp. 74f.

43 RAL, XI/109J/J/34, James, Paris, to Nathan and his nephews, London, July 5, 1834; RAL,

XI/109J/J/34A, same to same, July 21; RAL, XI/109J/J/34B, July 21; RAL, T22/606, XI/109/32/3/38B, Lionel, Paris, to his parents, July 14; RAL, T22/608, XI/109/32/3/38B, same to same, July 21.

44 RAL, XI/109J/J/34, James, Paris, to Nathan and his nephews, London, July 19, 1834; same to same, July 22; July 23; July 24; RAL, XI/109J/J/34A, July 26; RAL, XI/109J/J/34B, July 26; RAL, XI/109J/J/34, July 30; Aug. 3; Aug. 11; RAL, XI/109/32/4/26, deRF to Toreno, July 22; RAL, XI/109/32/1/72, Lionel to his parents, July 29; RAL, T22/614, XI/109/32/3/38B, same to same, Aug. 12; RAL, XI/109J/J/34/A, James to Nathan, Aug. 13; RAL, XI/109J/J/34/B, same to same, Aug. 13; RAL, XI/109J/J/34, same to same, Aug. 14; Aug. 16; Aug. 18; Aug. 19; Aug. 20; Aug. 23; RAL, T22/615, XI/109/32/3/38B, Lionel to his parents, Aug. 14; RAL, XI/109/32/4/33, deRF to E. Costil, Madrid, Aug. 16.

45 RAL, XI/109J/J/34, James, Paris, to Nathan and his nephews, London, July 11, 1834.

46 RAL, XI/109J/J/34, James, Paris, to Nathan and his nephews, London, May 25, 1834; same to same, June 4. Costil, the agent sent in July, seems not to have been a success, though he could hardly have arrived in Spain at a less propitious time.

47 RAL, XI/109/32/1/82, Lionel, Madrid, to his parents and uncles, Sept. 30, 1834; RAL, XI/109/32/1/83, same to same, Oct. 1; RAL, XI/109/32/1/84, Oct. 2; RAL, XI/109/32/1/85, undated, Oct. 3; RAL, T7/4, Lionel to his mother, Oct. 3; RAL, XI/109/32/4/49, Lionel to his parents and uncles, Oct. 13. Cf. Bullen and Strong (eds.), *Palmerston: Correspondence with Villiers*, p. 216.

48 RAL, XI/109/32/2/11, James, Paris, to Lionel, Madrid, Oct. 22, 1834; RAL, XI/109/32/1/87, Lionel to his uncles and parents, Dec. 2; RAL, XI/109J/J/34, James to Nathan, Dec. 20; RAL, XI/109/31a/1/62, Anselm, Frankfurt, to his uncle, Paris, Dec. 29, 1834.

49 RAL, XI/109/33/4/4, Agreement signed by Toreno, Jan. 6, 1835; RAL, XI/109J/J/35, James, Paris, to Nathan, London, March 4; RAL, XI/109/33/1/7, Lionel, Madrid, to his uncles and parents, March 21.

50 RAL, XI/109/31a/1/31, Lionel, Paris, to his parents, March 11, 1834.

51 RAL, XI/109/32/4/50, Lionel, Madrid, to his uncles and parents, Dec. 13, 1834; RAL, T22/678, XI/109/33/1/2, Lionel, Madrid, to Anthony, Paris, Feb. 15, 1835; RAL, T22/678, XI/109/33/1/2, Lionel to his uncles and parents, May 25; RAL, XI/109J/J/35, James to Nathan and Nat, Feb. 28; same to same, March 9; RAL, XI/109/33/1/9, Lionel to his uncle and parents, March 25. Cf. Fontana, *Revolucion*, pp. 59f.; Corti, *Reign*, pp. 120f. In fact, the contract increased the Rothschilds' share of the business from a minority to a majority shareholding; they remained formally in partnership, as they had been since 1830, with Inigo.

52 RAL, XI/109/33/1/20, Lionel, Madrid, to his uncles and parents, June 6, 1835. Cf. Corti, *Reign*, p. 122; Fontana, *Revolucion*, pp. 59f.

53 Martin, *Minas de Almadén*, p. 260.

54 AN, 132 AQ 4311/1M13, NMR to deRF, May 4, 1847.

55 RAL, XI/109J/J/36, James, Paris, to Nathan, Anthony and his children, London, April 11, 1836; RAL, XI/109J/J/38, James to his nephews, April 18, 1838.

56 See e.g. RAL, XI/109J/J/36, James, Paris, to Nathan, London, Feb. 28, 1836; same to same, March 2.

57 Heine, *Sämtliche Schriften*, vol. VI/I, pp. 144, 146; trans. Draper, *Heine*, pp. 666ff.

58 RAL, XI/109/33/1/16, Lionel, Madrid, to his uncles and parents, April 13, 1835; RAL, XI/109J/J/35A, James, Paris, to Nathan and his nephew, April 27; RAL, XI/109J/J/35B, same to same, April 27; RAL, XI/109J/J/35, April 30; May 2; May 9.

59 RAL, XI/109/33/1/43, Anthony, Paris, to his parents, London, June 1, 1835.

60 RAL, RFamC/1/157, Hannah, Paris, to Nathan, London, undated, *c.* Oct. 1833; RAL, XI/109J/J/33, James and Betty, Boulogne, to Nathan, London, Oct. 7; James, Paris to Nathan, Nov. 5; same to same, Nov. 9; RAL, XI/109/30/1/48, Lionel, Paris, to his parents, Nov. 12.

61 RAL, T6/127, James Robertson to Nathan, June 13, 1835; RAL, T22/715, XI/109/33/1/21, Lionel, Madrid, to Anthony, Paris, June 13; RAL, T22/717, XI/109/33/1/22, Lionel, Arunjez, to his uncles and parents, June 29. Cf. Corti, *Reign*, p. 124.

62 Corti, *Reign*, pp. 125–9, 139.

63 *Ibid.*, pp. 131–5.

64 *Ibid.*, pp. 136f.

65 RAL, XI/109J/J/40B, James, Paris, to his nephews, Feb. 28, 1840.

66 Corti, *Reign*, pp. 168f.

67 Corti, *Reign*, pp. 138f.; Bullen and Strong (eds), *Palmerston: Correspondence with Villiers*, p. 316. According to Villiers, Mendizábal hoped for a "stroke of generosity" from "the Leviathan" (meaning

Nathan). The diplomatic correspondence shows how little contact there was between the Rothschilds and Palmerston at this time.

68 Corti, *Reign*, pp. 139–43; Gille, *Maison Rothschild*, vol I, p. 251f.; Bullen and Strong (eds), *Palmerston: Correspondence with Villiers*, pp. 352–8, 294f., 434, 448, 554.

69 RAL, XI/109J/J/36, James, Paris, to Nathan, London, Feb. 16, 1836; same to same, Feb. 17; Feb. 18; Feb. 20; Feb. 22; Feb. 23; Feb. 27; March 5; March 9; March 10; March 26; March 27; March 28; March 29; April 18; April 21; April 26; May 5; May 21; May 25; May 28; May 29. Compare the views of Apponyi and Disraeli: Apponyi, *Vingt-cinq ans*, vol. III, pp. 235, 253; Gunn *et al.* (eds), *Disraeli letters*, vol. I, no. 496.

70 RAL, XI/109J/J/36, James, Paris, to Nathan, London, May 30, 1836; James and Nathan, Paris, to Nat, London, June 1; James and Nathan, Brussels, to Nat and Anthony, June 6; James, Frankfurt, to Anthony and Nat, June 18; same to same, June 19; James to Anthony and Nat, June 21; James and Salomon, Frankfurt, to Anthony, July 1; RAL, XI/109J/J/36A, James to Anthony, July 8; RAL, XI/109J/J/36B, James and Salomon to Nat, July 8; RAL, XI/109J/J/36B, James to Anthony, July 9; RAL, RFamC/4/142, Lionel to Anthony and Nat, July 18.

71 RAL, XI/109J/J/36, James and Salomon, Paris, to their nephews, London, Sept. 14, 1836; James to his nephews, Sept. 18; same to same, Oct. 26; Nov. 2; Nov. 23; Dec. 5; Dec. 9; Dec. 13.

72 Corti, *Reign*, pp. 147–52, 156ff., 169–74. The title was bestowed on Lionel in 1837, despite Hummelauer's best efforts: RAL, XI/109J/J/37, James, Paris, to Lionel, London, Dec. 27, 1837.

73 RAL, XI/109J/J/36B, James, Paris, to Nathan and his nephews, March 19, 1836. Cf. RAL, XI/109J/J/36, same to same, March 17; March 18; March 22; March 24; March 30; April 4; April 9; April 10.

74 RAL, RFamC/4/133, Lionel, Frankfurt, to James, Kreuznach, July 12, 1836; RAL, XI/109J/J/36, James, Kreuznach, to his brothers and nephew, July 14; James to Nat and Anthony, Aug. 17; RAL, RFamC/4/146, Lionel to Anthony and Nat, July 22. "Every person here laughs at their want of decision and at their not knowing which cause they ought to take up. Why do they not interfere regularly and send 50,000 men; they would finish the war in three months, or why do not they propose to send some French Generals?" wrote Lionel angrily. "It is disgusting to see two powers like England and France so afraid of the despotic Government"—meaning Metternich. See also RAL, XI/109J/J/36, James, Paris, to his nephews, London, Sept. 11; same to same, Dec. 25. Palmerston made a similar point in arguing against a guaranteed loan of the sort urged by Villiers: "Men would say that if money was the chief want of the Queenites a loan might set them on their legs, but that the Rothschilds will not contract to supply military skill and willingness to fight and honesty of purpose, and common sense, and without all these things the loans would only enrich a few more generals." Cf. Webster, *Foreign policy of Palmerston*, vol. I, pp. 425, 460.

75 RAL, XI/109J/J/37, James, Paris, to his nephews, April 8, 1837; same to same, April 9; April 10; April 11.

76 RAL, XI/109J/J/36, James, Paris, to Nathan and his nephews, London, April 12, 1836; same to same, April 30; James to Nat, June 4; James, Frankfurt, to Anthony, Paris, June 14; RAL, RFamC/4/140, Lionel, Frankfurt, to Anthony and Nat, July 17. Cf. Corti, *Reign*, pp. 143–7; Martin, *Minas de Almadén*, ch. 4; Gille, *Maison Rothschild*, vol. I, pp. 252f. See also RAL, XI/109J/J/36, James to his nephews, March 22, 1837 [wrongly dated 1836]; RAL, XI/101/0–4/7, James to NMR, March 22.

77 RAL, XI/109J/J/36, James, Paris, to his nephews, London, Sept. 17, 1836; same to same, Dec. 24; Jan. 1, 1837 [wrongly dated 1836]; Jan. 3; Jan. 4; RAL, XI/101/0–2/1, deRF to Weisweiller, Jan. 2; RAL, XI/109J/J/37, James to his nephews, Jan. 10; same to same, Jan. 21; Jan. 22; Jan. 24; Jan. 31; Feb. 5; RAL, XI/101/0–2/9, Mendizábal, Madrid, to deRF and NMR, Jan. 18; RAL, XI/101/0–2/10, deRF to Weisweiller, Madrid, Jan. 25; RAL, XI/101/0–2/11, same to same, Jan. 26; RAL, XI/101/0–4/10, March 22. See also James to his nephews, Sept. 30.

78 RAL, XI/101/0–5/2, James to NMR, April 10, 1837; Corti, *Reign*, p. 157.

79 RAL, XI/109J/J/37, James, Paris, to his nephews, London, April 19, 1837; Salomon and James to their nephews, May 15; James to his nephews, May 20; same to same, May 24; RAL, T25/106/0/4, James to C. Poulett Thomson, Board of Trade, London, May 16; RAL, XI/101/0–6/1, deRF to Weisweiller, May 22; RAL, XI/109J/J/37, Salomon and James to their nephews, July 13; James to his nephews, July 24; same to same, July 25; July 31; Aug. 26; Aug. 30; Sept. 4; Sept. 6. Cf. Corti, *Reign*, p. 158.

80 RAL, XI/109J/J/37, James, Paris, to his nephews, London, Oct. 26, 1837; same to same, Oct. 28; Oct. 31; Nov. 2; Nov. 3; Nov. 6; Nov. 7; RAL, XI/101/0–1/2, deRF and NMR to Weisweiller, Madrid, Nov. 6; *The Times*, Nov. 8, 1837, p. 2. Cf. Corti, *Reign*, p. 161.

81 RAL, XI/109J/J/37, James, Paris, to his nephews, Sept. 9, 1837; same to same, Sept. 11; Sept. 13; Salomon to his nephews, Sept. 15; James to his nephews, Nov. 2; same to same, Nov. 7; Nov. 8; Nov. 25; Nov. 26; Dec. 10; RAL, XI/101/1–21/7, Anselm, Paris, to his cousins, London, Feb. 7, 1838; RAL, XI/109J/J/38, James to his nephews, Feb. 14; same to same, Feb. 17; March 4; March 7; RAL, XI/109J/J/38A, March 27. The advances which Gaviria expected them to pay grew steadily, reviving Austrian suspicions of Rothschild backing for Madrid. Weisweiller's deal with Gaviria was one of the principal Rothschild grievances against him, but they had by now become dependent on their agent and could see no way to replace him.

82 RAL, XI/109/36/2/4, Anselm, Frankfurt, to James and Anthony, Paris, Jan. 1, 1838; RAL, XI/101/1–14/3, Anthony, Paris, to his brothers, London, Jan. 29; RAL, XI/109J/J/38, James, Paris, to his nephews, Feb. 1; same to same, Feb. 3; Feb. 6; RAL, XI/101/1–15/1, Anselm, Paris, to his cousins, London, March 1; RAL, XI/109J/J/38, James to his nephews, March 10; same to same, March 14; March 15; RAL, XI/101/1–15/8, Anthony and Anselm to Lionel, March 22; RAL, XI/101/1–15/7, same to same, March 23; RAL, XI/101/1–15/16, Anthony to his brothers, March 24; RAL, XI/109J/J/38, James to his nephews, March 26; same to same, March 28; March 31; April 1; April 2; April 3; April 4; April 7; April 10; April 11; April 12; April 14; April 17; April 18; April 19; April 28; April 30; May 2; May 5; May 6; May 9; May 19; May 20; May 21; May 26; June 3; June 12; June 13; July 9; July 11; July 14; July 15; July 18; July 19; RAL, XI/101/1–15/18, Anthony to his brothers, March 27; RAL, XI/101/1–15/19, same to same, March 31; RAL, XI/101/1–15/22, April 1; RAL, XI/101/1–22/1, Anselm to his cousins, March 7; RAL, XI/101/1–22/2a, same to same, April 10; RAL, XI/101/1–22/2b, April 11; RAL, XI/101/1–16/17, Anthony to his brothers, undated, May; RAL, XI/101/23/2, Anselm to his cousins, May 2; RAL, XI/109/36/2/2, Anselm, Frankfurt, to James and Anthony, May 25; RAL, XI/101/1–17/3, Anthony to his brothers, undated, June; RAL, XI/101/1–17/5, same to same, undated, June; RAL, XI/101/1–17/1, June 2; RAL, XI/101/1–17/9, June 7; RAL, XI/101/1–17/12, June 10; RAL, XI/101/1–17/18, June 15; RAL, XI/101/1–18(July)/16, July 2; RAL, XI/101/1–18(July)/17, July 7; RAL, XI/109J/J/38, Salomon and James, Paris, to Carl and their nephews, London, July 21; James to Carl, July 22; RAL, XI/101/1–18(August)/10, Anthony to his brothers, Aug. 2; AN, 132 AQ 5901, James, St Sauveur, to his brothers and nephews, Aug. 2; RAL, XI/101/1–18(August)/8, Anthony to his brothers, Aug. 3; RAL, XI/101/1–18(August)/7, same to same, Aug. 5; AN, 132 AQ 5901, James, St Sauveur, to Weisweiller, Aug. 5; RAL, XI/101/1–18(August)/14, Anthony to his brothers, Aug. 13; RAL, XI/109J/J/38, James, St Sauveur, to Salomon and his nephews, Aug. 23; same, Eaux Bonner, to same, Aug. 27; Aug. 28; Aug. 29; RAL, XI/101/1–18(September)/7, Anthony to his brothers and Anselm, London, Sept. 12; RAL, XI/109J/J/38, James, Aix, to Salomon and his nephews, London, Sept. 19; James, Marseille, to his brothers and nephews, Sept. 30; James, Florence, to his brothers and nephews, Oct. 4; James, Nice, to Salomon and Anthony, Oct. 7; James, Genoa, to Salomon and Anthony, Oct. 16; James, Paris, to Lionel and Nat, London, Nov. 11; James, Naples, to Salomon and his nephews, Dec. 15. For the comments of somewhat baffled diplomatic observers, see Corti, *Reign*, p. 162; Gille, *Maison Rothschild*, vol. I, pp. 254–7.

83 For a useful integrated statement of Spanish business, see AN, 132 AQ 5401, NMR to deRF, Nov. 18, 1839.

84 AN, 132 AQ 5401, NMR to deRF, Jan. 29, 1839; same to same, Feb. 1; same to same, March 1; July 15; RAL, XI/109J/J/39, James, Naples, to his brothers and nephews, April 2; same to same, April 5; April 6; May 12; RAL, XI/101/2–10/3, deRF to NMR, July 17; RAL, XI/109J/J/39, James, Kissingen, to his nephews, Aug. 14; RAL, XI/109J/J/39B, same to same, Aug. 21; RAL, XI/101/2–7/16, James, Frankfurt, to Anthony, Paris, Sept. 2; RAL, XI/109J/J/39, same to same, Sept. 11; Sept. 13; James to his nephews, London, Sept. 15; Amschel and James to Anthony and Anselm, Sept. 22; RAL, XI/101/2–10/19, Anthony to NMR, Sept. 14; RAL, XI/109J/J/39, James to his nephews, Oct. 28; same to same, Nov. 23; Nov. 28; Dec. 21; RAL, XI/101/—10/47, deRF to NMR, Nov. 20. Ironically, their old enemy Toreno had now been recruited as an ally, in return for a "gift" of 50,000 francs.

85 RAL, XI/109J/J/38, James, Paris, to his nephews, London, March 3, 1838; RAL, XI/101/1–15/4, Anthony, Paris, to his brothers, London, March 5; RAL, XI/109J/J/38, James to his nephews, March 5; same to same, March 6.

86 RAL, XI/109J/J/40, James, Paris, to his nephews, Jan. 6, 1840; RAL, XI/109J/J/40B, same to same, Feb. 1; RAL, XI/109J/J/40A, Feb. 3; RAL, XI/109J/J/40, Feb. 12; RAL, XI/109J/J/40A, Feb. 23; RAL, XI/109J/J/40B, Feb. 26; RAL, XI/109J/J/40, Feb. 29; James and Salomon to their nephews, March 25;

James to his nephews, March 29; RAL, XI/101/3,4,5–3/10, deRF to NMR, Feb. 26, 1841; RAL, XI/101/3,4,5–3/64, deRF to NMR, April 21; RAL, XI/109J/J/41, James to his nephews, April 14; same to same, April 28; May 12; May 15; RAL, XI/101/3,4,5–5/30, deRF to NMR, July 16; RAL, XI/101/3,4,5–5/33, James, Gastein, to his nephews, Aug. 11; RAL, XI/109J/J/42A, James, Paris, to his nephews and Hannah, Feb. 22, 1842; RAL, XI/109J/J/42A, James to his nephews, March 30; RAL, XI/109/43a/2/83, Anthony, Paris, to his brothers, undated, late 1842; RAL, XI/109/43a/2/128, Nat to his brothers, Dec. 24; RAL, T18/88, XI/109/45/6/121, same to same, undated, 1843; RAL, T18/90, XI/109/ 45/6/122, undated 1843; RAL, XI/109/45b/123, undated, 1843; RAL, XI/109/45b/6/26, April 1; RAL, T18/118, XI/109/45/6/40, May 16; RAL, XI/109/45b/6/50, June 8; RAL, T18/130, XI/10940/6/51, June 9; RAL, XI/109/45b/6/57, June 25; RAL, XI/109/45b/6/65, July 18; RAL, XI/109/45b/6/70, Aug. 3; RAL, XI/109/45b/6/89, Dec. 2; RAL, XI/109/46/1/184, undated 1844; RAL, XI/109/47/1/99, April 29; RAL, XI/109/47/1/104, May 25; RAL, XI/109/47/1/107, May 30; RAL, T18/363, XI/109/47/1/109, June 1; RAL, XI/109/47/1/133, undated, *c.* June; RAL, XI/109/47/1/160, undated, *c.* July; RAL, T18/545, XI/109/48/1/40, Aug. 14; RAL, XI/109J/J/45, James to his nephews, Feb. 12, 1845; same to same, March 22; March 24; March 30; AN, 132 AQ 5407/1M9, NMR to deRF, July 22; RAL, XI/109/58b/2/103, Anthony to his brothers, undated, late 1846. See also Corti, *Reign,* pp. 243f.; Gille, *Maison Rothschild,* vol. I, pp. 325–30; Cameron, *France and Europe,* p. 90.

87 Haus-, Hof- und Staatsarchiv Wien, Vertrag des Hofkammerpräsidenten Freiherrn von Kübeck, October 20, 1843; Corti, *Reign,* pp. 231f. The import of Cuban cigars had previously been prohibited, but the Rothschilds made them available to the government monopoly at prices which allowed an irresistible profit on sales to the public. For details of a similar deal with Piedmont–Sardinia, see AN, 132 AQ 5403/1M5, NMR to dRF, Jan. 17, 1843; same to same, March 7. See also AN, 132 AQ 5408/1M10, Hanau to NMR, Nov. 3, 1845.

88 RAL, XI/109J/J/42, James, Paris, to his nephews, Feb. 23, 1842; RAL, XI/109J/J/42A, same to same, March 16; RAL, XI/109/42a/2/24, Nat, Paris, to his brothers, March 17; RAL, XI/109J/J/42, James to his nephews and Alphonse, April 12; same to same, April 16; RAL, XI/10/43a/2/145, Nat to his brothers, undated, late 1842; RAL, T18/143, XI/109/45/6/135, same to same, undated, 1843; RAL, T18/185, XI/109/45/6/147, undated, 1843; RAL, XI/109/45b/6/11, Feb. 12; RAL, XI/109/45b/6/37, April 13; RAL, XI/109/45b/6/140, June 30; RAL, XI/109/45b/6/68, July 20; RAL, T18/215, XI/109/46/1/52, Jan. 10, 1844; RAL, XI/109/47/1/95, April 14; RAL, T6/1200, B. Weisweiller, Madrid, to NMR, June 1, 1846; RAL, XI/109/57/4/51, Nat to his brothers, undated, *c.* July 1846; RAL, XI/109/57/1/82, Anthony to his brothers, July 12; RAL, XI/109/57/3/66, same to same, Sept. 16; RAL, XI/109J/J/46, James to Lionel, Sept. 15; RAL, XI/109/58b/2/29, Nat to his brothers, undated, late 1846; RAL, XI/109/58b/2/37, same to same, undated, late 1846; RAL, XI/109/58b/2/47, undated, late 1846; RAL, XI/109/58b/2/65, undated, late 1846. Cf. Guizot and Lieven, *Lettres,* vol. III, p. 255; Corti, *Reign,* pp. 244f.; Bullen, *Entente Cordiale,* p. 194.

89 RAL, T7/53, Lionel to Lord Palmerston, July 22, 1846; RAL, XI/109/57/3/66, Anthony, Paris, to his brothers, London, Sept. 16; RAL, T6/225, Spanish Bondholders' Association to NMR, March 4, 1847.

90 RAL, T6/185, Weisweiller, Madrid, to deRF, undated, *c.* Oct. 1846. See also RAL, T6/184, Weisweiller, Madrid, to NMR and deRF, March 7, 1847.

91 RAL, XI/109/58b/2/103, Anthony, Paris, to his brothers, undated, *c.* 1846; RAL, XI/109J/J/46, James, Paris, to his nephews, London, Oct. 27.

92 AN, 132 AQ 5404/1M6, NMR to deRF, May 25, 1843; AN, 132 AQ 5407/1M9, Lionel Davidson, Mexico, to NMR, April 20, 1845; same to same, June 20.

93 AN, 132 AQ 5411/1M13, NMR to deRF, March 5, 1847; RAL, XI/109J/J/47, James, Paris, to his nephews, London, March 6.

94 RAL, T6/185, Weisweiller, Madrid, to NMR, deRF, March 8, 1847; RAL, T6/189, same to same, March 15; RAL, T6/200, deRF to Weisweiller, March 16; RAL, XI/109J/J/47, James, Paris, to his nephews, London, March 31; RAL, XI/109/61/2/46, Nat, Paris, to his brothers, London, undated, *c.* April; RAL, XI/109/61/2/49, same to same, undated, *c.* April.

95 RAL, XI/109J/J/47, James, Paris, to his nephews, London, April 28, 1847; same to same, May 18; May 22; RAL, T7/115, Anselm, Frankfurt, to James, Paris, May 23; AN, 132 AQ 5411/1M13, NMR to deRF, June 20; RAL, XI/109/63/2/52, Nat to his brothers, undated, *c.* July; RAL, XI/109/63/2/86, same to same, undated, *c.* July; RAL, XI/109/63/1/174, Sept. 27; AN, 132 AQ 5412/1M14, NMR to deRF, Nov. 29.

96   Carosso, *Investment banking*, pp. 9f.; Kynaston, *City*, vol. I, pp. 94f. Barings had the advantage of an
      American-born partner in Joshua Bates and a reliable agent in Thomas Wren Ward of the bankers
      Prime, Ward & King. Typically, they were able to exclude the Rothschilds from a major loan issued by
      the state of Louisiana in 1832.

97   Hofstadter, *Age of reform*, pp. 75ff.

98   RAL, XI/109/21/1/28, Lionel, Paris, to his parents, London, June 25, 1831 ("It will be a good thing if
      we can come by this manner into the American connexion"); RAL, XI/109J/J/31, James, Paris, to
      Nathan, London, June 25; RAL, XI/109J/J/34B, James to Nathan and Anthony, March 29, 1834;
      RAL, XI/109J/J/36, James to Nathan and Lionel, March 21, 1836; RAL, XI/101/file 3 letter 1, James
      to his nephews, Feb. 3, 1837. Cf. Gille, *Maison Rothschild*, vol. I, p. 405; Davis, *English Rothschilds*, pp.
      130f.; Ziegler, *Sixth great power*, pp. 146f., 150. Hence the portrait of President Andrew Jackson which
      can still be seen at New Court.

99   See e.g. RAL, RFamC/4/131, Lionel, Frankfurt, to Anthony and Nat, July 11, 1836.

100   RAL, XI/109J/J/34, James, Paris, to Nathan, London, Aug. 16, 1834; RAL, RFamC/4/126, Lionel,
      Frankfurt, to Anthony and Nat, July 3, 1836; RAL, XI/109J/J/36, James, Kreuznach, to Haas and Mar-
      tini, Paris, Aug. 15; RAL, XI/109J/J/36, James and Salomon, Paris, to their nephews, London, Sept. 14;
      James to his nephews, Nov. 23; same to same, Dec. 14; Dec. 15. Cf. Gille, *Maison Rothschild*, vol. I, pp.
      283–7, 402–5. As early as November 1835 Rothschild holdings of American securities were put at £5
      million, though this was probably a substantial overestimate. When the banking crisis broke out in
      March 1835, they were owed between £80,000 and £112,000 by American houses.

101   RAL, XI/109J/J/37, James, Paris, to his nephews, London, March 1, 1837; same to same, March 4;
      March 6; March 8; March 21; March 23; April 18.

102   Katz, *Belmont*, pp. 4ff.

103   Glanz, "Rothschild legend," p. 19.

104   In fact, the Rothschilds pursued these remaining bad debts tenaciously: see e.g. RAL, XI/101/0–1/39,
      deRF to NMR, Nov. 22, 1837; RAL, XI/109J/J/38, James, Paris, to his nephews, London, April 8,
      1838; same to same, April 28.

105   RAL, XI/109J/J/37, James, Paris, to his nephews, London, March 28, 1837; RAL, XI/101/0–7/1, same
      to same, April 26; RAL, XI/109J/J/37, Salomon and James to their nephews and Anselm, April 23;
      RAL, XI/ 101/0–7/3, same to same, June 15.

106   RAL, XI/109J/J/37, James, Paris, to his nephews, London, April 22, 1837.

107   RAL, XI/109J/J/37, James, Paris, to his nephews, London, April 24, 1837; same to same, April 26.

108   RAL, XI/109J/J/37, James, Paris, to his nephews, London, May 25, 1837.

109   RAL, XI/109J/J/37, James, Paris, to his nephews, London, May 27, 1837; same to same, May 29; May
      31; June 12.

110   For attempts to send Mayer, see RAL, XI/109J/J/41, James, Salomon and Anselm, Gastein, to
      Nat, Paris, Aug. 17, 1841; James, Paris, to Lionel, Oct. 2; RAL, T25/104/1/6/144, Anthony, Paris,
      to his brothers, undated, 1841. For press rumours on the subject, see Glanz, "Rothschild legend,"
      p. 5.

111   RAL, XI/109J/J/37, James, Paris, to his nephews, London, May 25, 1837.

112   RAL, XI/101/0–7/3, James and Salomon, Paris, to their nephews, June 15, 1837; RAL, XI/109J/J/37,
      James, Paris, to his nephews, London, Sept. 13.

113   RAL, XI/109J/J/37, James, Paris, to his nephews, London, July 16, 1837.

114   RAL, XI/101/0–7/8, deRF to NMR, July 19, 1837; RAL, XI/101/0–1/11, deRF to Belmont, New
      York, Sept. 7; RAL, XI/101/0–1/39, deRF to NMR, Nov. 22; RAL, XI/101/0–15/5, deRF to Belmont,
      New York, Dec. 6; RAL, XI/101/0–15/2, same to same Dec. 31.

115   RAL, XI/109J/J/38, James, Paris, to his nephews, London, March 10, 1838; same to same, April 30.

116   AN, 132 AQ 5406/1M8, NMR to deRF, Aug. 6, 1844.

117   AN, 132 AQ 5406/1M8, NMR to deRF, Nov. 27, 1844.

118   RAL, XI/101/1–18(August)/18, Anthony, Paris, to his brothers, London, August 8, 1838.

119   RAL, XI/109J/J/38, James, Florence, to Salomon and Anthony, Paris, Oct. 2, 1838; same, Nice, to
      same, Oct. 7. See also RAL, XI/109J/J/39A, James, Naples, to his brothers and nephews, April 2, 1839.

120   RAL, T25/104/0/128, Nat, Paris, to his brothers, London, Nov. 20, 1840.

121   RAL, T24/157, X/109/52/90, Nat, Paris, to his brothers, London, undated, 1842.

122   RAL, XI/109J/J/41A, James, Paris, to his nephews, May 5, 1841.

123   RAL, T23/376, XI/109/42/3/88, Anselm, Frankfurt, to James and Nat, Paris, June 28, 1842.

124   RAL, T23/108, XI/109/37/2/1, Lionel Davidson, New York, to Nat, Paris, undated, 1839; RAL,

T17/126, XI/109/37/2/9, same to same, Feb. 24. See also RAL, XI/109/46/1/72, Nat, Paris, to his brothers, Feb. 19, 1844. In fact, Davidson ended up acting as the firm's West Coast agent: there is a mountain in Nevada named after him.

125 RAL, XI/109J/J/36, James, Paris, to Nathan and Nat, London, May 12, 1836; RAL, XI/109J/J/37, James to his nephews, Jan. 16, 1837; same to same, Jan. 23; April 1. Cf. Ziegler, *Sixth great power*, pp. 146f., 150.

126 RAL, XI/109J/J/37, James, Paris, to his nephews, London, May 27, 1837; same to same, May 31; June 1; July 22; Sept. 5; Sept. 15; Nov. 6; Nov. 13; Nov. 20; RAL, XI/109J/J/38, James, St Sauveur, to Salomon and their nephews, Aug. 31, 1838.

127 RAL, XI/109J/J/37, James, Paris, to his nephews, London, Oct. 6, 1837; RAL, XI/101/1–13/9, Nat, Paris, to Lionel, London, undated, Jan.; RAL, XI/109J/J/38, James to his nephews, Feb. 18, 1838; RAL, XI/101/1–15/12, Anthony, Paris, to his brothers, London, March 15; RAL, XI/109J/J/38, James to his nephews, March 19; RAL, T6/136, J. Bullock, New York, Secretary of the State of Kentucky, to NMR, May 11; AN, 132 AQ 5400, NMR to deRF, May 25; RAL, T6/137, J. D. Beers, New York, to NMR, July 7; RAL, XI/109J/J/38, James to Carl, July 22.

128 RAL, XI/109/36/1/19, Nat, Paris, to Lionel, London, Oct. 10, 1838; AN, 132 AQ 5400, NMR to deRF, Nov. 30; same to same. Dec. 7; RAL, XI/109J/J/38, James to his nephews, Dec. 27; AN, 132 AQ 5401, NMR to Benjamin Curtis, Jan. 2, 1839; NMR to deRF, Jan 2; same to same, Jan. 15; Jan. 30; Feb. 6; March 19; RAL, XI/101/2–9/22, deRF to NMR, March 19; AN, 132 AQ 5401, NMR to deRF, March 25; same to same, April 8; May 10; June 4; June 11; Aug. 29; RAL, XI/109J/J/39, James, Kissingen, to his nephews, London, Aug. 23.

129 Hammond, *Banks and politics*, pp. 504f.

130 RAL, XI/109J/J/39A, James, Kissingen, to his nephews, Aug. 16, 1839; same to same, Sept. 1; Sept. 15; RAL, XI/101/2–10/21, Anthony, Paris, to NMR, Sept. 17; RAL, XI/101/2–10/20, deRF to Jaudon, Sept. 17; RAL, 101/2–10/22, Schaumburg to NMR, Sept. 18; RAL, XI/101/2–10/23, Anthony to his brothers, Sept. 21; RAL, XI/101/2–10/26, Moulton, New York, to NMR, Oct. 4; RAL, XI/109J/J/39, James, Paris, to his nephews, Nov. 6; same to same, Nov. 8; Nov. 9; Nov. 13; Nov. 15; RAL, XI/101/2–10/40, deRF to NMR, Nov. 15; RAL, XI/101/2–10/55, Jaudon to deRF, Nov. 21; RAL, XI/109J/J/39, James to his nephews, Nov. 21, same to same, Nov. 23; RAL, XI/101/2–10/56, Nov. 23; RAL, XI/101/2–10/53, deRF to Jaudon, Nov. 23; RAL, XI/109J/J/39, James to his nephews, Nov. 25; same to same, Nov. 27; RAL, XI/109J/J/39, deRF to NMR, Nov. 28; RAL, XI/101/2–10/61, James to his nephews, Nov. 29; RAL, XI/109J/J/39, same to same, Nov. 30; AN, 132 AQ 5434/1M39, Lionel to James and Anselm, Dec. 1; RAL, XI/101/2–10/64, Hottinguer, Paris, to deRF, Dec. 4; RAL, XI/109J/J/39, James to his nephews, Dec. 4; same to same, Dec. 5; Dec. 7; Dec. 8; Dec. 9; AN, 132 AQ 5434/1M39, Nat, London, to James and Anselm, Dec. 13; RAL, XI/101/2–10/67, deRF to NMR, Dec. 16; RAL, XI/109J/J/39B, James to his nephews, Dec. 21; same to same, Dec. 22; AN, 132 AQ 5434/1M39, Nat to James and Anselm, Dec. 23; AN, 132 AQ 5401, NMR to deRF, Dec. 23; AN, 132 AQ 5434/1M39, Mayer, London, to James and Anselm, Dec. 27; RAL, XI/109J/J/39, James to his nephews, Dec. 28; same to same, Dec. 29; same to same, Dec. 30; AN, 132 AQ 5434/1M39, Lionel to James, Anselm and Anthony, Dec. 29. Cf. Hammond, *Banks and politics*, pp. 508ff.; Ziegler, *Sixth great power*, pp. 146f., 150; Gille, *Maison Rothschild*, vol. I, pp. 291–5; Davis, *English Rothschilds*, pp. 130f.

131 AN, 132 AQ 5434/1M39, Lionel, London, to James, Anselm and Anthony, Paris, Dec. 29, 1839.

132 AN, 132 AQ 5434/1M39, Nat, London, to James, Anselm and Anthony, Paris, Dec. 30, 1839.

133 RAL, XI/109J/J/40, James, Paris, to his nephews, London, Jan. 23, 1840; same to same, Feb. 3; James and Salomon to their nephews, March 7; James to his nephews, March 22; AN, 132 AQ 5402, NMR to deRF, March 4; AN, 132 AQ 5402, NMR to deRF, April 14; same to same, May 1; May 26; July 24; Aug. 13; Aug. 18; Sept. 15; NMR to Nat, Nov. 10; NMR to deRF, Nov. 17.

134 RAL, T25/104/1/2/37, Anselm, Frankfurt, to his cousins, London, March 21, 1841; RAL, XI/101/3,4,5–3/47, deRF to NMR, April 5; RAL, XI/109J/J/41, James, Gastein, to Nat and Lionel, July 24; RAL, XI/109J/J/41, James, Salomon and Anselm, Gastein, to Nat, Paris, Aug. 17; James, Paris, to his nephews, London, Dec. 25; RAL, T23/415, XI/109/43/2/136, Nat, Paris, to Lionel and Mayer, London, undated, 1842; AN, 132 AQ 5403/1M4, NMR to deRF, July 19; same to same, Sept. 23.

135 Ziegler, *Sixth great power*, p. 150. Cf. RAL, XI/109J/J/42A, James, Paris, to his nephews, Jan. 2, 1842; RAL, T6/167, US Treasury Department to NMR, March 14, 1843.

136 RAL, XI/101/3,4,5–3/34, James, Paris, to his nephews, London, March 24, 1841; RAL, XI/101/3,4,5–5/2, deRF to NMR, May 5; RAL, XI/109J/J/41, James, Paris, to his nephews, London, Nov. 30; RAL, XI/109J/J/42, same to same, Jan. 19, 1842.

137 RAL, XI/109/43a/2/35, Anthony, Paris, to his brothers, undated, c. June 1842; RAL, XI/109/43a/2/100, Nat, Paris, to his brothers, London, July 1.

138 RAL, XI/109J/J/36A, James, Frankfurt, to Nat, London, July 9, 1836; RAL, RFamC/4/137, Lionel, Frankfurt, to Anthony and Nat, July 14; RAL, RFamC/4/145, same to same, July 21.

139 Bank of England, G8 (Committee of Treasury) 28 1147/3 f. 128, Minutes of Committee, Dec. 30, 1835; Minutes, June 1, 1836; Bank of England, G8 (Committee of Treasury) 29 1148/1 f. 91, Oct. 5. See also Bank of England, G23/55 2876/4, [J. W.] Pattison, Bank of England, to NMR, Dec. 4, 1834; Bank of England, G8 (Committee of Treasury) 28 1147/3 f. 38, Minutes of the Committee, Aug. 13, 1835.

140 RAL, XI/109J/J/36, James, Kreuznach, to his nephews, Aug. 17, 1836; RAL, James, Paris, to his nephews, London, Oct. 18; same to same, Oct. 31; Nov. 12; Nov. 14; Nov. 21; Nov. 22.

141 RAL, XI/109J/J/37, James, Paris, to his nephews, London, Jan. 29, 1837.

142 RAL, XI/109J/J/37, James, Paris, to his nephews, London, July 31, 1837; same to same, Aug. 1.

143 RAL, XI/109J/J/37, James, Paris, to his nephews, London, Feb. 1, 1837; same to same, March 21.

144 RAL, XI/109J/J/37, James, Paris, to his nephews, London, Feb. 1, 1837; same to same, April 9.

145 RAL, T6/33, T. A. Curtis, Bank of England, to James, Paris, Aug. 4, 1837. Cf. RAL, XI/109J/J/37, James to his nephews, Nov. 6; same to same, Nov. 8; same to same, Nov. 20.

146 RAL, XI/109J/J/38, James, Paris, to his nephews, March 18, 1838.

147 Bank of England, G23/56 2877/1, ff. 150–52, T. A. Curtis, Bank of England, to NMR, Dec. 21, 1838; same to same, Dec. 29.

148 RAL, XI/109J/J/39, James, Heinrichsbad, to Nat, June 29, 1839. Cf. Ziegler, *Sixth great power*, p. 136.

149 RAL, T7/16, XI/103/0,1–35, Anselm, Paris, to his cousins, July 28, 1839.

150 RAL, RFamC/1/91, Hannah, Suresnes, to Lionel and Nat, London, Aug. 4, 1839.

151 RAL, XI/109J/J/39, James, Heinrichsbad, to Nat, Paris, July 29, 1839.

152 Clapham, *Bank of England*, vol. II, pp. 168f. Because the Banque could not directly lend money, the operation had to be done indirectly: Baring drew three-month bills to the value of 48 million francs on a syndicate composed of Hottinguer, Delessert, d'Eichthal and Périer and d'Argout, then discounted the bills; Baring then made the cash available to the Bank.

153 RAL, XI/109J/J/39, James, Kissingen, to Anthony and Anselm, Aug. 1, 1839; James, Heinrichsbad, to Amschel, Frankfurt, Aug. 2; James, Mannheim, to Amschel and Carl, Aug. 4; James, Kissingen, to his nephews, Aug. 15.

154 RAL, XI/109J/J/39, James, Kissingen, to his nephews, London, Aug. 23, 1839.

155 RAL, XI/109J/J/39, James, Paris, to Lionel, Nat and Anthony, Nov. 24, 1839; AN, 132 AQ 5434/1M39, Lionel, London, to James and Anselm, Dec. 1; RAL, XI/109J/J/39, James, Paris, to his nephews, London, Dec. 2; same to same, Dec. 5; Dec. 9.

156 Kynaston, *City*, vol. I, p. 117.

157 RAL, XI/109/43a/2/101, Nat, Paris, to his brothers, London, July 2, 1842.

FOURTEEN   *Between Retrenchment and Rearmament (1840)*

1 Bouvier, *Rothschild*, pp. 102f.; Gille, *Maison Rothschild*, vol. I, p. 487.

2 Fischer *et al.* (eds), *Sozialgeschichtliches Arbeitsbuch*, vol. I, pp. 200–204.

3 RAL, XI/109/46/2/76, Rother, Bekanntmachung, Jan. 2, 1844; RAL, XI/109/46/1/8, Anselm, Frankfurt, to his cousins, London, Jan. 10; RAL, XI/109/46/1/9, same to same, Jan. 10; RAL, XI/109/47/1/9, April 7; RAL, XI/109/47/1/29, May 7; RAL, XI/109/47/1/31, Anthony, Frankfurt, to his brothers, London, undated, c. May; RAL, XI/109/47/1/33, same to same, May 12; RAL, XI/109/47/1/38, May 15; RAL, XI/109/47/1/40, undated, c. May; RAL, XI/109/47/1/41, undated, c. May; RAL, XI/109/47/1/44, May 21; RAL, XI/109/47/1/49, undated, c. May; RAL, XI/109/47/1/69, undated, c. May; RAL, T18/340, XI/109/47/1/88, April 15; RAL, T18/333, XI/109/47/1/69, undated, c. May; RAL, XI/109/47/1/81, Lionel, London, to Anthony, undated, c. May; RAL, XI/109/47/1/37, same to same, May 15; RAL, XI/109/51a/1/201, Nat, Paris, to his brothers, Jan. 29, 1845.

4 Mitchell, *British historical statistics*, pp. 405–9.

5 RAL, XI/109/37/1/23, Salomon, Vienna, to Anselm and his nephews, April 20, 1839; RAL, XI/109J/J/39, James, Kissingen, to his nephews, London, Aug. 19; Ayer, *Century of finance*, pp. 38f.

6 Details in Buxton, *Finance*, vol. I, pp. 39–84.

7 Imlah, *Economic elements*, p. 152; Gash, *Mr Secretary Peel*, p. 616.

8 RAL, T37/186, Spottiswoode MS, Henry Goulborn, Downing Street, to Herries, Sept. 11, 1841; RAL,

T37/169, Spottiswoode MS, Herries, St Julian, to Goulborn, Sept. 17; RAL, T25/104/1/5/134, Nat, Paris, to his brothers, Sept. 23; RAL, T25/104/1/5/135, same to same, Sept. 28.

9   RAL, XI/109/45b/6/121, Nat, Paris, to his brothers, London, undated, early 1843.

10 RAL, XI/109/46/1/59, Nat, Paris, to his brothers, London, Feb. 7, 1844.

11 RAL, T18/261, XI/109/46/1/72, Nat, Paris, to his brothers, London, undated, 1844; RAL, T18/227, XI/109/46/2/53, E. Welch to NMR, Jan. 22.

12 RAL, XI/109/42a/2/21, Nat, Paris, to his brothers, undated, March 1842; RAL, XI/109/42a/2/21, same to same, undated, March; RAL, XI/109J/J/42A, James, Paris, to his nephews, London, March 13; RAL, XI/109/42a/2/25, same to same, March 19; RAL, T23/291, XI/109/42/2/13, Anselm to his cousins, March 20; RAL, T23/204, XI/109/42/2/14, same to same, March 21; RAL, XI/109/43a/2/108, Nat to Lionel, Aug. 4; RAL, T23/426, XI/109/43/1/32, Anselm, Frankfurt, to Lionel, Aug. 14; AN, 132 AQ 5403/1M4, NMR to deRF, Aug. 31.

13 Corti, *Reign*, p. 250.

14 Schremmer, "Public finance," p. 398.

15 RAL, XI/109J/J/37, James, Paris, to his nephews, London, Nov. 11, 1837; same to same, Nov. 14; Nov. 15; Nov. 16; Nov. 21; Nov. 23; Dec. 6; RAL, XI/109J/J/38, Feb. 7, 1838; Feb. 11; Feb. 20; Feb. 27; March 24; April 3; April 19; April 21; James, Genoa, to Salomon and Anthony, Paris, Oct. 16; James, Naples, to Salomon and his nephews, Nov. 22.

16 RAL, XI/109J/J/39, James, Naples, to his brothers and nephews, March 14, 1839; same to same, March 16; April 6; RAL, XI/101/2–9/26, Anselm to NMR, March 21; RAL, XI/109/37/1/18, Salomon, Vienna, to his brothers, son and nephews, March 30; RAL, XI/101/2–7/4, Amschel, Frankfurt, to his brothers, April 4.

17 RAL, XI/109/37/1/23, Salomon, Vienna, to his nephews, London, April 13, 1839.

18 RAL, XI/109J/J/41, James, Paris, to his nephews, London, June 17, 1841; James, Gastein, to Nat and Lionel, July 24; same to same, July 25; James, Paris, to his nephews, London, Aug. 8; RAL, XI/109/42a/3/93, Salomon, Vienna, to his brothers and nephews, Feb. 2; RAL, XI/109/42a3/9, Anselm, Frankfurt, to his cousins, London, Feb. 18; RAL, XI/109/42a/1/10, James, Paris, to NMR, Feb. 19; RAL, XI/109/42a/3/94, Salomon to NMR, deRF and MAR, Feb. 21; RAL, XI/109/42a/3/95, same to same, Feb. 23; RAL, XI/109/42a/3/10, Anselm, Frankfurt, to Nat, Paris, Feb. 21; RAL, XI/109/42a/3/11, Anselm to his cousins, March 2; RAL, XI/109/42a/2/25, Anselm to Nat, undated, early 1842; RAL, XI/109/42a/2/15, Nat, Paris, to his brothers, London, undated, early 1842; RAL T23/273, XI/109/42/2/16, same to same, Feb. 28; RAL, XI/109/42a/3/11, March 5; RAL, T23/285, XI/109/42/2/21, undated, early 1842; RAL, XI/109/42a/2/28, undated, early 1842; RAL, XI/109/42a/2/34, March 7; RAL, XI/109/42a/22, March 10; RAL, XI/109/42a/2/25, March 19; RAL, XI/109/42a/2/27, March 26; RAL, XI/109/42a/2/70, undated, early 1842; RAL, XI/109/42a/3/90, Carl, Naples, to Salomon, March 18; RAL, T23/299, XI/109/42/3/81, Anselm to James, March 26; RAL, XI/109J/J/42, James to his nephews, April 9; same to same, April 14; RAL, XI/109/42a/3/102, Salomon to NMR, deRF and MAR, April 18.

19 RAL, XI/109/49/2/65, Anselm, Frankfurt, to his cousins, undated, late 1844; RAL, XI/109/58b/2/64, Nat, Paris, to his brothers, London, undated, late 1846; RAL, XI/109/58b/1/75, Anselm to Lionel, Dec. 13.

20 A detailed list is provided in Berghoeffer, *Meyer Amschel*, pp. 224f.; Gille, *Maison Rothschild*, vol. I, pp. 431f.

21 The case of Baden is the best documented: RAL, XI/109/36/2/13, Anselm, Carlsruhe, to MAR, June 12, 1838; RAL, XI/109/36/2/9, same to same, July 9; RAL, XI/109/38/2/65, Blittersdorf, Carlsruhe, to Anselm, April 3, 1840; RAL, XI/109/43a/3/8, Anselm, Frankfurt, to Salomon, James and his cousins, Sept. 7, 1842; RAL, XI/109/43a/3/10, same to same, Oct. 8; RAL, XI/109/45a/1/60, Mayer Carl, Frankfurt, to his cousins, undated, 1843; RAL, XI/109/51a/2/73, Anselm to his cousins, Feb. 14, 1845; RAL, XI/109/51a/2/105, Anselm to Nat, Feb. 18. On Hesse-Cassel: RAL, T20/65, XI/109/48/2/94, Anselm, Frankfurt, to James and Nat, Sept. 13, 1844; RAL, XI/109/51b/2/10, Nat, Paris, to his brothers, undated, early 1845; HSM, Bestand 300 C 28 Nr 2, Nr 20, Hessisches Finanzministerium to Kurfürst, Jan. 1.

22 Huber, "Bayern und das Haus Rothschild," p. 12. See also Gille, *Maison Rothschild*, vol. II, pp. 47ff.

23 RAL, XI/109/52a/1/43, Anselm, Frankfurt, to his cousins, London, April 7, 1845; RAL, XI/109/52b/1/31, Anselm to Anthony, June 6; RAL, XI/109/53a/1/85, same to same, July 13; RAL, XI/109/56/3/20, June 7, 1846; RAL, T7/80, Anselm, Frankfurt, to MAR, June 7; RAL, XI/109/56/3/20, same, Carlsruhe, to same, June 7; RAL, XI/109/59b/1/30, Anselm, Frankfurt, to his

cousins, London, March 4, 1847; RAL, XI/109/59b/1/60, same to same, March 9; RAL, T7/117, Anselm, Frankfurt, to Anthony, June 8.

24 RAL, T7/77, Anselm, Frankfurt, to his father, uncle and cousins, May 12, 1846; RAL, T7/87, same to same, May 26.

25 RAL, XI/109/61/2/165, Nat, Paris, to his brothers, London, undated, c. April 1846; RAL, XI/109/57/3/129, Anselm, Frankfurt, to Lionel, London, Sept. 29; RAL, XI/109/58b/2/39, Nat, Paris, to his brothers, London, undated, late 1846; RAL, XI/109/58b/2/65, same to same, undated, late 1846; RAL, XI/109/58a/1/91, Anselm, Frankfurt, to his cousins, London, Oct. 16; RAL, XI/109J/J/46, James, Ferrières, to Lionel, Mayer and Salomon, London, Oct. 18; RFamC/1/103, Hannah, Frankfurt, to Lionel and Mayer, London, Nov. 13; RAL, T7/85, Anselm, Frankfurt, to Lionel, Nov. 15; RAL, XI/109/61/2/58, Nat to his brothers, undated, c. April 1847.

26 Ayer, Century of finance, pp. 38f. See RAL, XI/109J/J/39, James, Naples, to his brothers, March 16, 1839.

27 Tilly, Financial institutions, pp. 67, 164n.

28 Corti, Reign, p. 228.

29 Stüve (ed.), Briefwechsel, p. 396; Vogel (ed.), Briefe Stüves, vol. II, p. 694.

30 CPHDCM, 637/1/34/124, Pro Memoria [of loan to] Hugo, Graf Henckel von Donnersmarck [issued by] Arnstein & Eskeles, MAR, Simon G. Sina, undated, c. May 1846; CPHDCM, 637/1/32, Pro Memoria . . . Graf Henkel von Donnersmark, undated, c. May.

31 Berghoeffer, Meyer Amschel, pp. 224f. The other Hungarian nobles who raised loans through the Rothschilds and their Vienna associates were Károly, Adolf and Hedrik Vicza, Counts of Hédérvár, Joseph and Anton Szápáry and Christoph, Emanuel and Ludwig, Counts of Niczky. Cf. Barany, Stephen Széchenyi.

32 RAL, XI/109J/J/33, James, Aix, to Salomon, Carl and Lionel, Aug. 13, 1833; RAL, XI/109/33/1/30, Anthony, Paris, to his parents, London, March 15, 1835; RAL, XI/109J/J/3B, James, Paris, to Nathan, London, April 19, 1836; RAL, XI/109J/J/36A, James to Carl and his nephew, Naples, April 19; RAL, XI/109J/J/36, James to Nathan and Nat, May 1. For allegations that the Rothschilds spread rumours of Austrian intervention in Naples as part of a speculation in Neapolitan bonds, see Corti, Reign, pp. 159f.

33 RAL, XI/109J/J/39, James, Naples, to his nephews, London, April 13, 1839; same to same, April 22.

34 AN, 132 AQ 5901, James, Rome, to deRF, June 3, 1839; AN, 132 AQ 5901, James, Heinrichsbad, to deRF, July 11; RAL, XI/109J/J/39, James, Kissingen, to his nephews, Aug. 15; James to his brothers, Aug. 17. See also RAL, XI/109J/J/39, Nat, Paris, to his brothers, Jan. 1, 1843; RAL, XI/109/46/1/25, Anselm, Frankfurt, to Nat, Paris, Feb. 11, 1845.

35 RAL, XI/109J/J/39, James, Kissingen, to Amschel and Carl, Aug. 1, 1839. See also RAL, T18/185, XI/109/45/6/147, Nat, Paris, to his brothers, undated, early 1841.

36 See e.g. RAL, XI/109/33/1/30, Anthony, Paris, to his parents, London, March 15, 1835; RAL, XI/109J/J/37, James, Paris, to his nephews, April 10, 1837; same to same, April 11; RAL, XI/109J/J/39, James, Rome, to his brothers and nephews, Feb. 9, 1839; same to same, Feb. 19; AN, 132 AQ 13/Bilans, Comptes des profits et pertes, Dec. 31; AN, 132 AQ 5901, James, St Sauveur, to deRF, July 16, 1840. Cf. Scherb, Geschichte, p. 64; Reeves, Rothschilds, pp. 265–71; Balla, Romance, pp. 225–9. See in general Felisini, Finanze pontificie.

37 Corti, Reign, pp. 137–40, 176f.; Muhlstein, Baron James, p. 105.

38 RAL, XI/109/31/1/45, Lionel, Paris, to his parents, London, April 14, 1834; RAL, XI/109J/J/34B, James, Paris, to Nathan and Anthony, London, April 19; RAL, XI/109J/J/34, James to Nathan, April 20; James to Nathan and Anthony, April 21; James to Nathan, April 22; same to same, April 23; James to Nathan and Anthony, April 26; same to same, April 28.

39 RAL, XI/109/31a/1/49, Lionel, Turin, to his uncle, Paris, April 28, 1834; RAL, XI/109/32/1/19, same to same, May 3; RAL, XI/109J/J/34, James to Nathan, May 5; RAL, XI/109/32/2/7, James to Lionel, May 6.

40 RAL, XI/109/32/2/1, Lionel, Turin, to his uncle, Paris, May 10, 1834; RAL, T22/570, XI/109/32/1/37B, same to same, May 11; RAL, XI/109J/J/34, James to Nathan and Anthony, London, May 14; same to same, May 15; July 3.

41 AN, 132 AQ 5403/1M5, NMR to deRF, Jan. 17, 1843.

42 Reeves, Rothschilds, p. 101.

43 The possibility of renewed fighting could never be ruled out, however: RAL, XI/109J/J/33, James, Paris, to Nathan, London, Dec. 21, 1833; RAL, XI/109J/J/34, James to Nathan, March 26, 1834; RAL, XI/109J/J/34A, James to Nathan and Anthony, May 13; same to same, May 29; RAL,

XI/109J/J/36, James to his nephews, Oct. 3; RAL, XI/101/1–13/3, Nat, Paris, to Lionel, London, Dec. 28, 1837; RAL, XI/101/1–13/4, same to same, Dec. 30.

44   Corti, *Reign*, p. 114; Gille, *Maison Rothschild*, vol. I, pp. 235–8.

45   On the canalisation of the Sambre, Cameron, *France and Europe*, pp. 119ff.; Gille, *Maison Rothschild*, vol. I, pp. 277–82.

46   RAL, XI/109J/J/36, James, Paris, to Nathan and his nephew, London, May 2, 1836; same to same, May 12; James, Kreuznach, to his brothers and nephews, July 14; RAL, RFamC/4/147, Lionel to Anthony and Nat, July 22.

47   RAL, XI/109J/J/35, James, Paris, to Nathan and his nephews, London, Jan. 25, 1835; RAL, XI/109J/J/35, James, Brussels, to Nathan and Nat, Feb. 17; same to same, Feb. 21; RAL, XI/109J/J/36, James, Paris, to his nephews, Nov. 5; RAL, XI/109J/J/37, same to same, Jan. 2, 1837; Jan. 9; Jan. 16; Jan. 23; James, Frankfurt, to his nephews, March 15. Cf. Gille, *Maison Rothschild*, vol. I, pp. 285ff.; Cameron, *France and Europe*, p. 123.

48   Cameron, *France and Europe*, pp. 119–24, 347; Gille, *Maison Rothschild*, vol. I, pp. 389–92; Gille, *Banque et crédit*, pp. 231–4. Between 1835 and 1838 they created thirty-one new enterprises with combined capital of more than 100 million francs.

49   RAL, XI/109J/J/37, James, Paris, to his nephews, Sept. 25, 1837; RAL, XI/101/0–1/20, Constantin, Brussels, to deRF, Sept. 29; RAL, XI/101/0–1/43, same to same, Oct. 2; RAL, XI/109J/J/37, James, Brussels, to his nephews, Oct. 16; RAL, XI/109J/J/37, James to his nephews and Haas, Oct. 19; same to same, Oct. 21; Oct. 26; Oct. 28; RAL, XI/101/0–1/38, Richtenberger, Brussels, to deRF, Nov. 20; RAL, XI/109J/J/37, James, Paris, to his nephews, Nov. 21; same to same, Nov. 25; Nov. 29; Dec. 2; Dec. 5; Dec. 6; RAL, XI/109/36/2/5, Anselm, Frankfurt, to deRF, Jan. 1, 1838; RAL, XI/109J/J/38, James to his nephews, Feb. 11; same to same, Feb. 24; Feb. 28; March 7; March 12; March 13; March 27; March 31; RAL, XI/101/1–15/6, Anthony to his brothers, March 12; RAL, XI/101/1–15/9, same to same, March 21; RAL, XI/109J/J/38, James to his nephews, April 12. The plan was to convert some 180 million francs of 5 per cent into 3 per cent rentes; the sticking point was the price of the new rentes.

50   There is evidence that they continued to conduct private financial business for him. See e.g. RAL, T25/104/0/67, Anselm, Paris, to his cousins, London, undated, 1840; RAL, XI/109J/J/40, James, Brussels, to his nephews, Jan. 15.

51   Cameron, *France and Europe*, pp. 336ff.

52   RAL, XI/109J/J/38, James, Paris, to his nephews, May 4, 1838; same to same, May 18.

53   RAL, XI/109J/J/38, James, Paris, to his nephews, London, March 26, 1838; same to same, May 2; May 8; May 9; May 14; May 16; May 17; May 20; May 21; May 22; May 23; May 28; May 29; May 30; May 31; RAL, XI/101/1–16/20, Anthony, Paris, to his brothers, May 2; RAL, XI/109/36/2/44, deRF to NMR, June 2; RAL, XI/109J/J/38, James to his nephews, June 3; same to same, June 4; June 9; June 11; June 12; June 13; June 16; June 18; James, Brussels, to his nephews, June 23; same to same, June 26; June 30; RAL, XI/101/1–17/7, Anthony to his brothers, undated, early June; RAL, XI/101/1–17/18, same to same, undated, mid-June; RAL, XI/101/1–18(July)/9, undated, July; RAL, XI/101/1–18(July)/14, undated, July; RAL, XI/109J/J/38, James, Paris, to Carl and his nephews, London, July 7; James and Salomon to Carl and their nephews, July 9; same to same, July 11; James to Carl and his nephews, July 12; same to same, July 14; July 15; July 18.

54   Ayer, *Century of finance*, pp. 36f. The loan finally issued was for £2.75 million at a price to investors of 73.5.

55   Gille, *Maison Rothschild*, vol. I, pp. 287–90, 389–92; Gille, *Banque et crédit*, pp. 231–4; Cameron, *France and Europe*, p. 124; *idem, Banking in the early stages of industrialisation*, pp. 133ff., 145.

56   AN, 132 AQ 5901, James, St Sauveur, to deRF, Aug. 18, 1838; RAL, XI/101/1–18(September)/2, Anthony, Paris, to his brothers and Anselm, London, undated, Sept.; RAL, XI/101/1–18(September)/4, same to same, undated, Sept.; RAL, XI/101/1–19/13, undated, Oct.; RAL, XI/101/1–19/14, undated, Oct.; RAL, XI/109J/J/38, James, Florence, to his brothers and nephews, Nov. 5; James, Naples, to Salomon and his nephews, Nov. 20; same to same, Nov. 30; RAL, XI/101/1–20/17, Anthony to his brothers, Nov. 27; RAL, XI/101/1–20/18, same to same, Nov. 28; RAL, XI/101/1–20/25, undated, Dec.; RAL, XI/101/1–20/26, undated, Dec.

57   RAL, XI/109J/J/38, James, Naples, to his brothers and nephews, Dec. 27, 1838. Cf. Corti, *Reign*, pp. 188f.; Cameron, *France and Europe*, pp. 340–43.

58   RAL, XI/109J/J/39, James, Naples, to his brothers and nephews, Jan. 1, 1839; RAL, XI/101/2–831, Anthony, Paris, to his brothers, London, Jan. 9.

59   RAL, XI/109J/J/39, James, Rome, to his brothers and nephews, Feb. 2, 1839; RAL, XI/101/2–9/4, Salomon, Vienna, to NMR, Feb. 6.

60   Corti, *Reign*, pp. 185ff.; Bouvier, *Rothschild*, pp. 103–5; Gille, *Maison Rothschild*, vol. I, pp. 297f.

61   The April 1839 treaty bound the signatory powers to uphold Belgian neutrality; seventy-five years later, it was one of the decisive justifications for Britain's intervention in what became the First World War.

62   RAL, XI/109J/J/39, James, Rome, to his brothers and nephews, March 14, 1839; same, Naples, to same, March 25; AN, 132 AQ 5901, James, Naples, to Constantin and his nephews, March 26. Cf. Gille, *Maison Rothschild*, vol. I, pp. 298–301.

63   RAL, XI/109J/J/39, James, Naples, to his brothers and nephews, May 12, 1839; same, Venice, to same, June 17; James, Paris, to his nephews, London, Nov. 21; same to same, Dec. 10; Dec. 11; James to Amschel and Salomon, Dec. 21.

64   RAL, XI/109/38/1/32, James, Brussels, to NMR, Jan. 9, 1840. See also RAL, XI/109J/J/40, James, Brussels, to his nephews, Jan. 7; same to same, Jan. 8; Jan. 9; same, Paris, to same, Jan. 15; Jan. 20; Jan. 25; RAL, XI/109J/J/40A, Feb. 1; RAL, XI/109J/J/40A, Feb. 2; RAL, XI/109J/J/40A, Feb. 3.

65   RAL, XI/109/39/1/14, MAR and SMR to deRF, Nov. 4, 1840; RAL, T25/104/0/119, Nat, Paris, to his brothers, London, Nov. 6; RAL, T25/104/0/122, Anselm, Frankfurt, to James and Nat, Nov. 13. Cf. Gille, *Maison Rothschild*, vol. I, pp. 301–4; Cameron, *France and Europe*, pp. 340–43.

66   RAL, XI/109/43a/2/163, Nat, Paris, to his brothers, London, undated, *c.* July 1842; RAL, T24/80, XI/109/52/13, XI/109/43/3/17, Anselm, Carlsruhe, to his father, Oct. 10; RAL, XI/109/43a/2/111, Nat, Paris, to his brother, Oct. 10; RAL, XI/109J/J/42, James, Paris, to Anthony, London, Oct. 21; same to same, Oct. 23; James to his nephews, Oct. 28. Cf. Gille, *Maison Rothschild*, vol. I, pp. 310–13; Cameron, *France and Europe*, pp. 340–43.

67   RAL, XI/109/42a/2/67, Nat, Paris, to his brothers, London, June 23, 1842. Cf. RAL, XI/109/43a/2/77, Anthony, Paris, to his brothers, undated, *c.* July; RAL, XI/109J/J42, James, Paris, to his nephews, London, Nov. 3; same to same, Nov. 5.

68   Cameron, *France and Europe*, pp. 340–43.

69   RAL, T25/104/0/102, Anselm, the Hague, to Nat, Paris, Oct. 15, 1840; RAL, XI/109/39/2/8, Anselm to MAR, Oct. 17; RAL, XI/109/39/2/7, Anselm to his father and uncle, Oct. 17; RAL, T25/104/0/103, Anselm to Nat, Oct. 18; RAL, XI/109/39/1/13, Amschel, Frankfurt, to Anselm, Oct. 20; RAL, T25/104/0/107, Anselm to Nat, Oct. 24. See also RAL, T25/104/1/6/153, Anselm to Anthony, undated, 1841.

70   RAL, XI/109/45b/5/61, Anselm to his father, uncle and cousins, Jan. 5, 1842; RAL, XI/109/42a/2/25, Nat, Paris, to his brothers, March 19; RAL, XI/109/42a/2/31, same to same, undated, March; RAL, XI/109J/J/42, James, Paris, to his nephews and Alphonse, April 6; RAL, XI/109/45b/6/30, Agreement between Rochusen, Dutch Finance Minister, and deRF, represented by Anselm, undated, 1842; RAL, XI/109/43a/2/63, Anthony, Paris, to his brothers, undated, *c.* July; RAL, XI/109J/J/42, James, to his nephews, Sept. 12. As in the Belgian case, public financial arrangements were supplemented by private dealings with the respective monarchs: see e.g. RAL, XI/109/42a/2/46, Nat to his brothers, undated, *c.* May; RAL, T23/327, XI/109/42/3/67, Anselm, the Hague, to NMR, May 6; RAL, T23/331, XI/109/42/3/18, same to same, May 10; May 13; RAL, XI/109/42a/3/20, May 16; RAL, T23/341, XI/109/42/2/94, Anthony, Paris, to his mother, May 26; RAL, T23/330, XI/109/42/3/17, Anselm, the Hague, to Nat, Paris, May 8, 1843.

71   Deschamps, *Belgique*, pp. 142f. Cf. RAL, XI/109/43a/2/120, Nat, Paris, to his brothers, London, Nov. 17, 1842.

72   RAL, XI/109/43a/3/22, Anselm, the Hague, to his father, uncle and cousins, Nov. 2, 1842; RAL, XI/109/43a/3/33, Anselm, Frankfurt, to James, Nov. 22; RAL, XI/109/43a/2/17, Anthony, Paris, to his brothers, undated, late 1842; RAL, XI/109/43a/2/124, Nat, to his brothers, Dec. 12; RAL, XI/109/45a/1/17, Anthony to his brothers, undated, early 1843; RAL, XI/109/45a/1/27, same to same, undated, early 1843; RAL, XI/109/45a/1/29, undated, early 1843; RAL, XI/109/45a/1/36, 1843; RAL, XI/109/45b/6/184, Nat to his brothers, undated, early 1843; RAL, XI/109/45b/6/184, same to same, undated, early 1843; RAL, XI/109/44/1/99, Anselm, the Hague, to deRF, Jan. 10; RAL, XI/109/44/1/98, same to same, Jan. 11; RAL, XI/109/45b/5/63, Anselm to his father, uncle and cousins, Jan. 13; RAL, XI/109/45b/5/65, same to same, Jan. 15; RAL, XI/109/45b/5/66, Jan. 17; RAL, XI/109/45b/5/68, Jan. 21; RAL, T18/24, XI/109/45/4/24, Agreement with Rochusen, Jan. 23; RAL, XI/109/45b/5/69, Anselm, Frankfurt, to his father, uncle and cousins, Jan. 31; RAL, XI/109/45b/5/76, same to same, Feb. 20; RAL, XI/109/45b/5/15, Anselm to Anthony, Feb. 4; AN, 132 AQ 5901,

Anselm to deRF, March 3; RAL, XI/109/45b/6/22, Nat, Paris, to his brothers, March 15; RAL, XI/109/45b/5/18, Anselm to his cousins, March 17; RAL, XI/109/45b/6/23, Nat to his brothers, March 21. In a bid to secure the main conversion, Anselm made Rochusen an initial loan of 6 million guilders.

73 RAL, XI/109/45b/5/23, Anselm, the Hague, to his cousins, London, March 31, 1843; RAL, XI/109/45b/6/26, Nat, Paris, to his brothers, April 1; RAL, XI/109/45b/5/79, Anselm to his father, uncle and cousins, April 2; RAL, T18/35, XI/109/45/5/25, Anselm to his cousins, April 11; RAL, XI/109/45b/6/29, Nat to his brothers, April 11; RAL, XI/109/45b/5/28, Anselm, Frankfurt, to his cousins, London, May 9; AN, 132 AQ 5901, Anselm to deRF, May 13; RAL, XI/109/45b/6/44, Nat to his brothers, May 29; RAL, XI/109/45b/6/49, same to same, June 7.

74 AN, 132 AQ 5901, Anselm, the Hague, to deRF, Paris, June 14, 1843; RAL, T18/136, XI/109/45/5/33, Anselm to his cousins, London, June 20; RAL, T18/180, XI/109/45/5/49, Anselm, Frankfurt, to Anthony, London, Nov. 14.

75 RAL, XI/109/46/1/7, Nat, Paris, to his brothers, undated, 1844; RAL, XI/109/48/1/20, same to same, undated, 1844; RAL, T18/405, XI/109/48/1/24, undated, 1844; RAL, XI/109/48/1/25, undated, 1844; RAL, XI/109/48/1/30, undated, 1844; RAL, XI/109/48/1/32, June 27; RAL, XI/109/48/1/33, undated, 1844; RAL, XI/109/48/1/35, June 29; RAL, T18/399, XI/109/48/1/42, Anselm, Breda, to James, July 9; RAL, XI/109/48/1/43, Anselm, the Hague, to his cousins, July 10; RAL, T18/402, XI/109/48/1/45, Anselm to deRF, July 11; RAL, XI/109/48/1/46, Anselm to Lionel, July 12; RAL, T18/407, XI/109/48/1/47, Anselm to James, July 13; RAL, XI/109/48/1/49, Anselm to his cousins, July 15; RAL, XI/109/48/1/50, same to same, July 16; RAL, XI/109/48/1/52, July 19; RAL XI/109/48/1/53, July 20; RAL, XI/109/48/1/29, July 22; Nat to his brothers, July 22; RAL, XI/109/48/1/56, Anselm to deRF, July 29; RAL, XI/109/48/2/28, Nat to his brothers, undated, 1844; RAL, XI/109/48/2/59, same to same, undated, 1844; RAL, XI/109/48/2/64, undated, 1844; RAL, XI/109/49/1/55, Lionel, Brussels, to Nat, Paris, Oct. 12; RAL, XI/109/49/1/72, same, the Hague, to same, Oct. 14; RAL, XI/109/49/1/79, Lionel, the Hague, to his brothers, Oct. 15; RAL, XI/109/49/1/107, Lionel, Frankfurt, to Nat, Oct. 21; RAL, XI/109/49/1/106, Lionel to his brothers, London, Oct. 21; RAL, XI/109/49/1/113, Nat to his brothers, Oct. 22; AN, 132 AQ 5406/1M8, NMR to deRF, Oct. 22; RAL, XI/109/49/1/131, Nat to Anthony, Oct. 24; RAL, XI/109/49/2/14, Anselm, Frankfurt, to his cousins, Nov. 3; RAL, XI/109/49/2/23, same to same, Nov. 4; RAL, XI/109/51a/2/105, Anselm to Nat, Feb. 18, 1845. Cf. Ayer, *Century of finance*, pp. 36f.; Gille, *Maison Rothschild*, vol. I, pp. 310–20; Deschamps, *Belgique*, p. 516.

76 RAL, XI/109/58b/2/44, Nat, Paris, to his brothers, undated, 1846. Gille, *Maison Rothschild*, vol. I, pp. 320–23; vol. II, pp. 33f., 44ff.

77 RAL, XI/109J/J/37, James, Paris, to his nephews, London, April 8, 1837; same to same, April 9; April 10; April 11; April 15.

78 RAL, XI/109J/J/37, James, Paris, to his nephews, London, Nov. 7, 1837.

79 RAL, XI/109J/J/38, James, Naples, to his brothers and nephews, Dec. 4, 1838; same to same, Dec. 5.

80 RAL, XI/101/2–8/13, Anthony, Paris, to his brothers, undated, March 1839; RAL, XI/101/2–18/15, same to same, undated, March; RAL, XI/101/2–8/19, undated, March; RAL, XI/101/2–8/22, undated, March; RAL, XI/101/2–8/23, undated, March. Cf. James, Rome, to his brothers and nephews, March 14; RAL, XI/101/2–9/22, unidentified hand, possibly Anselm, Paris, to Lionel, London, March 19; RAL, XI/101/2–9/22a, same to same, March 22; RAL, XI, 101/2–9/22b, March 23.

81 RAL, XI/109J/J/40, James, Paris, to his nephews, London, Feb. 20, 1840; same to same, Feb. 22.

82 RAL, XI/109J/J/39, James, Naples, to his brothers and nephews, May 12, 1839; same to same, May 21.

83 RAL, XI/109J/J/40C, James, Paris, to his nephews, London, Feb. 27, 1840.

84 RAL, XI/109J/J/40, James, Paris, to his nephews, London, Feb. 29, 1840.

85 RAL, XI/109/25/1/10, Lionel, Paris, to his parents, Jan. 12, 1832; RAL, XI/109/27/3/24, Anselm, Frankfurt, to James, Oct. 25; RAL, XI/109J/J/32, James, Paris, to Nathan, London, Dec. 11; same to same, Dec. 20; RAL, XI/109J/J/32A, Dec. 22; RAL, XI/109J/J/32B, Dec. 22; RAL, XI/109J/J/32C, Dec. 22; RAL, XI/109/27/1/54, Lionel to his parents, Dec. 22; RAL, XI/109J/J/32, James to Nathan, Dec. 25; same to same, Dec. 27; RAL, XI/109/27/1/59, Lionel to his parents, Dec. 27; RAL, XI/109/27/1/60, same to same, Dec. 29; RAL, XI/109J/J/32, James to Nathan, Dec. 29; RAL, T22/315, XI/109/27/2/27, Anthony, Paris, to his parents, Dec. 29; RAL, XI/109/27/1/62, Lionel to his parents, Dec. 31; RAL, XI/109/29/2/38, Greek loan contract (copy), Jan. 2, 1833; RAL,

XI/109J/J/33, James to Nathan, Jan. 12; Jan. 14; RAL, XI/109/30/2/3, Anselm, Paris, to Anthony, Feb. 19. Cf. Cameron, *France and Europe*, p. 458; Ayer, *Century of finance*, pp. 36f.; Gille, *Maison Rothschild*, vol. I, pp. 140f. The sum issued was 60 million francs (£2,343,750) in 5 per cent bonds.

86 RAL, XI/109/26/1/12, Nat, Paris, to his parents, May 15, 1832; RAL, T22/375, XI/109/29/1/63, Salomon, Vienna, to his brothers, Jan. 15, 1833; RAL, T22/376, XI/109/29/1/65, same to same, Jan. 16; RAL, XI/109/29/1/69, Salomon to his brothers and Anselm, Feb. 12; RAL, T22/39, XI/109/29/1/70, Salomon to his brothers, Feb. 19; RAL, XI/109/30/2/42, same to same, March 8; RAL, T22/396, XI/109/29/1/71, same to same, March 3; RAL, XI/109J/J/33, James, Paris, to Nathan and his nephews, London, March 16; same to same, March 17; March 19; March 25; March 30; April 1; April 3; RAL, T22/398, XI/109/29/1/72, Salomon to his brothers, March 31. As usual, Metternich kept Salomon exceptionally well informed, while Salomon was able to relay the latest news to Paris ahead of diplomatic despatches.

87 RAL, T22/399, XI/109/29/1/73, Salomon, Vienna, to his brothers, April 6, 1833; RAL XI/109/30/2/40, same to same, April 7; RAL, XI/109J/J/33, James, Paris, to Nathan and his nephew, London, April 14; same to same, April 16; April 20; RAL, XI/109/29/1/77, Salomon to James, April 28. See also RAL, XI/109J/J/33A, James to Nathan, Nov. 9; RAL, XI/109/30/1/50, Lionel to his parents, Nov. 23.

88 RAL, XI/109J/J/33, James, Paris, to Nathan and his nephews, London, April 21, 1833; RAL, XI/109/29/1/15, Lionel, Paris, to his parents, May 2; RAL, XI/109J/J/33, James to Nathan, May 14; same to same, June 18; June 25; July 6; July 13; RAL, XI/109/30/1/11, Lionel to his parents, July 10; RAL, XI/109J/J/33, James and Salomon to Nathan, July 18; James to Nathan and Anthony, July 24; same to same, July 31; RAL, XI/109/30/1/18, Lionel to his parents, Aug. 1; RAL, XI/109/30/1/19, same to same, Aug. 3; RAL, XI/109J/J/33, James, Geneva, to Nathan, Lionel and Salomon, Aug. 4; RAL, XI/109/30/1/37, Lionel to his father, Sept. 26; RAL, XI/109J/J/33, James and Betty, Boulogne, to Nathan, Oct. 7; James, Paris, to Nathan, Oct. 19; James and Salomon to Nathan and Lionel, Oct. 22; James and Salomon to Nathan, Oct. 24.

89 RAL, T22/595, XI/109/32/1/37B, Nat, Constantinople, to his parents, London undated, 1834. Cf. RAL, T22/504, XI/109/31/1/69, same to same, Jan. 14, 1834; RAL, XI/109/32/2/23, March 4; RAL, T22/545, XI/109/32/1/37B, March 18; RAL, XI/109/32/1/52, Lionel, Paris, to his parents, July 2; RAL, XI/109/31a/1/73, Nat to his parents, Nov. 25; Davis, *English Rothschilds*, p. 54. For further details of Nat's trip to Greece and Constantinople, see RAL, T7/2.

90 RAL, XI/109J/J/36, James, Paris, to Nathan and his nephews, Feb. 17, 1836; same to same, Feb. 20; Feb. 21; Feb. 22; Feb. 25; Feb. 27; March 1; RAL, XI/109J/J/36B, James, Frankfurt, to Anthony, July 9; RAL, XI/109J/J/36, James, Kreuznach, to his nephews, Aug. 11; James to Haas and Martini, Aug. 15; RAL, XI/101/3/5, Molé to deRF, Feb. 17, 1837; RAL, XI/109J/J/37, James, Paris, to his nephews, London, Feb. 19; RAL, XI/101/3/7, Molé to deRF, Feb. 23; RAL, XI/101/3/6, Russian embassy to deRF, Feb. 23; RAL, XI/101/3/8, James to NMR, Feb. 25; RAL, XI/101/0–1/5, Labensky to deRF, undated, April; RAL 101/0–5/1, deRF to NMR, April 5; RAL, XI/109J/J/37, James to his nephews, April 5; same to same, April 24; RAL, XI/101/0–7/2, deRF to NMR, May 6; RAL, XI/109J/J/37, James to his nephews, May 20; same to same, May 25; Sept. 6; AN, 132 AQ 5901, James, Eaux Bonnes, to Constantin, Paris, Sept. 1, 1838; RAL, XI/101/2–10/17, Anthony to his brothers, Aug. 24, 1839.

91 RAL, T23/377, XI/109/42/3/110, Nat, Paris, to his brothers, undated, 1843; RAL, XI/109/45b/6/112, same to same, undated, 1843; RAL, XI/109/45b/6/80, Oct. 10; AN, 132 AQ 5901, James, Chatsworth, to deRF, Aug. 8; RAL, XI/109/46/1/91, Nat to his brothers, undated, 1844; RAL, XI/109/46/1/83, same to same, *c*. April; RAL, XI/109/46/2/73, Addington, Foreign Office, to NMR, Feb. 24. For a contemporary joke on the subject—at James's expense—see Apponyi, *Vingt-cinq ans*, vol. IV, p. 11.

92 Gille, *Maison Rothschild*, vol. I, pp. 418f., 437ff.

93 This development had been expected for over a year: RAL, XI/109J/J/38, James, Paris, to his nephews, June 4, 1838; same to same, June 7; June 11; RAL, XI/101/1–17/23, Anthony, Paris, to his brothers, London, June 14; RAL, XI/109J/J/38, James to his nephews, June 19; same to same, June 23; RAL, XI/109/37/1/17, Salomon, Vienna, to his brothers and nephews, March 28, 1839; RAL, XI/109/37/1/18, same to same, March 30; RAL, XI/109J/J/39, James, Naples, to his nephews, London, April 30.

94 As in the past, Salomon became Metternich's informal diplomatic channel, through which his arguments for unity between the great powers were relayed to Paris: RAL, XI/109/37/1/26, Salomon, Vienna, to his brother and nephews, Paris, May 21, 1839; RAL, XI/109/37/1/27, same to same, May

25; RAL, XI/109/37/1/30, June 10; RAL, XI/109/37/1/33, June 11; RAL, XI/109/37/1/42, June 24; RAL, XI/109/37/1/43, June 29; RAL, XI/109/37/1/57, Sept. 1; RAL, XI/109/37/1/60, Oct. 15. The reaction of the Paris house was initially sanguine: RAL, XI/101/2–10/2, deRF to NMR, July 4; RAL, XI/109J/J/39, James, Kissingen, to Anselm, Paris, Aug. 9; James to his nephews, London, Aug. 14. However, James soon came to realise the implications of the situation: James, Frankfurt, to Anthony, Paris, Sept. 1; same to same, Sept. 15.

95   RAL, XI/101/2–10/31, deRF to NMR, Nov. 1, 1839; RAL, XI/109J/J/39, James, Paris, to his nephews, London, Nov. 2. See also RAL, XI/101/2–9/53, Ibrahim Pasha to deRF, Nov. 4.

96   RAL, XI/109J/J/40, James, Paris, to his nephews, Jan. 21, 1840; same to same, Jan. 22; RAL, XI/109J/J/40B, Jan. 26; RAL, XI/109J/J/40, Jan. 29; Jan. 30; RAL, XI/109/38/1/4, Salomon, Vienna, to his brothers, son and nephews, Jan. 30.

97   Frankel, *Damascus affair*, pp. 102f. See also general Frankel, "Damascus blood libel," *passim*; Erb, "Damascus Affair," *passim*.

98   Muhlstein, *Baron James*, pp. 120f. Laurin had become friendly with James's brother Carl when serving in Naples: Frankel, *Damascus affair*, p. 105.

99   *Ibid.*, pp. 80ff.

100 Erb, "Damascus Affair," p. 107.

101 Corti, *Reign*, pp. 222ff.; Frankel, *Damascus affair*, pp. 135f. Metternich evidently objected. Although he shared Laurin's view on the matter, he was unhappy at the way the story had been leaked via Rothschild to the press.

102 *Ibid.*, pp. 85, 110f.

103 Corti, *Reign*, pp. 222ff.; Frankel, *Damascus affair*, pp. 120ff.

104 Frankel, *Damascus affair*, pp. 125ff.; Loewe (ed.), *Montefiore diaries*, vol. I, pp. 213ff.

105 RAL, T25/104/0/54, Nat, Paris, to his brothers, London, June 3, 1840; RAL, T25/104/0/55, same to same, June 4; RAL, T25/104/0/56, June 9. Cf. Frankel, *Damascus affair*, p. 216f.

106 Having already visited the Holy Land in 1839, Montefiore was the obvious choice to lead such a delegation: see RAL, T42/15, RFamC/30/22, Montefiore, Alexandria, to NMR, May 8, 1839; RAL, T6/143, Kilboc Heugh & Co., Beirut, to NMR, May 12. Another member of the Montefiore delegation was Salomon Munk, the Berlin philologist, whom James helped become librarian at the Bibliothèque Nationale and later Professor of Hebrew at the Collège de France. See in general Loewe (ed.), *Montefiore diaries*, vol. I, pp. 223–97.

107 RAL, XII/158/9, cheque drawn on NMR, signed by Montefiore, June 3, 1840; same, June 8; RAL, RFam AD/2 Box F, Minutes of a meeting of the London Committee of the Board of Deputies of British Jews, at New Synagogue, Vestry Chamber, Great St Helen's St, June 15; RAL, XII/158/9, cheques signed by Montefiore "on Account of Funds Jews of Damascus," June 29; July 3; July 6; RAL, XI/109/39, Secretary to the Committee of the Great Synagogue to Lionel, Aug. 11. On the raising of money in Paris, RAL, T25/104/0/60, Nat, Paris, to his brothers, London, June 22; RAL, T25/104/0/61, same to same, June 24. Cf. Frankel, *Damascus affair*, pp. 227f.

108 Erb, "Damascus Affair," p. 106.

109 Loewe (ed.), *Montefiore diaries*, vol. I, pp. 223, 249, 284f.; Frankel, *Damascus affair*, pp. 379ff. Carl had some relevant experience: as early as 1838, he and Laurin had acted together to give financial assistance to the Jewish community of Safed, which had come under Druze attack in 1838: Barnett, "Diary," pp. 149ff.

110 RAL, XI/109/39, Laurin, Alexandria, to Anselm, Aug. 5, 1840. See also RAL, XI/109/39, Emile de Wagner, Alexandria, to NMR, Aug. 25.

111 Heine, "Lutetia," in *Sämtliche Schriften*, vol. V, pp. 273f.; Corti, *Reign*, p. 225. Heine attributed James's commitment to Betty's influence: Frankel, *Damascus affair*, p. 234.

112 RAL, T25/104/0/54, Nat, Paris, to his brothers, London, June 3, 1840; RAL, T25/104/0/55, same to same, June 4.

113 RAL, T25/104/0/57, Nat, Paris, to his brothers, London, June 12, 1840.

114 See e.g. RAL, RFamC/1/160 [ex XI/109/38], Hannah to Lionel, undated, *c.* Sept. 1840; RAL, XI/109/39, Laurin, Alexandria, to Anselm, Paris, Oct. 3. Cf. Erb, "Damascus Affair," p. 109.

115 Liberles, "Aristocrat and synagogue," pp. 95ff. This diatribe had in fact been prompted by the Frankfurt Rothschilds" refusal to establish a rabbinical seminary under his direction.

116 Quoted in Glanz, "Rothschild legend," p. 20.

117 *Ibid.*

118 RAL, T22/110, XI/109/25/3/34, J. R. B[ishop?] to Nathan, Dec. 30, 1832.

119   Frankel, *Damascus affair*, p. 312.
120   In his *La fausse industrie* (1836): Poliakov, *Antisemitismus*, vol. VI, pp. 171f.
121   Frankel, *Damascus affair*, p. 367: "On David's throne, once it is restored, there will sit that financial dynasty which all European recognises and to which all Europe submits. . . ."
122   Webster, *Foreign policy of Palmerston*, vol. II, p. 761. See also Frankel, *Damascus affair*, p. 306, for a letter to *The Times* on the subject from an "English Christian."
123   Vincent, *Disraeli, Derby and the Conservative party*, p. 32: "He talked to me with great apparent earnestness on the subject of restoring the Jews to their own land . . . The country, he said, had ample natural capabilities: all it wanted was labour, and protection for the labourer: the ownership of the soil might be bought from Turkey: money would be forthcoming: the Rothschilds and leading Hebrew capitalists would all help: the Turkish empire was falling into ruin: the Turkish Govt would do anything for money."
124   I am grateful to Professor David Landes for this point.
125   See Corti, *Reign*, pp. 362f., for Amschel's comment in 1845 that the idea of a Jewish homeland in the US was merely a "stunt."
126   RAL, T25/104/0/57, Nat, Paris, to his brothers, London, June 12, 1840; RAL, T25/104/0/58, same to same, undated, *c.* June; RAL, T25/104/0/62, undated, *c.* June.
127   RAL, T25/104/0/66, Anselm, Paris, to his cousins, London, July 23, 1840.
128   RAL, T25/104/0/131, Anselm, Frankfurt, to his cousins, London, Nov. 24, 1840. Cf. RAL, XI/109/40/1/49, Lipmann Loewenstein, Frankfurt, to Anselm, Jan. 29, 1841, sending a copy of his book on the affair, one of numerous accounts published at the time; RAL, T25/104/1/1/21, Anselm to his cousins, Feb. 2.
129   RAL, T23/377, XI/109/42/3/110, Salomon, Vienna, to MAR, deRF and NMR, June 28, 1842; RAL, XI/109/46/2/50, Fränkel, Jerusalem, to Lionel, Oct. 31, 1843.
130   Schischa, "Saga of 1855," pp. 269ff. Significantly, the Mayer de Rothschild hospital set up then was wholly controlled by the Rothschilds, and had been established under the supervision of James's son Gustave.
131   See e.g. RAL, XI/109J/J/42, James, Paris, to his nephews, London, Feb. 13, 1842; RAL, XI/109/46/1/88, Nat, Paris, to his brothers, London, undated, 1844.
132   Frankel, *Damascus affair*, pp. 136, 191.
133   Muhlstein, *Baron James*, pp. 120f.
134   Frankel, *Damascus affair*, pp. 198f.
135   Scherb, *Geschichte*, p. 73; Palmade, *Capitalism*, pp. 105–9.
136   RAL, T25/104/0/76, Nat, Paris, to his brothers, London, undated, *c.* Aug. 1840; RAL, T25/104/0/84, same to same, Sept. 7; RAL, T25/104/0/88, Sept. 8.
137   Corti, *Reign*, p. 202.
138   Se e.g. RAL, T25/104/0/68, Anselm, Paris, to his cousins, London, Aug. 2, 1840; RAL, T25/104/0/71, same to same, Aug. 3; RAL, T25/104/0/87, Nat, Paris, to his brothers, Sept. 11; RAL, T25/104/0/92, same to same, Oct. 4; RAL, T5/104/0/94, undated, *c.* Oct.; RAL, T25/104/0/96, Oct. 10; RAL, T25/104/0/98, undated, *c.* Oct.; RAL, T25/104/0/117, undated, *c.* Oct.; RAL, T25/104/0/118, undated, *c.* Oct.
139   Corti, *Reign*, pp. 192–204; Deschamps, *Belgique*, pp. 72f.
140   RAL, T25/104/0/73, Nat, Bayonne, to his brothers, London, Aug. 2, 1840.
141   Guizot and Lieven, *Lettres*, vol. II, pp. 192, 194, 229, 255.
142   Heine, "Lutetia," *Sämtliche Schriften*, vol. V, p. 321, trans. Prawer, *Heine*, pp. 643f.
143   RAL, T25/104/0/89, Nat, Paris, to his brothers, London, undated, *c.* Sept., 1840.
144   Muhlstein, *Baron James*, p. 118; Frankel, *Damascus affair*, p. 369; Corti, *Reign*, pp. 204f.; Gille, *Maison Rothschild*, vol. I, p. 486; Bouvier, *Rothschild*, p. 102.
145   Corti, *Reign*, p. 206.
146   RAL, T25/104/0/101, Nat, Paris, to his brothers, London, Oct. 13, 1840; RAL, T25/104/0/110, same to same, Oct. 20. Cf. Corti, *Reign*, p. 208.
147   RAL, T25/104/0/137, Nat, Paris, to his brothers, London, undated, *c.* Nov. 1840; RAL, T25/104/0/133, Anselm, Frankfurt, to his cousins, London, Nov. 25; RAL, T25/104/1/1/1, same to same, Dec. 2; RAL, XI/101/3,4,5, deRF to NMR, Jan. 2, 1841; RAL, XI/109J/J/40, James, Paris, to his nephews, London, Feb. 9 [wrongly dated 1840]; RAL, XI/101/3,4,5–3/14, deRF to NMR, Feb. 27; RAL, XI/109J/J/40, James to his nephews, March 1 [wrongly dated 1840]; same to same, March 3 [wrongly dated 1840]; March 5 [wrongly dated 1840]; March 6 [wrongly dated 1840]; RAL,

XI/109J/J/40A, March 9 [wrongly dated 1840]; RAL, XI/109J/J/40, March 10 [wrongly dated 1840]; March 15 [wrongly dated 1840]; March 16 [wrongly dated 1840]; RAL, XI/101/3,4,5–3/22, deRF to NMR, March 9; RAL, XI/101/3,4,5–3/26, same to same, March 15; RAL, XI/101/3,4,5–3/33, March 22.

148 Prawer, *Heine*, pp. 644ff.

149 RAL, XI/101/3,4,5–3/2, deRF to NMR, Jan. 3, 1841; RAL, XI/101/3,4,5–1a/60a, Jan. 6; RAL, XI/101/3,4,5–3/5, Jan. 7; RAL, XI/101/3,4,5–3/1b, Jan. 18; RAL, XI/109J/J/40B, James, Paris, to his nephews, Jan. 24 [wrongly dated 1840]; same to same, Jan. 31 [wrongly dated 1840]; RAL, XI/101/3,4,5–3/6, unsigned, deRF to NMR, Feb. 13; RAL, XI/101/3,4,5–3/8, same to same, Feb. 18; RAL, XI/101/3,4,5–3/9, Feb. 24; RAL, 101/3,4,5–3/17, March 2; RAL, XI/101/3,4,5–3/20, March 8; RAL, XI/109J/J/40, James to his nephews, March 20 [wrongly dated 1840]; March 24 [wrongly dated 1840]; RAL, XI/101/3,4,5–3/45, deRF to NMR, April 2.

150 Apponyi, *Vingt-cinq ans*, vol. IV, p. 451.

151 RAL, XI/109J/J/40, James, Paris, to his nephews, London, March 23, 1841; RAL, XI/109J/J/41, same to same, April 2; April 12; April 13; April 17; April 19; April 20; April 22; April 24; May 1; RAL, XI/101/3,4,5–3/68, deRF to NMR, April 24; RAL, XI/109J/J/41B, James to his nephews, May 5; RAL, XI/109J/J/41, same to same, May 8; May 11; May 17; May 18; May 21; May 22; May 24; May 25; May 30; June 1; June 3; June 5; June 15; June 16; June 19; June 20; June 21; June 23; June 26; June 27; June 28; June 30; July 5; July 12; RAL, XI/101/3,4,5–5/12, deRF to NMR, May 18; RAL, XI/101/3,4,5–5/23, deRF to NMR, June 19; RAL, XI/101/3,4,5–5/35, same to same, undated, Aug.; RAL, XI/109J/J/41, James, Anselm and Salomon, Gastein, to Nat, Paris, Aug. 11; James to Nat, Aug. 13; same to same, Aug. 14; James, Salomon and Anselm to Nat, Aug. 17; James, Salomon and Anselm, Vienna, to Nat, Paris, Aug. 24; RAL, XI/101/3,4,5–5/39, deRF to NMR, Sept. 8; RAL, XI/109J/J/41, James, Paris, to his nephews, London, Sept. 21; same to same, Oct. 2; Dec. 20.

152 Ayer, *Century of finance*, pp. 40f.; Gille, *Maison Rothschild*, vol. I, pp. 306–9; Capefigue, *Grandes opérations*, vol. III, pp. 230f.; Marion, *Histoire financière*, vol. V, pp. 192f.; Corti, *Reign*, p. 243. Three per cent rentes were sold to the consortium of bankers led by Rothschilds at a price of 76.75 (75.25 according to Capefigue). The new rentes were trading at a price of around 82 by the middle of 1842.

153 RAL, XI/101/3,4,5–5, Anselm, Paris, to his cousins, London, undated, 1842.

154 RAL, T25/104/0/140, Nat, Paris, to his brothers, London, Dec. 7, 1841; RAL, XI/109/39/1/46, deRF to NMR, Dec. 14. Cf. Corti, *Reign*, pp. 201, 209ff.

155 RAL, XI/109J/J/40, James, Paris, to his nephews, London, March 8, 1841 [wrongly dated 1840].

156 RAL, XI/109J/J/42, James, Paris, to his nephews, London, Sept. 7, 1842; same to same, Sept. 10; Oct. 23; Oct. 29; Oct. 30; Nov. 2; Nov. 5; Nov. 6; Nov. 9; Nov. 12; Nov. 13; Nov. 14; Nov. 15; Nov. 16; Nov. 19; Nov. 20; Nov. 23; Nov. 24; Nov. 27; Nov. 29; RAL, XI/109J/J42A, Nov. 30; RAL, XI/109J/J42B, Nov. 30; RAL, XI/109J/J/42, Dec. 5; Dec. 7; Dec. 8; Dec. 10; Dec. 11; Dec. 12; Dec. 14; Dec. 18; Dec. 21.

157 RAL, XI/109/50/2/43, Nat, Paris, to his brothers, London, undated, 1844; RAL, XI/109/47/1/87, same to same, March 29; RAL, XI/109/47/1/100, undated, *c*. April; RAL, XI/109/47/1/115, undated, *c*. April; RAL, XI/109/47/1/117, undated, *c*. April; RAL, XI/109/47/1/89, April 3; RAL, T20/32, XI/109/48/2/53, undated, *c*. June; RAL, XI/109/48/2/61, undated, *c*. June; RAL, XI/109/48/2/64, undated, *c*. June; RAL, T18/307, XI/109/47/1/14, Anselm, Frankfurt, to his cousins, April 18; RAL, XI/109/49/1/9, Lionel, Paris, to his brothers, Oct. 2; RAL, XI/109/50/2/100, same to same, undated, *c*. Oct.; RAL, XI/109/48/2/48, Nat to his brothers, Sept. 25; RAL, XI/109/49/1/67, same to same, Oct. 14; RAL, XI/109/49/1/158, Oct. 29; RAL, XI/109/49/2/99, Nov. 13; RAL, XI/109/49/2/188, Nov. 27; RAL, XI/109/49/2/211, undated, *c*. Dec.; RAL, XI/109/50/1/35, Dec. 5; RAL, XI/109/50/2/44, undated, *c*. Dec.; RAL, XI/109/50/2/109, undated, *c*. Dec.; RAL, XI/109/50/2/113, undated, *c*. Dec.; RAL, XI/109/50/2/114, undated, *c*. Dec.; RAL, XI/109/50/2/121, undated, *c*. Dec.; AN, 132 AQ 5405/1M7, Anthony, London, to his uncle and brothers, Paris, Nov. 15; AN, 132 AQ 5405/1M7, same to same, Nov. 28; AN, 132 AQ 5405/1M7, Nov. 29; AN, 132 AQ 32 (A-12–2/4), Anselm, Paris, to Méeus, Nov. 25. For the unsuccessful attempts of Barings to get back into the French bond market, see Ziegler, *Sixth great power*, pp. 139ff.

158 RAL, T25/104/0/147, Anselm, Frankfurt, to his cousins, London, Dec. 16, 1840.

159 RAL, XI/109/40/2/17, MAR to NMR, May 16, 1841; RAL, XI/40/2/1, SMR to MAR. NMR and deRF, June 1; RAL, XI/109J/J/41, James, Paris, to his nephews, London, June 21. Cf. Corti, *Reign*, pp. 227f.; Gille, *Maison Rothschild*, vol. I, pp. 324f.; Cecil, *Metternich*, pp.154f. On this occasion, Metternich refused Salomon's request for a "war clause."

160   RAL, XI/109/45a/1/58, Mayer Carl, Frankfurt, to Lionel, London, undated, 1843. Cf. Corti, *Reign*, p. 231; Gille, *Maison Rothschild*, vol. I, p. 325.

161   Nesselrode, *Lettres et papiers*, vol. VIII, p. 95.

162   RAL, XI/101/3,4,5–5, James, Paris, to his nephews, London, undated, early 1842; RAL, XI/109J/J/42, same to same, Jan. 27; Feb. 2; Feb. 26; April 11; April 13; RAL, XI/109/42a/2/4, Anthony, London, to his brother, London, June 6; RAL, XI/109/43a/2/34, undated, *c.* July; RAL, XI/109/43a/2/86, undated, *c.* Aug.; RAL, RFamC/1/23, Hannah, Mainz, to Mayer, London, Sept. 26; RAL, XI/109/43a/2/113, Nat to his brothers, Oct. 27; RAL, T18/265, XI/109/46/1/74, Nat to his brothers, undated, Aug. 1844; RAL, T18/540, XI/109/48/1/37, same to same, undated, Aug.; RAL, T18/533, XI/109/48/1/36, undated, *c.* Aug.; RAL, T18/540, XI/109/48/1/37, undated, Aug.; RAL, T18/544, XI/109/48/1/39, Aug. 14; RAL, T18/545, XI/109/48/1/40, Aug. 14; RAL, T20/6, XI/109/48/2/39, Aug. 17; RAL, T20/10, XI/109/48/2/40, Aug. 20; RAL, XI/109/51b/2/13, undated, Aug.; RAL, T18/532, XI/109/48/1/114, deRF to NMR, Aug. 7; RAL, T18/548, XI/109/48/120, same to same, Aug. 14; RAL, XI/109/48/2/42, Sept. 4; RAL, T20/35, XI/109/48/2/43, Sept. 5; RAL, T20/36, XI/109/48/2/44, Sept. 6; RAL, T20/3, XI/109/48/2/4, Lionel, Frankfurt, to Nat, Paris, Aug. 17; RAL, T20/43, same to same, Sept. 3; RAL, XI/109/48/2/18, Sept. 7; RAL, T20/60, XI/109/48/2/20, Sept. 9; RAL, T20/70, XI/109/48/209, Landauer, Trieste, to SMR, Aug. 30; RAL, XI/109/53b/1/17, Anthony, Paris, to his brothers, undated, *c.* Sept. 1845. Cf. Ridley, *Palmerston*, pp. 404f.

163   RAL, T20/39, XI/109/48/2/47, Nat, Paris, to his brothers, London, Sept. 17, 1844. The crisis was occasioned by an over-zealous British missionary named Pritchard who challenged the French claim to the island.

164   RAL, T6/1200, Weisweiller, Madrid, to NMR, June 1, 1846; RAL, XI/109/57/1/82, Anthony, Paris, to his brothers, London, July 12; RAL, XI/109/57/4/51, Nat, Paris, to Lionel, London, undated, *c.* July; RAL, XI/109/57/4/67, Nat and Mayer, Paris, to Lionel, undated, *c.* July; RAL, T6/184, Adolphe to deRF, Sept. 19.

165   RAL, XI/109/57/3/66, Anthony to his brothers, Sept. 16, 1846; RAL, XI/109J/J/46, James, Paris, to his nephews, London, Sept. 16.

166   RAL, XI/109J/J/46, James, Paris, to his nephews, London, Sept. 26, 1846; RAL, XI/109J/J/46, same to same, Sept. 29. Cf. RAL, XI/109/58b/2/60, Natty, London, to his cousins, Paris, undated, *c.* Oct.

167   RAL, XI/109/58b/2/37, Nat, Paris, to his brothers, undated, *c.* Oct. 1846.

168   RAL, T7/64, Anthony, Paris, to Lionel, London, Oct. 1, 1846.

169   RAL, XI/109/58b/2/47, Nat, Paris, to his brothers, London, undated, *c.* Oct. 1846. Cf. RAL, XI/109/58b/2/29, same to same, undated, *c.* Oct.; RAL, XI/109/58b/2/65, undated, *c.* Oct.

170   RAL, XI/109J/J/46, James, Paris, to his nephews, London, Oct. 6, 1846; same to same, Oct. 8; Oct. 13; Oct. 17; Oct. 23.

171   RAL, XI/109J/J/46, James, Paris, to his nephews, London, Oct. 29, 1846.

172   RAL, XI/109J/J/46, James, Paris, to his nephews, London, Nov. 7, 1846; same to same, Nov. 12; RAL, XI/109/58a/2/110, Nat, London, to his brothers, Paris, Nov. 17; RAL, XI/109J/J/46, James to his nephews, Nov. 28; same to same, Dec. 1; RAL, XI/109/58b/1/31, Anthony to his brothers, Dec. 5; RAL, XI/109/59b/2/49, same to same, undated, *c.* Jan. 1847; RAL, XI/109J/J/47, James to his nephews, Feb. 20.

173   RAL, XI/109J/J/47, James, Paris, to his nephews, London, Feb. 23, 1847.

174   RAL, XI/109J/J/47, James, Paris, to his nephews, London, Feb. 24, 1847.

175   RAL, T7/154, Alphonse, Paris, to his cousin Anthony, undated, *c.* 1847.

176   RAL, RFamC/1/107, Hannah, Frankfurt, to Lionel, Jan. 16, 1847; RAL, RFamC/1/108, same to same, June 26.

177   RAL, T7/34, Anselm, Frankfurt, to James and Alphonse, Paris, Jan. 28, 1847.

178   RAL, XI/109J/J/47, James, Paris, to his nephews, London, Feb. 27, 1847; same to same, March 4.

179   RAL, XI/109J/J/47, James, Paris, to his nephews, London, March 31, 1847; RAL, XI/109/61/2/129, Nat, Paris, to his brothers, undated, *c.* April; RAL, XI/109/61/2/5, same to same, undated, *c.* April; RAL, XI/109/60/1/11, April 3; RAL, XI/109J/J/47, James to his nephews, April 3; RAL, T7/96, Salomon, Vienna, to MAR, deRF and NMR, May 8; RAL, XI/109J/J/47, James to his nephews, May 17.

FIFTEEN   *"Satan Harnessed": Playing at Railways (1830–1846)*

1   Ribeill, *Révolution ferroviaire*, p. 86. (Lecomte was director-general of the Orléans railway company.)

2   Osborne, *Rossini*, p. 89; Rothschild, "Musical associations," pp. 288f.

3 Eichendorff, *Deutsche Lustspiele*, pp. 61f.
4 Sheehan, *German history*, pp. 466ff.
5 *The Times*, Jan. 24, 1825, p. 3; Pollins, *Economic history of the Jews*, p. 91; Malchow, *Gentlemen capitalists*, p. 22. Emden, *Jews of Britain*, p. 108, states that Nathan was in some way involved with Grand Surrey Docks and Canal Co., but I have found no evidence to support this.
6 RAL, XI/109J/J/43, James, Doncaster, to his nephews, London, Sept. 13, 1843.
7 RAL, RFamC/1/31, Hannah, Brighton, to Lionel, London, Jan. 18, 1844.
8 RAL, T7/33, Hannah, Frankfurt, to Charlotte, Nov. 5, 1846.
9 RAL, XI/109/69B/2, Nat, Paris, to his brothers, London, undated, c. Sept. 1848.
10 Buxton (ed.), *Memoirs*, pp. 288–90.
11 Corti, *Reign*, pp. 85f.
12 Hawke and Higgins, "Britain," pp. 181ff.
13 Corti, *Reign*, pp. 180ff. For further examples of the continental Rothschilds" tapping of British capital and expertise, see RAL, XI/101/0–1/33, James to NMR, Nov. 11, 1837.
14 Dunham, *Industrial Revolution*, pp. 232–5; Gille, *Banque et crédit*, pp. 105–13; Cameron, *France and Europe*, pp. 112f.; Braudel and Labrousse, *Histoire économique*, vol. VIII, pp. 364–77. See also on the failure of schemes to finance improved water provision for Paris: Bertier de Sauvigny, *Paris*, pp. 91–3.
15 Gille, *Banque et crédit*, pp. 113–26.
16 Corti, *Reign*, pp. 174, 241f.; Gille, *Maison Rothschild*, vol. I, pp. 414f.
17 Gille, *Maison Rothschild*, vol. I, pp. 377–82.
18 O'Brien (ed.), *Railways and economic development*.
19 Laffut, "Belgium," pp. 203ff.
20 Pseudo-scientific racial definitions of Jewishness were of course primarily devised by anti-Semites in order to get at apostates or the issue of "mixed marriages." Because the Rothschilds remained Jewish in the religious sense, they could be attacked in traditional terms too.
21 RAL, T7/87, Anselm, Paris, to Lionel, London, Dec. 13, 1846.
22 Corti, *Reign*, pp. 86–91; Grunwald, "Europe's railways," pp. 170ff.; Heuberger, *Rothschilds*, pp. 130ff.
23 Haus-, Hof-und Staatsarchiv Wien, SMR to Austrian Kolowrat, April 15, 1835. Cf. Corti, *Reign*, pp. 88–91; Cameron, *France and Europe*, p. 209.
24 Corti, *Reign*, pp. 97–9.
25 *Ibid.*, pp. 92–4; Grunwald, "Europe's railways," pp. 170ff.; Macartney, *Habsburg Empire*, p. 259.
26 Corti, *Reign*, pp. 94–6. Sina later secured this concession, and began constructing track from Vienna south towards Gloggnitz and along the right bank of the Danube towards Raab.
27 Corti, *Reign*, pp. 100ff.
28 *Ibid.*, pp. 109–11.
29 Österr. Verkehrsarchiv, SMR to Kaiser Ferdinand, Feb. 20, 1836; Salomon to Hofkanzlei, March 7; Präsidial-Erinnerung Wien, March 21.
30 Corti, *Reign*, pp. 111f.; Heuberger, *Rothschilds*, p. 130; Jenks, *Iron Ring*, p. 142; Polisensky, *Aristocrats*, p. 53; Born, *International banking*, pp. 43f.
31 Corti, *Reign*, pp. 232–4.
32 Goldschmidt, *Erinnerungen*, pp. 33f.
33 Tapie, *Rise and fall*, p. 267. The Austrian government's inertia is well illustrated by the failure of a scheme to raze the city walls to ease the development of traffic between the centre and the suburbs: Barea, *Vienna*, p. 234.
34 Corti, *Reign*, p. 112.
35 Deak, *Lawful revolution*, p. 52.
36 Corti, *Reign*, pp. 239ff.
37 *Ibid.*, p. 232f; Carden, *Machine tool trade*, pp. 80f.; Heuberger, *Rothschilds*, pp. 132ff.
38 Berend and Ranki, *Economic development*, p. 100.
39 Corti, *Reign*, pp. 165, 182–5; Greenfield, *Economics and liberalism in the Risorgimento*, p. 75; Blum, "Transportation," p. 30.
40 Haus-, Hof- und Staatsarchiv, Vienna, contract between SMR and the Royal and Imperial Finanzverwaltung, April 14, 1845. Cf. Corti, *Reign*, p. 240.
41 Heuberger, *Rothschilds*, p. 119.
42 HSM, 4. Best. 16 Rep. XV Kl. 1 Nr 1 Vol. I, Nr. 144, du Thil, Darmstadt, to MAR, Jan. 3, 1836; HSM, 4. Best. 16 Rep. XV Kl. 1 Nr 1 Vol. I, Nr. 146f, MAR to kurfürstliche Staatsminister, Jan. 11; HSM, 4. Best. 16 Rep. XV Kl. 1 Nr 1 Vol. I, Nr 143, Auszug aus dem Protokolle des Finanzministeri-

ums, Cassel; HSM, 4. Best. 16 Rep. XV Kl. 1 Nr 1 Vol. I, Nr 305f., Gesetz über die Abtretung zu Eisenbahnen, June 18, 1837.

43   Grunwald, "Europe's railways," p. 174.
44   Stürmer et al., Striking the balance, pp. 77ff. Cf. Tilly, Financial institutions, pp. 104–5, 173n.
45   Schwemer, Geschichte, vol. III/1, pp. 56f., 387. Interestingly, Amschel is quoted in this anecdote speaking with a broad Frankfurt accent: "Der Kurprinz muß Geld hawwe. Das Land gibt ihm nix. Der Mann hat Kinner."
46   RAL, XI/109/36/2/3, Anselm, Frankfurt, to James and Anthony, Paris, May 29, 1838. See also RAL, T28/287, XI/109/42/3/72, same to same, March 14, 1842. For Bleichröder's struggle to persuade the Frankfurt house to invest in Prussian shares, see Stern, Gold and iron, p. 7.
47   Heyn, "Private Banking," pp. 291f., 308f., 381; Cameron, France and Europe, pp. 228–41.
48   RAL, XI/109/45a/1/61, Mayer Carl, Frankfurt, to Lionel, undated, 1843; RAL, XI/109/45a/1/69, same to same, undated, 1843.
49   RAL, XI/109/45a/1/53, Mayer Carl, Frankfurt, to Lionel, London, Feb. 27, 1843; RAL, XI/109/45a/1/56, same to same, Dec. 17; RAL, XI/109/48/1/66, Lionel, Frankfurt, to his brothers, London, Aug. 15, 1844; RAL, XI/109/48/2/11, same to same, Sept. 2; HSM, Bestand 300 C 28 Nr 2, Nr 20, Finanzministerium an Kurprinz von Hessen, Feb. 2, 1845; HSM, Bestand 300 C 28 Nr 2, Nr 20, Amschel to Kurfürst von Hessen, Nov. 22.
50   RAL, T18/346, XI/109/47/1/44, Anthony, Frankfurt, to his brothers, May 21, 1844; RAL, XI/109/47/1/69, same to same, undated, c. May.
51   RAL, XI/101/0–2/2, NMR to deRF, Jan. 6, 1837.
52   Gille, Maison Rothschild, vol. I, pp. 276f.; vol. II, p. 326; idem, Banque et crédit, p. 231.
53   Cameron, France and Europe, pp. 209f.; Metternich (ed.), Nachgelassenen Papieren, p. 495.
54   As in England, the first French railways strictly speaking were built to transport coal in mining areas: the Saint-Etienne line built in the early 1830s was the analogue of the Stockton—Darlington line built a decade previously. But the development of the railway network proper—in the sense of a service for both freight and passengers, and reliant on steam locomotives rather than horses—should be dated from the construction of the Paris–Saint-Germain line. Cf. Marion, Histoire financière, vol. V, pp. 177f.
55   Corti, Reign, p. 217.
56   Carlisle, "Chemins de fer"; Dunham, Industrial Revolution, pp. 59f.; Heuberger, Rothschilds, p. 134; Cameron, France and Europe, pp. 134ff.
57   Gille, Maison Rothschild, vol. I, p. 265.
58   Ratcliffe, "Origin"; Bowie, "Rothschilds, railways and urban form," p. 88. Cf. Cameron, "Crédit Mobilier," pp. 463f.; Ribeill, Révolution ferroviaire, p. 97.
59   Marion, Histoire financière, vol. V, pp. 177–81; Grunwald, "Europe's railways," pp. 172ff; Clough, France, p. 146f.; Gille, Maison Rothschild, vol. I, pp. 262–4.
60   Ribeill, Révolution ferroviaire, p. 434.
61   Ratcliffe, "Railway imperialism," pp. 66ff.
62   RAL, XI/109J/J/36, James to Anthony and Haas, Paris, June 8, 1836; James, Frankfurt, to Anthony, June 13; same to same, June 26.
63   Corti, Reign, pp. 113f.; Ratcliffe, "Railway imperialism," pp. 70ff.; Grunwald, "Europe's railways," pp. 173ff.; Gille, Maison Rothschild, vol. I, pp. 262–4; Dunham, Industrial Revolution, pp. 61f.; Ribeill, Révolution ferroviaire, p. 465. Saint-Germain shareholders were entitled to shares in the Versailles line in the proportion of two to one. Another planned line to Poissy, branching off the Saint-Germain near Colombes and running through Bezons, was never authorised.
64   RAL, XI/101/0–6/7, Shafenburg, Paris, to Lionel, London, undated, c. Feb. 1837; RAL, XI/109J/J/37, James, Paris, to his nephews, London, April 8; same to same, April 11; April 12.
65   RAL, XI/109J/J/36, James, Paris, to his nephews, London, April 22, 1836; same to same, May 12; May 17; May 25; June 3; Nov. 16; April 17, 1837; April 19; April 26.
66   Heine, "Lutetia," in Sämtliche Schriften, vol. V, pp. 273f.; Corti, Reign, p. 225.
67   Johnson, "Revolution of 1830," p. 175. The Rive Droite cost 16.8 million francs to build compared with a projected cost of 11 million, though it was significantly cheaper than the Rive Gauche: Ribeill, Révolution ferroviaire, pp. 434f.
68   Gille, Maison Rothschild, vol. I, pp. 295–7; idem, Banque et crédit, pp. 156–60.
69   RAL, XI/109J/J/37, James, Paris, to his nephews, London, Sept. 26, 1837. See also James, Brussels, to Anthony, Paris, Oct. 21.
70   RAL, XI/109J/J/38B, James, Florence, to his brothers and nephews, Oct. 2, 1838; same to same, Oct.

4; Nov. 5; same, Naples, to same, Nov. 15; Nov. 17; Nov. 20; Nov. 24; Dec. 11; RAL, XI/109J/J/39, James, Venice, to his nephews, June 15, 1839; same to same, June 17; RAL, XI/109J/J/41, James, Salomon and Anselm, Gastein, to Nat, Paris, Aug. 11, 1841; RAL, XI/101/3,4,5–13, Emile Pereire to James, Nov. 26.

71 Deschamps, *Belgique*, pp. 500f.; Gille, *Maison Rothschild*, vol. I, pp. 269–74; *idem, Banque et crédit*, pp. 234–42; Dunham, *Industrial revolution*, p. 354.

72 Gille, *Banque et crédit*, p. 236; Gille, *Maison Rothschild*, vol. I, pp. 271ff.

73 RAL, XI/109J/J/37, James, Paris, to his nephews, May 23, 1837; same to same, June 20; James to his brothers and nephews, Aug. 8; RAL, XI/101/0–1/20, Constantin, Brussels, to deRF, Sept. 29; RAL, XI/101/0–1/28, Haas, Paris, to Anthony, London, undated, *c.* Oct.; RAL, XI/101/0–1/43, Constantin to deRF, Oct. 2; RAL, XI/109J/J/37, James to his nephews, Oct. 3; same to same, Oct. 4; Oct. 11; same, Brussels, to same, Oct. 21; RAL, XI/101/0–1/1, Scharfenberg, Paris, to Anthony, London, Oct. 28; RAL, XI/109J/J/37, James to his nephews, Nov. 2; same to same, Nov. 14; RAL, XI/109/36/2/5, Anselm, Frankfurt, to deRF, Jan. 1, 1838; RAL, XI/109J/J/38, James to his nephews, April 1; same to same, April 16; May 12; May 16; May 17; May 19; May 20. Cf. Gille, *Maison Rothschild*, vol. I, pp. 269–71.

74 RAL, XI/109J/J/36, James, Paris, to his nephews, Dec. 21, 1836; same to same, Dec. 24.

75 RAL, XI/109J/J/37, James, Paris, to his nephews, Nov. 11, 1837; same to same, March 14, 1838; May 12.

76 RAL, XI/109J/J/37, James, Brussels, to his nephews and Haas, Oct. 19, 1837.

77 RAL, XI/109J/J/37, James, Rouen, to Salomon and Anthony, Paris, July 28, 1837; James, Paris, to his nephews, London, Aug. 2. Faucher, *Notes*, vol. I, p. 64, for allegations of "chicanery" by the government.

78 Marion, *Histoire financière*, vol. V, pp. 177–81. See also Clough, *France*, pp. 146f.

79 RAL, XI/109J/J/38, James, Marseille, to Salomon and Anthony, Sept. 25, 1838.

80 RAL, XI/109J/J/37, James to his nephews, July 25, 1837; RAL, XI/109J/J/38, same to same, March 15, 1838; RAL, XI/109J/J/38, same, Aix, to Salomon and nephews, Sept. 19; RAL, XI/109J/J/38, James, Nice, to Saloman and Anthony, Oct. 5; RAL, XI/109J/J/39, James, Rome, to Salomon and his nephews, March 4, 1839; RAL, XI/109J/J/39A, James, Paris, to Amschel and Salomon, Dec. 21; RAL, XI/109J/J/39, James to his nephews, Dec. 22. Cf. Dunham, *Industrial Revolution*, pp. 443–7; Gille, *Banque et crédit*, pp. 264–6; *idem, Maison Rothschild*, vol. I, pp. 266, 382–7.

81 RAL, XI/109J/J/38, James, Paris, to his nephews, London, March 10, 1838. Cf. Gille, *Maison Rothschild*, vol. I, pp. 265f.

82 RAL, XI/109J/J/38, James, Paris, to his nephews, London, May 16, 1838; same to same, May 26; James, Saint Sauveur, to Salomon and his nephews, Aug. 23; James, Eaux Bonner, to his brothers and nephews, Aug. 27. Cf. Dunham, *Industrial Revolution*, pp. 64f.

83 Ratcliffe, "Railway imperialism," pp. 71ff.; Dunham, *Industrial Revolution*, pp. 443–7. On the four major groups discernible in this period—the Rothschild group, the Laffitte—Blount group, the "Paris–Orléans group" and the Talabot group—see Ribeill, *Révolution ferroviaire*, pp. 99ff. As Ribeill notes, the last had to rely quite heavily on James for financial support.

84 RAL, XI/109J/J/39, James, Naples, to his nephews, London, May 21, 1839; same, Venice, to same, June 17; James, Kissingen, to Anselm, Paris, Aug. 9.

85 Ribeill, *Révolution ferroviaire*, pp. 140f.

86 The diplomatic crisis inevitably drew attention to the potential military significance of the Belgian rail link: see Deschamps, *Belgique*, p. 500.

87 RAL, XI/109J/J/40A, James, Paris, to his nephews, London, March 22, 1840; RAL, XI/109J/J/40, same to same, April 3; RAL, T25/104/0/20, Nat, Paris, to his brothers, April 5; RAL, XI/109J/J/40, James to his nephews, March 1, 1841 [wrongly dated 1840]; RAL, XI/101/3,4,5–3/73, unsigned proposal, undated, *c.* April. Cf. Ratcliffe, "Railway imperialism," pp. 75ff.

88 Johnson, "Revolution of 1830," pp. 157ff.; Kemp, *Economic forces*, pp. 126–8.

89 RAL, XI/109J/J/41B, James, Paris, to his nephews, London, Oct. 28, 1841; RAL, XI/101/3,4,5–5/57, deRF to NMR, Oct. 30; RAL, XI/109J/J/42, James to his nephews, Jan. 7, 1842; same to same, Jan. 10; RAL, XI/109J/J/42B, Jan. 16; RAL, XI/109J/J/42, Feb. 7; RAL, XI/109J/J/42B, March 16; RAL, XI/109J/J/42A, March 31. See Dunham, *Industrial Revolution*, pp. 76f.; Gille, *Maison Rothschild*, vol. I, pp. 340–44.

90 RAL, XI/109/42a/1/5, James, Paris, to Nat, London, April 15, 1842; RAL, XI/109J/J/42, same to same, April 30.

91 RAL, XI/109J/J/42, James, Paris, to his nephews, London, April 7, 1842; same to same, April 9; April 13; April 14; April 16; April 20; RAL, XI/109/42a/2/38, Nat, Paris, to his brothers, London, April 20; RAL, XI/109/42a/2/40, same to same, undated, c. May; RAL, XI/109/42a/2/42, May 7; RAL, XI/109/42a/2/43, undated, c. May; RAL, XI/109/44/2/29, deRF to NMR, June 9.

92 RAL, XI/109J/J42, James, Paris, to his brothers and nephews, Nov. 29, 1842; RAL, XI/109J/J42A, James to his nephews, London, Nov. 30; RAL, XI/109J/J42B, same to same, Nov. 30. See also RAL, T18/200, XI/109/45/6/151, Nat, Paris, to his brothers, London, undated, 1843; RAL, XI/109/45b/6/251, same to same, undated, 1843.

93 RAL, XI/109J/J/42A, James, Paris, to his nephews, London, Jan. 28, 1841; RAL, XI/109J/J/42, same to same, Jan. 29; RAL, XI/109J/J/42B, Jan. 31; RAL, XI/109J/J/42, Feb. 1; RAL, XI/109J/J/42B, Feb. 5.

94 Gille, *Maison Rothschild*, vol. I, pp. 340–44. Cf. Ribeill, *Révolution ferroviaire*, pp. 107f.

95 RAL, XI/109J/J/42, James, Paris, to his nephews, London, March 23, 1842; same to same, March 26; Dec. 5; RAL, XI/109J/J/42B, Dec. 21; RAL, XI/109J/J/42, Dec. 24; Dec. 26; Dec. 28; RAL, XI/109/45b/6/171, Nat, Paris, to his brothers, London, undated, c. Jan. 1843; RAL, XI/109/46/1/78, undated, c. Feb. 1844; RAL, XI/109/47/1/87, same to same, March 29; RAL, XI/109/47/1/115, undated, c. April; RAL, XI/109/47/1/117, undated, c. April; RAL, XI/109/50/1/23, Dec. 3; RAL, XI/109/50/1/163, Dec. 24; RAL, XI/109/50/1/187, Dec. 28; RAL, XI/109/50/2/113, undated, c. Dec.; RAL, XI/109/51b/2/16, undated, c. Jan. 1845; RAL, XI/109/53b/2/8, undated, c. July; RAL, XI/109/53b/2/9, undated, c. July; RAL, XI/109/53b/11, undated, c. July; RAL, XI/109/53b/1/1, Anthony to his brothers, undated, c. Sept. Cf. Dunham, *Industrial Revolution*, pp. 76f., 443–7; Gille, *Maison Rothschild*, vol. I, pp. 306–9, 358ff.; Deschamps, *Belgique*, pp. 506f.; Palmade, *Capitalism*, pp. 113–15; Ribeill, *Révolution ferroviaire*, p. 108. See Marion, *Histoire financière*, vol. V, pp. 215ff. for details of the concession: the law of July 15, 1845 specified a forty-one-year concession; this was later reduced to thirty-eight.

96 RAL, XI/109/44/2/10, James, Paris, to his nephews, London, Jan. 12, 1843; RAL, XI/109/45b/6/16, Nat, Paris, to his brothers, London, Feb. 24; RAL, XI/109/45b/6/29, same to same, April 11; RAL, XI/109/45b/6/34, April 24; RAL, XI/109/45b/6/37, May 13; RAL, XI/109/45b/6/105, undated, 1843; RAL, T18/80, XI/109/45/6/115, undated; RAL, XI/109/45b/6/117A, undated, 1843; RAL, XI/109/45b/6/127, undated, 1843; RAL, XI/109/45b/6/133, undated, 1843; RAL, XI/109/45b/6/137, undated, 1843; RAL, T18/85, undated, 1843.

97 RAL, XI/109/45b/6/80, Nat, Paris, to his brothers, London, Oct. 10, 1843; RAL, XI/109/44/2/44, deRF to NMR, Oct. 30; RAL, T18/14 , XI/109/44/2/46, James to Nat, London, Oct. 31; RAL, XI/109/44/2/58, deRF to Teste, Minister of Public Works, Nov. 1; RAL, XI/109/44/2/52, James to Nat, Nov. 11; RAL, XI/109/46/1/48, Nat to his brothers, Jan. 2, 1844; RAL, T18/253, XI/109/46/1/60, same to same, Feb. 13; RAL, T18/234, XI/109/46/1/68, undated, c. Feb.; RAL, XI/109/46/1/80, undated, 1844; RAL, XI/109/46/1/99, undated, 1844; RAL, XI/109/46/1/105, undated; RAL, XI/109/47/1/119, undated, 1844; RAL, XI/109/47/1/131, undated, 1844; RAL, T18/376, XI/109/48/1/15, undated, 1844; RAL, T18/440, XI/109/48/1/32, undated, c. June; RAL, XI/109/48/1/33, undated, c. June; RAL, T18/447, XI/109/48/1/34, June 28; RAL, T18/380, XI/109/48/1/4, Anthony to his brothers, June 19; RAL, XI/109/52a/2/120, May 19, 1845.

98 RAL, XI/109/47/1/114, Nat, Paris, to his brothers, Paris, undated, c. April 1844; RAL, XI/109/53a/1/116, same to same, July 19, 1845. Cf. Gille, *Maison Rothschild*, vol. I, pp. 355–63; *idem*, *Banque et crédit*, pp. 264–6; Bouvier, *Rothschild*, pp. 116f.

99 Ribeill, *Révolution ferroviaire*, pp. 108f. The Creil–St Quentin was originally intended to be for seventy-five years but this too was reduced to just twenty-five.

100 RAL, XI/109J/J/42, James to his nephews, March 12, 1842; RAL, XI/109J/J/42B, same to same, March 13; March 16; RAL, XI/109J/J/42, Sept. 9; Sept. 25; Oct. 17; RAL, XI/109/46/1/63, Nat, Paris, to his brothers, March 9, 1844; RAL, XI/109/46/1/76, same to same, undated; RAL, XI/109/46/1/94, undated; RAL, XI/109/47/1/95, April 14; RAL, XI/109/48/2/48, Sept. 25; RAL, XI/109/49/1/33, Oct. 7; RAL, XI/109/49/1/47, Oct. 9. Cf. Gille, *Maison Rothschild*, vol. I, pp. 347–54.

101 RAL, XI/109/51b/2/20, Nat, Paris, to his brothers, London, undated, 1845; RAL, XI/109/51b/2/35, same to same, undated, 1845; RAL, XI/109J/J/45, James, Paris, to his nephews, London, Feb. 3; RAL, XI/109/51a/2/134, Nat to his brothers, Feb. 24; RAL, XI/109J/J/45, James to his nephews, March 21. See also RAL, XI/109J/J/46, same to same, April 11, 1846; April 25.

102 RAL, XI/109/46/1/91, Nat to his brothers, undated, 1844; RAL, XI/109/53b/2/41, same to same,

undated, *c.* July 1845; RAL, XI/109/53b/2/50, undated, *c.* July; RAL, XI/109/54a/2/167, Sept. 24; RAL, XI/109/54/2/92, Nov. 13. Cf. Dunham, *Industrial Revolution*, pp. 443–7; Gille, *Maison Rothschild*, vol. I, pp. 365ff.

103   Ribeill, *Révolution ferroviaire*, pp. 109f.
104   *Ibid.*, p. 127. The words were used by the mayor of Bordeaux in 1844.
105   RAL, XI/109/50/2/107, Nat, Paris, to his brothers, London, undated, *c.* Oct. 1844.
106   RAL, XI/109/54b/1/17, Anselm, Paris, to his cousins, London, Dec. 4, 1845.
107   Gille, *Maison Rothschild*, vol. I, pp. 363–71, 426–7.
108   RAL, XI/101/1–16/21, Anthony, Paris, to his brothers, London, May 3, 1838.
109   RAL, XI/109/42a/2/21, Nat, Paris, to his brothers, London, undated, *c.* March 1842. Cf. RAL, T25/104/0/33, same to same, April 20, 1840; RAL, T24/122, X/109/52/55, Anthony, Paris, to his brothers, London, undated, 1842.
110   RAL, XI/109/42a/2/24, Nat, Paris, to his brothers, London, March 17, 1842; RAL, XI/109/42a/2/37, same to same, undated, *c.* April; RAL, XI/109/43a/2/149, undated, *c.* July; RAL, XI/109/43a/2/152, undated, *c.* July; RAL, XI/109/42a/2/52, undated, *c.* May; RAL, XI/109/43a/2/156, undated, *c.* July; RAL, XI/109/43/2/117, Nov. 13.
111   RAL, XI/109/42a/2/10, Anthony, Paris, to his brothers, London, undated, *c.* June 1842. But see also AN, 132 AQ 5405/1M7, Anthony, London, to James and Nat, Nov. 30, 1844.
112   RAL, XI/109/43a/3/27, Anselm, Frankfurt, to Nat, Nov. 13, 1842 with RAL, RFamC/1/40, Hannah, East Cliff Lodge, to Lionel, New Court, July 28, 1844.
113   RAL, XI/109/45b/6/180, Nat, Paris, to his brothers, London, undated, *c.* Jan. 1843.
114   RAL, XI/109/46/1/91, Nat, Paris, to his brothers, London, undated, 1844. See also RAL, XI/109/47/1/114, same to same, undated, *c.* April.
115   RAL, XI/109J/J/45, James, Paris, to his nephews, London, Jan. 3, 1845; same to same, Jan. 7; Jan. 10; Jan. 12; Jan. 15; Jan. 24; Jan. 26; Jan. 27; RAL, XI/109J/J/45A, Jan. 28; RAL, XI/109J/J/45B, Jan. 28; RAL, XI/109J/J/45, Feb. 4; Feb. 7; Feb. 10; RAL, XI/109J/J/45, March 14; March 16; March 24; March 28. As in England, the paper of companies was often traded by speculators months before concessions had been awarded: RAL, XI/109/51a/2/33, Nat, Paris, to his brothers, Feb. 5; RAL, XI/109/53b/1/57, Anthony to his brothers, Sept. 18 or 19; RAL, XI/109/54a/2/58, same to same, undated, *c.* Oct.; RAL, XI/109/54b/2/6, undated, *c.* Oct.
116   RAL, XI/109/45b/6/57, Nat, Paris, to his brothers, London, June 25, 1843.
117   RAL, XI/109/49/2/211, Nat, Paris, to his brothers, London, Oct. 31, 1844.
118   RAL, XI/109J/J/45, James, Paris, to his nephews, London, March 18, 1845. Sometimes James's exhortations clearly offended Lionel: RAL, XI/109/57/4/43, Nat, Paris, to his brothers, London, undated, *c.* July 1846.
119   Bouvier, *Rothschild*, p. 113.
120   RAL, XI/109/42a/2/28, Nat, Paris, to his brothers, London, undated, *c.* March 1842; RAL, XI/109/42a/2/34, same to same, March 7; RAL, XI/109/42a/2/19, March 8; RAL, XI/109/42a/2/39, April 30. See also RAL, XI/109/43a/2/84, Anthony, Paris, to his brothers, London, undated, *c.* July.
121   RAL, XI/109/42a/2/46, Nat, Paris, to his brothers, London, undated, *c.* May 1842; RAL, XI/109J/J/42, James, Paris, to his nephews, London, Dec. 3, 1842; RAL, T24/144, X/109/52/77, Nat, Paris, to his brothers, London, Dec. 14; RAL, XI/109/45b/6/2, same to same, Jan. 4; RAL, XI/109/45b/6/3, Jan. 5; RAL, XI/109/45b/6/6, Jan. 19; RAL, XI/109/45b/6/13, Feb. 15; RAL, XI/109/45b/6/14, Feb. 22; RAL, XI/109/45b/6/21, March 15; RAL, T18/100, XI/109/45/6/33, April 17; RAL, T18/116, XI/109/45/6/39, May 15; RAL, XI/109/45b/6/44, May 29; RAL, XI/109/45b/6/50, June 8; RAL, T18/34, XI/109/45/6/96, undated; RAL, XI/109/45b/6/97, undated; RAL, XI/109/45b/6/99, undated; RAL, XI/109/45b/6/117, Jan. 1; RAL, T18/135, XI/109/45/6/133, undated; RAL, XI/109/45b/156, undated; RAL, XI/109/45b/6/183, undated; RAL, XI/109/45b/6/184, undated; RAL, XI/109/45a/1/36, Anthony to his brothers, undated; RAL, XI/109/45a/1/37, same to same, undated; RAL, XI/109/45a/1/38, undated; RAL, XI/109/45a/1/40, undated (all undated letters 1843). See also RAL, XI/109/54b/2/75, Nat to his brothers, undated, *c.* Oct. 1845.
122   RAL, XI/109/45b/6/22, Nat, Paris, to his brothers, London, March 15, 1843; RAL, XI/109/45b/6/54, same to same, June 17.
123   AN, 132 AQ 5405/1M7, Mayer, London, to James and Nat, Paris, Nov. 29, 1844. Cf. Ayer, *Century of finance*, pp. 40f.
124   RAL, XI/109/53b/2/84, Anthony and Nat, Paris, to their brothers, London, Sept. 22 or 23, 1845.

125 RAL, T7/67, Mayer, Wildbad, to Lionel, London, undated, 1846.

126 RAL, XI/109J/J/46, James, Paris, to his nephews, London, Jan. 3, 1846; same to same, Jan. 5; Jan. 23; Jan. 25; April 7; April 14; April 18; April 20; April 22; May 2; May 6; May 12; RAL, XI/109/57/4/23, Anthony to his brothers, undated, c. June; RAL, XI/109/57/4/28, same to same, undated, c. June.

127 RAL, XI/109J/J/46, James, Paris, to his nephews, London, June 22, 1846; same to same, June 27; June 29; July 2; July 7; RAL, XI/109/57/1/4, Anthony, Paris, to his brothers, London, undated, c. July 1; RAL, T7/56, same to same, undated, c. July 1; RAL, XI/109/57/4/13, undated, c. July 1.

128 RAL, XI/109J/J/45, James, Paris, to his nephews, London, Feb. 19, 1845; same to same, March 4; RAL, T7/73, Anselm, Paris, to his cousins, London, Jan. 26, 1846; RAL, XI/109/55/3/149, same to same, March 27. On investments in iron and steel companies, see Caron, *Economic history*, p. 79; Gille, *Maison Rothschild*, vol. I, pp. 294–8, 392–4, 398–400; *idem, Banque et crédit*, pp. 231–4; Deschamps, *Belgique*, pp. 511f.; Cameron, *France and Europe*, p. 358.

129 Ribeill, *Révolution ferroviaire*, p. 270.

130 Caron, "France," p. 33; Pollard, *Peaceful conquest*, pp. 129ff., 153ff.

131 Ribeill, *Révolution ferroviaire*, pp. 114f., 464–9; Kindleberger, *Financial history*, pp. 207f., 221f.; Johnson, "Revolution of 1830," pp. 157ff. Limited-liability companies (*sociétés anonymes à responsabilité limitée*) were not legalised in France until 1863.

132 For example, twelve out of twenty-eight engines on the Paris–Saint-Germain line were British-made and three out of twelve on the Paris–Versailles line.

133 Lévy-Leboyer, "Capital investment," pp. 249ff.; Braudel and Labrousse, *Histoire économique*, pp. 364–71.

134 Hugelmann, *A Rothschild*, pp. 3ff.

135 Prawer, *Heine*, pp. 331–5.

136 Heine, "Lutetia," in *Sämtliche Schriften*, vol. V, pp. 448ff.

137 Prawer, *Heine*, pp. 655f.

138 Mérimée, *Correspondance générale*, vol. IV, pp. 422f.

139 Nesselrode, *Lettres et papiers*, vol. X, p. 228.

140 RAL, Moscow 224, Betty, Paris, to Alphonse, New York, Nov. 22, 1848.

141 Deschamps, *Belgique*, pp. 506f.

142 Toussenel, *Juifs*, pp. 22ff.

143 *Ibid.*, pp. 33ff. Toussenel also argued for a conversion of the national debt and a state monopoly on the canal system.

144 *Ibid.*, p. 40. Cf. Loménie, *Dynasties*, vol. I, pp. 118f.; Marion, *Histoire financière*, vol. V, pp. 215–19; Palmade, *Capitalism*, pp. 105–9.

145 Dairnvaell, *Histoire édifiante*, pp. 17ff., 22.

146 Chirac, *Rois de la république*, pp. 148ff.

147 Drumont, *France juive*, pp. 343ff. And see Ribeill, *Révolution ferroviaire*, pp. 140f.

148 See e.g. Colling, *Roman de la finance*, pp. 73f.

149 Pollard, *Peaceful conquest*, p. 160.

150 Bertaut, *Bourse*, p. 199.

151 RAL, XI/109J/J42, James, Paris, to his nephews, London, Nov. 24, 1842.

152 RAL, X1/109J/J/45, James, Paris, to his nephews, London, March 23, 1845; RAL, X1/109J/J/46B, James, Wildbad, to Salomon and Alphonse, July 26, 1846; RAL, X1/109J/J/47, James to his nephews, March 8, 1847.

153 Wiebe *et al.* (eds), *Disraeli letters*, vol. IV, pp. 201f.; RAL, RFamC/2/44, Disraeli, Carlton Club, to Lionel, Jan. 28, 1846; RAL, RFamC/2/51, same to same, March 21.

154 Balzac, *Correspondance*, vol. V, pp. 167f.; Gille, *Maison Rothschild*, vol. I, pp. 429f.; Ribeill, *Révolution ferroviaire*, p. 141.

155 Bouvier, *Rothschild*, p. 121.

156 Marion, *Histoire financière*, vol. V, pp. 217–19.

157 Mérimée, *Correspondance générale*, vol. IV, p. 463f. Women were not invited on the ground that they would be incapable of adhering to the strict timetable!

158 Ribeill, *Révolution ferroviaire*, p. 141.

159 Dairnvaell, *Histoire édifiante*, pp. 5ff.

160 Prawer, *Heine*, pp. 331–5.

161 Dairnvaell, *Histoire édifiante*, pp. 25ff.

162   *Ibid.*, pp. 9–19.

163   Although it seems unlikely that this pamphlet was authorised, Anselm later stated that the "vulgar abuse" directed at James had "emanated principally from a despicable person, to whom our Paris House had quite rightly refused a loan": Corti, *Reign,* p. 249.

164   Dairnvaell, *Guerre aux fripons,* pp. 3ff. This was essentially a development of his allegations that James had bribed politicians and the press to secure the Nord concession, and a more general attack on the financing of the railways.

165   Banquier, *Que nous veut-on avec ce Rothschild,* pp. 12ff.

166   Drumont, *France juive,* p. 355.

167   Anon., *Jugement rendu,* pp. 6ff. It is possible that the author *was* Toussenel.

168   *Ibid.*, pp. 20ff.; translated into German as Anon., *Rothschild: Ein Urtheilsspruch.*

169   Corti, *Reign,* p. 248.

170   RAL, XI/109J/J/46, James, Wildbad, to Salomon and Anthony, Paris, July 18, 1846; RAL, XI/109J/J/46B, James to Salomon, Anthony and Alphonse, July 20.

171   RAL, XI/109J/J/38A, James, Aix, to Salomon and his nephews, Sept. 27. 1838. Cf. RAL, XI/101/0–1/18, Scharfenberg, Paris, to Anthony, London, Sept. 28, 1837.

172   RAL, XI/109/42a/2/44, Nat, Paris to his brothers, London, undated, *c.* May 1842; RAL, XI/109/42a/2/48, same to same, May 14.

173   RAL, XI/109/57/4/8, Anthony, Paris, to his brothers, London, undated, *c.* July 10, 1846.

174   RAL, XI/109/57/1//85, Anselm, Frankfurt, to his cousins, London, July 12, 1846; RAL, XI/109J/J/46B, James, Wildbad, to Lionel, London, July 16.

175   RAL, XI/109/57/1/70, Anthony, Paris, to his brothers, London, undated, *c.* July 11, 1846.

176   RAL, T7/88, Salomon, Paris, to his nephews, London, July 19, 1846.

177   RAL, XI/109J/J/46A, James, Wildbad, to Salomon and Anthony, July 16, 1846.

178   RAL, XI/109/57/1/78, Anthony, Paris, to his brothers, London, July 11, 1846; RAL, XI/109/57/1/79, same to same, undated, *c.* July 11 or 12; RAL, XI/109/57/1/87, July 12; RAL, XI/109/57/1/89. See also RAL, XI/109/57/4/14, undated, *c.* July; RAL, XI/109J/J/46, James, Wildbad, to Salomon and Anthony, Paris, July 14.

179   RAL, XI/109/57/1/110, Anthony, Paris, to Lionel, London, July 17, 1846.

180   RAL, XI/109/57/1/135, Anthony, Paris, to Lionel, London, July 21, 1846; RAL, XI/109/57/2/2, same to same, Aug. 1; RAL, XI/109/57/4/15, undated, *c.* Aug.; RAL, XI/109J/J/46, James, Wildbad, to Salomon, Anthony and Alphonse, Paris, July 21; same to same, Aug. 3.

181   RAL, XI/109/57/4/46, Nat to Lionel, undated, *c.* Aug. 1846; RAL, T7/59, Anthony to his brothers, Aug. 8; RAL, T7/60, same to same, Aug. 9; RAL, T7/62, Aug. 13.

182   AN, 132 AQ 5410/1M12, NMR to deRF, Aug. 31.

183   RAL, RFamC/1/103 [ex XI/109/58], Hannah, Frankfurt, to Lionel and Mayer, London, Nov. 11, 1846; RAL, XI/109J/J/47, James, Paris, to his nephews, London, Jan. 9, 1847.

184   RAL, XI/109/57/4/67, Mayer to Lionel, undated, 1846.

185   RAL, RFamC/21, Charlotte, London, to Leo, Cambridge, Feb. 8, 1864. Naturally, their mother interpreted their survival as "providential." According to one account, however, Evelina and her unborn son died as a result of another railway crash two years later: Rothschild, Garton and Rothschild, *Rothschild gardens,* p. 32.

SIXTEEN   *1848*

1   RAL, XI/109/65/1/147, Anonymous [postmarked Mannheim] to "Messrs Rothschild Brothers, Bankers, London," March 17, 1848.

2   RAL, XI/109/66/1, Anselm to his cousins, London, April 5, 1848.

3   Disraeli, *Coningsby,* p. 238.

4   See also Zimmermann, *Marr,* pp. 27, 68.

5   "Du aber . . . rechnest und blätterst in Deinen Papieren;
      . . . Es werden die Länder, die Völker gezahlt,
      Und jeglicher Thron hat seine Nummer.
      Das Lied, was uns die Geister geboten,
      Du nennst es Hunger nach Ruhm und Broten.
      Ob muthig zum Kampf die Hörner blasen;
      Du willst, das friedlich die Völker grasen;

Drückst kalten Blutes mit Deinen Noten
Den Stahl in die Faust der gefürsteten Macht . . .
    . . .
Ob ewig auf zerbrochenen Achsen
Die deutsche Geschichte keuchend rollt;
Ob winzige Maulwurfshügel wachsen,
Wo Pyramiden stehn gesollt:
Sie küssen die Sohlen Deiner Schuhe,
Sie danken Dir die geheiligte Ruhe,
Die nur der Rede Blut versprützt . . .
Es danken die Fürsten im Süden und Norden
Mit Band und Stern und Baronat;
Es sendet der heilige Kirchenstaat
Sein Lob und seinen Erlöserorden."
Beck, *Lieder*, pp. 4ff.

6   Herzen, *Letters from France and Rome*, pp. 30, 55.

7   Marx, "On the Jewish Question," esp. pp. 169ff. Cf. Rose, *Revolutionary anti-Semitism*, pp. 298ff.;
     Wistrich, *Antisemitism*, pp. 51ff.

8   Heine, "Aufzeichnungen," in *Sämtliche Schriften*, vol. VI/1, p. 665, trans. Prawer, *Heine*, pp. 755f. For
     a version of the same joke in which the request for money comes from a rabbi, see Browne, *Baron Roth-
     schild of Frankfurt and the Rabbi*.

9   Zimmermann, *Marr*, p. 16.

10   Muhlstein, *Baron James*, p. 147.

11   Eichendorff, *Werke*, pp. 1443ff.

12   Corti, *Reign*, p. 166.

13   *Ibid.*, p. 177.

14   *Ibid.*, pp. 234–9.

15   *Ibid.*, p. 231; Prawer, *Heine*, pp. 329f.

16   Kübeck, *Tagebücher*, vol. I/2, pp. 779f.

17   Bäuerle, *Baron Rothschild und die Tischlerstochter*, esp. pp. 179–87.

18   Goldschmidt, *Erinnerungen*, pp. 12–33, 35f., 113. Goldschmidt specifically mentions his brother's dis-
     missal by Mayer Carl (see p. 3) as a reason for his animosity.

19   Werner, "Eine vergessene Tat"; *The Times*, June 3, 1847, p. 6.

20   RAL, XI/109/60/2/86, Anselm, Frankfurt, to Anthony, May 10, 1847.

21   RAL, I/218/3, Nathan to Liverpool, August 21, 1826.

22   RAL, T7/122, Alphonse, Paris, to Mayer Carl, Frankfurt, Jan. 31, 1846.

23   RAL, XI/109J/J/46, James, Paris, to his nephews, London, June 21, 1846; same to same, June 23; RAL,
     XI/109/61/2/42, Nat, Paris, to his brothers, London, undated, c. June.

24   RAL, RFamC/2/53, Disraeli to Baron Lionel, Feb. 25, 1847.

25   Weintraub, *Albert*, p. 175.

26   Wemyss Reid, *Life of Forster*, p. 186. Cf. Davis, *English Rothschilds*, p. 134. Arthur Kinnaird was a part-
     ner in the house of Ransom & Co.

27   *The Times*, June 5, 1879, p. 8. See also RAL, XI/109J/J/47, James, Paris, to his nephews, London, April
     23, 1847.

28   RAL, RFamC/1/105, Hannah, Frankfurt, to Mayer, London, Jan. 11, 1847; RAL, RFamC/1/108,
     Hannah to Lionel, Jan. 26. See chapter 17.

29   RAL, T7/147, Nat, Paris, to his brothers, London, undated, c. April 1847.

30   Calculated from Mitchell, *European historical statistics*, pp. 96ff.

31   AN, 132 AQ 5410/1M12, NMR to deRF, Jan. 6, 1846; RAL, XI/109J/J/46, James, Paris, to his
     nephews, London, Jan. 16; same to same, Jan. 21; Jan. 24.

32   AN, 132 AQ 5411/1M13, NMR to deRF, Feb. 2, 1847.

33   RAL, XI/109/61/2/153, Nat, Paris, to his brothers, London, undated, c. April, 1847. For details of pur-
     chases see AN, 132 AQ 5412/1M14, NMR to deRF, July 2; AN, 132 AQ 5411/1M13, same to same,
     Aug. 16; AN, 132 AQ 5412/1M14, July 19; AN, 132 AQ 5412/1M14, Aug. 10.

34   RAL, XI/109J/J/46, James, Paris, to his nephews, London, Nov. 2, 1846. See also RAL, XI/109J/J/47,
     same to same, Jan. 20; March 2; March 4; RAL, XI/109/59b/1/107, Anthony, Paris, to his brothers,
     London, March 17; RAL, T7/137, deRF to NMR, March 19.

35   AN, 132 AQ 5748/3M9, Salomon, Vienna, to James, April 11, 1847.

36   RAL, T6/233, B. Davidson, Paris, to Mayer, London, Feb. 16, 1847; RAL, XI/109J/J/47, James, Paris, to his nephews, March 8; same to same, March 15; May 12; RAL, XI/109/61/2/104, Nat, Paris, to his brothers, London, undated, *c.* April; RAL, XI/109/62/1/103, same to same, July 18; RAL, XI/109/62/2/106, Aug. 12. Cf. Gille, *Maison Rothschild*, vol. I, pp. 408–10.

37   RAL, XI/109/61/2/153, Nat, Paris, to his brothers, London, undated, *c.* April, 1847.

38   RAL, T7/139, Nat, Paris, to his mother, May 12, 1847.

39   Chirac, *Haute Banque*, pp. 256–9.

40   Heine, "Aufzeichnungen," in *Sämtliche Schriften*, vol. VI/1, p. 633.

41   Figures from Mitchell, *British historical statistics*.

42   RAL, T7/76, Anselm, Frankfurt, to his father, uncle and cousins, April 19, 1846; RAL, XI/109J/J/46, James, Wildbad, to Salomon, Anthony and Alphonse, July 20.

43   Cf. Rohr, *Origins*.

44   RAL, XI/82/9/1/127, Amschel and Mayer Carl, Frankfurt, to NMR, Jan. 13, 1847; RAL, XI/109/64/2/78, Nat to his brothers, undated, *c.* Oct.; RAL, XI/109/64b/2/100, same to same, undated, *c.* Oct.; RAL, XI/109J/J/48, Salomon, Vienna, to his brothers, son and nephews, Jan. 7, 1848; RAL, XI/109/65A, Anselm, Frankfurt, to Nat, Paris, Jan. 9; RAL, XI/109/65A, Anselm to James, Jan. 11; RAL, T8/2, Carl, Naples, to his nephews, Paris, Jan. 12; RAL, XI/109/65A/44, Anselm, Frankfurt, to Anthony, London, Jan. 13; RAL, XI/109/65A/52, same to same, Jan. 23.

45   RAL, XI/109/65A, Anselm, Frankfurt, to Nat, Paris, Jan. 9, 1848. Cf. Gille, *Maison Rothschild*, vol. II, p. 30; Droz, *Revolutions allemandes*, p. 110.

46   RAL, XI/109/65A/10, Anselm, Frankfurt, to Alphonse, Paris, Feb. 2, 1848.

47   Emden, *Money powers*, pp. 85ff. In the end, the Badenese government bailed the Habers out.

48   RAL, T7/135, James, Paris, to his nephews, London, Jan. 14, 1847. Cf. Corti, *Reign*, p. 242.

49   RAL, T7/101, Salomon, Vienna, to his son, Frankfurt, Sept. 18, 1847; RAL, T7/102, same to same, Sept. 19; RAL, T/103, Salomon to Metternich, Sept. 19; RAL, T7/49, Charlotte, wife of Anselm, Paris, to her mother, Hannah, Sept. 27.

50   RAL, T7/132, Salomon to MAR, Dec. 23, 1847.

51   RAL, XI/109/65A, Salomon, Vienna, to Anselm, Frankfurt, Jan. 1, 1848; RAL, XI/109/65A, same to same, Feb. 2; RAL, XI/109/65A/67, Salomon to his brothers, son and nephews, Feb. 12; RAL, XI/109/65A/93, Anselm, Frankfurt, to James, Feb. 17, 1848.

52   RAL, XI/109J/J/46, James, Paris, to his nephews, London, Oct. 22, 1846. Cf. Gille, *Maison Rothschild*, vol. II, pp. 27f.

53   RAL, XI/109/58a/2/27, Nat and Anthony, Paris, to their brothers, London, Nov. 14, 1846; RAL, XI/109/58b/2/32, Nat, Paris, to his brothers, London, undated. *c.* Nov.; RAL, XI/109/58b/2/45, same to same, undated, *c.* Nov.; RAL, XI/109/58b/2/50, undated, *c.* Nov.; RAL, XI/109/58b/2/57, undated, *c.* Nov.; RAL, XI/109/58b/2/60, undated, *c.* Nov.; RAL, XI/109/58b/2/62, undated, *c.* Nov.; RAL, XI/109/58b/2/70, undated, *c.* Nov.; RAL, XI/109/58a/2/110, Nov. 17; RAL, XI/109/58a/2/168, Nov. 21; RAL, XI/109J/J/46, James, Paris, to his nephews, London, Nov. 10, 1846; same to same, Nov. 13; Nov. 14; RAL, XI/109/58b/1/46, Anthony to his brothers, Dec. 6; RAL, XI/109J/J/46, James, Paris, to his nephews, London, Dec. 22, 1846; same to same, Dec. 30.

54   RAL, XI/109/59b/2/35, Anthony to his brothers, undated, early 1847; RAL, XI/109/59b/2/45, same to same, undated; RAL XI/109/59a/1/17, Jan. 4; RAL, XI/109J/J/47, James, Paris, to his nephews, London, Jan. 9, 1847; RAL, XI/109/59a/1/49, Nat, Paris, to his brothers, London, Jan. 9; RAL, XI/109J/J/47, James, Paris, to his nephews, London, Jan. 13; RAL, T7/144, Nat, Paris, to his brothers, London, undated; RAL, T7/145, same to same, undated; RAL XI/109/59b/2/73, undated; RAL, XI/109/61/2/156, undated, *c.* May.

55   RAL, T6/238, Davidson to NMR, March 6, 1847; RAL, T6/239, same to same, March 6; also RAL, T6/241, March 9; RAL, XI/109/61/1/179, Nat, Paris, to his brothers, London, June 30; RAL, T7/124, Carl, Naples, to his nephews, July 21.

56   RAL, XI/109/61/2/43, Nat, Paris, to his brothers, London, undated, *c.* April 1847. Cf. Kindleberger, *Financial history*, p. 281.

57   *Ibid.*, pp. 105ff.

58   RAL, XI/109/59a/1/49, Nat, Paris, to his brothers, London, Jan. 9, 1847.

59   RAL, XI/109J/J/47A, James, Paris, to his nephews, London, April 12, 1847.

60   Kynaston, *City*, vol. I, p. 154.

61   RAL, XI/109/60/2/27, Nat, Paris, to his brothers, London, May 4, 1847.

62   Conacher, *Peelites and the party system*, p. 42.

63   Figures for length of line constructed and investment show that it was not until 1851 that the trough was reached, four years after the financial crisis: there was, to use an apposite metaphor, a "runaway train" effect: see Caron, "France," p. 33. New concessions even continued to be granted during 1847: RAL, XI/109/59b/2/69, Nat to his brothers, undated, early 1847; RAL, XI/109/59b/2/70, same to same, undated; RAL XI/109/59b/2/92, undated.

64   Corti, *Reign*, pp. 246f.; RAL, T7/122, Alphonse, Paris, to Mayer Carl, Frankfurt, Jan. 31, 1846.

65   RAL, XI/109J/J/46, James, Wildbad, to Anselm, Frankfurt, Aug. 1, 1846.

66   RAL, XI/109/58b/2/46, Nat, Paris, to his brothers, London, undated, *c.* Oct. 1846; RAL, XI/109/58b/2/73, same to same, undated, *c.* Oct.; RAL, XI/109J/J/46, James, Paris, to his nephews, London, Oct. 17; same to same, Oct. 21; Oct. 27; Nov. 24; Dec. 5.

67   RAL, XI/109J/J/47, James, Paris, to his nephews, London, April 19, 1847.

68   RAL, XI/109/63/2/49, Nat, Paris, to his brothers, London, undated, *c.* July 1847. Cf. Gille, *Maison Rothschild*, vol. I, pp. 371–6.

69   RAL, T7/65, Anthony, Paris, to Lionel, London, March 27, 1847; RAL, XI/109J/J/47, James, Paris, to his nephews, London, March 27.

70   RAL, XI/109/60/1/138, Nat, Paris, to his brothers, London, April 22, 1847; RAL, XI/109J/J/47, James, Paris, to his nephews, London, April 27; same to same, April 28. Cf. Gille, *Maison Rothschild*, vol. II, p. 29.

71   RAL, XI/109/63/2/32, Anthony, Paris, to my dear brothers, London, undated, summer 1847.

72   Calculated from Mitchell, *European historical statistics*, pp. 370ff.

73   RAL, T7/94, Salomon, Vienna, to deRF, Feb. 15, 1847.

74   Fortunately, a secret paragraph stipulated that if the 5 per cents fell 5 per cent below the contract price of 98, the deal would have to be renegotiated. Cf. Corti, *Reign*, p. 251; Gille, *Maison Rothschild*, vol. I, pp. 324f.

75   AN, 132 AQ 5748/3M9, Salomon, Vienna, to Gasser, St Petersburg, April 4, 1847; Salomon to James and Anselm, Paris, May 1.

76   Corti, *Reign*, p. 256.

77   *Ibid.*, pp. 245ff.

78   Heyn, "Private Banking," pp. 358–72.

79   Sked, *Survival*, p. 113.

80   RAL, XI/109/65B/2/12, Nat, Paris, to his brothers, London, undated, *c.* Jan. 1848.

81   RAL, XI/109/65A/67, Salomon, Vienna, to his brothers, son and nephews, Feb. 12, 1848; RAL, XI/109/65A/93, Anselm, Frankfurt, to James, Feb. 17.

82   RAL, XI/109/70/3, Mayer Carl, Frankfurt, to his cousins, London, March 4, 1848.

83   RAL, T7/64, Anthony, Paris, to Lionel, London, Oct. 1, 1846; RAL XI/109/59b/2/37, Anthony to his brothers, undated, early 1847; RAL, XI/109/59b/2/88, Nat, Paris, to his brothers, London, undated; RAL, XI/109J/J/47, James, Paris, to his nephews, London, Feb. 2.

84   RAL, XI/109/61/2/47, Nat, Paris, to his brothers, London, undated, *c.* April, 1847; RAL, XI/109/61/2/53, same to same, undated, *c.* April; RAL, XI/109/61/2/105, undated, *c.* May; RAL, XI/109/61/2/116, *c.* May; RAL, XI/109/61/2/119, undated, *c.* May; RAL, XI/109/61/2/149, undated, *c.* May; RAL, XI/109J/J/47, James, Paris, to his nephews, London, May 19; same to same, May 27; May 29; June 2; RAL, XI/109/61/1/174, Nat to his brothers, June 30; RAL, XI/109/63/2/64, same to same, undated, *c.* July; RAL, XI/109/63/2/75, undated, *c.* July; RAL, XI/109/63/2/88, undated, *c.* July; RAL, XI/109/62/2/54, Aug. 5; RAL, XI/109/62/2/231, Aug. 30; RAL, XI/109/63/1/51, Anthony to his brothers, Sept. 8; RAL, XI/109/63/1/81, Nat to his brothers, Sept. 13; RAL, XI/109/63/1/97, Anthony to his brothers, Sept. 15; RAL, XI/109/64a/1/177, Nat to his brothers, Oct. 21; RAL XI/109/64a/1/227, same to same, Oct. 28; RAL, XI/109/64b/2/54, undated, *c.* Nov.

85   RAL, XI/109/64b/2/70, Nat, Paris, to his brothers, London, undated, *c.* Oct. 1847; RAL, XI/109/64b/2/85, same to same, undated, *c.* Oct.; RAL XI/109/64a/1/112, Oct. 12.; RAL, XI/109/64b/2/86, undated, *c.* Oct.; RAL, XI/109/64b/2/88, undated, *c.* Nov.; RAL, XI/109/64b/2/94, undated, *c.* Nov.; RAL, XI/109/64b/2/95, undated, *c.* Nov. Details of the public auction itself in *The Times*, Nov. 12, 1847, p. 4.

86   RAL, XI/109/64b/2/73, Nat, Paris, to his brothers, London, undated, *c.* Oct. 1847.

87   RAL, XI/109/64a/2/57, Nat, Paris, to his brothers, London, Nov. 6, 1847; RAL, T7/160, Anselm, Munich, to his uncle and cousins, Paris, Nov. 7; RAL, XI/109/64b/2/67, Nat to his brothers, undated, *c.* Nov.

88 AN, 132 AQ 32 A-12–2/5, Vroutschow, Ministry of Finance, St Petersburg, to James, Paris, Dec. 7; RAL, XI/109/65B/2/24, Nat, Paris, to his brothers, London, undated, *c.* Dec.; RAL [formerly CPHDCM], 58–1–404, James, Paris, to Heinrich *Heine*, Oct. 19.

89 Capefigue, *Grandes opérations*, vol. III, pp. 230f.; Chirac, *Haute Banque*, pp. 190, 208–10; Ponteil, *Institutions*, p. 198; Corti, *Reign*, p. 253; Gille, *Maison Rothschild*, vol. I, pp. 309ff.; vol. II, p. 42f.

90 RAL XI/109/59a/2/15, Nat, Paris, to his brothers, London, Feb. 3, 1847; RAL, XI/109/59a/2/137, same to same, Feb. 24; RAL XI/109/59b/2/15, Anthony to his brothers, undated, early 1847; RAL, XI/109J/J/47, James, Paris, to his nephews, London, March 2; RAL, XI/109J/J/47A, same to same, March 3; RAL, XI/109J/J/47B, March 3. Cf. Corti, *Reign*, pp. 252f.

91 RAL, RFamC/1/112, Hannah, Paris, to Lionel, London, March 8, 1847; RAL, RFamC/1/113, same to same, March 12. Cf. Kynaston, *Cazenove*, p. 36.

92 AN, 132 AQ 5886/4M9, Carl to deRF, July 3, 1847; AN, 132 AQ 5887/4M10, CMR to deRF, Jan. 5, 1848; AN, 132 AQ 5668/2M9, same to same, Jan. 12.

93 Figures in Felsini, *Finanze pontificie*, pp. 82, 107, 239.

94 RAL, XI/109J/J/46, James, Paris, to his nephews, London, June 20, 1846; RAL, XI/109J/J/46, James, Wildbad, to Salomon, nephews and sons, July 27.

95 RAL, T/92, 109/59, Salomon [to NMR?], March 6, 1847.

96 RAL, XI/109/58b/1/148, Anselm, Frankfurt, to Lionel, London, Dec. 30, 1846; AN, 132 AQ 5886/4M9, CMR to deRF, Jan. 10, 1847.

97 RAL, T8/8, XI/109/64–5, Adolph, Rome, to Lionel, London, Jan. 18, 1848.

98 RAL, XI/109/65A/49, Alphonse, Paris, to his cousins, London, Jan. 14, 1848.

99 RAL, XI/109J/J/46B, James, Ostend, to Lionel, London, Sept. 7, 1846; RAL, XI/109/58b/2/44, Nat, Paris, to his brothers, London, undated, *c.* Nov.; RAL, XI/109/58b/2/53, same to same, undated, *c.* Nov.; RAL, XI/109J/J/46, James, Paris, to his nephews, London, Nov. 25; RAL, XI/109/64b/2/53, Nat to his brothers, undated, *c.* Oct.

100 RAL, XI/109/57/4/42, Nat, Paris, to his brothers, undated, 1846; RAL, T7/31, Salomon, Vienna, to NMR; RAL, T7/90, same to same, Jan. 24, 1847. Cf. RAL, RFamC/1/106 [ex XI/109/59], Hannah, Frankfurt, to Lionel, London, undated, late Dec. 1846.

101 RAL, XI/109/65B/2/38, Nat, Paris, to his brothers, London, undated, Jan. 1848; RAL, XI/109/65B/2/43, same to same, undated, late Jan.; RAL, XI/109/65B/2/53, undated, *c.* Feb.; RAL, XI/109/65B/2/58, undated, *c.* Feb.

102 RAL, XI/109/66/1, Anselm, Vienna, to his cousins, London, Jan. 19, 1848; RAL, XI/109/65A/67, Salomon, Vienna, to his brothers, son and nephews, Feb. 12; AN, 132 AQ 5748/3M10, Salomon to deRF, Feb. 18. See also RAL, XI/109/65B/2/19, Nat, Paris, to his brothers, London, undated, *c.* Feb.; RAL, XI/109/65B/2/21, same to same, undated, *c.* Feb.

103 RAL, XI/109/65A/11, Anselm, Frankfurt, to Lionel, London, Feb. 2, 1848; RAL, XI/109/65A/10, Anselm, Frankfurt, to Alphonse, Paris, Feb. 2.

104 AN, 132 AQ 5887/4M10, CMR to deRF, Feb. 19, 1848.

105 RAL, XI/109/65A/70, Anselm, Frankfurt, to NMR, Feb. 13, 1848.

106 RAL, XI/109/43a/2/34, Anthony, Paris, to his brothers, London, undated, *c.* July 1842; RAL, XI/109/43a/2/59, same to same, undated, *c.* July; RAL, XI/109/43a/2/132, Nat, Paris, to his brothers, London, undated, *c.* July; RAL, XI/109/43a/2/106, same to same, July 14.

107 RAL, XI/109J/J/46D, James, Milan, to Nat and Anthony, Paris, Aug. 12, 1846; RAL, XI/109/60/1/127, Nat, Paris, to his brothers, London, April 20, 1847.

108 RAL, XI/109/65B/2/12, Nat, Paris, to his brothers, London, undated, *c.* Feb. 20, 1848; RAL, XI/109/65B/2/15, same to same, undated, *c.* Feb. 21; RAL, XI/109/65A/114, Feb. 21. See also RAL, XI/109/65A/80, Feb. 14; RAL, XI/109/65B/2/20, undated, *c.* Feb.; RAL, XI/109/65B/2/21, undated, *c.* Feb.; RAL, XI/109/65B/2/28, undated, *c.* Feb.; RAL, XI/109/65B/2/34, undated, *c.* Feb.; RAL, XI/109/65B/2/39, undated, *c.* Feb.; RAL, XI/109/65B/2/40, undated, *c.* Feb.; RAL, XI/109/65B/2/41, undated, *c.* Feb.; RAL, XI/109/65B/2/55, undated, *c.* Feb.; RAL, XI/109/65B/2/58, undated, *c.* Feb.; RAL, XI/109/65A/49, Alphonse, Paris, to his cousins, London, Jan. 14; RAL, XI/109/65A—41, same to same, Feb. 7.

109 RAL, XI/109/65A/124, Nat, Paris, to his brothers, London, Feb. 23, 1848.

110 RAL, XI/109/65A/130, Nat to his brothers, Feb. 24, 1848.

111 NLS, Ellice MS 15098 ff. 53–4, Charlotte to Miss [Marrion] Ellice, undated, 1848. The recipient was a niece of the former Minister for War, Edward Ellice, and corresponded regularly with both Charlotte and Louisa: Cohen, *Lady de Rothschild*, pp. 55ff.

112   RAL, T8/38, Anselm, Frankfurt, to his cousins, London, March 1, 1848; RAL, XI/109/65B/1/21, Anselm to deRF, March 3.

113   RAL, XI/109/65B/1/36, Anselm, Frankfurt, to James and Nat, March 5, 1848; RAL, XI/109J/J/48, Salomon, Vienna, to Amschel, Frankfurt, March 7.

114   Sheehan, *German history*, p. 662. Cf. RAL, T8/4, Salomon, Vienna, to MAR, March 2, 1848; RAL, XI/109J/J/48, Salomon to his brothers, son and nephew, March 11.

115   CPHDCM, 637/1/316, Metternich, Arnheim, to Salomon, Vienna, April 3, 1848. Cf. Palmer, *Metternich*, p. 313; Gille, *Maison Rothschild*, vol. II, pp. 37–40; Polisensky, *Aristocrats*, pp. 101f.

116   Goldschmidt, *Erinnerungen*, pp. 36f.

117   RAL, XI/109J/J/48, Salomon, Vienna, to his brothers, son and nephews, March 3; same to same, March 4; March 8; March 16; March 19; March 21; March 22; March 23; RAL, XI/109/67, Salomon to Amschel, Frankfurt, April 4; RAL, XI/109/67, same to same, April 6; Salomon to James, April 22; Salomon to Amschel, May 16. James had naturalised Alphonse and Gustave in February, so they were clearly eligible as French citizens: Prevost-Marcilhacy, *Rothschild*, p. 148.

118   See e.g. RAL, XI/109/65B/2/23, Nat, Paris, to his brothers, London, undated, *c.* March 1848; and RAL, RFamP/D/1/1, ff. 194f., Charlotte Diary, May 1; ff. 244–6, May 9; RAL, XI/109/67/1, Nat to his brothers, June 4.

119   See e.g. RAL, XI/109/65B/2/22, Amschel[?] to his nephews, undated, *c.* March, 1848; AN, 132 AQ 5887/4M10, Carl, Naples, to James, Paris, March 2. Cf. Corti, *Reign*, pp. 313–16.

120   RAL, XI/109J/J/48/15, James, Paris, to his nephews, London, April 18, 1848; RAL, XI/109J/J/48/29, same to same, May 5.

121   RAL, XI/109/65B/1/38, Anselm, Frankfurt, to James and Nat, March 4, 1848; RAL, XI/109/65B/1/66, same to same, March 10; RAL, XI/109/65B/1/81, March 12.

122   RAL, XI/109/65B/1/243, Anselm to James, Nat and Alphonse, March 31, 1848; RAL, XI/109/66/1, same to same, April 3; RAL, RFam P/D/1/1, ff. 47–50, Charlotte Diary, April 2; RAL, XI/109/65/1/233, Mayer Carl, Frankfurt, to James, Nat and Alphonse, Paris, May 30.

123   RAL, XI/109/70/3, Anselm, Vienna, to James, Paris, March 7, 1849.

124   RAL, XI/109/67/2, Anthony, Frankfurt, to his brothers, London, May 1848; RAL, XI/109/68A/2, same to same, Aug. 10.

125   RAL, RFamP/D/1/1, Charlotte Diary, March 28, 1848; RAL, T8/6, Gustave, Paris, to his cousins, London, March 29; RAL, XI/109/65/1/242, same to same, March 30; RAL, T8/17, Gustave to Salomon, London, undated, *c.* May; RAL, XI/109/66/2, Gustave to his cousins, London, undated, *c.* May.

126   RAL, Moscow 224, Betty, Paris, to Alphonse, New York, Nov. 15, 1848; same to same, Nov. 16; Nov. 17; undated, *c.* Nov. 26; Nov. 28; Nov. 29; May 24, 1849.

127   RAL, Moscow 224, Betty, Paris, to Alphonse, New York, undated, *c.* Dec. 1848.

128   RAL, RFam P/D/1/1, Charlotte Diary, March 20, 1848; March 30; April 4.

129   RAL, RFam P/D/1/1, Charlotte Diary, March 28, 1848.

130   Cohen, *Lady de Rothschild*, pp. 50ff.

131   RAL, Moscow 224, Betty, Paris, to Alphonse, New York, Nov. 23, 1848.

132   Nesselrode, *Lettres et papiers*, vol. IX, p. 145.

133   RAL, RFam P/D/1/1, Charlotte Diary, March 20, 1848.

134   RAL, RFamP/D/1/2, ff. 115f., Charlotte Diary, Aug. 20, 1848.

135   CPHDCM, 637/1/18/16, Extract from Metternich's current account, June 30, 1848.

136   CPHDCM, 637/1/11/1–16, Aufnahme [SMR] am 30. Nov. 1848, Nov. 30, 1848; CPHDCM, 637/1/12/34–7, Zusammenstellung [SMR], July 24, 1849.

137   Berghoeffer, *Meyer Amschel*, pp. 209ff.; Palmer, *Metternich*, p. 318.

138   CPHDCM, 637/1/3/316, Metternich, Arnheim, to Salomon, Vienna, April 3, 1848; RAL, T8/56, same, London, to same, Frankfurt, Sept. 8. Cf. Trentmann, "New sources," pp. 76ff.

139   RAL, XI/109/67, Anselm, Vienna, to Amschel, Frankfurt, April 22, 1848.

140   Feydeau, *Mémoires*, pp. 159–61.

141   Muhlstein, *Baron James*, p. 181.

142   RAL, XI/109J/J/48/36, James, Paris, to his nephews, London, May 18, 1848; RAL, XI/109J/J/48/37, same to same, May 19; RAL, T8/22, Gustave to his cousins, May 18; RAL, RFamP/D/1/1, ff. 315–16, Charlotte Diary, May 19; RAL, RFamP/D/1/1, ff. 335–7, May 28. Apponyi, *Vingt-cinq ans*, vol. IV, p. 275.

143   RAL, XI/109/67, James, Paris, to his nephews, London, June 23, 1848.

144 RAL, XI/109/65B/2/37, Nat, Paris, to his brothers, London, undated, *c.* March 1848.
145 RAL, Moscow 224, Betty, Paris, to Alphonse, New York, Nov. 25, 1848; same to same, Nov. 26.
146 RAL, XI/109/67, Anselm, Vienna, to Amschel, May 26, 1848; same to same, May 28; RAL, T8/54, Anselm to NMR, May 27; RAL, XI/109/67, Salomon to Amschel, June 8; RAL, XI/109/67/1, same to same, June 9; RAL, RFamP/D/1/2, ff. 132–3, Charlotte Diary, Aug. 21.
147 RAL, XI/109/69A/2, Anselm, Sensing, to Lionel and Anthony, Nov. 5, 1848; same to same, Nov. 6; Nov. 7; Goldschmidt, *Erinnerungen,* pp. 36f.; Corti, *Reign,* pp. 275ff.
148 RAL, RFamP/D/1/1, Charlotte Diary, March 20, 1848; RAL, XI/109/65/1/226, Anselm, Frankfurt, to James, Nat and Alphonse, March 29; RAL, XI/109/67, Amschel, Frankfurt, to James, Paris, May 26; RAL, XI/109/68B/1, Anselm, Frankfurt, to his cousins, London, Sept. 21.
149 RAL, XI/109/65/1/170A, Nat, Paris, to his brothers, London, March 24, 1848; RAL, XI/109/66/1, Carl, Naples, to his nephews, April 7; RAL, XI/109/66/2, Carl to his nephews, May 31. But cf. RAL, XI/109/66/1, Adelheid, Naples, to her daughter Charlotte, April 27. When Nat saw Adolph after the revolution, he found him "quite an altered man, he has become the steadiest fellow ever seen, he neither smokes nor shags nor dances": RAL, XI/109/71/4, Nat to his brothers, undated, *c.* April 1849.
150 RAL, RFamP/D/1/1, Charlotte Diary, March 28, 1848.
151 RAL, XI/109/66/1, Gustave, Paris, to his cousins, London, April 3, 1848; RAL, XI/109/66/2, Nat, Paris, to his brothers, London, May 20; same to same, May 21; RAL, T8/24, Gustave to his cousins, May 22.
152 Bocher, *Mémoires,* p. 99; Agulhon, *Republican experiment,* p. 29; Muhlstein, *Baron James,* p. 175f. According to the republican leader Garnier-Pagès, the attack on Suresnes was instigated by a local poultry merchant, Louis Frazier. The crowd pillaged the pheasant pens and the stables, stole horses and "with hatchets, iron bars and clubs they laid waste furniture, mirrors, and pictures." Those convicted were sentenced to between five and twenty years in prison: Prevost-Marcilhacy, *Rothschild,* pp. 80ff.
153 RAL, XI/109/66/1, Gustave, Paris, to his cousins and brother, London, April 24, 1848; Cohen, *Lady de Rothschild,* p. 52.
154 RAL, XI/109J/J/48/15, James, Paris, to his nephews, London, April 18, 1848; RAL, RFamP/D/1/1, ff. 129–36, Charlotte Diary, April 20. Apponyi, *Vingt-cinq ans,* vol. IV, p. 275.
155 RAL, T8/25, Gustave, Paris, to his cousins, London, June 10, 1848.
156 RAL, XI/109/66/1, Anselm, Frankfurt, to Alphonse, April 3, 1848; RAL, XI/109/67, Amschel, Frankfurt, to James, Paris, undated, *c.* April 9; RAL, XI/109/66/1, Mayer Carl, Frankfurt, to his cousins, London, April 9. Cf. Corti, *Reign,* p. 267.
157 Goldschmidt, *Erinnerungen,* pp. 36f.
158 On tax, see RAL, XI/109/66/1, Alphonse, Paris, to his cousins, London, April 1, 1848.
159 RAL, XI/109/65/1/122, Bleichröder, Berlin, to MAR, March 18, 1848. Cf. Stern, *Gold and iron,* p. 8.
160 RAL, XI/109J/J/48/18, James, Paris, to his nephews, London, April 23, 1848.
161 Rath, *Viennese revolutions,* p. 234.
162 Haus-, Hof- und Staatsarchiv Wien, SMR to Foreign Ministry, June 15, 1848. Cf. Corti, *Reign,* pp. 268f.
163 Girard, *Travaux publics,* p. 36.
164 RAL, XI/109/65B/2/18, Nat, Paris, to his brothers, London, undated, *c.* March 1848; RAL, XI/109/65/1/170A, same to same, March 24; RAL, XI/109/65/1/199, Gustave, Paris, to his cousins, London, March 27; RAL, XI/109/65/1/224, Gustave to his sister and cousins, March 27; RAL, XI/109/67/2, Nat to his brothers, undated, April; same to same, undated, *c.* May 13.
165 RAL, XI/109/67/2, Nat, Paris, to his brothers, London, undated, *c.* June, 1848. Cf. Girard, *Travaux publics,* pp. 49–55.
166 RAL, XI/109/65B/2/14, Nat, Paris, to his brothers, London, undated, *c.* March 1848; RAL, XI/109/65/1/160, Anselm, Paris, to Lionel and Anthony, London, March 23; RAL, XI/109/65/1/166, Alphonse, Paris, to his brother and cousins, London, March 23.
167 RAL, XI/109/65/1/182, Nat, Paris, to his brothers, London, March 25, 1848. Cf. Gille, *Maison Rothschild,* vol. II, pp. 37–41.
168 Apponyi, *Vingt-cinq ans,* vol. IV, pp. 153, 170, 172, 178.
169 RAL, XI/109/65/1/169, Salomon, Vienna, to MAR, March 24, 1848. Cf. Gille, *Maison Rothschild,* vol. II, p. 35; *The Times,* March 16, 1848, p. 7; Faucher, *Notes,* vol. I, p. 213.
170 RAL, XI/109J/J/48/22, James, Paris, to his nephews, London, April 27, 1848; RAL, XI/109J/J/48/23, same to same, April 28.
171 RAL, XI/109J/J/48, Salomon, Vienna, to his brothers, son and nephews, March 2, 1848; same to same,

March 10; RAL, XI/109/65, March 29; March 30; March 31; CPHDCM, 637/1/12/1–2, SMR to MAR, April 9.

172   CPHDCM, 637/1/11/1–16, Aufnahme, Nov. 30, 1848.
173   RAL, XI/109/65B/2/30, Nat, Paris, to his brothers, London, undated, *c.* March 1848; RAL, XI/109/67, Amschel, Frankfurt, to his nephews, London, April 2.
174   CPHDCM, 637/1/A167/1128–32, Salomon to Amschel, Aug. 28, 1853.
175   The Beyfuses nevertheless survived the crisis, though the firm later changed its name: Emden, *Money powers,* p. 87n.
176   RAL, XI/109/65B/1/3, Anselm, Frankfurt, to deRF, March 1, 1848; RAL, XI/109/65B/1/4, Anselm to NMR, March 1; RAL, T8/32, Salomon to MAR, March 6; RAL, XI/109/65B/1/52, Anselm, Frankfurt, to James and Nat, Paris, March 8; RAL, XI/109/65B/1/81, same to same, March 12; RAL, XI/109/65B/1/86, March 13; RAL, XI/109J/J/48/7, Anselm to his cousins, London, April 5; RAL, XI/109/67, Mayer Carl, Frankfurt, to James and his cousins, Paris, April 7; Amschel to Lionel, London, April 7; Amschel to James, April 9.
177   RAL, XI/109/67, Salomon, Vienna, to Amschel, Frankfurt, April 7, 1848; same to same, April 8; April 9.
178   RAL, RFamP/D/1/1, ff. 91–3, Charlotte Diary, April 12, 1848; see also ff. 105f., April 16.
179   See e.g. RAL, XI/109/65B/2/16, Nat, Paris, to his brothers, London, undated, *c.* March 1848; RAL, XI/109/65B/2/31, same to same, undated, *c.* March; RAL, XI/109/65B/2/32, undated, *c.* March; RAL, XI/109/65B/2/37, undated, *c.* March; RAL, XI/109/65B/1/10, Anselm, Frankfurt, to his uncle and Nat, March 2; RAL, XI/109/65B/1/27, Nat to his brothers, March 4.
180   Both Schleswig and Holstein were formally under Danish suzerainty, the former guaranteed by Britain, Russia and France under a treaty of 1720. However, the Salic law of succession applied in the duchies but not in Denmark, so that the failure of the Danish male line appeared to call the future of the duchies into question. The German claim was primarily an ethnic one. Holstein was already part of the German Confederation; the southern part of Schleswig was linguistically German. The Danes forced the issue by incorporating Schleswig into Denmark on March 21. The Confederation Diet in Frankfurt, encouraged by the nationalist pre-parliament, responded by sending a Prussian army to Schleswig. To the dismay of the nationalists in Frankfurt, on August 26 the Prussians bowed to British and Russian pressure and accepted an armistice which established a joint Danish—Prussian administration in the duchies.
181   AN, 132 AQ 13/Bilans, Dec. 31, 1846–Dec. 31, 1849. Cf. Gille, *Maison Rothschild,* vol. II, pp. 573f.
182   RAL, XI/109/67, Amschel, Frankfurt, to his nephews, London, April 2, 1848; RAL, XI/109/67, Mayer Carl, Frankfurt, to James and his cousins, Paris, April 3; RAL, RFamP/D/1/1, ff. 69–71, April 5.
183   RAL, XI/109/65/1/202, Nat, Paris, to his brothers, London, March 27, 1848; RAL, RFam P/D/1/1, Charlotte Diary, March 30; RAL, XI/109/66/1, Nat to his brothers, April 9; RAL, XI/109/66/2, same to same, May 10. The political anxieties of Albert's uncle, King Leopold of the Belgians, were such that he deposited 5 million francs with the Rothschilds as a contingency fund in the event of his losing his throne: Corti, *Reign,* pp. 273–5.
184   Interestingly, Barings fared relatively well in 1847, but saw profits slump in 1848: Ziegler, *Sixth great power,* pp. 373–8.
185   RAL, RFamP/D/1/1, Charlotte Diary, March 20, 1848; March 30.
186   RAL, RFamP/D/1/1, ff. 106–12, Charlotte Diary, April 17; RAL, RFamP/D/1/1, ff. 253–9, May 13; RAL, RFamP/D/1/1, ff. 265–9, May 14; RAL, RFamP/D/1/2, undated, *c.* June; Hedley, *Selected correspondence of Fryderyk Chopin.*
187   Wiebe *et al.* (eds), *Disraeli letters,* vol. V, p. 19.
188   RAL, XI/109/65B/1/82, Mayer Carl, Frankfurt, to his cousins, London, March 12, 1848; RAL, XI/109/65/1/100, Salomon, Vienna, to NMR, March 15; RAL, XI/109J/J/48, Salomon to his brothers, son and nephews, March 16; same to same, March 17. Details of payments from London to Paris in AN, 132 AQ 5413/1M15, NMR to deRF, March 17; RAL, XI/109J/J/48/4, James, Paris, to his nephews, London, April 1; RAL, XI/109/66/1, Anselm, Frankfurt, to Lionel, London, April 2; RAL, XI/109J/J/48/5, James, Paris, to his nephews, London, April 3; RAL, XI/109J/J/48/6, same to same, April 4; RAL, XI/109J/J/48/7, April 5; RAL, XI/109/67, Amschel, Frankfurt, to James, Paris, April 7; RAL, XI/109/66/1, Mayer Carl, Frankfurt, to Lionel, London, April 7; RAL, XI/109J/J/48/9, James to his nephews, April 10; RAL, XI/109/66/1, Anselm, Vienna, to his cousins, London, April 11; RAL, XI/109/67, Amschel to Lionel, April 14; RAL, XI/109/66/1, Mayer Carl to Lionel, April 14; RAL, RFamP/D/1/1, ff. 106–12, Charlotte Diary, April 17; RAL, XI/109J/J/48/22, James, Paris, to his

nephews, London, April 27; RAL, XI/109/67, Mayer Carl to James, May 1; RAL, XI/82/9/1/132, Lionel to Amschel [and Amschel's undated reply], May 15; RAL, XI/109/67/2, Anthony, Frankfurt, to his brothers, undated, c. June. Cf. Davis, *English Rothschilds*, pp. 136f.

189 RAL, XI/109/66/1, Anselm, Vienna, to James, Paris, April 10, 1848; Anselm to James, Nat and Alphonse, April 12; Anselm to Mayer Carl, April 16; Anselm to James, Nat and Alphonse, April 24; RAL, XI/109/67, Anselm to Amschel, May 5.

190 RAL, XI/109J/J/47, James, Paris, to his nephews, London, April 13, 1847; same to same, May 11; May 15.

191 RAL, XI/109J/J/48/1, James, Paris, to his nephews, London, undated, c. Feb. 1848; Muhlstein, *Baron James*, p. 173.

192 RAL, XI/109/65B/2/39, James, Paris, to his nephews, London, undated, c. Feb. 1848.

193 RAL, XI/109/65B/2/17, Nat, Paris, to his brothers, London, undated, c. March 1848; RAL, XI/109/65B/2/18, same to same, undated, c. March; RAL, XI/109/65B/2/30, undated, c. March; RAL, XI/109/65B/2/32, undated, c. March; RAL, XI/109/65B/2/35, undated, c. March; AN, 132 AQ 5415/1M17, NMR to Belmont, March 20; RAL, RFamP/D/1/1, Charlotte Diary, March 30; RAL, XI/109/65B/2/33, Nat and Alphonse, Paris, to NMR, undated, c. April; AN, 132 AQ 5415/1M17, Belmont to NMR, April 8; RAL, XI/109J/J/48/29, James, Paris, to his nephews, London, May 5; RAL, XI/109J/J/48/32, same to same, May 13; RAL, XI/109/68B/1, Nat to his brothers, Sept. 26.

194 RAL, XI/109/69B, Alphonse, New York, to his cousins, London, Dec. 5, 1848; RAL, XI/109/69B/1, Alphonse to Nat, Brighton, Dec. 5; RAL, RFamP/D/1/2, ff. 306–8, Charlotte Diary, Dec. 13.

195 RAL, XI/109/70/4, Nat, Paris, to his brothers, London, undated, c. April 1849; RAL, XI/109/71/2, Lionel Davidson, Paris, to NMR, May 2; RAL, XI/109/72/1, Alphonse, New York, to his cousins, London, July 11.

196 RAL, XI/109/69B/1, Belmont to NMR, Dec. 26, 1848; AN, 132 AQ 5420/1M24, Copy of Mexican indemnity agreement, Feb. 9, 1849. Cf. Gille, *Maison Rothschild*, vol. II, pp. 580–89.

197 RAL, XI/109/65B/1/66, Anselm, Frankfurt, to James and Nat, Paris, March 10, 1848; RAL, XI/109/67, Mayer Carl, Frankfurt, to James and his cousins, Paris, April 16.

198 RAL, XI/109/65/1/104, Alphonse, Paris, to his cousins, London, March 16, 1848; RAL, XI/109/65/1/129, Alphonse to his cousins and Gustave, March 19. Cf. Braudel and Labrousse, *Histoire économique*, pp. 371–7, 400–405; Palmade, *Capitalism*, p. 121.

199 RAL, XI/109/65/1/201, Salomon, Vienna, to his brother and nephews, March 27, 1848; RAL, XI/109/65/1/211, same to same, March 28; RAL, XI/109/65B/1/243, Anselm to James, Nat and Alphonse, March 31; RAL, XI/109/67, Salomon to Amschel, Frankfurt, April 1; RAL, XI/109/66/1, Salomon to MAR, NMR and deRF, April 1; RAL, XI/109/66/2, Anselm to deRF, May 21; RAL, XI/109/66/2, Anselm to his cousins, May 21; same to same, May 23. Cf. Huertas, *Economic growth*, pp. 41ff.

200 RAL, XI/109/66/1, Nat, Paris, to his brothers, London, April 10, 1848; RAL, XI/109/67/2, same to same, undated, c. April; RAL, XI/109J/J/48/11, James, Paris, to his nephews, London, April 12; AN, 132 AQ 122/151, NMR to deRF, April 14; Banque de France to NMR, April 15; NMR to Banque de France, April 17; Banque de France to deRF, April 18; NMR to Banque de France, April 18; NMR to deRF, April 19; same to same, April 20; deRF to Banque de France, April 21; NMR to deRF, April 22; same to same, April 24; April 25; Banque de France to deRF, April 25; NMR to deRF, April 26; same to same, April 27; April 28; May 2; May 3; Statement of silver sent to Banque from NMR, May 4; NMR to deRF, May 4; same to same, May 5; May 6; May 8; May 9; May 10; May 11; May 12 [and subsequent letters].

201 RAL, XI/109/66/1, Anselm, Vienna, to Nat, Paris, April 13, 1848; RAL, XI/109/67, Anselm to Amschel, Frankfurt, April 13; same to same, April 14; April 15; RAL, XI/109/66/1, Anselm to Lionel, London, April 16; RAL, XI/109/66/1, Anselm to his cousins, London, April 17; RAL, XI/109/67, Anselm and Salomon to Amschel, April 19; same to same, April 20; RAL, XI/109/66/1, Anselm to his cousins, April 21; same to same, April 22; Anselm and Salomon to Amschel, April 24; RAL, XI/109/66/1, Anselm to James, Nat and Alphonse, April 24; RAL, XI/109/67, Mayer Carl to James and his cousins, Paris, April 27; CPHDCM, 637/1/12/6, Übereinkommen [between] SMR, Wertheimstein and Arnstein & Eskeles, April 27; RAL, XI/109/67, Anselm to Amschel, April 27; RAL, XI/109/67/2, Nat, Paris, to his brothers, London, April 28; RAL, XI/109/66/1, Anselm to Amschel, undated, c. April 30; RAL, XI/109/66/2, Anselm to his cousins, May 3; RAL, XI/109/66/2, same to same, May 10; May 17; RAL, XI/109/67, Anselm to Amschel, May 20; RAL, XI/109/67/1, Anselm to his cousins, June 1; same to same, June 4.

202   RAL, XI/109/66/1, Anselm, Vienna, to his cousins, London, April 10, 1848.
203   RAL, XI/109/67, Mayer Carl, Frankfurt, to James and his cousins, Paris, April 12; same to same, April
      13; Anselm and Salomon to Amschel, April 17; Amschel to his nephews, April 20.
204   AN, 132 AQ 58887/4M10, CMR to deRF, April 14, 1848; same to same, April 25.
205   Capefigue, *Grandes opérations*, vol. III, p. 231. This may have been a way of testing to see whether in
      principle the new regime would honour the financial obligations of the old.
206   Muhlstein, *Baron James*, pp. 177ff.; Duveau, *1848*, p. 60.
207   Caussidière, *Mémoires*, pp. 210ff. Cf. the account in RAL, RFamP/D/1/1, Charlotte Diary, March 28,
      1848. See Corti, *Reign*, pp. 259–63; Gille, *Maison Rothschild*, vol. II, p. 34; Muhlstein, *Baron James*, p.
      180. A subsequent announcement in the *Moniteur* confirmed that James intended to stay in Paris: Gille,
      Maison Rothschild, vol. II, p. 36.
208   RAL, XI/109/66/1, Nat, Paris, to his brothers, London, April 4, 1848.
209   RAL, RFamP/D/1/1, ff. 64–7, Charlotte Diary, April 4, 1848.
210   Gille, *Maison Rothschild*, vol. II, p. 158.
211   RAL, XI/109/67, James, Paris, to his nephews, London, July 7, 1848.
212   RAL, XI/109J/J/48/12, James, Paris, to his nephews, London, April 13, 1848; RAL, XI/109J/J/48/19,
      same to same, April 24; RAL, XI/109J/J/48/24, April 30; RAL, XI/109/67/2, Nat, Paris, to his broth-
      ers, London, undated, *c.* May 1; RAL, XI/109/67/2, James to his nephews, undated, *c.* May 9; RAL,
      XI/109/67/2, Nat to his brothers, undated, *c.* May 12; RAL, XI/109J/J/48/41, James to his nephews,
      May 26; RAL, XI/109/66/2, Nat to his brothers, May 26; RAL, XI/109/67/2, same to same, undated,
      c. June. Gille, *Maison Rothschild*, vol. II, pp. 155–8.
213   RAL, XI/109/67, James, Paris, to his nephews, London, June 10, 1848; same to same, June 17; RAL,
      XI/109/67/2, Nat, Paris, to his brothers, London, undated, *c.* June 21; RAL, XI/109/67/1, Anthony,
      Paris, to his brothers, June 25; RAL, XI/109/67/1, Anthony and Nat to their brothers, June 25; RAL,
      XI/109/67, James to his nephews, June 25; Salomon to James, June 26; James to his nephews, June 27;
      Anselm to Salomon and Amschel, June 28; RAL, XI/109/67/1, Anthony to his brothers, June 30.
214   AN, 132 AQ 5748/3M10, Anselm, Vienna, to deRF, Nov. 14, 1848.
215   RAL, XI/109/68B/2, Nat, Paris, to his brothers, London, undated, *c.* Aug. 1848.
216   Barthélemy, "Banque," and related material in AN, 132 AQ 32 A-12–2/5, dossier compiled by R.
      Fillon.
217   Mérimée, *Correspondance générale*, vol. V, p. 291.
218   RAL, RFamC/4/49, Lionel, Paris, to Charlotte, London, July 16, 1848. Cf. RAL, RFamC/4/50, same
      to same, July 18; RAL, XI/109/68A/1, Anthony, Paris, to his brothers, London, July 29; Nat to his
      brothers, July 29; same to same, July 30.
219   RAL, XI/109/68A/2, Anthony, Paris, to his brothers, London, undated, *c.* Aug. 1848; AN, 132 AQ 32,
      A–12–2/5, Fillon dossier. Cf. Chirac, *Haute Banque*, pp. 208–10; Gille, *Maison Rothschild*, vol. II, pp.
      43f.; Muhlstein, *Baron James*, p. 183.
220   Muhlstein, *Baron James*, p. 178; Duveau, *1848*, p. 189.
221   RAL, XI/109/68A/2, Nat, Paris, to his brothers, London, Aug. 1, 1848; RAL, XI/109/68B/1, same to
      same, Sept. 12; Sept. 15.
222   RAL, XI/109/67/2, Charlotte, London, to Lionel, Paris, undated, *c.* May 1848. Cf. RAL,
      XI/109J/J/48/40, James, Paris, to his nephews, London, May 23.
223   RAL, XI/109/67/1, Nat, Frankfurt, to his brothers, June 9, 1848; Amschel to James, Paris, June 9;
      Anselm, Vienna, to his cousins, London, June 12; RAL, XI/109/67, Amschel to James, June 16; same
      to same, June 18; June 23; Anselm to Amschel and Salomon, June 23. However, of the 26 million
      gulden, 16 million consisted of Salomon's debts.
224   RAL, XI/109/66/1, Nat, Paris, to his brothers, London, April 7, 1848; AN, 132 AQ 5413/1M15,
      NMR to deRF, April 25; AN, 132 AQ 5415/1M17, Mayer, London, to James and Nat, Paris, May 10;
      RAL, XI/109/66/2, Nat to his brothers, May 18; RAL, XI/109/67, James to his nephews, June 15; same
      to same, June 17; June 21; RAL, XI/109/68A/1, Nat to his brothers, July 7; RAL, XI/109/68A/1, same
      to same, July 9; RAL, XI/38/81B, Davidson, Valparaiso, to NMR, Oct. 29; RAL, XI/109/69B/2, Nat
      to his brothers, undated, *c.* Nov.; AN, 132 AQ 5417/1M21, Itzel, London, to deRF, Feb. 6, 1849; RAL,
      XI/109/71/4, Nat to his brothers, May 16.
225   RAL, XI/109/68A/2, Nat, Paris, to his brothers, London, Aug. 28, 1848. Gustave was also present; Nat
      declined to attend on the grounds of ill health.
226   Corti, *Reign*, pp. 270ff.; Bouvier, *Rothschild*, p. 130f.; Gille, *Maison Rothschild*, vol. II, pp. 50f.

227 AN, 132 AQ 5748/3M10, Anselm, Vienna, to deRF, Nov. 17, 1848.

228 Interestingly, "the intention [was] to give Italy its freedom against an indemnity of 10 millions of gulden": RAL, XI/109/67, Anselm, Vienna, to Amschel, Frankfurt, April 28, 1848; RAL, XI/109/67, Mayer Carl, Frankfurt, to James, Paris, May 3; RAL, XI/109/67, Salomon to Amschel, May 8.

229 RAL, XI/109/67/1, Anselm, Vienna, to his cousins, London, June 6, 1848; RAL, XI/109/67, Mayer Carl, Genoa, to Amschel and Wilhelm Carl, June 7; RAL, XI/109/67/1, Anselm to his cousins, June 21; RAL, XI/109/68A/1, Anthony, Paris, to his brothers, London, July 30; RAL, XI/109/68A/2, Nat to his brothers, Aug. 1.

230 RAL, XI/109/68A/2, Nat, Paris, to his brothers, London, Aug. 2, 1848; same to same, Aug. 3; Aug. 4; Anthony, Frankfurt, to his brothers, Aug. 4; Nat to his brothers, Aug. 5; same to same, Aug. 7; Anthony to his brothers, Aug. 7; same to same, Aug. 10; Nat to his brothers, Aug. 29.

231 RAL, XI/109/69B/1, Mayer Carl, Frankfurt, to his cousins, London, Dec. 12, 1848; RAL, XI/109/70/3, same to same, March 22; March 26. Cf. RAL, XI/109/70/4, Nat, Paris, to his brothers, London, undated, c. April; RAL, XI/109/71/1, same to same, April 10.

232 RAL, XI/109/70/2, Anselm, Vienna, to James, Paris, Feb. 22, 1849; Anselm to his cousins, London, Feb. 27; RAL, XI/109/70/3, same to same, March 3.

233 RAL, XI/109/70/3, Anselm, Vienna, to his cousins, London, March 20, 1849; Anselm to James, March 21. It is a myth repeated in most books that Salomon never returned to Vienna after 1848.

234 See e.g. RAL, XI/109/67, Salomon, Vienna, to his brothers and nephews, April 8, 1848; RAL, XI/109/66/1, same to same, April 11; RAL, XI/109/67/2, Nat, Paris, to his brothers, London, undated, c. April; RAL, XI/109J/J/48/25, James, Paris, to his nephews, London, May 1; RAL, XI/109/67, Mayer Carl, Frankfurt, to James, Paris, May 8; RAL, XI/109/67, Anselm to Salomon and Amschel, June 25; RAL, XI/109/68A/1, Nat, Paris, to his brothers, London, July 7; AN, 132 AQ 5748/3M10, Salomon, Frankfurt, to James, Paris, Aug. 4; RAL, XI/109/68B/2, Anthony, Paris, to his brothers, London, Aug. 8; RAL, XI/109/68A/2, Anselm to Lionel, Aug. 13; AN, 132 AQ 5887/4M10, CMR to deRF, Sept. 4; same to same, Sept. 5; Sept. 12; Carl, Naples, to James, Sept. 12; SMR to deRF, Sept. 14.

235 RAL, XI/109/68B/1, Anthony, Paris, to his brothers, London, Sept. 28, 1848; RAL, XI/109/69B/2, Mayer Carl, Frankfurt, to Anthony and Lionel, London, Oct. 1; RAL, XI/109/69A/2, Anselm, Vienna, to his cousins, London, Nov. 27; RAL, XI/109/69B/1, same to same, Dec. 10. Cf. Scott, *Roman Question*, pp. 28f.; Mack Smith, *Mazzini*, p. 79.

236 RAL, XI/109/70/2, Anselm, Vienna, to his cousins, Feb. 22, 1849; RAL, XI/109/70/3, same to same, March 3; Anselm to James and Gustave, Paris, March 12; Anselm to Lionel, March 14.

237 RAL, XI/109/70/4, Anthony, Paris, to his brothers, London, undated, c. April 1849.

238 RAL, XI/109/70/1, Anselm, Vienna, to Lionel, London, Jan. 11, 1849; RAL, XI/109/70/4, Lionel, Frankfurt, to Anthony, Paris, undated, c. March; RAL, XI/109/71/2, Anselm to Nat, May 14. Cf. CPHDCM, 637/1/12/34–37, Zusammenstellung, June 30–July 24; RAL, XI/109/72/2, Anselm, Vienna, to James, Wildbad, Aug. 3; CPHDCM, 637/1/12/38–41, Zusammenstellung, Aug. 25–30; RAL, XI/109/72, James, Milan, to Amschel, Frankfurt, Sept. 22.

239 Prevost-Marcilhacy, *Rothschild*, p. 22.

240 RAL, XI/109/72/2, Lionel, Wildbad, to Mayer, London, Aug. 7, 1849.

241 RAL, RFamP/D/1/2, f. 338, Charlotte Diary, Jan. 4, 1849. An exception was Hannah: see her defence of "Pam" in RAL, XI/109/73/3, Hannah, Frankfurt, to her son, Lionel, Nov. 19.

242 RAL, XI/109/71/4, Nat, Paris, to his brothers, London, undated, c. April 1849; RAL, XI/109/70, James, Paris, to his nephews, London, Jan. 14.

243 RAL, Moscow 224, Betty, Paris, to Alphonse, New York, Dec. 30, 1848.

244 See e.g. RAL, XI/109/70/4, Mayer to his mother, undated, c. March 1849; same to his brothers, undated, c. March.

245 RAL, XI/109/68A/2, Nat, Paris, to his brothers, London, Aug. 31, 1848; RAL, XI/109/68B/2, same to same, undated, c. Sept.; RAL, XI/109/68B/1, Sept. 1; Sept. 8.

246 RAL, XI/109/71/2, Nat, Paris, to his brothers, London, May 11, 1849.

247 Castellane, *Journal*, vol. IV, p. 192; Persigny, *Mémoires*, p. 129; Luna, *Cavaignac*, p. 377; Corti, *Reign*, pp. 270–75. Cf. RAL, RFamP/D/1/2, Charlotte Diary, Nov. 15, 1848.

248 RAL, XI/109/70/4, Anthony, Paris, to his brothers, London, undated, c. April 1849; RAL, XI/109/72/2, same to same, July 29; RAL, XI/109/73/1, Anthony to Mayer, Oct. 20. For earlier derogatory Rothschild comments, see RAL, XI/109J/J/46, James, Paris, to his nephews, London, May 26, 1846.

249   RAL, XI/109/70, James, Paris, to his nephews, London, Jan. 16, 1849; same to same, Feb. 1. The press
        exaggerated the sum involved, which was said to be a million francs: see Gille, *Maison Rothschild*, vol. II,
        p. 53.

250   RAL, XI/109/70, James, Frankfurt, to Anthony, Jan. 21, 1849.

251   Swartz and Swartz (eds), *Disraeli's reminiscences*, p. 64. See also Muhlstein, *Baron James*, pp. 191ff.

252   RAL, Moscow 224, Betty, Paris, to Alphonse, New York, Nov. 15, 1848; same to same, Nov. 16; Nov.
        17; undated, *c.* Nov. 26; Nov. 28; Nov. 29; Dec. 6; Dec. 12. Cf. Prevost-Marcilhacy, *Rothschild*, pp. 81f.

253   RAL, XI/109/67, James, Paris, to his nephews, London, June 9, 1848; RAL, T8/25, Gustave, Paris, to
        his cousins, London, June 10; RAL, XI/109/67, James to his nephews, June 13; RAL, XI/109/67/2,
        Nat, Paris, to his brothers, London, undated, *c.* June; RAL, XI/109/67/1, same to same, June 14; RAL,
        XI/109/67/2, undated, *c.* June.

254   RAL, XI/109/68B/1, Nat to his brothers, Sept. 5, 1848; RAL, XI/109/69B/2, undated, *c.* Sept. [several
        letters]; RAL, XI/109/68B/1, Sept. 22; RAL, XI/109/68B/1, Sept. 26; RAL, XI/109/69A/1, Anthony
        to his brothers, Oct. 11; RAL, XI/109/67/2, Nat to his brothers, Oct. 20; RAL, XI/109/69A/1, same to
        same, Oct. 23; Oct. 26; RAL, XI/109/69B/2, undated, *c.* Nov.; RAL, XI/109/69A/2, Nov. 7; Nov. 8;
        Nov. 14; Nov. 21.

255   RAL, Moscow 224, Betty, Paris, to Alphonse, New York, Nov. 19, 1848; same to same, Nov. 22; Nov.
        29.

256   RAL, Moscow 224, Betty, Paris, to Alphonse, New York, Dec. 30, 1848.

257   RAL, XI/109/70/1, Anthony, Paris, to Lionel, London, Jan. 2, 1849; RAL, XI/109/70, James, Paris, to
        his nephews, London, Feb. 4; RAL, XI/109/70/4, Anthony to Mayer, London, undated, *c.* April.

258   RAL, XI/109/71, James, Paris, to his nephews, London, April 10, 1849.

259   RAL, XI/109/70, James, Paris, to his nephews, London, Jan. 5, 1849; same to same, Jan. 6; Jan. 16;
        Feb. 21; Feb. 26; March 15; March 22; March 29; May 22; May 23.

260   RAL, XI/109/71, James, Paris, to his nephews, London, June 9, 1849. See also RAL, XI/109/71/3, Nat,
        Paris, to his brothers, London, June 7; same to same, June 27; RAL, XI/109/72/1, Anthony to his
        brothers, July 23.

261   RAL, XI/109/70/1, Anthony, Paris, to his brothers, London, Jan. 6, 1849; RAL, XI/109/70/4, same to
        same, undated, *c.* April.

262   RAL, XI/109/71/2, Mayer Carl, Frankfurt, to his cousins, London, May 17, 1849; RAL, XI/109/71/4,
        same to same, undated, *c.* May.

263   RAL, XI/109/71/1, Anselm, Vienna, to James, Paris, April 13, 1849; Anselm to his cousins, London,
        April 23; RAL, XI/109/71/2, same to same, May 2; May 5; May 29.

264   RAL, XI/109/72/1, Anselm to James and Gustave, July 4, 1849.

265   RAL, XI/109/71/3, Anselm, Vienna, to James and Gustave, June 16, 1849; Salomon, Vienna, to James,
        Paris, June 30. See also RAL, XI/109/73/3, James, Paris, to his nephews, London, Nov. 8.

266   RAL, XI/109/72/2, Anselm, Vienna, to James, Homburg, Aug. 4, 1849; AN, 132 AQ 5749/3M11,
        SMR to deRF, Aug. 18; RAL, XI/109/72/3, Salomon, Vienna, to his brothers and nephews, Sept. 19;
        Lionel, Frankfurt, to Anthony, London, Sept. 21; Lionel to Mayer, London, Sept. 23; RAl,
        XI/109/73/1, Salomon, Vienna, to Anselm, Oct. 9. Cf. Gille, *Maison Rothschild*, vol. II, pp. 65f.

267   RAL [formerly CPHDCM], 58–1–403/2, Heinrich Heine, "Deutschland im Oktober 1849" [copy].

268   RAL, XI/109/71/3, Anselm, Vienna, to his cousins, London, June 28, 1849. Cf. RAL, XI/109/72/2,
        Lionel, Wildbad, to Mayer, London, Aug. 4; Anthony, Paris, to Mayer, Aug. 18; RAL, XI/109/72/4,
        same to same, undated, *c.* Aug. 25; RAL, XI/109/72/3, Lionel, Frankfurt, to Mayer, Sept. 14.

269   RAL, XI/109/72/4, Carl, Naples, to his nephews, London, July 4, 1849; same to same, Aug. 7.

270   Wilson, *Rothschild*, p. 117.

271   RAL, XI/109/72/2, Lionel, Wildbad, to his mother, London, Aug. 25, 1849.

272   RAL, XI/109/70, James, Paris, to his nephews, London, March 12, 1849; James, Homburg, to Mayer,
        London, Aug. 3.

273   RAL, XI/109/72, James, Homburg, to Anthony, Paris, Aug. 8, 1849; RAL, XI/109/72/2, same, Wild-
        bad, to same, Aug. 21; RAL, XI/109/72, Aug. 23; RAL, XI/109/72/4, Adolph, Naples, to Anthony,
        Paris, Sept. 1. Cf. Gille, *Maison Rothschild*, vol. II, pp. 69–72.

274   RAL, XI/109/72/3, Adolph, Naples, to Anthony, Paris, Sept. 9, 1849; RAL, XI/109/73/3, Gustave,
        Paris, to his cousins, Dec. 22; Alphonse to Anthony, Dec. 24. Cf. Corti, *Reign*, pp. 140–42; Coppa,
        Cardinal Antonelli, p. 82; Gille, *Maison Rothschild*, vol. II, pp. 68f.

275   RAL, XI/109/73/3, Anselm, Frankfurt, to James and his cousins, Paris, Dec. 23, 1849.

276   RAL, XI/109/73, James, Paris, to his nephews, London, Dec. 12, 1849; RAL, XI/109/73/3, Salomon

to Anselm, Frankfurt, Dec. 18; RAL, XI/109/73/3, Nat, Paris, to his brothers, London, Dec. 25; Anselm to James, Dec. 26. Cf. AN, 132 AQ 5479/3M11, Salomon to James and Alphonse, Nov. 11; same to same, Dec. 14; Dec. 17; AN, 132 AQ 5749/3M11, Dec. 17.

277   RAL, XI/109/70/3, Anselm, Vienna, to James, Paris, March 30, 1849; RAL, XI/109/71/1, Anselm to James and his cousins, April 3; Anselm to his cousins, London, April 3; same to same, April 4; Anselm to James, April 11; same to same, April 12; RAL, XI/109/71/1, Salomon, Vienna, to James, April 25; RAL, XI/109/71/2, Anselm to James, Nat and Gustave, May 3; RAL, XI/109/71/1, Landauer, Milan, to SMR, May 19; RAL, XI/109/71/2, Anselm to his cousins, May 24.

278   RAL, XI/109/71/4, Nat, Paris, to his brothers, London, undated, *c.* April 1849; RAL, RFamP/D/1/3, ff. 5–6, Charlotte Diary, June 18.

279   RAL, XI/109/72/2, Anselm, Vienna, to James, Wildbad, Aug, 3, 1849.

280   RAL, XI/109/72, James, Paris, to his nephews, London, April 17, 1849; same to same, June 14; June 21. Cf. Cavour, *Nouvelles lettres*, pp. 299, 307f.; Corti, *Reign*, p. 299; Gille, *Maison Rothschild*, vol. II, pp. 75f.

281   AN, 132 AQ 5901, James, Brussels, to Anthony and Gustave, Paris, July 22, 1849; RAL, XI/109/72, James, Homburg, to Anthony and Gustave, July 29; RAL, XI/109/72/1, Lionel, Wildbad, to Mayer, London, July 31; James, Homburg, to Anthony and Gustave, Aug. 3; RAL, XI/109/72/2, Anselm, Vienna, to James, Aug. 5; Lionel, Wildbad, to Mayer, London, Aug. 11; Anselm to James, Aug, 15; same to same, Aug. 17; Aug. 22; Aug. 23; AN, 132 AQ 5749/3M11, SMR to Landauer, Turin, Aug. 22 [two letters]; RAL, XI/109/72/2, Lionel to Mayer, Aug. 25; Lionel to Anthony, Aug. 27; Anthony to Mayer, Aug. 27.

282   RAL, XI/109/72/3, Alphonse, Vienna, to Anthony, Paris, Sept. 7, 1849; RAL, XI/109/72/3, James, Vienna, to Anthony, Paris, Sept. 8; same to same, Sept. 9; James, Trieste, to Amschel, Frankfurt, Sept. 12; RAL, XI/109/72/3, Anthony, Paris, to Mayer, London, Sept. 14; AN, 132 AQ 5479/3M11, SMR to deRF, Sept. 19; RAL, XI/109/72/3, Anthony, Paris, to Mayer, London, Sept. 24. In fact, he secured only a quarter per cent commission on this advance, which Anthony regarded as "stupid" and typical of the way his uncles "always want to show themselves great people." For James's efforts to increase the commission on a later advance, see AN, 132 AQ 5749/3M11, Salomon, Vienna, to James, Paris, Dec. 30.

283   RAL, XI/109/72/3, Gustave, Turin, to Anthony and Alphonse, Paris, Sept. 24, 1849; RAL, XI/109/72, James and Anselm, Turin, to Amschel, Frankfurt, Sept. 24; James to Anthony and Alphonse, Sept. 25; same to same, Sept. 27; Sept. 28; Sept. 29; RAL, XI/109/73, Oct. 3. Cf. Gille, *Maison Rothschild*, vol. II, p. 78.

284   Cavour, *Nouvelles lettres*, pp. 341ff.; Corti, *Reign*, p. 299; Gille, *Maison Rothschild*, vol. II, p. 77.

285   Cavour, *Nouvelles Lettres*, pp. 344–8, trans. Corti, *Reign*, pp. 300ff. James attempted to mollify Cavour by sending his agent Landauer to offer him "as many Rentes *au prix courant* as I wanted." Cavour refused, "but it gave me some idea of the way business is done in most of the European Cabinets."

286   As he put it, planning a visit to Florence later in the year, "Wenn einmal wir mit Italien verheiratet sind, so müssen wir oft die Geschäften erneuern": RAL, XI/109/72, James, Turin, to Anthony and Alphonse, Paris, Sept. 28, 1849. See also RAL, XI/109/73/1, Anselm, Frankfurt, to James, Anthony and Gustave, Oct. 14.

287   RAL, XI/109/72/1, Mayer Carl, Frankfurt, to Lionel, London, July 6, 1849; Stüve (ed.), *Briefwechsel*, pp. 394ff.; Vogel (ed.), *Briefe Stüves*, p. 694. Another disappointment was Amschel's failure to secure the Darmstadt loan in September: see RAL, XI/109/72/3, Lionel, Berlin, to Mayer, London, Sept. 13.

288   AN, 132 AQ 5901/2M43, James, Homburg, to Anthony and Gustave, July 29, 1849; RAL, XI/109/72, same to same, July 29; RAL, XI/109/72/2, Lionel, Wildbad, to Mayer, London, Aug. 27; RAL, XI/109/72/3, same, Frankfurt, to same, Sept. 20; Lionel to Anthony, Sept. 23; AN, 132 AQ 5417/1M21, NMR to deRF, Nov. 9; RAL, XI/109/73/2, Lionel Davidson, Paris, to NMR and deRF, Nov. 23; RAL, XI/109/73, James, Paris, to his nephews, London, Dec. 1; same to same, Dec. 3. On Nicaragua, RAL, XI/109/73/3, Lord Eddisbury, Foreign Office, to Lionel, Dec. 19; Marmaduke Sampson to Lionel, Dec. 24.

289   RAL, XI/109/71/1, Nat, Paris, to his brothers, London, April 6, 1849; RAL, Moscow 224, Betty, Paris, to Alphonse, New York, Dec. 30, 1848.

290   RAL, XI/109/71/4, Nat, Paris, to his brothers, London, undated, *c.* April, 1849; RAL, XI/109/71/1, same to same, April 19.

291   RAL, XI/109/70/3, Nat, Paris, to his brothers, London, March 20, 1849; same to same, undated, *c.* April; RAL, XI/109/71/2, May 14.

292   RAL, XI/109/72/3, Anthony, Paris, to Mayer, London, Sept. 7, 1849; same to same, Sept. 10; Sept. 11; RAL, XI/109/73/1, Oct. 4; Oct. 16; RAL, XI/109/73/2, Nov. 2; Nov. 3. See also Alphonse to Mayer, Oct. 18; RAL, XI/109/73/1, Lionel, Paris, to Mayer, Oct. 31; RAL, XI/109/73/2, Nat, Freywaldau, to Mayer, London, Nov. 4; RAL, XI/109/73/2, Lionel to Mayer, Nov. 5; same to same, Nov. 6; RAL, XI/109/73, James, Paris, to Mayer, Oct. 30.

293   RAL, XI/109/72, James, Paris, to his nephews, London, July 11, 1849; RAL, XI/109/72/1, Anthony, Paris, to his brothers, July 19.

294   RAL, XI/109/70, James, Paris, to his nephews, London, March 4, 1849; same to same, March 5.

295   RAL, Moscow 224, Betty, Paris, to Alphonse, New York, May 3, 1849.

296   RAL, XI/109/72, James, Homburg, to Anthony, Paris, Aug. 24, 1849; RAL, XI/109/73, same, Paris, to same, London, Nov. 18.

297   RAL, XI/109/72, James, Paris, to his nephews, London, July 10, 1849. Corti, *Reign*, p. 282.

298   RAL, XI/109/73, James, Paris, to Anthony and Mayer, London, Nov. 7, 1849; same to same, Nov. 14; Nov. 17; RAL, XI/109/73/3, Alphonse, Paris, to his cousins, London, Nov. 18.

299   RAL, XI/109/73, James, Paris, to his nephews, London, Dec. 3, 1849; RAL, XI/109/73/3, Alphonse to his cousins, Dec. 7; same to same, Dec. 15; RAL, XI/109/73, James to his nephews, Dec. 8; same to same, Dec. 9; Dec. 10; Dec. 13; Dec. 17; Dec. 19; Dec. 21; RAL, XI/109/73/3, Emile Pereire, Paris, to Anthony, London, Dec. 15; same to same, Dec. 19; RAL, XI/109/73/3, Alphonse to his cousins, Dec. 31. Cf. Girard, *Travaux publics*, pp. 58–68; Bouvier, *Rothschild*, pp. 134ff.

300   RAL, XI/109/72, James, Homburg, to Anthony, Paris, Aug. 5, 1849. For Nat's traditional pessimism about French railways, see RAL, XI/109/72/2, Nat, Gräfenberg, to James, Homburg, Aug. 8; RAL, XI/109/73/3, Nat to his brothers, London, Dec. 7, 1849; Nat, Berlin, to his brothers, Dec. 12: "How is it possible to embark one's good hard cash in anything that depends on the stability of matters in France—when the whole concern can be totally upset from one moment to another?—A loan is a different thing, a loan is immediately to be sold but a stinking railroad sticks to you for years like a millstone round yr. neck." Also RAL, XI/109/73/3, Nat, Paris, to his brothers, London, Dec. 26.

301   Herzen, *My past and thoughts*, vol. II, p. xix; Zimmerman, *Midpassage*, pp. 106, 127.

302   Herzen, *Letters from France and Rome*, p. 79; Partridge, *Herzen*, p. 53; Zimmerman, *Midpassage*, p. 101.

303   Herzen, *My past and thoughts*, vol. II, pp. 757f.

304   Zimmerman, *Midpassage*, pp. 99ff., 166; Malia, *Herzen and the birth of Russian socialism*, p. 389.

305   Herzen, *My past and thoughts*, vol. II, p. 761f.

306   *Ibid.*, vol. II, p. 762.

307   *Ibid.*, vol. II, pp. 762–5. See also Vuilleumier *et al.*, *Autour d'Alexandre Herzen*, p. 229; Goncourt, *Journal*, vol. I, pp. 1035f.

308   CPHDCM, 637/1/131–11, Bilan deRF, Dec. 31, 1851; Herzen, *My past and thoughts*, vol. II, pp. 769, 1475; Vuilleumier, *Autour d'Alexandre Herzen*, pp. 109, 187; Malia, *Herzen and the birth of Russian socialism*, p. 389.

309   Herzen, *My past and thoughts*, vol. III, p. 1232.

PRINCIPAL ARCHIVES, LIBRARIES AND
MANUSCRIPT COLLECTIONS USED

Anglo-Jewish Archives, University of Southampton
Archives Nationales, Paris
Bank of England, London
Bayerisches Hauptstaatsarchiv
Birmingham University Library
Bodleian Library, Oxford
British Library, London
Cambridge University Library
Centre for the Preservation of Historical
   Documentary Collections, Moscow
Geheimes Staatsarchiv Preussischer Kulturbesitz,
   Berlin-Dahlem
Hessisches Staatsarchiv, Marburg
House of Lords Record Office
Institut für Stadtgeschichte, Frankfurt

Jüdisches Museum, Frankfurt
Leo Baeck Institute, New York
London School of Economics Library
Mecklenburgisches Landeshauptsarchiv Schwerin
National Library of Scotland
Rhodes House, Oxford
Rosebery Papers, Dalmeny House and Barnbougle
   Castle, Edinburgh
Rothschild Archive, London
Royal Archives, Windsor Castle
Salisbury Papers, Hatfield House
The Times Archive, London
Thüringisches Hauptstaatsarchiv, Weimar
University College, London
Warburg Institute, London

SECONDARY SOURCES

Achterberg, Erich, *Frankfurter Bankherren* (Frankfurt am Main, 1956)

Acton, Harold, *The Bourbons of Naples* (London, 1956)

Adam, Andrew E., *Beechwoods and bayonets: The book of Halton* (Buckingham, 1983)

Adler, Hermann, "*Remember the Poor': A Sermon preached in memory of the late Baroness Lionel de Rothschild at the Central Synagogue, March 22, 1884* (London, 1884)

Agulhon, Maurice, *The Republican experiment, 1848–52* (Cambridge, 1983)

Albert, Harold A., *Queen Victoria's sister: The life and letters of Princess Feodora* (London, 1967)

Alderman, Geoffrey, *The Jewish community in British politics* (Oxford, 1982)

———, *The Federation of Synagogues, 1887–1987* (London, 1987)

———, *Modern British Jewry* (Oxford, 1992)

Alice, Countess of Athlone, *For my grandchildren: Some reminiscences of Her Royal Highness Princess Alice* (London, 1966)

Allfrey, Anthony, *Man of arms: The life and legend of Sir Basil Zaharoff* (London, 1989)

———, *Edward VII and his Jewish court* (London, 1991)

Alter, Peter, "German-speaking Jews as patrons of the arts and sciences in Edwardian England ," in Werner E. Mosse and Julius Carlebach (eds), *Second chance: Two centuries of German-speaking Jews in the United Kingdom* (Tübingen, 1991), pp. 209–19

Amery, Leopold, *Joseph Chamberlain and the Tariff Reform campaign: The life of Joseph Chamberlain*, vols V and VI (London, 1969)

Andrew, Christopher, *Théophile Delcassé and the making of the Entente Cordiale* (London, 1968)

Anon. [? Heinrich Doering], *Die Familie Rothschild und die Fugger: Lebensgeschichte der Gründer und der vorzuglichsten Glieder dieser Häusern* (Liepzig, 1837)

————, *The Hebrew Talisman* (London, 1840)

———— [David M. Evans], *The City or, the physiology of London business: with sketches on 'change, and at the coffee houses* (London, 1845)

————, *Jugement rendu contre Rothschild et contre Georges Dairnvaell, auteur de l'histoire de Rothschild 1er, par la Tribunal de la saine raison, accompagné d'un jugement sur l'accident de Fampoux* (Paris, 1846)

————, *Rothschild: Ein Urtheilsspruch vom menchlichen Standpunkt aus* (Herisau, 1846)

———— [F. A. Steinmann], *Das Haus Rothschild: Seine Geschichte und seine Geschäft. Aufschlüsse und Enthüllungen zur Geschichte des Jahrhunderts, insbesondere des Staatsfinanz -und Börsewesens* (Prague/Leipzig, 1857)

————, *M. Mirès et M. de Rothschild* (Paris, 1861)

———— [Charlotte de Rothschild], *Addresses to young children, originally delivered in the Girls' Free School, Bell Lane* (London, 1861, 2nd edn, 1864)

————, *Gewaltsachen: Eine Auswahl der besten jüdischen Anekdoten, illustriert von Wilhelm Scholz* (Berlin, 1866)

————, *Der Ruin des Mittelstandes* (n.p. [Vienna?], n.d. [1891?])

————, [Constance Battersea], *Light on the way* (London, 1900)

————, *Histoire d'une famille regnante: Les Rothschild, par un petit porteur de fonds russes, série I* (Paris, 1925)

————, *Le pillage par les allemandes des oeuvres d'art et des bibliothèques appartenant à des Juifs an France* (Paris, 1947)

Apostol, P. N., M. V. Bernatzky and A. M. Michelson, *Russian public finances during the war* (New Haven, 1928)

Apponyi, comte Rudolf, *Vingt-cinq ans à Paris (1826–50)*, 4 vols (Paris, 1914)

Aris, Stephen, *The Jews in business* (London, 1970)

Armstrong, John, and Stephanie Jones, *Business documents: Their origins, sources and use in historical research* (London/New York, 1987)

Arnaud, E. Baron de Vitrolles, *Mémoires et réflections politiques: Mémoires de Vitrolles*, 3 vols (Paris, 1951)

Arnsberg, Paul, *Die Geschichte der Frankfurter Juden seit der Französischen Revolution*, 3 vols (Frankfurt, 1983)

Aronson, Theo, *Victoria and Disraeli* (London, 1977)

Artz, Frederick B., *France under the Bourbon Restoration, 1814–30* (Cambridge, Mass., 1931)

Askew, William C., *Europe and Italy's acquisition of Libya, 1911–12* (Durham, North Carolina, 1942)

Aspey, Melanie, "Mrs Rothschild," in Victor Gray (ed.), *The life and times of N. M. Rothschild 1777–1836* (London, 1998), pp. 58–67

Aspinall, A. (ed.), *The letters of King George IV, 1812–30*, 3 vols (Cambridge, 1938)

———— (ed.), *Politics and the press*, c. 1780–1850 (London, 1949)

Atkins, H. G., *Heine* (London, 1929)

Aycard, M., *Histoire du Crédit Mobilier, 1852–67* (Bruxelles/Leipzig/Livorno, 1867)

Ayer, J., *A century of finance, 1804 to 1904: The London house of Rothschild* (London, 1904)

Backhaus, Fritz (ed.), *"Und groß war bei der Tochter Jehudas Jammer und Klage . . ." Die Ermordung der Frankfurter Juden im Jahre 1241* (Frankfurt am Main, 1991)

————, " '. . . da dergleichen Geschäfte eigentlich durch große Konkurrenz gewinnen": Meyer Amschel Rothschild in Kassel," in Stadtsparkasse Kassel, *". . . da dergleichen Geschäfte eigentlich durch große Konkurrenz gewinnen"* (Kassel, 1994), pp. 9–61

————, "Die Rothschilds und das Geld: Bilder und Legenden," in Johannes Heil and Bernd Wacker (eds), *Shylock? Zinsverbot und Geldverleih in jüdischer und christlicher Tradition* (Munich, 1997), pp. 147–70

————, "The last of the court Jews—Mayer Amschel Rothschild and his sons," in Vivian B. Mann and Richard I. Cohen (eds), *From court Jews to the Rothschilds: Art, patronage, and power, 1600–1800* (New York, 1997), pp. 79–95

————, "The Jewish ghetto in Frankfurt," in Victor Gray (ed.), *The Life and times of N. M. Rothschild 1777–1836* (London, 1998), pp. 22–33

———— and Heike Drummer, *Museum Judengasse: Katalog der Dauerausstellung* (Frankfurt am Main, 1992)

Bagehot, Walter, *Lombard Street: A description of the money market* (London, 1873)

Bahlman, Dudley W. R. (ed.), *The diary of Sir Edward Walter Hamilton, 1885–1906* (Hull, 1993)

Bairoch, Paul, "Europe's gross national product: 1800–1975," *Journal of European Economic History* (1976), pp. 273–340

Baker, Kenneth, *The turbulent years: My life in politics* (London, 1993)

Balderston, Theo, "War finance and inflation in Britain and Germany, 1914–1918," *Economic History Review* (1989), pp. 222–44

Balfour, Lady Frances, *The life of George, 4th Earl of Aberdeen*, vol. I (Paris, 1922)

Balla, I., *The romance of the Rothschilds* (London, 1913)

Balogh, Thomas, *Studies in financial organization*, National Institute of Economic and Social Research, Economic & Social Studies, vol. VI (Cambridge, 1947)

Balzac, Honoré de, *Lettres à l'étrangère, 1845–1846*, vol. III (Paris, 1933)

———, *Correspondance*, 5 vols, ed. Roger Pierrot (Paris, 1962)

———, *La comédie humaine*, vol. III: *Etudes de moeurs: Scènes de la vie privée. Le père Goriot* (Paris, 1976)

———, *La comédie humaine*, vol. VI: *Etudes de moeurs: Scènes de la vie parisienne: La maison Nucingen* (Paris, 1977)

———, *La comédie humaine*, vol. VI: *Un homme d'affaires* (Paris, 1914)

———, *La comédie humaine*, vol. VI: *Etude de moeurs: Scènes de la vie parisienne. César Birotteau* (Paris, 1976)

———, *La comédie humaine*, vol. VI: *Etudes de moeurs: Scènes de la vie parisienne. Splendeurs et misères des courtisanes* (Paris, 1977)

———, *La comédie humaine*, vol. VII: *Etudes de moeurs: Scènes de la vie parisienne (suite). La cousine Bette* (Paris, 1977)

Banquier [pseud.], *Que nous veut-on avec ce Rothschild Ier, roi des juifs et dieu de la finance?* (Bruxelles, 1846)

Barany, George, *Stephen Széchenyi and the awakening of Hungarian nationalism* (Princeton, 1968)

Barea, Ilse, *Vienna* (London, 1966)

Barnett, R. D., "A diary that survived: Damascus 1840," in Sonia and Vivian D. Lipman (eds), *The century of Moses Montefiore* (Oxford, 1985), pp. 149–70

Baron, Joseph L. (ed.), *A treasury of Jewish quotations* (London, 1965)

Bartetzko, Dieter, "Fairy tales and castles: On Rothschild family buildings in Frankfurt on Main," in Heuberger (ed.), *Essays*, pp. 221–44

Barth, Boris, *Die deutsche Hochfinanz und die Imperialismen: Banken und Außenpolitik vor 1914* (Stuttgart, 1995)

Barthélemy, *Le peuple Juif: A M. le Baron de Rothschild* (Paris, 1847)

Barthélemy, J., "La Banque, auxiliaire de l'Etat: I," *L'Information* (Dec. 13, 1932)

Battenberg, Friedrich, *Das europäische Zeitalter der Juden*, 2 vols (Darmstadt, 1990)

Battersea, Constance (ed.), *Lady de Rothschild: Extracts from the notebooks with a preface by her daughter* (London, 1912)

———, *Waifs and strays* (London, 1921)

———, *Reminiscences* (London, 1922)

Bauer, Hans-Peter, *Merchant banks*, Bankwirtschaftliche Forschungen, 57 (Bern/Stuttgart, 1979)

Bauer, Max, *Bismarck und Rothschild* (Dresden, 1891)

Bäuerle, Adolf, *Wien vor zwanzig Jahren: oder Baron Rothschild und die Tischlerstochter* (Pest/Wien/Leipzig, 1855)

Baumier, Jean, *Les grandes affaires françaises* (Paris, 1967)

———, *Ces banquiers qui nous gouvernent* (Paris, 1983)

Beales, Derek, *From Castlereagh to Gladstone, 1815–1885* (London, 1969)

Beck, Karl, *Lieder vom armen Mann, mit einem Vorwort an das Haus Rothschild* (Leipzig, 1846)

Beer, Adolf, *Die Finanzen Österreichs im IX. Jahrhundert* (Vienna, 1873, repr. 1877)

Bender [Johann Heinrich], *Ueber den Verkehr mit Staatspapieren in seinen Hauptrichtungen . . . Als Beylageheft zum Archiv für die Civilist[ische] Praxis*, vol. VIII (Heidelberg, 1825)

Benson, A. C. and R. Esher (eds), *The letters of Queen Victoria: A selection from Her Majesty's correspondence between the years 1837 and 1861*, 3 vols (London, 1908)

Berend, Ivan T. and Györgi Ranki, *Economic development in East-Central Europe in the 19th and 20th centuries* (New York/London, 1974)

Bergeron, Louis, *Banquiers, négociants et manufacturiers parisiens du Directoire à l'Empire* (Paris, 1978)

———, *Les Rothschild et les autres: La gloire des banquiers* (Paris, 1991)

———, "The myth of the banker in France in the 19th and 20th centuries," in Heuberger (ed.), *Essays*, pp. 297–306

Berghoeffer, C. W., *Meyer Amschel Rothschild: Der Gründer des Rothschildscher Bankhauses* (Frankfurt am Main, 1924)

Bermant, Chaim, *The Cousinhood: The Anglo-Jewish gentry* (London, 1971)

Bertaut, Jules, *La bourse anécdotique et pittoresque* (Paris, 1933)

Bertier de Sauvigny, Guillaume André de, *Metternich and his times* (London, 1962)

———, *Metternich et la France après le congrès de Vienne* (Paris, 1968)

————, *Nouvelle histoire de Paris: La Restauration, 1815–1830* (Paris, 1977)

Bethmann, Johann Philipp Freiherr von, " 'Er kannte keine größere Wonne als Wohltun'": Mayer Amschel Rothschild," in Hans Sarkowicz (ed.), *Die großen Frankfurter* (Frankfurt am Main/Leipzig, 1994)

Billig, Joseph, *Le Commissariat Général aux Questions Juives (1941–1944)*, vol. I (Paris, 1960)

Bismarck, Otto von, *Die Gesammelten Werke*, vol. XIV, 1 and 2: *Briefe 1822–1898* (Berlin, 1933)

Black, David, *The King of Fifth Avenue: The fortunes of August Belmont* (New York, 1981)

Black, Eugene C., *The social politics of Anglo-Jewry, 1880–1920* (Oxford, 1988)

Black, Gerry, *JFS: A history of the Jews' Free School, London, since 1732* (London, 1997)

Blake, Robert, *Disraeli* (London, 1966)

———— and Wm Roger Louis (eds), *Churchill* (Oxford, 1993)

Blakiston, Georgina, *Lord William Russell and his wife, 1815–1846* (London, 1972)

Blanchard, Marcel, *Le Second Empire* (Paris, 1950)

————, "The railway policy of the Second Empire," in F. Crouzet, W. H. Chaloner and W. M. Stern (eds), *Essays in European economic history* (London, 1969), pp. 98–112

Blewett, Neal, *The peers, the parties and the people: The general elections of 1910* (London, 1972)

Blount, Edward, *Memoirs of Sir Edward Blount KCB (1815–1902)* (London, 1902)

Blum, Jerome, "Transportation and industry in Austria, 1815–48," *Journal of Modern History* (1943), pp. 24–38

Blumberg, A., *A carefully planned accident* (London, 1990)

Blunt, Anthony (ed.), *The James A. de Rothschild collection at Waddesdon Manor*, 11 vols (Fribourg, Switzerland, 1967–)

Bocher, Charles, *Mémoires de Charles Bocher, 1816–1907: Précédés par des souvenirs de famille, 1760–1816* (Paris, 1907)

Boehme, H., *The foundation of the German Empire* (Oxford, 1971)

Boime, Albert, "Entrepreneurial patronage in nineteenth century France," in Edward C. Carter, Robert Forster and Joseph N. Moody (eds), *Enterprise and entrepreneurs in nineteenth and twentieth century France* (Baltimore/London, 1976), pp. 137–209

Bontoux, E., *L'Union Générale: Sa vie, sa mort, son programme* (Paris, 1888)

Borchardt, Knut "Währung und Wirtschaft in Deutschland," in Deutsche Bundesbank (ed.), *Währung und Wirtschaft in Deutschland, 1876–1975* (Frankfurt am Main, 1976), pp. 1–53

Born, Karl Erich, *International banking in the nineteenth and twentieth centuries* (Leamington Spa, 1983)

Börne, Ludwig, *Mittheilungen aus dem Gebiete der Länder -und Völkerkunde, zweiter Theil* (Offenbach, 1833)

Bosworth, R. J. B., "Italy and the end of the Ottoman Empire," in Kent, Marian (ed.), *The great powers and the end of the Ottoman Empire* (London, 1984), pp. 52–75

Bourne, Kenneth, *Palmerston: The early years, 1784–1841* (London, 1982)

Bouvier, Jean, *Les Rothschild* (Paris, 1960)

————, *Le krach de l'Union Générale (1878–1885)* (Paris, 1960)

————, *Le Crédit Lyonnais de 1863 à 1882* (Paris, 1961)

————, *Un siècle de banque française* (Paris, 1973)

Bower, Tom, *Maxwell: The final verdict* (London, 1995)

————, *The perfect English spy: Sir Dick White and the secret war, 1935–90* (London, 1995)

Bowie, Karen, "The Rothschilds, the railways and the urban form of 19th century Paris," in Heuberger (ed.), *Essays*, pp. 87–98

Bradford, Sarah, *Disraeli* (London, 1982)

Bramsen, Bo and Kathleen Wain, *The Hambros, 1779–1979* (London, 1979)

Brandenburg, Erich, *From Bismarck to the World War: A history of German foreign policy* (Oxford, 1933)

Brandt, Harm-Heinrich, "Public finances of neo-absolutism in Austria in the 1850s: Integration and modernisation," in Peter-Christian Witt (ed.), *Wealth and taxation in Central Europe* (Leamington Spa/Hamburg/New York, 1987), pp. 81–109

Brassey, Maria, "Visitors to Waddesdon Manor, 1881–1898," unpublished MS, RAL (n.d.)

Braudel, Fernand and Ernest Labrousse, *Histoire économique et sociale de la France*, vol. III: *L'avènement de l'ère industrielle, 1789–1880* (Paris, 1976)

Brewer, John, *The sinews of power: War, money and the English state, 1688–1783* (London, 1989)

Brewitz, Walther, *Die Familie Rothschild* (Stuttgart, 1939)

Bridge, F. R., *Great Britain and Austria–Hungary, 1906–14: A diplomatic history* (London, 1972)

Briggs, Asa, *The age of improvement, 1783–1867* (London/New York, 1959)

————, *Victorian things* (London, 1988)

———, *Victorian people* (Chicago, 1995)

Bright, John (ed.), *Speeches on questions of public policy, by Richard Cobden MP*, ed. James E. Thorold Rogers (London, 1880)

Brock, Michael, *The Great Reform Act* (London, 1973)

——— and Eleanor Brock (eds), *H. H. Asquith, letters to Venetia Stanley* (Oxford, 1982)

Brockhaus, F. A., *Allgemeine deutsche Real-Enzyklopädie für die gebildeten Stände: Conversations Lexikon*, 7th edn, vol. IX (Leipzig, 1827)

———, *Allgemeine deutsche Real-Enzyklopädie für die gebildeten Stände: Conversations Lexikon*, 8th edn, vol. IX (Leipzig, 1836)

———, *Allgemeine deutsche Real-Enzyklopädie für die gebildeten Stände: Conversations Lexikon*, 9th edn, vol. XII (Leipzig, 1847)

———, *Allgemeine deutsche Real-Enzyklopädie für die gebildeten Stände: Conversations Lexikon*, 11th edn, vol. XII (Leipzig, 1867)

Brogan, D. W., *The French nation from Napoleon to Pétain, 1814–1940* (London, 1957)

Brooks, David (ed.), *The destruction of Lord Rosebery: From the diary of Sir Edward Hamilton, 1894–1895* (London, 1986)

Browne, Cohen Goodman, *Baron Rothschild of Frankfurt and the Rabbi* (London, 1912)

Browne, Lewis Allen, *The House of Rothschild* (London, 1934)

Buckle, George Earle (ed.), *The letters of Queen Victoria*, vol. III, 3rd Ser. (London, 1932)

Buckman, Peter, *The Rothschild conversion* (London, 1979)

Buderus von Carlshausen, Lothar, "Carl Friedrich Buderus: Das Leben eines kurhessischen Beamten in schwerer Zeit," *Monatsschrift für Landes-und Volkskunde, Kunst und Literatur Hessens* (1931), pp. 33–103

Buist, Marten G., *At spes non fracta: Hope and Co., 1770–1815* (The Hague, 1974)

Bullen, Roger, *Palmerston, Guizot and the collapse of the Entente Cordiale* (London, 1974)

——— and Felicity Strong (eds), Palmerston, vol. I: *Private correspondence with Sir George Villiers* (London, 1985)

Burk, Kathleen, *The first privatisation: The politicians, the City and the denationalisation of steel* (London, 1988)

———, *Morgan Grenfell, 1838–1988: The biography of a merchant bank* (Oxford, 1989)

Bury, J. P. T., "The identity of "C. de B."," *French Historical Studies* (1964), pp. 538–41

Bussche, Albrecht von dem, *Heinrich Alexander von Arnim: Liberalismus, Polenfrage und deutsche Einheit. Das 19. Jahrhundert im Spiegel einer Biographie des preußischen Staatsmannes* (Osnabrück, 1986)

Bussiere, Eric, *Paribas, Europe and the world, 1872–1992* (Antwerp, 1992)

Butler, J. R. M., *The passing of the Great Reform Bill* (London, 1914)

Buxton, Charles (ed.), *Memoirs of Sir Thomas Fowell Buxton*, 3rd edn (London, 1849)

Buxton, Sydney Charles, *Finance and politics: an historical study, 1783–1885* (London, 1888)

Byron, Lord, *The complete poetical works*, vol. V: *Don Juan*, ed. Jerome J. McGann (Oxford, 1986)

Cabanis, Jose, *Charles X: Roi ultra* (Paris, 1972)

Cadoux, Gaston, *Les finances de la ville de Paris de 1798 à 1900* (Paris/Nancy, 1900)

Cain, P. J., *Economic foundations of British expansion overseas, 1815–1914* (London, 1980)

——— and A. G. Hopkins, *British imperialism: Innovation and expansion, 1688–1914* (London, 1993)

——— and ———, *British imperialism: Crisis and deconstruction, 1914–1990* (London, 1993)

Cameron, Rondo, "The Crédit Mobilier and the economic development of Europe," *Journal of Political Economy* (1953), pp. 461–89

———, "French financiers and Italian unity: The Cavourian decade," *American History Review* (1957), pp. 552–69

———, "Papal finance and the temporal power, 1815–71," *Church History* (1957), pp. 132–42

———, *France and the economic development of Europe, 1800–1914* (Princeton, 1961)

——— (ed.), *Banking in the early stages of industrialization* (New York/Oxford, 1967)

———, "France 1800–1870," in *idem* (ed.), *Banking in the early stages of industrialization* (New York/Oxford, 1967), pp. 100–128

———, "Belgium 1800–1875," in *idem* (ed.), *Banking in the early stages of industrialization* (New York/London/Toronto, 1967), pp. 129–50

Canfield, C., *Outrageous fortunes: The story of the Medici, the Rothschilds and J. P. Morgan* (New York, 1981)

Cannadine, David, *Aspects of aristocracy: Grandeur and decline in modern Britain* (New Haven/London, 1994)

Capdebièle, François, "Female Rothschilds and their issue," unpublished MS, RAL (n.d.)

Capefigue, M., *Histoire des grandes opérations financières, banques, bourses, emprunts, compagnies industrielles etc.*, 4 vols (Paris, 1855)

Carden, Godref L., *The machine tool trade in Austria–Hungary* (Washington, 1909)

Cardoso, Eliana A. and Rudiger Dornbusch, "Brazilian debt crises: Past and present," in Barry Eichengreen and Peter H. Lindert (eds), *The international debt crisis in historical perspective* (Cambridge, Mass./London, 1989), pp. 106–39

Carlisle, Robert B., "Les chemins de fer, les Rothschild et les saint-simoniens," *Economies et Sociétés, Cahiers de l'ISEA* (1971), pp. 647–76

Caron, François, *An economic history of modern France* (London, 1979)

———, "France," in Patrick O'Brien (ed.), *Railways and the economic development of Western Europe* (London/Basingstoke, 1983), pp. 28–48

Carosso, Vincent P., *Investment banking in America* (Cambridge, Mass., 1970)

———, *The Morgans: Private international bankers, 1854–1913* (Cambridge, Mass., 1987)

Carr, Raymond, *Spain, 1808–1939* (Oxford, 1966)

Carr, William, *The wars of German unification* (Harlow, 1991)

Carreras, A., *Industrializacion Espanola: Estudios de historia cuantitiva* (Florence, 1995)

Case, Lynn M., *French opinion on war and diplomacy during the Second Empire* (Philadelphia, 1954)

Cassis, Youssef, "Management and strategy in the English joint stock banks, 1890–1914," *Business History* (1985), pp. 301–15

———, "Bankers in English society in the late nineteenth century," *Economic History Review* (1985), pp. 210–29

———, *La City de Londres, 1870–1914* (Paris, 1987)

——— (ed.), *Finance and financiers in European history, 1880–1960* (Cambridge, 1992)

———, *English City bankers, 1890–1914* (Cambridge/New York, 1994)

——— and P. L. Cottrell, "Financial history," *Financial History Review* (1994), pp. 5–22

Castellane, Maréchal de, *Journal du Maréchal Castellane, 1804–1862* (Paris, 1895)

Castex, Pierre-Georges, "L'univers de la comédie humaine," in Balzac, Honoré de, *La comédie humaine* (Paris, 1976), pp. ix–lxxvi

Caussidière, Marc, *Mémoires de Caussidière, ex-prefet de police et représentant du peuple* (Paris, 1849)

Cavour, Count Camille Benso di, *La politique du Comte Camille de Cavour de 1852 à 1861: Lettres inédites avec notes* (Turin, 1885)

———, *Nouvelles lettres inédites* (Turin, 1889)

Cecco, M. de, *Money and empire: The international gold standard, 1890–1914* (Oxford, 1973)

Cecil, Algernon, *Metternich, 1773–1859: A study of his period and personality* (London, 1933)

Cesarani, David, *The Jewish Chronicle and Anglo-Jewry, 1841–1991* (Cambridge, 1994)

Chamberlain, Muriel E., *Lord Aberdeen: A political biography* (London, 1983)

Chandler, George, *Four centuries of banking* (London, 1964)

Chapman, Guy, *The Third Republic of France* (London, 1962)

Chapman, Stanley, "The international houses: The continental contribution to British economic development, 1800–1860," *Journal of European Economic History* (1977), pp. 5–48

———, *The foundation of the English Rothschilds: N. M. Rothschild as a textile merchant, 1799–1811* (London, 1977)

———, "The establishment of the Rothschilds as bankers," *Transactions of the Jewish Historical Society of England* (1982–6), pp. 177–93

———, *The rise of merchant banking* (London, 1984)

———, "British-based investment groups before 1914," *Economic History Review* (1985), pp. 230–51

———, "Rhodes and the City of London: Another view of imperialism," *Historical Journal* (1985), pp. 647–66

———, "The establishment of the Rothschilds as bankers in London," in Heuberger (ed.), *Essays*, pp. 71–86

Charnacé, Guy de, *Le Baron Vampire* (Paris, 1885)

Chastenet, Jacques, *Une époque de contestation: La monarchie bourgeoise, 1830–48* (Paris, 1976)

Chateaubriand, François René, vicomte de, *Correspondance générale de Chateaubriand,* 5 vols (Paris, 1913)

———, *Mémoires d'outre-tombe,* 2 vols (Paris, 1958)

Checkland, S. G., *The rise of industrial society in England, 1815–1885* (London, 1964)

Chekhov, Anton, "Rothschild's fiddle," in Ronald Wilks (ed.), *The fiancée and other stories* (Harmondsworth, 1986), pp. 52–61

Chernow, Ron, *The House of Morgan* (London/Sydney/New York/Tokyo/Toronto, 1990)

———, *The Warburgs* (London, 1993)

Childers, Spencer, *The life and correspondence of the Rt. Hon. Hugh C. E. Childers,* vol. II (London, 1901)

Chilvers, Hedley A., *The story of De Beers* (London, 1939)

Chirac, Auguste, *La Haute Banque et les révolutions* (Paris, 1876)

————, *Les rois de la République: Histoire des juiveries* (Paris, 1883)

————, *L'agiotage de 1870 à 1884* (Paris, 1887)

Christophe, Robert, *Le duc de Morny, "Empereur" des français sous Napoléon III* (Paris, 1951)

Christopher, John B., "The desiccation of the bourgeois spirit," in Edward Mead Earle (ed.), *Modern France: Problems of the Third and Fourth Republics* (Princeton, 1951), pp. 44–61

Churchill, Randolph S., *Winston S. Churchill*, vol. I (Boston, 1966)

————, *Winston S. Churchill*, vol. II (London, 1967)

Ciocca, Pierluigi and Ulizzi Adalberto, "I tassi di cambio nominali e "reali" dell'Italia dall'unità nazionale al sistema monetario europeo (1861–1979)," *Ricerche per la Storia della Banca d'Italia*, vol. I (Rome, 1990), pp. 341–68

Clapham, J. H., *The economic development of France and Germany, 1815–1914* (Cambridge, 1921)

————, *The Bank of England: A history*, 2 vols (Cambridge, 1944)

Clark, Chester W., *Franz Joseph and Bismarck before 1866* (Cambridge, Mass., 1934)

Clarke, Edward, *Benjamin Disraeli* (London, 1926)

Clerc, Christine, *Fondations Rothschild: 130 ans de solidarité* (Paris, 1982)

Clough, S. B., *France: A history of national economics* (New York, 1939)

————, *An economic history of modern Italy* (New York, 1964)

Cobban, Alfred, *A history of modern France*, vol. II: *1799–1871* (Harmondsworth, 1961)

————, *A history of modern France*, vol. III: *1871–1962* (Harmondsworth, 1965)

Cohen, Albert, *Mangeclous* (Paris, 1938, 2nd edn 1965)

Cohen, Lucy, *Lady de Rothschild and her daughters, 1821–1931* (London, 1935)

Cohen, S. J., *Musterhaftes Leben des verewigten Herrn Bankiers Meyer Amschel Rothschild, Mitglied des Großherzoglich-Frankfurtischer Wahlkollegiums* (Frankfurt am Main, 1813)

Cohen, Stuart A., *English Zionists and British Jews: The communal politics of Anglo-Jewry, 1895–1920* (Princeton, 1982)

Colby, Reginald, "The Waterloo Dispatch," in Drew Middleton (ed.), *The battle of Waterloo* (Westport, Connecticut, 1977), pp. 87–99

Collett-White, Ann and James, *Gunnersbury Park and the Rothschilds* (Hounslow, 1993)

Colling, Alfred, *Le roman de la finance* (Monaco, 1945)

Collins, Michael, "The banking crisis of 1878," *Economic History Review* (1989), pp. 504–27

Conacher, J. B., *The Aberdeen coalition, 1852–1855* (Cambridge, 1968)

————, *The Peelites and the party system, 1846–1852* (Newton Abbot, 1972)

Contador, Claudio R., and Claudio L. Haddad, "Produto real, moeda e preços: A experiênca Brasileira no periodo 1861–1970," *Revista Brasileira de Estatistica* (1975)

Cope, S. R., *Walter Boyd: A merchant banker in the Age of Napoleon* (Gloucester, 1983)

Coppa, Frank, *Cardinal Giacomo Antonelli and Papal politics in European affairs* (New York, 1990)

Corley, T. A. B., *Democratic despot: A life of Napoleon III* (London, 1961)

Corti, Count Egon, *The rise of the House of Rothschild* (London, 1928)

————, *The reign of the House of Rothschild* (London, 1928)

Costello, John and Oleg Tsarev, *Deadly illusions: The KGB secrets the British government doesn't want you to read* (London, 1993)

Coston, Henry, *Les financiers qui mènent le monde* (Paris, 1955)

————, *La Haute Banque et les trusts* (Paris, 1958)

Cottrell, P. L., "London financiers and Austria, 1863–75: The Anglo-Austrian Bank," *Business History* (1969), pp. 107–19

————, "Anglo-French financial co-operation, 1850–80," *Journal of European Economic History* (1974), pp. 54–86

————, "London, Paris and silver, 1848–1867," in Anthony Slaven and Derek H. Aldcroft (eds), *Business, banking and urban history: Essays in honour of S. G. Checkland* (Edinburgh, 1982), pp. 102–11.

————, "The business man and financier," in Sonia and Vivian D. Lipman (eds), *The century of Moses Montefiore* (Oxford, 1985), pp. 23–44

————, "The domestic commercial banks and the City of London, 1870–1939," in Youssef Cassis (ed.), *Finance and financiers in European history, 1880–1960* (Cambridge, 1992), pp. 39–62

Coudray, H. du, *Metternich* (London, 1935)

Courtney, Cathy and Paul Thomson, *City lives: The changing voices of British finance* (London, 1996)

Cowles, Virginia, *The Rothschilds: A family of fortune* (London, 1973)

Cox, E. M. and Charles Whibley (eds), *Letters of the King of Hanover to Viscount Strangford G.C.B.* (London, 1925)

Crewe, Marquess of, *Lord Rosebery*, 2 vols (London, 1931)

Crouchley, A. E., *The economic development of modern Egypt* (London, 1938)

Crouzet, François, "Wars, blockade and economic change in Europe, 1792–1815," *Journal of Economic History* (1964), pp. 567–88

Cyon, Elie de, *Histoire de l'entente franco-russe* (Paris, 1895)

Dairnvaell, Georges ['Satan" (pseud.)], *Histoire édifiante et curieuse de Rothschild Ier, roi des Juifs* (Paris, 1846)

———, *Guerre aux fripons: Chronique secrète de la Bourse et des chemins de fer* (Paris, 1846)

Damascène, Morgand and Charles Fatout, *Le Baron James de Rothschild, 1844–1881* (Paris, 1881)

Darmstadter, F., *Bismarck and the creation of the Second Reich* (New York, 1965)

Darmstädter, Paul, *Das Grossherzogtum Frankfurt: Ein Kulturbild aus der Rheinbundszeit* (Frankfurt am Main, 1901)

Dasent, Arthur Irwin, *Piccadilly in three centuries, with some account of Berkeley Square and the Haymarket* (London, 1920)

Davenport-Hines, R. P. T, *Capital, entrepreneurs and profits* (London, 1990)

Davis, Lance E. and R. A. Huttenback, *Mammon and the pursuit of empire: The political economy of British imperialism, 1860–1912* (Cambridge, 1986)

Davis, Richard, *Disraeli* (London, 1976)

———, "The Rothschilds and English Society," unpublished paper given to the Seeley Society, Christ's College, Cambridge, RAL (1981)

———, *The English Rothschilds* (London, 1983)

Dawson, Frank Griffith, *The first Latin American debt crisis* (London, 1990)

Dayer, Roberta Albert, *Finance and empire: Sir Charles Addis, 1861–1945* (Basingstoke, 1988)

Deak, Istvan, *The lawful revolution: Louis Kossuth and the Hungarians, 1848–9* (New York, 1979)

Demachy, J. (ed.), *Les Rothschild, une famille des financiers juifs au XIXe siècle* (Paris, 1896)

Dennett, Laurie, *Slaughter and May: A century in the City* (Cambridge, 1989)

Deschamps, Henry-Thierry, *La Belgique devant la France de Juillet: L'opinion et l'attitude françaises de 1839 à 1848* (Paris, 1956)

Deutsche Bank (ed.), *Studies on economic and monetary problems and on banking history* (Mainz, 1988)

Diamond, S. (ed.), *A casual view of America: The home letters of Salomon de Rothschild, 1859–1861* (London, 1962)

Diaper, S., "Merchant banking in the inter-war period: The case of Kleinwort, Sons & Co.," *Business History* (1986), pp. 55–76

Dickson, P. G. M., *The financial revolution in England: A study in the development of public credit, 1688–1756* (London, 1967)

Dietz, Alexander, *Frankfurter Handelsgeschichte*, vol. IV (Frankfurt, 1925)

———, *The Jewish community of Frankfurt: A genealogical study* (Camelford, 1988)

Dines, Michael, *The Jewish jokebook* (London, 1986)

Disraeli, Benjamin, *Novels and tales by the Earl of Beaconsfield, with portrait and sketch of his life*, vol. VI: *Coningsby or The New Generation* (London, 1881)

———, *Novels and tales by the Earl of Beaconsfield, with portrait and sketch of his life*, vol. IX: *Tancred or the New Crusade* (London, 1881)

———, *Novels and tales of the Earl of Beaconsfield, with portrait and sketch of his life*, vol. XI: *Endymion* (London, 1881)

Doering, Heinrich, *Das Haus Rothschild: Eine historische–biographische Skizze* (Jena, 1842)

———, *Des Handelshauses Rothschild: Ursprung, Wachstum und Schicksale* (Leipzig, 1851)

Dosne, Mme, *Mémoires de Madame Dosne, l'égérie de M. Thiers*, 2 vols (Paris, 1928)

Draper, Hal (ed.), *The complete poems of Heinrich Heine* (Oxford, 1982)

Droz, Jacques, *Les révolutions allemandes de 1848* (Paris, 1957)

———, *Europe between two revolutions, 1815–48* (New York, 1967)

Druck, David, *Baron Edmond de Rothschild: The story of a practical idealist* (New York, 1928)

Drumont, Edouard, *La France juive: Essai d'histoire contemporaine, 2 vols* (Paris, 1885)

———, *Gambetta et sa Cour: Barons juifs* (Paris, 1892)

———, *Le testament d'un antisémite* (Paris, 1894)

———, *Les juifs contre la France* (Paris, 1899)

Dugdale, Blanche E. C., *Arthur James Balfour, 1st Earl of Balfour, 1906–1930*, 2 vols (London, 1936)

Dugdale, E. T. S. (ed.), *German diplomatic documents, 1871–1914*, 4 vols (London, 1928)

Dumont, Marie-Jeanne, *Le logement social à Paris, 1850–1930: Les habitations à Bon Marché* (Paris, 1991)

Dunham, Arthur Louis, *The Industrial Revolution in France, 1815–48* (New York, 1955)

Dupeux, Georges, *French society, 1789–1970* (London, 1976)

Dupont-Ferrier, Pierre, *Le marché financier de Paris sous le Second Empire* (Paris, 1925)

Duveau, Georges, *1848: The making of a revolution* (London, 1967)

Ebstein, Georges, *Etude sur la crise financière de 1882* (Paris, 1882)

Edelstein, M., *Overseas investment in the age of high imperialism* (London, 1982)

Egremont, Max, *Balfour* (London, 1980)

Ehrenberg, Richard, *Große Vermögen*, vol. I: *Die Fugger, Rothschild, Krupp* (3rd edn, Jena, 1925)

Ehrman, John, *The Younger Pitt*, vol. III: *The consuming struggle* (London, 1996)

Eichendorff, Joseph von, *Werke in einem Band* (Munich, 1955)

———, *Deutsche Lustspiele vom Barock bis zur Gegenwart: Das Incognito*, ed. Helmut von Arntzen and Karl Pestalozzi (Berlin, 1968)

Eichengreen, Barry, *Golden fetters: The gold standard and the great depression, 1919–1939* (New York/Oxford, 1992)

———, Marc Flandreau, "The geography of the gold standard," *International Macroeconomics*, 1050 (October 1994)

Einzig, Paul, *The history of foreign exchange* (London/New York, 1962)

Eliot, George, *Daniel Deronda* (Oxford, 1984)

Elliot, A. R. D., *Life of Lord Goschen*, 2 vols (London, 1911)

Ellis, Aytoun, *Heir of adventure: The story of Brown, Shipley & Co. merchant bankers, 1801–1960* (London, 1960)

Ellmann, Richard, *Oscar Wilde* (Harmondsworth, 1988)

Elon, Amos, *Founder: Meyer Amschel Rothschild and his time* (London, 1996)

Elston, D. R., *Israel: The making of a nation* (London, 1963)

Emden, Paul H., "The brothers Goldsmid and the financing of the Napoleonic Wars," *Transactions of the Jewish Historical Society of England* (1935–39), pp. 225–46

———, *Money powers of Europe in the nineteenth and twentieth centuries* (New York, 1938)

———, *Jews of Britain: A series of biographies* (London, 1944)

Einaudi, Luca, "Money and politics: European Monetary Union and the international gold standard (1865–1873)," unpublished PhD thesis (Cambridge University, forthcoming)

Endelman, Todd M., *The Jews of Georgian England, 1714–1830: Tradition and change in a liberal society* (Philadelphia, 1979)

———, *Radical assimilation in English Jewish history, 1656–1945* (Bloomington/Indianapolis, 1990)

Erb, Rainer, "The "Damascus Affair" 1840: The role of the Rothschilds in mobilising public opinion," in Heuberger (ed.), *Essays*, pp. 99–112

Ernouf, le Baron A. A., *Paulin Talabot: Sa vie et son oeuvre, 1799–1885* (Paris, 1886)

Escott, Beryl E., "The Story of Halton House," unpublished MS, RAL (1984)

Evans, Richard J., *Proletarians and politics: Socialism, protest and the working class in Germany before the First World War* (London, 1990)

Farrer, David, *The Warburgs* (London, 1974)

Fase, Martin M. G., Gerald D. Feldman and Manfred Pohl (eds), *How to write the history of a bank* (Aldershot, 1995)

Faucher, Léon, *Notes et correspondance*, 2 vols (Paris, 1867)

Feaveryear, Sir Albert, *The pound sterling: A history of English money* (Oxford, 1963)

Feis, Herbert, *Europe, the world's banker, 1870–1914* (New York, 1930)

Feldman, David, *Englishmen and Jews: Social relations and political culture, 1840–1914* (New Haven/London, 1994)

Felisini, Daniela, *Le finanze pontificie e i Rothschild, 1830–1870*, Collona di ricerche in Storia Economica (IUN) (Naples, 1990)

Ferguson, Niall, "Public finance and national security: The domestic origins of the First World War revisited," *Past & Present* (1994), pp. 141–68

———, "The Kaiser's European Union: What if Britain had stood aside in August 1914?," in *idem* (ed.), *Virtual history: Alternatives and counterfactuals* (London, 1997), pp. 228–80

Fernández-Armesto, Felipe, *Millennium: A history of the last thousand years* (London, 1995)

Feydeau, Ernest Aymé, *Mémoires d'un coulissier* (Paris, 1873)

Fieldhouse, D. K., *Economics and empire, 1830–1914* (London, 1973)

Finestein, Israel, *Jewish society in Victorian England: Collected essays* (London, 1993)

Fischer, W., J. Krengel and J. Wietog (eds), *Sozialgeschichtliches Arbeitsbuch: Materialien zur Statistik des Deutschen Bundes 1815–1870* (Munich, 1982)

Flandreau, Marc, *L'or du monde: La France et la stabilité du système monétaire international, 1848–1873* (Paris, 1995)

———, "An essay on the emergence of the international gold standard, 1870–80," *International Macroeconomics*, 1210 (1995)

Flint, John, *Cecil Rhodes* (London, 1976)

Fontana, J., *La revolucion liberal* (Madrid, 1977)

Ford, J. A. (ed.), *The correspondence of William I and Bismarck*, 2 vols (London, 1903)

Forrest, D. M, *A hundred years of Ceylon tea* (London, 1967)

Forstmann, Wilfried, *Simon Moritz Bethmann, 1768–1826: Bankier, Diplomat und politischer Beobachter*, Studien zur Frankfurter Geschichte, ed. Frankfurter Verein für Geschichte und Landeskunde (Frankfurt am Main, 1973)

———, "Frankfurt am Main—Ein europäisches Finanzzentrum. Aspekte zu Banken -und Bankpolitik in Frankfurt am Main im 18. und 19. Jahrhundert," in Johannes Heil and Bernd Wacker (eds), *Shylock? Zinsverbot und Geldverleih in jüdischer und christlicher Tradition* (Munich, 1997), pp. 101–12

Foster, R. F., *Lord Randolph Churchill* (Oxford, 1981)

Fournier-Verneuil, M., *Paris: Tableau moral et philosophique* (Paris, 1826)

Fraenkl, Josef, "Herzl and the Rothschild family," *Herzl Family Yearbook* (1960), pp. 217–36

———, "The Chief Rabbi and the visionary," in *idem* (ed.), *The Jews of Austria: Essays on their life, history and destruction* (London, 1967), pp. 11–129

Frankel, Jonathan, "A historiographical oversight: The Austrian consul-general and the Damascus blood libel (with the Laurin–Rothschild correspondence, 1840)," unpublished MS, RAL (n.d.)

idem, The Damascus affair: "Ritual murder," politics and the Jews in 1840 (Cambridge, 1997)

Fraser, Peter, *Joseph Chamberlain: Radicalism and empire, 1868–1914* (London, 1966)

Freimann, Aron, *Stammtafeln der Freiherrlichen Familie von Rothschild* (Frankfurt am Main, 1906)

——— and I. Kracauer, *Frankfort: Jewish community series* (Philadelphia, 1929)

Friedman, I., *Germany, Turkey and Zionism, 1897–1918* (Oxford, 1977)

Friedman, Régine Mihal, "The Rothschilds: One family—two films," in Heuberger (ed.), *Essays*, pp. 333–50

Fritsch, Wilson, *External constraints on economic policy in Brazil, 1889–1930* (Basingstoke, 1988)

Fritsche, Victor von, *Bilder aus dem österreichischen Hof -und Gesellschaftsleben* (Vienna, 1914)

Froude, J. A., *Lord Beaconsfield* (London, 1890)

Fuchs, Edouard, *Die Juden in der Karikatur: Ein Beitrag zur Kulturgeschichte* (Berlin, 1985)

Fulda, Bernhard, "The Prussian loan in London 1818: Politics and finance in the late stages of the Prussian Reform period," unpublished BA thesis (Oxford University, 1998)

Fulford, Roger, *Glyn's, 1753–1953* (London, 1953)

——— (ed.), *Darling Child: Private correspondence of Queen Victoria and the German Crown Princess, 1871–1878* (London, 1976)

Galbraith, J. A., *Crown and charter* (London, 1974)

Gall, Lothar, *Bismarck, the white revolutionary*, vol. I: *1815–71* (London, 1986)

———, Gerald D. Feldman, Harold James, Carl-Ludwig Holtfrerich and Hans E. Büschgen, *The Deutsche Bank, 1870–1995* (London, 1995)

Garrard, John A., *The English and immigration, 1880–1910* (London/New York/Toronto, 1971)

Gartner, Lloyd P., *The Jewish immigrant in England, 1870–1914* (London, 1973)

Gash, Norman, *Mr Secretary Peel* (London, 1961)

Gatrell, Peter, *Government, industry and rearmament in Russia, 1900–1914: The last argument of Tsarism* (Cambridge, 1994)

Gay, Ruth, *The Jews of Germany* (New Haven/London, 1992)

Gebhard, Louis A. Jnr, "Austria's dreadnought squadron and the naval outlay of 1911," *Austrian History Yearbook* (1968–9), pp. 245–58

Gentz, Friedrich von, *Briefe von Friedrich von Gentz an Pilat: Ein Beitrag zur Geschichte Deutschlands im XIX. Jahrhundert*, 2 vols, ed. Karl von Mendelssohn Bartholdy (Leipzig, 1868)

———, *Tagebücher von 1829–1831* (Vienna, 1920)

Gerber, J., "The Damascus blood libel: Jewish perceptions and responses," in *Proceedings of the Eighth World Congress of Jewish Studies: Division B* (Jerusalem, 1982), pp. 105–10

Gerloff, Wilhelm, "Der Staatshaushalt und das Finanzsystem Deutschlands, 1820–1927," in *idem* (ed.), *Handbuch der Finanzwissenschaft*, vol. III (Tübingen, 1929), pp. 4–69

Germanicus, *Die Frankfurter Juden und die Aussaugung des Volkswohlstandes: Eine Anklage wider die Agiotage und wider den Wucher* (Leipzig, 1880)

Germanicus, *Die Rothschild-Gruppe und der "monumentale" Conversions-Schwindel von 1881* (Leipzig, 1881)

Gerretson, F. C., *History of the Royal Dutch*, 4 vols (Leiden, 1953–7)

Gerschenkron, Alexander, *Economic backwardness in historical perspective* (Cambridge, Mass., 1962)

Gilam, Abraham, *The emancipation of the Jews in England, 1830–1869* (New York, 1982)

Gilbert, B. B., *David Lloyd George: A political life*, vol. I: The architect of change, 1863–1912 (Columbus, 1987)

———, *David Lloyd George. A political life*, vol. II: *Organizer of victory, 1912–1916* (London, 1992)

Gilbert, Felix, *Bankiers, Kunstler und Gelehrte* (Tübingen, 1975)

Gilbert, Martin, "*Never Despair': Winston S. Churchill*, vol. VIII: *1945–1965* (London, 1990)

Gille, Bertrand, *La banque et le crédit en France de 1815 à 1848* (Vendôme, 1959)

——— (ed.), *Lettres adressées à la Maison Rothschild de Paris par son représentant à Bruxelles* (Louvain/Paris, 1961)

———, *Histoire de la Maison Rothschild*, vol. I: *Des origines à 1848* (Geneva, 1965)

———, *Histoire de la Maison Rothschild*, vol. II: *1848–70* (Geneva, 1967)

Gillett Brothers Discount Co. Ltd, *The bill on London or, The finance of trade by bills of exchange* (London, 1964)

Girard, Louis, *La politique des travaux publics du Second Empire* (Paris, 1952)

Girault, René, *Emprunts russes et investissements français en Russie* (Paris, 1973)

Giuffrida, Romualda, *I Rothschildi e la finanza pubblica in Sicilia (1849–1955)* (Caltanessitta/Rome, 1968)

Glanz, Rudolf, "The Rothschild legend in America," *Jewish Social Studies* (1957), pp. 3–28

Glyn, Mills & Co., *Glyn, Mills & Co.* (London, 1933)

Goethe, Johann Wolfgang von, *Dichtung und Wahrheit, Werke, Kommentare und Register*, Hamburger Ausgabe in 14 Bänden, vol. IX: *Autobiographische Schriften I* (Munich, 1981)

Goldschmidt, Hermann von, *Einige Erinnerungen aus längst vergangenen Tagen* (Vienna, 1917)

Goncourt, Edmond and Jules de, *Journal: Mémoires de la vie littéraire*, 2 vols (Paris, 1956)

Gooch, G. P., and Harold Temperley (eds), *British documents on the origins of the War, 1898–1914*, 9 vols (London, 1926–27)

Good, David F., *The economic rise of the Habsburg Empire, 1750–1914* (Berkeley/Los Angeles, 1984)

Gower, Sir George Leveson, *Years of endeavour, 1886–1907* (London, 1942)

Gray, Denis, *Spencer Perceval: The Evangelical prime minister, 1762–1812* (Manchester, 1963)

Gray, Victor (ed.), *The Life and times of N. M. Rothschild 1777–1836* (London, 1998)

Green, Edwin, *Debtors to their profession: A history of the Institute of Bankers, 1879–1979* (London, 1979)

Green, Timothy, "Precious heritage: The three hundred years of Mocatta & Goldschmid," unpublished MS, RAL (n.d.)

———, *The new world of gold* (London, 1981)

Greenfield, Kent Roberts, *Economics and liberalism in the Risorgimento: A study of nationalism in Lombardy, 1814–48* (Baltimore, 1934)

Greville, Charles C. F., *The Greville memoirs: A journal of King George IV and King William IV*, vol. I, ed. Henry Reeve (London, 1875)

———, *The Greville memoirs (second part): A journal of the reign of Queen Victoria from 1837 to 1852*, vol. II, ed. Henry Reeve (London, 1885)

Grigg, John, *Lloyd George: The people's champion, 1902–1911* (London, 1978)

———, *Lloyd George: From peace to war, 1912–1916* (London, 1985)

Grunwald, Kurt, "Europe's railways and Jewish enterprise: German Jews as pioneers of railway promotion," *Leo Baeck Institute Year Book* (1967), pp. 163–209

Guedalla, Philip, *Palmerston* (London, 1926)

Guillen, Pierre, "The Entente of 1904 as a colonial settlement," in Prosser Gifford and Wm Roger Louis (eds), *France and Britain in Africa: Imperial rivalry and colonial rule* (New Haven/London, 1971), pp. 333–69

Guizot, François and Princess Dorothea Lieven, *Lettres de François Guizot et de la Princesse de Lieven*, 3 vols (Paris, 1963)

Gunn, J. A. W., John Matthews, Donald M. Schurman and M. G. Wiebe (eds), *Benjamin Disraeli: Letters*, vols I and II (Toronto, 1982)

Gutzkow, Karl, *Öffentliche Charaktere: Erster Theil* (Hamburg, 1835)

Haldane, Richard Burdon, *An autobiography* (London, 1929)

Halévy, Elie, *The rule of democracy* (London, 1952)

Hall, Michael, "The English Rothschilds as collectors," in Heuberger (ed.), *Essays*, pp. 265–86

———, "Nathan Rothschild as an owner of paintings," in Victor Gray (ed.), *The Life and times of N. M. Rothschild 1777–1836* (London, 1998), pp. 68–78

Hambros Bank Ltd, *Hambros Bank Ltd., 1839–1939* (London, 1939)

Hammond, Bray, *Banks and politics from the Revolution to the Civil War* (Princeton, 1957)

Hamon, Augustin and X.Y.Z., *Les maitres de la France* (Paris, 1936)

Handelskammer zu Frankfurt, *Geschichte der Handelskammer zu Frankfurt, 1707–1908* (Frankfurt, 1908)

Hansard, T. C. (ed.), *The parliamentary debates: forming a continuation of the work entitled "The parliamentary history of England from the earliest period to the year 1803". New Series; commencing with the accession of George IV*, vol. XVIII (January 29–April 22, 1828) (London, 1828)

Hansen, B. and K. Tourk, "The profitability of the Suez Canal as a private enterprise, 1859–1956," *Journal of Economic History* (1978), pp. 938–58

Hansert, Andreas, "The dynastic power of the Rothschilds: A sociological assessment," in Heuberger (ed.), *Essays*, pp. 165–78

Harcourt Williams, Robin (ed.), *Salisbury–Balfour correspondence: Letters exchanged between the 3rd Marquess of Salisbury and his nephew Arthur James Balfour, 1869–1892* ([Ware], 1988)

Hardach, Gerd, *The First World War, 1914–1918* (Harmondsworth, 1987)

Hardwick, Molly, *Mrs Dizzy: The life of Mary Anne Disraeli, Viscountess Beaconsfield* (London, 1972)

Hargreaves, Eric Lyde, *The national debt* (London, 1930)

Harman, A., *Metternich* (London, 1932)

Harper, Martin, *Mr Lionel: An Edwardian episode* (London, 1970)

Harvey, C. E., *The Rio Tinto Company: An economic history of a leading international mining concern* (London, 1981)

Harvey, William H., *Coin's financial school*, ed. Richard Hofstadter (Cambridge, Mass., 1963)

Hawke, G. and J. Higgins, "Britain," in Patrick O'Brien (ed.), *Railways and the economic development of Western Europe* (London/Basingstoke, 1983), pp. 170–202

Hawtrey, Sir Ralph George, *A century of bank rate* (2nd edn, London, 1962)

Healey, Edna, *Coutts & Co., 1692–1992: The portrait of a private bank* (London, 1992)

Heckscher, Eli F., *The continental system: An economic interpretation* (Oxford, 1922)

Hedley, Arthur, *Selected correspondence of Fryderyk Chopin* (London, 1962)

Heffer, Simon, *Moral desperado: A life of Thomas Carlyle* (London, 1995)

Heilbrunn, Rudolf M., "Das Haus Rothschild: Wahrheit und Dichtung," Vortrag gehalten am 6. März 1963 im Frankfurter Verein für Geschichte und Landeskunde (1963)

———, "Die wirtschaftliche und politische Bedeutung des Hauses Rothschild," Vortrag gehalten vor dem Lions Club Frankfurt-Goethestadt (1965)

———, "Der Anfang des Hauses Rothschild: Wahrheit und Dichtung," *Jahrbuch des Instituts für deutsche Geschichte* (1973), pp. 209–38

Heimann-Jelinek, Felicitas, "The 'Aryanisation' of Rothschild assets in Vienna and the problem of restitution," in Heuberger (ed.), *Essays*, pp. 351–64

Heine, Heinrich, *Sämtliche Schriften*, vols. II–VI (Munich, 1971)

Helleiner, Karl F., *Free trade and frustration: Anglo-Austrian negotiations, 1860–1870* (Toronto, 1963)

———, *The imperial loans: A study in financial and diplomatic history* (Oxford, 1965)

Hémont, L'Abbé, *Les juifs et Bazaine* (Paris, 1899)

Henderson, W. O., *The Zollverein* (London, 1939)

Henrey, R., *A century between* (London/Toronto, 1937)

——— (ed.), *Letters from Paris: Written by C. de B., a political informant, to the head of the London house of Rothschild, 1870–1875* (London, 1942)

Henriques, Robert, *Bearsted: A biography of Marcus Samuel, 1st Viscount Bearsted and founder of "Shell" Transport and Trading Company* (New York, 1960)

Henriques, U. R. Q., "The Jewish emancipation controversy in nineteenth century Britain," *Past & Present* (1968), pp. 113–43

Herding, Klaus, "Die Rothschilds in der Karikatur," in Cilly Kugelmann and Fritz Backhaus (eds), *Jüdische*

Figuren in Film und Karikatur. Die Rothschilds und Joseph Süß Oppenheimer (Sigmaringen, 1996), pp. 13–64

Herries, Edward, *Memoirs of the public life of the Rt Hon. John Charles Herries* (London, 1880)

Hershlas, Z. Y., *Introduction to the modern economic history of the Middle East* (Leiden, 1964)

Hertz, J. H., *The Rt. Hon. Lord Rothschild: Memorial sermon* (London, 1915)

Herzen, Alexander, *My past and thoughts: The memoirs of Alexander Herzen*, 4 vols (London, 1968)

———, *Letters from France and Italy, 1847–1851* (Pittsburgh, 1995)

Herzl, Theodor, *Tagebücher, 1895–1904*, 3 vols (Berlin, 1922)

Heseltine, William, *A family scene during the panic at the Stock Exchange in May 1835* (2nd edn, Canterbury, 1848)

Hessen, Rainer von, " 'You did not recommend a fool to me'—Elector William II of Hesse and Meyer Amschel Rothschild," in Heuberger (ed.), *Essays*, pp. 21–36

———, *Wir Wilhelm von Gottes Gnaden: Die Lebenserinnerungen Kurfürst Wilhelms I. von Hessen 1743–1821* (Frankfurt/New York, 1996)

Heuberger, Georg, *The Rothschilds: A European family*, Catalogue of the exhibition "The Rothschilds—A European Family" in the Jewish Museum of the City of Frankfurt am Main, October 11, 1994–February 27, 1995 (Sigmaringen, 1994)

——— (ed.), *The Rothschilds: Essays on the history of a European family* (Sigmaringen, 1994)

———, "The Rothschilds: Family history in the museum context," in *idem* (ed.), *Essays*, pp. 15–20

Heuberger, Rachel and Helga Krohn, *Hinaus aus dem Ghetto . . . Juden in Frankfurt am Main, 1800–1950* (Frankfurt am Main, 1988)

Heyn, Udo, "Private banking and industrialization: The case of Frankfurt am Main, 1825–1875," unpublished DPhil thesis (University of Wisconsin, 1969)

Hidy, R. W., *The House of Baring in American trade and finance: English merchant bankers at work, 1763–1861*, Harvard Studies in Business History, XIV (Cambridge, Mass., 1949)

Hilton, Boyd, *Corn, cash and commerce: The economic policies of Tory governments, 1815–1830* (Oxford, 1977)

Hoare, Philip, *Wilde's last stand: Decadence, conspiracy and the First World War* (London, 1997)

Hoare's Bank, *Hoare's Bank: A record, 1672–1955. The story of a private bank* (London, 1955)

Hobson, J. A., *Imperialism: A study* (London, 1988 [1st edn 1902])

Hobson, J. M., "The military-extraction gap and the wary Titan: The fiscal sociology of British defence policy, 1870–1913," *Journal of European Economic History* (1993), pp. 461–506

Hoffmann, W. G., F. Grumbach and H. Hesse, *Das Wachstum der deutschen Wirtschaft seit der Mitte des 19. Jahrhunderts* (Berlin, 1965)

Höffner, Corinna, "Frankfurter Privatsammlungen: Stifter und Bestände—Eigenart und Umfang," unpublished Staatsexamen für das Lehramt an Haupt -und Realschulen thesis (J. W. Goethe-Universität Frankfurt, 1992)

Hofstadter, Richard, *The age of reform from Bryan to F.D.R.* (London, 1962)

Holmes, A. R. and Edwin Green, *Midland: 150 years of banking business* (London, 1986)

Holmes, Derek, *The triumph of the Holy See* (London, 1972)

Homer, Sidney, *A history of interest rates* (2nd edn, New Brunswick, 1977)

Hood, Clifton, *722 Miles: The building of the subways and how they transformed New York* (Baltimore/London, 1993)

Howard, Michael, *The Franco–Prussian War* (London, 1961)

Howe, Irving and Ruth R. Wisse (eds), *The best of Shalom Aleichem* (Washington, DC, 1979)

Huber, Heinrich, "Fürstprimas Karl von Dalberg und das Haus Rothschild: Ein Beitrag zur Geschichte der Judenemanzipation in Frankfurt a.M.," *Weltkampf* (1943), pp. 19–27

———, "Bayern und das Haus Rothschild: Eine geschichtliche Betrachtung," *Allgemeine Zeitung der Juden in Deutschland* (March 15, 1957)

Hübner, comte de, *Neuf ans de souvenirs d'un ambassadeur d'Autriche à Paris sous le Second Empire, 1851–59*, 2 vols (Paris, 1904)

Huertas, Thomas, *Economic growth and economic policy in a multi-national setting: The Habsburg Monarchy, 1841–1865* (New York, 1977)

Hugelmann de Vegny Saint-Salmon, M. Gabriel, *A Rothschild: L'inauguration du chemin de fer du Nord* (Paris, 1846)

Hunt, Herbert J., *Balzac's Comedie Humaine* (London, 1964)

Hurst, Michael, *Joseph Chamberlain and Liberal reunion* (London, 1967)

Hüttl, Ludwig, *Ludwig II. König von Bayern: Eine Biographie* (Munich, 1986)

Hyamson, Albert M., *David Salomons* (London, 1939)

———, *Jews College London, 1855–1955* (London, 1955)

Icke, David, . . . *And the truth shall set you free* (Ryde, Isle of Wight, 1995)

Iliowzi, Henry, "*In the Pale': Stories and legends of the Russian Jews* (Philadelphia, 1897)

Imlah, Albert H., *Economic elements in the Pax Britannica* (Cambridge, Mass., 1958)

Ingrao, C., *The Hessian mercenary state* (Cambridge, 1987)

Israel, Jonathan I., *European Jewry in the Age of Mercantilism, 1550–1750* (Oxford, 1985)

Issawi, C., *Economic history of the Middle East, 1800–1914* (Chicago, 1966)

Jäckel, Eberhard and Axel Kuhn (eds), *Hitler: Sämtliche Aufzeichnungen, 1905–1924* (Stuttgart, 1980)

Jackson, Patrick, *The last of the Whigs: A political biography of Lord Hartington, later 8th Duke of Devonshire (1833–1908)* (Rutherford, New Jersey/London, 1994)

Jackson, Stanley, *The Sassoons: Portrait of a dynasty* (London, 1968)

Jacobson, Jacob, "Die Auflösung des Rothschildarchivs in Frankfurt a.M.," *Zeitschrift für die Geschichte der Juden in Deutschland* (1931), p. 279

Jacquemyns, G., *Langrand-Dumonceau: Promoteur d'une puissance financière catholique*, 5 vols (Brussels, 1960)

Jahrbuch für die Statistik des Preussischen Staates, ed. Königliches Statistisches Bureau (Berlin, 1869)

James, Robert Rhodes, *Lord Randolph Churchill* (London, 1959)

———, *Rosebery* (London, 1963)

Janik, A. and S. Toulin, *Wittgenstein's Vienna* (London, 1973)

Jardin, André and André-Jean Tudesq, *Restoration and reaction, 1815–1848* (Cambridge, 1983)

Jay, Richard, *Joseph Chamberlain: A political study* (Oxford, 1981)

Jenkins, Roy, *Mr Balfour's Poodle: An account of the struggle between the House of Lords and the government of Mr Asquith* (London, 1968)

———, *Asquith* (London, 1986)

Jenkins, T. A., *Gladstone, Whiggery and the Liberal Party, 1874–1886* (Oxford, 1988)

Jenks, Leland Hamilton, *The migration of British capital to 1875* (New York/London, 1927)

Jenks, William A., *Francis Joseph and the Italians* (Charlottesville, 1978)

———, *Austria under the Iron Ring* (Charlottesville, 1965)

Jennings, Louis J. (ed.), *Correspondence and diaries of John Wilson Croker, Secretary to the Admiralty 1809–1830*, vol. III (London, 1884)

Jewish Theological Seminary of America, *The Jew as Other: A century of English caricature, 1730–1830* (New York, 1995)

Johnson, Christopher H., "The revolution of 1830 in French economic history," in John Merriman (ed.), *1830 in France* (New York/London , 1975), pp. 139–89

Johnson, Nancy E. (ed.), *The diary of Gathorne Hardy, later Lord Cranbrook, 1866–1892: Political selections* (Oxford, 1981)

Johnston, Thomas, *The financiers and the nation* (London, 1934)

Joll, James, *The origins of the First World War* (London, 1992)

Jones, Steve, *In the blood: God, genes and destiny* (London, 1996)

Joslin, David, *A century of banking in Latin America* (Oxford, 1963)

Jullian, Philippe, *Les styles* (Paris, 1961)

Jurk, Michael, "The other Rothschilds: Frankfurt private bankers in the 18th and 19th centuries," in Heuberger (ed.), *Essays*, pp. 37–50

Kadish, Sharman, *Bolsheviks and British Jews: The Anglo-Jewish community, Britain and the Russian Revolution* (London, 1992)

Kaplan, Marion A., *The making of the Jewish middle class: Women, family and identity in imperial Germany* (Oxford, 1991)

Kapp, Freidrich, *Der Soldatenhandel deutscher Fürsten nach Amerika, 1775–1783* (Berlin, 1884)

Kapralik, C. I., *Reclaiming the Nazi loot* (London, 1962)

Katz, David, *Philosemitism and the readmission of the Jews to England* (Oxford, 1982)

Katz, David S., *The Jews in the history of England, 1485–1850* (Oxford, 1994)

Katz, Irving, *August Belmont: A political biography* (New York, 1968)

Katz, Jacob, *Tradition and crisis: Jewish society and the end of the Middle Ages* (New York, 1961)

———, *Jews and Freemasons in Europe, 1723–1939* (Cambridge, Mass., 1970)

———, *Out of the ghetto: The social background of Jewish emancipation, 1770–1870* (New York, 1978)

Katzenstein, Peter J., *Disjoined partners: Austria and Germany since 1815* (Berkeley/Los Angeles, 1976)

Kehr, Eckart, "Zur Genesis der preußischen Bürokratie und des Rechtsstaats," in Hans-Ulrich Wehler (ed.),

Der Primat der Innenpolitik. Gesammelte Aufsätze zur preußisch-deutschen Sozialgeschichte im 19. und 20. Jahrhundert (Berlin, 1970), pp. 31–52

———, "Biographische Skizzen: Fugger; Carnot und Scharnhorst; Rothschild," in Wehler (ed.), *Primat der Innenpolitik*, pp. 284–92

Kemp, Tom, *Economic forces in French history* (London, 1971)

Kennan, George F., *The decline of Bismarck's European order: Franco-Russian relations, 1875–1890* (Princeton, 1979)

———, *The fateful alliance: France, Russia and the coming of the First World War* (Manchester, 1984)

Kennedy, Paul M., *The rise of Anglo-German antagonism, 1860–1914* (London, 1982)

Kent, Marian (ed.), *The great powers and the end of the Ottoman Empire* (London, 1984)

Kessler, David, "The Rothschilds and Disraeli in Buckinghamshire," *Transactions of the Jewish Historical Society of England* (1982–86), pp. 231–52

Kindleberger, Charles P., *Economic growth in France and Britain, 1851–1950* (Cambridge, Mass., 1964)

———, *A financial history of Western Europe* (London, 1984)

Kipping, E., *Die Truppen von Hessen-Kassel im amerikanischen Unabhängigkeitskrieg 1776–1783* (Darmstadt, 1965)

Kirke Rose, T., *The metallurgy of gold* (London, 1896)

Kissinger, Henry, *Diplomacy* (London, 1994)

Kitchen, Martin, *The political economy of Germany, 1815–1914* (London, 1978)

Klein, Ernst, "Preußens 30–Million-Anleihe in London vom 31. März 1818," *Zeitschrift für Geschichtwissenschaft*, (1956), pp.

Knapp, Vincent J., *Europe in the era of social transformation: 1700 to the present* (Englewood Cliffs, New Jersey, 1976)

Knight, G. A., "Das Rothschildsche Banken -und Wirtschaftsarchiv in London: Empfängerüberlieferung in Überblick," *Bankhistorisches Archiv* (1979), pp. 61–6

———, "The Rothschild–Bleichröder axis in action: An Anglo-German co-operative, 1877–1878," *Leo Baeck Year Book* (1983), pp. 43–57

Koch, Gertrud, "Tabuen oder Falken—die Rothschild-Filme im Vergleich," in Cilly Kugelmann and Fritz Backhaus (eds), *Jüdische Figuren in Film und Karikatur: Die Rothschilds und Joseph Süß Oppenheimer* (Sigmaringen, 1996), pp. 65–95

Koch, Rainer, *Grundlagen bürgerlicher Herrschaft: Verfassungs-und sozialgeschichtliche Studien zur bürgerlichen Gesellschaft in Frankfurt am Main (1612–1866)*, Frankfurter Historische Abhandlungen, 27 (Wiesbaden, 1983)

Kolb, Louis, "The Vienna Jewish Museum," in Josef Fraenkl (ed.), *The Jews of Austria: Essays on their life, history and destruction* (London, 1967), pp. 147–59

Komlos, John, *The Habsburg Monarchy as a customs union: Economic development in Austria–Hungary in the nineteenth century* (Princeton, 1983)

Kopper, Christopher, "The Rothschild family during the Third Reich," in Heuberger (ed.), *Essays*, pp. 321–32

Kracauer, Isidor, "Die Geschichte der Judengasse in Frankfurt am Main," in *Festschrift zur Jahrhundertfeier der Realschule der israelitischen Gemeinde (Philanthropin) zu Frankfurt am Main 1804–1904* (Frankfurt am Main, 1904), pp. 303–464

———, *Geschichte der Juden in Frankfurt am Main (1150–1824)*, 2 vols (Frankfurt, 1925, 1927)

Kriegel, Abraham D. (ed.), *The Holland House diaries, 1831–40: Diary of Henry Richard Vassall Fox, 3rd Lord Holland* (London, 1977)

Kriegk, Georg Ludwig, *Geschichte von Frankfurt am Main* (Frankfurt am Main, 1871)

Kropat, Wolf Arno, *Frankfurt zwischen Provinzialismus und Nationalismus: Die Eingliederung der "Freien Stadt" in den preußischen Staat (1866–1871)* (Frankfurt am Main, 1971)

———, "Die Emanzipation der Juden in Kurhessen und in Nassau im 19. Jahrhundert," in Christiane Heinemann (ed.), *Neunhundert Jahre Geschichte der Juden in Hessen: Beiträge zum politischen, wirtschaftlichen und kulturellen Leben* (Wiesbaden, 1983), pp. 325–50

Kübeck von Kübow, Carl Friedrich, *Tagebücher des Kübeck von Kübow* (Vienna, 1909)

———, *Aus dem Nachlaß des Freiherrn Carl Friedrich Kübeck von Kübow: Tagebücher, Briefe, Aktenstücke 1841–55*, Veröffentlichungen der Kommission für neuere Geschichte Österreichs, 45 (Graz/Cologne, 1960)

Kubicek, R.V., *Economic imperialism in theory and practice: The case of South African gold mining, 1886–1914* (Durham, 1979)

Kynaston, David, *Cazenove and Co.: A history* (London, 1991)

———, *The City of London, vol. I: A world of its own, 1815–90* (London, 1994)

———, *The City of London, vol. II: Golden years, 1890–1914* (London, 1996)

———, "The City of London in Nathan Rothschild's time," in Victor Gray (ed.), *The Life and times of N. M. Rothschild 1777–1836* (London, 1998), pp. 42–9

Laffitte, Jacques, *Mémoires de Laffitte* (Paris, 1932)

Laffut, "Belgium," Patrick O'Brien (ed.), *Railways and the economic development of Western Europe* (London/Basingstoke, 1983), pp. 203–26.

Lancaster, Osbert, *From here of all places* (London, 1959)

Landes, David S., *Bankers and pashas: International finance and economic imperialism in Egypt* (London, 1958)

———, "The old bank and the new: The financial revolution of the nineteenth century," in F. Crouzet, W. H. Chaloner and W. M. Stern (eds), *Essays in European economic history, 1789–1914* (London, 1969), pp. 112–27

———, "The spoilers foiled: The exclusion of Prussian finance from the French Liberation Loan of 1871," in Charles P. Kindleberger and Guido di Tella (eds), *Economics in the long view: Essays in honour of W. W. Rostow* (London/Basingstoke, 1982), pp. 67–110

Landmann, Salcia, *Der jüdische Witz: Soziologie und Sammlung* (Olten/Freiburg im Breisgau, 1963)

Lane, Barbara Miller and Leila J. Rupp (eds), *Nazi ideology before 1933: A documentation* (Manchester, 1978)

Lang, Jochen von, *Der Adjutant. Karl Wolff: Der Mann zwischen Hitler und Himmler* (Berlin, 1985)

Lant, Jeffrey L., *Insubstantial pageant: Ceremony and confusion at Queen Victoria's court* (New York, 1980)

Launay, vicomte de [Gay, Delphine, later Mme de Girardin], *Lettres parisiennes*, 3 vols (Paris, 1856)

Lawson, Nigel, *The view from No. 11: Memoirs of a Tory radical* (London, 1992)

Lears, Rufus, *Filled with laughter: A fiesta of Jewish humor* (New York, 1961)

Lee, A. G. (ed.), *The Empress Frederick writes to Sophie her daughter, Crown Princess and later Queen of the Hellenes, 1889–1901* (London, 1955)

Lee, Samuel J., *Moses of the New World: The work of Baron de Hirsch* (New York/South Brunswick/London, 1970)

Lefebvre, René, "Les Rothschild," *Crapouillot* (n.d. [1951?]), pp. 6–20

Lefèvre, André, *Sous le Second Empire: Chemins de fer et politique* (Paris, 1951)

Lenarz, Michael, *Der alte jüdische Friedhof zu Frankfurt am Main* (Frankfurt am Main, 1996)

Letcher, Owen, *The gold mines of Southern Africa* (London, 1936)

Levene, Mark, *War, Jews and the new Europe: The diplomacy of Lucien Wolf, 1914–1919* (Oxford, 1992)

Levy, Maria Barbara, "The Brazilian public debt: domestic and foreign," in Reinhard Liehr (ed.), *La dueda pùblican en América en perspectiva historica* (Frankfurt am Main, 1995), pp. 209–54

Lévy-Leboyer, Maurice, "Capital investment and economic growth in France, 1820–1930," in Peter Mathias and M. M. Postan (eds), *The Cambridge economic history of Europe*, vol. VII: *The industrial economies: Capital, labour and enteprise, part I* (Cambridge, 1978), pp. 231–395

Lewnsohn, Solomon, *Die treue Anhänglichkeit zu Jerusalem und die Liebe zu Zion* (n.p., 1858)

Liberles, Robert, *Religious conflict in social context: The resurgence of Orthodox Judaism in Frankfurt am Main, 1838–1877* (Westwood, Conn., 1985)

———, "The world of Dietz's *Stammbuch*: Frankfurt Jewry, 1349–1870," in Alexander Dietz (ed.), *The Jewish community of Frankfurt: A genealogical study* (Camelford, 1988), pp. i–xxxi

———, "The Aristocrat and the synagogue: the Rothschilds and Judaism," in Heuberger (ed.), *Essays*, pp. 195–204

Lieven, Princess Dorothea, *The private letters of Princess Lieven to Prince Metternich, 1820–1826* (London, 1948)

Lindemann, Albert S., *The Jew accused: Three anti-Semitic affairs (Dreyfus, Beilis, Frank), 1894–1915* (Cambridge, 1991)

Lipman, Edward, "The City and the 'People's Budget,'" unpublished MS (1995).

Lipman, Sonia, "The making of a Victorian gentleman," in Sonia and Vivian D. Lipman (eds), *The century of Moses Montefiore* (Oxford, 1985), pp. 3–22

Lipman, Vivian D., *A century of social service, 1859–1959: The Jewish Board of Guardians* (London, 1959)

———, *A history of the Jews in Britain since 1858* (Leicester, 1990)

List, Friedrich, *Grundlinien einer politischen Ökonomie und andere Beiträge der amerikanischen Zeit, 1825–1832,* Friedrich List, Schriften/Reden/Briefe, vol. II, im Auftrag der Friedrich List-Gesellschaft e.V., ed. Erwin von Beckerath, Karl Goeser, Freidrich Lenz, William Notz, Edgar Salin, Artur Sommer (Berlin, 1931)

Litvinoff, Barnet (ed.), *The essential Chaim Weizmann: The man, the statesman, the scientist* (London, 1982)

Lloyd George, David, *War memoirs of David Lloyd George*, 2 vols (London, 1933)

Locke, Robert R., "A method for identifying French corporate businessmen (the Second Empire)," *French Historical Studies*, 10, 2 (1977), pp. 261–93

Loewe, Louis (ed.), *Diaries of Sir Moses and Lady Montefiore*, 2 vols (Oxford, 1983)

Loménie, E. Beau de, *Les responsabilités des dynasties bourgeoises*, 5 vols (Paris, 1954)

Longford, E., *Wellington: The years of the sword* (London, 1969)

———, *Wellington: Pillar of state* (London, 1972)

——— (ed.), *Darling Loosy* (London, 1991)

Lord, Robert H., *The origins of the War of 1870* (Cambridge, Mass., 1924)

Losch, Philipp, *Geschichte des Kurfürstentums Hessen, 1803 bis 1866* (Marburg, 1922)

———, *Kurfürst Wilhelm I, Landgraf von Hessen* (Marburg, 1923)

Lottman, Herbert R., *Return of the Rothschilds* (London/New York, 1995)

Luna, Frederick A. de, *The French Republic under Cavaignac* (Princeton, 1969)

Lyons, F. S. L., *Internationalism in Europe 1815–1914* (Leyden, 1936)

Macartney, C. A., *The Habsburg Empire, 1790–1918* (London, 1969)

———, *The House of Austria* (Edinburgh, 1978)

McCagg, William O., Jr, *Jewish nobles and geniuses in modern Hungary* (New York, 1972)

———, "Vienna and Budapest around 1900: The problem of Jewish influence," in György Ránki and Attila Pok (eds), *Hungary and European civilisation* (Budapest, 1989), pp. 241–64

———, "The Jewish position in interwar Central Europe: A structural study of Jewry at Vienna, Budapest and Prague," in Victor Karady and Yehuda Don (eds), *A social and economic history of Central European Jewry* (New Brunswick, New Jersey, 1989), pp. 47–81

———, *A history of the Habsburg Jews* (Bloomington, Indiana, 1989)

Mace, Simone, "The archives of the London Merchant Bank of N. M. Rothschild & Sons," *Business Archives* (1992), pp. 1–14

———, "From Frankfurt Jew to Lord Rothschild: The ascent of the English Rothschilds to the nobility," in Heuberger (ed.), *Essays*, pp. 179–94

McGrath, William J., *Dionysian art and populist politics in Austria* (New Haven, 1974)

Mack Smith, Denis, *Italy: A modern history* (Ann Arbor, Michigan, 1959)

———, *Victor Emmanuel, Cavour and the Risorgimento* (Oxford, 1971)

———, *Cavour* (London, 1985)

———, *Mazzini* (New Haven, 1994)

McKay, John, "Baku oil and Transcaucasian pipelines, 1883–1891: A study in Tsarist economic policy," *Slavic Review* (1984), pp. 604–23

———, "The House of Rothschild (Paris) as a multinational industrial enterprise, 1875–1914," in A. Teichova, M. Lévy-Leboyer and H. Nussbaum (eds), *Multinational enterprise in historical perspective* (Cambridge, 1986), pp. 74–86

Mackay, Ruddock F., *Balfour: Intellectual statesman* (Oxford, 1985)

Mackenzie, Compton, *Realms of silver* (London, 1954)

Maggs, Christopher, *A century of change: The story of the Royal National Pension Fund for Nurses* (London, 1987)

Magnus, Lady Katie, *Jewish portraits* (London, 1897)

Malchow, Howard Le Roy, *Gentleman capitalists: The social and political world of the Victorian businessman* (London, 1991)

Malia, Martin, *Alexander Herzen and the birth of Russian socialism* (Cambridge, 1961)

Mann, Golo, *Secretary of Europe: The life of Friedrich von Gentz, enemy of Napoleon* (New Haven, 1946)

Marcus, Joseph, *Social and political history of the Jews in Poland* (Amsterdam, 1983)

Margoliouth, Rev. Moses, *The history of the Jews of Great Britain*, 3 vols (London, 1851)

Marion, Marcel, *Histoire financière de la France depuis 1715*, vol. V: *1819–1875* (Paris, 1928)

Marks, Lara V., *Model mothers: Jewish mothers and maternity provision in East London, 1870–1939* (Oxford, 1994)

Marsh, Peter T. *Joseph Chamberlain: Entrepreneur in politics* (New Haven/London, 1994)

Martel, Gordon, *Imperial diplomacy: Rosebery and the failure of foreign policy* (Kingston, Ontario/London, 1986)

Martin, V. M., *Los Rothschild y las Minas de Almadén* (Madrid, 1980)

Marx, Julius, *Die wirtschaftliche Ursachen der Revolution von 1848 in Österreich* (Graz/Cologne, 1965)

Marx, Karl, "On the Jewish question," in *idem* and Friedrich Engels (eds), *Collected works*, vol. III: *1843–1844* (London, 1975), pp. 146–74

März, Eduard, *Österreichische Bankpolitik in der Zeit der großen Wende 1913–1923: Am Beispiel der Creditanstalt für Handel und Gewerbe* (Munich, 1981)

———, "The Austrian Crédit Mobilier in a time of transition," in John Komlos (ed.), *Economic development in the Habsburg monarchy in the nineteenth century: Essays* (New York, 1983), pp. 117–36

Matthew, H. C. G. (ed.), *The Gladstone diaries with Cabinet minutes and prime ministerial correspondence*, 14 vols (Oxford, 1968–94)

———, "Disraeli, Gladstone and the politics of mid-Victorian budgets," *Historical Journal* (1979), pp. 615–643

———, *Gladstone, 1809–1874* (Oxford, 1986)

———, *Gladstone, 1875–1898* (Oxford, 1995)

Maurois, André, *Disraeli* (London, 1927)

May, Arthur J., *The Habsburg monarchy* (Cambridge, Mass., 1951)

Mayer, Arno J., *The persistence of the old regime* (New York, 1971)

Mayeur, Jean-Marie, *Les débuts de la Troisième République, 1871–98* (Paris, 1973)

Mayorek, Yoram, "Between East and West: Edmond de Rothschild and Palestine," in Heuberger (ed.), *Essays*, pp. 129–46

Melville, Lewis, *The life and letters of William Cobbett in England and America, based upon hitherto unpublished family papers*, 2 vols (London/New York/Toronto, n.d.)

Mende, Fritz, *Heinrich Heine: Chronik seines Lebens u. Werkes* (Berlin, 1970)

Merimée, Prosper, *Correspondance générale*, 6 vols (Paris, 1945)

———, *Correspondance générale*, 2e série, 9 vols (Paris, 1953–61)

Metternich, R. (ed.), *Aus Metternichs nachgelassenen Papieren*, 8 vols (Vienna, 1880–84)

Meyer, Michael, *Response to modernity: The Reform movement in Judaism* (New York, 1988)

Mezerey, Jean de, "Les origines de la famille Rothschild," *La Revue* (1901), pp. 186–91

Michel, Bernard, *Banques et banquiers en Autriche au début de XXe siècle* (Paris, 1976)

Michie, R. C., *The London and New York Stock Exchanges, 1850–1914* (London, 1987)

Michon, Georges, *L'alliance Franco-Russe, 1891–1917* (Paris, 1927)

Milward, A. and S. B. Saul, *The development of the economies of continental Europe, 1850–1914* (London, 1977)

Minchton, Walter, "Patterns of demand, 1750–1914," in C. M. Cipolla (ed.), *The Fontana economic history of Europe: The Industrial Revolution* (Glasgow, 1973), pp. 77–186

Mirès, Jules Isaac, *A mes juges: Ma vie et mes affaires* (Paris, 1861)

Mitchell, B. R., *European historical statistics, 1750–1975* (London, 1975)

———, *Abstract of British historical statistics* (Cambridge, 1976)

Modder, Frank Montagu, *The Jew in the literature of England to the end of the nineteenth century* (New York/Philadelphia, 1939)

Monypenny, W. F. and G. E. Buckle, *The life of Benjamin Disraeli, Earl of Beaconsfield*, 6 vols (London, 1910–20)

Moreau, Emile, *Souvenirs d'un gouverneur de la Banque de France (1926–1928)* (Paris, 1954)

Morgan, E. Victor, *The theory and practice of central banking, 1797–1913* (Cambridge, 1943)

——— and W. A. Thomas, *The Stock Exchange* (London, 1962)

Morgan Grenfell & Co. Ltd, *George Peabody & Co., J. S. Morgan & Co., Morgan Grenfell & Co., Morgan Grenfell & Co. Ltd* (Oxford, 1958)

Morley, John, *The life of William Ewart Gladstone*, vols II and III (London, 1903)

Morris, Susannah, "Voluntary action and the housing of the working classes in London, 1840–1914," unpublished DPhil thesis (Oxford University, forthcoming)

Morton, Frederick, *The Rothschilds: A family portrait* (London, 1961)

Moss, David J., *Thomas Attwood: The biography of a Radical* (Montreal/London, 1990)

Mosse, Werner, *Jews in the German economy: The German-Jewish economic elite, 1820–1935* (Oxford, 1987)

Mount, Ferdinand, *Umbrella* (London, 1995)

Muhlstein, Anka, *Baron James: The rise of the French Rothschilds* (London, 1983)

Murray, B. K., *The People's Budget, 1909/10: Lloyd George and liberal politics* (Oxford, 1980)

Murray, D. L., *Disraeli* (London, 1927)

Nash, W. G., *The Rio Tinto mine* (London, 1904)

BIBLIOGRAPHY 617

Neal, Larry, *The rise of financial capitalism: International capital markets in the age of reason* (Cambridge, 1990)

Nesselrode, comte Charles de, *Lettres et papiers du Chancelier comte de Nesselrode, 1760–1850*, 11 vols (Paris, 1904–11)

Newbury, Colin, "Out of the pit: the capital accumulation of Cecil Rhodes," *Journal of Imperial and Commonwealth History* (1981), pp. 25–49

———, "Technology, capital and consolidation: the performance of De Beers Mining Company Limited, 1880–1889," *Business History* (1987), pp. 1–42

———, *The Diamond Ring: Business, politics and precious stones in South Africa, 1867–1947* (Oxford, 1989)

Newman, Aubrey, *The United Synagogue, 1870–1970* (London, 1976)

Nicholas, Lynn, *The rape of Europa: The fate of Europe's treasures in the Third Reich and the Second World War* (London, 1994)

Nicolle, André, *Comment la France a payé après Waterloo* (Paris, 1929)

Nicholls, David, "Fractions of capital: The aristocracy, the City and industry in the development of modern British capitalism," *Social History* (1988), pp. 71–83

Nichols, Irby C., Jnr, "Britain and the Austrian war debt, 1821–3," *The Historian* (1958), pp. 328–46

———, *The European pentarchy and the Congress of Vienna* (The Hague, 1971)

Nichols, J. Alden, *Germany after Bismarck: The Caprivi era, 1890–1984* (Cambridge, Mass., 1958)

Nicolson, Harold, *The Congress of Vienna: A study in allied unity, 1812–1822* (London, 1946)

Nicolson, Nigel, (ed.), *Vita and Harold: The letters of Vita Sackville-West and Harold Nicolson* (London, 1992)

Niecks, Frederick, *Frederick Chopin as a man and musician* (London, 1890)

Nipperdey, Thomas, *Germany from Napoleon to Bismarck, 1800–1866* (Dublin, 1996)

Obenaus, Herbert, "Finanzkrise und Verfassungsgebung. Zu den sozialen Bedingungen des frühen deutschen Konstitutionalismus," in Gerhard A. Ritter (ed.), *Gesellschaft, Parlament und Regierung: Zur Geschichte des Parlamentarismus in Deutschland* (Düsseldorf, 1974), pp. 57–75

O'Brien, P. K. (ed.), *Railways and the economic development of Western Europe* (London/Basingstoke, 1983)

———, "The costs and benefits of British imperialism, 1846–1914," *Past & Present* (1988), pp. 163–200

———, "Power with profit: The state and the economy, 1688–1815," Inaugural lecture, University of London (1991)

O'Brien, Terence H., *Milner: Viscount Milner of St. James's and Cape Town, 1854–1925* (London, 1979)

Offer, Avner, *Property and politics, 1870–1914: Landownership, law, ideology and urban development in England* (Cambridge, 1981)

Oppenheim, Moritz, *Erinnerungen*, ed. Alfred Oppenheim (Frankfurt am Main, 1924)

Osborne, Richard, *Rossini* (London, 1986)

Otazu, Alfonso de, *Los Rothschild y sus Socias en Espana, 1820–1850* (Madrid, 1987)

Ouvrard, Gabriel-Julien, *Mémoires sur sa vie et ses diverses operations financières*, 3 vols (Paris, 1825)

Overy, Richard, "Göring's "multi-national" empire," in A. Teichova and P. L. Cottrell (eds), *International business and Central Europe, 1919–1939* (Leicester, 1984), pp. 269–98

Owen, R., *The Middle East and the world economy, 1800–1914* (London, 1981)

Oxaal, Ivor, "The Jews of the young Hitler's Vienna," in *idem*, M. Pollack and G. Botz (eds), *The Jews, anti-semitism and culture in Vienna* (New York/London, 1987), pp. 11–38

Palin, Ronald, *Rothschild relish* (London, 1970)

Palmade, Guy P., *French capitalism in the nineteenth century* (Newton Abbot, 1972)

Palmer, Alan, *Metternich: Councillor of Europe* (London, 1972)

———, *The chancelleries of Europe* (London, 1983)

Pamlenyi, E. (ed.), *A history of Hungary* (London, 1975)

Paret, Peter, *Art as history: Episodes in the culture and politics of nineteenth century Germany* (Princeton, 1988)

Parfitt, T., " 'The Year of the Pride of Israel': Montefiore and the Damascus blood libel of 1840," in Sonia and Vivian D. Lipman (eds), *The century of Moses Montefiore* (Oxford, 1985), pp. 131–48

Park, Joseph H., *British Prime Ministers of the nineteenth century, policies and speeches* (New York, 1950)

Parry, J. P., *Democracy and religion: Gladstone and the Liberal Party, 1867–1875* (Cambridge, 1986)

Partridge, Monica, *Alexander Herzen, 1812–1870* (Paris, 1984)

Paucker, Pauline, "The image of the German Jew in English fiction," in Werner E. Mosse and Julius Carlebach (eds), *Second Chance: Two centuries of German-speaking Jews in the United Kingdom* (Tübingen, 1991), pp. 315–33

Payard, Maurice, *Le financier G.-J. Ouvrard, 1770–1846* (Rheims, 1958)

Perkin, Harold, *The rise of professional society: England since 1880* (London, 1989)

Peron, Jean, *Les Rothschild* (Paris, 1942)

Perry, Roland, *The Fifth Man* (London, 1994)

Persigny, duc de, *Mémoires du duc de Persigny* (Paris, 1896)

Peter, Roland, "Geburt einer Geldmacht: 250 Jahre Rothschild," *Damals: Das aktuelle Geschichtsmagazin* (1993), pp. 56–9

Petit, Henri-Robert, *Rothschild: Roi d'Israël et les Américains* (Paris, 1941)

Peyrefitte, Roger, *Les juifs* (Paris, 1965)

Pflanze, Otto, *Bismarck and the development of Germany*, vol. I: *The period of unification, 1815–71* (Princeton, 1990)

——, *Bismarck and the development of Germany*, vol. II: *The period of consolidation, 1871–1880* (Princeton, 1990)

Phiebig, Albert J., *The descendants of Mayer Amschel Rothschild* (n.p., 1948[?])

Phillips, David Graham, "The empire of Rothschild," *Cosmopolitan* (1905), pp. 501–15

Piatigorsky, Jacqueline, *Jump in the waves: A memoir* (New York, 1988)

Picciotto, J., *Sketches of Anglo-Jewish history* (London, 1875)

Pinkney, David H., *Napoleon III and the rebuilding of Paris* (Princeton, 1958)

Pinney, Thomas (ed.), *The letters of Thomas Babington Macaulay*, 6 vols (Cambridge, 1974–81)

Platel, Baron Félix, *Les hommes de mon temps* (Paris, 1878)

Platt, D. C. M., *Finance, trade and politics in British foreign policy, 1815–1914* (London, 1968)

——, *Foreign finance in continental Europe and the United States, 1815–1870: Quantities, origins, functions and distribution* (London, 1984)

Plender, John and Paul Wallace, *The Square Mile: A guide to the new City of London* (London, 1985)

Plenge, Johann, *Gründung und Geschichte des Crédit Mobilier* (Darmstadt, 1976)

Plessis, Alain, *La Banque de France*, vol. I: *La Banque de France et ses deux cents actionnaires sous le Second Empire* (Geneva, 1982)

——, *La Banque de France*, vol. II: *Régents et gouverneurs de la Banque de France sous le Second Empire* (Geneva, 1985)

——, *La Banque de France*, vol. III: *La politique de la Banque de France de 1851 à 1870* (Geneva, 1985)

——, *The rise and fall of the Second Empire, 1852–71* (Cambridge, 1985)

Plumb, Sir John, *Vintage Memories* (Cambridge, 1988)

Plutarch, *Plutarchi chaeronensis apophthegmata Regium et Imperatorum, eiusdem Apophthegmata Laconica, Raphaële Regio interprete* (Paris, 1530)

Pohl, Manfred, *Einführung in die deutsche Bankengeschichte* (Frankfurt, 1976)

——, "From court agent to state financier—the rise of the Rothschilds," in Heuberger (ed.), *Essays*, pp. 51–70

Poidevin, Raymond, *Les relations économiques et financières entre la France et l'Allemagne de 1898 à 1914* (Paris, 1969)

——, *Finances et relations internationales, 1887–1914* (Paris, 1970)

Poliakov, Léon, *Jewish bankers and the Holy See* (London, 1977)

——, *Geschichte des Antisemitismus*, 8 vols (Frankfurt am Main, 1989)

Polisensky, Josef V., *Aristocrats and the crowd in the revolutionary year 1848* (Albany, New York, 1980)

Pollard, Sidney, *European economic development, 1815–70* (London, 1974)

——, *Peaceful conquest: The industrialization of Europe, 1760–1970* (Oxford, 1981)

——, "Capital exports, 1870–1914: Harmful or beneficial?," *Economic History Review* (1985), pp. 489–514

Pollins, Harold, *Economic history of the Jews in England* (East Brunswick, New Jersey, 1982)

Ponteil, Félix, *Les institutions de la France de 1814 à 1870* (Paris, 1966)

Ponting, Clive, *Churchill* (London, 1994)

Pool, Bernard (ed.), *The Croker papers, 1808–1857* (London, 1967)

Pope-Hennessy, John (ed.), *Baron Ferdinand de Rothschild's livre d'or* (Cambridge, 1957)

Porter, Andrew, *Victorian shipping, business and imperial policy: Donald Currie, the Castle Line and Southern Africa*, Royal Historical Society Studies in History, 49 (Woodbridge/New York, 1986)

Pose, Alfred, *La monnaie et ses institutions: Histoire, théorie et technique*, 2 vols (Vendôme, 1942)

Pottinger, E. Ann, *Napoleon III and the German crisis, 1865–1866*, Harvard Historical Studies, LXXV (Cambridge, Mass., 1966)

Powell, Ellis T., *The evolution of the money market, 1385–1915* (London, 1966)

Prawer, S. S., *Heine the tragic satirist: A study of the later poetry, 1827–1856* (Cambridge, 1961)

——, *Heine's Jewish comedy: A study of his portraits of Jews and Judaism* (Oxford, 1983)

————, *Israel at Vanity Fair* (Leiden/New York/Copenhagen/Cologne, 1992)

Preissler, Dietmar, *Frühantisemitismus in der Freien Stadt Frankfurt und im Großherzogtum Hessen (1810 bis 1860)* (Heidelberg, 1989)

Prevost-Marcilhacy, Pauline, *Les Rothschild: Bâtisseurs et mécènes* (Paris, 1995)

————, "Rothschild architecture in England, France, Germany, Austria and Italy," in Heuberger (ed.), *Essays*, pp. 245–64

Pringle, Robin, *A guide to banking in Britain* (London, 1975)

Priouret, Roger, *La Caisse des Dépôts: Cent cinquante ans d'histoire financière* (Paris, 1966)

Proust, Marcel, *A la recherche du temps perdu*, vol. II: *A l'ombre des jeunes filles en fleurs* (Paris, 1988)

————, *A la recherche du temps perdu*, vol. III: *Le côté de Guermantes 1* (Paris, 1988)

————, *A la recherche du temps perdu*, vol. III: *Le côté de Guermantes 2* (Paris, 1988)

————, *A la recherche du temps perdu*, vol. V: *La prisonnière* (Paris, 1989)

————, *A la recherche du temps perdu*, vol. IV: *Sodomme et Gomorrhe* (Paris, 1989)

Pückler [-Muskau], Hermann Fürst von, *A tour in England, Ireland and France in the years 1826, 1827 and 1829, with remarks on the manners and customs of the inhabitants, and anecdotes of distinguished characters. In a series of letters by a German prince*, trans. Sarah Taylor Austin (Philadelphia, 1833)

————, *Briefe eines Verstorbenen: Vollständige Ausgabe*, ed. Heinz Ohff (Kupfergraben, 1986)

————, *Pückler's Progress: The adventures of Prince Pückler-Muskau in England, Wales and Ireland as told in letters to his former wife, 1826–9* (London, 1987)

Puder, H., *Das Haus Rothschild: Die internationalen verwandtschaftlichen Beziehungen der judischen Hochfinanz* (Leipzig, 1933)

Pulzer, Peter, *The rise of political anti-Semitism in Germany and Austria* (London, 1964)

————, *The Jews and the German state: The political history of a minority, 1848–1933* (Oxford, 1992)

Quinn, Dermot, *Patronage and piety: The politics of English Roman Catholicism, 1850–1900* (Basingstoke, 1993)

Raikes, Thomas, *A portion of the journal kept by Thomas Raikes, Esq. from 1831 to 1847: Comprising reminiscences of social and political life in London and Paris during that period*, 4 vols. (London, 1856)

Ramm, Agatha (ed.), *The political correspondence of Mr. Gladstone and Lord Granville, 1868–1876*, Camden 3rd Ser., LXXXI and LXXXII (London, 1952)

———— (ed.), *The political correspondence of Mr. Gladstone and Lord Granville, 1876–1886*, 2 vols (Oxford, 1962)

————, *Sir Robert Morier: Envoy and ambassador in the age of imperialism, 1876–1893* (Oxford, 1973)

Ramon, Gabriel, *Histoire de la Banque de France* (Paris, 1929)

Ramsden, John (ed.), *Real old Tory politics: The political diaries of Sir Robert Sanders, Lord Bayford, 1910–35* (London, 1984)

Ratcliffe, Barrie M., "The origin of the Paris–Saint-Germain railway," *Journal of Transport History* (1972), pp. 197–219

————, "Railway imperialism: The example of the Pereires" Paris–Saint-Germain Company, 1835–1846," *Business History* (1976), pp. 66–84

Rath, R. John, *The Viennese revolutions of 1848* (Austin, 1957)

Ravage, M[arcus] E[li], *Five men of Frankfort: The story of the Rothschilds* (London/Bombay/Sydney, 1929)

Ray, Cyril, *Lafite: The story of Château Lafite-Rothschild* (London, 1978)

————, *Mouton-Rothschild: The wine, the family, the museum* (London, 1980)

Read, Donald, *The power of news: The history of Reuters, 1849–1989* (Oxford, 1992)

Reader, W. J., *A house in the City: A study of the City and of the Stock Exchange based on the records of Foster and Braithwaite, 1825–1975* (London, 1979)

Reeves, John, *The Rothschilds: The financial rulers of nations* (London, 1887)

Reid, Stuart J., *Lord John Russell* (London, 1895)

Reinerman, Alan J., *Austria and the Papacy in the Age of Metternich, vol. II: Revolution and reaction, 1830–38* (Washington, DC, 1989)

Reinharz, Jehuda and W. Schatzberg, *The Jewish response to German culture* (Boston, 1986)

Reitlinger, Gerald, *The economics of taste*, vol. I: *The rise and fall of picture prices, 1760–1960* (London, 1961)

————, *The economics of taste*, vol. II: *The rise and fall of objets d'art prices since 1750* (London, 1963)

Rémond, René, *The right wing in France* (Philadelphia, 1966)

Remusat, Charles de, *Mémoires de ma vie*, 4 vols (Paris, 1959–67)

Renouvin, Pierre, *Histoire des relations internationales*, vol. V: *1815–1871* (Paris, 1954)

————, *Histoire des relations internationales*, vol. VI: *1871–1914* (Paris, 1955)

Ribeill, Georges, *La révolution ferroviaire: La formation des compagnies de chemins de fer en France (1823–1870)* (Paris, 1993)

Rich, N. and M. H. Fisher (eds), *The Holstein papers: The memoirs, diaries and corrrespondence of Friedrich von Holstein, 1837–1909*, vol. I: *Memoirs and political observations* (Cambridge, 1955)

———— and ———— (eds), *The Holstein Papers: The memoirs, diaries and correspondence of Friedrich von Holstein, 1837–1909*, vol. III: *Correspondence, 1861–96* (Cambridge, 1961)

———— and ———— (eds), *The Holstein papers: The memoirs, diaries and corrrespondence of Friedrich von Holstein, 1837–1909*, vol. IV: *Correspondence, 1897–1909* (Cambridge, 1961)

Richman, Jacob, *Laughs from Jewish lore* (New York, 1926)

Richter, Werner, *Bismarck* (London, 1964)

Ridley, Jane, *The young Disraeli* (London, 1995)

Ridley, Jasper, *Lord Palmerston* (London, 1972)

Riker, T. W., *The making of Roumania: A study of an international problem 1856–1866* (London, 1931)

Riley, James C., *International government finance and the Amsterdam capital market, 1740–1815* (Cambridge, 1980)

Rintoul, M. C., *Dictionary of real people and places in fiction* (London/New York, 1993)

Robb, Graham M., *Balzac: A biography* (London, 1994)

Robert, S. Paul [Raben, L. F.], *La verité sur la maison Rothschild* (Paris, 1846)

Roberts, Richard, *Schroders: merchants and bankers* (Basingstoke, 1992)

Rohr, Donald G., *The origins of social liberalism in Germany* (Chicago, 1963)

Roqueplan, Nestor, *Le Baron James de Rothschild* (Paris, 1868)

Rose, Norman, "Churchill and Zionism," in Robert Blake and Wm. Roger Louis (eds), *Churchill: A major new assessment of his life in peace and war* (Oxford, 1993), pp. 147–66

Rose, Paul Lawrence, *Revolutionary anti-Semitism in Germany from Kant to Wagner* (Princeton, 1990)

Rosenbaum, E. and A. J. Sherman, *M. M. Warburg and Co, 1798–1938: Merchant bankers of Hamburg* (London, 1979)

Rosenberg, Alfred, *Der Mythus des 20. Jahrhunderts: Eine Wertung der seelisch-geistigen Gestaltenkämpfe unserer Zeit* (Munich, 1935)

Rosenberg, Edgar, *From Shylock to Svengali: Jewish stereotypes in English fiction* (Stanford, 1960)

Rößler, Carl, *Die fünf Frankfurter: Lustspiel in drei Akten* (Berlin, 1923)

Rössler, Hellmuth, *Graf Johann Philipp Stadion: Napoleons deutscher Gegenspieler*, vol. II: *1809 bis 1824* (Vienna/Munich, 1966)

Rotberg, Robert I., *The Founder: Cecil Rhodes and the pursuit of power* (New York/Oxford, 1988)

Roth, Cecil, *The magnificent Rothschilds* (London, 1939)

————, *A history of the Jews in England* (Oxford, 1949)

————, *The Great Synagogue London, 1690–1940* (London, 1950)

Rothschild, A. Freiherr von, *Offenes Sendschreiben. Von A. Frhr. v[on] Rothschild in Wien an Hofprediger Stöcker in Berlin. Übers. in's Hebräische von A. Rudoll* (Pressburg, 1880)

Rothschild, Alain de, *Le Juif dans la cité* (Paris, 1982)

Rothschild, Arthur de, *Histoire de la poste aux lettres: Depuis ses origines les plus anciennes jusqu'à nos jours* (Paris, 1873)

Rothschild, Charlotte de [Baroness Lionel], *Prayers and meditations: For daily use in the House of Israelites* (London, 1876)

Rothschild, Charlotte de, "A brief history of the Rothschild family and their musical associations," *Family Connections* (compact disk), (1994), pp. 3–7

————, "The musical associations of the Rothschild family," in Heuberger (ed.), *Essays*, pp. 287–96

Rothschild, C[onstance] and A[nnie] de, *The history and literature of the Israelites, according to the Old Testament and the Apocrypha*, 2 vols (London, 1870)

Rothschild, Edmund de, *Window on the world* (London, 1949)

————, *A gilt-edged life: Memoir* (London, 1998)

Rothschild, Guy de, *The whims of fortune* (London, 1985)

————, *Mon ombre siamoise* (Paris, 1993)

Rothschild, Henri de, *Croisières autour de mes souvenirs* (Paris, 1932)

————, *Tour du monde* (Paris, 1936)

Rothschild, Lord [Victor], *Meditations of a broomstick* (London, 1977)

————, "*You have it, Madam*": *The purchase, in 1875, of Suez Canal shares by Disraeli and Baron Lionel de Rothschild* (London, 1980)

————, *The shadow of a great man* (London, 1982)

————, *Random variables* (London, 1984)

Rothschild, Miriam, "Nathaniel Charles Rothschild, 1877–1923," MS (1979)

————, *Dear Lord Rothschild: Birds, butterflies and history* (London, 1983)

————, "The Rothschilds and the original EEC—family reflections I: The men," in Heuberger (ed.), *Essays*, pp. 147–54

————, "The silent members of the first EEC—family reflections II: The women," in Heuberger (ed.), *Essays*, pp. 155–64

————, Kate Garton and Lionel de Rothschild, *The Rothschild gardens* (London, 1996)

Rothschild, Mrs James de, *The Rothschilds at Waddesdon Manor* (London, 1979)

Rothschild, Nadine de, *La Baronne rentre à cinq heures* (Paris, 1984)

Rothschild, Philippe de, *Milady Vine: The autobiography of Philippe de Rothschild* (London, 1984)

Rousseau, Jean-Claude, "La mésaventure Rothschild: Fevrier 1848 à Suresnes," *Bulletin de la Société Historique de Suresnes* (1972)

Rowland, Peter, *The last Liberal governments: The promised land, 1905–1910* (London, 1968)

Rozenblit, Marsha L., *The Jews of Vienna, 1867–1914: Assimilation and identity* (Albany, New York, 1983)

Rubens, Alfred, "The Rothschilds in caricature," *Transactions of the Jewish Historical Society* (1968–69), pp. 76–87

————, *Anglo-Jewish Portraits* (London, 1935)

Rubin, Abba, *Images in transition: The English Jew in English literature, 1660–1830* (Westport, Conn./London)

Rubinstein, W. D., "British millionaires, 1809–1989," *Bulletin of the Institute of Historical Research* (1974), pp. 203–23

————, *A history of the Jews in the English-speaking world: Great Britain* (Basingstoke, 1996)

Rudolph, Richard R., "Austria, 1800–1914," in Rondo Cameron (ed.), *Banking and economic development: Some lessons of history* (New York/London/Toronto, 1972), pp. 26–57.

Rumney, J., "Anglo Jewry as seen through foreign eyes," *Transactions of the Jewish Historical Society of England* (1932–5), pp. 323–40

Rurüp, Reinhard, "Emanzipation—Anmerkungen zur Begriffsgeschichte," in *idem, Emanzipation und Antisemitismus: Studien zur "Judenfrage" der bürgerlichen Gesellschaft* (Göttingen, 1975), pp. 159–66

————, "The tortuous and thorny path to legal equality: "Jew Laws" and emancipatory legislation in Germany from the late 18th century," *Leo Baeck Institute Year Book* (1986), pp. 3–33

Russell, Henry Benajah, *International monetary conferences: their purposes, character, and results; with a study of the conditions of currency and finance in Europe and America during intervening periods and in their relations to international action* (New York/London, 1898).

Russo-Jewish Committee, *Russian atrocities, 1881: Supplementary statement issued . . . in confirmation of* The Times *narrative* (London, 1882)

Sabouret, Anne, *MM. Lazard Frères et Cie.* (Paris, 1987)

Salbstein, M. C. N., *The emancipation of the Jews in Britain: The question of the admission of Jews to Parliament, 1828–1860* (Rutherford, New Jersey, 1982)

Sammons, Jeffrey L., *Heinrich Heine: A modern biography* (Manchester, 1979)

Samson, Jim, *The music of Chopin* (London, 1985)

————, *Chopin* (Oxford, 1996)

Sauer, J., *Finanzgeschäfte des Landgrafen von Hesse-Kassel: Ein Beitrag zur Geschichte des Kurhessischen Haus und Staatschatzen und zur Entwicklungsgeschichte des Hauses Rothschild* (Fulda, 1930)

Saxe-Coburg-Gotha, Duke of, *Memoirs of Ernest II Duke of Saxe-Coburg-Gotha*, 4 vols (London, 1888)

Sayers, Richard Sidney, *Bank of England operations, 1890–1914* (London, 1936)

————, "The development of central banking after Bagehot," *Economic History Review* (1951), pp. 109–16

————, *Central banking after Bagehot* (Oxford, 1957)

————, *Modern banking* (7th edn, Oxford, 1967)

————, *The Bank of England, 1891–1944*, 3 vols (Cambridge, 1976)

Schachar, Isaiah, *The Judensau: A medieval anti-Jewish motif and its history* (London, 1974)

Schama, Simon, *Two Rothschilds and the state of Israel* (London, 1978)

Schembs, Hans-Otto, " 'For the care of the sick, the good of the community, the embellishment of their home town": The charitable Rothschild foundations in Frankfurt am Main," in Heuberger (ed.), *Essays*, pp. 205–20

Scherb, Friedrich Edlen von, *Geschichte des Hauses Rothschild* (Berlin, 1893)

Schimpf, Dorothea, *Emanzipation und Bildungswesen der Juden im Kurfürstentum Hessen 1807–1866: Jüdische Identität zwischen Selbstbehauptung und Assimilationsdruck*, Schriften der Kommission für die Geschichte der Juden in Hessen, 13 (Wiesbaden, 1994)

Schischa, A., "The Saga of 1855: A study in depth," in Sonia and Vivian D. Lipman (eds), *The century of Moses Montefiore* (Oxford, 1985), pp. 269–346

Schnee, Heinrich, *Die Hoffinanz und der moderne Staat*, 3 vols (Berlin, 1953)

———, *Rothschild: Geschichte einer Finanzdynastie* (Göttingen/Berlin/Frankfurt, 1961)

Schneider, Georg, *Die Schlüsselliteratur* (Stuttgart, 1951)

Schnerb, Robert, *Rouher et le Second Empire* (Paris, 1949)

Schnur, Harry S., *Jewish humour* (London, 1945)

Schooling, Sir William, *Alliance Assurance, 1824–1924* (London, 1924)

Schorske, Carl, *Fin-de-siècle Vienna: Politics and culture* (London, 1979)

Schremmer, D. E., "Taxation and public finance: Britain, France and Germany," in Peter Mathias and Sidney Pollard (eds), *The Cambridge economic history of Europe*, vol. VIII: *The industrial economies: The development of economic and social policies* (Cambridge, 1989), pp. 315–494

———, *Steuern und Staatsfinanzen während der Industrialisierung Europas: England, Frankreich, Preußen und das deutsche Reich 1800 bis 1914* (Berlin, 1994)

Schroeder, Paul W., *Metternich's diplomacy at its zenith, 1820–2* (Austin, 1962)

Schwemer, Richard, *Geschichte der Freien Stadt Frankfurt a.M.* (1814–1866), 3 vols (Frankfurt am Main, 1910–18)

Scott, Ivan, *The Roman question and the powers, 1848–1865* (The Hague, 1969)

Serre, comte Pierre François Hercule de, *Correspondance du comte de Serre 1796–1824, annotée et publiée par son fils*, 6 vols (Paris, 1876)

Seton-Watson, Christopher, *Italy from liberalism to fascism* (London, 1967)

Seton-Watson, Hugh, *The Russian Empire, 1801–1917* (Oxford, 1967)

Shannon, Catherine B., *Arthur J. Balfour and Ireland, 1874–1922* (Washington, DC, 1988)

Shaw, S. J., "Ottoman expenditures and budgets in the late nineteenth and twentieth centuries," *International Journal of Middle East Studies* (1978), pp. 373–8

Sheehan, James J., *German history, 1770–1866* (Oxford, 1989)

Sherwig, John M., *Guineas and gunpowder: British foreign aid in the wars with France, 1793–1815* (Cambridge, Mass., 1969)

Sievers, Leo, *Juden in Deutschland* (Hamburg, 1977)

Sigurd, Paul Scheichl, "Contexts and nuances of anti-Jewish language," in Ivor Oxaal, M. Pollac and G. Botz (eds), *The Jews, anti-Semitism and culture in Vienna* (London and New York, 1987), pp. 89–110

Sington, Derrick and Arthur Weidenfeld, *The Goebbels experiment: A study of the Nazi propaganda machine* (London, 1942)

Sked, Alan, *The survival of the Habsburg Monarchy* (London/New York, 1979)

———, *The decline and fall of the Habsburg Empire, 1815–1918* (London/New York, 1989)

Skolnik, Esther Simon, *Leading ladies: A study of eight late Victorian and Edwardian political wives* (New York/London, 1987)

Slinn, Judy, *A history of Freshfields* (London, 1984)

Smith, E. A., *The House of Lords in British politics and society, 1815–1911* (London, 1992)

Smith, Philip, *Brinco: The story of Churchill Falls* (Toronto, 1975)

Sokolow, Nahum, *History of Zionism, 1600–1918*, 2 vols (London/New York, 1919)

Sombart, Werner, *Die Juden und das Wirtschaftsleben* (Leipzig, 1911)

Somervell, D. C., *Disraeli and Gladstone* (London, 1925)

Sorkin, David, *The transformation of German Jewry, 1780–1840* (New York, 1987)

Sotheby Parke Bernet & Co., *Mentmore sale catalogues*, 5 vols (London, 1977)

Souhami, Diana, *Bakst: The Rothschild panels of The Sleeping Beauty* (London, 1992)

Southgate, D., *The passing of the Whigs, 1832–1886* (London, 1962)

Spalding, Henry D., *Encyclopaedia of Jewish humour* (London/New York, 1972)

Spalding, William F., *Tate's modern cambist, centenary edition: A manual of the world's monetary systems, the foreign exchanges &c.* (28th edn, London, 1929)

Sparr, Thomas, "The Rothschilds in literature," in Heuberger (ed.), *Essays*, pp. 307–20

Speitkamp, Winfried, "Restauration als Transformation: Untersuchungen zur kurhessischen Verfassungsgeschichte, 1813–1830," in Uwe Schultz (ed.), *Die Geschichte Hessens* (Stuttgart, 1983), pp. 160–70

Spencer-Silver, Patricia, *Pugin's builder: the life and work of George Myers* (Hull, 1993)

Spiegelberg, Richard, *The City: Power without accountability* (London, 1973)

Spiel, Hilde, *Fanny von Arnstein* (Oxford, 1991)

Spinner, Thomas J., Jr, *George Joachim Goschen: The transformation of a Victorian Liberal* (Cambridge, 1973)

Srbik, Heinrich Ritter von, *Metternich: Der Staatsman und der Mensch*, 3 vols (Munich, 1925–54)

Stapleton, Augustus Granville, *George Canning and his times* (London, 1859)

Stapleton, Edward J. (ed.), *Some official correspondence of George Canning*, 2 vols (London, 1887)

Steed, Henry Wickham, *Through thirty years, 1892–1922*, 2 vols (London, 1924)

Steefel, Lawrence D., "The Rothschilds and the Austrian loan of 1865," *Journal of Modern History* (1936), pp. 27–40

Steele, E. D., *Palmerston and Liberalism, 1855–65* (Cambridge, 1991)

Steiner, Zara S., *The Foreign Office and foreign policy, 1898–1914* (Cambridge, 1969)

Stendhal [Henri Beyle], *A life of Rossini* (London, 1956)

———, *Lucien Leuwen* (Paris, 1973)

Stengers, Jean, "King Leopold and Anglo-French rivalry, 1882–1884," in Prosser Gifford and Wm Roger Louis (eds), *France and Britain in Africa: Imperial rivalry and colonial rule* (New Haven/London, 1971), pp. 121–66

Stephen, Leslie and Sidney Lee (eds), *Compact edition of the dictionary of national biography*, 2 vols (Oxford, 1975)

Stern, Fritz, *Gold and iron: Bismarck, Bleichröder and the building of the German Empire* (Harmondsworth, 1987)

Stern, Selma, *The court Jew: A contribution to the history of the period of absolutism in Central Europe* (Philadelphia, 1950)

Stiefel, D., "The reconstruction of Credit-Anstalt" in Herbert Matis (ed.), *The economic development of Austria since 1870* (Aldershot, 1994), pp. 511–28

Stürmer, Michael, Gabriele Teichmann and Wilhelm Treue, *Striking the balance: Sal. Oppenheim jr & Cie: A family and a bank* (London, 1994)

Stüve, Gustav (ed.), *Briefwechsel zwischen Stüve und Detmold in den Jahren 1848 bis 1850*, Quellen und Darstellungen zur Geschichte Niedersachsens ed. Historischen Verein für Niedersachsen, XIII (Hanover/Leipzig, 1903)

Supple, Barry, *The Royal Exchange Assurance: A history of British insurance, 1720–1970* (Cambridge, 1970)

Surtees, Virginia, *Coutts Lindsay, 1824–1913* (Norwich, 1993)

Sutton, Denys *et al.*, *Waddesdon Manor: Aspects of the collection* (London, 1977)

Swartz, Helen M. and Marvin (eds), *Disraeli's reminiscences* (London, 1975)

Swartz, Marvin, *The politics of British foreign policy in the era of Disraeli and Gladstone* (London, 1985)

Sweet, Paul R., *Friedrich von Gentz* (Westport, Conn., 1970)

Tait, Hugh, *The Waddesdon bequest: The legacy of Baron Ferdinand Rothschild to the British Museum* (London, 1981)

Talleyrand, Prince de, *Memoirs of the Prince de Talleyrand*, ed. the duc de Broglie (London, 1891)

Tapie, Victor L., *The rise and fall of the Hapsburg Monarchy* (London, 1971)

Taylor, A. J. P., *The Habsburg Monarchy, 1815–1918* (London, 1948)

———, *The struggle for mastery in Europe, 1848–1918* (Oxford, 1954)

Teichova, Alice and P. L. Cottrell (eds), *International business and Central Europe, 1918–1939* (Leicester, 1983)

Thackeray, William Makepeace, *The history of Pendennis* (London, 1904)

———, "The book of snobs," in George Saintsbury (ed.), *The Oxford Thackeray, vol. IX* (London/New York/Toronto, 1908), pp. 257–493

———, *The letters and private papers of William Makepeace Thackeray*, 4 vols, ed. Gordon N. Ray (London, 1945)

Thane, Pat, "Financiers and the British state: The case of Sir Ernest Cassel," *Business History* (1986), pp. 35–61

Thatcher, Margaret, *The Downing Street years* (London, 1993)

The Times, The history of The Times, vol. II: *The tradition established, 1841–1884* (London, 1939)

———, *The history of The Times*, vol. III: *The twentieth century test, 1884–1912* (London, 1947)

———, *The history of The Times*, vol. IV: *The 150th anniversary and beyond, 1912–1948* (London, 1952)

Thielen, Peter Gerrit, *Karl August von Hardenberg, 1750–1822* (Cologne/Berlin, 1967)

Thompson, Neville, *Wellington after Waterloo* (London, 1986)

Thompson, Paul, *Socialists, Liberals and Labour: The struggle for London, 1885–1914* (London, 1967)

Tilly, Richard, *Financial institutions and industrialisation in the Rhineland, 1815–70* (Madison, Wis., 1966)

Tilney Bassett, A. (ed.), *Gladstone to his wife* (London, 1936)

Timberlake, R. R., "Hastoe near Tring: Recollections of life on the Rothschild Estate in the time of the first Baron Rothschild," *Hertfordshire's Past* (1995), pp. 11–21

Tombs, Robert, *The war against Paris, 1871* (Cambridge, 1981)

Torido, Gianni, *An economic history of liberal Italy, 1850–1918* (London, 1990)

Tortella, Gabriel, "Spain 1829–1874," in Rondo Cameron (ed.), *Banking and economic development: Some lessons of history* (New York/London/Toronto, 1972), pp. 91–121.

Toussenel, Alphonse, *Les juifs, rois de l'époque: Histoire de la féodalité financière* (Paris, 1847)

Trebilcock, Clive, *The industrialisation of the continental powers, 1780–1914* (London, 1981)

Trentmann, Frank, "New sources on an old family: The Rothschild papers at the Special Archive, Moscow— and a letter from Metternich," *Financial History Review* (1995), pp. 73–9

Treskow, A. von, *Nathan Meyer Rothschild. Biographische Skizze (Nebst seinem Testament). Nach englischen Quellen* (Quidlinburg/Leipzig, 1837)

Trevelyan, G. M., *The life of John Bright* (London, 1913)

Trollope, Mrs Frances, *Vienna and the Austrians*, vol. II (London, 1838)

Turrell, Robert Vicat, "Rhodes, De Beers and monopoly," *Journal of Imperial and Commonwealth History* (1982), pp. 311–43

———, " 'Finance . . . the Governor of the imperial engine': Hobson and the case of Rothschild and Rhodes," *Journal of Southern African Studies* (1987), pp. 417–32

——— and Jean-Jacques van Helten, "The Rothschilds, the Exploration Company and mining finance," *Business History* (1986), pp. 181–205

Tyson, Geoffrey, *100 years of banking in Asia and Africa, 1863–1963* (London, 1963)

Ude-Meier, Klaus and Valentin Senger, *Die jüdischen Friedhöfe in Frankfurt* (Frankfurt am Main, 1985)

Valentin, Veit, *1848: Chapters of German history* (London, 1965)

Verity, William, "The rise of the Rothschilds," *History Today* (1968), pp. 225–33

Viel-Castel, comte Horace Salviac de, *Mémoires du comte Horace de Viel-Castel sur la règne de Napoleon III*, 6 vols (Paris, 1883)

Villèle, Jean Baptiste de, *Mémoires et correspondance du comte de Villèle*, 5 vols (Paris, 1888–90)

Vincent, John (ed.), *Disraeli, Derby and the Conservative party: Journals and memoirs of Edward Henry, Lord Stanley, 1849–1869* (Hassocks, 1978)

——— (ed.), *The later Derby diaries: Home rule, Liberal Unionism and aristocratic life in late Victorian England* (Bristol, 1981)

——— (ed.), *The Crawford papers: The journals of David Lindsay, 27th Earl of Crawford and 10th Earl of Balcarres, 1871–1940, during the years 1892–1940* (Manchester, 1984)

——— (ed.), *A selection from the diaries of Edward Henry Stanley, 15th earl of Derby (1826–93), between September 1869 and March 1878*, Camden 5th Ser., vol. IV (London, 1994)

Vogel, Walter (ed.), *Briefe Johann Carl Bertram Stüves*, vol. II: *1848–1872*, Veröffentlichungen der Niedersächsischen Archivverwaltung, XI (Göttingen, 1960)

Völker, H. (ed.), *Die Stadt Goethes: Frankfurt am Main im 18. Jahrhundert* (Frankfurt, 1932)

Vuilleumier, Marc, Michel Aucouturier, Sven Stelling-Michaud and Michel Cadot, *Autour d'Alexandre Herzen: Révolutionaires et exilés du XIXe siècle* (Geneve, 1973)

Wake, Jehanne, *Kleinwort Benson: The history of two families in banking* (Oxford, 1997)

Waller, Bruce, *Bismarck at the crossroads, 1878–80: The reorientation of German foreign policy after the Congress of Berlin* (London, 1974)

Walpole, Spencer, *The life of Lord John Russell* (London, 1889)

Ward, Mrs Humphrey [Mary Augusta], *Marcella* (London, 1894)

———, *Sir George Tressady* (London, 1909)

Warnke-Dakers, Kerstin, "Lord Rothschild and his poor brethren—East European Jews in London, 1880–1906," in Heuberger (ed.), *Essays*, pp. 113–28

Wasson, Ellis Archer, *Whig renaissance: Lord Althorp and the Whig Party, 1782–1845* (London, 1987)

Watson, J. Steven, *The reign of George III, 1760–1815* (Oxford, 1960)

Wawro, Geoffrey, *The Austro-Prussian War: Austria's war with Prussia and Italy in 1866* (Cambridge, 1996)

Weber, Max, *The Protestant ethic and the spirit of capitalism*, transl. Talcott Parsons (London, 1991)

Webster, Sir Charles, *The foreign policy of Palmerston*, 2 vols (London, 1951)

Weil[l], Alexandre, "L'état des Juifs en Europe," *La revue indépendante*, vol. XVI (1844), pp. 481–518

——, "Rotschild et les finances de l'Europe," *La revue indépendante*, vol. XVII (1844), pp. 424–9

Weinberg, David H., *Les juifs à Paris de 1933 à 1939* (Paris, 1974)

Weinstock, Herbert, *Rossini: A biography* (London, 1968)

Weintraub, Stanley, *Disraeli: A biography* (London, 1993)

——, *Albert: Uncrowned king* (London, 1997)

Weizmann, Chaim, *Trial and error: The autobiography of Chaim Weizmann* (New York, 1949)

Welch, David, *Propaganda and the German cinema, 1933–1945* (Oxford, 1983)

Wemyss Reid, T., *Life of the Rt. Hon. W. E. Forster* (London, 1888)

Werner, Moritz, "Eine vergessene Tat des Barons Amschel: Dokumente Rothschildschen Geimeinsinns aus dem Frankfurter Stadtarchiv," *Frankfurter Israelitisches Gemeindeblatt* (1934)

Whale, P. Barrett, *Joint stock banking in Germany: A study of the German Creditbanks before and after the War* (London, 1930)

Whibley, Charles, *Lord John Manners and his friends*, vol. II (London, 1925)

White, Benjamin, *Silver: Its history and romance* (London, 1917)

White, Jerry, *Rothschild buildings: Life in an East End tenement block, 1887–1920* (London, 1980)

Whyte, A. J. (ed.), *The life and letters of Cavour, 1849–61* (Oxford, 1930)

Wiebe, M. G., J. B. Conacher and John Matthews (eds), *Benjamin Disraeli: Letters*, vol. III: *1838–1841* (Toronto, 1987)

——, *Benjamin Disraeli: Letters*, vol. IV: *1842–1847* (Toronto, 1989)

——, *Benjamin Disraeli: Letters*, vol. V: *1848–1851* (Toronto, 1992)

Wilde, Oscar, *The works of Oscar Wilde*, ed. with an introduction by G. F. Maine (London/Glasgow, 1952)

Williams, Bill, *The making of Manchester Jewry, 1740–1875* (Manchester, 1976)

——, "Nathan Rothschild in Manchester," in Victor Gray (ed.), *The Life and times of N. M. Rothschild 1777–1836* (London, 1998), pp. 34–41

Williamson, Edwin, *The Penguin history of Latin America* (London, 1992)

Wilson, Derek, *Rothschild: A story of wealth and power* (London, 1988)

Wilson, J. S. G., *French banking structure and credit policy* (London, 1957)

Winter, James, *Robert Lowe* (Toronto, 1976)

Winton, J. R., *Lloyd's Bank, 1918–1969* (Oxford, 1982)

Wippermann, Wolfgang, *Das Leben in Frankfurt zur NS-Zeit: Darstellung, Dokumente und didaktische Hinweise* (Frankfurt am Main, 1986)

Wirth, Max, *A history of banking in all the leading nations*, vol. IV (New York, 1896)

Wiskemann, Elizabeth, *Czechs and Germans: A study of the struggle in the historic provinces of Bohemia and Moravia* (Oxford, 1938)

Wistrich, Robert S., *Socialism and the Jews: The dilemmas of assimilation in Germany and Austria–Hungary* (Rutherford, New Jersey, 1982)

——, *The Jews of Vienna in the age of Franz Joseph* (Oxford, 1989)

——, *Between redemption and perdition: Modern antisemitism and Jewish identity* (London/New York, 1990)

Witte, S. I., *Memoirs of Count Witte* (London, 1921)

Wohl, Anthony S., *The eternal slum: Housing and social policy in Victorian London* (London, 1977)

Wolf, Lucien, "Rothschildiana," in *idem, Essays in Jewish History*, ed. Cecil Roth (London, 1934), pp. 261–308

Wolf, Siegbert, *Liberalismus in Frankfurt am Main: Vom Ende der Freien Stadt bis zum Ersten Weltkrieg*, Studien zur Frankfurter Geschichte, 23 (Frankfurt am Main, 1987)

Wolff, Otto, *Ouvrard: Speculator of genius, 1770–1846* (London, 1932, 2nd edn 1962)

Woodward, E. L., "Economic factors making for peace or war," in *idem, War and peace in Europe 1815–1870 and other essays* (London, 1931), pp. 70–113

Wulf, Joseph, *Literatur und Dichtung im Dritten Reich* (Frankfurt am Main/Berlin, 1989)

Yellen, Sherman, Jerry Bock and Sheldon Harnick, "The Rothschilds: A musical legend," unpublished MS, RAL (1969)

Yergin, Daniel, *The prize: The epic quest for oil, money and power* (2nd edn, London, 1993)

Yogev, Gedaliah, *Diamonds and coral: Anglo-Dutch Jews and eighteenth century trade* (Leicester, 1978)

Yonge, Charles Dilke, *Life and administration of Robert Banks, 2nd Earl of Liverpool* (London, 1868)

Zetland, Marquis of (ed.), *The letters of Disraeli to Lady Bradford and Lady Chesterfield*, vol. I: *1873 to 1875* (London, 1929)

Ziegler, Philip, *The sixth great power: Barings, 1762–1929* (London, 1988)

———, *King Edward VIII: The official biography* (London, 1990)

Zielenziger, Kurt, *Juden in der deutschen Wirtschaft* (Berlin, 1930)

Zimmerman, Judith E., *Midpassage: Alexander Herzen and European revolution* (Pittsburgh, 1989)

Zimmermann, Moshe, *Wilhelm Marr: The patriarch of anti-Semitism* (New York/Oxford, 1986)

Zola, Emile, *Les Rougon Macquart*, vol. V: *Histoire naturelle et sociale d'une famille sous le second Empire: L'Argent* (Paris, 1967)